THE ENCYCLOPEDIA OF
the French Revolutionary
and Napoleonic Wars

A Political, Social, and Military History

The Encyclopedia of

the French Revolutionary

and Napoleonic Wars

A Political, Social, and Military History

VOLUME THREE

Entries R–Z
Primary Source Documents

Gregory Fremont-Barnes, Editor

A B C CLIO

Santa Barbara, California   Denver, Colorado   Oxford, United Kingdom

Library of Congress Cataloging-in-Publication Data

The encyclopedia of the French revolutionary and Napoleonic Wars : a political, social, and military history / editor, Gregory Fremont-Barnes.

   p.   cm.

Includes bibliographical references and index.

ISBN 1-85109-646-9 (hard cover : alk. paper) — ISBN 1-85109-651-5 (ebook)

1. First Coalition, War of the, 1792–1797—Encyclopedias.   2. Second Coalition, War of the, 1798–1801—Encyclopedias.   3. France—History—Revolution, 1789–1799—Encyclopedias.   4. Napoleonic Wars, 1800–1815—Encyclopedias.   5. France—History, Military—1789–1815—Encyclopedias.   6. Europe—History—1789–1815—Encyclopedias.   I. Fremont-Barnes, Gregory.

DC220.E53   2006

944.0403—dc22

                                                                                                            2006019409

08 07 06   10 9 8 7 6 5 4 3 2 1

This book is also available on the World Wide Web as an eBook. Visit abc-clio.com for details.

ABC-CLIO, Inc.

130 Cremona Drive, P.O. Box 1911

Santa Barbara, California 93116–1911

This book is printed on acid-free paper.

Manufactured in the United States of America

Submissions Editor	Alexander Mikaberidze
Project Assistant	Wendy Roseth
Production Editor	Martha Ripley Gray
Editorial Assistant	Alisha L. Martinez
File Management Coordinator	Paula Gerard
Map Production	George Barile, Accurate Art, Inc.; George Zirfas, Chez D'Art, Inc.
Production Manager	Don Schmidt
Media Image Coordinator	Ellen Brenna Dougherty
Media Editor	Ellen Rasmussen
Media Manager	Caroline Price
Typesetting and Interior Design	Andrew Berry, Letra Libre, Inc.

Contents

List of Entries

Primary Source Documents

List of Maps

Key to Military Map Symbols

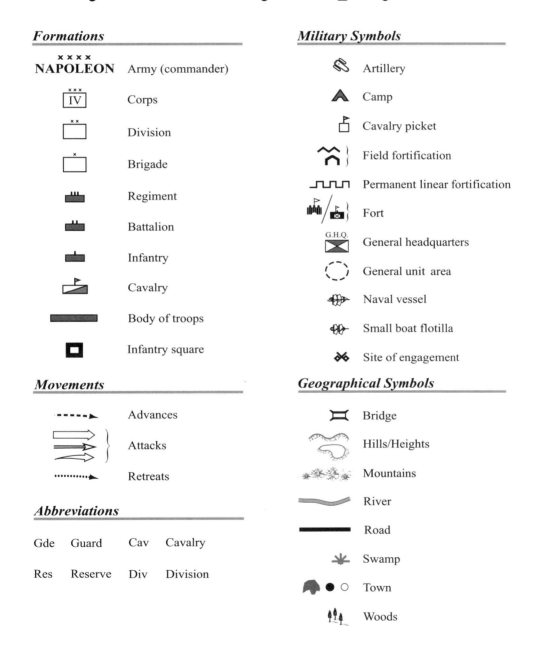

Formations

× × × ×
NAPOLEON   Army (commander)

× × ×
IV   Corps

× ×   Division

×   Brigade

Regiment

Battalion

Infantry

Cavalry

Body of troops

Infantry square

Movements

- - - - ►   Advances

⟹   Attacks

········►   Retreats

Abbreviations

Gde   Guard   Cav   Cavalry

Res   Reserve   Div   Division

Military Symbols

Artillery

Camp

Cavalry picket

Field fortification

Permanent linear fortification

Fort

G.H.Q.   General headquarters

General unit area

Naval vessel

Small boat flotilla

Site of engagement

Geographical Symbols

Bridge

Hills/Heights

Mountains

River

Road

Swamp

Town

Woods

Chronology

July

17   Battle of Perpignan on the Pyrenean front

21   Allies capture Mainz

August

28   Toulon surrenders to an Anglo-Spanish expeditionary force; start of siege of Quesnoy in the Austrian Netherlands

29   Siege of Dunkirk, Austrian Netherlands, begins

September

8   Battle of Hondschoote, Austrian Netherlands; siege of Dunkirk lifted

11   Allied forces accept surrender of Quesnoy

22   Battle of Truillas, on the Pyrenean front

October

8   Royalist rebellion in Lyon ends

15–16   Battle of Wattignies, in the Austrian Netherlands

December

19   Allies evacuate Toulon, taking Royalist civilians with them

23   Vendéan revolt ends

26   Battle of the Geisberg, on the Rhine front

1794

April

1   British capture St. Lucia, in the West Indies

20   British capture Guadeloupe, in the West Indies

26   Battle of Landrecies, in the Austrian Netherlands

29–30   Battle of Le Boulou, on the Pyrenean front

May

11   Battle of Courtrai, in the Austrians Netherlands

18   Battle of Tourcoing, Austrians Netherlands

23   Battle of Tournai, Austrian Netherlands

June

1   Battle of the Glorious First of June, off Ushant

6   French assume new offensive in Italy

26   Battle of Fleurus, Austrian Netherlands

July

27   Coup of Thermidor in Paris; Robespierre executed the following day

August

1   Battle of San Marcial, on the Pyrenean front

10   British forces capture Corsica

25   French invade Holland

29   French retake Valenciennes

October

5   Battle of Maciejowice, during the Polish revolt

6   French reconquest of Guadeloupe complete

9   French troops occupy Cologne, on the Rhine

November

4–5   Battle of Praga, during the Polish revolt

18   French capture Nijmegen, in Holland

26   French capture Figueras on the Pyrenean front

December

10   French retake Guadeloupe

1795

January

3   Third and final partition of Poland

20   French troops occupy Amsterdam

30   French cavalry captures the Dutch fleet at Texel

February

3   French troops capture Rosas on the Pyrenean front

March

13–14   Battle of the Gulf of Genoa

25   British expeditionary force to Flanders is evacuated by sea at Bremen

April

5   Treaty of Basle concluded between France and Prussia

25   French begin offensive along the river Fluvia on the Pyrenean front

June

17   Battle of Belle Isle

19   French recapture St. Lucia, in the West Indies

23   Battle of the Ile de Groix

27   British land French royalist troops at Quiberon Bay on the coast of France

July

17   Battle of Hyères

21   French republican forces defeat the royalists at Quiberon

22   French and Spanish conclude peace at Basle

August

1   British invade Ceylon

September

6   French open offensive along the Rhine

14 British expeditionary forces conquers the Dutch
    Cape Colony in southern Africa

October
1   France annexes Belgium
5   Bonaparte uses artillery in the streets of Paris to
    quell the coup of Vendémiaire
27 New French government, the Directory, takes
    power in Paris

November
23 Battle of Loano

1796
February
14 British expeditionary force captures Dutch
    colony of Ceylon

March
2   Bonaparte assumes command of French troops
    in Italy
9   Bonaparte and Josephine marry

April
11 Napoleon opens offensive on the Italian front
12 Battle of Montenotte
14–15 Second Battle of Dego
16–17 Battle of Ceva
21 Battle of Mondovi
28 Piedmont and France conclude peace at Cherasco

May
8   Action at Codogno
10 Battle of Lodi
13 French forces occupy Milan
26 British troops retake St. Lucia in the West Indies
30 Battle of Borghetto; first siege of Mantua begins

June
3   British capture St. Vincent in the West Indies
4   First Battle of Altenkirchen, Rhine front
28 Fortress at Milan capitulates to the French

July
5   Battle of Rastatt, Rhine front
9   Battle of Ettlingen, Rhine front
14 Battle of Haslach, Rhine front
31 French abandon siege of Mantua

August
3   Battle of Lonato, Italian front
5   Battle of Castiglione, Italian front

7   Battle of Forcheim, Rhine front
11 Battle of Neresheim, Rhine front
17 Dutch surrender their fleet to British forces at
    Cape Colony
19 French and Spanish conclude Treaty of San
    Ildefonso
24 Battle of Friedberg, Rhine front; Battle of
    Amberg, Rhine front; French resume siege of
    Mantua

September
3   Battle of Würzburg, Rhine front
4   Battle of Rovereto, Italian front
8   Battle of Bassano, Italian front

October
2   Battle of Biberach, Rhine front
8   Spain declares war on Britain
10 Peace concluded between France and Naples
19 Battle of Emmendlingen, Rhine front
23 Battle of Schliengen, Rhine front

November
2   French reoccupy Corsica after British evacuation
12 Battle of Caldiero, Italian front
15–17 Battle of Arcola, Italian front
17 Tsarina Catherine II of Russia dies

December
22 French naval force appears off Bantry Bay on the
    Irish coast

1797
January
14–15 Battle of Rivoli, Italian front

February
2   Mantua surrenders to the French, Italian front
14 Battle of St. Vincent off the coast of Spain
17 British take Trinidad in the West Indies
19 Peace concluded between France and the Papal
    States
22 French expeditionary force lands on the Welsh
    coast
24 French troops in Wales capitulate

April
16 Mutiny breaks out among British naval crews at
    Spithead
17 Preliminary peace concluded between France and
    Austria at Leoben
18 Second Battle of Altenkirchen, Rhine front

20 Battle of Diersheim, Rhine front

May

12 Mutiny breaks out among British naval crews at the Nore

15 End of naval mutiny at Spithead

June

15 End of naval mutiny at the Nore

July

9 French establish the Cisalpine Republic in northern Italy

October

11 Battle of Camperdown between the British and Dutch naval squadrons

17 France and Austria conclude Treaty of Campo Formio

1798

May

19 French expeditionary force departs from Toulon bound for Egypt

24 Outbreak of rebellion in Ireland

June

12 French occupy Malta en route to Egypt

July

1 French expedition arrives in Egypt

13 Battle of Shubra Khit

21 Battle of the Pyramids

22 French enter Cairo

August

1–2 Battle of the Nile

22 French expeditionary force disembarks at Kilala Bay on the Irish coast

September

8 French troops in Ireland surrender to British

9 Turkey declares war on France

October

12 Battle of Donegal, off the Irish coast

November

19 British troops capture Minorca

23 Neapolitan forces invade central Italy

29 Neapolitan troops occupy Rome

December

13 Neapolitan troops evacuate Rome

1799

January

23 French establish the Parthenopean Republic in the former Kingdom of the Two Siclies (Naples)

February

10 French troops begin campaign in Syria

March

12 France declares war on Austria

17 French besiege Acre on the Syrian coast

21 Battle of Ostrach, Rhine front

25 Battle of Stockach, Rhine front

30 Battle of Verona, Italian front

April

5 Battle of Magnano, Italian front

15 Russian army under Suvorov arrives at the Italian front

26 Battle of Cassano, Italian front

29 Allied occupation of Milan

May

20 French lift siege of Acre in Syria

June

4–7 First Battle of Zürich, on the Swiss front

18–19 Battle of the Trebbia, Italian front

21 Battle of San Giuliano, Italian front

July

15 Ottoman troops land in Aboukir Bay, Egypt

25 French attack Turkish positions at Aboukir

August

2 French capture Aboukir from the Turks

15 Battle of Novi, Italian front

24 Bonaparte leaves Egypt for France

26 French offensive near Mannheim, Rhine front

27 British expeditionary force disembarks from North Holland; Suvorov's army begins march from Italy to Switzerland; Tsar Paul I forms League of Armed Neutrality against Britain

30 British squadron seizes Dutch fleet at the Helder

September

18 French surrender Mannheim, Rhine front

19 Battle of Bergen, in Holland

25–26   Second Battle of Zürich, Swiss front

October
- 9   Bonaparte lands in France
- 10   By a convention with the French, Anglo-Russian forces to be withdrawn from North Holland

November
- 9–10   Coup of Brumaire in Paris; Consulate comes to power

December
- 25   Bonaparte appointed First Consul

1800

January
- 24   Convention of El Arish concluded between British and French in Egypt

March
- 20   Battle of Heliopolis, in Egypt

April
- 20   Allies lay siege to Genoa in northern Italy

May
- 15   French forces enter the Great St. Bernard Pass in the Alps

June
- 2   French forces occupy Milan
- 4   French surrender Genoa
- 9   Battle of Montebello
- 14   Battle of Marengo; Kléber assassinated in Cairo
- 15   Austrians conclude armistice by which they agree to evacuate northern Italy
- 19   Battle of Höchstädt on the Rhine front

July
- 28   Truce agreed between French and Austrians on the Rhine front

September
- 5   French garrison on Malta capitulates

December
- 3   Battle of Hohenlinden, Rhine front
- 16   Denmark and Sweden join Russia in League of Armed Neutrality against Britain
- 18   Prussia joins League of Armed Neutrality
- 25   French and Austrians sign armistice

1801

January
- 1   Act of Union joins Ireland to Britain

February
- 4   William Pitt, British prime minister, resigns, to be replaced by Henry Addington
- 8   Peace concluded between France and Austria by Treaty of Lunéville

March
- 8   British expeditionary force lands in Egypt
- 20–21   Battle of Alexandria
- 23   Tsar Paul I of Russia assassinated
- 28   Peace concluded between France and Naples by Treaty of Florence

April
- 2   Battle of Copenhagen

July
- 6, 12   First and Second Battles of Algeciras, off Spanish coast
- 15   Bonaparte concludes Concordat with Pope Pius VII

August
- 31   French army in Egypt capitulates

October
- 1   Preliminary treaty of peace concluded by Britain and France at Amiens

1802

February
- 5   French expeditionary force lands in St. Domingue, in the West Indies

March
- 25   Definitive version of Treaty of Amiens concluded

August
- 2   Bonaparte proclaimed Consul for life

October
- 15   French troops invade Switzerland

1803

May
- 2   United States agrees to purchase Louisiana Territory from France

1807

February
3   Battle of Jankovo, East Prussia
7–8   Battle of Eylau, East Prussia
19   British fleet enters the Dardanelles

March
18   French lay siege to Danzig, in East Prussia

May
27   Danzig surrenders

June
10–11   Battle of Heilsberg, East Prussia
14   Battle of Friedland, East Prussia
25   Napoleon and Tsar Alexander meet on the River Niemen

July
7   France and Russian conclude peace at Tilsit
9   France and Prussia conclude peace at Tilsit
19   French issue ultimatum to Portugal demanding conformance with Continental System

September
2–5   British naval force bombards Copenhagen

October
27   France and Spain conclude Treaty of Fontainebleau

November
23   Napoleon issues first Milan Decree
30   French troops enter Lisbon

December
17   Napoleon issues second Milan Decree

1808

February
16   Beginning of French invasion of Spain

March
17   King Charles IV of Spain abdicates
24   French troops enter Madrid

April
17   Conference at Bayonne opens

May
2   Popular uprising in Madrid

June
6   Joseph Bonaparte proclaimed King of Spain
15   First siege of Saragossa begins

July
14   Battle of Medina del Rio Seco
20   French surrender at Bailén

August
1   Murat becomes King of Naples; British troops land in Portugal
16   Action at Roliça
17   French abandon siege of Saragossa
21   Battle of Vimiero
22   Convention of Cintra concluded

September
27   Congress of Erfurt between Napoleon and Tsar Alexander

November
5   Battle of Valmeseda
10   Battles of Espinosa de los Monteros and Gamonal
23   Battle of Tudela
29–30   Action at Somosierra

December
20   Second siege of Saragossa begins
21   Battle of Sahagún
29   Action at Benevente

1809

January
16   Battle of Corunna

February
20   Saragossa surrenders to the French

March
28   Battle of Medellín

April
11–16   British naval attack on the Basque and Aix Roads
16   Battle of Sacile, Italian front
20   Battle of Abensberg
21   French troops capture Landshut
22   Battle of Eggmühl; Wellesley assumes command of British forces in Portugal
23   Storming of Ratisbon

May

3 Battle of Ebersberg
12 Battle of Oporto
13 French occupy Vienna
21–22 Battle of Aspern-Essling

June

14 Battle of Raab

July

5–6 Battle of Wagram
10–11 Battle of Znaim
12 Austrians conclude armistice with the French
27–29 Battle of Talavera

October

14 Treaty of Schönbrunn concluded between France and Austria

November

19 Battle of Ocaña

December

15 Napoleon and Josephine divorce

1810

February

5 French begin investment of Cádiz
20 Execution of Tyrolean rebel leader Andreas Hofer

April

2 Napoleon and Marie Louise of Austria marry in Paris

July

1 Louis Bonaparte abdicates as King of Holland
9 France annexes Holland

September

27 Battle of Busaco

October

10 French troops arrive before the Lines of Torres Vedras

November

16 French retreat from the Lines of Torres Vedras

1811

January

26 French besiege Badajoz

March

5 Battle of Barrosa
9 Badajoz surrenders to the French
11 Birth of a son to Napoleon and Marie Louise

May

7 British lay siege to Badajoz
16 Battle of Albuera

June

20 French relieve Badajoz

September

25 Battle of El Bodón

1812

January

20 Wellington captures Ciudad Rodrigo

March

16 Wellington begins third siege of Badajoz

May

28 Treaty of Bucharest ends Russo-Turkish War

June

19 United States declares war on Britain
22 Grande Armée invades Russia
28 French occupy Vilna

July

8 French occupy Minsk
22 Battle of Salamanca
25–26 Battle of Ostronovo
28 French occupy Vitebsk

August

8 Battle of Inkovo
12 Wellington enters Madrid
14 First Battle of Krasnyi
16–18 Battle of Polotsk
24 French abandon siege of Cádiz
26 Kutuzov appointed Russian commander-in-chief

September

7 Battle of Borodino
14 French army occupies Moscow
19 Wellington lays siege to Burgos

October

18 Battle of Vinkovo

19 French army abandons Moscow and begins to retreat west
21 Wellington retreats from Burgos
24 Battle of Maloyaroslavets
30 Wellington abandons Madrid

November
17 Second Battle of Krasnyi
25–29 French forces cross the Berezina River

December
5 Napoleon leaves the Grande Armée for Paris
8 French troops reach Vilna
14 Last French troops reach the Niemen River
28 Convention of Tauroggen between Prussian and Russian forces

1813
February
7 Russian troops enter Warsaw

March
12 French troops abandon Hamburg
13 Prussia declares war on France
27 Allied troops occupy Dresden

April
3 Battle of Möckern

May
2 Battle of Lützen
8 French troops occupy Dresden
20–21 Battle of Bautzen
27 French abandon Madrid

June
2 British lay siege to Tarragona
4 Armistice agreed between French and Allies in Germany
12 British abandon siege of Tarragona; French evacuate Burgos
21 Battle of Vitoria
28 Siege of San Sebastian begins
30 Siege of Pamplona begins

July
7 Sweden joins the Sixth Coalition
19 Austria agrees to join the Allies
28–30 Battle of Sorauren

August
12 Austria declares war on France

23 Battle of Grossbeeren
26 Battle of Pirna
26–27 Battle of Dresden
30 Battle of Kulm
31 British capture San Sebastian; Battle of Vera; Battle of San Marcial

September
6 Battle of Dennewitz

October
7 Wellington crosses the Bidassoa River
9 Battle of Düben
14 Action at Liebertwolkwitz
16–19 Battle of Leipzig
18 Saxony defects to the Allies
30 Battle of Hanau
31 French surrender Pamplona

November
10 Battle of the Nivelle
11 French surrender Dresden

December
9–12 Battle of the Nive
13 Battle of St. Pierre

1814
January
11 Naples joins the Allies
14 Denmark concludes peace with the Allies at Kiel
27 Battle of St. Dizier
29 Battle of Brienne

February
1 Battle of La Rothière
3 Negotiations for peace begin at Châtillon-sur-Seine
10 Battle of Champaubert
11 Battle of Montmirail
12 Battle of Château-Thierry
14 Battle of Vauchamps
17 Battle of Valjouan
18 Battle of Montereau
26 British lay siege to Bayonne
27 Battle of Orthez
27–28 Battle of Meaux

March
7 Battle of Craonne
9 Allies conclude Treaty of Chaumont
9–10 Battle of Laon

13   Battle of Rheims

20   Battle of Arcis-sur-Aube

25   Battle of La-Fère-Champenoise

31   Action at Montmartre; Paris surrenders

April

6   Napoleon abdicates unconditionally

10   Battle of Toulouse

14   Action at Bayonne

17   Marshal Soult surrenders to Wellington, ending the Peninsular War

28   Napoleon leaves for Elba

30   (First) Treaty of Paris concluded between France and the Allies

May

27   French forces surrender Hamburg

July

5   Battle of Chippewa

25   Battle of Lundy's Lane

November

1   Congress of Vienna convenes

December

24   Treaty of Ghent concludes war between Britain and the United States

1815

January

8   Battle of New Orleans

February

26   Napoleon leaves Elba for France

March

1   Napoleon lands in France

15   Naples, still under Murat's rule, declares war on Austria

19   Bourbons leave Paris

20   Napoleon reaches Paris and returns to power

25   Allies form Seventh Coalition

May

2–3   Battle of Tolentino

June

9   Congress of Vienna closes

16   Battles of Ligny and Quatre Bras

18   Battle of Waterloo; Battle of Wavre

22   Napoleon abdicates

September

26   Holy Alliance concluded between Russia, Prussia, Austria and other powers

November

20   (Second) Treaty of Paris concluded between France and the Allies; Quadruple Alliance agreed between Britain, Austria, Russia, and Prussia

Glossary of Military Terms

The terminology associated with warfare on land and at sea during the period 1792–1815 is very large and can fill several books. Siege warfare alone produced a unique language of its own, mainly connected with the parts of fortifications and the craft associated with their defense or reduction. Below are some of the technical terms referred to in this work, as well as others commonly associated with the period.

à cheval: mounted

à pied: on foot

abatis: barricade of felled trees or interwoven branches

adjutant-general: staff colonel sometimes assigned to serve as a chief of staff at division or corps level

Afrancesados: Spanish Francophiles, associated with those who supported the French occupation of Spain from 1808

aide-de-camp: junior staff officer attached to a general or marshal

Amalgame: amalgamation of regular French infantry regiments and volunteer units to form a composite units

approaches: trenches or siege lines dug toward the enemy positions

arme blanche: generic term for cavalry

ataman: senior Cossack officer

Bashkirs: primitively armed and equipped light cavalry from Asiatic Russia

bastion: four-sided fortification

battery: gun emplacement or company of artillery; batteries could number six, eight or twelve guns

breaking ground: beginning a siege

breastplate: steel plate worn by cuirassiers to protect their fronts; badge worn on the shoulder-belt

breastwork: parapet, usually on a field fortification, to protect the defenders

brigade: tactical formation consisting of two or more battalions of infantry or regiments of cavalry

cadre: important officers, enlisted men and other staff needed to organize and train a unit

caisson: ammunition wagon

caliber the internal diameter of the barrel of the weapon, and approximately the diameter of the projectile fired

canister: artillery ammunition consisting of small lead balls encased in a tin

cannon: informal term for artillery piece

carbine: short cavalry musket

carabinier: type of heavily-armed cavalryman, similar to a cuirassier

carbine: type of musket carried by cavalry, shorter and lighter than the standard infantry musket

carriage: wooden frame which supports the barrel of a cannon

cartouche: cartridge box

case shot: type of artillery ammunition, effectively the same as canister

chasseurs à cheval: light cavalry

chasseurs à pied : light infantry

chef: colonel-proprietor of a regiment in the Russian Army

chef de bataillon: major; commander of a French battalion

chef d'escadron: major; commander of a cavalry squadron

cheval-de-frise: planks or beams studded with spikes or blades, used as a barricade

chevauléger/chevau-léger: light cavalry, usually French

chevauxléger: light cavalry, usually German

chouan: Royalist insurgent from Brittany

citadel: component of a fortification, consisting of four or five sides

class: annual proportion of the population liable

cockade: rosette bearing the national colors worn on a hat or helmet

color/colour: infantry flag, battalion or regimental

commissariat: army department responsible for supply

company: small tactical unit of infantry or cavalry, or battery of artillery; a subdivision of a battalion

cornet: lowest officer rank in the cavalry; second lieutenant corps: self-contained formation, and the largest tactical unit in an army, containing elements of infantry, cavalry, artillery, and staff; a corps consisted of two or more divisions

Cortes: the parliament of Spain

Cossack: generic name for irregular Russian cavalry

court-martial: military court

cuirass: metal breastplate or backplate worn by heavy cavalry

cuirassier: heavy cavalrymen wearing a steel cuirass and helmet

debouch: to issue from a ravine or wood into open ground

defile: narrow way through which troops can only march on a very confined front

demi-brigade: French unit of the Revolutionary period consisting of one regular and two volunteer or conscript battalions

department/*département:* geographical sub-division of France used for administrative purposes

division: military formation comprising two or more brigades, comprising several thousand infantry and cavalry supported by artillery

dragoon: medium cavalry capable of fighting mounted or on foot, though almost invariably playing the former role

eagle: standard consisting of an bronze Imperial eagle mounted on a staff and presented to most units of the French Army from 1804

embrasure: opening of a parapet of a fortress or field fortification through which artillery (or small arms) could be fired

émigrés: Royalists who fled France after the outbreak of Revolution in 1789

enfilade: to fire on the flank of an opponent

ensign: the lowest rank in the infantry; second lieutenant

Erzherzog: Archduke; an Austrian title

escadron: squadron of cavalry

esplanade: open area separating a citadel from surrounding buildings

état-major: regimental staff

evolution: drill movement, including marching and weapons handling

facings: distinctive colors on a uniform, usually the collar and cuffs, which differentiate units

fascine: bundle of brushwood used to fortify a position or to fill ditches during an assault

field marshal: highest rank in the British, Russian, and Prussian armies

foot: infantry

flêche (modern spelling, *flèche*): V-shaped fortification whose rear is left open, from the French for "arrow"

flintlock: most common form of musket of the eighteenth and early nineteenth centuries

forlorn hope: advance storming party, usually that sent ahead of the main assault into the breach of a city or fortress wall

Freiherr: title used throughout German-speaking territories, roughly equivalent to *Baron*

Freikorps: independently-raised units, usually from Prussia or Austria; bands of volunteers

Fürst: title used in German-speaking territories, roughly equivalent to *Prince*

fusil: musket

gabion: wicker basket filled with earth used in fortification

général de brigade: rank in the French army usually accorded to the senior officer commanding a brigade; brigadier general

général de division: rank in the French army usually accorded to the senior officer commanding a division; major general

glacis: slope leading up to a fortification

Graf: Title used in German-speaking territories, roughly equivalent to *Count*

Grapeshot: type of artillery ammunition, only effective at short range, consisting of a cloth bag filled with musket balls which spread on leaving the barrel

grand battery: tactical amalgamation of several artillery batteries in order to produce a massive concentration of fire

Grande Armée: From 1805, the main body of the French army and any allied forces serving under Napoleon's personal command

grenadier: elite infantry, no longer armed with hand grenades, often used to spearhead an attack; they could operate as entire units or form a single company of a battalion

Grenzer: troops serving on the Austrian frontiers with the Ottoman Empire

guard: term accorded to elite troops, usually regarded as the best in the army; in both French and German, spelled "Garde"

guerrilla: irregular fighter

guidon: cavalry standard

gun: an artillery piece (cannon); not to be confused with small arms, which were known by type, that is, musket, fusil, rifle, pistol, etc.

handspike: metal lever used to manhandle a cannon into a desired position

haversack: bag carried by an infantryman containing food and personal effects, usually worn slung on the hip, as opposed to a knapsack

hornwork: part of a fortification comprising the front of a bastion and two side extensions horse artillery: light caliber guns drawn by horse teams whose crew either rode on the limbers or on horseback, thus giving them greater speed over the foot artillery

howitzer: short-barrelled cannon used to lob shells using a high trajectory

Hundred Days, The: term used to describe the period of Napoleon's short reign between March and June 1815

hussar: type of elaborately costumed light cavalry; originally Hungarian

Imperial Guard: elite formation of the French and Russian armies, in the case of the former divided into the Young, Middle, and Old Guard. This formed Napoleon's tactical reserve and was seldom committed to battle until the campaign of 1813

invest: in siege warfare, to surround a town or city in preparation for the establishment of formal siege works

Insurrection: militia from Hungary and Croatia

Jäger/jäger: literally, huntsman, in German; rifleman or other type of light infantryman, usually from a German-speaking area

Junker: East Prussian aristocracy

Kalmuk: type of light cavalry from Asiatic Russia

knapsack: pack wore by infantry on the back

Korps: Austrian army corps

Krümper: Prussian reservist serving between 1808 and 1812

lancer: light cavalryman armed with a lance

Landwehr: militia or newly-recruited infantry unit, from German-speaking states

légère: light, indicating types of infantry or cavalry

legion/*légion:* a military formation usually consisting of a combination of infantry, cavalry and artillery, often of foreign troops forming part of another army

levée en masse: universal male conscription introduced by the French during a period of national emergency in 1793

light dragoon: type of light cavalry

ligne: line; standard form of (usually) infantry meant to fight in the battle line

light infantry: equipped like line infantry, but employed in a more mobile capacity on the battlefield, especially by operating in open, or skirmish, order

limber: two-wheeled carriage with ammunition box which connects a team of horses to a cannon to facilitate movement

limber up: to attach a cannon to a limber in order to move the former

line: in French, ligne; for example, standard form of (usually) infantry meant to fight in the battle line

"line infantry" or "infantry of the line" (*infanterie de la ligne*)

line of communication: route behind an army, either by road or river or both, by which supplies, reinforcements, and couriered messages traveled

line of march: general route taken by an army on the march

line operations: as with line of march, but normally applied to enemy territory

line of retreat: general route of withdrawal taken by a (usually defeated) army

loophole: opening made in a wall to enable the defenders to fire through with small arms

lunette: triangular fortification atop a glacis or beside a ravelin

magazine: place of storage for ammunition

Mameluke: from the Turkish *mamluk* (slave), a type of Egyptian horseman, variously and elaborately armed, though also referring to those serving in the French Imperial Guard

marines: troops specifically trained to fight at sea

marshal: highest rank in the French Army from May 1804

militia: forces raised for home defense

National Guard: troops raised in France (*Garde Nationale*) for home defense

Oberst: colonel

opolchenye: untrained Russian militia

Ordenança: Portuguese militia

outpost: infantry or cavalry occupying an advanced position to facilitate observation of the enemy or early warning of its approach

palisade: sharpened wooden stakes used mainly for defense against cavalry

parallel: large trench dug during siege operations which runs parallel to the enemy fortification; manned by troops and supplies in anticipation of the assault

parapet: stone wall or bank of earth offering protection to troops occupying a fortified position

partisans: guerrillas; irregular troops

piece: a cannon, regardless of caliber

picket/*picquet:* sentry or a small outpost

pioneer: regimental carpenter or other skilled craftsman

pontoon: boats specifically designed to be laid adjacent to one another to form a bridge

pontonnier: engineer trained to build pontoons or temporary bridges

quarters: soldiers' accommodation, whether barracks or civilian lodgings

rampart: wall of earth or stone comprising the main part of a fortress

ravelin: detached, triangular-shaped fortification positioned in front of a fortress wall redoubt: field fortification, usually dug just prior to battle, armed with infantry and often artillery

representative on mission/*représentant en mission:* deputy of the Convention or other Revolutionary government official, armed with sweeping powers, sent on specific missions to various regions or armies; political commissars

rifle: infantry firearm with a grooved or "rifled" bore, thus providing spin—and therefore greater accuracy—than its smooth-bore counterpart, the ordinary musket

round shot: the most common form of artillery ammunition, consisting of a solid cast-iron sphere, now commonly referred to as a "cannonball"; the weight of the ball varied according to the caliber of the gun from which it was fired

saber/sabre: cavalry sword with a curved blade, generally used by light cavalry and general officers

sap: narrow siege trench

sapper/*sapeur:* combat engineer; often used to construct or demolish field fortifications, and to dig saps during siege operations

sans-culottes: extremist revolutionaries in France, generally associated with Paris

Schützen: German riflemen

shako: cylindrical military headdress, usually of leather, with a peak and usually a chin-strap

shell: explosive projectile

shot: abbreviation for round shot, the most common form of artillery ammunition

shrapnel: type of artillery ammunition, unique to the British Army, consisting of a hollow sphere packed with musket balls and powder, which when detonated in the air by a fuse showered its target with its contents

skirmisher: soldier operating in open or extended order to snipe at the enemy individually or as part of a screen to mask friendly troops

spiking: the means by which a cannon can be made inoperable by the hammering of a spike down the touchhole

squadron: subdivision of a cavalry regiment, usually consisting of two companies or troops

square: infantry formation assumed as a defense against cavalry

standard: cavalry flag, usually rectangular in shape

sutler: camp-follower who sells food and drink to soldiers, either on the march or in camp

tirailleur: skirmisher or light infantryman, usually French and serving together as a unit rather than in the light company of a line regiment

train: transport service of an army, responsible for conveying supplies, artillery, bridging equipment, and all the other paraphernalia of war

Tricolor: French national flag, adopted during the Revolution, consisting of blue, white and red bands

troop: unit of cavalry smaller than a squadron, usually the equivalent of an infantry company

uhlan: Polish for *lancer,* usually applied to those serving in German-speaking states or in the Russian Army

vedette: cavalry sentry or scout

vivandière: female sutleress who accompanies an army on campaign and provides food and sundry services, such as cooking and clothes washing, for a fee

voltigeur: from the French for "vaulter," a light infantryman usually serving in the light company of a line regiment, usually deployed in extended order to form a skirmisher screen ahead of infantry or cavalry

winter quarters: the quarters occupied by an army during that season, when fighting usually entered a period of hiatus until spring

Glossary of Naval Terms

aloft: up in the masts or rigging

amiral: admiral in the French Navy

astern: behind the vessel

boarding: coming aboard an enemy vessel by force

bow: the forward (front-most) part of a vessel

brig: a lightly-armed (ca. 14 guns), maneuverable, square-rigged, two-masted vessel, smaller than a sloop

broadside: the simultaneous firing of all the guns positioned on one side of the ship

canister shot: a type of ammunition consisting of a cylindrical tin case packed with many iron balls which when fired from a cannon at short range spread out to kill and maim enemy personnel

carronade: a short-barrelled, heavy calibre gun used only at close range for devastating results against the enemy's hull and crew; only the Royal Navy carried such weapons, which were not counted in the rating of vessel

chain shot: a type of ammunition comprising two iron spheres or half-spheres, connected by a short length of chain, mainly used to damage rigging and sails

contre-amiral: rear admiral in the French Navy

double: to attack an enemy vessel from both sides simultaneously

fireship: vessel packed with combustibles, steered into the enemy, and set on fire

flagship: the ship of the officer commanding a squadron or fleet, usually a vice- or rear-admiral, and flying his flag

fleet: a force of more than ten warships

flotilla: a force of small vessels, sometimes troop ships and gun boats

frigate: a single-decked warship mounting between 24 and 44 guns

grapeshot: a type of ammunition consisting of a canvas bag filled with small iron balls which when fired from a cannon spread out to kill and maim enemy personnel

grog: drink made from a mixture of rum and water

gun: a cannon; these fired round shot weighing between 12 and 36 lbs; small arms, technically speaking, were not "guns," but referred to by their specific type, for example, musket, pistol, etc.

line ahead: formation by which all vessels follow one another in a line, bow to stern; the standard formation for attack

line of battle: the positioning of warships in a line with their broadsides facing an enemy against whom they intend to engage in battle

line of battle ship: ship of the line; vessels carrying at least 64 guns and thus large enough to sail in the line of battle, as opposed to frigates and other, smaller vessels

magazine: place of storage for ammunition

marines: troops specifically trained to fight at sea

port: the lefthand side of a ship when looking toward the bow; opposite of "*starboard*"

prize: a captured enemy vessel

rake: to fire at an enemy ship's bow or stern when it is at right angle to one's one vessel, so enabling the shot to travel down the length of the enemy ship

ship: in distinction from a boat, a square-rigged vessel with three masts

ship of the line: warship carrying a minimum of 64 guns that by virtue of its size and armament could fight in a line of battle; the standard type was the 74

sloop: a single-decked warship slightly smaller than a sixth-rate (frigate) but larger than a brig

starboard: the right-hand side of a vessel as one looks forward; opposite of "*port*"

stern: the rear-most part of the hull, usually ornamented and especially vulnerable to enemy fire

strike (one's colors): to haul down the national flag to indicate a desire to surrender

tack: to change course by turning the bow through the wind

vice-amiral: vice admiral in the French Navy

wear: to change a ship's course by turning her stern to windward; opposite of tacking

R

Raab, Battle of (14 June 1809)

A decisive victory for the (French) Army of Italy over the (Austrian) Army of Inner Austria near the city of Raab (now Györ) in Hungary during the War of the Fifth Coalition. The victory enabled the French under Napoleon's 28-year-old stepson, Prince Eugène de Beauharnais, Viceroy of Italy, to reinforce Napoleon prior to the Battle of Wagram.

When the 1809 Franco-Austrian war began, Archduke John led the Austrian Army of Italy into northern Italy to engage the French Army of Italy, composed largely of Italian troops, under Eugène de Beauharnais. After initial success, John was ordered to retire to Austria to join Archduke Charles's retreating army. Eugène pursued him into Hungary, where the two armies met outside Raab, where John had been joined by Archduke Joseph, Palatine (Viceroy) of Hungary, with 20,000 insurrection troops (poorly equipped militia called out in emergencies).

After some skirmishing on 13 June, John took up a defensive position south of Raab, near the river Danube along the higher ground behind the Páncza stream, whose marshy banks made it largely impassable to artillery and cavalry. In the center, the stone-built Kismegyer farm complex guarded the main crossing. John deployed most of his cavalry on the southern flank under *Feldmarschalleutnant* Johann Freiherr von Mecsèry; *Feldmarschalleutnant* Hieronymus Graf Colloredo-Mansfeld's mixed infantry held the Kismegyer village area, with *Feldmarschalleutnant* Franz Jellacic Freiherr von Buzim's Reserve behind them. The right flank under *Feldmarschalleutnant* Johann Freiherr von Frimont was comprised of the regular cavalry and some insurrection troopers.

Eugène's Franco-Italian army enjoyed a significant artillery advantage with about 70 guns, alongside 28,000 infantry and 12,000 cavalry. General Emmanuel, marquis de Grouchy, who commanded the right wing (dragoons and General Louis-Pierre Montbrun's light cavalry), was to force a crossing over the southern Páncza, while Eugène directed generals Jean Seras and Paul Grenier's infantry assault in the center, and General Jacques, comte Lauriston guarded the northern section of the stream.

After Grouchy's first attack was beaten off, the French artillery pounded the Austrian positions, and from 2:00 P.M. Grenier's corps launched a series of assaults during which Kismegyer farm changed hands five times before Jellacic's reserve finally repulsed the attack around 4:00 P.M. However, in the south, Montbrun's cavalry had outflanked and defeated Mecsèry's insurrection cavalry. Grouchy had located a ford and threw the rest of his cavalry across into the left of the Austrian center to support Grenier's renewed assault. John drew in his left wing, but by 4:15 P.M. the farm had fallen to the infantry of the Italian Guard. Lauriston now crossed the stream to enage Frimont and, in danger of encirclement, John was forced to order a general retreat eastward. Both sides sustained about 3,000 casualties, but the Austrians also lost a similar number of prisoners.

Rohan Saravanamuttu

See also Beauharnais, Eugène Rose de; Charles, Archduke of Austria, Duke of Teschen; Eggmühl, Battle of; Fifth Coalition, War of the; Grouchy, Emmanuel, marquis de; John, Archduke; Lauriston, Jacques Alexandre, comte; Montbrun, Louis-Pierre; Wagram, Battle of

References and further reading
Petre, F. Loraine. 1990. *Napoleon and the Archduke Charles: A History of the Franco-Austrian Campaign in the Valley of the Danube in 1809*. London: Greenhill.
Wöber, Ferdi I. 2001. *1809 Schlacht bei Raab* [Battle of Raab]. Maria Anzbach: Self-published.

Radetzky von Radetz, Johann Joseph Wenzel Graf (1766–1858)

Chief of the general staff of the Austrian armies against Napoleon and commanding general of Austrian forces during the revolution of 1848 in Italy. In his youth, Radetzky proved his bravery as a soldier; he was wounded numerous times, and he was noted for his intelligence and initiative. As a commander, he demonstrated concern for his soldiers and proposed innovations such as officer training schools, peacetime army maneuvers, and the use of militia (*Landwehr*). He hated bureaucracy and battled the rigid regulations and stagnation of the Habsburg imperial court. His strategic sense, however, led to the victories in 1813 and 1848–1849 that saved the faltering Habsburg Empire.

Radetzky was born on 2 November 1766 at Trebnice, south of Prague, on the holdings of his father, Peter Graf Euseb. He enlisted in a cuirassier regiment in 1784 and saw his first action in the war against Turkey in 1788–1789. During the French Revolutionary Wars, he led a cavalry charge at Fleurus (26 June 1794) and was promoted to captain. In 1796, he was a member of Jean de Beaulieu's staff facing Bonaparte's French army in northern Italy. During the War of the Second Coalition, he attained the rank of colonel and served at the Trebbia, Novi, Marengo, and Hohenlinden. In 1805, he was a *Generalmajor* under Archduke Charles in Italy. After assisting the archduke in reform efforts for the Austrian Army, in 1809 he commanded *Feldmarschalleutnant* Johann von Hiller's rear guard. For service at and after the Battle of Wagram (5–6 July 1809), he was promoted to *Feldmarschalleutnant*. As chief of the general staff, he tried again to reorganize and modernize the Austrian Army, but he faced an impossible task in the face of conservative opposition in Vienna.

Before Austria joined the Sixth Coalition in 1813, the forty-six-year-old Radetzky helped to assemble and organize an army of over 200,000 men under *Feldmarschall* Karl Fürst zu Schwarzenberg. He authored the Trachenberg Plan (12 July 1813), which guided Allied strategy during the autumn campaign in Germany. While Allied commanders were instructed to avoid battles in which Napoleon himself commanded, they were to seize the offensive against the French emperor's line of communications and any detached corps. This method led to Napoleon's expulsion from Germany after the Battle of Leipzig (16–19 October).

Radetzky urged Emperor Francis I to have Schwarzenberg's army lead the invasion of France in 1814, but Austria's chancellor, Klemens Fürst Metternich, for political reasons, did not endorse this strategy. Radetzky was not allowed to contribute further to the overall Austrian planning. Thus, Field Marshal Gebhard von Blücher's Prussians led the Allied advance toward Paris, prompting Napoleon's abdication in April, while Schwarzenberg's army crept securely along the Aube and Seine rivers.

After Napoleon's defeat at Waterloo and his second abdication in 1815, Radetzky held minor posts in the Austrian Empire while the Habsburg army was allowed to deteriorate. However, as a result of nationalistic revolts in Italy in 1830, he was sent to quell the unrest as commanding general of Lombardy-Venetia. He was promoted to field marshal in 1836. Milan rebelled against Austrian authority on 18 March 1848, and after five days of street fighting, Radetzky withdrew his army of 50,000 men to the Quadrilateral, the complex of fortresses at Legnano, Mantua, Peshciera, and Verona. Although Venice fell, Radetzky's forces held firm and routed the coalition of Italians at Custozza on 24–25 July, a victory that may have saved the Austrian Empire and turned the tide of revolutions in Europe. Radetzky recaptured Milan and, in a masterful campaign, invaded Piedmont, ending the Italian revolt with a decisive victory over the armies of King Charles Albert at Novara (23 March 1849). Thereafter, he served as governor-general of Lombardy-Venetia, harshly repressing Italian nationalism, until 1857. Following his death on 5 January 1858, he was honored by Johann Strauss the Elder's *Radetzky March*, the musical tribute to the savior of imperial Austria.

Llewellyn D. Cook Jr.

See also Austrian Army; Blücher von Wahlstatt, Gebhard Lebrecht Fürst; Charles, Archduke of Austria, Duke of Teschen; Fifth Coalition, War of the; Fleurus, Battle of; France, Campaign in; Francis I, Emperor; Germany, Campaign in; Leipzig, Battle of; Marengo, Battle of; Metternich, Klemens Wenzel Lothar Fürst; Novi, Battle of; Quadrilateral, The; Schwarzenberg, Karl Philipp Fürst zu; Second Coalition, War of the; Trebbia, Battle of the; Wagram, Battle of

References and further reading
Rothenberg, Gunther E. 1982. *Napoleon's Great Adversary: Archduke Charles and the Austrian Army, 1792–1814.* London: Batsford.
Sked, Alan. 1979. *The Survival of the Habsburg Empire: Radetsky, the Imperial Army, and the Class War of 1848.* New York: Longman.

Rapp, Jean, comte (1771–1821)

French general Jean Rapp survived numerous wounds and served as one of Napoleon's most valued aides. His reputation is one of courage and physical resilience, but Rapp was an intelligent and able administrator as well.

Rapp was born in Colmar on 27 April 1771. His father was a devout Lutheran and had hopes that Jean would someday become a pastor. The young Rapp did receive a good education in preparation for a pastoral career, but his physical strength and adventurous nature led him to join a French cavalry regiment in 1788. He worked his way up the noncommissioned ranks while establishing a reputation for toughness in battle. In two separate actions in 1793, Rapp suffered a saber cut and a bullet wound. He was made lieutenant in 1794. At Ligenfeld on 28 May 1795 Rapp received several saber cuts on his head and left arm.

His conspicuous gallantry made him a desirable aide-de-camp, and he was soon on the staff of General Louis Desaix. In this role, he was wounded at Kehl in 1797, and was promoted to captain. Later that same year, Rapp accompanied Desaix to Italy and met General Bonaparte. Rapp was part of the expedition to Egypt in 1798, fighting in virtually every engagement there. He was wounded in the left shoulder at Samahoud, 22 January 1799. Promoted to colonel, he helped in negotiations with the British for the evacuation of French troops remaining in Egypt after Bonaparte's departure in August 1799. Rapp and Desaix returned to France in May 1800, and both men fought at the Battle of Marengo, 14 June 1800. Desaix was mortally wounded in the battle, and died on the field in Rapp's arms.

Napoleon made Rapp one of his own aides after the death of Desaix. Rapp served in a variety of roles from 1800 to 1805. He was an intelligence officer, a military inspector, and a diplomatic envoy, and he organized a squadron of Mamelukes in Marseilles for service in Napoleon's Imperial Guard. Rapp was promoted to general in 1803. As part of Napoleon's inner circle, he was a friend of Josephine, although plans for a marriage with one of her nieces fell through. Instead, in 1805 Napoleon arranged a marriage for Rapp with fourteen-year-old Rosalie Vanlerberghe, the daughter of an important manufacturer of munitions. Later in 1805, Rapp accompanied Napoleon on his famous Austerlitz campaign. At the Battle of Austerlitz, 2 December 1805, Rapp led a charge at the head of the Mamelukes and other Imperial Guard cavalry against a counterattack by the Russian Imperial Guard cavalry. Despite receiving several saber cuts, Rapp repulsed the Russians, capturing many of them, including Prince Repnin.

After Austerlitz, Rapp was promoted to *général de division,* and continued gathering intelligence and inspecting military formations. He accompanied Napoleon on the Jena campaign of 1806, and led a charge at Schleiz on 9 October. During the campaign in Poland against the Russians, he was wounded at Golymin on 26 December. The bullet wound almost necessitated the amputation of his left arm, but Rapp refused the operation. In 1807 he became governor of Danzig. Rapp's organizational abilities were put to use in raising the Polish light cavalry regiment for Napoleon's Imperial Guard. In 1809 the Emperor made Rapp a count and allowed him to leave his duties in Danzig temporarily, in order to serve with the staff in the campaign against Austria. The general distinguished himself at Aspern-Essling. Also in 1809 Rapp helped stop an assassination attempt on Napoleon by a knife-wielding young German named Staps. The following year, Rapp was briefly out of favor with Napoleon. The general feigned illness in

order to avoid attending the marriage of the Emperor and his second wife, Marie Louise. As a friend of Josephine, Rapp did not favor Napoleon's divorce from her. Rapp's own arranged marriage ended in divorce in 1811, a process facilitated by the general's relationship with Julie Boettcher, who bore him two children.

When Napoleon invaded Russia in 1812, Rapp initially fulfilled his duties as governor of Danzig, but later rejoined the Emperor's staff at Smolensk. Rapp fought at Borodino on 7 September, and received three minor wounds and one serious bullet wound in his thigh. During the retreat from Moscow, Cossacks ambushed Napoleon and his staff. Rapp's horse was killed in the ensuing melee, and the Emperor narrowly escaped being killed or captured. Later in the retreat, Rapp, though suffering badly from frostbite, fought alongside Marshal Michel Ney in the rear guard. Rapp resumed his duties at Danzig after the Russian campaign, and prepared to defend it against imminent attack. Prussian and Russian forces besieged Danzig from January through November of 1813. His garrison decimated by disease, Rapp finally surrendered on terms. He and his men were held as prisoners in and around Kiev until Napoleon's first abdication in the spring of 1814.

Rapp commanded French forces guarding the Rhine during the Hundred Days in 1815. Napoleon had great faith in his former aide-de-camp, for Rapp had less than 30,000 men with which to face a gathering Allied army of around 200,000 troops. While Napoleon took the main French army into Belgium, Rapp organized a remarkably effective defense in Alsace, using a combination of fortified garrisons and limited counterattacks. He was able to claim a small victory at La Suffel on 28 June. Napoleon had already been defeated at Waterloo ten days earlier. Rapp resigned himself to the Bourbon restoration after Napoleon's second abdication and exile. Rapp remarried (Mademoiselle Rotberg) and had two more children. He was given some ceremonial posts, but developed cancer and died at the age of fifty on 8 November 1821.

Ralph Ashby

See also Aspern-Essling, Battle of; Austerlitz, Battle of; Borodino, Battle of; Cossacks; Desaix, Louis-Charles-Antoine, chevalier de Veygoux; Fifth Coalition, War of the; Fourth Coalition, War of the; Germany, Campaign in; Golymin, Battle of; Imperial Guard (French); Jena-Auerstädt Campaign; Josephine, Empress; Marengo, Battle of; Marie Louise, Empress; Middle East Campaign; Ney, Michel; Russian Campaign; Third Coalition, War of the; Waterloo, Battle of
References and further reading
Austin, Paul Britten. 1993. *1812: The March on Moscow.* London: Greenhill.
———. 1995. *1812: Napoleon in Moscow.* London: Greenhill.
———. 1996. *1812: The Great Retreat.* London: Greenhill.

Lachouque, Henry. 1997. *The Anatomy of Glory: Napoleon and His Guard.* Trans. Anne S. K. Brown. London: Greenhill.

Rapp, Jean, comte. *Memoirs of General Count Rapp, First Aide-de-Camp to Napoleon.* Cambridge: Ken Trotman. (Orig. pub. 1823.)

Rastatt, Battle of (5–9 July 1796)

Also known as the Battle of Malsch, this was the first (indecisive) engagement of the 1796 campaign in Germany between the (French) Army of the Rhine and Moselle under General Jean Moreau and the (Austrian) Army of the Upper Rhine under *Feldmarschalleutnant* Maximilian Graf Baillet von Latour, reinforced by troops brought from the lower Rhine by the overall Austrian commander, Archduke Charles.

After crossing the Rhine, Moreau marched his main force north to circumvent the Black Forest to reach the main road network. Pushing his central column through the forest, Moreau marched north and engaged the Austrians around Rastatt and Malsch until the advance of the French center threatened Austrian communications and forced Charles to withdraw. The Austrian retreat led quickly to the Holy Roman Empire's southern princelings making peace with the French.

The campaign had opened on the central Rhine, as French general Jean-Baptiste Jourdan's Army of the Sambre and Meuse was defeated at Wetzlar on 15 June by Archduke Charles and his Army of the Lower Rhine. To the south, Moreau's Army of the Rhine and Moselle had mounted diversions around Mannheim in mid-June to draw in the (Austrian) Army of the Upper Rhine under Latour. Suddenly on 23 June, Moreau's right under General Laurent Gouvion St. Cyr led the French army of 53,000 across the Rhine at Strasbourg. Moreau then marched north with General Louis Desaix's column down into the Rhine valley; General Pierre Marie Ferino marched south to cut off the Austrian left wing under *Feldmarschalleutnant* Michael Frieherr von Fröhlich around Freiburg. Between them, St. Cyr went east into the Black Forest and destroyed the Swabian District contingent of Holy Roman Empire troops to take Freudenstadt on 3 July. Latour had hastily marched south from Mannheim to the Murg River crossing at Rastatt with 10,000 Austrian troops. When news reached the archduke on 26 June, he left the Army of the Lower Rhine under *Feldzeugmeister* Wilhelm Ludwig Graf Wartensleben and marched south with 20,000 troops. The cautious Moreau moved slowly toward the northern end of the Black Forest and reached Rastatt on 5 July. Latour withdrew 15 kilometers east to Malsch, where Charles joined him the following day.

Moreau delayed his attack until he knew St. Cyr was approaching. This French column had turned north and marched down the Murg, forcing Charles to deploy *Generalmajor* Konrad Valentin Freiherr von Kaim's division to face him. The Austrian army was positioned around Malsch with about 38,000 troops facing a slightly larger French force. On 9 July, Desaix attacked Charles's right and after a desperate struggle, took the village. At the head of his troops, Charles led them forward and swept back into Malsch. The success was short-lived, as French troops again took the village and it was late afternoon before Austrian infantry could finally secure it. As Charles pushed Moreau toward Rastatt, news arrived of Kaim's defeat by St. Cyr around Rothenzholl in the Murg-Enz gap about 15 kilometers south of Malsch. St. Cyr could now cut Charles off from his communications in the Neckar valley. Both sides had suffered heavy casualties, so the next morning Charles withdrew toward Pforzheim.

David Hollins

See also Charles, Archduke of Austria, Duke of Teschen; Desaix, Louis-Charles-Antoine, chevalier de Veygoux; Gouvion St. Cyr, Laurent, comte; Holy Roman Empire; Jourdan, Jean-Baptiste; Moreau, Jean Victor; Rhine Campaigns (1792–1797)
References and further reading
Charles, Archduke. 1816. *Grundsätze der Strategie.* 2 vols. Vienna: Anton Strauss. Vol. 2 trans. George Nafziger as *Archduke Charles's 1796 Campaign in Germany* (West Chester, OH: Self-published, 2004).
Phipps, Ramsay Weston. 1980. *The Armies of the First French Republic and the Rise of the Marshals of Napoleon I.* Vol. 2, *The Armées de la Moselle, du Rhin, de Sambre-et-Meuse, de Rhin-et-Moselle.* London: Greenwood. (Orig. pub. 1926–1939.)

Ratisbon, Storming of (23 April 1809)

Scene of the last engagement of the Bavaria phase of the campaign of 1809, when Napoleon's Franco-Allied army seized the important city of Ratisbon (now Regensburg) on the Danube from Archduke Charles's retreating Austrian army. The brief defense of the city and installation of a pontoon bridge to the east enabled the Austrian army to escape into Bohemia. During the assault, Marshal Jean Lannes led his troops up ladders onto the walls, and Napoleon was wounded by a small artillery round.

Following his victory at Eggmühl on 22 April Napoleon summoned his first ever council of war, which decided to halt the army about 18 kilometers south of the city of Ratisbon (which the Austrians had captured two days earlier). That night, the main Austrian army (I–IV Korps and I Reserve Korps) began moving its heavy equipment over the city's vital stone bridge over the Danube, while a pontoon bridge was thrown 2 kilometers downstream to the east for the troops. Five battalions from II Korps defended the city, while 6,000 cavalry and some infantry battalions held the hilly ground outside.

At dawn on 23 April the French advance continued in a pincer movement toward Ratisbon, with General Louis-Pierre Montbrun coming from the southwest and Napoleon moving up from the south. Around 9:00 A.M. 10,000 French cavalry, led by General Etienne Nansouty's two cuirassier divisions, began to engage the Austrian cavalry, who despite poorly coordinated charges were able to hold them for almost three hours to facilitate the army's escape, before they slipped away. Only then did the French discover the pontoon bridge, but its last defenders were able to hold on and cut the securing ropes to prevent the French from using it.

By noon the French infantry had arrived and formed up around the city's medieval defenses. Lannes was given charge of its capture and opened up an artillery bombardment, while light infantry engaged the Austrian troops in the suburbs. Two infantry assaults on the main gates had already failed with heavy losses, when at 3:00 P.M. General Henri-Gatien, comte Bertrand, head of the engineers, smashed a breach in the wall with heavy artillery near the Straubing gate. Walking to observe the gap, Napoleon was struck by a small canister round in the left foot but was able to mount his horse and ride around, reassuring his anxious troops. Three small parties with siege ladders failed to scale the damaged wall until Lannes seized a ladder and led his men up to secure the lightly defended walls. A street-by-street battle raged for several hours until the French could secure and begin looting the southern part of the city. The bridge was determinedly defended by the 1st battalion of Infanterie Regiment 15 from the northern gatehouse until around 9:00 P.M., when they abandoned their positions and the French could reach the northern suburb of Stadt-am-Hof. The last 300 defenders surrendered soon after.

David Hollins

See also Bertrand, Henri-Gatien, comte; Charles, Archduke of Austria, Duke of Teschen; Eggmühl, Battle of; Fifth Coalition, War of the; Lannes, Jean; Montbrun, Louis-Pierre; Nansouty, Etienne Marie Antoine Champion
References and further reading
Arnold, James. 1990. *Crisis on the Danube: Napoleon's Austrian Campaign of 1809.* London: Arms and Armour.
Castle, Ian. 1998. *Eggmühl 1809.* Oxford: Osprey.
Petre, F. Loraine. 1991. *Napoleon and the Archduke Charles: A History of the Franco-Austrian Campaign in the Valley of the Danube in 1809.* London: Greenhill.

Rayevsky, Nikolay Nikolayevich, Count (1771–1829)

Russian general and army commander. Rayevsky was born to a prominent Russian family, nephew of Prince Gregory Potemkin. He was enlisted in the Life Guard Preobrazhensk Regiment at the age of three (thus guaranteeing him a place in the ranks when he came of age) in 1774, becoming a sergeant on 11 May 1777, an ensign on 12 January 1786, a sub-lieutenant on 12 January 1788, and a lieutenant in 1789. During the Russo-Turkish War of 1787–1792, he transferred as a premier major to the Nizhegorod Dragoon Regiment on 11 April 1789 and served in Moldavia and Wallachia, fighting at Akkerman and Bender. Rayevsky was promoted to lieutenant colonel on 12 September 1790, and at the age nineteen, he took command of the Great Hetman Bulava (*Bulavy Velikogo Getman*) Cossack Regiment.

Promoted to colonel on 11 February 1792, Rayevsky served in Poland in the same year, distinguishing himself at Gorodische and Daragosta. In 1793 he took part in the operations around Mogilev. In 1794 he commanded the Nizhegorod Dragoon Regiment in the Caucasus and took part in the Persian campaign in 1796, fighting at Derbent. However, Rayevsky was discharged from the army during Tsar Paul's purges in May 1797. He was restored to the army with the rank of major general only after Paul's assassination on 27 March 1801, but he took another discharge on 31 December of the same year due to poor health and family problems. Rayevsky returned to service in 1805, when he was appointed to the Imperial Retinue and served under Prince Peter Bagration during the Russian retreat from Braunau to Austerlitz. In April 1807 he took command of a *Jäger* brigade in Bagration's advance guard in Poland. He distinguished himself at Guttstadt, Quetz, Deppen, Heilsberg (where he was wounded in the leg), and Friedland.

Rayevsky participated in the Russo-Swedish War in 1808, commanding a detachment in Bagration's 21st Division. In the spring of 1808 he took part in the actions at Kumo, Bjorneborg, Normark, Christianstadt, and Vaasa, earning promotion to lieutenant general on 26 April 1808 and command of the 21st Division two days later. Rayevsky then fought at Gamle-Kalerby, Lappo, Kuortaine, Brahestadt, and Uleaborg. In 1809, during the Russo-Turkish War, he led the 11th Division in the Danubian Principalities, distinguishing himself at Silistra and Shumla. On 12 April 1811 he took command of the 26th Division. In 1812, during the campaign in Russia, he commanded the 7th Corps of the 2nd Western Army. On 22–23 July he distinguished himself in the battle at Saltanovka (near Mogilev), where he engaged French forces under Marshal Nicolas Davout. He resolutely defended Smolensk on 15–16 August, allowing the Russian armies to regroup and retreat to Borodino.

On 7 September 1812, Rayevsky took part in the Battle of Borodino, where he defended a strong field entrenchment manned by artillery in the center of the Russian positions, sometimes referred to as the Rayevsky, or Great, Redoubt. At the council of war at Fili, he urged the abandonment of Moscow. In October–November 1812, he participated in the battles of Tarutino, Maloyaroslavets, and Krasnyi. However, he became seriously ill and had to take a furlough in December. He returned to the army in late April 1813. During the campaigns of 1813–1814, Rayevsky commanded the Grenadier Corps, fighting at Koenigswartha, Bautzen, Dresden, Kulm, and Dohna. At the Battle of Leipzig he was seriously wounded in the neck but remained on the battlefield and later was promoted to general of cavalry on 20 October 1813. After the battle he left the army to recuperate from his wound and returned in early 1814, when he replaced General Peter Graf zu Wittgenstein on 20 February.

In 1814 Rayevsky fought at Arcis-sur-Aube, Vitry, La-Fère-Champenoise, and Montmartre. In 1815 he led his corps to France during the Hundred Days and attended a military parade at Vertus. After the war, he commanded the 3rd Corps (25 January 1816) and then the 4th Corps before retiring on 7 December 1824. He was surprised and anguished when in December 1825, his two sons, Alexander and Nikolay, his brother Vasily Davydov, and two sons-in-law, Mikhail Orlov and Sergey Volkonsky, took part in the Decembrist Uprising and were arrested and exiled to Siberia. Despite his family involvement in the uprising, Rayevsky was appointed a member of the State Council on 7 February 1826, and over the next four years he tried in vain to secure amnesty for the members of his family. However, he became seriously ill and died on 28 September 1829. He was buried in the village of Boltyshka in the Kiev *gubernia* (province). During the Napoleonic Wars, Rayevsky was celebrated for leading an attack with his two sons, Alexander (sixteen years old) and Nikolay (ten years old) during the action at Saltanovka in 1812.

Alexander Mikaberidze

See also Arcis-sur-Aube, Battle of; Bagration, Peter Ivanovich, Prince; Bautzen, Battle of; Borodino, Battle of; Davout, Louis Nicolas; Dresden, Battle of; Fourth Coalition, War of the; France, Campaign in; Friedland, Battle of; Germany, Campaign in; Heilsberg, Battle of; Krasnyi, Second Battle of; Kulm, Battle of; La-Fère-Champenoise, Battle of; Leipzig, Battle of; Maloyaroslavets, Battle of; Montmartre, Action at; Paul I, Tsar; Russian Campaign; Russo-Swedish War; Russo-Turkish War; Smolensk, Battle of; Third Coalition, War of the; Wittgenstein, Peter Khristianovich Graf zu (Sayn-)

References and further reading
Arkhiv Rayevskhikh. 1908–1915. 5 vols. St. Petersburg: Raevskago.
Borisevich, A. 1912. *General ot kavalerii N. N. Rayevsky.* St. Petersburg: Raevskago.
Shenkman, Gregory. 2003. *General Raevskii i ego semia.* St. Petersburg: Aleteiia.
Yepanchin, Yu. 1999, "N. N. Rayevsky," *Voprosi istorii,* no. 3.

Rebolledo de Palafox y Melzi, José (1775–1847)

By far the most famous Spanish general of the Peninsular War, José Rebolledo de Palafox y Melzi joined the Guardias de Corps in 1792, and by 1808 was a second lieutenant (a post which gave him the rank of brigadier in the rest of the army). A supporter of the aristocratic faction that overthrew Charles IV and Manuel de Godoy at Aranjuez, Palafox was given command of the escort that took Godoy, the former favorite, to France when Napoleon ordered that he should travel to Bayonne. Hearing of the Dos de Mayo (Madrid uprising of 2 May 1808), he decided to make use of it to further the traditionalist assault on enlightened absolutism, and to this end organized an insurrection in his home city of Saragossa (Zaragoza). In brief, the aim of this affair was to establish himself as regent and unleash a war against the French that would sweep away Bourbon reformism, but the plan miscarried on account of the simultaneous organization of other uprisings in many other cities.

For the next two years Palafox (and, following his capture, his supporters) made repeated efforts to take control of the Spanish uprising and discredit their opponents. These efforts seriously compromised the war effort, and it is therefore ironic that Palafox is seen as one of the greatest heroes of Spain's resistance to Napoleon. In part a reflection of the general's skills as a propagandist—his bombastic and grandiloquent pamphlets reached every part of Spain—this image is also the result of events at Saragossa, which withstood two terrible sieges before finally falling to the enemy in February 1809 (whereupon Palafox was taken prisoner).

How much of the credit for withstanding the sieges should go to Palafox is a moot point, however. In both sieges his personal courage is open to question, while in the second one in particular he crammed the city with so many troops that it was left devoid of hopes of relief and exposed to an epidemic of typhus that wiped out thousands of its defenders. Nor did he show much grasp as a field commander: In the campaign of October–November 1808, his insistence on an offensive in Navarre exposed the forces of both himself and General Francisco Javier de Castaños to catastrophic disaster. That said, he did inspire great courage among his men, and was unique among Spanish commanders in his ability to reach out to the common people.

Released by Napoleon as a peace emissary in 1814, Palafox rallied to the cause of absolutism in 1814 and was rewarded with the post of Captain General of Aragón. Thereafter, however, he played no role in politics, serving a succession of regimes in a variety of posts in the royal bodyguard and the military administration until his death in 1847.

Charles J. Esdaile

See also Bayonne, Conference at; Castaños, Francisco Javier
de; Charles IV, King; Godoy y Alvarez de Faria, Manuel de,
Príncipe de la Paz, Duque de Alcudia; Madrid Uprising;
Peninsular War; Saragossa, Sieges of
References and further reading
Esdaile, Charles J. 2002. *The Peninsular War: A New History.*
    London: Penguin.
Rudorff, Raymond. 1974. *War to the Death: The Twin Sieges
    of Zaragoza, 1808–1809*. London: Hamilton.

Regency, The

See Prince Regent and the Regency Period

Reichenbach, Convention of (27 June 1813)

The Convention of Reichenbach is the name given to a series of agreements reached at the town of Reichenbach in
the Kingdom of Saxony between Austria, Britain, Prussia,
and Russia during the 1813 summer armistice. What is
usually referred to as the Convention or Treaty of Reichenbach was an agreement between Austria, Prussia, and Russia on the minimum terms for a preliminary peace with
the Emperor Napoleon. Other agreements arising out of
the meetings at Reichenbach included unilateral treaties
between Britain and Prussia, and between Britain and Russia. Some sources also refer to the convention as the articu-
lation of Austria's terms for armed mediation with Napoleon's representatives, principally the diplomat Louis,
comte de Narbonne.

In the summer of 1813, Klemens Graf Metternich, the
Austrian foreign minister, finalized the creation of the
grand coalition that was to defeat Napoleon at Leipzig that
fall. Metternich had first visited Napoleon at Dresden on
26 June, where in a stormy interview the French emperor
angrily rejected Austria's demands that Napoleon essentially withdraw to France's natural frontiers along the
Rhine, Alps, and Pyrenees. Metternich's demands were
codified the next day in a secret treaty at Reichenbach between Austria, Prussia, and Russia, with neither Britain nor
Sweden being a party to this treaty. The demands included
Napoleon's withdrawal from Germany, the return of Illyria
to Austria, the independence of the Hanse cities of Hamburg and Lübeck, and the enlargement of Prussia by the
dissolution of the Duchy of Warsaw, Napoleon's satellite
Polish ally. Napoleon's acceptance of these terms would
only guarantee Austrian neutrality and mediation.

Metternich had already established that Napoleon
would reject these demands at Dresden. He pledged Austria to join the coalition once Napoleon's rejection of the
terms became known. The Allies additionally agreed not to
make a separate peace with Napoleon under any circumstances. After Reichenbach, Napoleon again attempted negotiation at Prague beginning on 30 June, but only agreed
to the return of Illyria in order to buy Austrian neutrality,
and these negotiations were in any event broken off on 4
August. The Austrian emperor, Francis I, convinced that
Napoleon was not serious about negotiation, determined
on war against his son-in-law on 12 August.

There are two schools of thought about Metternich's
diplomacy. The first, best represented by Henry Kissinger,
claims that Metternich subtly set a trap for Napoleon at
Dresden, which he codified at Reichenbach. Another view,
held by Felix Markham, sees Metternich as less interested
in painting Napoleon as a warmonger and more interested
in establishing the basis for a general peace. Whatever Metternich's actual motives, Reichenbach's direct effect was to
add Austria's military might to the Sixth Coalition.

John T. Kuehn

See also Armistice of 1813; Austria; Francis I, Emperor;
Germany, Campaign in; Leipzig, Battle of; Metternich,
Klemens Wenzel Lothar Fürst
References and further reading
Chandler, David G. 1995. *The Campaigns of Napoleon.*
    London: Weidenfeld and Nicolson.
Hamilton-Williams, David. 1999. *The Fall of Napoleon: The
    Final Betrayal.* London: Arms and Armour.
Kissinger, Henry A. 1964. *A World Restored: Metternich,
    Castlereagh and the Problems of Peace, 1812–22.* New
    York: Grosset and Dunlap.
Markham, Felix. 1963. *Napoleon.* New York: New American
    Library.
Schroeder, Paul. 1994. *The Transformation of European
    Politics, 1763–1848.* New York: Oxford University Press.
Stewart, Charles William Vane, Marquess of Londonderry.
    1830. *Narrative of the War in Germany and France in 1813
    and 1814.* London: Colburn and Bentley.

Reichsdeputationshauptschluss

See Imperial Recess

Reille, Honoré Charles Michel Joseph, comte (1775–1860)

Reille was a talented member of the younger generation of
French military leaders, one of those whose careers began
after the Revolution of 1789. Entering the army as a volunteer in 1791, he reached the rank of brigadier general in
1803 at the age of twenty-eight. Reille served for many
years as aide-de-camp and staff officer under the future
marshal, André Masséna, whose daughter he married in
1814. The young officer fought throughout Europe during

the French Revolutionary and Napoleonic Wars, from his first campaign in Belgium in 1793 to Poland in 1807, and he then saw extensive duty in Spain from 1808 to 1813. Reille commanded one of the three corps that Napoleon led in the Waterloo campaign of 1815, and he returned to the army in 1818, three years after the restoration of Louis XVIII to the French throne.

Reille was born in Antibes on 1 September 1775, the son of a judicial official in the royal administration. After service in the National Guard, he responded to the call for volunteers for the army in 1791. As a lieutenant in the infantry, the young man saw action at the Battle of Neerwinden in the spring of 1793, then participated in the capture of Toulon.

Fighting with the (French) Army of Italy from 1794 onward, Reille began his long association with Masséna. He served as that general's aide-de-camp during the campaign of 1796–1797, was wounded during the river crossing at Lodi, and led a cavalry charge at Arcola. Reille continued his role as a valuable subordinate to Masséna in Switzerland in 1799, and he played a significant part in the siege of Genoa in 1800. Both of these campaigns established Masséna as one of the leading figures on the French military scene.

While Genoa was under siege from Austrian forces on land and the Royal Navy at sea, Reille slipped through the blockading forces carrying a crucial message from Bonaparte to Masséna. As a result of Reille's daring, Masséna now learned that Bonaparte intended to cross the Alps in order to strike Austrian forces in Italy from the north. The longer Masséna could tie down enemy forces in northwestern Italy, the greater the chances of a spectacular French success.

After Bonaparte achieved his victory over the Austrians at the Battle of Marengo, Colonel Reille received the delicate task of negotiating a line of demarcation between French and enemy forces. Bonaparte found Reille so impressive that he asked to have the young soldier transferred to his own staff.

On the battlefield as a brigade commander at Jena (1806) and Pultusk (1807), Reille won promotion to the rank of *général de division*. He served at that rank as aide-de-camp to Napoleon at the Battle of Friedland (1807). The young general then spent most of the years from 1808 through 1813 in the Iberian Peninsula, although he was called away from Spain to lead a division at the Battle of Wagram in 1809.

From the time he returned to Spain in 1810, Reille had no successes comparable to those he had achieved as a more junior leader. Rather than fighting a conventional opponent in the open field, Reille had to deal with fortified Spanish cities and irrepressible local guerrilla units. In

early 1812, by now Napoleon's most experienced general in fighting Spanish irregulars, he took command of the newly formed Army of the Ebro. His assignment was to wipe out resistance in northeastern Spain. Inadequate numbers of troops, the continuing shortage of supplies, and the difficulties of the terrain combined to produce complete failure. Reille's problems were compounded by unrealistic orders sent from Napoleon's faraway headquarters.

In 1813, Reille, now a full general, led the former Army of Portugal, which was transformed into one of the three French corps that fought in northern Spain. By the summer, French forces under King Joseph and General Jean-Baptiste Jourdan were hard-pressed by the Marquis of Wellington, in a campaign that culminated with the Battle of Vitoria in June 1813. Although Reille's units fought heroically, Joseph and Jourdan were nonetheless defeated, and the French, now under the command of Marshal Nicolas Soult, were pushed back across the Pyrenees. Reille's forces distinguished themselves by conducting a series of orderly retreats from northern Spain all the way back to France.

Barely forty years old, Reille commanded one of the three corps that Napoleon took into Belgium during the Waterloo campaign. On 16 June 1815, Reille advanced cautiously against the Duke of Wellington at Quatre Bras when a bolder approach might have thrown the enemy into disarray. Reille's experiences fighting in Spain made him wary of British forces concealed behind the crests of hills and ready to pounce on a rapidly advancing French army.

Two days later at Waterloo, he had a more useful insight into the situation: he urged the Emperor to avoid a frontal attack on Wellington's formidable defenses in favor of a maneuver on the enemy flank. Napoleon rejected the advice, and Reille's corps initiated the Emperor's final battle with ferocious attacks against the farmhouse at Hougoumont on the west side of the Allied line.

The defeat of Napoleon and the dissolution of the remnants of the former Grande Armée brought Reille a brief period in retirement. In 1818, however, he returned to active duty, and, in September 1847, he was named a Marshal of France. He lived to see Napoleon III, the nephew of his former commander, become ruler of France. Reille died in Paris on 4 March 1860, at the age of eighty-five, and he was laid to rest alongside Masséna in the Père-Lachaise cemetery.

Neil M. Heyman

See also Arcola, Battle of; Bonaparte, Joseph; Fifth Coalition, War of the; Flanders, Campaigns in; Fourth Coalition, War of the; Friedland, Battle of; Genoa, Siege of; Italian Campaigns (1792–1797); Jena, Battle of; Jourdan, Jean-Baptiste; Lodi, Battle of; Marengo, Battle of; Masséna,

André; National Guard (French); Neerwinden, Battle of;
Peninsular War; Pultusk, Battle of; Quatre Bras, Battle of;
Soult, Nicolas Jean de Dieu; Switzerland, Campaign in;
Toulon, Siege of; Vitoria, Battle of; Wagram, Battle of;
Waterloo, Battle of; Waterloo Campaign; Wellington, Arthur
Wellesley, First Duke of

References and further reading

Alexander, Don W. 1985. *Rod of Iron: French
    Counterinsurgency Policy in Aragon during the Peninsular
    War.* Wilmington, DE: Scholarly Resources.
Chandler, David G. 1995. *The Campaigns of Napoleon.*
    London: Weidenfeld and Nicolson.
Esdaile, Charles J. 2003. *The Peninsular War: A New History.*
    New York: Palgrave Macmillan.
Hamilton-Williams, David. 1993. *Waterloo: New Perspectives:
    The Great Battle Reappraised.* New York: Wiley.
Hayman, Peter. 1990. *Soult: Napoleon's Maligned Marshal.*
    London: Arms and Armour.
Horrocks, Raymond. 1982. *Marshal Ney: The Romance and
    the Real.* New York: Hippocrene.
Marshall-Cornwall, James. 1965. *Marshal Massena.* London:
    Oxford University Press.

Republican Calendar

The Republican calendar was used in France from 1793 to
1806 as a secular and Revolutionary alternative to the
Gregorian calendar.

The Republican calendar was adopted by the National
Convention on 24 October 1793. Its proponents hoped to
devise a rational decimal system for the measurement of
time, as they had done for the measurement of weights and
lengths. They also hoped to symbolize the beginning of a
new era in which the values and symbols of the Republic
would replace those of the *ancien régime* (called the "vul-
gar era" in the act that created the new calendar).

Mathematicians Gaspard Monge and Charles Gilbert
Romme devised a scheme intended to be as simple as the
metric system, yet compatible with the uneven cycle of the
seasons. The Republican calendar year still numbered 365
to 366 days, but it was divided into 12 months of equal
length (30 days), followed by 5 to 6 additional days. A complex system of leap years would have kept the calendar in
sync with the solar year over several millennia, though the
calendar was abandoned long before it could be of any use.
Each month was divided into 3 weeks of 10 days each. In
addition, days were to be divided into ten hours of 100
minutes each, which were themselves divided into 100 seconds. The implementation of this last clause was not to
take effect for two years because it demanded extensive
modifications of existing clocks.

Poets André Chénier and Philippe Fabre d'Eglantine
were responsible for replacing all references to Christian
and Roman deities with Revolutionary symbols. The calendar's first day was set retroactively on 22 September 1792
(1 Vendémiaire Year I), the day on which the Republic was
proclaimed following the French victory at Valmy. The
names of the twelve months were based on Greek and
Latin names and referred to each season's typical weather
and crops: Vendémiaire (grape harvest), Brumaire (fog),
Frimaire (cold), Nivôse (snow), Pluviôse (rain), Ventôse
(wind), Germinal (seed), Floréal (flower), Prairial
(meadow), Messidor (wheat harvest), Thermidor (heat),
and Fructidor (fruit). The ten days of each week, or *décade*,
were called Primidi, Duodi, Tridi, Quartidi, Quintidi, Sex-
tidi, Septidi, Octidi, Nonidi, and Décadi, based on the
Latin root for the numbers one through ten. In addition,
each day of the year was assigned a name inspired by farming. The month of Vendémiaire, for example, included
such days as Safran (saffron), Chataîgne (chestnut), Cheval
(horse), Carotte (carrot), Potiron (pumpkin), Tonneau
(barrel), Chanvre (hemp), and Boeuf (ox).

The last day of each ten-day week, or Décadi, was set
aside as a day of rest. In addition, the five or six comple-
mentary days that closed off the year were labeled "Sans-
Culottides" after the sans-culottes, as the working-class
urban Revolutionaries were called (changed to the neutral
"Jours Complémentaires" during the Directory) and became annual feast days. These were the feasts of Virtue, Genius, Work, Opinion, Rewards, and (in leap years only)
Revolution.

The Republican calendar never had the lasting influence, both in France and abroad, that the metric system
had. Its secular nature offended the Roman Catholic
Church. The ten-day week was unpopular with workers,
who now had to wait nine days before resting. The general
public found the 22 September starting date confusing, for
it did not coincide with existing months and years. Napoleon abolished the calendar on 1 January 1806. It was revived briefly during the Commune (1871) and is still used
occasionally by anticlerical Frenchmen.

Philippe R. Girard

See also Convention, The; Directory, The; French
Revolution; Valmy, Battle of
References and further reading
Dershowitz, Nachum, and Edward Reingold. 2002.
    Calendrical Calculations. New York: Cambridge
    University Press.
Richards, Edward G. 1999. *Mapping Time: The Calendar and
    its History.* New York: Oxford University Press.

Reynier, Jean Louis Ebénézer, comte
(1771–1814)

Reynier was born into a Huguenot family in Switzerland in
1771. His training was in civil engineering, but in 1792 he

volunteered for the artillery, in which he served in the early part of the French Revolutionary Wars and fought at Jemappes. In January 1795 he was promoted to *général de brigade* after initially declining the promotion while serving under General Charles François Dumouriez.

In 1796 he was promoted to *général de division* after serving as General Jean Moreau's chief of staff for the Army of the Rhine and Moselle. In this capacity, Reynier showed his talent for planning. In 1798 he went with Bonaparte to Egypt, where he commanded a division and fought in the Battle of the Pyramids and then in the Syrian campaign. After a heated argument with General Jacques-François Menou, to whom he was second in command, Reynier was arrested and sent back to France to be put on trial, though he was cleared of all charges. Reynier continued his assault on his fellow officers and finally engaged in a duel outside Paris with General Jacques-Zacharie Destaing, whom Reynier killed; as a result of the duel, Reynier was exiled from Paris. During this period he served in Italy, where he was defeated by a British expeditionary force at Maida. In 1808 he became minister of war and marine for the Kingdom of Naples. In 1809 he was recalled for service in the Grande Armée in central Europe.

Reynier fought in the latter part of the Wagram campaign, in which he commanded the Saxon corps in the French army. In March 1810 he led II Corps in the (French) Army of Portugal commanded by Marshal André Masséna. His command covered the sieges of Ciudad Rodrigo and Almeida during 1810. Later in the year he commanded the left wing at the Battle of Busaco. He continued with the army when it advanced to the Lines of Torres Vedras. In 1811 he won a victory at Sabugal while covering the army's retreat. Later he fought at Fuentes de Oñoro. His skills as an organizer were reflected in his detailed planning of the army's marches and countermarches. He was also critical of Masséna's conduct. In May 1811 he was made a Count of the Empire.

Reynier served in the Russian campaign of 1812 on the southern flank commanding VII Corps, which was composed almost entirely of Saxon troops. In the 1813 campaign in Germany he continued as commander of VII Corps, which fought at Bautzen, Dresden, Grossbeeren, Dennewitz, and, finally, at Leipzig, where the corps defected to the Allies and Reynier was taken prisoner. While in captivity, Reynier was offered a commission in the Russian Army, which he refused. He returned to France in February 1814 after a prisoner exchange, but died from exhaustion and fatigue two weeks after his arrival.

Dallace W. Unger Jr.

See also Almeida, Sieges of; Bautzen, Battle of; Busaco, Battle of; Ciudad Rodrigo, First Siege of; Dennewitz, Battle of; Dresden, Battle of; Dumouriez, Charles François

Dupérier; Fifth Coalition, War of the; Fuentes de Oñoro, Battle of; Germany, Campaign in; Grossbeeren, Battle of; Jemappes, Battle of; Leipzig, Battle of; Maida, Battle of; Masséna, André; Menou, Jacques-François de Boussay, baron; Middle East Campaign; Moreau, Jean Victor; Naples; Peninsular War; Pyramids, Battle of the; Russian Campaign; Saxon Army; Torres Vedras, Lines of

References and further reading
Bowden, Scott. 1990. *Napoleon's Grande Armée of 1813*. Chicago: Emperor's.
Chandler, David G. 1995. *The Campaigns of Napoleon*. London: Weidenfeld and Nicolson.
Smith, Digby. 2001. *1813 Leipzig: Napoleon and the Battle of the Nations*. London: Greenhill.
Zamoyski, Adam. 2004. *1812: Napoleon's Fatal March on Moscow*. London: HarperCollins.

Rheims, Battle of (13 March 1814)

Rheims was among the last battles of Napoleon's famous defensive campaign of 1814. It can be counted as the Emperor's final victory prior to his abdication and is noteworthy for that fact alone. Napoleon's situation in early March 1814 seemed grim. His army had been severely mauled at the bloody battles of Craonne and Laon against Field Marshal Gebhard von Blücher's forces, and the enormous Austro-Russian army of *Feldmarschall* Karl Philipp Fürst zu Schwarzenberg was edging ever close to Paris from the south. All that was needed was for Blücher's army to unite with Schwarzenberg's and march on Paris. Facilitating this juncture, an independent Russian corps under the French émigré general Louis de St. Priest seized the key city of Rheims on 12 March. Rheims was also important symbolically as the ancient coronation site for French kings.

Napoleon reacted quickly to this danger. Early on the thirteenth, he set out for Rheims with Marshal Auguste Marmont's corps, elements of Marshal Michel Ney's corps, and portions of his Old Guard—about 13,500 men. St. Priest had approximately the same number of men. Napoleon used Marmont as his advance guard and approached the city from the west. Once there, Marmont immediately began to skirmish, while Antoine, comte Drouot set up the artillery of the Guard on the hill near St. Pierre. At 4:00 P.M. Drouot opened fire with devastating effect, mortally wounding St. Priest almost immediately. Marmont's main columns now advanced, supported by generals Louis Colbert and Isidore Exelmans's light cavalry. Of note, the relatively new Guard of Honor cavalry regiments, which had been somewhat ineffective during earlier battles, performed exceptionally well in the street fighting. It is thought that the residents of Rheims hung out lanterns after the sun set to aid the French cavalry in its pursuit of the beaten Russian troops.

Napoleon was welcomed as a liberating hero by the city's residents, and by 9:30 P.M. the battle was effectively over, with St. Priest's corps in flight, having lost 6,000 men to the French 700. The immediate result of the battle, aside from the destruction of St. Priest's corps, was that Napoleon had interposed himself between Blücher and Schwarzenberg at a decisive point. Once Blücher heard the news of St. Priest's defeat, he kept his army in the vicinity of Laon. Schwarzenberg and Tsar Alexander, too, were anxious and put a temporary halt to their offensive.

John T. Kuehn

See also Alexander I, Tsar; Blücher von Wahlstatt, Gebhard Lebrecht Fürst; Craonne, Battle of; Drouot, Antoine, comte; France, Campaign in; Imperial Guard (French); Laon, Battle of; Marmont, Auguste Frédéric Louis Viesse de; Ney, Michel; Schwarzenberg, Karl Philipp Fürst zu

References and further reading

Chandler, David G. 1995. *The Campaigns of Napoleon.* London: Weidenfeld and Nicolson.

Craig, Gordon A. 1965. *Problems of Coalition Warfare: The Military Alliance against Napoleon, 1813–1814.* The Harmon Memorial Lectures in Military History, no. 7. Colorado Springs, CO: United States Air Force Academy.

Dederfield, R. F. 2001. *Imperial Sunset: The Fall of Napoleon, 1813–1814.* New York: Cooper Square Press.

Lachouque, Henri. 1961. *The Anatomy of Glory.* Trans. Anne S. K. Brown. Providence, RI: Brown University Press.

Lawford, James. 1977. *Napoleon: The Last Campaigns, 1813–1815.* London: Roxby.

Petre, F. Loraine. 1994. *Napoleon at Bay, 1814.* London: Greenhill.

Rhine Campaigns (1792–1797)

When war began in 1792, the French Revolutionary government's key aim was to secure the nation's "natural frontiers" of the Alps, the Pyrenees, and the Rhine, so the river Rhine—being the only of these three natural features not yet identifying the French frontier—became their primary strategic objective. By 1794 the French had conquered the Austrian Netherlands (Belgium and Luxembourg) but had only secured the left bank of the central Rhine following their victory in Italy. The first French incursions into the Holy Roman Empire in Germany met with a combined Austro-Prussian response, but after that alliance's collapse in 1795—with Prussia signing a separate peace at Basle on 5 April—French forces marched across the Rhine into southern Germany in 1796.

From the outset of hostilities on 20 April 1792 between France and the German monarchies, the French Revolutionaries planned to seize the Austrian Netherlands and the Palatinate (German states on the left bank of the Rhine). The Prussians favored a rapid march on Paris to restore the Bourbon monarchy, so the army commander,

Feldmarschall the Duke of Brunswick, planned a steady advance against the belt of fortresses before marching into France. In August, 40,000 Prussians under Brunswick entered France, marching along the Moselle. The (Austrian) Army of the Upper Rhine would advance in the south, while a second advanced from the Austrian Netherlands on Lille. The Prussians took the fortresses of Longwy and Verdun, but badly afflicted by dysentery, the weakened Prussian army was halted at Valmy on 20 September by a French army under General Charles Dumouriez. Although there was little fighting, the French steadiness and Brunswick's retreat caused a sensation and gave the French the confidence to commence their own advances.

The (French) Army of the Rhine under General Adam de Custine invaded the Palatinate, taking Speyer on 30 September and the fortress city of Mainz on 21 October. Having reached the Rhine, he advanced up the Main valley to take Frankfurt. However, Brunswick's army had recovered and defeated Custine at Frankfurt on 2 December, forcing the French army into a difficult retreat on Strasbourg by March 1793. A French garrison under General Francisco Miranda held out in Mainz against a Prussian siege, but the city fell on 23 July.

As Allied armies evicted the French from the Austrian Netherlands, the Austrians and Prussians returned to the offensive in the Palatinate. *Feldzeugmeister* Dagobert Graf Würmser's Army of the Upper Rhine, which defeated Custine at Offenbach in July, smashed through the supposedly impregnable Weissenburg defensive lines in a series of bloody battles during September and October. Brunswick's two victories over the (French) Army of the Moselle under General René Moreaux at Pirmasens on 22 July and 14 September cleared the French from the German left bank of the Rhine. However, amid growing mistrust, Austro-Prussian relations broke down and, despite a victory over the Army of the Moselle, now under General Louis Hoche, at Kaiserslautern on 28 November, Brunswick failed to advance into French Alsace.

As the Prussians reduced their forces along the Rhine to improve their position in Poland, the French regrouped for a renewed effort in 1794. They concentrated on the Austrian Netherlands and had defeated the Allies by June, forcing the British into Holland and the Austrians east to the Rhine. The reduction in French troops along the Rhine had enabled the Prussians to take Kaiserslautern in May, but once reinforced, the French were able to take Trier in August. After success in the Austrian Netherlands, General Jean-Baptiste Jourdan turned east with his Army of the Sambre and Meuse to cross the river Roer (Ruhr) in October to chase the Austrians from Maastricht, Coblenz, and Cologne that month, effectively securing the Rhine as the line of separation between the hostile forces. On 5 April

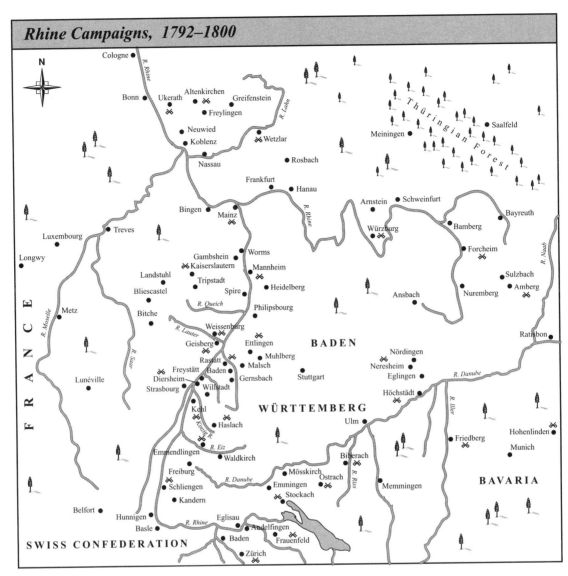

Adapted from Pope 1999, 547–548.

1795 the Prussians withdrew from the war after signing the Peace of Basle. In August, Jourdan crossed the Rhine, while General Jean Charles Pichegru's Army of the Rhine and Moselle took Mannheim, before Pichegru commenced armistice negotiations with the Austrians in September. Isolated, Jourdan was routed outside Mainz in October by Würmser, who retook Mannheim the following month.

In June 1796 the French launched a two-pronged attack across the Rhine into southern Germany to engage the combined (Austrian) Armies of the Upper and Lower Rhine under *Feldmarschall* Archduke Charles. Jourdan's advance was halted in the north by the archduke at Wetzlar on 16 June, but after indecisive fighting at Rastatt, General Jean Moreau's Army of the Rhine and Moselle was able to push the archduke's southern forces back to Neresheim, where they fought an indecisive action over 1–3 August.

However, the archduke was then able to march north to combine with his northern troops under *Feldzeugmeister* Wilhelm Graf Wartensleben to defeat Jourdan at Amberg before driving him westward to crush him at Würzburg on 3 September. Although Moreau had driven the southern Austrian troops under *Feldmarschalleutnant* Maximillian Graf Baillet von Latour back to Munich, defeating him at Friedberg on 24 August and Biberach on 2 October, Jourdan's defeat forced him to withdraw hastily westward. Defeated by Charles at Emmendingen, Moreau withdrew over the Rhine on 24 October.

Brief French incursions were launched over the Rhine in April 1797 in support of Bonaparte's advance on Vienna, in which General Louis Lazare Hoche defeated *Feldmarschalleutnant* Franz Freiherr von Werneck at Neuwied on 18 April and two days later, Moreau defeated *Feldzeug-*

meister Anton Sztáray Graf von Nagy-Mihaly at Diersheim before the armistice of Leoben concluded hostilities. The subsequent Peace of Campo Formio secured the left bank of the Rhine for France, although Austria had achieved its policy objective of swapping the Austrian Netherlands for contiguous territory in the former Venetian Republic.

David Hollins

See also Amberg, Battle of; Basle, Treaties of; Biberach, Battle of; Brunswick, Charles William Ferdinand, Duke of; Campo Formio, Treaty of; Charles, Archduke of Austria, Duke of Teschen; Emmendingen, Battle of; Dumouriez, Charles François Dupérier; First Coalition, War of the; Flanders, Campaigns in; Friedberg, Battle of; Hoche, Louis Lazare; Holy Roman Empire; Jourdan, Jean-Baptiste; Leoben, Preliminaries of; Mainz, Siege of; Mannheim Offensive; Moreau, Jean Victor; Neresheim, Battle of; Pichegru, Jean-Charles; Rastatt, Battle of; Rhine Campaigns (1799–1800); Valmy, Battle of; Venetian Republic; Würmser, Dagobert Sigismund Graf; Würzburg, Battle of

References and further reading
Blanning, Tim C. W. 1996. *The French Revolutionary Wars, 1787–1802*. New York: St. Martin's.
Chuquet, Arthur. 1886–1896. *Les guerres de la révolution*. 11 vols. Paris: Léopold Cerf.
Griffiths, Paddy. 1998. *The Art of War of Revolutionary France 1789–1802*. London: Greenhill.
Lynn, John A. 1984. *The Bayonets of the Republic: Motivation and Tactics in the Army of Revolutionary France, 1791–94*. Urbana: University of Illinois Press.
Phipps, Ramsay Weston. 1980. *The Armies of the First French Republic and the Rise of the Marshals of Napoleon I*. Vol. 2, *The Armées de la Moselle, du Rhin, de Sambre-et-Meuse, et de Rhin-et-Moselle*. London: Greenwood. (Orig. pub. 1926–1939.)
Wagner, A. 1981. *Der Feldzug der K. Preussischen Armee am Rhein im Jahre 1793*. Wiesbaden: LTR. (Orig. pub. Berlin, 1831.)

Rhine Campaigns (1799–1800)

After a pause, the war between France and Austria, which had ended in 1797 with the Treaty of Campo Formio, resumed in 1799 with the formation of the Second Coalition, including Britain, Austria, and Russia, while Prussia remained neutral. Having secured its "natural frontiers," the French planned renewed offensives into southern Germany and Austrian-held Italy, but both were defeated in early 1799. The Austrians expelled the French from southern Germany but failed to exploit the opportunity to evict them from strategically important Switzerland. In September an Anglo-Russian force landed in Holland but was forced to withdraw in late October. When Russia left the coalition shortly thereafter, France, now under First Consul Napoleon Bonaparte, decided to continue the war. The French marched across the upper Rhine into southern

Germany, and by the time of Bonaparte's victory at Marengo, on 14 June 1800, they had almost reached Munich. A short-lived ceasefire failed in November, and the French finished off the war by defeating the Austrians at Hohenlinden in December.

Fighting on the Continent during the War of the Second Coalition resumed in early in 1799. The new coalition was based around Russia and Austria. Tsar Paul I of Russia intended to halt the flow of revolutionary enthusiasm, while Holy Roman Emperor Francis II (later Francis I of Austria) wanted to restore Habsburg influence in Germany and recover control of northern Italy. While Switzerland was the key to control of central Europe as it held the strategic transalpine roads, only Britain wished to prioritize it as an objective, mainly as a base for émigré activity and intelligence gathering.

The French, who had created satellite republics in Switzerland, Holland, and Piedmont, looked to expand eastward and planned to attack both in Germany and Italy before Russian troops could reinforce the Austrians. The Rhine campaign began on 1 March 1799 as the (French) Army of the Rhine under General Jean-Baptiste Jourdan crossed the Rhine into southern Germany without a declaration of war, while his left wing under General Jean-Baptiste-Jules Bernadotte took Mannheim on the middle Rhine. As Jourdan emerged through the Black Forest on 6 March, General André Masséna with the (French) Army of Helvetia commenced his march across the upper Rhine toward Feldkirch in the Austrian Tyrol.

The Austrian army under *Feldmarschall* Archduke Charles responded quickly. While *Feldmarschalleutnant* Anton Sztáray Graf von Nagy-Mihaly led an independent *korps* against Bernadotte and *Feldmarschalleutnant* Johann Freiherr von Hotze defended Feldkirch with the left wing, Charles moved his main force across the river Lech to defeat Jourdan at Ostrach on 21 March. The archduke then followed Jourdan to the main strategic objective in southern Germany, Stockach, which stood at the junction of the roads connecting Germany and Switzerland. There, the Austrians decisively defeated the French on 25 March. Meanwhile, Hotze had defeated Masséna around Feldkirch and was pushing westward to Zürich, outflanking Jourdan's position and forcing him to withdraw back to the Black Forest, where he resigned his command to Masséna on 26 March. Bernadotte likewise abandoned his march into Germany and recrossed the Rhine.

Anxious about his losses, Charles blamed the government in Vienna for detaching troops to Italy and the Tyrol, but he pressed for a rapid advance into Switzerland to force Masséna from Zürich by threatening the French commander's rear. However, Vienna required him to march westward to Rastatt at the northern end of the Black

Forest, where the peace conference that had commenced in 1798 was winding up. During the night of 28 April, as they tried to leave the town, two French ambassadors were murdered and another injured by cavalry of the Austrian advance guard. Charles took the opportunity created by the subsequent political furor to leave the area and march into Switzerland to defeat Masséna at the first Battle of Zürich over 4–6 June. However, as Russian troops marched from Italy to secure Switzerland, the archduke was ordered north in late August to recapture the key fortress of Mannheim and besiege Phillipsburg in support of the Anglo-Russian invasion of Holland. The French then renewed their offensive: Masséna overwhelmed the Austro-Russian force under Hotze and General Alexander Rimsky-Korsakov at the second Battle of Zürich on 25 September, as General Guillaume Brune halted the Allied invasion in Holland and General Claude Lecourbe advanced from Mainz to retake Mannheim.

When war resumed in late April 1800, *Feldzeugmeister* Paul Kray Freiherr von Krajova had taken command of the Austrian army in Germany but was outnumbered by the (French) Army of the Rhine, now under General Jean Moreau. The French crossed the upper Rhine to defeat Kray in a series of battles between 3–16 May at Engen, second Stockach, Mösskirch, and Biberach, forcing the Austrians to withdraw toward their base on the Danube at Ulm, which they reached on 11 May. Moreau's victory at Erbach on 16 May cut the main road to Munich, so when he was victorious at the Danube crossing at Höchstädt on 19 June, Kray was forced to abandon Ulm and withdraw in a northern loop toward Munich and on 10 July to cross the Iller. News of Bonaparte's victory at Marengo prompted the two commanders to agree to the armistice of Parsdorf on 15 July.

The truce broke down and fighting resumed in late November. Moreau advanced from Munich to engage the Austrian army now under Archduke John's command. At Hohenlinden on 3 December the French held their positions against a multi-column Austrian assault from the forest to the east, before counterattacking to crush the Austrian left and comprehensively defeating John's army. Three weeks later, Austria signed an armistice with France at Steyr on 25 December, which led to the Peace of Lunéville in February 1801.

David Hollins

See also Bernadotte, Jean-Baptiste-Jules; Biberach, Battle of; Brune, Guillaume-Marie-Anne; Campo Formio, Treaty of; Charles, Archduke of Austria, Duke of Teschen; Francis I, Emperor; Höchstädt, Battle of; Hohenlinden, Battle of; Holy Roman Empire; Italian Campaigns (1799–1800); John, Archduke; Jourdan, Jean-Baptiste; Kray, Paul Freiherr von Krajova; Lunéville, Treaty of; Marengo, Battle of; Masséna, André; Moreau, Jean Victor; North Holland, Campaign in (1799); Ostrach, Battle of; Paul I, Tsar; Rhine Campaigns (1792–1797); Rimsky-Korsakov, Alexander Mikhailovich; Second Coalition, War of the; Stockach, First Battle of; Stockach, Second Battle of; Switzerland, Campaign in; Zürich, First Battle of; Zürich, Second Battle of

References and further reading
Blanning, Tim C. W. 1996. *The French Revolutionary Wars, 1787–1802.* New York: St. Martin's.
Dean, Martin C. 1993. *Austrian Policy during the French Revolutionary Wars, 1796–1802.* Vienna: Military History Institute.
Esdaile, Charles J. 2001. *The French Wars, 1792–1815.* New York: Routledge.
Phipps, Ramsey Weston. 1980. *The Armies of the First French Republic and the Rise of the Marshals of Napoleon I.* Vol. 2, *The Armées de la Moselle, du Rhin, de Sambre-et-Meuse, et de Rhin-et-Moselle.* London: Greenwood. (Orig. pub. 1926–1939.)
Rodger, A. B. 1964. *The War of the Second Coalition: A Strategic Commentary.* New York: Oxford University Press.
Ross, Steven T. 1963. *The War of the Second Coalition.* Princeton: Princeton University Press.

Rifle

The rifle as a weapon was not commonplace in Europe during the Napoleonic Wars. Rifled muskets, loaded from the muzzle just like common muskets, were issued to four British rifle battalions in the Iberian Peninsula, but the common practice was for a few members of every battalion to be issued rifles.

The term *rifle* comes from an archaic verb, *to rifle,* meaning "to cut spiral grooves in," referring to the way in which the barrel had grooves cut in it to impart spin to the projectile fired. The spin increased range and accuracy. However, such weapons were costly to produce and slow to load, and they required the user to be better trained than the average infantryman of the period. Further, the British Army, despite the successful experiments conducted by Colonel Patrick Ferguson with his breech-loading rifled muskets, was averse to change, and for many decades resisted the rifling concept. Interestingly, although the invention of rifling seems to have been German, the Prussian Army followed the British lead in issuing only a few rifled muskets within companies. The same applied in the Russian Army, but the French seemed to have little time for rifled muskets and discontinued their issue in 1807. The main arguments against the rifle were that it was too costly to issue to every rifleman, and it took far longer to train riflemen individually than it took to train a company or even a battalion of musket users.

The few riflemen that existed were issued with prepared ammunition, but also often carried separate powder and ball for the sake of security. Their exploits were well known. The accuracy of the rifled musket was far greater than that of the common musket, so that marksmen were able to pick individual men as targets, whereas the normal line infantry were hard-pressed to hit anything at any range greater than about 80 yards. The rifle issued to the British Army was designed by Ezekiel Baker, who, when he fired 34 shots at 100 yards and 24 at 200 yards at a man-sized target, hit the target every time.

The Baker rifle had its problems: although much easier to reload than earlier forms of the weapon, even in the prone position, the rifling grooves were soon filled with powder deposits, and reloading became difficult, if not impossible. Riflemen were issued a mallet with which to hit the ramrod to force the ball down the barrel past the fouling. This meant that the ball was often badly misshapen on firing, which rendered vain any hope of improved accuracy. Other armies were frequently forced to use civilian rifled weapons.

At the Battle of Waterloo the British 95th Regiment had fourteen companies armed with rifles, and more than half of the men of the light companies of battalions of the King's German Legion, as well as the *Jäger* battalions in the Hanoverian, Netherlandish, and Prussian armies, also carried rifles. Little is said of this in the histories of the battle, but it is an important point, marking the service debut of the rifle.

David Westwood

See also Infantry; Musket
References and further reading
Blackmore, Howard L. 1994. *British Military Firearms, 1650–1850.* London: Greenhill.
Haythornthwaite, Philip J. 1979. *Weapons and Equipment of the Napoleonic Wars.* Poole, UK: Arms and Armour.
———. 1990. *The Napoleonic Source Book.* London: Guild.
———. 2002. *British Rifleman, 1797–1815.* Oxford: Osprey.
Hughes, B. P. 1974. *Firepower: Weapons Effectiveness on the Battlefield, 1630–1850.* London: Arms and Armour.
Urban, Mark. 2004. *Rifles: Six Years with Wellington's Legendary Sharpshooters.* London: Faber.
Westwood, David. 2004. *The Military Rifle.* Santa Barbara, CA: ABC-CLIO.

Rimsky-Korsakov, Alexander Mikhailovich (1753–1840)

Prominent Russian military commander. Born to a Russian noble family on 24 August 1753, Rimsky-Korsakov enlisted as a corporal in the Life Guard Preobrazhensk Regiment in 1768, rising to sub-ensign in 1769, to sergeant in 1770, to ensign in 1774, and to lieutenant in 1775. Promoted to lieutenant colonel in 1778, he transferred to the Chernigov Infantry Regiment and served in Poland from 1778 to 1779. During the Russo-Turkish War of 1787–

1792, he was assigned to the Austrian *Korps*, fighting at Khotin and Gangur in 1788. The following year, he commanded a detachment at Byrlad, Maximeni, on the Siret River and at Galati. He had the honor of delivering the news of the Russian victories to Catherine II, who promoted him to brigadier.

Rimsky-Korsakov transferred to the Life Guard Semeyonovsk Regiment on 25 July 1789 and served during the Russo-Swedish War on the galley flotilla against the Swedes at Friedrichsham, Neischlodt, and Julaksioki. He became a major general in 1793 and briefly visited Britain in 1794. He joined the Austrian army in the Austrian Netherlands and took part in various actions against the French in late 1794. He returned to Russia in 1795 and the following year participated in the Persian expedition along the Caspian Sea, distinguishing himself at Derbent and Gandja. Under Tsar Paul, Rimsky-Korsakov became the infantry inspector for the St. Petersburg Inspection and received promotion to lieutenant general on 15 January 1798. He became *chef* (colonel-proprietor) of the Rostov Musketeer Regiment on 28 September 1798.

In 1799 Rimsky-Korsakov commanded a corps against the French in Switzerland and was decisively defeated at the second battle of Zürich in September. He was removed from command and discharged from the army that November. He returned to service in March 1801, receiving the rank of general of infantry that month with seniority dating from December. In 1802 he became governor of Byelorussia and, one year later, was appointed the infantry inspector in Moscow. In 1805–1806 he commanded the Russian reserves in the western provinces. He became military governor of Lithuania on 1 October 1806 and organized local militias during the campaigns in Poland in 1806–1807. He took a discharge on 15 July 1809 following a disagreement with General Aleksey Arakcheyev. In 1812 he was again appointed military governor of Lithuania, serving in this position for the next eighteen years. He became a member of the State Council in 1830 and died in St. Petersburg on 25 May 1840.

Alexander Mikaberidze

See also Arakcheyev, Aleksey Andreyevich, Count; Catherine II "the Great," Tsarina; Fourth Coalition, War of the; Paul I, Tsar; Switzerland, Campaign in; Zürich, Second Battle of
References and further reading
Mikaberidze, Alexander. 2005. *The Russian Officer Corps in the Revolutionary and Napoleonic Wars, 1792–1815.* New York: Savas Beatie.
Mikhailovsky-Danilevsky, Alexander, and Dmitri Miliutin. 1852. *Istoriia voini Rossii s Frantsiei v 1799 godu.* St. Petersburg: Tip. Shtaba voenno-uchebnykh zavedenii.
Russkii biograficheskii slovar [Russian Biographical Dictionary]. 1896–1918. St. Petersburg: Izdanie Imperatorskago Russkago istoricheskago obshchestva.

River Plate, Expeditions to the

See Buenos Aires, Expeditions to

Rivoli, Battle of (14–15 January 1797)

Fought on the hilly ground between Lake Garda and the Adige River, a dozen miles northwest of Verona, the Battle of Rivoli was Bonaparte's most decisive victory in his first Italian campaign. The defeat at Rivoli led to the failure of the last Austrian attempt at relieving Mantua. After the capitulation of the fortress at the beginning of February 1797, Bonaparte could move his army to the Austrian borders, thus speeding up the chain of events leading to the end of the war in Italy and the Peace of Campo Formio.

After the Battle of Arcola in November 1796, both armies, tired, depleted, and worn to rags, would have welcomed a period of rest in winter quarters. Their hopes were to remain unfulfilled. After recent French defeat in Germany, the Directory looked toward peace and sent Minister Henri Clarke to Italy for armistice talks. Expecting Mantua to surrender very soon, Bonaparte opposed a cease-fire. It was the Aulic Council in Vienna, however, that entertained stronger reasons for reopening hostilities in Italy as soon as possible. The first was to make a new attempt at rescuing Mantua before lack of supplies and malarial disease forced *Feldmarschall* Dagobert Graf Würmser to capitulate. Political reasons were also at work. To the lower social classes supporting the *ancien régime,* the fall of Mantua would mean the final victory of the French Revolutionary cause in Italy. Moreover, the pope might be forced to consent to wage war against Revolutionary France by a new show of Austrian military enterprise. Such pressing needs led Vienna to send orders to the Austrian commander in Italy, *Feldzeugmeister* Joseph Alvinczy Freiherr von Berberek, for a new campaign that—rather unusually—was to begin in winter.

Beginning in December, a constant inflow of replacements started filling the gaps in the Austrian army. Admittedly, the quality of the new troops—recruits, Vienna volunteers, depot units—was on the average poor. By the new year, however, Alvinczy could field about 47,000 men for campaign service, the Mantua garrison (about 20,000) and some thousands for rear duties not included.

Once again, the Austrian plan to relieve Mantua, devised by the same Colonel Franz Weyrother later responsible for the plan at Austerlitz, provided for two separate lines of advance. A diversionary force, in two columns under *Feldmarschalleutnant* Adam Freiherr von Bajalich (6,000 men) and *Feldmarschalleutnant* Giovanni Marquis di Provera (9,000), would, respectively, push westward over the plain toward Verona and Legnago. By feinting operations on the Adige, they intended to draw Bonaparte's attention. Despite the approaching winter, however, the main thrust was to be delivered from the Alps. Under the direct command of Alvinczy, about 28,000 men in six columns would move from Trento down the Adige valley and through the chain of mountains (collectively called Monte Baldo) between the Adige and Lake Garda. After breaking through the bottleneck at Rivoli, they would make for Mantua.

This plan apparently rested on some uncertain assumptions: (1) that a substantial part of Bonaparte's army was south of the Po preparing to invade the Papal States; (2) that Bonaparte would mistake the diversionary force for the main army and would concentrate most French troops behind the Adige from Verona to Legnago; (3) that consequently only minor forces would be left at the strong defensive position of Rivoli in the upper Adige valley and, once attacked, they would not be able to receive immediate support; (4) that the Austrian columns could advance over mountain roads and tracks covered with snow in a coordinated way and with relatively small manpower consumption; and (5) that Würmser could actively cooperate by launching sorties from Mantua. None of these assumptions turned out to be valid.

The (French) Armée d'Italie had also received some replacements. Its general situation, however, did not look good. Besides the chronic lack of equipment and supplies, after nine months of campaigning Bonaparte had run short of capable generals and knew that the fighting quality of his troops was declining. The French deployment in January 1797 was as follows: General Pierre Augereau's division (9,000 men) behind the Adige between Verona and Legnago; André Masséna's (9,000) around Verona; Barthélemy Catherine Joubert's (10,250) at Rivoli and on Monte Baldo; General Antoine Rey's (4,100) at Brescia and along the western shore of the Garda; a reserve under General Claude Victor (2,400) at Castelnuovo and Villafranca; and General Thomas Alexandre Dumas's and Claude Dallemagne's blockading corps (10,200) around Mantua. To the south of the Po, there was only a small column under General Jean Lannes, with 2,000 French and several thousand Italian troops.

On 7 January Bonaparte left for Bologna, where three days later he received the news that Provera's column had appeared before Legnago. He immediately ordered Lannes back to the Adige, and rushed to his headquarters at Roverbella, just north of Mantua, where he arrived probably early on the twelfth. As Alvinczy had hoped, by that time Bonaparte still believed that the main threat was on the lower Adige and thus made his dispositions accordingly. Later that day, however, he started receiving reports announcing that Joubert was under attack at La Corona, a steep defile on Monte Baldo, five miles north of Rivoli. To ascertain the real magnitude of this new threat, Bonaparte asked Joubert for more information. Early on the thirteenth, Joubert realized that he was facing a strong and determined army (actually, 28,000 men). While three of Alvinczy's columns were marching down the valley roads along the Adige (Prince Reuss's and Ocksay's on the western, Vukassovich on the eastern bank), three other columns (Köblös's, Lipthay's, and Lusignan's) trudged along the tracks of Monte Baldo covered with snow. Later in the afternoon, fearing being outflanked, Joubert withdrew to Rivoli.

By 3:00 P.M., thanks to Joubert's reports, Bonaparte knew that the main attack was coming from the north. He reacted swiftly, rushing Masséna with three demi-brigades and some cavalry to Rivoli. Rey's division was also ordered to move to Rivoli, a brigade under General Joachim Murat being ferried across Lake Garda.

At Rivoli, where now both Bonaparte and Alvinczy were expecting to fight a decisive battle, less than four miles separated the Adige from Lake Garda. Over this ground, a two-layer amphitheater facing the southern slopes of Monte Baldo formed one of the strongest defensive positions anywhere in the Italian Alps. The village of Rivoli lay (and still lies) in the center of this hilly semicircle that stretches to the north, the west, and the south, with the steep bank of the Adige to the east. The outward and higher layer of the amphitheater has a diameter of about three miles, starting from the Chapel of San Marco to the north, and ending at Monte Pipolo to the south. A mile-wide plateau runs throughout its extension. Three villages, San Giovanni, Caprino, and Pesina (from east to west), are located on the plateau along the banks of a small stream called the Tasso. The inner layer has a diameter of a mile and a half.

A peculiar feature made Rivoli an excellent defensive position. While the defender could easily undertake operations with all three arms (infantry, cavalry, and artillery), a network of relatively good roads being available to approach the battlefield from the south, the attacker had no such facility, as the northern accesses from Monte Baldo, even in more favorable weather, were only practicable to infantry. This suggested that Alvinczy's field artillery and cavalry should file along the roads on either side of the Adige. From the river valley bottom, the only exit to the Rivoli amphitheater was by the road on the western bank. It led to the Dogana Inn and the main village, after winding up to an inner plateau through a steep, narrow, and easily defensible defile.

By the evening of 13 January, Joubert had deployed his troops over a restricted area along the edges of the inner

plateau, where they could take advantage of some entrenchments. Three Austrian columns (from east to west, under Ocksay, Köblös, and Lipthay, respectively) had encamped for the night on the heights north of the Tasso. Lusignan was farther to the west, with orders to make a long outflanking detour and reach the southern side of the amphitheater at Monte Pipolo, thus cutting off Joubert's line of retreat and preventing Bonaparte from sending him support. Lusignan's column was, however, considerably behind schedule because of the snow and the bad dirt tracks.

Bonaparte joined Joubert during the night, rushing ahead of Masséna's troops. From Bonaparte's recollections and most French sources, we learn that once on the spot he immediately recognized the enemy plan and took adequate countermeasures. As a matter of fact, later that night Joubert's division advanced to regain control of the outward plateau south of the Tasso. In this sector, about 9,000 French were now facing 12,000 Austrians, the latter being short of artillery and rations.

Following the French advance, skirmishes broke out at daybreak on the fourteenth. The combat rapidly escalated along the line, ebbing and flowing, but with no decisive outcome. After a couple of hours, around 9:00 A.M., Lipthay managed to outflank the French left and routed two demi-brigades (the 29th and 85th). By that time, however, the awaited reinforcements appeared on the southern edge of the battlefield. Masséna brought the 32nd forward, and by 10:30 A.M. the French left was restored. Farther east, the 14th demi-brigade, under General Louis-Alexandre Berthier, were gallantly resisting Ocksay's attack. Meanwhile, Prince Reuss's column had started climbing up the road leading from the valley bottom to the inner plateau, receiving substantial support from the guns Vukassovich had deployed on the eastern bank of the Adige. On higher ground, the 39th demi-brigade put up fierce resistance against an enemy that was numerically superior, but was forced to advance uphill in long road columns. With great perseverance, Reuss's troops eventually succeeded in pushing the French out of their entrenchments and started streaming over the inner plateau.

The prospect of a junction between the column from the Adige and those coming down the ridge posed a serious threat to the French right flank and rear. Joubert and Berthier set to work, however, to rally their men for a counterattack against Reuss. Meanwhile, about 250 cavalry under generals Charles-Victor Leclerc and Antoine Lasalle charged the troops under Köblös and Ocksay, which after hours of fighting lay scattered on the plateau. Some Austrian units apparently panicked and started retreating, partly uphill, partly down the road to the Adige valley bottom, the latter causing some disorder in Reuss's tightly packed column. It is believed that at this crucial point two

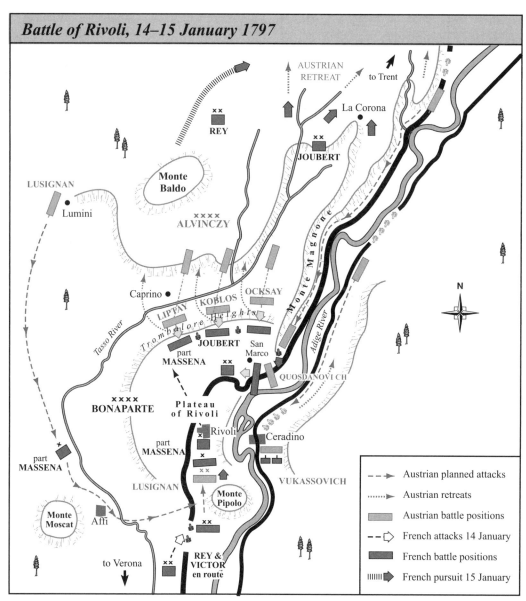

Battle of Rivoli, 14–15 January 1797

Austrian planned attacks
Austrian retreats
Austrian battle positions
French attacks 14 January
French battle positions
French pursuit 15 January

Adapted from Chandler 1966, 117.

Austrian ammunition wagons exploded, thus spreading further chaos among the infantry ranks. Certainly it is a fact that most of Reuss's units broke and fled down the road to the Adige. With effective cavalry and artillery support, Joubert and Masséna moved forward again and took definitive control of the outward plateau and the villages, repulsing the Austrians toward Monte Baldo.

As the main action was being fought, around 11:00 A.M. Lusignan's column appeared on Monte Pipolo, at the southern edge of the amphitheater. It was, however, too late for Lusignan's force to influence the battle's outcome. Even worse, he found himself trapped between the French army at Rivoli and the reinforcements approaching from the south. Attacked from many sides, Lusignan's men retreated in great disorder, leaving hundreds of prisoners be-

hind. By late afternoon, the Battle of Rivoli was over and Alvinczy's army in full retreat.

Bonaparte did not sleep on the battlefield. Being informed that Provera was now in sight of Mantua, he entrusted Joubert with the pursuit of the Austrian army (which Bonaparte's subordinate duly embarked on, clashing again with Alvinczy on the fifteenth) and then himself rushed with Masséna's and Victor's divisions to face the new threat. Austrian losses at the Battle of Rivoli and in the following pursuit are estimated at 14,000 dead, wounded, stragglers, and prisoners. The French had 5,000 losses. On this figure, however, sources are obscure, as usual.

At Rivoli Bonaparte showed most of his superior military skills at their best. The concentration of his army at Rivoli was executed at an exceptional speed, the night march of Masséna's division being one of the keys to victory. During the battle, Bonaparte succeeded in always keeping his numerically inferior army concentrated in a central position. He was, moreover, also favored by the excellent defensive ground, some faulty assumptions made by his opponents, the poor general quality of the Austrian army, and the lack of coordination between Alvinczy and his subordinates.

Had Provera succeeded in arriving at Mantua on 13 January, he would have forced Bonaparte to choose between two alternatives: to rush in support of Joubert, thus risking Mantua being rescued; or to reinforce the French forces around the fortress, thus abandoning Joubert to his fate. In either case, the outcome of the campaign would have not been the same.

Marco Gioannini

See also Alvinczy, Joseph Freiherr von Berberek; Arcola, Battle of; Augereau, Pierre-Charles-François; Berthier, Louis-Alexandre; Campo Formio, Treaty of; Clausewitz, Karl Maria von; Directory, The; Italian Campaigns (1792–1797); Joubert, Barthélemy Catherine; Lannes, Jean; Lasalle, Antoine Charles Louis, comte; Leclerc, Charles-Victor Emmanuel; Mantua, Sieges of; Masséna, André; Murat, Joachim; Papal States; Pius VI, Pope; Victor, Claude Perrin; Würmser, Dagobert Sigismund Graf

References and further reading
Boycott-Brown, Martin. 2001. *The Road to Rivoli: Napoleon's First Campaign.* London: Cassell.
Esposito, Vincent J., and John R. Elting. 1999. *A Military History and Atlas of the Napoleonic Wars.* London: Greenhill.

Robespierre, Maximilien François Marie Isidore (1758–1794)

Maximilien Robespierre has been cast as both hero and villain of the Revolution, his name inextricably associated with the Terror of 1793–1794, for which he has served as a scapegoat. For some he was a great idealist, for others an appalling hypocrite; it is almost impossible to reconcile the apparently conflicting aspects of his brief, but momentous, political career. Yet in many respects he reflected the general fortunes of a Revolution that lurched dramatically from idealistic expectations to violent extremism. On account of his admiration for Rousseau, it is tempting to regard Robespierre as an ideologue who sought to make others conform to his vision, driving the Revolution in an authoritarian direction. Yet Robespierre's ideals were inevitably affected by changing circumstances, above all in the hothouse atmosphere created by internal rebellion and foreign war, where the very survival of the Republic became paramount for its leaders. As such, he incarnated both the triumphs and the tragedy of the Revolution.

Robespierre, who hailed from the northern town of Arras, where he was born in 1758, in modest circumstances (the original "de" in his name was a pre-Revolutionary affectation later abandoned), made his local reputation as a champion of the poor. Practicing as a barrister in his native town, he defended impecunious clients, a reputation that secured him election to the Estates-General in 1789. There he first emerged from obscurity when he demanded that all adult males be admitted to the franchise; restrictions on the vote were an affront to the Rights of Man. His distinction as a "man of the people" grew apace, chiefly via the Jacobin Club of Paris. Following the collapse of the monarchy in 1792, he was elected to the National Convention summoned to draw up a republican constitution, at the head of the list of deputies for the capital.

Yet, as an impeccable dresser, in wig and silk stockings, he was for, rather than of, the populace. In 1793, having condemned participants in a grocery riot, he was reminded that "citizen Robespierre" had never experienced pangs of hunger. Unlike Jean-Paul Marat, or indeed Georges Danton, who were capable of haranguing the crowd on street corners, Robespierre excelled in carefully crafted speeches, delivered to more orderly assemblies (when shouted down on 9 Thermidor—27 July 1794—and subsequently arrested, he was immobilized and took no action to secure his release). Nonetheless, he was totally dedicated to the Revolutionary cause, living simply in lodgings and leaving little in the way of personal wealth, hence his sobriquet, "the incorruptible."

Such puritanism, combined with single-mindedness, rendered him ready to sacrifice all to the cause, including himself. The acid test came with the exercise of real power in 1793. Condemnation of king and government (he was a ferocious regicide) was coherently pursued, but the year Robespierre spent on the great Committee of Public Safety inevitably proved much more demanding. Robespierre has become synonymous with the committee and its policies because he was its chief spokesman, justifying the course taken in a great series of speeches made between the autumn of 1793 and the early summer of 1794. As a consequence, he has been accused of great hypocrisy: the individual who had opposed the war that broke out in 1792 now demanded it be pursued with the utmost vigor; the deputy who made a celebrated speech against the death penalty in 1790 became willing to strike down opponents of the Revolution without mercy; the scourge of the clergy sponsored the Cult of the Supreme Being and appeared to regard himself as its pontiff.

In view of the great crisis facing the fledgling French Republic, few of Robespierre's colleagues had expressed misgivings about the establishment of the Terror, deemed necessary to strengthen government and punish rebels.

Maximilien Robespierre, the leading member of the infamous Committee of Public Safety that ruled France during the Terror of 1793–1794. Thousands were guillotined as alleged enemies of the Revolution. (Library of Congress)

Success in defeating internal insurrection and rolling back the foreign armies, however, led many to ask how much longer these draconian measures should remain in place. At this point Robespierre's judgment appeared to desert him, as those proposing a slackening of repression, notably his erstwhile colleague Danton, were put down as counter-revolutionaries. At Paris the Terror intensified instead of diminishing.

Was this an inexorable momentum, as power became concentrated in fewer hands, difficult to relinquish, and dissent still harder to tolerate? Or had Robespierre in particular come to regard terror not simply as a means of defeating enemies but of creating a utopian order, where all base passions would cease to exist? Robespierre contended that democracy could only flourish among virtuous citizens, but was the Terror becoming a shortcut to fashioning new people, forcing them to be free? Though it is anachronistic to talk of totalitarianism, Robespierre seems to have succumbed to the temptation of using violence as a means of effecting thoroughgoing political and cultural change.

Historians still debate Robespierre's demise in the early summer of 1794. Ill for a month, the strain of office taking its toll, he had perhaps become out of touch, even deluded. His call on 8 Thermidor for yet more heads to roll, when "guillotine sickness" was spreading alarm among members of the Convention on whom his authority ultimately rested, was a profound error, almost a suicidal gesture. He had never led an organized party, but the next day those most closely associated with him, such as Louis Antoine de Saint-Just, were arrested along with him. The people of Paris, themselves disciplined by the Terror, failed to offer assistance, and he was either shot, or shot himself through the jaw in a vain attempt to end his life. He was guillotined the next day, 10 Thermidor (28 July). His execution did not represent the end of the Revolution, nor even the immediate termination of the Terror, but there was a reassertion of both the liberal and limited goals of the Revolution.

Malcolm Crook

See also Convention, The; French Revolution; Jacobins; Public Safety, Committee of; Terror, The; Thermidor Coup
References and further reading
Andress, David. 2005. *The Terror: Civil War in the French Revolution.* London: Little, Brown.
Cobb, Richard. 1998. *The French and their Revolution: Selected Writings.* London: Murray.
Gough, Hugh. 1997. *The Terror in the French Revolution.* Basingstoke, UK: Palgrave Macmillan.
Hampson, Norman. 1974. *The Life and Opinions of Maximilien Robespierre.* London: Duckworth.
Hardman, John. 1999. *Robespierre.* London: Longman.
Higonnet, Patrice. 1998. *Goodness beyond Virtue: Jacobins during the French Revolution.* Cambridge, MA: Harvard University Press.
Jordan, David P. 1985. *The Revolutionary Career of Maximilien Robespierre.* New York: Free Press.
Kennedy, Michael L. 1982–2000. *The Jacobin Clubs in the French Revolution.* 3 vols. Princeton: Princeton University Press.
Palmer, R. R. 2005. *Twelve Who Ruled: The Year of the Terror in the French Revolution.* Princeton: Princeton University Press. (Orig. pub. 1941.)
Rudé, George, ed. 1967. *Robespierre.* Englewood Cliffs, NJ: Prentice-Hall.
Scurr, Ruth. 2006. *Fatal Purity: Robespierre and the French Revolution.* London: Chatto and Windus.
Thompson, J. M. 1988. *Robespierre.* Oxford: Blackwell.

Roer, Battle of the (2 October 1794)

The Battle of the Roer resulted in the Austrians being forced out of Flanders and back across the Rhine. It may have been one of the most effectively fought battles of the French Revolutionary armies, well planned and executed by commanders and troops who had learned their military craft through bitter experience.

The summer of 1794 saw the end of the Terror under Maximilien Robespierre and the abandonment of the policy of executing unsuccessful generals, or even those suspected of royalist leanings. The season also saw the enormous expansion of the French armies, thanks to the mobilization of the nation under Lazare Carnot, and an improvement in the weapons that those armies wielded. Through experience and training, the new drafts became more proficient in the use of their arms as well. Although the French still practiced a more open order of battle, with emphasis on skirmishing, they had learned to move large bodies of men rapidly and to fight in the more traditional, formal manner.

The Army of the Sambre and Meuse was one of the chief beneficiaries of the improvements. As the principal army at this stage in the war, it was charged with completing the conquest of the Low Countries. General Jean-Baptiste Jourdan, who commanded the army, was a politically active general, but a somewhat cautious one, as well. Jourdan opened his autumn campaign with an attack on Ayvaille, from which he quickly drove the Austrian defenders. *Feldzeugmeister* Franz Sebastian de Croix Graf von Clerfayt retreated with his forces to the river Roer, approximately 40 kilometers west of the Rhine, where he hoped to establish a defensive line behind the river to await reinforcements and hold onto part of the Low Countries. The Austrians destroyed the bridges over the Roer, and rendered many fords uncrossable. Other crossings were covered by field fortifications and artillery.

Jourdan was ordered by Carnot to pause in his pursuit of Clerfayt until he had captured the important city of Maastricht. Jourdan realized that the strategically proper course was to push the Austrians over the Rhine, to prevent them from relieving Maastricht. Therefore, ignoring his orders, Jourdan left a small covering force around Maastricht, then pushed his entire army on toward the Roer. He had around 100,000 men, opposed by 76,000 Austrians. The Austrians were established on the right bank of the Roer, with the exception of a bridgehead at Aldenhoven at the center of their line. Having conducted a detailed reconnaissance of the line, Jourdan ordered an attack on 2 October. Fog delayed the opening of the battle from 5:00 A.M. to 10:00 A.M. Several divisions on the right were to make a frontal attack on the Austrians at Duren, while another division was to sweep round the Austrian open flank and over the Roer.

In the event, the flanking attack went too wide and did not arrive until the end of the day. Even so, the Austrians were forced back by hard fighting. On Jourdan's left, the attack was held up for a while by well-sited Austrian artillery. Eventually, General Jean-Baptiste Kléber massed his own artillery and covered an attack by divisions under generals

Michel Ney and Jean-Baptiste Bernadotte. French troops swam across the river and established a bridgehead on the eastern bank, despite heavy fire from the Austrians. By the end of the day, Ney and Bernadotte had achieved their goals. When night fell, they were constructing bridges to bring the rest of the left wing across the Roer. In the center, the French launched a frontal attack on Aldenhoven. They overran the fortifications guarding the city and soon captured it. The Austrians evacuated their bridgehead and destroyed the bridge behind them, preventing Jourdan from crossing. By nightfall on 2 October, the French were victorious all along the line. Clerfayt ordered his men to retreat to the Rhine, which they crossed by the sixth.

Tim J. Watts

See also Bernadotte, Jean-Baptiste-Jules; Carnot, Lazare Nicolas Marguerite; Flanders, Campaigns in; Jourdan, Jean-Baptiste; Kléber, Jean-Baptiste; Ney, Michel; Robespierre, Maximilien François Marie Isidore; Terror, The
References and further reading
Phipps, Ramsay Weston. 1980. *The Armies of the First French Republic and the Rise of the Marshals of Napoleon I.* Vol. 2, *The Armées de la Moselle, du Rhin, de Sambre-et-Meuse, de Rhin-et-Moselle.* London: Greenwood. (Orig. pub. 1926–1939.)
Ross, Steven T. 1973. *Quest for Victory: French Military Strategy, 1792–1799.* New York: Barnes.

Roliça, Battle of (17 August 1808)

The first major encounter between British forces under Lieutenant General Sir Arthur Wellesley and the French in Portugal. The French under General Henri François Delaborde had taken up a strong position around the village of Roliça, but they were forced back by the British and Portuguese. Delaborde withdrew to join the main French force under General Jean Andoche Junot, leading to the Battle of Vimeiro.

After landing in Portugal, Wellesley quickly led his forces southward toward Lisbon. Junot needed time to gather as many troops as possible to meet this threat and deployed Delaborde to delay the advance of the Anglo-Portuguese army. Having been pushed back in a skirmish at Obidos, Delaborde deployed his force around the village of Roliça. On the morning of 17 August 1808, Wellesley advanced to attack in three columns. On the left Brigadier General Ronald Ferguson had 4,500 men. The right flank was under the command of Colonel Nicholas Trant, leading 1,300 Portuguese troops. Wellesley himself took control of the central force of 9,000 men. Delaborde quickly realized that the enemy force was three times his own strength and that the Anglo-Portuguese attempt to outflank him would succeed if he remained in position. The

French fought a skilful action allowing them to retreat to a ridgeline one mile to the rear of Roliça. This position could be approached using four gullies.

Having re-formed his force, Wellesley was determined to attack the new position using the same tactics as before, relying on his flank attacks to make the enemy position untenable. Trant and Ferguson, however, were slowed down by the terrain, and the central force attacked first. The central gully was attacked by the 29th and 9th Foot. The 29th Foot was in the lead; when it reached the top it was met by disciplined fire from a Swiss regiment. This fire disorganized the front of the column. The British were then attacked in the flank by a French force that had been positioned in the ground between the gullies. This attack was successful, resulting in the death of the colonel of the 29th and the capture of the regimental colors.

The 9th Foot now advanced in support of their comrades, and they were able to launch a counterattack, which retook the colors, though in the process their commander was killed. For the next two hours, Delaborde skillfully held off the British attacks with a series of charges once the British tried to deploy from the tops of the gullies. Delaborde was nevertheless under pressure. Wounded, aware that Ferguson was now on his flank, and threatened by a large force of Portuguese cavalry, Delaborde used his small cavalry force to delay this attack. The Portuguese proved to be no match for the French, who were able to withdraw with the loss of around 700 men. Wellesley had suffered nearly 500 casualties. Delaborde had fought a valiant action, allowing Junot to prepare his forces for the next confrontation, at Vimeiro.

Ralph Baker

See also Junot, Jean Andoche, duc d'Abrantès; Peninsular War; Vimeiro, Battle of; Wellington, Arthur Wellesley, First Duke of
References and further reading
Chartrand, René. 2001. *Vimeiro 1808*. London: Osprey.

Romana, Pedro de la

See Caro y Sureda, Pedro, Marqués de la Romana

Romanticism

Romanticism may be defined as a self-conscious artistic movement directed against the rationalism, mechanistic materialism, and classicism of the Enlightenment and the hegemony of France between 1789 and 1815. Romanticism means expressing one's emotion and intuition as sources of truth. The love of nature, the quest for new experience,

the view of society as an organism rather than as a machine—all these are characteristics of Romanticism.

Romanticism involved every aspect and genre of the arts: poetry, prose, drama, the visual arts, and music (opera in particular). Although a diverse movement in art, literature, and music, the chief characteristics of Romanticism in the arts include emotion, sensitivity, imagination, self-expression, the exotic, the dramatic, and a return to the medieval. According to Romantics, the chief weakness in the Enlightenment was its neglect of the imagination, emotions, aesthetics, and mystery. The origins of Romanticism date from the 1750s with the work of Jean-Jacques Rousseau and Immanuel Kant. Although both philosophers are often considered to be Enlightenment thinkers, they were forerunners of the Romantic movement. Rousseau stressed sensibility in his writings, while Kant, although a rationalist, believed that knowledge was subjective rather than objective in nature.

The Romantic movement flourished in parts of Europe that had opposed French Revolutionary and Napoleonic rule, particularly in the German states and Britain. Initially many Romantics, both poets and musicians, had been supporters of the Revolutionary upheaval in France. But as the Revolution grew more extreme and Napoleon began conquering Europe and subjecting occupied populations to the French worldview, they turned against all things French, including its Neoclassical aesthetic.

Napoleon and the French Revolution were catalysts in the Romantic movement. This is particularly evident in the writings of Byron, Shelley, Coleridge, Keats, and Wordsworth. The poet William Wordsworth introduced Romanticism to Britain. Like many Romantics, Wordsworth welcomed the French Revolution, as is evidenced in his poem *The Prelude*, but turned against it when liberty became terror. In drama, Romanticism meant departing from classical rules; in poetry it meant, to Wordsworth at least, using simple rather than literary language and writing about ordinary people. His poems evoke a mystical adoration of nature.

German Romantics were tremendously affected by the Napoleonic era, and the movement was intimately connected to the nascent German sense of nationality, stemming from the humiliation of the Napoleonic Wars. Before Napoleon, German Romantics had not been concerned with a German identity and generally had supported the liberal gains of the French Revolutionaries. But all this changed with Napoleon's conquests. German Romantic writers such as Johann Gottfried von Herder, often referred to as cultural nationalists, looked to the Middle Ages for a sense of German history and collective identity. He identified the *Volkgeist* (national spirit), objected to French dominance of German manners, and urged Germans to focus on their own culture.

Napoleon's influence is unquestionable in the music of Ludwig van Beethoven, who had been an admirer of Napoleon until 1804, the year he crowned himself Emperor. It was in this year that Beethoven had actually written a dedication of his Third Symphony, the *Eroica,* to Napoleon, but when he learned of the coronation, he tore the page out of the score. The great transitional figure between the Classic and Romantic eras in music, Beethoven is still a figure who, both in his person and through his achievement, has come to typify Romantic notions of individual genius and the transcendent expression of the freedom of the human spirit. These values survived to underpin nascent democratic and antiauthoritarian political movements around the world.

Leigh Whaley

See also Beethoven, Ludwig van; Byron, George Noel Gordon, Lord; Coleridge, Samuel Taylor; Goethe, Johann Wolfgang von; Kant, Immanuel; Keats, John; Kleist, Heinrich Wilhelm von; Literature and the Romantic Movement (contextual essay); Schiller, Friedrich von; Shelley, Percy Bysshe; Wordsworth, William
References and further reading
Bainbridge, Simon John Julian. 1995. *Napoleon and English Romanticism.* Cambridge: Cambridge University Press.
Murray, Christopher John, ed. 2003. *Encyclopedia of the Romantic Era, 1760–1850.* New York: Dearborn.

Roncesvalles, Battle of (25 July 1813)

Engagement fought between the French and Anglo-Spanish forces in July 1813, which formed part of what is sometimes known as the Battles of the Pyrenees, together with the battles of Sorauren and Maya, during the Peninsular War. When Marshal Nicolas Soult began his counteroffensive through the Pyrenees in July 1813, he ordered generals Honoré Reille and Bertrand Clausel with the 40,000 men under their command to advance from St. Jean-Pied-de-Port and to attack the Allied forces at the pass at Roncesvalles.

The pass itself was held by Major General John Byng's British brigade, supported by the Spanish regiment of León. The Marquis of Wellington had reinforced the position eight days before by ordering a division commanded by Lieutenant General Sir Lowry Cole to advance from Pamplona. At 6:00 A.M. on 25 July, the French attacked, led by the troops of Clausel. They advanced on the high ground on either side of the road running through the pass. Byng's brigade was holding the eastern side of the pass. Due to the steep, grass-covered slopes, they were in a strong position. There now followed a period of fierce skirmishing, which held up the French advance for three hours until Clausel was able to move three battalions onto the flank of the British position. Byng then retreated to the heights at Altobiscar, which Clausel did not attempt to attack.

While Clausel was making limited progress, Reille had tried to advance in the west and had begun to move onto the Lindus plateau, where they were met by Major General Robert Ross commanding troops from Cole's division. Ross had heard the noise of the fighting between Byng and Clausel and ordered his Brunswick light troops forward to watch the activity of the enemy to his front. In a short time they made contact with French troops under the command of General Maximilen Foy. Ross was deploying his forces on the plateau and in order to complete this maneuver, he ordered a company of the 20th Foot to charge the French. A short melee took place until Ross ordered the company to withdraw. The terrain forced Reille to deploy on a narrow frontage, and as the French columns tried to break onto the plateau they were stopped by the fire of the British lines.

By now Cole had been able to bring up fresh troops and by 2:00 P.M. could deploy a further three brigades against the French. Despite the fact that the Allied troops were heavily outnumbered, the French were unable to make any headway, and the battle ended at around 5:00 P.M., due to a heavy fog covering the battlefield. Portuguese infantry arrived to reinforce Cole further, but he took the decision to withdraw during the night. Wellington was critical of this order, as he had instructed that the passes were to be held if at all possible. Cole's force had suffered the loss of about 450 men, but he had held up Reille's advance for almost a day.

Ralph Baker

See also Foy, Maximilen Sebastien, comte; Maya, Battle of; Peninsular War; Reille, Honoré Charles Michel Joseph, comte; Sorauren, Battle of; Soult, Nicolas Jean de Dieu; Wellington, Arthur Wellesley, First Duke of
References and further reading
Robertson, Ian. 2003. *Wellington Invades France.* Mechanicsburg, PA: Stackpole.

Rosas, Siege of

See Pyrenean Campaigns (1793–1795)

Rosetta Stone

The Rosetta stone is a damaged granodiorite *stela* (inscribed slab) 112 centimeters tall, weighing three-quarters of a ton, and is probably the most important find in the history of Egyptology. It provided the key to deciphering Egyptian hieroglyphics.

It was made in 196 B.C. in Memphis and bears a decree in two languages written in three scripts: one text is written in Greek (the governmental language); the second in Coptic, using the demotic script, that is, the everyday script of literate Egyptians; and the third in Coptic as well, but using hieroglyphics (the script that was 3,000 years old then and used for religious documents). The decree is in honor of the boy king, Ptolemy V Epiphanes (205–180 B.C.) and records the decision of the Egyptian priests to establish a royal cult in return for concessions to the temples. The stone was probably originally erected at the temple city of Sais. Copies were intended to be erected at every temple. Its rough back indicates that it had its back to a wall. It is likely to have been moved to Rosetta in medieval times to be used as a building block.

When Bonaparte invaded Egypt in 1798, he took with him a party of 167 scientists and artists, called the savants, who studied the antiquities they found. Thus Bonaparte could be said to be the father of Egyptology. One of the party, Dominique Vivant, baron Denon, wrote an account of the campaign. In July 1799 French soldiers under the command of the engineer officer, Pierre François Bouchard, were dismantling a house to prepare the defenses of el-Rashid (Rosetta), when they discovered the stone. Its significance was quickly realized because it was clear from the Greek text that the other texts were the same, making it possible to use the stone as the first significant step in deciphering hieroglyphics. The French took copies of the text, using the stone as a printing block. Traces of the ink survive today. In 1801 the French, now commanded by General Louis Desaix, surrendered to the British and Turks. Under the Treaty of Alexandria, they surrendered the antiquities they had collected to the British. In 1802 these antiquities were donated to the British Museum, where the stone is exhibited.

Even with the stone, deciphering hieroglyphics took more than twenty years. A number of scholars worked on the puzzle including Johann Akerbad, Sylvestre de Saey, the English polymath Thomas Young, and the brilliant Frenchman Jean-François Champollion. Hieroglyphs were originally thought to be picture symbols rather than symbols of sounds (phonetic symbols). A number of cartouches containing royal names had been translated with the help of Greek and Roman sources. The translation of these names established that the hieroglyphs within the cartouches were phonetic symbols. Thomas Young used the stone and a large obelisk brought from Pilae to Kingston Lacey, Dorset, to translate a few symbols, including those which spell out phonetically the name for Ptolemy.

Champollion realized in 1822 that even hieroglyphics outside the cartouches used phonetic as well as picture symbols. He also realized that Coptic, which was written in an adapted Greek alphabet called the demotic script, was a form of the language of ancient Egypt. In other words, two of the inscriptions were in Coptic, simply using different scripts. Putting this information together enabled hieroglyphics to be translated.

Rohan Saravanamuttu

See also Desaix, Louis-Charles-Antoine, chevalier de Veygoux; Egypt; Middle East Campaign; Savants
References and further reading
Denon, Baron Vivant. 1986. *Travels in Egypt.* London: Darf. (Orig. pub. 1802.)
Meyerson, Daniel. 2005. *The Linguist and the Emperor: Napoleon and Champollion's Quest to Decipher the Rosetta Stone.* New York: Random House.
Sole, Robert, and Dominique Vabelle. 2001. *The Rosetta Stone: The Story of the Decoding of Hieroglyphics.* London: Profile.

Rovereto, Battle of (4 September 1796)

Fought in the autumn of 1796 during *Feldmarschall* Dagobert Graf Würmser's second campaign to rescue besieged Mantua, the so-called Battle of Rovereto was less a full-scale battle than a sequence of small and somewhat separated combats that allowed Bonaparte's army to break through a row of narrow defiles in the upper Adige valley on their way to Trento.

After Würmser's first failure at relieving Mantua, in August 1796, the Austrian army retreated to the Tyrol. While Bonaparte set about reorganizing his worn-out army and preparing a new blockade of Mantua, the strategic situation quickly developed in a rather peculiar fashion. The Directory in Paris urged the unwilling commander of the Armée d'Italie to push northward through the Tyrol in an attempt to link up with General Jean Moreau in Germany. Meanwhile, the Aulic Council in Vienna ordered Würmser to prepare for a second attempt to relieve Mantua—a strategic decision taken partly for political reasons, in order to reassure Naples and the pope of Austria's will to continue the war against France.

According to the Austrian plan, *Feldzeugmeister* Paul Freiherr von Davidovich was to defend the access to Tyrol with a force of about 14,000 men in the area between Trento, Rovereto, and Lake Garda, with another 11,000 regulars and *Schützen* (rifle-armed militia) being scattered over the alpine valleys in the Austrian rear. Meanwhile, Würmser, with two divisions (about 9,500 men), would proceed from Trento down the Sugana valley, join with *Feldmarschalleutnant* Johann Freiherr Mészáros's division (10,000) in Bassano and make for Mantua via Vicenza. His leading division (that of *Feldmarschalleutnant* Karl Freiherr von Sebottendorf) left Trento on 1 September. The very same day Bonaparte determined his final dispositions. The left wing under General Claude-Henri, comte de Vaubois (11,000) was to reach Mori at the northern end of Lake Garda by either following the western shore of the lake or crossing it by boat. The center column under General André Masséna (13,000) was to move up the Adige valley, pushing the enemy outposts from Ala and Serravalle. General Pierre Augereau's division (9,000) would cover Masséna's right flank, trudging its way through the Monti Lessini between the Adige and the Sugana valley. The French columns had orders to concentrate before Rovereto, south of Trento.

On 3 September, Masséna made progress in the Adige valley, dislodging *Generalmajor* Joseph Philipp Freiherr von Vukassovich's detachments (2,700) from Ala and Serravalle. Primitive mountain tracks, however, considerably delayed Augereau's movement. On being informed of the French advance, Würmser ordered Davidovich to counterattack at dawn. It was Bonaparte, however, who kept the initiative on the fourth. To force the defile at Marco, Masséna sent a strong detachment of light troops under General Jean-Joseph Pijon to the heights, as his main body pushed forward along the main road. Fearing being outflanked, the Austrians retreated to Rovereto and, after a short and unsuccessful defense of this city, back to Calliano. Meanwhile, Vaubois attacked the entrenched camp at Mori, defeating Prince Reuss's brigade and thus establishing a link with Masséna.

Situated in a very narrow defile between the river and a steep mountain wall, the Austrian entrenchments at Calliano were held by about 4,800 men (Vukassovich's and *Generalmajor* Johann Graf Spork's brigades). A sudden massed charge by three of Masséna's demi-brigades, with the support of heavy artillery fire, broke the discouraged defenders. The Austrians soon withdrew to Trento in great disorder, after losing in two days of fighting about 6,000 men and many guns. Figures for French casualties are uncertain.

Marco Gioannini

See also Augereau, Pierre-François-Charles; Directory, The; Italian Campaigns (1792–1797); Mantua, Sieges of; Masséna, André; Moreau, Jean Victor; Würmser, Dagobert Sigismund Graf
References and further reading
Boycott-Brown, Martin. 2001. *The Road to Rivoli: Napoleon's First Campaign.* London: Cassell.
Esposito, Vincent J., and John R. Elting. 1999. *A Military History and Atlas of the Napoleonic Wars.* London: Greenhill.

Royal Navy

Introduction
During the whole period of the French Revolutionary and Napoleonic Wars, Britain maintained the largest and most effective navy in the world. This circumstance came about by reason of necessity, for the strategic realities of a small island nation, unable to raise a large standing army by dint of tradition and size of population, demanded that the country's resources for defense should be allocated to its navy. The Royal Navy was superior to its rivals in practically every sphere except for ship design. The quality and training of its crews, the fitness of its officers, the skills attained by its men in navigation and gunnery, all combined to render the Royal Navy practically unbeatable. Until well into the Peninsular War in Spain, successive British governments allocated far greater sums for the navy than for the army, for the simple reason that its seamen could perform many more essential services for the nation than could its soldiers. Whereas Britain's continental allies could be relied upon to supply the vast numbers of troops needed to fight France on land, which Britain was itself incapable of raising, the Royal Navy could oppose the Revolutionary and Napoleonic navies to an extent impossible for Britain's continental allies.

The Royal Navy not only ensured the nation's defense against invasion—unquestionably its primary task—but it also protected the British merchant fleet, upon which the country depended for its overseas trade. Conversely, the navy actively preyed on the enemy's commercial shipping, so reducing French maritime-based revenue. The navy's war against French commerce also served as a counterweight to Napoleon's Continental System, which closed the French-controlled ports of Europe to British vessels as early as the end of 1806. Unlike France, which in addition to drawing on its internal resources could plunder western and central Europe as compensation for gradually decreasing access to overseas markets, Britain was not self-sufficient, and its economy depended heavily on foreign commerce, not only with the Continent but with its empire. A powerful navy ensured the empire's preservation.

The Royal Navy also played an important offensive role, seeking out and destroying the enemy's naval forces, whether in the numerous ship-to-ship actions of the period, or in the less frequent encounters involving squadrons or fleets, such as at the famous battles of St. Vincent, the Nile, Copenhagen, and Trafalgar. Less dramatic, but also important, was the task of blockading enemy fleets and ports, thus denying the enemy (always France, and periodically its allies, the Spanish and Dutch) the ability to strike at British trade, colonies, and naval assets. The Royal Navy also seized enemy colonies and overseas bases and disrupted whatever wider strategic plans France might have in view, whether in European waters or across the world's oceans. The navy played a vital role in conveying troops by water for operations on the Continent, in the West Indies and South America, and as far off

Ships of the Royal Navy in action against the French at the Battle of the Nile. British crews enjoyed the unbeatable advantages of superior gunnery, training, and morale. (Unsigned print, ca. 1900)

as the East Indies. Having disembarked British troops, the navy was then required to supply and reinforce them in the theater of operations and, ultimately, to return them to Britain. Small expeditionary forces were landed by the navy on numerous occasions during the period 1793–1815, but the large-scale operations undertaken by Sir Arthur Wellesley, the future Duke of Wellington, in Portugal and Spain—the Peninsular War—could not have occurred without the essential services provided by the Royal Navy.

Ship Construction and Design

Ships were constructed of wood, with the most preferred type being oak, which was both durable and resilient. Teak, grown in India, also proved excellent material, and fir was sometimes used for hulls, though it was best for deck planks. Elm was also sometimes used for hulls. Very large quantities of wood were required for even the smaller-sized vessels, not to mention ships of the line, with the largest ships requiring over 5,000 cartloads of timber, each of 50 cubic feet (the equivalent of approximately one full-grown oak). There was never enough timber, with shortages of oak being particularly acute. Pine was also important, as it functioned well for the masts.

The rigging, though complex, served well its purpose of extracting power from the wind and supporting the masts. The warship of the late eighteenth century was in fact fairly simple in design and function, constructed of wood, canvas, and rope, yet its design enabled a captain to execute a large number of maneuvers, including sailing with a wind dead ahead by having the ship tack, that is, zigzag its way in the direction intended. A captain did not have to depend entirely on the wind, for he could also make use of the current or tide to reach his destination, even with an adverse wind. A ship contained a large number of types of sails, which, when combined with the power of the wind and the muscle of the crew, could propel the vessel across the Atlantic in as little as four weeks.

This rate of speed was enhanced by a distinct advantage enjoyed by ships of the Royal Navy over most foreign vessels: copper sheathing. The longer a ship had been in commission, especially if it served in tropical waters such as those surrounding the West Indies, the more it was likely to have small sea creatures and vegetation attached to its bottom. As this marine life grew, so the ship slowed in its progress through the water, owing to the resistance caused by friction. The underside of a ship could also be attacked by a small burrowing creature known as the Teredo worm, which would bore its way into the ship from beneath, gradually eating away the timber and thus weakening the ship's structure.

Copper sheathing protected ships from such pests, thereby increasing a ship's longevity and preventing the decrease in its speed. Coppering a ship's bottom also decreased the time a vessel had to be laid up in dock in order to scrape and burn off the growth clinging to the underside. Although this innovation was expensive, it was effective against marine growth and boring animals, for copper in contact with water soon forms a layer of oxide, which is poisonous to most marine animals and is too slick to allow adhesion for plants. It also provided the advantage of superior speed over vessels not outfitted in this way.

Ship design naturally depended on the function for which the ship was intended, and always constituted a compromise between various conflicting requirements, including speed, seaworthiness, carrying capacity, strength, and maneuverability. Whatever the ship's function, it had at least to provide space for its crew and the supplies on which it depended, together with weapons and ammunition and other cargo. Guns were exceedingly heavy and inaccurate, and they offered a very limited range. Needless to say, the more guns a ship could accommodate the better, and the only feasible method of carrying them was in rows along each deck, that is to say, on the broadside. This was the most efficient method of deploying them for battle, and, in any event, a ship would capsize with any other configuration.

Shipbuilders understood the practical limits that could be placed on the length of a vessel and the need for sufficient strength to protect it from enemy fire. They also had to consider a ship's ability to carry itself and its cargo—in good as well as bad weather—which, together with its stability at sea, dictated the number of decks a ship could contain. Everything was a compromise: the heavier the ship, the slower she moved. The longer the ship, the faster she sailed, but the more space required to turn. A smaller ship, equipped with plenty of sails, would have an advantage in speed over a larger vessel, but in adverse weather conditions the larger vessel could sustain the strain of the wind longer and was slowed down less by the effect of the waves. Thus, ship types were specialized, with larger vessels boasting strength, size, and the ability to mount more guns, and smaller vessels displaying superiority in maneuverability and speed.

Although no perfect system of standardization of ship types existed, such types can be broken down into categories and readily distinguished. Ships of the line carried 64 guns or more; frigates usually 36 or 44 guns; brigs and sloops carried fewer guns still. Ships of the line and frigates were three-masted vessels with square sails on all three masts, that is, square-rigged, though most ships also carried a number of sails fore and aft as well.

Warships of this era mounting at least 20 guns carried a "rating." There were six rates, each defined by the number of guns carried. First rates carried 100 guns or more; second rates mounted 90 to 98 guns and normally served as flagships for admirals. There were very few of these two rates in commission, but they were particularly powerful and deployed their guns on three decks. The most common vessel intended to take its place in the line of battle was the third rate, which had between 64 and 84 guns, with almost all ships of this rate having guns on two decks. First-, second-, and third-rate vessels were called "line-of-battle ships" or "ships of the line," and were those that stood end-to-end in battle delivering their broadsides to the enemy in the principal formation employed in combat. The kind of ship whose complement of guns fell below 64 did not normally take a place in the line of battle, since its armament was considered too light and its hull insufficiently strong to bear up against fire delivered by larger vessels.

Two-deckers, which were seldom seen in the line, were mostly used as escorts for larger warships or for troop transports and merchant vessels. Such ships were sometimes classed as fourth rates of 50 to 60 guns or fifth rates of 30 to 44 guns. Frigates, which generally fell into the category of fifth rates, were used extensively at this time. They contained a single gun deck and carried between 28 and 40 guns. They were built for speed, though powerful enough to defend themselves even against ships of the line for a short period. The larger types were fifth rates, and the smaller ones sixth rates, with 20 to 28 guns. Sixth rates were usually known as "post ships." Below these were the unrated sloops, which carried between 8 and 20 guns. Unrated vessels also included a variety of other types, such as brigs, schooners, bomb ships, fire ships, and transports.

Weaponry and Its Use

The principal weapons aboard ships of this period were smoothbore cannon mounted on carriages. These items of naval ordnance amounted to little more than iron tubes, closed at one end, down which were loaded various forms of ammunition. Guns were classified according to the weight of the shot they fired: 32-pounder, 24-pounder, and so on. Guns were shifted into position by a system of ropes and pulleys, together with handspikes that enabled the crew to manhandle the weapon into position, particularly after discharge. The gun carriage sat on wheels, or trucks, enabling the crew to run the gun back inboard for loading.

The barrel first had to be cleaned of any burning fragments left by the previous powder cartridge. A bag containing gunpowder packed in the form of a cartridge was then pushed down the barrel from the muzzle, followed by a felt wad. The shot was then pushed after it, followed by another wad meant to hold the shot in place. After ramming all these materials home, a member of the gun crew used a spike to pierce the cartridge bag by inserting it into the touch hole near the breech of the gun. Next, a small amount of fine grain gunpowder was inserted into the touch hole. The men then "ran out" the gun through the port, the position adjusted for proper elevation and aim. Then, when a slow match was applied, the flame was transmitted down to the cartridge and ignition achieved. The weapon discharged and violently recoiled, but the force was partly controlled by the weight of the gun itself and the rope "breechings," which stopped the gun from rolling back further than was necessary to reload it.

The heaviest piece of ordnance, a 32-pounder, required a crew of fifteen men to operate it, though it could be fired by fewer men once losses were incurred. A gun crew underwent constant and repetitive training in order to perfect the routine of loading and firing their weapon as rapidly and as accurately as possible—no mean feat when performed under battle conditions, complete with thick swirling smoke, cramped conditions, deafening noise, and the cries of the wounded. A crew could certainly be trained to execute their functions quickly; having them fire their weapon accurately took rather more time to perfect.

A skilled gun crew, firing with the right type of ammunition and in good weather conditions, could hit a target more than a mile away, but the effective range of typical gunners was closer to a quarter of a mile. Ideally, ships would be within "pistol shot," where hitting the target was more or less guaranteed. In such a case, rate of fire took precedence over accuracy, and a good crew could fire an average of every 90 seconds. A great psychological effect could be achieved by firing a broadside simultaneously, but inevitably, different standards of gunnery between different gun crews, together with the effect of casualties, made this very difficult after a few discharges. Simultaneous firing, moreover, took a toll on the ship itself. More commonly, crews fired in quick succession down the deck, creating a kind of ripple of fire. Depending on the purpose to be achieved, crews fired at the enemy above the bulwarks to slow down their speed by damaging masts and rigging, or at the hull to create holes beneath the waterline or to disable the opponent's guns and kill their crews.

Several forms of projectile were available to gunners. For short ranges, grapeshot, consisting of a bundle of musket shot secured together in canvas, could be fired to create the effect of a shotgun when they left the barrel. Similarly, canister or case shot consisted of a tin containing small shot, which burst after emerging from the muzzle. Where

the objective was to disable an enemy vessel's masts and rigging, many types of shot were available, including bar shot and chain shot. Bar shot consisted of two halves of an iron ball attached to a bar, making the shape of a dumbbell. When fired, this projectile did great damage to ropes and spars. Chain shot consisted of two balls connected by several inches of chain. These cut and tangled ropes.

Such projectiles were very effective against the motive power of a ship and against men, but they were inaccurate and traveled only a short distance. For greater distance, crews used round shot—what is often referred to now as a cannonball. This was spherical, iron, and solid, and meant to smash the enemy's hull. The heaviest type, of 32 pounds, had a velocity of 1,600 feet per second on leaving the muzzle and could crash through two and a half feet of oak planking. Where round shot hit thinner planking, the resulting shower of splinters could disable and kill men, not to mention dismount a gun or destroy its carriage. Any man unfortunate enough to find himself in its path was either badly mauled or killed. Limbs were commonly lost through such fire. Even the "wind" produced by a closely passing shot was capable of killing a man, queerly, without leaving so much as a mark on his body.

Even more effective at close range were double-shotted guns—those loaded with two shots. Normally, opponents fought in parallel lines, thus exposing only their strongest sides. Great damage could, however, be achieved if a captain could maneuver his ship so as to cross the bow or stern of his opponent, thus enabling him to "rake" the target with most of his broadside guns while himself suffering comparatively little from the few guns that the enemy had mounted on his bow and stern. These were the most vulnerable parts of the ship, and shot fired along the whole length of the decks often dismounted guns.

The accepted, conventional method of fighting was in "line of battle," that is, with both squadrons or fleets deployed in more or less parallel lines (whether on the same or opposite courses) so that their broadsides could be brought to bear against the enemy. Ships were said to be "in line ahead," that is one behind the other in single file. Once the lines passed one another, they maneuvered in an oval or elliptical formation and returned to engage their opponent once again. Such methods rarely led to decisive victories, since the quality of the various fleets were not as distinguishable in the late eighteenth century as they became a generation later. The idea of "breaking the line" (deliberately driving through the line and forcing the opponent to fight individual ship-to-ship actions when one possessed an advantage in numbers, seamanship, and morale) had come into notice at the Battle of Saintes in 1782, during the American Revolutionary War, and was used again very successfully at St. Vincent in 1797 and, most famously, at Trafalgar in 1805.

Whether fleet actions or single-ship actions, most encounters were fought at close range, so close in fact that small arms were regularly employed, together with edged weapons carried by boarding parties. The most common form of firearm at sea, as on land, was the musket, though the blunderbuss could still be seen during this period, and the Americans sometimes used rifles. "Sea service" muskets were of a very similar type to the land version, though slightly shorter. Blunderbusses, with a bell-shaped mouth and firing irregular-sized objects such as bits of iron, were used with deadly effect at close range, particularly against boarders. Muskets were discharged from across rival decks, particularly by marines, but could be wielded by boarding parties. Once discharged in hand-to-hand fighting, however, there was no time to reload, so the weapon was usually reversed to make use of its butt end as a club.

If rival crews actually confronted one another face to face in a boarding action, then recourse was most often had to boarding pikes; pistols; tomahawks or boarding axes; and knives or daggers. Boarding pikes were about six feet long, made of ash and tipped with a triangular steel blade that narrowed to a point. They were most effective in defending against boarders attempting to mount the side of an enemy vessel. Boarding pikes came in long and short versions, depending on the area on the ship where they were to be used. As there was little room on the cramped decks of a ship to employ long weapons, short pikes were therefore designed for such conditions.

The cutlass was short, heavy, and bereft of unnecessary ornamentation, with a strong hand guard on the hilt, both to protect the hand and to use as a knuckle-duster, in the event that lack of space prevented its user from swinging the blade. Officers' swords were similar, very unlike the straight dress swords seen in portraits, which were only used for ceremonial purposes on land. Midshipmen, who were generally only in their teens, often employed a simple dirk, much like a dagger, or a very short sword. Pistols were very similar to the patterns used ashore, but plainer and sturdier, and sometimes modified with a belt hook to enable a sailor to carry more than one slung across his front and to prevent his dropping it in combat. Hand grenades were also used (though much less frequently than in the past), particularly by sailors positioned in the fighting tops (platforms mounted on the masts about halfway up). Grenades were of simple design, consisting of hollow spheres filled with gunpowder and lit with a slow match.

The Royal Navy also had use of a special naval gun known as a carronade, a weapon not employed in any other navy except that of the United States. It was shorter than a standard "great gun," as cannon were officially designated, and fired a 68-pound shot for larger ships, and

smaller weights for smaller vessels. Employing a small charge and a short barrel, the benefit of the carronade derived from the smashing power produced by the weight of its shot rather than from the velocity at which it traveled. The Royal Navy's preferred method of fighting was at close quarters, and its sailors generally aimed at the enemy hull, as opposed to the rigging, which was the traditional target sought by the French. Once a ship could be maneuvered into close range, the more rapid broadsides produced by the superior efficiency of a British crew, now further enhanced by the devastating power of the carronade, gave the British a distinct advantage. The carronade had numerous other advantages, including the fact that the gun was mounted on a slide carriage, rather than on trucks (small wheels). The recoil was absorbed by the slide, whereas in ordinary guns this was absorbed by a series of ropes. Carronades were lighter, required fewer men to operate, and could be aimed more easily by using a screw to elevate and depress the barrel. No other European navy employed carronades, and this technological innovation showed its worth in several actions.

Higher Direction and Support

The Royal Navy was backed by a complex organization, made necessary by the fact that warships, though relatively simple in design and function, were in other ways the most complicated man-made objects in existence, whose maintenance and construction required a complex system of officials, dockyards, and skilled workers to manage, direct, and support. The navy employed more men than any other occupation or institution in the country and was not unnaturally the most expensive to maintain. The navy was managed by the Admiralty in London and maintained at various dockyards, the six major ones being Portsmouth, Plymouth, and Chatham, all on the south coast of England, Deptford and Woolwich on the Thames; and Sheerness in Scotland. Such yards constructed ships and refitted them, though, with its worldwide responsibilities, the navy had also to rely on overseas dockyards that maintained and refitted local squadrons. Gibraltar in the Mediterranean, Antigua and Jamaica in the West Indies, Halifax on the Canadian coast, and Bombay in India were the principal overseas ports of the Royal Navy. Ships requiring repairs or resupply could usually depend on such yards, which contained shipwrights, carpenters, and other skilled craftsmen, to stock their needs and make necessary repairs.

Recruitment

Manning the Royal Navy was a perennial problem, as there was never enough available manpower to satisfy the navy's needs. Conscription largely brought in men already connected with the sea, but landsmen were sometimes drafted as well. Many others were obtained by the more ruthless method of the press gang, by which seamen—desirable recruits because they were already acquainted with life aboard ship—were in effect seized from merchant ships or abducted from the streets of port towns and compelled to serve aboard a vessel of the Royal Navy. Men already serving the navy or in possession of a certificate of exemption could avoid "the press," but this unjust method of manning the fleet was a legal, if unofficial, means at the government's disposal. Pressed men, like convicts, were held aboard ships until the end of the war.

About half the sailors in the Royal Navy were pressed, the remainder being volunteers (who themselves may have been pressed to the extent that once caught they may have been offered the opportunity to "volunteer" and receive higher pay rather than protest at the injustice of their predicament). Those who genuinely volunteered often did so with dreams of glory and adventure, but for the most part their motivation lay in acquiring "prize money"—a specified payment made to every officer and seaman as a reward for the capture of an enemy vessel in reasonable enough condition for the navy to commission for its own use. Men sometimes "volunteered" under the influence of drink, only afterward realizing that they had become virtual prisoners in the hands of their captain.

The strength of the Royal Navy in the year of Trafalgar (1805) was slightly over 100,000 men, of whom a quarter were marines, men specially trained to serve aboard ships on sentry duty, to maintain discipline, and to provide musket fire in battle and landing parties in amphibious operations. Their chief function was to prevent mutiny aboard ship. The navy expanded rapidly during the French Revolutionary and Napoleonic Wars, but while Parliament voted for impressive numbers of sailors and ships on a yearly basis, these figures were never reached.

Discipline and Conditions of Service

Discipline aboard ship was strict and sometimes harsh. Landsmen, in particular, with no experience of the rigors of life at sea, had to be blended into the existing team, a team that had to be capable of carrying out a variety of difficult and often complex functions under all conditions, especially combat. Petty officers encouraged the quick fulfillment of orders with the use of a rope's end or cane, with which they would strike men perceived as too slow. But it was the captain, as supreme authority aboard the ship, with absolute command over the officers and men, who, whether benign or despotic, possessed the power of life and death over the crew.

Most captains were strict, but essentially reasonable, despite the fact that the lash was used regularly. The harshness of this method of punishment must be seen in the context of the time; life on land was fraught with poverty, illness, and crime, and punishments for civilians were at least as severe as for those in the navy. Men subjected to a lashing with the cat-o'-nine-tails were tied to a grating and flogged with a whip consisting of nine cords, all of them knotted. In short order this removed the skin from a man's back, leaving it a bloody mass of pulp. The number of lashes was specified by the captain, and usually did not exceed two dozen, with the punishment being carried out by the bosun's mate. The captain could always employ the death sentence for serious offenses, such as mutiny. At a time when capital punishment was regularly handed down by the courts for what today would be considered a minor offense (such as petty theft), the use of the death penalty aboard ship was relatively rare. Whatever the punishment prescribed by a captain, the crew generally accepted it as a matter of course. It was abuse of the system of discipline by the occasionally sadistic officer to which the men might object, rather than the system as it then existed.

Desertion was severely punished, but it is not surprising that many men, especially those who had been pressed, should have resorted to it. Leave was seldom given during wartime, for the simple reason that many men might simply abscond once ashore or be taken aboard other ships, especially when in for a refit or at the end of a commission. On the occasions when men were granted leave, they often spent all their money in a drunken spree or in the pursuit of women, having been confined aboard ship often for months at a time. Once the war ended, most sailors were discharged from the service with the usual ruthless cutbacks in naval expenditure. There were no pensions for the aged or injured, and men found themselves back in society without immediate means of food, accommodation, and work.

The functions of a ship's crew were necessarily varied in complexity and skill. The men were divided into several groups, the two main ones being able seamen and landsmen. The first were skilled men; the latter were unskilled. Able seamen were employed in the rigging and were extremely fit, able to climb the masts, spars, and lines with remarkable agility and speed so as to enable them to take in the sails—all tasks performed high above the deck. This was necessarily dangerous work, especially for the "topmen," who worked amid the higher sails and masts. Older men or those with fewer skills might be in charge of a gun or perform other tasks not requiring the same degree of strength or agility.

Landsmen usually worked on the deck, manhandling ropes to fix the sails in place, raising the anchor, and doing other work for which no machinery then existed to replace simple, brute strength. Such men were known as "waisters," being employed in the center of the ship, and were generally incapable of working in the rigging because of age, lack of fitness, or low intelligence.

Living conditions aboard ship were cramped, smelly, and uncomfortable. The men slept in hammocks slung between the decks, stowing them each day. They ate at a mess table erected at mealtimes between the guns and then stowed again, leaving the deck free for the use of the guns. The whole purpose of the ship was for fighting; the comfort and convenience of the men was not an issue aboard warships at this time. The men's diet consisted of hard tack (a sort of biscuit), salted meat, and various beverages, including beer and grog (watered-down rum). Fresh meat and fruit were rare, and poor nutrition and scurvy were a constant problem.

Officers and Men

Noncommissioned officers were in charge of the guns, and the men performing their respective tasks in the rigging. The more senior of the NCOs were the warrant officers. The boatswain held responsibility for the seamen and the carpenter for the ship's structure; the purser managed the system of pay and the provision of food and clothing aboard ship. The navigation of the ship fell largely to the master. Officers held commissions from the king authorizing them to hold a position of command, either lieutenant, captain, or admiral. Prior to becoming an officer, a boy aged between thirteen and eighteen would serve for a number of years as a sort of apprentice or cadet, known as a midshipman, though older men could remain midshipmen if they failed their lieutenant's examination or were unable to secure promotion through patronage.

The system of patronage was extremely important at the time, not only within the armed forces, but in politics. Receiving a post or promotion in the navy usually came as the result of distinguished service or, more frequently, through the assistance of a friend or family member with influence within the service. A patron might wish to support a young man's professional aspirations, have a family or political connection with him, or need to return a political or financial favor performed by the aspirant's family.

Having passed his lieutenant's examination as a midshipman, a man had to rely on patronage to rise to a captaincy or depend on the fate of circumstances. Battle might disable or kill off those of higher rank, thereby opening up more senior positions. Distinguished conduct in combat might also secure the rank of captain, giving the independent command of a ship to an ambitious lieutenant. Beyond captain came the rank of admiral, divided into rear admiral, vice admiral, and admiral, the last rank itself divided into three parts to distinguish them according to seniority. After becoming a captain, promotion was achieved by seniority, and though this was more or less a simple waiting game, patronage could still make the difference between a desirable or undesirable posting, whether in terms of the quality of the squadron or fleet one commanded or the station (theater of operations) to which one was assigned. During peacetime a ship was usually "paid off," which meant that her crew was released from service and the captain placed on half pay, unless he could find another ship into which he could immediately transfer.

Conclusion

The Royal Navy easily surpassed all other contemporary navies for size, efficiency, and power. Well before the end of the Napoleonic Wars in 1815, the navy had achieved maritime supremacy over all contenders and enabled this small island nation, in the remaining period of the nineteenth century, to establish an empire on a scale not seen since ancient Rome.

Gregory Fremont-Barnes

See also Artillery (Naval); Blockade; British Army; Continental System; Copenhagen, Battle of; Dutch Navy; French Navy; Marines; Naval Warfare; Nelson, Horatio, First Viscount; Nile, Battle of the; Ottoman Navy; Peninsular War; Privateering; Prize Money; Russian Navy; Spanish Navy; St. Vincent, Battle of; Trafalgar, Battle of; United States Navy

References and further reading
Blake, Nicholas, and Richard Lawrence. 2003. *The Illustrated Companion to Nelson's Navy.* London: Chatham.
Clowes, William Laird. 1997. *The Royal Navy: A History from the Earliest Times to 1900.* 7 vols. London: Chatham. (Orig. pub. 1898.)
Cordingly, David. 2004. *Billy Ruffian.* London: Bloomsbury.
Fremont-Barnes, Gregory. 2005a. *Nelson's Sailors.* Oxford: Osprey.
———. 2005b. *Trafalgar 1805: Nelson's Crowning Victory.* Oxford: Osprey.
Gardiner, Robert. 2003. *Warships of the Napoleonic Era.* London: Chatham.
Goodwin, Peter. 2004a. *Men O'War: The Illustrated Story of Life in Nelson's Navy.* London: National Maritime Museum.
———. 2004b. *Nelson's Victory: 101 Questions and Answers about HMS Victory, Nelson's Flagship at Trafalgar 1805.* London: Brassey's.
———. 2005. *The Ships of Trafalgar: The British, French and Spanish Fleets, 21 October 1805.* London: Conway Maritime.
Hall, C. D. 2004. *Wellington's Navy: Sea Power and the Peninsular War, 1807–1814.* London: Chatham.
Haythornthwaite, Philip. 1999. *Nelson's Navy.* Oxford: Osprey.
Heathcote, T. A. 2005. *Nelson's Trafalgar Captains and Their Battles.* London: Cooper.
Henry, Chris. 2004. *Napoleonic Naval Armaments, 1792–1815.* Oxford: Osprey.
Herman, Arthur. 2005. *To Rule the Waves: How the British Navy Shaped the Modern World.* London: Hodder and Stoughton.
Ireland, Bernard. 2000. *Naval Warfare in the Age of Sail: War at Sea, 1756–1815.* New York: Norton.
James, William. 2002. *The Naval History of Great Britain.* London: Conway Maritime.

Konstam, Angus. 2001. *British Napoleonic Ship-of-the-Line.* Oxford: Osprey.

Lambert, Andrew. 2000. *War at Sea in the Age of Sail.* London: Cassell.

Lavery, Brian. 1989. *Nelson's Navy: The Ships, Men and Organisation, 1793–1815.* London: Conway Maritime.

———. 2003. *Jack Aubrey Commands: An Historical Companion to the Naval World of Patrick O'Brian.* London: Conway Maritime.

LeFevre, Peter. 2004. *Nelson's Fleet at Trafalgar.* Annapolis, MD: Naval Institute Press.

LeFevre, Peter, and Richard Harding, eds. 2005. *British Admirals of the Napoleonic Wars: The Contemporaries of Nelson.* London: Chatham.

Lewis, Michael A. 2004. *A Social History of the Navy, 1793–1815.* London: Chatham.

Lyon, David. 1996. *Sea Battles in Close-up: The Age of Nelson.* Annapolis, MD: Naval Institute Press.

Macdonald, Janet. 2004. *Feeding Nelson's Navy: The True Story of Food at Sea in the Georgian Era.* London: Chatham.

Masefield, John. 2002. *Sea Life in Nelson's Time.* Annapolis, MD: Naval Institute Press.

Maynard, C., ed. 2004. *A Nelson Companion: A Guide to the Royal Navy of Jack Aubrey.* London: O'Mara.

McGowan, Alan. 1999. *HMS* Victory: *Her Construction, Career and Restoration.* London: Chatham.

Morriss, Roger. 1983. *The Royal Dockyards during the Revolutionary and Napoleonic Wars.* Leicester, UK: Leicester University Press.

Parkinson, C. Northcote. 1954. *War in the Eastern Seas.* London: Ruskin House.

———. 1977. *Britannia Rules: The Classic Age of Naval History, 1793–1815.* London: Book Club Associates.

Pivka, Otto von. 1980. *Navies of the Napoleonic Era.* New York: Hippocrene.

Pope, Dudley. 1997. *Life in Nelson's Navy.* London: Chatham.

Pope, Stephen. 1998. *Hornblower's Navy: Life at Sea in the Age of Nelson.* London: Welcome Rain.

Rodger, N. A. M. 1988. *The Wooden World: An Anatomy of the Georgian Navy.* London: Fontana.

———. 2005. *The Command of the Ocean: A Naval History of Britain, 1649–1815.* London: Penguin.

Tracy, Nicholas. 1996. *Nelson's Battles: The Art of Victory in the Age of Sail.* London: Chatham.

———. 2006. *Who's Who in Nelson's Navy: 200 Naval Heroes.* London: Chatham.

Tunstall, Brian. 1990. *Naval Warfare in the Age of Sail: The Evolution of Fighting Tactics, 1650–1815.* Annapolis, MD: Naval Institute Press.

Winfield, Riff. 2005. *British Warships in the Age of Sail, 1792–1815: Design, Construction, Career and Fates.* London: Chatham.

Russia

The Russian Empire was the largest state that participated in the French Revolutionary and Napoleonic Wars. The international status of the Russian Empire was transformed during the wars. Russia was a junior partner in the early coalitions; by 1815 Russia was recognized as the strongest military power on the Continent.

In the late eighteenth century, the empire's borders had expanded westward, as a consequence of the three partitions of Poland-Lithuania in 1772, 1793, and 1795, to incorporate Lithuania, Belarus, and the Western Ukraine, and southward, as a consequence of two Russo-Turkish Wars of 1768–1774 and 1787–1792 (which ended by the Treaty of Jassy on 9 January 1792), to the northern shores of the Black Sea. The period of the Napoleonic Wars saw further significant territorial acquisitions in the north, south, and west, namely the Grand Duchy of Finland (as a result of the Russo-Swedish War of 1808–1809), Bessarabia (as a result of the Russo-Turkish War of 1806–1812), and the Congress Kingdom of Poland (ceded to Russia at the Congress of Vienna in 1815). The Russian Empire extended to the Bering Sea and the Pacific Ocean in the east, and inroads had been made into the Caucasus in the late eighteenth and early nineteenth centuries.

The population of the Empire (excluding the Caucasus, the Polish provinces, and Finland) rose from 37.2 million in 1795 to 43.1 million in 1815. The Grand Duchy of Finland comprised some 1.4 million inhabitants in 1843; the population of the Congress Kingdom of Poland numbered approximately 3.3 million. The expansion of the Empire resulted in a fall in the percentage of ethnic Russians in the population. In 1782 (at the fourth census), the Russian population was 48.9 percent of the total population of the Empire; by 1833 (the seventh census), it had fallen to 45.32 percent. Non-Russians included Ukrainians, Poles, Belarusans, Lithuanians, Latvians, Estonians, Finns, Romanians, Jews, Tatars, Bashkirs, Chuvash, Mordvins, Mari, Votiaks, Kalmyks, and Komi. When Napoleon invaded Russia in 1812, he crossed through Lithuanian and Belarusan lands before entering Russia proper after the Battle of Smolensk. He was unable, however, to gain any military or diplomatic advantages from his presence in nonethnic Russian territory. Non-Russians, with the exception of Jews, served in the imperial Russian Army.

It was the Russian peasants who had to bear the major burden of war, either directly, as recruits, or indirectly, as payers of the poll tax. Some 90 percent of the Russian population (as opposed to the population of the Russian Empire as a whole) were peasants. The peasantry was not a homogeneous group. Over half the peasants were legally categorized as serfs, that is, seigneurial peasants who lived on land owned by nobles. The rest were loosely categorized as state peasants, comprising court peasants (who lived on land owned by members of the imperial court); Cossacks (of Russian or Ukrainian ethnic origin who lived mainly in what had been or still were the outposts of the Empire in the south, the north Caucasus, and Siberia); so-called economic peasants, who had lived on church or monastic lands until the secularization of Church lands in 1764; so-called black peasants, who lived on land, mainly in the north and in Siberia, where there had never been noble landowners; and various smaller categories of former servitors, military settlers, and non-Russian peasants.

Peasants—either serfs or state peasants—were largely self-governing, through the village commune, or *mir*. It was the commune that selected unfortunate young men as recruits for the army (who were often either work shy, trouble makers, or simply impoverished), and who supplied and dispatched the recruits and handled the requests by the army for supplies, quarters, and transport. These latter burdens fell most heavily on peasants in the western and southern borderlands, where the bulk of the Russian Army was quartered. Once a peasant was recruited, he rarely returned to his village, unless he was found to be medically unfit or unless he was wounded very early in the campaign. Contact between soldiers and peasants was therefore rather limited under normal circumstances; the military activities of 1812, of course, had a far more direct impact on peasant lives along the route of the invasion and the retreat.

The other main source of conscripts to the army consisted of artisans and day laborers in towns. Townspeople, though, only made up a small percentage of the Russian population (although the number of people living in towns was always considerably higher than the number in legally defined urban groups). In 1795, the number of males in various urban groups was estimated as 771,317, which rose to 1,208,600 in 1815. The elite category of the urban groups—the merchants—were excluded from the recruit levy (although they paid a special tax in its place), so that the pool for recruits was limited. Officers and soldiers were billeted on towns, and most large towns had garrisons, but apart from the large military presence in the major cities of St. Petersburg and Moscow, most troops were quartered on the southern and western borderlands.

The nobles provided the bulk of the officer corps. It has been estimated that the number of male Russian nobles rose from 362,574 in 1795 to 429,226 in 1816. This comprises about 2 percent of the Russian population—a nobility rather larger proportionally than that of Sweden, but small compared with other east European states such as Hungary or Poland. Nobles had been obliged to serve the state—in a military or, far more rarely, in a civil capacity—in the reign of Peter the Great. But in 1762, during the short reign of Peter III, nobles were freed from compulsory service to the state. In practice, this change had only a limited effect, and nobles continued to serve,

partly because by this time service had become the raison d'être of the nobility, and, more prosaically, because the majority of noble families needed a state income to support themselves.

Nobles were not, of course, taxpayers, and there was no attempt in Russia to introduce property tax or any other form of direct taxation of the privileged classes during the Napoleonic Wars. Service in the army was consistently more popular and more prestigious than civil service, and entry into the elite Guard regiments was only possible for young nobles who had wealth and connections. The elite military schools helped to foster an esprit de corps among the officer class, although this feeling of solidarity may also have helped the spread of reformist and revolutionary ideas after 1815.

Russia was backward economically in the late eighteenth and early nineteenth centuries. Grain yields (only twice or three times the grain sown) were consistently lower than those of western and northwestern Europe. This disproportion can partly be explained by climatic conditions, but there were other factors that perpetuated economic backwardness. Peasants were slow to adopt innovations in technology, field rotation, or experiment with new crops. Serfdom acted as a brake on innovation, not least because serfs traditionally worked noble lands, so that the kind of commercial agriculture found in Britain in the seventeenth and eighteenth centuries, where the nobility took a more direct interest in their own lands, failed to develop. The other major problem was poor transportation. It was particularly difficult in the spring, when the thaw made swollen rivers impassable and turned roads into quagmires. Nevertheless, the grain market had expanded from the second half of the eighteenth century, aided by the abolition of internal customs, rising grain prices, the development of the southern port of Odessa, and further development of the canal system that facilitated transportation of goods to the Baltic ports.

Russian industry developed late, but major advances, particularly in the metallurgy and textile manufactories, had taken place from the time of the reign of Peter the Great in the first quarter of the eighteenth century. The most successful area of development was iron production; by 1800 Russia had become the greatest producer of pig iron in the world (although thereafter it was rapidly overtaken by Britain). Iron was used for cannon and armaments, and the center of the armaments industry was the town of Tula, south of Moscow. The main shipbuilding centers were in St. Petersburg, on Kronstadt (an island in the Gulf of Finland), and in the Crimea. Moscow was the center of the textile industry and the silk-weaving industry, but there were other important regional centers. A major economic weakness for Russia was the slow development of towns and of the urban elites. Traditions of urban self-government were weak, and an imposed western-style guild system had failed to take root. As a result, urban goods and artisans were constantly undercut by peasant traders, and the majority of towns remained small and predominantly peasant in social composition.

The relative economic backwardness of Russia was exposed during the French Revolutionary and Napoleonic Wars. Russia had the industrial capacity to supply troops with arms and uniforms and, at least in principle, had sufficient grain to feed the troops and sufficient fodder for horses. Russian soldiers were in effect conscripted for life (twenty-five years) and were paid very little, nor were salaries for officers generous. But Russia lacked the resources or the income to sustain the largest army in Europe during almost constant warfare, particularly when its territory was invaded in 1812. Industry was not sufficiently advanced to benefit from the increased needs by the military for textiles and armaments. Attempts to increase the state's income through rises in direct and indirect taxation foundered because the tax-paying population was too small (nobles, clergy, and merchants being excluded) and too impoverished to be further exploited, and the mechanisms of tax collection remained inefficient. The consequence was that arrears rose alarmingly.

Budgeting mechanisms and the banking and credit systems were underdeveloped (there was no national bank), so that the rising national debt could not be underwritten or consolidated in a sinking fund. Customs revenues declined sharply during the time that Russia adhered to the Continental System by which Napoleon sought to close continental markets to Britain. Extensive subsidies, particularly from Britain, could not make up this shortfall in income. The Russian government therefore resorted to printing paper money (assignats), which in turn led to inflation and devaluation of the ruble (the value of the ruble fell by 24 percent between 1806 and 1810). By 1810, Russia was facing a financial crisis, but new regulations to stabilize the currency were wrecked by the experience of invasion, which destroyed towns (most notably Moscow and Smolensk), villages, and agriculture along the path of the invasion route.

The Russian tsar is often described as an autocrat; however, it is not the case that there were no practical restrictions on the tsar's power. Tsars were conscious that they could be victims of military or palace coups (as was Paul I, father of Alexander I) or that their policies could provoke popular revolt (as in the Pugachev Revolt during the reign of Catherine II). But there were no formal legal or institutional restrictions on tsarist power—no national representative institution, no powerful body of social elites or regional interest groups, no administrative institution

with powers to block tsarist policy, no separate legal body or codified set of laws that could be used against arbitrary tsarist action.

The tsar had sole control over foreign and military policy, although tsars rarely took part in battle (Alexander learned his lesson after he participated in the Battle of Austerlitz in 1805). While this complete control gave the ruler great freedom of action, it also meant overreliance on individual ministers, army commanders, and friends, and in practice meant that the central government apparatus was inefficient, cumbersome, and overly dependent on the personal views and whims of the ruler. Some restructuring of central government took place during Alexander's reign, most notably the reform of the Senate and the introduction of ministries, including the ministry of finance and the ministry of war. These newly established institutions proved inadequate in dealing with the strains of war.

The acquisition of new lands and a new great-power status in the Vienna settlement of 1815 could not disguise the fact that war left the Russian Empire with an enormous debt, an inflated currency, impoverished western provinces, its largest city in ruins, and an empty treasury. As Russia continued to maintain the bulk of its army in peacetime after 1815 (only the temporary militias were demobilized), and war had not resulted in technological advances in industry or agriculture or substantial improvements in banking and credit facilities, let alone any fundamental change in the structure of society or the form of government, there was no obvious remedy for reducing the financial crisis.

Thus, by the end of the era the vast Russian Empire posed an extraordinary paradox, possessing by far the largest army in Europe, and benefiting substantially from the settlement reached at the Congress of Vienna, yet with little to show for itself in terms of social, political, scientific, or economic development.

Janet Hartley

See also Alexander I, Tsar; Austerlitz, Battle of; Catherine II "the Great," Tsarina; Continental System; Cossacks; Finland; Paul I, Tsar; Poland; Poland, Partitions of; Russian Army; Russian Campaign; Russian Navy; Russo-Swedish War; Russo-Turkish War; Vienna, Congress of

References and further reading
Dixon, S. 1999. *Russia in the Age of Modernization, 1676–1825.* Cambridge: Cambridge University Press.
Duffy, Christopher. 1981. *Russia's Military Way to the West:Origins and Nature of Russian Military Power, 1700–1800.* London: Routledge.
Dziewanowski, M. 1990. *Alexander I: Russia's Mysterious Tsar.* New York: Hippocrene.
Hartley, J. M. 1994. *Alexander I.* London: Longman.
———. 1999. *A Social History of the Russian Empire, 1650–1825.* London and New York: Longman.

Kagan, F. W. 1999. *The Military Reforms of Nicholas I: The Origins of the Modern Russian Army*. London: Macmillan.

McConnel, Allen. 1970. *Alexander I: Paternalistic Reformer*. New York: Crowell.

McGrew, Roderick. 1992. *Paul I of Russia, 1754–1801*. Oxford: Clarendon.

Moon, David. 1999. *The Russian Peasantry, 1600–1900: The World the Peasants Made*. London and New York: Longman.

Niven, Alexander C. 1978. *Napoleon and Alexander I: A Study in Franco-Russian Relations, 1807–12*. Washington, DC: University Press of America.

Palmer, Alan. 1972. *Russia in War and Peace*. London: Weidenfeld and Nicolson.

Puryear, V. 1951. *Napoleon and the Dardanelles*. Cambridge: Cambridge University Press.

Ragsdale, Hugh, ed. 1979. *Paul I: A Reassessment of his Life and Reign*. Pittsburgh: University Center of International Studies.

———. 1980. *Détente in the Napoleonic Era: Bonaparte and the Russians*. Lawrence: Regents Press of Kansas.

———. 1988. *Tsar Paul and the Question of Madness: An Essay in History and Psychology*. New York: Greenwood.

Saul, Norman E. 1970. *Russia and the Mediterranean, 1797–1807*. Chicago: University of Chicago Press.

Saunders, David. 1992. *Russia in the Age of Reaction and Reform 1801–1881*. London: Longman.

Seton-Watson, Hugh. 1967. *The Russian Empire, 1801–1917*. Oxford: Clarendon.

Thaden, Edward C. 1971. *Russia Since 1801: The Making of a New Society*. New York: Wiley-Interscience.

Russian Army

Russia was at war for virtually the entire period between 1789 and 1815. The Russian Army participated in seven campaigns against France, in 1799, 1805, 1806–1807, and 1812–1814; fought two wars against the Turks in 1787–1792 and 1806–1812; a war with Persia in 1804–1813; two wars with Sweden in 1789–1791 and 1808–1809; in the Partition of Poland in 1792–1794; and in the annexations of principalities in Georgia and the northern Caucasus.

Recruitment

Able to draw on a population of almost 40 million by the late eighteenth century, Russian sovereigns drew conscripts from the servile population of an empire that included serfs, state and church peasants, and townspeople. Every year the sovereign or the Senate acting in the imperial name issued a decree (*ukaz*) specifying a levy to be raised. The number of recruits fluctuated with military need, and each decree stipulated how many individuals were to be recruited from a given number of men, what procedures were to be followed, and which groups were to be exempt. In 1724, the system was modified, and levies were imposed based on the number of souls, not households. While under Peter the Great all estates had to provide specified levy quotas, the system later gradually changed. In 1736 new regulations allowed nobles to keep one son at home to take care of the family property; other male children could study until the age of 20, at which time they had to be enlisted in the army for twenty-five years. After 1737–1739 clergy and merchants were exempted from recruitment if they paid a special fee. Finally, in 1762 Tsar Peter III promulgated the Charter of Liberties, which abolished mandatory military service for the nobles. After 1811 landowners could pay a fee of 2,000 rubles in lieu of providing a recruit. Thus, the burden of recruitment lay heavily on serfs, townspeople, and peasants. In total, between 1705 and 1825, there were over 90 levies raised, yielding more than 4,000,000 men for the Russian armies. During the period 1805–1815 Russia raised levies every year except 1814, drafting over 1.2 million men.

In time of emergency, Russian sovereigns often issued heavier levies or resorted to militia mobilizations. During the 1806–1807 campaigns in Poland, Tsar Alexander issued a special levy for "temporary internal militia" that yielded some 200,129 men. The heaviest levies were held in 1812, when three emergency levies were issued within six months calling for over 400,000 men, excluding militia.

Age limits for recruits were initially restricted to those between 15 and 30, inclusive, but they were eventually raised by 5 years. Catherine the Great raised the minimum age requirement to 17. During the Napoleonic Wars, age requirements went through various changes: the maximum age for a recruit was raised to 36 in 1806, age limits were set at 19 to 37 in 1808, the minimum age was lowered to 18 in 1811, and the maximum increased to 40 in 1812. In practice, officials often ignored regulations and accepted underage boys or older men. Height regulations also gradually evolved, starting with 2 arshins and 4 vershkis (5 ft. 3 in.) in the 1730s. During the Napoleonic Wars, requirements were lowered by half an inch in 1805, 1808, and 1809, an entire inch in 1806 and 1811, and two inches in 1812. Shorter men were usually recruited anyway and assigned to garrison duty or to the navy. Soldiers initially had to serve in the army for life. However, following the successful war against the Ottomans in 1787–1792, Catherine rewarded her troops with a reduction in their term of service to twenty-five years in 1793. Tsar Alexander considered proposals to reduce military service to twelve years but could not implement them in wartime.

Peter the Great initially forced the nobility into mandatory military service, beginning their term as ordinary soldiers with eventual promotion to officer's rank. However, the nobles exploited a loophole in the system by

Table R.1 Levies during the Napoleonic Wars

Levy	Year	Levy Quota	Recruits	
			Expected	Actual
73rd	1802	2 per 500 souls	52,523	46,491
74th	1803	2 per 500 souls	60,379	54,855
75th	1804	1 per 500 souls	n/a	38,437
76th	1805 (first call-up)	4 per 500 souls	n/a	110,000
	1805 (second call-up)	n/a	n/a	58,205
77th	1806–1807 (militia recruitment)	5 per 500 souls	612,000	200,129
78th	1808	5 per 500 souls	118,300	38,906
79th	1809	5 per 500 souls	82,146	ca. 60,000
80th	1810	3 per 500 souls	n/a	94,589
81st	1811	4 per 500 souls	135,000	120,000
82nd	1812 (first call-up)	2 per 500 souls	70,000	166,563
83rd	1812 (second call-up)	8 per 500 souls	181,585	n/a
84th	1812 (third call-up)	8 per 500 souls (1 per 50 souls in Lifland)	167,686	n/a
85th	1813	8 per 500 souls (1 per 50 souls in Estland)	n/a	ca. 200,000
86th	1815	1 per 500 souls (Ukraine, Bessarabia, and Georgia exempt)	n/a	33,417

Sources: Data from Beskrovny 1996; Geisman 1902; Kersnovskii 1992; Ulianov 1997; V. Zwegintsov, *Russkaia armia*, vol. 4 (Paris: N.p., 1973).

Note: n/a = Data not available.

enlisting their children in the Imperial Guard at the time of their birth or infancy; by the time the children grew up, they already had officer's rank without the benefit of any experience or training. Initially, the length of service for nobles was not established, which often meant they served for life. Although in 1762 Tsar Peter III had abolished mandatory military service for the nobles, the army nevertheless remained the only honorable career for young noblemen. The total size of the officer corps is estimated as some 12,000 in 1803, over 14,000 in 1805–1807, and between 15,000 and 17,000 in 1812–1815.

After enlisting, a nobleman was usually given the rank of a noncommissioned officer but had to serve as a soldier for three months before actually receiving the rank. Of course, patronage and nepotism played an important role in advancement. Many senior officers made sure their sons or relatives served in their units and received promotions in a timely or expedited fashion. Civilians who transferred to military service usually had their officer epaulettes within one to three years, depending on their previous civilian rank and position. The wait was considerably longer for nonnobles, who usually had to serve between five and seven years to become officers. Noncommissioned officers were in the worst position, because they had usually served over ten years before receiving an officer's rank.

Despite the perennial problem of incompetent officers in the army, the Russian system of military education was surprisingly multifaceted. The highest institutions were the Page Corps, the Tsarskoe Selo Lycée, and the 1st and 2nd Cadet Corps, followed by the Corps of Foreign Fellow Believers, the Grodno (later Smolensk) Cadet Corps, the Imperial Military Orphan Home, and the Regiment of the Nobility. The quality of instructors and graduates, however, remained poor. Most junior officers came untrained and illiterate, while senior command was largely restricted to the senior aristocracy. A number of relatively competent foreign officers served in the Russian Army throughout the period, but they often had a divisive influence and generated mistrust among the Russian officers and troops. Criminal profiteering in the commissariat and among suppliers was rampant. Medical services were primitive at best.

Army Command

Under Tsar Paul I, the overall command of military forces was in the hands of the War College. The tsar also had effective command of the army through the War Chancellery. Such duplication of authority often confused matters, and Alexander I considered several proposals to reorganize the command structure. In 1802 the Ministry of Military Land Forces was formed, and the War College was turned into an executive bureau within the ministry. The Imperial War Chancellery continued to operate until 1808. Between 1803 and 1808, the ministry was reorganized and divided into provisioning, commissariat, accounting, legal, engineers, artillery, and medical departments. In 1808–1810 the Ministry of Military Land Forces expanded its authority, subordinating the Imperial War Chancellery. In 1810, the Imperial State Council was established, which in-

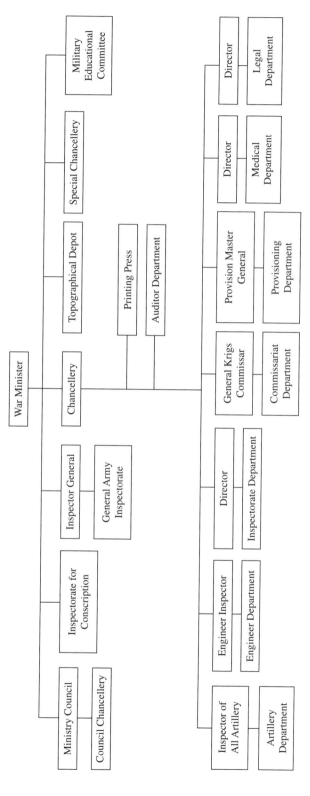

Fig R.1 Command Structure of the Russian Ministry of War, 1811–1815

Source: Data from Beskrovny 1996 and Bezotosny 2000.

cluded the Department of Military Affairs. On 27 January 1812 the ministry was renamed the Ministry of War. A new statute freed the ministry from numerous petty responsibilities and gave wider powers to divisional commanders. The new ministry was governed through the chancellery and the council and was divided into seven departments: artillery, engineers, inspectorate, legal, provisioning, commissariat, and medical.

Throughout the Napoleonic Wars, the Russian Army operated without a separate general staff, and His Imperial Majesty's Suite on Quartermaster Service performed these functions. Organized in 1797, the suite was commanded by the quartermaster general, General Aleksey Arakcheyev, in 1797–1799 and General Paul Sukhtelen in 1801–1808. In 1804, the suite staff comprised 5 generals, 39 staff, and 62 junior officers, as well as 45 column guides (*kolonova-zhatii*), who were assigned to local headquarters. After 1807 foreign officers, including Karl von Clausewitz, Karl von Pfuel, and Ludwig Wolzogen, were accepted into the suite. Under General Peter Volkonsky's leadership, the suite was reorganized in November 1810 and divided into the archive, the Suite Depot (led by General Karl Oppermann), and a chancellery of four sections: the first responsible for current affairs, the second for topography, the third for routes, and the fourth for treasury affairs.

The functions of the suite were further determined during the reforms of 1810–1812. Two main sections were established under the direction of the quartermaster general: the first section was responsible for intelligence gathering; the second section directed the drafting of dispositions, the movement of troops, the selection of positions, and instructions to local commanders. In 1812 the suite staff consisted of 10 generals, 58 staff, and 99 junior officers; over the next two years, the number of officers serving in the suite increased to over 130. In December 1815 Alexander issued a decree establishing the General Staff, which incorporated the suite.

Organization

Upon his accession to the throne, Tsar Paul launched a series of reforms aimed at transforming the Russian Army. His Gatchina Troops (the tsar's personal guard at the palace of that name), trained in the Prussian manner, became the pattern for the rest of the imperial army. New drill regulations were introduced in December 1796, while new uniforms were issued in the Prussian style, and soldiers were required to wear their hair pulled back behind their heads in tightly braided queues. The officer corps was purged, and 7 field marshals, over 300 generals, and more than 2,000 officers were expelled between 1796 and 1799. Regiments went through a major transformation, as regimental commanders lost their power and regimental *chefs*

(colonel-proprietors) gained virtually unlimited authority over the units. For the duration of Paul's rule, units were designated after the chefs. Ten *Jäger* corps and three separate battalions were soon transformed into separate regiments. Under the 1796 Regulations, heavy cavalry regiments comprised five squadrons, while the light cavalry was organized into two regiments of five squadrons each.

Paul's reforms were most beneficial for the artillery. Lighter artillery pieces were introduced, and specific regulations were adopted for barrels and carriages. New artillery was armed with 12-pounder (medium and small) and 6-pounder guns, and 20-pounder and 10-pounder unicorns (a type of artillery piece unique to the Russians, the unicorn was a compromise between an ordinary cannon and a howitzer). Russian artillery was organized into one horse and ten field battalions, each consisting of five companies. Each field artillery company included four medium 12-pounder guns, four small 12-pounder guns, and four 20-pounder unicorns. The horse artillery company consisted of six 6-pounder guns and six 10-pounder unicorns. Infantry regiments were also assigned artillery pieces.

The Russian Army was divided between fourteen military inspectorates (*inspektsia*). Two inspectors (one each for infantry and cavalry) regularly examined troops in each inspection, while the Inspector of All Artillery supervised the whole branch of the service. Emphasis was put on drilling and parade appearance, rather than on actual tactical maneuvers. In January 1801, the Russian Army consisted of 446,059 men: 201,280 infantrymen, 41,685 cavalrymen, 36,500 artillerymen, 96,594 garrison troops, and 70,000 men in special forces (for example, the corps of Louis-Joseph de Bourbon, prince de Condé, a French emigré).

On the accession of Tsar Alexander, the main military forces comprised the following forces: infantry—three Imperial Guard, thirteen grenadier, sixty-nine musketeer, and nineteen Jäger regiments; cavalry—four Imperial Guard, thirteen cuirassier, eleven dragoon, eight hussar, two horse, and three regular Cossack regiments; and the artillery and engineer service—four field and one horse artillery regiments, one pioneer regiment, and eight pontoon companies. The first several years of Alexander's reign saw the gradual transformation of Russian military forces. After the 1802 reforms, an infantry regiment was organized into three battalions of four companies each, and the average strength of units varied between 1,500 and 1,700 men. Although the Russian Army had ad hoc divisions on campaign, the conversion to a divisional system was only initiated in 1806, when the first eighteen divisions were formed. The normal strength of a division was 18,000–20,000 men. By 1812 Russian forces increased to almost 700,000 men, including 362,000 infantry, 86,920 cavalry,

52,500 artillerymen, 75,000 garrison troops, and up to 120,000 irregulars.

The Russian infantry included heavy and light infantry and garrison troops. In 1812, the heavy infantry included four Guard, fourteen grenadier, ninety-six infantry, and four marine regiments, and the Caspian Sea Marine Battalion. The garrison infantry comprised the Life Guard Garrison Battalion, twelve garrison regiments, twenty garrison battalions, and forty-two battalions and four half-battalions of the Internal Guard. Infantry forces also included invalid companies. Each regiment included two to four battalions, each composed of four companies. Regimental *chefs* commanded the regiments, and the 1st battalion was designated as the *chef bataillon* (*shefskii*) and carried the chef's name. In the chef's absence, the regimental commander or commanding officer led the unit. After October 1810 a regular infantry regiment consisted of two active battalions (1st and 3rd) and one replacement (2nd, or *zapasnoi*) battalion; after November 1811 the 4th reserve (*rezervnii*) battalion was assigned to the recruitment depots. The grenadier companies of the 2nd battalions were often combined to establish combined grenadier battalions. The light infantry regiments did not carry flags, while the line infantry units usually had six flags (two for each battalion, except for the 4th battalion). One of the flags was considered regimental and often referred to as "white," while the other were known as "colored."

Infantry regiments were organized into brigades, divisions, and corps. Two regiments comprised a brigade; three brigades (1st and 2nd infantry, 3rd Jäger) made a division. In a grenadier division, all three brigades were composed of grenadiers. Each division had field artillery consisting of one battery and two light companies. Divisions were designated by numbers, and by mid-1812 there were one Guard infantry division, two grenadier divisions, and twenty-four infantry divisions. Later, additional divisions were established to reinforce the army, including the 28th and 29th divisions from the Orenburg and Siberia garrisons forces; the 30th through the 37th divisions were raised from the 2nd battalions of the first twenty-seven divisions and the 38th to 48th divisions from the 4th battalions of the remaining divisions. The light infantry gradually increased throughout the Napoleonic Wars. In 1812 it consisted of two Guard and fifty Jäger regiments and the Guard *ekipazh* (crew). In addition, during the Russian campaign, special jäger regiments and battalions were organized within the *gubernia Opolchenyes* (provincially based, virtually untrained militia). The Jäger regiments had similar organization to the line infantry units. Each infantry division had one Jäger brigade, usually the third.

After the 1801 reorganization, Russian heavy cavalry comprised five squadrons, of which four were active and one stood in reserve. In 1803, the number of cuirassier regiments was set at six, while the dragoons increased to twenty-two. By 1805 there were four Guard regiments, six cuirassier, thirty dragoon, eight hussar, and three uhlan (lancer) regiments, while in 1812, cavalry included six Guard, eight cuirassier, thirty-six dragoon, eleven hussar, and five uhlan regiments. The Russian Guard cavalry consisted of four regiments of five squadrons each, two heavy (Chevalier Guard and Life Guard Horse) and two light (Hussar and Cossack).

Unit strengths varied greatly; on average, a heavy cavalry regiment consisted of one commanding officer, forty officers, seven NCOs, seventeen trumpeters, and 660 privates. Light cavalry regiments were divided into two battalions of five squadrons each; each regiment included one commanding officer, sixty-seven officers, 120 noncommissioned officers, twenty-one trumpeters, and 1,320 privates. One squadron from each battalion was designated as in reserve, while the remaining units were on active duty. On campaign, the reserve squadron remained in depot and trained recruits for the replacements. The regimental chef commanded each cavalry regiment, and the 1st squadron was usually named after him. In his absence, the regimental commander led the unit. Two or three cavalry regiments were often organized into a brigade, and three brigades (two heavy and one light) were united into a cavalry division. In 1812 divisions were further organized into cavalry corps. Cuirassier brigades had a separate designation from the general cavalry brigades. By 1812 there were one Guard cavalry division, two cuirassier divisions, and eight cavalry divisions. In March 1812 eight new cavalry divisions were formed; the 9th through 12th Divisions were organized from the replacement squadrons, while the 13th through 16th Divisions were raised from the cavalry recruitment depots.

After the 1812 campaign the cavalry underwent major reorganization. Two dragoon regiments were transformed into cuirassier regiments, one dragoon regiment into a hussar regiment, seven dragoon regiments into uhlans, and eight dragoon regiments into horse Jägers. In late December 1812 new cavalry divisions were formed—one Guard cavalry division, three cuirassier divisions, four dragoon divisions, two horse-Jäger divisions, three hussar divisions, and three uhlan divisions. Each division now included four regiments, with each regiment composed of six active and one replacement squadron.

Tsar Alexander also continued his father's reforms of the artillery. Starting in 1802 a special commission supervised its modernization. In 1803 the artillery train, which was previously manned by civilians, was placed under military control. New aiming devices (*dioptre* and *quadrant*) and caissons (ammunition wagons) were introduced in

1802–1803. In 1803, 3-pounder unicorns were distributed to Jäger units. The field artillery was reorganized. Regimental artillery was detached from units and formed into separate light artillery companies. In 1804 the regimental artillery was organized into regiments composed of two battalions of four companies each (two heavy and two light). In 1805 the inspector of all artillery, Aleksey Arakcheyev, launched a series of reforms to modernize the artillery. Known as the 1805 System, these measures introduced standardized equipment, ammunition, and guns. Following the Russian defeat at Austerlitz, however, further changes were introduced in the artillery. In 1806 artillery regiments were reorganized into brigades of two heavy, one horse, and two light artillery companies. Brigades were attached to infantry divisions. New artillery regulations prescribed specific instructions on artillery deployment and firing. By 1812 the artillery comprised the Guard and (regular) army branches. The regular artillery consisted of twenty-seven field artillery brigades (972 guns), ten reserve brigades (492 guns), and four replacement brigades (408 guns). Each brigade included one heavy and two light companies of 12 guns each. Cossack forces also included two horse artillery companies, with a third added in 1813. Artillery companies were armed with 12-pounder and 6-pounder guns, and 20-pounder and 10-pounder unicorns. A squad comprised two guns (*vzvod*) commanded by a noncommissioned officer. Two squads formed a division, and three divisions made one company, led by a staff officer.

Alexander Mikaberidze

See also Alexander I, Tsar; Arakcheyev, Aleksey Andreyevich, Count; Austerlitz, Battle of; Catherine II "the Great," Tsarina; Clausewitz, Karl Maria von; Corps System; Cossacks; Division; Fourth Coalition, War of the; France, Campaign in; Germany, Campaign in; Paul I, Tsar; Pfuel, Karl Ludwig August von; Russia; Russian Campaign; Russo-Polish War; Russo-Swedish War; Russo-Turkish War; Second Coalition, War of the; Third Coalition, War of the
References and further reading
Begunova, A. 1992. *Sabli ostri, koni bistri . . . Iz istorii russkoi kavalerii.* Moscow: Molodaia gvardiia.
Beskrovny, L. 1974. *Russkoe voennoe iskusstvo XIX v.* Moscow: Nauka.
———. 1996. *The Russian Army and Fleet in the Nineteenth Century.* Gulf Breeze, FL: Academic International.
Bezotosny, V. 2000. *Russkaia armia, 1812–1814.* Moscow: Vlados
Bogdanov, L. 1979. *Russkaia armia v 1812 g.* Moscow: Voennoe izd-vo Ministerstva oborony.
Duffy, Christopher. 1981. *Russia's Military Way to the West: Origins and Nature of Russian Military Power, 1700–1800.* London: Routledge.
Gabaev, G. 1912. *Rospis rus. Polkam 1812 g.* Kiev: N.p.
Geisman, P. 1902. "Istoricheskii ocherk vozniknovenia i razvitia v Rossii General'nogo shtaba do kontsa
tsarstvovania Aleksandra I." In *Stoletie Voennogo Ministerstva,* vol. 4, part 2: sect. 1. St. Petersburg: Voennoe Ministerstvo.
Glinoetskii, N. 1874. *Russkii Generalnii Shtab v tsarstvovanie Aleksandra I.* St. Petersburg: V Tip. Departamenta udielov.
Haythornthwaite, Philip. 1987a. *The Russian Army of the Napoleonic Wars.* Vol. 1, *Infantry, 1799–1814.* London: Osprey.
———. 1987b. *The Russian Army of the Napoleonic Wars.* Vol. 2, *Cavalry.* London: Osprey.
Kersnovskii, A. 1992. *Istoriia russkoi armii.* Moscow: Golos.
Partridge, Richard, and Michael Oliver. 1999. *Napoleonic Army Handbook.* Vol. 1, *The British Army and Her Allies.* London: Constable.
Seaton, Albert. 1979. *The Russian Army of the Napoleonic Wars.* London: Osprey.
Smith, Digby. 2002. *Armies of 1812: The Grande Armée and the Armies of Austria, Prussia, Russia and Turkey.* Staplehurst, UK: Spellmount.
Spring, Laurence. 2002. *Russian Grenadiers and Infantry, 1799–1815.* Oxford: Osprey.
———. 2003. *The Cossacks, 1799–1815.* Oxford: Osprey.
Taylor, Brian D. 2003. *Politics and the Russian Army: Civil-Military Relations, 1689–2000.* Cambridge: Cambridge University Press.
Ulianov, I. 1997. *Reguliarnaia pekhota. 1801–1855.* Moscow: OOO Izd-vo AST.
Viskovatov, A. V. 1841–1862. *Istoricheskoe opisanie odezhdi i vooruzheniia Rossiiskikh voisk.* 30 vols. St. Petersburg: Voennaya.

Russian Campaign (1812)

Decisive campaign between France and Russia, known as the Patriotic War of 1812 in Russia. Following the Treaty of Tilsit of 1807, relations between France and Russia became increasingly tense, and the possibility of another war loomed over the Continent. Tsar Alexander I had not forgotten the painful lessons of the Wars of the Third and Fourth Coalitions (1805 and 1806–1807, respectively) and was aware of the widespread displeasure prevailing in Russia, particularly in the army, over the "ignominious" Peace of Tilsit. Within a year of Tilsit, there was a marked deterioration in Franco-Russian relations. Although Napoleon and Alexander seemed to improve their relations at Erfurt in 1808, the fissures became evident the following year, when Russia took virtually no steps to support France against Austria in the War of the Fifth Coalition.

Russia was particularly concerned by Napoleon's aggressive policy in Europe, after, in 1810, France annexed Holland, the Hanseatic cities, and the North German states all the way to the river Elbe, including the Duchy of Oldenburg, whose duke was Alexander's brother-in-law. The Continental System, which Russia was forced to join in

1807, proved extremely disadvantageous to Russian merchants and led to a sharp decrease in Russian overseas trade. The major issue of contention between France and Russia was the Polish question. The ink was hardly dry on the Tilsit agreement when Napoleon created the Duchy of Warsaw under the nominal control of the king of Saxony; the French abolished serfdom and introduced the French civil code, actions that appeared to threaten the Russian Empire. Napoleon's interest in consolidating his control over the Poles was further revealed when, after the defeat of Austria in 1809, he incorporated western Galicia into the Duchy of Warsaw, which, in effect, threatened the western frontiers of Russia.

In early 1811 Napoleon began preparing for war against Russia and took special care in preparing for the "Second Polish Campaign" (the first being in 1806–1807) attempting to ensure rapid victory over Russia. The enormous Grande Armée, of over 600,000 troops and 1,372 field guns, was created. More than half of its troops were furnished by Napoleon's allies, including Austria, Prussia, Saxony, Spain, Bavaria, Poland, and Italy. Anticipating war, both countries sought allies. Each hoped for the support of Austria and Prussia, but the presence of the Napoleonic armies in Germany and the recent defeat of Austria in 1809 left little choice for these states but to submit to the French.

Napoleon's overall strategy for the war ideally included the use of troops from Sweden and the Ottoman Empire to form his extreme flanks. However, Napoleon was unable to exercise influence on either state. Sweden, protected from the French army by the sea, formed an alliance with Russia (April 1812) in return for the promise of Russian assistance in annexing Norway, then in Denmark's possession. As for the Ottomans, by the spring of 1812 they still were at war with Russia and appeared to be natural allies of Napoleon. But their war had been a failure, with their armies defeated by the Russians and their national finances exhausted. By the spring, Alexander managed to achieve a significant diplomatic success by concluding the Treaty of Bucharest (28 May 1812) with the Turks.

By the spring of 1812 Napoleon's gigantic army was deployed in three groups along the Vistula River stretching from Warsaw to Könisgberg. The main forces consisted of I Corps under Marshal Louis Nicolas Davout, II Corps under Marshal Nicolas Charles Oudinot, III Corps under Marshal Michel Ney, I and II Reserve Cavalry Corps under Marshal Joachim Murat, and the Imperial Guard under marshals François Joseph Lefebvre and Adolphe Edouard Mortier, totaling about 220,000 men and 628 guns. This force was under Napoleon's direct command. The Central Army, under the command of Napoleon's stepson, the Viceroy of Italy, Eugène de Beauharnais, consisted of IV Corps under Eugène and VI Corps under Marshal Laurent Gouvion St.

Cyr, supported by General Emmanuel, marquis de Grouchy's III Reserve Cavalry Corps and the Italian Royal Guards, for a total of 70,000 men and 208 guns. The army on the right wing consisted of V Corps under General Józef Poniatowski, VII Corps under General Jean Louis Reynier, VIII Corps under General Dominique Vandamme, and IV Cavalry Corps under General Marie-Victor Latour-Maubourg. These forces amounted to 75,000 men and 232 guns. Napoleon's brother, Jérôme Bonaparte, King of Westphalia, commanded these troops. Marshal Jacques Etienne Macdonald's X Corps guarded the left flank of the army, and 30,000 Austrians under *Feldmarschall* Karl Philip Fürst zu Schwarzenberg covered the right flank.

Russia fielded more than 900,000 men, but these forces were scattered in Moldavia, the Crimea, the Caucasus, Finland, and the internal regions, leaving some 250,000 men with over 900 guns to face Napoleon's army during the initial stages of the invasion. The 1st Western Army of General Mikhail Barclay de Tolly (120,000 men and 580 guns) was deployed on the Rossyena-Lida Line in the direction of St. Petersburg. The 2nd Western Army under General Peter Bagration (49,000 men and 180 guns) was assembled in the area of Volkovysk and Belostock, covering the route to Moscow. General Alexander Tormasov commanded the 3rd Observational Reserve Army (later renamed the 3rd Western Army) of 44,000 men and 168 guns in the vicinity of Lutsk, covering the route to Kiev. Besides these three major armies, the Russians also arranged two lines of defense. Along the first line, General Peter Essen's corps was deployed at Riga. Two Reserve Corps under General Egor Muller-Zakomelsky (27,473 men) and General Fedor Ertel (37,539 men) were assembled in a second line in the Toropets and Mozyr regions. The Russian extreme flanks were covered by General Baron Fadey Steingell (19,000 men) in the north and Admiral Pavel Chichagov's Army of the Danube (57,526 men) in the south.

On the eve of the war, the Russian Army considered a few strategic plans and adopted one by General Karl von Pfuel. Pfuel's plan involved a withdrawal maneuver by the 1st Western Army to the Drissa camp on the Zapadnaia Dvina River, where it was supposed to contain the enemy while the 2nd Western Army struck the enemy in the flank and rear from the Volkovysk-Mir region. This plan was flawed for several reasons. It did not take into account the possibility of the French simultaneously attacking from two directions. The Russian armies were divided into several units, each isolated from the others by the almost impassable bogs of Polesye. The limited strength of the 2nd Western Army made an attack on the flank and rear of the enemy unrealistic. Napoleon had only to oppose it with an equivalent force to halt its advance. Another problem facing Russian

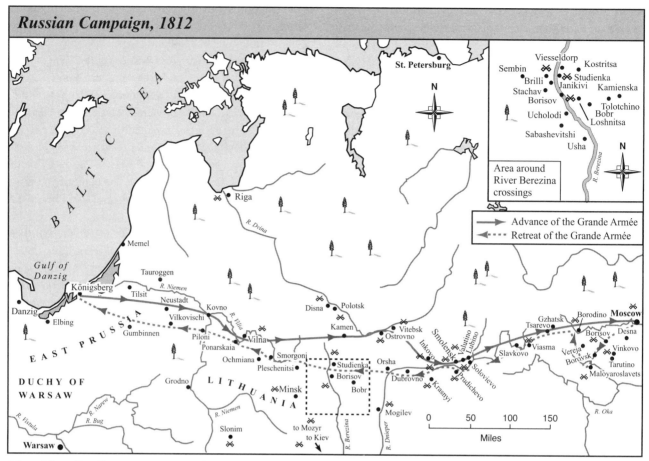

Russian Campaign, 1812

Adapted from Chandler 1966, 772–773; and Fremont-Barnes and Fisher 2004, 165.

forces was the failure to establish a centralized command. No commander in chief had been appointed, and generals Bagration and Tormasov were independent commanders only nominally subordinate to the minister of war, Barclay de Tolly, who could issue orders only in the name of the tsar. Moreover, according to the Statute for the Administration of the Large Active Army, the tsar also assumed supreme command whenever he joined the army.

During the night of 23 June Napoleon's army crossed the Russian border at the Niemen River. Despite increasing criticism of Pfuel's plan, the Russian armies began to withdraw toward the Drissa camp. The 1st Western Army reached the Drissa camp on 8 July, where Alexander finally discarded Pfuel's strategy. Urged by his advisers, Alexander then left the army without appointing a commander in chief. Barclay de Tolly then fulfilled the functions of commander in chief, based on his position as war minister. On 14 July Barclay de Tolly abandoned the Drissa camp, leaving General Peter Graf zu Wittgenstein with some 20,000 men to cover the area in the direction of St. Petersburg. Barclay withdrew toward Smolensk, fighting rearguard actions at Vitebsk and Ostrovno. In the south, Bagration's

2nd Western Army withdrew first toward Minsk and then to Nesvizh and Bobruisk, eluding Napoleon's enveloping maneuvers and gaining minor victories at Mir and Romanov. When Davout's forces finally intercepted the 2nd Western Army at Mogilev, Bagration made a diversion to Saltanovka on 23 July and, with a skillful maneuver, withdrew toward Smolensk through Mstislavl. On 2 August he arrived at Smolensk to join the 1st Western Army. The two armies totaled 120,000 men, facing some 180,000 men in Napoleon's main forces.

Simultaneously, the 3rd Western Army defeated Reynier's corps at Kobryn and then pinned down Schwarzenberg and Reynier's corps in the Volhynia region. On 31 July Chichagov's Army of the Danube moved from Moldavia to support Tormasov's army. In the north, Oudinot's corps attacked Wittgenstein, who protected the route to St. Petersburg, and took Polotsk on 26 July. However, in minor actions at Klyastitsy on 30 July–1 August, the French suffered a defeat and withdrew toward Polotsk. Napoleon had to divert St. Cyr to support Oudinot's operations. In the Baltic provinces, Macdonald's corps was pinned down near Riga. Thus, by August 1812, Napoleon's initial plan to destroy the Russian army in a decisive battle had been frustrated; the Grande Armée suffered heavy losses from strategic consumption (the reduction of forces due to the deployment of garrisons, establishment of depots, protection of lines of communications, and other duties) and desertion.

As their armies united at Smolensk, the Russians faced a crisis of command. This conflict stemmed from political discord between the old Russian aristocracy and the "foreigners," who had gradually gained power at the court and in the army. The specific reason for the tension was the difference in views on strategy among the senior officers and army commanders who represented opposing parties. Barclay de Tolly was the focal point of the so-called German party, who supported his defensive plans. Opposing them, the "Russian party," led by Bagration, represented the majority of the Russian army and urged an immediate counteroffensive against Napoleon. Anti-Barclay sentiments were so strong among the senior officers that they openly loathed the commander in chief and intrigued for the appointment of Bagration to supreme command. Some even encouraged Bagration to replace Barclay de Tolly by force. Giving in to pressure, Barclay de Tolly agreed to an offensive from Smolensk to Rudnia and Porechye to attempt to break through the French center and then destroy the remaining corps piecemeal.

However, because of differences of opinion among the commanders and Barclay de Tolly's vacillation, precious time was lost in futile maneuvering. That gave Napoleon enough time to recognize Russian intentions and counteract them accordingly. In a brilliant maneuver, Napoleon unexpectedly crossed the Dnieper and threatened to capture Smolensk. General Dmitry Neverovsky's resolute rearguard action at Krasnyi on 14 August enabled General Nikolay Rayevsky to prepare the defense of Smolensk while the two Russian armies rushed back to the city. On 15–16 August the Russians repulsed French assaults on Smolensk but were nonetheless forced to abandon the city. As the Russians withdrew to Moscow, Napoleon attempted to cut their line of retreat. However, in the Battle of Valutina Gora on 19 August, Barclay de Tolly's army succeeded in clearing its way to Dorogobuzh.

The surrender of Smolensk further aroused discontent in the army and society. On 20 August, Alexander replaced Barclay de Tolly with General Mikhail Kutuzov, who took command on 29 August at Tsarevo Zaimische. Kutuzov withdrew the troops farther to the east, deploying them near the village of Borodino, where he decided to give battle. On 5 September, the French attacked the Russians at Shevardino and drove them back after a fierce night engagement. The Russians received reinforcements under General Mikhail Miloradovich as well as *opolchenye* (un-

trained militia) forces, increasing their strength to 155,000 troops, of whom 115,000 men were regulars, and 640 guns. Napoleon had some 135,000 men with 587 guns.

The Battle of Borodino took place on 7 September. Napoleon chose frontal attacks on fortified Russian positions (Bagration's *flêches*—field fortifications in the shape of arrow heads—and the Great Redoubt, also known as the Rayevsky Redoubt, which was a large-scale field fortification built in the center of the Russian positions) instead of flanking maneuvers. In savage and bloody fighting, both sides displayed great bravery and steadfastness. Although the French controlled the battlefield at the end of the day, the Russian army withdrew in good order and remained battle ready. French losses were between 30,000 and 35,000 men, including 49 generals. The Russians lost some 44,000 men, including 29 generals.

During his retreat to Moscow, Kutuzov still considered engaging the enemy in front of Moscow. However, at the military council at Fili on 13 September, Kutuzov ordered that Moscow be abandoned without a fight. The following day, Napoleon's troops entered the city. However, the same day fires began in Moscow and continued until 18 September, destroying two-thirds of the city. Meanwhile, Wittgenstein achieved an important victory at Polotsk on 20 October and secured the northern approaches to St. Petersburg. Macdonald spent August–December unsuccessfully besieging Riga in the Baltic provinces.

While the French remained in Moscow, the Russian army skillfully maneuvered from the Ryazan road to the Kaluga road, where Kutuzov established the Tarutino camp. Through this maneuver, Kutuzov protected the southern provinces that had abundant supplies and manufacturing enterprises. The Russians also threatened Napoleon's rear and lines of communication. At Tarutino, Kutuzov began intensive preparations for future operations and increased his army to 110,000–120,000 men, with additional militia forces to come. Kutuzov also encouraged guerrilla operations against the invaders and organized several regular cavalry detachments under Denis Davydov, Alexander Figner, Alexander Seslavin, and Ivan Dorokhov to harass French communications and supply lines. Napoleon made several peace proposals to Alexander, but they were all rejected.

On 18 October Murat's advance guard suffered a sudden defeat on the Chernishnya River, north of Tarutino. Hearing this news, Napoleon realized he had to abandon devastated Moscow before winter arrived. The French finally commenced their retreat on 19 October. Napoleon's forces dwindled to some 100,000 men, accompanied by thousands of noncombatants and an enormous train with supplies and loot. He planned to move his forces to the western provinces of Russia, where supply stores had been prepared in advance. However, the route from Moscow to Smolensk, via Gzhatsk, had been devastated after French forces had fought their way to the Russian capital in August–September. Napoleon therefore decided to advance by the Kaluga route, which would take the army through unharmed regions to the southwest.

Initially, Napoleon successfully deceived the Russian forces about his plan; however, heavy rains made the roads almost impassable and considerably delayed French movements on 21–22 October. During the night of the twenty-third, Russian scouts finally realized that Napoleon was moving his entire army southward. Kutuzov, promoted to field marshal on 11 September, immediately dispatched General Dmitry Dokhturov's corps from Tarutino to the little town of Maloyaroslavets, the only point where Kutuzov could join the new Kaluga road and block the French advance.

In a savage battle on 23–24 October, the French captured the town of Maloyaroslavets but failed to break through the main Russian army. After a council of war on the evening of 25 October, Napoleon began a withdrawal to Smolensk by way of Borodino and Gzhatsk. The Battle of Maloyaroslavets had a crucial impact on Napoleon's campaign in Russia. The French were prevented from

reaching the rich provinces in southeastern Russia and were forced to return to the devastated route to Smolensk. The marching and fighting at Maloyaroslavets consumed seven crucial days; a week after the battle, the snow began to fall, and frost struck.

Kutuzov dispatched Ataman Matvei Platov's Cossacks and General Mikhail Miloradovich's advance guard to pursue the French, while the main Russian army slowly followed behind. In addition, the flying detachments of generals Adam Ozharovsky, Denis Davydov, Paul Golenishchev-Kutuzov, and Peter Volkonsky constantly harassed the French lines of communication. Meanwhile, in the south, Chichagov merged his forces with Tormasov's army and took command of some 60,000 men. Containing Schwarzenberg's corps in Volhynia and leaving General Fabian Osten-Sacken's corps to oppose the Austrians, Chichagov moved north to intercept Napoleon, taking Minsk on 16 November and Borisov on the twenty-second.

In early November the French army finally reached Smolensk, where huge supply depots had earlier been established. However, discipline broke down, and looting became rampant. Napoleon hoped to rally his forces there, but Kutuzov's advance toward Krasnyi threatened to cut

The retreat from Moscow. Remnants of the Grande Armée struggle through subzero temperatures and blinding snow in an epic march of misery and death that claimed the lives of countless thousands. (Print by J. Rousset from *Illustrierte Geschichte der Befreiungskriege* by Julius von Pflugk-Harttung, 1913)

Marshal Ney, musket in hand, leads the rear guard of the Grande Armée during Napoleon's catastrophic retreat from Moscow. (Engraving by Henry Wolf after Adolphe Yvan from *Life of Napoleon Bonaparte* by William M. Sloane. New York: Century, 1906, vol. 4)

his route. On 3 November Miloradovich and Platov attacked Davout near Viazma and captured the town. Napoleon soon abandoned Smolensk, and as the French withdrew, the superior Russian forces attacked three French corps (Eugène, Davout, Ney) while they were marching from Smolensk to Krasnyi. Each corps was temporarily cut off, and Ney's corps even surrounded, but none of them were forced to lay down their arms; Ney was cut off from the main army, but conducted a heroic retreat across the Dnieper River and earned the nickname "the Bravest of the Brave." Nevertheless, French losses were horrendous due to constant skirmishes, cold weather, and lack of supplies. The inadequately clothed French troops began to suffer and die from frostbite and hypothermia and thousands of stragglers were killed or captured by Russian guerrillas. By mid-November only some 49,000 French troops remained under arms, but they were accompanied by tens of thousands of stragglers. The Russian army also suffered severely in the harsh winter conditions, losing some 80,000 men.

As Napoleon retreated westward the Russians had a unique chance of trapping him on the Berezina River. The main Russian army under Kutuzov closely pursued Napoleon's forces, while Wittgenstein's corps converged from the northeast and Chichagov's army from the southwest. However, Napoleon demonstrated his dazzling military talents by diverting Russian attention to Uchlodi, while his forces crossed the river at Studienka. In desperate fighting, Napoleon extricated part of his army, but suffered 25,000 battle casualties and lost some 30,000 noncombatants. Although Chichagov was held responsible for the Berezina failure, Wittgenstein and Kutuzov also acted indecisively; Kutuzov's faltering actions at Krasnyi and the Berezina served as a basis for the so-called golden-bridge or parallel-march thesis in Soviet historiography, which argued that Kutuzov had refrained from attacking the French in order to preserve his armies and let the winter and hunger do their business.

As the retreat continued, the Grande Armée ceased to exist as an organized military force. On 5 December Napoleon appointed Murat in charge of the army and left for Paris. Five days later, the Russian army captured Vilna and halted its pursuit. By 25 December the last remnants of the Grande Armée crossed the Niemen River.

The Russian campaign had disastrous consequences for Napoleon. His military might was shattered following the loss of up to a half million men in Russia. The French cavalry was virtually wiped out and never fully recovered during the subsequent campaigns in 1813–1814. Furthermore, Napoleon's allies, Austria and Prussia, took advantage of the moment to break the alliance with France and joined their efforts to the Russian war against Napoleon. The campaign is particularly interesting for its gigantic scope and intensity, as well as the variety of tactics employed. The campaign also had important effects on Russia. The Russian army became the main force in the subsequent struggle for Germany. The war deeply influenced cultural and social life in Russia. Twelve years later, the Decembrists declared themselves "The children of 1812," as their ideology was influenced by the events of that year.

Alexander Mikaberidze

See also Alexander I, Tsar; Bagration, Peter Ivanovich, Prince; Barclay de Tolly, Mikhail Andreas; Beauharnais, Eugène Rose de; Bennigsen, Levin August, Baron; Berezina, Actions and Crossing at the; Bonaparte, Jérôme; Borodino, Battle of; Camp Followers; Chichagov, Pavel Vasilievich; Continental System; Cossacks; Davout, Louis Nicolas; Davydov, Denis Vasilievich; Dokhturov, Dmitry Sergeyevich; Erfurt, Congress of; Fifth Coalition, War of the; Fourth Coalition, War of the; Gouvion St. Cyr, Laurent, comte; Grouchy, Emmanuel, marquis de; Guerrilla Warfare; Imperial Guard (French); Krasnyi, First Battle of; Krasnyi, Second Battle of; Kutuzov, Prince Mikhail Golenischev-, Prince; Lefebvre, François Joseph; Macdonald, Jacques Etienne Joseph Alexandre; Maloyaroslavets, Battle of; Miloradovich, Mikhail Andreyevitch, Count; Mogilev, Action at; Mortier, Adolphe Edouard Casimir Joseph; Moscow, Occupation of; Murat, Joachim; Neverovsky, Dmitry Petrovich; Ney, Michel; Osten-Sacken, Fabian Vilgelmovich, Prince; Osterman-Tolstoy, Alexander Ivanovich, Count; Ostrovno, Battle of; Oudinot, Nicolas Charles; Pfuel, Karl Luwdwig August von; Platov, Matvei Ivanovich, Count and Ataman; Poland; Polotsk, Battle of; Poniatowski, Józef Anton, Prince; Rayevsky, Nikolay Nikolayevich, Count; Reynier, Jean Louis Ebénézer, comte; Rimsky-Korsakov, Alexander Mikhailovich; Russo-Turkish War; Schwarzenberg, Karl Philipp Fürst zu; Smolensk, Battle of; Tauroggen, Convention of; Third Coalition, War of the; Tilsit, Treaties of; Tormasov, Alexander Petrovich, Count; Vandamme, Dominique Joseph René; Vilna, Battle of; Vitebsk, Battle of; Wittgenstein, Peter Khristianovich Graf zu (Sayn-)

References and further reading

Austin, Paul Britten. 1993. *1812: Napoleon's Invasion of Russia*. London: Greenhill.
Belloc, Hilaire. 1926. *Napoleon's Campaign of 1812 and the Retreat from Moscow*. New York: Harper.
Brett-James, Antony. 1966. *1812: Eyewitness Accounts of Napoleon's Defeat in Russia*. New York: St. Martin's.
Cate, Curtis. 1985. *The War of the Two Emperors: The Duel between Napoleon and Alexander—Russia, 1812*. New York: Random House.
Duffy, Christopher. 1972. *Borodino*. London: Sphere.
Hereford, George B. 2002. *Napoleon's Invasion of Russia*. London: Empiricus.
Nafziger, George F. 1988. *Napoleon's Invasion of Russia*. Novato, CA: Presidio.
Nicolson, Nigel. 1985. *Napoleon, 1812*. London: Weidenfeld and Nicolson.
Riehn, Richard K. 1990. *1812: Napoleon's Russian Campaign*. New York: McGraw-Hill.
Smith, Digby. 2002. *Armies of 1812: The Grande Armée and the Armies of Austria, Prussia, Russia and Turkey*. Staplehurst, UK: Spellmount.
Zamoyski, Adam. 2004. *1812: Napoleon's Fatal March on Moscow*. London: HarperCollins.

Russian Navy

After its creation by Peter the Great at the beginning of the eighteenth century, the Russian Navy became an important part of Russian military forces, establishing glorious traditions that are honored to the present day. Throughout the eighteenth century, Russia waged a series of wars to gain access to major seas: In the Great Northern War (1700–1721), Russia gained a coastline on the Baltic Sea, and the Russo-Turkish Wars in the 1760s and 1770s turned Russia into a major power in the Black Sea. Thus, in the late eighteenth century, Russia's naval force comprised two major fleets, the Baltic and the Black Sea fleets, as well as the White Sea and Caspian Sea flotillas. Each fleet was organized into divisions and brigades; each division comprised three squadrons, the 1st (main), the 2nd (advance-guard), and the 3rd (rearguard) squadrons.

During the Napoleonic Wars, the Baltic Fleet consisted of three divisions and the Black Sea Fleet of two divisions. From 1808 each squadron had ship and rowing crews, and each crew numbered eight companies of 100 men. The Baltic Fleet had 52 ships and eight rowing crews, while the Black Sea Fleet included 31 ships and four rowing crews. In 1810 further changes were made when the Guards Naval Crew was created comprising four (later eight) companies. Naval personnel were not recruited separately: During regular army levies, a specific quota of conscripts was assigned to the navy. Sailors were trained under the 1720 Naval Regulations with emphasis on constant drill and strict discipline. Officers and noncommissioned officers were trained in naval institutions and navigational colleges, including the Naval Academy, Artillery College, Naval Architectural College, and Baltic College in Kronstadt, and the Black Sea Navigational College in Kherson. In addition, Russian rulers sought assistance from abroad by hiring foreign officers, including Samuel Greig, Johann Heinrich von Kingsbergen, Roman Crown, and John Paul Jones. A number of young Russians were regularly sent abroad, mainly to Britain, for training. Throughout the Napoleonic Wars, the length of service in the navy was twenty-five years. By 1812 there were 28,408 sailors and officers serving in the Baltic Fleet and some 12,000 men in the Black Sea Fleet.

The strength of the Russian Navy varied throughout the period. In 1797–1798 the Baltic Fleet included 45 ships of the line, 19 sail frigates, 12 oared frigates, and 132 ships of other classes; while the Black Sea Fleet was composed of 15 ships of the line, 6 sail and 15 oared frigates, and 72 vessels of other classes. The Caspian flotilla consisted of 3 frigates and 24 vessels of lesser class. In 1802 a special Committee to Improve the Condition of the Navy was established to reorganize and modernize the naval forces. Despite finding many flaws, however, the committee made only superfluous changes in the navy. Based on its recommendations, by 1803 the Baltic Sea Fleet included 32 ships of the line, 28 frigates, 4 gunboats, 3 corvettes, 6 brigs, 35 light ships, and almost 300 oared boats. The Black Sea Fleet was limited to 21 ships of the line, 10 frigates, 5 brigs, 20 light ships, and some 190 oared boats.

In reality, however, the navy was often in such poor condition that many fewer ships were actually able to put to sea. In 1807 the Black Sea Fleet, engaged in operations against the Turks, comprised 12 battle-ready ships of the line, 82 gunboats, 1 yacht, and 27 lesser ships. In 1812 the Baltic Fleet officially comprised 41 ships of the line, but only 9 of them actually served in the Baltic Sea, while 11 were in Archangel and 9 in Britain, 9 were unfinished, and 3 were converted to blockships for use in preventing enemy vessels from entering Russian ports.

During the Napoleonic Wars the Russian Navy was involved in several major campaigns. In 1798–1799 the Black Sea Fleet was dispatched to support the Allies in the Mediterranean Sea. Operating under the command of the famous Admiral Fedor Ushakov, the Russian Fleet achieved considerable success, capturing the Ionian Islands and the island of Corfu. In August 1805 the Russian naval squadron in the Adriatic Sea landed Allied troops in Italy and supported them against the French at Cattaro (now Kotor) and Ragusa in 1806. During the Russo-Turkish War of 1806–1812 the Russian squadron under Vice Admiral Dmitry Senyavin annihilated the Turkish Fleet in actions at the Dardanelles, Tenedos, and Mount Athos. However, the Treaty of Tilsit in 1807 undermined Senyavin's successes and forced him to seek neutral ports at Trieste and Lisbon, where he was blockaded by the (British) Royal Navy in 1808 and forced to transfer his ships to the British. In the north, a Russian fleet helped transport troops to Holland in 1799 and to northern Germany in 1805.

The navy also participated in the Russo-Swedish War of 1808–1809, but its operations were restricted, since the Baltic Sea could be navigated for only a limited time of the year. In addition, animosity between army commanders and the minister of the navy sometimes caused additional difficulties; thus in the spring of 1808, the Swedes recaptured the key islands of Gotland and Aland after the Russian navy failed to support its land forces. Furthermore, following the Treaty of Tilsit, the Royal Navy directly threatened its Russian counterpart in the Baltic Sea in 1808–1810 and engaged in occasional minor engagements with it. In the east, the Caspian flotilla held firm control of the Caspian Sea and supported the Russian armies during the Russo-Persian War of 1803–1813, which ended by the Treaty of Gulistan on 12 October 1813.

Alexander Mikaberidze

See also Artillery (Naval); French Navy; Frigates; Ionian Islands; Naval Warfare; North Holland, Campaign in (1799); Royal Navy; Russian Army; Russo-Swedish War; Russo-Turkish War; Senyavin, Dmitry Nikolayevich; Ships of the Line; Sloops; Tilsit, Treaties of

References and further reading
Alekseyev, Vladimir. 1976. *Russkie i sovetskie moriaki na Sredizemnom more*. Moscow: Voeniszdat.
Bestuzhev, N. A. 1961. *Opyt istorii rosiiskogo flota*. Leningrad: Gos. soiuznoe izd-vo sudostroit. Promyshl.
Krotkov, A. 1889. *Russkii flot v tsarstvovanie imperatritsy Ekateriny II s 1772 g. po 1783 God*. St. Petersburg: Morskago ministerstva.
Mitchell, Donald W. 1974. *A History of Russian and Soviet Sea Power*. New York: Macmillan.
Mordvinov, R. N. 1951. *Admiral Ushakov*. Moskva: Voenno-morskoe izd-vo Voenno- morskogo ministerstva Soiuza SSR.
Pivka, Otto von. 1980. *Navies of the Napoleonic Era*. New York: Hippocrene.
Tarle, Eugene. 1956. *Tri ekspeditsii russkogo flota*. Moscow: Voennoe izd-vo.

Russo-Polish War (1792–1794)

The Russo-Polish War was one of the last efforts of independent Poland-Lithuania to retain its independence and self-governance. Yet the Polish-Lithuanian armies were no match for the huge Russian war machine. Badly trained, not numerous enough, and badly equipped, Polish soldiers showed incredible bravery and heart for fighting, only to be overwhelmed by their more numerous Russian foes. After the war, Russia and Prussia staged the Second Partition of Poland.

On 3 May 1791 the Four Years' Parliament (*Sejm*) passed the first Polish Constitution. Although not as democratic as the French constitution of September 1791, the Polish Constitution was also influenced by the Enlightenment and promised a well-ordered state. This new, modern document promised important reforms and the strengthening of the Polish-Lithuanian state. At the same time it deprived the nobility of numerous privileges and freedoms that class had hitherto enjoyed. Such changes were not to be accepted by many Polish nobles, nor by Poland's neighbors, in particular by Russia. A group of Polish aristocrats, with Russian support, signed in St. Petersburg the Act of Confederation against the constitution on 27 April 1792. The act, announced on 14 May in the town of Targowica, declared the constitution void and called for military assistance from the Russian tsarina, Catherine II.

On 18 May Russian troops crossed the Polish-Lithuanian border, aiming to restore the old form of government. They were divided into two groups: General Mikhail Kakhovskii's army invading from Moldavia and Kiev in the south, and General Mikhail Krechetnikov's army entering Lithuania from the north. The former consisted of four corps numbering 64,000 troops and 136 guns, and the latter, 33,000 men and 58 guns. Kakhovskii's plans were to surround the Polish Crown army based in Ukraine near Bracław and destroy it, or push it back across the Bug River toward central Poland. Krechetnikov's task was to defeat the Lithuanian army, cross the Bug, and possibly cut the Crown army's route of retreat.

The Polish-Lithuanian army was smaller and less experienced than its adversaries, but also divided into smaller groups. Shortly after the war started, Polish strength had risen to 70,000 men, but many were unarmed and ill-trained. In the end only about 40,000 men took part in the struggle. In addition to these disadvantages, the Polish treasury was empty, and all negotiations to secure a loan failed. Prussia, which was obliged to come to Poland's help according to a bilateral alliance, failed to do so. In the Ukraine, a Crown force numbering 17,000 troops under Prince Józef Poniatowski retreated toward central Poland. They were called to do so by the king, Stanisław August Poniatowski, who hoped to negotiate peace conditions with the Russians. The Crown troops managed to avoid being outflanked by the numerous Russian army, and on 17 June the first major battle took place at Zieleńce, where the Polish troops defeated the Russian corps.

Despite the victory, the Crown army, facing massive Russian forces, continued its retreat toward the Bug, which it reached on 7 July. It was along this river, between Dubienka and Włodawa, that the united Crown army numbering 25,000 decided to put up a defense. The north wing was defended by Wielhorski's division, the center by Poniatowski, while the south wing, stretching between the river and the Austrian border, was covered by an army under the command of Tadeusz Kościuszko, an experienced general and veteran of the American Revolutionary War.

The engagement, which began with Kakhovskii's attack on 13 July, is known as the Battle of Dubienka. Two of Kakhovskii's corps (General Levanidov's 9,000 troops and Tormasov's 8,000) attacked the northern wing and the center, tying Poniatowski's and Wilehorski's troops in position. The main Russian army under General Mikhail Kutuzov and General Dunin (25,000 strong) crossed the Bug on the seventeenth and attacked Kościuszko's 5,300-strong division. Kościuszko managed to hold off the Russian attacks, but at the end of the day, on learning that the other Polish divisions had started to retire toward Warsaw, he ordered a retreat. The Battle of Dubienka remained unresolved—without a victor. Kościuszko had managed to hold back an army five times stronger than his own and retreat in good order.

Yet the campaign was practically lost. Although over 30,000 men stood ready in central Poland, the king, hoping to preserve some of the rights granted by the Four Years' Parliament, decided to join the Confederation of Targowica and cease military operations. The king's decision meant that the war had ended.

The war in the north, in Lithuania, ended even more rapidly. The small Lithuanian force of 10,000 men was badly commanded by Prince Ludwig of Württemberg, who was a traitor and was soon replaced. These scattered troops, lacking proper command, were no match for the stronger and better-trained Russian army. There were no major battles in Lithuania, except for the action at Mir on 11 June, where the defeated Lithuanian army retreated first toward Grodno and then toward the Bug, hoping to join with the Polish Crown armies.

Following the Second Partition of Poland in 1793, and the Russian attempt to diminish by more than half the size of the Polish army, Polish politicians and generals decided to open a new military campaign. An uprising against Russian rule in Polish territories started on 24 March 1794 under Kościuszko's command. The first battle, fought on 4 April at Racławice, brought victory to the Polish army. Part of the army consisted of peasants armed with scythes. Kościuszko's troops managed to win several minor clashes and Warsaw was liberated from Russian occupation. Yet in May the Russian army, accompanied by Prussian troops, began a counteroffensive. In June and July, insurgent armies lost the battles of Szczekociny and Chełmn. Soon thereafter Prussian troops occupied Kraków, and together with Russian forces began an initially unsuccessful siege of Warsaw.

In August, insurrection in Lithuania died out, while a decisive battle was fought on 10 October at Maciejowice. Kościuszko, who was wounded, was taken prisoner by the Russians. Between 4 and 9 November, General Alexander Suvorov stormed the Warsaw district of Praga, where the civilian population was eventually overwhelmed, with more than 10,000 being massacred by the troops. The last insurgent troops surrendered to the Russian army at Radoszyce on 17 November.

Jakub Basista

See also Catherine II "the Great," Tsarina; Kutuzov, Mikhail Golenischev-, Prince; Maciejowice, Battle of; Poland; Poland, Partitions of; Poniatowski, Józef Anton, Prince; Suvorov, Alexander Vasilievich

References and further reading
Dedrej, Piotr. 2000. *Zieleńce-Mir-Dubienka 1792*. Warsaw: Bellona.
Gierowski, Józef Andrzej. 1996. *The Polish-Lithuanian Commonwealth in the XVIIIth Century*. Krakow: Polska Akademia Umiejętności.
Lukowski, Jerzy. 1990. *Liberty's Folly*. New York: Routledge.
———. 1999. *The Partitions of Poland*. New York: Longman.
Wandycz, Piotr. 1975. *The Lands of Partitioned Poland, 1795–1918*. Seattle: University of Washington Press.

Russo-Swedish War (1808–1809)

The Baltic Sea, dominated by Sweden for centuries, was important to Russia for both strategic and commercial reasons. In a series of wars between 1700 and 1791, Russia succeeded in annexing territories in eastern Finland and along the southern Baltic coastline. However, Russian sovereigns sought to secure the free navigation of the Baltic and to protect their capital, St. Petersburg, by annexing Finland, then in Swedish possession. Following the Peace of Tilsit on 7 July 1807, Napoleon consented to the Russian takeover of Finland. Meanwhile, Britain, concerned about the Franco-Russian rapprochement, pressured Sweden to contain Russian interests in the region. In 1807, to prevent the French from acquiring the Danish fleet, a British fleet bombarded Copenhagen on 2–5 September and forced the Danes to surrender their fleet. Tsar Alexander was infuriated by Britain's aggression against Denmark, his ally. In addition, this attack violated the Russo-Swedish agreement on closing Baltic ports to British ships. Concerned about the British presence in the Baltic Sea, Alexander requested King Gustavus IV to expel the British from Swedish ports. Receiving a Swedish rejection on 21 January 1808, Russia considered it a casus belli.

Russian preparations for war had already begun in December 1807. A corps of three infantry divisions was deployed near the Russo-Finnish frontiers. General Fedor Buxhöwden assumed overall command, while General Peter Bagration led the 21st Infantry Division, General Nikolay Tuchkov commanded the 5th Division, and Count Nikolay Kamenski led the 17th Division. The Russian divisions were understrength and exhausted by the previous campaign in Poland during the War of the Fourth Coalition. Their combined strength amounted to some 24,000 men. The initial Russian strategy called for the occupation of as much territory as possible before opening negotiations. The 1st Column under Tuchkov was to march from Neschlodt and Sulkava toward Rantasalmi to prevent the Swedish forces deployed around Outokumpu from supporting their comrades at Tavastheus (Hämeenlinna). Bagration was ordered to Keltis (Kouyola), moving in the general direction of Tavastheus. The 3rd Column under Kamenski was to advance from Fredrikshamn (now Hamina) along the coast toward Helsingfors (Helsinki) to occupy Sveaborg.

The Swedes were able to mobilize some 50,000 men, but of these only some 19,000 men (14,984 regular troops and 4,000 militia [*vargering*]) were under the command of General Carl Nathanael Klercker in Finland. A strong garrison of some 7,000 men protected the fortress of Sveaborg, known as the Gibraltar of the North, on the coast of the Gulf of Finland. Despite all the intelligence on Russian troop movements they received, the Swedish government failed to make any preparations to repel an attack.

On 21 February 1808, the Russian army invaded Finland in three columns. The troops spread proclamations urging the local population not to oppose the occupation and promising to observe order and make payment for requisitions. Russian forces advanced quickly, capturing Kuopio, Tavastheus, Tammerfors, and Åbo, as well as the shoreline between Åbo and Vaasa in March. In addition, the Russian advance guard seized the Åland Islands and the Island of Gotland. As Swedish forces withdraw northward, the Russians also took possession of Jacobstad, Gamlakarleby, and Brahestad.

However, the strategic situation soon changed. The Swedes concentrated their forces in the north, where they were well supplied and reinforced from the mainland. Russian columns, on the other hand, were extended along lengthy lines of communication and supply. Considerable Russian forces were tied up at Sveaborg, and the Finnish population displayed increasing discontent with the Russian presence in the region. In early April, Karl Johan Adlerkreutz, a young and energetic Swedish commander, was appointed second in command to Marshal Klingspor and attacked the dispersed Russian forces, defeating them at Gamlakarleby, Brahestad, Siikajoki, and Revolax.

These successful engagements improved Swedish morale and increased anti-Russian sentiments among the local population. In late April, the Swedes launched an offensive: Colonel Sandels with 3,000 men marched into the Savolax region, where he captured an entire Russian detachment at Pulkkila on 2 May and then seized Kuopio. In the south, the Swedes recaptured both Gotland and the Åland Islands after the Russian navy failed to support its land forces, partly because of animosity between Buxhöwden and the Minister of the Navy, Admiral Pavel Chichagov. On 6 May, however, the Russians captured Sveaborg.

By late spring 1808 the Russian army was organized into three army corps. General Nikolay Rayevsky commanded the first corps in the north covering the approaches to Vaasa. General Mikhail Barclay de Tolly's corps was to advance into the Savolax region and occupy Kuopio. Bagration commanded the troops on the shores of the Gulf of Bothnia protecting the coastline between Björneborg and Åbo. As the Russians launched another offensive in June, Barclay de Tolly occupied Kuopio on 19 June and engaged the Swedish forces around Toivola, suffering from constant attacks by Finnish guerrillas. In the northwest, Rayevsky found himself isolated from Russian reinforcements. As the Swedes counterattacked, Rayevsky resolutely defended Nykarleby and Vaasa before suffering defeat at Lappo (Lapua) in central Österbotten on 14 July.

The same month, Kamenski turned the tide of success. Taking over Rayevsky's corps, he defeated the Swedish army under Lieutenant Colonel Otto von Fieandt at Karstula on 21 August and then achieved a series of victories at Lappfjärd (29 August), Ruona and Salmi (1–2 September), and Oravais on 14 September. The Swedes were in full retreat, pursued by Kamenski. Infuriated by these reverses, Gustavus IV personally led a landing force on the southeast shore of the Gulf of Bothnia to divert Russian forces in the north. However, Bagration successfully repulsed incursions between 15 and 27 September.

An armistice was concluded on 29 September 1808. However, as he traveled to meet Napoleon at Erfurt, Alexander disapproved the cease-fire and ordered a new offensive. In October, the Russian army advanced northward to Uleåborg and, by late December, all of Finland was finally under Russian control. To bring a quick conclusion to the war, Alexander appointed General Bogdan von Knorring to command Russian forces in Finland. The Russians considered a three-pronged offensive into Sweden: Bagration was to cross the frozen gulf to the Åland Islands and then advance directly to the Swedish capital, Stockholm; simultaneously, Barclay de Tolly was to proceed with his corps across the gulf from Vaasa to Umeå, while another Russian corps marched along the gulf shore to Torneå. Bagration advanced his corps of some 17,000 men to the Åland Islands in early March 1809. The Swedes had some 10,000 men (6,000 regulars and 4,000 militia) under an energetic commander, General Georg Carl von Döbeln, who resolutely defended the islands before abandoning them on 18 March. The Russian advance guard under Jacob Kulnev made a daring raid on the Swedish coastline, capturing the town of Grisslehamn, near Stockholm.

Simultaneously, dramatic events occurred at the royal court in Stockholm. Gustavus was unpopular even before the war started, and the military defeats were largely blamed on his ineffective command. With Russian forces crossing the Gulf of Bothnia, the agitation among the soldiers exploded, and Swedish officers organized a coup d'état on 13 March 1809, establishing a regency under Duke Charles of Sudermania (Charles XIII, 1809–1818).

Meanwhile, Barclay de Tolly and Pavel Shuvalov marched toward Umeå. In late March, Barclay de Tolly undertook a hazardous march across the frozen Östra Kvarken and captured Umeå. In the north, Shuvalov marched with his corps along the gulf coast from Uleåborg and occupied Torneå, forcing the surrender of a Swedish detachment of 7,000 men at Kalix.

With two Russian corps converging at Umeå and Bagration's troops already in the vicinity of Stockholm, the Swedes began diplomatic negotiations to halt the invasion. However, as negotiations dragged on, Alexander appointed Barclay de Tolly as commander in chief and ordered another invasion of Sweden. The Russians resumed hostilities in early May, advancing from Torneå toward Luleå and Skellefteå. On 2 May, General Ilya Alekseyev's advance guard undertook a daring crossing of the Gulf of Bothnia at Skellefteå, where his detachment marched for twenty-six miles up to their knees in the melting ice to surprise the Swedish garrison and capture the town. On 1 June the Russians captured Umeå, defeating Swedish detachments at Savar and Ratan. Diplomatic negotiations began on 15 August 1809 and resulted in the Treaty of Fredrikshamn (now Hamina) on 17 September. Sweden acknowledged the loss of all of Finland as well as the Åland Islands, and Russia secured its position on the Baltic Sea.

Alexander Mikaberidze

See also Alexander I, Tsar; Bagration, Peter Ivanovich, Prince; Barclay de Tolly, Mikhail Andreas; Buxhöwden, Fedor Fedorovich, Count; Chichagov, Pavel Vasilievich; Copenhagen, Attack on; Denmark; Erfurt, Congress of; Finland; Fourth Coalition, War of the; Gustavus IV, King; Kamenski, Nikolay Mikhailovich, Count; Kulnev, Jacob Petrovich; Rayevski, Nikolay Nikolayevich, Count; Sweden; Tilsit, Treaties of; Tuchkov, Nikolay Alekseyevich

References and further reading
Borodkin, Mikhail. 1909. *Istoriia Finliandii: Vremia Imperatora Aleksandra I* [History of Finland: The Reign of Emperor Alexander I]. St. Petersburg: Gosudarstvennaia.

Danielson, Johann Richard. 1896. *Suomen sota ja Suomen sotilaat vuosina 1808–1809*. Helsinki: Weilin ja Göös.

Hornborg, Erik. 1955. *När Riket Sprängdes: Fälttågen I Finland och Västerbotten, 1808–1809*. Stockholm: Norstedt.

Sukhtelen, Paul. 1854. *Narrative of the Conquest of Finland by the Russians in the Years 1808–9: From an Unpublished Work by a Russian Officer of Rank*. Ed. Gen. Monteith. London: Booth.

Sweden Armen, Generalstaben. 1890–1922. *Sveriges krig åren 1808 och 1809*. 9 vols. Stockholm: Kongl. boktryckeriet P.A. Norstedt.

———. 1906. *Krigshistoriska avdelningen. Shveidskaia voina 1808–1809 g.g. sostavlena voenno-istoricheskim otdelom Shvedskogo Generalnogo Shtaba* [The Swedish Campaign of 1808–1809, Compiled by the Military History Section of the Swedish General Staff]. 2 vols. St. Petersburg: Izd. Glavnago upravleniia General'nago shtaba.

Russo-Turkish War (1806–1812)

The conflict between Russia and Turkey originated in the late sixteenth century, when the rising Russian state clashed with the Ottoman Empire over the sphere of influence in the Danube valley, the Caucasus, and the Black Sea. Over the next two centuries, they fought six wars, and under Tsarina Catherine the Great, the Russian army achieved considerable successes, annexing the Crimea and a small strip between the Bug and Dniester rivers. In the Caucasus, Russia expanded its influence to the Georgian principalities as well. However, the major goals of establishing Russian influence in the Balkans and the Straits of the Bosporus and the Dardanelles (also known as the Black Sea Straits) were not achieved. In 1796 Tsar Paul changed his foreign policy and joined his forces with the Turks against France. After his accession to the throne in 1801, Alexander gradually reversed his father's policy.

Russo-Turkish relations soon became strained, particularly after Napoleon approached Sultan Selim III with a proposal of alliance. The possibility of French domination of the Balkans and the Straits concerned Alexander. In addition, Russia sympathized with the Slavic peoples under Turkish domination. When the Serbs began an uprising in 1803, they turned to Russia for protection and received moral and financial support over the next three years. When the sultan expressed his readiness to renew the alliance of 1799, Alexander proposed to expand it to satisfy Russian interests in the region.

Although a new treaty was signed on 23 September 1805, Selim carefully watched the struggle between France and the Third Coalition. After the defeat of the Allied army at Austerlitz in 1805, Selim decided to join the winning side, hoping to recover lost territories from Russia. He acknowledged Napoleon's imperial title and began negotiations for an alliance with France. Furthermore, he declared his intention to close the Black Sea Straits to Russian vessels and replaced the current *hospodars* (princes) of Moldavia and Wallachia with more pro-French princes. He thus violated one of the articles of the Treaty of Jassy of 1792, which had concluded the previous Russo-Turkish war, that required Russia's consent to dismiss or appoint the hospodars.

As diplomatic relations ended in stalemate, Russia and the Ottoman Empire began concentrating their troops on their borders. In October 1806 Alexander ordered the invasion and occupation of Bessarabia, Moldavia, and Wallachia (also known as the Danubian Principalities). Over the next three months, a Russian army of some 40,000 men under General Ivan Michelson quickly advanced through the Principalities and drove Turkish forces toward the Danube River. As his army secured control of the Principalities, Alexander reinstated Constantine Ipsilanti as hospodar of Wallachia, announcing that Russian troops had come to protect the local Slav population against the Turks. The Russians also provided substantial financial and military support to the Serbian insurgents. Russian troops laid siege to the fortress of Ismail, while General Mikhail Miloradovich advanced to Bucharest, defeating Turkish detachments at Turbat and Giurgiu in late March.

The Turks meanwhile mobilized their forces and counterattacked. Grand Vizier Ibrahim Hilmi Pasha personally led the Turkish army across the Danube in May 1807. In the same month, however, the Janissaries revolted in Constantinople to overthrow Selim, and this development paralyzed the Turkish army. On 13 June 1807 Miloradovich easily defeated the Turkish advance guard under Ali Pasha at Obilesti, forcing the main Turkish army to retreat beyond the river Danube.

On the Serbian front, joint Russo-Serbian forces defeated the Turks at Malanica and forced them to withdraw to Negotin. A formal agreement between the Russians and the Serbs was signed in July 1807, and Alexander officially recognized the Serbian state. On the naval side, Vice Admiral Dmitry Senyavin, whose squadron operated in the Ionian Islands in 1805–1806, defeated the Turkish fleet in a series of naval engagements at Tenedos, in the Dardanelles, and at Mount Athos in the Aegean Sea to establish Russian dominance over the eastern Mediterranean. In Transcaucasia, the Russians also achieved a series of successes, securing the southern regions of Georgia.

Meanwhile, the Russians suffered a major setback at the hands of Napoleon at the Battle of Friedland on 14 June 1807. The two emperors soon signed a peace treaty at Tilsit, which called for a halt to military operations in the Danube valley while Napoleon offered to act as a mediator. Napoleon's agreement with Russia only exasperated the Turks, who felt betrayed by the French and eventually refused to support French plans against Russia. The Russian commander in chief General Ivan Meyendorff, without Tsar Alexander's knowledge, signed an armistice between Russia and Turkey on 4 September at Slobozia. The treaty called for Russian withdrawal from the principalities of Moldavia and Wallachia within a month, while the Turks agreed to remain south of the Danube. Enraged by his general's unauthorized diplomatic negotiations, Alexander appointed as the new commander in chief Field Marshal

Alexander Prozorovsky, with instructions to open an offensive immediately.

By the spring of 1809 Russian forces in the Danubian Principalities had been increased to 80,000 men, spread all over the region. Prozorovsky concentrated his efforts on capturing the fortresses of Giurgiu and Braila; however, both assaults were badly organized and executed. At Braila alone, the Russians lost 2,229 killed and 2,550 wounded. After these failures, Prozorovsky became depressed and refused to take any action for over two months. He then withdrew his forces to the left bank of the Danube and concentrated his resources on capturing the fortresses of Isaccea, Tulcea, and Babadag. The Turks exploited Russian inactivity and quickly launched a brutal reprisal against the Serbs.

In July Tsar Alexander, eager to bring a quick conclusion to the war, dispatched Prince Peter Bagration to assume command of the Army of Moldavia. Bagration, with an army of some 25,000 men, immediately launched an offensive across the Danube, capturing the fortresses of Macin, Constanta, and Girsov, and reaching Cavarna and Bazardjik. On 16 September, he defeated the Turkish army at Rassevat, and on 22 September, he besieged Silistra, one of the key fortresses in the Danube valley. Russian victories forced the Grand Vizier Yussuf to halt his invasion of Serbia and Wallachia and direct his army of 50,000 men to Silistra. Bagration stopped the vizier's advance to Silistra, fighting to a draw a superior Turkish army at Tataritsa on 22 October. However, shortages of ammunition and supplies forced him to lift the siege of Silistra and return to the left bank of the Danube. Nevertheless, in late 1809 he succeeded in taking the fortresses of Ismail and Braila. In March 1810 Bagration resigned his command after a disagreement with Alexander on overall Russian strategy in the region.

On 16 February 1810 Alexander appointed General Nikolay Kamenski as commander in chief of the Army of Moldavia. In the opening of the campaign against the Turks, Kamenski moved his army across the Danube, capturing the fortresses of Silistra, Razgrad, and Bazardjik. He then encircled the main Turkish army of 40,000 men under the grand vizier at Shumla and besieged it after unsuccessful initial assaults. Simultaneously, Kamenski made a disastrous assault on Ruse on 3 August, losing almost 9,000 men. To rescue the grand vizier's army in Shumla, the Turks dispatched reinforcements of approximately 50,000 troops, but Kamenski intercepted and routed them at Batin on 7–8 September 1810. Between September 1810 and February 1811 he captured the fortresses of Ruse, Turnu, Plevna, Lovech, and Selvi. Yet, despite these resounding victories, Kamenski had to withdraw his army to winter quarters on the left bank of the Danube. He became seriously ill in March 1811 and left the army to recuperate in Odessa.

With the threat of a French invasion looming over Russia, Alexander was concerned about his southern frontiers. In March 1811 he appointed General Mikhail Kutuzov to bring a victorious conclusion to the war as quickly as possible. Kutuzov withdrew garrisons from most of the fortresses and concentrated his army near Ruse on the right bank of the Danube. In June 1811 the Turkish army under Ahmed Pasha launched an offensive against the Russians, but was defeated near Ruse on 4 July. However, concerned about a flanking maneuver by Ismail Bey from Vidin, Kutuzov abandoned Ruse and withdrew his army to the left bank of the river.

In July and August, Turkish forces made several unsuccessful attempts at crossing the Danube. Kutuzov then devised an operation to surround and destroy the entire Turkish army. On 10 September 1811 he allowed the Turkish army under Ahmed Pasha to cross the Danube at Slobodzea, near Ruse. He then dispatched a corps of some 11,000 men under General Yevgeny Markov, who secretly crossed the river downstream and captured the Turkish camp and fortress of Ruse on the right bank. The main Turkish army under Ahmed Pasha was thus surrounded on the riverbank and gradually starved into submission, surrendering on 5 December.

Although diplomatic negotiations had begun in October, the Turks prolonged the process, hoping Napoleon's invasion of Russia would change the political situation. However, thanks to Kutuzov's diplomatic skills, the Turks finally signed a peace treaty at Bucharest on 28 May 1812, relinquishing their claims to Bessarabia and Georgia. The conclusion of the Russo-Turkish War secured the southern frontiers of Russia and allowed Alexander to move the Army of the Danube from the Principalities into the main theater of operations against Napoleon.

Alexander Mikaberidze

See also Alexander I, Tsar; Austerlitz, Battle of; Bagration, Peter Ivanovich, Prince; Catherine II "the Great," Tsarina; Dardanelles, Expedition to the; Friedland, Battle of; Ionian Islands; Janissaries; Kamenski, Nikolay Mikhailovich, Count; Kutuzov, Mikhail Golenischev-, Prince; Miloradovich, Mikhail Andreyevitch, Count; Ottoman Empire; Paul I, Tsar; Senyavin, Dmitry Nikolayevich; Third Coalition, War of the; Tilsit, Treaties of
References and further reading
Mikhailovsky-Danilevsky, Alexander. 2002. *Russo-Turkish War of 1806–1812*. Ed. Alexander Mikaberidze. 2 vols. West Chester, OH: Nafziger Collection.
Petrov, A. 1885–1887. *Voina Rossii s Turtsiei, 1806–1812* [Russia's War against Turkey, 1806–1812]. 3 vols. St. Petersburg: Voennaia.
Shirokorad, A. 2000. *Russko-Turetskie voini, 1676–1918 gg* [Russo-Turkish Wars, 1676–1918]. Moscow: AST.

S

Saalfeld, Action at (10 October 1806)

The first major confrontation in the 1806 campaign between French and Prussian forces. Marshal Jean Lannes, faced by a smaller force under the command of Prince Louis Ferdinand of Hohenzollern, was given the task of taking Saalfeld. A combination of French tactical initiative and poor Prussian deployment led to the defeat of the Prussian force and to the death of Prince Louis.

Early in the Prussian campaign, Prince Louis commanded the advance guard of Frederick Louis, Prince Hohenlohe's corps of the Prussian army and was given orders to hold Saalfeld. Lannes, conversely, had instructions to take Saalfeld, provided the enemy were discovered to be numerically inferior to his forces. Lannes duly sent out cavalry patrols to ascertain the strength of the enemy. Prince Louis had deployed his force in three lines, outside the town, but he had made little attempt to occupy the villages on his flanks. The ground was also broken up by a number of streams running in steep ravines down to the river Saale. The river itself was directly to the rear of the Prussian position. As Lannes advanced from the wooded hills to the south of Saalfeld, he was able to observe the entire enemy position. Initially he deployed in skirmish order the first of his troops to arrive on the battlefield, and they quickly advanced under the cover of the ravines. He also deployed a battalion composed entirely of the elite companies (grenadiers and *voltigeurs*) of his infantry to pin down the Prussians defending Saalfeld.

The French then seized the villages that flanked the Prussian line and began to issue an effective fire on the exposed lines of troops. This bombardment continued for about two hours. By now Lannes had received reinforcements and was determined to attack the Prussian right wing. Prince Louis, realizing that his line of communications was threatened, weakened his center in order to deploy troops onto a low ridge to the right of his main line, called the Sandberg. He then took the decision to launch an attack in the center against a screen of French skirmishers. The troops in the center were Saxons, and despite their bravery in attack they were repulsed by the skirmishers on their flanks and fresh French troops to their front. Having blunted the enemy advance, Lannes began an artillery bombardment before launching his own assault. French troops attacked the Sandberg, which allowed a combined infantry and cavalry assault to be delivered against the Prussian center. The four Saxon battalions there quickly broke.

In an attempt to stabilize the situation, Prince Louis led five squadrons of his own cavalry forward, in the course of which he was killed in single combat by a French sergeant of hussars. The Prussian force was now broken, and in the cavalry pursuit that followed nearly thirty guns were taken, together with 1,500 prisoners. The Prussian survivors were forced to rally 4 miles to the north of Saalfeld. The French victory began to dispel the myth of Prussian invincibility and provided a vital morale boost for the French army prior to the decisive battles to be fought at Jena and Auerstädt only days later.

Ralph Baker

See also Auerstädt, Battle of; Fourth Coalition, War of the; Jena, Battle of; Jena-Auerstädt Campaign; Lannes, Jean
References and further reading
Petre, F. Loraine. 1993. *Napoleon's Conquest of Prussia, 1806.* London: Greenhill.

Sacile, Battle of (16 April 1809)

This battle was the first large-scale engagement between the French and Austrians during the 1809 campaign. Prince Eugène de Beauharnais attacked Archduke John near the town of Sacile after the Austrians had launched a rapid invasion of northern Italy. The French were outnumbered, and with the Austrians threatening their rear, Eugène chose to withdraw over the river Piave. Eugène lost around 6,000 troops, with the Austrians suffering considerably fewer losses.

At the start of the War of the Fifth Coalition, Eugène, commanding the Army of Italy, had been surprised by the rapid advance of the forces of Archduke John. Eugène decided to concentrate his forces at Sacile. Early on 15 April John advanced on the French positions, and his cavalry was able to capture a number of French infantry. On the following day, Eugène planned to attack the Austrians. Although he was outnumbered, he believed that he would receive reinforcements during the day and hoped that a resolute attack on the Austrian line would force them back.

The assault began at dawn against the Austrian left. The initial attack against the town of Porcia failed. The Austrian defenders were then attacked in the flank by the newly arrived troops of General Gabriel Barbou's division. However, Archduke John sent reinforcements to the sector of the field around Porcia, and it was not until noon that the French could claim to have Porcia completely under their control. The terrain around Porcia was quite broken by watercourses and crops, and this slowed up the French assault. Up until this point, Archduke John had been convinced that the attack on Porcia was not the main French objective, but that it was just intended to make him commit his reserves. It was now clear, however, that the Austrians had a numerical advantage and that for the moment no more attacks threatened.

As a result, in the middle of the afternoon Archduke John ordered his forces to launch an offensive to retake Porcia. At the same time he sent a flanking attack to threaten the rear of Eugène's position. This attack was carried out with great spirit, and despite the fact that Eugène sent further reinforcements to the flank, the French could not hold onto Porcia. Eugène realized that he would not receive his expected reinforcements and ordered a general withdrawal. By ordering his cavalry forward to cover this movement and taking advantage of the Austrians' disorganization from the day's fighting, the main French army was able to withdraw unmolested, though around Porcia they had lost a number of prisoners. Eugène marched his army back to Sacile in divisional squares. The French had lost around 6,000 men, over half of whom had been captured, and fifteen guns. The Austrians had lost around 4,000 men and continued to pursue Eugène until he reached the river Adige.

Ralph Baker

See also Beauharnais, Eugène Rose de; Fifth Coalition, War of the; John, Archduke
References and further reading
Epstein, Robert. 1984. *Prince Eugene at War, 1809.* Arlington, TX: Empire Games.
Schneid, Frederick C. 2002. *Napoleon's Italian Campaigns, 1805–1815.* Westport, CT: Greewood.

Sahagún de Campos, Action at (21 December 1808)

This engagement took place between British cavalry under Lord Henry Paget and French cavalry who were billeted in the Spanish village of Sahagún. The action saw the destruction of much of the French cavalry, with almost no British loss.

Late in 1808, Lieutenant General Sir John Moore was attempting to advance on Burgos. He had received reports that enemy troops under the command of Marshal Nicolas Soult were in dispersed positions. Moore hoped to surprise them with a rapid advance. It had been reported that two regiments of French cavalry were bivouacked at Sahagún under the command of General César Alexandre Debelle. This force totaled around 500 troops. Paget, commanding the 15th and 10th Hussars, decided to attack this force. He planned to make a night march from his position 12 miles from Sahagún and to fall upon the enemy at dawn. The 10th Hussars under Brigadier General Sir John Slade with two artillery pieces were to attack the village from the west. Paget and the 15th Hussars would place themselves to the east and south of the village in order prevent the French from retreating. The plan was ambitious, and given the poor weather conditions its implementation depended on good leadership and the discipline of the British. The march was conducted in snowstorms, and at times the troopers had to dismount to continue.

Paget arrived at Sahagún just as dawn was breaking, but there was no sign of Slade. At this point the British were seen by French sentries, who raised the alarm. Paget was forced to move his regiment further to the east and discovered that Debelle's force was trying to evacuate the village. Debelle was unsure of whether he was facing Spanish or British cavalry and was slow in responding to Paget's attack. The charge of the British cavalry broke through the first line of the French, which was composed of chasseurs. The second line consisted of dragoons, who withstood the initial charge, and the action now broke down into a series of small combats. Having gained the initial advantage, however, Paget's hussars slowly pushed the French away from Sahagún to the east.

The French retreat now began to dissolve into a rout, and the hussars took many prisoners. In total thirteen officers and 150 men were captured. During the fighting over 120 Frenchmen became casualties, and the chasseurs were effectively destroyed as a unit. British losses were very slight, amounting to two killed and twenty wounded. Slade arrived with his force at the end of the fighting and was criticized for his tardiness. If he had been present earlier, even fewer of the enemy would have escaped. Moore arrived at Sahagún toward the end of the day. When news came two days later of a massing of French troops north of Madrid, Moore began his disastrous retreat toward Corunna, on the northwest coast of Spain.

Ralph Baker

See also Corunna, Retreat to; Moore, Sir John; Peninsular War; Soult, Nicolas Jean de Dieu; Uxbridge, Henry William Paget, Second Earl of
References and further reading
Fletcher, Ian. 1999. *Galloping at Everything. The British Cavalry in the Peninsular War and at Waterloo.* Staplehurst, UK: Spellmount.

Salamanca, Battle of (22 July 1812)

The year of 1812 had begun well for the Earl of Wellington's army, and Sir Rowland Hill's attack on the forts at Almaraz set the seal on a remarkably successful five-month period. British successes were to continue, for in July Wellington achieved one of his and the British army's greatest victories.

The spectacular gains achieved by Wellington during the first half of the year became all the more significant when news began to filter through to him of the steady withdrawal from Spain of a large number of French troops, including the Imperial Guard, who were destined to take part in the fateful invasion of Russia that year. Hereafter, the already hard-pressed and harassed French armies would fight with an increased disadvantage, one which the Spanish guerrillas in particular were quick to seize upon.

The French armies in Spain were placed under the command of Napoleon's brother, Joseph, and it was Marshal Auguste de Marmont's Army of Portugal, some 52,000 strong, that posed the more immediate problem for Wellington, whose own troops numbered just over 60,000. During the first days of June, Wellington began to concentrate his army for a thrust into central Spain against Marmont, a move that would both threaten the main French communications and almost certainly bring French reinforcements rushing to Marmont's assistance. Wellington hoped to prevent this latter eventuality by planning a series of concerted moves and concentrations elsewhere in Spain to keep the French forces occupied. Having satisfied himself that all these arrangements had been made, Wellington, on 13 June, began his advance from Ciudad Rodrigo with 48,000 men and fifty-four guns.

Four days later the Allied army entered Salamanca unopposed, although Marmont had left garrisons in three small forts in the western suburbs of the town. These were besieged and fell on 27 June. For the next three weeks, the two armies were in close proximity to each other, and on

18 July they marched parallel with one other on opposite sides of the river Guarena, the bands of the two armies playing as they marched. This close marching continued for the next two days, and by the night of the twenty-first, both armies had crossed the river Tormes and camped within a few hundred yards of each other.

That night a violent storm broke overhead, and when the moon disappeared behind the inky black clouds, it was left to the silver streaks of lightning to illuminate the surrounding countryside. Several troopers of the 5th Dragoon Guards were killed by lightning, while dozens of horses bolted, charging over their riders as they lay on the ground. A torrential downpour, from which there was little shelter, added to the confusion. These kinds of weather conditions were to be repeated at Sorauren and, more famously, at Waterloo, by which time Wellington's men had come to look upon such storms before battle as an omen of victory.

On the morning of 22 July, both armies resumed their march south, still parallel with each other, the rays of the sun warming the troops on both sides after their soaking the night before. The two armies marched across flat and rolling countryside, with no remarkable features other than two distinctively shaped hills, the first, a rounded ridge to the northeast of the village of Los Arapiles called the Lesser Arapil, and the second, called the Greater Arapil, a box-shaped hill some 100 feet high about half a mile to the south of the Lesser Arapil. These two hills lay in the middle of an undulating plain, about 9 miles long, stretching from the small village of Calvarasa de Arriba in the east, to Miranda de Azan in the west. The village of Los Arapiles lay just to the left of center of the plain.

Marmont's intention was to sever the road leading to Ciudad Rodrigo, along which Wellington had begun to send his baggage and supplies. To accomplish this, Marmont needed to outstrip his opponents and turn west across the head of the leading British columns. At around eight o'clock on the morning of the twenty-second, Marmont's troops became involved in a race with a Portuguese brigade to occupy the Greater Arapil. Some brief but heavy fighting occurred here, but the Portuguese were driven back, and Marmont was left in possession of the Greater Arapil, while Wellington occupied the Lesser Arapil.

Little fighting occurred the rest of the morning as both armies continued their march southwest. Marmont, meanwhile, watched from his lofty position on the Greater Arapil and spotted a cloud of dust rising from behind the Lesser Arapil in the direction of Ciudad Rodrigo, which seemed to confirm his belief that Wellington was retreating. The column was, in fact, Major General Sir Edward Pakenham's 3rd Division, which Wellington had brought forward to Aldea Tejada, either to protect his right flank or to act as an independent force. The French columns were

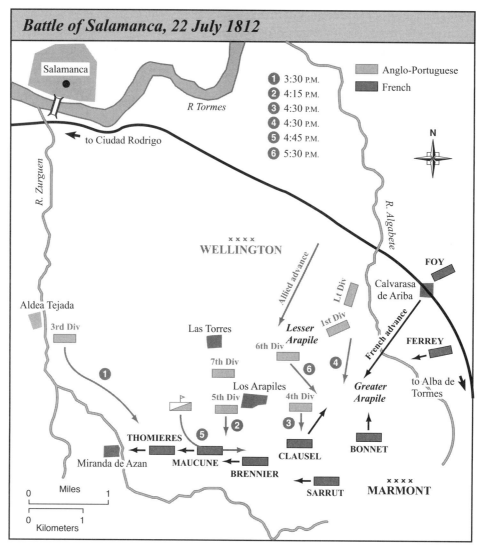

Battle of Salamanca, 22 July 1812

- ① 3:30 P.M.
- ② 4:15 P.M.
- ③ 4:30 P.M.
- ④ 4:30 P.M.
- ⑤ 4:45 P.M.
- ⑥ 5:30 P.M.

Anglo-Portuguese
French

Adapted from Fremont-Barnes 2002A, 62.

moving faster than Wellington's own men, who had halted around the village of Los Arapiles, and by early afternoon the divisions of generals Jean Guillaume Thomières, Antoine Lewis Maucune, and Bertrand, baron Clausel were well on their way heading west to the Rodrigo road and were strung out in a long line some 4 miles long.

It soon became apparent that the leading French division, that of Thomières, was outstripping Maucune's division, which was following behind, and a considerable gap opened up between them, something that did not go unnoticed by Wellington, who galloped off to Aldea Tejada to order Pakenham to attack immediately.

It was about 3:30 P.M., and the long, dusty columns of French troops were hurrying across the Ciudad Rodrigo road to cut off Wellington's escape route. Thomières himself must have felt fairly safe and secure, and he was certainly unaware of the storm that was about to break around him. That storm arrived in the shape of Paken-

ham's 3rd Division, which suddenly appeared on Thomières's right flank, supported by 1,100 cavalry who scattered the leading French companies. The shock of seeing Pakenham's battalions just a few hundred yards away must have been immense. One moment the French were grasping the initiative, the next they had it wrenched violently from them by nearly 6,000 British and Portuguese infantry who smashed into them, unleashing volley after volley into their packed and panicking ranks.

Thomières's leading column was ripped apart by the ferocity of the attack, which saw hundreds killed and wounded in minutes. Thomières himself was killed, and the casualty figures for the two leading battalions are comparable with those sustained by Lieutenant Colonel John Colborne's brigade at Albuera the previous year; the leading regiment lost 1,031 of its 1,449 men, while the second regiment lost 868 out of 1,123 men. With Thomières gone and the leading regiments destroyed, the rest of Thomières's division disintegrated and fled in panic to the southeast.

Lieutenant General Sir James Leith's 5th Division, supported by Brigadier General Thomas Bradford's Portuguese, had been launched into the attack about 40 minutes after Pakenham. Advancing directly south from Los Arapiles, the 8,500 Allied troops struck at Maucune's division, which had been following Thomières at a distance. The French, numbering about 5,000 men, were outnumbered, but they expected help shortly from General Antoine Brennier's division, which was hurrying to their support. Maucune had seen the damage that the Allied cavalry had done to Thomières's division and so formed his nine battalions into squares. Unfortunately, on this occasion it was the wrong formation, and when Lieutenant Colonel Charles Greville's and Major General William Pringle's brigades came up, after having advanced through a heavy French artillery barrage, they simply leveled their muskets and unloaded them into the dense French ranks, sweeping away the French squares with three devastating volleys.

The French troops who survived this onslaught broke and fled in the same direction as the survivors of Thomières's division. It was now, more than ever, that they needed to be in square formation, for as they looked back they saw, to their horror, Major General John Le Marchant's brigade of heavy dragoons thundering after them. The fugitives tried to defend themselves as best they could, but the dragoons swept over them with ease, chopping and hacking all around them. Five French battalions were left totally destroyed in the wake of Le Marchant's men, who now saw before them, running to aid Maucune's men, the 4,300 men of Brennier's division.

Brennier's men were exhausted by their hurried, mile-long dash to aid Maucune, and even though they had time to form square, they were not steady enough to resist the power of the dragoons. A ragged volley brought a few horses and riders crashing to the ground, horses that smashed into the squares, causing great confusion and panic. Other dragoons came charging in, and in a few minutes Brennier's division, too, was streaming away toward the woods to the southeast.

Le Marchant's dragoons soon became drunk with success and got completely out of control. Even Le Marchant could not hold them in check. The French ran around in all directions as the dragoons struck wildly in every direction. Unlike other cavalry misadventures during the Peninsular War, there was no effective enemy cavalry force to take advantage of the disorder, and Le Marchant's men went about their business unopposed. Le Marchant himself did manage to keep one squadron in check, however, which engaged some French infantry close to the woods to the southeast of the battlefield. Here Le Marchant met his

death when he was hit by a single musket ball that broke his spine. It was a bitter blow to Wellington, who had seen one of the few capable cavalry commanders taken from him. Le Marchant died knowing his men had done their job, and when they returned, breathless and excited, to their own lines, they could look back over a trail of devastation that had contributed to the destruction of no less than three whole French divisions—all in just 40 minutes.

Farther to the east of Los Arapiles, Wellington's men were not so successful, for when Lieutenant General Lowry Cole's 4th Division advanced to the east of the Greater Arapil, it was flung back in bloody disorder by two fresh French divisions, but not before having engaged a numerically superior enemy in a furious firefight. On the Greater Arapil itself, Brigadier General Denis Pack's Portuguese brigade met with a similar fate. There the French successes combined to provide Clausel—now in command following serious wounds to first Marmont and then General François Antoine Bonnet, who was killed—with the prospect of being able to stem the tide of the battle and possibly even retrieve the situation for the French.

Clausel's counterattack was intelligently planned and executed with flawless precision by 12,000 men of the French 2nd and 8th Divisions who strode doggedly across the plain between the two Arapiles while General Jacques Thomas Sarrut's division held Pakenham's victorious 3rd Division in check on their left flank.

The bold French maneuver was thwarted, however, for Wellington had correctly anticipated the move. He had deployed the two British brigades of Major General Henry Clinton's 6th Division in the by-now standard two-deep line, with Rezende's Portuguese in line behind them. On Clinton's right were Spry's Portuguese, while Anson's brigade, from Cole's 4th Division, was brought up alongside on Clinton's left.

Clausel's men advanced under heavy fire from the Allied artillery on and behind the Lesser Arapil, which mowed down whole files of men. When their columns had got halfway across the plain between the two hills, they came face to face with Clinton's lines, which opened up a rolling volley that engulfed the heads of the columns, sending them staggering backward. For a few brief minutes, the French returned the fire, but their formation was against them. Although numerically superior to Clinton's men, their columns could not match the firepower of the British lines, and they were driven back in disorder.

All but three of Marmont's eight infantry divisions had been swept away, and Wellington's men pressed forward on all sides to complete their victory. The sun had begun to set when Wellington ordered Clinton forward in pursuit of the fleeing French fugitives, but when they had passed the Greater Arapil, Clinton's men came up against

The Battle of Salamanca, where Wellington, finally able to assume the offensive, inflicted a crushing blow against the principal French army in Spain. (Mansell/Time & Life Pictures/Getty Images)

General Claude François Ferey's division, some 5,500 men who had yet to see any serious action during the day. Ferey formed his seven battalions into a three-deep line and, for a change, it was the turn of the red-jacketed British to experience the firepower of such a formation. The French checked the British advance and even forced them back. In fact, Ferey was only forced to retreat when threatened on his flank. Unfortunately for him, Ferey was not among those who fled the battlefield, as he was cut in two by a round shot from an Allied gun.

The battle was as good as over, and thousands of defeated French troops streamed away to the woods to the southeast and to the bridge at Alba de Tormes. After several days of hard marching and due to the rigors of the battle itself, Wellington's men were too exhausted to effect a serious pursuit. However, since the bridge over the Tormes at Alba de Tormes was held by Spanish troops under Carlos de España, Wellington was quietly confident of being able to capture the whole. Unfortunately, de España had withdrawn his troops, much to the annoyance of an exasperated

Wellington, and the French were able to make good their escape, although hundreds of isolated and scattered fugitives were taken by Allied cavalry during the next few days.

The victory at Salamanca had cost Wellington 5,214 casualties, of which 3,176 were British. The exact French casualty figure is hard to determine, although it is fairly certain to have been around 14,000. Twenty guns were also taken. The Battle of Salamanca demolished the belief that Wellington was just an overcautious and defensive-minded commander, and when news of the victory spread throughout Europe, his reputation as one of the great commanders was assured.

On 12 August Wellington's army entered Madrid amid much rejoicing by the people, who could experience the feeling of freedom from French occupation for the first time since December 1808. The following month, Wellington headed northeast to lay siege to Burgos, but here the magic was to desert him, during an operation that he himself was to call the worst scrape he was ever in.

Ian Fletcher

See also Albuera, Battle of; Bonaparte, Joseph; Burgos, Siege of; Guerrilla Warfare; Hill, Sir Rowland; Imperial Guard (French); Marmont, Auguste Frédéric Louis Viesse de; Pakenham, Sir Edward; Peninsular War; Wellington, Arthur Wellesley, First Duke of

References and further reading
Esdaile, Charles J. 2003. *The Peninsular War: A New History.* London: Palgrave Macmillan.
Fletcher, Ian. 1997. *Salamanca 1812: Wellington Crushes Marmont.* Oxford: Osprey.
Gates, David. 2001. *The Spanish Ulcer: A History of the Peninsular War.* New York: Da Capo.
Glover, Michael. 1996. *Wellington's Peninsular Victories: The Battles of Busaco, Salamanca, Vitoria and the Nivelle.* London: Weidenfeld and Nicolson.
———. 2001. *The Peninsular War, 1807–1814: A Concise Military History.* London: Penguin.
Lawford, J. P., and Peter Young. 1972. *Wellington's Masterpiece: The Battle and Campaign of Salamanca.* London: Allen and Unwin.
Muir, Rory. 2001. *Salamanca 1812.* New Haven, CT: Yale University Press.
Napier, W. F. P. 1992. *A History of the War in the Peninsula.* 6 vols. London: Constable. (Orig. pub. 1828.)
Oman, Sir Charles. 2005. *A History of the Peninsular War.* 7 vols. London: Greenhill. (Orig. pub. 1902–1930.)
Paget, Julian. 1992. *Wellington's Peninsular War: Battles and Battlefields.* London: Leo Cooper.
Uffindell, Andrew. 2003. *The National Army Museum Book of Wellington's Armies: Britain's Triumphant Campaigns in the Peninsula and at Waterloo, 1808–1815.* London: Sedgwick and Jackson.
Weller, Jac. 1992. *Wellington in the Peninsula.* London: Greenhill.

Sambre, Battles of the (May–June 1794)

The Battles of the river Sambre were part of the main French campaign of 1794. They culminated in the victory of Fleurus, which removed the most direct threat to Paris, forced the Allies out of Belgium, and laid Holland open to conquest by the Revolutionary armies. The victories on the Sambre also vindicated the *levée en masse* (universal conscription) and the amalgamation of regular troops with those raised by the Revolutionary government.

The failure of French armies to force the Allied armies out of the country in 1793 caused the Convention to declare universal conscription on 23 August. The levée en masse was intended to make France a nation in arms. One result of universal conscription was that Revolutionary France created the largest army in European history. By January 1794 about 800,000 men had been called to the colors and were ready for battle. One problem caused by the massive influx of recruits was the tension between the new citizen-soldiers and the old regular army. Many times, the two groups failed to see themselves as part of the same

army. Defeats in 1793 had led to decreased cooperation and mutual blame between them. One solution was to brigade two battalions of volunteers with one of regulars to form a demi-brigade. Progress was slow during 1793. On 10 January 1794 the Convention decreed that amalgamation of volunteers and regulars would be the rule throughout the army. By April, about one-third of the units in the northern theater had been amalgamated. When that summer's campaign began, the French armies were much larger, better trained, and better armed than ever before.

The Committee of Public Safety had the task of deciding how to use this large body of men. Revolutionary doctrine called for a policy of attack wherever possible. The Committee viewed the Belgian theater as key, and a major offensive was planned. French forces along the river Sambre constituted the southern arm of this offensive. Beginning in late April, the Army of the Ardennes under General Louis Charbonnier and the right wing of the Army of the North under General Jacques Desjardins advanced together toward Austrian positions along the Sambre below Charleroi. The Austrian commander, Prince Wenzel Anton Graf Kaunitz, had approximately 30,000 men to the French 50,000.

On 12 May, the united French force captured the Austrian outpost at Thuin on the south bank, then crossed over the Sambre. Kaunitz retreated toward Charleroi and assumed defensive positions. A French frontal assault on 13 May collapsed in disorder, and the invaders were driven back across the Sambre by Austrian cavalry. Representatives of the Committee of Public Safety refused to accept defeat, however, and ordered Charbonnier and Desjardins to attack once more. Neither general was in overall command, and the arrangements were inept. On 20 May they forced a passage over the Sambre once again, but this time Austrian attempts to drive them back on 21 May were unsuccessful. When two divisions under General Jean-Baptiste Kléber were detached to outflank the Austrian positions, Kaunitz attacked again on 24 May. The French were driven back in disorder against the Sambre, and were only saved from disaster by Kléber. Learning of the attack, he returned to the field and fought a creditable rearguard action while the remainder of the army crossed the river.

Remarkably, the combined French force continued to return to fight. After losing 8,000 men in two unsuccessful assaults over the Sambre, Charbonnier and Desjardins wanted to rest their men and await reinforcements. Instead, they were ordered to try again. On 26 May, they surged across once more. After taking a single outpost, the French attack came to a halt. However, the Austrians were in the midst of redeploying. Their new commander, the Prince of Orange, ordered his left wing to fall back on Charleroi. On 29 May, the French pushed forward and overran the Austrian forward defenses, surrounding Charleroi, their next objective, the next day. A counterattack by Austrian troops on 3 June broke the siege of Charleroi and cost the French 2,000 more casualties.

General Jean-Baptiste Jourdan arrived the next day with a large part of the Army of the Moselle. Jourdan had been originally directed to march on Namur or Liège, but the indecisive fighting on the Sambre caused a change in plans. Jourdan brought 50,000 men with him, giving him a substantial advantage over the opposing Austrians. At the urging of Louis Antoine Léon de Saint-Just, the Committee of Public Safety agreed to unite Jourdan's, Charbonnier's, and Desjardins's troops into one army, with Jourdan as commander on 8 June. The new force became the Army of the Sambre and Meuse.

On 12 June Jourdan led his army across the Sambre to attack Charleroi. Four days later, a smaller Austrian army defeated him and hustled the French back across the river. On 18 June Jourdan tried again. This time he managed to besiege Charleroi while the Prince of Orange gathered reinforcements. The 2,800 men garrisoning Charleroi capitulated on 25 June after a heavy bombardment, this surrender releasing the besieging force for the upcoming battle and furnishing Jourdan with an important reserve.

On 26 June the French and Austrian armies fought the decisive Battle of Fleurus. Jourdan had about 76,000 troops, while the Prince of Orange had only 52,000. Jourdan arranged his men in a convex line to cover Charleroi. Orange believed the city was still holding out, and planned to drive the French back onto it, relieving the place once more. At first, the French left under Kléber was driven back nearly to Charleroi. Kléber managed to mount a furious counterattack that brought the Austrians to a halt. Elsewhere, the Austrians made slow progress, but by early afternoon the line had stabilized, thanks to the presence of the French reserves formerly besieging Charleroi. Around this time, Orange learned that Charleroi had surrendered. Without any further reason for continuing the battle, he broke off the fighting and withdrew.

Although it had been a near-run thing, Fleurus proved to be a decisive French victory. The French were firmly established on the northern bank of the Sambre. Under orders to keep his army concentrated, Orange withdrew to the east. Communications for the Allied forces in Belgium were threatened, forcing them to withdraw to the north. Jourdan quickly followed up his advantage and pushed further into Belgium, where in July and August he quickly occupied the key cities and fortresses. By September, the Army of the Sambre and Meuse had grown to over 160,000 men. The French advanced further north, invading Holland, most of which was conquered by the end of the year, leaving the coalition against France on the verge of collapse.

Tim J. Watts

See also Convention, The; First Coalition, War of the; Flanders, Campaigns in; Fleurus, Battle of; Jourdan, Jean-Baptiste; Kléber, Jean-Baptiste; Levée en Masse; Public Safety, Committee of
References and further reading
Blanning, T. C. W. 1996. *The French Revolutionary Wars, 1787–1802*. London: Arnold.
Phipps, Ramsay Weston. 1980. *The Armies of the First French Republic and the Rise of the Marshals of Napoleon I*. Vol. 2, *The Armées de la Moselle, du Rhin, de Sambre-et-Meuse, de Rhin-et-Moselle*. London: Greenwood. (Orig. pub. 1926–1939.)
Wetzler, Peter. 1985. *War and Subsistence: The Sambre and Meuse Army in 1794*. New York: Lang.

San Giuliano, Battle of (16 May 1799)

Sometimes called the First Battle of Marengo, the engagement at San Giuliano was fought on the plain east of Alessandria, in northern Italy, as French commander in chief General Jean Moreau ordered General Claude Victor to reconnoiter in force the area between the Bormida and Scrivia rivers. In the ensuing action, the French surprised and severely mauled the Austro-Russian advanced guard, before safely retreating back behind the walls of Alessandria.

After the liberation of Lombardy in April 1799, Field Marshal Alexander Suvorov's next goal was Piedmont. According to the plan developed by his chief of staff, *Generalmajor* Johann Marquis Chasteler de Courcelles, two Allied bodies (Prince Peter Bagration with 6,000 and *General der Kavallerie* Michael Freiherr von Melas with 14,000 men) were to cross the river Po at different points between two of its northern tributaries, the Adda and the Ticino. Once on the southern bank, they would move west along the main road from Piacenza, making for the fortresses of Tortona and Alessandria. Two other Austrian columns were to remain on the northern bank of the Po, one operating in Lomellina under *Generalmajor* Fürst Franz von Rosenberg-Orsini, the other, under *Feldmarschalleutnant* Joseph Freiherr von Vukassovich, cautiously pushing into northeastern Piedmont. Two smaller columns (Klenau and Ott) were detached on the Tuscan Apennines to protect the army's left flank against the pending threat of General Jacques Macdonald's Armée de Naples from central Italy. On 12 May, the Allies suffered an unexpected reverse at Bassignana, as Rosenberg's hazardous attempt at crossing the Po just east of Valenza was repulsed by Victor. By 15 May, however, Melas's main body arrived before Tortona, with Bagration's advance guard watching the Bormida, just east of Alessandria.

During the night of 15 and 16 May, Victor's infantry division, with some supporting cavalry (in total 7,500), crossed the Bormida over a flying bridge and advanced eastward. The Allied outposts in Marengo, Spinetta, and Cascina Grossa—some Austrian infantry and two Cossack regiments (*sotnia*) under Colonel Adrian Denisov—rapidly gave way before the determined 74th demi-brigade. Later in the morning, Victor's battalions ran into *Feldmarschalleutnant* Michael Freiherr von Frölich's Austrian division, temporarily led by *Generalmajor* Franz, Marquis de Lusignan. This general deployed his seven infantry battalions across the road to Tortona, some hundred meters west of the village of San Giuliano. Some squadrons of Austrian dragoons were also at hand to oppose the French momentum. Bagration soon arrived with his Russian forces, which he placed under the command of Lusignan. Victor, realizing that he was now facing far superior enemy forces and being satisfied with the results of his reconnaissance, retreated back to Alessandria in good order.

A month later, on 16 June, another engagement took place on the same battlefield, as General Emmanuel, marquis de Grouchy's division (4,500), spearheading Moreau's attempt at regaining the Po plain to relieve Alessandria and link with Macdonald, pushed *Feldmarschalleutnant* Heinrich Graf Bellegarde's Austrians from Spinetta and San Giuliano back across the Bormida. Just after this combat, however, Moreau received news of Macdonald's defeat at the Battle of the Trebbia and hastily retraced his steps back into the Ligurian Apennines.

Marco Gioannini

See also Bagration, Peter Ivanovich, Prince; Bellegarde, Heinrich Graf; Cossacks; Grouchy, Emmanuel, marquis de; Italian Campaigns (1799–1800); Macdonald, Jacques Etienne Joseph Alexandre; Marengo, Battle of; Melas, Michael Friedrich Benedikt Freiherr von; Moreau, Jean Victor; Sardinia; Second Coalition, War of the; Suvorov, Alexander Vasilievich; Trebbia, Battle of the; Victor, Claude Perrin

References and further reading
Denisov, Adrian. 2000. *Zapiski donskogo atamana Denisova.* St. Petersburg: VIRD.
Duffy, Christopher. 1999. *Eagles over the Alps: Suvorov in Italy and Switzerland, 1799.* Chicago: Emperor's Press.
Mikaberidze, Alexander. 2003. "Lion of the Russian Army: Life and Military Career of General Prince Peter Bagration." 2 vols. Ph.D. diss., Florida State University.
Zhurnal Voennikh Deistvii Otriada Kn. P.I. Bragationa (s 9 Aprelia po 28 Sentiabria 1799). 1903. St. Petersburg: N.p.

San Ildefonso, Treaty of (1 October 1800)

Signed between France and Spain in 1800 and not to be confused with an earlier agreement of the same name con-

cluded in May 1796, the Treaty of San Ildefonso was intended to pave the way for what the First Consul, Napoleon Bonaparte, hoped would be a new colonial empire in the Western Hemisphere.

Of chief importance here was the territory of Louisiana. Ceded to Spain by France in 1762 at the close of the Seven Years' War (1756–1763), it stretched from the Gulf of Mexico to the present-day Canadian frontier and from the Mississippi River to the Rocky Mountains. Though largely unexplored, and colonized by Europeans only in the extreme south, where New Orleans was a major port and the center of a rich plantation economy, it was quite clear that this vast region was potentially of immense importance. Thus, a valuable source of colonial produce though it was, it was also a convenient source of food and raw materials for France's colonies in the West Indies, all of which Bonaparte was determined to see restored to French rule. And, last but not least, there was the issue of global strategy, for a base in the American West would allow Bonaparte both to apply pressure to the British in Canada and to threaten the United States, which was not the friend and ally of France as France had hoped.

On the contrary, in fact, disputes over French privateering had by 1798 produced intermittent fighting at sea between American and French warships and privateers, known as the Quasi-War, which lasted until 1800. Greatly alarmed at the threat to Louisiana, which was inadequately garrisoned by France's ally Spain, and being defended only by its colonial militia, the French backed down. Conciliatory messages were sent to President John Adams, and on 30 September 1800, relations were put back on a normal footing by the Treaty of Mortefontaine. For the time being, then, the United States was quiescent, but such were the contradictions between the French and American positions that it was clear that trouble was likely to erupt once again in the future. In short, the strategic imperative for the acquisition of Louisiana remained. At the very time, then, that negotiations were in train with regard to the agreement of 30 September 1800, parallel talks were being held in Madrid with regard to Louisiana.

In obtaining the retrocession of Louisiana to France there was little difficulty: the Spanish government regarded Louisiana as more trouble than it was worth and was happy to see France take over the territory, while it also recognized that giving France what she wanted in the Western Hemisphere was a necessary quid pro quo for concessions in Europe (in particular, Charles IV was looking for an Italian throne for his eldest daughter, who was married to the son of the Duke of Parma). On 1 October 1800, then, the Treaty of San Ildefonso handed Louisiana back to France. For the time being, the new arrangement remained secret, while for a variety of reasons the actual transfer of power did not take effect until 15 October 1802.

Charles J. Esdaile

See also Charles IV, King; Louisiana Purchase; Spain; United States
References and further reading
Bemis, Samuel. 1936. *A Diplomatic History of the United States.* Holt: New York.
Esdaile, Charles J. 2007. *From Amiens to Waterloo: An International History of the Napoleonic Wars.* London: Penguin.

San Marcial, First Battle of (1 August 1794)

The First Battle of San Marcial was the most important battle fought during the Franco-Spanish Pyrenean campaigns of 1793–1795 in the western Pyrenees. French forces had been increasing, thanks to the mobilization overseen by minister of war Lazare Carnot. The Army of the Western Pyrenees used the resulting superiority in men and artillery to expel the Spanish forces from France and to threaten key points in the south of the country. The victory ensured that there would be no further invasion in this area and that the important city of Bayonne would be secure.

Shortly after the French Revolutionary government declared war on Spain on 7 March 1793, Spanish forces advanced over the Pyrenees. The theater naturally divided itself into two parts—the eastern and western Pyrenees. French forces were outnumbered, poorly trained, and badly equipped. The Spanish occupied a number of border towns and fortified positions before grinding to a halt. For most of 1793 and 1794, both sides in the western Pyrenees watched each other and diverted their best soldiers to more active theaters. The demands of the brutal campaign against the counterrevolution in the Vendée, for example, imposed a constant drain on the Army of the Western Pyrenees. Minor sparring between the two sides continued, with the French concentrating on training and building up their forces.

In late 1793 General Jacques-Leonard Muller, who had proven himself in fighting in Flanders and northern France, was appointed to command the Army of the Western Pyrenees. Muller was a courteous, almost timid man, but he recognized the need to reorganize the army. He completed the amalgamation of volunteer with regular units and appointed commanders who had acquitted themselves well in battle. His most outstanding subordinate was General Bon Adrien Jannot de Moncey, a future marshal under Napoleon. Muller was under considerable pressure to attack the Spanish forces opposite him in order to complement the successful advance of the Army of the Eastern Pyrenees at the other end of the front.

Muller opened his campaign on 24 July 1794, with approximately 30,000 men at his disposal. The Spanish forces were considerably inferior, totaling a mere 20,000 men, half of them poorly trained militia. The Spanish general recognized that Muller would soon launch an offensive. When his request to retreat was refused, he resigned and was replaced by an elderly and feeble favorite of the court. Muller's plan was simple. By night, he marched one column under Moncey toward the center of the Spanish line. The following day, diversionary attacks began to pin Spanish forces on the coast and on the landward flank. Moncey then proceeded on 27 July to move from Elizondo in the Baztan valley and cross the mountains to join a second column at Lesaca in the Spanish rear. The hard-marching Moncey covered over 20 miles through the mountains in only 32 hours. The Spanish fell back to San Marcial, to cover the important town of Irun. By the thirty-first, the French had surrounded San Marcial on three sides. When they opened an assault on 1 August, the garrison quickly retreated. More than 200 guns were captured, along with large quantities of supplies and provisions. Muller's army thereafter poured across the Spanish frontier, capturing San Sebastian on 4 August and Tolosa on the ninth. Although French casualties were light, Muller ceased his pursuit, bringing operations in this sector to a halt for the remainder of the year.

Tim J. Watts

See also Carnot, Lazare Nicolas Marguerite; Moncey, Bon Adrien Jannot de; Pyrenean Campaigns (1793–1795); Vendée, Revolts in the
References and further reading
Ducere, Edouard. 1881. *L'Armée des Pyrénées Occidentales avec éclaircissements historiques sur les campagnes de 1793, 1794, 1795.* Bayonne: Hourquet.
Phipps, Ramsay Weston. 1980. *The Armies of the First French Republic and the Rise of the Marshals of Napoleon I.* Vol. 3, *The Armies in the West, 1793–1797, and the Armies in the South, 1792 to March 1796.* London: Greenwood. (Orig. pub. 1926–1939.)

San Marcial, Second Battle of (31 August 1813)

Practically the last field action fought on Spanish soil in the Peninsular War, the second Battle of San Marcial was the result of a last-minute French attempt to relieve the beleaguered fortress of San Sebastian. In brief, the plan adopted by Marshal Nicolas Soult, who held command of all French forces in the western Pyrenees, was to smash through their Spanish counterparts that blocked the main road to San Sebastian at the heights of San Marcial with four divisions, while three other divisions were to cross the river Bidassoa (which marks the frontier) further inland

and break through the mixed force of British, Portuguese, and Spanish infantry that linked the position at San Marcial with those held by the Light Division further south.

In theory, it was a good plan, but many French troops had to be held back to keep watch on the many Anglo-Portuguese units further up the Bidassoa, while the rough terrain also greatly favored the defense. On top of this, the Allied forces also had copious reserves: behind San Marcial were two full divisions of British infantry, together with some other troops. In the event, then, Soult was unsuccessful. Two assaults on San Marcial were beaten off with heavy losses, while at Salain, having initially pushed back the defenders, the French abandoned their advance when Anglo-Portuguese forces that had been stationed further south began to threaten their left flank and rear.

The fighting, however, did not end here. At San Marcial, the attackers had been able to fall back across the Bidassoa without difficulty, but at Salain they had marched deeper into Spain, and by the time they got back to the river they found that a sudden thunderstorm had made the fords by which they had crossed very hazardous. Some troops still got through, but eventually the passage became completely blocked. With four brigades still to cross, the French were in real trouble, but in the end they all escaped. Thus, feeling their way along the river bank, they eventually came to the bridge at Vera. The way was blocked by a company of the 95th Rifles, which put up a fierce fight from the shelter of a house overlooking the crossing, but no reinforcements were forthcoming, and in the end the French burst through. Behind them, however, lay nearly 4,000 dead and wounded; Allied losses, by contrast, scarcely coming to 2,500.

Charles J. Esdaile

See also Peninsular War; San Sebastian, Siege of; Soult, Nicolas Jean de Dieu; Vera, Battles of
References and further reading
Oman, Charles. 2005. *A History of the Peninsular War.* 7 vols. London: Greenhill. (Orig. pub. 1902–1930.)

San Sebastian, Siege of (28 June–31 August 1813)

The siege of San Sebastian was the third of the three great successful sieges carried out by the Marquis of Wellington's army during the Peninsular War. The siege operations on this occasion were conducted by Lieutenant General Sir Thomas Graham while Wellington was based at his headquarters in the Pyrenees at Lesaca.

With Marshal Nicolas Soult having been thrown back across the French border, there was no real reason to hurry the siege. Interference from any relieving enemy force was unlikely, and Graham was able to carry on the operations at a more leisurely pace than at Ciudad Rodrigo and Badajoz. (On these latter two occasions, the close proximity of French relieving armies had forced Wellington to commit his troops to the assault before he was entirely satisfied with the condition of the breaches, and as a result heavy casualties were sustained.)

San Sebastian was rather a small town, situated on a low, sandy peninsula, dominated by a rocky mountain called Monte Orgullo, upon which was built a castle. The town was bordered on three sides by the waters of the Bay of Biscay and could only be approached by land from the south. To the east of the town flowed the river Urumea, which at high water formed a sort of wide estuary. The town itself lay at the southern foot of Monte Orgullo and was separated from the castle by a line of defensive works. This meant that even in the event of the town falling to the Allies, the castle was still defensible.

Graham chose the eastern wall of the town, standing about 27 feet high, as the target for his siege guns, which were positioned upon the Chofre Sand Hills away to the east. Having blasted suitable breaches, Graham's men would have to storm the place by crossing the Urumea at low tide.

Graham's 10,000-strong force began its siege operations on 28 June but it was not until 25 July that the first assault was made, by Major General John Oswald's 5th Division and Brigadier General Thomas Bradford's Portuguese brigade, neither of which were able to get inside the place, defended as it was by a brave and determined garrison of about 3,000 French troops under the command of General Emmanuel Rey.

During the next few days, Soult launched his attack across the passes in the Pyrenees, but with the attack having been repulsed, the Allies were able to turn their attention to San Sebastian once more. On 26 August more siege guns arrived from Britain, Wellington now being able to supply his army through the ports along the coast of northern Spain.

After four days of accurate, sustained fire, the eastern wall of San Sebastian was reduced to a crumbling wreck and a practicable breach made, with another, smaller breach being effected farther to the north. Rey's artillery also suffered and was practically silenced, although both the garrison and the Spanish population were kept busy all day and night clearing the rubbish from the walls and repairing defenses in the breaches.

On 30 August Graham was satisfied with the state of the two breaches and gave orders that the place was to be stormed at noon the following day. The timing of the attack was thus quite a departure from the normal practice of storming a town after dark. On this occasion, of course, the timing was purely dependent on the tide, but what it meant was that Graham's stormers would attack in full view of the defenders and in broad daylight. It was not a pleasing prospect, but the storming of a town afforded the British troops the chance of plunder and drink and of release from army discipline. They had acquired a taste for such things at Ciudad Rodrigo and Badajoz, and no matter what obstacles were placed in their way they were not to be put off, nor would there be any shortage of volunteers for the forlorn hope, as the initial assault party was called in siege warfare.

Graham's plan involved an attack on the main breach by the 5th Division and Bradford's Portuguese, who were supported by 750 volunteers from the 1st and Light Divisions. Further to the north, some 800 Portuguese volunteers were to wade through the shallow waters of the Urumea and attack the smaller breach.

The morning of 31 August dawned bright and fresh after a night of heavy rain and thunderstorms, and as the columns of British and Portuguese stormers formed up ready to begin the assault, crowds of local people wearing their holiday clothes began to congregate in order to watch. When the signal for the assault was fired, the Allied troops began to pick their way across the beach through shallow rocky pools to make their way toward the breaches, which yawned silent, intimidating, and inviting before them. When the forlorn hope approached the walls, the watching French gunners opened up with a devastating blast of grapeshot that swept away half of the attackers in an instant.

For the next hour or so, Graham watched helplessly as his men were smashed against the defenses while the spectators elsewhere watched in awe. The garrison proved as tenacious as those at Ciudad Rodrigo and Badajoz, and all manner of shells, grenades, and other combustibles were thrown down to explode amid the columns of Allied infantry. The defenders lined the ramparts and opened up a withering fire into the attacking columns, bringing them grinding to a halt.

At this point Graham issued an order to Colonel Alexander Dickson, commanding the Allied artillery, an order based partly on inspiration and partly on desperation. Graham asked Dickson to open fire over the heads of the stormers and onto the French guns in the town. It was perhaps one of the earliest examples of a creeping barrage and was certainly a gamble, but it worked. The astonished British stormers pushed their faces to the ground as shot and shell screamed just a few feet overhead to crash into the French guns and defenders behind the ramparts. The stormers lay listening to this terrifying but pleasing symphony for about 20 minutes, and when the guns lifted, they stormed forward to carry the defenses, which had been torn apart by the guns. The breaches had all but been abandoned by the defenders, and when a magazine exploded, killing and wounding a large number of Frenchmen, the town was as good as taken. As Graham watched from the sand hills, he saw with relief his men disappear into the smoke as they drove the remaining French troops from the breaches.

San Sebastian was taken soon afterward, although the castle of La Mota held out until 8 September. Allied casualties were 856 killed and 1,520 wounded. The aftermath of the storming of San Sebastian was much the same as that at Ciudad Rodrigo and Badajoz, as the victorious troops embarked upon an orgy of destruction, which was made worse by a fire that engulfed the whole town. There were fierce accusations afterward that Wellington himself had ordered the town to be put to the torch, as it had been continuing to trade with France, accusations that Wellington denied, although he might well have felt justified in resorting to such a measure.

Ian Fletcher

See also Badajoz, Third Siege of; Ciudad Rodrigo, Second Siege of; Graham, Sir Thomas; Peninsular War; Siege Warfare; Soult, Nicolas Jean de Dieu; Wellington, Arthur Wellesley, First Duke of
References and further reading
Esdaile, Charles J. 2003. *The Peninsular War: A New History.* London: Palgrave Macmillan.
Fletcher, Ian. 2003. *Fortresses of the Peninsular War, 1807–14.* Oxford: Osprey.
Gates, David. 2001. *The Spanish Ulcer: A History of the Peninsular War.* New York: Da Capo.
Glover, Michael. 2001. *The Peninsular War, 1807–1814: A Concise Military History.* London: Penguin.
Myatt, Frederick. 1987. *British Sieges of the Peninsular War, 1811–13.* Staplehurst, UK: Spellmount.
Napier, W. F. P. 1992. *A History of the War in the Peninsula.* 6 vols. London: Constable. (Orig. pub. 1828.)
Oman, Sir Charles. 2005. *A History of the Peninsular War.* 7 vols. London: Greenhill. (Orig. pub. 1902–1930.)
Paget, Julian. 1992. *Wellington's Peninsular War: Battles and Battlefields.* London: Leo Cooper.
Uffindell, Andrew. 2003. *The National Army Museum Book of Wellington's Armies: Britain's Triumphant Campaigns in the Peninsula and at Waterloo, 1808–1815.* London: Sedgwick and Jackson.
Weller, Jac. 1992. *Wellington in the Peninsula.* London: Greenhill.

Sánchez García, Julián (1774–1832)

A peasant from Muñoz who had from 1793 to 1801 served as a soldier, on 15 August 1808 Julián Sánchez García joined the militia raised to defend Ciudad Rodrigo in the aftermath of the Spanish uprising. Experienced and courageous, within a few months he was in command of a squadron of cavalry—the genesis of what was to become the 1st Regiment of Lancers of Castile—and at the head of these men he led a series of raids against the French, his most notable success coming on 21 June 1809 at Almeida de Sayago, where he defeated a much stronger party of French dragoons.

Range far and wide though he and his men did, however, they remained part of the army that was then based at Ciudad Rodrigo under the Duque del Parque: Indeed, when Del Parque went on the offensive in October 1809, Sánchez and his lancers were called in to assist with reconnaissance and outpost duty as "army-level" troops. Badly beaten at Alba de Tormes, Del Parque then went into winter quarters, Sánchez in the meantime busying himself with such tasks as rounding up deserters, gathering in supplies, and skirmishing with the French forces based at Salamanca. In the spring, though, the army moved south and took up positions around Badajoz.

Left behind as part of the garrison of Ciudad Rodrigo, Sánchez then fought a series of actions with the enemy troops that were closing in on the city. However, no amount of skirmishing could prevent the French from commencing siege operations. Cavalry being of only limited use in this situation, the governor ordered Sánchez to break out, which he did by means of a sudden charge launched at one o'clock in the morning on 23 June 1810. Left to his own devices, Sánchez, or El Charro as he had come to be known, turned guerrilla, and spent his time harassing the communications of the French army that had invaded Portugal following the fall of Ciudad Rodrigo. With the reappearance of Allied troops in the region in 1811, however, this period of independence came to an end. With his forces swollen to a full cavalry brigade, Sánchez was absorbed into the Spanish 5th Army and fought with the Earl of Wellington in the campaigns of Burgos and Salamanca in 1812, before spending the rest of the war in garrison at Ciudad Rodrigo.

Despite being made governor of Santoña, he felt he was never adequately rewarded by Ferdinand VII, and he therefore sided with the liberals in 1820. Captured by the French in 1823, he escaped immediate retribution, but a year later he was accused of conspiracy and imprisoned without trial. Released in 1826, he spent what remained of his life in comfortable retirement.

Charles J. Esdaile

See also Alba de Tormes, Battle of; Burgos, Siege of; Ciudad Rodrigo, First Siege of; Ferdinand VII, King; Guerrilla Warfare; Peninsular War; Salamanca, Battle of; Wellington, Arthur Wellesley, First Duke of
References and further reading
Esdaile, Charles J. 2002. *The Peninsular War: A New History*. London: Penguin.
———. 2004. *Fighting Napoleon: Guerrillas, Bandits and Adventurers in Spain, 1808–14*. London: Yale University Press.

Santo Domingo

Santo Domingo was the name of the Spanish colony that occupied the eastern portion of the island of Hispaniola in the Caribbean Sea. Originally inhabited by the Arawaks, the island was controlled by the Spanish after the arrival of Christopher Columbus in 1492. Columbus had established the settlement of Navidad on the north coast, but the native inhabitants destroyed the initial colony. In 1493 Columbus established Isabela, the first true Spanish town on the island. This effort also failed, and by 1499 Isabela was all but abandoned. Then, in 1496, the Spanish founded the city of Santo Domingo at a site with a good harbor, fertile land, and a large native population to exploit. For the next several decades, Santo Domingo served as the center of Spanish exploration and colonization of the Caribbean.

By the middle of the sixteenth century, Santo Domingo began to decline in importance, as the native population decreased dramatically and Spain turned to the conquest of mainland North and South America. Many Spanish settlers left the island. The remaining Spanish concentrated on the eastern end of the island, largely ignoring the western half of Hispaniola. Soon, Dutch, English, and French pirates established themselves in the western part of the island. The French then began to colonize the area, as French settlers developed plantations and began to import African slaves. In 1697, despite British opposition, the Spanish government recognized the French claim to the western one-third of the island. Renamed St. Domingue (later Haiti), the French colony continued to prosper. By the 1780s St. Domingue produced nearly half of the sugar and coffee consumed in Europe and the Americas. It was also a significant producer of other products, such as cotton and indigo. St. Domingue's population surpassed 500,000. At the same time, Spanish Santo Domingo continued to decline. A subsistence economy and contraband supported a population of less than 100,000, as many colonists abandoned the island.

In 1795 Spain ceded Santo Domingo to France as a result of Spanish military defeat in Europe. The former Spanish colony continued to decline under French rule. The advent of French rule marked the beginning of a period of intervention and conflict that lasted until the 1840s. The uprising led by blacks and mulattoes in French St. Domingue greatly affected Santo Domingo. Between 1804 and 1809 the Spanish, French, Haitians, and British fought for control of Santo Domingo. The Haitians occupied much of the eastern part of the island. However, the Spanish colonists, with the aid of the British, drove out the Haitians. By 1809 Santo Domingo was again under Spanish control. Then, in 1821, a group of colonists deposed the Spanish authorities and declared their independence. Weeks after independence, Haitian troops again invaded Santo Domingo. This time, Haiti, led by Jean Pierre Boyer, occupied the eastern portion of the island until 1842. Santo Domingo did not actually achieve its independence until 1844 under the leadership of Juan Pablo Duarte. The country then became known by its present name, the Dominican Republic.

Ronald Young

See also Haiti; Toussaint Louverture; West Indies, Operations in the
References and further reading
Rodman, Selden. 1964. *Quisqueya: A History of the Dominican Republic.* Seattle: University of Washington Press.
Wiarda, Howard J., and Michael J. Kryzanek. 1982. *The Dominican Republic: A Caribbean Crucible.* Boulder, CO: Westview Press.

Santo Domingo, Battle of (6 February 1806)

The naval battle fought off the island of Hispaniola in the West Indies came in the aftermath of the French navy's defeat at Trafalgar. After Napoleon called off the invasion of England, he ordered attacks on British colonies and commerce. Two naval squadrons were dispatched from Brest, both of which initially escaped unobserved by the British in December 1805.

Six ships led by Rear Admiral Jean Willaumez headed for the South Atlantic. Another five ships under the command of Rear Admiral Corentin Urbain Leissègues made their way to the West Indies. Leissègues's orders were to disembark 1,000 troops at Santo Domingo to relieve the French garrison there, which was still holding out. After stopping at Santo Domingo, Leissègues was to attack Britain's West Indian trade.

Initially, two British squadrons attempted to stop the French squadron, but both failed. In the meantime, British vice admiral Sir John Duckworth got word of a French squadron near the island of Madeira. Duckworth had been leading the British blockade of Cádiz in southern Spain. Believing the French squadron to be that of another French commander, Duckworth raised the blockade and set out for Madeira. He briefly pursued Willaumez's squadron, but the French ships outsailed the British. Short of water, Duckworth later steered for the West Indies, stopping first at Barbados and then making his way to the Leeward Islands, where he joined with Rear Admiral Alexander Cochrane. In the Caribbean, Duckworth watered and refitted his squadron.

At first, there was no news of the French squadron, and Duckworth prepared to return to Europe. Soon, Duckworth received word that the French ships had also arrived in the Caribbean. The British initially believed the squadron to be that of Willaumez, whom Duckworth had earlier pursued. In reality, however, it was Leissègues's squadron, which had made the difficult winter passage across the Atlantic.

On 6 February 1806 the British sighted the French squadron anchored at the eastern end of the island of Hispaniola, where they were landing troops and supplies for the French garrison. The French were nearly ready to weigh anchor when the British discovered them. When the ship on lookout signaled that enemy ships were in sight, Leissègues ordered his squadron to make sail. A battle soon ensued. The British approached the French squadron in two columns. Leissègues sailed across the front of the two columns, hoping to concentrate his attack on the nearer column. This strategy failed, however, when the rudder failed on the lead French ship, the *Alexandre.* Duckworth's flagship the *Superb,* supported by the *Northumberland* and *Agamemnon,* closed in on the helpless *Alexandre.* Later, Leissègues's flagship, the *Impérial,* was badly damaged by the *Northumberland.* The *Superb* then engaged and defeated the French flagship. The British succeeded in driving two of the French ships ashore, including the *Impérial.* The British burned both of these ships. Three other French ships were captured. Only the French frigates were able to escape.

British casualties were relatively light, with 74 dead and 264 wounded. The French suffered much heavier casualties, with approximately 1,500 killed or wounded.

Ronald Young

See also England, French Plans for the Invasion of; Santo Domingo; Trafalgar, Battle of; West Indies, Operations in the
References and further reading
Clowes, William Laird. 1996. *The Royal Navy: A History from the Earliest Times to 1900.* Vol. 5. London: Chatham. (Orig. pub. 1898.)
Jenkins, E. H. 1973. *A History of the French Navy: From Its Beginnings to the Present Day.* Annapolis: Naval Institute Press.
Marcus, Geoffrey Jules. 1971. *The Age of Nelson: The Royal Navy, 1793–1815.* New York: Viking.
Woodman, Richard. 2003. *The Victory of Seapower: Winning the Napoleonic War, 1806–1814.* London: Chatham.

Saragossa, Sieges of (28 June–13 August 1808; 21 December 1808–20 February 1809)

A major city on the southern bank of the river Ebro in Aragón possessed of no defenses other than a medieval

Amid bitter street fighting in which quarter was neither given nor received, French infantry assault the grim defenders of a church during the siege of Saragossa. (Print after Jules Girardet from *Life of Napoleon Bonaparte* by William M. Sloane. New York: Century, 1906, vol. 3.)

wall, Saragossa was a leading center of the Spanish insurrection of 1808. As such, it was an early target of the French, who mounted their first attempt at its capture on 15 June. A simple escalade, it was driven off by the inhabitants with 700 French casualties, and on 28 June regular siege operations therefore began against the city under General Jean Antoine Verdier. With the defenders distracted by a catastrophic explosion in their main powder magazine, the invaders drove the Spaniards off the heights that dominated the city from the south. With this preliminary move out of the way, on 2 July 3,000 troops attacked the walls, only to find that the defenders, who had by now been reinforced by a regiment of line infantry from Catalonia, again put up a desperate resistance. Indeed, the invaders were once again repelled with 500 killed and wounded, their defeat being accompanied by the emergence of one of the greatest popular icons of the Spanish struggle in the person of Agustina of Aragón—more precisely, Agustina Zaragoza Domenech—a Catalan girl who single-handedly saved a key position from the enemy by seizing a linstock from a dying gunner (reputedly her lover) and firing a cannon into the very faces of the advancing French.

Much discouraged, Verdier now resigned himself to engaging in conventional siege operations. Despite a se-

ries of sorties, by 31 July all was ready for the bombardment of the city. With sixty guns in place, whole sections of the city's flimsy defenses were swept away, and on the afternoon of 4 August the French attacked again. This time there was no mistake: protected until the last minute by their trenches, the assault columns scrambled through the various breaches and poured into the streets. Yet, inspired by the demagoguery of their commander, General José Palafox, the defenders remained as defiant as ever. In the face of furious opposition, the attackers were forced to fight their way yard by yard toward the heart of the city. Had they been able to keep going, they might well have triumphed, but the attack ran out of steam, and the end of the day found the French confined to a narrow finger of territory stretching from the walls deep into the city.

What might have happened next is difficult to say: Verdier's forces were in no fit state to do much more, but the Spaniards were too disorganized to do more than keep up a steady fusillade and make spasmodic rushes at one French position or another. In short, fresh troops might yet have won the day for Verdier, but on 12 August he received news of the French defeat at Bailén and decided to abandon the siege forthwith. By 13 August, then, the invaders were gone, having lost 3,500 men compared to perhaps 5,000 Spanish.

The French did not, however, forget Saragossa, and on 20 December, 40,000 men appeared before the city. Facing them was a defending force of 32,000 troops, while the city's medieval defenses had been strengthened by a line of earthworks and entrenchments that linked together the various convents and monasteries that lay just outside the walls. Inside the city, meanwhile, streets had been barricaded, doors and windows blocked by obstacles, walls loopholed, and houses linked by tunnels and passageways. But neither these preparations nor the continued braggadocio of Palafox could save the city. By the close of the year it had been closely blockaded on both banks of the river, and considerable progress made on the attackers' trenches and gun emplacements. Nor was much done to stop their progress: Though plenty of troops were available, the only sorties that took place consisted of suicidal rushes by mere handfuls of men.

Very soon, in fact, Palafox was exposed as a mediocre commander. All the troops in Aragón having been concentrated in Saragossa, it was found that there were none left for a relief force, while such was the overcrowding in the city that populace and troops alike soon fell prey to a devastating epidemic of typhus. To the misery of disease was soon added that of bombardment, for on 10 January 1809 the French opened up on the city with their siege batteries. After seventeen days of bombardment, moreover, the walls were stormed. As before, the defenders fought on, but the city was doomed. Despite scenes of desperate heroism—in a foretaste of battles far in the future, the French had to advance into the city house by house, blowing holes in partition walls and methodically slaughtering the defenders of each room—the invaders could not be checked, while the ravages of typhus and starvation very soon brought the city to its knees. On 20 February, then, the guns at last fell silent, the whole dreadful affair having cost the French 10,000 casualties and an unknown number of Spanish. With the fall of the city, the entire population of 54,000 fell into French hands.

Charles J. Esdaile

See also Bailén, Battle of and Capitulation at; Peninsular War; Rebolledo de Palafox y Melzi, José; Siege Warfare
References and further reading
Esdaile, Charles J. 2002. *The Peninsular War: A New History.* London: Penguin.
Rudorff, Raymond. 1974. *War to the Death: The Sieges of Saragossa, 1808–1809.* London: Hamilton.

Sardinia

At the outbreak of the French Revolutionary Wars, the Kingdom of Sardinia included Piedmont in northwestern Italy, Savoy and the port of Nice in geographical France, and the Mediterranean island of Sardinia. Ruled by the House of Savoy, Sardinia participated in the First Coalition against France. After defeat in 1796, Piedmont fell under French influence and, later in 1802, under French administration, while the rulers of Savoy retired to Sardinia until the kingdom's restoration after the Congress of Vienna.

In 1789 the Kingdom of Sardinia was the most powerful *ancien régime* state in Italy and an ally of monarchical France. Not an enlightened reformist sovereign, King Victor Amadeus III ruled his 3.2 million subjects according to the principles of a military-bureaucratic absolutism and drove the state finances into dire straits. The economic crisis of those years brought social discontent in Piedmont, particularly among the peasant masses, who nevertheless in general remained faithful to the Crown. Here and there, Jacobin ideals found supporters among the citizens, to a lesser extent, however, than elsewhere in Italy.

A rapid deterioration of diplomatic relations with France followed the Revolution and led to war in 1792, during which the French occupied the long-coveted territories of Savoy and Nice. With the less than enthusiastic support of Austria, for four years the small, but professional and well-trained Sardinian (often called Piedmontese) army succeeded in keeping the more numerous enemy forces at bay in the northwestern and Maritime Alps.

In April 1796, however, Bonaparte began his first Italian campaign and, by attacking inland from the western Ligurian coast, managed to separate the Piedmontese from the Austrian army. Defeated at Mondovì, Victor Amadeus signed an armistice at Cherasco on 28 April (ratified in Paris on 15 May), whereby Sardinia renounced Savoy and Nice, and allowed the French armies free transit across Piedmont. Victor Amadeus died in October, and two years later King Charles Emmanuel IV gave up Piedmont to the French Directory, abdicated, and sailed to Sardinia. A manipulated plebiscite in February 1799 ratified the French annexation of Piedmont, which played a role in igniting several popular uprisings throughout the country in the following months.

In 1799, the French were defeated, and Piedmont was occupied by Field Marshal Alexander Suvorov's Austro-Russian army. The Allies, however, did not allow the king of Savoy back on the throne, and after the Battle of Marengo (14 June 1800), Piedmont returned to French control. In 1802, Charles Emmanuel IV abdicated in favor of his brother Victor-Emmanuel I, who remained in Sardinia. On 11 September of the same year, Bonaparte, now First Consul, decided to turn Piedmont into six French departments (Dora, Marengo, Po, Sesia, Stura, and Agogna, later suppressed) and the 27th Military District. Alessandria was to become the most important French military depot in northern Italy. Throughout the Napoleonic years, many units recruited in Piedmont fought in the Grande Armée, some restoring their previous martial fame with distinguished records of service.

After the fall of the Napoleonic Empire, the second Treaty of Paris (November 1815) restored Victor-Emmanuel I to his former possessions of Piedmont, Savoy, and Nice, with Genoa and Liguria as welcome additions. On such an enlarged territorial basis, the Kingdom of Sardinia was to reestablish itself as the most important Italian state and ultimately was to take the lead in the movement for national independence.

Marco Gioannini

See also Cherasco, Armistice at; Directory, The; First Coalition, War of the; Italian Campaigns (1792–1797); Italian Campaigns (1799–1800); Jacobins; Marengo, Battle of; Mondovi, Battle of; Paris, Second Treaty of; Suvorov, Alexander Vasilievich; Vienna, Congress of

References and further reading

Broers, Michael. 1997. *Napoleonic Imperialism and the Savoyard Monarchy, 1773–1821: State Building in Piedmont.* Lampeter, UK: Mellen.

Ilari, Virgilio, Piero Crociani, and Ciro Paoletti. 2001. *Storia militare dell'Italia giacobina* [A Military History of Jacobin Italy], *1796–1802.* Vol. 1. Rome: Stato Maggiore dell'Esercito-Ufficio Storico.

Saumarez, Sir James (1757–1836)

British admiral and general of Royal Marines. From 1793 to 1814, Saumarez served in the Channel Fleet, the Mediterranean Fleet, and the Baltic Fleet, distinguishing himself in several actions.

Saumarez was born at St. Peter Port, Guernsey, on 11 March 1757. He first saw active service in August 1770 in the Mediterranean, where he served until April 1775. During the American Revolutionary War, Saumarez served off the American coast from 1775 to 1778. Following the war, he remained on half pay until the conflict with Revolutionary France began in 1793.

Saumarez thereupon returned to active service and was given command of the frigate *Crescent* (36 guns), in which he defeated and captured the French frigate *Réunion* (36) on 20 October 1793. He remained in the Channel Fleet through 1798, where he was primarily employed on blockade duty off Brest and Rochefort. Joining Sir John Jervis (later Earl St. Vincent) in February 1797, he commanded *Orion* (74) at the Battle of St. Vincent on 14 February. Following this action, he remained with Jervis in the blockade of Cádiz, alternating command of the inshore squadron with (the newly promoted and knighted) Vice Admiral Sir Horatio Nelson. In May 1798, Saumarez accompanied Nelson into the Mediterranean in pursuit of the expedition bound for Egypt under Bonaparte. The fleets met at the Battle of the Nile on 1 August, and although no second in command was specifically designated, Saumarez was the senior captain present and was chosen by Nelson to escort the prizes back to Gibraltar. Afterward, he rejoined St. Vincent in the blockade of Brest.

Saumarez was promoted to rear admiral on 1 January 1801 and on 13 June of that year was made a baronet. Afterward, he was ordered to command the blockade of Cádiz, where he remained until he learned of a French squadron of three ships of the line and one frigate under the command of *contre-amiral* (rear admiral) Charles Durand, comte de Linois, anchored in the Bay of Gibraltar under the guns of their Spanish allies at Algeciras. On 6 July 1801, Saumarez attacked with six ships of the line, but due to Linois's superior defensive position and a lack of wind, he was forced to retreat to Gibraltar after losing one ship to the French. Both squadrons required extensive repairs; Saumarez refitted at Gibraltar, and Linois sent for reinforcements from Cádiz to escort his ships through the straits.

Six Spanish ships arrived early on 12 July, and the Franco-Spanish squadron departed that evening. Saumarez pursued, and in the ensuing encounter off Algeciras he destroyed two Spanish first rates of 112 guns each and captured a French 74. For his turn-around victory, Saumarez was made a Knight of the Bath. Following the rupture of the Peace of Amiens, he commanded the Guernsey station until 1807, when he was promoted to vice admiral and made second in command of the fleet off Brest. In March 1808, he was given command of the Baltic Squadron, a command he held until 1813. He was promoted to admiral on 4 June 1814.

Following the peace, he held the command at Plymouth from 1824 to 1827; he was raised to the peerage as Baron de Saumarez of Saumarez in Guernsey and was made general of marines in February 1832. He died on 9 October 1836.

Jason Musteen

See also Algeciras, First Battle of; Algeciras, Second Battle of; Amiens, Treaty of; Blockade; Middle East Campaign; Nelson, Horatio, First Viscount; Nile, Battle of the; St. Vincent, Battle of; St. Vincent, John Jervis, First Earl of

References and further reading

Clowes, William Laird. 1997. *The Royal Navy: A History from the Earliest Times to 1900.* 7 vols. Vol. 4. London: Chatham. (Orig. pub. 1898.)

Gardiner, Robert, ed. 2001. *Nelson against Napoleon: From the Nile to Copenhagen, 1798–1801.* London: Chatham.

Kennedy, Ludovic. 2001. *Nelson and His Captains.* London: Penguin.

Savants

Group of 167 civilian scholars and engineers who accompanied the French army to Egypt during the campaign of 1798–1801. Collectively they made up the Institute of Egypt, a learned society modeled on the French National Institute, which Napoleon Bonaparte established in August 1798 to facilitate research concerning Egypt. Because the purpose of the military campaign was to secure Egypt as a French colony, the savants undertook a detailed, systematic study of all aspects of the region and its inhabitants. Some of the civilians were engineers and students from the Ecole Polytechnique, while others were distinguished scholars. Among the noted luminaries were Dominique Vivant Denon, a prominent antiquarian and art historian; Gaspard Monge, famed for his contribution to descriptive geometry; Joseph Fourier, a mathematician known for his work in calculus; Claude-Louis Berthollet, an eminent chemist; Guy-Sylvain Dolomieu, the mineralogist for whom dolomite was later named; and Etienne Geoffry St. Hilaire, a talented young zoologist from the Museum of Natural History. The various civilian researchers constituted the Scientific and Artistic Commission.

The Institute of Egypt was a separate body that promoted scholarship by creating an administrative structure for conducting and organizing research, and providing meeting rooms, a library, a printing press, and, importantly, various workshops. Because most of the scientific and technical equipment was destroyed at the Battle of the Nile (1 August 1798) or in the uprising in Cairo (21–22 October 1798), Nicolas Conté, an inventor and chief of the army's balloonists, who managed the workshops, had to produce new equipment for the scholars' work. The more established savants and some of the army generals were made members of the institute, but all who were part of the Scientific and Artistic Commission were welcome to attend meetings and submit research to be reviewed for publication. The institute published two periodicals, *La Décade Egyptienne*, a journal, and the *Courrier d'Egypte,* a newspaper.

The work of the savants was extensive and varied. Projects relevant to health, population, agriculture, manufacturing, geography, cartography, and political and social organization were clearly intended to ease military occupation and build the foundations of colonial administration. Researchers concluded that contemporary Egypt was similar to pre-Revolutionary France, oppressed and enervated by inefficient, corrupt rule, stifled by religious dogma, and very much in need of enlightened government. Investigations of the natural history, flora, fauna, and antiquities were intended to illuminate what Europeans viewed as an exotic and relatively little-known civilization. St. Hilaire collected and preserved birds, fish, and crocodiles, while Monge explained the nature of the mirage. Berthollet explored the chemical properties of natron.

Excavating the remains of pharaonic temples and tombs captured the imaginations of most of the savants, and served the ideological purpose of attaching some of the grandeur and mystique of a powerful, "lost" ancient civilization to contemporary France and Bonaparte. Denon, the first civilian to accompany the army into Upper Egypt, became known for his enthusiastic description and spontaneous sketches of ancient ruins. Subsequently, contingents of engineers excavated, surveyed, and illustrated various sites along the Nile in Upper Egypt. Because they had military support and resources as well as technical training, they were able to provide architectural drawings and imagined reconstructions of ancient monuments more extensively and accurately than earlier travelers.

The most significant artifact unearthed was the Rosetta Stone, which a military engineer discovered accidentally in the course of work on fortifications at el-Rashid (Rosetta) in the Delta. The savants immediately recognized that the inscription would provide the key to the decipherment of hieroglyphic script. They translated the Greek version of the inscription and made copies of the stone. Its cultural value made the Rosetta Stone so famous that the British claimed it as a trophy of war when the French withdrew from Egypt in 1801. Though the Institute of Egypt disbanded when French occupation ended, the French Ministry of the Interior published the work of the Scientific and Artistic Commission in the elaborately illustrated, oversized, multivolume *Description of Egypt*. This magnum opus was one of the first comprehensive surveys of Egyptology.

Melanie Byrd

See also Cairo, Uprising in; Egypt; Middle East Campaign; Nile, Battle of the; Rosetta Stone

References and further reading
Beaucour, Fernand, Yves Laissus, and Chantal Orgogozo. 1990. *The Discovery of Egypt: Artists, Travelers and Scientists.* Translated from the French by Bambi Ballard. Paris: Flammarion.
Gillispie, Charles Coulston, and Michel Dewachter, eds. 1987. *The Monuments of Egypt: The Napoleonic Edition.* Princeton: Princeton Architectural Press.
Solé, Robert. 1998. *Les savants de Bonaparte.* Paris: Du Seuil.

Savary, Anne Jean Marie René, duc de Rovigo (1774–1833)

French general and statesman. He was born at Marcq in the Ardennes on 26 April 1774 and educated at the college of St. Louis at Metz. Savary enlisted in the army in 1790 and took part in actions against Prussian forces in 1792. He later served under generals Charles Pichegru and Jean Moreau on the Rhine River, rising to *chef de escadron* in 1797. He joined Bonaparte's expedition to Egypt in 1798 and left an interesting account of the French conquest of that country. Returning to France, Savary supported the coup d'état of 18–19 Brumaire (9–10 November 1799) and served as Bonaparte's aide-de-camp in the Italian campaign of 1800, distinguishing himself at Marengo on 14 June of that year. For his actions, Bonaparte, as First Consul, appointed Savary commander of the elite *gendarmes* unit in charge of his security in 1801. Two years later, Savary rose to *général de brigade* and was employed by Bonaparte in several political missions.

In 1804 he traveled to the western departments of France to investigate Georges Cadoudal's conspiracy and was later involved in the infamous kidnapping of the duc d'Enghien, playing a crucial role in his execution. In February 1805 he was promoted to *général de division* and participated in the campaign of that year against the Third Coalition. That November Savary was sent on a mission to the Allies and used the opportunity to gather intelligence on their forces. In 1806 he distinguished himself at Jena and later that year temporarily commanded Marshal Jean Lannes's V Corps. After the Treaty of Tilsit (July 1807) Savary briefly served as the French envoy to St. Petersburg before being replaced by General Armand-Augustin-Louis, marquis de Caulaincourt in 1808. Napoleon then employed him in Spain, where Savary persuaded King Charles IV and his son Ferdinand VII to accept Napoleon's mediation and escorted them to Bayonne, where the Spanish royal family was arrested. In May 1808 Savary was given the title of duc de Rovigo and accompanied the Emperor to Erfurt, where he took part in negotiations with the Russians.

Following the 1809 campaign, Savary replaced Joseph Fouché as the minister of police on 3 June 1810 and became notorious for his strict enforcement of the law. Nevertheless, General Claude-François de Malet's conspiracy (October 1812) demonstrated that Savary, who was arrested by conspirators in his bed, also lacked the acumen of his predecessor. Savary's reputation never recovered from this debacle, though he continued to serve in his position until the fall of the Empire.

In 1814 he accompanied Empress Marie Louise to Blois. A year later, he welcomed Napoleon's return and became the inspector general of gendarmerie and a peer of France. After Waterloo, Savary accompanied Napoleon to Rochefort and sailed with him to Plymouth on board HMS *Bellerophon*. The British authorities refused to allow him to accompany Napoleon to St. Helena and imprisoned him

for several months on Malta. After his escape in April 1816, Savary settled in Smyrna (now Izmir, Turkey) and spent several years traveling. Despite being on the proscription list and sentenced to death, Savary returned to France in 1819, though the Bourbons refused his offers of service. He later settled in Rome, where he remained for almost a decade. The July Revolution of 1830 enabled him to return to France. In 1831, King Louis Philippe appointed him commander in chief of the French army in Algeria. However, the ailing Savary soon had to return to France, where he died in Paris on 2 June 1833.

Alexander Mikaberidze

See also Bayonne, Conference at; Brumaire, Coup of; Caulaincourt, Armand-Augustin-Louis de, marquis de, duc de Vicence; Charles IV, King; Enghien, Louis Antoine Henri de Bourbon-Condé, duc d'; Erfurt, Congress of; Ferdinand VII, King; Fouché, Joseph, duc d'Otrante; Fourth Coalition, War of the; Italian Campaigns (1799–1800); Jena, Battle of; Lannes, Jean; Malet Conspiracy; Marengo, Battle of; Marie Louise, Empress; Middle East Campaign; Pichegru, Jean-Charles; St. Helena; Third Coalition, War of the; Tilsit, Treaties of

References and further reading
Arnold, Eric A. 1979. *Fouché, Napoleon, and the General Police.* Washington, D.C.: University Press of America.
Esquer, G., ed. 1914. *Correspondance du duc de Rovigo, commandant en chef le corps d'occupation d'Afrique (1831–1833).* Algiers: Carbonel.
Gotteri, Nicole. 1997. *La police secrète du Premier Empire.* Paris: Perrin.
Lenz, Thierry. 2001. *Savary: Le séide de Napoléon.* Paris: Fayard.
Melchior-Bonnet, Bernadine. 1961. *Un policier dans l'ombre de Napoléon: Savary, duc de Rovigo.* Paris: Perrin.
Rovigo, Duc de. 1828a. *Mémoires du Duc de Rovigo: Pour servir à l'histoire de l'empereur Napoléon.* 8 vols. Paris: Bossange.
———. 1828b. *Memoirs of the Duke of Rovigo.* 4 vols. London: Colburn.
———. 1892. *La mission du Général Savary à Saint-Pétersbourg: Sa correspondance avec l'empereur Napoléon et les ministres des relations extérieures, 1807.* St. Petersburg: N.p.

Savoy

Savoy was a duchy owned by the king of Sardinia whose territory is now divided between the departments of Haute-Savoie and Savoie in southeastern France. Between 1789 and 1791 Savoyard émigrés gathered in Paris and conspired to overthrow "Sardinian tyranny." Secretly funded by the minister of foreign affairs, Charles François Dumouriez and François-Amédée Doppet created the Légion des Allobroges of around 2,000 men in July 1792. During the night of 21–22 September a French army under

General Anne Pierre Montesquiou and the Légion des Allobroges invaded Savoy. The outnumbered Sardinians evacuated Savoy without fighting. In October, the short-lived Assemblée Nationale des Allobroges voted to join France as the 84th Department, under the name "Mont-Blanc." Upset by the anticlerical measures taken by the Revolutionary government and the *levée en masse* (universal conscription), the inhabitants of the valley of Thônes, east of Annecy, rose up in revolt in early May 1793. Local troops and National Guard units were able to quickly suppress this revolt.

In August 1793 Sardinian forces invaded and drove out the French. In September, French forces under General François Kellermann returned to liberate the department. Minor unrest continued throughout the region. By the Armistice of Cherasco and the subsequent treaty of peace in 1796, King Victor-Amédée renounced his claim to Savoy.

In 1797 Mont-Blanc was one of the forty-nine departments to elect royalists. In August 1798 Savoy was divided in half. The northern portion was combined with Geneva and annexed to the French Republic in April to create the new Département du Léman. Although the concordat between Bonaparte and Pope Pius VI reduced local opposition to the French government, tension still existed between the rural and urban populations. In addition, in the department of Léman, there was tension between the Genevois and the Savoyards.

Initially protected by the neighboring neutral Helvetian (Swiss) Republic, Savoy became threatened once Austria reached an agreement with Britain (partners in the Second Coalition) by which the former could violate the Helvetian Republic's neutrality, though this was not to come to pass for more than a decade. In late December 1813 an Austrian army of 12,000 men under *Feldmarschalleutnant* Ferdinand Bubna Graf von Litic captured Geneva, moving into northern Savoy in January 1814. In February Marshal Pierre Augereau led a counterattack that drove the Austrians back to Geneva. The following month, the Austrians launched a new offensive, capturing all of Savoy by April. By the first Treaty of Paris of May 1814, most of Savoy was returned to Sardinia, leaving Chambéry and Annecy to France. During the Hundred Days, Marshal Louis Suchet invaded Savoy, driving out the Sardinians by mid-June. In late June an Austrian-Sardinian army of 30,000 men under Bubna in turn pushed Suchet back, occupying all of Savoy by early July. With the second Treaty of Paris of November 1815, all of Savoy was returned to Sardinia.

Kenneth G. Johnson

See also Augereau, Pierre-François-Charles; Cherasco, Armistice at; Concordat; Dumouriez, Charles François

Dupérier; Kellermann, François Etienne Christophe "the Elder"; Levée en Masse; National Guard (French); Paris, First Treaty of; Paris, Second Treaty of; Pius VI, Pope; Sardinia; Suchet, Louis-Gabriel

References and further reading
Nicolas, Jean. 1989. *La Révolution française dans les Alpes, Dauphiné et Savoie, 1789–1799*. Toulouse: Privat.
Palluel-Guillard, André. 1999. *L'Aigle et la Croix: Genève et la Savoie, 1798–1815*. Saint-Gingolph: Cabédita.
Rabut, Elisabeth. 1989. *La Savoie du Nord et la Révolution*. Annecy: Archives départementales de la Haute-Savoie.
Roux, Xavier. 1892. *L'invasion de la Savoie et du Dauphiné par les autrichiens en 1813 et 1814*. Grenoble: Baratier.

Saxon Army

Generally regarded as a mediocre fighting force, the Saxon Army fought extensively throughout the Napoleonic Wars, almost entirely in the capacity of an ally of the French. The army of this impoverished central European electorate played only a minor role in the War of the First Coalition, in which it served on the Rhine front. It did not see action again until 1806, and then only as an uneasy ally of Prussia. Like the army of its much more powerful neighbor, the Saxon Army continued to wear uniforms and employ tactics practically unchanged since the end of the Seven Years' War (1756–1763). In 1806 the army numbered 19,000 men, organized into one battalion of the elite Leib-Grenadier Garde and twelve regiments of the line, all dressed in white coats, belts, and breeches, with black gaiters and bicorn hats—straight out of the age of Frederick the Great. The cavalry was variously composed between 1806 and 1815, but at the beginning of this period comprised four heavy (cuirassier) and five light (*chevauléger*, uhlan, and hussar) cavalry regiments. There were also foot and horse artillery batteries, a corps of engineers, and garrison infantry.

The Saxons fought at the decisive Battle of Jena, where they acquitted themselves well, but changed sides after the campaign, joining the group of central European states bound in alliance with France known as the Confederation of the Rhine. As a newly created kingdom, Saxony sent a small contingent to fight in the 1807 campaign against Prussia and Russia, where it performed well at the siege of Danzig, and at the battles of Heilsberg and Friedland.

In 1809 the army expanded with the raising of two battalions of light infantry and one of *Jägers* (riflemen). The entire Saxon Army participated in the campaign of that year against Austria, forming IX Corps of the Grande Armée, and consisting of 15,500 infantry, 2,500 cavalry, and 38 guns, under Marshal Jean-Baptiste Bernadotte. The Saxons fought at Linz and at Wagram, where on the first day of action, 5 July, in conjunction with French units, Saxon infantry ejected the Austrians from Raasdorf before proceeding to Aderklaa, where they were confronted by Austrian cuirassiers deployed for a charge. Inexplicably, while the whole of the Saxon cavalry prepared to counter this threat, about 400 men of the Prinz Clemens Chevauxlégers galloped forward alone, only to be repulsed by their opponents, who met them with pistols at 30 meters. When the remaining Saxon cavalry attacked, the Austrians received them in similar fashion, but were driven off. Curiously, one squadron of Saxon chevauxlégers and a regiment of Austrian cuirassiers shared the same regimental proprietor (*Inhaber*), Duke Albrecht.

Around sundown, however, the infantry ran into trouble. As dusk fell, men from a retreating French division accidentally mistook two Saxon battalions in General Pierre Louis Dupas's division for Austrians (both sides wearing white uniforms) and fired on them, inflicting severe casualties. The two units broke up, some scattering into buildings near Wagram and others fleeing to the rear. This precipitated a rout of both French and Saxon units, which only ended when the retreating mass reached Raasdorf, the position held by Napoleon's Imperial Guard.

When Bernadotte later attacked with IX Corps around 9:00 P.M., great confusion ensued when Saxon units, sent into the streets of Wagram amid burning buildings—dressed in white and calling out in German like their foes—were frequently fired on by friendly units. More Saxon units were sent in at 10:30 under *Generalmajor* Hartitzsch, but, unaware that his countrymen were already fighting in the village, his men, as before mistaking them for Austrians, spent several minutes shooting down friendly troops emerging from the village as fresh Austrians engaged the beleaguered Saxons from the other side. Convinced that they were under attack from both front and rear, cohesion among the Saxons broke down entirely, and they fled in panic to Aderklaa around 11:00, leaving large numbers of their wounded comrades behind.

On the second day of the battle, on 6 July, things deteriorated even further for the Saxons. Before dawn Bernadotte had, without orders, withdrawn IX Corps from its vulnerable position at Aderklaa to a more secure position southeast of the village. This enabled the Austrians to occupy the undefended village around 3:00 A.M. without opposition. Napoleon, furious with Bernadotte for abandoning the place, ordered Marshal André Masséna to retake it. The Saxon element of the attack was to advance between Aderklaa and Wagram. Masséna's attack was initially successful, but the second Austrian line remained steadfast, and issued such devastating musket fire that both French and Saxons retreated for the rear, some taking cover in Aderklaa. Farther to the right, as the

Saxons were withdrawing, Austrian light cavalry charged, causing a panic and flight toward Raasdorf, where the Saxons halted only after Napoleon's personal intervention. The Emperor and Bernadotte proceeded to argue furiously over the circumstances of the retreat, and Napoleon became livid when Bernadotte, in a declaration made to his troops after the battle, not only failed to mention their retreat, but congratulated them on their part in the victory, dubious though it was. Notwithstanding Bernadotte's assertions, the Saxons' reputation was badly damaged by their conduct at Wagram.

In 1810 the Saxon Army was reduced in size to about 14,000 men, including the disbanding of one heavy cavalry regiment. However, 20,000 men took part in the Russian campaign in 1812, nearly all in French general Jean Reynier's VII Corps, with detached units in IX Corps. The superb heavy cavalry—regarded as among the best mounted formations in Europe, consisting of the Garde du Corps and Zastrow Cuirassiers—were brigaded with Poles under General Johann von Thielmann in General Jean Thomas Lorge's 7th Cuirassier Division. A light cavalry regiment of chevauxlégers was brigaded with Bavarians in General Emmanuel, marquis de Grouchy's III Reserve Cavalry Corps. The Saxon infantry of Klengel's brigade, numbering about 2,400 men, fought a fierce action on 27 July at Kobryn, where they were surprised and overwhelmed amid the fiery ruins of the town by 12,000 Russians to whom they surrendered when their ammunition was exhausted. Other units fought at Pruszana and Gorodeczno from 10 to 12 August, but it is the conduct of the heavy cavalry three weeks later that is best remembered.

The Garde du Corps and Zastrows greatly distinguished themselves on 7 September at the exceedingly bloody Battle of Borodino, where they lost half their number of 850 men when most of the squadrons charged directly over the breastworks of General Nikolay Rayevsky's "Great" Redoubt, many falling into the ditch or forcing their way through the embrasures. Other squadrons entered the redoubt by the southern entrance and charged Russian infantry in the ravine behind it. When one of Napoleon's staff officers declared the Saxons to be inside the redoubt, the Emperor indignantly attributed victory to the 5th (French) Cuirassiers—almost certainly an unfair verdict.

As VII Corps did not penetrate deep into Russia, the Saxons did not suffer the horrendous losses experienced by most of the Grande Armée. The regiments of heavy cavalry, being attached to other corps, however, were reduced to a mere 20 officers and 7 men, and another 48 lost as prisoners, while the light cavalry lost all but 26 officers and men, the survivors being captured together while attempting to cross the Berezina River.

Rain having rendered small arms fire impossible, Saxon infantry (left) use musket butts and bayonets to defend the churchyard at Grossbeeren against a Prussian onslaught on 23 August 1813. (Painting by Richard Knötel from *Die deutschen Befreiungskriege* by Hermann Müller-Bohn, 1913)

Saxony was unable to field a force for the spring campaign of 1813, Reynier's VII Corps comprising only a single weak French division, even though most of the campaign of that year was fought on Saxon soil. However, by the time the armistice of 1813 was over in mid-August, the 24th Division had been reconstituted under General von Lecoq, still a part of VII Corps, comprising ten battalions of infantry, totaling 5,967 men, plus 12 guns and 452 artillerists. Action came swiftly for the Saxons, when at Grossbeeren on 23 August in a heavy downpour the Franco-Saxon VII Corps (18,000) under Marshal Nicolas Oudinot was overwhelmed by General Friederich von Bülow's 38,000 Prussians. Sahr's division of Saxons stormed the burning village and forced out three defending Prussian battalions. Perceiving action then to be at an end, Reynier pitched camp, only to find Bülow's artillery raining shot down on him. After a lengthy exchange of fire, two Prussian divisions, well exceeding Reynier's force, attacked Grossbeeren, forcing back the French and engaging some of the Saxons in hand-to-hand fighting near the town's windmill, the rain making musket fire difficult. The Saxon defense collapsed, encouraging French divisions to retreat as well. Reynier retreated, but the Prussians were

too exhausted to pursue. Saxon morale never recovered from Grossbeeren, and their conduct influenced Oudinot's decision to abandon his offensive against Berlin.

The Saxons next saw action against the Prussians at a particularly fierce battle at Dennewitz on 6 September. In the course of the battle, Bülow took the village of Göhlsdorf, which was retaken by the French around 3:30, but when Marshal Michel Ney ordered Oudinot to shift some of his men to Rohrbeck to support Ney's right flank, Reynier strongly objected and called for reinforcements. This call was ignored. Bülow consequently retook Göhlsdorf and drove out the Saxons. The arrival of fresh Russians and Swedes later in the day obliged Reynier to retreat toward Oehna where, together with the rest of Oudinot's army, the retreat disintegrated into a rout, with Saxon morale completely broken.

Reynier's report of 15 September called for considerable reinforcements, emphasizing a particular need for French, rather than Saxon, troops, while Ney warned that the Saxons were likely to switch sides as soon as an opportunity presented itself. As a result of high rates of desertion and heavy losses, the 24th Division was disbanded, and its remnants merged with the survivors of the 25th Division.

Notwithstanding the generally poor quality of line regiments, there was also present the elite Grenadier Guard battalion and the reconstituted Zastrow Cuirassiers and Garde du Corps, who possessed a special attachment to Napoleon, quite in contrast to their compatriots in the infantry and light cavalry.

At the Battle of Leipzig, the resurrected 24th Division (VII Corps), totaling 3,679 men under General von Zeschau, consisted of ten battalions of infantry and sixteen guns. General Lessing commanded the heavy cavalry brigade of eight squadrons of Zastrows and Garde du Corps. The Saxons arrived at the battle on the second day (17 October) from Düben, to be deployed in and around the village of Paunsdorf, between the northern and southern sectors of the battle area. On the eighteenth, without warning, most of the 24th Division, together with the light cavalry in VII Corps, defected to the Allies, soon followed by the Württemberg cavalry and the remaining Saxons. This obliged the French to try to control the damage with a series of cavalry attacks, but the situation could not be stabilized, and the remaining French units in the area withdrew to Stötteritz. This episode did little to affect what had already become a clear Allied victory, but it marked the end of Saxony's military role as a French ally—a decision the Saxons had made two days before—and signaled the collapse of the Confederation of the Rhine.

On 19 October General von Ryssel assumed command of the Saxon division, which was ordered to Torgau, where it blockaded the city with a Prussian corps under General Tauentzien. The city capitulated on 14 November, after which the Saxons marched to Merseburg for reorganization. Thereafter Saxon forces took part in a few minor operations in Germany until the end of the war in April 1814. It must nevertheless be noted that the Saxon heavy cavalry regiments remained fiercely loyal to Napoleon. The Allies' resulting severe reprisals against Saxony in answer to the heavy cavalry's continued service to the Emperor left Napoleon little choice but to discharge the men, who eventually agreed to return home, but not before strong protests and dramatic scenes of lamentation.

After Napoleon returned from Elba the Saxon Army was mobilized, but trouble erupted when Saxon soldiers who had found themselves serving in the Prussian army as a result of the division of Saxony by the Congress of Vienna began to organize a rebellion on 2 May 1815, demanding reunification. To avoid further trouble between Prussian and Saxon units, the latter were reassigned to the (Austrian) Army of the Upper Rhine where, after performing minor services, they returned to Saxony on 20 November.

Gregory Fremont-Barnes

See also Armistice of 1813; Berezina, Actions and Crossing at the; Bernadotte, Jean-Baptiste-Jules; Borodino, Battle of; Bülow von Dennewitz, Friedrich Wilhelm Graf; Confederation of the Rhine; Dennewitz, Battle of; Fifth Coalition, War of the; First Coalition, War of the; Fourth Coalition, War of the; Friedland, Battle of; Germany, Campaign in; Grossbeeren, Battle of; Grouchy, Emmanuel, marquis de; Heilsberg, Battle of; Jena, Battle of; Jena-Auerstädt Campaign; Leipzig, Battle of; Masséna, André; Ney, Michel; Oudinot, Nicolas Charles; Rayevsky, Nikolay Nikolayevich, Count; Reynier, Jean Louis Ebénézer, comte; Rhine Campaigns (1792–1797); Russian Campaign; Saxony; Thielmann, Johann Amadeus Freiherr von; Vienna, Congress of; Wagram, Battle of

References and further reading
Bowden, Scott. 1990. *Napoleon's Grande Armée of 1813*. Chicago: Emperor's.
Gill, John. 1992. *With Eagles to Glory: Napoleon and His German Allies in the 1809 Campaign*. London: Greenhill.
Nafziger, George. 1991. *Poles and Saxons of the Napoleonic Wars*. Chicago: Emperor's.
Partridge, Richard, and Michael Oliver. 2002. *Napoleonic Army Handbook*. Vol. 2, *The French Army and Her Allies*. London: Constable.
Pivka, Otto von. 1979. *Napoleon's German Allies*. Vol. 3, *Saxony, 1806–1815*. London: Osprey.
Smith, Digby. 2001. *1813 Leipzig: Napoleon and the Battle of the Nations*. London: Greenhill.

Saxony

At the outbreak of the great struggle between Revolutionary France and the German states of the Holy Roman Empire in 1792, Saxony was a state of 15,185 square miles with a population of nearly 2 million, comprising several territories that did not form a homogeneous entity. It included two parts of Lusatia, as well as Querfurt, Hennenberg, Naumburg, and Mesremburg; each territory had a separate government and diet (parliament). Its ruler, Frederick Augustus, assumed the throne in 1763 as Elector of Saxony, but only started to rule personally in 1768 when he turned eighteen.

In 1785 Saxony joined the Fürstenbund, a German League of Princes under the leadership of the king of Prussia directed against the Holy Roman Emperor, Joseph II, but remained neutral during the clash between Austria and Prussia in 1790. The following year Frederick Augustus declined the crown of Poland.

In February 1792 Saxony refused to join the league established by Austria and Prussia that sought to restore absolute monarchy in France. Yet after the war broke out in April, the 6,000-strong Saxon Army joined the struggle in October, fulfilling its duty to the Holy Roman (or German) Empire. Even after the Peace of Basle was signed in April 1795, Frederick Augustus continued the war until the Saxons were forced to retreat by the advance of French forces under General Jean-Baptiste Jourdan, which moved into central Germany in August 1796.

Saxony remained neutral in 1805 during the War of the Third Coalition between France and her allies on the one hand, and Austria, Russia, Sweden, and Britain on the other. A year later, in 1806, Saxon troops joined Prussia in the new coalition against France. Both German powers suffered badly in the battles of Jena and Auerstädt, and large parts of Saxony were occupied by the French army, which enforced the introduction of numerous French reforms there. On 11 December Saxony signed the Treaty of Posen with Napoleon, by which Saxony agreed to pay a contribution of 25 million francs and joined the Confederation of the Rhine. Saxony also promised a contingent of 20,000 men to Napoleon. At the same time, thanks to Napoleon, Frederick Augustus was elevated to the title of King of Saxony. In territorial terms, Saxony annexed Cottbus from Prussia, while losing minor lands in the west to the new Kingdom of Westphalia. It is estimated that Saxony's population numbered 2.27 million in 1810.

After the Peace of Tilsit in July 1807, when the Polish state was restored by Napoleon in the rump form of the Duchy of Warsaw, Frederick Augustus became its grand duke. As a loyal ally of Napoleon, Saxony provided troops for his campaign against Russia and Prussia in 1807 and against Austria in 1809. However, Frederick Augustus's loyalty was tried when Napoleon emerged defeated from the Russian campaign in 1812 and the Allied armies entered Saxony—which became the main battleground of the new campaign—in the spring of the following year. Even then the king refused to fight against Napoleon and fled to Prague, although he withdrew his troops from the French army. Following Napoleon's victory at Lützen in May, the Saxon army once more stood at the side of the French emperor. During the Battle of Leipzig in October 1813 a number of Saxon regiments deserted and joined the Allies. The king himself was taken prisoner in Leipzig after the battle.

Thereafter, Saxony was ruled by a provisional government under the Russian prince Nikolay Grigorievich Repnin-Volkonsky, and later the Prussian generals Eberhard Friedrich Freiherr von der Recke and von Gaudi. At the Congress of Vienna, Frederick Augustus was allowed to retain his royal title and rule Saxony, which lost three-fifths of its territory to Prussia. About 7,800 square miles with 864,400 inhabitants were incorporated by Prussia, leaving 5,790 square miles and 1,182,750 inhabitants with Saxony.

Jakub Basista

See also Auerstädt, Battle of; Basle, Treaties of; Confederation of the Rhine; Fifth Coalition, War of the; Fourth Coalition, War of the; Germany, Campaign in; Holy Roman Empire; Jena, Battle of; Jourdan, Jean-Baptiste; Leipzig, Battle of; Lützen, Battle of; Poland; Russian Campaign; Saxon Army; Third Coalition, War of the; Tilsit, Treaties of; Vienna, Congress of; Westphalia

References and further reading
Blackbourn, David. 2002. *History of Germany, 1780–1918: The Long Nineteenth Century.* Oxford: Blackwell.
Carsten, F. L. 1959. *Princes and Parliaments in Germany.* Oxford: Oxford University Press.
Gill, John H. 1992. *With Eagles to Glory: Napoleon and His German Allies in the 1809 Campaign.* London: Greenhill.
Hofschröer, Peter. 1993. *Leipzig 1813: The Battle of the Nations.* London: Osprey.
Pivka, Otto von. 1979. *Napoleon's German Allies: Saxony, 1806–15.* London: Osprey.

Scharnhorst, Gerhard Johann David von (1755–1813)

Prussian general whose work to reform his nation and its army and whose service as chief of staff to Gebhard Lebrecht von Blücher helped to vanquish Napoleon and to establish Prussia as the most formidable military power of the late nineteenth century. A liberal intellectual, Scharnhorst sought to bring modernity to Prussia and its army. Although he was unable to accomplish the loftiest of his goals, he managed to take an antiquated army and institutionalize the means by which it regained its vitality and served as a model to future generations of military professionals.

Neither Prussian nor noble by birth, Scharnhorst did not develop the proclivities that prevented the development of a professional outlook in so many Junker officers. Born 12 November 1755 at Bordenau, near Hanover, Scharnhorst had a soldier as a father, but not a commissioned officer. After formal education at the cadet school of Wilhelm Graf von Schaumburg-Lippe, Scharnhorst was commissioned into the Hanoverian Army. As a young officer, he gained a good reputation as a military essayist and as a competent leader. Campaigning in Flanders in 1793–1794 during the French Revolutionary Wars, he won acclaim for his conduct in the defense of Menin. He was rewarded for his services with a promotion to major and the position of chief of staff to the commander in chief of the Hanoverian Army.

In 1801 Scharnhorst sought greater opportunities than the Hanoverian Army could offer and took a commission as a lieutenant colonel in the Prussian Army. Posted to the staff of the quartermaster general, he was fittingly assigned the task of overseeing and improving institutions of military education. In addition to his formal duties, Scharnhorst quickly established the Militärische Gesellschaft (a military discussion society) as a forum for serving officers to contemplate the state of their profession. A keen observer of military developments, Scharnhorst was quick to recognize that the French were at the forefront of a revolution in military affairs. Thus, even before Napoleon had reached the apex of his power, Scharnhorst was aware that Prussia's security was based on a host of outdated practices.

Despite gaining a patent of nobility as a condition of his joining the Prussian Army, Scharnhorst had difficulty gaining wide acceptance for his ideas. Advocating such revolutionary concepts as combined arms divisions, a popular militia, and an expandable national army, Scharnhorst put himself at odds with many of Prussia's career soldiers. To an officer corps dominated by Junkers committed to preserving their place of honor in the army made famous by Frederick the Great, Scharnhorst was an interloper who championed unwelcome changes to the system. Lacking the physical stature or family name requisite for gaining instant respect, he needed the battles of Jena and Auerstädt to give currency to his ideas.

When Prussia went to war in 1806, it did so with a proud martial heritage and little else. The senior command was dominated by old men who were either unwilling or unable to note that the world had changed around them. The army, as Scharnhorst had observed, was mired in antiquated practices and in no way ready for a contest with the most capable fighting force of the time. On 14 October, Scharnhorst was at Auerstädt, serving as chief of staff to Charles William, Duke of Brunswick. Despite commanding the largest portion of the Prussian army and fighting against the numerically inferior corps of Marshal Louis Davout, Brunswick's Prussians were ultimately routed. Scharnhorst had exercised little, if any, influence on the duke, who fell mortally wounded in the fighting.

When the battle ended, however, Scharnhorst was given the opportunity to display his genius for operational matters by assuming the role of chief of staff to General Gebhard von Blücher. The partnership proved effective, and Blücher's retreating force acquitted itself far better than most of the other remnants of the Prussian army. When Blücher surrendered at Ratkau, in the vicinity of Lübeck, on 24 November, both he and Scharnhorst were marched off into a brief period of captivity. Scharnhorst was later repatriated in a prisoner exchange and saw further action at the Battle of Eylau on 8 February 1807. Indeed, in that battle he played a key role in delivering the Prussian attack that prevented the French from achieving a clear-cut victory.

Scharnhorst's most dramatic contribution to the Prussian Army was not his valor in battle, but rather the work he undertook as the leader of the Military Reorganization Commission. After the battles of Jena and Auerstädt, the defects of the Prussian military system were painfully obvious to even the most casual observer. In July 1807, King Frederick William III appointed Scharnhorst, now a major general, to preside over a general reform of the Prussian Army. Scharnhorst, along with Colonel August von Gneisenau, Major Karl von Grolman, Major Her-

mann von Boyen, and the civilian Heinrich Freiherr vom und zum Stein, led a process that reinvigorated the army and established the institutions needed to make it effective. As Prussia abolished serfdom, the reformers sought to appeal to the common man's nascent sense of Prussian nationalism as a means to motivate an army of citizen-soldiers. The reformers abolished the harsh disciplinary measures of the old army and endeavored to end the stifling influence of the Junkers by opening the officer corps to men of talent and basing promotions on merit. They reorganized the various branches of the army into effective combined arms brigades and created the *Landwehr,* a national militia. With the establishment of what would become the Berlin *Kriegsakademie* (War College), Scharnhorst and his followers also set the foundation for the development of a trained and truly modern general staff.

When Prussia returned to war in 1813, it fielded a vastly improved army from the one that had been humiliated in 1806. As chief of staff to Blücher in 1813, Scharnhorst was able to direct the efforts of the force he had essentially created. Although his tenure as chief of staff was brief, he established the standard for the future conduct of that most important post. Wounded during an assault at Grossgörschenon 2 May 1813, at the Battle of Lützen, Scharnhorst died on 8 June from infection.

Charles Steele

See also Auerstädt, Battle of; Blücher von Wahlstatt, Gebhard Lebrecht Fürst; Brunswick, Charles William Ferdinand, Duke of; Davout, Louis Nicolas; Eylau, Battle of; Fourth Coalition, War of the; Frederick William III, King; Germany, Campaign in; Gneisenau, August Wilhelm Anton Graf Neidhardt von; Jena, Battle of; Jena-Auerstädt Campaign; Lützen, Battle of; Prussia; Prussian Army; Stein, Heinrich Friedrich Karl Freiherr vom und zum

References and further reading
Chandler, David G. 1995. *The Campaigns of Napoleon.* London: Weidenfeld and Nicolson.
Craig, Gordon A. 1964. *The Politics of the Prussian Army: 1640–1945.* London: Oxford University Press.
Dupuy, Colonel T. N. 1984. *A Genius for War: The German Army and General Staff, 1807–1945.* Fairfax, VA: Hero.
Goerlitz, Walter. 1953. *History of the German General Staff: 1657–1945.* New York: Praeger.
Paret, Peter. 1966. *Yorck and the Era of Prussian Reform: 1807–1815.* Princeton: Princeton University Press.
Rosinski, Herbert. 1966. *The German Army.* New York: Praeger.

Schérer, Barthélemy Louis Joseph (1747–1804)

A French Revolutionary general, tactician, and war minister, Schérer was victorious at Loano in 1795 and laid the basis for Bonaparte's first Italian campaign.

Born in Alsace, Schérer volunteered for the Austrian Army in 1760 as an infantry *kadett* (cadet). Wounded at Torgau that November, he rose to lieutenant by 1764. After serving as an aide-de-camp (ADC) from 1770, he resigned in 1775, but joined the French Army as a captain in the Strasbourg Provincial Artillery regiment in April 1780. Permitted to join the Dutch Army in February 1785, he was appointed a major in the Maillebois Legion before becoming an ADC to the Dutch chief of staff from February 1789. Despite promotion to lieutenant colonel, he resigned in March 1790 and rejoined the French Army. Appointed a captain in the 82nd Infantry regiment in January 1792, he was employed as an ADC by General Jean Etienne de Prez de Crassier in the Armée du Midi from May and then by Prince Eugène de Beauharnais in the Armée du Rhin, where he was promoted to *chef de bataillon* and made a staff *adjutant général* in July 1793.

Promoted to *général de brigade* that September, Schérer advanced to *général de division* in January 1794. Transferred to the Armée du Nord in April, he participated in the victory at Mont Palisel on 1 July, before commanding a division in the Armée de Sambre-et-Meuse, which took Landrecies, Quesnoy, Valenciennes, and Condé during July and August. Commanding a division, Schérer led the right wing in the victory at Spiremont on 18 September. He led the Armée d'Italie from November 1794 to May 1795, when he took command of the Armée des Pyrénées Orientales (Eastern Pyrenees). After victory over the Spanish at the river Fluvia on 15 June, he was reappointed commander of the Armée d'Italie in September. His autumn advance brought victory against the Austro-Piedmontese army at Loano on 23–29 November. He resigned, but was only relieved by Bonaparte in March 1796, following which he was appointed inspector of cavalry in the Armée d'Intérieur in June and in the Armée du Rhin-et-Moselle from February 1797. During his tenure as minister of war (July 1797–February 1799), he was widely accused of corruption and drunkenness, until he returned to the Armée d'Italie in March 1799. He was victorious at Pastrengo on 26 March, but was defeated in April by the Austrians at Verona and Magnano. On 26 April, defeat by Field Marshal Alexander Suvorov on the Adige River brought his retirement.

His army instructions, drafted over the winter of 1795–1796, formed the basis of Bonaparte's system in 1796. Following General Jean-Baptiste Kléber, he emphasized attacks in massed battalion columns with bayonets lowered. In line, the infantry would fight in two ranks, supported by small flank columns. Schérer was the first French general to establish a formalized military espionage system, directed by an *adjoint* (assistant staff officer).

David Hollins

See also Beauharnais, Eugène Rose de; Espionage; Fluvia, Battles of the; Italian Campaigns (1792–1797); Italian Campaigns (1799–1800); Kléber, Jean-Baptiste; Loano, Battle of; Magnano, Battle of; Pyrenean Campaigns (1793–1795); Suvorov, Alexander Vasilievich; Verona, Battle of
References and further reading
Griffith, Paddy. 1998. *The Art of War in Revolutionary France, 1789–1802*. London: Greenhill.
Six, Georges. 1937. *Les généraux de la Révolution et l'Empire*. Paris: Bordas.

Schill, Ferdinand Baptista von (1776–1809)

A Prussian patriot who rebelled against Napoleon's occupation of his country, Ferdinand von Schill was born on 5 June 1776 at Wilsdorf-bei-Dresden, Saxony, to Johann Georg von Schill, a Prussian Army officer who had served in the Seven Years' War (1756–1763). Schill attended school in Breslau, in Silesia. He exhibited severe behavioral problems due to his excessive energy and introvert personality. In his boyhood he demonstrated talent with his poetry; he lived in his own rather romanticized world. To rectify this condition, he joined the Brown Hussars of the Prussian Army at age twelve.

As a second lieutenant of the Ansbach-Bayreuther Dragoons, Schill suffered a severe head wound at the Battle of Jena on 14 October 1806 against the French. He escaped and convalesced at Kolberg (Kołobrzeg in present-day Poland), near the Baltic coast. His lengthy convalescence provided Schill with an acute knowledge of the area.

After his recovery, Schill reported to the commander of the fortress at Kolberg, who concurred with Schill's wish to remain in the vicinity to observe and familiarize himself with the area in order to be of use in a future military context. Schill became commander of the Hussar Volunteers. He took part in the heroic siege of Kolberg against the French from 20 March to 2 July 1806.

On 9 July 1807 France and Prussia signed the Peace of Tilsit, France and Russia having concluded their own treaty of peace two days earlier. This humiliating and detrimental treaty led to a loss of over 50 percent of Prussia's territory. Moreover, Prussia had to pay a financially crippling war indemnity. The once-mighty kingdom became a vassal of France.

Schill was promoted to major in 1809 and received command of the 2nd Hussar Regiment, which he formed with his Kolberg troops. Meanwhile, Prussians underwent enlightened social, economic, and military reforms under Heinrich Freiherr vom und zum Stein and General Gerhard von Scharnhorst. These reforms instilled patriotic sentiments throughout Prussia and created a widely held belief in the imminence of a war of liberation that would free all Germans from the hated French occupation.

Not realizing that this belief was erroneous, Schill left Berlin on 28 April with his 600-strong Brandenburg Hussar Regiment, telling his troops they would aim to reestablish Prussia's glory and engage in a war of liberation against the French. Schill had not received the consent of King Frederick William III, who ordered his return to Berlin. When Schill refused, the king declared Schill and his men deserters. While marching to the river Elbe through Saxony, he frightened the locals, who offered scant support. However, Schill was joined on 2 May by 300 Prussian infantry from Berlin who were disillusioned with the slow evolution of the political situation.

Schill notified the Duke of Anhalt-Coethen that his regiment was an advance guard for the 14,000 troops under General Gebhard von Blücher, whose fanatical hatred of the French was well known. The duke wrote to the King of Westphalia, Jérôme Bonaparte, who in turn ordered General François Kellermann to prepare for a widening revolt. Jérôme later discovered that Blücher was not going to arrive and that Schill had been declared a traitor by the Prussian king.

Meanwhile Schill seized the town of Halle, where the troops stole the payroll. Jérôme was determined that Schill should be stopped. He sent 4,000 Dutch troops to Magdeburg and a Dutch division to Göttingen, while 1,500 troops were stationed between Lübeck and Hamburg.

On 5 May 1809, Schill's troops engaged in a military encounter near Dodendorf with the Westphalian and French garrisons that protected the fortress of Magdeburg. Schill was confronted by 400 Westphalian troops and a French light infantry company. The Prussians gained the upper hand, taking 200 prisoners, but losing 13 officers and 70 men of their own.

On 24 May, however, Schill's men were completely surrounded by 5,000 Dutch and Danish troops at Damgarten near Wismar. After some ferocious fighting, Schill and his force escaped to Stralsund, in Pomerania (an originally Swedish province ceded to France in 1807), which they captured. Jérôme ordered his generals to pursue Schill. On the thirty-first, Schill's regiment was almost completely annihilated during vicious street fighting against Dutch forces. Schill himself was killed by a saber blow. Recapturing Stralsund was an important strategic victory for Napoleon; it prevented the British from using it as a base for a landing.

Only a few of Schill's men escaped to Prussia. The majority of his remaining troops were caught, and many were imprisoned in France. Eleven of Schill's officers endured a military tribunal that found them guilty of desertion. They were shot at Wesel on 16 September.

Schill's body was buried at St. Jürgen Cemetery in Stralsund. However, there had been a 10,000-franc price on Schill's head. It was severed from his body, preserved, and delivered to Jérôme. In 1837 Schill's head was found in the Anatomical Museum in Leiden and returned to Prussia, where it was buried among his officers in Braunschweig. Schill's family name died out after the death of his niece. After Germany was unified, Schill's reputation was rehabilitated, and he was deemed a patriot. His deserter status was revoked. The 1st Silesian Leib-Hussar Regiment was named after him in 1889, and plays were written in his honor. Three monuments to him can be found in Wesel, Brunswick, and Stralsund, respectively. His exploits are remembered in a folk song learned by German schoolchildren.

Annette E. Richardson

See also Blücher von Wahlstatt, Gebhard Lebrecht Fürst; Bonaparte, Jérôme; Fourth Coalition, War of the; Frederick William III, King; Jena, Battle of; Kellermann, François Etienne "the Younger," comte; Scharnhorst, Gerhard Johann David von; Stein, Heinrich Friedrich Karl Freiherr vom und zum; Tilsit, Treaties of

References and further reading
Ernstberger, Anton. 1957. "Ferdinand von Schills Nachlass." *Bayerische Akademie der Wissenshaften,* no. 11.
Ferdinand von Schill: Freiheitskämpfer und Held: Dramtisches Gedicht in fünf Akten. N.d. Breslau: Lützow.
Joubert, André. 1873. *Révolte du Major Schill d'après de documents noveaux et inédits.* Angers. N.p.
Lamar, Glenn J. 2000. *Jérôme Bonaparte: The War Years, 1800–1815.* Westport, CT: Greenwood.
Lilencro. L. K. C. von. 1810. *Schilliana: das ist, Züge und Thatsachen aus dem Leben und Charakter des preussischen Major von Schill. Von einem Unpartheischen.* Hamburg: Herold.
Treitschke, Heinrich von. 1975. *History of Germany in the Nineteenth Century: Selections from the Translation of Eden and Cedar Paul.* Chicago: University of Chicago Press.

Schiller, Friedrich von (1759–1805)

Poet, historian, and philosopher; celebrated as the greatest German playwright; along with his friend Goethe, the leading exponent of Weimar Classicism.

When, in 1792, the National Assembly awarded French citizenship to Schiller and other foreign friends of humanity, the gesture acknowledged a shared ideal and concealed a gulf in understanding. Schiller was known for having championed the spirit of rebellion and struggle for liberty in his dramas and historical narratives. Yet, like many German intellectuals who viewed the Revolution as the triumph of enlightened philosophy, he was soon disgusted by its violence. Rather than adopting a more conservative political outlook, however, he rejected political action as the solution to political problems.

The *Aesthetic Education of Man* (1795) argued that the attempt to proceed directly from the absolutist state based on force to the ideal state based on reason had produced only social collapse and barbarism. In the modern world of specialization and alienation, political conflict arose from the division of human nature into its sensual and rational components. Only the aesthetic could mediate between them and produce the harmonious human being capable of moral action and therefore of living in true freedom. Schiller returned to the problem of the Revolution in several major poems, notably the "Song of the Bell" (1800), which praised industrious order and warned against upheaval. Some commentators have seen allusions to Napoleon (whom Schiller distrusted) in the historical dramas devoted to the rebellious General Wallenstein and the false Dimitri I. At the least, leaders convinced of their own destiny provided a perfect vehicle for his continuing reflections on power, legitimation, ethics, and freedom, a process that contemporary politics may have stimulated.

Schiller's idealism and passion for liberty made him an icon for both liberals and socialists in the nineteenth century, and the centennial of his birth was marked by international celebrations. At the same time, his emphasis on inner rather than political freedom allowed appropriation by conservatives, and the "Song of the Bell" was for generations part of the canon in authoritarian German schooling.

Although Schiller's poetry has declined in popularity, his hymn "To Joy" (1785) has retained its appeal, since Beethoven employed it in the choral movement of the Ninth Symphony (1823). An instrumental setting is today the anthem of the European Union, but the humanitarianism of the text—evoking the spirit of fraternity that Schiller, like Beethoven, at first found so attractive in the Revolution—underlies the choice and is present by implication.

James Wald

See also Beethoven, Ludwig van; Goethe, Johann Wolfgang von; Kant, Immanuel; Staël, Mme Germaine de
References and further reading
Berghahn, Klaus L. 1992. "*Gedankenfreiheit.* From Political Reform to Aesthetic Revolution in Schiller's Works." In *The Internalized Revolution: German Reactions to the French Revolution, 1789–1989,* ed. Ehrhardt Bahr and Thomas P. Saine, 99–118. New York: Garland.
Schiller, Friedrich. 1959. *An Anthology for Our Time.* Trans. Jane Bannard Greene, Charles E. Passage, and Alexander Gödevon Aesch. Ed. Frederick Ungar. New York: Ungar.

Schimmelpenninck, Rutger Jan (1761–1825)

Leader of the Patriot Party and grand pensionary (president) of the Batavian Republic (formerly the Dutch Re-

public) from 1805 to 1806, Schimmelpenninck was born on 31 October 1761 in Deventer (in present-day Netherlands). His father, Gerrit, and his mother, Hermanna Koolhas, were Mennonites. The studious young Schimmelpenninck attended the elite Atheneum Illustre at Deventer. He became involved with the Patriot Party while studying Roman and contemporary law in Leiden. Schimmelpenninck graduated on 11 December 1784 and thereafter practiced law in Amsterdam. He married Catharina Nahuys on 26 August 1788. They had a son, Gerrit, and a daughter, Catharina.

By 1794 Schimmelpenninck chaired the Committee of Revolution of the Patriot Party, which was headed by Joan Derk van der Capellen, based in Zwolle, Overijssel. Van der Capellen had written a revolutionary pamphlet that spread Enlightenment ideas and French Revolutionary thought. These were readily accepted and quickly pervaded the Dutch Republic. In the 1794–1795 revolution, the Patriot Party, supported by popular sentiment, ousted William V, Prince of Orange, the Dutch Republic's general hereditary *stadtholder.*

Schimmelpenninck became president of the Amsterdam city government in 1796 and was an elected delegate to the First and Second National Assemblies (1796–1798) of the newly proclaimed Batavian Republic. In charge of creating a new constitution, he led the moderate group, which fell between the Unitarians and the Federalists. Neither group accepted the new constitution, a circumstance that led to a coup d'état in June 1798 and the establishment of a unitary government.

Schimmelpenninck served as the Batavian Republic's ambassador to France from 13 June 1798 until December 1802 and then as ambassador to Britain from 8 December 1802 until 14 June 1803, when war broke out between the two countries. He was distraught that he had failed to keep the Francophile Batavian Republic neutral, and on the resumption of war Schimmelpenninck once again became ambassador to France. Napoleon, concerned about political developments and mounting debts in the nearly bankrupt country, and wanting tighter control, forced the creation of a new government. On 29 April 1805, Napoleon appointed Schimmelpenninck councilor pensionary or grand pensionary (president) of the newly named Batavian Commonwealth for a five-year period.

Schimmelpenninck took up residence in Huis ten Bosch (the present-day palace of the queen of the Netherlands) and lived very regally, almost like a monarch, while he worked on numerous reforms. Although he was going blind and had a few other ailments, Schimmelpenninck instituted major reforms that modernized the country. He created a tax system and introduced a general tax to address the dire financial situation. He enacted expansive, beneficial health reforms, and major agricultural reforms, and he enforced water regulations and sea reclamation guidelines. His principal reform was the very advanced Education Act of 1805, which allowed equal recognition of Protestant, Catholic, and Jewish schools.

On 4 June 1806 Napoleon instigated Schimmelpenninck's resignation; the following day Louis Bonaparte was proclaimed King of Holland. He was popular and reigned until 1810, when he was also removed by Napoleon. The country became a satellite of France and adopted French reforms.

Napoleon gave Schimmelpenninck a French baronial title and appointed him to the Senate in France. In 1813 he returned to Holland and served as a member of the First Chamber from 1815 to 1820. He then retired to his estates in Overijssel province. Schimmelpenninck died in Amsterdam on 15 February 1825.

Annette E. Richardson

See also Bonaparte, Louis; Netherlands, The
References and further reading
Israel, Jonathan I. 1998. *The Dutch Republic: Its Rise, Greatness, and Fall, 1477–1806.* Oxford: Clarendon.
Palmer, R. R. 1954. "Much in Little: The Dutch Revolution of 1795." *Journal of Modern History* 26 (March): 15–35.
Schama, Simon. 1992. *Patriots and Liberators: Revolution in the Netherlands, 1780–1813.* London: Fontana.
Schuchart, Max. 1972. *The Netherlands.* New York: Walker.

Schliengen, Battle of (24 October 1796)

The Battle of Schliengen was the final major engagement during the French campaign in southern Germany in 1796. Archduke Charles made one final attempt to prevent the (French) Army of the Rhine and Moselle from escaping across the Rhine, but he was unsuccessful. With the close of the battle, campaigning ended in Germany for 1796.

When Charles defeated General Jean-Baptiste Jourdan at Amberg on 24 August, he was forced to retreat back toward the Rhine River. Charles made sure that Jourdan would be unable to return to Germany during the autumn of 1796, then turned on the southern French army under General Jean Moreau. Moreau was uncertain whether Jourdan had been defeated until 10 September, when he read newspaper accounts of the battle. He realized that he was in danger of being cut off and ordered his army to move back toward the Rhine and safety. Charles ordered various Austrian detachments to try to cut Moreau off. They succeeded in preventing all further supplies from reaching the Army of the Rhine and Moselle, forcing Moreau's men to live off the land and limit their ammunition. Moreau, however, was able to brush off several small-scale attacks. The most serious fighting occurred at Biber-

ach on 2 October. The outnumbered Austrians under *Feldmarschalleutnant* Maximillian Graf Baillet von Latour were routed by the more numerous French, opening the way for the French to pass through the Black Forest. Despite some hesitation by Moreau in deciding which route to take, the French were able to pass without incident through the Black Forest and into the Rhine River valley by 12 October.

When Moreau reached the Rhine at Breisach, he would have been able to pass over without interference, but he wanted to cross farther downstream, near Strasbourg, to block an Austrian attack into French territory. He moved slowly, allowing Charles to concentrate his entire force. While Moreau had been able to escape a few days earlier, he now was in danger of being destroyed. Several days of skirmishing, beginning on 19 October, convinced Moreau that he could not force his way through on the right, or east, bank of the Rhine. Instead, he sent one corps under General Louis Desaix across the Rhine, with orders to move on Strasbourg and threaten Charles's rear. With the rest of the army, Moreau moved upriver toward Schliengen. On 24 October, Charles's pursuit caught up with Moreau at Schliengen. Charles attacked all along the line. On the left, he managed to force the French back. The French right, however, was posted in the nearby hills, preventing the Austrians from making the best use of their well-trained troops. The right gave ground slowly during the day. Fighting ended in the early evening when pouring rain made it impossible for the soldiers to keep their powder dry. A thick fog covered the field and allowed Moreau to break away from the pursuit. His army crossed the Rhine at Hunningen on 26 October, marking the end of the campaign.

Tim J. Watts

See also Amberg, Battle of; Biberach, Battle of; Charles, Archduke of Austria, Duke of Teschen; Desaix, Louis-Charles-Antoine, chevalier de Veygoux; Jourdan, Jean-Baptiste; Moreau, Jean Victor; Rhine Campaigns (1792–1797)
References and further reading
Phipps, Ramsay Weston. 1980. *The Armies of the First French Republic and the Rise of the Marshals of Napoleon I.* Vol. 2, *The Armées de la Moselle, du Rhin, de Sambre-et-Meuse, de Rhin-et-Moselle.* London: Greenwood. (Orig. pub. 1926–1939.)
Ross, Steven T. 1973. *Quest for Victory: French Military Strategy, 1792–1799.* New York: Barnes.

Schönbrunn, Treaty of (14 October 1809)

The agreement, also known as the Treaty of Vienna, between the French and Austrian empires that concluded the War of the Fifth Coalition in 1809. Austria ceded western parts of its empire to France and France's allies in the Confederation of the Rhine, as well as ceding northeastern parts to the Duchy of Warsaw and Russia. Austria agreed to join the Continental System (the French-imposed embargo on continental trade with Britain), reduce its army to 150,000 troops, and pay an indemnity of 85 million francs.

Following the French victory over Austria at Wagram in July 1809, peace negotiations dragged on for three months until the treaty was signed at Schönbrunn Palace on 14 October. Austria ceded the provinces of Salzburg and Berchtesgaden, together with the western tip of Upper Austria, to France for subsequent transfer to Bavaria. The territories France acquired from Austria were added to the former Venetian possessions along the eastern Adriatic Sea (which France had taken from Austria under the Treaty of Pressburg in 1805) to form the Illyrian Provinces as part of the French Empire. These territories were in two parts: First, the county of Görz, the small territory of Montefalcone, the city of Trieste, the province of Carniola with its enclaves on the Adriatic, and the Villach district of Carinthia. Secondly, all the Austrian territories west of the river Save: part of Civilian Croatia, Fiume and the Hungarian Littoral, Austrian Istria and the Adriatic islands, together with the two Military Frontier Districts (Karlstadt and Banal). In addition to the territory, Napoleon gained the six Austrian *Grenzer* infantry regiments based in these Military Districts.

Austria also ceded the Lordship of Razuns, an enclave within the Graubunden (eastern Switzerland) to Napoleon. To Saxony, Austria ceded small Habsburg enclaves inside Saxony, while her gains under the Third Partition of Poland were transferred to the king of Saxony as ruler of the Duchy of Warsaw: western Galicia, except Kraków, together with the district of Zamosc in eastern Galicia, acquired by Austria under the First Partition. The most powerful French ally, Russia, was awarded the Galician district of Tarnopol (around Brody).

Obliged to break relations with Britain and, by joining the Continental System, close her ports to British trade, Austria recognized the changes of monarch in Italy and Spain, together with any future changes in Portugal. Austria was to pay the outstanding balance on the contributions of 200 million francs levied on its territories—set as an indemnity by Napoleon at 85 million francs. The Austrian Army was reduced to 150,000 men for the duration of Anglo-French hostilities, prompting the disbandment of eight infantry regiments.

The French emperor guaranteed Austria's remaining territorial integrity. The treaty was the prelude to the Austro-French alliance of 1810 and Napoleon's marriage to the Austrian emperor's daughter, Maria Ludovika

(Marie Louise). The Russian tsar, however, became anxious about an enlarged Duchy of Warsaw as a base for Polish nationalism.

David Hollins

See also Austria; Bavaria; Confederation of the Rhine; Continental System; Fifth Coalition, War of the; Marie Louise, Empress; Poland; Poland, Partitions of; Pressburg, Treaty of; Saxony; Venetian Republic; Wagram, Battle of
References and further reading
La Paix de Vienne conclué entre la France, ses Allies, et l'Autriche le 14 octobre 1809. [The Peace of Vienna concluded between France, her Allies and Austria on 14 October 1809]. 1809. Weimar.
Schroeder, Paul. 1994. *The Transformation of European Politics, 1763–1848.* New York: Oxford University Press.

Schwarzenberg, Karl Philipp Fürst zu (1771–1820)

Born into one of the most powerful noble families in the Habsburg Empire, Schwarzenberg initially pursued a distinguished military career before becoming involved in state diplomacy. More a politician than a military commander, by 1813 he was the ideal choice as both Austrian and Allied supreme commander. His victory at Leipzig in October 1813, followed by a steady advance to reach Paris in March 1814, sealed the fate of Napoleon's empire.

Born in Vienna on 18 April 1771, Karl Fürst zu Schwarzenberg came from one of the richest Austrian noble families. From an early age, he was enthusiastic about military skills and training, building up his own physique while also studying scientific subjects, including mathematics, history, and languages, but he suffered from a weak constitution. Under *Feldmarschall* Moritz Freiherr von Lacy's sponsorship, he bought an *Unterleutnant*'s commission in Infantry Regiment 10 in 1787, fighting courageously and actively in the first year of the war with Turkey in 1788 to win promotion to *Hauptmann*. Joining *Feldmarschall* Gideon Freiherr von Loudon's headquarters in 1789, he soon fell ill; when he was promoted to *Major* in 1790, Schwarzenberg briefly was on lighter duties as an officer in the Netherlands Arcieren Ceremonial Guard before returning to Vienna to expand his scientific education. After recovering, he was appointed to the Latour Dragoons in 1791 when aged just 20, but he was coolly received, as the regimental officers considered service in its ranks to be a well-earned honor, rather than a post for the well connected. Nevertheless, he managed to win some respect with his military skills and keen eye.

Promoted to *Oberstleutnant*, Schwarzenberg transferred to the Uhlan Freikorps in the following year. He led his regiment as part of the advance guard of the army com-

Prince Schwarzenberg. Although commander in chief of Allied forces in Germany during the crucial campaign of 1813, he found his authority restricted by the presence of Allied monarchs at his headquarters. (Engraving by Hassell and Rickards, 1814. The David Markham Collection)

manded by *Feldmarschall* Friedrich Josias Graf Saxe-Coburg-Saalfeld, notably at Neerwinden in March 1793 and on raids against the French. He proved his cavalry skills as the *Oberst* commanding the Zeschwitz Kurassier at the Anglo-Austrian victory at Le Cateau-Cambrésis in 1794. At the head of his regiment, he led them and twelve British cavalry squadrons in a daring charge through fog to shatter a French corps, inflicting 3,000 casualties and capturing thirty-two guns.

Fighting in Germany in 1796, Schwarzenberg led his regiment in Archduke Charles's victories at Amberg and Würzburg. Following promotion to *Generalmajor*, Schwarzenberg led formations of light infantry and cavalry in raids against the French. During the War of the Second Coalition, he again fought under Archduke Charles in 1799, leading the advance guard of the army's center at Ostrach and Stockach, before playing a key part in the storming of Mannheim. After several actions against the French general Michel Ney, he was again afflicted by illness and only returned to military service in late 1800 after promotion to *Feldmarschalleutnant*. In the defeat of Hohenlinden on 3 December, Schwarzenberg commanded a division on the right wing and courageously led them in breaking out

of imminent encirclement by the French. His prompt action led to his appointment as rearguard commander, once Archduke Charles had taken over the remains of the army later that month, but it was rather wrecked by the defeat at Hohenlinden and Charles felt he could do nothing much with it. Schwarzenberg's leadership of this rear guard, which included rescuing the artillery park, was rewarded with an additional appointment as *Inhaber* (honorary colonel) of the 2nd Uhlan Regiment.

Back in Vienna, he rejoined the diplomatic circle and on the accession of the new Russian tsar, Alexander I, in 1801, Schwarzenberg was sent to St. Petersburg as representative of Emperor Francis II (from 1806 changed to Francis I of Austria) for the Holy Roman Empire and Austria. Briefly appointed vice president of the Hofkriegsrat (the supreme military administration) in March 1805, he commanded a korps in Germany in the War of the Third Coalition, fighting at Günzburg and the victory at Haslach on 11 October, which was decided by his charge with two regiments of cuirassiers. Three days later, as Napoleon's Grande Armée began to encircle the Austrian army under the de facto command of *Feldmarschalleutnant* Karl Mack Freiherr von Leiberich, Schwarzenberg commanded twelve cavalry squadrons when the nominal army commander, Archduke Ferdinand d'Este, abandoned Mack and led what cavalry he could muster away from the imminent disaster. In a difficult march through enemy lines, Schwarzenberg commanded the rear guard until the survivors reached Cheb in Bohemia on 21 October. Summoned to Vienna from his sickbed, Schwarzenberg accompanied Emperor Francis II to Moravia, where he often spoke out against any hasty plans for an early battle and was vindicated by the Allied defeat at Austerlitz.

In virtual retirement because of ill health until late 1808, Schwarzenberg supported Archduke John in creating the *Landwehr* (reserve militia), which he believed was vital to raise enough manpower to defeat the French. Later that year, his political career again came to the fore as he returned to St. Petersburg as ambassador. His mission was to persuade Alexander either to join an alliance with Austria or to at least remain neutral in any future war between Austria and France. Despite his persuasive skills and tact, Schwarzenberg was only able to return with a message from the tsar advising Austria to act with caution.

When war broke out again in 1809 with Russia and France, Schwarzenberg returned from St. Petersburg in June, reaching the emperor's headquarters two days before the Battle of Wagram (5–6 July), in which he was assigned the command of a Reserve Korps cavalry division. His expert handling of the rearguard actions in the subsequent retreat to Znaim won him promotion to *General der Kavallerie* on 22 September. Selected as Austrian ambassador to

Paris, he deployed his natural charm to ingratiate himself with Napoleon and assist the new Austrian foreign minister, Klemens Graf Metternich, in negotiating the marriage of the French emperor to Emperor Francis's eldest daughter, Maria Ludovika (Marie Louise). Schwarzenberg hosted a ball at his Paris residence in honor of the bride on 1 July 1810, but the event tragically ended in a fire, which killed his sister-in-law.

After negotiating the arrangements for the 30,000-strong (Austrian) Auxiliary Korps to join Napoleon's 1812 invasion of Russia, Schwarzenberg was the natural choice as its commander after Archduke Charles refused the appointment. Commanding the korps on the southern flank of the Grande Armée, Schwarzenberg was promoted to *Feldmarschall* on Napoleon's recommendation and would be the only Austrian general ever to use a French-style baton. He was soon given additional command over the defeated VII (Saxon) Corps by Napoleon and rallied his forces to beat the Russians under General Alexander Tormasov at Podubnic (Gorodechnya) on 12 August. After holding larger Russian forces at bay that autumn, Schwarzenberg led his men back across the Pripet Marshes on the retreat following Napoleon's disaster at the Berezina River. Reinforced by reserve Austrian troops, Schwarzenberg counterattacked and was able to winter at Pultusk to protect Warsaw. After withdrawing on Kraków in February 1813, he handed over command to *Feldmarschalleutnant* Johann Freiherr von Frimont and returned to Paris as Austrian ambassador.

Austria initially hesitated over its next move following Napoleon's catastrophic defeat in Russia. In April 1813 Schwarzenberg attempted to dissuade Napoleon from continuing the war, but he was unable to prevent the conflict from resuming, involving Russia and Prussia against France, and returned to Vienna to join the negotiations with the Allied powers. As Austria's participation in this, the War of the Sixth Coalition, looked likely, Schwarzenberg was on 13 May appointed commander of the (Austrian) Army of Bohemia, with *Feldmarschalleutnant* Johann Joseph Graf Radetzky von Radetz as his chief of staff and the Saxon *Generalmajor* Friedrich von Langenau as head of the Operations Directorate. When Austria opted for war on the Allied side, in August, Schwarzenberg was again the natural political choice as commander in chief of the Allied armies, holding the rank of *Feldmarschall*. However, having to please three sovereigns attached to his headquarters, while leading his own army in accordance with the Austrian political policy of defeating—but not destroying—the French army, was a tricky task.

The actual operational planning had to be left to Radetzky and Langenau, who with their Allied counterparts devised the Trachenberg Plan: Each Allied army would try to defeat in succession the smaller French formations without a direct confrontation with Napoleon until the armies could mass together with total forces of about 250,000 men. Napoleon initially advanced toward the Prussians under General Gebhard von Blücher, but then turned south to engage Schwarzenberg's army as it advanced into Saxony. The Allies assembled 80,000 men outside Dresden in late August, but the cumbersome council of war of 25 August prevented Schwarzenberg from mounting anything more than five poorly coordinated columns in demonstration attacks. Napoleon, who had arrived in the city that evening, was able to counterattack and defeat Schwarzenberg in a two-day battle over 26–27 August. Napoleon then tried to defeat the Prussian and Swedish armies, giving Schwarzenberg the opportunity to guide his own army, now reinforced with Russian troops, northward and with the other Allied armies, concentrate against Napoleon at Leipzig in mid-October.

On 14 October a large French cavalry force engaged the Austro-Russian advance guard cavalry in an indecisive action at Liebertwolkwitz. Schwarzenberg's army faced the Grande Armée alone two days later in several actions, which halted the French counterattack, while Blücher arrived from the north with the (Prussian) Army of Silesia. Reinforced by Crown Prince Jean-Baptiste-Jules Bernadotte and his 60,000 Swedish troops from the Army of the North, Schwarzenberg tightened his grip around Leipzig and resumed the battle on 18 October to achieve a decisive victory. The overwhelming Allied onslaught forced the Grande Armée to retreat on 19 October, leaving 33,000 prisoners.

Showered with honors, Schwarzenberg pressed for a determined pursuit but was slowed by Metternich's political policies, which attempted to bring Napoleon to terms. Nevertheless, in late December, the Allies crossed the Rhine and advanced into France. By 23 January 1814 Schwarzenberg's troops had occupied Langres, Chaumont, and Châtillon-sur-Seine. On 1 February Schwarzenberg and Blücher launched a successful combined attack at Brienne, but Napoleon recovered to win three victories during 10–14 February against the Allies. Meanwhile, Schwarzenberg had defeated Marshal Claude Victor at Bray-sur-Seine but was then defeated by Napoleon at Montereau on 17 March, which forced him to retreat to Troyes. Napoleon continued to pursue Schwarzenberg, but left Paris open to Blücher. The French emperor divided his forces, which allowed Schwarzenberg to resume his advance. His victory at Arcis-sur-Aube over 20–21 March led to the capture of Paris on 31 March and forced Napoleon's abdication on 6 April.

Appointed president of the Hofkriegsrat in May, Schwarzenberg led the (Austrian) Army of the Rhine during the Hundred Days in 1815. Soon after, following the death of his beloved sister Caroline, he fell ill. A stroke causing severe paralysis disabled him in 1817. In 1820, while revisiting the Leipzig battlefield, he suffered a second stroke and died on 15 October.

In his book *On War,* Clausewitz praised Blücher for his willingness to take risks with a smaller force, while criticizing Schwarzenberg for his timidity and hesitation in failing to pursue Napoleon in 1813 and bring about the final defeat of the French. However, Schwarzenberg's primary mission was to work within the political objectives set for him by Metternich and Emperor Francis. His army comprised most of the forces that Austria could field in central Europe and so he could not take risks. As a diplomat, Schwarzenberg had been less successful, but he had proved to be the right "political" field commander and raised Austrian prestige by his victory at Leipzig and the capture of Paris.

David Hollins

See also Alexander I, Tsar; Amberg, Battle of; Arcis-sur-Aube, Battle of; Armistice of 1813; Austerlitz, Battle of; Berezina, Actions and Crossing at the; Bernadotte, Jean-Baptiste-Jules; Blücher von Wahlstatt, Gebhard Lebrecht Fürst; Brienne, Battle of; Charles, Archduke of Austria, Duke of Teschen; Clausewitz, Karl Maria von; Dresden, Battle of; Ferdinand d'Este, Archduke; Fifth Coalition, War of the; First Coalition, War of the; Flanders, Campaigns in; France, Campaign in; Francis I, Emperor; Germany, Campaign in; Hohenlinden, Battle of; John, Archduke; Leipzig, Battle of; Liebertwolkwitz, Action at; Mack, Karl Freiherr von Leiberich; Mannheim Offensive; Marie Louise, Empress; Metternich, Klemens Wenzel Lothar Fürst; Montereau, Battle of; Neerwinden, Battle of; Ney, Michel; Ostrach, Battle of; Radetzky von Radetz, Johann Joseph Wenzel Graf; Rhine Campaigns (1792–1797); Rhine Campaigns (1799–1800); Russian Campaign; Second Coalition, War of the; Stockach, First Battle of; Third Coalition, War of the; Tormasov, Alexander Petrovich, Count; Ulm, Surrender at; Victor, Claude Perrin; Wagram, Battle of; Würzburg, Battle of

References and further reading
Arnold, James. 1990. *Crisis on the Danube: Napoleon's Austrian Campaign of 1809.* New York: Paragon.
Bancalari, Gustav. 1882. *Feldmarschall Carl Philip Fürst Schwarzenberg.* Salzburg: Dieter.
Clausewitz, Carl von. 1976. *On War.* Trans. Michael Howard and Peter Paret. Princeton: Princeton University Press.
Hollins, David. 2004. *Austrian Commanders of the Napoleonic Wars.* Oxford: Osprey.
Kerchnawe, Hugo, and Alois Veltze. 1913. *Feldmarschall Karl Fürst Schwarzenberg, der Führer der Verbündeten in den Befreiungskriegen* [FM Karl Prince Schwarzenberg, the leader of the Allies in the Wars of Liberation]. Vienna: Gesellschaft für neuere Geschichte Österreichs.
Prokesch-Osten, Anton von. 1823. *Denkwurdigkeiten aus dem Leben des Feld-marschall's Fürsten Schwarzenberg* [Notable events from the life of FM Prince Schwarzenberg]. Vienna: Strauss.

Scott, Sir Walter (1771–1832)

Poet, editor, critic, and translator, Sir Walter Scott initiated the writing of Romantic narrative historical novels, mainly about Scotland. Scott was born in Edinburgh on 15 August 1771. He was the third son and ninth child of lawyer Walter Scott and Anne Rutherford, whose father, John Rutherford, was chair of Medicine at the University of Edinburgh. At age 18 months Scott suffered from infantile paralysis in his right leg, which left him lame for the rest of his life. His parents sent him to his grandparents' farm Sandy Knowe, where young Scott grew up listening to Scottish ballads and stories, which instilled him with nationalistic pride as well as with enthusiasm for romance and history.

In 1779 Scott returned to his family in Edinburgh and studied at local schools. From the age of 15, Scott worked as an apprentice in his father's law office and studied for the bar at the University of Edinburgh, where he passed exams and was accepted to the Faculty of Advocates in 1792; he remained a practicing lawyer for the next four decades.

While vacationing in the English Lake District, Scott met the daughter of a French royalist émigré Marguerite Charlotte Charpentier, whom he married in December 1797. The couple eventually had four children: Sophie, Walter, Anne, and Charles. In 1799 Scott was appointed sheriff deputy of the county of Selkirk, which brought an annual salary of £300.

Scott was a firm Tory and supported the Act of Union of 1801. He abhorred popular insurrection and opposed the French Revolution. However, he also believed individuals were entitled to dignity that was denied many people during the Industrial Revolution. Scott's memories of childhood stories became the basis of his future novels.

Scott's passion for collecting ballads led to his first translations of German ballads that appeared in 1796 and 1799. In 1802 he established his literary reputation with his two-volume *Minstrels of the Scottish Border,* a collection of Scottish Border stories and ballads. In 1805 appeared the wildly popular *The Lay of the Last Minstrel,* whose success determined Scott to make literature his principal undertaking. Thereafter he wrote historical novels such as *Rob Roy, Ivanhoe,* and *Heart of Midlothian*—all hugely popular. *Marmion* and *The Works of John Dryden* were published in 1808, and the *Lady of the Lake* in 1810. He also edited the works of Jonathan Swift, John Dryden, and other writers. In 1814 he began his series of *Waverley* novels, which were published anonymously before Scott acknowledged his authorship in 1827. He completed *Ivanhoe* in 1819, *Kenilworth* in 1821, *Quentin Durward* in 1823, and *Woodstock* in 1826. In 1827 he published *The Life of Napoleon Buonaparte* in nine volumes, followed by *The Maid of Perth* in

1828, *Anne of Geierstein* in 1829, and *Count Robert of Paris* and *Castle Dangerous* in 1832.

The success of his novels brought great fame to Scott, who became by far the most popular of Scottish poets. He was given a baronetcy in 1818. He helped found the boys' school, Edinburgh Academy, in 1823 and managed the state visit of George IV to Edinburgh. However, Scott's fortunes changed with his wife's death in 1826. His involvement in his friends James and John Ballantyne's publishing house led to near bankruptcy in 1826. The debt was only cleared in 1847 when Scott's copyrights to his novels were sold. In 1831 Scott sailed to the Mediterranean to improve his health but suffered a severe stroke in Naples. Returning to Scotland, he died on 2 September 1832 and was buried beside his wife at Dryburgh Abbey.

Annette E. Richardson

See also Blake, William; Byron, George Noel Gordon, Lord; Coleridge, Samuel Taylor; Keats, John; Romanticism; Union, Act of; Shelley, Percy Bysshe; Southey, Robert; Wordsworth, William
References and further reading
Daiches, David. 1971. *Sir Walter Scott and his World.* London: Thames and Hudson.
Johnson, Edgar. 1970. *Sir Walter Scott: The Great Unknown.* London: Hamish Hamilton.
Mayhead, Robin. 1973. *Walter Scott.* Cambridge: Cambridge University Press.
Stalker, Archibald. 1921. *The Intimate Life of Sir Walter Scott.* London: Black.
Sutherland, John. 1995. *The Life of Walter Scott: A Biography.* Oxford: Blackwell.
Wilson. A. N. 1982. *The Lord of Abbotsford: A View of Sir Walter Scott.* Oxford: Oxford University Press.

Second Coalition, War of the (1798–1802)

After the Peace of Campo Formio (17 October 1797), Bonaparte, the victor of the Italian campaigns of 1796–1797, received orders to prepare to invade Britain. He, however, suggested an alternative campaign. He realized the very great challenges in crossing the English Channel in the face of a superior enemy navy. Egypt, on the other hand, seemed to him to be the crossroads of the world, and a hinge for the British Empire in the East. He therefore proposed taking a force across the Mediterranean to invade the land of the pharaohs. In mid-May 1798, Bonaparte left the port of Toulon with some 36,000 men. The French managed to evade a British naval force, and landed at Malta where, on 10 June, they took the island from the Order of the Knights of St. John. Shortly thereafter, Bonaparte left a small garrison force and with the majority of his army proceeded to Egypt where his troops landed near Alexandria on 1 July.

Bonaparte then fought a series of battles with the Mameluke rulers of Egypt. On 2 July, he seized Alexandria, and nearly three weeks later, on the twenty-first, the French fought a force of 6,000 Mameluke cavalry, together with a large army of local levies—perhaps as many as 54,000 infantry, though many of these sat out the battle. The Mamelukes attacked the French on the west side of the river Nile near the Pyramids. The French infantry, deployed in squares, held fast, and their firepower easily repulsed the repeated charges of their opponents. Bonaparte was so impressed with the Mamelukes' courage that he recruited some of them into his own units. Thereafter the French took Cairo. Bonaparte seemed to have achieved his goals.

As an aside, Napoleon and his troops made a remarkable discovery in the form of what was to become known as the Rosetta Stone, which later enabled scholars to understand Egyptian hieroglyphics, the language of official and religious writing in ancient Egypt.

At the height of this seemingly triumphant campaign, the fleet that had transported Bonaparte's's army to Egypt suffered a catastrophic defeat on 1 August in Aboukir Bay by a British force commanded by Commodore Sir Horatio Nelson. The French ships had anchored in this bay, one of the entrances to the Nile delta, where Nelson brilliantly divided his force of thirteen ships in two, sending four vessels to attack on the landward side of the French and the remainder to attack on the seaward side, thus subjecting his enemy to bombardment from the port and starboard sides simultaneously. When the night battle ended, the British had captured or destroyed all but two ships in the French fleet. The victory at the Nile cut off Bonaparte's communications with France, and thus condemned his troops to ultimate defeat.

Bonaparte tried to escape the consequences of the naval defeat in Aboukir Bay and to preempt a Turkish offensive after Sultan Selim III declared war on France. He moved out of Egypt to invade Syria, brushing aside ineffective Turkish resistance at Jaffa and besieging the port city of Acre. The small garrison, led by the British admiral Sir Sidney Smith, and buoyed by two British ships anchored offshore, held on despite the presence of superior French forces outside the town. For a month, from mid-March to mid-April 1799, the French tried but failed to break into the city, and when plague struck his troops, Bonaparte had no choice but to raise the siege.

Meanwhile, once Austrian armies in Italy had largely reversed the gains Bonaparte had made in his brilliant campaigns of 1796–1797, Bonaparte decided to abandon his troops in Egypt. Moving secretly by frigate, he, several senior officers, some scientists, and about 200 troops, sailed for France on 22 August. The small group reached

Contending Powers in the Second Coalition, 1798–1802

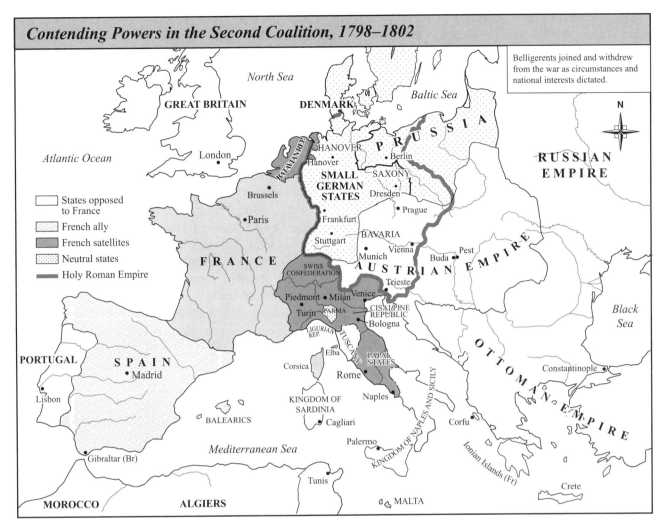

Belligerents joined and withdrew from the war as circumstances and national interests dictated.

Legend:
- States opposed to France
- French ally
- French satellites
- Neutral states
- Holy Roman Empire

Adapted from Fremont-Barnes 2001, 51.

France on 9 October, and within a week Bonaparte had reached Paris to review the situation.

The military situation in Europe was in a fluid state. While Napoleon had been fighting in Egypt, the Second Coalition had come into being. Austria, Russia, Turkey, the Papal States, Portugal, Naples, and Britain had joined together to try to contain Revolutionary France. Despite its combined military power, the coalition's fundamental weakness proved to be its failure to compel all coalition partners to remain faithful to the alliance and not conclude a separate peace. In time, Bonaparte was able to pick apart the coalition, exposing its lack of genuine unity.

While Bonaparte was campaigning in Egypt, fighting had resumed on the European continent in 1799. There were three main theaters of conflict. A combined Anglo-Russian army was threatening North Holland, while Austrian armies with Russian support were moving through southern Germany to the Rhine and across northern Italy to reverse Bonaparte's great victories in the campaign for

Mantua of 1796–1797. The center of gravity of this broad campaign was northern Italy, and its outcome determined the fate of the Second Coalition. At first, the French assumed the offensive when Lazare Carnot, in charge of the overall French military effort, formulated a strategy that called for an attack on all three fronts. After some early successes, it seemed that Carnot's plan had proven overambitious. On 25 March 1799, at Stockach in southern Germany, the Austrians defeated a French army led by General Jean-Baptiste Jourdan, who first retreated across the Rhine, and then conceded his command to General André Masséna. As part of the Allies' strategy, another Austrian army commanded by *Feldmarschalleutnant* Paul Kray Freiherr von Krajova moved into northern Italy and on 5 April, at Magnano, south of Verona, it met General Barthélemy Schérer's army, halted its attack, and broke the French right flank, whereupon Schérer's troops retreated westward, followed closely by the Austrians reinforced with a Russian army.

At Cassano, just east of Milan, the combined Austro-Russian army attacked on 27 April. Troops under Russian field marshal Alexander Suvorov stormed the French position along the river Adda, and, despite hard-fought resistance from the badly outnumbered French, the Austrians seized the position, and soon thereafter occupied Milan and, later, Turin in late May. The French, for their part, retreated across northern Italy to Genoa.

To assist General Jean Moreau, whose army had retreated, the French government sent another force, commanded by General Jacques Macdonald, to northern Italy. Suvorov, realizing he could become trapped between the converging French armies, moved to attack Macdonald at the Trebbia River on 18–19 June. After two days of savage fighting, Macdonald retreated toward Moreau near Genoa, and it appeared that the Allies had reconquered Italy. The final battle took place north of Genoa at Novi, as General Barthélemy Joubert tried to stop Suvorov on 15 August. The larger Allied army seized the heights from the entrenched French defenders, leaving Joubert and four divisional commanders among the dead. Moreau then led the retreat back to France.

French forces managed to resist the Allied offensive on the northern front. A combined Anglo-Russian army landed in North Holland, and French forces under General Dominique Vandamme attacked on 19 September at Bergen op Zoom. While the British resisted the French surge, the Russians broke, and the Duke of York had to retreat north, ending the Allied threat from that theater.

The Allies also threatened southern Germany and Switzerland in the third offensive of its three-pronged assault. Between 4 and 7 June 1799, the Austrians and French clashed at Zürich in French-controlled Switzerland in a four-day battle that caused many casualties and forced the French under Masséna to retreat. The Austrian commander, Archduke Charles, became ill, and command devolved upon Suvorov, who continued the advance. He divided his army, sending different parts through the various mountain passes, where Masséna managed to hold up some columns while savagely beating others. As he maneuvered back and forth near Zürich on 25–26 September, Masséna dealt Suvorov such a terrible defeat that, disgusted with the strength of France's resistance and the weak Allied effort, Tsar Paul I withdrew Russia from the Second Coalition in late October.

By this point Bonaparte had returned from Egypt and sought to restore France's crumbling position in northern Italy. He helped to engineer a coup, claiming that the Directory, which had led France, was not up to the challenge. What became known as the coup of Brumaire took its name from the date in the short-lived Republican calendar on which it occurred: 9–10 November (1799), or 18–19 Brumaire, Year VIII. The new government, the Consulate, first established three consuls in emulation of the Roman Republic, with Bonaparte ultimately establishing himself as First Consul. Now firmly in charge of the government at home, he moved to gain control of the war effort. He realized that the Austrians were the key, and the Italian front was the center of gravity. He intended to have French forces hold back the Allies on the other two fronts while he fought for decisive victory in northern Italy.

As Masséna tried to defend Genoa, Bonaparte gathered forces, and moved from Switzerland through the Alpine passes in late spring 1800. Masséna surrendered Genoa on 4 June, and Austrian troops under *General der Kavallerie* Michael von Melas occupied the city. Meanwhile, Bonaparte began a rapid march through the St. Bernard Pass to confront Melas who, though cheered by his victory at Genoa, remained concerned about Bonaparte's approach. The French vanguard fought the Austrian rear guard near Montebello on 9 June and forced the Austrians back, as more and more French troops moved to concentrate east of Alessandria and south of the river Po.

The result was the Battle of Marengo, fought on 14 June 1800. Realizing that Bonaparte had concentrated on his rear—his line of retreat and communications through Italy to Vienna—Melas attacked, surprising Bonaparte and driving the outnumbered French back several miles throughout the morning and early afternoon. As more forces arrived, Bonaparte continued to commit troops to halt the attack. Meanwhile, Melas retired to Alessandria that afternoon and turned over command to a subordinate. The Austrians then paused, giving Bonaparte time to reorganize his troops, and to commit 6,000 late-arriving French cavalry, whom he sent crashing into the Austrians' flank. The reinvigorated and strengthened French army transformed a near defeat into a decisive victory: Melas agreed to a truce, and withdrew north of the Mincio River and east of the Po, while Bonaparte returned to France.

As Bonaparte was reestablishing French supremacy in northern Italy, and as the fighting stalled in Holland, the French regained the initiative in southern Germany. Moreau followed up his victory, the second Battle of Stockach, on 3 May, moving from Baden into Bavaria. Pursuing the retreating Austrians, Moreau attacked on 19 June with such determination that his opponents, though outnumbering his own forces, could not organize a coordinated defense below Höchstädt, on the Danube, and after eighteen hours had to abandon the town.

Bonaparte's victory at Marengo led to six months of armistice talks between France and Austria. Fighting had ended in Holland, and both Bonaparte and Moreau halted after their victories at Marengo and Höchstädt. As negotia-

tions ebbed and flowed, the Austrians built up their army facing Moreau to more than 130,000, while Bonaparte reinforced Moreau to 119,000. On 3 December, the Austrian commander, Archduke John, seeking to turn Moreau's left flank, attacked him east of Munich, near Hohenlinden, only to be decisively defeated. In the course of fifteen days, the Austrians retreated nearly 200 miles, all the way to Vienna.

Two other French armies maintained the pressure on Austria. Macdonald moved from Switzerland into the Tyrolean Alps, and another army commanded by General Guillaume Brune completed the task of pushing the Austrians out of northern Italy. By this point, the Austrian emperor, Francis I, realized the futility of his position, and signed the Treaty of Lunéville on 8 February 1801, which meant that Britain remained France's only significant opponent.

Undaunted, Britain took advantage of Bonaparte's preoccupation with the fighting in northern Italy to confront the remaining French forces in Egypt. On 8 March 1801, Lieutenant General Sir Ralph Abercromby landed an army at Aboukir Bay, site of Nelson's great naval victory several years before. As the British force marched to Alexandria, French general Jacques Menou (successor of General Jean Kléber, who had been assassinated) came out to oppose it. Ferocious fighting on 20–21 March resulted in a British victory, and the subsequent French surrender of Cairo and Alexandria, in June. All other French forces followed suit and were returned to France in British ships.

Britain also maintained its control of the seas. As the Second Coalition teetered toward defeat, many of the Baltic countries came together in the League of Armed Neutrality (consisting of Denmark, Sweden, Prussia, and Russia) in order to protect themselves from Royal Navy vessels sent to the Baltic to interdict neutral commerce with France and her allies. On 2 April 1801, a British fleet under Nelson sailed into Copenhagen harbor, severely damaging twelve Danish warships in a fierce struggle. Denmark quickly agreed to peace with Britain and a withdrawal from the league, and when Tsar Paul was assassinated, his successor, Alexander I, adopted a decidedly pro-British policy. Thus ended any further threat posed by the Baltic states.

After about a year of inaction, during which time Britain found itself powerless to contest French power on the Continent, and France, conversely, proved itself unable to challenge Britain's mastery of the seas, the two belligerents signed a treaty at Amiens on 25 March 1802, ending the War of the Second Coalition. This peace was to last a mere fourteen months before Britain and France once more went to war in what contemporaries in Britain called "the Great War," now known as the Napoleonic Wars (1803–1815).

Charles M. Dobbs

See also Abercromby, Sir Ralph; Aboukir, Battle of; Acre, Siege of; Albeck, Battle of; Alexander I, Tsar; Alexandria, Battle of; Algeciras, First Battle of; Algeciras, Second Battle of; Amiens, Treaty of; Armed Neutrality, League of; Bergen, Battle of; Brumaire, Coup of; Brune, Guillaume-Marie-Anne; Cairo, Uprising in; Campo Formio, Treaty of; Carnot, Lazare Nicolas Marguerite; Cassano, Battle of; Charles, Archduke of Austria, Duke of Teschen; Consulate, The; Copenhagen, Battle of; Directory, The; El Arish, Convention of; England, French Plans for the Invasion of; Francis I, Emperor; Genoa, Siege of; Heliopolis, Battle of; Höchstädt, Battle of; Hohenlinden, Battle of; Italian Campaigns (1799–1800); John, Archduke; Joubert, Barthélemy Catherine; Jourdan, Jean-Baptiste; Kléber, Jean-Baptiste; Kray, Paul Freiherr von Krajova; Lunéville, Treaty of; Macdonald, Jacques Etienne Joseph Alexandre; Magnano, Battle of; Malta, Operations on; Mannheim Offensive; Marengo, Battle of; Masséna, André; Melas, Michael Friedrich Benedikt Freiherr von; Menou, Jacques-François de Boussay, baron; Middle East Campaign; Montebello, Battle of; Moreau, Jean Victor; Nelson, Horatio, First Viscount; Nile, Battle of the; North Holland, Campaign in; Novi, Battle of; Ostrach, Battle of; Paul I, Tsar; Pyramids, Battle of the; Rhine Campaigns (1799–1800); Rosetta Stone; San Giuliano, Battle of; Schérer, Barthélemy Louis Joseph; Shubra Khit, Action at; Smith, Sir William Sidney; Stockach, First Battle of; Stockach, Second Battle of; Suvorov, Alexander Vasilievich; Switzerland, Campaign in; Trebbia, Battle of the; Vandamme, Dominique Joseph René; Verona, Battle of; York and Albany, Frederick Augustus, Duke of; Zürich, First Battle of; Zürich, Second Battle of

References and further reading
Arnold, James. 2005. *Marengo and Hohenlinden.* London: Leo Cooper.
Blanning, T. C. W. 1986. *The Origins of the French Revolutionary Wars.* New York: Longman.
———. 1996. *The French Revolutionary Wars, 1787–1802.* London: Hodder Arnold.
Brindle, Rosemary. 2003. *Guns in the Desert: General Jean-Pierre Doguereau's Journals of Napoleon's Egyptian Expedition.* New York: Praeger.
Chandler, David G. 1995. *The Campaigns of Napoleon.* London: Weidenfeld and Nicolson.
Duffy, Christopher. 1999. *Eagles over the Alps: Suvorov in Italy and Switzerland, 1799.* Chicago: Emperor's Press.
Esdaile, Charles J. 2001. *The French Wars, 1792–1815.* New York: Routledge.
Esposito, Vincent J., and John R. Elting. 1999. *A Military History and Atlas of the Napoleonic Wars.* London: Greenhill.
Fremont-Barnes, Gregory. 2001. *The French Revolutionary Wars.* Oxford: Osprey.
Gardiner, Robert, ed. 1997. *Nelson against Napoleon: From the Nile to Copenhagen, 1798–1801.* London: Chatham.
Grainger, John D. 2004. *The Amiens Truce: Britain and Bonaparte, 1801–1803.* Rochester, NY: Boydell.
Herold, Christopher. 2005. *Bonaparte in Egypt.* London: Greenhill.
Hollins, David. 2000. *The Battle of Marengo.* Oxford: Osprey.
Lavery, Brian. 1998. *Nelson and the Nile: The Naval War against Napoleon, 1798.* Annapolis, MD: United States Naval Institute Press.

Lefebvre, Georges. 1969. *Napoleon from 18 Brumaire to Tilsit, 1799–1807*. Translated from the French by Henry F. Stockhold. New York: Columbia University Press.

Mackesy, Piers. 1974. *Statesmen at War: The Strategy of Overthrow, 1798–1799*. London: Longman.

———. 1984. *War without Victory: The Downfall of Pitt, 1799–1802*. Oxford: Clarendon.

———. 1995. *British Victory in Egypt, 1801: The End of Napoleon's Conquest*. London: Routledge.

Marshall-Cornwall, James. 2002. *Napoleon as Military Commander*. New York: Penguin.

Phipps, Ramsay Weston. 1980. *The Armies of the First French Republic and the Rise of the Marshals of Napoleon I*. Vol. 5, *The Armies on the Rhine in Switzerland, Holland, Italy, Egypt, and the Coup d'Etat of Brumaire, 1797 to 1799*. London: Greenwood. (Orig. pub. 1926–1939.)

Rodger, A. B. 1964. *The War of the Second Coalition: A Strategic Commentary*. New York: Oxford University Press.

Ross, Steven T. 1963. *The War of the Second Coalition: A Strategic Commentary*. Princeton: Princeton University Press.

Rothenberg, Gunther. 1982. *Napoleon's Great Adversaries: Archduke Charles and the Austrian Army, 1792–1814*. London: Batsford.

Schur, Nathan. 1999. *Napoleon in the Holy Land*. Mechanicsburg, PA: Stackpole.

Sherwig, John M. 1969. *Guineas and Gunpowder: British Foreign Aid in the Wars with France, 1793–1815*. Cambridge: Harvard University Press.

Ségur, Philippe Paul, comte de (1780–1873)

French general, diplomat, and historian, Philippe Paul Ségur wrote the first widely published eyewitness account of Napoleon's invasion of Russia, *History of Napoleon and the Grand Army in 1812*. The book's accuracy has been called into question ever since it first appeared. Ségur may have been prone to exaggeration, but in action he was a brave officer, and he was wounded several times in the service of Napoleon.

Born 4 November 1780 into a noble military family, Ségur joined the cavalry in 1800, enlisting in the Bonaparte Hussars. The fact that he was the grandson of a marshal and the son of a general smoothed the path of promotion, and he was quickly made an officer. Ségur ultimately proved himself capable on his own merits. When the Bonaparte Hussars were disbanded in 1801, Ségur became an aide-de-camp to General Jacques Etienne Macdonald. He was attached to General Géraud Duroc's staff serving Napoleon in 1804. Ségur negotiated the terms of *Feldmarschalleutnant* Karl Mack Freiherr von Leiberich's surrender to Napoleon at Ulm in 1805. In 1806 he served at the siege of Gaeta in Naples. In 1807, while with Napoleon's main army in Poland, Ségur was wounded and taken prisoner by the Russians. Released after the Treaty of Tilsit, Ségur again served as an aide-de-camp. He received two wounds at Somosierra in Spain, on 30 November 1808, courageously charging along with the Polish light cavalry of Napoleon's bodyguard against strong enemy positions. Promoted to colonel for his gallantry, he was made a count in 1809, and was then sent on diplomatic missions to St. Petersburg and Vienna.

Ségur was promoted to general in 1812 and accompanied Napoleon on his disastrous invasion of Russia, thus gaining inspiration for the famous book. In early 1813, Ségur helped to organize new cavalry regiments for the Imperial Guard, and fought at Leipzig and Hanau later that year. In 1814, he served in the defense of France during the Allied invasion. Commanding a brigade of Imperial Guard cavalry, he fought at Montmirail on 11 February. Leading his brigade at Rheims, on 13 March, he was in the thick of the fight, suffering musket ball and bayonet wounds.

Ségur rallied to Napoleon during the Hundred Days and retired from service when the Bourbons returned again, despite his status as a member of the old nobility. He reentered the army in 1818, and in 1824 published his memoirs on the Russian campaign. The book was very successful, but many veterans of the campaign fiercely criticized the work. The controversy resulted in a duel fought between Ségur and General Gaspard Gourgaud, during which Ségur was wounded. Ségur embraced the Revolution of 1830, and was made a peer of France by King Louis-Philippe. He retired from the army after the Revolution of 1848. He wrote several histories, none as popular as his work on the 1812 campaign. Ségur died on 25 February 1873.

Ralph Ashby

See also Duroc, Géraud Christophe Michel, duc de Frioul; Fourth Coalition, War of the; France, Campaign in; Gaeta, Sieges of; Germany, Campaign in; Hanau, Battle of; Imperial Guard (French); Leipzig, Battle of; Macdonald, Jacques Etienne Joseph Alexandre; Mack, Karl Freiherr von Leiberich; Montmirail, Battle of; Peninsular War; Rheims, Battle of; Russian Campaign; Somosierra, Action at; Third Coalition, War of the; Tilsit, Treaties of; Ulm, Surrender at

References and further reading
Lachouque, Henry. 1997. *The Anatomy of Glory: Napoleon and His Guard*. Trans. Anne S. K. Brown. London: Greenhill.

Ségur, Philippe de. 2003. *Napoleon's Expedition to Russia: The Memoirs of General de Ségur*. London: Constable and Robinson.

Semaphore

The French Revolution has long been hailed for its scientific and technological advances, but one that impressed contemporaries is today virtually forgotten. The sema-phore, or optical telegraph, of Claude Chappe solved the age-old problem of quick and accurate communication over long distances, and moreover permitted bidirectional and secure transmission of complex messages of unanticipated content. The Revolution provided the demand and thus the resources for the experiment, which flourished and spawned imitations in other countries until the advent of electrical telegraphy more than half a century later.

In the mature system, highly disciplined pairs of operators transmitted a sophisticated code between elevated stations (on natural heights, existing structures such as churches, or towers built for the purpose) spaced 8 to 10 kilometers apart along painstakingly chosen routes. At the top of each station, a post supported a crossbar, or "regulator," at each end of which was a shorter "indicator." By means of pulleys, the operator rotated the three arms so as to form any of ninety-eight configurations, ninety-two of which carried content. Each of these two-part signals referred to one of ninety-two codes on one of ninety-two pages in a codebook (a vocabulary of 8,464 terms, which supplements tripled by 1799). Chappe achieved speed and accuracy by encoding words or phrases rather than letters and sending them down the line one at a time rather than all at once. Security was ensured because only the "directors" at either end of the line knew the codes.

Ideological as much as technical factors persuaded the Convention to authorize funding in 1793. By shrinking social and geographical distance, the telegraph, like the departmental system, promised to unite the disparate groups and regions of the new nation. Above all, though, the system administered by Chappe and his brothers provided valuable military information in real time. In the summer of 1794, the first line carried news of victories from Lille to Paris in an hour. New lines gradually radiated outward from the capital to the major cities of France and its conquered territories. Under ideal conditions (daylight and clement weather), one signal could travel 760 kilometers to Toulon in 12 minutes, versus three days for a rider and more than a week for a coach. Napoleon, who for a time demanded to review every transmission in advance, extended the system even to Amsterdam and Venice. In response, the British created a counterpart for the Admiralty (1796–1814) and one in Spain during the Peninsular War.

After the Restoration, the Chappe network continued to grow within the reduced borders of France, but as before, it remained under the control of the state. By the 1830s it comprised over 1,000 employees and 500 stations along some 4,800 kilometers of lines between twenty-nine cities.

James Wald

See also Chappe, Claude; Convention, The; Peninsular War

References and further reading
Field, Alexander J. 1994. "French Optical Telegraphy, 1793–1855: Hardware, Software, Administration." *Technology and Culture* 35: 315–347.
Holzman, Gerard J., and Björn Pehrson. 1995. *The Early History of Data Networks.* Los Alamitos, CA: IEEE Computer Society Press.

Senyavin, Dmitry Nikolayevich (1763–1831)

Russian admiral. Born to a noble family from the Kaluga *gubernia* (province), he studied in the Naval Cadet Corps and began service in the Baltic Fleet in 1778, becoming a midshipman in 1780. He took part in a cruise to Portugal in 1780–1781 and transferred to the Black Sea Fleet, where he commanded a packetboat in 1786. He participated in the Russo-Turkish War of 1788–1792, becoming adjutant general in 1788 and commanding the ship of the line *Navarkhia* in the Battle of Cape Kaliakria. In the 1790s, he served under Admiral Fedor Ushakov and took command of the ship of the line *St. Peter* in 1796. In 1798–1799, he took part in Ushakov's expedition in the Mediterranean. Returning to Russia, he became the commandant of the Black Sea port of Kherson and later rose to rear admiral and commandant of Revel, on the Baltic. In August 1805 he became a vice admiral and took command of the Russian naval squadron in the Adriatic. He fought the French at Cattaro (Kotor) and Ragusa (Dubrovnik) in 1806.

During the Russo-Turkish War of 1806–1812, he defeated the Turkish Fleet at the Dardanelles, Tenedos, and Mt. Athos. However, the Treaty of Tilsit undermined his successes and forced him to seek neutral ports at Trieste and Lisbon, where he was blockaded by the Royal Navy in 1808. Senyavin was forced to place his ships in British custody and returned to Russia in 1809, where he was reprimanded for losing his ships. Senyavin served as commandant of the port of Revel in 1810 before retiring three years later. Tsar Nicholas I recalled him to active duty in 1826–1829, when Senyavin commanded the Baltic Fleet.

Alexander Mikaberidze

See also Russian Navy; Russo-Turkish War; Tilsit, Treaties of
References and further reading
Mikaberidze, Alexander. 2005. *The Russian Officer Corps in the Revolutionary and Napoleonic Wars, 1792–1815.* New York: Savas Beatie.

Sérurier, Jean Mathieu Philibert, comte (1742–1819)

Sérurier was one of four officers to receive the honorific title of Marshal of the Empire. He had been a soldier during the Seven Year's War (1756–1763), and it seemed his military career had ended before the French Revolution had begun. During the Revolutionary period, however, he fought in Italy from 1795 and helped Bonaparte in the coup d'état of Brumaire (9–10 November 1799). From this point he entered political life and was governor of the Invalides.

Sérurier's early career had led him through the Seven Years' War, and at the start of the Revolution he commanded a regiment stationed in Corsica. In 1791 he was moved to Perpignan, in southeastern France on the Pyrenean front, and was employed in putting down royalist elements. In the political climate of the time he was accused of royalist sympathies and was only saved from imprisonment or worse by the intervention of Paul Barras, a prominent member of the Convention. Having avoided arrest, he was recommended for promotion, and by 1794 he was a *général de division* in Italy. In 1795 he fought under the command of General André Masséna at Loano. He then captured Ceva early in 1796 and at the Battle of Mondovi effectively put Piedmont out of the coalition against France.

Sérurier then fought at Borghetto and was given the responsibility by Bonaparte of conducting the siege of Mantua. He was ordered to break the siege in response to the attack by the Austrian *Feldmarschall* Dagobert Graf Würmser, but did not take part in the Castiglione campaign due to illness. In 1797 Sérurier defeated an Austrian force commanded by *Feldmarschalleutnant* Giovanni, Marquis di Provera at La Favorita during his attempt to relieve Mantua. Sérurier had the honor of accepting the surrender of Mantua on 16 January 1797. He fought at the Piave and Tagliamento later in the year, and then ill health returned and rendered him unable to hold a field command. He managed to return to Italy in August 1798, but was forced to surrender to the Russian field marshal Alexander Suvorov at Verderio in April 1799.

Sérurier was granted parole, and on returning to Paris he played a part in the coup d'état of Brumaire. In recognition of his help, Bonaparte made him a senator, recognizing the fact that active command was now beyond him. He was vice president of the Senate in 1802 and in 1804 was appointed governor of the Invalides. In May of that year he was made a Marshal of the Empire; in Sérurier's case this was effectively an honorific title. In 1808 he became a Count of the Empire. He carried out the duties of governor of the Invalides to the best of his capacity, and when Paris was in imminent danger of occupation in 1814 he ordered the destruction of many trophies of war and captured colors. Upon the restoration of the monarchy, he was made a peer, a title recognized by Napoleon on his return from exile in 1815. However, in the second restoration he was replaced at the Invalides and died in 1819.

Ralph Baker

See also Borghetto, Battle of; Brumaire, Coup of; Castiglione, Battle of; Ceva, Battle of; France, Campaign in; Italian Campaigns (1792–1797); Italian Campaigns (1799–1800); Loano, Battle of; Mantua, Sieges of; Marshalate; Masséna, André; Mondovi, Battle of; Sardinia; Second Coalition, War of the; Standards, Flags, and Eagles; Suvorov, Alexander Vasilievich; Würmser, Dagobert Sigismund Graf
References and further reading
Chandler, David G., ed. 1987. *Napoleon's Marshals*. London: Weidenfeld and Nicolson.
Delderfield, R. F. 2004. *The March of the Twenty-Six*. London: Leo Cooper.
Macdonell, A. G. 1996. *Napoleon and His Marshals*. London: Prion.

Seventh Coalition

See Waterloo Campaign

Shelley, Percy Bysshe (1792–1822)

British Romantic poet, author, Classical scholar, and philosophical Revolutionary.

Shelley was born in West Sussex on 4 August 1792, during the infancy of the French Revolution. Too young to experience the change it ushered in, his emergence into adulthood coincided with Napoleon's defeat, making him witness to the conservative backlash that accompanied it. Shelley became one of the greatest members of what may be considered the second generation of the Romantic movement, the one that flourished after the reestablishment of conservative political and religious rule throughout Europe following the Congress of Vienna. Purportedly representing the triumph of reason over superstition, the French Revolution built upon the Enlightenment and defeated the last vestiges of feudalism that had once supported Romanticism and chivalry. Nevertheless, Revolutionary art and literature celebrated Romanticism, and for many, Shelley defines the Romantic movement.

Shelley began his education at Eton College at the age of twelve, where he discovered the works of the anarchist philosopher and Revolutionary author, William Godwin, and developed an affinity for the ideals of the French Revolution. In 1810, he began his studies at Oxford, but the tradition and conformity he found there proved too confining for the young poet, and he was eventually expelled for publishing *The Necessity of Atheism*, condemning compulsory state Christianity.

Following his expulsion, Shelley married Harriet Westbrook and spent two years in various places, including Ireland, where Shelley's Revolutionary tendencies grew even stronger and where he published a *Declaration of Rights.* In 1813, Shelley wrote the radical *Queen Mab: A Philosophical Poem,* reflecting his socialist tendencies and his disdain for political and religious authority. The poem was not published until 1821, long after the British Revolutionary fervor of the 1790s had waned, but its impact as a mixture of romance and Revolutionary utopianism could not be ignored, particularly by the increasingly radical working class.

Shelley left Harriet and his two children in 1814 for Godwin's daughter, Mary, and the two fled to the Continent, where they met Lord Byron and began a strong attachment that continued until Shelley's death. Three weeks after Harriet's apparent suicide in December 1816, Shelley and Mary Godwin were married. The couple soon became a part of the great corps of British Romantics in Italy, including Byron, Leigh Hunt, and the ailing John Keats. During this last phase of his life, Shelley published many of his most important works, including the lyrical *Laon and Cythna, or The Revolt of Islam,* which advocated radical, yet bloodless reform and *Prometheus Unbound,* a celebration of the individuality of man, who serves no master, political or religious.

After four productive years in Italy, Shelley drowned in July 1822 at the age of thirty, already arguably the greatest of the Romantic poets of his generation. For Shelley and his circle, unlike earlier authors such as Sir Walter Scott, who were drawn to the romance of the chivalry of the Middle Ages but repelled by revolutionary politics, revolution and romance were intertwined; the politics of the one were present in the language of the other. They drew their utopian vision of what should be from what Shelley called "the master theme of the epoch—the French Revolution," and sought through words and action to bring about their own revolution.

Jason Musteen

See also Blake, William; Byron, George Gordon Noel, Lord; Coleridge, Samuel Taylor; Keats, John; Romanticism; Scott, Sir Walter; Southey, Robert; Vienna, Congress of; Wordsworth, William

References and further reading
Bieri, James. 2004. *Percy Bysshe Shelley, A Biography: Youth's Unextinguished Fire, 1792–1816.* Newark, DE: University of Delaware Press.
———. 2005. *Percy Bysshe Shelley, A Biography: Exile of Unfulfilled Renown, 1816–1822.* Newark, NJ: University of Delaware Press.
Gilmour, Ian H. 2002. *The Making of the Poem: Byron and Shelley in Their Time.* London: Chatto and Windus.
Haines, Simon. 1997. *Shelley: The Divided Self.* Basingstoke, UK: Macmillan.
Höhne, Horst. 2000. *In Pursuit of Love: The Short and Troublesome Life and Work of Percy Bysshe Shelley.* New York: Peter.

Ships of the Line

In the age of fighting sail, ships of the line constituted the most powerful warships, those capable of taking up a position in the main battle line in a sea fight and absorbing the punishment from enemy fire, as well as making a contribution to destroying the opposing line. Such ships were also known as line-of-battle ships, a designation that gave the name to the modern battleship. Heavily armed and manned, they conveyed great national prestige. They were square-rigged ships with three masts and two or three gun decks. They were rated according to the number of guns they carried, from 64 to 120 guns or more. Ships of the line consisted of first through third rates. First rates mounted 100 guns or more, second rates had 90–98 guns, and third rates carried 64–80 guns.

When large, long-range guns were introduced aboard warships, boarding and ramming declined as tactics. The first guns at sea had been positioned high in the ship, but naval architects soon discovered that the safest way to arrange the heavier cannon was to place them low in the hull, complete with gunports, to facilitate fire in the form of broadsides. Since the ships' most powerful guns were mounted in their sides, the most effective tactic in battle was a line ahead formation (ships placed end to end following the same course). Battles at sea between squadrons and fleets became stately affairs with the opposing sides proceeding in parallel lines and blasting away at one another. The line ahead tactic also had the advantage of protecting the vulnerable, more lightly armed bow and stern and preventing the ship from being "raked" by an opponent, during which enemy shot could conceivably travel down the entire length of a deck.

By the time of the French Revolutionary Wars, the smallest ship deemed capable of standing in the battle line was the third-rate 64-gun warship, although many held that the 74-gun should be the smallest warship in a battle line. The British kept their 64s in service longer than did the French because, given their extensive empire, numbers of ships were more important than their individual strength. The 64-gun ship was also cheaper to build and maintain than the 74.

The 74-gun ship of the line, developed first by the French and Spanish, was actually the most numerous of its type in the Royal Navy during the Revolutionary and Napoleonic Wars. An excellent compromise, it combined superior sailing ability with strong firepower (it was the smallest ship capable of carrying 32-pounders on its lower gun deck). In addition to service in the battle line, it performed numerous other duties, including detached service and convoy protection. In many respects, it was the workhorse of this period at sea. The French had larger two-deckers in 80-gun ships of the line, but they were expensive to build and maintain, and they were at the limit of ship length possible with the wooden construction of the period.

The largest ships of the line were the first rates with three-gun decks, mounting 100 guns or more. They were usually the fleet flagships. They tended to be ponderous vessels (the 100-gun HMS *Victory* could make only 8 knots), but this was not a serious drawback when a fleet moved at the speed of its slowest vessels. The French initiated the construction of even larger first rates of 110 guns or more, which the British were then obliged to follow.

Ships of the line required the largest pieces of timber, were immensely complex and technologically challenging, and took years to build. As such, they were the most expensive ships per ton to construct. The *Victory*, Vice Admiral Viscount Horatio Nelson's flagship at the Battle of Trafalgar (21 October 1805), displaced about 3,500 tons. To build her took about 100 acres of woodland (principally oak), and her standard and running rigging alone ran about 27 miles in length. Although such ships required large crews (the *Victory* at Trafalgar had 821 officers and men) and were costly to maintain, they were generally well maintained and tended to have long service lives. The *Victory* was begun in 1759, launched in 1765, and commissioned in 1778. She went through extensive repairs during 1800–1803 but remained in active service until 1813 (and technically is still a commissioned Royal Navy warship).

The French produced some excellent ships and lengthened them to allow them to carry more guns, leading the British to follow suit. The *Ville de Paris,* completed in 1795, was 190 feet long on her gun deck, compared to 186 feet for the *Victory*. The largest ship of the line of the period, however, was the Spanish *Santísima Trinidad,* which carried 130–136 guns on four decks. She displaced some 4,000 tons and had a crew of approximately 1,100 men. Attacked by four British ships of the line at Trafalgar, she was badly damaged and forced to strike her colors, but sank in the great storm following the battle.

Armament of ships of the line varied considerably. By the Napoleonic period, ships rated at 110 and 120 guns each usually mounted 32-pounders on their lower deck, 24-pounders on their middle deck, and 18-pounders on the upper deck. Carronades, including 68-pounders—only in use by the British and Americans—were not included in the rating armament but were often mounted on the forecastle and quarterdeck, along with a few long guns. At Trafalgar, for example, the *Victory* mounted thirty 32-pounders, twenty-eight 24-pounders, thirty 12-pounders, twelve quarterdeck 12-pounders, and two 68-pounder carronades.

Spencer C. Tucker

See also Artillery (Naval); Blockade; French Navy; Frigates; Naval Warfare; Nelson, Horatio, First Viscount; Royal Navy; Sloops; Spanish Navy; Trafalgar, Battle of

References and further reading
Blake, Nicholas. 2005. *Steering to Glory: A Day in the Life of a Ship of the Line.* London: Chatham.
Cordingly, David. 2003. *Billy Ruffian: His Majesty's Ship "Bellerophon" and the Downfall of Napoleon: A Biography of a Ship of the Line, 1782–1836.* London: Bloomsbury.
Howard, Frank. 1979. *Sailing Ships of War, 1400–1860.* London: Conway Maritime.
Konstam, Angus. 2001. *British Napoleonic Ship-of-the-Line.* Oxford: Osprey.
Lavery, Brian. 1983. *The Ship of the Line: Design, Construction, and Fittings.* 2 vols. London: Conway Maritime.
———. 1989. *Nelson's Navy: The Ships, Men and Organisation, 1793–1815.* London: Conway Maritime.
———. 1992. *The Line of Battle: The Sailing Warship, 1650–1840.* London: Conway Maritime. 2 vols.

Shrapnel

Innovative form of antipersonnel ammunition employed by the Royal Artillery. Officially known as spherical case, shrapnel soon came to bear the name of its inventor, Lieutenant Henry Shrapnel, who invented this novel device in 1784. Shrapnel was accepted into British service in 1803 and first used in action against the Dutch in Surinam the following year. From 1804, when its inventor was appointed senior assistant inspector of the artillery, the Royal Artillery adopted shrapnel as a standard form of ammunition, along with existing forms of ammunition: round shot, canister, grape-, and case shot.

The shrapnel shell consisted of a hollow metal sphere or casing, with a thinner body than that of an ordinary exploding shell, which it resembled. It could be fired from ordinary field pieces or howitzers, and in its original form, it was packed with carbine balls mixed with a charge of gunpowder, though it could also contain scraps of metal. With the use of a timed fuse, explosion could be delayed until the shell arrived over its target, and on bursting it would shower its contents at high speed and with theoretically devastating results, especially against tight formations of infantry and cavalry. A 6-pound shrapnel shell had a spread of 250 yards at point-blank range.

Nevertheless, shrapnel's effectiveness very much depended on, above all, the gunner's meticulous care and skill in timing, which meant correctly adjusting the length of the fuse, so calculated to explode above the target. Failure could produce two different, equally disappointing, results: the trajectory might be correct, but the fuse might be set too short, in which case the explosion cast the contents in front of the target. Conversely, the timing of the fuse could be correct, but the trajectory might be incorrect, in which case the shell burst behind the target. There were also all-too-frequent occurrences of shells exploding in the barrel when gunners used too much powder in the charge, though this did not result when they fired shrapnel from howitzers or mortars. Shrapnel could also be used in Congreve rockets, which when fired took an erratic flight path and exploded, causing considerable alarm to the enemy.

The British enjoyed exclusive use of shrapnel during the Napoleonic Wars, and widely employed it in the Peninsular War, from the Battle of Vimeiro (21 August 1808) onward. It was, however, the focus of initial skepticism from a number of officers, including Viscount (later the Duke of) Wellington, who after the Battle of Busaco (27 September) questioned its effectiveness until gunners substituted musket balls, with satisfactory results, inflicting far higher casualties than any other form of ammunition effective at an equivalent range (over 600 yards). Shrapnel was particularly employed at long ranges in order to compensate for the lighter field pieces usually employed by the British Army, which had a shorter range than their heavier French counterparts. Indeed, over time shrapnel became an important component of Royal Artillery ammunition, and it continued to be used in Spain and in the Waterloo campaign, by which time it accounted for 15 percent of all stocks of field piece ammunition and as much as half of howitzer ammunition. The French remained ignorant of this novel weapon until after the Napoleonic Wars.

Gregory Fremont-Barnes

See also Artillery (Land); British Army; Busaco, Battle of; Congreve Rockets; Peninsular War; Vimeiro, Battle of; Waterloo Campaign; Wellington, Arthur Wellesley, First Duke of

References and further reading
Haythornthwaite, Philip. 1999. *Weapons and Equipment of the Napoleonic Wars*. London: Arms and Armour.
Henry, Chris. 2002. *British Napoleonic Artillery, 1793–1815.* Vol. 1, *Field Artillery*. Oxford: Osprey.
Hogg, O. F. 1970. *Artillery: Its Origin, Heyday, and Decline.* Camden, CT: Archon.
Hughes, B. P. 1974. *Firepower: Weapons Effectiveness on the Battlefield, 1630–1850.* New York: Scribner's.
Kiley, Kevin. 2004. *Artillery of the Napoleonic Wars*. London: Greenhill.

Shubra Khit, Action at (13 July 1798)

A minor engagement between French forces under General Napoleon Bonaparte and Mameluke troops under Murad Bey near the town of Shubra Khit, in Egypt.

The (French) Army of the Orient landed in Egypt on 2 July 1798 and quickly captured the city of Alexandria. After resting his troops, Bonaparte led five divisions under generals Jean Reynier, Louis Desaix, Charles Dugua, Honoré Vial, and Louis Bon across the desert to the Egyptian capital of Cairo, while a flotilla under Captain Jean-Baptiste Perrée sailed upstream on the Nile. French troops suffered severely from heat, sickness, and thirst before reaching El Rahmaniya on 10 July and resting on the banks of the Nile, where they eagerly threw themselves into the river to satisfy their burning thirsts and feasted on watermelons that later spread diarrhea in the army. That same day, Desaix's advance elements had a skirmish with a Mameluke detachment led by Muhammed Bey el-Elfi. Bonaparte soon learned that a Mameluke force of some 4,000 cavalrymen and several thousand infantry supported by a flotilla was approaching the town of Shubra Khit, 8 miles south of El Rahmaniya.

All French forces therefore marched at once to Shubra Khit, where they arrived at dawn on 13 July. Bonaparte deployed each division in square, six ranks deep on each side and with artillery at the corners. The Mamelukes, meanwhile, formed a semicircle around the French squares and waited for an opportune moment to attack. The action initially began on the Nile, where the French and Mameluke flotillas engaged in an artillery duel around 9:00 A.M. Soon after, the Mameluke cavalry charged the French, but, unfamiliar with European-style tactics, they suffered heavy casualties every time they approached the squares. After over an hour of indecisive attacks, the French division switched to the offensive and forced the Mamelukes to return to their initial positions. Bonaparte diverted part of his troops to the Nile, where the Mameluke flotilla threatened to overwhelm the French ships by 10:30 A.M. French reinforcements arrived in time to contain enemy attacks. Finally, Perrée's flagship (a *xebec*, a shallow-draft, three-masted vessel, often with lateen sails, commonly used in the Mediterranean and on the Nile) *Le Cerf* scored a hit on the main Mameluke ship, which, as it was carrying ammunition, exploded and forced the remaining ships to flee. The Mameluke cavalry also withdrew in their wake. Bonaparte resumed his advance on Cairo the following day.

The French infantry divisions suffered no casualties, while the French flotilla lost some 30 men, mostly wounded. Precise Mameluke casualties remain unclear and are estimated at some 400–500 men. The location of the battle is often referred to as Chebreiss in French.

Alexander Mikaberidze

See also Desaix, Louis-Charles-Antoine, chevalier de Veygoux; Middle East Campaign; Murad Bey; Ottoman Army; Reynier, Jean Louis Ebénézer, comte
References and further reading
Desvernois, Nicolas Philibert. 1898. *Mémoires du General Bon. Desvernois*. Paris: Plon.
Herold, Christopher. 2005. *Bonaparte in Egypt*. London: Greenhill.

La Jonquiere, C. F. de. 1889–1902. *L'expédition d'Egypte.* 5 vols. Paris: H. Charles-Lavauzelle.

Niqula ibn Yusuf al-Turk [Nicolas the Turk]. 1950. *Chronique d'Egypte, 1798–1804.* Cairo: Institut français d'archéologie orientale.

Vertray, Captain. 1883. *L'armée française en Egypte, 1798–1801: Journal d'un officier de l'Armée d'Egypte.* Paris: Charpentier.

Shuvalov, Pavel Andreyevich, Prince (1776–1823)

Russian general and corps commander. Shuvalov was born to a noble family and enlisted as a cornet in the Life Guard Horse Regiment in 1786. He became a sub-lieutenant in January 1793. Shuvalov served in the Russo-Polish War, distinguishing himself at Pragain in 1794. Promoted to colonel on 29 August 1798, Shuvalov was discharged from the army on 16 April 1799. However, he volunteered for the campaign of 1799 in Italy and Switzerland, where he distinguished himself at the St. Gotthard Pass. He was officially restored to the army with the rank of major general on 27 September 1801.

Shuvalov became *chef* (colonel-proprietor) of the Glukhovsk Cuirassier Regiment on 23 June 1803, *chef* of the Serpukhov Dragoon Regiment on 5 September 1806, and again *chef* of the Glukhovsk Cuirassier Regiment on 17 October 1806. During the 1806–1807 campaigns in Poland, he served with the 9th Division in General Ivan Nikolayevich Essen's 1st Corps. During the Russo-Swedish War of 1808–1809, Shuvalov commanded a corps and captured Torneo in the spring of 1809, for which he was promoted to lieutenant general on 1 April 1809 and adjutant general on 19 July 1808. He completed several diplomatic missions to Vienna between December 1809 and May 1811.

During the 1812 campaign, Shuvalov commanded the 4th Corps in the 1st Western Army but was replaced because of poor health by General Alexander Osterman-Tolstoy on 13 July 1812. After recuperating, he attended Tsar Alexander I during the campaigns in Germany and France in 1813–1814 and distinguished himself at Kulm, Leipzig, Brienne, Arcis-sur-Aube, La-Fère-Champenoise, and Montmartre. Shuvalov took part in the negotiations for the surrender of Paris in March 1814 and, as the Russian representative, accompanied Napoleon to Elba. After the war, he resumed his work in the diplomatic service until his death on 13 December 1823.

Alexander Mikaberidze

See also Alexander I, Tsar; Arcis-sur-Aube, Battle of; Brienne, Battle of; Elba; Fourth Coalition, War of the; France, Campaign in; Germany, Campaign in; Italian Campaigns (1799–1800); Kulm, Battle of; La-Fère-Champenoise, Battle of; Leipzig, Battle of; Montmartre, Action at; Osterman-Tolstoy, Alexander Ivanovich, Count; Russian Campaign; Russo-Polish War; Russo-Swedish War; St. Gotthard Pass, Actions at the; Switzerland, Campaign in

References and further reading

Mikaberidze, Alexander. 2005. *The Russian Officer Corps in the Revolutionary and Napoleonic Wars, 1792–1815.* New York: Savas Beatie.

Shilder, N. 1897. "Graf Shuvalov i Napoleon v 1814 g." *Russkaia Starina*, no. 5.

Sicily

Since 1738, the political fate of the realm of Sicily had been linked to that of Naples under the Spanish House of Bourbon. King Ferdinand III (IV of Naples) ruled Sicily throughout the Napoleonic years, with a short interlude under his son Francis from January 1812 to July 1814. The Napoleonic Wars in Italy exacerbated preexisting political tensions on the island between the Neapolitan court and the autonomist bent of Sicilian feudal barons. At the same time, the key role of Sicily in the Mediterranean theater led the British government to keep the island under military control and heavily interfere in her domestic affairs.

At the end of the eighteenth century, the seeds of discontent were flowering among Sicilian noble landowners, who felt menaced by bleak economic prospects and Neapolitan centralizing policies, with restrictions on their feudal privileges and tax immunities. Such tensions grew stronger in 1799 and from 1806 to 1815, when the French occupation of Naples forced the king and his court to flee to Sicily, under the protection of the British fleet. Ferdinand did not abandon his profligate lifestyle and spent most of his time at the royal hunting lodge near Corleone. His wife Maria Carolina, daughter of the Austrian empress Maria Theresa, possessed a much more active interest in politics, sometimes with a pro-French bias. Both, however, continued to ignore Sicilian particularism, the recovery of Naples being their only concern. Toward this end, new taxes were imposed, which considerably reduced the profits the barons were expecting from the British military occupation of the island (1806–1815) as well as from the exploitation of Sicily's sulfur mines. At various stages, the princes of Cassaro, Belmonte, and Castelnuovo took the lead in the baronial political revolt against the court.

After 1806, the nobles actively cooperated with British diplomatic representatives, who were suspicious of the Bourbon intrigues and wanted to keep a tight hold on Sicily. By maintaining a garrison of over 17,000 men on the island, the British discouraged any French landing. The British also employed local manpower to raise new units, notably the Sicilian Light Infantry Regiment, which in 1807 fought against the Turks in Egypt, and the Calabrian Free Corps, which distinguished itself in Catalonia, in eastern Spain, in 1812–1813. Three other regiments of Italian levies were formed in Sicily; all saw action in Spain in 1812 and in Italy in 1813–1814.

In 1811, Major General Lord William Bentinck was appointed military commander of Sicily. In the course of pursuing his own ambitions—which often put him at odds with the British government's instructions—Bentinck feared that the conflict between the barons and the court could threaten British control of the island. Politically a Whig, he caused growing concern among the local feudal lords over the issue of constitutional rights. With Bentinck's support, the barons summoned a new parliament in 1812 to approve a "liberal" constitution. According to the Constitution of July 1812, the king of Naples allowed Sicily a greater degree of political and fiscal autonomy, while the barons renounced most feudal privileges, a rather paradoxical conclusion to a process that had begun with the claim of constitutional rights in defense of those very privileges.

The Sicilian constitutional experiment did not, however, last long. After the Congress of Vienna (1814–1815), King Ferdinand was allowed to return to Naples. In 1816, the Neapolitan and Sicilian realms were reunited under the name of the Kingdom of the Two Sicilies.

Marco Gioannini

See also Ferdinand IV, King; Naples; Vienna, Congress of
References and further reading
Acton, Harold. 1998. *The Bourbons of Naples.* London: Trafalgar Square.
Croce, Benedetto. 1970. *History of the Kingdom of Naples.* Chicago: University of Chicago Press.
Flayhart, William. 1992. *Counterpoint to Trafalgar: The Anglo-Russian Invasion of Naples, 1805–06.* Columbia: University of South Carolina Press.
Ghirelli, Antonio. 1981. *Storia di Napoli* [History of Naples]. Torino: Einaudi.
Gregory, Desmond. 1988. *Sicily: The Insecure Base: A History of the British Occupation of Sicily, 1806–15.* Madison, NJ: Fairleigh Dickinson University Press.
Ilari, Virgilio, Piero Crociani, and Ciro Paoletti. 2001. *Storia militare dell'Italia giacobina* [A Military History of Jacobin Italy] *1796–1802.* Vol. 2, *La guerra peninsulare.* Rome: Stato Maggiore dell'Esercito-Ufficio Storico.
Johnston, Robert M. 1904. *The Napoleonic Empire in Southern Italy and the Rise of the Secret Societies.* 2 vols. London: Macmillan.
Mack Smith, Denis. 1968. *Modern Sicily after 1713.* London: Chatto and Windus.
Rosselli, John. 1956. *Lord William Bentinck and the British Occupation of Sicily, 1811–1814.* Cambridge: Cambridge University Press.
Schneid, Frederick C. 2002. *Napoleon's Italian Campaigns, 1805–1815.* Westport, CT: Greenwood.

Sickness and Disease

Sickness and disease killed and incapacitated far more soldiers than did enemy fire during the French Revolutionary and Napoleonic Wars. Even soldiers wounded in battle were at greater risk of dying through infection than of the wound itself. The principles of hygiene were not fully understood, and the science of microbiology did not emerge until later in the nineteenth century; thus the spread of infection was a mystery to medical practitioners of the period. Conflicting theories as to the source of disease included an imbalance in the body's humors and a miasma emanating from marshy and foul-smelling areas. The sheer scale of disease within an army often overwhelmed the medical services, and army doctors often succumbed to the illnesses they were treating.

Of all soldiers who died during the period between 1792 and 1815, two of every three died of disease, and these diseases were many and varied. However, while armies suffered greatly from sickness and disease, it should not be forgotten that civilians also succumbed to life-threatening illnesses, exacerbated by poor living conditions, poor hygiene, and lack of effective antibiotics. Epidemics of disease swept through both military and civilian populations.

Dysentery was present in all the armies involved, and one estimate is that in the late eighteenth century, 30 percent of an army would be suffering from this disease at any one time. It was a problem for armies that spent long periods encamped in one place, as water supplies became contaminated with the sewage from thousands of men and horses. This illness killed and incapacitated troops in all theaters of the war.

Next to dysentery, typhus was a major killer of soldiers, a disease spread via the body louse. Close bodily contact and the sharing of infested clothing and bedding disseminated this infection throughout the armies of the period. The disease was known as gaol fever and ship fever, and during the Peninsular War there is no doubt that Spanish fever was in fact typhus. Typhus was a significant killer of French troops during Napoleon's retreat from Moscow in 1812.

The West Indies was a major theater of conflict, and many thousands of soldiers went to their graves there. Of 89,000 British officers and men who served there between 1793 and 1801, nearly 45,000 died, mainly from yellow jack or black vomit, descriptive names for yellow fever. The West Indies was a posting that inspired dread in soldiers, and some British units even mutinied on being told they were going there in 1795. It was noted that black soldiers had a much lower sickness rate from the disease than did those of European origin, undoubtedly due to an acquired immunity. A French army under General Charles-Victor Emmanuel Leclerc was sent to St. Domingue (Haiti) in 1801, but both the French commander and 25,000 of his troops succumbed to yellow fever. The mortality rate for the disease in this theater was undoubtedly increased by the soldier's propensity for alcohol, as yellow fever affects the liver, and so alcohol abuse may have increased the mortality rate.

Malaria was a disease described at the time under the general term *fever* or *ague*, but one that also had a significant impact upon armies. It was present in the West Indies, but was also prevalent in the Iberian Peninsula and the Low Countries. In 1809, a British expedition sailed to the island of Walcheren in the Scheldt estuary, where an army of 40,000 men was defeated, not by the enemy, but by "Walcheren fever." Of this army, over 40 percent were struck down by the disease, resulting in 3,900 deaths and many thousands more permanently debilitated. Only 100 were killed by enemy action. Modern medical opinion suggests that Walcheren fever was a combination of malaria, typhus, typhoid, and dysentery, acting together upon a susceptible soldiery.

Other diseases that Napoleonic troops encountered included bubonic plague in Egypt during Bonaparte's campaign there in 1799, a disease that had a considerable effect on the morale of the French army as well as a physical effect. Both British and French troops suffered from ophthalmia in this theater, many becoming blind. Throughout the wars, epidemics of measles and smallpox ravaged armies, especially those troops in barracks. The latter infection, however, could be controlled by vaccination, introduced by Edward Jenner in 1796, and this preventative measure was enthusiastically embraced by many nations at the time, particularly France. Venereal disease and alcohol caused problems for soldiers with little education, and scurvy appeared among some troops, despite it being known that citrus fruits and vegetables would combat this disease, caused as it was by a deficiency of Vitamin C. Lack of access to such foods still caused outbreaks, as the Grande Armée found on its retreat out of Russia in 1812.

Lack of understanding about hygiene and antisepsis meant that wounds became infected and soldiers died of gangrene or tetanus. In many military hospitals, especially on campaign, soldiers with simple wounds were placed in the same wards (and often the same beds) as men with infectious diseases.

Despite the lack of knowledge about disease, treatments were available, although many of these were based upon local folklore and "quack" medicine. Peruvian bark, or cinchona bark, was used to combat fevers. This bark contains quinine and so is effective in cases of malaria.

Mercurous chloride (calomel) was used to treat syphilis, and other commonly used agents included acetate of lead, antimony, camphor, arsenic, and ammonia, either administered singly or in combination. Less toxic treatments included warm baths, clean clothing and bedding, and improved diet. Bleeding and the administration of purgatives were still popular among the medical profession, although these treatments were more injurious than beneficial.

Paul Chamberlain

See also Haiti; Leclerc, Charles-Victor Emmanuel; Losses (French); Medical Services; Middle East Campaign; Peninsular War; Russian Campaign; Santo Domingo; Walcheren, Expedition to; West Indies, Operations in the
References and further reading
Blanco, Richard L. 1974. *Wellington's Surgeon General: Sir James McGrigor.* Durham, NC: Duke University Press.
Bond, Gordon C. 1979. *The Grand Expedition: The British Invasion of Holland in 1809.* Athens: University of Georgia Press.
Cantlie, Sir Neil. 1974. *A History of the Army Medical Department.* London: Longmans.
Gabriel, Richard A., and Karen S. Metz. 1992. *A History of Military Medicine.* Vol. 2, *From the Renaissance through Modern Times.* New York: Greenwood.
Howard, Dr. Martin. 2002. *Wellington's Doctors: The British Army Medical Services in the Napoleonic Wars.* Staplehurst, UK: Spellmount.
———. 2006. *Napoleon's Doctors.* Staplehurst, UK: Spellmount.
Keevil, John, Christopher Lloyd, and Jack Coulter. 1957–1963. *Medicine and the Navy, 1200–1900.* 4 vols. Edinburgh: E. & S. Livingstone.
McGrigor, Mary, ed. 2000. *The Scalpel and the Sword: The Autobiography of the Father of Army Medicine.* Dalkeith, Scotland: Scottish Cultural Press.
Richardson, Robert G. 1974. *Larrey: Surgeon to Napoleon's Imperial Guard.* London: Purnell.

Siege Warfare

Form of combat based on the attack and defense of fixed points. These points may be various population centers, such as towns, cities, and fortifications. This type of warfare dates back to ancient times, and has developed an entire lexicon of its own terminology. The practice of siege warfare, however, underwent a series of profound changes with the introduction of gunpowder and artillery at the end of the Middle Ages. While siege warfare is not commonly associated with the French Revolutionary or Napoleonic Wars, some major sieges did take place during both series of conflicts.

Siege warfare is based on the encirclement of one force (the besieged) by another (the besieger). Though an ancient form of fighting, siege warfare underwent a series of important developments in the sixteenth and seventeenth centuries, a period often described as the Military Revolution, which influenced the way this method of warfare was conducted between 1792 and 1815. These changes reflected the development of workable gunpowder weaponry, and fundamentally transformed the architecture of military and civic defenses. Briefly, these changes included lower and thicker walls, built on a more angular as opposed to a linear pattern. The use of angles was important for two reasons. First, it presented a smaller target for the attacker's artillery than linear walls. Second, it allowed for the use of crossfire between two of the bastions. Thus the defenses were mutually supporting, making assault in the open suicidal on the part of the attacker. This design came to be known as the *trace italien,* since it was first developed in Italy in the sixteenth century. In order to attack a fortress or town surrounded by this sort of defense, it became necessary to dig a fairly intricate series of trenches. The development of this architecture came in response to the French use of artillery during their invasions of northern Italy.

French siege warfare developed to its highest points during the reign of Louis XIV. His chief engineer, Sébastien le Prestre de Vauban, mastered siege warfare in both its offensive and defensive aspects. He was known to have designed several fortresses deemed impregnable by contemporaries. Likewise, he conducted some of the most successful sieges of the period, and he established the methods by which a later generation of French commanders conducted sieges during the French Revolutionary and Napoleonic Wars.

In the form of siege warfare that had emerged by the late eighteenth century, artillery played the predominant role. French artillery, after the reforms of Count Jean-Baptiste Vaquette de Gribeauval, which were put into effect in 1776, was recognized as the best in Europe.

If a siege followed the prescribed methods of the day, the first step was for the besiegers to surround the point they wished to capture. Often, two lines were used to surround the point. One, referred to as a line of circumvallation, encompassed the outer reaches of the area under siege. The line of circumvallation protected the entire besieging army from attack. Then an internal line was established, known as a line of contravallation. This line faced toward the besieged, and served as the launching point for the siege. Laying out the lines for a siege was the work of the engineers. Once both lines were established, a process made more difficult by Frederick the Great of Prussia, who began the practice of building forts outside the walls, the defenders were called upon to surrender. If they refused, the besiegers began to entrench their positions.

The first parallel approach trench was opened at night. Speed and secrecy were of paramount importance in this operation, so as to prevent the besieged from launching a counterattack or sortie while those who were digging the trench were exposed. Once the first parallel was complete, the garrison was again asked to surrender. If they refused, the process of moving the parallels closer to the besieged continued. Each parallel was connected to the one behind it via a communications trench, often dug in a zigzag pattern so as to reduce the danger of the besiegers coming under concentrated enemy fire, or being enfiladed while moving forward.

As the lines continued to approach the besieged, thousands of sandbags, gabions, and planks had to be brought forward as well. These would be used in the final assault on the besieged in order to fill in their outer ditch defense. Likewise, the heavy artillery used in a siege was moved forward at night, and had to be in position to begin a fresh bombardment by daybreak.

When the artillery was considered to be close enough, the work of blasting a breach in the defender's walls began in earnest. Usually, 24-pounder cannon were utilized in the work of blasting gaping holes in the defenses. Eighteen-pounder guns, while considered useful for dismounting a defender's guns, were considered too light to make an effective breach in the walls. Once the artillery created a breach large enough to make an assault practical, a storming party was assembled. This body of men was referred to as the forlorn hope. The party usually consisted of a subaltern, two sergeants, and about twenty-five privates. One last call to surrender was issued to the besieged. If this were refused, the forlorn hope attacked, usually at night so as to minimize casualties.

The mission of the forlorn hope was to capture the breach and hold it until the main assault party could move in and support them. Even under the best of circumstances, this presented no easy task. If the attackers took the breach and succeeded in taking the town, the town and its garrison could expect no mercy. However, up to this point—prior to the storming of the city itself—if the besieged surrendered, the civilians could expect some protection from the worst ravages an army could unleash.

Knowing this, the garrison fought furiously. Once the forlorn hope captured the breach, the main assault force moved in with scaling ladders, bags of leaves, and grass to fill the defenders' ditch, and axes to cut through any obstacles laid in the path of the attackers. For their part, the defenders did their utmost to make the breach and ditch a death trap. They rained hand grenades and small-arms fire down on the attackers, and rolled barrels of powder with lit fuses down the walls. If they had the time while waiting for the forlorn hopes to get in position, the defenders cleared the ditch of rubble and placed obstacles in it such as *chevaux-de-frise.* These were long poles with

British infantry attempt to scale the walls of Badajoz, the site of one of several horrific sieges conducted during the Peninsular War. (Unsigned engraving from *British Battles on Land and Sea* by James Grant. London, Paris & New York: Cassell, Petter & Galpin, n.d.)

blades attached to impale the attackers as they attempted to take the ditch. Mines were likewise set to detonate when the assault parties had gained control of a certain area.

The savagery of combat could escalate further if the garrison fought house to house within the town. This type of combat was always bloody and chaotic, with houses burning and brutal combat raging in narrow streets, further heightening the level of destruction.

Considering the violence often associated with the final stages of a siege, it is little wonder that some of the worst atrocities came in the wake of storming a town that refused to surrender. This was particularly the case after the British stormings of Ciudad Rodrigo and Badajoz, in January and April 1812, respectively. As the above makes clear, the final stages of a siege could be extremely violent and confused. Some historians of this period have discussed how this could bring about a psychotic state, due to the heightened stress of combat. The indiscriminate rape and bloodshed that occurred afterward constituted a stress release for the attackers, who had undergone such intense fighting.

It has often been said that the French Revolutionary and Napoleonic Wars witnessed the abandonment of the type of positional warfare that had lent itself to sieges in favor of a more mobile form of campaigning. While there is some truth to this observation, it can be misleading if taken to extremes. Furthermore, it is worth recalling that Bonaparte first gained the attention of the Committee of Public Safety for his work at the siege of Toulon in 1793, though it must be stressed that he was not himself a senior commander and did not initiate the siege.

With respect to sieges conducted during the period 1792–1815, each operation developed in its own manner, and no general description can completely and accurately explain the process. Still, some fundamental observations are possible. In general, sieges were costly in lives both to the attackers and to the defenders. French armies did not, as a general practice, carry with them the large and cumbersome siege trains (vehicles carrying specialized equipment and ammunition for this type of warfare) that so often burdened the armies of Louis XIV. Over time, the various powers opposing the French followed the example of their enemy and abandoned their siege trains as well. This meant, however, that important points were often besieged using much more makeshift means.

The practice of conducting sieges was not abandoned altogether, but it was certainly less frequently employed as a method of war than in the past, and it was employed in a more haphazard fashion. In some cases, heavier caliber guns were taken from naval vessels when available in order to provide the firepower necessary to form breaches in the walls. Likewise, the lack of a proper siege train often meant that, when important points had to be taken, the attackers had to resort to various ruses and subterfuges. Sometimes the gates of a fortress were simply rushed, in the hope that the attackers could gain entrance before the guards shut them out. This naturally could lead to excessively high casualties on the part of the attackers. At other times, garrisons were subjected to intense bombardment, in the hope that this would frighten the defenders into surrender. Likewise, the bombardment could inflict heavy casualties on the defenders, as well as any civilians unfortunate enough to be caught in it. The British often used rockets for this purpose, and they were known to create quite a stir among the defenders and civilians within a garrison.

James McIntyre

See also Acre, Siege of; Almeida, Sieges of; Artillery (Land); Badajoz, First Siege of; Badajoz, Second Siege of; Badajoz, Third Siege of; Burgos, Siege of; Cádiz, Siege of; Ciudad Rodrigo, First Siege of; Ciudad Rodrigo, Second Siege of; Congreve Rockets; Gaeta, Sieges of; Genoa, Siege of; Gerona, Siege of; Gribeauval System; Lyons, Siege of; Magdeburg, Siege of; Mainz, Siege of; Mantua, Sieges of; Pamplona, Siege of; Public Safety, Committee of; San Sebastian, Siege of; Saragossa, Sieges of; Stralsund, Siege of; Tarragona, Sieges of; Torgau, Siege of; Toulon, Siege of; Valencia, Siege of

References and further reading
Augoyat, Antoine. 1860–1864. *Aperçu historique sur les fortifications, les ingénieurs, et sur le corps du génie en France.* 3 vols. Paris: Dumaine.
Belmas, Jacques. 1836–1837. *Journaux des sièges faites ou soutenus par les français dans la Peninsule de 1807 à 1814.* 4 vols. Paris: Didot Frères.
Blanning, T. C. W. 1996. *The French Revolutionary Wars 1787–1802.* London: Arnold.
Chandler, David G. 1995. *The Campaigns of Napoleon.* London: Weidenfeld and Nicolson.
Duffy, Christopher. 1979. *Siege Warfare: The Fortress in the Early Modern World, 1494–1660.* London: Routledge.
———. 1985. *The Fortress in the Age of Vauban and Frederick the Great, 1660–1789.* London: RKP.
———. 1996. *Fire and Stone.* London: Greenhill.
Elting, John R. 1988. *Swords around a Throne.* New York: Free Press.
Fletcher, Ian. 2003. *Fortresses of the Peninsular War, 1808–14.* Oxford: Osprey.
Griffith, Paddy. 1998. *The Art of War of Revolutionary France, 1789–1802.* London: Greenhill.
Henry, Chris. 2003. *British Napoleonic Artillery, 1793–1815.* Vol. 2, *Siege and Coastal Artillery.* Oxford: Osprey.
Muir, Rory. 1998. *Tactics and the Experience of Battle in the Age of Napoleon.* New Haven: Yale University Press.
Myatt, Frederick. 1987. *British Sieges of the Peninsular War.* Staplehurst, UK: Spellmount.
Rothenberg, Gunther E. 1978. *The Art of Warfare in the Age of Napoleon.* Bloomington: Indiana University Press.

Sieyès, Emmanuel Joseph, comte (1748–1836)

Sieyès played an important role in both the French Revolution and the rise of Napoleon. A former clergyman taken by the idealistic ideas that formed the intellectual basis of the Revolution, Sieyès promoted the use of those ideas to improve conditions for common Frenchmen.

"The Abbé Sieyès," as he was generally known, was elected a representative of the Third Estate of Paris in the Estates-General convened by King Louis XVI. In a pamphlet he published in early 1789, he voiced the concerns of the day: "What is the Third Estate? Everything. What was it until today? Nothing. What does it want? To become something" (quoted in Sewell 1995). He later helped form the radical Jacobin Club and played a major role in writing the Declaration of the Rights of Man and the Citizen, the basic statement of rights and protections that is often compared with the Bill of Rights in the U. S. Constitution.

Sieyès voted for the death of the king, became a member of the Convention, survived the Terror by keeping a low profile, and helped bring about the downfall of Maximilien Robespierre. He then held a succession of important positions in and for the government, including the presidency of the Council of Five Hundred. He became a member of the Directory in early 1799.

Sieyès was greatly concerned for the stability—indeed, the survival—of a government that could withstand the forces of both the Left and the Right. He had little use for the Directory of which he was a member, and became involved in a number of plots to bring about its overthrow. He understood that any successful coup needed the support of the army, and planned to have General Barthélemy Joubert serve as his "sword," but Joubert's death at the Battle of Novi left Sieyès looking for another "sword." He found one in the young General Napoleon Bonaparte, fresh back from what was generally conceived to have been a successful campaign in Egypt and the Holy Land.

Sieyès was an idealistic but shrewd politician, determined to save the nation from itself. Bonaparte was an ambitious and astute politician, convinced that only he was capable of saving the nation. They collaborated in the coup d'état of Brumaire (9–10 November 1799) along with Joseph Fouché, Charles-Maurice de Talleyrand, and others. Bonaparte and Sieyès, along with Pierre Roger

Ducos, became the ruling consuls of the new government, known as the Consulate.

Sieyès had been the mastermind of the coup, but Bonaparte quickly became the most powerful man in France, with the other consuls playing largely ceremonial roles. Sieyès was eased into retirement, where he lived in luxury. During the period of the First Empire (1804–1814), after Bonaparte assumed an imperial title and became known as Napoleon I, the Emperor always recognized Sieyès's importance and later made him a count. But having been instrumental in ushering in both the Revolution and Bonaparte, Sieyès's active role was over, and he lived the rest of his life in relative obscurity.

J. David Markham

See also Barras, Paul Jean François Nicolas, vicomte de; Brumaire, Coup of; Consulate, The; Convention, The; Council of Five Hundred; Directory, The; Fouché, Joseph, duc d'Otrante; French Revolution; Jacobins; Joubert, Barthélemy Catherine; Louis XVI, King; Middle East Campaign; Novi, Battle of; Robespierre, Maximilien François Marie Isidore; Talleyrand-Périgord, Charles-Maurice de, Prince; Terror, The

References and further reading
Asprey, Robert. 2000. *The Rise of Napoleon Bonaparte.* New York: Basic Books.
Doyle, William. 2003. *The Oxford History of the French Revolution.* Oxford: Oxford University Press.
Sewell, William H. 1995. *A Rhetoric of Bourgeois Revolution: The Abbé Sieyes and* What Is the Third Estate? Durham, NC: Duke University Press.

Six Days Campaign (February 1814)

The Six Days campaign refers to a series of battles fought in the second week of February 1814 during the campaign in France, namely, Champaubert, Montmirail, Château-Thierry, and Vauchamps. French victories in all of these battles rallied Napoleon's forces and reignited Allied resolve to defeat Napoleon in the subsequent weeks.

In the Battle of Champaubert on 10 February, Napoleon's troops routed the outnumbered forces of General Zakhar Dmitrievich Olsufiev and captured the general as well. That victory divided the (Russo-Prussian) Army of Silesia and allowed Napoleon to push on to Montmirail to defeat generals Johann von Yorck and Fabian Osten-Sacken, while leaving Field Marshal Gebhard von Blücher isolated to the east. The Battle of Montmirail on 11 February was lost by the Allies, largely because Sacken did not meet up with Yorck's forces near Château-Thierry before the battle, and because Yorck was subsequently slow to come to Osten-Sacken's rescue. The Battle of Château-Thierry followed soon after on 12 February, too soon for the Allied forces to be able to regroup properly, although it

was not the absolute victory that Napoleon sought. The campaign changed direction after Napoleon received word that the (Austrian) Army of Bohemia under *Feldmarschall* Karl Philipp Fürst zu Schwarzenberg was making inroads along the Seine. After sending part of his forces south to bolster the French line near Montereau, Napoleon and General Emmanuel Grouchy faced Blücher, who had advanced from the east in order to prevent Napoleon from assisting his forces on the Seine. The subsequent Battle of Vauchamps on 14 February broke up the whole of Blücher's forces, and Blücher fled east toward Châlons.

Later commentators noted that in this campaign Napoleon achieved unexpected and extraordinary results, including the elimination of approximately 20,000 troops of the enemy total—which nearly halved the forces in opposition. This was partly due to the nature of the campaign: Napoleon's troops were greatly outnumbered, and so he fought by means of careful maneuvers and tactics, rather than using the sort of brute force characteristic of earlier French victories. For Napoleon, the victories improved his troops' morale and ensured the support of Paris a while longer.

But the campaign rallied the fractious Allies and helped to end their bickering among themselves: they rediscovered their joint purpose to fight France until Napoleon was defeated. They also confirmed this commitment in the Treaty of Chaumont, dated 1 March. The treaty pledged that no nation would sign a separate peace with Napoleon, and that the Allies sought both the 1791 French borders and, potentially, Napoleon's abdication. Success in the Six Days campaign indicated that Napoleon would not give up without fighting to the end, but it also ensured that the Allies would not halt until they reached Paris.

Korcaighe P. Hale

See also Blücher von Wahlstatt, Gebhard Lebrecht Fürst; Champaubert, Battle of; Château-Thierry, Battle of; Chaumont, Conference and Treaty of; France, Campaign in; Grouchy, Emmanuel, marquis de; Montmirail, Battle of; Osten-Sacken, Fabian Vilgelmovich, Prince; Schwarzenberg, Karl Philipp Fürst zu; Vauchamps, Battle of; Yorck von Wartenburg, Johann David Ludwig Graf

References and further reading
Chandler, David G. 1995. *The Campaigns of Napoleon.* London: Weidenfeld and Nicolson.
Delderfield, R. F. 2001. *Imperial Sunset: The Fall of Napoleon, 1813–1814.* Lanham, MD: Cooper Square.
Lawford, James. 1977. *Napoleon: The Last Campaigns, 1813–1815.* London: Roxby.
Petre, F. Loraine. 1994. *Napoleon at Bay, 1814.* London: Greenhill.

Sixth Coalition, War of the

See France, Campaign in; Germany, Campaign in

Slave Trade

The French Revolutionary and Napoleonic Wars mark a watershed in the history of the Atlantic slave trade. Originating in the sixteenth century, the trade had reached its high point during the dramatic expansion of the Atlantic economy in the eighteenth century, and for slaving nations like France, it was thriving as never before. At the same time, abolitionist movements in Britain and France, nurtured by the universalist ideas of human liberty and dignity espoused by the Enlightenment, were exerting increasing pressure on public opinion. This movement, along with the specific military-diplomatic conjuncture of the wars, enabled Britain—the international leader of abolitionism—to press the European slaving nations to take action against the practice. While Britain's efforts did not result in an immediately effective abolition of the actual trade, they did bring about, at the Congress of Vienna in 1815, its first unequivocal and public denunciation on humanitarian grounds. This declaration, signed by all participants of the Congress, was to pave the way for more successful efforts during the course of the nineteenth century, ultimately leading to general abolition.

The main European slaving nations on the eve of the French Revolution were the old colonial powers Spain and Portugal, and the colonial newcomers of the seventeenth century, Britain and France. Only the latter, however, had by this time genuinely developed any significant abolitionist societies. The British Society for Effecting the Abolition of the Slave Trade, having obtained abolition of the trade within the British Empire by 1807, was more effective than the French Société des Amis des Noirs (Society of the Friends of the Blacks), that, though counting influential members in the National Assembly, was hampered by the even more powerful colonial lobby of the Club Massiac, many of whose members owned West Indian plantations. Later, under Napoleon, the so-called Creole Party, led by Empress Josephine, represented the interests of sugar planters and shippers, so that pragmatic economic considerations continued to dominate the politics of the French slave trade.

The National Convention had abolished the bounty system in 1793, a minor victory for the Société. The 1794 abolition of slavery was, however, rather more an ex post facto recognition of the reality of the St. Domingue uprising than an initiative taken on true humanitarian grounds, and it was never implemented. With the French abolitionist movement resting on such a shaky foundation, it comes as no surprise that Napoleon—who himself appears never to have had any strong convictions on the matter—reconsidered the issue and shifted policy, for a combination of economic and strategic reasons. He was ever the pragma-

tist, and first planter interests, then the changing diplomatic situation, dictated his decisions. Thus, after a brief period of vacillation during which he attempted to introduce an unworkable mixed regime of free and slave islands, on 12 May 1802, Napoleon not only restored slavery and the slave trade throughout the French colonies, but also reinstituted much of the Code Noir (Black Code), the old colonial slave code dating back to the days of Louis XIV. As a final symbolic gesture, St. Domingue's former *ancien régime* administrator was even returned as governor of that island.

With Napoleon's defeat and abdication in 1814, Britain was able to bring pressure on France to move against the trade. The issue was complicated by the fact that British abolitionists adopted a hard-line position, demanding that the British representatives at Paris, and later at the Congress of Vienna, make French abolition of the trade a requirement for the return of their lucrative West Indian colonies. The Foreign Office, in contrast, took the position that forced abolition would destabilize the restored French monarchy and with it the newly won peace. Aware of these difficulties, France—aided by Spain and Portugal—strung Britain out as long as possible, in the hope of gaining maximum concessions. In the end, France regained its key islands and, in Article I of the five "Additional Articles between France and Great Britain" in the first Treaty of Paris, merely undertook to abolish the trade within five years, giving the French ample time to replenish their depleted slave stock. These terms were a clear victory for the wily French diplomat, Prince Charles Maurice de Talleyrand. France, finally, further pledged to work with the British for general abolition, at the upcoming congress to be held at Vienna.

On 8 February 1815, the Declaration of the Powers relative to the Universal Abolition of the Slave Trade was signed by Britain, Russia, Sweden, France, Spain, Portugal, Austria, and Prussia and annexed to the General Treaty of the Vienna Congress as Act XV. It denounced the trade in no uncertain moral terms as an utterly repugnant bane to humanity that needed to be eradicated for the benefit of all mankind. Important qualifications were made, however, respecting the right of individual nations to determine their own timetable for actual abolition. Still, even though in practical terms the declaration was little more than a moral statement, it contributed greatly to raising public awareness of the issue, and made the position of those powers that persisted in the trade increasingly untenable on ethical grounds.

On 29 March 1815—less than a month after his return from Elba—Napoleon abolished the slave trade in the French colonies not only for French, but also foreign traders. This astonishing about-face from his previous policy was, in the view of most scholars, probably no more than a cynical attempt to play on British opinion and divide Britain from the other Allies, though some argue he may have been motivated by a desire to punish the rather Anglophile French ports. After Waterloo, the British were able to invoke not only the terms of the first Treaty of Paris and the Vienna declaration, but also, ironically, Napoleon's 1815 abolition, against the again-restored Louis XVIII. Still, while Talleyrand had been more or less coerced into honoring Napoleon's decree, the second Treaty of Paris only foresaw further discussions on abolition. So the French (clandestine) trade continued, and the British renewed their efforts at the Congress of Verona in 1822.

William L. Chew III

See also Convention, The; Haiti; Martinique; Paris, First Treaty of; Paris, Second Treaty of; Santo Domingo; Slavery; Talleyrand-Périgord, Charles-Maurice de, Prince; Vienna, Congress of; Wilberforce, William

References and further reading
Blackburn, Robin. 1988. *The Overthrow of Colonial Slavery, 1776–1848*. London: Verso.
Hochschild, Adam. 2006. *Bury the Chains: The British Struggle to Abolish Slavery*. London: Pan.
Hurst, Michael, ed. 1972. *Key Treaties for the Great Powers, 1814–1914*. 2 vols. Vol. 1, *1814–1870*. Newton Abbot, UK: David and Charles.
Morgan, Kenneth. 2001. *Slavery, Atlantic Trade and the British Economy, 1660–1800*. Cambridge: Cambridge University Press.
Putney, Martha. 1975. "The Slave Trade in French Diplomacy from 1814 to 1815." *Journal of Negro History* 60, no. 3: 411–427.
Reich, Jerome. 1968. "The Slave Trade at the Congress of Vienna—A Study in English Public Opinion." *Journal of Negro History* 53:129–143.
Rodriguez, Junius P., ed. 1997. *The Historical Encyclopedia of World Slavery*. 2 vols. Santa Barbara, CA: ABC-CLIO.
Walvin, James. 2001. *Black Ivory: Slavery in the British Empire*. Oxford: Blackwell.

Slavery

By the time of the French Revolutionary and Napoleonic Wars, slavery in the New World had already existed for more than two centuries, above all in the West Indies, the majority of whose islands—the most lucrative being Jamaica—were controlled by Britain, and in the southern states of America, specifically Virginia, the Carolinas, and Georgia. By 1790 some 700,000 slaves lived in the United States.

At the same time, there was also an important French presence in the Caribbean, most notably perhaps in the plantation colony of St. Domingue, present-day Haiti. St. Domingue was home to approximately 40,000 Frenchmen and about half a million blacks, the majority of whom were slaves. They provided labor for sugar, coffee, and cotton plantations on the island. Connections with trade and investment, including the slave trade, made many Frenchman back in their home country interested in the political situation in St. Domingue and the question of slavery in general. There were also about 28,000 free blacks and mulattoes in St. Domingue, most of whom owned slaves of their own.

Before the French Revolution, slaves and their owners were subject to the Code Noir (literally, "Black Code"), a slave code written in 1685. The code provided for the education and baptism of slaves into Catholicism, as well as excluding Jews from the colonies. Slave status, according to the code, was to be passed down through the mother rather than father. While most of the code dealt with religious, heritage, or punishment issues, it also placed responsibility for the care of sick and elderly slaves on the slaveholder.

Even before the Revolution, the Société des Amis des Noirs (Society of Friends of the Blacks) had been agitating for the abolition of slavery. Pamphlets were one of the main methods used by abolitionists to spread their message, arguing either for full abolition, or for improvement in the situation of slaves. Olympe de Gouges wrote one of the most famous pamphlets on this subject, *Reflections of Black People*. The Amis des Noirs based their arguments for abolition on the Declaration of the Rights of Man and the Citizen and the granting of political rights to religious minorities. Their membership included prominent revolutionaries such as Jacques-Pierre Brissot, the marquis de Condorcet, the marquis de Lafayette, the comte de Mirabeau, and Emmanuel Sieyès, among others. Perhaps the best-known champion of the abolitionist movement of the time was Abbé Henri-Baptiste Grégoire.

In some cases abolitionists argued not for full abolition of the slave trade, but rather for abolition of that segment of the slave trade that transported Africans to the French colonies. They also suggested that a slave revolt might take place in St. Domingue, an insinuation that would later lead some to accuse them of fomenting the revolt.

Despite the efforts of these abolitionist groups, the French public was largely uninterested in the question of abolition, since slavery had already been abolished in France and the slavery of the French West Indies was both distant and profitable.

The shift in the political mood of the Revolution in France led both slaves and their colonial owners to approach the National Assembly to argue for their respective positions regarding the repeal of slavery in the colonies. As they discussed the issue in Paris, unrest in the colonies became more pronounced, with blacks and mulattoes agitating for full rights, and slave owners and colonists opposed abolition for fear of losing their livelihood.

The first major agitation was seen among black slaves on the islands of Guadeloupe and Martinique. Inspired by tales of white slaves' freedom in France, in late 1789 black slaves on the islands unsuccessfully staged their own revolt. In October 1790, the first major slave revolt on the island of Haiti began with 350 mulattoes. The rebellion was suppressed relatively quickly and the organizers executed, including Vincent Ogé, one of the most outspoken leaders and mulatto property owners on the island.

On 15 May 1791, the National Assembly voted to award full political rights to free blacks and mulattoes born of free mothers and fathers. While the law only affected a few hundred individuals on the island, the planters and slave owners were so opposed to it that they refused to follow the new edict. Several months later, on 22 August 1791, a second, larger revolt took place in St. Domingue, commonly recognized as the first successful slave revolt in history. In response, the National Assembly revoked the rights of free blacks and mulattoes in September 1791. This move only increased the violence of the revolt, as slaves burned plantations and murdered their owners. The revolt brought to the fore the talented Toussaint Louverture, who stood as the leader of the black slaves in St. Domingue during their struggle.

In order to maintain order in their most lucrative colony, the Legislative Assembly dispatched commissioners to St. Domingue. The Montagnard Convention followed up the move in September 1792 with the dispatch of commissioners and troops to the island in the face of continuing unrest. These commissioners and troops provided support to those slaves opposing those white plantation owners who were willing to accept British intervention to restore their positions. Sonthonax, the Jacobin delegate, offered partial emancipation of the slaves in August 1793, which was confirmed by the Convention in February 1794.

As First Consul, Bonaparte attempted to restore the colony to its productive past through the reimposition of slavery in a failed military expedition to the island in 1802–1803. A force under General Charles-Victor Leclerc arrived and tricked Toussaint Louverture into returning to France, where he was confined to prison and left to die of cold and starvation. The slave revolt continued on the island, despite the death of Toussaint Louverture. Bonaparte then sent a larger force to the island, but the ravages of yellow fever left a mere 7,000 alive by the time they arrived. General Donatien Rochambeau, head of the mission, chose to surrender to the Royal Navy, which was supporting the slave insurrection. After a bloody vengeance on the remaining French on the island, St. Domingue declared its independence as Haiti on 1 January 1804. Bonaparte did, however, reestablish slavery in France's remaining colonies by a law of May 1802, which was written into the Civil Code of 1807. After his return from exile on Elba, however, Napoleon outlawed slavery in the colonies in support of his more liberal imperial policy. After Napoleon's downfall in 1815, the Congress of Vienna condemned slavery in the French West Indies, and by doing so contributed to its ultimate demise.

Christine Grafton

See also Civil Code; Convention, The; Haiti; Leclerc, Charles-Victor-Emmanuel; Martinique; Sieyès, Emmanuel Joseph, comte; Slave Trade; Toussaint Louverture; Vienna, Congress of; Wilberforce, William

References and further reading
Cooper, Anna Julia. 1988. *Slavery and the French Revolutionists.* New York: E. Mellen.
Davis, David Brion. 1999. *The Problem of Slavery in the Age of Revolution, 1770–1823.* New York: Oxford University Press.
Dubois, Laurent. 2004. *A Colony of Citizens: Revolution and Slave Emancipation in the French Caribbean, 1787–1804.* Chapel Hill: University of North Carolina Press.
Hochschild, Adam. 2006. *Bury the Chains: The British Struggle to Abolish Slavery.* London: Pan.
Hunt, Lynn, ed., trans. 1996. *The French Revolution and Human Rights: A Brief Documentary History.* New York: St. Martin's.
Jeanneney, John R., ed. 1995. *The French Revolution of 1789 and Its Impact.* Westport, CT: Greenwood.
Lambert, David. 2005. *White Creole Culture, Politics and Identity during the Age of Abolition.* Cambridge: Cambridge University Press.
Morgan, Kenneth. 2001. *Slavery, Atlantic Trade and the British Economy, 1660–1800.* Cambridge: Cambridge University Press.
Walvin, James. 2001. *Black Ivory: Slavery in the British Empire.* Oxford: Blackwell.

Sloops

Ships of the Royal Navy were divided into rates that reflected the size of the ship. These ran from first rate down to sixth rate. Below the last rate were numerous unrated ships, and it was in this broad unrated category that sloops were found. A sloop was the largest type of unrated vessel, with a "master and commander," or simply "commander" in charge, rather than a captain. The rank was between lieutenant and post captain commanding a rated vessel. All navies had ships classed as sloops.

The term sloop covered a range of vessels, but generally meant a ship carrying from ten to eighteen guns. The largest resembled miniature frigates, with a quarterdeck and forecastle, three masts, an armed upper deck and unarmed lower deck. These ships were armed with fourteen or sixteen 6-pounder guns. In the early years of the French Revolutionary Wars, they were also armed with twelve or fourteen swivel guns. Later sloops of this type were armed with carronades, usually 12-pounders, but later vessels were armed with 32-pounders.

Most sloops were flush-decked, that is, with no quarterdeck or forecastle, because sloops with this design were considered more weatherly than quarterdeck sloops. They were often as large as the quarterdeck vessels, and carried the same amount of armament, usually 24- or 32-pounder carronades. Brig sloops were similar but had only two masts. A number of captured French vessels of that type were employed as sloops in the Royal Navy.

Sloops were not usually employed by the main fleets, and were certainly not used in front-line roles. They were not weatherly enough to be used for blockade duties, and they were not fast enough or sufficiently armed to act as scouts for main battle fleets. Sloops were regarded as the smallest viable ship for independent cruising and patrol work, and were often used to escort merchant convoys. The war in the Iberian Peninsula necessitated large supply convoys, which were attacked by French and American privateers, and here the brig sloop was used very successfully for escort and inshore support duties. They were also considered especially useful in defending the southern coast of England against the threatened French invasion, and they often captured enemy privateers and merchantmen.

Captain Lord Cochrane, in the *Speedy* with a crew of eighty-four men and six officers, armed with 12-pounders, cruised successfully in the Mediterranean and captured a mass of enemy shipping; the war with Denmark in 1807 was fought in the narrow coastal waters of the Baltic between Danish gunboats and British brig sloops, and during the War of 1812, both the Royal Navy and the United States Navy employed sloops on the Great Lakes. The Americans used sloops in the Atlantic, and one, the *Wasp*, was sent to operate in the English Channel, where she captured a number of British merchantmen.

Paul Chamberlain

See also Artillery (Naval); Blockade (Naval); Danish Navy; England, French Plans for the Invasion; French Navy; Frigates; Naval Warfare; Peninsular War; Privateering; Privateers (French); Royal Navy; Ships of the Line; United States Navy; War of 1812

References and further reading
Gardiner, Robert, ed. 1996. *Fleet Battle and Blockade: The French Revolutionary War, 1793–1797*. London: Chatham.
Lavery, Brian. 1989. *Nelson's Navy: The Ships, Men and Organisation, 1793–1815*. London: Conway Maritime.

Smith, Sir William Sidney (1764–1840)

One of the most colorful and charismatic naval figures of his age, Smith is comparatively unknown, eclipsed by the deeds of Nelson. A man of unbounded vanity, he was daring to the point of recklessness, blindly arrogant, tirelessly energetic, self-promoting, petulant, a superb leader of men, and dismissive of higher authority. Exceedingly ambitious, and a masterful self-publicist, Smith was not only admired but loved by his men.

He was born William Sidney Smith (though he generally referred to himself by his second forename) on 21 June 1764 into a military and naval family with connections through marriage to the great family of Pitt. Smith joined the Royal Navy at the age of thirteen and first saw action in the *Unicorn* in 1778 against an American frigate off Boston. A year later the *Unicorn* captured or destroyed three French frigates. On 25 November he went aboard Sir George (later Lord) Rodney's flagship, the *Sandwich*, on the Channel station. On 8 January 1780, while the fleet was escorting a large convoy to Gibraltar, Minorca, and the West Indies, it fell in with a Spanish convoy and took one ship of the line from the escort and all twenty-three merchant ships. Later, on 16 January, he served at the Battle of Cape St. Vincent (not to be confused with the action of the same name, fought in 1797). Smith also fought in three encounters with Admiral Luc Urbain de Bouexic, comte de Guichen, including Dominica (17 April 1780), and two other actions on 15 and 19 May.

Although still short of the required age of nineteen, Smith passed his examination and was commissioned a lieutenant aboard the *Alcide* on 25 September of that year, and served at the Battle of the Chesapeake (9 September 1781). He later fought at St. Kitts (25–26 January 1782), at Dominica (9 April 1782), and at Les Saintes (12 April). In February 1784 he was placed on half pay and, like many other officers, decided to go abroad and study a foreign language that might be of use in his future career. From the spring of 1785 until 1787 Smith lived in France, where he perfected his command of the language and conducted amateur espionage. Peace with France precluded active service, so Smith looked for adventure elsewhere.

In 1787 he traveled through Spain to Gibraltar, and on surmising that, owing to the emperor's belligerent threats, a war with Morocco was likely, Smith traveled through that country gathering intelligence on the coasts, harbors, and military and naval strength, without any hindrance from the authorities. On the completion of his tour in May 1788, he submitted his findings to the Admiralty, including a description of the emperor's naval force. Smith then decided to fight as a mercenary in a country not at war with Britain. He therefore took six months' leave of absence and went to Stockholm in the summer of 1789, for Sweden had been at war with Russia since July the previous year; this was principally a naval affair fought in the Baltic, and Sweden was after experienced leaders. Without any authorization from his government, Smith served in an undefined capacity as a volunteer, sailing a yacht that trailed the king's galley, the *Seraphim*. Gustavus soon granted him command of a squadron of small frigates, floating batteries, and oared galleys, and addressed him as "colonel."

At Styrsudden on 3–4 June, the Russians drove the Swedes into the Bay of Viborg and blockaded them, and within a few days the king gave Smith command of a squadron that numbered eight small vessels, twenty galleys with 4,000 marines, and seventy-two gunboats. With this force, Smith took part in bitter hand-to-hand fighting with the Russians inside the bay. When, on 9–10 July at Svenskund, the Swedish fleet emerged from the bay and, partly with oared vessels that harked back to Lepanto two centuries before, directly confronted the Russians, the Swedes emerged victorious, in part due to Smith's contributions in training and raising the morale of his crews. He returned to Britain with the sincere thanks of Gustavus and a knighthood in the Order of the Sword, formally conferred on him by George III on 16 May 1792. As Smith was granted permission to use this title, he assumed the name "Sir Sidney," which his naval colleagues often belittled by calling him "the Swedish knight."

War between Austria and Prussia on the one hand and France on the other appeared imminent in early 1792, and as the British government desired an officer to gather intelligence in the Near East, the Admiralty and Foreign Office sent Smith to Constantinople. He was to carry out intelligence gathering in the waters around the Black Sea, the Bosporus, the Sea of Marmora, the Dardanelles, and the Ionians, with freedom to do so by a naval commission from the Turks, who were then at war with Russia. Yet a far greater threat emerged when in February 1793 Britain declared war on Revolutionary France, an event of which Smith did not even become aware until the end of the year, while he was at the port of Smyrna (now Izmir, Turkey). He, in common with all British military and naval officers abroad, was immediately recalled home to report for duty.

With his own resources, he bought a small lateen-rigged vessel, which he renamed the *Swallow,* and took aboard about forty men. He proceeded to sail for the principal French naval base in the Mediterranean, Toulon, that, along with Lyons and Marseilles, had declared for the monarchy and appealed to Britain for help. Lord Hood duly arrived with a fleet and began a blockade of Toulon by sea, landing a force of mixed nationalities to defend the perimeter of this vital anchorage. When, however, the overwhelming presence of forces loyal to the Republic concentrated against the perimeter defenses rendered further Allied operations untenable—sealed by the young captain Napoleon Bonaparte's strategic placement of artillery to command both roadsteads—Hood ordered an evacuation of Allied troops and as many royalists as possible. Of vital importance was the fate of the French fleet moored or penned up in the dockyard, including thirty-two ships of the line and fourteen frigates. As most of the sailors, now imprisoned in the harbor, were sympathetic to the Revolution, Hood lacked enough crews to take away the ships.

The only alternative, Smith observed while a guest aboard Hood's flagship, was to burn them, a thought that had already occurred to Horatio Nelson, then captain of the *Agamemnon,* only a fortnight before. Hood issued Smith orders to burn every ship that could not be carried away, together with the arsenal, the enterprise to be achieved with a flotilla of gunboats and twenty-four officers and men. Spanish gunboats reluctantly followed him, but by the time Smith reached the shore, all these save one had abandoned the scene. Many of the prisoners, no longer under guard, had by this time freed themselves, threatening Smith's mission. Some of his vessels had to train their guns on the French while parties went ashore under fire in order to place combustibles among the stores and ships.

By nightfall republican forces were well within musket range and had to be kept at bay with grapeshot. By the time the charges had been laid to the combustibles and a fire ship towed into position, the French were at the dockyard gates. When the time agreed on with the governor arrived, the fuses and fires were set, the powder train to the fire ship was lit, and the landing parties were brought off. However, two of Smith's gunboats were sunk by the explosion of a French frigate supposed to have been sunk by the Spanish. Other Spanish parties had failed to penetrate the boom (a heavy chain laid across a harbor entrance to bar access to enemy vessels) to the inner harbor where lay further French ships, and though Smith joined the Spanish in a second attempt to get past, by then musketry from the docksides and the French flagship rendered this impossible. Instead, Smith and his men made for the ships of the line anchored in the inner roadstead, and set fire to a number of these.

Meanwhile, as the harbor began to be consumed in flames and clouds of smoke, fuelled by burning tar, hemp, oil, and the ships themselves, another explosion sent a mass of debris into the air, though this one caused no damage to his little vessels. Having set fire to everything possible in light of the enemy's presence, and having exhausted their supplies of combustibles, Smith and his weary men now evacuated some of the troops of the rear guard and rejoined the fleet, past the fire of forts now under enemy possession. Despite his original plan, Smith was unable to evacuate any more civilians in addition to those thousands already aboard Hood's fleet. The remainder were, immediately and in the days of fury that lay ahead, massacred in their thousands, as republican troops entered the town shooting and bayoneting as they went, driving others into the sea or executing them after brief imprisonment.

All told, Hood had preserved and sailed off with four ships of the line, eight frigates, and seven corvettes. Smith and his men had burned or sunk ten ships of the line, two frigates, and two corvettes. However, this left eighteen ships of the line, four frigates, and three corvettes intact and reserviceable. Most of these the Spanish had been assigned to destroy, and there is strong evidence that treachery lay behind their preservation. Nevertheless, Smith's achievement was impressive, destroying as he did more ships than could be expected in a major fleet action. Still, though Hood praised him in his dispatches, Smith's great ego, the fact that he enjoyed no official capacity, and, of course, his failure to complete the task, left him open to criticism from many in the navy who desired a convenient scapegoat. In fact, blame should have fallen on Hood and the Spanish commander, Admiral Don Juan de Langara.

Smith's exploit met with only partial success, but the mere fact that Hood had accepted his services—in a purely voluntary capacity—combined with Smith's own vainglorious ego and campaign of self-promotion, generated considerable antagonism against him in the fleet. Nevertheless, he had served Hood's purpose, and in recognition the admiral sent Smith back to the Admiralty with dispatches announcing the destruction of at least a portion of the Toulon fleet. This distinction led to Smith's appointment to the frigate *Diamond* (38 guns), attached to the Channel Fleet. At about this time he spoke to Lord Spencer, the first lord of the Admiralty, and wrote to William Windham, the secretary of state for war, outlining the need for flat-bottomed boats that could be used to harass the French coast. He also laid out plans for a full-scale invasion to take an army all the way to Paris, using the Seine as the principal line of communication.

He spent most of 1794 in the North Sea, and much of 1795 and 1796 cruising off the north coast of France, where, in command of a small number of vessels in the squadron of Commodore Sir John Warren, he managed to capture or destroy so many French naval and merchant vessels as to bring a virtual end to local seaborne commerce. Smith entered the mouth of the harbor and closely monitored the major naval base at Brest. At the beginning of 1795 he disguised his ship as a French frigate, made modifications to his officers' uniforms, and approached the port for observation, passing several enemy frigates in the process and narrowly escaping detection by a suspicious vessel by boldly offering it assistance (it had sprung a leak). In March 1795 he was given command of an inshore flotilla of small craft to be used to harry French coastal shipping, and with these he caused havoc among French ships attempting to shelter in shallow water and among shoals along the Norman and Breton coasts. He also sent in a number of landing parties.

In March 1796 he followed a convoy into the harbor at Herqui, on the coast of Britanny, stormed the batteries covering the harbor, spiked the guns, and burned the ships. By this time he had acquired a reputation among the French, who suspected that he maintained connections with the royalist Chouans, then in revolt, as well as with royalist émigrés in England. To many he was little more than an arsonist, owing to his feat at Toulon, while on half pay and holding no official appointment. Lying off Le Havre, at the mouth of the Seine, on 18 April 1796, Smith learned that a privateer lugger, the *Vengeur*, with a particular reputation for its destruction of British trade, lay at anchor within the harbor. In this cutting-out expedition Smith took with him nine officers and twenty-four ratings. Although he and his men succeeded in surprising and seizing the vessel in a hand-to-hand struggle, Smith found his escape downriver prevented by the flood tide that had carried the vessel into the estuary. There he sat helpless for lack of sufficient wind. When dawn broke, Smith and his prize were overwhelmed by French vessels of all descriptions, and Smith had no choice but to surrender, along with his officers and crew. Though well treated, Smith was sent to Paris and imprisoned in the Temple, where Louis XVI and the royal family had been held before their execution. French authorities flatly refused all attempts by the British government to secure his release by exchange.

His captors and the French public at large had particular cause for reviling Smith, for his incendiary exploits at Toulon were regarded as little more than an act of piracy conducted by a man holding no commission and therefore not subject to the laws that governed the treatment of prisoners of war. His eighteen months' campaign waged against commerce certainly endeared him to no one, and some went so far as to claim that his object at Le Havre was in fact the destruction of that city by fire. He spoke fluent French and was known to have royalist émigré connections back home. To the French it seemed that he must be a counterrevolutionary, landing royalist agents on the coasts. As a spy, he would not be exchanged, even though he had been captured armed and in uniform. His reputation and the enmity he had aroused cost Smith two years of his liberty, and even when Lord Spencer offered to exchange 1,000 French prisoners for him, the French government demanded no fewer than 4,000, which the Admiralty refused. At first some of Smith's friends attempted to tunnel under the walls of the prison from the cellar of a nearby house, but their work was discovered by a sentry in the exercise yard. Eventually he befriended the prison governor and obtained parole to walk the streets of Paris on occasional evenings. With the aid of a former royalist officer of engineers, Colonel Antoine le Picard de Phélypeaux, Smith managed to escape, and royalists masquerading as soldiers with forged orders to transfer Smith to Fontainebleau whisked him away in a coach. Though the coach crashed in the streets of Paris, Smith was secreted in a royalist safehouse before proceeding to Le Havre, via Rouen, dressed as a French seaman. He boarded the frigate *Argo* (44) by means of a chartered fishing boat, and arrived safely at Portsmouth on 7 May 1798.

Smith reached London the following day, where he was received in triumph at a time when British fortunes were at a particularly low point, and presented to the king. At this time the French were assembling a large fleet at Toulon, with a destination unknown to the British. Bonaparte, commanding the troops on board, arrived at the port just as Smith was reaching London. This activity naturally concentrated British naval attention on the Mediterranean theater, under the command of Admiral Sir John Jervis, the newly ennobled Earl of St. Vincent, with Rear Admiral Sir Horatio Nelson as a subordinate commander. St. Vincent, blockading the Spanish fleet at Cádiz, decided to detach Nelson and send him into the Mediterranean in search of the French fleet.

For several months nothing was heard from Nelson and his three-month search for the French, although it was known that they had not passed Gibraltar into the Atlantic. Then, on 2 October, news reached London of the victory at the Battle of the Nile and the destruction of the French fleet there on 1–2 August. Still, the French army threatened the integrity of the Ottoman Empire, and the prime minister, William Pitt, needed all the diplomatic influence he could muster to keep Turkey in alliance with Britain. In October Smith embarked for the south of Spain in command of the *Tigre* (80), with orders to join St. Vincent at either Cádiz or Gibraltar, and bearing authority from the Foreign Office to undertake a diplomatic mission to Turkey. There he was to hold the unique position of joint minister with his brother, Spencer Smith, already in situ. One of his principal tasks was to convey a military mission, complete with advisers, to Constantinople, to aid the Turkish defense of their empire.

St. Vincent duly sent him on his way east, but owing to the vague and dual nature of Smith's responsibilities, he neglected explicitly to place Smith, with local naval responsibilities in the eastern Mediterranean, under the rightful authority of the theater commander in chief, Nelson. Smith, whose independent spirit naturally inclined him to assume greater powers than naval precedent permitted, interpreted his orders to suit himself, operated in the manner of an independent commander, adopted for himself the rank of commodore, and flew a broad pennant aboard his vessel, assuming for himself command over those of Nelson's ships that remained at Alexandria while the victor of the Nile was at Naples.

The result may be imagined. Nelson, with a delicate ego of his own, heightened by the victories at St. Vincent and the Nile, interpreted Smith's conduct as a gross violation of the chain of command and refused to recognize Smith's assumed rank. A compromise was forged, with St. Vincent as the mediator: Nelson acknowledged Smith's authority to undertake the blockade of Alexandria and the naval defense of Ottoman territory, but not to do so without requesting permission from Nelson and acknowledging Nelson as his superior. Smith, for his part, acknowledged his error in adopting a broad pennant without authority, and though he continued as the ranking officer in the Levant, thereafter recognized Nelson as senior commander in the Mediterranean theater and acknowledged that he therefore fell under Nelson's direct command.

On 26 December, Smith arrived at Constantinople where Sultan Selim III concluded a treaty with Russia and Britain, to which both Smith and his brother put their names. The Turks had already declared war, and Smith had authority to take command of any Turkish or Russian warships in the Levant, to which the sultan added command of all Turkish military and naval forces being assembled to oppose the French, then based at Cairo. Smith advised a concentration of troops on Rhodes in preparation for a counteroffensive against the French in Egypt. With authorization from London, he began to recruit Albanian troops to sail gunboats on the Nile delta, and proposed amphibious landings on the river to coincide with the summer flooding. Aboard the *Tigre* Smith had brought shipwrights to instruct the Turks in building vessels of all descriptions, from gunboats to ships of the line.

In the meantime, he learned with shock in early 1799 that Lord Elgin was being sent out to replace his brother and him in their diplomatic capacities. Shortly thereafter, Nelson ordered Smith to replace Captain Thomas Troubridge in the blockade of Alexandria, leaving him two ships of the line and other vessels. Smith planned to harass the French at sea while the Turks struck by land, but these plans were changed when news arrived of Bonaparte's march north from Egypt into Palestine (at the time officially known as Syria). This news prompted Smith to send an officer to warn the Turks and to prepare the defenses of the old crusader fort at Acre on the Syrian coast. The French first took El Arish, then Gaza, and then, on 7 March, Jaffa, en route to Syria.

Smith immediately dispatched his friend Colonel Phélypeaux in the *Theseus* to Acre, where he and Captain Ralph Willett Miller of that ship undertook defensive measures. Smith, following in the *Tigre*, arrived on 15 March, and three days later he struck a decisive blow at sea by capturing the entire French siege train, including artillery, stores, and ammunition, not to mention the eight gunboats that carried these essential elements of Bonaparte's impending operations. Smith made maximum use of his prizes: he mounted the siege guns on the walls of the fortress, while the gunboats, with the *Tigre* and *Theseus* in support, assumed positions from which they could enfilade the trenches of the besieging forces.

Without proper siege equipment, the French were left with ordinary field guns, and more heavy guns were not brought to the city until 25 April, by which time, under Smith's direction, the state of the city's defenses had been greatly improved. For the next six weeks, the besiegers dug trenches, extended their saps, and undertook mining operations, while the defenders countermined and delivered sorties. Finally, on 4 May, after considerable activity and a good deal of hand-to-hand fighting, the French succeeded in creating a practicable breach in the fortress wall, laid a mine beneath it, and ordered a general assault for the following day. The Turks, however, managed to defuse the mine during the night, so delaying the attack. On the night of the seventh, a large body of Turkish reinforcements arrived off the coast from Rhodes, obliging Bonaparte to anticipate their landing by ordering an immediate assault. Ferocious fighting lasted until morning, by which time the French had taken one of the towers, while the Turks offshore could not land owing to becalmed conditions.

Realizing that time was running short, Smith ordered ashore a strong contingent of seaman armed with pikes who manned the breach until the Turks could land. Fierce fighting continued that day, but by dusk the French had retired, and twelve days later they lifted the siege and marched off. Smith, while displaying his usual vanity and pomposity, showed immense personal courage and intelligence and may rightly be credited with having saved the city, thereby terminating further French conquests in the Middle East. Nevertheless, he was gracious enough to give credit where it was due and demonstrated that his qualities as a leader functioned as well ashore as at sea.

The British public and government received news of the French withdrawal before Acre with great enthusiasm, and Smith was singled out for praise and reward. Both houses of Parliament voted him thanks, and the following year he was granted an annual pension of £1,000. He also received the thanks of the City of London and of the Levant Company, which eventually gave him a piece of plate and a grant of £1,500. In common with Nelson in the wake of the victory at the Nile, Smith received from the sultan a pelisse and the *chelingk*—a special plume of victory to be worn in his hat.

However well deserved these accolades, Smith's triumph again went to his head, and he resumed his arrogant assumption of a rank and level of responsibility that were not rightly his own. He resumed his pretensions as station commander in chief and diplomatic joint representative to Turkey—subordinate only to his brother, who of course was a great distance away at Constantinople—and as such presumed to interpret explicit orders from home as he saw fit. While the Foreign Office specifically forbade any negotiations that stipulated for the surrender of French forces in Egypt except as prisoners of war, on his own authority Smith concluded on 24 January 1800 the Convention of El Arish, whose terms granted the French, together with their weapons and effects, free passage back to their own country in Allied ships, the cost to be borne by Britain and Turkey. By this time Nelson had been replaced as commander in chief in the Mediterranean by Lord Keith, who by refusing to approve these terms reopened hostilities, which did not cease until after Lieutenant General Sir Ralph Abercromby's forces (including seamen dispatched ashore under Smith, still in command of the *Tigre*) landed in Egypt in 1801 and defeated General Jacques, baron Menou. Following the capitulation of Alexandria on 2 September, Smith was sent back to England, and on 10 November he arrived in London, bearing dispatches announcing the fall of French power in Egypt.

In 1802 Smith was elected Member of Parliament for Rochester, in Kent, and the following year, under Lord Keith, he commanded a squadron of small vessels off the Belgian and Dutch coasts. He was promoted to rear admiral on 9 November 1805, and the following January he was appointed to the *Pompée,* in which he served under Vice Admiral Cuthbert, Baron Collingwood with a detached command off the Neapolitan coast. Between May and August 1806, Smith waged a highly successful campaign against French shipping in the area, while simultaneously antagonizing colleagues in the army with whom he was to meant to cooperate, not least Lieutenant General Sir John Moore, of later Peninsular fame.

Notwithstanding the friction that followed in his wake, Smith proved extremely adept at fulfilling his naval responsibilities. He saw to it that arms and ammunition were delivered to local resistance fighters in the mountains of Calabria, he harassed and often drove off small French contingents guarding the shores, and he successfully attacked a number of fortified points along the coast with local partisan forces, backed by British seamen and marines. Smith's squadron patrolled the coast from Scylla to the Bay of Naples, not only destroying French vessels, but taking Capri and threatening Salerno and Policastro. He succeeded in fomenting risings across the Basilicata and throughout Calabria generally, even if the various guerrilla forces seldom cooperated with one another or acted in force.

In August 1806 the Admiralty sent Smith instructions to join the command under Vice Admiral Sir John Duckworth in the eastern Mediterranean, where between February and March 1807 the fleet made an unsuccessful attempt to threaten the Turkish government and was forced to pass the Dardanelles under fire. In the summer of that year Smith returned home, but by November he was back at sea, this time in the *Hibernia* as senior officer off the coast of Portugal. As French forces approached Lisbon, Smith evacuated the prince regent, the royal family, and government officials, and detached several of his own ships to convoy the Portuguese squadron that took the refugees to Brazil. In February 1808 the Admiralty appointed Smith to command the South American station and sent him to Rio de Janeiro. There Smith's irascible temper soon brought him into conflict with Lord Strangford, the British minister to Brazil, and the resulting abusive correspondence exchanged between them resulted in Smith's peremptory recall in the summer of 1809.

He was promoted to vice admiral on 31 July 1810, and in October of that year he married Caroline Rumbold, widow of the diplomat Sir George Rumbold. In July 1812 he was appointed second in command to Vice Admiral Sir Edward Pellew (later Viscount Exmouth), commander in chief in the Mediterranean. In March 1814, on grounds of extremely poor health, Smith was permitted to return to Britain, which he did in the *Hibernia*. His active service terminated on his arrival at Portsmouth in July. Smith's coincidental presence in Brussels in June 1815 enabled him to meet the Duke of Wellington, albeit as a civilian, at the end of the Battle of Waterloo. Afterward Smith rode with the army into Paris, where on 29 December Wellington invested him with the insignia of Knight Commander of the Bath (KCB), the nomination for which Smith had received at the beginning of the year. On 19 July 1821 he was promoted to full admiral.

For many years afterward he lived in Paris, where he founded and appointed himself president of a society known as the Knights Liberators, which sought to appeal to the Barbary States for the release of Christian slaves. His efforts, such as they were, apparently achieved nothing, apart from some amusingly worded correspondence with various North African rulers. Smith was nominated for a Grand Cross of the Order of the Bath (GCB) on 4 July 1838. He died in Paris, without children, having outlived his wife by fourteen years, on 26 May 1840. Smith was buried in Père-Lachaise Cemetery.

Gregory Fremont-Barnes

See also Abercromby, Sir Ralph; Acre, Siege of; Alexandria, Battle of; Calabria, Uprising in; Chouans; Collingwood, Cuthbert, Viscount; Dardanelles, Expedition to the; El Arish, Convention of; Hood, Alexander, First Viscount Bridport; Menou, Jacques-François de Boussay, baron; Middle East Campaign; Moore, Sir John; Nelson, Horatio, First Viscount; Nile, Battle of the; Phélypeaux, Antoine le Picard de; Pitt, William; Russo-Swedish War; St. Vincent, John Jervis, First Earl of; Toulon, Siege of; Waterloo, Battle of

References and further reading
Clowes, William Laird. 1997. *The Royal Navy: A History from the Earliest times to 1900.* Vols. 4–5. London: Chatham. (Orig. pub. 1898.)

Crook, Malcolm. 1991. *Toulon in War and Revolution: From the Ancien Regime to the Restoration, 1750–1820.* Manchester: Manchester University Press.

Forczyk, Robert A. 2005. *Toulon 1793: Napoleon's First Great Victory.* Oxford: Osprey.

Mackesy, Piers. 1995. *British Victory in Egypt, 1801: The End of Napoleon's Conquest.* London: Routledge.

Pocock, Tom. 1998. *A Thirst for Glory: The Life of Admiral Sir Sidney Smith.* London: Pimlico.

Russell of Liverpool, Lord. 1964. *Knight of the Sword: The Life and Letters of Admiral Sir William Sidney Smith.* London: Gollancz.

Shankland, Peter. 1975. *Beware of Heroes: Admiral Sir Sidney Smith's War against Napoleon.* London: Purcell.

Sparrow, Elizabeth. 1999. *Secret Service: Secret Agents in France, 1792–1815.* Woodbridge, UK: Boydell.

Smolensk, Battle of (17 August 1812)

The Russian city of Smolensk lies some 280 miles east of Moscow. The battle marked the first time that Napoleon faced a united Russian army; the encounter was indecisive for both sides, though Napoleon held the city.

When Napoleon planned his 1812 campaign against Russia, Smolensk was the farthest point that he expected to reach. He had hoped to force a decisive battle long before reaching that city, and had brought with him an enormous army of some half a million men. The very size of that army worked against it, however, as it was difficult to move quickly. Napoleon pursued the Russians and won numerous skirmishes, but the two Russian armies led by generals Mikhail Barclay de Tolly and Peter Bagration managed to elude him. Napoleon thought he had them trapped at Vilna in late June and then again a month later at Vitebsk. Each time, however, unnecessary delays on the part of the French, together with effective rearguard tactics by the Russians, allowed the Russians to withdraw toward Smolensk.

At both Vilna and Vitebsk, Napoleon delayed rather than pursued the withdrawing Russians. At Vilna he hoped to hear offers of peace from Tsar Alexander, but there was never any real chance of that happening. At Vitebsk his army was greatly reduced in fighting effectiveness due to the extremely hot weather it had endured. The Russian climate was already taking its toll in men and horses, and

French supply lines were longer than ideal. Nevertheless, Napoleon decided to pursue the Russians, and they left Vitebsk for Smolensk on 13 August.

The French delay had allowed the two Russian armies to combine forces in Smolensk, presenting a force of some 50,000 men. Napoleon had spent much of 15 August, his birthday, idle, which allowed the Russians to prepare their defenses in Smolensk. On the sixteenth, the French and Russian armies clashed in the suburbs, each sustaining significant casualties. The city walls provided good defensive strength, and the French were unable to move forward with much success: The Russians had deployed their forces effectively. The French forces probed but did not attack in force. On the seventeenth, Napoleon sent three corps against the Russian defenses, but gained little for his effort. Russian casualties were as much as 14,000, but the French suffered losses nearly that high, an unfavorable circumstance for an invading army. The fighting had done great damage to the city, much of which was in flames during most of the day.

On the eighteenth, Bagration and Barclay de Tolly agreed to have the 2nd Western Army moved to the east to prevent a possible French flanking movement. Barclay de Tolly then had little choice but to begin his own withdrawal later in the day. Had the French pressed their attack on the eighteenth, they might have destroyed at least a large portion of the Russian army opposing them. Instead, the French were exposed to the sight of a burning city that surpassed even the spectacle of Moscow's fires, not far in their future. By the nineteenth, the French were in control of the city, but Napoleon's orders to block the retreating Russians were not effectively carried out by General Jean Junot. The Russians escaped with their army mostly intact.

During the battle, Napoleon had indicated that he would likely stay in Smolensk for the winter, which was in keeping with his original plans. The fires had not destroyed the entire city. Though his supply lines were even longer than they had been at Vitebsk, they were still not so long that they could not be maintained. He could organize the territory he had conquered, call for fresh troops and supplies, and renew the fight against the tsar in the spring. He could even simply declare victory, maintain the conquered territory, and leave the next step up to Alexander. He could recognize Poland as an independent nation, which would assure him of its loyalty and give him a new cadre of dedicated soldiers. Organizing this new Polish territory would take time, but the benefits were potentially very important. It was a good option, and one that Napoleon seriously considered.

Withdrawing to Vitebsk was another possibility. That city had troops and adequate provisions for the upcoming winter. Napoleon's commanders and advisers were in favor of calling a halt to the campaign, and Napoleon gave strong consideration to the option of not moving forward, but he ultimately feared inaction more than the possibility of being lured further into Russia. He could have moved against the tsar at St. Petersburg, the capital, but when the Russian army retreated toward Moscow, Napoleon had little choice but to follow it. Within the week, Napoleon left Smolensk along the road to Borodino and Moscow.

Smolensk figured one more time in the 1812 campaign. When Napoleon decided to leave Moscow and was forced into a northern route, he hoped to return only as far as Smolensk. He had left a garrison in the city and presumed there would be adequate supplies to enable him to establish his winter quarters there. When he reentered that city, however, he discovered that the expected supplies did not exist, and the withdrawal from Russia, with all its terrible consequences, continued.

J. David Markham

See also Alexander I, Tsar; Bagration, Peter Ivanovich, Prince; Barclay de Tolly, Mikhail Andreas; Borodino, Battle of; Junot, Jean Andoche, duc d'Abrantès; Poland; Russian Campaign; Vilna, Battle of; Vitebsk, Battle of
References and further reading
Austin, Paul Britten. 1993. *1812: The March on Moscow.* London: Greenhill.
Chandler, David G. 1995. *The Campaigns of Napoleon.* London: Weidenfeld and Nicolson.
Clausewitz, General Carl von. 1992. *The Campaign of 1812 in Russia.* London: Greenhill.
Markham, J. David. 2003. *Imperial Glory: The Bulletins of Napoleon's Grande Armée 1805–1814.* London: Greenhill.
Nafziger, George F. 1988. *Napoleon's Invasion of Russia.* Novato, CA: Presidio.
Riehn, Richard K. 1991. *1812: Napoleon's Russian Campaign.* New York: Wiley.
Zamoyski, Adam. 2004. *1812: Napoleon's Fatal March on Moscow.* London: HarperCollins.

Somosierra, Action at (30 November 1808)

One of the very few actions of the Peninsular War in which Napoleon was in personal command of the French forces, the combat that took place at Somosierra was an important moment in the campaign launched by the French emperor to avenge the defeat of Bailén. Massing a large army behind the river Ebro, early in November he moved forward to attack the (Spanish) Army of Extremadura, which was coming up to defend Burgos. Defeating this force at Gamonal on 10 November 1808, he burst through the Spanish center and headed straight for Madrid. Before reaching the Spanish capital, however, he had to cross the Somosierra Pass, where the main road from the French frontier to Madrid climbs over the imposing Sierra de

Guadarrama. In the process it provided the Spaniards with an excellent defensive position: before reaching the summit of the pass, the highway snaked its way along a three-mile-long cleft in the mountains, and was in consequence overlooked from all sides, while the ascent was also both very steep and very narrow.

That said, however, the defenders did not make the most of their opportunities. A large part of their forces was detached to hold the outlying town of Sepúlveda, which lay some miles to the west of the Madrid highway just beyond the northern fringes of the Sierra de Guadarrama, while no advantage was taken of the excellent flanking positions offered by the pass itself. Still worse, no attempt was made to hold the heights that lay to east and west of the road. All that was done, indeed, was to throw up an entrenchment at the summit of the pass and arm it with sixteen cannon. To clear the way, then, was an easy matter: As Napoleon saw, all he had to do was to clear the Spaniards from Sepúlveda—a simple matter that was accomplished on 29 November—and send infantry to scale the hills that overlooked the pass.

For reasons that have never been entirely clear, this did not satisfy the Emperor, however. Notwithstanding the fact that the French infantry was making steady progress—though steep, the heights they were scaling could easily be climbed by troops operating in open order—he ordered the regiment of Polish light horse that constituted his personal bodyguard to charge the Spanish positions head on. With exemplary courage, the Poles did so, only to receive discharge after discharge from the Spanish cannon. With many men shot from their saddles, the survivors at first could take no more, and fell back in disorder. Rallied by General Louis-Pierre Montbrun, however, they returned to the attack, and this time burst through the Spanish positions. Badly shaken, the defenders turned and ran, leaving Napoleon free to close in on Madrid two days later.

Charles J. Esdaile

See also Bailén, Battle of and Capitulation at; Gamonal, Battle of; Madrid, Action at; Montbrun, Louis-Pierre; Peninsular War
References and further reading
Esdaile, Charles J. 2002. *The Peninsular War: A New History.* London: Penguin.
Oman, Charles. 2005. *A History of the Peninsular War.* 7 vols. London: Greenhill. (Orig. pub. 1902–1930.)

Sorauren, Battle of (28, 30 July 1813)

Engagement fought during the Peninsular War between the French and Anglo-Portuguese forces on 28 and 30 July 1813, which formed part of what is known as the Battles of the Pyrenees, together with the battles of Roncesvalles and

Maya. Marshal Nicolas Soult's defeat here led to the failure of his counteroffensive in the Pyrenees to relieve the city of Pamplona, which was under siege.

Having forced the Anglo-Spanish armies back from the passes in the Pyrenees, Soult continued his march toward Pamplona. The Marquis (later Duke of) Wellington ordered the concentration of his forces to prevent Soult's advance. Within a matter of days, Wellington had 24,000 men at his disposal to face around 36,000 French troops. Wellington had deployed his force along a ridge to the north of the village of Oricain before the plain of the Arga River and Pamplona itself was reached. Despite the fact that Soult outnumbered Wellington at this point, he chose to delay his attack, having little cavalry or artillery available. On the morning of 28 July, Soult ordered General Bertrand Clausel to attack on the right flank, while in the center and left General Honoré Reille sent his columns forward. The French attack ground up the slope, but despite the fact that in places they gained the crest, Wellington was able to launch counterattacks to force the enemy back.

Seeing the repulse of the French, Brigadier General Denis Pack on the left of the British line decided to launch an attack on the village of Sorauren. This position was, however, strongly held, and Wellington saw that success was unlikely. He ordered the attack to end, but not before Pack had been severely injured and the British had lost 300 casualties. By the end of the day, both sides had been reinforced. The French general, Jean-Baptiste Drouet, comte d'Erlon was facing Lieutenant General Sir Rowland Hill near the village of Lizaso to the northwest, and Lieutenant General George Ramsay, of the Earl of Dalhousie's division, had reached Sorauren and was able to extend the British line.

On 29 July Soult ordered his generals to march to the northwest. His plan was to exploit the gap between Wellington, who was deployed around Pamplona, and the force under Lieutenant General Sir Thomas Graham besieging San Sebastian. He hoped to cut the main line of communication between the two. However, Wellington's position provided him with two advantages; first, he could clearly see the movements of the French; and second, he deployed artillery on the ridge. On 30 July d'Erlon, under Soult's supervision, attacked Hill and was able to force him back. Despite this French success, around Sorauren the French had been unable to extricate themselves from the British and came under heavy fire from the guns that Wellington had positioned on the ridge. Wellington now ordered an attack to be launched on Sorauren itself. In the ensuing fighting, the French suffered around 3,000 casualties. Soult was forced to conduct a withdrawal toward France, leaving San Sebastian and Pamplona eventually to fall into British hands.

Ralph Baker

See also Drouet, Jean-Baptiste, comte d'Erlon; Graham, Sir
Thomas; Hill, Sir Rowland; Maya, Battle of; Pamplona,
Siege of; Peninsular War; Reille, Honoré Charles Michel
Joseph, comte; Roncesvalles, Battle of; San Sebastian, Siege
of; Soult, Nicolas Jean de Dieu; Wellington, Arthur
Wellesley, First Duke of
References and further reading
Robertson, Ian. 2003. *Wellington Invades France.*
    Mechanicsburg, PA: Stackpole.

Souham, Joseph, comte (1760–1837)

Joseph Souham was born at Lubersac on 30 April 1760 into
the family of nine children of Joseph and Marie Dandaleix
de Frémont. His father died when Souham was ten years
old. The child developed a pronounced stutter, preventing
advanced study, but he did learn to read and write. On 17
March 1782 Souham enlisted as a private in Louis XVI's
elite 8th Cavalry Regiment. He served in this unit, where
exceptional height was a prerequisite, from 1782 to 1790.
Souham was 6 feet 6 inches tall.

Once Souham realized in 1792 that war was imminent, he joined the 2nd Volunteer Battalion of Corrèze,
which fought against Prussia and Austria. He was promoted to second lieutenant colonel on 16 August 1792 and
participated in the Battle of Jemappes on 6 November 1792
and at the siege of Dunkirk in 1793. On 30 July of that year,
Souham was appointed as *général de brigade.* Three weeks
later he became commander of a 30,000-strong division
under General Jean-Charles Pichegru, who commanded
the Army of the North. Souham served alongside General
Jean Victor Moreau, who commanded 20,000 men. The
two commanders became fast friends.

On 29 April 1794, accompanying Pichegru during the
campaign in the Austrian Netherlands (present-day Belgium), Souham showed initiative and audacity at Courtrai.
A four-hour battle, ending with a French bayonet charge,
secured Souham's victory over the Austrians. On 16 May
the Austrian, British, and Hanoverian forces merged into
one large command. Two days later they attacked the
French positions near Tourcoing, the town itself being the
headquarters of Frederick Augustus, Duke of York. The
British were repulsed by Souham's brilliant strategy, and
the Austrian commander *Feldzeugmeister* Franz de Croix
Graf von Clerfayt retreated with 20,000 troops after losing
5,500 men and six guns. Souham lost 3,000 men and six
guns. The French went on to take all the areas west of the
Rhine. The Austrians were pushed across the river Meuse.

In October 1794 Souham defeated the British at
's Hertogenbosch (Bois le Duc). The following month
Pichegru and Souham captured the Dutch fortress of Nijmegen, an encounter during which Souham's troops

fought with distinction. Pichegru and Souham captured
the Dutch fleet at Texel, as well as Amsterdam, which in reality was ready to accept the French "liberators." The Dutch
Republic was renamed the Batavian Republic and became
a satellite of France. In all, the Army of the North won ten
victories in its campaign to occupy the Dutch Republic, in
the course of which it took 2,500 prisoners, 2,000 pieces of
artillery, a dozen flags, and six fortresses.

Souham joined Moreau and the Army of the Rhine in
1798, and he was instrumental in preventing the treachery
of Pichegru from affecting the French cause. He defeated
the Allies at Pfullendorf and Stockach in March 1799, but
soon thereafter was suspected of involvement in royalist
schemes, as a result of which he was exiled to his estate.
When the courts found no evidence of complicity, Souham
was restored to command in 1800, serving under Moreau
in the campaign in Germany, where he acquitted himself
honorably at Blaubeuren.

In 1804 Souham fell afoul of Napoleon. He was imprisoned for three days in the Temple (the medieval prison
in Paris that had held the royal family) and implicated in
royalist intrigues, specifically, as a co-conspirator in the
duplicities of Moreau and Pichegru. He endured further
disgrace for allegedly participating in the revolt of Chouan
leader Georges Cadoudal. After Napoleon had Cadoudal
executed, Souham remained on his estates, where he hos-
pitably welcomed anyone who came to visit.

He was reinstated in 1808 and played a notable role in
the Peninsular War, serving under Marshal Laurent Gouvion St. Cyr in Catalonia. Souham distinguished himself at
Lampoudan in November 1808, the siege of Rosas (7
November–4 December), Cardedeu (16 December), and
Molins de Rey (21 December). He fought admirably at
Valls and Reus on 25 February 1809, at Vich and San
Colona in April 1809, and at the siege of Gerona in December of that year. In 1810 he served at Rippol in January and
at Vich on 20 February, where he received a severe wound
on the left temple. His participation in so many actions
earned him the title of count. In 1812 Souham received
command of the army formerly under Marshal Auguste de
Marmont after the latter's defeat at Salamanca in July 1812,
and greatly bolstered his reputation when he forced the
Earl (later Duke) of Wellington to retreat from Burgos.
Souham also recaptured Salamanca.

During the campaign in Germany in 1813, Souham
distinguished himself at Weissenfels on 29 April and
fought honorably at the Battle of Lützen on 2 May. He was
wounded at the decisive Battle of Leipzig (16–19 October).
Souham was awarded the title of Grand Officer of the Legion of Honor for his services to France. In the closing period of the 1814 campaign in France, Souham was expected to guard Paris with the 2nd Reserve Division, which

had been reduced to a contingent of a mere 500 men, although he had been promised 2,000. He was unfairly held responsible for the ensuing fiasco.

Souham sided with the royalists after Napoleon's first abdication. Louis XVIII was pleased to welcome Souham to his cause and offered him highly sought-after commands. Souham lost these when Napoleon returned to power; they were reinstituted after Napoleon's final abdication in July 1815. Souham retired in 1832, and died on 28 April 1837. His name is inscribed on the Arc de Triomphe in Paris.

Annette E. Richardson

See also Burgos, Sieges of; Chouans; Courtrai, Battle of; First Coalition, War of the; Flanders, Campaigns in; France, Campaign in; Germany, Campaign in; Gerona, Siege of; Gouvion St. Cyr, Laurent, comte; Jemappes, Battle of; Leipzig, Battle of; Louis XVIII, King; Lützen, Battle of; Marmont, Auguste Frédéric Louis Viesse de; Moreau, Jean Victor; Peninsular War; Pichegru, Jean-Charles; Rhine Campaigns (1799–1800); Salamanca, Battle of; Second Coalition, War of the; Stockach, First Battle of; Texel, Capture of the Dutch Fleet off; Tourcoing, Battle of; York and Albany, Frederick Augustus, Duke of

References and further reading
Chandler, David G. 1995. *Campaigns of Napoleon.* London: Weidenfeld and Nicolson.
Connelly, Owen. 1991. *The French Revolution and Napoleonic Era.* 2nd ed. London: Holt, Rinehart Winston.
Glover, Michael. 1978. *The Napoleonic Wars: An Illustrated History, 1792–1815.* New York: Hippocrene.
Hutt, Maurice. 1983. *Chouannerie and Counter-Revolution: Puisaye, the Princes and the British Government in the 1790s.* 2 Vols. Cambridge: Cambridge University Press.
Israel, Jonathan I. 1998. *The Dutch Republic: Its Rise, Greatness, and Fall, 1477–1806.* Oxford: Clarendon.
Palmer, R. R. "Much in Little: The Dutch Revolution of 1795." *Journal of Modern History* 26 (March 1954): 15–35.
Rose, J. Holland. 1911. *The Revolutionary and Napoleonic Era: 1789–1815.* Cambridge: Cambridge University Press.
Schama, Simon. 1992. *Patriots and Liberators: Revolution in the Netherlands, 1780–1813.* London: Fontana.

Soult, Nicolas Jean de Dieu (1769–1851)

Soult was one of Napoleon's most senior and experienced lieutenants. The product of a modest family background and years of service in the pre-Revolutionary army, he fought with distinction under General André Masséna in Switzerland and Italy, played a key role in the construction of the Grande Armée, and contributed in a crucial way to Napoleon's greatest battlefield victory, at Austerlitz in December 1805. A prolonged period of service in Spain removed him from Napoleon's side, but he returned to central and western Europe for the last of the Emperor's campaigns. From 1830 to 1847 Soult had a distinguished career in government during the reign of King Louis-Philippe.

Although Soult led his forces with skill and determination, his reputation has suffered from two alleged defects in his character. After being severely wounded at the siege of Genoa in the spring of 1800, Soult supposedly lost his lust for combat and remained conspicuously far from the fighting when battle was underway. Soult was also charged with a taste for looting during his campaigns. Although other senior French leaders also looted, his greed for plunder has become notorious for its sheer scale.

Nicolas Soult was born at St.-Amans-Labastide in the Languedoc region of southern France on 29 March 1769. His given name was Jean de Dieu, but the name "Nicolas," employed by his soldiers, has become the one historians conventionally use. Soult's father was a local notary, who died when his son was only ten. Without much formal education, Soult entered the army in 1786 and rose to the rank of sergeant before the Revolution of 1789. In early 1792, after moving from his old regular regiment to a unit of newly raised volunteers, Soult received the temporary rank of junior lieutenant and took up duties as a drill master. Throughout his career, Soult maintained the crude but effective manner of a pre–1789 drill sergeant. His methods served him and his new company of grenadiers effectively as the campaign of 1792 approached.

In 1793 Soult began his participation in years of fighting along France's borders with the Rhineland states and Belgium. He first distinguished himself in late March in a rearguard action against a Prussian attack near Mainz. Recognized by commanders such as generals Adam Philippe de Custine and Louis Lazare Hoche as a promising young officer, he received assignments for dangerous scouting missions and lightning attacks against enemy lines. In moments when good officers were in short supply, Captain Soult was employed as temporary commander of a brigade. He became renowned for his skill in training the units under his command. In 1794 Soult became chief of staff to General François Lefebvre's division in the legendary Army of the Sambre and Meuse. He participated as a staff officer in the decisive victory of that army over the Austrians at Fleurus in July 1794. His efforts, often marked by his presence at the front line in the thick of the fighting, brought him a distinctive reward: In October 1794, at the age of twenty-five, he was named a *général de brigade* and awarded his own brigade. Service with the Army of the Sambre and Meuse also brought Soult his first contact with General Michel Ney, another future marshal and one of Soult's most bitter rivals.

Marshal Soult. A corps commander during the campaigns of 1805–1807, he is best known for the prominent part he played in the Peninsular War in Spain and Portugal. (Engraving by Rouillard and Demare, 19th c. The David Markham Collection)

The following years found Soult fighting on numerous occasions in western Germany. His most notable achievement came at the Battle of Stockach in late March 1799. The overall offensive under General Jean-Baptiste Jourdan through the Black Forest and into the Danube valley failed, and the French forces were compelled to retreat to the Rhine. But Soult led his brigade with panache and determination during the French advance against the Austrians. He was even more effective in directing the skillful retreat of several French divisions. In the aftermath of the campaign, Soult rose to the rank of *général de division.*

A crucial turning point in Soult's career came in April 1799, when he received a command in General André Masséna's Army of Switzerland. This posting gave him the opportunity to distinguish himself while leading a division in combat; eventually, he commanded an entire army corps of three divisions.

With France's eastern frontier defenses tottering in 1799, only Masséna's forces staved off invasion. Two important battles around Zürich proved decisive for the campaign, and Soult played an important role in each. In early June, Soult's division bolstered Masséna's defenses in the fighting east of Zürich. When Masséna took the offensive in late September, Soult fought heroically against the Austrians and Russians at the eastern end of Lake Zürich. In this action, Soult planned a surprise attack after a daring personal reconnaissance in which he dressed as a private soldier on sentry duty. He carried off a complex offensive movement across the Linth River involving swimmers, rapid road construction, and bridging operations. Placed in command of three divisions, Soult pursued Russian forces down the Rhine, and then turned part of his sizable force northward to reinforce Masséna.

By now a key lieutenant under Masséna, Soult joined the senior general in northern Italy in February 1800. One of Soult's first tasks was to restore discipline to the force of 18,000 neglected and hungry men Masséna placed under his command. As Austrian armies advanced, Masséna's forces were driven apart. On Masséna's left, General Louis Suchet was forced westward to Nice and beyond. Soult's men, comprising the right wing of Masséna's army, tried to assume the offensive but were forced backward. Finally, Masséna himself, along with Soult, took refuge in Genoa, beginning a legendary siege that pinned down the Austrians and enabled Bonaparte to cross the Alps and strike at their rear.

Soult performed with his usual front-line heroism and initiative. The French hold on Genoa was imperiled by Austrian pressure on two powerful fortresses in the mountains ringing the city. With Soult at their head, his troops recaptured one of the strong points and pushed the enemy besiegers away from the second. Soult continued such sorties to keep the army confronting Genoa off balance until, during one such venture in May, he was badly wounded in the leg and captured. Although his wound eventually healed, Soult limped for the remainder of his life.

With his recovery and return to duty, Soult entered a period of more relaxed service. He became the military administrator in Piedmont, and then led a French army into southern Italy as Bonaparte consolidated his control there. In these venues, the veteran young general began to acquire a taste for plundering the people and places under his control.

Bonaparte's hopes of invading England provided Soult with an unprecedented opportunity for distinction and promotion. He had not had a personal relationship with Bonaparte, but a strong recommendation from Masséna helped Soult advance rapidly. In August 1803 he took charge of the forces at St. Omer, one of the major military camps for Bonaparte's army stationed on the English Channel. He soon received command of IV Corps, the largest in the Grande Armée. With 46,000 men under him, the former drill sergeant now had an unprecedented number of troops upon whom to lavish his energies as a military trainer. He drove his men ferociously, taking them on maneuvers three times each week and drilling them for twelve hours at a time. With his headquarters at Boulogne, he seemed destined to have the central role in any assault on France's main adversary. Having quickly emerged as a key figure in the newly constructed Grande Armée, Soult received the distinction of marshal on 19 May 1804, the first on the list of generals to get the award.

Soult led the superbly trained IV Corps during the series of victorious campaigns stretching from the summer of 1805 through the summer of 1807. When Napoleon marched the Grande Armée eastward in August 1805, Soult led his troops in the sweeping advance that isolated *Feldmarschalleutnant* Karl Mack Freiherr von Leiberich's Austrians at Ulm. The energetic young corps commander then pushed his forces eastward to Vienna and thereafter northward in pursuit of the retreating enemy. Napoleon finally drew the Austrians and their Russian allies toward Austerlitz, in western Bohemia. On the morning of 2 December, when Napoleon's masterful direction of the battle had led the enemy to weaken the center of their line, the Emperor chose IV Corps to strike the decisive blow. Austerlitz was Soult's most memorable success on the battlefield, but it has given rise to a shadow over his reputation. As a corps commander, Soult no longer played the role of combat leader that he had at Genoa, and some subordinates began to comment on the general's alleged habit of remaining well away from any point of danger.

Nonetheless, Soult and IV Corps again took a leading role during the Jena campaign against Prussia in the fall of 1806. Soult's forces, along with the corps of marshals Jean Lannes and Pierre Augereau, defeated the Prussians at Auerstädt, while the main body of the enemy lost at Jena to Louis Davout. Soult then helped to conduct a devastating pursuit of the defeated Prussians. A highpoint of his performance here was in helping to trap and capture General Gebhard von Blücher, the enemy's most aggressive leader, at Lübeck along with a large remnant of the Prussian army.

In the campaign in Poland the following year, Soult led his corps at the Battle of Eylau (7–8 February 1807) and captured the enemy stronghold of Königsberg (June). Following the Treaty of Tilsit in July, Soult spent more than a year commanding an army of occupation in Prussia. During this time, he shared in the military and financial honors Napoleon bestowed on the Emperor's most successful military subordinates. An income of 300,000 francs per year made Soult a wealthy man, and the title of duc de

Dalmatie put him in the ranks of Napoleon's newly created nobility.

Soult then served in the Iberian Peninsula for more than five years. Like most of his colleagues in the upper ranks of the French military system, he found the experience diminished rather than enhanced his reputation. Soult led II Corps during Napoleon's offensive of November 1808, destroying a Spanish army at Gamonal on 10 November and capturing the key urban center of Burgos. At Napoleon's direction, Soult moved northward against the Spanish forces under General Joaquín Blake. After Blake's defeat, Soult remained in northern Spain in preparation for a thrust into Portugal. Isolated in northern Spain, Soult was in danger of being defeated by the substantial British forces under Lieutenant General Sir John Moore and Lieutenant General Sir David Baird approaching him from the west and north. Soult was saved by Napoleon's ability to shift substantial French forces northward. The Emperor then decided to return to France and left his distinguished subordinate to lead the pursuit of the British, who were retreating to the northern port of Corunna.

On 16 January 1809 Soult and Moore met in battle at Corunna, on the northwest coast of Spain. The French leader became the first of his peers to encounter the effectiveness of a trained British army in the Iberian Peninsula. Soult saw his attacking forces shattered by the steadiness and firepower of the British battleline. Soult could take credit, however, for forcing the seaborne evacuation of the enemy's troops, as well as for the death of Moore in the last stages of the battle.

In response to Napoleon's orders, now coming from the Emperor back in France, Soult took part in a set of offensives to secure control of the Iberian Peninsula. While other forces moved into Galicia and Catalonia, Soult advanced into Portugal in order to seize the capital city of Lisbon. The difficulty of consolidating his position near Corunna as well as coping with emerging guerrilla forces delayed Soult's progress. Having established himself at Oporto in northern Portugal, the French leader developed a sweeping set of political ambitions. Soult appealed to local Portuguese officials in a possible attempt to establish himself as the monarch of the northern part of the country. His dreams were soon shattered, however, when a British force under Lieutenant General Sir Arthur Wellesley (the future Duke of Wellington) defeated Soult, on 12 May 1809, and expelled the French leader and his army from Oporto. Soult conducted a humiliating retreat back to Galicia, with the loss of all his guns, after this initial defeat at the hands of Wellesley.

Soult faced another frustration in August 1809. Rushing his troops from northern Spain, he failed to cut off

Wellesley's retreat westward after the Battle of Talavera. Napoleon put the blame for the failure on his brother Joseph, whom he had made King of Spain, and on Joseph's key military adviser, General Jean-Baptiste Jourdan. On 16 September Soult replaced Jourdan. He now faced the problem of coordinating operations for the fractious, independent-minded generals who controlled the various provinces of Spain. And Soult's task was not made easier by his long-standing difficult relations with Joseph. Nevertheless, he achieved a significant victory over the Spanish at Ocaña on 19 November.

Soult's term in the Peninsula featured the French offensive southward into Andalusia in early 1810, his destruction of a Spanish army under General Gabriel Mendizabal at the Gebora River on 19 February 1811, and his success in capturing the key border fortress of Badajoz the following month. He remained in Andalusia for two years, but sustaining his position there proved impossible in the summer of 1812. By the time he evacuated Andalusia, his relations with Joseph had grown so acrimonious that the French general was writing Napoleon to suggest that Joseph had treasonous dealings with Spanish authorities. Recalled for service in Germany in 1813, Soult fought at the Battle of Bautzen on 20–21 May. With a corps of Napoleon's army under his command, he tried to emulate his success eight years earlier at Austerlitz by crushing the center of the Allied line. But this time, the French failed to weaken their adversary by attacks elsewhere on the battlefield, and Soult succeeded only in driving the opposing Prussians and Russians into an orderly retreat.

In June 1813 Wellington's defeat of the French army at Vitoria placed Napoleon's entire position in Spain in jeopardy. Soult returned to stabilize the situation. Arriving at Bayonne, he restored order and discipline in the shaken ranks of the French forces. He then undertook a series of offensives to block Wellington from moving through the Pyrenees. Soult failed in efforts to relieve the besieged French garrisons at Pamplona and San Sebastian, and on 7 October Wellington led an Anglo-Portuguese army onto French soil. Although both sides suspended military operations for several months in the winter of 1813–1814, Soult found himself pushed from one defensive line after another. He encountered Wellington in the final losing battle of the campaign at Toulouse on 10 April 1814. Both sides were unaware that by this time Napoleon had already abdicated his throne.

Soult accepted the Bourbon Restoration under King Louis XVIII with a degree of enthusiasm that disturbed many of his former comrades-in-arms. He took the position of minister of war in December 1814, and his policies, such as restoring royalist officers while retiring former officers from Napoleon's army, caused lasting resentment.

With Napoleon's return to power in March 1815, Soult shifted sides once again. Napoleon appointed him chief of staff for the newly formed Army of the North. The Emperor may have distrusted Soult too much to award him a field command, but with the flight of General Louis-Alexandre Berthier, Napoleon's longtime chief of staff, the French army required a prestigious figure with experience in moving large numbers of troops.

Soult's performance in the Waterloo campaign added little to his military reputation. Unlike the superbly efficient Berthier, he failed on several occasions to produce lucid and timely orders. Nor did he always send out messages by several couriers—one of Berthier's practices—to ensure orders got through. Thus, on 16 June, Marshal Michel Ney did not receive firm instructions to engage the British at Quatre Bras, an error enabling Wellington to make an orderly withdrawal. Soult also failed to reconnoiter the direction of the Prussian retreat after the Battle of Ligny. On the other hand, just before the Battle of Waterloo, Soult wisely advised Napoleon to recall Marshal Emmanuel, marquis de Grouchy from his pursuit of the Prussians in order to concentrate French strength against Wellington. He also advised against a frontal assault on the Allied lines. Napoleon rejected these sound suggestions from the one French general who had faced Wellington repeatedly.

In the aftermath of Napoleon's fall, Soult was forced into exile in Germany for several years. But he returned in 1819, and, after the fall of the Bourbons in 1830, he began a final era of service to the French government. Under King Louis-Philippe, Soult twice returned to his old position of minister of war and twice served as prime minister. While representing the French government at the coronation of Queen Victoria in 1838, he received a warm official welcome, had a reunion with his old adversary, the Duke of Wellington, and was applauded by the British public.

Soult received a final—and rare—honor from the French government when he was elevated to the rank of marshal-general in 1847. The old soldier died at his birthplace, St-Amans-Labastide, on 26 November 1851. He had lived to the age of eighty-two.

Neil M. Heyman

See also Auerstädt, Battle of; Augereau, Pierre-François-Charles; Austerlitz, Battle of; Badajoz, First Siege of; Bautzen, Battle of; Berthier, Louis-Alexandre; Blake, Joaquín; Blücher von Wahlstatt, Gebhard Lebrecht Fürst; Bonaparte, Joseph; Corunna, Battle of; Corunna, Retreat to; Davout, Louis Nicolas; England, French Plans for the Invasion of; Eylau, Battle of; Flanders, Campaigns in; Fleurus, Battle of; Fourth Coalition, War of the; Genoa, Siege of; Germany, Campaign in; Grouchy, Emmanuel, marquis de; Hoche, Louis Lazare; Italian Campaigns (1799–1800); Jena, Battle of; Jena-Auerstädt Campaign; Jourdan, Jean-Baptiste; Lannes, Jean; Lefebvre, François

Joseph; Ligny, Battle of; Louis XVIII, King; Mack, Karl
Freiherr von Leiberich; Marshalate; Masséna, André;
Moore, Sir John; Ney, Michel; Ocaña, Battle of; Oporto,
Battle of; Orthez, Battle of; Pamplona, Siege of; Peninsular
War; Quatre Bras, Battle of; Rhine Campaigns
(1799–1800); San Sebastian, Siege of; Stockach, First Battle
of; Suchet, Louis Gabriel; Switzerland, Campaign in;
Talavera, Battle of; Third Coalition, War of the; Tilsit,
Treaties of; Toulouse, Battle of; Ulm, Surrender at; Vitoria,
Battle of; Waterloo, Battle of; Waterloo Campaign;
Wellington, Arthur Wellesley, First Duke of; Zürich, First
Battle of; Zürich, Second Battle of

References and further reading
Chandler, David G., ed. 1987. *Napoleon's Marshals.* London:
    Weidenfeld and Nicolson.
———. 1995. *The Campaigns of Napoleon.* London:
    Weidenfeld and Nicolson.
Connelly, Owen. 1968. *The Gentle Bonaparte: A Biography of
    Joseph, Napoleon's Elder Brother.* New York: Macmillan.
———. 1987. *Blundering to Glory: Napoleon's Military
    Campaigns.* Wilmington, DE: Scholarly Resources.
Delderfield, R. F. 2004. *The March of the Twenty-Six.*
    London: Leo Cooper.
Elting, John. 1988. *Swords around a Throne: Napoleon's
    Grande Armée.* New York: Free Press.
Esdaile, Charles J. 2003. *The Peninsular War: A New History.*
    New York: Palgrave Macmillan.
Glover, Michael. 1963. *Wellington's Peninsular Victories.* New
    York: Macmillan.
Hamilton-Williams, David. 1993. *Waterloo—New
    Perspectives: The Great Battle Reappraised.* New York:
    Wiley.
Hayman, Peter. 1990. *Soult: Napoleon's Maligned Marshal.*
    London: Arms and Armour.
Humble, Richard. 1973. *Napoleon's Peninsular Marshals.*
    New York: Taplinger.
Macdonell, A. G. 1996. *Napoleon and His Marshals.* London:
    Prion.
Marshall-Cornwall, James. 1965. *Marshal Massena.* London:
    Oxford University Press.
Phipps, Ramsay Weston. 1980. *The Armies of the First French
    Republic and the Rise of the Marshals of Napoleon I.* Vol. 2,
    *The Armées de la Moselle, du Rhin, de Sambre-et-Meuse,
    de Rhin-et-Moselle.* London: Greenwood. (Orig. pub.
    1926–1939.)
Young, Peter. 1973. *Napoleon's Marshals.* London: Osprey.
———. 1973. *Napoleon's Marshals.* New York: Hippocrene.

South America

The French Revolutionary and Napoleonic Wars had a
profound effect on the Spanish and Portuguese colonies in
South America. In 1793 Spain joined those countries fighting against France. Spanish colonial trade continued, but
at lower levels. In 1795, by the terms of the Treaty of Basle,
Spain unilaterally ended hostilities with the French, an act
of desertion that angered Britain. When Spain and Britain
went to war in 1796, Spain's transatlantic trade collapsed,

as the British attacked Spanish shipping. The British clearly
controlled the seas after their victory at Trafalgar in 1805,
further damaging Spain's relationship with its South
American colonies.

The port of Buenos Aires (in present-day Argentina)
was especially hard hit by the decline in commerce. In June
1806 a British force occupied the city. This force, led by
Commodore Sir Home Riggs Popham, who was not authorized by the British government to undertake the expedition, easily defeated the Spanish militia and took the city.
The viceroy, the Marquis de Sobremonte, fled to the interior city of Córdoba. When a second expedition arrived in
early 1807, however, the residents of Buenos Aires defeated
it, and the British surrendered. The result for the colony
was that the viceroy was deposed and an interim viceroy
was named, paving the way for independence.

In 1806 France implemented Napoleon's Continental
System (the French-imposed embargo on continental
trade with Britain). The French saw Portugal as a potential
weak link in the system and invaded in 1807, sending the
Portuguese prince regent, John (João), into exile in Brazil.
More than 10,000 people made the journey, escorted by a
British naval squadron. John then ruled his empire from
Rio de Janeiro until 1821. He went so far as to elevate
Brazil's status to that of a kingdom. After John returned to
Portugal, his son Pedro led the Brazilian independence
movement in 1822.

France then invaded Spain in 1808, and Napoleon
placed his brother Joseph on the Spanish throne, leading to
revolts in Spain and later to the independence movements
in the Spanish colonies. The earliest revolt occurred in the
Audiencia de Charcas (in present-day Bolivia), where infighting among government officials about events in Spain
allowed some colonists to take political power and declare
self-rule. In 1809, in the city of La Paz (in present-day Bolivia), colonists arrested the governor and bishop, formed a
governing council, and declared independence. However,
Spanish loyalists put down this first attempt at South
American independence.

South American colonists took further action in 1810
as French troops advanced southward through Spain. On
19 April 1810 the city council of Caracas (in modern-day
Venezuela) called a *cabildo abierto,* or open town meeting.
The colonists created a governing junta to rule in the name
of deposed king Ferdinand VII. Caracas and its surround-
ings then suffered through more than a decade of warfare,
as patriots and loyalists fought for control of the colony. To
the south, colonists in Buenos Aires called a *cabildo abierto*
in May 1810 in response to the fall of Seville to the French.
They created a junta to replace the local Spanish authorities and arrested the viceroy. Unlike Caracas, Buenos Aires
never again came under Spanish rule. In July 1810,

colonists in New Granada (present-day Colombia) deposed the viceroy in Bogotá. In Chile, colonists created a ruling junta in September. By that time most of South America, with the exception of the Spanish colonial heartland of Peru, had assumed some degree of self-rule in response to the French invasion of Spain. Spain, however, later fought back and regained control of much of its South American empire before colonists achieved final independence in the 1820s.

The British used their navy in the South Atlantic to keep the French out of the Spanish colonies. The British also sought to act as intermediaries between Spain and the revolutionaries in the colonies who had declared independence. Spain, however, refused such mediation. Despite the fact that many British merchants pressured the government to aid the independence movements in Latin America, British authorities did not officially assist the patriots. Instead, the British government received guarantees from most European powers that none of them would send troops to interfere in the wars of independence in Spanish America. Nevertheless, by the time the British issued the 1819 Foreign Enlistment Act, prohibiting British nationals from entering foreign service, more than 5,000 British soldiers were already serving in the New World.

Ronald Young

See also Basle, Treaties of; Bolívar, Simón; Bonaparte, Joseph; Buenos Aires, Expedition to; Continental System; Ferdinand VII, King; Peninsular War; Portugal, Invasions of (1807–1808); Spain; Trafalgar, Battle of

References and further reading

Burkholder, Mark A., and Lyman L. Johnson. 2001. *Colonial Latin America.* 4th ed. Oxford: Oxford University Press.

Bushnell, David, and Neil Macaulay. 1994. *The Emergence of Latin America in the Nineteenth Century.* 2nd ed. Oxford: Oxford University Press.

Harvey, Robert. 2000. *Liberators.* London: Constable and Robinson.

Kaufmann, William. 1967. *British Policy and the Independence of Latin America, 1804–1828.* Hamden, CT: Archon.

Keen, Benjamin, and Keith Haynes. 2000. *A History of Latin America.* 6th ed. New York: Houghton Mifflin.

Lynch, John. 1986. *The Spanish American Revolutions, 1808–1826.* 2nd ed. New York: Norton.

———, ed. 1994. *Latin American Revolutions, 1808–1826: Old and New World Origins.* Norman: University of Oklahoma Press.

Robertson, William S. 1967. *France and Latin-American Independence.* New York: Octagon.

Slatta, Richard W., and Jane Lucas De Grummond. 2003. *Simón Bolívar's Quest for Glory.* College Station: Texas A & M University Press.

Wilcken, Patrick. 2004. *Empire Adrift: The Portuguese Court in Rio de Janeiro, 1801–1821.* London: Bloomsbury.

Southey, Robert (1774–1843)

English poet and writer. The son of a linen draper, Southey studied at Corston and Bristol before enrolling at the prestigious Westminster School, where he began to write his first works. However, he was expelled from the school for publicly condemning the practice of whipping. In 1792 he entered Balliol College at Oxford and showed sympathy with the ideals of the French Revolution in his early poems *The Fall of Robespierre* (1794) and *Joan of Arc* (1796). At this period, Southey met Samuel Taylor Coleridge, with whom he established a writing partnership and shared radical political and religious viewpoints. They even collaborated on establishing a commune in America, though it came to no avail. Southey secretly married Edith Fricker (whose sister was married to Coleridge) in 1795 and joined his uncle in Portugal.

In 1797 Southey published *Letters Written During a Short Residence in Spain and Portugal* (1797) and produced two volumes of his collected *Poems* (1795–1799). These works were followed by *The Inchcape Rock* and *The Battle of Blenheim,* the latter an antiwar tract. After serving as editor of two volumes of contemporary verse in the *Annual Anthology,* Southey translated the latter part of Jacques Necker's *On the French Revolution,* the wide-ranging reviews of which increased his political and literary notoriety.

In 1803 Southey and his wife visited the Coleridges at Great Hall, Keswick, where they remained for the rest of their life. During the Napoleonic Wars, Southey renounced his youthful radicalism and fascination with the French Revolution. To maintain his family, he produced a variety of works, including criticism, history, biography, translations, and journalism. In 1809 Southey began writing for the Tory *Quarterly Review,* which eventually published some ninety-five of his articles. In 1810 Southey started writing a history of Brazil, which was published in three volumes in 1819. In 1813 he was appointed poet laureate through the influence of Sir Walter Scott, which provided him with economic security. He published the two-volume *Life of Nelson* in 1813 and completed *Life of Wesley* and the *Rise and Progress of Methodism* in 1820, *The Book of the Church* in 1824, and *Sir Thomas More* in 1829. *Essays Moral and Political* followed in 1832, and the next year he published *Lives of British Admirals.*

In 1817 Southey was accused of republicanism and radicalism following an unauthorized publication of his early work *Wat Tyler.* He became involved in a bitter quarrel with Lord Byron, who criticized Southey in *English Bards and Scotch Reviewers* in 1809 and dedicated to Southey the first cantos of his satiric masterpiece *Don Juan* in 1819. In response, Southey denounced Byron in *A Vi-*

sion of Judgement (1821), which only intensified their animosity, as Byron produced a brilliant parody of Southey's poem under the title *The Vision of Judgment* in 1822.

In addition to literary infighting, Southey endured the mental illness of his first wife, who died in 1837, and family quarrels with his second wife, Caroline Anne Bowles. He died from a fever on 21 March 1843 and was buried in the churchyard at Crosthwaite.

Annette E. Richardson

See also Blake, William; Byron, George Noel Gordon, Lord; Coleridge, Samuel Taylor; Keats, John; Romanticism; Scott, Sir Walter; Shelley, Percy Bysshe; Wordsworth, William
References and further reading
Carnall, Geoffrey. 1960. *Robert Southey and His Age: The Development of a Conservative Mind.* Oxford: Clarendon.
Curry, Kenneth. 1974. *Southey.* London: Routledge and Keegan Paul.
Dowden, Edward. 1879. *Southey.* London: Macmillan.
Madden, Lionel. 1972. *Robert Southey: The Critical Heritage.* London: Routledge and Keegan Paul.
Storey, Mark. 1997. *Robert Southey: A Life.* Oxford: Oxford University Press.

Spain

The period of the French Revolution and the rule of Napoleon was a time of great trauma for Spain. In 1789 the country was a world power second only to Britain. A powerful fleet secured Spain's control of the greatest empire in the world; several decades of enlightened absolutism under the rule of Charles III (reigned 1759–1788) had strengthened the administration, increased the power of the state, undermined the control of the Catholic Church, and stimulated intellectual life; the introduction of free trade with America had led to considerable economic growth, and, in particular, the emergence of a nascent cotton industry in Catalonia; and a permanent alliance with France known as the Family Compact brought Spain both safety in Europe and the ability to stave off British rivalry in the Atlantic.

Look at 1815, however, and the picture is very different. Much of the country was in ruins; the state was in eclipse; the navy was nonexistent; economic life was at a standstill; large parts of its American empire had either broken away from Spain or were in a state of revolt; and there was a very real risk of civil war. Conventionally, much of the blame for this transformation has been laid at the door of Charles IV (reigned 1788–1808) and his favorite and chief minister, Manuel de Godoy, but this is unfair: the former was certainly not possessed of the same vision and energy as his predecessors, while the latter was a man of dubious probity, but in the last resort Spain was faced by

circumstances that would have tested the strongest of administrations.

The first problem faced by Charles IV on his accession to the throne in 1788 was, of course, the French Revolution. The Revolution was a frightening spectacle for the court of Madrid, and its response was to impose an absolute blackout on all news from across the Pyrenees. Yet no move was made to attack France, and it increasingly began to be felt that the best way forward was to adopt a policy of conciliation. Early in 1792, then, the chief minister, José Moñino, Conde de Floridablanca, was replaced by the Conde de Aranda and friendly overtures made to France. With the establishment of the Republic in September 1792, however, Aranda was discredited, with the result that power passed to Godoy. The latter was no more bellicose than Aranda, but on 7 March 1793, the French assembly declared war. There followed the so-called War of the Convention of 1793–1794. Quickly invading Roussillon, a Spanish army briefly blockaded Perpignan, but a French victory at Peyrestortes forced it to retreat to entrenched positions just north of the Spanish frontier.

At the beginning of May 1794, meanwhile, a further French victory at Le Boulou drove it back across the frontier. Crossing the Pyrenees into Catalonia in July, the French then closed in on Figueras, which was protected by a large citadel that stood on a height overlooking the town. In a three-day battle fought on 17–19 November, the French drove the Spaniards away from the position, and the garrison then surrendered without further resistance. Both armies then went into winter quarters, while the guns had also fallen silent at the other end of the Pyrenees, where another French army had made a small lodgment in Navarre. When the fighting was renewed, the Spanish forces defending Catalonia beat back no fewer than three French offensives and even managed to outflank the invaders and recapture the frontier town of Puigcerda, but in the west operations went less well: Defeating the troops opposing them at Irurzun, the (French) Army of the Western Pyrenees penetrated deep into Spain and occupied both Vitoria and Bilbao.

These French successes coincided with the end of the war. Fighting the Republic had proved ruinously expensive and had led to a major financial crisis, thanks to the depreciation of the government bonds issued to finance the struggle. Forced to impose heavy conscription, Godoy had found himself facing great resentment on the home front. Stirred up by an aristocratic clique opposed to the reforms of the Bourbons, talk of a Spanish revolution had been heard. Much alarmed, Charles IV therefore ordered Godoy to open peace negotiations with France, the war being ended on 12 July 1795 by the Treaty of Basle. The terms were moderate enough—Godoy was actually rewarded by

Charles with the title Prince of the Peace—but even so the war had sounded a clarion call. In the dangerous new world that had emerged, a world in which Spain could count on continued British hostility without necessarily being able to rely on France coming to its assistance, the only hope was to intensify the pace of reform. Yet it was not as simple as that. With French armies triumphant on all fronts, France was unlikely to remain inactive in the face of the emergence of a significant threat in Madrid. To allay Paris's suspicions, and at the same time to regain the services of the French navy in the never-ending rivalry with Britain, it was therefore decided to seek an alliance with France; hence the Treaty of San Ildefonso of May 1796, and, shortly afterward, Spain's reentry into the war as a member of the French camp.

This switch in Spain's foreign policy has frequently been castigated as the origin of all the country's later ills, but in assessing Godoy's actions, one needs to take three vital points into account. In the first place, the desire for reform that underpinned San Ildefonso was entirely sincere: over the next few years the favorite was to push the cause of enlightened reform further than any other statesman in Europe. In the second place, it is quite clear that Godoy was well aware that France was not to be trusted: Far from thrusting Spain ever deeper into the French embrace, he was therefore from the very beginning awaiting the moment when he could restore Spain's freedom of action. And in the third, caught as it was between Britain and France, Spain could not stand alone: an alliance with Britain having been found wanting, there was simply no alternative but a deal with Paris. At all events, reform was certainly essayed: A commission of generals was established to consider the needs of the army and a variety of concrete measures introduced to improve its efficiency; the Church and the aristocracy were taxed more heavily; the Bourbon attempt to "civilize" the Spanish populace (and thereby to increase levels of productivity, education, and public order) was continued, most notably by the abolition of bullfighting; and a very considerable start was made on the expropriation and sale of the lands of the Church.

However, the net effect was hardly great. In the first place, Godoy was entirely dependent on royal favor, which was something that was not to be relied upon (in 1798, for example, French pressure led to him losing the post of chief minister). In the second, many of his plans were sabotaged by the resistance of his many enemies within the administration. In the third, the favorite's undoubted venality cost him the support of many officials and intellectuals who might otherwise have supported his policies. And in the fourth, Godoy's efforts were simply nullified by the size of the crisis facing Spain. Most important here was the impact of the war with Britain.

Costly enough in itself—the Spanish navy, for example, suffered serious reverses at St. Vincent in 1797 and Algeciras in 1801—the war had indirect effects that were even worse. The many sectors of the economy associated with the transatlantic trade were badly hit, while revenue from the Americas also declined dramatically. A brief respite was provided by the Treaty of Amiens of 1802, but the balance sheet was hardly positive for the regime—the gain of the insignificant Portuguese frontier district of Olivença in the so-called War of the Oranges hardly balanced the loss of Trinidad—and the two years that intervened before Spain was once again forced to enter the war on the side of France in 1804 (something that Godoy struggled desperately to avoid) were marked by both a terrible famine and an epidemic of yellow fever that decimated the population of Andalucía.

Given the miseries endured by the populace, not to mention the fact that the regime's attack on the Church stripped the poor of their only source of relief, popular unrest grew enormously—there were serious revolts in both Valencia and Bilbao—and this provided the many elements in the Church, the nobility, and the army who felt threatened by Godoy's policies with a means of putting pressure on the regime. By means of a clever campaign of black propaganda, they painted a picture of decadence, corruption, and incompetence that has survived unchallenged to this day, and at the same time won them the support of the crowd. Meanwhile, seizing upon the crown prince, Ferdinand, as a useful figurehead whom they would be able to manipulate at will, they promoted him as a "prince charming" who would put an end to all Spain's ills, and they also began to intrigue for the support of Napoleon. With things going from bad to worse—in 1805, of course, came the dramatic defeat of Trafalgar, while in 1807 the British invaded modern-day Uruguay and Argentina—Godoy responded by a variety of diplomatic twists and turns, not to mention some intrigues of his own, but these only served to destabilize the situation still further, and the end result was French intervention, the overthrow of Charles IV and Godoy by a hastily organized military coup, the removal of the entire Bourbon dynasty, and the overwhelming upsurge of popular feeling that precipitated the Peninsular War of 1807–1814.

The military events of this conflict are dealt with elsewhere. In brief, however, after some initial reverses—most notably, the Battle of Bailén—forced them to evacuate most of the territory that they had been occupying when the war broke out, the French counterattacked and retook Madrid, whereupon Joseph Bonaparte was installed as King of Spain. Between then and the beginning of 1812, there followed a long struggle to reduce the rest of the country. However, aided by a variety of factors—British intervention, rough terrain, and the sheer size of the country—the so-called Patriot forces clung on. So heavy were Spain's losses that her military capacity was eventually reduced to almost nothing, but Napoleon's invasion of Russia destabilized his position in the Peninsula, and Wellington's Anglo-Portuguese army was at last enabled to take the offensive. Even then it took another two years' hard fighting, but by April 1814 the Bonaparte Kingdom of Spain was little more than a memory.

The significance of the Peninsular War in terms of the general history of Spain cannot be underestimated. Hamstrung by the collapse of its naval power in the period 1796–1808, Spain was confronted by the loss of most of its American colonies: Faced by the inability of the mother country either to provide for their defense or to meet their economic needs, from 1810 onward the Creoles of one territory after another rose in revolt. Meanwhile, at home, dissatisfaction with the Bourbons, economic self-interest, and the demands of the war against France had produced the rise of a revolutionary movement that gave birth to the English terms *liberal* and *liberalism*. From this movement there emerged the Constitution of 1812, and with it the definitive end of both feudalism and the Spanish Inquisition, while in response there came together a powerful counterrevolutionary party whose aim it was to restore absolutism, and in many cases reverse the reforms introduced by the Bourbon monarchy in the eighteenth century. Add to all this an army that had been deeply politicized by the events of 1808–1814, and it will be appreciated that Spain was set for a nineteenth century that would be deeply disturbed.

Charles J. Esdaile

See also Algeciras, First Battle of; Algeciras, Second Battle of; Amiens, Treaty of; Bailén, Battle of and Capitulation at; Basle, Treaties of; Bayonne, Conference at; Bonaparte, Joseph; Buenos Aires, Expedition to; Cádiz, Cortes of; Charles IV, King; Ferdinand VII, King; Godoy y Alvarez de Faria, Manuel de, Príncipe de la Paz, Duque de Alcudia; Guerrilla Warfare; Junta Central; Le Boulou, Battle of; Moñino, José, Conde de Floridablanca; Oranges, War of the; Peninsular War; Pyrenean Campaigns (1793–1795); San Ildefonso, Treaty of; South America; Spanish Army; Spanish Navy; St. Vincent, Battle of; Trafalgar, Battle of; Trinidad, Capture of; Wellington, Arthur Wellesley, First Duke of

References and further reading

Anna, Timothy E. 1983. *Spain and the Loss of America.* Lincoln: University of Nebraska Press.
Callahan, William J. 1984. *Church, Politics, and Society in Spain, 1750–1874.* Cambridge, MA: Harvard University Press.
Costeloe, Michael P. 1986. *Response to Revolution: Imperial Spain and the Spanish American Revolutions, 1810–1840.* Cambridge: Cambridge University Press.
Esdaile, Charles J. 2002. *The Peninsular War: A New History.* London: Penguin.
Glover, Michael. 1971. *The Legacy of Glory: The Bonaparte Kingdom of Spain, 1808–1813.* New York: Scribner.
Herr, Richard. 1958. *The Eighteenth-Century Revolution in Spain.* Princeton: Princeton University Press.
———. 1989. *Rural Change and Royal Finances in Spain at the End of the Old Regime.* Berkeley: University of California Press.
Hilt, Douglas. 1987. *The Troubled Trinity: Godoy and the Spanish Monarchs.* Tuscaloosa: University of Alabama Press.
Lovett, Gabriel H. 1965. *Napoleon and the Birth of Modern Spain.* 2 vols. New York: New York University Press.
Lynch, John. 1989. *Bourbon Spain, 1700–1808.* Oxford: Blackwell.

Spain, Campaigns in

See Peninsular War

Spanish Army

Traumatic in the extreme, the Spanish Army's experience of the French Revolutionary and Napoleonic Wars deeply affected its outlook and had a lasting impact on the history of Spain.

In 1789 the army was a conventional late eighteenth-century force, whose only distinguishing feature was an exceptionally strong royal guard. Recruited by a mixture of voluntary enlistment and a limited system of conscription that was generally imposed only in wartime and affected only the urban and rural poor, it consisted of a typical array of conventionally organized infantry and cavalry regiments. A number of the infantry regiments were foreign—Irish, Italian, Swiss, and Walloon—and there were separate corps of artillery and engineers, both of which enjoyed considerable administrative independence. Officers, meanwhile, came primarily from the nobility; promotion from the ranks was possible and quite widespread, but such men rarely advanced beyond the rank of captain: By 1800 perhaps one-third of the officer corps consisted of ex-rankers. With favor at court very important in securing advancement, promotion was in general highly inequitable, and so the army suffered from having a minority of well-connected officers, who were promoted rapidly and often rose far beyond their capacity, and a majority of perpetual captains and lieutenants, who were both aging and embittered.

Hardly conducive to professional solidarity, this situation was to have serious results in 1808. As for other defects, Spain being desperately short of horses, there were too few cavalry, while the army was entirely dependent on the population for its transport: Horses, oxen, mules, and wagons all had to be hired at the start of each campaign, while they were left in the charge of civilian teamsters who were prone to abscond at the first opportunity. Above all, however, in the reign of Charles III (1759–1788), the army had been run down in favor of the navy, the latter being of far greater importance in a situation where a permanent alliance with France ensured that Spain's only major foreign opponent would be Britain. The result of all this was that the war against France of 1793–1795 was a difficult experience. The Spaniards fought well, but they were unable either to respond effectively to the tactics employed by their French opponents, or to build up a large army. Under the influence of the royal favorite, Manuel de Godoy, the period from 1795 to 1808 was therefore marked by a serious attempt at military reform. Thanks to the opposition of vested interests in the army and a variety of other problems, this effort had little effect, however: The royal guard was cut in half, the number of light infantry greatly increased, and the army given some horse artillery, but otherwise all remained much as before.

When war broke out with France in 1808, Spain was therefore at a serious disadvantage, while the army's problems were rendered still worse by the circumstances of the Spanish uprising. For a variety of reasons, the army was deeply unpopular, and the result was that many leading generals were overthrown or even murdered. At the same time there was a breakdown of authority, and a failure to establish adequate systems of command and control, while the officer corps itself split: Denied promotion, many of the humbler subaltern officers collaborated enthusiastically with the insurgents and made no attempt to rally round their superiors, even when the latter were demonstrably loyal to the rebellion. And finally, in the general confusion, many regular units disintegrated, while those that survived had hastily to be brought up to strength with large numbers of raw recruits. On top of this, many new regiments were formed under the leadership of improvised officers who were frequently lacking in talent, training, and experience. For obvious reasons, meanwhile, the vast majority of these new forces were composed of infantry: It was simply quicker and cheaper to turn out foot soldiers than it was to train fresh cavalrymen or to equip new batteries of artillery.

In consequence, the Spanish Army had little chance. Thus, the single lucky victory obtained at Bailén was followed by a series of terrible defeats—good examples are Tudela, Uclés, Medellín, Alba de Tormes, and Ocaña—for the Spanish levies could barely maneuver or change formation on the battlefield, while their lack of artillery and, more especially, cavalry support placed them at a still greater disadvantage. Nor was there ever any chance of remedying these problems. One way forward would have

been to avoid battle and adopt a defensive strategy: Spread around the periphery of the country, the Spanish armies were sheltered by massive chains of mountains, such as the Sierra Morena. However, this strategy was not an option: the provisional government that ruled Spain from 1808 to 1810 needed military victories, while generals that jibbed at taking the field were liable to be replaced and on occasion even killed as traitors.

Yet going over to the attack was not easy either, for the Spanish field armies were necessarily operating on exterior lines, while their starting positions were often hundreds of miles apart. In consequence, it was easy for the French to defeat them in detail, while the disadvantages under which the generals were laboring were frequently increased by the meddling of their political superiors and the hesitation engendered by the deep dilemmas that they faced (damned if they did not fight, they knew that they would be defeated if they did). Finally, since the chief theater of operations could only be the open plains of the *meseta* (the country's central plateau), defeat was invariably accompanied by enormous casualties and the loss of large numbers of guns and other impedimenta. At the same time, as military service was deeply unpopular, the army impossible to supply in an adequate manner, and joining the guerrillas a constant temptation, desertion was enormous. In consequence, with each defeat the generals—who were, it has to be said, hardly a galaxy of talent—had to start virtually from scratch, only for their efforts almost immediately to be lost in some fresh catastrophe.

In fairness it ought to be observed that the Spaniards often actually fought with great courage, particularly in the defense of besieged cities and fortresses and in situations where the French could not bring their massive superiority to bear (a good example is the Battle of Albuera, where four battalions of Spanish infantry held off two French divisions and thereby saved Sir William Beresford from complete disaster). But gallantry was not enough: By the beginning of 1810, Spain's soldiers had lost so much ground to the French that they had literally run out of resources. From 1810 to 1812, then, all that the army could do was to seek to hang on to such enclaves of territory as the Patriot cause still possessed, while at the same time harassing the French with raids and skirmishes. In this manner the struggle against Napoleon was sustained, but the military were never able to regain even such strength as they had possessed in 1808, with the result that the liberation of Spain in 1812–1813 saw only a limited degree of Spanish participation. Indeed, even the organizing genius of Wellington, who became commander in chief of the Spanish Army in January 1813, proved insufficient to the task of rebuilding the army, and it was not until the autumn of that year, by which time the French had almost been cleared from the Peninsula, that substantial bodies of troops were once again available for service.

All this had a deep impact on the army's psychology. Reduced to a secondary role in the ejection of the French, it had also been forced to endure the open scorn of many British soldiers (scorn that is echoed in much British writing on the Peninsular War to this very day). At the very time that it had been fighting the invaders with such devotion, moreover, it had seen itself stripped of most of the legal privileges that the military estate had enjoyed in 1808 by the Cortes of Cádiz. Rather than a source of pride, the war against Napoleon therefore became a source of humiliation—humiliation, moreover, which was in large part blamed on the civilian politicians who had actually run the war effort—and the result was a propensity toward military intervention in politics that was to mar the course of Spanish history until well into the twentieth century. In brief, the army became obsessed by the need to maintain law and order, the unity of Spain, and the primacy of the armed forces, and in this fashion it was drawn deeper and deeper into the camp of political reaction. In consequence, it may be said that the victims of General Franco's firing squads in the Spanish Civil War of 1936–1939 were the last casualties of the struggle against Napoleon.

Charles J. Esdaile

See also Alba de Tormes, Battle of; Albuera, Battle of; Bailén, Battle of and Capitulation at; Beresford, Sir William Carr; Cádiz, Cortes of; Godoy y Alvarez de Faria, Manuel de, Príncipe de la Paz, Duque de Alcudia; Medellín, Battle of; Ocaña, Battle of; Peninsular War; Pyrenean Campaigns (1793–1795); Spain; Spanish Navy; Tudela, Battle of; Wellington, Arthur Wellesley, First Duke of

References and further reading
Chartrand, René. 1998. *Spanish Army of the Napoleonic Wars.* Vol. 1, *1793–1808.* Oxford: Osprey.
———. 1999. *Spanish Army of the Napoleonic Wars.* Vol. 2, *1808–1812.* Oxford: Osprey.
Esdaile, Charles J. 1988. *The Spanish Army in the Peninsular War.* Manchester, UK: Manchester University Press.
———. 1990. *The Duke of Wellington and the Command of the Spanish Army, 1812–1814.* London: Macmillan.
Pivka, Otto von. 1975. *Spanish Armies of the Napoleonic Wars.* London: Osprey.

Spanish Navy

The French Revolutionary and Napoleonic Wars witnessed a dramatic transformation in the position of the Spanish Navy. Thus, in 1792 Spain was, on paper at least, one of Europe's leading naval powers—indeed, Spain's navy was ranked behind only those of Britain and France—whereas in 1814 the few Spanish warships that still remained could barely be put to sea.

At the beginning of the struggle, however, no one could have predicted this transformation. For most of the eighteenth century, the Spanish Navy had been in the ascendant. Under Charles III, in particular, the number of ships had been greatly expanded, as were Spain's naval dockyards and other shipbuilding facilities. Meanwhile, Spanish shipbuilders were given the best training available, and their ranks strengthened by imported foreign experts. The training of naval officers was reformed, and a comprehensive system of naval conscription instituted in maritime provinces. In the 1780s, a regular program of fleet maneuvers was instituted. And, above all, money was lavished on the navy: Between 1776 and 1784, for example, spending averaged 28 percent of the national budget.

All this produced an impressive force. Aided not just by rapid naval building but the construction of the many ships built in Cuba from long-lasting colonial hardwoods, in 1792 the navy amounted to 76 ships of the line, 41 frigates, and 109 smaller vessels. Spanish ship design, meanwhile, was excellent: With some exceptions, Spanish warships were immensely strong, eminently sea-worthy, and highly maneuverable, while they had also been growing ever bigger and could carry more guns than British warships of a comparable size. Indeed, the Spanish Navy was the proud owner of the *Santísima Trinidad*, which was the largest warship in the world and carried 136 guns. And, last but not least, the naval officer corps was first rate: not only had men such as Alejandro Malaspina played a major part in the voyages of exploration and discovery characteristic of the eighteenth century, but commanders such as José de Mazarredo, Federico Gravina, Cosmé Churruca, Dionisio Alcalá Galiano, and Cayetano Valdés were widely known for courage and professionalism.

What, then, wrecked the Spanish Navy? According to tradition, the answer lies in the incompetence and corruption endemic in the Spanish administration, and, in particular, the misdeeds of the Spanish royal favorite, Manuel de Godoy. This verdict, however, is unfair. It is certainly true that full-scale naval construction effectively ceased in Spain in 1796, that the Spanish Navy was dogged by a variety of logistical problems, and that every Spanish fleet that put to sea was defeated, but the reasons for this are far more complicated than the "black legend" tends to assume. In the first place, the outbreak of war with France in 1793 completely transformed Spain's strategic situation. Even though peace was made with the Republic in 1795, and a military alliance forged in 1796, Madrid could no longer depend on Paris's friendship (as it had been able to do throughout the eighteenth century). With the recent naval expansion only achieved at the cost of the army, which had generally been allowed to run down, a certain reallocation of resources was now inevitable, and all the more so, given the soaring inflation that had gripped Spain since 1780 and was forcing up the cost of construction and maintenance.

Beyond, this, meanwhile, the navy was affected by serious shortages of raw materials. Thus, by the 1790s the oak forests on which shipbuilding in Spain depended had been seriously depleted, while war with Britain from 1796 onward meant that the Baltic pine on which her shipbuilders increasingly relied for masts could not be obtained (initially much pine had come from Mexico, but by the 1790s the most accessible forests had all been cut down there, too). Manpower also was at a premium. Larger ships required larger crews, but the supply of sailors was affected by a series of epidemics of yellow fever that gutted entire communities along the south coast of Spain: between 1803 and 1805, for example, fully 25 percent of the population of Málaga were struck down by this disease.

And, last but not least, war with Britain meant that Spain's ships were forced to remain cooped up in harbor for long periods, with serious results for both shiphandling and gunnery practice. Though corruption doubtless played its part (along, perhaps, with want of imagination: There was, for example, no attempt to copy the British innovation of supplementing the sailor's diet with citrus fruit), Spain's naval decline must therefore be attributed to other issues. Yet decline the Spanish Navy did. Despite great courage and devotion, Spanish fleets were worsted at Cape St. Vincent and Trafalgar, while by 1808 the struggle against Britain had cost 25 men-of-war shipwrecked or lost in battle. As a further 15 had been stricken or broken up since 1792 and still others lost in the war of 1793–1795 or transferred to France, Spain's striking power had been more than halved, while those ships that remained could hardly put to sea for want of crews, naval stores, and other supplies, the problems experienced in this area being greatly increased by the loss of much of the country to enemy occupation and the complete devastation of the economy. Spanish ships did participate in the Peninsular War, helping, for example, to transport troops around the coast and participating in amphibious operations, but all the while rotting and obsolescent men-of-war were having to be stricken from the service, while others again were lost to shipwreck. For all this destruction there was no replacement, save for a few French ships captured at Cádiz in 1808, and the end result was that by 1814 Spanish naval power was no more.

Charles J. Esdaile

See also French Navy; Godoy y Alvarez de Faria, Manuel de, Príncipe de la Paz, Duque de Alcudia; Naval Warfare; Peninsular War; Royal Navy; Ships of the Line; Spain; Spanish Army; St. Vincent, Battle of; Trafalgar, Battle of

References and further reading
Gardiner, Robert. 2003. *Warships of the Napoleonic Era.* London: Chatham.
Harbron, John. 2004. *Trafalgar and the Spanish Navy.* London: Conway Maritime.
Henry, Chris. 2004. *Napoleonic Naval Armaments, 1792–1815.* Oxford: Osprey.
Pivka, Otto von. 1980. *Navies of the Napoleonic Wars.* Newton Abbott: David and Charles.

Speransky, Mikhail Mikhailovich, Count (1772–1839)

Prominent Russian statesman and reformer, secretary to Tsar Alexander I. He was born on 12 January 1772, the son of the village priest from Cherkutino in central Russia, and studied at the seminary in Vladimir. In 1788 he enrolled in the Main Seminary in St. Petersburg, from which he graduated in 1792 and at which he stayed for four years as instructor of philosophy and prefect. In January 1797 he left the seminary for the civil service and was granted the rank of titular counselor, becoming a secretary to powerful Prince Aleksey Kurakin, procurator general of the Senate. He was promoted to college assessor on 16 April 1797 and court counselor on 12 January 1798. In December 1798, Speransky became the herald of the Order of St. Andrew the First Called. Promoted to state counselor in December 1799, he became the secretary of the Order of St. Andrew the First Called in July 1800.

Under Paul's successor, Tsar Alexander I, Speransky quickly advanced through lower bureaucratic ranks. In 1801, he was appointed the head of the Third Division of the Inevitable Council (*Nepremenii Sovet*) in May and promoted to the rank of actual state counselor. In 1802, he was assigned, on V. P. Victor Pavlovich Kochubey's recommendation, to the new Ministry of the Interior, where he directed one of the departments after February 1803. He gained experience in drafting legislation (1802–1804) and facilitated the establishment of the *St. Peterburgskii zhurnal* (1804–1809), where he regularly published reports on the ministry's activities. In May 1806 Speransky became the head of the Second Expedition of the Ministry and gained the confidence of Alexander through his regular reports. In November 1807 he became administrative secretary and assistant to the tsar himself. Speransky was promoted to privy counselor on 15 August 1808. On 28 December, he was appointed *tovarish* (deputy) minister of justice and chair of the commission drafting legislation. He reorganized the seminaries and secured the establishment of the first Russian lycée, and he attempted to reform the bureaucracy by requiring the nobles to perform actual service to the state and pass examinations. In 1809, Speransky prepared a plan of major government restructuring that divided the population into three classes with varying degrees of political and civil rights, called for the creation of elective assemblies, and established the State Council in January 1810.

Speransky actively supported Franco-Russian rapprochement after Tilsit, and in 1808 he accompanied Alexander to his meeting at Erfurt with Napoleon, who described him as "the only clear head in Russia." Speransky's pro-French leanings, aloof personality, and nonnoble origins added to the hostility of the nobles, who vigorously intrigued against him. In 1810, anticipating a new war with France, Speransky prepared an extensive plan to revive the Russian economy that provided for drastic cuts in state expenditure and an increase in state taxes. Alexander approved the plan, but Minister of Finances Dmitri Aleksandrovich Guriev effectively sabotaged it. In 1811 Speransky effectively supervised the economic struggle with France and established a new series of tariffs that deprived France of trade privileges with Russia.

Speransky's influence and actions further exasperated his enemies. In March 1811, he found himself attacked by his high-placed enemies at court, where the renowned historian Nikolay Karamzin disparaged him in his new work *Of Old and New Russia* and Guriev accused him of corruption. Alexander even had his personal agent Jacob (Yakov) Ivanovich de Sanglen assigned to spy on Speransky. On 29 March 1812 Speransky was summarily dismissed after a two-hour conversation with the tsar. Returning to his home at midnight, he found a police carriage waiting at his door and was immediately taken to exile in Nizhny Novgorod, and then to even more distant Perm. In September 1814, he was allowed to return to his estate of Velikopolie, near Novgorod. Two years later, he was pardoned, after his appeals to powerful Count Aleksey Andreyevich Arakcheyev, and appointed provincial governor in Penza on 11 September 1816. Three years later, he became governor-general of Siberia, where he introduced a series of reforms and established effective administration.

On 29 July 1821 he was appointed a member of the State Council and worked in the Legislative Department. Tsar Nicholas I, Alexander's successor, initially appointed him a member of the special tribunal that tried and sentenced the Decembrists; later Speransky wrote a letter that secured a significant reduction of the sentences imposed by the tribunal. In February 1826 he directed the Second Division of Nicholas's personal chancellery and supervised the codification of laws. He oversaw the gargantuan task of publishing the Russian laws in the *Complete Collection of the Laws of the Russian Empire* (*Polnoye sobraniye zakonov Rossiyskoy imperii*) and supervised preparation of a *Digest of the Laws* (*Svod zakonov Rossiyskoy imperii*). He was pro-

moted to privy counselor on 14 October 1827. For his dedicated service on the codification of laws, Speransky was decorated in 1833 and 1837, while he was awarded the title of count on 12 January 1839. He died in St. Petersburg on 23 February 1839 and was buried at the Tikhvin cemetery of the Alexander of Neva Monastery.

Alexander Mikaberidze

See also Alexander I, Tsar; Erfurt, Congress of; Paul I, Tsar; Tilsit, Treaties of
References and further reading
Chibiryaev, S. A. 1989. *Velikii russkii reformator. Zhizn, deyatelnost, politicheskie vzgliadi M.M. Speranskogo.* Moscow: N.p.
Fedorov, V. A. 1997. *M. M. Speransky and A. A. Arakcheyev.* Moscow: N.p.
Raeff, Marc. 1956. *Siberia and the Reforms of 1822.* Seattle: University of Washington Press.
———. 1969. *Michael Speransky: Statesman of Imperial Russia, 1772–1839.* The Hague: Nojhoff.
Tomsinov, V. A. 1991. *Svetilo russkoi biurokratii. Istoricheskii portret M.M. Speranskogo.* Moscow: N.p.
Valka, S. N., ed. 1961. *M. M. Speranskii: Proiekty i zapiski.* Moscow: N.p.

Spithead, Mutiny at (15 April–15 May 1797)

The mutiny at Spithead was carried out as a protest against the conditions of service endured by British sailors in the Royal Navy. By 1797 the navy had been at war for a decade. Its size had increased from 45,000 men in 1793 to 110,000 at the turn of the century. Only 20 percent of the navy consisted of volunteers. Ships of the line were huge workplaces and constantly required fresh recruits. The Impress Service lawfully apprehended men from age eighteen to fifty-five to involuntarily serve in the navy. Those with seafaring experience were more highly valued and were seized before those less qualified.

Conditions aboard ship were, at least by today's standards, inhumane; sailors were treated little better than animals. The crews lived in very cramped quarters. On many Royal Navy ships, some 500 seamen were forced to sleep in a confined area with minimal personal space, much like slave ships. Their poor diet sometimes resulted in typhus and scurvy. Medical attention was often inept, and many died through the ignorance—and sometimes the neglect—of the doctors. The meager food was atrocious, largely inedible, and inadequate for the labor expended. Severely cruel, often unearned, punishment for the slightest infraction was the norm; brutal discipline rather than earned respect was all too often the officers' method of control. Many sailors despised those of their officers whom they regarded as vindictive, though animosity for the higher ranks and contempt for the lower ranks was certainly not universal within the navy. There had been no pay increase since 1658. Wages were intermittently paid and always in arrears, the sailors' families suffering accordingly. The army had received a pay increase in 1795, so sailors believed it was their turn. The war was so unrelenting that the men were often refused shore leave and could not return home for several—sometimes many—years. By 1797 the sailors were war weary, as was the country.

Eleven petitions regarding the sailors' grievances had been sent to the First Lord of the Admiralty, John Spencer, second Earl Spencer. Although he had occupied his post for three years at the time of the mutiny, Spencer was unfamiliar with life aboard ship and unsympathetic to the mutineers; he ignored their demands.

This situation, brewing since 1795, exploded on 15 April 1797, when the crews of sixteen ships of the line of the Channel Fleet at Spithead, near Portsmouth, refused to obey orders to sail from Admiral Alexander Hood, Lord Bridport. The mutiny was serious because the ships at Spithead constituted the main defense against the French. Valentine Joyce, the 26-year-old leader of the mutiny, hosted two delegates from each of the sixteen ships aboard the *Queen Charlotte* to discuss strategy. The firmly united group agreed that no ship would sail until all of their grievances were met. When the orderly, peaceful mutineers insisted on parliamentary approval of their pay demands and a signed and written royal pardon, Spencer was forced to confer with King George III and the prime minister, William Pitt, at Windsor Castle. Meanwhile, for fear the French might take advantage of the situation and appear in the Channel, Spencer ordered some ships to sea. They refused.

Spencer returned with 100 copies of a royal pardon. The untrusting mutineers insisted on seeing the original pardon. By mid-May, Parliament agreed to the pay increase. The Admiralty offered lengthier periods of leave on shore, regular and increased pay, better medical attention, better victuals, and overall improvements in shipboard conditions. The 100 offending officers were permanently removed, and the sailors ended their mutiny.

This relatively peaceful mutiny—as opposed to the other disturbance at the Nore—was successful, for there was no loss of life. The government kept its word, and no one was hanged for the offense.

Annette E. Richardson

See also Hood, Alexander, First Viscount Bridport; Nore, Mutiny at the; Royal Navy; Ships of the Line
References and further reading
Bullocke, John Greville. 1938. *Sailors' Rebellion: A Century of Naval Mutinies.* London: Eyre and Spottiswood.
Dugan, James. 1965. *The Great Mutiny.* New York: Putnam.
Gardiner, Robert, ed. 1996. *Fleet Battle and Blockade: The French Revolutionary War, 1793–1797.* London: Chatham.
Gill, Conrad. 1913. *The Naval Mutinies of 1797.* Manchester: Manchester University Press.
Guttridge, Leonard F. 1992. *Mutiny: A History of Naval Insurrection.* New York: Berkley.
Manwaring, George. 1935. *The Floating Republic: An Account of the Mutinies at Spithead and the Nore in 1797.* London: Bles.

St. Cyr, Laurent Gouvion

See Gouvion St. Cyr, Laurent, comte

St. Dizier, Battle of (26 March 1814)

One of the last engagements of the 1814 campaign in France, the Battle of St. Dizier (not to be confused with the two-day action of the same name fought on 26–27 January between the Prussians under Gebhard von Blücher and the French under Marshal Claude Victor on the first day, and Napoleon and the Prussian rear guard on the second) was part of an attempt by Napoleon to lure the Allied troops to attack him instead of advancing to Paris. In retreat after his loss in the Battle of Arcis-sur-Aube on 20–21 March, Napoleon entered St. Dizier on 22–23 March, with plans to add its garrison strength to his field forces of 34,000 men in order to disrupt communications between the Armies of Silesia (largely Prussian) and Bohemia (largely Austrian) and force them to respond to his actions. Unbeknownst to Napoleon, however, details regarding his plans (contained in part in his uncoded correspondence to the empress) had been intercepted by the Allies. So, too, had information that Paris was in an uproar and unprepared to defend itself against the invading armies.

After some discussion among the Allied leaders, General Ferdinand Winzegorode's forces were sent east toward St. Dizier to hold off Napoleon, while the bulk of the Allied forces in the area continued along the Marne toward Paris. Although technically a victory for Napoleon, who routed Winzegorode's troops on 26 March, the Battle of St. Dizier did not halt the advance to the capital. In the wake of his nominal success, Napoleon then had to race the Allies to Paris for a final stand.

Korcaighe P. Hale

See also Arcis-sur-Aube, Battle of; Blücher von Wahlstatt, Gebhard Lebrecht Fürst; Brienne, Battle of; France, Campaign in; Winzegorode, Ferdinand Fedorovich, Baron
References and further reading
Chandler, David G. 1995. *The Campaigns of Napoleon.* London: Weidenfeld and Nicolson.
Delderfield, R. F. 2001. *Imperial Sunset: The Fall of Napoleon, 1813–1814.* Lanham, MD: Cooper Square.

Lawford, James. 1977. *Napoleon: The Last Campaigns, 1813–1815*. London: Roxby.

Petre, F. Loraine. 1994. *Napoleon at Bay: 1814*. London: Greenhill.

St. Domingue

See Haiti

St. Gotthard Pass, Action at the (24 September 1799)

The Russian field marshal Alexander Suvorov chose the St. Gotthard Pass as the way in which he would enter Switzerland at the start of his campaign in September 1799. The French held the pass, but their forces were spread thinly. The assault was carried out by Russian troops on 24 September and succeeded in pushing the French back. For the loss of around 1,000 men, Suvorov had gained entrance to Switzerland.

Suvorov had chosen the St. Gotthard Pass as the way into Switzerland for his forces because it had a paved road, which would make supplying his forces easier. However, he knew that the French would be in a strong position, and he tried to combine his frontal assault on the pass with an attack on the lines of communication of the French at the village of Andermatt, by forces under the command of *Feldmarschalleutnant* Franz Fürst von Rosenberg. General Charles Etienne Gudin defended the pass, with about 3,800 men. Suvorov planned to attack the pass using three columns. The flanking columns were to advance first to secure high ground on either side of the road, after which the central column would then drive up the road. The attack was to begin at 3:00 A.M. However, due to various delays the attack did not begin until 2:00 P.M. The first troops to advance were Russian *Jägers* under the command of Prince Peter Bagration. These light infantry were met by French troops manning rough defenses made of rocks and logs. The French fire inflicted a significant number of casualties, and the Russians were halted. This attack should have been supported, but the Russians were unused to the mountain terrain, and the advance was consequently very slow. Suvorov was furious at this delay and bullied his troops forward.

Austrian troops now reinforced Bagration, and the initial enemy positions were taken. The French withdrawal toward the hospice at the head of the pass was very ordered. At this point, however, after a difficult climb, a Russian force composed of one infantry regiment, Jägers, and dismounted Cossacks led by General Mikhail Semenovich

Baranovsky outflanked the French defenders. The hard-pressed French were now forced back past the hospice and retreated to the village of Hospental, about 3 miles to the north of the pass. The pursuit of the Russians was now quite vigorous, and the attack pressed into the village. By now it was becoming dark, and Suvorov was unaware that Gudin had massed his remaining forces on the outskirts of the village. However, Gudin was aware that more forces were climbing the pass and took the decision to escape under the cover of darkness. He left behind his three guns but succeeded in withdrawing, due to the laxness of Russian pickets. Suvorov had taken the pass, but the earlier delays meant that the enemy had been given time to prepare their defenses further along the routes into Switzerland.

Ralph Baker

See also Bagration, Peter Ivanovich, Prince; Second Coalition, War of the; Suvorov, Alexander Vasilievich; Switzerland, Campaign in

References and further reading

Duffy, Christopher. 1999. *Eagles over the Alps: Suvorov in Italy and Switzerland, 1799*. Chicago: Emperor's Press.

St. Helena

A British island possession in the South Atlantic Ocean, site of Napoleon's final exile and death.

St. Helena is located at 16 degrees south latitude, 5 degrees 40 minutes east longitude, and about 1,200 miles from the west coast of Africa. It is 10 miles long and 7 miles wide at its greatest extent. It has a temperate climate despite its tropical latitude and rises to a maximum altitude of 2,690 feet above sea level. The soil is poor and has never been especially productive agriculturally, but St. Helena's economy has nonetheless always been heavily dependent on farming, with fishing and livestock as supplements.

When Napoleon first sighted the island from HMS *Northumberland* on 15 October 1815, St. Helena maintained a population of about 5,000, mostly concentrated in the capital of Jamestown, and a garrison of about 3,000.

A limited number of companions accompanied Napoleon into exile. These included Doctor Barry O'Meara, formerly surgeon aboard the *Northumberland*; the Counts Henri Bertrand, Gaspard Gourgand, Emmanuel Las Cases, and Charles Montholon; and a small domestic staff, several of whom brought wives and children. While none of Napoleon's family accompanied him into exile, it is possible he was the father of Madame Albine de Montholon's daughter, Napoléone, who was later born on the island.

After landing on 16 October 1815, Napoleon lodged with the Balcombe family. He initially appeared to treat exile as a vacation, sharing practical jokes with the family's

Longwood, Napoleon's residence on St. Helena from 1815 until his death six years later. (Unsigned engraving, 19th c. The David Markham Collection)

daughters, Jane (sixteen) and Betsy (fourteen). He soon moved to a private estate, Longwood, approximately 6 miles from Jamestown. At Longwood, Napoleon had personal use of six rooms: an antechamber for receiving visitors, a parlor, a bedroom, a study, a library to house the many books he either brought with him or had sent, and a large dining room. Moderate as it was, Longwood certainly provided adequate accommodation for the exiles, who lived quite comfortably at the expense of the British government. This consideration notwithstanding, the residents were sure to always retain full court etiquette and always addressed Napoleon as "your majesty."

Napoleon's exile turned sour following the arrival of a new governor, Sir Hudson Lowe. Not only was Lowe a former commander of Corsican and French exiles and émigrés, and therefore by his very presence an insult to Napoleon, but he also bore with him more restrictive rules from the British government concerning the conditions of Napoleon's exile. Even more offensive, Lowe firmly maintained the British policies of addressing Napoleon as "General Bonaparte" and rejecting any correspondence that arrived for the prisoner bearing an imperial or royal title. He also, in accordance with policy, censored Napoleon's outgoing correspondence, which ultimately prevented Napoleon from drawing on his private funds lest the details of his financial correspondence be examined by the governor.

Insistent on retaining his imperial dignity, Napoleon withdrew into Longwood. The withdrawal, prompted by pride and furthered by stubborn determination, was to become rather extreme. The constant supervision and visible escorts required of him any time he left Longwood prompted him to suspend his outdoor activities. He gave up his horseback riding and, other than a brief gardening craze among the exiles, generally spent more and more time inside, with one stretch totaling more than 100 days. He also sought to secure relief, launching a final campaign to portray the conditions of his exile as intolerable and cruel. He instructed his fellow exiles to complain vociferously about conditions, and refused to see commissioners sent by the Allied powers to verify his presence and the conditions of his captivity.

The most productive use of his time was in the dictation of his memoirs to several of the exile community. Largely factually accurate, the recollections on St. Helena do include a few self-serving omissions and distortions. Napoleon, however, freely admitted his errors, both in dealing with Prince Charles-Maurice de Talleyrand, formerly the foreign minister, and with respect to his invasions of Russia and Spain. Regardless, more important than the facts, maxims, admissions, or distortions recorded by the exiles was the deliberate creation of a Napoleonic myth which depicted the ruler as a champion of the common people, a creation intended to replace his image as dictator. Combined with his attempts to portray himself as an exiled martyr suffering under the heel of Lowe and the British government, these efforts succeeded in arousing some sympathy in Europe, though never enough for the Allies to consider releasing him or transferring him to a less remote location. Having broken his pledge to remain on Elba during his 1814–1815 exile, Napoleon was not to be trusted again.

Though only forty-five years old when he arrived on St. Helena, Napoleon increasingly suffered symptoms of hiccupping, vomiting, and bowel dysfunction. Doctor Francesco Antommarchi, who replaced O'Meara in 1818, diagnosed a liver ailment and treated his patient with medications that only inflamed his stomach conditions. Napoleon's health worsened, and he died at 5:49 P.M. on 5 May 1821, attended by sixteen witnesses. An autopsy, previously ordered by Napoleon, revealed cancerous lesions in his stomach; as a result, the examiners listed stomach cancer as the official cause of death. The post mortem revealed no liver ailments, though Antommarchi dissented from this report. What is certain is that arsenic poisoning played a role in Napoleon's death, either accidentally, as the medications prescribed by Antommarchi contained arsenic or, as some commentators have suggested, deliberately, though the evidence for this is far from conclusive.

Burial took place on 9 May 1821. The remaining exiles (O'Meara and Las Cases had departed earlier) left the island shortly thereafter. Napoleon's body was disinterred and returned to France in 1840 where, after public exposure, it was reburied 6 February 1841.

Deprived of its most famous resident, St. Helena returned to obscurity. It remained a stop on the sailing route from Britain to South Africa, but greatly declined in importance as steam replaced sail. Today, St. Helena remains a British-dependent territory, with about 7,000 inhabitants engaged in fishing, farming, and ranching, as well as providing limited support for the military base on Ascension Island. Access is largely limited to infrequent and expensive berths on ships, so few admirers or historians of the fallen emperor ever visit the scene of his final exile.

Grant Weller and Marie H. Weller

See also Antommarchi, Francesco; Balcombe, Betsy; Bertrand, Henri-Gatien, comte; Elba; Lowe, Sir Hudson; Montholon, Charles Tristan, comte de; O'Meara, Barry Edward; Talleyrand-Périgord, Charles-Maurice de, Prince; Verling, James Roch

References and further reading
Antommarchi, Francesco. 1826. *The Last Days of Napoleon: Memoirs of the Last Two Years of Napoleon's Exile.* London: Colburn.
Blackburn, Julia. 1993. *The Emperor's Last Island: A Journey to St. Helena.* New York: Vintage.
Chaplin, Arnold. 1919. *A St. Helena Who's Who, or a Directory of the Island During the Captivity of Napoleon.* London: Humphrey's.
Croker, John Wilson. 1823. *An Answer to O'Meara's Napoleon in Exile, or, A Voice from St. Helena: From the Quarterly Review for February, 1823.* N.p.: T. and J. Swords.
Forshufvud, Sten, and Ben Weider. 1995. *Assassination at St. Helena Revisited.* London: Wiley.
Forsyth, William. 1853. *History of the Captivity of Napoleon at St. Helena; From the Letters and Journals of the Late Lieut.-Gen. Sir Hudson Lowe, and Official Documents Not Before Made Public.* 3 vols. London: John Murray.
Giles, Frank. 2001. *Napoleon Bonaparte: England's Prisoner.* New York: Carroll and Graf.
Gregory, Desmond. 1996. *Napoleon's Jailer: Lt. Gen. Sir Hudson Lowe: A Life.* Madison, NJ: Farleigh Dickinson University Press.
Kauffman, Jean-Paul. 1999. *The Black Room at Longwood: Napoleon's Exile on Saint Helena.* London: Four Walls Eight Windows.
Las Cases, Marie Joseph. 1823. *Mémorial de Sainte-Hélène, ou journal se trouve consigné, jour par jour, ce qu'a dit et fait Napoléon durant dix-huit mois, du 20 juin 1815–25 novembre 1816.* 8 vols. Paris: L'Auteur.
Markham, J. David. 2005. *Napoleon and Doctor Verling on St. Helena.* London: Pen and Sword.
O'Meara, Barry Edward. 1819. *An Exposition of Some of the Transactions, that Have Taken Place at St. Helena, Since the Appointment of Sir Hudson Lowe as Governor of that Island . . . Various Official Documents, Correspondence, &c.* 2nd ed. London: Ridgway.
———. 1822. *Napoleon in Exile, or, A Voice from St. Helena: The Opinion and Reflections of Napoleon on the Most Important Events of his Life and Government, in His own Words.* Philadelphia: Jehu Burton.
Royle, Stephen. "Attitudes and Aspirations on St Helena in the Face of Continued Economic Dependency." *Geographical Journal* 158, no. 1 (March 1992): 31–39.

St. Hilaire, Louis Vincent Joseph le Blond, comte de (1766–1809)

One of the Empire's outstanding divisional generals, Louis Vincent Joseph le Blond St. Hilaire was instrumental in a number of Napoleon's victories. He rose from the rank of enlisted soldier in the *ancien régime*'s army to one of the highest-ranking officers under the Empire. Napoleon publicly promised him a marshal's baton shortly before his death. His loss in 1809 was keenly felt during the subsequent campaigns.

St. Hilaire joined the French Army in 1777 under the Bourbons. He was posted to the West Indies and served during the American Revolutionary War against the British. His abilities were recognized, and St. Hilaire received an officer's commission in 1783. As with many other regular soldiers, the French Revolution offered him new opportunities for advancement. In the war against the First Coalition, St. Hilaire served in the Alps, and by September 1795, he was promoted to *général de brigade.* He proved to be an aggressive and tough fighter, who was often among the heaviest action. During the Battle of Loano, St. Hilaire lost two fingers. He served under the various commanders of the Army of Italy, including generals Amédée Emmanuel La Harpe, André Masséna, Pierre Augereau, and Claude-Henri Belgrand de Vaubois. In 1796 he fought at Bassano. Several days afterward, St. Hilaire was wounded in both legs and returned to France to recover.

St. Hilaire was assigned to a number of training and administrative posts during his recovery. In 1798 he accompanied Bonaparte on his Egyptian expedition, but later returned to France. In 1799 he was promoted to *général de division.* St. Hilaire joined the army preparing to invade England in 1803. He was appointed one of the division commanders in Marshal Nicolas Soult's IV Corps when the Grande Armée was assembled for the War of the Third Coalition in 1805. During the campaign, St. Hilaire performed creditably, but not spectacularly, though at Austerlitz his division performed the vital task of storming the Pratzen Heights to break the Allied line. He was once again wounded while leading his men.

By October 1806 St. Hilaire had returned to duty to lead his division, which performed well at the Battle of Jena, and participated in the pursuit across Prussia. On 8 February 1807 St. Hilaire led his division forward in a snowstorm against the Russians at Eylau. Unable to break their line, St. Hilaire was lucky to hold his own. Four months later, on 10 June, his division fought in the bloody Battle of Heilsberg, which was a technical French victory.

In 1808 St. Hilaire was ennobled (made a count) by Napoleon for his work. His division was stationed in Germany, as a part of Marshal Louis Davout's III Corps, and missed the invasion of Spain. When it became obvious that the Austrians were preparing for war in 1809, St. Hilaire concentrated his division and joined Davout on his march toward the Danube. His division was one of the few divisions in Napoleon's army that included large numbers of veterans. On 22 April they fought in the Battle of Eggmühl. Napoleon was pleased with St. Hilaire's conduct during the battle. Afterward, the division paraded before the Emperor, who proclaimed that St. Hilaire had earned his marshal's baton and would receive it shortly.

The Austrians under Archduke Charles retreated from Vienna, leaving it an open city. Napoleon followed, crossing the Danube near the villages of Aspern and Essling. Only a part of the French army had crossed before Archduke Charles attacked. After heavy fighting on 21–22 May, the French were forced to retreat. During the fighting, St. Hilaire's left foot was nearly shot away. He refused to let the surgeons amputate it, and the operation to repair it was bungled. An infection set in, and he died on 5 June 1809 in Vienna.

Tim J. Watts

See also Aspern-Essling, Battle of; Augereau, Pierre-François-Charles; Austerlitz, Battle of; Bassano, Battle of; Charles, Archduke of Austria, Duke of Teschen; Davout, Louis Nicolas; Eggmühl, Battle of; England, French Plans for the Invasion of; Eylau, Battle of; Fifth Coalition, War of the; Fourth Coalition, War of the; Heilsberg, Battle of; Italian Campaigns (1792–1797); Jena, Battle of; Loano, Battle of; Masséna, André; Middle East Campaign; Soult, Nicolas Jean de Dieu; Third Coalition, War of the

References and further reading
Chartrand, René. 1996. *Napoleonic Wars, Napoleon's Army.* London: Brassey's.
Rothenberg, Gunther E. 1982. *Napoleon's Great Adversaries: The Archduke Charles and the Austrian Army, 1792–1814.* Bloomington: Indiana University Press.

St. Laurent, Battle of (13 August 1794)

The Battle of St. Laurent was the last major offensive by the Spanish army during the Pyrenean campaign of 1794. The Spanish defeat led to the fall of the last French city held by the Spanish and the shifting of operations into Spain.

Most of the Spanish forces had been driven out of France by the early summer of 1794. The (French) Army of the Eastern Pyrenees spent the summer besieging small forts along the Mediterranean coast. The main action, however, centered on the fortress of Bellegarde, which guarded the main road into Spain. A garrison of around 1,000 Spanish troops held out against a force of approximately 16,000 French. Other French divisions stood to the east and west of Bellegarde. The Spanish army around St. Laurent was under the command of the Conde de la Union. They had been routed in the Battle of Le Boulou at the beginning of May, but de la Union had been busily rebuilding his strength. He sparred with the detached French forces, trying to cut off a division under General Pierre Augereau at San Lorenzo-de-la-Muga on 19 May. Augereau held his ground, despite some desperate fighting, and the Spanish were forced to retreat. French army commander General Jacques Dugommier pulled his left and right divisions closer to the center at Bellegarde. During the rest of the summer, both sides jockeyed, with de la Union concerned mostly with relieving Bellegarde.

On 13 August de la Union launched his attack. His forces totaled 45,000 men, including 4,000 cavalry, an arm in which the French were notably weak. He again concentrated especially against Augereau, who was positioned around the city of St. Laurent. Augereau had only about 9,000 men, but they were the cream of the French army. Augereau had established himself as a drillmaster, and his men were well trained and devoted to their commander, and considered themselves an elite group.

De la Union massed 22,000 men against Augereau. He hoped to turn Dugommier's flank and force him to retreat from Bellegarde. As was often the custom during the time, the Spanish were divided into six columns. They were to converge on a foundry at the center of Augereau's line. Timing and coordination were difficult, and several columns became lost or delayed. Augereau once again distinguished himself as a determined leader, rallying troops with personal examples of bravery. Future marshal of the Empire Jean Lannes distinguished himself, leading a battalion of grenadiers. After fighting that lasted all day, the Spanish were driven back to their original positions. Their losses were over 1,300 men killed and wounded, with similar numbers for Augereau's forces. Only 140 prisoners were taken, perhaps because Augereau had recently instituted a policy of "war to the death" because of Spanish refusal to permit a prisoner exchange.

While the main attack had been made against Augereau, a diversionary attack was launched against the French left wing, but the 5,000 assailants were quickly driven off. Spanish gunboats attempted to land another force along the coast, but the single French battalion defending the area repulsed the landing.

By the end of the day, de la Union was forced to pull his army back to its original positions. Dugommier was thus able to concentrate his army more closely around Bellegarde. The city surrendered on 17 September, marking the end of Spanish occupation of French territory in the south of the country.

Tim J. Watts

See also Augereau, Pierre-François-Charles; Lannes, Jean; Le Boulou, Battle of; Pyrenean Campaigns (1793–1795)
References and further reading
Fervel, N. N. 1861. *Campagnes de la Révolution française dans les Pyrénées-Orientales.* Paris: Dumaine.
Phipps, Ramsay Weston. 1980. *The Armies of the First French Republic and the Rise of the Marshals of Napoleon I.* Vol. 3, *The Armies in the West, 1793–1797, and the Armies in the South, 1792 to March 1796.* London: Greenwood. (Orig. pub. 1926–1939.)

St. Lucia

One of the Windward Islands in the Caribbean, located between Martinique and St. Vincent, 52 kilometers long, 17 kilometers across, and 616 square kilometers, its main port is Castries. St. Lucia had been a prosperous French colony before the French Revolution, producing sugar, coffee, cotton, and cocoa.

In 1791, two representatives from France seized power from the royalist governor, Jean-Joseph Soubader de Gimat. In 1792, when Martinique and Guadeloupe had risen up in counterrevolution, the new governor sent from France, Jean-Baptiste Lacrosse, used St. Lucia as his base of operations, from which he restored republican control over Martinique and Guadeloupe through the distribution of republican pamphlets. On 1 April 1794, a large British invasion force of over 4,000 men led by Vice Admiral Sir John Jervis and Lieutenant General Sir Charles Grey landed, following their recent conquest of Martinique. The 100-man garrison of Morné Fortune, led by General Nicolas Xavier de Ricard, quickly surrendered on 3 April after a strong show of force by the British. The French troops were transported to France, while Ricard made his way to the United States.

Although the British nominally gained control of the island, they still needed to pacify the interior, as groups of republican soldiers and insurgent slaves led a guerrilla war against the British. This was known as the Brigand's War, or Guerre des Bois. Led by the republican commissioner Gaspard Goyrand and supplied with weapons and reinforcements from Guadeloupe by that island's civil commissioner, Victor Hugues, the insurgents continued to harass the British and eventually controlled most of the island by mid-April 1795. Under increasing pressure, the British evacuated the island on 19 June 1795. In April 1796 a new British expedition of 9,000 troops and 2,000 black pioneers, commanded by Admiral Hugh Cloberry Christian and Major General Ralph Abercromby, arrived to reconquer the island.

To face this invasion, Goyrand had only a 2,000-man garrison, all but 100 of which were black troops. Unable to oppose the multiple British landings, the French put up a stiff resistance, fighting the British as they retreated back to the fortifications around Morné Fortune. Goyrand refused to surrender, and his disciplined black troops defeated a number of British attacks, forcing Abercromby to besiege the French positions. Reinforced by another 5,500 men, Abercromby encircled Morné Fortune and moved to establish his batteries. Continuing to fend off the British assaults, the French garrison held out until late May. Running out of water and gunpowder, Goyrand knew that the fortifications could not withstand a close-range bombardment, as the British had pushed their lines to within 500 yards. On 25 May, Goyrand surrendered St. Lucia on the condition that he and his men be given safe conduct back to France. The tenacity and determination of Goyrand's black soldiers cost the British nearly 600 casualties and, more importantly, a month of valuable campaign time.

Continuing his campaign in the Caribbean, Abercromby left Brigadier General John Moore in command with around 4,000 men, as a number of insurgents were still fighting in the interior. Fighting continued until 1799, but waned with the death of the insurgent leader Stanislaus in October 1797. The island remained British until the Peace of Amiens in 1802, when it was returned to France. In June 1803, a small British expedition of 3,000 men, commanded by Lieutenant General William Grinfield, quickly overwhelmed the French garrison of 100 men commanded by General Antoine Noguès. St. Lucia remained a British colony under the terms of the Treaty of Paris in 1814.

Kenneth Johnson

See also Abercromby, Sir Ralph; Amiens, Treaty of; Martinique; Moore, Sir John; Paris, First Treaty of; St. Vincent, John Jervis, First Earl of; West Indies, Operations in the
References and further reading
Clowes, William Laird. 1997. *The Royal Navy: A History from the Earliest Times to 1900.* Vol. 4. London: Chatham. (Orig. pub. 1898.)
Duffy, Michael. 1987. *Soldiers, Sugar, and Seapower: The British Expeditions to the West Indies and the War against Revolutionary France.* Oxford: Clarendon.
Fortescue, Sir John. 2004. *A History of the British Army.* 13 vols. Vol. 4. Uckfield, UK: Naval and Military.
Gardiner, Robert, ed. 1997. *Fleet Battle and Blockade: The French Revolutionary War, 1793–1797.* London: Chatham.

St. Michael, Battle of (25 May 1809)

Forty kilometers northwest of Graz, the French army of Prince Eugène de Beauharnais crushed an Austrian division under *Feldmarschalleutnant* Franz Jellacic Freiherr von Buzim, who was attempting to join Archduke John's army. General Paul Grenier's Corps (15,000 men) intercepted Jellacic (8,000 men) in the Mur valley, capturing nearly 5,000 prisoners and inflicting 1,560 casualties for 700 losses.

Cut off from the main Austrian army during the retreat from Germany in April 1809, Jellacic marched into the Tyrol, and on 19 May, he received orders from Archduke John (withdrawing from Italy) to continue to Graz. Prince Eugène with his Franco-Italian army was heading down the Mur valley from Klagenfurt (southern Austria) toward Vienna. Although he received reports of French cavalry around Judenburg, 20 kilometers to the south, Jellacic marched toward Leoben, and the next day his tired troops reached Mautern. Further reports arrived of French troops within 20 kilometers of St. Michael, where Jellacic planned to enter the Mur valley and march 8 kilometers to Leoben. His division marched early on 25 May, led by a *Grenzer* (frontier infantry) battalion and a small squadron of light cavalry, followed by seven and a half infantry battalions, a *Landwehr* (militia) battalion, and four light guns. Meanwhile Eugène in Unzmarkt ordered Grenier's Corps (twenty-four battalions, eight cavalry squadrons, and twelve guns) to intercept the Austrians.

The advance guards clashed near the village of St. Michael around 9:00 A.M. on 25 May, confirming Jellacic's belief that he only faced weak French forces. However, *général de division* Jean Mathieu Seras's division (eight battalions, four cavalry squadrons, and ten guns) was steadily marching up onto the western end of the *Platte* (high flat ground) above St. Michael, which commanded the Austrians' escape route. On the Austrian left, *Oberst* Ludwig Eckhardt with two battalions secured the vital bridge over the Leising, while *Generalmajor* Ettingshausen's two battalions formed the Austrian right. A *Grenzer* battalion with the Landwehr assaulted Seras's right flank, supported by Eckhardt, and by 11:00 A.M., they had driven the French from the Platte. Jellacic extended his line along 1.5 kilometers, with the Grenzers and Landwehr on the right to defend the wooded Fresenberg hill, the center (two and a half battalions) under *Generalmajor* Ignaz Freiherr von Legisfeld, and on the left Ettingshausen with three battalions. General Pierre Durutte arrived with the rest of Grenier's Corps, and the French attacked in overwhelming numbers. Two battalions assaulted the Austrian left, while six under General Nicolas-François, vicomte Roussel d'Hurbal attacked the right and two headed for the Austrian rear. At 4:00 P.M., Eugène ordered Seras to lead six battalions against the Austrian center, with another eight following. They were supported by the cavalry, who scattered the Austrian infantry and reached the vital river bridges. The battle was decided in

about 10 minutes, as Jellacic's troops fled in disorder, pursued by Seras. Just 2,000 reinforcements eventually reached Archduke John at Graz, and Eugène marched on to Vienna.

David Hollins

See also Beauharnais, Eugène Rose de; Fifth Coalition, War of the; John, Archduke
References and further reading
Epstein, Robert. 1984. *Prince Eugène at War, 1809*. Chicago: Emperor's Headquarters.
Wagner, Anton H. 1984. *Militärhistorische Schriftenreihe 51: Das Gefecht bei St. Michael-Leoben am 25. Mai 1809* [The Battle of St. Michael-Leoben on 25 May 1809]. Vienna: Heeresgeschichtliches Museum [Army Museum].

St. Pierre, Battle of (13 December 1813)

The Battle of St. Pierre was fought between Anglo-Portuguese forces under the command of Lieutenant General Sir Rowland Hill and French forces under the overall command of Marshal Nicolas Soult along the southern approaches to the city of Bayonne between the Nive and Adour rivers, in southwestern France.

Soult had for some time been planning a spoiling attack against exposed portions of the Marquis of (later the Duke of) Wellington's army as it approached Bayonne. Wellington, on the other hand, had been aware of that possibility and had warned his subordinates, Lieutenant General Hill and Marshal (his rank in the Portuguese Army) Sir William Beresford, of the danger and directed their preparations for such an attack. Heavy rains swelled the Nive River and threatened the two bridges linking the two wings of the Allied army. One of the two bridges, a pontoon bridge at Villafranque, had only been completed on 11 December. The other was a permanent stone bridge at Ustaritz. If the two were to wash out, Wellington would be forced to march troops 13 miles to reinforce Hill's forces. As it happened, on the twelfth both bridges were washed out. Soult therefore took the opportunity to launch an attack on the nearly isolated wing under Hill.

Hill had under his command approximately 14,000 men, including the two divisions that had distinguished themselves under his command at Albuera, to cover a front of about 3 miles. However, following Wellington's warnings and orders to strengthen his position, he had advanced until his flanks were totally protected by the uncrossable Nive and Adour rivers. In addition, his position was anchored on a series of hills between the two rivers, with several small villages and large farmsteads as strongpoints. The position had one serious drawback: It was effectively split into three separate sectors by two deep ravines, both filled with water. Nevertheless, that fact had its advantages: the ravines also effectively split the attacking French force into three separate avenues of approach.

Although Soult had overwhelming strength available to him, much of it was in the form of recently arrived drafts of conscripts, ill-trained and not terribly eager to die in what was increasingly looking like a lost cause. In addition, Soult failed to mass his forces and failed to press home attacks that were on the verge of succeeding with the use of his reserves. Hill managed the fight well, though he was hard pressed at times in the center and on the right flank. Uncharacteristically in Wellington's army, two of Hill's regimental commanders displayed cowardice in the face of the enemy, which was the direct cause of much of the crisis in the center. British reinforcements arrived in time to prevent potential disaster, but by the time they reached the scene of action, Hill had the situation well in hand, and Wellington took no direct role in the conduct of the action after he arrived, preferring to let his stalwart subordinate "Daddy" Hill finish and win the battle on his own. Wellington also allowed Hill to take full credit for the victory.

Although, the Battle of St. Pierre was not in any way a decisive Allied victory—Hill and Wellington merely hustled the retreating French troops back into their lines of defense south of Bayonne, due to the proximity of the fortified positions of that city—it did have significant consequences. In addition to the fighting of the previous week on the western approaches to Bayonne, where the Allies suffered from some rough handling by Soult's repeated attacks, the Battle of St. Pierre demonstrated to both Soult and Wellington that the French army was no longer capable of successfully launching major offensive operations. How much of this was due to the increasingly exhausted and demoralized French soldiers, how much of it was due to the declining quality of French leadership, including that of Soult himself, how much of it was due to the now nearly invincible attitude of the British and Portuguese veterans of Wellington's Allied army, is unclear. What is clear, however, is that after St. Pierre, Soult made no further major attempts to conduct substantial offensive operations. The end of the Peninsular War—and with it the end of the Napoleonic Empire—was in sight.

John T. Broom

See also Albuera, Battle of; Beresford, Sir William Carr; Hill, Sir Rowland; Peninsular War; Soult, Nicolas Jean de Dieu; Wellington, Arthur Wellesley, First Duke of

References and further reading

Esdaile, Charles J. 2003. *The Peninsular War: A New History.* New York: Palgrave Macmillan.

Gates, David. 1986. *The Spanish Ulcer: A History of the Peninsular War.* New York: Norton.

Robertson, Ian. 2003. *Wellington Invades France: The Final Phase of the Peninsular War, 1813–1814.* London: Greenhill.

St. Vincent, Battle of (14 February 1797)

A significant British naval victory achieved by Admiral Sir John Jervis over the Spanish at the end of the War of the First Coalition; best known for the unorthodox tactics employed by Commodore Horatio Nelson.

Having temporarily abandoned the Mediterranean in 1796 owing to the unexpected alliance concluded between the Spanish and French, Admiral Sir John Jervis lay in the Tagus with eleven line-of-battle ships until January 1797. On the eighteenth of that month he left Lisbon with orders to protect a convoy bound for Brazil. Having escorted it to a sufficiently safe distance into the Atlantic, he was to meet up off Cape St. Vincent with Rear Admiral William Parker, who had left the Channel with reinforcements for Jervis's station. Jervis's force was reduced through an accident occurring to the *St. George* (98 guns), which had to remain behind for repairs, but having safely escorted the convoy out to sea and proceeding for the cape, Jervis fell in with Parker's ships on 6 February, thereby increasing his fleet to fifteen ships of the line, as well as frigates. Three ships were undergoing repairs: the *St. George* and *Zealous* (98) at Lisbon, and the *Plymouth* (80) at Gibraltar.

Meanwhile, at Cartagena lay the main Spanish fleet, consisting of twenty-seven ships of the line, twelve frigates, a brig-corvette, and several smaller vessels, the whole under Admiral Don José de Cordova. Franco-Spanish strategy directed that Cordova's fleet sail to Brest, where it would rendezvous with the combined French and Dutch fleets for operations leading to the invasion of England. Before reaching Brest, however, Cordova was first to stop at Cádiz in order to take on food and supplies.

Jervis, who held responsibility for ensuring that Cordova did not join the fleet under Morard de Galles, not only possessed inferior numbers to his opponent, but was unaware that Cordova was initially bound for Cádiz. Moreover, as Jervis naturally expected to confront him off Cape St. Vincent, a good deal west of Cádiz, he would almost certainly never have sighted, much less engaged, the Spanish commander that month, had the weather not confounded Cordova's intention of proceeding straight to Cádiz. Rather than fighting a major battle, in all probability Jervis would have missed the Spanish fleet altogether, or discovered it at Cádiz and there established a lengthy blockade. But strong and persistent winds near Gibraltar, moving east and southeast, were to bring the two fleets together.

While Jervis, now reinforced, made his way toward Cape St. Vincent, Cordova was proceeding toward Cádiz, having left Cartagena on 1 February. He passed the Strait of Gibraltar on the fifth, and on doing so detached some of his gunboats and transports, escorted by a number of larger vessels, to make sail for Algeciras. One ship of the line rejoined the fleet soon thereafter. Two others left port on the tenth, and on the following day discovered and chased the 38-gun *Minerve*, with Commodore Nelson aboard. Having escaped his larger pursuers, Nelson joined the fleet early on the thirteenth, bringing Jervis intelligence that the Spanish were now at sea.

Cordova would have reached the safety of Cádiz by that time, but for a gale that drove him considerably west of that port, right into Jervis's vicinity. When, finally, on the evening of the thirteenth, the wind shifted to the southwest, the Spanish made for land in some disorder. Yet their presence was already known to Jervis, whose ships heard the Spanish signal guns. Before dawn on the fourteenth, moreover, Jervis received news from a Portuguese vessel that the Spanish were to windward of his position, only five leagues distant.

Mist and darkness shrouded the two fleets on the morning of 14 February, with Jervis's force arranged in two columns sailing on the starboard tack, with Cape St. Vincent 25 miles to the northeast. The first sighting of the Spanish occurred around 6:30 A.M., when five ships were seen to the southwest on the starboard tack. After sending a ship to reconnoiter, Jervis signaled the fleet to form in close order at 8:15. He repeated the previous night's signal to prepare for action, and at 9:30 sent three ships of the line, followed 20 minutes later by three more, to pursue.

At that point the strengths of each side were unknown to the other. Incorrect intelligence led Cordova to believe Jervis had only nine ships of the line, and by 9:00 A.M. Jervis had only perceived twenty line-of-battle ships when in fact there were twenty-six. Two hours later Cordova counted Jervis's force at fifteen. Jervis still did not have complete information on Spanish strength—which totaled twenty-seven ships of the line, two of which had recently joined from Algeciras.

At this point Jervis's fleet, arranged in two parallel lines, was making for a gap that divided Cordova's fleet into two unequal divisions. To windward lay twenty-one ships, all but two of which were sailing in a group under full sail, the wind on the starboard quarter. The remaining two were a considerable distance to the southwest. The second group, composed of only six ships, was to leeward. These were close-hauled on the port tack in an effort to link up with the larger force before Jervis could interpose his ships between them.

Just before 11:00 A.M. some of the lead Spanish ships of the weather division began to wear and trim on the port tack, apparently intending to form line and to proceed down Jervis's weather column. This maneuver would allow them to fire on eight ships with at least twenty of their own, while simultaneously preventing Jervis's lee column from firing without risk of striking friendly vessels. At 11:00 A.M. Jervis issued orders to obviate this danger, signaling his ships to form in a single column ahead, with the *Victory* (Jervis's flagship) in the lead and to proceed south-southwest, so as to keep Cordova's lee division on Jervis's lee or port bow.

Soon after his ships formed into a single column of line ahead, Jervis ordered his vessels to pierce the Spanish line. At nearly the same moment, five out of the six ships composing Cordova's lee division, believing that they were not the object of attack and, in addition, unable to cross the bows of Jervis's line, hauled up on a starboard tack with an apparently uncertain purpose, before adopting a definite course to the northeast. The sixth ship fled, at full sail and unaccompanied, to the southeast and shortly thereafter was lost from view. Yet even as this temporary confusion and the desertion of one ship seemed to reveal a weakening in the Spanish lee division, the five remaining vessels were almost immediately joined by three more ships, probably the *Conde de Regla* (112), the *Principe de Asturias* (112) and *Oriente* (74).

With these maneuvers completed, the Spanish weather division had declined in number to eighteen ships of the line, including the two ships then closing from Algeciras. Firing commenced at long range at 11:30 A.M., when the *Culloden* ran abreast of the ships leading the Spanish weather division. The British vessels following the *Culloden* did the same as they came within range, and just after 12:00 noon, immediately after the *Culloden* passed the last Spanish vessel, Jervis issued orders for her to tack.

The *Blenheim* followed suit shortly thereafter, and in turn the *Prince George*, which was considerably out of the line to leeward. Around this time, Cordova's lee division came about on the port tack, perhaps in hopes of breaking Jervis's column at the place where his ships were tacking in succession. The *Orion* nevertheless came about, while in her wake, the *Colossus*, which was herself in the course of coming about, suffered serious damage to some of her yards, obliging her to wear rather than tack. She was in serious danger while her stern pointed to leeward, exposing her to raking fire from the lead vessel of the Spanish lee division; but the *Orion*, realizing the predicament, slowed by backing her main topsail and offered cover to the *Colossus*, who, in the event, was not raked.

Jervis then made a bold decision: The van was to alter its course slightly and cut through the Spanish line. Just as

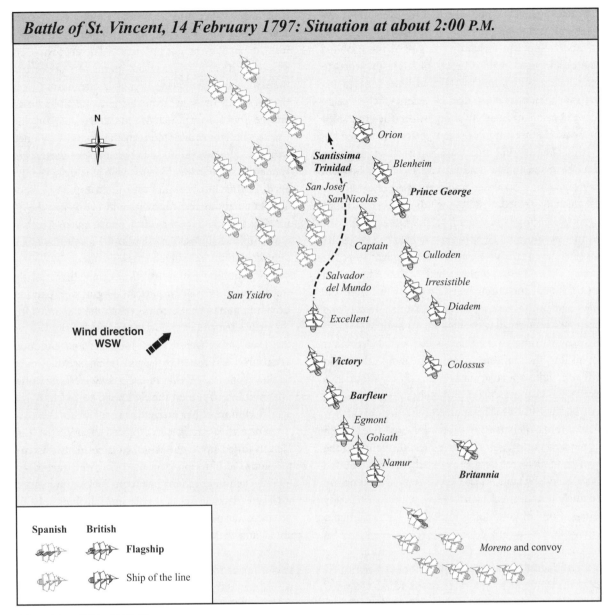

Battle of St. Vincent, 14 February 1797: Situation at about 2:00 P.M.

N

Orion

Santissima
Trinidad

Blenheim

San Josef
San Nicolas

Prince George

Captain

Culloden

Salvador
del Mundo

Irresistible

San Ysidro

Diadem

Wind direction
WSW

Excellent

Victory

Colossus

Barfleur

Egmont

Goliath

Namur

Britannia

Moreno and convoy

Spanish	British	
		Flagship
		Ship of the line

Adapted from White 2001, 61.

she was preparing to tack, the *Irresistible*, directly ahead of the *Victory*, became heavily engaged with the Spanish lee division. While the *Irresistible* had tacked in order to follow the van, the Spanish continued their course, thereby attempting to pierce the British line ahead of the *Victory*. Yet Jervis's flagship advanced fast enough to foil the attempt, and the lead Spanish ship, obliged to tack near the lee of the *Victory*, was raked in the process before bearing up. The seven vessels that followed then attempted to overtake or pass astern of the *Egmont* and *Goliath*, but were foiled and, apart from the *Oriente*, all had to bear up. This last vessel proceeded on the port tack, passed Jervis's rear while obscured by smoke, and managed to reach the Spanish weather division.

By 1:00 P.M. the British line had proceeded to the point where they had entirely cleared the Spanish weather division and, in altering course on the starboard tack, left Cordova with a means of linking his two divisions together by steering the weather division to leeward. The ships of the Spanish weather division took the opportunity thus afforded them by bearing up in a mass and advancing northeast. The battle now reached its crucial stage, for so far contact had been minimal, and had the Spanish succeeded in joining together their two divisions, the action would have terminated shortly thereafter, either with no decisive conclusion or as little more than a British pursuit of a faster-sailing opponent fleeing under all sail for the safety of Cádiz. At best Jervis might have hoped to catch and engage the rearmost vessels, but the bulk would almost certainly have eluded him.

It was Nelson who instantly recognized the problem and the unique opportunity before him. He intended to seize it. The British column was at that time doubled up, and Nelson knew that it was too far astern of the fleeing Spanish to be able to intercept them before they made for the open sea. He therefore wore the *Captain* and passed between the *Diadem* and the *Excellent*, seeking to come athwart the bows of the leading vessels of the Spanish weather division, still massed and composed of a number of very heavily armed vessels, including the enormous four-decker, *Santísima Trinidad* (130). Other ships included the *San Josef* (112), *Salvador del Mundo* (112), *San Nicolas* (80), *San Ysidro* (74), and a vessel thought to be the *Mexicano* (112). The *Captain* reached its desired position at about 1:30 P.M. and commenced firing. By this time, the *Culloden* had overtaken the rearmost Spanish vessels and had been lightly engaged with them for 10 minutes.

Before this time, at 1:20, Jervis had signaled the last ship in his line, the *Excellent*, to alter course radically to aid the *Captain*. Taking a sharp larboard tack, by about 2:15 the *Excellent* had assumed a position ahead of the leading ships of the British line. The Spanish were then prevented from combining their two divisions, for now five British vessels blocked their further progress: the *Captain* and the *Excellent* in their direct path, supported thereafter by the *Culloden*, *Blenheim*, and *Prince George*. In fact, even before the Spanish found their plans foiled, they had already abandoned hope of combining forces and had assumed a new course on the starboard tack.

Around 2:00 P.M., the *Culloden* had advanced far enough ahead so as to draw off some of the intense fire directed at the *Captain* by the massive *Santísima Trinidad* and her consorts, who by now had hauled up so as to employ the full weight of their broadsides. This gave the *Captain* a brief respite, during which time she brought up additional ammunition from below and carried out essential repairs to her damaged rigging. Soon thereafter the *Blenheim* also approached and passed to windward of the *Captain*, giving Nelson further protection from fire.

Meanwhile, two other Spanish ships had been engaging the *Captain* and *Culloden*—the *San Ysidro* and *Salvador del Mundo*. These vessels were so heavily damaged aloft as to be virtually dead in the water and received several broadsides not only from the *Blenheim*, but also, as they came up, from the *Prince George*, *Orion*, and other vessels astern. Shortly thereafter, at about 2:35, the *Excellent*, in response to the signal to bear up, came alongside the crippled *Salvador del Mundo* and fought her on her weather bow for a short time before advancing toward and

engaging the next opponent, the *San Ysidro*, which by that time had lost her three topmasts. Collingwood, in the *Excellent*, exchanged a close fire with her on the lee beam until at 2:53; having put up a spirited defense while entirely disabled, the *San Ysidro* struck her colors and exchanged them for the Union Jack in signal of surrender.

At about the same time as the *Excellent* had ceased to engage the *Salvador del Mundo* and taken on the *San Ysidro*, the *Irresistible* stood on the enemy's weather bow while the *Diadem* stood on the enemy lee quarter. The *Salvador del Mundo* was by this time already severely damaged, having lost her fore and main topmasts. Soon she also lost her mizzen topmast, and on seeing the *Victory* moving toward her stern and preparing to fire her bow guns—followed closely by the *Barfleur*—the captain of the *Salvador del Mundo* surrendered his ship.

At around 3:15 the *Excellent* came abreast of the leeward side of the *San Nicolas*, an 80-gun ship that had lost her fore topmast in her contest with the *Captain*. On coming within ten feet of the starboard side of the *San Nicolas*, the *Excellent* delivered a crushing fire and continued on her course, as directed by Jervis's signal. Seeking some protection from the *Excellent*'s fire, the *San Nicolas* luffed up, but in doing so fouled the *San Josef*, herself heavily damaged and short of her mizzenmast.

Once the *Excellent* had passed clear of the *Captain*, Nelson luffed up to the wind, causing his badly damaged fore topmast to topple over the side. The vessel was in fact in a stricken state, having lost her wheel and sustained considerable damage to her sails and shrouds. No further progress was possible, and with the *Blenheim* immediately ahead and the *Culloden* struggling behind, Nelson had no choice but to board the *San Nicolas*. Before he did so, the two ships returned broadsides for several minutes at 20 yard's distance. On shifting to starboard, the *Captain* fouled the *San Nicolas* in two places, locking the two vessels together.

Nelson then ordered his men to board the *San Nicolas*, whose rigging remained fouled with that of the *Captain*. Leading his men through the stern windows of the Spanish 80, Nelson and his party fought their way to the forecastle, where they accepted the surrender of the ship from the commander. On the port side of the *San Nicolas* stood the *San Josef*, from which Nelson's men then began to receive small arms fire. Ordering forward reinforcements, Nelson proceeded to cross the deck on to the *San Josef*, which, after a brief struggle, also surrendered. The boarding of an enemy vessel from the deck of another, newly captured, was virtually unprecedented, and established Nelson's reputation as a bold and fearless officer.

By Nelson's reckoning, it was his audacious action of crossing the decks of the *San Nicolas* and boarding the *San*

Josef that led the latter vessel to surrender. Yet the evidence suggests that the two vessels may have succumbed on account of the continuous fire to which they were subjected by the *Prince George,* which continued until the moment of actual surrender. Whatever the case, Nelson's conduct was exemplary, and in both instances he boarded enemies that were not yet vanquished.

It will be recalled that, shortly after 3:00 P.M., the *Excellent* passed the *San Nicolas* and began to pound the *Santísima Trinidad,* then receiving fire from the *Blenheim, Orion,* and *Irresistible.* The immense Spanish ship struck her colors but eluded actual capture, for two friendly ships of the van came to her aid, together with two others, which had in the course of the day been approaching from the west-southwest. In addition, the impending union between the Spanish lee and weather divisions enabled her to sail beyond the reach of the British vessels that had reduced her to ruin.

At 3:52, on observing the approach of so many as-yet unengaged Spanish ships, Jervis ordered his ships to prepare to bring to, thus putting them in a position to protect the four prizes and his own severely damaged ships. At 4:15 the signal for the frigates to take the prizes into tow was hoisted by Jervis's flagship, and at 4:39 the fleet was directed to form into close line ahead, astern of the *Victory.* By that time the battle was effectively over, though even at 4:50 the *Britannia* and *Orion* fired at the ships escorting the crippled *Santísima Trinidad.* Shortly thereafter, Nelson moved his broad pennant from his stricken *Captain* to the *Irresistible.*

The British suffered about 400 wounded, of whom 227 were in a serious state; 73 officers and men were killed. Of Jervis's ships, only the *Captain* lost a mast, though the *Colossus, Culloden, Egmont,* and *Blenheim* all suffered severe damage to their masts and spars. Apart from the prizes, only perhaps ten of the Spanish ships were seriously damaged, the *Santísima Trinidad* having received the highest losses with 200 killed and wounded. Spanish losses are not known, apart from the prizes, all of which lost masts. The *Salvador del Mundo* had 42 killed and 124 wounded; the *San Ysidro,* 29 killed and 63 wounded; the *San Josef,* 46 killed and 96 wounded; and the *San Nicolas,* 144 killed and 59 wounded.

Though Jervis's victory was undeniably a great one, it is also true that circumstances always favored him except in point of numbers, and it would have been unforgivable had he not inflicted a significant defeat on the Spanish. Cordova's numerical superiority was overwhelming: twenty-seven ships to Jervis's fifteen; in terms of guns and men the advantage was still greater. The greater disparity, however, lay in the quality of the respective officers and crews. Jervis led men displaying a high degree of discipline and training, while the Spanish were mostly untrained landsmen or soldiers. In many vessels, seamen made up a distinct minority of the crew, so that, when action began, many of the men succumbed to panic and therefore were worse than useless.

The *San Josef* provides a telling example of how ill-prepared the Spanish were to fight any opponent, much less one of high standards. After this vessel was captured, it was discovered that some of the guns that had faced their opponents during the battle had not been fired and still had their tompions affixed. The Spanish officers, themselves deficient compared to their British counterparts, could do nothing with such men, and in the chaos that reigned in Cordova's fleet, Spanish guns were as likely to injure vessels carrying their own men as they were those carrying their opponents. However determined and brave the Spanish officers may have been, they were simply no match for Jervis's, who possessed a superior grasp of navigation and tactics.

Nevertheless, Jervis did not take proper advantage of his victory. He only captured four ships when he might have taken three or four more—those that were severely disabled in the fighting. Perhaps the onset of darkness explains this, for at 5:00 P.M. Jervis halted the pursuit. Yet it would have been in darkness that numbers would have mattered less. As Jervis was superior at maneuver, he almost certainly could have kept pace with his opponent, and having already suffered considerable damage in the battle, the Spanish probably would have lost their weakened vessels to the pursuers.

Both sides spent the night repairing their ships, and when the sun rose on the morning of 15 February, both fleets could see one another arrayed in line of battle ahead, sailing on opposite tacks. As the Spanish had the weather gauge, they were in a position to resume fighting, but instead bore away at 2:30 P.M., hauling the wind when they perceived Jervis doing the same. They soon sailed from view and reached the safety of Cádiz. Jervis made for Lagos Bay, on the Portuguese coast, where he anchored with his prizes on the afternoon of the sixteenth. When the news arrived in London, Jervis was raised to the peerage as Earl of St. Vincent, while Nelson was knighted. Unbeknownst to him, Nelson had been promoted to rear admiral just prior to the battle; he returned home a popular hero and went on to achieve great victories in his own right at the Nile, Copenhagen, and Trafalgar.

Gregory Fremont-Barnes

See also Copenhagen, Battle of; England, French Plans for the Invasion of; First Coalition, War of the; Naval Warfare; Nelson, Horatio, First Viscount; Nile, Battle of the; Royal Navy; Spanish Navy; St. Vincent, John Jervis, First Earl of; Trafalgar, Battle of

References and further reading

Clowes, William Laird. 1997. *The Royal Navy: A History from the Earliest Times to 1900.* Vol. 4. London: Chatham. (Orig. pub. 1898.)

Gardiner, Robert, ed. 1997. *Fleet Battle and Blockade: The French Revolutionary War, 1793–1797.* London: Chatham.

Lloyd, Christopher. 1963. *St. Vincent and Camperdown.* London: Batsford.

Tracy, Nicholas. 1996. *Nelson's Battles: The Art of Victory in the Age of Sail.* London: Chatham.

Warner, Oliver. 1958. *A Portrait of Lord Nelson.* London: Chatto and Windus.

White, Colin. 2001. *1797: Nelson's Year of Destiny.* Stroud, UK: Sutton.

St. Vincent, John Jervis, First Earl of (1735–1823)

Born on 9 January 1735 to an old but impoverished family in Stone, Staffordshire, John Jervis was educated at a grammar school at Burton-on-Trent and at a private school in Greenwich, where his family moved in 1747. In January 1749 he entered the Royal Navy as an able seaman. Jervis became a midshipman in 1752. He passed his examination in January 1755 and the next month was promoted to lieutenant. After holding a number of routine sea assignments, he made commander in May 1759.

Two months later Jervis became acting commander of the sloop *Porcupine* and took part in the expedition against Quebec. That September he took command of the sloop *Scorpion,* returning in her to Britain with dispatches. He made post captain in October 1760. He then held assignments in the North Sea and the West Indies and in the expedition that recovered Newfoundland. In the spring of 1763, at the end of the Seven Years' War, he was paid off (released from service on half pay).

Jervis returned to active employment in 1769 in command of the frigate *Alarm* (32 guns) in the Mediterranean. When the ship was paid off in 1772, Jervis spent a year in France. He then traveled in the company of Captain Samuel Barrington to Russia, Sweden, Denmark, and Holland, where he studied the arsenals and navies of northern Europe. Again with Barrington, he cruised in a yacht along the French coast.

In June 1775 Jervis returned to naval command in the *Kent* (74), but in September he took command of the *Foudroyant* (80), at the time the largest two-decker in the Royal Navy. He was in her at Ushant on 27 July 1778, and he participated in two relief expeditions to Gibraltar, in 1780 and 1781. In April 1782 the *Foudroyant* fell in with a French convoy off Brest and in the process captured the largest French ship, the *Pégase* (74), which was, however, newly commissioned, short of officers, and carrying an untrained crew. Jervis, slightly wounded in the action, was knighted for his success. At the end of the year his ship was paid off, but an appointment to the West Indies was annulled with the conclusion of peace in 1783.

Jervis then entered Parliament. He was promoted to rear admiral in September 1787 and to vice admiral in February 1793. He was then appointed to command the naval expedition to the West Indies in the fall of 1793 with his flag in the *Boyne* (93). His squadron took the French islands of Martinique and Guadeloupe in March and April 1794. Ill, Jervis received permission to return to Britain, where he arrived in February 1795. Made admiral in July, Jervis sailed to the Mediterranean as commander in chief of the British fleet there in November.

At the end of 1796 Britain lost control of the Mediterranean. This was a consequence of French control of Italy, which forced Naples into neutrality, and of Spain's cooperation with France. Faced with vastly superior numbers, Jervis withdrew his ships to Gibraltar. In early February 1797 he posted his ships off Cape St. Vincent, determined to prevent enemy ships from the Mediterranean from sailing north to join those at Brest, preparing the way for a possible invasion of England. On 14 February his fifteen ships of the line fell in with twenty-seven Spanish ships. Although they enjoyed far superior numbers, the Spanish vessels were newly commissioned and had untrained crews. In the resulting Battle of St. Vincent, the British captured four Spanish ships and roughly handled others. The threat of invasion of England was ended, and Jervis was voted a pension of £3,000 a year and raised to the peerage as Earl of St. Vincent. He continued to command in the Mediterranean, blockading the Spanish at Cádiz and maintaining rigid discipline that prevented mutinies similar to those that occurred in the Royal Navy at Spithead and the Nore during 1797.

A detachment of Jervis's fleet under Rear Admiral Sir Horatio Nelson defeated the French at the Nile on 1–2 August 1798, and another element under Commodore John Thomas Duckworth assisted with the capture of Minorca in late 1798. Jervis's health continued to deteriorate, abetted by the strain of his own tyrannical nature, and he asked to resign his command. In June 1799 he sailed home to recuperate.

In 1800, not fully recovered, Jervis took command of the Channel Fleet, an appointment that displeased many officers because of his reputation as a harsh and dictatorial commander. Jervis immediately instituted stringent measures and kept the fleet sailing almost continually off Brest. Although many officers disliked his orders and regulations, these brought a new standard of efficiency in blockade operations. Jervis kept the fleet continuously off Brest for 121 days from May to September 1800.

In the spring of 1801, in the ministry of Henry Addington, St. Vincent was appointed First Lord of the Admiralty. In this post he endeavored to impose his system on the entire navy. Although a number of his reforms were salutary, including efforts to end corruption and improve efficiency, his methods alienated many. With the collapse of the Addington government and the return of William Pitt in May 1804, St. Vincent was replaced. Returned to command of the Channel Fleet in March 1806 as acting admiral of the fleet, he maintained the blockade of Brest until April 1807, when he asked to be relieved. The years of service had broken St. Vincent's health, and he never held another command. Among British naval officers of the period he is second only to Nelson. He had a lasting impact on Royal Navy discipline and organization, and on the mechanics of blockade operations. On the coronation of George IV, St. Vincent was promoted to admiral of the fleet in July 1821. He died at his home in Sussex on 14 March 1823.

Spencer C. Tucker

See also Addington, Henry; Blockade; England, French Plans for the Invasion of; Martinique; Minorca; Naval Warfare; Nelson, Horatio, First Viscount; Nile, Battle of the; Nore, Mutiny at the; Pitt, William; Royal Navy; Spithead, Mutiny at; St. Vincent, Battle of; West Indies, Operations in the

References and further reading
Arthur, Charles B. 1986. *The Remaking of the English Navy by Admiral St. Vincent: The Great Unclaimed Naval Revolution (1795–1805)*. Lanham, MD: University Press of America.
Berckman, Evelyn. 1962. *Nelson's Dear Lord: A Portrait of St. Vincent*. London: Macmillan.
Crimmin, P. K. 2000. "John Jervis, Earl of St. Vincent." In *Precursors of Nelson: British Admirals of the Eighteenth Century*, ed. Peter Le Fevre and Richard Harding, 325–350. London: Chatham.
Smith, David Bonner. 1922–1927. *Letters of Admiral of the Fleet the Earl of St. Vincent, 1801–1804*. 2 Vols. London: Navy Records Society.
Tucker, Jedediah Stephens. 1844. *Memoirs of the Right Hon. the Earl of St. Vincent*. 2 Vols. London: Bentley.

Stadion-Warthausen, Johann Philipp Graf (1763–1824)

Austrian diplomat, foreign and finance minister. A career diplomat, Stadion led important negotiations with Britain during the French Revolutionary Wars and with the Allies at the end of the Napoleonic Wars. As foreign minister from 1806 to 1809, he directed foreign policy toward German nationalism.

From the minor Austrian nobility, Stadion was a keen student of history and international relations from an early age, especially the history of the development of France. Under the sponsorship of the chancellor (foreign minister), Wenzel Anton Fürst von Kaunitz, he joined the imperial diplomatic service and in 1787 was appointed ambassador to Sweden. Two years later, he transferred to London, where he developed a keen interest in commerce, maritime trade, and world events outside of Europe. His promotion to ambassador extraordinary with ministerial status by Emperor Leopold II reflected his key role in Anglo-Austrian relations, persuading Britain to join the War of the First Coalition in 1793. His dislike of deputy foreign minister Johann Freiherr von Thugut was mutual, and quickly led to his removal; after marrying a distant cousin in 1794, he spent several years on his estates. After the government overhaul of 1801, Stadion became ambassador to Berlin, charged with improving relations with Prussia. After two difficult years, he was sent as ambassador to St. Petersburg, where he directed the negotiations that led to the Austro-Russian alliance of 1804 and then accompanied Tsar Alexander during the early part of the campaign of 1805.

Stadion's appointment as foreign minister in 1806 on Archduke Charles's recommendation represented a radical policy shift from alliances with Russia toward supporting growing German nationalism. Decisive and energetic, he deployed his mastery of both Czech and Magyar to further a policy of centralizing the Austrian Empire by establishing greater control over the provinces. Patriotic societies for Germans and Czechs were encouraged, but unauthorized newssheets were controlled. "*Volle Freiheit für die Bücher, keine Freiheit für die Blätter!*" (Freedom for books, no freedom for propaganda sheets!) was his motto as he sought to encourage popular support for renewed war against France. With Archduke John, he established the *Landwehr* (militia) in 1808 and pushed the decision for war through the imperial councils. Following the defeat at Eggmühl in April 1809, he pressed for Archduke Charles's replacement.

Following the unsuccessful campaign of 1809, Stadion was sacked and withdrew to his estates. Recalled to Vienna as a foreign ministry adviser in 1813, he was sent as the Austrian emissary to the Russo-Prussian headquarters after their defeat at Lützen (2 May). There he negotiated and signed the Convention of Reichenbach, agreeing to Austria's participation in the war should Napoleon refuse Vienna's terms. He then served as Austria's main representative in various Allied policy meetings until Napoleon was defeated. Appointed finance minister in 1815 to try to bring order to the empire's shattered treasury, Stadion established a national bank and a sinking fund (reserves) to deal with the imperial debt, withdrew much of the paper money from circulation, and reformed taxation.

David Hollins

See also Alexander I, Tsar; Austria; Charles, Archduke of Austria, Duke of Teschen; Cobenzl, Johann Ludwig Graf; Eggmühl, Battle of; Fifth Coalition, War of the; First Coalition, War of the; Francis I, Emperor; John, Archduke; Lützen, Battle of; Reichenbach, Convention of; Third Coalition, War of the; Thugut, Johann Amadeus Freiherr von
References and further reading
Rössler, Hellmuth. 1966. *Graf Johann Phillip Stadion, Napoleons deutsche Gegenspieler* [Napoleon's German opponent]. Vienna: Herold.
Wurzbach, Constant von. 1856–1891. *Biographisches Lexikin des Kaiserthums Osterreich* [Biographical dictionary of the Austrian empire]. 60 vols. Vienna: Zamarski.

Staël, Mme Germaine de (1766–1817)

Swiss writer and critic; leader of liberal opposition to Napoleon. Madame de Staël was born Anne-Louise Germaine Necker, the daughter of the Swiss banker, Louis XVI's director general of finances, Jacques Necker, and Suzanne Corchod. She grew up in the intellectual atmosphere of her mother's salon. As an adolescent, she read the works of Montesquieu, Rousseau, and Voltaire. In 1786 she married Baron de Staël-Holstein, the Swedish ambassador to France. This was an arranged marriage, planned by her parents, which produced one child, a daughter, Gustavine, who died before she reached age two. Madame de Staël and her husband established separate households after their first two years of marriage.

Madame de Staël may be best characterized as a woman of letters, political propagandist, and conversationalist, who epitomized European thought and culture in her time. Her first publication, *Lettres sur le caractère et les écrits de Jean-Jacques Rousseau* (Letters on the Character and Writings of Jean-Jacques Rousseau, 1788), revealed a commitment to the rationalism of the Enlightenment that would remain with her throughout her life. During the French Revolution, she was a supporter of the liberal constitutional monarchy, and her next work, *Refléxions sur le procès de la reine* (Reflections on the Queen's Trial, 1793), was a plea to save Queen Marie Antoinette from the guillotine. She condemned the excesses of the Terror in her subsequent *De l'influence des passions sur le bonheur des individus et des nations* (On the Influence of the Passions on the Happiness of Individuals and Nations, 1796).

Initially an admirer of Napoleon, she soon turned against him when he revealed his true colors: an insatiable lust for power, authoritarianism, and antifeminist views. She remained one of his strongest opponents and a thorn in his side until her death. With her lover Henri-Benjamin Constant de Rebecque, also a proponent of ideas of freedom, she led the liberal opposition to Napoleon from the

Necker château of Coppet in Switzerland. There she hosted a salon that was attended by diplomats and politicians, including two of Napoleon's brothers, Lucien and Joseph. Her salon was famous throughout Europe as a center of progressive political and intellectual discussions.

Her writings during the Napoleonic era reflected her opposition to Napoleon. Her first novel, *Delphine* (1802), which dealt with intellectual women, prompted him to ban her from France. *Corinne, ou l'Italie* (Corinne, or Italy, 1807) further antagonized him, as it concerned an independent female poet. Her greatest anti-Napoleonic work, however, was not a novel, but her study *De l'Allemagne* (On Germany, 1810), a book based on her experiences of living in various German cities, which praised a German culture that Napoleon denied existed. At the printing press, the plates were smashed and burned, but a few copies were salvaged, and it was published in England.

Madame de Staël died in Paris after suffering from a stroke on Bastille Day, 14 July 1817. Her last work, *Dix Années d'exil* (Ten Years of Exile), which chronicled her attack on Napoleon and his regime, was published posthumously in 1821. Of all her children, only Albertine, her daughter with Constant and later the duchess of Broglie, left descendants.

Leigh Whaley

See also Bonaparte, Joseph; Bonaparte, Lucien; Constant de Rebecque, Henri-Benjamin; French Revolution; Terror, The
References and further reading
Fairweather, Maria. 2006. *Madame de Staël*. London: Constable and Robinson.
Herold, J. Christopher. 1964. *Mistress to an Age: A Life of Madame de Staël*. New York: Time.
Staël, Germaine de. 2000. *Ten Years of Exile*. Trans. Avriel H. Goldberger. De Kalb: Northern Illinois University Press.
Winegarten, Renée. 1985. *Mme. de Staël*. Dover, NH: Berg.

Standards, Flags, and Eagles

The military standard is as ancient as warfare itself and has been carried into battle by almost every culture in recorded history. In essence, it was simply a recognizable emblem, often a flag or an effigy, that served to distinguish the identities of opposing forces and to mark the position of the commander on the field of battle. Yet over the course of European history, the standard came to represent far more than a simple matter of tactical expediency. It evolved into a semisacred manifestation of regimental honor—the symbolic embodiment of each soldier's duty, both to his comrades and to his country.

The flag was the predominant military standard used by European armies throughout the medieval and early modern periods, and the national and military flags of the

Napoleonic era evolved from these amazingly diverse ensigns. The army of the Middle Ages was essentially a collection of private soldiers who, in order to function as a coherent military unit, were largely dependent upon the unambiguous leadership of a nobleman. Thus, personal aristocratic banners were used to mark the identity and position of each commander and his retinue on the field of battle. The art of heraldry was created in order to ensure the uniqueness of each flag.

The establishment of national standing armies in the seventeenth century was followed by the adoption of both uniform dress and the systemization of flags in the eighteenth and nineteenth centuries. Rather than merely representing the commander's identity, flags were increasingly used in order to distinguish between specific types of soldiers in an increasingly specialized military. By the Napoleonic period, European armies were commonly divided into three main branches, and each carried a specific type of flag. The first was the cavalry standard. Emerging from the largest flags flown by the knightly armies of the Middle Ages, the cavalry standard was usually square and, as its name implies, had initially been designed to "stand" in one place rather than to be carried into battle. The second type was the guidon: a rectangular, swallow-tailed pendent carried by dragoons (mounted infantry). The fluid nature of cavalry warfare placed both guidon and cavalry standards in constant danger of capture by the enemy—an unacceptable disgrace for any unit. Though standards retained their symbolic importance, mounted units of the Napoleonic period often found it prudent to leave their standards behind the lines. Indeed, during the entire 1803–1815 period, no British cavalry units carried flags into the field.

The last and most important type of flag was known as the infantry color. The exact source of the name remains uncertain, though Sir John Fortescue in his *History of the British Army* states that "Before the end of the [sixteenth] century the flags of infantry, from their diversity of hues, had gained the name of Colours" (quoted in Edwards 1953, 7). Each infantry regiment or battalion typically carried two colors; the first was known as the Royal, King's, or Sovereign's Color, and served to mark the unit's allegiance to nation and ruler. Its design was consequently based on the national flag or the coat of arms of the monarch. The King's Color for all British infantry units of the Napoleonic Wars, for example, consisted of the Union flag, containing the regimental number or badge at its center. The second infantry flag was known as the Regimental or Battalion Color. This flag was unique to each unit and differed widely in style and color, though it typically incorporated a distinctive badge, number, or name of the regiment or battalion in question.

Perhaps the most famous standard of the Napoleonic Wars was the French imperial eagle. Modeled after the eagle of the Roman legions, the new symbol of the French military was intended to be carried atop the pike from which the color flew. It was first presented to the French army by Napoleon himself at the Champ de Mars in 1804. From this point on, unit flags became secondary to the symbolic value of the eagle itself. Regiments often neglected their flags entirely, preferring instead to carry the eagle alone into combat.

The color and imperial eagle served an important tactical role throughout the Napoleonic Wars. They acted as a natural rallying point, and the sight of the colors during desperate battles strengthened the morale of the men and testified to the continued resistance and continuity of the unit. But perhaps their most important role was as the symbolic heart of each regiment. Infantry colors and the imperial eagle were almost always carried into combat and formed a conspicuous target for enemy guns, as well as a natural focal point of attack by both infantry and cavalry. Yet the soldiers of all nations fought tenaciously and gave their lives in defense of their standards for reasons that were often more symbolic than strategic. The standard was a semisacred object, often consecrated in an elaborate ceremony by a member of the royal family or in the case of France by the Emperor. Before receiving its flags or eagle, each unit would swear to defend them to the death. Additionally, at a time when monuments recognizing the sacrifice of individual soldiers were rare, soldiers saw their standards as the only memorial for fallen comrades. To abandon the color to the enemy was to dishonor, not only the contemporary regiment, but the memory of every man who had given his life in defense of his unit and his country.

The military standard continued to play an important, though increasingly ceremonial, role after 1815. The industrialization of warfare during the late nineteenth and early twentieth century—and above all the conspicuousness of flags and standards in the field— changed the very nature of armed conflict, finally rendering the romance and pageantry of the standard obsolete.

Samuel Cohen

See also Cavalry; Infantry
References and further reading
Charrié, Pierre. 1982. *Drapeaux et Étendards de la Révolution et de l'Empire* [Flags and Standards of the Revolution and the Empire]. Paris: Copernic.
Edwards, Thomas Joseph. 1953. *Standards, Guidons and Colours of the Commonwealth Forces.* Aldershot, UK: Gale and Polden.
Haythornthwaite, Philip J. 1998. *Weapons and Equipment of the Napoleonic Wars.* London: Arms and Armour.
Lemonofides, Dino. 1971. *British Infantry Colours.* London: Almark.

Over, Keith. 1976. *Flags and Standards of the Napoleonic Wars*. London: Bivouac.

Wise, Terence. 1977. *Military Flags of the World, 1618–1900*. Poole, UK: Blandford.

———. 1978. *Flags of the Napoleonic Wars*. 2 vols. London: Osprey.

Stein, Heinrich Friedrich Karl Freiherr vom und zum (1757–1831)

A liberal-conservative statesman, Stein is often regarded as Germany's leading reformer of the early nineteenth century. Coming from an old family of landowning imperial knights in the Rhineland, he studied law, political science, and history at Göttingen, before undertaking practical training in Regensburg, Vienna, and Hungary, while traveling around central Europe for several years. In 1772 he first met Karl August von Hardenberg, who was later to become a major reformer in Prussia alongside Stein.

Stein joined the Prussian service in 1780. Regarded as a great specialist in economics, in 1784 he was appointed head of the Prussian State Mines Administration in the western provinces. By 1796 he had risen to head of the central administration authority of the western parts of Prussia, and was based in Minden. In 1785 he undertook a diplomatic mission to the court of the Prince Elector of Hesse and spent some months in England in 1786–1787 studying mining technology. He was also involved in the defense of the central Rhineland from the French invasion in autumn 1792, when General Adam de Custine first took the German fortress-city of Mainz.

In 1793 Stein married Wilhelmine, Gräfin von Wallmoden-Gimborn. The union produced two daughters. The elder, Henriette, married Hermann Graf von Giech; the younger, Therese, married Ludwig Graf von Kielmansegg, of the Hanoverian nobility.

The French occupation of large parts of western Germany from then onward forced Stein to relocate on a number of occasions. The inability of the Holy Roman Empire to defend itself against such encroachments on its territory made its mark on Stein. The resulting exchanges of territory and the secularization of ecclesiastical territories made it necessary for him to devote much of his time to administrative reorganization. The loss of the left bank of the Rhine to France meant that Stein lost family property. He did not support the French Revolution, but later became one of the leading lights in the struggle against Napoleon.

Following the Peace of Basle in 1795, Prussia made peace with Revolutionary France. Stein spent this time as president of the Westphalian Chambers at Wesel, Hamm, and Minden, along the Line of Demarcation with France. He encouraged investment in infrastructure and reformed the administration. In Minden, he first met and befriended the gifted Prince Louis Ferdinand, a nephew of Frederick the Great, who fell at Saalfeld in the Jena-Auerstädt campaign of 1806.

In 1798 Stein called for Prussia to modernize its constitution and territorial administration to face the threat from France and to secure the independence of Germany. He also gave his support to the military reformers, in due course particularly to Gerhard von Scharnhorst and Augustus von Gneisenau. Stein also became a close friend of General Gebhard von Blücher, who symbolized Prussia's struggle against France.

Having lost property to the French in the Rhineland, Stein purchased the estate of Birnbaum on the Wartha River in eastern Germany in 1802. He was now a landowner in Prussia proper, an act of considerable symbolism.

The principality of Münster was added to Prussia's western territories following the secularization of the German ecclesiastical states in the Principal Resolution of the Imperial Deputation (Imperial Recess) of 1803. Stein did much to ensure a smooth transition. He favored Prussia's territorial aggrandizement at the expense of the minor German principalities because a strong Prussia could unite at least northern Germany and oppose France's ambitions.

In October 1804 Stein left Westphalia for Berlin, moving from local to central government. Once in Berlin, he became minister of finance and the economy in Prussia and played a leading role in national politics. Prussia's primitive banking system also attracted Stein's attention. He discovered a number of frauds in the autumn of 1805 and replaced the bank's directors. The practice of securing mortgages in south Prussia was forbidden, and speculation was threatened with greater penalties.

In April 1806 Stein published his first important memorandum on the reform of central government, which caused considerable friction with King Frederick William III. Stein cast his eye on the eastern provinces, and particularly the newly acquired Polish territories, wanting their new administration to follow the pattern of that of the western provinces. He ran into determined resistance from the local squirearchy.

It was, however, events involving France that weighed most heavily on Stein's mind at this time. The defeat of Austria and Russia at the Battle of Austerlitz in December 1805 isolated Prussia. With the creation of the Confederation of the Rhine on 12 July 1806, hegemony over the German states passed to France. The abdication of Emperor Francis II on 6 August 1806 ended the first German (or Holy Roman) Empire. Two months later, Napoleon's veterans were victorious over the much-vaunted Prussian army at the twin battles of Jena and Auerstädt. Prussia paid the price for the decade of neutrality.

The years following this catastrophic defeat were just as turbulent for Stein. He left Berlin with his monarch when the government was transferred to Königsberg in East Prussia. He was opposed to the current system of central government, in which the ministers were not formed into any council and the king ruled through a cabinet of advisers not consisting of ministers. Stein's vociferous activities as a reformer led to conflict with the king, resulting in his dismissal in January 1807. That June, Stein wrote his most famous political document, the Nassau Memorandum, which called for a decentralized administration and the participation of the citizen in government.

Stein returned to government in October 1807 as Prussia's chief minister, a post he held until November 1808. Frederick William had begun to reform his government along the lines suggested earlier by Stein. Indeed the post of chief minister was newly created, and Hardenberg had held it for only two months before Stein replaced him. Stein's name is closely linked with reforms in the system of government, in social structures, in local government, in the army, and in education. He is particularly known for the Emancipation Edict of October 1807, which freed the peasants from the last vestiges of personal serfdom, and the Towns Act of 1808, which gave Prussia's towns a considerable degree of self-government. These reforms emphasized the strengthening of the state through the cooperation of its citizens and their assumption of responsibilities, as well as the breaking down of the class system.

As chief minister, it was Stein's responsibility to negotiate reparations for the recent war with the French intendant general, Pierre Antoine Bruno Daru, a matter fraught with difficulties, as the occupiers were most rapacious and Prussia was not in a position to raise loans to cover the amount demanded. Known as an active and leading patriot, Stein became the focus of attention for French spies. His letter of 15 August 1808 to Prince Wittgenstein was intercepted. It discussed the possibility of a national uprising, following the example set by Spain.

The twenty-fourth of November, 1808, was a day that Stein would never forget. His reform bill for central government was finally implemented, but his behind-the-scenes activities had come to Napoleon's attention. The letter to Wittgenstein forced the king to dismiss his controversial minister. On 16 December, Stein went into exile in Bohemia, then part of the Austrian Empire, from where he continued to plot Napoleon's overthrow.

Although he was forced to observe events from outside Prussia, Stein nevertheless continued to play a major role in the political proceedings of 1809–1812. He was closely connected to the underground nationalist organi-

zation known as the Tugendbund, the "League of Virtue." When Austria went to war with France in 1809, many in Prussia reached for their sabers, and a rebellion under Major Ferdinand von Schill took place in northern Germany. Stein called for an anti-Napoleonic insurrection in Germany and for the liberation of Germany by Germans. Napoleon's first defeat at the hands of the Austrian Archduke Charles at the Battle of Aspern-Essling that May raised the political temperature. Stein's hopes were dashed when Napoleon reimposed his will over the Austrians at Wagram in July.

When in exile in Austria, Stein also took the opportunity to write a book on the history of France and the Revolution from 1789 to 1799.

In the spring of 1812, Tsar Alexander I of Russia, anticipating war with Napoleon, called on Stein to serve him as an adviser on German affairs. From this advantageous position, Stein was able to pull strings throughout Europe, acting as the dynamo in the German liberation movement. He not only wrote a number of important memoranda on the German question, he also played an active role in the German Committee that plotted an anti-French uprising. Furthermore, he assisted in the formation of the Russo-German Legion, which was formed from prisoners of war from Napoleon's invading army and intended to be the spearhead of a new national German army.

Stein returned to Germany with the advancing Russian army at the beginning of 1813 and was appointed head of the military administration of the occupied territories. He acted as an intermediary between Tsar Alexander and Frederick William, negotiating their military alliance for the war against Napoleon. General Johann David von Yorck supported him in these negotiations. He was commander of the Prussian Auxiliary Corps that had gone to Russia with Napoleon, but later went over to the Russians. Stein's endeavors were rewarded that October at the Battle of Leipzig, in which Napoleon was decisively defeated and driven out of Germany.

Stein also acted as chief of administration of the provisional government of the liberated German territories, and later of occupied France. Although he did not play a decisive role in the first Peace of Paris in 1814, or at the Congress of Vienna, Stein nevertheless continued to advise the tsar and in that way influenced the shape of post-Napoleonic Europe. He also advised the Prussian delegation at the Congress and later declined offers from both Austria and Prussia to serve as an ambassador in the Federal German Diet in Frankfurt.

Once the Congress of Vienna had completed its business, Stein returned to his native Nassau for the first time in seven years. He participated in the conferences that prepared the treaty for the second Peace of Paris. In 1816, he acquired the castle of Cappenberg in Westphalia, in exchange for his estate of Birnbaum, an act marking his return home to western Germany. It had formerly been ecclesiastical property and had been secularized in 1803. He made this castle his main place of residence, although he also had residences in Nassau and in Frankfurt. His personal contacts and his extensive correspondence kept him in touch with developments in society, politics, and science. He did not hold public office, but took an effective part in the political life of the newly formed Prussian province of Westphalia, as well as in the movement for constitutional monarchy and political representation in Prussia.

His days as a politician were now coming to an end. In 1819 Stein founded the Early German Historical Society and, largely from his own means, began the collection of medieval German historical sources that has continued to the present. He was very active in both the organization and research of the sources he gathered. From July 1820, he spent a year traveling in Switzerland and Italy, before returning home.

As a septuagenarian, Stein received his last public appointment, as marshal of the Provincial Chambers in the first three parliaments of the province of Westphalia, in 1826, 1828, and 1830–1831. He was active until six months before his death and died in 1831, aged seventy-three, in Cappenberg. He was laid to rest in the family graveyard in Frücht, near Bad Ems, in the Rhineland. Although he had spent much of his life as an administrator in Prussian service, Stein helped lay the foundation stones of modern Germany and is seen as a symbol of German patriotism.

Peter Hofschröer

See also Alexander I, Tsar; Aspern-Essling, Battle of; Auerstädt, Battle of; Austerlitz, Battle of; Basle, Treaties of; Blücher von Wahlstatt, Gebhard Lebrecht Fürst; Charles, Archduke of Austria, Duke of Teschen; Confederation of the Rhine; Emancipation Edict; Fifth Coalition, War of the; Francis I, Emperor; Frederick William III, King; Germany, Campaign in; Gneisenau, August Wilhelm Anton Graf Neidhardt von; Hardenberg, Karl August Fürst von; Holy Roman Empire; Imperial Recess; Jena, Battle of; Leipzig, Battle of; Mainz, Siege of; Paris, First Treaty of; Paris, Second Treaty of; Prussia; Rhine Campaigns (1792–1797); Saalfeld, Action at; Scharnhorst, Gerhard Johann David von; Schill, Ferdinand Baptista von; Tugendbund; Vienna, Congress of; Wagram, Battle of; Yorck von Wartenburg, Johann David Ludwig Graf

References and further reading
Botzenhart, Erich. 1931–1937. *Freiherr vom Stein: Briefwechsel, Denkschriften und Aufzeichnungen.* Berlin: Heymann.
Ford, Guy S. 1922. *Stein and the Era of Reform in Prussia, 1807–15.* Princeton: Princeton University Press.
Gray, Marion W. 1986. *Prussia in Transition: Society and Politics under the Stein Reform Ministry of 1801.* Philadelphia: American Philosophical Society.
Hubatsch, Walter and Erich Botzenhart, eds. 1957–1974. *Freiherr vom Stein: Briefe und amtliche Schriften.* 10 vols. Stuttgart: Kohlhammer.
Lehmann, Max. 1902–1905. *Freiherr vom Stein.* 3 vols. Leipzig: Hirzel.
Pertz, Georg Heinrich. 1848. *Denkschriften des Ministers Freiherrn vom Stein.* Berlin: E. S. Mittler.
———. 1849–1854. *Das Leben des Ministers Freiherrn vom Stein.* 6 vols. Berlin: Mittler.
Raack, R. C. 1965. *The Fall of Stein.* Cambridge, MA: Harvard University Press.
Raumer, Kurt von. 1960. *Die Autobiographie des Freiherrn vom Stein.* Münster: Aschendorff.
Ritter, Gerhard. 1958. *Stein—Eine politische Biographie.* Stuttgart: Deutsche Verlagsanstalt.
Seeley, J. R. 1879. *Life and Times of Stein.* 2 vols. Boston: Roberts.
Simon, Walter M. 1955. *The Failure of the Prussian Reform Movement, 1807–1819.* Ithaca, NY: Cornell University Press.

Stendhal (1783–1842)

Marie-Henri Beyle, known to the world as Stendhal, became one of the modern age's most important literary figures. Living as he did in the transitional period from the *ancien régime* through the age of Napoleon and into the period of the Bourbon Restoration and the July Revolution of 1830, Stendhal witnessed France's and Europe's movement into the modern era. His diary, letters, and fiction are vivid reflections of his life in this fascinating time.

Many careers were made in the footsteps of Napoleon's glory, including Stendhal's. The reader is struck by the central role played by Napoleon in the lives of Stendhal's literary characters, and this is no accident. Stendhal's career would rise and fall with the fortunes of Napoleon. Indeed, in his autobiographical work, *The Life of Henry Brulard,* Stendhal stated: "I fell when Napoleon did in April 1814" (Stendhal 1986a, 8).

Stendhal was a native of Grenoble, but he longed for the adventures of Paris. Thus, when he moved to the capital in November 1799 the day after Bonaparte seized power during the coup of Brumaire (9–10 November 1799), he was filled with great hopes for a new, more exciting life.

In Paris Stendhal came under the protection of his father's cousin, Noël Daru, who was important politically in both Grenoble and Paris and who had connections with many members of the government, including Charles-Maurice de Talleyrand, Bonaparte's foreign minister. The elder Daru and his sons, Pierre and Martial, would serve as Stendhal's benefactors throughout the period of his life under the Consulate and Empire. Stendhal was given a job as one of the clerks at the ministry of war, working under the direction of Pierre Daru. When Bonaparte crossed the Alps in 1799, Stendhal eagerly accepted a commission as a second lieutenant in the 6th Dragoons and followed Bonaparte to Italy. He soon adopted the general as his hero, writing of an earlier campaign in the opening lines of *The Charterhouse of Parma:* "On 15 May 1796, General Bonaparte made his entry into Milan at the head of that youthful army which but a short time before had crossed the Bridge of Lodi, and taught the world that after so many centuries Caesar and Alexander had a successor" (Stendhal 1958, 19).

Stendhal was eventually appointed provisional deputy war commissar for Brunswick. Shortly thereafter, he was raised to full war commissar, and in 1808 he became the intendant of the imperial domains. This position was one of considerable power and prestige and allowed Stendhal to live the kind of life he had once dreamed of living. His travels through Germany and Austria in 1809, however, opened his eyes to the true horrors of war, a disillusionment that would be reflected in both his later literary work and the letters and diary that he maintained.

Back in Paris, Daru arranged for Stendhal's appointment as auditor of the Council of State, one of the top government officials in the Empire. He was soon given the additional appointment of inspector of the accounts, buildings, and furniture of the crown. These responsibilities included managing the Palace of Versailles, the Château of Fontainebleau, and the Musée Napoléon, now known as the Louvre.

In 1812 Stendhal, ever anxious for adventure, joined Napoleon's army for the campaign in Russia. As a sign of his importance and his closeness to the court, he first stopped to pay a visit to Empress Marie Louise and her infant son, Napoleon, the King of Rome. The journey into and out of Russia provided Stendhal with images of war and life that would never leave him. More than ever before he would become involved in the dirty business of war, and more than ever before he would be threatened by it.

In 1814 Allied forces were moving into France from several directions. Stendhal organized the defense of Grenoble in 1814, for which he earned the respect and admiration of all who were with him. He returned to Paris and witnessed the departure of Marie Louise and the King of Rome as the Allies approached the capital.

After the final fall of Napoleon, Stendhal did not wish to live in a France that was intent on returning to the days before the Revolution. The Bourbons executed or imprisoned those who had served Napoleon and sought to slander his image. Stendhal, in disgust, moved to Milan, where he remained until 1821.

The Restoration left Stendhal and his literary characters longing for the Emperor and his past glories. While Stendhal is careful to point out Napoleon's faults, he nevertheless makes his love of the Emperor clear. In his most fa-

mous work, *Scarlet and Black,* the main character Julien has but one hero: Napoleon. Julien's most treasured reading material consisted of the bulletins of Napoleon's army and Napoleon's memoirs, written during his exile on St. Helena. Stendhal's own feelings about the man who so influenced his life and literature are probably summed up in his *Life of Napoleon:* "I am writing this Life of Napoleon to refute a slander" (Stendhal 1956, 7).

J. David Markham

See also Brumaire, Coup of; France, Campaign in; Italian Campaigns (1799–1800); Marie Louise, Empress; Napoleon II, King of Rome; Russian Campaign; St. Helena; Talleyrand-Périgord, Charles-Maurice de, Prince
References and further reading
Markham, J. David. 1994. "Following in the Footsteps of Glory: Stendhal's Napoleonic Career." In *Selected Papers of the Twenty-Fourth Consortium on Revolutionary Europe,* 415–425. Tallahassee, FL: Institute on Napoleon and the French Revolution.
May, Gita. 1977. *Stendhal and the Age of Napoleon.* New York: Columbia University Press.
Stendhal [Marie-Henri Beyle]. 1953. *Scarlet and Black: A Chronicle of the Nineteenth Century.* Trans. Margaret Shaw. London: Penguin.
———. 1954. *The Private Diaries of Stendhal.* Ed. and trans. Robert Sage. New York: Doubleday.
———. 1956. *A Life of Napoleon.* London: Rodale.
———. 1958. *The Charterhouse of Parma.* Trans. Margaret Shaw. London: Penguin.
———. 1986a. *The Life of Henry Brulard.* Trans. Jean Steward and B. C. J. G. Knight. Chicago: University of Chicago Press.
———. 1986b. *To the Happy Few: Selected Letters.* Trans. Norman Cameron. London: Soho.

Stettin, Capture of

See Lasalle, Antoine Charles Louis, comte

Stockach, First Battle of (25 March 1799)

Decisive Austrian victory over the French during the War of the Second Coalition.

When the French restarted the war in March 1799, Archduke Charles with his Austrian army engaged the Army of the Danube under General Jean-Baptiste Jourdan at Stockach, a key crossroads at the northwestern end of the Bodensee (Lake Constance), which controlled the road south into Switzerland. Charles counterattacked against the main French assault, but suffered heavy losses. The victory secured Austrian control of southern Germany, but politicians in Vienna prevented the archduke from exploiting his success for two months. The archduke's strategy was focused on retaking Switzerland from French control, as Switzerland controlled the central position between Germany and Italy. He did not want to waste troops annihilating Jourdan's small force.

On 1 March, Jourdan's 40,000-strong force advanced into southern Germany to support General André Masséna's Army of Helvetia in Switzerland, although war was not declared until 12 March. They faced an Austrian army under Archduke Charles numbering about 60,000. From 15 March, the two sides fought running skirmishes until Charles defeated Jourdan at Ostrach on 21 March, forcing the French to withdraw westward. On 24 March, Charles's advance guard under *Feldmarschalleutnant* Friedrich Graf Nauendorff drove the French out of Stockach town, and Charles planned to press the attack the next day. The Austrian advance guard covered the whole front, with the left wing under *Feldmarschalleutnant* Joseph Staader Freiherr von Adelsheim based defensively around Wahlweis and the right under *Feldzeugmeister* Oliver Graf Wallis around Mahlspuren, with a reserve under *Feldmarschalleutnant* Johann Graf Kolowrat-Krakowsky at Stockach.

The French deployed General Pierre Marie Ferino's 1st Division near Muhlhausen, General Joseph Souham's 2nd Division on his left near the Stockach-Engen road; northwest of Engen was General Nicolas Soult's advance-guard division, while General Laurent Gouvion St. Cyr's 3rd Division was in the nearby forest; General Dominique Vandamme's small Flanquers force guarded the left wing on the Danube, with General Jean Joseph d'Hautpoul's Reserve at Immendingen on the Danube. The Austrian advance guard's reinforced right wing under *Generalmajor* Maximillian Graf von Merveldt's command was to split St. Cyr and Vandamme from the main French army, while the rest of Nauendorff's advance guard would screen the rest off and push it back westward. Charles could thereby secure the main road into Switzerland and advance into Masséna's rear to force his withdrawal.

Based at Engen, Jourdan believed Charles had dispatched forces to the Tyrol to halt Masséna's advance. Knowing he would nevertheless lose another defensive action, Jourdan massed his army on the left to mount a surprise counterattack. St. Cyr, Soult, and the reserve would attack the Austrian right, attempting to outflank them and reach the Austrian rear by moving through Mösskirch. Ferino and Souham would attack frontally, join up around Nenzingen, and march on Stockach to secure the main road east. The French attack began at dawn on 25 March in the south, as Ferino advanced against Nauendorff's left under *Generalmajor* Karl Fürst zu Schwarzenberg and pushed it back on Nenzingen, but Ferino could not get any farther that afternoon, as Souham had been halted by

Nauendorff's central units around Aach. Ferino made some further progress by late evening toward Wahlweis, where there was street fighting until late evening.

The battle, however, was decided in the north. Vandamme, Soult, and the French reserve had headed for Emmingen that morning to support the inactive St. Cyr, who was engaged by Merveldt down the Liptingen-Stockach road. The Austrian advance troops were soon put to flight, causing a general panic around Liptingen when the French advance guard approached. As Vandamme and Soult closed in from the flanks by 9:00 A.M., Merveldt's retreat fell into disorder, and his men fell back down the road toward Neuhaus. Believing he had destroyed the whole Austrian right, Jourdan fatally split his forces at 10:00 A.M.: Soult and Vandamme were to pursue Merveldt along the Stockach road, while St. Cyr's fairly fresh troops made an extended march around the northern flank to cut Austrian communications, and the Reserve cavalry remained at Liptingen.

When news arrived, Charles had initially ordered a general slow retreat by Schwarzenberg and Nauendorff, while the position was stabilized. The archduke then took some of Nauendorff's troops to reinforce the right, leaving Staader to fight a holding action in the south, which would isolate Ferino's French division around Stockach, while the Austrian counterattack destroyed Jourdan's left. Covering Merveldt, Wallis's main right wing established a position south of the Graue Wald (Grey Forest) and in two hours' ferocious fighting, halted the head of Soult's column as it emerged from the forest, before launching their attack back up the road toward Liptingen around 2:00 P.M. Charles had sent his grenadiers and Reserve cavalry to the Austrian right wing, and they joined Wallis's advance through the Graue Wald to emerge near Neuhaus around 4:00 P.M., where Soult had been able to reorder his men. The Austrians quickly took the Homburg hill and deployed three regiments and two grenadier battalions to engage Soult's infantry.

Meanwhile, *Feldmarschalleutnant Generalmajor* Franz Freiherr von Petrasch had moved into the gap between Soult and Vandamme, whose own advance had been halted. Knowing his left was being overwhelmed, Jourdan ordered St. Cyr to hasten his march on Mösskirch and moved his Reserve cavalry forward to support Soult. The light cavalry failed to dislodge the Austrians from the Homburg hill, while the heavy cavalry were destroyed by *Feldmarschalleutnant* Johann Graf von Riesch's Reserve around 5:00 P.M. Jourdan had nothing left and withdrew on Liptingen. Charles now swung his right wing to attack this village from the flank, while his left advanced up the road. St. Cyr had driven a small Austrian force through Mösskirch by 4:00 P.M., but withdrew on receiving news of Soult.

The Austrians suffered heavy losses of about 5,000 men, nearly double those of the French. Jourdan evacuated the area as night fell and recrossed the Rhine on 5 April. Charles was ordered not to Switzerland, but to the central Rhine.

David Hollins and Roland Kessinger

See also Charles, Archduke of Austria, Duke of Teschen; Gouvion St. Cyr, Laurent, comte; Jourdan, Jean-Baptiste; Masséna, André; Rhine Campaigns (1799–1800); Schwarzenberg, Karl Philipp Fürst zu; Second Coalition, War of the; Souham, Joseph, comte; Soult, Nicolas Jean de Dieu; Switzerland, Campaign in; Vandamme, Dominique Joseph René

References and further reading

Charles, Archduke. 1893. *Geschichte des Feldzuges in Deutschland in Ausgewählte Schriften.* Vol. 3. Vienna: Braumüller.

Kessinger, Roland. 2002. "The Battle of Stockach." *First Empire.*

Phipps, Ramsay Weston. 1980. *The Armies of the First French Republic and the Rise of the Marshals of Napoleon I.* Vol. 5, *The Armies on the Rhine, in Switzerland, Holland, Italy, Egypt, and the Coup d'Etat of Brumaire, 1797 to 1799.* London: Greenwood. (Orig. pub. 1926–1939.)

Stockach, Second Battle of (3 May 1800)

Also known as the Battle of Engen, this decisive French victory in southern Germany prevented Austrian interference with Bonaparte's advance through Switzerland into Italy.

General Jean Moreau's (French) Army of the Rhine crossed the Rhine in early May to attack *Feldzeugmeister* Paul Kray Freiherr von Krajova's Austrian army. The main attack came across the Rhine near Basle to draw Kray west, while Moreau's right advanced from Zürich to threaten Kray's communications with Ulm. The main French army defeated Kray at Engen, while Moreau's right under General Claude Jacques Lecourbe overwhelmed an Austrian division at Stockach, forcing Kray to withdraw.

Moreau's 120,000-strong army was divided into four corps: the left wing under General Gilles Bruneteau, vicomte de Sainte-Suzanne, the center under General Laurent Gouvion St. Cyr and the right under Lecourbe, with Moreau commanding the Reserve. Kray deployed 80,000 men in eight divisions between Kehl and the Bodensee (Lake Constance). Moreau's plan was to draw Kray toward Donaueschingen, while Lecourbe marched north from Zürich into Kray's rear around the key crossroads at Stockach. Over 25–30 April, Ste. Suzanne, St. Cyr, and Moreau crossed the Rhine between Strasbourg and Basle. As Kray massed his troops to support *Feldmarschalleutnant* Friedrich Graf Nauendorff's division in opposing them,

Lecourbe crossed the Rhine at Schaffhausen (near the Bodensee) on 1 May and drove Lothringen's small division back on Stockach. Moreau and St. Cyr attacked Nauendorff, who fell back to Engen. Kray ordered *Generalmajor* François-Joseph-Louis Freiherr de Klinglin and *Generalmajor* Carl von Lindenau to take their divisions to Engen and keep control of the road through to Stockach and the Austrian base at Ulm.

On 3 May, Lecourbe attacked Prinz Joseph von Lothringen near Stockach. General Gabriel Jean Molitor's division attacked frontally and on the left flank, while General Joseph de Montrichard tackled the Austrian right and General Dominique Vandamme cut their communications to Kray. Overwhelmed by 3:00 P.M., Lothringen withdrew on Mösskirch. The Austrian cavalry attempted to protect them north of Stockach, but were scattered by General Etienne Nansouty's Reserve cavalry. Meanwhile, Nauendorff engaged Moreau's Reserve at Engen, but around noon, Moreau assaulted the hills south of Welschingen. Attacked on both flanks, Nauendorff fell back to join *Feldmarschalleutnant* Johann Graf Kolowrat-Krakowsky's Reserve division. An Austrian attack on Welschingen failed, but their gunners pinned the French into the village until nightfall. General Jean Thomas Lorge's division had taken Muhlhausen, threatening Kray's links to Lothringen. St. Cyr approached Engen around 4:00 P.M. His 1st Division under General Baraguey d'Hilliers drove the Austrian rear guard back on Archduke Ferdinand's division positioned in the hills 7 kilometers west of Engen, where they joined Lindenau's right flank. Once General Michel Ney's 3rd Division arrived, St. Cyr assaulted the archduke's lines, forcing him on Stetten, a small village 4 kilometers east of Engen, where fighting continued, but General Antoine Richepance's division could make no progress against Lindenau. The Austrians lost 6,400 men against French casualties of 2,000. Kray was forced to withdraw on Mösskirch, where Moreau defeated him on 5 May. With the Austrians driven from the Swiss border, Moreau dispatched part of Lecourbe's corps to Milan to support Bonaparte.

David Hollins and Roland Kessinger

See also Ferdinand d'Este, Archduke; Gouvion St. Cyr, Laurent, comte; Italian Campaigns (1799–1800); Kray, Paul Freiherr von Krajova; Moreau, Jean Victor; Nansouty, Etienne Marie Antoine Champion; Ney, Michel; Rhine Campaigns (1799–1800); Vandamme, Dominique Joseph René

References and further reading

Azan, Paul, and Ernest Picard. 1907–1909. *Campagne de 1800 en Allemagne* [Campaign of 1800 in Germany]. Paris: Chapelot.

Kessinger, Roland. 2001. "The Battle of Engen." *First Empire* 61: 8–16.

Stokoe, John (1775–1852)

Stokoe entered the navy at the age of nineteen and was present at the battles of Copenhagen and Trafalgar. He joined the crew of the HMS *Conquerant* as surgeon, and went with it to St. Helena. At some point he was introduced by Dr. Barry O'Meara to Napoleon, and soon began to engage in some secret correspondence to Longwood, Napoleon's residence on the island. When Sir Hudson Lowe, the island's governor, became anxious to provide Napoleon a doctor after O'Meara's departure, Stokoe was a natural choice, as Napoleon had refused to see Lowe's first choice, James Verling. Stokoe began to serve as Napoleon's doctor on 17 January 1819, and between that date and 21 January he visited Napoleon five times.

Lowe became convinced that Stokoe was going to be at least as close to Napoleon as O'Meara had been. When Stokoe went home on leave, immediately upon arrival in Britain he was ordered back to St. Helena, where he was court-martialed for disobedience to Lowe. Convicted on most counts, Stokoe was thrown out of the navy. Stokoe's court-martial is well documented in Verling's journal.

Like so many others in the cast of characters on St. Helena during Napoleon's exile, Stokoe kept notes and wrote his recollections of his time there. Many years later these memoirs were discovered and published, after heavy editing, by Paul Frémeaux as *With Napoleon on St Helena*. The treatment of Stokoe was not one of Lowe's finer moments, and contributed greatly to his image as a man overcome with suspicion.

J. David Markham

See also Copenhagen, Battle of; Lowe, Sir Hudson; O'Meara, Barry Edward; St. Helena; Trafalgar, Battle of; Verling, James Roch

References and further reading
Markham, J. David. 2005. *Napoleon and Dr. Verling on St. Helena.* Barnsley: Pen and Sword.
Stokoe, Dr. John. 1902. *With Napoleon at St. Helena: Being the Memoirs of Dr. John Stokoe, Naval Surgeon.* Translated from the French of Paul Frémeaux by Edith S. Stokoe. London: Lane.

Stralsund, Siege of (30 January–19 April 1807)

In early 1807 Marshal Adolphe Mortier was ordered to subdue Pomerania, Swedish territory situated on the European mainland, an objective that necessitated the capture of the town of Stralsund and its formidable defenses. The fortress was invested by the end of January, and the siege was to last until April, principally because in March much of the French force was withdrawn, allowing the Swedish garrison to launch a major counterattack. However, an armistice was signed on 19 April when the fortress effectively surrendered.

In January 1807, Mortier deployed his corps along the line of the river Peene in Pomerania and shortly thereafter received orders to complete the occupation of the province. In order to do this, it was necessary to take the fortress of Stralsund. Mortier began his advance in two columns on 28 January with General Charles Grandjean on the right and General Pierre Louis Dupas on the left. Grandjean took the town of Greifswalde with little difficulty, defeating the Swedish outposts stationed there. Within two days, Mortier's corps was outside Stralsund, and the investment of the town began. However, the blockade could not be completed, first because Mortier could not cut off communications to the Swedish garrison by sea, and second because the Swedes were able to fire on the French siege lines by sailing gunboats out from the port.

For the following two months the French settled into their siege lines. A number of small-scale engagements took place, as Pierre, Count Essen, commanding the Swedish garrison, conducted an active defense. How active was shown to the full when on 29 January Mortier was ordered to move most of his troops to Kolberg, leaving only Grandjean to maintain the siege lines. Essen quickly tried to take advantage of this. Outnumbered by a Swedish force of around 13,000 troops, Grandjean was forced to fall back through the town of Greifswalde and then across the Peene. He then moved to Anklam, where he was attacked by Essen on 3 April. The situation seemed serious, and Mortier decided that he had to intervene to safeguard the French position. Mortier moved to Stettin and reached the city on 13 April, being met there by reinforcements from Berlin. The arrival of these troops brought Mortier's command up to equal strength with that of Essen. Mortier, thus strengthened, counterattacked and obliged the Swedish army to fall back on Anklam.

Despite poor weather, Mortier was able to build on this success, and by 17 April Essen's force was back across the Peene. Napoleon had instructed Mortier to attempt to negotiate an armistice with Essen and thus free up his troops to be used elsewhere. These negotiations proved successful after ten days of talks, and on 29 April an armistice was signed. It guaranteed that the Swedes would remain beyond the line of the river Peene, and a month's notice was required for termination of the armistice. Mortier's troops could now be released to operate with the main French army on the Vistula, in Poland, against the Russians.

Ralph Baker

See also Fourth Coalition, War of the; Mortier, Adolphe Edouard Casimir Joseph

References and further reading
Petre, F. Loraine. 2001. *Napoleon's Campaign in Poland, 1806–1807.* London: Greenhill.

Studienka, Action at

See Berezina, Actions and Crossing at the

Subservie, Jacques Gervais, baron (1776–1856)

Jacques Gervais, baron Subservie, was born on 1 September 1776 in the southwestern part of France. Hailing from the prominent Subservie family, Jacques attended some of the most illustrious schools in the years preceding the collapse of the *ancien régime.* After his schooling, Subservie, inspired by the vigor and dynamism of the Revolutionary Wars, decided to join the French Army, serving at Malta during the expedition to Egypt. He remained on the island due to illness and was captured by the British in 1800. He became aide-de-camp to Marshal Jean Lannes and served in the campaigns of 1805–1807 before being sent to the Peninsula, where he fought at Medellín on 29 March 1809. He led the 10th Cavalry Brigade at the Battle of Talavera on 27–28 July 1809, and on 28 November of that year, Napoleon ennobled him as baron Subservie. As a result of this promotion, Subservie became one of the most trusted generals on Napoleon's staff.

On 6 August 1811 Subservie became *général de brigade* under Marshal Louis Suchet. He was badly wounded at Borodino during the Russian campaign, but recovered sufficiently to serve in Germany in 1813 and in the campaign in France, where he was present at Brienne, Champaubert, and Montereau. He received a second severe wound near Paris in March 1814 and was promoted to *général de division* the following month. During the First Restoration, the Bourbons annulled his new rank, though he was made a lieutenant general in July 1814. In 1815, as Napoleon prepared for his final campaign, Subservie again served in the cavalry, under General Claude Pajol, and fought at Waterloo. On the second return of the Bourbons, Subservie took a leading role in French politics and served as inspector of cavalry until his death on 10 March 1856.

Jaime Ramón Olivares

See also Borodino, Battle of; Brienne, Battle of; Champaubert, Battle of; Fourth Coalition, War of the; France, Campaign in; Germany, Campaign in; Lannes, Jean; Malta, Operations on; Medellín, Battle of; Middle East Campaign; Montereau, Battle of; Pajol, Claude Pierre; Peninsular War; Russian Campaign; Suchet, Louis Gabriel; Talavera, Battle of; Third Coalition, War of the; Waterloo, Battle of

References and further reading
Chandler, David G. 1995. *The Campaigns of Napoleon.* London: Weidenfeld and Nicolson.
Fregosi, Paul. 1990. *Dreams of Empire: Napoleon and the First World War, 1792–1815.* Secaucus, NJ: Carol.
Ropes, John Codman. 1893. *The Campaign of Waterloo: A Military History.* New York: Scribner's.

Suchet, Louis-Gabriel (1770–1826)

Louis-Gabriel Suchet emerged as the most successful of Napoleon's generals in coping with the difficulties of fighting in the Iberian Peninsula. After campaigning in Italy and Switzerland during the War of the Second Coalition, he fought with distinction as a divisional commander in the successful campaigns of 1805, 1806, and 1807. Although his early career brought him numerous laurels in conventional warfare, Suchet received no training in the complex task of fighting simultaneously against both guerrillas and regular enemy forces. But in 1808, Napoleon promoted the rising young leader to command a corps in Spain. There Suchet had a run of successes, pacifying the province of Aragón for several years and extending French control for a time into neighboring Catalonia and Valencia. His single greatest achievement, for which he won his marshal's baton, was capturing the Spanish fortress of Tarragona in May 1811. Only when the Earl (later Duke) of Wellington had defeated other French leaders and driven them from Spain into southern France was Suchet compelled to agree to an armistice with the enemy. Rallying to Napoleon in the spring of 1815, he held a high-ranking post in the defense of France's eastern border. Suchet survived the end of the Napoleonic era in France by a little more than a decade, dying in 1826.

Louis-Gabriel Suchet was a child of privilege, born at his father's country estate near Lyons on 2 March 1770. The son of a wealthy silk manufacturer, the young man joined the National Guard, then entered a volunteer battalion as a private soldier in 1792. Within a year, his fellow soldiers had chosen him as lieutenant colonel of the same unit. Suchet's battalion participated in the siege of the port of Toulon, where his battlefield exploits brought him to the attention of General Napoleon Bonaparte. During the 1796–1797 campaign in Italy, Suchet served at times in General André Masséna's division, at other times in the division led by General Pierre Augereau. He was wounded in battle several times, displayed both tactical skill and bravery, and rose to the rank of colonel. When the French army left Italy to pursue the Austrian enemy into their homeland, Suchet commanded the advance guard of Bonaparte's forces.

Although he reached the rank of *général de brigade* in 1798 and *général de division* in 1799, the years following

Marshal Suchet. A divisional commander in the campaigns against the Third and Fourth Coalitions, he numbered among the few senior French officers serving in Spain who managed to preserve his reputation intact. (Drawing by Jean Baptiste Guerin from *Life of Napoleon Bonaparte* by William M. Sloane. New York: Century, 1906, vol. 3)

the Italian campaign saw Suchet's career lose some of its upward momentum. His personal relationship with Bonaparte was cool: Suchet exhibited no affection for his commander, and Bonaparte reciprocated by excluding the young officer from the list of associates marked for promotion to the top of the military hierarchy. Moreover, a paradoxical combination of political traits made him suspect to the government back in Paris. Suchet's family background gave him the appearance of a sympathizer with the deposed aristocracy. At the same time, Suchet's extravagant rhetoric in favor of deepening the effect of the Revolution was seen as too radical for the post-Jacobin era.

Nonetheless, Suchet saw his reputation rise in the eyes of several senior commanders. Serving as a brigade commander under Masséna in Switzerland in the spring of 1799, he pulled his unit out of a perilous position after the

bold French advance into eastern Switzerland. After returning safely to French lines, the young general received the post of Masséna's chief of staff. Later that year, he served as chief of staff to General Barthélemy Joubert in Italy. In that capacity, Suchet advised his commander to avoid fighting a superior Russian force at Novi in August. When Joubert ignored the advice and was killed in the subsequent battle, Suchet helped to lead the defeated French army home.

Masséna's 1800 campaign in northwestern Italy, which culminated in the siege of Genoa, brought Suchet mixed success. As commander of the northern segment of the French line, Suchet was unable to hold back an Austrian force, being pushed as far westward as Nice and beyond. His failure forced Masséna into a defensive position behind the walls of the important Italian port city. Suchet redeemed himself, however, by halting the Austrian offensive along the river Var west of Nice, thereby safeguarding the route into southern France. By holding down some 30,000 Austrian troops in Provence during May with his own meager force of only about 8,000 men, Suchet contributed to Bonaparte's successful crossing of the Alps and subsequent victory at the Battle of Marengo.

In the years following, Suchet received only modest rewards. Named the French army's inspector general of infantry in 1801, he was passed over when several of his contemporaries received the title of marshal on 19 May 1804. With the formation of the Grande Armée, Suchet got the relatively lowly post of divisional commander. Fighting in V Corps under Marshal Jean Lannes, Suchet had a string of exceptional successes. His division advanced rapidly into Germany in the summer of 1805, thereby helping to confine and capture the Austrian army under *Feldmarschalleutnant* Karl Mack Freiherr von Leiberich at Ulm. At the subsequent Battle of Austerlitz in early December, Suchet's troops held the French army's northern flank against Russian attacks, permitting Napoleon to concentrate his forces in the center for the victorious strike against the enemy's lines. In October 1806, Suchet's division was the first to encounter the Prussian army and achieve a French victory in the fighting at Saalfeld; in the ensuing Battle of Jena, Suchet's men again spearheaded the French advance.

In the subsequent offensive into Poland in late 1806 and early 1807, Suchet received orders to guard the area around Warsaw. Although his troops saw action at Pultusk and Ostrolenka, Suchet had no role to play in the great battlefield dramas of Eylau and Friedland. Nonetheless, his solid, sometimes brilliant leadership now brought him appropriate rewards. In March 1808, Napoleon granted him several large estates and named him a Count of the Empire. Moreover, after fifteen years of service, Suchet ascended to command of an army corps. In September 1808, he received orders to take this force into Spain.

Suchet had never fought guerrillas as he was to do so often in Spain. But he had experienced enough leadership challenges to help him cope better than many of his contemporaries in the French army with the problems of both conventional and irregular warfare in the Peninsula. Campaigning in an area in which he was unlikely to receive reinforcements, Suchet saw the need to preserve the strength of his army at all costs. Ever since his service with the ragged troops of Bonaparte's Army of Italy in 1796–1797, Suchet had been a stickler for obtaining adequate supplies of food for his men. And he insisted on suitable medical care for them. At the same time, he had become convinced of the advantages of unwavering discipline in the army. He was also equipped by experience for the delicate task of occupying a hostile area. As military governor of Toulon back in 1793, he had begun to acquire experience in ruling over a civilian population, and he had served as military governor of the Italian city of Padua in early 1801.

Suchet arrived in Spain in December 1808. He was ordered to Aragón to join other commanders like Marshal Adolphe Mortier and General Jean Andoche Junot in besieging the key Spanish fortress of Saragossa. Dispatched to northeastern Spain at this early stage in the Peninsular War, Suchet was to spend most of the following five years here.

In helping with the siege of Saragossa, a major city on the river Ebro, the young general soon faced the problems of guerrilla warfare. His role was to hold the road center of Calatayud, to the southwest of Saragossa, thus maintaining the besiegers' supply line with Madrid. In dealing with the local population, Suchet tested some of the policies that served him well throughout his posting in the Peninsula. In particular, he worked to win over the Spanish under his jurisdiction by avoiding the harsh requisitioning policies that elsewhere provoked fierce popular resistance.

With the fall of Saragossa in February 1809, Suchet replaced Junot as commander of V Corps and received the assignment of pacifying Aragón. Although the three divisions he now led were notoriously ill-disciplined, Suchet transformed them into a potent fighting force that later received the title of the Army of Aragón. The French leader shook off an initial defeat at the hands of General Joaquín Blake at Alcañiz in late May. Dismissing incompetent officers and reconstituting his forces, he led his troops to victories over Blake in battles at Maria and Belchite the following month, thereby freeing Aragón of conventional Spanish forces.

Suchet's next task was to cope with insurgents within the Aragonese population. His success came from a mixture of conciliation and firmness. He capitalized on sepa-

ratist feeling in Aragón and the willingness of the local population to disavow allegiance to the old Spanish monarchy. He saw no need to harass local religious leaders, and he was comfortable calling on representatives of the population to offer him advice and suggestions. In forming a police force, he tried to rely on the local population for recruits, and he had some modest success in bringing local notables into the French administration. Meanwhile, Suchet made every effort to maintain discipline among his own troops by paying them regularly and providing them with adequate rations. By employing an entire army corps in controlling the people of Aragón, Suchet assured that local insurgents, who had not yet organized effectively, could not get a foothold in the region. He soon gained a reputation for unmitigated harshness in dealing with guerrillas who fell into his hands.

Success in counterinsurgency received a boost from the fact that, starting in mid-1809 after defeating the Austrians at Wagram, Napoleon did not face organized opposition elsewhere. Since the Emperor had no need to draw troops from Spain for a number of years, Suchet was allowed to keep his forces intact. He even received a stream of reinforcements from across the Pyrenees. On the other hand, cooperation among the generals in charge of individual provinces in Spain was conspicuous by its absence. While Suchet could clear Aragón of insurgent opposition, the elusive enemy could easily slip over into a neighboring province. Nor was Suchet, for all his abilities, willing to cooperate with his fellow French generals.

Pursuing a policy certain to rouse popular feeling against the occupiers, Napoleon insisted on draining away the resources of the Spanish countryside. The Emperor directed Suchet to undertake other responsibilities that undercut the successes in Aragón. By requiring Suchet to advance into the neighboring provinces of Catalonia and Valencia in February 1810, Napoleon began to spread Suchet's troops perilously thin. Insurgents in Aragón took notice.

Suchet failed in an initial attempt to take the port city of Valencia in April 1810, but he then produced a series of dramatic successes. His troops captured two main Spanish strongholds in southern Catalonia—Lérida and Tortosa—and Suchet became recognized as one French commander who could produce good results against both enemy regulars and enemy insurgents.

The highpoint of Suchet's command in Spain came in 1811 with the capture of Tarragona; on 8 July he received the baton of Marshal of the Empire as a reward for this achievement, becoming the only French general to win this distinction in the Peninsula. As a major port and key fortress, Tarragona enabled regular Spanish forces to maintain themselves in lower Catalonia. A difficult siege began in early May, with the defenders aided by the presence of a Royal Navy squadron. British warships directed artillery fire against the French attackers, and British transports brought Spanish forces by sea to reinforce Tarragona's garrison. By the close of June, Suchet's Army of Aragón had breached the fortress walls, fought through the streets of the city, and captured a garrison of 9,000. But even Suchet, the disciplinarian and advocate of moderate treatment for Spanish civilians, found himself helpless to control his victorious French forces. Filled with excitement and postbattle exhilaration, Suchet's troops sacked the city and murdered thousands of Tarragona's population.

Suchet faced a new challenge when Napoleon ordered him to move against the city of Valencia. The city was the last base of support for Spanish regular forces in eastern Spain, and it provided crucial supplies for guerrillas operating in that part of the country. In October, a new victory over Blake at Sagunto, north of Valencia, put the Army of Aragón in a position to advance on Valencia itself. Suchet took the city in January 1812, capturing his longtime adversary Blake along with 18,000 troops. Napoleon recognized the feat of arms by naming Suchet duc d'Albufera, after a small body of water near the captured city.

But Suchet's success at Valencia had negative consequences. For one thing, concentrating the army for a conventional campaign enabled insurgents back in Aragón to renew their activities. Moreover, Napoleon diverted troops from the Army of Portugal in western Spain in order to reinforce Suchet. With the shrinkage in French troops there, Wellington received a golden opportunity to strike at his enemy's border fortresses at Ciudad Rodrigo and Badajoz. With these in his hands, the British commander in chief was able to advance into the center of Spain and even to take temporary possession of Madrid.

Reconstructing the Grande Armée in 1813 after his disastrous Russian campaign, Napoleon desperately needed troops in Germany. The Emperor transferred units from Italy to Germany, leaving a gap that Napoleon filled by drawing troops from Suchet's command. Thus, Italian regiments serving under Suchet were reconstituted as a single division and sent back to Italy. Besides his diminished resources, Suchet found himself confronted with the potent opposition of the Royal Navy. In the spring, a landing force of British and Sicilian troops tried to recapture Tarragona. He was able to bring sufficient forces together to relieve the city in August, but by then the overall situation in Spain was growing increasingly unstable.

After the defeat of French forces at Vitoria in June 1813, and Wellington's invasion of French territory in October, Suchet realized that holding extensive territory in northeastern Spain was no longer possible. He withdrew to northern Catalonia, and, in a controversial decision, refused to join Marshal Nicolas Soult in a counteroffensive Soult had planned against Wellington. In early 1814, Suchet was pushed northward to Gerona and then to the approaches to the Pyrenees at Figueras. At this time, new demands from Napoleon that troops leave Spain for the campaign in France deprived Suchet of over 20,000 troops, leaving barely 12,000 soldiers under his command.

Suchet's troops remained a disciplined, if small fighting force in southwestern France when Napoleon's resistance to the invading Allies collapsed in the spring of 1814. With his headquarters at Narbonne, Suchet negotiated an armistice with Wellington. It was his only important contact with the distinguished British commander. Alone among the senior French military leaders who served years in Spain, Suchet never faced Wellington on the battlefield. The French marshal also declared his allegiance to the restored monarchy of Louis XVIII and received a number of rewards. Elevated to the peerage, Suchet obtained a succession of prestigious military commands. Napoleon's return from exile in March 1815 found Suchet as commander of the 5th Division stationed at Strasbourg.

Suchet joined several of the other marshals in rallying to Napoleon's service. Although Suchet had not seen the Emperor since 1808, Napoleon showed that he was aware of the talents of this Peninsular veteran, awarding him a significant independent command. Suchet was sent to Lyons as Napoleon prepared to thrust his army into Belgium, and he was given the mission of defending southeastern France. His "Corps of Observation of the Alps" consisted of some 8,000 regulars and 15,000 members of the National Guard. With this meager force, Suchet had to shield France from an Austrian and Piedmontese attack expected to advance from Switzerland or Savoy.

Suchet took the initiative away from the enemy by driving into Savoy and seizing the key military routes through the Alps. His offensive began on 14 June, the day before Napoleon's troops entered Belgium. Facing a well-led, veteran Austrian army of some 48,000 men, however, Suchet was compelled to order a retreat, which most of the army carried out in a disciplined manner. More than a week after Waterloo, he learned about Napoleon's defeat and abdication, and he followed orders from the provisional government in Paris to negotiate an armistice with the enemy.

As a penalty for having renewed his ties with Napoleon, Suchet was deprived of both his peerage and his military post at Strasbourg. His peerage was restored in 1819, but he never again received any military responsibilities. After living his last decade in obscurity, Suchet died at his chateau near Marseilles on 3 June 1826.

Neil M. Heyman

See also Augereau, Pierre-François-Charles; Austerlitz, Battle of; Badajoz, Third Siege of; Blake, Joaquín; Ciudad Rodrigo, Second Siege of; Eylau, Battle of; Fourth Coalition, War of the; Friedland, Battle of; Genoa, Siege of; Guerilla Warfare; Italian Campaigns (1792–1797); Italian Campaigns (1799–1800); Jena, Battle of; Joubert, Barthélemy Catherine; Junot, Jean Andoche, duc d'Abrantès; Lannes, Jean; Louis XVIII, King; Mack, Karl Freiherr von Lieberich; Marengo, Battle of; Marshalate; Masséna, André; Mortier, Adolphe Edouard Casimir Joseph; National Guard (French); Novi, Battle of; Peninsular War; Pultusk, Battle of; Saalfeld, Action at; Saragossa, Sieges of; Soult, Nicolas Jean de Dieu; Switzerland, Campaign in; Tarragona, Sieges of; Third Coalition, War of the; Toulon, Siege of; Ulm, Surrender at; Valencia, Siege of; Vitoria, Battle of; Wagram, Battle of; Waterloo Campaign; Wellington, Arthur Wellesley, First Duke of

References and further reading
Alexander, Don W. 1985. *Rod of Iron: French Counterinsurgency Policy in Aragon during the Peninsular War.* Wilmington, DE: Scholarly Resources.
Chandler, David G., ed. 1987. *Napoleon's Marshals.* London: Weidenfeld and Nicolson.
———. 1995. *The Campaigns of Napoleon.* London: Weidenfeld and Nicolson.
Delderfield, R. F. 2004. *The March of the Twenty-Six.* London: Leo Cooper.
Elting, John. 1988. *Swords around a Throne: Napoleon's Grande Armée.* New York: Free Press.
Esdaile, Charles J. 2003. *The Peninsular War: A New History.* New York: Palgrave Macmillan.
———. 2004. *Fighting Napoleon: Guerrillas, Bandits and Adventurers in Spain, 1808–1814.* New Haven: Yale University Press.
Hayman, Peter. 1990. *Soult: Napoleon's Maligned Marshal.* London: Arms and Armour.
Humble, Richard. 1973. *Napoleon's Peninsular Marshals.* New York: Taplinger.
Macdonnell, A. G. 1996. *Napoleon and His Marshals.* London: Prion.
Phipps, Ramsay Weston. 1980a. *The Armies of the First French Republic and the Rise of the Marshals of Napoleon I.* Vol. 4, *The Army of Italy, 1796 to 1797; Paris and the Army of the Interior, 1792 to 1797; and the Coup D'Etat of Fructidor, September 1797.* London: Greenwood. (Orig. pub. 1926–1939.)
———. 1980b. *The Armies of the First French Republic and the Rise of the Marshals of Napoleon I.* Vol. 5, *The Armies on the Rhine, in Switzerland, Holland, Italy, Egypt, and the Coup d'Etat of Brumaire, 1797 to 1799.* London: Greenwood. (Orig. pub. 1926–1939.)
Reynaud, Jean-Louis. 1992. *Contre-guerilla en Espagne (1808–1814): Suchet pacifie l'Aragon.* Paris: Economica.
Rodger, A. B. 1964. *The War of the Second Coalition: A Strategic Commentary.* Oxford: Clarendon.
Schneid, Frederick C. 2002. *Napoleon's Italian Campaigns, 1805–1815.* Westport, CT: Praeger.
Suchet, Louis-Gabriel, duc d'Albufera. 1828. *Mémoires du maréchal Suchet: duc d'Albufera, sur ses campagnes en Espagne, depuis 1808 jusqu'en 1814, écrits par lui-même.* Paris: Adolphe Bossange.
Tone, John Lawrence. 1994. *The Fatal Knot: The Guerrilla War in Navarre and the Defeat of Napoleon in Spain.* Chapel Hill: University of North Carolina Press.
Young, Peter. 1973a. *Napoleon's Marshals.* London: Osprey.
———. 1973b. *Napoleon's Marshals.* New York: Hippocrene.

Suvorov, Alexander Vasilievich (1729–1800)

Russian military commander notable for his achievements in the Russo-Turkish War of 1787–1792 and in the French Revolutionary Wars.

His father, Vassily Suvorov, a senator, had been secretary to Peter the Great, and rose to the rank of lieutenant general in 1758. At the age of twelve, Alexander Suvorov was enlisted in the Life Guard Semeyonovsk Regiment, then granted a leave of duty to study at home. In the eighteenth century, it was common for the nobility to enroll their sons in the Guards as children: As the children grew up, they climbed the ranks, enabling them to begin their later, true service in possession of an officer's rank.

In January 1748 at the age of eighteen, Suvorov began a military career that spanned five decades, as a corporal in the third company of the Life Guard Semeyonovsk Regiment. From the very beginning, he was a zealous soldier, volunteering for dreaded sentry duty, even in bad weather. Not only did he excel at the expected military disciplines of fortification and mathematics, but he also delved deeply into philosophy and history, as well as languages. From his early education he spoke and wrote German and French. In later years he picked up Italian, Spanish, and Latin, reading classical literature in the original.

In 1754 Suvorov transferred from the Guard to the regular army and was promoted to the rank of lieutenant in the New Ingermanland Infantry Regiment. By 1758 he had been further promoted to lieutenant colonel. During the Seven Years' War (1756–1763), on 14 July 1759, eleven and a half years after entering military service, Suvorov fought his first battle, against Prussian troops, near Krossen in Silesia. A month later he fought at Kunersdorf, where Russian and Austrian troops crushed Frederick the Great's forces, and on 28 September 1760 he was among the Russian troops who entered Berlin under the leadership of Count Peter Saltykov.

On 5 September 1762 Suvorov was promoted to colonel and appointed commander of the Astrakhan, then, in 1763, the Suzdal Infantry Regiment. It was at this time that he wrote his *Suzdal Regimental Code*, outlining the organization of service and training in a regiment. Suvorov set forth three basic military precepts: First, measure and assess; second, value the element of surprise; third, focus on close combat. Suvorov's first victory in battle came on

Alexander Suvorov, a Russian field marshal who established a fearsome reputation in operations against the Turks and Poles before the wars with Revolutionary France. He performed well on the Italian and Swiss fronts in 1799. (By George Dawe [1781–1929] from Grand Duke Nikolay, 1905–1909. *Russkie portrety XVIII i XIX stol I et ii*, St. Petersburg, Izd: Velikago Kniazia Nikolaia Mikhailovicha)

13 September 1769, when he commanded three regiments to put down the Bar Rebellion for Polish independence. The victory led to a promotion to the rank of major general in 1770. More victories followed. On 26 April 1772 he accepted the surrender of the Polish garrison at the castle at Kraków.

Meanwhile, in the south, Russia and Turkey had been at war since 1768. Suvorov asked to be transferred to Field Marshal Peter Rumyantsev's army, in which he quickly scored victories at Karasu and Küçük Kaynarca. In May 1773 he led 3,000 Russian troops against 12,000 Turks and captured the Ottoman fortifications and town of Turtukai. In June 1773 he undertook a second successful raid and received the very prestigious Order of St. George (2nd degree), awarded only for major military victories. His victory over the much larger Turkish army of Abder-Rezak Pasha at Kozludji, in June 1774, established Suvorov's reputation for tactical brilliance.

Recalled to Russia in 1774 to deal with the peasant revolt of Emelian Pugachev, Suvorov arrived too late to suppress the rebellion, but he escorted its leader into captivity. In January 1774, on a furlough from the army, he married

Varvara Prozorovskaya, a tall, pretty girl twenty years his junior, and entered into the well-connected Golitsyn family. The marriage, which had been arranged by her father, was a total disaster, though the couple had a daughter, whom Suvorov adored. Between 1774 and 1786 Suvorov commanded various divisions and corps in the Kuban, the Crimea, Finland, and Russia itself. In 1778 he prevented a Turkish landing in the Crimea, thus obviating another Russo-Turkish War.

From 1787 to 1792, Suvorov participated in the new Russo-Turkish War during which he defended the coastal fortress of Kinburn against two Turkish seaborne assaults in September and October 1787. He then stormed and captured Ochakov in the Crimea in December 1788, and joined forces with the Austrian general Friedrich Josias Graf Saxe-Coburg-Saalfeld to defeat Osman Pasha at Focsani in August 1789. On 22 September 1789 Suvorov routed the Ottoman army under Yusuf Pasha on the Rimnic River and, for this decisive victory, he was rewarded with the title of Count of Rimniksky (of Rimnic) by Catherine the Great, while the emperor Joseph II made him a count of the Holy Roman Empire.

On 22 December 1790 Suvorov gained fame as a consequence of the storming of the fortress of Izmail, but also notoriety for the subsequent slaughter of most of its defenders. In 1793 he commanded the Russian forces that suppressed the Polish revolt of Tadeusz Kościuszko (Thaddeus Kosciusko) and won more victories at Knupshchitse, Brest-Litovsk, Kobila, Praga, and Warsaw. He was promoted to field marshal in 1794, but the slaughters that followed the captures of Ochakov, Izmail, Praga, and Warsaw tainted his reputation in Western eyes. He was warmly greeted as a victor and national hero when he returned to St. Petersburg on 3 December 1795.

Less than a year later, on 6 November 1796, Catherine II died, succeeded by her son, Paul I. Paul was enamored of all things Prussian, as part of his allegiance to his German-born father, Peter III. Suvorov had nothing but scorn for Prussian parade-ground drilling and their heavy, tight uniforms, which Paul greatly admired. Suvorov was forced to retire and spent the next two years exiled to the village of Konchanskoe. Tsar Paul, meantime, became involved in the Second Coalition and mobilized his forces against France. A Russian squadron under the command of Admiral Fyodor Ushakov was sent to the Mediterranean, where it coordinated its actions with the British and Turkish fleets. Paul also committed the Russian army to military operations in Europe, where a combined Austro-Russian army was sent to drive the French out of Italy and Switzerland and put an end to the Revolutionary threat.

In February 1799 Paul summoned Suvorov from his estate and ordered him to take command of the army destined for Italy. Suvorov was placed at the head of a united Austro-Russian army and reached Verona by mid-April. Later that month he launched an offensive against the French, who were defeated at Cassano on the river Adda, opening up the road to Milan. Turning westward, Suvorov then occupied Turin, the capital of Piedmont, in mid-May. In one month of campaigning he was able to secure all of Lombardy and large portions of Piedmont. As the French armies counterattacked, Suvorov made a prodigious fifty-mile, thirty-six-hour forced march to rout the French forces led by General Etienne Macdonald in a three-day battle on the Trebbia River on 17–19 June. Then, on 15 August, Suvorov scored the greatest victory of the campaign, at the town of Novi, where he crushed another French army led by generals Jean Moreau and Barthélemy Joubert. For this spectacular victory, Suvorov was conferred the title of Count of Italy. The victory at Novi opened a clear path for Allied forces into southern France; Suvorov began drafting plans for the invasion. However, the Austrian Military Council, which sought to reap the fruits of this victory for itself, demanded that Suvorov leave the Austrian troops in Italy and lead his Russians to Switzerland, to link up with the forces under General Alexander Rimsky-Korsakov.

Suvorov, now sixty-eight years old, proceeded to lead his 20,000 battle-weary men over the Alps to take on four times as many French troops. In a sixteen-day march in September–October, Russian troops struggled through treacherous mountain passes, overcoming intermittent French resistance. In the most astonishing feat, while under fire, Russian troops repaired Devil's Bridge, which spanned a narrow gorge, and fought their way to the other side. The army's descent, however, was blocked by a French army under General André Masséna, who had just defeated Rimsky-Korsakov's corps at Zürich and now sought to entrap Suvorov in the Alps. Not one to balk at difficult odds, Suvorov ordered his starving troops to break out of the French encirclement, which they did with heavy casualties. In early October, Suvorov finally met up with Rimsky-Korsakov in Austria. Three-quarters of his army had survived the grueling march and battles.

Suvorov's heroic passage through the Alps was the most remarkable exploit of an already-remarkable military career. The Swiss were so impressed that they erected a monument in his honor, which still stands along the route of his march. For his outstanding military achievement Suvorov was given the highest possible military rank by the Russian tsar—generalissimo—a rank that required troops to salute him even in the presence of the tsar.

On his return trip to Russia, Suvorov was initially promised by Tsar Paul a grand welcome and reception in the capital. Relations between them rapidly deteriorated,

however, after Paul was told that Suvorov had revoked some of the Prussian-style reforms he had introduced, and, further, that he had a general serving as his duty officer—a privilege reserved for members of the imperial family. Incensed at this insubordination, Paul prohibited Suvorov from entering St. Petersburg in daylight, and it was said that he even wanted to deprive the field marshal of his titles.

Already in bad health after an exhausting campaign, Suvorov was shaken by this disgrace. He arrived at St. Petersburg late at night on 20 April 1800, unheralded and unwelcome. An imperial courier informed him that he was forbidden to visit the imperial palace. After almost a month of agony, Suvorov died on 18 May. Paul persecuted him even in death: the newspapers were not allowed to publish obituaries on Suvorov, and the military honors accorded to him were listed one grade below his rank. Suvorov nevertheless was laid to rest in one of the most venerated places of burial in Russia: the Lower Church of the Annunciation of Alexander-Nevsky Lavra.

Irena Vladimirsky

See also Cassano, Battle of; Catherine II "the Great," Tsarina; Italian Campaigns (1799–1800); Joubert, Barthélemy Catherine; Macdonald, Jacques Etienne Joseph Alexandre; Masséna, André; Moreau, Jean Victor; Novi, Battle of; Paul I, Tsar; Rimsky-Korsakov, Alexander Mikhailovich; Russo-Polish War; Second Coalition, War of the; Switzerland, Campaign in; Trebbia, Battle of the; Zürich, Second Battle of

References and further reading
Duffy. Christopher. 1981. *Russia's Military Way to the West: Origins and Nature of Russian Military Power, 1700–1800.* London: Routledge and Kegan Paul.
———. 1999. *Eagles over the Alps: Suvorov in Italy and Switzerland, 1799.* New York: Emperor's Press.
Ekshtut, Semyon. 2000. "Suvorov." *Russian Life* 43, no. 3: 40–48.
Longworth, Philip. 1966. *The Art of Victory: The Life and Achievements of Field Marshal Suvorov, 1729–1800.* New York: Holt, Rinehart and Winston.
Lopatin, V. S. 2001. *Zhizn' Suvorova, rasskazannaia im samim i ego sovremennikami: Pis'ma, dokumenty, vospominaniia, ustnye predaniia.* Moscow: Terra-Knizhnyi klub.
Menning, Bruce W. 1986. "Train Hard, Fight Easy: The Legacy of A. V. Suvorov and his 'Art of Victory.'" *Air University Reviews.* November–December: 79–88.
Osipov, K. 1944. *Alexander Suvorov: A biography.* London: Hutchinson.
Savinkin, A. E., ed. 2001. *Ne chislom, a umeniem!: voennaia sistema A. V. Suvorova.* Moscow: Russkii put'.
Semanov, S. N., ed. 2000. *Aleksandr Vasil'evich Suvorov.* Moscow: Russkii Mir.

Sweden

Like the rest of Europe, Sweden was caught up in the revolutionary upheaval and, later, the Napoleonic Wars that were unleashed by France. During the late eighteenth century, the ideas of the Enlightenment made their way into Sweden and were being transformed into government policy, creating what in Sweden is known as the Age of Liberty. Gustavus III instituted reforms abolishing censorship and encouraged free trade. By 1781, religious freedom was granted for all Christian denominations, and in 1782, Jews were given toleration. Culture flowered in Sweden under Gustavus, who was considered one of the most enlightened monarchs of Europe.

In promulgating reforms, Gustavus put himself in conflict with the aristocracy, who considered some of his actions to be unconstitutional. Through his enlightened reforms, Gustavus had become more autocratic, which alarmed the aristocracy. In 1788, he went to war against Russia, in hopes of gaining some Finnish provinces lost in 1721 by the Treaty of Nystad and in 1743 by the Treaty of Åbo. The aristocracy opposed this war and the further erosion of their privileges.

In 1792 Gustavus III was assassinated and succeeded by Gustavus IV. The new king was equally as autocratic as his father had been. His abhorrence of the French Revolution and Napoleon led Sweden to offer troops to the Third Coalition with Britain, Russia, and Austria on 31 August, supplemented by a formal treaty signed on 3 October. Austria was knocked out in December 1805, but Sweden remained in alliance with Russia, later joined by Prussia in the War of the Fourth Coalition in the autumn of 1806. On 17 June 1807, a treaty was signed between Sweden and Britain, in accordance with which Sweden sent 10,000 troops along the river Oder, though these saw virtually no action. Even before Napoleon's decisive defeat of the Russians at Friedland on 14 June, Sweden called for a cease-fire on 18 April. Nevertheless, Gustavus terminated the cease-fire, precipitating a French attack on 13 July, which overran Swedish Pomerania after the siege of Stralsund. The Treaty of Tilsit between Napoleon and Tsar Alexander I of Russia, who abandoned the Fourth Coalition, stipulated that Sweden must break off its alliance with Britain and join the Continental System, which was intended to cut off British trade. As Gustavus refused to end his relationship with Britain, his country's major trading partner, Russia attacked Swedish Finland in 1808. By the following year the Russians had occupied Finland, a possession Sweden had controlled for almost 700 years.

The loss of Finland caused political reverberations for Sweden. Gustavus, by this time indisputably insane, was overthrown on 13 March 1809 in a coup that was staged by officers and members of the aristocracy. In December he went into exile in Germany, and then Switzerland, where he died penniless in February 1837. The Swedish parliament drafted a new constitution based on the Enlighten-

ment ideals of Montesquieu and on Swedish precedent. The 1809 constitution, which survived until 1975, limited the power of the monarchy by giving power to the Riksdag (parliament) and to the Royal Council. Subsequently, Gustavus IV's younger brother was elected king as Charles XIII on 5 June 1809. The problem of succession, however, was not resolved, for Charles XIII was childless. In addition to the problem of who would next occupy the Swedish throne, the greater problem lay in where the next king would lead Sweden. Because of the Napoleonic ascendancy in Europe, a Francophile faction gained influence in the government and believed that the best course for Sweden was to make an alliance with France.

The pro-French faction considered several candidates among Napoleon's marshals. The name that stood out particularly was Marshal Jean-Baptiste-Jules Bernadotte, for his genuine interest in the affairs of the Baltic nations and for the kindness he had shown to Swedish prisoners in 1807. Napoleon, his commanding officer and friend, encouraged him to pursue his candidacy to the Swedish throne, on the basis that he would close the Baltic ports to Britain, enhance French influence in Europe, and possibly ally his country to France—though the Emperor released him from his oath of allegiance and allowed him to foreswear his French nationality. In 1810 Bernadotte was elected Prince Royal of Sweden by the Riksdag and took the name Charles John, and in effect, became the power behind the throne. Sweden played a small part in the Allied coalition of 1813 in Germany, where the former French marshal-turned-king consistently declined to commit his troops in battle for fear of sustaining heavy casualties and risking disapprobation at home.

When Bernadotte assumed his new position and name—Crown Prince Charles John—he assured Russia that Sweden would not make any attempt to retake Finland. Instead, he looked westward to Norway, which was under Danish rule. Charles John believed that Norway would be better compensation for Sweden because of their long common frontier and because of Norway's long coastline with the North Sea. To forward his designs on Norway, Charles John concluded an alliance with Tsar Alexander in 1814 obtaining Russia's support, in exchange for territorial concessions regarding Finland. Napoleon's disastrous invasion of Russia gave Charles John the opportunity to act. In doing so, he turned his back on Napoleon by attacking Denmark, an ally of France. A combined Russo-Swedish force overwhelmed Danish troops in December 1813. On 14 January 1814, King Frederick VI of Denmark signed the Treaty of Kiel, which ceded Norway to Sweden. On 4 November, the Norwegian parliament voted to create a dynastic union with Sweden, with Charles John as king, but retaining its parliament and legal systems.

These arrangements were confirmed when, during the Congress of Vienna, Napoleon's victors accepted the union with Norway.

On 5 February 1818, Charles XIII died, and Jean-Baptiste-Jules Bernadotte, Crown Prince (Charles John) was proclaimed Charles XIV John, King of Sweden, of Norway, of the Goths, and of the Vandals. During the early years of his reign, Charles XIV John worked to secure the foundations of the new House of Bernadotte. He was constantly on his guard for assassination attempts by supporters of the descendants of Gustavus IV. During his coronation, he made sure of giving the appearance of continuity with the previous House of Vasa, which had ruled Sweden for almost 300 years. One of Charles XIV John's first actions as king was to secure a dynastic marriage in 1823 for his son, Oscar, to Josphine de Beauharnais, the granddaughter of Napoleon's first wife, the Empress Joseephine, who was also related to the Wittelsbach dynasty of Bavaria. On domestic policies, the reign of Charles XIV John was marked by conservatism on the part of the former Jacobin and by growing calls for liberalization, such as free speech, free trade, and civil liberties, among his subjects. Swedish foreign policy during the post-Napoleonic era was to take a neutral course between Britain and Russia. Charles XIV John died on 26 January 1844, beloved by his people. Peace and prosperity marked the reign of the first Bernadotte, whose ruling house was accepted by the Swedish people.

Dino E. Buenviaje

See also Alexander I, Tsar; Bernadotte, Jean-Baptiste-Jules; Continental System; Denmark; Finland; Fourth Coalition, War of the; Friedland, Battle of; Gustavus IV, King; Josephine, Empress; Norway; Russian Campaign; Russo-Swedish War; Stralsund, Siege of; Swedish Army; Swedish Navy; Third Coalition, War of the; Tilsit, Treaties of; Vienna, Congress of

References and further reading
Andersson, Ingvar. 1956. *A History of Sweden.* London: Weidenfeld and Nicolson.
Barton, H. Arnold. 2003. *Sweden and Visions of Norway: Politics and Culture 1814–1905.* Carbondale: Southern Illinois University Press.
Carr, Raymond. 1945. "Gustavus IV and the British Government, 1804–09." *English Historical Review* 60:36–66.
Elgström, Ole. 2000. *Images and Strategies for Autonomy: Explaining Swedish Security Policy Strategies in the 19th Century.* Dordrecht, Netherlands: Kluwer.
Jörgensen, Christer. 2004. *The Anglo-Swedish Alliance against Napoleonic France.* New York: Palgrave Macmillan.
Nordstrom, Byron. 2002. *The History of Sweden.* Westport, CT: Greenwood.
Palmer, Alan. 1990. *Bernadotte: Napoleon's Marshal, Sweden's King.* London: John Murray.
Scott, Franklin D. 1988. *Sweden: The Nation's History.* Carbondale: Southern Illinois University Press.
Weibull, Jörgen. 1997. *Swedish History in Outline.* Trelleborg, Sweden: Skogs Boktryckeri AB.

Swedish Army

The Swedish Army was small but generally well equipped. At the start of the Napoleonic Wars, the army was hampered by the use of outdated tactics, and it was defeated in the 1808–1809 war against Russia. From 1813 Swedish forces formed part of the (Allied) Army of the North and fought at Leipzig.

The Swedish Army was composed of two parts: the regular army and regiments that could be called up in case of war. These regiments generally had regular officers and noncommissioned officers. There were twenty-four infantry regiments in total throughout the period. In general, the light troops were the best in the army. However, many of these skirmishing troops came from Finland and were not available to the army after 1808, when Finland was lost to Russia. The Swedish cavalry was made up of thirteen regiments, of which ten were dragoons, the rest hussars and guard units. The artillery was composed of four regiments with twenty batteries in total.

The Swedish army was first involved in Swedish Pomerania in 1805. Here the army was seeking to hold the city of Stralsund. In 1806 Swedish troops were captured in an engagement with Prussian troops retreating from the advancing French. In 1808 the army fought a major campaign against the Russians in Finland. The Swedish army at this point had a strength of around 13,000 men. Although it won a series of small engagements, the army was not able to prevent the superior Russian forces from taking most of Finland. Swedish commanders relied on outdated tactics and were very conscious of protecting their supply lines, as a result of which their advances were always slow. The Swedes also possessed a poor system of intelligence, which led to their overestimation of the strength of the Russian forces. The war ended in 1809 and left Finland in Russian hands.

The next engagement of the Swedish army was in 1813, under the command of the former French marshal and new King of Sweden, Jean-Baptiste-Jules Bernadotte. Bernadotte led the Army of the North, of which the Swedes formed a part. It has often been suggested that Bernadotte deliberately protected the Swedish army from serious fighting—including at the great battle at Leipzig—an assertion generally borne out by the infrequency with which the Swedes were actually committed to battle. At Grossbeeren on 23 August, only the horse artillery commanded by Colonel Charles von Cardell were fully engaged, while the Swedish cavalry led by General Anders Frederik

Skjoldebrand fought at Dennewitz. At Roslau on 28 September, however, the Swedish army did fight an independent action. In this engagement, they showed that their tactical skills had considerably improved since 1808, so enabling them to force the French back. At Leipzig in October, the Swedish army was committed in the attack on Leipzig itself but only suffered about 200 casualties. Bernadotte thereafter employed Swedish forces in clearing northern Germany of the enemy and then turned his attentions toward Denmark. At Bornhöved, the Swedish cavalry led by Skjoldebrand made a fierce attack against a Danish force, and later Swedish troops were used to intimidate Norway into a union with Sweden.

Ralph Baker

See also Bernadotte, Jean-Baptiste-Jules; Dennewitz, Battle of; Finland; Germany, Campaign in; Grossbeeren, Battle of; Leipzig, Battle of; Norway; Russo-Swedish War; Stralsund, Siege of; Sweden

References and further reading
Cassin-Scott, Jack. 1976. *Scandinavian Armies in the Napoleonic Wars.* London: Osprey.
Nafziger, George. 1997. *Napoleon at Leipzig: The Battle of Nations, 1813.* Chicago: Emperor's.
Partridge, Richard, and Michael Oliver. 1999. *Napoleonic Army Handbook.* Vol. 1, *The British Army and Her Allies.* London: Constable and Robinson.
Petre, F. Loraine. 1992. *Napoleon's Last Campaign in Germany, 1813.* London: Greenhill.
Smith, Digby. 2004. *Armies of the Napoleonic Era.* Atglen, PA: Schiffer.

Swedish Navy

By the 1790s the previously renowned Swedish Navy was a shadow of its former self. The Baltic Sea is often shallow, has many dangerous rocks, and is bordered by a coastline of inlets, ideal for amphibious warfare. The Swedes had possessed two fleets: one was for high seas operations, the other for combined operations with the army. The high seas fleet (*Orlogs Flottan*) of 1808 consisted of seventeen men-of-war, of which eleven carried 64 guns or more. The ships for the coastal fleet (the army fleet, *Armens Flottan*) were shallow draught galleys and similar rowed boats.

The galleys were able to sail, but the oars were a necessary addition for the type of war contemplated: moving troops along the Baltic coast for raiding purposes. This fleet was to fight the equivalent Russian force, to support Swedish land forces with men, guns, and supplies, and to transport the army when needed. The fleet comprised two squadrons in 1788 (one at Stockholm, one at Helsingfors), with a total of some 143 galleys and similar vessels plus support craft.

The war against Russia of 1788–1790 was the result of King Gustavus III's need to increase his popularity at home: It was a dismal failure from the start, when the fleet ran away from the Russians at Hogland. Peace followed in 1790, and the Swedish fleet saw no further action until 1808–1809, once more against Russia. After the loss of much of their fleet after the capitulation of Sveaborg, the Swedes decided to build a new fleet.

Russia had, in agreeing to the Treaty of Tilsit in 1807, accepted the task of persuading the Swedes to join the Napoleonic anti-British blockade known as the Continental System, but Sweden refused to agree, and remained opposed to Napoleon. This unwillingness to comply with the Russians resulted in the war of 1808. In the war the Swedes attempted to retake the Åland Peninsula, but they lost to the Russians, despite putting up a good fight. They lost again in the Battle of Sandström after two days of fighting. The Russians also defeated the army, and Russian occupation of Finland became a fact. Interestingly, the Swedes then engaged in guerrilla warfare, the units sometimes cooperating with the Swedish fleet and the army. With the winter of 1808–1809, however, guerrilla resistance ended.

The only time that the Swedish navy encountered any success was when operating with the Royal Navy in 1808, when the Russians were bottled up in Baltischport in Estonia for a time.

Because of this disastrous war against the Russians and extra conscription, King Gustavus IV (who ascended the throne in 1792) was ousted from power in a coup d'état, and Sweden also lost control over Finland. The result was that Sweden no longer had any military power to speak of and spent the rest of the Napoleonic Wars reordering itself internally, especially after the French marshal Jean-Baptiste Bernadotte was elected king.

David Westwood

See also Bernadotte, Jean-Baptiste-Jules; Continental System; Finland; Gustavus IV, King; Russo-Swedish War; Sweden; Swedish Army; Tilsit, Treaties of

References and further reading
Haythornthwaite, Philip J. 1990. *The Napoleonic Source Book.* London: Guild.
Smith, Digby. 2004. *Navies of the Napoleonic Era.* Atglen, PA: Schiffer.
Stenzel, Alfred. 1911. *Seekriegsgeschichte.* 5 vols. Hannover: Pemsel.

Swiss Forces

Fighting on the side of the French, the Swiss provided Napoleon with the services of four infantry regiments plus various other units during his various campaigns. They were widely known for their excellent discipline and marksmanship, and particularly distinguished themselves during the Russian campaign in 1812.

Swiss regiments had historically fought as mercenaries in the armies of other nations, including that of France, long before the French Revolution. During the Revolution, the Swiss Guards of Louis XVI were massacred at the Tuileries on 10 August 1792. Eventually the Swiss took the side of the Revolution, forming the Helvetic Republic. Napoleon negotiated a convention with the Swiss in 1803. The agreement stated that the Swiss would provide four regiments to France, but no troops to any other nation. Swiss troops would be paid the same rate as French troops, and enjoy the same privileges. In addition, each Swiss regiment would have one Catholic and one Protestant chaplain, an unusual arrangement unknown in most of Napoleon's forces. The uniforms of the Helvetic Republic had been blue, but the Swiss reverted to red uniforms, which they had traditionally worn. The style, cut, and insignia of the uniforms would be the same as for French uniforms, except for the basic red color of the jackets. Each regiment would be distinguished by contrasting colors on collars and cuffs, yellow for the 1st, royal blue for the 2nd, black for the 3rd, and sky blue for the 4th.

The 1st Regiment was fully organized by 1805. The other three regiments were ready in 1806. Napoleon also had a separate agreement with the canton of Valais, which provided him with one infantry battalion wearing red uniforms faced with white. This battalion served in Spain until 1810, when Valais was incorporated into the French Empire. In addition, Napoleon's chief of staff, Marshal Louis-Alexandre Berthier, was given the principality of Neuchâtel, and formed a battalion of troops wearing chamois uniforms faced with red. The Neuchâtel battalion (nicknamed "the Canaries") saw service in Spain and guarded Berthier's headquarters on other campaigns. The other Swiss regiments fought mostly in Spain, and also in Naples.

The Swiss regiments formed part of Marshal Nicolas Oudinot's corps for the invasion of Russia in 1812. They fought well in several engagements, but were not at Borodino. The Swiss joined the main column during the retreat from Moscow, and helped save the survivors of Napoleon's army at the crossing of the Berezina River. The Swiss fought stubbornly there as part of the rear guard, making bayonet charges after expending their ammunition. Almost wiped out by the campaigns of 1812 and 1813, there were still some Swiss troops fighting in defense of France during the Allied invasion of 1814. One Swiss battalion fought at Wavre in 1815. Consistently neutral since the Napoleonic Wars, Switzerland no longer provides troops to other nations, with the exception of the Swiss Guard of the Vatican.

Ralph Ashby

See also Berezina, Actions and Crossing at the; Berthier, Louis-Alexandre; France, Campaign in; Germany, Campaign in; Louis XVI, King; Oudinot, Nicolas Charles; Peninsular War; Russian Campaign; Switzerland; Wavre, Battle of

References and further reading
Dempsey, Guy. 2002. *Napoleon's Mercenaries: Foreign Units in the French Army under the Consulate and Empire, 1799–1814*. London: Greenhill.
Elting, John R. 1988. *Swords around a Throne*. New York: Free Press.
Smith, Digby. 2004. *Armies of the Napoleonic Era*. London: Schiffer.

Switzerland

On the eve of the French Revolution, the Swiss Confederation constituted a loose federation of thirteen virtually sovereign cantons, "allied districts," and "subject districts," ruled by various cantons. That confederation possessed no central government, no uniform administration, no army, and no unified law. Each province had its own government, legal system, and administration. Urban oligarchies dominated the cantons, possessing feudal privileges. A diet, with representatives from various cantons and their allies, met to discuss common interests such as war and commercial treaties.

The Swiss Confederation remained neutral during the War of the First Coalition. However, after 1795, the Directory began interfering in its internal affairs. Swiss expatriate liberals such as Frederick Laharpe and Peter Ochs, who supported the French Revolution and the formation of a united Swiss state, favored French intervention. Bonaparte, who visited Switzerland in 1797, urged the Directory to intervene in that country to gain control over the mountain passes. He also called for the formation of a united Switzerland.

In early 1798, revolts in a number of cantons, most notably the uprising in Vaud against Berne, provided France with an excuse to intervene and "liberate" those areas. The French invaded Switzerland in support of Vaud, and in March 1798 General Guillaume Brune occupied Berne. The French used Berne's sizable treasury to finance Bonaparte's Egyptian expedition. In April, Geneva was annexed to France. Berne's collapse marked the dissolution of the Swiss Confederation. A new Helvetic Republic, "one and indivisible," was proclaimed in April 1798. From then until 1813, Switzerland was a French protectorate.

A new liberal constitution, modeled on the 1795 French constitution, laid the foundation of modern Switzerland. It set up a Directory and a bicameral legislature and proclaimed legal equality, civic liberties, and the right of private property. It established, for the first time, a common Swiss citizenship and universal manhood suffrage. Internal tolls and customs were removed. The cantons lost their traditional independence and became administrative units run by prefects. The number of cantons rose to eighteen when the former subject regions became cantons. The new Helvetic government abolished feudal dues and ecclesiastical privileges and confiscated Church possessions. The authorities created a single currency, the Swiss franc, reorganized the tax system, rescinded guild restrictions, and secularized education.

The Helvetic Republic, however, experienced economic difficulties and faced political opposition. French impositions and heavy requisitions caused fiscal hardships. A revolt by several cantons was crushed by French troops. In August 1798, France compelled Switzerland to sign a treaty of alliance, forcing it to supply troops, financial support, and free passage through its territory.

In 1799, Switzerland became a theater of operations during the War of the Second Coalition. That coalition aimed at expelling France from Switzerland, a goal supported by Swiss aristocrats. In early June, the Austrian Archduke Charles forced General André Masséna to evacuate Zürich and occupied the city. The Austrians were reluctant, however, to get involved in internal Swiss politics, and Charles withdrew to Germany. Masséna then defeated the Russian general Alexander Rimsky-Korsakov in the second Battle of Zürich (September 1799), thereby saving the Helvetic Republic. Yet the invading armies ravaged much of its territory, and heavy French taxes aggravated the economic crisis. Deep divisions between the pro-French Unitarians and the federalists, the latter of whom favored a weak central government and the restoration of the cantons' powers, caused considerable instability. A series of coups and constitutional changes marked that period.

Following the Treaty of Amiens (March 1802), Bonaparte ordered French troops to withdraw temporarily from Switzerland. The French evacuation weakened the Helvetic government, and a federalist revolt forced it to evacuate Berne. Twelve rebelling cantons formed a new federal diet. In September 1802, Bonaparte ordered his army back to Switzerland in support of the government, forcing the rebel diet to disperse.

Bonaparte was now determined to impose a settlement to guarantee stability and French control. He summoned a Helvetic committee of delegates of both parties to Paris to discuss a new constitution. The outcome was the Mediation Act, which Bonaparte ratified on 19 February 1803. The Mediation Act ended the Helvetic Republic and restored the federal system, comprising nineteen nearly sovereign cantons. A feeble federal diet constituted the central government. The chief magistrate, the *Landamman,* was in charge of foreign policy and internal security. Each canton provided a quota of troops and paid its share of military costs. Freedom of speech and faith disappeared, yet the Mediation Act reaffirmed legal equality and the freedom of Swiss citizens to dwell and own property anywhere. Bonaparte endorsed the principle of cantonal autonomy and the restoration of the former ruling elites who, in return, recognized his supremacy.

The Mediation Act period (1803–1813) was marked by stability and conservatism. The urban aristocracies secured their power in the major cities of Berne, Lucerne, Fribourg, Solothurn, Basle, and Zürich. The authorities returned confiscated church land, reopened monasteries, and reestablished internal tolls. Various cantonal authorities regulated the morals of their citizens' lives. Internal stability and autonomy enabled cantonal governments to launch reform programs. They set up uniform administrative and judicial structures, established local police, maintained roads, stabilized finances, and managed welfare programs. Swiss education was viewed as a principal task of the state and became a model throughout Europe. The school founded in Yverdun by Henry Pestalozzi gained considerable esteem. The authorities also launched important public works.

While Switzerland remained officially independent and neutral, in reality it was a Napoleonic satellite. Napoleon ran its foreign and military policy and controlled the Landamman. In 1809, Napoleon became "Mediator of the Swiss Confederation." Switzerland had to abide by the Continental System (the French-imposed embargo of continental trade with Britain), despite the grave damage to its economy, especially to its textile industry. The Emperor also reduced the Confederation's territory. He gave Neuchâtel to Marshal Louis-Alexandre Berthier as a fief, ordered Italian troops to occupy the canton of Ticino, and annexed the Valais to his empire. Out of 9,000 Swiss troops who marched into Russia, only 700 survived.

The Swiss government sided with Napoleon until his defeat at Leipzig. Switzerland then declared its neutrality and withdrew from the Continental System. In December 1813, a large Austro-Bavarian army invaded Switzerland, bringing to an end the Mediation Act's regime and French influence. In September 1814, with the admission of Valais, Neuchâtel, and Geneva to the Confederation, the number of cantons rose to twenty-two. A few days before Waterloo, Switzerland formally joined the coalition against Napoleon. In August 1815, after lengthy discussions, a new constitution, the so-called Federal Pact, was proclaimed, restoring much of the old system. It endowed the cantons with full sovereignty and established a diet with limited power. The Congress of Vienna recognized Swiss neutrality and ratified the cantonal borders.

Alexander Grab

See also Amiens, Treaty of; Berthier, Louis-Alexandre; Brune, Guillaume-Marie-Anne; Charles, Archduke of Austria, Duke of Teschen; Continental System; Directory, the; Leipzig, Battle of; Masséna, André; Middle East Campaign; Rimsky-Korsakov, Alexander Mikhailovich; Russian Campaign; Second Coalition, War of the; Swiss Forces; Switzerland, Campaign in; Vienna, Congress of; Zürich, First Battle of; Zürich, Second Battle of

References and further reading
Chapuisat, Edouard. 1908. Le commerce et l'industrie à Genève pendant la domination française, 1798–1813. Geneva: Julien.
Guillon, Edouard. 1910. Napoléon et la Suisse, 1803–1815. Paris: Lausanne Plon.
Suratteau, Jean. 1969. "Occupation, occupants et occupés en Suisse de 1792 à 1814." In Occupants, Occupés, 1792–1815. Brussels: Université Libre de Bruxelles.

Switzerland, Campaign in (1799)

The series of battles fought in the area in 1799 formed part of the War of the Second Coalition. The fighting centered on French attempts to control Zürich. There were a number of separate engagements at this city. The Austrians and French were the main protagonists in the area, but in late 1799 Field Marshal Alexander Suvorov led a Russian army into the theater.

The war in Switzerland began as a result of the activities of the Second Coalition formed against the French. The coalition was formally completed in June 1799 with an Austro-British alliance, though it had begun the previous December with an Anglo-Russian alliance. Ranged against the French were the states of Britain, Austria, Russia, Naples, and the Ottoman Empire (Turkey). Marshal André Masséna, in his first independent command, led the 34,000-strong (French) Army of Switzerland. It was intended that Masséna should attack the Austrian commander Feldmarschalleutnant Johann Freiherr von Hotze. General Barthélemy Schérer with the (French) Army of Italy was to support the right of Masséna's advance. Masséna advanced to the upper Rhine in order to threaten Vorarlberg. He assembled his forces near Sargans on 2 March in order to cross the river. He ordered sappers to build a bridge and attacked across the river on 6 March.

Masséna then ordered the storming of the fort at St. Luzisteig. Advancing further, the French took the town of Chur and around 3,000 Austrian prisoners. However, Masséna was finding it difficult to supply his troops and was unable to advance farther. His position was made worse by the fact that Archduke Charles had defeated General Jean-Baptiste Jourdan at Stockach on 25 March and the Austrian general Feldmarschalleutnant Paul Kray Freiherr von Krajova had pushed Schérer back around Verona.

The Allies were then reinforced by a Russian army led by Suvorov, totaling around 25,000. Due to his reputation, Suvorov assumed command of the Allied forces in the area. Masséna was given command of the remnants of Jourdan's and Schérer's armies.

In May Archduke Charles attacked Masséna's forces. He first retook Chur and then crossed the Rhine, threatening the communications of the French. Masséna launched a successful counterattack, but then withdrew his forces to a defensive position around Zürich, which he had fortified earlier. By the start of June, the Austrians were in a position to attack. The main attack came on 4 June against the 650-meter Zürichberg hill. The Austrian assault failed with Hotze, one of the Austrian generals, wounded. Masséna believed that he could not hold Zürich and withdrew to higher ground to the north. The Allies occupied Zürich and now dominated northern Switzerland. However, Masséna gradually received reinforcements and more importantly a formidable array of aggressive junior officers. Principal among these were generals Adolphe Mortier and Nicolas Soult, both future marshals under Napoleon.

At Novi in Italy, the French were once more defeated, which meant that a new strategy could be formulated. The Allies decided that Russian forces would unite in Switzerland and then strike westward into France. From the south, Suvorov was to march through the southern alpine passes, while General Alexander Rimsky-Korsakov was to advance into Switzerland from the north, having moved through Germany. Suvorov was not convinced that this was the best strategy, but offered no resistance, due to the fact that he believed that the morale of the French armies was weakening. Archduke Charles left Switzerland, leaving only Hotze before Zürich until Rimsky-Korsakov arrived. Masséna saw his chance to strike at the Allied armies before they were able to unite against him. Masséna ordered a division to contest Suvorov's advance through the St. Gotthard Pass and turned the full weight of his army against Rimsky-Korsakov.

On 25 September Masséna attacked the Russians, Mortier's division leading the main attack. The French division commanded by General Jean Thomas Lorge was ordered to cross the river Limmat and sweep round to the north of Zürich to threaten any Russian retreat. By the early afternoon, the Russian forces were mainly crowded in front of the gates of Zürich, making a perfect target for the French. Rimsky-Korsakov withdrew his forces inside the walls, though he soon decided that the town could not be held and continued to withdraw. Masséna ordered his forces to pursue the enemy, and Rimsky-Korsakov's withdrawal degenerated into a rout. This attack effectively destroyed Rimsky-Korsakov's command, with the Russians losing many guns and over 8,000 men.

Soult had also attacked the Austrians under Hotze at the eastern end of Lake Zürich on the same day. His target was Uznach, which formed the junction between the Russian and Austrian forces. The heavy mist that filled the valleys helped the French attack. In the middle of the attack, while Hotze was leading reinforcements to strengthen the Austrian line, he was shot dead. The disheartened Austrians were defeated, with the loss of almost 6,000 men.

Suvorov meanwhile had stormed the St. Gotthard Pass on 25 September. The French then fought a number of delaying actions to impede Suvorov's advance. He joined an Austrian force at Glarus led by *Generalmajor* Fürst Franz von Rosenberg-Orsini and *Feldmarschalleutnant* Franz Xavier Auffenberg. It was at this point that Suvorov heard of the defeats that had been suffered at Zürich. In a council of war it was decided that the Allied forces must strike to the east before they were surrounded. Rosenberg fought a two-day battle in the Muotatal valley against forces under Mortier's command. However, his victory did little to improve the situation of the Allies. Three French columns were now advancing on Glarus, and Suvorov had to extricate his forces once more. The Russians reached Chur by 10 October, but had lost almost one-fifth of the force that had begun the campaign in September. This was effectively the end of the campaign, as the tsar ordered the return of Suvorov's army.

Ralph Baker

See also Charles, Archduke of Austria, Duke of Teschen; Jourdan, Jean-Baptiste; Kray, Paul Freiherr von Krajova; Masséna, André; Mortier, Adolphe Edouard Casimir Joseph; Novi, Battle of; Rimsky-Korsakov, Alexander Mikhailovich; Schérer, Barthélemy Louis Joseph; Second Coalition, War of the; Soult, Nicolas Jean de Dieu; St. Gotthard Pass, Action at the; Stockach, First Battle of; Suvorov, Alexander Vasilievich; Switzerland; Zürich, First Battle of; Zürich, Second Battle of

References and further reading
Blanning, Tim. 1996. *The French Revolutionary Wars, 1787–1802.* London: Hodder and Arnold.
Duffy, Christopher. 1999. *Eagles over the Alps: Suvorov in Italy and Switzerland, 1799.* Chicago: Emperor's.
Nafziger, George. 1996. *Imperial Bayonets.* London: Greenhill.
Nosworthy, Brent. 1997. *Battle Tactics of Napoleon and his Enemies.* London: Constable and Robinson.
Rothenberg, Gunther. 1995. *Napoleon's Great Adversaries: The Archduke Charles and the Austrian Army, 1792–1814.* London: Spellmount.

Swords

See Cavalry; Infantry

T

Talavera, Battle of (27–28 July 1809)

The first major encounter for the British in Spain during the Peninsular War, Talavera was fought between French forces under the nominal command of King Joseph Bonaparte—with de facto command resting with Marshal Jean-Baptiste Jourdan—and a British and Spanish force under Lieutenant General Sir Arthur Wellesley (later the Duke of Wellington) and General Gregorio García de la Cuesta, respectively. The Allies achieved a defensive victory, albeit one expensively bought.

Having driven Marshal Nicolas Soult from Portugal, Wellesley (who became Viscount Wellington after this battle) looked to the south, toward Marshal Claude Victor, whose force was concentrated in and around the old Roman town of Mérida. His Spanish allies were frustratingly difficult to get on with, as Lieutenant General Sir John Moore had found to his cost the previous year. In spite of this it was agreed that the British army should cooperate with the Spaniards in a joint operation against Victor's force. In fact, so eager were the Spaniards about the plan that they agreed not only to feed Wellesley's army but also to provide much-needed transport for it. This having been agreed upon, Wellesley crossed the border into Spain and marched his army to a prearranged area of concentration, north of the Tagus at Plasencia.

Victor's 20,000 men, meanwhile, had moved northeast from Mérida to Talavera, where he hoped to unite with other French forces under General Horace Sébastiani, who had 22,000 men at Madridejos, and Joseph Bonaparte, king of Spain, in command of a further 12,000 men at Madrid. In theory, this move would allow the French to field a combined army of around 50,000 men, all of whom were tried and tested soldiers. Against this Wellesley and Cuesta, the Spanish commander, could field 55,000, of whom 35,000 were Spanish.

Wellesley's doubts as to the merits of the Spaniards surfaced fairly soon, as did his frustrations when they failed to fulfill any of their promises regarding transport and supplies. And when he rode south to Almaraz to inspect the Spanish army, Wellesley was more than a little disillusioned when he saw the poor condition of their arms and equipment.

The seventy-year-old Cuesta himself gave little cause for optimism, and he adopted a singularly belligerent attitude toward his British ally as a result of which many hours were lost as the two men argued over the strategy to be employed against the French. Eventually, Wellesley and Cuesta agreed to unite their armies at Oropesa, about 30 miles west of Talavera.

The two forces duly met as planned on 20 July, and three days later had a perfect opportunity to attack Victor, who had yet to meet either Sébastiani or Joseph and who was outnumbered by just over two to one. Cuesta refused to move, however, and the chance was lost. He did agree to attack at dawn on the twenty-fourth, although by then, of course, Victor had retired toward Madrid.

Wellesley was naturally furious, and when a buoyant Cuesta decided to set off in pursuit of Victor, it was Wellesley's turn to refuse to budge. He had good reason, as intelligence reports showed that the French were only days away from uniting, which would give them a combined strength of 50,000 men. Nonetheless, Cuesta gave chase and was predictably mauled by Victor's veterans on the twenty-fifth.

By 27 July Wellesley had positioned his army a few miles to the west of the Alberche River, which flows north from the Tagus just east of Talavera. Later that day, he narrowly avoided capture while carrying out a reconnaissance from the top of the Casa de Salinas, a semifortified building on the left bank of the Alberche. As he peered out in the direction of the French army, he just caught sight of a party of French light infantry, stealing around the corner of the building. He rushed down the stairs, mounted his horse, and rode hell for leather away from the building, followed by a couple of volleys from the enemy infantry. It was the first of a couple of occasions in the Peninsular War when Wellesley narrowly avoided capture, the other notable occasion being at Sorauren in 1813.

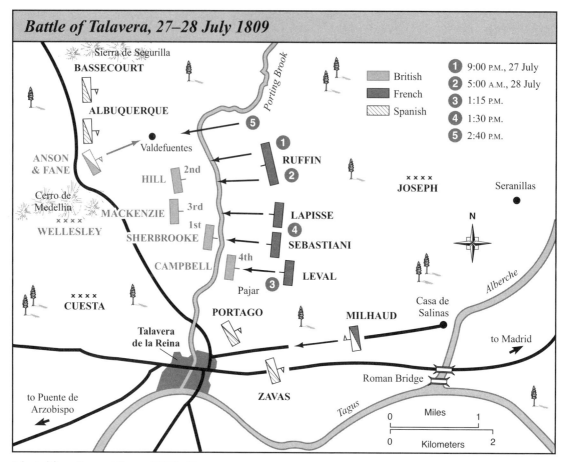

Adapted from Fremont-Barnes 2002A, 43.

There was some skirmishing throughout the rest of the day, including the celebrated incident during the evening involving four battalions of Spanish infantry who, when "threatened" by some distant French cavalry, let loose a shattering volley before running away at the sound of their own muskets, stopping only to plunder the British baggage train.

That night Wellesley had drawn his army up along a front stretching north to south from the heights of Segurilla to Talavera itself. On the right were positioned Cuesta's 35,000 Spaniards, the right flank resting upon Talavera, being the strongest part of the line. The left flank of the British line rested upon the Cerro de Medellín, a large hill that dominated the landscape, separated from the heights of Segurilla by a wide, flat valley nearly a mile wide. In front of the Allied position, and directly opposite the Cerro de Medellín, was the Cerro de Cascajal, which was soon to become the center of the French position, and between the two hills, running along the valley between them, was a small stream called the Portina.

The sun had long since gone down when, at around ten o'clock, under the cover of darkness, an entire French division stole across the Portina and fell upon the British and King's German Legion troops (Hanoverians, abbreviated as KGL), on and at the foot of the Medellín, who were dozing off after a hard day in the field. The French advanced in three columns, one of which got lost and, failing to find any of its objectives, returned to the main French line. The other two columns, however, caused a great deal of panic in the British lines and at one point even occupied the summit of the Medellín after managing to completely pass by Colonel Rufane Shaw Donkin's brigade, which occupied the forward slopes of the hill.

It was during this confusion that Major General Rowland Hill almost got himself captured when, riding forward to investigate with his brigade major, he found himself confronted by a number of French skirmishers, one of whom tried to drag Hill from his horse. The two British officers quickly turned tail and rode off, but the brigade major was killed when the French opened fire. Hill then brought forward Brigadier General Richard Stewart's brigade of the 2nd Division, among which was the 29th Foot, which drove the French from the summit amid a blaze of musketry. The situation was eventually restored, and the French returned to their original positions having lost about 300 men, the British losing a similar number.

A single French gun, fired in the gloom at about five o'clock on the morning of 28 July, signaled the beginning of the main French attack. The gun triggered off a rippling fire that rolled along the French position from about sixty of their guns. On the Medellín, Wellesley's men were ordered to lie down as enemy cannonballs came bouncing in among them, while on the slopes of the hill British gunners worked at their own guns in reply.

From his position high on the Medellín, which was shrouded in smoke, Wellesley could see nothing of what was going on below, but the sounds—soon to become so familiar to him and his army—were unmistakable. Large numbers of French sharpshooters were pushing back his own skirmish lines, though Wellesley's light companies and riflemen disputed every yard of broken ground. The French came on in three columns, each three battalions strong, altogether numbering nearly 4,500 men from General François Ruffin's division. The most northerly of the columns, moving to the north of the Medellín, exchanged fire at long range with the 29th but went no farther. The other two columns, however, hit that part of the British line on the Medellín that was held by Stewart's and Major General Christopher Tilson's brigades. As at Vimeiro, the French attack was hampered by its formation, and the outnumbered British brigades easily outgunned the French columns, sweeping them with fire and forcing them to a standstill. French attempts to deploy into line proved futile and impossible amid the concentrated, controlled platoon fire from the 29th and 48th Regiments. After just a few minutes, those at the back and in the middle of the French columns, unable to see what was happening up front but aware that something very unpleasant was occurring to their comrades, decided not to wait and see for themselves but simply melted away to the rear, very few of them having fired any shot in anger. Ruffin's attack had ended in failure, and his beaten battalions were pursued for a short distance across the Portina, having suffered over a thousand casualties.

The initial French attack having been repulsed by 7:00 A.M., the battle lapsed into a duel between the two sides' artillery. This lasted for just an hour, and no more serious fighting occurred for another five hours, during which both sides quenched their thirst at the Portina brook and took advantage of the lull to collect their wounded.

At one o'clock in the afternoon, the peace was shattered by another French artillery barrage, which heralded a large-scale infantry assault on the right of Wellesley's line around the Pajar, a semifortified farmhouse that marked the junction of the British and Spanish sectors of the Allied line. Laval's division numbered 4,500 men, who began to advance across the broken ground and through the olive groves to begin their attack on that part of Wellesley's line held by Campbell's 4th Division.

Again Laval's men attacked in three columns, each three battalions strong and supported by guns, but as had happened earlier in the day, his men found Campbell's musketry too hot to handle, and the French columns broke and fled before they did too much damage, having abandoned seventeen of their guns. Laval's attack was only the prelude to the main French attack, however, and shortly afterward, some eighty French guns were blazing away at the right center of the British line in an attempt to soften it up before the main infantry assault, which was delivered by no less than 15,000 seasoned troops under Sebastiani and General Pierre Lapisse.

It sounds rather repetitive to say that the French columnar formation gave the British line a distinct advantage, but that is exactly what happened—again. The twelve French battalions could bring only 1,300 muskets to bear on their British adversaries, some 6,000 men of Sherbrooke's 1st Division, among which were some of the best troops in the army, the Foot Guards and the King's German Legion. The irresistible and pulverizing firepower of these troops was turned on the French to devastating effect, and soon enough the French veterans were streaming back across the Portina. However, three of the brigades who had seen them off, including the Guards and the Hanoverians, were carried away with their success and, pursuing them too far, were in turn severely mauled by the French, large numbers of whom were still fresh. Sherbrooke's men returned to the British line in a sorry state, particularly the Foot Guards, who had lost 611 men.

This misadventure caused a large gap in the Allied center upon which some 22,000 French cavalry and infantry bore down with relish. There was no second Allied line, and Wellesley could spare only a single battalion to plug the gap. It was a major crisis. Fortunately, the battalion, the 1/48th (first battalion, 48th Foot), was the strongest in the army, but it still had to face a French attack of overwhelming numerical strength. The 48th was supported by the three battalions of Major General Alexander Mackenzie's brigade, which were moved slightly to their left to join the 1/48th. These battalions, numbering around 3,000 men, opened their ranks to let in the survivors of the Guards who formed up behind them and with a great cheer announced their intention to rejoin the battle.

The British troops waited silently in line as the French came noisily on, British 6-pounder guns tearing gaps in their columns as they did so. Lapisse's battalions had advanced to within just fifty yards when nearly 3,000 nervous British fingers twitched on the triggers of their Brown Bess muskets and whole files of Frenchmen came crashing to the ground amid rolls of thick gray smoke. The shattered French columns shuddered to a halt in the face of the savage onslaught. A series of withering volleys ripped into them at the rate of four every minute, and although they stood to exchange fire with Mackenzie's men the French could not match the firepower of their enemies. In the face of such an onslaught, in which the Guards and the 14th Light Dragoons joined in, Lapisse's battalions broke and fled back across the Portina, leaving some 1,700 of their comrades behind them to mark their failure.

All French attacks to the south of and directly at the Medellín had resulted in bloody failure, and the French troops watching from the Cascajal did not wish to renew the attack in this part of the field. It was decided, therefore, to test the mettle of Wellesley's left flank to the north of the Medellín, Ruffin's infantry division being the instrument of this test. The nine battalions of Ruffin's division had already been heavily engaged the night before and on the morning of the twenty-eighth itself, and the men showed little inclination to attack in any positive manner, a reluctance not unnoticed by Wellesley, who decided to launch his cavalry against them.

Ruffin's columns advanced amid heavy shelling from the Allied artillery, and when Brigadier General George Anson's cavalry brigade, consisting of the 23rd Light Dragoons and 1st KGL Light Dragoons, was spotted advancing along the floor of the valley to the north of the Medellín, the French formed square, which provided an even better target for the guns. Anson's cavalry advanced in a controlled manner against the French, who were still a good distance away. However, this disciplined ride was not to last for too long, for the 23rd Light Dragoons were about to provide the British army with the second of its great cavalry fiascos of the war.

For no apparent reason, the British light dragoons suddenly broke into a full gallop, whereas the KGL light dragoons held back, keeping up a gentle pace. The 23rd Light Dragoons, under the command of Major Frederick Ponsonby, suddenly came up against a small, dry river bed, which was a tributary of the Portina. The cutting was deep and wide, and, while not the sort of ravine that it has often been called, it was nonetheless a serious obstacle for a cavalry regiment to negotiate at full speed. The first ranks crashed headlong into the cutting, while others tried in vain to leap across to the other side. It was a classic "steeplechase," in which scores of men and horses were lost, the majority with badly broken arms and legs. Those who were lucky enough to negotiate the cutting then found themselves vastly outnumbered by French chasseurs, who set about the blown and disorganized light dragoons with relish. Ponsonby's men rallied and fought as best they could, but they were overwhelmed and forced back to their own lines having lost half of their number. The 1st KGL Light Dragoons, on the other hand, had come on at an easier pace and took the cutting in their stride. Their own attack failed to break any of the French infantry squares, and they too retired to their original position. However, the two cavalry attacks, combined with the constant shelling from the Allied artillery, caused Ruffin's wavering division to turn about and return to the Cascajal.

Although there were still three hours of daylight left, there was no further serious fighting, and as darkness fell, Wellesley's men camped on the ground they occupied around the Medellín, expecting a resumption of the battle the next day. However, when dawn broke on the twenty-ninth, the British troops peered out across the valley to see that Victor's army had retired, leaving Wellesley in possession of the field.

It had been a bloody battle, which had resulted in some 5,365 British casualties. The French themselves had lost 7,268. Cuesta's Spaniards had held the right flank of the Allied position throughout the day but had hardly been involved in any of the fighting, and their loss was trifling.

The victory at Talavera had earned for Wellesley the title Baron Douro and Viscount Wellington. There were few other comforts to be derived from the battle, however, as captured dispatches showed the French to be far more numerous than had been thought. On 3 August Wellington and his army were at Oropesa, but news that Soult was close by at Navalmoral, threatening to cut him off from Portugal, prompted a quick retirement upon Badajoz on the Spanish-Portuguese border.

Ian Fletcher

See also Bonaparte, Joseph; García de la Cuesta, Gregorio; Hanoverian Army; Hill, Sir Rowland; Jourdan, Jean-Baptiste; Moore, Sir John; Peninsular War; Soult, Nicolas Jean de Dieu; Victor, Claude Perrin; Vimeiro, Battle of; Wellington, Arthur Wellesley, First Duke of

References and further reading
Edwards, Peter. 2005. *Talavera: Wellington's Early Peninsula Victories, 1808–09.* Ramsbury, UK: Crowood.
Esdaile, Charles J. 2003. *The Peninsular War: A New History.* London: Palgrave Macmillan.
Gates, David. 2001. *The Spanish Ulcer: A History of the Peninsular War.* New York: Da Capo.
Glover, Michael. 2001. *The Peninsular War, 1807–1814: A Concise Military History.* London: Penguin.
Napier, W. F. P. 1992. *A History of the War in the Peninsula.* 6 vols. London: Constable. (Orig. pub. 1828.)
Oman, Sir Charles. 2005. *A History of the Peninsular War.* 7 vols. London: Greenhill. (Orig. pub. 1902–1930.)
Paget, Julian. 1992. *Wellington's Peninsular War: Battles and Battlefields.* London: Leo Cooper.
Uffindell, Andrew. 2003. *The National Army Museum Book of Wellington's Armies: Britain's Triumphant Campaigns in the Peninsula and at Waterloo, 1808–1815.* London: Sedgwick and Jackson.
Weller, Jac. 1992. *Wellington in the Peninsula.* London: Greenhill.

Talleyrand-Périgord, Charles-Maurice de, prince (1754–1838)

French foreign minister and statesman. Talleyrand was born to an ancient noble family of Périgord on 2 February 1754. Neglected by his family, he suffered a crippling accident in infancy when he broke his left foot, which remained deformed and forced him to wear a heavy brace to support his leg for the rest of his life. The accident also prevented him from pursuing a military career and compelled him to enter the church. He studied at the Collège de Harcourt and the Seminary of Saint-Sulpice and rapidly advanced through the church hierarchy; he became sub-deacon in 1775 and was ordained a priest in December 1779. In 1780 the Assembly of the Clergy chose him as one of the two agents general to manage ecclesiastical property. Using family influence, he later secured the position of vicar general of the diocese in Rheims, and in January 1789 he became the bishop of Autun. Throughout his service in the church, Talleyrand showed himself an independent spirit, enjoying worldly pleasures and sharing the ideas of the Enlightenment, even paying respect to one of the chief opponents of the Church, Voltaire himself. In April 1789 he was elected a representative of the clergy of Autun to the Estates-General and helped to prepare the cahiers of his constituency.

In the National Assembly Talleyrand took part in the committee working on the constitution and was instrumental in proposing the nationalization of Church lands in October 1789. Furthermore, he supported the Civil Constitution of the Clergy and was among the first to swear the civil oath. Denounced by the Church, he resigned his see in January 1791. The following year, Talleyrand made his debut in international politics, when he served on a diplomatic mission to London (January–May 1792). Returning to France, he witnessed the September Massacres of 1792 and obtained documents from Georges Danton to seek refuge in Britain. His property was confiscated in December 1792, and the British government expelled him from Britain in 1794. For the next two years, Talleyrand found refuge in the United States, where he lived in Philadelphia and was involved in various business transactions.

He was able to return to France only under the Directory in September 1796. Through his connections with Paul Barras, the most important member of the Directory, Talleyrand received the post of minister of foreign affairs in July 1797. He soon became notorious for his venality and his involvement in the infamous XYZ Affair, which resulted in the rupture of diplomatic relations with the United States and a two-year undeclared naval conflict known as the Quasi-War (1798–1800). In spite of this reputation Talleyrand proved himself a very capable and cun-

Prince Talleyrand. His exceptional capacity for intrigue and double-dealing enabled him to serve as foreign minister to both Napoleon and his successor, the restored Bourbon king, Louis XVIII. (Print after Henri Dupray, ca. 1890)

ning diplomat. Early on, he took notice of the rising star of General Napoleon Bonaparte and established close relations with him. In 1797–1798 he supported Bonaparte's plans for the expedition to Egypt and even promised to resign his post and travel on a peace mission to the Ottoman Empire.

In July 1799 Talleyrand tried to dissociate himself from the unpopular Directory and resigned his post of minister of foreign affairs. After Bonaparte's return from Egypt in October 1799, Talleyrand actively participated in the preparations for the coup d'état of 18–19 Brumaire (9–10 November) and personally persuaded Barras to resign. As First Consul, Bonaparte rewarded him with the position of minister of foreign affairs in December 1799. Talleyrand remained at this post for the next eight years and played an important role in conducting foreign policy in the service of Bonaparte (from 1804 known as Napoleon). He became the grand chamberlain of the Empire in 1804 and was granted the title of prince de Bénévent in 1806. Talleyrand actively took part in various business machinations that gained him huge financial advantage; he often demanded and received considerable kickbacks from the governments with which he negotiated. Talleyrand was involved in the duc d'Enghien incident in

1804, which involved the kidnapping and murder of a member of the Bourbon family, though he later denied any role in it. After 1807, in the wake of the Tilsit agreements, he disapproved of Napoleon's conquests and began secretly conspiring against him.

He resigned from the foreign ministry in 1807, but retained his titles; Napoleon, recognizing the value of Talleyrand's skill, continued to consult him on various issues, so Talleyrand remained actively involved in foreign policy. In 1808 he encouraged the overthrow of the Spanish Bourbon royal family, later confined at Talleyrand's château of Valençay. At Erfurt, Napoleon relied on Talleyrand to persuade Tsar Alexander to support France against Austria, but Talleyrand did exactly the opposite, urging him to oppose Napoleon. Furthermore, thereafter Talleyrand was on the payroll of the tsar, whom he secretly provided with crucial information on Napoleon's plans. In 1809 he clandestinely intrigued with Joseph Fouché, the minister of police, in Napoleon's absence from Paris. In 1810 he helped arrange Napoleon's marriage to Austrian princess Marie Louise.

Two years later, following the disastrous campaign in Russia, Napoleon offered Talleyrand the post of foreign minister, but the latter declined it. In 1814, as the Allies approached Paris, Talleyrand deftly maneuvered against Napoleon and persuaded the Senate to establish a provisional government, over which he presided. Talleyrand then convinced the government members to declare Napoleon deposed. After the Allies entered the capital, Alexander stayed at Talleyrand's house, and the latter convinced him that only the restoration of the Bourbons could guarantee peace in Europe. The Bourbon monarchy appointed him foreign minister in May 1814 and later the chief representative of France at the Congress of Vienna, where he fully demonstrated his diplomatic skills in an unequal struggle against the other European powers. He skillfully played off the Allies against each other, created a secret alliance between Austria, Britain, and France, and secured considerable concessions for France. During the Hundred Days in 1815, Talleyrand supported the Bourbons, and he was appointed president of the governing council, while retaining the office of foreign minister. However, he clashed with the ultra-royalists and resigned his post in September 1815.

For the next fifteen years, Talleyrand led a private life and worked on his memoirs. In 1817 he was granted the title of duc de Dino, which he transferred to his cousin. During the Revolution of 1830 he returned to politics one more time, helping Louis-Philippe to ascend the throne. At the age of seventy-six, he was appointed ambassador to London, where he played an important role in negotiations over the creation of Belgium in 1830. His last diplomatic achievement was the signing of an alliance between France, Britain, Spain, and Portugal in April 1834. After his return to France,

his health rapidly deteriorated, and he died in Paris on 17 May 1838. He was buried at his château at Valençay.

Talleyrand was an extraordinary diplomat, and his career continues to amaze. He served successive French regimes for over four decades and successfully outmaneuvered most of them. He led the French foreign ministry for more than a decade and played a crucial role throughout the Empire and Restoration. In his memoirs, he claimed that his changes in allegiance always served the interests of France, though he also profited greatly. Napoleon had once believed Talleyrand was the most capable minister he had, but he later changed his opinion, describing him as "*merde dans un bas de soie*" (s— in a silk stocking; quoted in Cooper 2001, 187) on a famous occasion in 1809.

On a minor note, in 1785 Talleyrand had a liaison with Adelaïde de Flahaut and sired a son, Charles de Flahaut. Charles later became a lover of Queen Hortense de Beauharnais of Holland and fathered a son, the duc de Morny, the half-brother of Emperor Napoleon III.

Alexander Mikaberidze

See also Alexander I, Tsar; Barras, Paul Jean François Nicolas, vicomte de; Bayonne, Conference at; Consulate, The; Directory, The; Enghien, Louis Antoine Henri de Bourbon-Condé, duc d'; Erfurt, Congress of; Ferdinand VII, King; Fouché, Joseph, duc d'Otrante; Louis XVIII, King; Marie Louise, Empress; Middle East Campaign; Russian Campaign; Tilsit, Treaties of; Vienna, Congress of

References and further reading
Beau, André. 1998. *Talleyrand: L'apogée du sphinx: La Monarchie de Juillet.* Paris: Royer.
Bernard, Jack F. 1973. *Talleyrand: A Biography.* New York: Putnam.
Cooper, Duff. 2001. *Talleyrand.* London: Weidenfeld and Nicolson.
Dwyer, Philip G. 1996. *Charles-Maurice de Talleyrand, 1754–1838: A Bibliography.* Westport, CT: Greenwood.
Lacour-Gayet, G. 1928–1934. *Talleyrand, 1754–1838.* 4 vols. Paris: Payot.
Pallain, G. 1891. *Correspondance diplomatique: Talleyrand sous le Directoire.* Paris: Plon.
———. 1889. *La mission de Talleyrand à Londres en 1792.* Paris: Plon.
Poniatowski, Michel. 1982. *Talleyrand et le Directoire, 1796–1800.* Paris: Perrin.
Talleyrand-Périgord, Charles-Maurice de. 1967. *Lettres de Talleyrand à Napoléon.* Ed. Pierre Bertrand. Paris: Bonnot.
———. 1989. *Mémoires complets et authentiques de Charles-Maurice de Talleyrand, prince de Bénévent: texte conforme au manuscrit original. Contenant les notes de Monsieur Adolphe Fourier de Bacourt, légataire des manuscrits de l'auteur.* 6 vols. Paris: Bonnot.

Tamames, Battle of

See Peninsular War

Tarbes, Battle of (20 March 1814)

The Battle of Tarbes was fought between French forces under Marshal Nicolas Soult retreating toward Toulouse and Anglo-Allied forces under the Marquis of (later the Duke of) Wellington in pursuit.

As Soult attempted to withdraw to the fortified and well-supplied city of Toulouse, Wellington repeatedly used his newfound strength in cavalry and his overall superiority to encircle Soult's forces, pinning them against the Pyrenees. Elements of Wellington's forces repeatedly engaged Soult's retreating troops, lending a fairly modern texture to the closing days of the campaign. The largest of these engagements occurred along the river Adour at the town of Tarbes. By 20 March Wellington's forces had already cut off Soult's troops from the shortest and most direct route to Toulouse and were attempting to cut the remaining two routes and thus force Soult's army against the mountains. Soult continued to withdraw with three of his six divisions, leaving the divisions of generals Jean Isidore Harispe and Eugène Casimir Villatte of Bertrand, baron Clausel's corps and Eloi Charlemagne Taupin's division of General Honoré, comte Reille's corps to defend from the heights above the river and the town of Tarbes. Taupin's division was to make a show of defending the town before withdrawing across the narrow bridge to the high ground beyond.

The pursuing British were organized in two columns under Marshal Sir William Beresford and Lieutenant General Sir Rowland Hill. Beresford's column was attempting to turn the French right and thus force a retreat into the Pyrenees, while Hill applied direct pressure on the French rear. Hill's task was to attack the town of Tarbes and the heights above it on the eastern side of the Adour River. His attack progressed slowly, as he had to fight through the town and then try to cross the river using the narrow bridge. He did not succeed until Beresford's turning movement had taken effect and forced Taupin's division to withdraw, almost too late to make its escape.

Beresford's troops, led by the Light Division, included the 6th Division, a Spanish force under Lieutenant General Manuel Freire, and several brigades of cavalry, with the 4th Division under Lieutenant General Sir Lowry Cole following. Beresford attacked Clausel's corps on the French right, that is, the northern end of the line, along a high, steep, and heavily wooded ridge, known as the Heights of Oleac, which was crowned with a windmill. It was on the wooded steep slope of the Heights of Oleac that the bulk of the fighting took place. Rather than attempt a conventional infantry assault, Beresford directed the Light Division under Major General Charles, Baron von Alten to send the entire 95th Rifles, consisting of three battalions in skirmish order, up the ridge. After reaching the top of the ridge and emerging from the

woods, the 95th was counterattacked by Harispe's division, which presumably thought the dark-coated riflemen were Portuguese troops. After a fierce fight on top of the ridge, the French withdrew, as Lieutenant General William Clinton's division began to outflank them from the right.

The British forces then began an advance, which drove the three divisions from the heights above the Adour back toward the three divisions Soult had earlier withdrawn behind the next stream that formed an obstacle, the Larret. The British forces now faced the whole of Soult's army arrayed to their front. They had successfully pushed the French away from the second of the three routes to Toulouse. Wellington, noting that it was late afternoon and that the strength of Soult's forces made his position on the Larret unassailable, chose not to press the attack further. Had he done so, especially on the French right, it is possible that the French army would have had no choice but to withdraw against the Pyrenees, away from their third and final escape route to Toulouse. However, Wellington's decision not to attack permitted Soult to withdraw.

Even though Soult's forces were forced to take the longest route to Toulouse, a route almost 50 miles longer than that taken by the British, he was able to successfully withdraw to Toulouse. Although the British forces had roughly handled the three divisions Soult had left to delay the British advance, they were unable to prevent Soult from moving the bulk of his forces back toward Toulouse and safety. In the end, the longer route Soult was obliged to take proved the better one, as the two roads that Wellington used to approach Toulouse were low-lying routes and slow going for the Allied army. In the final analysis, the Battle of Tarbes must be considered a tactical success for Soult, because even though his forces were compelled to retreat, their delay ensured the survival of his forces and his continued resistance at the city of Toulouse.

John T. Broom

See also Beresford, William Carr; Hill, Sir Rowland; Peninsular War; Reille, Honoré Charles Michel Joseph, comte; Soult, Nicolas Jean de Dieu; Toulouse, Battle of; Wellington, Arthur Wellesley, First Duke of
References and further reading
Esdaile, Charles J. 2003. *The Peninsular War: A New History.* New York: Palgrave Macmillan.
Gates, David. 1986. *The Spanish Ulcer: A History of the Peninsular War.* New York: Norton.
Robertson, Ian. 2003. *Wellington Invades France: The Final Phase of the Peninsular War, 1813–1814.* London: Greenhill.

Tarragona, Siege of (8 May–29 June 1811)

A major fortress and seaport, Tarragona was from 1808 onward the chief bastion of Spanish resistance in Catalonia.

As such, it was always a major target for the French, but it was not until May 1811 that they were able to move to its capture. Led by General Louis Suchet, some 22,000 men marched against the city, and on 16 May operations began against the city's western front. Meanwhile, a further attack was launched against an outlying redoubt known as Fuerte Olivo, which crowned the heights that overlooked Tarragona from the north. Ten thousand strong, the garrison, which was commanded by the head of Spanish forces in Catalonia, the Marqués de Campoverde, put up a fierce fight, but on 29 May Fuerte Olivo was stormed in a desperate night action. On 3 June, Campoverde therefore left the city by sea to organize a relief force. In this, however, he proved ineffectual, while on 21 June the French stormed the main part of the city.

All that was left to the defenders, who were now led by General Juan Senen de Contreras, was the hill occupied by the old Roman town and the cathedral. Protected by city walls and steep slopes, this was a good place for a last stand, but no help was forthcoming, either from Campoverde, whose operations at this time were utterly incompetent, or from a small British expeditionary force that had just appeared off the coast. In consequence, Senen de Contreras resolved to break out, but in the event the French attacked his positions much sooner than he had anticipated. Thus, on 28 June a ferocious bombardment smashed a breach in the walls. No sooner had the last stones fallen, meanwhile, than three columns of attackers headed for the walls. There followed a desperate fight—300 soldiers, for example, held out to the last man in the cathedral—but by dawn on 29 June all resistance was at an end. In all, Spanish casualties numbered at least 15,000, including 2,000 civilians murdered in the course of the fighting on 28 June, and in recognition of his achievements, Suchet was awarded a marshal's baton.

Charles J. Esdaile

See also Peninsular War; Siege Warfare; Suchet, Louis-Gabriel
References and further reading
Esdaile, Charles J. 2002. *The Peninsular War: A New History.* London: Penguin.
Oman, Charles. 2005. *A History of the Peninsular War.* 7 vols. London: Greenhill. (Orig. pub. 1902–1930.)

Tauroggen, Convention of (30 December 1812)

The signing of the Convention of Tauroggen between the Prussian general in Russian service, Hans Karl von Diebitsch, and the Prussian general Johann David von Yorck neutralized the Prussian contingent in Napoleon's Grande Armée of 1812, which had invaded Russia earlier that year. This act symbolized the end of the campaign in Russia and the beginning of the campaign in Germany, which was to conclude with Napoleon being thrown back across the Rhine into France.

The Prussian Auxiliary Corps of 1812 that marched into Russia in June was 20,000 men strong. It was deployed to the left of the main body of Napoleon's army and was part of the force under the command of the French marshal Jacques Etienne Macdonald. It marched up the Baltic coast toward Riga, engaging Russian forces on several occasions.

Capturing Moscow did not achieve victory for Napoleon. As he was in danger of being isolated in Russia's great city, he evacuated it that October. His army disintegrated on its retreat toward the Prussian border, and Napoleon left the army to return to Paris. Macdonald's force also fell back toward the Prussian border, receiving orders to break off the siege of Riga on 18 December. Russian forces moved to cut off his line of retreat. Yorck allowed his corps to become separated from Macdonald, with Russian troops interposing themselves between them. From 25 December Yorck was no longer in contact with his chief, and he took this opportunity to engage the Russians in negotiations. The tsar was astute enough to send three native Prussians to conduct these talks: generals Diebitsch, Karl von Clausewitz, and Karl Friedrich Graf zu Dohna. On 30 December they met in the mill of Poscherun, near Tauroggen, just on the Russian side of the border with Prussia. Here, they agreed on and signed the Convention of Tauroggen, in which Yorck's corps declared itself neutral and in return was allowed to withdraw unmolested to the area around Tilsit, Memel, and the Haff, in the north of East Prussia. Yorck was to await further instructions from his king, Frederick William III.

It has been a subject of debate ever since whether Yorck was acting on secret instructions from Berlin, or whether he simply used his own initiative. In either case, this event dramatically altered the situation, making it impossible for the French to hold East Prussia. Macdonald abandoned Königsberg (now Kaliningrad) on 4 January 1813, the Russians entering the capital city of the province the same day. The tsar sent the German patriot Heinrich Freiherr vom und zum Stein to Königsberg to take control of the province. He arrived there on 22 January and set about assembling the provincial estate, or governing council.

These events instigated an uprising in which, on 6 February 1813, the Estates of East Prussia declared themselves against Napoleon without waiting for instructions from the king. The next day, they set about raising armed forces for the forthcoming war, including a militia. These acts, although initially condemned by Frederick William, were repeated throughout Prussia a month later. The Convention of Tauroggen sparked off what became known as the War of Liberation.

Peter Hofschröer

See also Clausewitz, Karl Maria von; Frederick William III, King; Germany, Campaign in; Macdonald, Jacques Etienne Joseph Alexandre; Russian Campaign; Stein, Heinrich Friedrich Karl Freiherr vom und zum; Yorck von Wartenburg, Johann David Ludwig Graf
References and further reading
Droysen, Johann Gustav. 1913. *Das Leben des Feldmarschalls Grafen Yorck von Wartenburg.* 2 vols. Leipzig: Insel.
Hamilton-Williams, David. 1994. *The Fall of Napoleon: The Final Betrayal.* London: Arms and Armour.

Tengen, Battle of

See Teugn-Hausen, Battle of

Teplitz, Treaty of (9 September 1813)

The small town of Teplitz-Schönau in the western part of the Czech Republic is currently best known as a health resort, though it was the site of one of the turning points in the campaign of 1813 between Prussia, Russia, and Austria on the one hand and Napoleon on the other. At this small and strategic village, on 9 September 1813, officers and diplomats from Prussia, Russia, and Austria met and reached an agreement known as the Treaty of Teplitz, which promised unity between Allied forces and pledged to restore Prussia and Austria to their 1805 boundaries.

Napoleon, who had remained the master of Europe throughout the first decade of the nineteenth century, had become vulnerable in the years leading up to the Teplitz agreement. Napoleon's fortunes began to turn with the beginning of the costly Peninsular War in the Iberian Peninsula against British, Spanish, and Portuguese forces led by the Marquis of Wellington. Later, with the failure of his Continental System—intended to cripple British trade with the Continent—Napoleon's dominance over Europe began to wane. Tsar Alexander of Russia was particularly skeptical of Napoleon's intentions and often acted in violation of the Continental System by conducting trade with Britain. In order to punish the tsar for his failure to honor the Treaty of Tilsit, concluded on 7 July 1807 and binding Alexander to the Continental System, Napoleon planned his massive and ill-fated invasion of Russia in 1812.

For the invasion, Napoleon assembled a force that totaled over 600,000 men, most of whom were not French, but citizens of French satellite states who were sometimes unwillingly conscripted. Due to the vast size of the force and the enormous distances to be covered, the army's supply system struggled from the beginning. Compounding such problems, the Russians' scorched-earth policy denied the French access to vital local supplies.

Napoleon knew that he had to strike fast, but he did not achieve the decisive victory he desired at Borodino on 7 September 1812. Instead, the battle ended in stalemate, and produced some of the highest casualties ever suffered in action by Napoleon's forces. The Emperor was able to occupy Moscow, but it proved a hollow victory. Napoleon remained in the city for five weeks in September and October, hoping to reach terms with Alexander, who did not pursue negotiations since he knew the dire condition of Napoleon's troops. After suffering horribly at the hands of Russia's famous "General Winter," Napoleon's army left Moscow and began its horrific retreat at only a quarter of its original strength. Napoleon had never been more vulnerable than at this time.

Seizing the opportunity, Russia signed the Convention of Kalisch on 28 February 1813, allying itself with Prussia and inviting Austria and Britain to join the coalition against Napoleon. On 27 March the combined Russian and Prussian forces occupied Dresden, the capital of Saxony, but were soon after defeated by Napoleon at Lützen. Both sides were exhausted, so an Austrian-brokered cease-fire was reached on 4 June 1813.

A serious attempt at achieving a lasting peace followed, known as the Congress of Prague. Napoleon, however, angrily rejected all terms offered. Austria therefore declared war on France, joining Prussia and Russia, while Britain pledged financial and material support. On 26–27 August Napoleon again defeated his opponents, this time at Dresden, but the end was near. It was his last victory on German soil.

On 9 September officials representing Prussia, Russia, and Austria concluded the Treaty of Teplitz, which was to play an important part in sealing Napoleon's ultimate defeat. In the debates at Teplitz and in the treaty, the three countries strengthened their coalition, acknowledged the need to fight Napoleon's subordinates while avoiding him in major battles (the Trachenberg Plan), and pledged to restore the boundaries of Prussia and Austria as they stood in 1805.

In mid-October, at the Battle of Leipzig, also known as the "Battle of the Nations," Napoleon's forces were decisively defeated and forced to retreat all the way back across the Rhine into France proper. During the course of the battle and in the wake of this retreat, his former satellite states joined with the Allies and augmented their forces substantially.

On 9 November the Allies offered Napoleon terms for peace, but he again angrily refused them. In response, the

Allies resolved on 1 December to invade France. After a final campaign on French soil, the Allies occupied Paris on 31 March 1814, forcing Napoleon to abdicate and to accept exile on the island of Elba, off the western coast of Italy.

Arthur Holst

See also Alexander I, Tsar; Armistice of 1813; Borodino, Battle of; Continental System; Dresden, Battle of; Elba; France, Campaign in; Germany, Campaign in; Kalisch, Convention of; Leipzig, Battle of; Lützen, Battle of; Peninsular War; Russian Campaign; Tilsit, Treaties of

References and further reading
Delderfield, R. F. 2001. *Imperial Sunset: The Fall of Napoleon, 1813–1814.* New York: Cooper Square.
Hamilton-Williams, David. 1994. *The Fall of Napoleon: The Final Betrayal.* London: Arms and Armour.
Lawford, James P. 1977. *Napoleon: The Last Campaigns, 1813–15.* New York: Crown.

Terror, The (1793–1794)

Though restricted to a single year of the French Revolution, from 1793 to 1794, the Terror (*la Terreur*) has become emblematic of the Revolution, with the guillotine as its symbol. There is no doubt it was a terrible phenomenon, with perhaps 35,000 to 40,000 official victims of summary justice, not to mention those who died in prison or were killed in the civil war that accompanied this *annus horrendus* (horrible year). The cause of liberty and equality was fatally compromised by association with this bloodletting, which should nonetheless be kept in perspective. The Terror was a means of saving the Revolution and strengthening the war effort as France faced imminent defeat; it was a bundle of exceptional measures aimed at combating the great crisis that threatened the Revolution's very existence in 1793. Major cities and many parts of the countryside (notably in the west of France) had risen in revolt against the government in Paris, while the infant French Republic was facing invasion on all frontiers. The Terror was thus a mechanism for mobilizing resources and organizing the country for war, applying coercion where persuasion was no longer effective.

The Revolution was violent from beginning to end, but the official repression known as the Terror should be distinguished from the spontaneous violence that preceded and succeeded it. The overthrow of the *ancien régime* was essentially bloodless, but order was hard to restore, especially in the context of war after 1792. That summer, as the monarchy fell and invasion seemed imminent, numerous atrocities occurred, notably the September prison massacres at Paris. When crisis returned in the spring of 1793, the Terror represented an attempt to prevent such outrages by giving government more power to contain it. The machinery comprised Revolutionary tribunals to judge political cases; the dispatch of representatives on mission to the provinces, where they took executive action (and administered most of the executions); and a Committee of Public Safety, which ruled by decree, though it was elected by, and was ultimately answerable to, the National Convention. As the situation worsened, other institutions such as watch committees, which arrested perhaps 200,000 people over the next year, and an infamous Law of Suspects, carrying a wide-ranging catalog of political crimes, were introduced in September. It was declared that *terreur* was the order of the day.

As these emergency measures began to bite, in order to implement the *levée en masse,* military requisitioning, and economic controls known as the Maximum, the repressive side of the Terror came into play. If nobles and priests were more likely victims than ordinary people, peasants were the largest group to succumb. Indeed, this was no class war, for sans-culottes were also on the receiving end, their anarchic activities brought to book. The Terror hit hardest in areas of unrest and revolt, in the rebel cities of Lyons, Marseilles, and Toulon, and in the Vendée, in the west of France, where a vast rural region was enflamed. Yet, though it is true that the punishment was often far in excess of the crime, it is also true that many quiet areas did not witness a single execution during this period.

A recent trend in writing on the Revolution has suggested that the Terror was not so much the product of extraordinary circumstances as the result of a flawed political culture. The Revolutionaries were as incapable of tolerating dissent and accepting pluralism as the *ancien régime* monarchy. Talk of regeneration encouraged illusions about the ability of politics to reshape individuals as well as its institutions. Attempts to enforce a secular, republican culture wreaked havoc on the Church. Social aspects of the Terror, such as ambitious schemes for land redistribution, education, or poor relief, were pursued in a climate of severe intimidation. With the constitution suspended, nomination superseded election, and lower-class citizens enjoyed local office, pushing through exceptional measures their superiors were reluctant to embrace.

Yet equally significant is the reluctance with which the Terror was initially embraced and the fact that, once it appeared to be working, there were demands for its relaxation. That it continued into the early summer of 1794 is not easily explained, though perhaps the very momentum it had acquired kept the juggernaut rolling. In fact, the legislation became even more draconian, with the passage of the law of 22 Prairial (10 June 1794), which dispensed with defense counsel and the presentation of evidence, and offered only two verdicts: acquittal or death. There was a final surge of executions in Paris, where many prisoners were now being sent: 200 a day on average between June and July. Yet this paroxysm only hastened the end, compelling the deputies of the Convention to reassert their authority and bring down Maximilien Robespierre, who seemed incapable of accommodating to the less demanding situation.

After 9 Thermidor (27 July), the machinery of the Terror was gradually dismantled: The Committee of Public Safety and the Revolutionary Tribunal were remodeled in August; the Maximum was abolished in December. It was now the turn of those who exercised power during the Terror to fear for their lives, though most of the killings that followed were the result of personal vendettas and mob violence. Government-sponsored violence on this scale was not to be repeated.

The Terror was not so much a deliberate choice by bloodthirsty Jacobins as a desperate response to the breakdown of government in the midst of an overwhelming situation. Resources were mustered, armies raised, inflation curbed, civil war ended, and invasion halted. In this sense the Terror might be termed a success. It was a relatively short-lived phase in the Revolution, but it did make the longer-term task of stabilization more difficult. Above all, it left an indelible mark on the French, indeed European consciousness, and it retains considerable resonance even today.

Malcolm Crook

See also Constitutions (French); Convention, The; French Revolution; Jacobins; Levée en Masse; Lyons, Siege of; Public Safety, Committee of; Robespierre, Maximilien François Marie Isidore; Thermidor Coup; Toulon, Siege of; Vendée, Revolts in the

References and further reading
Andress, David. 2005. *The Terror: Civil War in the French Revolution.* London: Little, Brown.
Aulard, F. A., ed. 1889–1951. *Recueil des Actes du Comité de Salut Public.* Paris: Impr. nationale.
Baker, Keith Michael, ed. 1994. *The Terror: The French Revolution and the Creation of Modern Political Culture.* Vol. 4. Oxford: Pergamon.
Bouloiseau, Marc. 1968. *Le Comité de Salut Public.* Paris: Presses universitaires de France.
Gough, Hugh. 1998. *The Terror in the French Revolution.* Basingstoke, UK: Macmillan.
Greer, Donald. 1935. *The Incidence of the Terror in the French Revolution: A Statistical Study.* Cambridge, MA: Harvard University Press.
Hardman, John. 1999. *Robespierre.* London: Longman.
Higonnet, Patrice. 1998. *Goodness beyond Virtue: Jacobins during the French Revolution.* Cambridge, MA: Harvard University Press.
Kennedy, Michael L. 1982–2000. *The Jacobin Clubs in the French Revolution.* 3 vols. Princeton: Princeton University Press.
Palmer, R. R. 2005. *Twelve Who Ruled: The Year of the Terror in the French Revolution.* Princeton: Princeton University Press. (Orig. pub. 1941.)
Wright, D. G. 1991. *Revolution and Terror in France, 1789–95.* London: Longman.

Teugn-Hausen, Battle of (19 April 1809)

In the opening battle of the Bavarian campaign of the War of the Fifth Coalition, Marshal Louis Davout's 17,000 French troops defeated an equally strong Austrian corps under *Feldmarschalleutnant* Prinz Friedrich Hohenzollern-Hechingen (generally known as Hohenzollern) 15 kilometers southwest of Ratisbon (present-day Regensburg). Davout was able to escape encirclement by the Austrian army and reach Napoleon's Franco-German army, massing near Ingolstadt.

When the Austrian army invaded Bavaria in April 1809, Davout's III Corps was isolated at Ratisbon, while Napoleon's main army assembled 45 kilometers to the southwest, around Ingolstadt. The Austrian army commander, Archduke Charles, was attempting to catch Davout's corps in a three-pronged march northward over wooded, ridge-lined hills toward the upper Danube, as Davout withdrew southwest down the single riverside road. On 19 April around 8:00 A.M. *Feldmarschalleutnant* Fürst Franz von Rosenberg-Orsini's IV Korps (the central column) began an inconclusive engagement with Davout's rear guard under General Louis-Pierre Montbrun, 5 kilometers to the east, around Dünzling.

At about the same time the left column, Hohenzollern's III Korps, seized lightly defended Hausen village, while Archduke Charles held his reserve of twelve grenadier battalions at Grub, 4 kilometers to the southeast. Hohenzollern's advance-guard infantry crossed the heavily wooded Hausnerberg, and its skirmishers descended toward Teugn village, through which ran the crucial riverside road. About half of Davout's column had already marched through, but as *Feldmarschalleutnant* Franz Marquis de Lusignan deployed his brigade on the Hausnerberg, Davout dispatched three regiments from General Louis St. Hilaire's division up the Buchberg (a small hill to the west of the road) to repel this Austrian advance, while another regiment engaged the advance guard infantry on the higher ground to the west around Roith, on the Austrian left.

As the lead units of General Louis, comte Friant's division arrived, they were directed to attack the Austrian right, forcing Lusignan to withdraw into the woods on the Hausnerberg ridge, pursued by Friant's infantry. Hohenzollern had sent forward *Generalmajor* Alois Fürst Liechtenstein's brigade from Hausen, and they arrived as Lusignan's men came tumbling out of the trees. Liechtenstein led his men and Lusignan's re-formed infantry forward, but they could make little headway in the woods against the French infantry, who now had artillery support. Hohenzollern, who had deployed his artillery and some hussars at Hausen, led his last infantry reserve in a final attack on the wooded ridge, but to his left the advance guard infantry was already being driven back.

By 3:00 P.M. the attack had failed, forcing him to withdraw to Hausen, while the exhausted French secured their positions in the woods. To the southeast, Archduke Charles had remained at Grub, awaiting news of developments, as the wooded ridges made it impossible to see far beyond Hausen. The archduke only committed his grenadiers to Hausen as the fighting died away, around 4:00 P.M., amid a huge thunderstorm. Davout's victory passed the strategic initiative from the Austrians to Napoleon, who would launch his counterattack at Abensberg the next day.

David Hollins

See also Abensberg, Battle of; Charles, Archduke of Austria, Duke of Teschen; Davout, Louis Nicolas; Fifth Coalition, War of the; Friant, Louis, comte; Montbrun, Louis-Pierre; St. Hilaire, Louis Vincent Joseph le Blond, comte de
References and further reading
Arnold, James. 1990. *Crisis on the Danube.* London: Arms and Armour.
Castle, Ian. 1998. *Eggmühl 1809: Storm over Bavaria.* Oxford: Osprey.

Texel, Capture of the Dutch fleet off (23–29 January 1795)

Incident during the winter of 1794–1795, toward the end of the invasion of the Dutch Republic by General Jean-Charles Pichegru, during which the Dutch fleet, icebound before Den Helder in the strait between North Holland and the island of Texel (the Marsdiep), was forced to surrender.

Traditionally, the capture of the Dutch fleet has been characterized as an extraordinary, even somewhat heroic event. A small French detachment consisting of a squadron of hussars, three battalions of infantry, and horse artillery, under the command of one Lieutenant Colonel Louis Joseph de Lahure, marched from Amsterdam to Den Helder, secured the city on the evening of 22 January 1795, and hastened through the icy cold night the seven or eight miles over land to the fleet, marching over the thickly frozen sea that surrounded the icebound ships. They then proceeded to board and capture the fleet by surprise and prevent it from sailing off to Britain or Zeeland, which was still in the hands of those loyal to the House of Orange, which had been ousted from power as a result of the French invasion. Fifteen Dutch ships of the line were captured, of which eleven were in a ready state. In addition, a few merchantmen and a fleeing British vessel were cap-

tured, and some French prisoners held on Texel were released. This version of events, however, is disputed, and the event seems to have been somewhat less spectacular.

According to other sources, after Dutch resistance was broken and William V, Prince of Orange and *stadtholder* (de facto ruler, but de jure subordinate to the legislature, the States-General) of the United Provinces, had fled to Britain on 8 January, Pichegru quickly sent a regiment of hussars under General Johan Willem de Winter to Den Helder to prevent the port from being captured by the British and to capture the Dutch fleet. De Winter was a former Dutch naval officer who served in the French army in the Batavian Legion, a regiment of anti-Orangist "Patriot" sympathies. He seems to have arrived in Den Helder a few days later than his troops, and in consequence it is possible that de Lahure was in fact the actual commander in the field. There is no mention of artillery.

On 22 January the hussars reached Den Helder, and on the morning of the twenty-third, a trooper was reported looking through the gun port of one of the ships, having reached the vessels by riding over the thick frozen ice. The hussars seem to have been received aboard the ships in rather a friendly fashion; indeed, no mention is made of actual fighting. The senior fleet officer at the time of the attack, a certain Reyntjes, seems already to have been ordered not to resist the French, and it was agreed to await a clarification of orders, which arrived soon thereafter and confirmed the order not to resist. Five days later, officers and men aboard the ships vowed to retain naval discipline and comply with French orders, although the fleet remained under the Dutch flag. De Winter later became admiral of the Batavian fleet and held senior command at the Battle of Camperdown (Kamperduin) where, despite his defeat, he fought—as indeed did the crews generally—with distinction.

M. R. van der Werf

See also Camperdown, Battle of; Dutch Navy; First Coalition, War of the; Flanders, Campaigns in; Pichegru, Jean-Charles; Winter, Johan Willem de
References and further reading
Fehrmann, C. N. 1969. *Onze vloot in de Franse Tijd, de admiralen De Winter en Ver Heull.* The Hague: Kruseman.
Jonge, J. C. de. 1869. *Geschiedenis van het Nederlandse Zeewezen.* Zwolle: Hoogstratenen Gorter.
Phipps, Ramsay Weston. 1980. *The Armies of the French Republic and the Rise of the Marshals of Napoleon I.* Vol. 1, *The Armée du Nord.* London: Greenwood. (Orig. pub. 1926–1939.)

Thermidor Coup (27 July 1794)

The overthrow of Maximilien Robespierre on 9 Thermidor (27 July 1794) that ended the Reign of Terror. In the

French Republican calendar, Thermidor was the eleventh month; it began on 19–20 July, and its name, from the Greek word for "hot," alluded to the midsummer heat.

Maximilien Robespierre, a solitary-minded and principled lawyer from Arras with considerable oratorical skills, gained control over the Jacobin Club, and by July 1793 he had become the leading member of the twelve-man Committee of Public Safety (CPS), the National Convention's executive body. With Robespierre its prime mover, the committee's word was law, as it issued decrees, administered France, and controlled finances, the military, and the Popular Societies throughout the country. The committee instigated a deliberate Reign of Terror in the name of safeguarding the principles of the Revolution and protecting the nation from foreign threats. However, the Terror soon turned into a political tool wielded in the hands of the CPS to deal ruthlessly with its rivals. Among those who became its victim was Jacques Hébert, a journalist and voice of the sans-culottes, and Georges Danton, who had served in the first CPS from April to July 1793 but who now disagreed with Robespierre.

By early summer 1794 the policies of the CPS led to thousands of executions and established an atmosphere of terror and fear. However, the French successes against the armies of the First Coalition led some Jacobins, who also feared becoming the next victims of the CPS, to oppose its policies. In June and July, Paul Barras, Joseph Fouché, and Jean Lambert Tallien covertly rallied the deputies of the Convention to oppose the CPS. On 27 July, as he was delivering a speech to the Convention, Louis Antoine de Saint-Just, a member of the CPS, came under attack by deputies who accused the CPS and Robespierre in particular of dictatorship. Led by Tallien, François Louis Bourdon, and Jean-Nicholas Billaud-Varenne, the deputies proceeded to declare Robespierre an outlaw and had the members of the CPS arrested at the Hôtel de Ville. After a hasty trial, which effectively (and ironically) employed the system earlier established by the CPS itself, Robespierre and his fellow members of the CPS were found guilty and guillotined.

Historians usually acknowledge the Thermidor coup as one of the turning points in the French Revolution. It marked the end of the radical stage of the Revolution, which seemed to stagnate as the bourgeoisie sought stability and peace. The Directory, with a five-member executive, was established and governed France until 9–10 November 1799, when Bonaparte staged the coup of Brumaire and established the Consulate.

Annette E. Richardson

See also Barras, Paul Jean François Nicolas, vicomte de; Brumaire, Coup of; Consulate, The; Convention, The; Directory, The; First Coalition, War of the; Fouché, Joseph, duc d'Otrante; French Revolution; Girondins; Jacobins; Public Safety, Committee of; Republican Calendar; Robespierre, Maximilien François Marie Isidore; Terror, The

References and further reading
Bienvenue, Richard. 1970. *The Ninth of Thermidor.* Oxford: Oxford University Press.
Hardman, John. 1981. *The French Revolution: The Fall of the Ancien Régime to the Thermidorian Reaction, 1785–1795.* London: Arnold.
Lefebvre, Georges. 1964. *The Thermidorians and the Directory: Two Phases of the French Revolution.* New York: Random House.
Mathiez, Albert. 1931. *After Robespierre: The Thermidorian Reaction.* New York: Knopf.
Palmer, R. R. 2005. *Twelve Who Ruled: The Year of the Terror in the French Revolution.* Princeton: Princeton University Press.
Woronoff, Denis. 1984. *The Thermidorean Regime and the Directory: 1794–1799.* Cambridge: Cambridge University Press.

Thielmann, Johann Adolph Freiherr von (1765–1824)

Saxon, Russian, and Prussian general. As a reward for his service in the Battle of Borodino, he was made a Saxon *Freiherr* (baron) on 8 October 1812. In spring 1813 he was commander of the important Saxon fortress at Torgau. In the combat at Wavre (18 June 1815) against superior French forces, the Prussian III Corps under his command secured the rear of Field Marshal Gebhard Fürst Blücher von Wahlstatt's main forces, which were advancing toward Waterloo on the same day.

Thielmann entered military service in 1780 and became a corporal (7 June 1782); cornet (30 March 1784); second lieutenant (13 July 1791); premier lieutenant (3 May 1798); captain 2nd class (15 January 1807); captain (5 February 1807); major (1 March 1809); lieutenant colonel (12 April 1809); colonel (17 July 1809); major general (26 February 1810); and lieutenant general (12 May 1813). He entered Russian service as a lieutenant general on 19 March 1815 before transferring to Prussian service as a lieutenant general (the patent later being postdated to 10 June), which made him junior to generals Ernst Julius Freiherr Schuler von Senden, Karl Christian von Elsner, Levin Karl von Heister, Ludwig Mathias von Brauchitsch, and Friedrich Erhard von Roeder. His final promotion was to general of cavalry on 30 May 1824 (the patent being postdated to 31 May). During the French Revolutionary Wars, he served in the campaigns of 1793–1795. During the Napoleonic Wars he fought in the campaigns of 1806 in Saxony, 1807 in East Prussia, 1812 in Russia, and 1813–1815 in Germany, France, and Belgium, respectively.

Born 27 April 1765, the son of a Saxon high official, Thielmann early on developed a love for the military and joined the Saxon cavalry at a young age, remaining in the line until 1806. Not being a nobleman, his advancement was slow. Nevertheless, his intelligence and abilities were recognized. After the Battle of Jena (14 October 1806), he was sent to French headquarters to discuss the terms of peace. Advancement followed, and on 1 April 1807, Thielmann became adjutant to General Georg Friedrich von Polenz, who commanded the Saxon auxiliary corps. On 15 June 1808, he became the Saxon military representative and adjutant to the French marshal Louis Nicolas Davout.

On 28 April 1809 Thielmann was made commander of the (weak) Saxon army corps defending Saxony against a corps of émigré Brunswick troops (the "Black Legion") commanded by the Duke of Brunswick. On 26 February 1810, he became commander of a brigade of cuirassiers, which he also led to Russia in 1812, assigned to IV Reserve Cavalry Corps. His brigade distinguished itself at the Battle of Borodino (7 September 1812) but suffered extremely heavy losses, which were compounded by the ravages of the retreat from Moscow; only a handful of men returned with Thielmann to Saxony in December 1812. On 2 January 1813 Thielmann was made commander of the cavalry in Torgau, becoming governor of this fortress on 24 February. He resigned from Saxon service on 10 May, after his king decided to hand the fortress over to the French.

Entering Russian service on 1 September 1813, he was made leader of a raiding corps. On 26 October he was charged with the organization of a new Saxon army corps, which on 1 December formed the principal part of III Federal German Corps under the Duke of Saxe-Weimar. On 9 June 1814 Thielmann became commander of this corps.

During the Waterloo campaign, he was assigned command of III Corps of the Prussian army on 9 April 1815, and fought at Wavre, on the same day as the Battle of Waterloo. After the peace, he became commanding general in Westphalia on 3 October. On 3 April 1820 he was transferred as commander to VIII Corps. Thielmann died from a sudden stroke of apoplexy on 10 October 1824.

Oliver Schmidt

See also Blücher von Wahlstatt, Gebhard Lebrecht Fürst; Borodino, Battle of; Davout, Louis Nicolas; Fourth Coalition, War of the; France, Campaign in; Germany, Campaign in; Jena, Battle of; Russian Campaign; Saxon Army; Waterloo, Battle of; Waterloo Campaign; Wavre, Battle of

References and further reading
Priesdorff, Kurt von. 1937–1942. *Soldatisches Führertum* [Military Leadership]. 10 vols. Vol. 3, pp. 458–466 (no. 1215). Hamburg: Hanseatische Verlagsanstalt.

Third Coalition, War of the (1805)

Although the Treaty of Amiens, concluded in March 1802, returned peace to the European continent after a decade of war, it proved no more than a fragile peace, and was broken within fourteen months of its signature when Britain declared war on 18 May 1803. Britain immediately reimposed a naval blockade of French ports, while Bonaparte (a year later to become the Emperor Napoleon I) resumed the preparations to cross the English Channel and invade Britain that had been interrupted by Amiens. Invasion would be impossible without either the defeat of the Royal Navy or the diversion of sufficient numbers of British ships away from the Channel so that the French could effect a crossing. But apart from the French occupation of Hanover in 1803, a British patrimony as a result of George III's German ancestry, there were no operations on the European continent until 1805, the war being confined to minor naval operations between Britain and France.

Britain would not acquiesce to a French-controlled Europe and, by 1805, had found allies for a new coalition against Napoleon. Russia, Austria, and Sweden joined with Britain in April, August, and October, respectively, making circumstances apparently auspicious for the Allies. The bulk of French forces, some 200,000 men in the Grande Armée, were encamped along the English Channel, near Boulogne, preparing for the long-awaited invasion of Britain. Marshal André Masséna had 50,000 men in northern Italy, and, of course, there remained reserve forces in France. The Allies had a simple and seemingly effective plan. They would move first to destroy Masséna's army, and then move north of the Alps, cross the Rhine, and invade France while Napoleon and his main army remained in quarters along the Channel.

When Napoleon realized his enemies' plan, he moved swiftly. On 27 August the Grande Armée quietly left its camps around Boulogne, and, marching swiftly, crossed the Rhine by 26 September. Continuing its rapid advance, Napoleon's army reached the Danube by 6 October, the speed of its advance upsetting Allied calculations and putting the bulk of the Grande Armée in the rear of an Austrian army commanded by *Feldmarschalleutnant* Karl Leiberich von Mack near Ulm. In so doing, Napoleon managed to cut Mack's lines of communications, supply, and retreat to Vienna.

As Napoleon moved swiftly, the Allies continued with their original plan, unaware of the trap that awaited. Mack's 50,000 men moved toward Ulm, with the purpose of guarding the northern flank of the main advance into northern Italy that was to seek to defeat Masséna's army. The Archduke Charles of Austria had 100,000 men, and he intended to move against Masséna as a prelude to a subse-

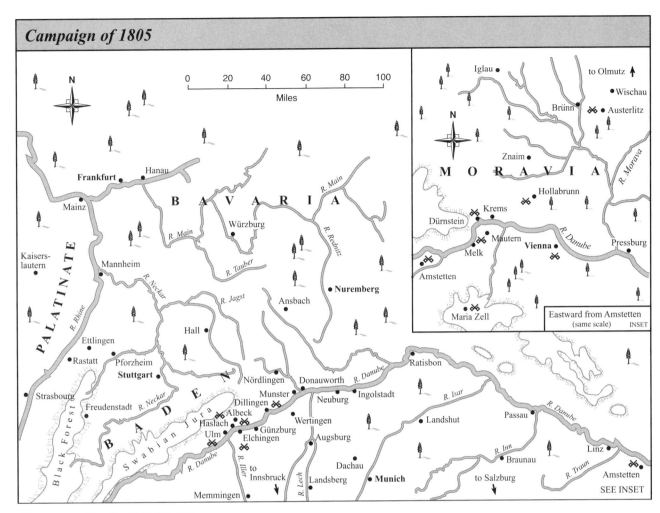

Campaign of 1805

Adapted from Chandler 1966, 388–389.

quent advance north of the Alps, across the Rhine, and into France. Meanwhile, a Russian army of 120,000 men was moving westward into Germany, while to the north, Sweden was preparing to send an army to Pomerania, Sweden's only continental possession. All these offensives, operating along different lines of advance into eastern France, were designed to overwhelm Napoleon's forces.

As the Allies moved at a somewhat leisurely pace but with superior numbers, Napoleon raced to the critical point. As French cavalry emerging from the Black Forest in southern Germany demonstrated in front of Mack's Austrians at Ulm (the French moved back and forth out of the Black Forest, confusing the Austrians, who seemed unaware of the approaching trap), Napoleon's infantry advanced in six great columns in a wide arc around to the north and then east of Mack's position. The French infantry averaged some 18 miles a day—an astounding speed of advance.

By 30 September Mack, realizing that he was in danger of being encircled, tried to break out of the trap and open a line of retreat toward Vienna. He attacked the French twice: at Haslach and again at Elchingen. At Haslach 4,000 French troops commanded by General Pierre Dupont managed to withstand an assault by 25,000 Austrians, while at Elchingen Marshal Michel Ney sought to regain the town the French had only recently abandoned. As French reinforcements arrived, the Austrians retreated. Napoleon's unexpected advance demoralized Mack and his army, a demoralization made more complete by the fact that the promised Russian support was too slow in coming. Two groups, however, did break out of the encirclement, only to surrender later: the Archduke Ferdinand, with 13,000 cavalry eventually capitulated at Trochtelfingen, while another 12,000 men wound up laying down their arms at Neustadt. Mack surrendered his army, consisting of some 30,000 men and 65 pieces of artillery, at Ulm on 20 October. For Napoleon this constituted a great strategic rather than tactical victory, demonstrating the value of superior use of the principles behind maneuver and surprise.

Napoleon moved quickly to follow up this overwhelming success. He detached troops to prevent Archdukes Charles and John from moving across the Alps from northern Italy, and himself drove eastward toward Vienna. Masséna in Italy followed Charles and sought to keep him engaged, to prevent Charles from concentrating on moving through the Alps to contest Napoleon for the Austrian capital. On 30 October Masséna's and Charles's armies met at Caldiero. Charles made a spoiling attack to create time for his baggage and slowly moving forces to retreat farther eastward. After the battle, he and the main body of his army safely retreated across the Julian Alps into the broad Hungarian plain.

Driving back the Russians under General Mikhail Kutuzov in front of him, Napoleon gained the Austrian capital on 14 November, though the Russian army had fought an effective delaying action at Dürnstein on the eleventh and later under Prince Peter Bagration at Hollabrunn on the fifteenth and sixteenth. With only 7,000 men, Bagration held off the advancing French and, although he lost half his men, enabled the main body of the Russian army to escape.

Napoleon continued north, his army becoming progressively weaker as it moved away from Vienna. He had to detach troops to guard an ever-lengthening line of communications back to France, and other units to occupy Vienna. He began to concentrate his men around Brünn, several days' march north of the capital. When troops from the formations under marshals Jean-Baptiste Bernadotte and Louis Davout, respectively, joined Napoleon's army, the Emperor commanded about 73,000 men.

The Allies were not idle. To Napoleon's northwest was the Archduke Ferdinand with 18,000 men at Prague; to the northeast, Tsar Alexander of Russia and Emperor Francis of Austria had some 90,000 men near Olmütz; and the Archdukes Charles and John were still trying to break through the French units defending the southern Alps. The Allied plan was clear—to concentrate their superior forces and trap Napoleon far from France. The French, therefore, needed to strike before the opposing armies could combine to overwhelm him.

The result was a tactical masterpiece (as opposed to the strategic masterpiece of Ulm), achieved on 2 December. Napoleon was setting a trap, as he concentrated his army just east of the village of Austerlitz. He deployed his men on low ground, which normally would be a disastrous decision, and greatly extended his right wing in plain sight of his gathering opponents. He wanted them to concentrate their attention on the apparent vulnerability of his overextended right wing, and to fix in their minds a sense of the weakness of the overall French position. The French right wing seemed an irresistible target, for, if the combined Austro-Russian army could break Napoleon's right, the Allies could sever his line of retreat to Vienna and then to France and trap him for the winter in Bohemia. Napoleon, on the other hand, was betting that late-arriving reinforcements would strengthen his right sufficiently to enable it to hold while he delivered the decisive blow elsewhere.

Napoleon initially had placed his men on the hills to the east, the Pratzen heights, for he recognized that this position was the critical point for the battle. When he moved westward to lower ground, he deliberately weakened and overextended his right, although he would have Davout's 8,000 men help strengthen the right in the event of the expected Austrian attack. Further, he planned for a coup de main to destroy the critical hinge of the Allied position. The Austrian attack began early on 2 December on a battlefield shrouded in mist, and by midmorning it had succeeded in bending the French position.

At this point Napoleon struck the overstretched Allied center. In retreating from the hills, he had his men stamp the snow on the slope to allow for an easier climb when they returned. He waited as perhaps a third of the Allied army moved across his front to attack the French right. In doing so, the Allied center was stretched and weakened to maintain the tempo of the attack on the French right.

At the critical moment, around 9:30 A.M., Napoleon sent Marshal Nicolas Soult's corps forward. The mist burned off, and the so-called Sun of Austerlitz lit the battlefield as the French troops seized the heights. As the French split the Allies in two, the French right now moved around the Austrian left to surround it. To further complicate matters, French artillery sent round shot onto the frozen ponds behind the Russian position on the Allied right, breaking through the ice and thus making movement and retreat difficult. There were many desperate and furious attacks and counterattacks, including those by the Russian Imperial Guard and by the French Imperial Guard—together some of the best infantry and cavalry in the world. The French, including the Mameluke cavalry Napoleon had incorporated into his forces after his campaign in Egypt in 1798, held the vital center, eventually driving the Russians off.

Napoleon had outmaneuvered his opponents and gained a great victory. At a cost of 9,000 French casualties, he inflicted more than 27,000 casualties on the Allies. In the course of the fighting, Napoleon had caused his enemies to divide their larger army in two, which he had then been able to overwhelm by seizing the central position—the Pratzen heights. He had destroyed the Austrian left, and had driven off the Russian right in what was to become one of the greatest battlefield victories of the Napoleonic Wars, and perhaps of all military history.

Two days after Austerlitz, the Austrian emperor agreed to an armistice, and the Russian armies marched east. On 26 December, Austria made clear the extent of its defeat by signing the Treaty of Pressburg. By the terms of that treaty, Austria withdrew from the Third Coalition and accepted French control over northern Italy and western and southern Germany. Pressburg marked the high point of Napoleon's domination on the European continent until the Treaties of Tilsit were concluded with Russia and Prussia, respectively, eighteen months later.

Austerlitz notwithstanding, French victories on the Continent did not affect British mastery of the seas. Britain maintained its naval superiority with Nelson's great victory at Trafalgar on 21 October 1805. In the spring and summer of 1805 a French fleet commanded by Admiral Pierre de Villeneuve eluded the British blockade of the French port of Toulon, rendezvoused with a small Spanish fleet, and made for the West Indies.

The Franco-Spanish fleet had a complex task, which likely exceeded the capacity of its commanders. Napoleon wanted to combine this fleet with another at Brest (which, in the event, never broke through the British blockade of that port). Villeneuve's sailing to the West Indies was merely diversionary—to draw off British squadrons from the Atlantic and Mediterranean—so that Villeneuve could return to European waters, combine with other squadrons, escort Napoleon's army across the English Channel, and land his troops in England.

Vice Admiral Horatio, Viscount Nelson, in command of the British fleet in the Mediterranean, pursued Villeneuve's fleet to the West Indies and back to Europe, where it sought shelter in Cádiz on the southwestern coast of Spain. By late August, with Austria and Russia confronting him, Napoleon broke up the invasion camp at Boulogne and marched his army to the Danube. He then ordered Villeneuve to leave Cádiz and steer for the Mediterranean in order to provide flank protection for Masséna's army in northern Italy.

When Villeneuve emerged from Cádiz, Nelson confronted him on 21 October off Cape Trafalgar. While Villeneuve's fleet of thirty-three ships was arranged in a single file (line ahead), Nelson divided his smaller fleet, of twenty-seven ships, into two squadrons that he used to pierce the Franco-Spanish line—a risky maneuver, but one that in the event worked extraordinarily well. A weak wind meant the British had to approach very slowly, allowing French gunners to pummel the lead British ship in each squadron, Nelson's *Victory* and the *Royal Sovereign,* under the second in command, Vice Admiral Cuthbert Collingwood. Yet the British held their course, and the two columns drove into the long line of Franco-Spanish ships. For five hours the battle raged, in the course of which Nelson was killed by a musket shot. Seventeen ships of the Combined Fleet were captured and one was destroyed; no British ship was lost. Nelson's flagship returned his body to Britain for a lavish ceremonial burial in St. Paul's Cathedral. France never again contested British control of the seas.

Nevertheless, the Third Coalition lay in tatters, for Napoleon stood as the most powerful individual on the European continent.

Charles M. Dobbs

See also Alexander I, Tsar; Amiens, Treaty of; Austerlitz, Battle of; Bagration, Peter Ivanovich, Prince; Bernadotte, Jean-Baptiste-Jules; Blockade; Caldiero, Second Battle of; Charles, Archduke of Austria, Duke of Teschen; Davout, Louis Nicolas; Dupont de l'Etang, Pierre-Antoine, comte; Dürnstein, Battle of; Elchingen, Battle of; Enghien, Louis Antoine Henri de Bourbon-Condé, duc d'; England, French Plans for the Invasion of; Ferdinand d'Este, Archduke; Francis I, Emperor; George III, King; Hanover; Hollabrunn, Action at; Imperial Guard (French); John, Archduke; Kutuzov, Mikhail Golenischev-, Prince; Mack, Karl Freiherr von Leiberich; Masséna, André; Nelson, Horatio, First Viscount; Ney, Michel; Pressburg, Treaty of; Soult, Nicolas Jean de Dieu; Tilsit, Treaties of; Trafalgar, Battle of; Ulm, Surrender at; Villeneuve, Pierre Charles Jean Baptiste Silvestre de

References and further reading
Adkins, Roy. 2004. *Trafalgar: The Biography of a Battle.* London: Little, Brown.
Alombert, Paul Claude. 2002. *La campagne de 1805 en Allemagne.* 3 vols. Paris: Editions historiques Teissèdre.
Bowden, Scott. 1997. *Napoleon and Austerlitz.* Chicago: Emperor's Press.
Chandler, David G. 1990. *Austerlitz 1805: Battle of the Three Emperors.* Oxford: Osprey.
———. 1995. *The Campaigns of Napoleon.* London: Weidenfeld and Nicolson.
Clayton, Tim, and Phil Craig. 2004. *Trafalgar: The Men, the Battle, the Storm.* London: Hodder and Stoughton.
Connelly, Owen. 1999. *Blundering to Glory: Napoleon's Military Campaigns.* Wilmington, DE: Scholarly Resources.
Duffy, Christopher. 1977. *Austerlitz.* London: Seeley Service.
Dupuy, Trevor N. 1968. *The Battle of Austerlitz: Napoleon's Greatest Victory.* New York: Macmillan.
Esdaile, Charles J. 2001. *The French Wars: 1792–1815.* New York: Routledge.
Esposito, Vincent J., and John R. Elting. 1999. *A Military History and Atlas of the Napoleonic Wars.* London: Greenhill.
Fisher, Todd. 2001. *The Napoleonic Wars: The Rise of the Emperor, 1805–1807.* Chicago: Fitzroy Dearborn.
Gardiner, Robert, ed. 1997. *The Campaign of Trafalgar, 1803–1805.* London: Chatham.
Gates, David. 1997. *The Napoleonic Wars, 1803–1815.* New York: Arnold.
Hayward, Joel. 2003. *For God and Glory: Lord Nelson and His Way of War.* Annapolis, MD: Naval Institute Press.
Horne, Alistair. 1979. *Napoleon: Master of Europe, 1805–1807.* London: Weidenfeld and Nicolson.

Hourtoulle, François G. 2003. *Austerlitz: The Empire at its Zenith.* Paris: Histoire et Collections.

Manceron, Claude. 1966. *Austerlitz: The Story of a Battle.* Trans. George Unwin. New York: Norton.

Marshall-Cornwall, James. 2002. *Napoleon as Military Commander.* New York: Penguin.

Pope, Dudley. 1999. *Decision at Trafalgar.* New York: Henry Holt.

Rothenberg, Gunther. 1982. *Napoleon's Great Adversaries: Archduke Charles and the Austrian Army, 1792–1814.* London: Batsford.

Schneid, Frederick C. 2005. *Napoleon's Conquest of Europe: The War of the Third Coalition.* Westport, CT: Praeger.

Schom, Alan. 1992. *Trafalgar: Countdown to Battle, 1803–1805.* New York: Oxford University Press.

Sherwig, John M. 1969. *Guineas and Gunpowder: British Foreign Aid in the Wars with France, 1793–1815.* Cambridge, MA: Harvard University Press.

Thugut, Johann Amadeus Freiherr von (1736–1818)

Austrian diplomat and foreign minister; known as the War Baron for his implacable opposition to the instability caused by the French Revolutionaries. From 1793 he worked to create alliances to defeat successive French governments, but once Bonaparte had restored stability in late 1799, he was keen to make peace. Defeat in the War of the Second Coalition led to Thugut's dismissal on 1 January 1801. Skillful and cunning, he was too inclined to intrigue, but despite being grasping, he rarely indulged in financial irregularities. Genuinely praised by his allies, he was passionately loathed by his opponents, who included most of the military establishment.

The son of an army paymaster, his linguistic abilities led to sponsorship by Empress Maria Theresa (reigned 1740–1780) at the Oriental Languages Academy. He joined the diplomatic service in 1754, working as a translator in Constantinople, before Chancellor (foreign minister) Wenzel Anton Fürst Kaunitz made him ministry secretary, in which capacity he accepted bribes from France. Again in Constantinople, he secured the Turkish cession of the Bukovina in 1775 and was ennobled as a *Freiherr* (baron). After fruitless negotiations with Frederick the Great and service in various embassies, Thugut was appointed director general of the Haus-, Hof- und Staatskanzlei (deputy foreign minister) in 1793 and promoted to minister of foreign affairs in 1794.

Moving Austria away from its traditional focus on Germany to create a centralized, consolidated empire, Thugut aimed to contain both growing Prussian power and the impact of the French Revolution, while seeking opportunities for gains in southern and eastern Europe. In 1795 he signed an offensive-defensive treaty with Russia to participate in the Third Partition of Poland and gain a free hand in the Balkans. Supporting the religious rulers of the Holy Roman Empire as a bulwark of Austrian influence in Germany, he had to concede the loss of the Rhineland to France under the Peace of Campo Formio on 17 October 1797, which led to pressure to secularize these territories to compensate the German princes, though he secured Venetia and Dalmatia in return.

As the only official with individual access to the emperor, Francis I, he could place his supporters in key positions. Ferdinand Graf Tige was made head of the Hofkriegsrat (War Ministry) in 1796, which appointed the powerful army chiefs of staff, so Thugut could ensure his candidates were selected and thus direct military strategy. After concluding alliances with Turkey and Russia in 1798, Thugut pushed Austria into the War of the Second Coalition, focusing Austrian armies on securing southern Germany and northern Italy. This policy led to Russian withdrawal from the war in late 1799. Frosty relations with Britain meant no subsidies were agreed on until June 1800, and Thugut was sacked as minister when the war ended. Awarded a substantial estate in Croatia and a 7,000-florin pension, he left Vienna for Pressburg on 27 March 1801. Although he later returned to Vienna, Thugut remained in retirement and unmarried until his death on 28 May 1818.

David Hollins

See also Austria; Campo Formio, Treaty of; Francis I, Emperor; Holy Roman Empire; Poland, Partitions of; Second Coalition, War of the

References and further reading
Roider, Karl A. 1987. *Baron Thugut and the Austrian Response to the French Revolution.* Princeton: Princeton University Press.

Vivenot, Alfred Ritter von. 1870. *Thugut und sein politisches System* [Thugut and His Political Philosophy]. Vienna: K. Gerold's Sohn.

Wurzbach, C. von. 1856–1891. *Biographische Lexikon des Kaiserthums Österreich* [Biographical Encyclopedia of the Austrian Empire]. 60 vols. Vienna: Zarmarski and Dillmarsch.

Tilsit, Treaties of (7 and 9 July 1807)

Two peace treaties that ended the War of the Fourth Coalition, which had pitted France against Russia and Prussia. These latter two powers, which had allied against Napoleon in July 1806, were forced to ask for terms when Russia, the stronger of the two states, was decisively defeated at Friedland on 14 June 1807. The terms of both treaties were dictated by Napoleon, the first being that with Russia. On 25 June, Napoleon and Tsar Alexander I met on a raft in the middle of the Niemen River near the French-occupied

Napoleon meets Tsar Alexander and the King and Queen of Prussia at Tilsit in 1807. This historic conference marked a dramatic shift in Russian policy and confirmed French supremacy in Europe. (Library of Congress)

town of Tilsit in Poland. Negotiations unfolded over the next two weeks and concluded with the signing of an agreement on 7 July 1807.

The terms were not wholly disadvantageous for Russia, as the treaty established an alliance between the two powers and virtually divided Europe into western and eastern spheres of influence controlled by France and Russia. This division was accomplished through territorial concessions and diplomatic guarantees. Many of the territorial terms that benefited France came at the expense of Prussia. Russia agreed to the creation of the Duchy of Warsaw from formerly Prussian-controlled Polish lands and accepted that King Frederick Augustus of Saxony, an ally of Napoleon, would govern it. Russia also acquiesced in the French creation of the Kingdom of Westphalia in northern Germany and its eventual rule under Jérôme Bonaparte, Napoleon's brother. In addition, the Duchy of Berg, founded by Napoleon in 1806, was expanded. The creation of these new bodies, coming only a year after the formation of the Confederation of the Rhine, firmly es-

tablished Napoleon's control in central Europe while greatly weakening Prussia, which also lost the port of Danzig (now Gdansk), as the Treaty of Tilsit established it as a free city. France also gained influence through Russia being forced to withdraw from Romania and accept the rule of Napoleon's brothers Joseph in Naples and Louis in Holland.

Finally, in secret articles, Russia was made to cede the port town of Cattaro (now Kotor, Montenegro) and the Ionian Islands to France. Russia outwardly gained only a small portion of East Prussia, but diplomatic guarantees offered by Napoleon held the promise for much greater territorial aggrandizement. Napoleon agreed not to impede Russian operations to expand into Swedish-controlled Finland. He also offered to mediate for peace between Russia and the Ottoman Empire, as the two powers had been at war since the previous year. If the Ottomans refused the gesture, Napoleon implied that France would help Russia expand into the European portion of the Ottoman Empire, with the exception of Constantinople. This provision concerning the Ottoman Empire was vaguely worded, but was a step for Russia toward the goal of expansion at the expense of Turkey.

Further measures solidified the military alliance between the two powers. Alexander agreed to try and negotiate peace between France and Britain. If this measure did not produce positive results by 1 November 1807, Russia was compelled to declare war. In the event of hostilities against the British, the treaty stated that Russia and France would force Denmark, Sweden, and Portugal to close their ports to British shipping. This measure was an expansion of Napoleon's Continental System, which was an effort to deny European markets to British commerce and thus bankrupt Britain, which relied on overseas trade for its economic well-being, and to force the country to make peace with France. In seeking to achieve this end, the Treaty of Tilsit also stipulated that Russia join the Continental System and use its naval power against British trade in the Mediterranean.

The second Treaty of Tilsit, with Prussia, concluded on 9 July 1807, was much harsher than that between France and Russia, as many of the terms in the initial agreement were concluded at the expense of Russia's former ally. In return for peace with France, King Frederick William III of Prussia had to agree to all of the territorial losses stipulated by the treaty between Napoleon and Alexander. All Prussian lands west of the river Elbe were lost in order to create the Kingdom of Westphalia, while the Duchy of Warsaw consumed most of the Prussian-controlled Polish lands. Frederick William was also forced to surrender the port city of Danzig.

In effect, Prussia lost nearly half of its territory, which decreased from about 89,000 square miles to just over 46,000 square miles. Prussia was also required to formally recognize all of Napoleon's newly created kingdoms. Additional measures were as harsh as the territorial terms. Napoleon compelled Prussia to enter into a military alliance with France and Russia in the event of war against Britain, a situation that he had already engineered in the terms with Russia. Frederick William also had to bring Prussia into compliance with the Continental System. Finally, additional legislation, signed on 12 July 1807, forced Prussia to agree to the occupation of all of its remaining territory by French troops pending the payment of a war indemnity. The amount of the indemnity was set in 1808 at 140 million francs.

Although Napoleon succeeded in bringing western and central Europe under his control through the Treaties of Tilsit, the agreements did not produce the desired result of a lasting peace in a French-dominated Europe. The treaty with Prussia guaranteed that the Prussians would remain openly hostile to Napoleon. The agreement with

Russia also contained problematic terms. Not only would disagreement later arise between France and Russia over the status of Polish lands, but the Continental System proved a vexing issue. The economic hardship it later created in Russia led to Russian defiance of the system as early as 1810, and contributed directly to the breakdown in Franco-Russian relations that led to war in 1812.

Eric W. Osborne

See also Alexander I, Tsar; Bonaparte, Jérôme; Bonaparte, Joseph; Bonaparte, Louis; Confederation of the Rhine; Continental System; Fourth Coalition, War of the; Frederick William III, King; Friedland, Battle of; Ionian Islands; Poland; Prussia; Russia; Russo-Swedish War; Russo-Turkish War; Saxony; Sweden; Westphalia

References and further reading
Butterfield, Herbert. 1929. *The Peace Tactics of Napoleon, 1806–1808.* Cambridge: Cambridge University Press.
Casaglia, Gherardo. 1998. *Le Partage du Monde: Napoleon et Alexandre à Tilsit, 25 juin 1807.* Paris: S.P.M.
Connelly, Owen. 1991. *The French Revolution and Napoleonic Era.* New York: Harcourt Brace.
Horne, Alistair. 1979. *Napoleon, Master of Europe, 1805–1807.* London: Weidenfeld and Nicolson.
Ross, Steven T. 1969. *European Diplomatic History, 1789–1815: France against Europe.* Garden City, NY: Anchor.
Schroeder, Paul. 1994. *The Transformation of European Politics, 1763–1848.* New York: Oxford University Press.
Troyat, Henri. 1982. *Alexander of Russia, Napoleon's Conqueror.* Trans. Joan Pinkham. New York: Dutton.

Tolentino, Battle of (2–3 May 1815)

Fought at Tolentino, a small city in the Italian Marche (a region abutting the eastern coast of central Italy), this was an Austrian victory against the Neapolitan army. The main and final clash of the war waged by King Joachim Murat to keep his throne, it led to the Treaty of Casalanza (20 May) whereby Murat abdicated, thus paving the way for the Bourbon restoration in Naples.

Murat declared war on Austria on 15 March 1815, marching northward from central Italy and gaining some minor successes. In mid-April, however, the course of the war quickly turned in favor of the Austrians, as Murat failed to force the line of the river Po in Emilia. He then retreated southward to the Marche, with two Austrian armies in pursuit. While *Feldmarshalleutnant* Adam Graf von Neipperg's 11,000 troops were on Murat's heels down the Adriatic coast road, *Feldmarschalleutnant* Vincenz Ritter von Bianchi's force (about 12,000 infantry, 1,500 cavalry, and twenty-eight guns) followed a more westerly route under the cover of the Apennines. On 30 April the latter column reached the walled city of Tolentino, in the narrow and impenetrable valley of the Chienti River, stretching eastward from the mountains down to the sea. By that time Murat was in Macerata, 10 miles east of Tolentino. The Neapolitan army could field about 15,000 infantry, 3,800 cavalry, mostly raw conscripts, and twenty-eight guns, with substantial reinforcements on the way.

On 2 May at 11:00 A.M. two Neapolitan columns marched on Tolentino. The first column, with most of the artillery and the cavalry, advanced along the valley-bottom road, pushing back the Austrian outposts at Sforzacosta. The battle raged for many hours, the Neapolitan momentum being eventually checked at the bridge at Rancia. Meanwhile, the second Neapolitan column, trudging over rough tracks across the left hillside, had taken Monte Milone, a village dominating Tolentino, and threatened the Austrian left flank at Cantagallo. In the late afternoon, however, an infantry counterattack repulsed the Neapolitans behind Monte Milone. As night fell, Bianchi strove to strengthen his defensive line between Monte Milone and Rancia, while Murat awaited reinforcements at Macerata.

On the second day Murat ordered his army forward in three columns. General Giuseppe Lechi's left wing advanced over the hills on the southern bank of the Chienti. The central column under Murat moved up the main road to take Rancia, while General Principe Francesco Pignatelli-Strongoli's right wing attacked Cantagallo. Though outnumbered, the Austrian right did not give way before Lechi. In the other sectors, the Neapolitans were more successful, dislodging the enemy from Rancia, Cantagallo, and Il Casone. At noon, Murat ordered his reserve (General Carlo d'Ambrosio's division and the Royal Guard, about 8,000 men) forward. As soon as they emerged from the woods, the Neapolitan infantry spotted some enemy cavalry and immediately formed four big squares. Under strong artillery fire and pressed at close quarters by enemy infantry and cavalry, the slow-moving and dense formations started wavering and soon retreated in disorder.

Despite this unexpected reverse, at this junction Murat was still strong enough to gain the day. It was the poor morale of his troops, together with Neipperg's upcoming threat from the north and political concerns about the kingdom's domestic situation that convinced him to give up the fight. At Tolentino the Neapolitans lost 1,100 killed and wounded, and 2,200 prisoners. Austrian losses were 700 and 450.

Marco Gioannini

See also "Italian Independence," War of; Murat, Joachim; Naples

References and further reading
Colletta, Pietro. 1982. *La campagna d'Italia di Gioacchino Murat (1815)* [Joachim Murat's Italian Campaign]. Turin: Utet.
Villar, Constant. 1821. *Campagne des Autrichiens contre Murat en 1815*. Brussels: Wahlen.

Tolstoy, Alexander Ivanovich, Count

See Osterman-Tolstoy, Alexander Ivanovich, Count

Tone, Wolfe (1763–1798)

The eldest son of Peter and Margaret Lamport Tone, Wolfe Tone was born in Dublin on 20 June 1763. Although Peter's carriage-making business failed, patronage from Theobald Wolfe, a prominent barrister and politician and Tone's godfather, allowed the family to survive. Tone entered Trinity College in 1781, and despite a raffish career, which included dueling, went on to the Inner Temple in London, returning to Ireland in 1789 as a lawyer. In 1785 he married Matilda Witherington, against the wishes of her family.

In 1791 Tone took part in founding the United Irishmen, simultaneously writing pamphlets for the Catholic Committee as well, advocating religious toleration, parliamentary power and reform, and ultimately, independence for Ireland. After 1793 British crackdowns on the United Irishmen, as well as the revelation that Tone had written material for William Jackson, a French Revolutionary agent, prompted him to flee Ireland in June 1795 for the United States. Tone and his family languished in Philadelphia and Princeton before getting support from the French ambassador to the United States to petition the French government. With introductions from James Monroe, Tone made contact with Lazare Carnot and General Louis Lazare Hoche, who agreed that Ireland could serve as a staging area for an attack on Britain.

Unfortunately, the December 1796 invasion led by Hoche and Tone floundered when a storm off the Irish coast scattered the French fleet and forced a return to Brest. Tone spent the next year at Hoche's command on the Rhine and touring the Netherlands, whose government he admired. The deaths of both Hoche and Carnot, as well as the advent of Bonaparte, prevented Tone from succeeding in pushing for a second invasion, which would have been in competition for resources with Bonaparte's Egyptian expedition. Rebellion broke out in Ireland during the summer of 1798, and Tone was hastily recalled by the Directory and dispatched with 8,000 French troops. Poor planning guaranteed that the fleet was followed by a British naval squadron, which attacked off the Irish coast near Donegal, capturing the flagship *Hoche* and arresting Tone.

Tone claimed the protections of his French uniform, but was treated as a revolutionary and criminal, imprisoned at Derry, and then transferred to Dublin for trial on 10 November. He was found guilty of treason and sentenced to hang, but Tone cut his throat in his cell, dying from those injuries on 17 November. His wife and surviving son William lived in France on a pension, and William was a Napoleonic officer during the Hundred Days.

Margaret Sankey

See also Carnot, Lazare Nicolas Marguerite; Directory, The; Donegal, Battle of; Hoche, Louis Lazare; Ireland; Irish Rebellion; Middle East Campaign
References and further reading
Elliott, Marianne. 1982. *Partners in Revolution: The United Irishmen and France.* New Haven: Yale University Press.
———. 1989. *Wolfe Tone, the Prophet of Irish Independence.* New Haven: Yale University Press.
Wilson, David A. 1998. *United Irishmen, United States: Immigrant Radicals in the Early Republic.* Ithaca: Cornell University Press.

Torgau, Siege of
(8 October 1813–10 January 1814)

The fortress city of Torgau was situated at an important crossing of the river Elbe in the Kingdom of Saxony. Being of strategic significance in both the spring and fall campaigns of 1813, its possession was contested until it finally fell to the Allies in January 1814.

Torgau was a fortress of the first order and had been well maintained. Its defenses consisted of a strong outer wall, fosses, and external works. There were seven bastion fronts along the perimeter of the wall. There was no wall along the eastern side, as that side ran along the Elbe. A bridgehead of considerable strength stood on the eastern bank, covering the bridge. Three bastions ran along the front of this bridgehead. Its ditches could be flooded; the bridge was wooden and covered. In the city itself there were 557 dwellings. Two external forts, Fort Zinna and Fort Mahla, had been built on the hills to the northeast of Torgau, and there were also two lunettes on each bank.

This fortress town was garrisoned by Saxon troops under the command of General Johann Adolph Freiherr von Thielmann. In the immediate aftermath of the campaign of 1812 in Russia, Frederick August, the king of Saxony, maintained a policy of neutrality. Thielmann had been ordered to deny access to the fortress to any foreign power. He refused to hand it over to Prusso-Russian forces in the spring of 1813, when they advanced into Saxony.

The French victory over the Allies at Lützen, on 2 May 1813, materially altered the situation. While Napoleon pressured Frederick August to join him, he sent General Jean Reynier's corps toward Torgau. General Pierre François Durutte's division arrived there on 7 May, but Thielmann refused entry to it. Frederick August acceded to Napoleon's demands, and on 12 May, Thielmann received orders to join forces with Reynier. He complied, opening the city and fortress to the French, but went over to the Allies with his staff.

For the remainder of the campaign in Germany, Torgau remained in French hands. On 14 September the comte de Narbonne was made governor. Additional defenses were constructed to protect the bridge from fire ships.

After the Battle of Dennewitz on 6 September, a Prussian observation corps took up positions on the east bank, harassing shipping along the great river. On 3 October, the Prussians forced a crossing of the Elbe at Wartenburg and moved along the west bank toward Torgau. On the eighth, Narbonne declared the city in a state of siege. The garrison was around 25,000 men strong, with 199 guns. The Saxon troops left Torgau on 22 October. At the end of the month, a Prussian force under General Friedrich von Tauentzien sealed off the western side. The siege of Torgau now commenced. Throughout November, sorties, raids, and bombardments were undertaken. The besiegers started the construction of a mine. A plague of typhus broke out.

Narbonne attempted to negotiate surrender from 4 to 7 December, but Tauentzien did not accept his proposals. Further talks were held that month, before agreement was finally reached on 20 December. On 10 January 1814 the survivors of the garrison departed. Their losses numbered around 15,000 men.

Peter Hofschröer

See also Dennewitz, Battle of; Germany, Campaign in; Lützen, Battle of; Reynier, Jean Louis Ebénézer, comte; Siege Warfare; Thielmann, Johann Adolph Freiherr von
References and further reading
Augoyat, Antoine Marie. 1840. *Rélation de la défence de Torgau par les troupes françaises en 1813.* Paris: Leneveu.
Petre, F. Loraine. 1992. *Napoleon's Last Campaign in Germany, 1813.* London: Greenhill.

Tormasov, Alexander Petrovich (1752–1819)

Russian general and army commander. Born into an ancient Russian noble family, Tormasov began his career as a page at the imperial court in February 1762 and enlisted as a lieutenant in the Vyatka Infantry Regiment on 13 March 1772. He was promoted to captain in May 1772 and served as adjutant to Count Bruce, who was appointed commander of the Finland Division in 1774. Tormasov became lieutenant colonel and commander of the Finland *Jäger* Battalion in 1777. He served in the Crimea in 1782–1783 and commanded the Aleksandria Light Horse Regiment in 1784. From 1788 to 1791, he participated in the Russo-Turkish War, commanding a cavalry brigade that remained in reserve at Ochakov. Tormasov was promoted to brigadier general on 5 April 1789 and to major general on

1 April 1791. He distinguished himself at Babadag and Macin.

From 1792 to 1794, Tormasov served against the Polish insurgents, fighting at Vishnepol, Mobar, Warsaw, Maciejowice, and Praga. He was appointed *chef* (colonel proprietor) of the Military Order Cuirassier Regiment on 14 December 1796 and promoted to lieutenant general on 18 February 1798. However, Tormasov had an argument with Tsar Paul in 1799 and was discharged from the army on 23 July 1799. He returned to service on 28 November 1800 and was restored as *chef* of the Life Guard Horse Regiment on 18 December. Two days later, he was appointed commander of the Life Guard Horse Regiment. Tormasov was promoted to general of cavalry on 27 September 1801 and enjoyed a rapid succession of promotions, including to cavalry inspector of the Dniester Inspection on 23 July 1801 and cavalry inspector of the Lifland Inspection on 20 February 1802.

After briefly retiring in late 1802, Tormasov became military governor of Kiev on 7 February 1803. In 1804 he was awarded an estate in the Courland *gubernia* (province), and in 1805 he began organizing the Army of the Dniester against the Turks. He took a prolonged furlough because of poor health in 1806. After recuperating, Tormasov was appointed military governor of Riga on 28 March 1807 but retired again because of poor health that December. After the death of his wife, Tormasov returned to the army on 21 June 1808 and was appointed commander in chief of the troops in Georgia and the Caucasus in September 1808 during the Russo-Turkish War.

Tormasov secured the Russian administration in the Transcaucasia, defeating several Persian raids into Georgia and launching a successful offensive against the Turks in western Georgia. Simultaneously, he forced the remaining independent Georgian principalities, including the Kingdom of Imereti, into submission to Russia. He captured the fortresses of Poti and Akhaltsikhe and negotiated with the Persians at the fortress of Askoran in early 1810. He crushed the Persian Prince Abbas Mirza at Migri and Akhalkalaki in September 1810. During October, November, and December, Tormasov suppressed an uprising in Daghestan, then engaged King Solomon of Imereti at Akhaltsikhe and prevented a Turkish invasion of southern Georgia. Tormasov was appointed commander in chief of the 3rd Reserve Army of Observation in Volhynia on 27 March 1812.

During the Russian campaign of 1812, Tormasov engaged Austrian and French troops at Brest, Kobryn, and Gorodechnya. He took command of the 2nd Western Army after Prince Peter Bagration's death in late September, but he arrived at the camp at Tarutino after the two Russian armies were merged. Tormasov thereupon assumed command of the main Russian forces, excluding the advance guard. In November, he fought at Maloyaroslavets and Krasnyi, and pursued the French to Vilna. In early 1813 he briefly commanded the Russian army after Field Marshal Mikhail Kutuzov's death and took part in the Battle of Lützen during the spring campaign in Germany. However, he had to leave the army because of poor health, and, on being appointed a member of the State Council, he returned to St. Petersburg. He became military governor of Moscow on 11 September 1814 and was awarded the title of Count of the Russian Empire on 11 September 1816. Tormasov died on 25 November 1819 and was buried in the Don Monastery in Moscow.

Alexander Mikaberidze

See also Bagration, Peter Ivanovich, Prince; Germany, Campaign in; Krasnyi, Second Battle of; Kutuzov, Prince Mikhail Golenischev-, Prince; Lützen, Battle of; Maciejowice, Battle of; Maloyaroslavets, Battle of; Paul I, Tsar; Russian Campaign; Russo-Polish War; Russo-Turkish War

References and further reading
Mikaberidze, Alexander. 2005. *The Russian Officer Corps in the Revolutionary and Napoleonic Wars, 1792–1815.* New York: Savas Beatie.

Torres Vedras, Lines of

An enormous network of forts, batteries, and redoubts, built into the natural terrain, constructed in secret approximately 40 miles north of Lisbon, which could be used by Viscount (later the Duke of) Wellington, if needed, as a last line of defense. Construction of the Lines of Torres Vedras was ordered by Wellington in November 1809, and, when completed, the network included three separate defensive lines rendering a French invasion down the Peninsula into Lisbon impossible.

The Lines, 30 miles long at their widest, took a year to build, utilizing over 10,000 Portuguese laborers, supervised by fewer than twenty British and Allied engineers, at a total cost of nearly £100,000. The construction teams dammed rivers to form inundations, scarped whole hillsides to create precipices, and blocked numerous valleys with vast stone walls. When completed, the Lines included approximately 150 redoubts and earthworks of various descriptions mounting over 600 cannon. Even including the Portuguese militiamen supported by the British, Wellington's force was far too small to garrison the Lines. To deal with this problem, his engineers built lateral roads behind the hills, making it possible to concentrate troops rapidly at any threatened point. All the roads on the French side of the hills were destroyed, making it difficult for Marshal André Masséna to move troops into position for an attack.

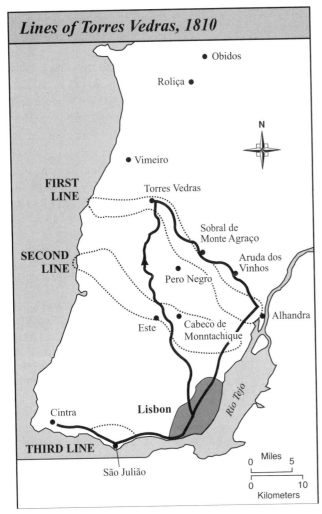

Lines of Torres Vedras, 1810

Obidos

Roliça

N

Vimeiro

FIRST LINE

Torres Vedras

Sobral de
Monte Agraço

SECOND LINE

Aruda dos
Vinhos

Pero Negro

Este

Cabeço de
Monntachique

Alhandra

Rio Tejo

Cintra

Lisbon

THIRD LINE

São Julião

Miles 0 — 5

Kilometers 0 — 10

Adapted from Paget 1997, 112.

In April 1809, when Lieutenant General Sir Arthur Wellesley (shortly to be raised to the peerage as Viscount Wellington) took command of the British expeditionary force in Portugal, he understood the need to conserve his army. Unlike the French, the British could not lose entire armies and return months later with larger ones. Additionally, the key to success for Wellington, as for all generals, was protecting his supply lines. For Wellington, that meant always having access to the sea through a good port, which also provided an escape route, both of which were available through Lisbon. Wellington was certainly mindful of what had happened to Lieutenant General Sir John Moore and the army during the disastrous retreat to Corunna earlier the same year. The Lines of Torres Vedras helped Wellington to meet these strategic objectives.

In the summer of 1810, the French, under Masséna, were in the early stages of an invasion of Portugal. The British and their Portuguese and Spanish allies suffered a series of setbacks: The French captured the great Spanish fortress of Ciudad Rodrigo (10 July); the British were

forced to withdraw during the action at the Coa (24 July); and, as a result of a huge accidental explosion that destroyed the magazine, the Portuguese fortress at Almeida surrendered to the French (26 August). The pursuing French forced Wellington to fight a major rearguard action at Busaco (27 September).

Although the British completely and bloodily repulsed a series of French assaults, many historians have criticized Wellington for not counterattacking in order to drive Masséna back toward Spain. Wellington, however, was interested in more than a small tactical victory; his overall scheme was to pull the French further into Portugal. Predictably, the French found a way around the British right flank and continued to push Wellington back toward Lisbon, unknowingly falling deeper into Wellington's strategic trap.

Wellington, knowing that the Torres Vedras defensive positions were ready, continued to retreat, instituting a policy of "scorched earth" (burning crops in his wake) as he moved toward Lisbon. The British entered the Lines in early October. On Wellington's orders, the British left nothing behind as they headed south; all the Portuguese were forced to move with the British army, and any food that could not be transferred behind the Lines was destroyed. The French continued to follow the retreating British, but suddenly, to their complete shock, they encountered the Lines of Torres Vedras. Masséna halted his troops, gazed at this military feat, and knew his 65,000 men were insufficient to breech Wellington's defenses. As Masséna pondered what to do, he sent General Maximilien, comte Foy to Napoleon with news of the campaign and a request for reinforcements.

The French made a couple of half-hearted attempts to force the Lines (12–14 October), but the superior defensive positions afforded by the Lines enabled the British to repulse them with ease. Wellington's strategy was simple: Do not lose men in battle, and let starvation and illness destroy the French army. With winter fast approaching and no Portuguese peasants to plunder, the French troops suffered terribly. Finally, in November, with no other viable option, Masséna began a slow retreat back to Spain. By the time the French returned to Spain in April 1811, they had lost over 30,000 men, most to starvation and illness, as a result of Wellington's scorched-earth policy.

Unfortunately, the French were not the only casualties. In order to make the land north of the defenses bare of supplies for the marauding French, Wellington forced 300,000 Portuguese to relocate behind the Lines. Most of the refugees lived in shantytowns in and around Lisbon. Over 40,000 died during the winter of 1810–1811 from the effects of exposure, malnutrition, and disease, in spite of the best efforts of the British and Portuguese governments. Many British soldiers and officers made substantial voluntary contributions of food and money to aid the refugees, and Wellington himself wrote several letters back to London requesting assistance.

The Lines of Torres Vedras epitomized Wellington's style of strategic thinking. Not only did he focus upon his major priorities; protecting Britain's only field army in Europe, protecting his supply route through Lisbon, and providing his army a place to disembark in case of disaster, but he used the defensive lines as a jumping-off point for a major offensive. Throughout the Peninsular War, Wellington was at his best utilizing a defensive position to gain the advantage before shifting to the offensive. Wellington saw the possibilities the topography north of Lisbon afforded him, and his military brilliance enabled him to develop a strategy encompassing all eventualities, good or ill. Once the Lines proved impenetrable to the enemy, he could then plan and launch an offensive campaign for the liberation of the whole Iberian Peninsula.

Craig T. Cobane

See also Almeida, Sieges of; Busaco, Battle of; Ciudad Rodrigo, First Siege of; Corunna, Retreat to; Foy, Maximilien Sebastien, comte; Masséna, André; Moore, Sir John; Peninsular War; Wellington, Arthur Wellesey, First Duke of

References and further reading
Esdaile, Charles J. 2003. *The Peninsular War: A New History.* New York: Palgrave Macmillan.
Fletcher, Ian. 2003. *The Lines of Torres Vedras, 1809–11.* Oxford: Osprey.
Grehan, John. 2004. *The Lines of Torres Vedras: The Cornerstone of Wellington's Strategy in the Peninsular War, 1809–1812.* Staplehurst, UK: Spellmount.
Oman, Sir Charles. 2005. *A History of the Peninsular War.* 7 vols. Vol. 3. London: Greenhill. (Orig. pub. 1902–1930.)

Toulon, Siege of
(7 September–19 December 1793)

Napoleon Bonaparte initially came to national attention after the siege of Toulon, where he, a mere captain in the artillery, played a decisive role in dislodging British and Allied forces from the great Mediterranean naval port. Bonaparte was the latest in a succession of military leaders entrusted with the task. He owed his appointment partly to Corsican deputy-on-mission Antonio Salicetti, sent from Paris to oversee operations, but also to his support for the dominant Jacobins, who were attempting to crush the widespread urban revolts of summer 1793, which their seizure of power had provoked. Bonaparte's success was due to his vigorous pursuit of an obvious strategy to end the siege, by seizing a vital promontory (the so-called Petit-Gibraltar) dominating the bay of Toulon, thus threatening the escape of the enemy fleet.

The Toulonnais inhabitants, like their counterparts in larger towns elsewhere, notably Lyons and Marseilles, had withdrawn allegiance from the Jacobin-led government. Their new town council denounced the National Convention, from which provincial deputies had been purged on 2 June 1793, and compromise seemed unlikely. The Army of the Alps was diverted to deal with rebels in Provence, and when Marseilles surrendered on 25 August, Toulon was isolated. Its leaders turned to the British fleet, then blockading the Mediterranean coast, for assistance in resisting "the wrath of Robespierre." Vice Admiral Samuel, Lord Hood, the British commander working with allied Spanish and Neapolitan contingents, responded positively, but only in return for surrender of the naval base and a declaration in favor of the infant pretender to the throne, Louis XVII. The Toulonnais reluctantly accepted this gross act of treason to avoid imminent defeat and bloody reprisals, admitting their former adversaries to the port on 27–28 August, though all they achieved was a stay of execution.

The Allied forces proved unable to exploit this unanticipated windfall. A potential bridgehead for the invasion of southern France required reinforcements, which failed to materialize. In their absence, preparations were made to withstand a siege, unsustainable once the maritime escape route was removed. That it took three months for republican forces to break the resistance at Toulon was a reflection of inefficiency, overcome once Captain Bonaparte was given command of the artillery in November. He led the successful assault on the key redoubt on 17 December, and with republican artillery rendering their position untenable, the Allies began to withdraw the day after. In doing so, they removed or destroyed much of the French Mediterranean fleet, inflicting a naval disaster worse than Trafalgar, though the dockyards remained virtually undamaged. Many rebels fled with the Allies, but repression was severe for those left behind—over 1,000 executions followed. For Bonaparte, who played no part in this punishment, the siege represented a vital stepping-stone to renown; rewarded with promotion to brigadier general, his name (then Buonaparte) appeared in the newspapers for the first time.

Malcolm Crook

See also Convention, The; Jacobins; Lyons, Siege of; Robespierre, Maximilien François Marie Isidore; Siege Warfare

References and further reading
Clowes, William Laird. 1996. *The Royal Navy: A History from the Earliest Times to 1900.* Vol. 4. London: Chatham. (Orig. pub. 1898.)
Crook, Malcolm. 1991. *Toulon in War and Revolution: From the Ancien Regime to the Restoration, 1750–1820.* Manchester, UK: Manchester University Press.
Forczyk, Robert A. 2005. *Toulon 1793.* Oxford: Osprey.

994

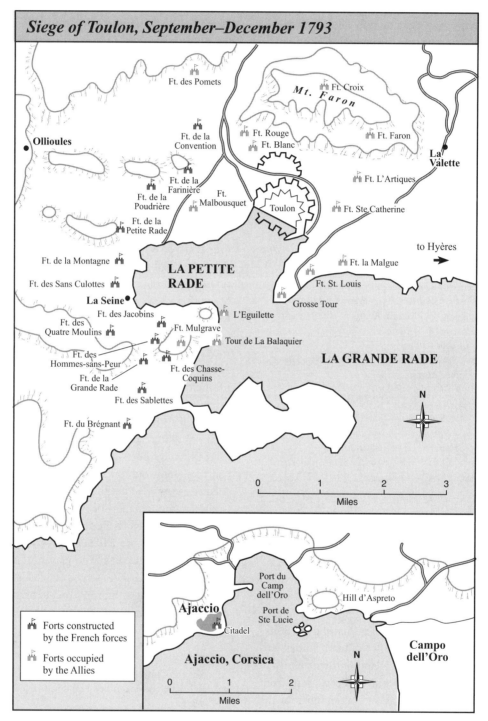

Adapted from Chandler 1966, 18.

Ireland, Bernard. 2005. *The Fall of Toulon: The Royal Navy and the Royalist Stand against the French Revolution.* London: Weidenfeld and Nicolson.

Rose, John Holland. 1922. *Lord Hood and the Defence of Toulon.* Cambridge: Cambridge University Press.

Toulouse, Battle of (10 April 1814)

The last major engagement of the Peninsular War, fought between the Marquis of Wellington's Allied army of approximately 50,000 men, and Marshal Nicolas Soult's 42,000 French troops. Unbeknownst to the combatants, Napoleon had already abdicated in Paris a few days before, thus rendering the Battle of Toulouse a pointless bloodletting.

Wellington's victorious army was too tired to give immediate chase to the defeated French after the Battle of Orthez, but on 2 March 1814 caught up with it at Aire, at which engagement the Allies lost 150 men before hastening the French on their way. The pursuit stalled here, however, due to political expediency, for Bordeaux was known to have royalist sympathies and, as such, Marshal Sir William Beresford, with the 4th and 7th Divisions, marched north to that city, which was given up to him on 12 March. The 7th Division remained in Bordeaux while Beresford returned with the 4th Division to rejoin Wellington on the sixteenth.

There were further clashes between the two armies as Soult continued his retreat to Toulouse, notably at Vic Bigorre on the nineteenth and at Tarbes the following day, an action that Wellington later called the sharpest fight of the war.

Soult finally entered Toulouse on 24 March. His first task was to issue fresh arms and ammunition, clothes, and supplies to his men. Eight thousand French troops were without shoes, and thousands more lacked even the most basic of equipment, much of it having been abandoned during the pursuit from Orthez. Fortunately for him, Toulouse was a main French Army depot, and stocks and supplies were plentiful. Reinforcements were also to be found here, which made good some of the losses of the previous few weeks.

The city of Toulouse was surrounded by a high wall, flanked with towers, but the defenses were not constructed along the lines laid down by Vauban and were nowhere near as strong as those at any of the other main towns besieged by Wellington. The wide river Garonne flows to the west of Toulouse, and it was a major obstacle. On the left bank of the river was the fortified suburb of St. Cyprien, while to the east lay the suburbs of St. Etienne and Guillemerie. To the north and east of the city flowed the Langue-doc Canal, and even farther still to the east was the river Ers. The key to the city, however, was the Calvinet ridge, which ran between the Ers and the canal to the east of the city. In fact, the feature called the Calvinet was two ridges, the second actually being Mont Rave. The ridge, standing some 600 feet high, overlooked the city, and once it was taken, Wellington's siege guns would be able to pound away at the place with ease. A series of redoubts were therefore constructed upon the ridge, notably the Augustins and the Sypière, while other entrenchments were dug also.

On 27 March an attempt was made to bridge the Garonne, but the pontoons fell some 80 feet short. On the thirtieth another attempt was made, about a mile farther south, but this too proved unsatisfactory, as the roads were not of sufficient quality to allow the passage of wheeled vehicles. The bridge was therefore taken up and laid some fifteen miles north of the city, and on the evening of 4 April Beresford crossed with 19,000 men. Unfortunately, heavy rain swept the bridge away—in a repeat of the episode during the crossing of the Nive in December 1813 when part of Wellington's forces had been stuck on one side beyond immediate support—leaving Beresford stranded on the right bank of the river. On this occasion, Soult chose not to attack, and three days later the bridge was operational once more.

On 8 April the rest of Wellington's army crossed the Garonne, leaving Lieutenant General Sir Rowland Hill's corps on the left bank, from where it was to threaten the suburb of St. Cyprien. Elsewhere, the 3rd and Light Divisions were to attack the line of the canal along the northern front, with the main attack being delivered by Beresford with the 4th and 6th Divisions, who were to advance along the left bank of the Ers before wheeling to the right and moving against the French positions on the southern end of the Calvinet ridge. The northern end of the ridge was to be attacked by Major General Manuel Freire's Spaniards, who, having a much shorter distance to cover, were to begin their attack only when Beresford was in position in front of the ridge.

The Allied offensive got underway at 5:00 A.M. with Hill's diversionary attack west of the Garonne against the defenders at St. Cyprien. Several battalions worked their way around the French works here, but the object of the game was to keep Soult from withdrawing his men to the area of the main Allied attack against the Calvinet ridge. Hill's attack petered out with skirmishing and artillery fire between the two sides, but no attempt was made to storm the suburb. Soult soon recognized the ruse and withdrew General Claude Pierre Rouget's brigade to assist in the defense of Mont Rave.

To the north, meanwhile, Lieutenant General Sir Thomas Picton began his feint with an effective attack on

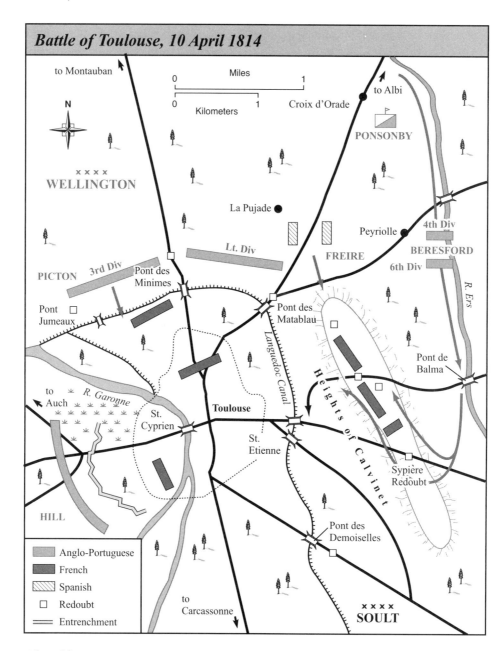

Battle of Toulouse, 10 April 1814

Adapted from Fremont-Barnes 2002A, 83.

the French positions close to the canal. However, Picton got carried away and ordered Major General Thomas Brisbane's brigade to storm the bridge over the canal and take some French positions in and around some farm buildings and orchards. This was against Wellington's express orders, and the attack was driven back with loss. Major General Charles, Baron von Alten's Light Division, on the other hand, on Picton's left flank, acted precisely in accordance with the commander in chief's wishes and restricted itself to skirmishing with French pickets at the Matabiua bridge.

To the east of Toulouse, Freire's Spaniards waited while these attacks progressed. Beresford's two divisions had still not arrived opposite Mont Rave, owing to the

boggy nature of the ground over which they marched. They were still out of range of the enemy guns, and so in spite of the slow pace of their march there was little danger. However, when they had got to within a mile of the position from which they would wheel to their left, they came under fire from the guns on Mont Rave. This prompted Beresford into abandoning his guns, as they sank deep into the mud and slowed the columns down. The guns were left on a knoll, from which they commenced firing on the guns on Mont Rave.

The impatient Freire appears to have mistaken the fire from Beresford's guns as the signal for his own infantry attack to begin, and at once ordered his two brigades for-

British infantry exchanges fire with the French across the Languedoc Canal during the Battle of Toulouse. (Print after Henri Dupray, ca. 1890)

ward in line with two others in support. Freire's Spaniards came on bravely in the face of a heavy artillery barrage from the Calvinet ridge, but when they came within musket range the defenders opened up a withering fire, which brought the Spaniards to a halt just sixty yards from the French. At this point tragedy struck, for the disordered Spaniards sought the shelter of a sunken road that gave them some relief from the storm of lead being turned on them. Unfortunately, they were reluctant to leave the security of the lane, and when the French defenders left their trenches and came forward, Freire's men were trapped. The French just fired blindly into the helpless target before them, and they were joined by other French troops and by two heavy guns that poured out a shower of grape into the Spaniards. It was only with great difficulty that the survivors managed to extricate themselves, and they fled in panic back to their original positions.

Wellington acted quickly to ease the plight of the Spaniards and sent orders to Beresford telling him to wheel right and begin his attack, irrespective of where he was. Beresford, however, had also seen the result of Freire's attack and decided, as he could be of little use there, to ignore the order and continue his march south. Finally he

reached his position; the 4th and 6th Divisions wheeled to their left and formed in line to begin their assault on Mont Rave. The British troops set off with a front of over a mile and a half but had gone only a short distance when two French brigades, under General Eloi Charlemagne Taupin, appeared to their west attacking in column. Six years of fighting the British had taught the French little of the disadvantage of sending column against line, and in the ensuing firefight Beresford's men swept the French before them, killing Taupin himself. Soon afterward, the two British divisions reached Mont Rave and cleared the defenders from it. Beresford then waited while he had his guns brought up.

At about 4:00 P.M., the 6th Division advanced north to clear the French from the Calvinet ridge, but it succeeded in driving them from the southern end of the ridge only, and even that was achieved only after heavy fighting, during which the Augustins redoubt changed hands five times.

While the 6th Division struggled for possession of the ridge, Picton launched another attack to the north of the city. Once again he was beaten back with heavy casualties, including Brisbane, who was wounded, and Lieutenant Colonel Thomas Forbes, of the 45th Foot, who was killed.

Altogether, Picton's division suffered 354 casualties in his vain assaults north of the canal.

At about 4:30 P.M. Soult finally ordered the Calvinet ridge to be abandoned. The remaining defenders there had come under increasing pressure, not only from the 6th Division but also from a battery of horse artillery that Wellington had sent forward. With the withdrawal from the ridge, all French troops were now within the perimeter defined by the canal, and at 5:00 P.M., with the light beginning to fade, the fighting died down. Both armies slept that night on the blood-soaked ground they had fought so hard for during the day, a day that had cost Wellington some 4,558 casualties, against Soult's 3,236.

The following morning, Soult began to prepare to abandon Toulouse, and at nightfall on the eleventh his troops began to file out of the city along the road south toward Carcassone. The whole tragedy of the battle was that it need never have been fought in the first place, for even as Soult's men headed south, Wellington received news of Napoleon's abdication, which had taken place on 6 April, four days before the battle. Toulouse, therefore, had been a tragic and needless waste of life.

Even so, there was still one last pointless postscript to the war. On 14 April, four days after Toulouse and a full eight days after Napoleon's abdication, General Pierre Thouvenot, commanding the garrison at Bayonne decided, either out of ignorance or malice, to launch a sortie against the besieging Allied troops. In the resulting fight, 843 British troops became casualties, including Lieutenant General Sir John Hope, who was wounded and taken prisoner, and Major General Andrew Hay, who was killed. The French themselves lost 891 men in this futile action.

Ian Fletcher

See also Beresford, Sir William Carr; Hill, Sir Rowland; Orthez, Battle of; Peninsular War; Picton, Sir Thomas; Soult, Nicolas Jean de Dieu; Tarbes, Battle of; Wellington, Arthur Wellesley, First Duke of

References and further reading

Beatson, F. C. 1995. *Wellington: The Bidassoa and the Nivelle.* London: Donovan.
Esdaile, Charles J. 2003. *The Peninsular War: A New History.* London: Palgrave Macmillan.
Gates, David. 2001. *The Spanish Ulcer: A History of the Peninsular War.* New York: Da Capo.
Glover, Michael. 2001. *The Peninsular War, 1807–1814: A Concise Military History.* London: Penguin.
Napier, W. F. P. 1992. *A History of the War in the Peninsula.* 6 vols. London: Constable. (Orig. pub. 1828.)
Oman, Sir Charles. 2005. *A History of the Peninsular War.* 7 vols. London: Greenhill. (Orig. pub. 1902–1930.)
Paget, Julian. 1992. *Wellington's Peninsular War: Battles and Battlefields.* London: Leo Cooper.
Robertson, Ian. 2003. *Wellington Invades France: The Final Phase of the Peninsular War, 1813–1814.* London: Greenhill.
Uffindell, Andrew. 2003. *The National Army Museum Book of Wellington's Armies: Britain's Triumphant Campaigns in the Peninsula and at Waterloo, 1808–1815.* London: Sedgwick and Jackson.
Weller, Jac. 1992. *Wellington in the Peninsula.* London: Greenhill.

Tourcoing, Battle of (17–18 May 1794)

The Battle of Tourcoing halted the Allied advance from Flanders into northwest France during the campaign of 1794. The fighting was scattered and confused, and did not produce a decisive victory for either side. The Allies, however, decided to take up defensive positions and make their main effort farther south.

The French plan for 1794 called for an advance by the Army of the North on Brussels, capital of the Austrian Netherlands. The Allies hoped to make their main effort around Landrecies. By the second week of May several French divisions under General Joseph Souham had advanced in the midst of the Allied right wing. *Generalmajor* Karl Mack Freiherr von Leiberich recognized the opportunity to cut off Souham and crush his force by means of a concentric attack by Allied forces around Tourcoing. Mack's plan called for six separate columns, but their movements were hampered by lack of communications and coordination. Although the Allies had 80,000 men in the area, only 62,000 were able to participate in the battle.

Souham recognized the situation as well. In the absence of General Jean-Charles Pichegru, he planned to throw most his forces against the Allied right under *Feldzeugmeister* Franz Sebastian de Croix Graf von Clerfayt. Reports of movements by Austrian and British troops on 16 May caused Souham to scrap that plan and concentrate his forces on the two columns advancing against him in the center. When the Allied attack began on 17 May, things quickly fell apart. Clerfayt's column on the right was held up by an unexpectedly fierce French defense on the river Lys. Columns on the left under Archduke Charles and *Feldzeugmeister* Franz Kinsky Graf von Wichinitz und Tettau were hampered by fog and moved more slowly than expected. Only the central columns, consisting mostly of British and Hessian troops under the Duke of York, achieved their goals for 17 May. The Guards Brigade particularly distinguished itself in overrunning several French defensive positions.

By the morning of 18 May Souham had massed his forces. Archduke Charles and Kinsky ignored orders to move faster, and Clerfayt was diverted by General Dominique Vandamme's brigade. Souham's main attack quickly captured Tourcoing and forced the British from their advanced positions. Showing remarkable discipline, the British Guards cut their way out of several encirclements, though the British cavalry and artillery suffered great losses. During the retreat on 18 May the civilian drivers cut the traces and abandoned most of the guns and caissons, and thus the cavalry regiments following on the same road were not able to pass easily. Needless losses of horses and men resulted.

By 19 May most of the Allied forces were back at their starting point. French losses were approximately 3,000 men killed and wounded, and 7 guns lost. Allied losses were heavier, with 4,000 men killed and wounded, and another 1,500 captured. As many as 50 guns were captured.

Tourcoing was a moral defeat for the Allies. The Austrians, who were the dominant partners, decided to remain on the defensive in Flanders. The Battle of Tournai on 22 May confirmed this decision. The French, on the other hand, saw Tourcoing as a victory, confirming their method of warfare as superior to prevailing orthodox tactics.

Tim J. Watts

See also Charles, Archduke of Austria, Duke of Teschen; First Coalition, War of the; Flanders, Campaigns in; Landrecies, Battle of; Mack, Karl Freiherr von Leiberich; Pichegru, Jean-Charles; Souham, Joseph, comte; Tournai, Battle of; Vandamme, Dominique Joseph René; York and Albany, Frederick Augustus, Duke of
References and further reading
Belloc, Hilaire. 1912. *Tourcoing.* London: Swift.
Phipps, Ramsay Weston. 1980. *The Armies of the First French Republic and the Rise of the Marshals of Napoleon I.* Vol. 1, *The Armée du Nord.* London: Greenwood. (Orig. pub. 1926–1939.)

Tournai, Battle of (22 May 1794)

In the spring of 1794, French forces in the Austrian Netherlands (Belgium) fought several large-scale battles against the troops of the opposing Allied coalition. On 22 May, after its success at the Battle of Tourcoing, General Jean-Charles Pichegru's Army of the North failed in an assault on the fortress city of Tournai in western Belgium. Although Austrian and British troops under *Feldmarschall* Friedrich Josias Graf Saxe-Coburg-Saalfeld (generally known as Saxe-Coburg) fended off the French attack, the Battle of Tournai showed the ability of French units to maintain their cohesiveness in difficult circumstances. It also forced Saxe-Coburg to pull reinforcements from the southern sector of the Allied front, thereby setting the stage for the decisive French victory at Fleurus in late June.

The French and their Austrian, British, and Hanoverian opponents launched offensives starting in April 1794. After two years of fighting, each side hoped to seize the initiative in this new campaign. The French forces that took

the field reflected the growing strength of their country's military system. The amalgamation of units of volunteers and conscripts had been completed by February, and the conscription law of the previous year—the famous *levée en masse*—provided a military manpower pool of unprecedented size. Tactical training in the newly formed field armies produced units that could attack with skill and élan, as well as remain steady in adversity.

By late May the French had gained the initiative, and in the northern sector in Belgium, they compelled Saxe-Coburg and his army to retreat to the fortified city of Tournai. French attacks there lasted from early morning until the evening of 22 May. Saxe-Coburg defeated Pichegru's efforts to take Tournai, and the French lost 6,000 men in the battle compared to only 4,000 Allied casualties. Nonetheless, the French fought well. General Jacques Macdonald, a future Marshal of the Empire, directed his brigade's complex movements on the battlefield with particular skill.

Tournai proved only a temporary French setback. In the aftermath of the battle, Pichegru besieged and eventually took the city of Ypres. Moreover, Saxe-Coburg felt compelled to draw reinforcements northward from Allied units on the Sambre. In the face of weakened enemy forces in the south, General Jean-Baptiste Jourdan was able to attack and take the key Allied stronghold of Charleroi. Saxe-Coburg attempted to counter this French offensive, and as a result, he was defeated by Jourdan at the decisive Battle of Fleurus. The French now occupied all of Belgium.

Neil M. Heyman

See also Flanders, Campaigns in; Fleurus, Battle of; Jourdan, Jean-Baptiste; Levée en Masse; Macdonald, Jacques Etienne Joseph Alexandre; Pichegru, Jean-Charles; Tourcoing, Battle of
References and further reading
Lynn, John A. 1984. *The Bayonets of the Republic: Motivation and Tactics in the Army of Revolutionary France, 1791–1794.* Urbana and Chicago: University of Illinois Press.
Phipps, Ramsay Weston. 1980. *The Armies of the First French Republic and the Rise of the Marshals of Napoleon I.* Vol. 1, *The Armée du Nord.* London: Greenwood. (Orig. pub. 1926–1939.)
Ross, Steven T. 1975. *Quest for Victory: French Military Strategy, 1792–1799.* South Brunswick, NJ: Barnes.
Weigley, Russell F. 1991. *The Age of Battles: The Quest for Decisive Warfare from Breitenfeld to Waterloo.* Bloomington and Indianapolis: Indiana University Press.

Toussaint Louverture (1743–1803)

Toussaint Louverture (born François-Dominique Toussaint, and generally referred to as Toussaint) was the leader of a thirteen-year struggle for the abolition of slavery in St.

Domingue (present-day Haiti). He strongly opposed Napoleon's ambitions to reinstate slavery. Toussaint's defiant stance was instrumental in Haiti gaining independence from France.

Pierre Dominique Toussaint Breda was born a slave around 1743 on L'Habitation Breda, a plantation near Cap-Haïtien. He served as a house servant and coachman. Toussaint's grandfather had been an African king from present-day Benin who had been enslaved and transported to St. Domingue. Toussaint had four living siblings. As a gifted youngster, Toussaint acquired a self-taught education, nurtured by his liberal and humane owner, the comte de Noé. Toussaint became literate and read all of the books in de Noé's library. He taught himself Latin and French. Toussaint's interest in healing herbs and his people's history was supplemented by his awareness of Enlightenment thought, which framed his liberal ideals. The comte de Noé freed him in 1777; in the same year, he married single mother Suzanne Simone Baptiste, with whom he had two sons.

At the outbreak of the French Revolution, St. Domingue was the most lucrative of the French colonies. The prosperous island produced nearly 70 percent of France's overseas trade. The class structure had three tiers: whites, who were the masters and owners; 28,000 former black slaves and mulattoes; and 500,000 black slaves; this structure was regulated by the Code Noir, the slave labor code. The slaves sustained the sugar, cotton, and coffee plantations. Their horrendous living and working and conditions and the appallingly inhumane treatment they received resulted in countless deaths, requiring constant replenishment of their numbers by new slaves from Africa.

St. Domingue endured considerable political upheaval under successive Spanish, British, and then French colonial governments, all of which represented slave-trading nations. Trouble began when French troops sympathetic to the Revolution encouraged the St. Domingue troops to mutiny in 1790. The St. Domingue Colonial Assembly of white plantation owners declared their loyalty solely to the king of France, rather than the Revolutionaries who controlled the French government. In February 1791, an unsuccessful mulatto uprising resulted in the public torture and execution of organizer Vincent Ogé. In May 1791 the French National Assembly decreed that colored people of free parents would have equality. However, the National Assembly reversed the May decree, rescinding it on 24 September 1791.

Slaves, angered that their petition for an extra day to work their own parcels of land was refused, began a revolt at the Turpin plantation. They burned entire plantations, massacred masters and owners, and attacked various towns. This uprising was exacerbated by a civil war between the mulattoes and whites on one side and the Revolutionaries and rebel slave groups on the other. Toussaint felt betrayed by the French and joined the latter group as a medical aide in September 1791. The newly arrived civil commissioners from France were given responsibility for the mulattoes and free blacks; however, they refused to negotiate with the leaders of the uprisings. On 4 April 1792, the French Legislative Assembly reversed their September decision when King Louis XVI signed a decree of universal equality for property-owning free men.

The second group of civil commissioners, which included lawyer Léger Félicité Sonthonax, arrived on 18 September 1792 to enforce the April decree. Sonthonax was caught in the maelstrom of events. To gain a fighting force, he freed 15,000 blacks. Louis XVI was executed on 21 January 1793. France became a republic, and the French declared war on Britain on 1 February. After France declared war on Spain in March, Toussaint took service in the Spanish army in neighboring Santo Domingo, which occupied the eastern side of the island of Hispaniola, with a colonel's commission. After an unsuccessful revolt was waged against the commissioners in June, Sonthonax emancipated all the slaves on 21 August.

From the outset of the war with France, Britain, with its dominant naval presence in the Atlantic and Caribbean, began to pursue its traditional strategy of seizing French colonial possessions in the West Indies. A British expeditionary force led by Brigadier General Thomas Maitland arrived to aid the Spanish, and it occupied the coastal areas. By this time, owing to his formidable leadership and organizational skills, Toussaint had risen through the ranks in the Spanish army. Adept at finding weaknesses in his opponents' strategies, he earned the sobriquet of "L'Ouverture" (now generally spelled "Louverture"), meaning "the opening." His strategic network of shelters and weapons caches proved eminently valuable to the troops, whose privations, trials, and tribulations he shared in the early stages of the conflict. By such conduct, Toussaint earned his troops' implicit trust.

On 4 February 1794, the French National Convention abolished slavery in the French colonies. This action caused Toussaint to defect from the Spanish side on 6 May. The Spanish ceded Santo Domingo (the present-day Dominican Republic) to the French under the Treaty of Basle on 22 July 1795, although in practice they retained possession. Toussaint, by now a French general, was proclaimed lieutenant governor of St. Domingue on 1 April 1796. The French general Etienne-Maynard Laveaux, whom Toussaint had rescued from an earlier insurrection, appointed Toussaint as commander in chief of the French forces in May 1797.

By October, the exceptionally disciplined and often harsh Toussaint was in complete charge. He expelled all the

French officials, renounced French authority, and governed on his own. St. Domingue prospered under his rule; he brought peace and restored stability. He reinstated the Roman Catholic Church, wrote a new, if hastily contrived, constitution, and changed to the Gregorian calendar. Although Toussaint's main focus was the well-being of his countrymen, discontent prevailed. He forced the amicable Maitland to withdraw completely in September 1793, but the two countries maintained trade relations.

The tightly disciplined Toussaint practiced a strict, confining military dictatorship, which created enemies. On 16 June 1799 Toussaint defeated mulatto general André Rigaud in the exceptionally cruel "War of the Knives." In January 1801 Toussaint successfully conquered the Spanish side of the island. As well as requiring forced labor to repair the damage to the island, devastated by continuous warfare, he also made notable public improvements. On 8 July a new constitution was promulgated; it declared nominal independence and approved Toussaint's role as governor for life. The constitution was published, and copies appeared throughout the Western world.

Bonaparte, who had overthrown the Directory in Paris in November 1799 to become First Consul and, in 1804, Emperor, continued the West Indian policy of his predecessors. He personally disliked Toussaint, whom he called "this gilded African." Bonaparte's ultimate long-term goal was to return St. Domingue to its pre-1791 state of production, using slave labor, on the premise that only free men had the right to equality as promised by the Revolution. He believed that the French should hold dominion over large areas of the New World. Bonaparte fully realized that the events in St. Domingue could serve as a rallying cry for other countries subjugated by France.

To that end, in January 1802, Bonaparte sent his brother-in-law, General Charles-Victor Leclerc, who was married to Pauline Bonaparte, to St. Domingue with a sizable fleet and 25,000 men to subjugate and defeat Toussaint. During the conflict, the French were initially defeated by Toussaint's guerrilla tactics and scorched-earth strategy, and later by dysentery, yellow fever, and a shortage of food. Yet the French replenished their losses, even though they eventually lost approximately 50,000 men to war and disease. Toussaint capitulated on 1 May 1802 and retired to his plantation. However, Leclerc then had the elderly Toussaint seized and shipped in chains to France, where he was imprisoned in the French Alps near Besançon. He died there of neglect on 27 April 1803.

Despite the death of Toussaint Louverture, the struggle for independence continued, and Haiti, the "Land of Mountains," the basis of French trade in the West Indies, was established as an independent state on 1 January 1804.

Annette E. Richardson

See also Basle, Treaties of; Bonaparte, Pauline; Convention, The; Directory, The; Haiti; Leclerc, Charles-Victor Emmanuel; Louis XVI, King; Santo Domingo; Slave Trade; Slavery; West Indies, Operations in the
References and further reading
Brown, Gordon S. 2005. *Toussaint's Clause: The Founding Fathers and the Haitian Revolution.* Jackson: University Press of Mississippi.
Cauna, Jacques de, ed. 2004. *Toussaint Louverture et l'indépendance d'Haïti: Témoignages pour un bicentenaire.* Paris: Karthala; Saint-Denis: Société française d'histoire d'outre-mer.
Heinl, Robert Debs, Jr., and Nancy Gordon Heinl. 1978. *Written in Blood: The Story of the Haitian People, 1792–1971.* Boston: Houghton Mifflin.
Hoobler, Thomas, and Dorothy Hoobler. 1990. *Toussaint Louverture.* New York: Chelsea House.
James, Cyril L. 1963. *The Black Jacobins.* 2nd ed. New York: Vantage.
Korngold, Ralph. 1945. *Citizen Toussaint.* Boston: Little, Brown.
Moïse, Claude. 2001. *Le projet national de Toussaint Louverture et la Constitution de 1801.* Montréal: CIDIHCA.
Ott, Thomas. 1973. *The Haitian Revolution: 1789–1804.* Knoxville: University of Tennessee Press.
Parkinson, Wenda. 1978. *"This Gilded African": Toussaint Louverture.* London: Quartet.
Ros, Martin. 1994. *The Night of Fire: The Black Napoleon and the Battle for Haiti.* Trans. Karin Ford-Treep. New York: Sarpedon.
Stephen, Alexis. 1949. *Black Liberator: The Life of Toussaint Louverture.* Trans. William Stirling. London: Benn.
Tyson, George F. 1973. *Toussaint Louverture.* Englewood Cliffs, NJ: Prentice-Hall.
Waxman, Percy. 1931. *The Black Napoleon: The Story of Toussaint Louverture.* New York: Harcourt, Brace.

Trachenberg Plan

See Armistice of 1813

Trafalgar, Battle of (21 October 1805)

Decisive British naval victory over a combined Franco-Spanish fleet, which in the short term ended all prospect of a Napoleonic invasion of England and in the long term established Britain as undisputed mistress of the seas for the remainder of the nineteenth century.

The campaign in which the Battle of Trafalgar was fought constituted only a short period in the naval conflict between Britain and France that had begun in 1793 and ended in 1815. It was, however, the most decisive, demonstrating not only Britain's naval power, but the country's significance as a major participant in a war

The Battle of Trafalgar. Nelson's overwhelming triumph over the combined Franco-Spanish fleet ensured Britain's protection from invasion for the remainder of the Napoleonic Wars. (Print after W. L. Wyllie, 1905)

waged on an unprecedented scale that was not to be surpassed until the First World War. Within that campaign, Trafalgar itself stands as one of history's greatest naval encounters and the last significant battle fought between wooden navies. In the course of a few hours, Vice Admiral Horatio, Viscount Nelson, with a fleet of twenty-seven ships, eliminated forever the threat of French invasion, and made Britain secure at sea for the next hundred years. It was a victory marred only by his death, although the fact that Nelson's demise coincided with his crowning achievement made possible his legendary status, which persists to this day.

Napoleon realized by the summer of 1804 that, while his traditional emphasis on land operations had resulted in great territorial acquisitions for France in the campaigns of the 1790s, at sea Britain remained dominant. With French squadrons sitting idle, blockaded in every port, Britain stood between Napoleon and French hegemony over the Continent. Blessed with lucrative colonial goods and secure sea-lanes, Britain could continue to finance any nation opposing Napoleonic rule with massive subsidies. These subsidies were made possible by a combination of levies on imported goods, domestic taxation, and loans secured by Parliament. British control of the sea, moreover, left France unable to pursue any colonial ambitions, thus further reducing France's ability to increase its revenue through maritime trade. Finally, and most importantly, the protection afforded by the Royal Navy prevented the possibility of a direct invasion of England by French forces sent across the Channel.

In July 1804, therefore, Napoleon developed a grand strategy that, though it underwent half a dozen variations before the spring of 1805, never changed in its basic objectives: that of breaking the blockades of its ports, combining as many French and Spanish ships of the line as possible, and sailing them in overwhelming force to the English Channel. There they would escort an invasion flotilla—the most formidable one assembled opposite the English coast since 1066—that by the beginning of 1805 was intended to carry six army corps, totaling 160,000 men borne in over 2,000 craft. Success depended on control of the Channel—even if only for a few days—in order for the flotilla, otherwise defenseless against warships, to make the short crossing to the coast of Kent.

In April 1805, with plans to coordinate the union of various French squadrons from Brest, Rochefort, and elsewhere, French admiral Pierre de Villeneuve eluded the British blockade off the Mediterranean port of Toulon and met up with a Spanish fleet under Admiral Don Federico Gravina at Cádiz. Thus reinforced, Villeneuve, now in command of what was known as the Combined Fleet, sailed for the West Indies in an attempt both to rendezvous with other naval forces and to divert the attention of British ships keeping watch in the Channel. Villeneuve was not initially aware that Nelson, commander in chief of the Mediterranean Fleet, had followed him to the West Indies, albeit some weeks behind. The British admiral, while he made up the lost time, narrowly missed Villeneuve who, immediately upon learning of Nelson's proximity, promptly returned to European waters, which he reached in July, in hopes of clearing the Channel. When this plan failed, partly owing to an unexpected though indecisive encounter with a British squadron off the northwest coast of Spain, Villeneuve took refuge, first in Ferrol, and then in Cádiz, far to the south, where he was blockaded by Vice Admiral Cuthbert Collingwood.

By August, however, Villeneuve's fate fell rapidly down the list of Napoleon's strategic priorities, with a fundamental change in French grand strategy instituted by the Emperor. With war looming with Austria and Russia, Napoleon broke up his invasion camp at Boulogne and began marching his army to the Danube. The invasion of England was consequently postponed, and the Combined Fleet was ultimately ordered to leave port and assist in diversionary operations in the Mediterranean. Villeneuve did not in fact venture out of Cádiz again until 20 October, heading south for the Strait of Gibraltar. Yet on learning that some British ships were watering at Gibraltar and aware of Nelson's presence, Villeneuve decided to reverse course and return north to Cádiz. His pursuer, however, intercepted him and forced an engagement off Cape Trafalgar.

The Battle of Trafalgar was an exceedingly complex affair, with sixty ships of the line engaged, several bearing the same names on both sides, but the basic outlines of the action may be broadly sketched here. On sighting his opponents early on the morning of 21 October, Nelson, in his flagship the *Victory* (100 guns), gave the signal to prepare for battle. His opponent's fleet consisted of thirty-three ships of the line, carrying 30,000 officers and men and 2,632 guns, plus five frigates and two smaller vessels. The British fleet, though numerically inferior—twenty-seven ships of the line, carrying 17,000 officers and men and 2,148 guns, plus four frigates and two auxiliary vessels— was decidedly superior in terms of training and morale.

By 11:40 A.M. Nelson, leading the weather column, and his second in command, Collingwood, in the *Royal Sovereign* (100), leading the lee column, both on parallel courses, were proceeding at right angles straight for the Franco-Spanish line. Nelson's plan was to pierce Villeneuve's line about a third of the way down from the van, or leading squadron, engaging the center squadron, while Collingwood's column would pierce the enemy's line farther south, confronting vessels belonging to the center and rear. By this bold maneuver, the Franco-Spanish van, thus separated from the main body, would require considerable time to change course and come to the aid of its outnumbered consorts, while the rearmost vessels in Villeneuve's line would also take time to reach the action. Nelson calculated that in so isolating the Franco-Spanish center, he could overwhelm it with superior numbers. The battle would then develop into a series of small actions between individual ships or groups of ships, actions in which the British could rely on their superior gunnery, seamanship, and morale to prevail over their divided and despondent adversaries.

Just before noon, Nelson hoisted the famous signal, "England expects that every man will do his duty," and shortly thereafter the *Royal Sovereign*, slightly ahead of the *Victory*, reached the enemy line near the Spanish flagship, Vice Admiral Don Ignacio de Alava's 112-gun *Santa Ana*. Firing at the *Fougueux* (74) as he approached, Collingwood came alongside the *Santa Ana* and delivered several broadsides. The two ships then spent the next two hours engaging one another at close range, in the course of which the Spaniard was badly mauled.

The *Royal Sovereign* was not alone in confronting the Spanish flagship. The *Belleisle* (74) fired a broadside into her port side and others into the starboard of the *Fougueux* before proceeding to take on the *Indomptable* (80), which Collingwood managed to rake. In the meantime, the *Fougueux* had returned fire on the *Belleisle*, and the two began a vicious exchange. The third ship in Collingwood's column, the *Mars* (74), under Captain George Duff, also took on the *Fougueux*, which raked her. Shortly after 1:00 P.M. Duff was killed, but the vessels in Collingwood's column continued to engage the enemy line with considerable vigor, bringing on the individual ship-to-ship actions that Nelson had wanted.

Meanwhile, in Nelson's column, the *Victory* began to receive fire at about noon from the French 74-gun *Héros*. The British flagship, unable due to light winds to reach the enemy line for another half an hour, was left unable to reply. In the course of her slow progress, the *Victory* lost the use of her wheel—smashed by a round shot—while her sails began to tatter. Thereafter the *Victory* was steered from the gunroom below deck. On reaching the Franco-Spanish line, the *Victory* passed across the stern of the *Bucentaure* (80), Villeneuve's flagship, firing her broadside at

Battle of Trafalgar, 21 October 1805

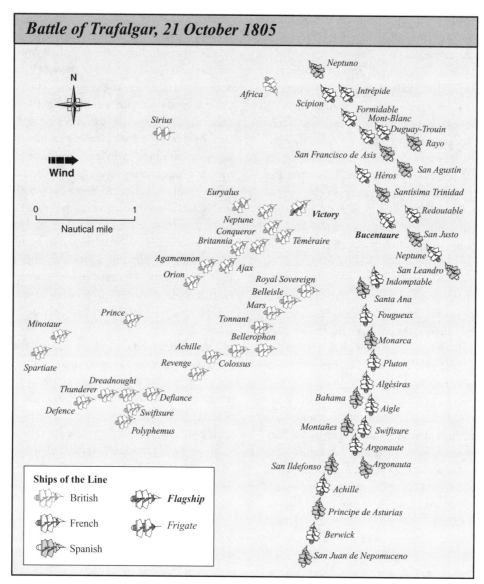

Adapted from Fremont-Barnes 2005B, 46.

point-blank range through the *Bucentaure*'s stern windows, causing massive damage to her interior and inflicting horrendous casualties. Soon thereafter, the French *Neptune* (80) began to fire on the *Victory*, which then collided with the *Redoutable* (74), the rigging of both vessels becoming entangled.

A short time later, about 1:15 P.M., a marksman positioned in the mizzen top of the *Redoutable* fired at and hit Nelson in the left shoulder, the musket ball puncturing his lung before lodging in his spine. The admiral was carried below to the orlop deck and attended by Dr. William Beatty, the *Victory*'s surgeon, who soon discovered that the wound was mortal. Command devolved first on Captain Thomas Hardy and then on Collingwood.

The *Redoutable*'s captain, Jean-Jacques Lucas, had made use of his time in port to train his crew in boarding tactics, small-arms drill, and the use of grenades. Thus, no sooner had the *Victory* run on board his ship than Lucas ordered his men to use grappling irons to lock the vessels together. Broadsides were exchanged from just a few feet away, with predictably devastating effect, and from the fighting tops of the French 74, sailors and marines fired down on to the decks of the *Victory*, picking off, in addition to Nelson, many of her gunners, officers, and marines. Having left the *Victory*'s upper deck practically deserted, Lucas then attempted to board, only to discover that the curve of the vessels' hulls left them too far apart at the bulwarks to make the enterprise viable. The powerful HMS *Téméraire* (98) under Captain Eliab Harvey then approached the port side of the *Redoutable* and began a heated exchange. When a third British vessel came within easy range of the *Redoutable*, the French vessel's mainmast collapsed and fell across the deck of the *Téméraire*, knocking down that ship's topmasts. Despite terrific punishment and heavy losses, Lucas refused to surrender, until at last his stricken vessel, having engaged at least three British ships, began to founder. While Nelson lay mortally wounded below decks aboard the *Victory*, the battle raged on as before, with no signals issued—for fear of adversely affecting the morale of the British crews—to indicate that the fallen admiral could no longer exercise command.

To return to Collingwood's column, around 2:00 P.M. the frigate *Euryalus* tied a line to that admiral's battered *Royal Sovereign* and took her in tow. The struggle between the *Belleisle* and *Fougueux* had meanwhile abated, enabling Captain William Hargood of the former to take on the French *Neptune* (80) under Commodore Esprit-Tranquille Maistral. The two ships exchanged broadsides for nearly an hour before the *Neptune* was obliged to move off when the *Polyphemus* (64) arrived to give relief to the beleaguered *Belleisle*. Against all the odds, she had survived successive broadsides from the *Pluton*, *Aigle*, *San Justo*, all 74s, and the *San Leandro*, with 64 guns, as well as from the *Fougueux* and *Neptune*. Undaunted, Hargood now took on the Spanish *Argonauta* (80), as well, though Commodore Don Antonio Pareja's ship had in earlier fighting already sustained severe damage of her own—so much so that she soon surrendered to the still defiant but now mastless, motionless, and scarcely floating *Belleisle*. The long ordeal suffered by Hargood's crew finally came to an end when HMS *Swiftsure* (74) appeared on the scene and engaged the French *Achille* (74), so diverting that vessel's attention. Thus the *Belleisle* was saved, to be taken in tow by the frigate *Naiad*.

The *Tonnant* (80), the fourth ship in the lee column to reach Villeneuve's line, engaged the Spanish *Monarca* (74) before taking on the French *Algésiras*, also of 74 guns, against which the *Tonnant* issued such a devastating broadside that she did not reply for several minutes, and then only feebly. Nevertheless, French marksmen in the fighting tops killed many of the gunners on *Tonnant's* upper deck, as well as her captain, Charles Tyler, as a prelude to boarding. In the event, the French were repulsed by grapeshot from *Tonnant's* starboard guns. Paradoxically, the situation soon became reversed; when the *Algésiras* lost all three of her lower masts, shot through below the deck, the crew of the *Tonnant* leapt over the gunwales and carried her, finding Admiral Charles Magon dead at the foot of the poop ladder.

The *Monarca*, which had lowered her colors as a sign of surrender, but found no British ship in a position to take possession of her, thereupon rehoisted her colors and prepared to fight on. The British reply was immediate: *Bellerophon* (74), fresh from action with the *Aigle*, which

had made two attempts to board her, not only reopened the contest with the *Monarca*, but issued such a destructive fire that the *Aigle*, unable to reply in kind, cleared off, her starboard side dreadfully battered. The *Bellerophon* then proceeded to engage the Spanish *Montanez* and *Bahama* and the French *Swiftsure*, all 74s.

The *Colossus* and British *Achille*, also 74s, approached from astern of the *Bellerophon*, the *Achille* exchanging fire with two vessels before taking on the French *Berwick*, which struck to her after fierce resistance. The *Swiftsure* and *Bahama* later surrendered to the *Colossus*. Meanwhile, the *Revenge* (74) passed the *Dreadnought* (98) and *Polyphemus* and fired on the Spanish *San Ildefonso* (74). *Polyphemus* also dismasted the *Achille* and went on to engage the Spanish flagship under Gravina, the 112-gun *Principe de Asturias*. Gravina's men prepared to board the *Polyphemus*, but small-arms fire issued by Captain Robert Redmill's marines, together with close-range blasts from carronades, kept them at bay. Soon after, the *Principe de Asturias* bore away, her decks strewn with dead.

The *Defiance* (74) then engaged the *Aigle*, boarding her for a short period before the men were recalled and the cannonade resumed. Within half an hour, however, the French vessel, suffering from severe casualties and accepting the inevitable, raised her colors in token of surrender and received a prize crew. Astern of the *Defiance* came the *Dreadnought*, which came alongside the Spanish *San Juan de Nepomuceno* (74), which surrendered after a few minutes' fighting. The *Dreadnought* then sought out Gravina's ship, which was heading for the safety of Cádiz. As for the remaining ships in Collingwood's column, these suffered far fewer casualties and received considerably less damage than the leading vessels.

The same was true in the case of Nelson's column. The initial actions of the *Victory* and *Téméraire* have been considered. The third ship to go into action was the *Neptune* (98), not to be confused with the French vessel of the same name. The *Neptune* passed between the *Victory* and *Bucentaure*, firing as she went, and approached the massive four-decker, the *Santísima Trinidad* (130), whose stern she raked. At 1:50 P.M. the Spanish behemoth's main and mizzen masts crashed overboard, followed fifteen minutes later by her foremast, upon which she surrendered to the *Neptune*. Meanwhile, the *Leviathan* (74) was busily engaged with the *San Augustín* (74), which she boarded and captured. The *Conqueror* (74), coming into action, took on Villeneuve's already crippled *Bucentaure* and the *Santísima Trinidad*, while the *Intrépide* (74) surrendered to the *Orion* (74).

At the same time, Rear Admiral Pierre Dumanoir Le Pelley, commanding the Franco-Spanish van from aboard the *Formidable* (80), had spent the action adhering strictly to the letter of his instructions from Villeneuve to proceed north. Whether he had deliberately ignored Villeneuve's subsequent frantic signals to come about, or had failed to notice the commander in chief's signals through the smoke of battle, Dumanoir had continued on his course while the battle raged to the south. The only British vessel that saw action far to the north was the 64-gun *Africa,* which entered the fray around noon, fighting the Spanish 80-gun *Neptuno* before proceeding to assist her consort, the *Neptune,* then exchanging fire with the *Santísima Trinidad.* By 3:00 P.M. Dumanoir Le Pelley finally obeyed Villeneuve's repeated signals for the van to come about and assist the center and rear, but by then the opportunity to restore Franco-Spanish fortunes had passed. The best that Villeneuve's ships could hope for was that individual vessels could somehow disengage themselves from the disaster and make their way to Cádiz. If some of his ships still stood a chance to save themselves, for Villeneuve, personally, it was too late: The *Bucentaure,* a floating wreck, struck her colors and surrendered with the French commander in chief on board.

Nelson, meanwhile, aware that death was imminent, asked that financial provision be made by the nation for Lady Hamilton, his wife in all but name and mother of their daughter, Horatia. Soon thereafter, learning that victory was assured, Nelson died around 4:00 P.M.

In less than five hours of savage fighting, the Combined Fleet had been comprehensively defeated, with eighteen out of thirty-three ships of the line either captured or destroyed, and no British vessels lost. Spanish losses amounted to approximately 1,000 killed or drowned and slightly more wounded. French losses are estimated at approximately 3,300 killed or drowned and over 1,000 wounded. Twenty-six of the flag officers and captains of the Combined Fleet were killed or wounded, and approximately 7,000 French and Spanish became prisoners, representing a loss of almost 25 percent of their total. British losses were remarkably small: 449 officers and men killed and 1,214 wounded, or approximately 10 percent of the total force. The greatest loss for the British, of course, was that of their revered admiral, who had saved the nation through brilliant leadership and bold fighting tactics.

The battle had important consequences in the short, and the long, term. Within three months of Trafalgar, British troops were ensconced on Sicily, securing that island as a permanent British station until Napoleon's fall. With Malta also in British hands, and with the Mediterranean under the control of the Royal Navy, French expansion into the eastern Mediterranean was considerably less likely than ever before. The French fleet was unable to pose any significant threat for the remainder of the Napoleonic Wars. Having defeated France decisively, Britain was enabled to assume the offensive in the struggle against Napoleon, making it possible only three years after Trafalgar to land troops and supplies in the Iberian Peninsula, so opening a new front against the French Empire. The Peninsular campaigns, led by the Marquis of Wellington (his most senior of many titles in Iberia), placed heavy demands on the French Army between 1808 and 1814, whereas British command of the sea enabled Wellington to receive reinforcements and supplies completely unmolested. In short, Trafalgar confined Napoleonic rule to the European continent, at the same time enabling Britain to oppose France in what became by 1812 a major theater of conflict on land.

In the longer term, Trafalgar stands as the most decisive naval battle of modern times. It marked both the beginning and the end of an era: the beginning of over a century of British naval mastery, and the end of fleet actions fought under sail, as well as to two centuries of maritime rivalry between Britain, France, and Spain. Nelson's objective—to destroy the Franco-Spanish fleet in order to eliminate the threat of invasion to the British Isles—had been achieved, and with overwhelming success. For a hundred years after the Napoleonic Wars, Britain's control of the seas went undisputed. The battle came at a time when the Industrial Revolution was gaining momentum; with Britain undisputed mistress of the seas, the nation was assured of raw materials for export and home consumption, and of food for a population too large to be fed by domestic production alone. The routes to markets overseas remained uncontested, and the foundation was laid for imperial expansion on a scale not seen since the height of the Roman Empire. In short, the naval supremacy that Britain won at Trafalgar laid the basis for the country's position as a world power in the Victorian era and beyond.

Gregory Fremont-Barnes

See also Artillery (Naval); Blockade; Collingwood, Cuthbert, Viscount; England, French Plans for the Invasion of; French Navy; Frigates; Naval Warfare; Nelson, Horatio, First Viscount; Peninsular War; Royal Navy; Ships of the Line; Spanish Navy; Third Coalition, War of the; Villeneuve, Pierre Charles Jean Baptiste Silvestre de

References and further reading
Adkin, Mark. 2005. *The Trafalgar Companion: The Complete Guide to History's Most Famous Sea Battle and the Life of Admiral Lord Nelson.* London: Aurum.
Adkins, Roy. 2004. *Trafalgar: The Biography of a Battle.* London: Little, Brown.
Bennett, Geoffrey. 2004. *The Battle of Trafalgar.* Barnsley, UK: Wharncliffe.
Best, Nicholas. 2005. *Trafalgar: The Untold Story of the Greatest Sea Battle in* History. London: Weidenfeld and Nicolson.
Clayton, Tim, and Phil Craig. 2004. *Trafalgar.* London: Hodder and Stoughton.
Clowes, William Laird. 1997. *The Royal Navy: A History from the Earliest Times to 1900.* Vol. 5. London: Chatham.
Corbett, Julian. 1976. *The Campaign of Trafalgar.* 2 vols. New York: AMS.

Davies, Paul. 1972. *The Battle of Trafalgar*. London: Pan.

Desbrière, Edouard. 1933. *The Naval Campaign of 1805: Trafalgar*. Trans. and ed. Constance Eastwick. 2 vols. Oxford: Clarendon.

Fabb, John, and Jack Cassin-Scott. 1977. *The Uniforms of Trafalgar*. London: Batsford.

Fraser, Edward, Marianne Cznik, and Michael Nash. 2004. *The Enemy at Trafalgar: Eyewitness Narratives, Dispatches and Letters from the French and Spanish Fleets*. London: Chatham.

Fremont-Barnes, Gregory. 2005a. *Nelson's Sailors*. Oxford: Osprey.

———. 2005b. *Trafalgar 1805: Nelson's Crowning Victory*. Oxford: Osprey.

Gardiner, Robert, ed. 1997. *The Campaign of Trafalgar, 1803–1805*. London: Chatham.

Glover, Richard. 1973. *Britain at Bay: Defence against Bonaparte, 1803–14*. London: Allen and Unwin.

Goodwin, Peter. 2004. *Nelson's Victory: 101 Questions and Answers about HMS* Victory, *Nelson's Flagship at Trafalgar 1805*. London: Brassey's.

———. 2005. *The Ships of Trafalgar: The British, French and Spanish Fleets, 21 October 1805*. London: Conway Maritime.

Harbron, John. 2004. *Trafalgar and the Spanish Navy: The Spanish Experience of Sea Power*. London: Conway Maritime.

Hart, Roger. 1972. *England Expects*. London: Wayland.

Heathcote, T. A. 2005. *Nelson's Trafalgar Captains and their Battles*. London: Pen and Sword.

Lavery, Brian. 2004. *Nelson's Fleet at Trafalgar*. Annapolis, MD: Naval Institute Press.

Lee, Christopher. 2005. *Nelson and Napoleon: The Long Haul to Trafalgar*. London: Headline.

Legg, Stuart. 1966. *Trafalgar: An Eyewitness Account of a Great Battle*. London: David.

Lyon, David. 1996. *Sea Battles in Close-up: The Age of Nelson*. Annapolis, MD: Naval Institute Press.

Mackenzie, Robert Holden. 2004. *The Trafalgar Roll: The Officers, the Men, the Ships*. London: Chatham.

Maine, René. 1957. *Trafalgar: Napoleon's Naval Waterloo*. London: Thames and Hudson.

McGowan, Alan. 1999. *HMS* Victory: *Her Construction, Career and Restoration*. London: Chatham.

Nicolas, Sir Nicholas Harris, ed. 1998. *The Dispatches and Letters of Vice Admiral Lord Viscount Nelson*. 7 vols. Vols. 5–7. London: Chatham.

Nicolson, Adam. 2005. *Men of Honour: Trafalgar and the Making of the English Hero*. London: HarperCollins.

Pocock, Tom. 2003. *The Terror before Trafalgar: Nelson, Napoleon and the Secret War*. London: John Murray.

Pope, Dudley. 1999. *England Expects: Nelson and the Trafalgar Campaign*. London: Chatham.

Robson, Martin. 2005. *Battle of Trafalgar*. London: Conway Maritime.

Schom, Alan. 1992. *Trafalgar: Countdown to Battle, 1803–1805*. London: Penguin.

Terraine, John. 1998. *Trafalgar*. London: Wordsworth.

Tracy, Nicholas. 1996. *Nelson's Battles: The Art of Victory in the Age of Sail*. London: Chatham.

Warner, Oliver. 1965. *Nelson's Battles*. London: Batsford.

———. 1966. *Trafalgar*. London: Pan.

Warwick, Peter. 2005. *Voices from Trafalgar*. London: David and Charles.

White, Colin, ed. 2005. *The Trafalgar Captains: Their Lives and Memorials*. London: Chatham.

Trebbia, Battle of the (17–19 June 1799)

A three-day major engagement in northern Italy between the Austro-Russian and French armies during the War of the Second Coalition. In the spring of 1799, the Allied army under Field Marshal Alexander Suvorov launched a successful offensive, driving the French armies out of Lombardy and Piedmont. In response, the French prepared for a counterattack involving General Jacques Macdonald from southern Italy and General Jean Moreau from Genoa.

Hearing about Macdonald's advance, Suvorov decided to destroy the French forces separately. Leaving *Feldmarschalleutnant* Heinrich Graf Bellegarde to keep an eye on Moreau, Suvorov marched with some 24,000 men, moving with the remarkable speed of over thirty miles in twenty-four hours. As he approached the river Tidone on 17 June, Suvorov received urgent news from Austrian *Feldmarschalleutnant* Karl Ott Freiherr von Bartokez, who was attacked by superior French forces. The Allied army arrived on the battlefield at a crucial moment, when the French forces were spread out and vulnerable to a flank attack. The fighting was particularly savage on the right flank, where Cossacks attacked the Polish Legion, yelling "Praga, Praga," in reference to the brutal Russian assault on Praga, a suburb of Warsaw, in 1794. By late afternoon the French held their ground on the right flank, but the Russians threatened their left flank and forced them to withdraw across the river. Both armies took up positions between the rivers Tidone and Trebbia. The French received reinforcements under generals Jean-Baptiste Olivier and Joseph de Montrichard, bringing the French strength to 33,500 men.

The Allies attacked early on the morning of 18 June, and by late afternoon they had cleared the left bank of the Trebbia, while the French occupied their positions on the right. During the night of 19 June, Suvorov received reinforcements, bringing his forces to almost 35,000 men.

On the French side, Macdonald decided to thwart Allied plans by attacking first. After a brief cannonade, the French advanced at around 10:00 A.M. on 19 June. The Poles made a flanking maneuver against the Allied right flank and created a gap of some 1,500 yards in the Russian line, which the French immediately exploited. Suvorov personally led the reinforcements that drove the French back across the Trebbia. Meantime, Montrichard and Olivier attacked General Ivan Förster's division in the center of the

Allied position. The French moved without coordination and exposed themselves to an attack by *General der Kavallerie* Johannes Fürst zu Liechtenstein's cavalry, which charged the left flank of Montrichard's division. Liechtenstein then continued his advance and engaged generals Olivier and Jean-Baptiste Salme to the north. At the same time, General François Watrin reached Calendasco and threatened to overwhelm the Allied left flank from the rear. However, with Olivier and Montrichard retreating, he was in danger of being cut off from the main forces, and he withdrew his troops across the Trebbia. By 6:00 P.M. the Allies regained the left bank of the river, and the belligerent armies stood in the same positions as the night before. Late on the evening of 19 June, the French retreated across the river Nure, ending the two-day battle on the Trebbia. The Allies' total casualties in the actions on the Tidone and Trebbia were some 5,500 men killed and wounded. French casualties were even higher, with some 2,000 killed and over 7,000 men wounded, including two *généraux de division* and two *généraux de brigade*. In addition, the Allies entered Piacenza, where they captured over 7,000 wounded.

Alexander Mikaberidze

See also Bellegarde, Heinrich Graf; Cossacks; Italian Campaigns (1799–1800); Liechtenstein, Johannes Joseph Fürst zu; Macdonald, Jacques Etienne Joseph Alexander; Moreau, Jean Victor; Second Coalition, War of the; Suvorov, Alexander Vasilievich

References and further reading
Blanning, T. C. W. 1996. *The French Revolutionary Wars, 1787–1802.* London: Arnold.
Clausewitz, Karl von. 1833. *Die Feldzüge von 1799 in Italien und der Schweiz.* Berlin: Ferdinand Dümmler.
Duffy, Christopher. 1999. *Eagles over the Alps: Suvorov in Italy and Switzerland, 1799.* Chicago: Emperor's Press.
Gachot, Edouard. 1903. *Les Campagnes de 1799: Souvarow en Italie.* Paris: Perrin.
Longworth, Philip. 1965. *The Art of Victory: The Life and Achievements of Generalissimo Suvorov, 1729–1800.* London: Constable.
Mikhailovsky-Danilevsky, Alexander, and Dmitri Miliutin. 1852. *Istoriia voini Rossii s Frantsiei v 1799 godu.* St. Petersburg: Tip. Imp. Akademii nauk.
Orlov, Nikolay. 1895. *Suvorov na Trebbii v 1799 g.* [Suvorov on Trebbia in 1799]. St. Petersburg: N.p.
———, ed. 1898. *Pokhod Suvorova v 1799 g.: Po zapiskam Gryazeva* [Suvorov's Campaign of 1799: Gryazev's Notes]. St. Petersburg: N.p.
Suvorov, A. V. 1952. *Dokumenti* [Documents]. Moscow: [Military Press of the Ministry of War].

Trianon Decree (5 August 1810)

Implemented in 1810 as an element of Napoleon's Continental System, the Trianon Decree imposed tariffs on imported goods including colonial and American products.

Napoleon had implemented what is known as the Continental System on 16 May 1806, with the passage of the Berlin Decrees. The basic purpose behind the System was to blockade Britain and bring the country to its knees economically. However, the Continental system tended to affect all of Europe, as well as the United States, by imposing trade restrictions on continental ports. Many countries, including the United States, believed that neutral ships should be able to carry the goods of both neutral and belligerent states to and from Europe—that is to say, to trade without restriction—a principle of free trade known by the contemporary concept of "free ships make free goods."

The Continental System did not function as Napoleon envisioned, and as a result, the French emperor attempted to tighten the economic noose around Europe, issuing, on 5 August 1810, the Trianon Decree. This proclamation imposed stiff import tariffs on twenty-one (or twenty-four, depending upon how one categorizes the products) colonial items, including cinnamon, cloves, cochineal, cocoa, coffee, cotton, dyewoods, indigo, mahogany, nutmeg, pepper, sugar, and tea. The tariffs ranged greatly for each item, depending upon its origin and method of transportation to France. For example, the tariff on cotton from the Americas reached 800 percent. Cotton from the Middle East was taxed at 400 percent if carried by sea and 200 percent if transported overland. The French confiscated goods all over Europe and even sequestered American vessels, citing the Trianon Decree.

Napoleon's rationale for the Trianon Decree apparently was based on his belief that all colonial goods entering Europe were British in origin or intended for purchase in Britain, even if carried aboard the vessels of other countries. In line with mercantile theory, the high tariffs would increase the flow of currency into France, render British businesses less profitable, and encourage the growth of French industry and agriculture.

The Trianon Decree has received considerable criticism by scholars. Napoleon lacked a keen understanding of political economy, and the Trianon Decree constituted one of many related declarations issued by the French emperor in his attempt to patch and modify the failing Continental System. It was, moreover, very unpopular on the Continent. Tsar Alexander of Russia refused to comply with the stipulations of the Trianon Decree when requested to do so by Napoleon, for the tsar did not view the decree's provisions as consistent with Russian national interests. The decree also angered merchants in Frankfurt, Berlin, Leipzig, and Vienna, resulting in the establishment of *zollverein*s (customs unions) and serving as an impetus to anti-French sentiment across Germany.

Terry M. Mays

See also Alexander I, Tsar; Berlin Decrees; Mercantilism; Milan Decrees; Continental System
References and further reading
Broers, Michael. 1996. *Europe under Napoleon, 1799–1815.* London: Arnold.
Crouzet, François. 1958. *L'Economie britannique et le blocus continental, 1806–1813.* Paris: Presses universitaires de France.
Ellis, Geoffrey J. 1991. *The Napoleonic Empire.* Atlantic Highlands, NJ: Humanities Press International.
Heckscher, E. F. 1964. *The Continental System: An Economic Interpretation.* Gloucester, MA: Peter Smith.
Melvin, Frank Edgar. 1919. *Napoleon's Navigation System: A Study of Trade Control during the Continental Blockade.* New York: AMS.

Trinidad, Expedition to (January–February 1797)

Following Spain's declaration of war on Britain in October 1796, Henry Dundas, the British secretary of state for war and the colonies, decided to launch another offensive against Spain's possessions in the West Indies, particularly Trinidad and Puerto Rico. In January 1797, 3,750 troops stationed on Barbados were loaded aboard three ships of the line, two frigates, and smaller craft. This expedition was under the joint command of Lieutenant General Sir Ralph Abercromby and Rear Admiral Henry Harvey. On 16 February, as the British made their way around Trinidad, they spotted a Spanish squadron anchored in Chaguaramas Bay, 8 miles west of Puerto de España. With only four undermanned ships of the line and a frigate, Rear Admiral Sebastian Ruiz de Apodaca decided to burn his ships to deny them to the British. All of the vessels were successfully burned except the *San Domaso* (74 guns), which the British quickly captured. Apodaca and approximately 2,400 men made their way overland back to Puerto de España. Meanwhile, the Spanish governor, José Maria Chacon, had a garrison of only about 600 men to protect Puerto de España. While Royal Navy ships bombarded Puerto de España, the British troops landed at three different points along the shore, a little over a mile from the city.

Still awaiting the arrival of Apodaca and his men, Chacon could not oppose the landing with his small force. Only in the evening, once Apodaca had arrived, did Chacon attempt to impede the British advance. After a brief skirmish, the Spanish were forced back into the city. Even though many British troops took to plunder and got drunk, the British were able to take control of Puerto de España. Abercromby offered Chacon the possibility of capitulation. While negotiations were underway, Abercromby restored order among his troops. On the morning of 18 February, both sides agreed to a capitulation in which the British obtained possession of the island, while the Spanish forces were to be transported back to Spain, pledging not to serve until properly exchanged. The British took the island, as well as a ship of the line, and caused the destruction of three ships of the line and a frigate for the paltry cost of seven men. Abercromby decided to retain possession of Trinidad and left a garrison of 1,000 men under the command of Lieutenant Colonel Thomas Picton. This decision, in turn, delayed until April the British attack on Puerto Rico, which ultimately proved unsuccessful. Trinidad remained a British colony following the Congress of Vienna in 1815.

Kenneth Johnson

See also Abercromby, Sir Ralph; Picton, Sir Thomas; Vienna, Congress of; West Indies, Operations in the
References and further reading
Clowes, William Laird. 1997. The Royal Navy: A History from the Earliest Times to 1900. 7 vols. Vol. 4. London: Chatham.
Duffy, Michael. 1987. *Soldiers, Sugar, and Seapower: The British Expeditions to the West Indies and the War against Revolutionary France.* Oxford: Clarendon.
Fortescue, Sir John. 2004. *History of the British Army.* Vol. 4. Uckfield, UK: Naval and Military.
Gardiner, Robert, ed. 1997. *Fleet Battle and Blockade: The French Revolutionary War, 1793–1797.* London: Chatham.

Tripolitan War (1801–1805)

No sooner had the United States achieved its independence, in 1783, than American merchant vessels lost the protection they had formerly enjoyed while sailing under the British flag. This new circumstance had particular significance in the Mediterranean, where the territories along the North African coast, known as the Barbary States, preyed upon the merchant shipping of vulnerable nations, especially those of southern Europe, confiscating vessels and enslaving their crews. The Barbary States consisted of, from west to east, Morocco, Algiers, Tunis, and Tripoli (now Morocco, Algeria, Tunisia, and Libya, respectively), all but Morocco being *de jure* dependencies of the Ottoman Empire, but in reality effectively autonomous by the end of the eighteenth century.

The United States, possessing no navy to speak of until at least 1797 and thus utterly unable to defend its merchantmen in the Mediterranean, pursued the expedient—if not craven—policy long since adopted by several other minor powers: the payment of tribute to various Barbary States in exchange for immunity from seizure for its commercial vessels, as well as ransom for the release of sailors already in Barbary hands. In April 1800, however, Tripoli threatened war within six months if the United

States refused to pay it tribute on the same exhorbitant terms as Algiers, to whom America had become a tributary in 1796. With the addition of several powerful frigates to its standing force, and with its young navy encouraged by its recent success against France in the undeclared Quasi-War (1798–1800), the new administration under Thomas Jefferson refused to comply with Tripoli's extortionate demands, and on 26 February 1801 the pasha opened hostilities.

Commodore Richard Dale, leading a squadron of three frigates and a schooner, was duly dispatched to the Mediterranean on 24 July with orders to blockade Tripoli. The first encounter with the enemy took place on 1 August when the 12-gun schooner *Enterprise* captured the 14-gun cruiser *Tripoli*. Yet thereafter Dale unaccountably dithered at Gibraltar and other friendly ports, and was replaced in April 1802 with Commodore Richard Morris. He, too, was eventually recalled as ineffective, to be replaced by the dynamic Commodore Edward Preble, who arrived off Tripoli in September 1803. By this time the American squadron had grown to two frigates, two brigs, and three schooners.

Although he sought to infuse a new offensive spirit into the American effort, Preble's operations got off to an inauspicious start when, on 31 October, the 36-gun frigate *Philadelphia* accidentally ran aground on rocks in the uncharted waters of Tripoli harbor while pursuing an enemy craft. With the frigate listing severely to one side, she was unable to train her guns on the enemy gunboats racing to overwhelm her, and Captain William Bainbridge was forced to surrender his ship and crew of 307 men. Preble, though furious at the loss of so important an element of his small force, remained undaunted, and though he concluded that recapturing the *Philadelphia* was impossible, nevertheless devised a strategy intended to deny her use to the enemy. In a daring raid conducted on the night of 16 February 1804, Lieutenant Stephen Decatur and 75 volunteers entered the harbor aboard the ketch *Intrepid*, overcame the Tripolitan sentries aboard the *Philadelphia*, and set the prize alight. Decatur's exploit, performed without the loss of a single man, instantly raised the prestige of the nascent U.S. Navy and heartened Preble's squadron.

Thus emboldened, Preble launched a series of seaborne attacks against Tripoli on 3, 7, and 25 August, and again on 3 September, employing the 44-gun heavy frigate *Constitution* and a host of smaller vessels. In a celebrated gunboat action on 3 August, Decatur, since promoted a captain—at twenty-five, the youngest ever in the U.S. Navy—captured two Tripolitan craft, contributing further to the hero status that he had attained earlier that year. Nevertheless, the war could not be won by boarding actions alone, and as Preble's bombardment of the harbor defenses failed to inflict significant damage, he had to devise an alternative strategy. This came in the form of yet another raid, conducted by Master Commandant Richard Somers and 12 others aboard the *Intrepid*, which had been converted into an explosion vessel. On the night of 4 September 1804 she sailed into Tripoli harbor with the object of damaging the walls of the pasha's castle. In the event, the *Intrepid* exploded prematurely, her crew dying in the impressive, yet totally ineffective, inferno. With this setback and Preble's replacement by Commodore Samuel Barron, the active naval phase of the war came to an end, though the blockade of Tripoli continued.

Notwithstanding the strangulating effect that the blockade was having on Tripoli's waterborne supply of food—all the Barbary States being heavily dependent on imports of grain and other products—the four-year conflict in fact came to an end as a result of a plot to overthrow the pasha, Yusuf Karamanli. In an unprecedented diplomatic move, Jefferson agreed to support a plan, formulated by Yusuf's exiled brother, Hamet, involving American financial backing and naval support for a mercenary army to be raised by Hamet in Egypt. This force was to capture the Tripolitan port city of Derna, 500 miles to the west, before moving on to Tripoli, a further 400 miles west. Once Yusuf was overthrown, Hamet was to assume power and reestablish peace between his country and the United States. Despite initial reservations concerning the morality of backing such a scheme—which amounted to the subversion of a foreign government—the president approved it, placing in command William Eaton, a former U.S. Army officer and consul to Tunis.

Eaton, with a small party of U.S. Marines and navy midshipmen, joined forces near Alexandria with the several hundred Arab mercenaries Hamet managed to raise in Egypt. With this unlikely polyglot force, Eaton began his march on 8 March 1805, proceeding across the burning wastes of the Libyan Desert, staving off heat exhaustion, Bedouin attacks, and even a mutiny by Hamet's forces, before storming and capturing Derna on 28 April. The garrison successfully resisted Tripolitan counterattacks on 8 May and 10 June, respectively, and before Eaton's expedition could proceed further news arrived that the war had ended as a result of a treaty concluded on 4 June.

While the Tripolitan War ranks as little more than a minor episode in the larger context of early-nineteenth-century warfare, it held considerable political and military significance for the United States. Politically, the Tripolitan War set two important precedents concerning the powers of the presidency. First, Congress had from the outset of hostilities authorized Jefferson to dispatch forces abroad to fight without a formal declaration of war; and second, the president established the principle that the United States could remove a foreign government from power not merely by military means, but through subversion—in this instance by supporting domestic opposition and dissident émigrés. Many presidents have since made use of these powers, particularly the first, such as during the Korean and Vietnam wars.

Apart from these key political features, the Tripolitan War had important implications for the infant U.S. Navy, for the conflict stimulated warship construction and provided a useful training ground for navy personnel, many of whom, with a few years' experience in Mediterranean waters, would later distinguish themselves in the War of 1812 against Britain. Finally—and perhaps most significantly—the Tripolitan War marked the first instance of the United States extending its (albeit still limited) power well beyond its shores, establishing a pattern in its foreign policy that, though not fully matured until 1917, has continued to the present day.

Gregory Fremont-Barnes

See also United States; United States Navy; War of 1812
References and further reading
Allison, Robert J. 2000. *The Crescent Obscured: The United States and the Muslim World, 1776–1815.* Chicago: University of Chicago Press.
Fremont-Barnes, Gregory. 2006. *The Wars of the Barbary Pirates.* Oxford: Osprey.
Kitzen, Michael L. 1993. *Tripoli and the United States at War: A History of American Relations with the Barbary States, 1785–1805.* Jefferson, NC: McFarland.
Lambert, Frank. 2005. *The Barbary Wars: American Independence in the Atlantic World.* New York: Hill and Wang.
London, Joshua. 2005. *Victory in Tripoli: How America's War with the Barbary Pirates Established the U. S. Navy and Shaped a Nation.* Hoboken, NJ: John Wiley.
Parker, Richard. 2004. *Uncle Sam in Barbary: A Diplomatic History.* Tallahassee: University Press of Florida.
Wheelan, Joseph. 2004. *Jefferson's War: America's First War on Terror, 1801–1805.* New York: Carroll and Graf.
Whipple, A. B. C. 1991. *To the Shores of Tripoli: The Birth of the U. S. Navy and Marines.* Annapolis, MD: Naval Institute Press.
Zacks, Richard. 2005. *The Pirate Coast: Thomas Jefferson, the First Marines, and the Secret Mission of 1805.* New York: Hyperion.

Troyes, Agreement at (22 February 1814)

An agreement reached between the Allied powers during the opening phase of the 1814 campaign in France. Following a series of victories between 10 and 14 February, Napoleon marched with his army against *Feldmarschall* Karl Philipp Fürst zu Schwarzenberg, who, although he had superior forces, retreated to Troyes and asked Napoleon for an armistice, which the latter scornfully rejected. The

Army of Bohemia soon linked up with General Gebhard von Blücher's forces at Méry on 21 February. The following day, the Allies summoned a council of war at Troyes to discuss a new strategy against Napoleon. Tsar Alexander of Russia and King Frederick William III of Prussia wanted to engage the French army, but Schwarzenberg persuaded them to agree to a further withdrawal. Napoleon expected a major battle against the Austrians near Troyes on 23 February, but, following the Allied agreement reached at that town, the Allies deprived him of this opportunity; Schwarzenberg's army quickly retreated on Vandeuvre, while Blücher had to withdraw back to the Marne.

Alexander Mikaberidze

See also Alexander I, Tsar; Blücher von Wahlstatt, Gebhard Lebrecht Fürst; France, Campaign in; Frederick William III, King; Schwarzenberg, Karl Philipp Fürst zu
References and further reading
Chandler, David G. 1995. *The Campaigns of Napoleon.* London: Weidenfeld and Nicolson.
Hamilton-Williams, David. 1994. *The Fall of Napoleon: The Final Betrayal.* London: Arms and Armour.

Truillas, Battle of (22 September 1793)

The Battle of Truillas marked the high-water point of the Spanish invasion of southern France in 1793. The Spanish army had been forced back from their positions around the fortified city of Perpignan, and the (French) Army of the Eastern Pyrenees hoped to drive them out of France. Instead, because of French inexperience, interference from the Committee of Public Safety's representatives, and animosity between the French commanders, the French were routed and forced to resume their positions at Perpignan.

The Spanish army under General Don Antonio Ramón Ricardos threatened to cut Perpignan completely off from reinforcements by September 1793, having established a series of fortified camps around the city. On 17 September, a column advanced from the camp at Peyrestortes and took the village of Vernet. A French counterattack from Perpignan routed the Spanish column and drove them out of Peyrestortes. Five hundred prisoners and forty-three guns were captured, and Ricardos concentrated his army on a new line centered on the town of Truillas. On the nineteenth, General Luc Siméon Dagobert arrived with reinforcements to take command of the Army of the Eastern Pyrenees. He was pressured by representatives of the Committee of Public Safety to make a frontal assault on the Spanish position. Dagobert would have preferred to outflank Ricardos and threaten his communications, but his position was uncertain.

The plan agreed upon called for three columns to attack in echelon. Dagobert commanded the central column, but the left- and right-hand columns were commanded by his rivals. One he criticized for being too young and impulsive, while the other had formerly been a doctor rather than a soldier. Although the French forces totaled 16,000 men, many were poorly trained, and 3,000 were armed only with pikes. Dagobert also erred by making each column nearly equal in strength, failing to concentrate enough men to force a breakthrough.

The French attacked on 22 September. At first the turning movement on the French right went well. The Spanish were driven back, but the French then stopped to bombard a small fort. Ricardos rushed his reserves to block the French. The poorly trained French broke and fled. Meanwhile, the French left column crawled slowly toward the Spanish, held up by a thin screen of skirmishers. Dagobert, an aggressive commander, threw his forces at the Spanish center around Truillas. Ricardos rushed his reserves back to the center and managed to throw back Dagobert's assault. Dagobert then made a tactical error by marching his command to the right in another attempt to turn the Spanish left. The flanking march exposed the column's left flank to the Spanish. The crafty Ricardos swiftly launched a counterattack that routed the French and drove them from the field.

Spanish casualties totaled about 1,500 men. Dagobert, however, lost close to 6,000. He accused his two lieutenants of jeopardizing success because of their rivalry. Furious, he resigned his command of the Army of the Eastern Pyrenees.

Tim J. Watts

See also First Coalition, War of the; Perpignan, Battle of; Public Safety, Committee of; Pyrenean Campaigns (1793–1795)
References and further reading
Fervel, N. N. 1861. *Campagnes de la Revolution Française dans les Pyrénées-Orientales.* Paris: Dumaine.
Phipps, Ramsay Weston. 1980. *The Armies of the First French Republic and the Rise of the Marshals of Napoleon I.* Vol. 3, *The Armies in the West, 1793–1797, and the Armies in the South, 1792 to March 1796.* London: Greenwood. (Orig. pub. 1926–1939.)

Tuchkov (Tuchkov I), Nikolay Alekseyevich (1765–1812)

Russian general and corps commander. Tuchkov was enrolled in the Engineer Corps in 1773 and began active service as a sergeant in the artillery in 1778. He transferred as a sub-lieutenant to the Cannonier Regiment in 1783 and became adjutant general to *General-Feldzeugmeister* Ivan Müller-Zakomelsky in 1785. Tuchkov was promoted to captain of the Bombardier Regiment in 1787 and partici-

pated in the Russo-Swedish War in 1788–1790. He transferred as a major to the Muromsk Infantry Regiment in 1791 and served in Poland in 1792–1794, fighting at Nesvizh, Zelva, Brest-Litovsk, and Warsaw. At Maciejowice, he commanded a battalion of the Velikolutsk Musketeer Regiment and captured the local castle and an artillery piece. He was promoted to colonel and transferred to the Belozersk Infantry Regiment on 15 October 1794.

Tuchkov became a major general and *chef* (colonel-proprietor) of the Sevsk Musketeer Regiment on 15 October 1797. Between 11 November 1798 and 9 April 1801, this regiment was named after its chef as Tuchkov I's Musketeer Regiment. In 1799 he served in General Alexander Rimsky-Korsakov's corps and distinguished himself at the second Battle of Zürich. For his actions, he was promoted to lieutenant general on 24 September 1799 and was later appointed infantry inspector in the Lifland Inspection on 2 October 1800. Tuchkov served in the Lifland Inspection for the next four years, joining Baron Levin Bennigsen's corps during the 1805 campaign. His troops reached Silesia by December 1805, but had to return to Russia after the Battle of Austerlitz. In 1806 he was given command of the 5th Division in General Fedor Buxhöwden's corps. Tuchkov remained in reserve during the battles of Pultusk and Golymin. He took part in the council of war at Novgorod and commanded the Russian right wing during the offensive in early January 1807.

Tuchkov assumed command of Buxhöwden's corps on 26 January 1807 and covered the right flank at Eylau. In April Tuchkov was given command of General Ivan Nikolayevich Essen's corps and fought on the Narew River. After the Treaty of Tilsit, Tuchkov participated in the invasion of Finland during the Russo-Swedish War and operated in the north. He occupied Kuopio in early March and advanced to Vaasa. He was unable to halt the Swedish offensive in April 1808 and was recalled to headquarters at Åbo, where he arrived in time to command troops against the Swedish landing force. Tuchkov then led the Russian troops in the Savolax region and fought at Idensalmi in October 1808. He took a prolonged furlough because of poor health in November 1808. Tuchkov was appointed military governor of Kamenets-Podolsk on 20 January 1811 and took command of the 3rd Corps in the 1st Western Army in early 1812.

During the 1812 campaign Tuchkov took part in the actions at Ostrovno, Vitebsk, and Smolensk. He and his brother, Pavel Tuchkov III, distinguished themselves in the battle at Valutina Gora (Lubino). At Borodino, Tuchkov's corps was deployed on the extreme left flank and repulsed Prince Józef Poniatowski's attacks at Utitsa. Leading a bayonet attack of the Pavlovsk Grenadier Regiment, Tuchkov was severely wounded in the chest. He was transported to

Jaroslavl, where he died on 11 November 1812 and was buried at Tolgsk Monastery.

Alexander Mikaberidze

See also Austerlitz, Battle of; Bennigsen, Levin August, Baron; Borodino, Battle of; Buxhöwden, Fedor Fedorovich; Eylau, Battle of; Fourth Coalition, War of the; Golymin, Battle of; Maciejowice, Battle of; Ostrovno, Battle of; Poniatowski, Józef Anton, Prince; Pultusk, Battle of; Rimsky-Korsakov, Alexander Mikhailovich; Russian Campaign; Russo-Polish War; Russo-Swedish War; Smolensk, Battle of; Switzerland, Campaign in; Third Coalition, War of the; Tilsit, Treaties of; Tuchkov (Tuchkov III), Pavel Alekseyevich; Vitebsk, Battle of; Zürich, Second Battle of
References and further reading
Gavrilov, I. 1998. *Tuchkovy.* Moscow: N.p.
Mikaberidze, Alexander. 2005. *The Russian Officer Corps in the Revolutionary and Napoleonic Wars, 1792–1815.* New York: Savas Beatie.

Tuchkov (Tuchkov II), Sergey Alekseyevich (1767–1839)

Russian general and corps commander. Tuchkov enlisted in the 2nd Fusilier Regiment in 1773 and began active service as a sergeant in 1783, rising to sub-lieutenant in 1785. In 1788–1790, during the Russo-Swedish War, Tuchkov served in a galley fleet and participated in several naval actions. In the Battle of Rochensalmi he was wounded. In 1794 he commanded a horse artillery battalion in Poland and distinguished himself at Vilna and Praga, receiving promotion to premier major. In 1796 Tuchkov participated in the campaign against Persia, fighting at Derbent. For his services, he was promoted to lieutenant colonel on 22 December 1797 and appointed commander of the Fanagoria Grenadier Regiment on 19 July 1798.

Tuchkov was promoted to major general and appointed *chef* (colonel-proprietor) of the Caucasus Grenadier Regiment on 22 November 1798. He remained in the Transcaucasia for the next six years, fighting the Chechens, Circassians, Turks, and Persians. He retired on 30 November 1804 but returned to service two years later, becoming chef of the Kamchatka Musketeer Regiment on 5 September 1806. In 1808 he was sent to the (Russian) Army of Moldavia and took part in operations in the Danube valley during the war against the Turks. However, he was accused of abandoning the siege of Silistra in 1810 and was under investigation for the next four years. He served as a duty officer in the headquarters of the Army of the Danube in 1811 and commanded the 2nd Reserve Corps at Mozyr in 1812. Tuchkov took part in operations on the Berezina River in November 1812 and later served at the sieges of Modlin and Magdeburg in 1813. He be-

came the military governor of Babadag in 1826, rose to lieutenant general on 26 April 1829, and became the commandant of Ismail on 8 January 1830. He founded the small town of Tuchkov near Ismail and retired in 1836.

Alexander Mikaberidze

See also Berezina, Actions and Crossing at the; Germany, Campaign in; Russian Campaign; Russo-Polish War; Russo-Turkish War
References and further reading
Aleksandrov, G. 1874. "Cherti iz zhizni S.A. Tuchkova." *Russkii Arkhiv,* no. 5.
Gavrilov, I. 1998. *Tuchkovy.* Moscow: N. p.
Mikaberidze, Alexander. 2005. *The Russian Officer Corps in the Revolutionary and Napoleonic Wars, 1792–1815.* New York: Savas Beatie.
Tuchkov, Sergey. 1908. *Zapiski.* St. Petersburg: N.p.

Tuchkov (Tuchkov III), Pavel Alekseyevich (1776–1858)

Russian general and corps commander. Tuchkov enlisted as a sergeant in the Bombardier Regiment on 29 December 1785 and served as an adjutant to his father in 1787. He became a captain of the 2nd Bombardier Regiment on 4 August 1791. He was promoted to major in early 1797 and served in von Mertens's (later Baturin's) artillery battalion. At a military parade in 1798 he was promoted to lieutenant colonel and appointed to the Life Guard Artillery Battalion. He became a colonel in 1799. Tuchkov was promoted to major general and appointed *chef* (colonel-proprietor) of the 1st Artillery Regiment on 20 October 1800. Three years later he became chef of the 9th Artillery Regiment on 30 June, but retired on 18 November 1803. He returned to service on 23 March 1807 and was appointed chef of the Wilmandstrand Musketeer Regiment.

Tuchkov commanded the 1st Brigade of the 17th Division in 1807 but did not participate in operations in Poland. In 1808 he participated in the Russo-Swedish War and commanded a detachment of the 17th Division. He took part in the actions at Kuskoski, Helsingfors, Tavastheus, Sveaborg, and Gangud (Hango), and defended the coastline of southern Finland. Tuchkov defended the islands of Sando and Kimiton in the summer of 1808, commanded a corps at Uleaborg in late 1808, and participated in Prince Peter Bagration's advance across the frozen Gulf of Bothnia to the Åland Islands in March 1809. In 1810 Tuchkov commanded a brigade of the 17th Division attached to the 1st Western Army and took part in the construction of the fortress of Dünaburg. In early 1812 his brigade was attached to the 2nd Corps in the 1st Western Army.

During the Russian campaign of 1812 Tuchkov fought at Orzhishki and Koltyniani and commanded the Russian rear guard during the retreat of the 1st Western Army to Smolensk. After the Battle of Smolensk, Tuchkov was dispatched ahead of his brother General Nikolay Tuchkov's corps to defend the road junction at Lubino (Valutina Gora). He anticipated the French troops there and resolutely defended his positions against superior French forces. In the evening, he led a counterattack with the Ekaterinoslavl Grenadier Regiment, but he was captured after receiving a bayonet wound to the abdomen and several saber cuts to the head. He was well treated by Marshal Louis-Alexandre Berthier, who kept him at his quarters and lent him 6,000 francs. Napoleon interviewed Tuchkov on 25 August and offered to deliver a peace proposal to Tsar Alexander through Tuchkov, who however declined to accept that role to do so.

In the fall of 1812 Tuchkov was transported to Metz and remained in captivity for the next two years. He received an allowance of 2,000 francs from the French government and was transferred to Brittany in January 1814. He was released in April 1814 and, after a six-month leave, returned to the army. Tuchkov served under General Nikolay Rayevsky during the Russian advance to France in 1815 and took command of the 8th Division on 16 December 1815. He retired on 21 February 1819 after twenty-five years of distinguished service. Tuchkov was appointed to the Senate in 1828 and chaired various charitable societies. He became privy counselor in 1840 and died on 5 February 1858 in St. Petersburg.

Alexander Mikaberidze

See also Alexander I, Tsar; Bagration, Peter Ivanovich, Prince; Berthier, Louis-Alexandre; Rayevsky, Nikolay Nikolayevich, Count; Russian Campaign; Russo-Swedish War; Smolensk, Battle of; Tuchkov (Tuchkov I), Nikolay Alekseyevich
References and further reading
Gavrilov, I. 1998. *Tuchkovy.* Moscow: Rus.
Mikaberidze, Alexander. 2005. *The Russian Officer Corps in the Revolutionary and Napoleonic Wars, 1792–1815.* New York: Savas Beatie.
Tuchkov, P. 1873. "Moi vospominania o 1812 g." *Russkii Arkhiv*, no. 10.

Tuchkov (Tuchkov IV), Alexander Alekseyevich (1777–1812)

Russian general and corps commander. Tuchkov was born to a prominent Russian noble family. His ancestors had immigrated from Prussia in the thirteenth century, and Tuchkov's father, Aleksey, had served as senator and lieutenant general of engineers under Tsarina Catherine II. Tuchkov was enlisted in the Bombardier Regiment in 1788, served as a *flügel*-adjutant and adjutant general to his fa-

ther in 1789–1791, and was appointed captain of the 2nd Artillery Battalion on 8 July 1794. In 1795–1797 he served in succession in Mertens's artillery battalion, the 6th Artillery Regiment, the 12th Artillery Regiment, and the 1st Artillery Battalion (promoted to major in 1797). He became a lieutenant colonel in 1798 and a colonel on 6 May 1799, and was appointed commander of the 6th Artillery Regiment on 27 November 1800.

Tuchkov retired in 1801 and traveled throughout Europe. He returned to military service in 1804 and was appointed to the Murom Musketeer Regiment. In 1806 he transferred to the Tavrida Grenadier Regiment and fought the French at Golymin. Tuchkov became *chef* (colonel-proprietor) of the Revel Musketeer regiment on 15 December 1806. In early 1807 he was attached to the 6th Division in Poland but did not take part in the Battle of Eylau. In June 1807 he served in Prince Peter Bagration's advance guard at Guttstadt and distinguished himself at Deppen, Heilsberg, and Friedland. In 1808, during the Russo-Swedish War, he was attached to General Mikhail Barclay de Tolly's corps and operated in the Savolax region in north Finland, fighting at Kuopio and Idensalmi. He was promoted to major general on 24 December 1808 and commanded the advance guard of Prince Pavel Shuvalov's corps operating at Tornea in March 1809.

In May 1809 Tuchkov led a daring march across the thawing ice in the Gulf of Bothnia to capture Skelleftea. In June he became a duty general to Barclay de Tolly and remained in Finland until April 1810. During the Russian campaign of 1812 he commanded the 1st Brigade of the 3rd Division of the 3rd Corps of the 1st Western Army and fought at Vitebsk, Smolensk, and Lubino. At Borodino, Tuchkov commanded a brigade in his brother General Nikolay Tuchkov's corps at Utitsa, at the southern end of the battlefield. During the fighting, he personally led the counterattack of the Revel Musketeer Regiment but was killed when several cannonballs ripped him apart. His body was never found, and his remains were presumably buried in a common grave. His wife, Margarita Tuchkov, built a church on the site of Tuchkov's death in 1820.

Alexander Mikaberidze

See also Bagration, Peter Ivanovich, Prince; Barclay de Tolly, Mikhail Andreas; Borodino, Battle of; Catherine II "the Great," Tsarina; Fourth Coalition, War of the; Friedland, Battle of; Heilsberg, Battle of; Russian Campaign; Russo-Swedish War; Shuvalov, Pavel Andreyevich, Prince; Smolensk, Battle of; Tuchkov (Tuchkov I), Nikolay Alexeyevich; Vitelbsk, Battle of
References and further reading
Gavrilov, I. 1998. *Tuchkovy.* Moscow: Rus.
Mikaberidze, Alexander. 2005. *The Russian Officer Corps in the Revolutionary and Napoleonic Wars, 1792–1815.* New York: Savas Beatie.

Tudela, Battle of (23 November 1808)

A major French victory, the Battle of Tudela took place during the counteroffensive that Napoleon mounted in Spain following the surrender of General Pierre Dupont at Bailén on 21 July 1808. In the wake of this event, the French forces in central Spain had fallen back behind the river Ebro. Concentrated around Vitoria and Pamplona, they were there joined by thousands of reinforcements, some of Napoleon's best marshals, and the Emperor himself. Against this array, the Spaniards had no chance. Political problems had delayed the concentration of their own armies on the Ebro, while they were in any case badly outnumbered. When Napoleon attacked at the beginning of November, the French therefore quickly broke through. With several French corps heading for Madrid, the correct move for the (Spanish) Army of the Center, which had been stationed around the city of Logroño, would have been to retire on New Castile in the hope of protecting Andalucía. Instead, however, its commander, General Francisco Castaños, allowed himself to be persuaded that he should rather help protect Zaragoza (Saragossa), and he therefore retreated no further than a position stretching between the Navarrese town of Tudela and the Sierra de Moncayo. Much too long for Castaños's forces to hold by themselves, this line could only have been held with the aid of General José Palafox's Army of Reserve (in essence, the troops raised since the uprising in Aragón, together with a mixture of levies and regulars sent up from Valencia).

For a variety of reasons, however, Palafox hated Castaños and was scheming to secure his overthrow. In consequence, there was a considerable delay before any of his troops joined the Army of the Center, and they were in fact still filing into position when the French attacked under Marshal Jean Lannes on the morning of 23 November 1808. Lannes's blow fell on the Spanish right, which rested on the river Ebro around Tudela. Caught by surprise, the three Spanish divisions in this sector fought bravely, but a large force of French cavalry penetrated an unguarded gap in their line and then fanned out so as to take them in the rear, while at the same time almost capturing Castaños, who was cut off from his men and forced to hide in an olive grove. With their left wing and center too far away to affect the course of the fighting, the result was that the Spaniards were completely beaten. Most of the Aragonese forces got back to Zaragoza, where they were besieged by the French a month later, while Castaños's own troops escaped encirclement at the hands of Marshal Michel Ney, who had been dispatched from Old Castile to take them in the rear, and got away to New Castile. But Spanish casualties had still been very heavy, while Castaños's reputation had been dealt a blow from which it never recovered.

Charles J. Esdaile

See also Bailén, Battle of and Capitulation at; Castaños, Francisco Javier de; Lannes, Jean; Ney, Michel; Peninsular War; Rebolledo de Palafox y Melzi, José

References and further reading
Esdaile, Charles J. 2002. *The Peninsular War: A New History.* London: Penguin.
Oman, Charles. 2005. *A History of the Peninsular War.* 7 vols. London: Greenhill. (Orig. pub. 1902–1930.)

Tugendbund

This association, founded to encourage the moral regeneration of Prussia after the catastrophes of Jena and Auerstädt in October 1806, was called the Moral and Scientific Society. Better known as the Tugendbund (League of Virtue), it was founded in Königsberg (now Kaliningrad) in East Prussia early in 1808 and was one of a number of such groups formed at this time. Its activities included the alleviation of the suffering caused by the recent war and the French occupation, the patriotic education of youth, and the exertion of pressure on the government to continue its military reforms. Its objective was to bring about the end of the French occupation of Germany.

Among its founders were professors Wilhelm Traugott Krug, Georg Baersch, and others. Its members included pro-reform army officers, men of letters, and sons of landowners belonging to the Königsberg lodge of Freemasons. They intended to seek "the revival of morality, religion, serious taste, and public spirit." It was not a formal organization, but a loose body of men sharing these ideals. The influence of this group spread to the provinces of Silesia and Pomerania, but did not enjoy so much support in the Mark of Brandenburg and Berlin.

It attracted around 300 to 400 supporters, including senior army officers such as generals Hermann von Boyen and Karl von Grolman, but not the leading military reformers Gerhard von Scharnhorst and August von Gneisenau. Many a nervous senior public servant and army officer did not allow his subordinates to be associated with it. Although Heinrich Freiherr vom und zum Stein was known to disapprove of this society, comparing the anti-French statements of its members to the "rage of dreaming sheep," he had frequent secret contact with people involved in such organizations.

There was considerable disquiet at the effects of the French occupation of Germany. The philosopher Johann Fichte published his *Addresses to the German Nation* at the end of 1807 and was one of a number of intellectuals expressing ideas on German nationalism.

The war between Austria and France in 1809 led to considerable unrest in Germany. After the Austrian defeat at the Battle of Wagram that July, a backlash against the supporters of this disorder was inevitable. Indeed, the Tugendbund was blamed for instigating Major Ferdinand von Schill's rebellion, in which this Prussian army officer led his squadron of cavalry across northern Germany, hoping to spark a popular uprising. Fearing the French reaction to what amounted to a secret society, and under pressure from Napoleon, Frederick William III issued a decree dissolving this group in December 1809. Nevertheless, this group of like-minded people continued to play an influential role behind the scenes, with its members joining other similar associations.

These groups included organizations such as the Deutsche Gesellschaften, or German Patriotic Societies, the Burschenschaften, or German Students Associations. The most effective of these bodies was the Turngesellschaft, or Fitness Society, founded by Friedrich Jahn in Berlin. Aimed at academic youth, this organization prepared both the body and the mind for the forthcoming war against France, and many of its members became militarily active in the campaigns in Germany (1813) and France (1814). This movement is said to have inspired the founding of Adolf Lützow's Freikorps in 1813.

Peter Hofschröer

See also Auerstädt, Battle of; Fichte, Johann Gottlieb; Fifth Coalition, War of the; Fourth Coalition, War of the; France, Campaign in; Frederick William III, King; Germany, Campaign in; Gneisenau, August Wilhelm Anton Graf Neidhardt von; Jena, Battle of; Lützow, Adolf; Prussia; Scharnhorst, Gerhard Johann David von; Schill, Ferdinand Baptista von; Stein, Heinrich Friedrich Karl Freiherr vom und zum; Wagram, Battle of

References and further reading
Lehmann, Hans Friedrich Gottlieb. 1867. *Der Tugendbund, aus den hinterlassenen Papieren des Mitstifters Professor Dr. Hans Friedrich Gottlieb Lehmann, herausgegeben von Professor Dr. August Lehmann.* Berlin: Weidling.

Turkey

See Ottoman Empire

Turkish Navy

See Ottoman Navy

Turner, Joseph Mallord William (1775–1851)

Leading English Romantic painter, forerunner of the Impressionist movement.

Joseph Turner was born on 23 April 1775 to William and Mary Turner in London, where his father was a wig-maker and barber. Turner was largely self-taught. After a successful probationary term, he enrolled as a student at the Royal Academy Schools on 11 December 1789. He studied with Thomas Malton and specialized in drawing and watercolors. He became a voracious traveler, touring to make sketches in England, Wales, and Scotland, and on the Continent, nearly every year of his life.

He exhibited *Fishermen at Sea* at the Royal Academy in 1790. He received a three-year position as copyist of drawings in 1794. Turner added oil painting as a specialty in 1796, the year his first oil painting was exhibited. His vibrant seascapes had no worthy competition. On 4 November 1799 he was elected an associate of the Royal Academy of Art based on his interpretation of Norham Castle. This learning stage, during which he copied the Old Masters in oils and watercolors, proved successful. He sold nearly all his works to numerous patrons who supported all his endeavors.

Although Turner showed little curiosity about the opposite sex, his mistress Sarah Danby had at least one child by him, and he may have had other children by other relationships. Although he never acknowledged them as his, Turner supported his children and Sarah financially, though he was not an affectionate father.

On 12 February 1802, Turner became a full member of the Academy and moved into his own home at 64 Harley Street. He added a studio in 1803 and exhibited there throughout his career, while also continuing to exhibit at the Royal Academy. His father became his business manager. Turner was appointed Professor of Perspective at the Academy in 1807 and gave his first lecture in 1811.

Turner's style changed considerably over the course of his career. From 1800 to 1820 he painted historical and mythological works with subdued coloring and a strong emphasis on contour and detail. *Calais Pier* was painted in 1803 and well received. The influence of French painter Claude Lorrain was evident in *Dido Building Carthage* and *Crossing the Brook*. He also worked on the seventy drawings of *Liber Studiorum* from 1807 to 1819. *Sun Rising through Vapor* is also representative of this period. After 1820, Turner used enhanced coloring effects and variations of light, as represented by *Bay of Baiae* and *Ulysses Deriding Polyphemus*. He drastically changed his style by constructing the object of his work with a vibrant sense of color and misty masses, as seen in *Rain, Steam and Speed*, and *The Sun of Venice Going to Sea*. This revolutionary, visionary, misty style infuriated Turner's critics. He was staunchly defended by the respected Sir Thomas Lawrence and John Ruskin, who realized that Turner had laid the groundwork for future art movements. His watercolors were universally admired and never garnered criticism.

As he aged, the wealthy Turner became increasingly reclusive. In 1856, five years after his death, his estate left for the nation almost 300 paintings and nearly 30,000 watercolors and drawings, plus his £140,000 fortune, the whole known as the Turner Bequest, now held by the Tate Britain Gallery in London. All told he had sold approximately 1,000 paintings and drawings.

Annette E. Richardson

See also Blake, William; Constable, John; David, Jacques-Louis; Goya y Lucientes, Francisco José de; Lawrence, Sir Thomas; Romanticism

References and further reading
Bailey, Anthony. 1997. *Standing in the Sun: A Life of J. M. W. Turner.* London: Sinclair-Stevenson.
Butlin, Martin, and Evelyn Joll. 1977. *The Paintings of J. M. W. Turner.* New Haven: Yale University Press.
Lindsay, Jack. 1971. *J. M. W. Turner: His Life and Work: A Critical Biography.* New York: Harper and Row.
Rodner, William S. 1997. *J. M. W. Turner: Romantic Painter of the Industrial Revolution.* Berkeley and Los Angeles: University of California Press.
Townsend, Joyce. 1973. *Turner's Painting Techniques.* London: Tate Gallery.
Wilton, Andrew. 1987. *Turner in His Time.* London: Thames and Hudson.

Two Sicilies, Kingdom of the

See Naples

Tyrol, Uprising in the (April–November 1809)

The Tyrolean uprising was a revolt of local peasants against the Bavarian government. Instigated by Austria, it kept Bavarian troops away from the Battle of Wagram and lasted from April through November 1809. The Tyroleans lost in spite of Austrian efforts, and the province remained in Bavarian hands until the Congress of Vienna in 1815. The most lasting result of the uprising was the legacy of

The revolt in the Tyrol. Encouraged by the Austrians to throw off the yoke of Napoleon's Bavarian allies, the people of this Alpine region took up arms in 1809 in a futile act of resistance. (Ridpath, John Clark, *Ridpath's History of the World*, 1901)

Andreas Hofer, whose memory served as an emblem for national independence thereafter.

The uprising had its foundations in the Treaty of Pressburg (26 December 1805), which forced Austria to cede the Tyrol to Bavaria. The new Bavarian government closed the provincial estates, instituted conscription and taxes, and closed several monasteries. Thus, when Hofer and a delegation of Tyrolese were invited to Vienna in January 1809, they readily pledged their support against the French and Bavarians.

The rebellion began in the marshes around Sterzing, where a small Bavarian force was captured on 11 April, and at Hall, where Joseph Speckbacher and his militia captured the Bavarian garrison on 12 April. These two victories allowed the Tyrolean forces to invest Innsbruck. At the same time, Archduke John was leading an Austrian army against the forces of the Kingdom of Italy, which were commanded by Napoleon's stepson, Prince Eugène de Beauharnais. Encouraged by Eugène's successes, Bavarian and French forces retook Innsbruck. They underestimated the support for Hofer's rebellion, however, and the small detachment of Bavarians, left to defend the city, was defeated at the Battle of Berg Isel on 29 May. They retreated and left Innsbruck open to Hofer's troops. Soon after, Josef von Hormayer, an Austrian administrator, took charge of the city, and Hofer returned to his home. The rebellion continued in other parts of the province, however, as Speckbacher undertook a siege from 23 June to 16 July that resulted in the capture of Castle Kufstein.

Despite these local successes, the French victory at Wagram (5–6 July) sounded the death knell for the Tyrolean insurrection. In the armistice of Znaim on 12 July, Archduke Charles agreed to evacuate the Tyrol. The Austrians withdrew, leaving the Tyrolese to their fate. Marshal François Lefebvre, with 40,000 Franco-Bavarian troops, arrived to end the uprising. Choosing the same terrain that had brought them victory before, the local militia achieved initial success at Sterzing (6–9 August) and a second encounter at Berg Isel (13 August), forcing the invaders to withdraw. During this lull, Hofer's troops once again took Innsbruck and established him as the governor of the province from 15 August to late November. At an engagement at Lofer on 25 September, Speckbacher forced the Franco-Bavarian troops to withdraw, but suffered heavy losses himself. These losses contributed to his defeat on 16 October at Melleck, where the Tyrolese were routed. Meanwhile, the Treaty of Schönbrunn, concluded on 14 October, had confirmed Bavarian control of the Tyrol, except for the Italian-speaking southern Tyrol, which went to the Kingdom of Italy, and the eastern Tyrol, which was added to the French province of Illyria. Following the action at Melleck, Eugène offered amnesty to the rebels on 25 October. His offer was followed by a final battle at Berg Isel (1 November), which resulted in Hofer's surrender on the eighth. Hofer nevertheless called for another insurrection four days later. This action forfeited his amnesty and also branded him as a hothead. He was captured and executed at the direct order of Napoleon on 10 February 1810.

Doug Harmon

See also Bavaria; Beauharnais, Eugène Rose de; Charles, Archduke of Austria, Duke of Teschen; Fifth Coalition, War of the; Hofer, Andreas; John, Archduke; Lefebvre, François Joseph; Pressburg, Treaty of; Schönbrunn, Treaty of; Vienna; Congress of; Wagram, Battle of; Znaim, Battle of

References and further reading
Junkelman, Marcus. 1985. *Napoleon und Bayern den Anfängen des Königreiches*. Regensburg: F. Pustet.
Paulin, Karl. 1996. *Andreas Hofer und der Tiroler Freiheitskampf 1809*. Vienna: Tosa-Verl.

U

Ucles, Battle of

See Peninsular War

Ulm, Surrender at (20 October 1805)

At the Bavarian city of Ulm on the river Danube, an Austrian army, surrounded and isolated by the rapid advance of Napoleon's Grande Armée, surrendered on 20 October 1805. This French success ended the ambitious offensive strategy of the Third Coalition and opened the road for a French advance on Vienna, leading ultimately to the climatic Battle of Austerlitz in December 1805.

The nervous peace that existed in Europe in the years following the signing of the Treaty of Amiens in March 1802 broke down in May 1803 with a resumption of war between Britain and France, a conflict that widened in 1805 when Russia, Austria, and Sweden formed the Third Coalition to oppose France. As part of the grand strategy of the alliance, a joint Austro-Russian force was to attack France through Bavaria. Napoleon's army, encamped along the English Channel coast, had been training hard for an invasion of England. Now, with war renewed on the Continent, Napoleon turned his army to face this new threat.

On 25 August the first elements of the 190,000-strong French army commenced marching for the river Rhine. On the same day, a Russian army led by General Mikhail Kutuzov crossed the Russian border to begin the long march to join the Austrian army in Bavaria. This force, nominally commanded by Archduke Ferdinand d'Este, was in reality under the direction of *Feldmarschalleutnant* Karl Mack Freiherr von Leiberich, who held direct authority from Emperor Francis to overrule Ferdinand. About 72,000 strong, the army left Austrian territory on 8 September, entered Bavaria, and took up a position on the river Lech, about 35 miles west of Munich, to await the Russians. Almost immediately Mack suffered a setback, when he learned that the 22,000-man Bavarian army had withdrawn to the north, instead of joining the coalition, and was now allied with France. Even more worrying news followed, however, causing Mack to reconsider his position: French troops were already on the Rhine.

In preparation for an advance on the Danube, three formations, Marshal Jean Lannes's V Corps, the Imperial Guard, and the Cavalry Reserve converged on Strasbourg, while marshals Louis Davout (III Corps), Nicolas Soult (IV), and Michel Ney (VI) centered on Landau. Marshal Auguste de Marmont's II Corps marched for Mainz at the junction of the Rhine and Main rivers, while Marshal Jean-Baptiste Bernadotte (I Corps) headed for Frankfurt am Main.

At this point Napoleon was uncertain as to the position occupied by the Austrians but anticipated intercepting them in Bavaria between the Inn and Lech rivers, for which purpose the French army was directed to points along a 30-mile stretch of the Danube between Ulm and Dillingen. On 25 September, just one month after the first orders were issued, the leading elements of the French army crossed the Rhine, completing the first stage of this extraordinary realignment from the shores of the English Channel.

Reports that the French were on the Rhine prompted Mack to advocate a rapid advance on to the line of the Iller River between Ulm and Memmingen, from where he could block any attempt by the French to debouch from the defiles of the Black Forest. Archduke Ferdinand strongly objected to this forward movement, but Mack overruled him and occupied the line of the Iller. Mack's confidence received a boost from assurances he received from Emperor Francis that the Prussian territory of Ansbach would block any French advance against his rear. But the army did not share his confidence, and dissension among senior officers caused command difficulties. However, Francis approved Mack's orders and informed Ferdinand that he was not to oppose Mack's decisions.

While senior Austrian officers bickered, Napoleon took the decision to risk the wrath of Prussia and with it

General Mack surrenders his army at Ulm, 20 October 1805. Napoleon's strategic encirclement of the Austrians, in conjunction with the Battle of Austerlitz six weeks later, sealed the fate of the Third Coalition. (Print by Bousson, Valadon, Paris, after E. Boutigny from *Life of Napoleon Bonaparte* by William M. Sloane, New York: Century, 1906, vol. 2)

the danger that it would come into the coalition against him by ordering Bernadotte to march with I and II Corps through Ansbach. He felt the risk worthwhile, considering that Prussia would be slow to react and that falling on Mack's right and rear before the arrival of the Russians could be crucial to the success of the campaign. In the event, Prussia did fail to oppose the move.

To shroud his movements, Napoleon ordered Marshal Joachim Murat's Cavalry Reserve to advance through the Black Forest, forming an extended cavalry screen probing toward the Danube. The Imperial Guard and V Corps followed. Farther north the other five corps began their southeasterly march in appalling weather—rain, sleet, and even snow. It was a fraught time, with food in short supply and tensions between corps commanders high. As the columns continued their advance, Napoleon heard, on 4 October, that Mack was at Ulm, necessitating a realignment of the line of advance.

On that same day Mack recognized that the French troops issuing from the Black Forest constituted a feint and that his line on the Iller was redundant. Instead he ordered

the army to re-form along the line of the Danube from Ulm to Donauwörth. On 6 October, advanced elements of Soult's corps stormed the bridge at Donauwörth before the Austrian garrison was able to complete its destruction, and by the early hours of the following morning, Soult's men and some of Murat's cavalry were across the river. As Mack received this news, he also heard of Bernadotte's violation of Ansbach. Although now separated by this French move from *Feldmarschalleutnant* Michael Freiherr von Kienmayer's 12,000 men, who formed the extreme right of his army, Mack remained confident. He felt it important to hold his position, offering protection to Austrian possessions in the Tyrol and Vorarlberg that retreat eastward would uncover. At the same time he considered that a retreat southward through the Tyrol would expose the Russians to the full weight of the French army. Therefore Mack held his position, intending to tie down a great number of French troops, by presenting a threat to their communications, until Kutuzov's arrival.

On 8 October an outnumbered Austrian column, intercepted at Wertingen, about 10 miles south of Donauwörth, gave up the prisoners Napoleon needed—now he had a more accurate impression of the situation around Ulm. Meanwhile Lannes, Davout, Marmont, and Bernadotte completed their crossing of the Danube, leaving only Ney on the north bank. Delighted to find he now held a position of strength in the rear of the Austrians and with no sign of the Russians, Napoleon determined to prevent Mack from escaping, considering his most likely routes to be eastward through Augsburg or south toward the Tyrol. But Mack had no intention of retreating. Instead he determined to strike a blow at French communications and any troops on the north bank of the Danube; however, the subsequent capture of a bridge over the Danube at Günzburg by French troops under Ney on 9 October delayed the move and forced the Austrians back on Ulm.

Napoleon now occupied the major towns on the eastern and southern routes from Ulm, gradually tightening the noose around the city. However, a breakdown in communications resulted in only General Pierre-Antoine Dupont's division of Ney's corps remaining on the north bank of the Danube after Günzburg.

With his relationship with Ferdinand becoming ever more strained, Mack now planned a northeast breakout toward Bohemia. At the same time, Napoleon continued his movements to prevent a southern breakout. On 11 October some 25,000 Austrian troops emerged on the north bank of the Danube and encountered Dupont's isolated division of about 6,000 men at Haslach. The French put up an outstanding defense against the overwhelming Austrian numbers, before finally retreating under cover of darkness. Mack was unable to locate Ferdinand during the battle, and thus Austrian command and control suffered, resulting in the army retiring back to Ulm. Even so, Mack hoped to exploit this success, but senior officers vigorously objected, claiming the exhaustion of their troops, leading to further confrontations between Mack and Ferdinand. As a result the Austrian army rested on 12 October.

A new attempt the following day called for about 35,000 men, divided into two columns, to march from the city, with the rest of the army to follow later. The right column struggled slowly through ground destroyed by weather and earlier troop movements, only reaching Elchingen, about 7 miles, by the end of the day. The left column, on much better ground, covered about 20 miles. Meanwhile, the troops still at Ulm, awaiting the order to follow on, had their orders cancelled. A French agent passed information to Mack that caused him to change his plan again. The concentration of the French army to the south of the city and its westward movement puzzled him, as the city lay mainly on the north bank. The information he received told him that a British force had landed at Boulogne and a revolt broken out in France. The news was

false, but for Mack it explained the confusing French movements—they were retreating. He canceled his previous orders to follow up the breakout; now he needed as many men as possible to pursue the French. Even before fresh orders were issued from headquarters, however, the situation changed once more.

News of the action at Haslach alerted Napoleon to his weakness on the north bank, and he issued orders to support Dupont. On the morning of 14 October the Austrian column at Elchingen was attacked by Ney and fell back on Ulm. The other column, 20,000 strong under *Feldmarschalleutnant* Franz Freiherr von Werneck, unaware of developments, pushed on alone. Tensions in Ulm between Mack and Ferdinand now reached the breaking point. It appeared that the last chance of a breakout had evaporated, and while Mack still maintained the importance of defending the city and tying down the French, Ferdinand refused to accept the possibility of his own capture. That night, with *Feldmarschalleutnant* Karl Philipp Fürst zu Schwarzenberg and twelve squadrons of cavalry, he abandoned the city, hoping to locate Werneck's column.

On 15 October the French completed the encirclement and began to bombard the city. Mack received a summons to surrender but refused. He still had about 23,000 men with which to tie down the French, gaining valuable time for the arrival of the Russians. But it was not to be. The lead elements of the Russian army had only just reached the Bavarian border, 160 miles away—and it would be another two weeks before they regrouped and were ready for action. Two days later Mack received another call to surrender, and, demoralized by dissension among his officers, he agreed to do so on 25 October if there was still no sign of Russian intervention. This agreement granted limited French access to the city, quickly lowering still further the already-shattered morale of the garrison.

Mack met Napoleon on 19 October, suffering a further setback with the news of Werneck's interception and surrender two days earlier (although his cavalry did escape, eventually joining Ferdinand). With this news and a written assurance from Marshal Louis Berthier that the Russians could not arrive by the stated deadline, Mack agreed to surrender at once. The following morning, the garrison at Ulm marched into captivity. Of the 72,000 men that had advanced into Bavaria, almost 50,000 were now prisoners, taken at Ulm and in the battles around the city. Another column of 6,000 men, operating on the Iller, failed to make good their escape into the Tyrol and later swelled the catch.

For the Grande Armée it had been an extraordinary achievement. But there was no time for the army to rest on its laurels. Four days later the whole army, except for Ney's corps, prepared to march to face Kutuzov's Russians. The campaign concluded with the decisive Battle of Austerlitz on 2 December.

Ian Castle

See also Amiens, Treaty of; Austerlitz, Battle of; Bernadotte, Jean-Baptiste-Jules; Berthier, Louis-Alexandre; Davout, Louis Nicolas; Dupont de l'Etang, Perre-Antoine, comte; England, French Plans for the Invasion of; Ferdinand, d'Este, Archduke; Francis I, Emperor; Kutuzov, Mikhail Golenishev-, Prince; Lannes, Jean; Mack, Karl Freiherr von Leiberich; Marmont, Auguste Frédéric Louis Viesse de; Murat, Joachim; Ney, Michel; Schwarzenberg, Karl Philipp Fürst zu; Soult, Nicolas Jean de Dieu; Third Coalition, War of the

References and further reading
Bowden, Scott. 1997. *Napoleon and Austerlitz.* Chicago: Emperor's.
Burton, R. G. 2003. *From Boulogne to Austerlitz.* Cambridge: Trotman. (Orig. pub. 1912.)
Castle, Ian. 2002. *Austerlitz 1805: The Fate of Empires.* Oxford: Osprey.
———. 2005. *Austerlitz: Napoleon and the Eagles of Europe.* London: Leo Cooper.
Chandler, David G. 1995. *The Campaigns of Napoleon.* London: Weidenfeld and Nicolson.
Duffy, Christopher. 1977. *Austerlitz 1805.* London: Seeley Service.
Furse, George A. 1995. *Campaigns of 1805—Ulm, Trafalgar and Austerlitz.* Tyne and Wear: Worley. (Orig. pub. 1905.)
Maude, F. N. 1912. *The Ulm Campaign 1805.* London: Allen.
Maycock, F. W. O. 1912. *The Napoleonic Campaign of 1805.* London: Gale and Polden.
Willbold, Franz. 1987. *Napoleons Feldzug um Ulm.* Ulm: Süddeutsche Verlagsgesellschaft.

Uniforms

The era of the French Revolutionary and Napoleonic Wars witnessed a remarkable combination of styles and colors in the uniforms of troops represented by dozens of combatant nations. These variations and the general sartorial splendor associated with the age were not simply the product of armies seeking to attire their men as peacocks for the sake of vanity; in spite of ostentatious design and endless variation in dress, several practical considerations were at play. First and foremost, uniforms helped distinguish friend from foe; second, they provided a sense of *esprit de corps* within the unit, thus bolstering the soldiers' morale; and third, the more ornamental and imposing aspects of a uniform, such as tall headdress and epaulettes, served—or at least were intended to serve—to intimidate one's adversary, not simply to add to the pageantry of war.

The uniforms of this period have been and continue to be the objects of copious research, and no attempt will be made here to cover the minutiae associated with a study that, though peripheral to most military historians, remains absolutely essential to the pursuits of wargamers and historical reenactors. The broad features, however, can be outlined.

At the start of the French Revolutionary Wars (1792–1802), most armies arrayed their troops in similar uniforms. The colors varied, certainly, as well as much of the ornamentation, including buttons, lace, and badges, but generally speaking, soldiers wore a close-fitting coat in the national colors—dark blue for France and Prussia, white for Austria, green for Russia, scarlet for Britain—with lapels that revealed the waistcoat from the neck to the waist, and a long tail at the back. Regimental distinctions, particularly in the infantry, came in the form of "facings": colored collars, cuffs, and sometimes lapels, or colored trim to the coat, especially the rear of the coattail, which was often turned back at the bottom. Throughout the 1790s, infantry wore breeches (generally white or buff in summer and dark in winter) and stockings or gaiters, with trousers—both more practical and comfortable—only gradually replacing after the turn of the century. Most troops, whether infantry, cavalry, or artillery, wore a bicorn (that is, a two-cornered) hat, with the peaks worn on either side of the head (that is, transversely, as opposed to front and back, like naval officers of the period), thus replacing the tricorn (three-cornered) version so characteristic of the eighteenth-century armies of Frederick the Great and those that fought in the American Revolutionary War. On top of all this, infantry generally wore a stock around the neck, consisting of a leather or stiff fabric collar that obliged the soldier to keep his head constantly upright.

The soldier's uniform and equipment—the latter consisting of canteen, haversack, blanket, ammunition pouch, and other items—were kept firmly in place by tight-fitting leather belts and cross-straps, these last dyed in black or white. Cavalry generally wore a cocked hat and heavy riding boots. When to this apparatus and attire was added a musket and bayonet for an infantryman, or a sword and pistol for a cavalry trooper, it is clear that the fighting man constituted something of an overdressed beast of burden.

During the Napoleonic Wars (1803–1815), coats grew progressively shorter in the back, and headgear evolved into many more forms, including the peaked-bell or cylindrical-shaped leather shako or helmet, usually bearing a badge or brass plate to identify the unit and chin-scales to hold the headgear in place. As before, each country sported its own variations in headdress and coat, though the lesser states allied to more powerful neighbors generally outfitted their troops in similar styles. Thus, Dutch and Italian troops, as well as most of those hailing from the German states of the Confederation of the Rhine, wore French-style dress, while during the Peninsular War the Portuguese received their uniforms from their British allies. In contrast to the infantry, cavalry, especially hussars, tended to favor fashion over function, sometimes wearing tufts or fur on their caps that, apart from some of the light cavalry, generally appeared in a completely different form from that of the infantry. Indeed, headgear varied much more widely among the cavalry, who, according to their role on the battlefield and national preferences of dress, might wear the steel helmet common to the cuirassiers, the square-topped Polish-style "czapka" popular with many lancer units, or the tall, imposing bearskin cap often worn by elite heavy cavalry.

In all armies, especially those of Naples and Spain, officers—above all mounted senior ranks such as the French marshals and Allied corps and army commanders—favored varying degrees of ornamentation, generally gold or silver lace and plumes to their hats, not to mention medals, ribbons, and decorations emblazoned across their chests. Virtually the only exception to this rule could be found among the British officer corps, where generals serving in Iberia tended to wear more sober dress, though the scarlet coat (hence the term "Redcoat" coined by the American colonists more than a generation earlier) so characteristic of the army in general was perhaps flamboyant enough on its own. Some senior officers contented themselves with the plainest of uniforms or even actual civilian clothes, a trend begun, though by no means insisted upon, by the Duke of Wellington, who, for instance, declined to wear gloves, and fought the Waterloo campaign wearing a simple dark blue coat covered by a cloak and cape of the same color.

Uniforms were unquestionably attractive, but were not always particularly functional, and never comfortable, with often no thought in their design given to the practicalities of life on campaign, including conditions of combat or climate. Hence, it is not surprising that many soldiers adapted their uniforms to suit circumstances, their commanding officers generally accepting the necessity of, or turning a blind eye to, such improvisations. Indeed, a "full dress" or "regulation dress" uniform, which when originally issued to a soldier might conform in every respect to regulations and present an imposing spectacle on the parade ground, quickly wore out on campaign when—as was so often the case—no replacement items could be procured from a local depot or regimental headquarters back home. Indeed, a soldier might serve through an entire campaign with no new articles of clothing issued to him apart from perhaps undergarments and shoes or boots. Even footwear sometimes had to be acquired in the aftermath of battle from the dead or wounded. As men naturally cannot march far in bare feet, footwear was thus prized above all things except food. Once dilapidation of

one's uniform set in, "campaign dress" became the norm, with soldiers resorting to whatever methods they could devise to hold their clothing together—patches, string, bandages—or seeking replacements with equivalent items through purchase or plunder. Numerous firsthand accounts relate how uniformity could be sometimes lost altogether as a result of the rigors of campaign, the most notable examples being in Russia, where during the retreat of the Grand Armée from Moscow in 1812 no two soldiers in a unit might be dressed exactly alike.

In general, the uniforms of rival armies were sufficiently distinct that, even amid the thick smoke of battle, troops were still able to distinguish their comrades from their adversaries. The distinctions of national colors disappeared entirely if a soldier wore "service dress" to protect him from the elements: a gray or brown greatcoat over himself and a waterproof covering (usually oilskin) over his shako or helmet, the latter of which hid badges and other identifying features both of unit and nationality. Where troops wore very similar uniforms, such as the French and Spanish in the Peninsular War, the Saxons and Austrians in the campaign of 1809, and the Prussians and Nassauers at Waterloo, "friendly fire" was almost inevitable. Under such conditions, particularly when visibility was poor, troops thus attired and seen from a distance or in silhouette could easily cross swords or bayonets.

Gregory Fremont-Barnes

See also Artillery (Land); Cavalry; Confederation of the Rhine; Infantry; Musket; Peninsular War; Rifle; Standards, Flags, and Eagles; Waterloo Campaign
References and further reading
Funcken, Liliane, and Fred Funcken. 1984. *The Napoleonic Wars: Arms and Uniforms.* 2 vols. New York: Prentice-Hall.
Haythornthwaite, Philip. 1976. *Uniforms of the Retreat from Moscow, 1812, in color.* New York: Hippocrene.
———. 1981. *Uniforms of the French Revolutionary Wars, 1789–1802.* Poole, UK: Blandford.
———. 1985. *Uniforms of the Napoleonic Wars, 1796–1814.* Poole, UK: Blandford.
———. 1995. *Uniforms of the Peninsular War, 1807–1814.* London: Weidenfeld Military.
———. 1996. *Uniforms of Waterloo.* London: Weidenfeld Military.
———. 1999. *Weapons and Equipment of the Napoleonic Wars.* London: Arms and Armour.
Smith, Digby. 2006. *Uniforms of the Napoleonic Wars: An Illustrated Encyclopedia.* London: Lorenz.

Union, Act of (1 January 1801)

The constitutional union between Great Britain and Ireland that took effect on 1 January 1801, so forming the United Kingdom. Before then, Great Britain (itself formed by the union of England and Scotland in 1707) and Ireland had had separate parliaments, although the Irish Parliament was subordinated to the British. Uniting the two kingdoms into one was part of the prime minister, William Pitt's, plan to suppress revolutionary activity in Ireland while exploiting the kingdom's resources more efficiently to carry on the conflict with Revolutionary France. The Irish Rebellion and French invasion of 1798 had demonstrated that the Irish Anglican landowning class, the "Protestant Ascendancy," was no longer able to suppress the Catholics and Protestant Dissenters who made up the vast majority of the Irish population. It was also hoped that removing the artificial commercial barriers between the two kingdoms would contribute to economic growth.

Pitt and the Chief Secretary for Ireland, Lord Castlereagh, hoped that Irish Protestants would be reassured by the fact that, while they were in a minority in Ireland itself, as subjects of the United Kingdom they would be part of a majority. For Irish Catholics, Pitt and Castlereagh planned to follow union with emancipation, removing most of the remaining restrictions on Catholic political rights and the freedom of the Roman Catholic Church as an institution. Pitt hoped that the Catholic elite would prefer incorporation into the new United Kingdom to both continued subjection to the Protestant Ascendancy and the dangers emanating from Revolutionary and anti-clerical France. (Irish Catholic bishops supported union.)

Creation of the union required passage in both the British and the Irish parliaments. Although Pitt's government faced some resistance in the British Parliament, caused mostly by English dislike of the idea of Irish representatives in Westminster, the real challenge was in the Irish Parliament, the political expression of the Protestant Ascendancy, which was being asked to vote its own extinction. Forcing the Act of Union through Parliament required the generous distribution of bribes. Although the issue of union provoked a voluminous pamphlet debate, there was little popular political opposition, unlike a previous occasion in 1759 when a rumor that union was being considered brought angry mobs onto the streets of Dublin.

Under the new arrangement, Ireland was represented in the House of Lords (the upper house of Parliament in Westminster) by 32 peers, including 4 bishops of the Church of Ireland, and in the House of Commons by 100 Members of Parliament. The administration of Ireland, however, was virtually unchanged. Pitt's plan of combining union with Catholic emancipation proved a failure, due to the opposition of George III. The king believed that Catholic emancipation would be a violation of his coronation oath. The opposition of the king not only delayed Catholic emancipation for decades, but forced Pitt's resignation as prime minister on 3 February 1801 (Castlereagh also resigned). In Ireland, the union without emancipation was unpopular, and resentment over it contributed to the brief rebellion of Robert Emmet in 1803.

William E. Burns

See also Castlereagh, Robert Stewart, Viscount; Catholic Emancipation; George III, King; Great Britain; Ireland; Irish Rebellion; Pitt, William

References and further reading

Brown, Michael, Patrick M. Geoghegan, and James Kelly, eds. 2003. *The Irish Act of Union 1800: Bicentennial Essays.* Dublin: Irish Academic.

Ehrman, John. 1996. *The Younger Pitt: The Consuming Struggle.* London: Constable.

Geoghegan, Patrick M. 1999. *The Irish Act of Union: A Study in High Politics, 1798–1801.* Dublin: Gill and Macmillan.

Keogh, Dáire, and Kevin Whelan, eds. 2001. *Acts of Union: The Causes, Contexts, and Consequences of the Acts of Union.* Dublin: Four Courts.

Lydon, James. 1998. *The Making of Ireland: From Ancient Times to the Present.* London: Routledge.

United Kingdom

See Great Britain

United States

As the French Revolutionary Wars began, American sympathies were deeply divided between Britain and France. The Franco-American alliance of 1778 was still in effect in 1793, but the revolutionary change in government in France gave President George Washington the excuse he needed to declare neutrality in April. He indicated that he expected the warring parties to accord the new United States all the rights of neutral nations. Washington had asked his cabinet a series of questions, and replies from secretary of the treasury Alexander Hamilton and secretary of state Thomas Jefferson revealed that the existing Franco-American treaty raised some thorny questions, such as whether the United States was obliged to help defend French possessions in the West Indies or to deny ports and supplies to the British.

As the French Revolution turned more violent, the United States proclaimed its neutrality. The Act of 1794 forbade American citizens to enlist in foreign armies and prohibited the outfitting of foreign vessels in American ports. The act showed some of the difficulties the United States would face in containing French efforts to arm and outfit American privateers to attack British shipping and in withstanding British pressure as well. As a reaction to U.S. reluctance to support France, an undeclared war arose between France and the United States known as the Quasi-War, fought at sea from 1798 to 1800, as U.S. Navy warships protected American shipping and seized French privateers.

Americans also harbored a number of grievances against Britain. The Treaty of Paris ending the American Revolutionary War in 1783 had granted the new United States land west of the Appalachian Mountains but obliged the new government to compensate colonists who had been loyal to the king during the Revolution and who had left America under pressure. The United States charged Britain with arming Native Americans and failing to vacate frontier forts now in U.S. territory, while Britain insisted on payment to loyalists. The result was Jay's Treaty on 19 November 1794, named for the American ambassador to Britain, John Jay. Soon thereafter, the American minister in Spain, Thomas Pinckney, negotiated Pinckney's Treaty on 27 October 1795, strengthening U.S. commercial rights to use New Orleans in Spanish Louisiana and to gain access to the Caribbean from the Mississippi River.

The long conflict in Europe provided the United States with a splendid opportunity, which it used to negotiate the Louisiana Purchase. After Napoleon Bonaparte gained power in France, Spain retroceded the vast Louisiana Territory to France in 1801. Fear of French intentions in the New World caused the new U.S. president, Thomas Jefferson, to instruct his ministers to purchase New Orleans and secure control of the Mississippi River. A slave revolt in St. Domingue and the difficulty in suppressing it may have convinced Bonaparte to set aside his dreams of empire in the Americas. Or, perhaps, Bonaparte recognized his power on the European continent could not be translated into power across the Atlantic. He surprised the American negotiators and offered to sell the entire territory, about one-third of the present continental forty-eight states, for $15 million.

The Louisiana Purchase (3 May 1803) could not compensate for problems in international trade. The United States had a large merchant marine but a small navy, and it wanted to trade with the belligerents. With the outbreak of war between Britain and France in May 1803, however, Britain began to blockade French-controlled ports on the Continent, thereby limiting American access.

Perhaps more importantly, the Royal Navy made the United States cognizant of its weakness as a result of the practice of impressment. British naval vessels would stop American merchant ships to ensure they were not bound for blockaded ports, and they would remove sailors they claimed had deserted from the Royal Navy. The United States charged Britain with kidnapping, but British naval records claimed some 42,000 Royal Navy seamen had jumped ship.

The real issue was international respect, and President Jefferson announced the Embargo Act on 22 December 1807. It was repealed fifteen months later, for it failed miserably to pressure Britain into halting the practice of impressment by reducing trade with Britain and limiting the sale of important naval stores. More importantly, American merchantmen violated the act in order to continue to sell goods to the British. Prices were good, and violating the act was easy, as for example by simply moving goods across the poorly defended border with British-controlled Canada or falsifying cargo manifests.

The eventual result was that the United States declared war on Britain in 1812, although this new conflict had virtually no effect on the course of the fighting in Europe. After the failure of the Embargo Act, Congress had approved the Non-Intercourse Act on 1 March 1809, which lifted the embargo on American shipping, save for those vessels bound for British- or French-controlled ports. It too had little effect, as did its successor, Macon's Bill Number 2, which promised to lift the embargo against Britain or France if either stopped its search and seizure of American shipping. France, needing U.S. trade and not in a position to interdict U.S. trade with Britain, agreed, while Britain did not; this constituted the immediate cause of the War of 1812.

The American declaration of war on 18 June did not materially affect the British effort against Napoleon. There were three main phases to the War of 1812. In the first phase, the Royal Navy and the British army were mostly concentrating against Napoleon in the Iberian Peninsula, and the United States failed to press its demographic advantage against outnumbered British troops and Canadian militia in 1812 and 1813. Later, in 1813, the Royal Navy diverted increasing numbers of ships for duty in North American waters. In the third and final phase, in 1814, once Napoleon was finally defeated, Britain began transferring troops, mostly from southern France, to Canada and withstood American attacks across the Niagara frontier. The British launched an ill-fated offensive from Montreal south, and then, to compensate for the American seizure and burning of York (modern Toronto), British forces took Washington, burned the White House, unsuccessfully attacked Baltimore, and proceeded south to the Gulf Coast in an abortive effort to seize New Orleans.

Nine months after France had been defeated, Britain accepted a peace based on the status quo ante bellum (the situation as it existed before the war). Although the Treaty of Ghent was concluded on 24 December 1814, word of peace did not reach Washington until the British had already been disastrously defeated at the Battle of New Orleans, fought on 8 January 1815—two weeks after the signature of the treaty. Having won the war's last battle, Americans naturally believed they had also won the peace, though in reality the conflict with Britain ended as a stalemate. The United States was indeed fortunate even for this result, for had the conflict in Europe terminated earlier, Britain might well have released far larger forces for service in North America, enabling it to occupy, rather than merely raid, U.S. territory and so shifting the balance of power at the negotiating table.

Charles M. Dobbs

See also Continental System; Fontainebleau, Treaty of; France; Great Britain; Louisiana Purchase; New Orleans, Battle of; Peninsular War; United States Army; United States Navy; War of 1812
References and further reading
Blumenthal, Henry. 1970. *France and the United States: Their Diplomatic Relations, 1789–1914.* Chapel Hill: University of North Carolina Press.
DeConde, Alexander. 1958. *Entangling Alliance: Politics and Diplomacy under George Washington.* Durham, NC: Duke University Press.
———. 1966. *The Quasi-War: The Politics and Diplomacy of Undeclared War with France, 1797–1801.* New York: Scribner.
Egan, Clifford L. 1983. *Neither Peace nor War: Franco-American Relations, 1803–1812.* Baton Rouge: Louisiana State University Press.
Hill, Peter P. 2005. *Napoleon's Troublesome Americans: Franco-American Relations, 1804–1815.* Washington, DC: Potomac.
Hitsman, J. MacKay. 1966. *The Incredible War of 1812: A Military History.* Toronto: University of Toronto Press.
Horsman, Reginald. 1962. *The Causes of the War of 1812.* Philadelphia: University of Pennsylvania Press.
Mahon, John K. 1972. *The War of 1812.* Gainesville: University of Florida Press.
Perkins, Bradford. 1955. *The First Rapprochement: England and the United States, 1795–1805.* Philadelphia: University of Pennsylvania Press.
———. 1961. *Prologue to War: England and the United States, 1805–1812.* Berkeley: University of California Press.
———. 1964. *Castlereagh and Adams: England and the United States, 1812–1823.* Berkeley: University of California Press.
Stinchcombe, William. 1981. *The XYZ Affair.* Westport, CT: Greenwood.
Updyke, Frank A. 1965. *The Diplomacy of the War of 1812.* Gloucester, MA: Smith.
Wright, J. Leitch, Jr. 1975. *Britain and the American Frontier, 1783–1815.* Athens: University of Georgia Press.

United States Army

Before the outbreak of hostilities with the British in 1812, the role of the U.S. Army had been one of providing security for the borders of the new republic, mainly against Native American forces. After 1812 the army expanded quickly, and after a number of reverses developed into an efficient force capable of contributing effectively, in conjunction with militia forces, in winning the Battle of New Orleans (8 January 1815) against veteran British troops.

The army was virtually disbanded after independence in 1783, its role limited to duties along the frontier. However, when tension rose with France as a result of the seizure of neutral shipping, Congress authorized a force in 1799 amounting to 30,000 men and given the title of the Eventual Army. By 1801, however, the likelihood of war with France had faded, and President Thomas Jefferson reduced the army to almost skeletal strength. By 1808, with increased resentment against the British and a threat from Native American forces being organized by Chief Tecumseh, leader of the Shawnee, the strength of the army was increased. For the next three years, the army was deployed to defend the frontiers of the young nation, and it was thus spread very thinly in a large number of garrisons.

Although the army was generally successful in containing the attacks of the confederation of tribes organized by Tecumseh, it was ill-prepared to meet its next challenge in the War of 1812. It was rare for all elements of a regiment to be stationed together, and senior officers did not have the opportunity to drill large formations. Many of these officers were still tied to military doctrine dating from the period of the Revolutionary War and had not assimilated the advances that had been made in Europe. The army also lacked a staff corps and had no organized quartermaster or ordnance departments.

Despite the fact that in January 1812 Congress increased the size of the army once more, on the outbreak of war with Britain six months later, the nation had to rely on volunteers and militia to bring the field forces up to an effective strength. The early part of the war witnessed a series of defeats for the U.S. Army, when it failed in its planned invasion of Canada. This failure was mainly due to the inexperience of officers in commanding substantial forces, which led to a lack of coordination on the battlefield and a lack of aggressiveness, which meant that the initiative often passed to smaller British forces. Nevertheless, the success of officers like General Winfield Scott proved that if U.S. troops were well led, they were a match for British regulars. By 1814 the regular army had established the support services that it required and was able to fight the British to a standstill at Lundy's Lane (25 July 1814). The army nevertheless still maintained its strong tradition of relying on volunteer forces, who performed poorly in the defense of Washington in August 1814, yet were to prove their worth in the victory at New Orleans, where General Andrew Jackson commanded a mixed force of regular troops and Kentucky, Tennessee, and Louisiana militia.

Ralph Baker

See also Bladensburg, Battle of; British Army; Chippewa, Battle of; Lundy's Lane, Battle of; New Orleans, Battle of; United States; War of 1812

References and further reading

Bluhm, Raymond K. 2005. *U.S. Army: A Complete History.* Westport, CT: Hugh Lauter Levin Associates.

Borneman, Walter. 2004. *1812: The War That Forged a Nation.* London: HarperCollins.

Kochan, James. 2000. *The United States Army, 1812–1815.* Oxford: Osprey.

Palmer, Dave R. 2001. *Provide for Common Defense: America, Its Army, and the Birth of a Nation.* New York: Presidio.

Quimby, Robert S. 1997. *The U.S. Army in the War of 1812: An Operational and Command Study.* East Lansing: Michigan State University Press.

Skeen, Carl E. 1999. *Citizen Soldiers in the War of 1812.* Lexington: University Press of Kentucky.

Stewart, Richard Winship, ed. 2005. *American Military History.* Vol. 1, *The United States Army and the Forging of a Nation, 1775–1917.* Washington, DC: Department of the Army.

United States Navy

While the United States Navy did not take part in hostilities in European waters during this period, it played an important role in the Anglo-American War of 1812, which broke out as a result of the maritime policies adopted by both Britain and France with respect to neutral trade. When the administration of President George Washington assumed office under the new Constitution in 1789, it was faced almost immediately with the need to create a navy, initially to protect its commerce, but later increasingly to implement foreign policy with the backing of a competent naval force. A series of conflicts—the Quasi-War with France (1798–1800), the Tripolitan War (1801–1805), and the War of 1812 with Britain—posed a variety of challenges to the new navy. They also, however, provided valuable experience in suppressing piracy, patrol and blockade, the convoying of merchantmen, shore bombardment, support of land operations, single-ship engagements, and even actions involving whole squadrons (these last on the Great Lakes).

From its birth on 27 March 1794, the navy was under the control of the War Department, but it was later established as a separate department on 30 April 1798. The first secretary of the navy was Benjamin Stoddert. The customs, traditions, and basic policies of the navy were born and shaped during this era.

The Quasi-War with France began in 1798 after French seizures of a large number of American ships. In response, the Naval Act (May 1797) allowed the president to construct and employ three new frigates, which had been projected earlier. These were duly launched as the *United States, Constellation,* and *Constitution.* They were of a new design and heavier than their counterparts in other navies, but fast enough to outrun the more formidable ships of the line of foreign powers. They were to patrol the long Atlantic coastline and deal with French privateers and naval vessels. Hostilities came to a focus in the Caribbean, where the French waged war on both British and American commerce. By early 1799 the navy had grown to twenty-two ships, nineteen of which were deployed in West Indian waters. With the appointment of Bonaparte as First Consul in November 1799, French efforts to conciliate the United States, in order to isolate Britain, began, and hostilities between the two countries ended on 30 September 1800 by the Treaty of Mortefontaine. In the same year Congress approved retaining a navy of thirteen frigates, with six on active duty at any one time.

The next adversaries against which the United States Navy was opposed were the Barbary States (Morocco, Algiers, Tunis, and Tripoli) which occupied the western Mediterranean coast of North Africa. A large part of their economies was based on raiding the commerce of the weaker European nations—that is, those without powerful navies—enslaving the captives taken, and extorting both tribute and ransom. These largely helpless states found it expedient to pay off the Barbary powers rather than chastise them by military action, a practice that had persisted for centuries. America's considerable commerce with the Mediterranean region had, until independence, flown the British flag, and thus enjoyed the protection of the Royal Navy. After 1783, of course, that had changed, and Algiers seized American ships beginning in 1785, demanding tribute in exchange for protection from future attacks and ransom for the release of their prisoners. A treaty was eventually concluded with Algiers that obliged the United States to pay tribute in the form of naval stores, among other goods, and even to supply a small frigate and several other vessels.

Further difficulties with the Barbary States continued with subsequent administrations, including that of Thomas Jefferson, who came to office in February 1801. The new president chafed at the idea of tribute and instituted a policy of resistance to Barbary demands. No sooner was he installed in office than Tripoli declared war on the United States, which responded by dispatching a succession of squadrons to the Mediterranean to blockade the port of Tripoli. The frigate *Philadelphia* grounded in Tripoli harbor and was captured, but in a daring raid led by Lieutenant Stephen Decatur, the vessel was burned. American ships bombarded Tripoli in August and September 1804, but with little success, and the war did not come to an end until a American-backed overland expedition captured the port of Derna with a mixed American and Arab force. Participation by the U.S. Marines in this campaign explains the line "to the shores of Tripoli" in their hymn. Troubles with the Barbary States were not finally resolved until 1815, when Decatur visited various ports, negotiating treaties backed with the threat of naval bombardment.

Continual friction with Britain over interference with American shipping and, especially, Britain's impressment of American seamen into the Royal Navy intensified matters to the point that war was declared on 18 June 1812. The naval part of the war included frigate duels, squadron actions on the Great Lakes, naval support of operations on land, and the repulse of British incursions onto United States territory.

The frigate duels, in which the Americans often prevailed, were epitomized by Captain Isaac Hull's victory over the British ship *Guerrière* (19 August 1812), which added luster to the record of the *Constitution*, also known as "Old Ironsides."

Two battles involving fleets built and employed exclusively on inland waters played important roles in the success of land operations. On 10 September 1813 Commodore Oliver Hazard Perry engaged a British squadron on Lake Erie and defeated and captured the entire British force. His victory assured the water-borne supply route to General William Harrison's army and contributed to its success. Later, on 11 September 1814, Lieutenant Thomas Mcdonough defeated the British on Lake Champlain as they attempted to attack the American position at Plattsburg.

At various times during the war, the British put landing forces ashore at a number of points on the long American coastline. The largest of these operations took place in Chesapeake Bay in August 1814, when the British defeated the Americans at Bladensburg (24 August) and burned the new government buildings in Washington. Later, an attack on Baltimore's Fort McHenry between 12 and 14 September was repulsed, inspiring the poem by Francis Scott Key that became the words of the U.S. national anthem. American gunboats also contested British landings made during the attempt to seize New Orleans, which failed as a result of General Andrew Jackson's notable victory on 8 January 1815.

The naval aspects of the War of 1812 received serious scholarly attention at the turn of twentieth century. Theodore Roosevelt produced a lengthy history of the war, and the prophet of sea power, Captain Alfred Thayer Mahan, extended his analysis of its influence on war and national policy.

The long peace in Europe following the general settlement of 1815 allowed for the strengthening of the United States Navy, which in time evolved into one of the world's best and most experienced. The experience of the Civil War (1861–1865) brought the United States Navy into the modern age.

Kenneth Vosburgh

See also Bladensburg, Battle of; French Navy; New Orleans, Battle of; Royal Navy; Tripolitan War; United States; War of 1812

References and further reading
Canney, Donald L. 2001. *Sailing Warships of the U.S. Navy.* London: Chatham.
de Kay, James T. 2004. *A Rage for Glory: The Life of Commodore Stephen Decatur, USN.* New York: Free Press.
Dudley, William S. 1985. *The Naval War of 1812: A Documentary History.* Washington, DC: Naval Historical Center, Department of the Navy.
Fowler, William M. 1984. *Jack Tars and Commodores: The American Navy, 1783–1815.* Boston: Houghton Mifflin.
Fremont-Barnes, Gregory. 2006. *The Wars of the Barbary Pirates.* Oxford: Osprey.
Gardiner, Robert, ed. 1998. *The Naval War of 1812.* London: Chatham.
Kitzen, Michael L. 1993. *Tripoli and United States at War: A History of American Relations with the Barbary States, 1785–1805.* Jefferson, NC: McFarland.
Lambert, Frank. 2005. *The Barbary Wars: American Independence in the Atlantic World.* New York: Hill and Wang.
Lardas, Mark. 2003. *American Heavy Frigates, 1794–1826.* Oxford: Osprey.
Mahan, Alfred Thayer. 1905. *Sea Power in its Relation to the War of 1812.* Boston: Little, Brown.
Malcomson, Robert. 1998. *Lords of the Lake: The Naval War on Lake Ontario, 1812–1814.* Annapolis, MD: Naval Institute Press.
Palmer, Michael A. 1987. *Stoddert's War: Naval Operations during the Quasi-War with France, 1798–1801.* Columbia: University of South Carolina Press.
Tucker, Spencer. 1993. *The Jeffersonian Gunboat Navy.* Columbia: University of South Carolina Press.
———. 2005. *Stephen Decatur: A Life Most Bold and Daring.* Annapolis, MD: Naval Institute Press.
Welsh, William Jeffrey, and David Curtis, eds. 1991. *War on the Great Lakes: Essays Commemorating the 175th Anniversary of the Battle of Lake Erie.* Kent, OH: Kent State University Press.
Wheelan, Joseph. 2003. *Jefferson's War: America's First War on Terror, 1801–1805.* New York: Carroll and Graf.
Whipple, A. B. C. 1991. *To the Shores of Tripoli: The Birth of the U.S. Navy and Marines.* New York: Morrow.

Uvarov, Fedor Petrovich, Count (1773–1824)

Prominent Russian cavalry commander. Uvarov was born on 23 April 1773 to a petty noble family in Khruslavka in the Tula *gubernia* (province). He was enlisted as a sergeant in the artillery in 1776 at the age of three, transferred to the Life Guard Preobrazhensk Regiment in 1780, and rose to *vakhmistr* (noncommissioned officer) in the Life Guard Horse Regiment in late 1786. His active service began as a captain of the Sofia Infantry Regiment on 12 January 1788, and he served in the Olonetsk Horse *Jäger* Squadron from 1789 to 1790. He became a second major in the Smolensk Dragoon Regiment in September 1790. Uvarov served in Poland in 1792–1794, fighting at Stolbtsy, Mir, Natsybov, Warsaw (promoted to premier major), Sali, and Vilna, becoming a lieutenant colonel in May 1795. During the reign of Tsar Paul I, he rapidly achieved promotions: He transferred to His Majesty's Life Guard Cuirassier Regiment in March 1797, became colonel in April 1798, briefly served in Zorn's Cuirassier Regiment, transferred to the Life Guard Horse Regiment on 14 September 1798, and was promoted to major general and appointed adjutant general, concurrently, on 30 September 1798.

Uvarov transferred to the Chevalier Guard Corps in January 1799 and, after the reorganization of the corps, became *chef* (colonel-proprietor) of the Chevalier Guard Regiment in August 1799. He was promoted to lieutenant general on 17 November 1800. He took part in the conspiracy against Paul but did not play an active role in his assassination. He distinguished himself commanding the Russian cavalry at Austerlitz in December 1805. In 1807 he fought at Guttstadt, Heilsberg, and Friedland. After Tilsit, he commanded the Chevalier Guard Regiment in St. Petersburg and was given command of the advance guard of the (Russian) Army of Moldavia in April 1810, during the war against the Turks. Uvarov took part in the actions at Silistra, Shumla, Ruse, and Batin.

In late 1811 Uvarov was recalled to St. Petersburg and appointed commander of the 1st Reserve Cavalry Corps of the 1st Western Army in April 1812. He participated in the retreat to Smolensk and fought at Kolotsk Monastery. During the Battle of Borodino, he and Cossack commander Ataman Matvei Platov led a famous failed cavalry attack on the French left flank, referred to variously as Uvarov's Diversion or Platov's Raid. Technically, both Uvarov and Platov failed to accomplish the assigned mission at Borodino and thus received no awards after the battle. Ironically, however, the attack had a dramatic effect on Napoleon, causing him to worry about his flank enough to hold back his Imperial Guard. After the battle, Uvarov and his command covered the retreat to Moscow and, at the council of war at Fili, he urged that the army fight another battle in defense of the city. In October Uvarov's corps remained in reserve and did not fight at Maloyaroslavets and the first action at Krasnyi, but it was involved in the battle at Vyazma and the second action at Krasnyi.

In 1813–1814 Uvarov attended Tsar Alexander I at Lützen, Bautzen, Dresden, Kulm, Leipzig, Brienne, Arcis-sur-Aube, La-Fère-Champenoise, and Montmartre. He was promoted to general of cavalry on 20 October 1813 for his services at Leipzig. Returning to Russia, Uvarov was involved with the committee that assisted invalid Russian soldiers of the Napoleonic Wars and accompanied Alexander to the congresses in Vienna (1815), Aix-la-Chapelle (1818), and Laibach (1821). He became commander of the Guard Corps in November 1821 and a member of the State Council in September 1823. Uvarov became seriously ill in the summer of 1824 and died on 2 December of that year in St. Petersburg.

Alexander Mikaberidze

See also Alexander I, Tsar; Arcis-sur-Aube, Battle of; Austerlitz, Battle of; Bautzen, Battle of; Borodino, Battle of; Brienne, Battle of; Cossacks; Dresden, Battle of; Fourth Coalition, War of the; France, Campaign in; Friedland, Battle of; Germany, Campaign in; Heilsberg, Battle of; Imperial Guard (French); Krasnyi, Second Battle of; Kulm, Battle of; La-Fère-Champenoise, Battle of; Leipzig, Battle of; Lützen, Battle of; Maloyaroslavets, Battle of; Montmartre, Action at; Paul I, Tsar; Platov, Matvei Ivanovich, Count and Ataman; Russian Campaign; Russo-Polish War; Russo-Turkish War; Smolensk, Battle of; Third Coalition, War of the; Tilsit, Treaties of; Vienna, Congress of

References and further reading

Mikaberidze, Alexander. 2005. *The Russian Officer Corps in the Revolutionary and Napoleonic Wars, 1792–1815.* New York: Savas Beatie.

Uxbridge, Henry William Paget, Second Earl of (1768–1854)

A lifelong military leader, with a distinguished political career, Uxbridge was considered by most to be Britain's best cavalry commander and served as the Duke of Wellington's second in command at Waterloo, leading the decisive charge that smashed Napoleon's first major attack of the battle.

Lord Henry Paget began his career in the infantry, raising a regiment and receiving the temporary rank of lieutenant colonel in 1793, and participating in the Flanders campaign the following year. During the expedition, Paget had his first experience with the cavalry, with which he was thereafter associated. In a very short time he was in command of the 7th Light Dragoons (later known as the 7th Hussars), which was considered one of the best cavalry regiments in the army.

In 1808 the now lieutenant general led the British cavalry in the Peninsular War at the actions at Sahagún de Campos and Benavente during the Corunna campaign. At Sahagún, Paget's daring surprise attack resulted in his dragoons defeating a numerically superior French cavalry force—inflicting more than 150 casualties to less than 20 for the British. Paget's tactical skills were demonstrated eight days later at Benavente, where he maneuvered the cavalry of the French Imperial Guard into a trap leading to the capture of its commanding officer, General Charles, comte Lefebvre-Desnouëttes. Again the French cavalry suffered, this time more than 130 casualties to less than 50 in Paget's force. Unfortunately, his Peninsular service was ended as a result of his scandalous liaison with, and later marriage to, Henry Wellesley's wife (Lady Charlotte Wellesley, Wellington's sister-in-law), which made it impossible for him to serve under Wellington. Paget's absence was to prove a major disadvantage to the British army during the remainder of the Peninsular War.

From 1809 to 1815 Paget's only military service was in the disastrous Walcheren expedition (1809), in which he commanded a division. His duties as a Member of Parliament occupied him during most of this time period. In 1812 his father's death required that Paget take the family seat in the House of Lords, as the second Earl of Uxbridge.

In 1815, with Napoleon's escape from Elba and the subsequent Waterloo campaign, Uxbridge was recalled to duty by Wellington. Initially placed in command of British cavalry, he was later put in charge of all the Anglo-Allied cavalry and horse artillery. On 17 June, when the French under Marshal Michel Ney pushed into Quatre Bras, Uxbridge covered the Anglo-Dutch strategic withdrawal in a fashion consistent with his performances of 1808–1809. The following day, Uxbridge gained the crowning distinction of his military career in leading the great cavalry charge that checked, and in part routed, the massive infantry attack of General Jean-Baptiste Drouet, comte d'Erlon. During the charge, Uxbridge repeatedly exposed his own life without injury, but at the end of the day he was severely wounded by one of the last cannon shots fired, which prompted a notable exchange of British understatement: "By God! I've lost my leg!" exclaimed Uxbridge, to which Wellington, atop his own horse beside him, retorted, "Have you, by God?" (Longford 1973, 480). The severe wound to Uxbridge's right knee necessitated the amputation of his leg.

He finished his military and political career with the rank of field marshal in 1846.

Craig T. Cobane

See also Benavente, Action at; Corunna, Retreat to; Drouet, Jean-Baptiste, comte d'Erlon; Flanders, Campaigns in; Imperial Guard (French); Lefebvre-Desnouëttes, Charles, comte; Ney, Michel; Peninsular War; Quatre Bras, Battle of; Sahagún de Campos, Action at; Walcheren, Expedition to; Waterloo, Battle of; Waterloo Campaign; Wellington, Arthur Wellesley, First Duke of

References and further reading
Fletcher, Ian. 1999. *Galloping at Everything: The British Cavalry in the Peninsular War and at Waterloo 1808–1815.* Mechanicsburg, PA: Stackpole.
Longford, Elizabeth. 1973. *Wellington: The Years of the Sword.* London: Weidenfeld and Nicolson.

V

Valencia, Siege of
(25 December 1811–8 January 1812)

One of the greatest Spanish disasters in the Peninsular War, the fall of Valencia marked the high tide of French conquest in the conflict. Having received orders from Napoleon in autumn 1811 to occupy the Levant, the commander of the French forces in Aragón and Catalonia, Marshal Louis-Gabriel Suchet, opened operations against Valencia by advancing to Murviedro. Here he was held up for some time by a Spanish force entrenched in the ruins of the Roman town of Saguntum, which occupied a bluff high above the town, but on 25 October an attempt to relieve the defenders was destroyed in sight of the walls, whereupon they surrendered in despair. Suchet, however, had been much impressed by their resistance, and therefore elected not to resume his march on Valencia until he had called up reinforcements from Aragón.

Not until late December, then, did the French appear before the city. At first sight they appeared to be confronted by a difficult target. Commanded by General Joaquín Blake, the Spaniards were entrenched in a series of defensive positions that stretched along the south bank of the river Turia all the way from the sea to the mountains that fringed the coastal plain. Yet Suchet was undaunted. Blake's forces were, as he was well aware, distinctly variable in terms of their quality, whilst he quickly spotted that the western section of their line was comparatively weak. At the same time, meanwhile, the close nature of the terrain—a mass of orange groves—made it almost impossible for the defenders to observe his movements.

The way forward, then, was obvious. Massing his troops on the western edge of the coastal plain, on the morning of 25 December Suchet launched a surprise attack on Blake's left flank. Taken entirely by surprise, the defenders were overwhelmed, and within a few hours the bulk of Blake's forces were shut up inside Valencia, the victorious French troops having quickly cut the road to the south and reached the sea. Valencia, however, was in no position to withstand a formal siege. Food supplies were limited; the city's defenses consisted only of earthworks; and both army and population were thoroughly demoralized, as, indeed, was Blake. An attempt at a mass break-out on 29 December was foiled by bungling and irresolution, while on 5 January 1812 Suchet commenced a general bombardment of the city. Three days later, it was all over: With the populace on the verge of revolt, Blake capitulated. At 20,000 men and more than 500 guns, Spanish losses were immense, but the French victory was at best Pyrrhic.

Thanks to the impending invasion of Russia, Napoleon had ceased to send fresh troops to the Peninsula, and the result was that the offensive against Valencia pulled large numbers of men away from central and western Spain and in the process enabled the Earl of (later the Duke of) Wellington to take the offensive on the Portuguese frontier. Victory in Valencia, in short, cost Napoleon the war.

Charles J. Esdaile

See also Blake, Joaquín; Peninsular War; Siege Warfare; Suchet, Louis-Gabriel; Wellington, Arthur Wellesley, First Duke of

References and further reading
Esdaile, Charles J. 2002. *The Peninsular War: A New History.* London: Penguin.
Oman, Charles. 2005. *A History of the Peninsular War.* 7 vols. London: Greenhill. (Orig. pub. 1902–1930.)

Valenciennes Offensive

See Belgium, Campaign in (1792); Flanders, Campaigns in

Valjouan, Action at

See France, Campaign in

Valmaseda, Action at (5 November 1808)

This minor engagement was fought during the Peninsular War between Spanish forces under General Joaquín Blake and French troops under General Eugène Casimir Vilatte that formed part of Marshal Claude Victor's corps. Following his defeat near the Portuguese-Spanish border in late October 1808, Blake was in the course of retreating when he turned to regroup his forces at Valmaseda and inflicted a reverse on a pursuing French division. Only competent leadership and discipline saved the French from serious loss.

Just prior to the full-scale invasion of Spain by Napoleon's army in 1808, Spanish forces under Blake had been attacked by Marshal François Lefebvre on 31 October. Although Blake was defeated, Napoleon was angry at this somewhat premature attack, as he had hoped to destroy the Spanish force rather than simply oblige it to retreat to the west. Nevertheless, Bilbao was captured, and Napoleon therefore ordered that the defeated Spanish be pursued by marshals Lefebvre and Victor. The Spanish forces soon became strung out along their line of retreat, and Victor pursued them vigorously over difficult terrain. On 4 November Napoleon himself crossed into Spain with his main army. Blake decided to counterattack at this point. He knew that he was about to be reinforced by the troops of the Marqués de la Romana. The total Spanish force now amounted to approximately 24,000 men, with about thirty guns.

Blake decided to halt his retreat near Valmaseda; when his rear guard came under pressure from the French while crossing a narrow valley, he launched an attack early on the morning of 5 November. The French force that bore the brunt of this attack was a division under the command of Vilatte, detached from Victor's corps. Vilatte had twelve battalions of infantry amounting to just over 10,000 men, but he had little in the way of cavalry or artillery. During the initial attack, Vilatte was quickly expelled from the village of Valmaseda, and his force thrown into confusion. Though able to rally his troops, Vilatte was aware that he was heavily outnumbered and ordered a withdrawal. The French formed a large divisional square to protect themselves during their retreat and fell back eastward. With the discipline of his troops sufficient to prevent the Spanish from closing with them, Vilatte was able to withdraw, with only around 300 casualties and leaving one gun in Spanish hands. Blake attempted to follow up his victory, but was prevented from doing so by Napoleon's approach. Thus, once again, Blake was forced to retreat. As a consequence of his conduct prior to and during the action at Valmaseda, Victor was reprimanded by the Emperor. Nonetheless, Victor was to defeat Blake at the Battle of Espinosa de los Monteros a few days later.

Ralph Baker

See also Blake, Joaquín; Caro y Sureda, Pedro, Marqués de la Romana; Espinosa de los Monteros, Battle of; Lefebvre, François Joseph; Peninsular War; Victor, Claude Perrin
References and further reading
Esdaile, Charles J. 2002. *The Peninsular War: A New History*. London: Penguin.
Gates, David. 2002. *The Spanish Ulcer: A History of the Peninsular War*. London: Pimlico.
Oman, Charles. 2005. *A History of the Peninsular War*. 7 vols. London: Greenhill. (Orig. pub. 1902–1930.)

Valmy, Battle of (20 September 1792)

Important battle of the War of the First Coalition (1792–1797), usually identified as one of the decisive battles in world history. In July 1792 an Allied Austrian and Prussian force assembled at Coblenz in the Rhineland with the aim of marching on Paris, rescuing King Louis XVI, and crushing the French Revolution. Charles William (Karl Wilhelm), Duke of Brunswick, had command. Although accounts vary, the invasion force probably numbered about 84,000 men: 42,000 Prussians, 29,000 Austrians, 5,000 Hessians, and 8,000 French émigrés. The invaders planned a movement in which the main force under Brunswick, accompanied by Prussian King Frederick William II, would be protected on its flanks by two Austrian corps, one each to the north and south. The attackers planned to move west between the two principal French defending armies: the Armée du Nord under General Charles François Dumouriez (from 16 August) and the Armée du Centre under General François Etienne Christophe Kellermann (after 27 August). Once the invaders had taken the poorly provisioned French border fortresses, they could move to Châlons, and from there they would have fertile and open territory to Paris.

The Allied invasion of France began in late July and moved at a leisurely pace. On 19 August the Allies crossed the French frontier. Longwy fell on 23 August and Verdun on 2 September. With the fall of the two fortresses, the way to Paris seemed open. Brunswick's forces then moved into the thick woods, narrow defiles, and marshy lowlands of the Argonne, terrain that favored the defender. Torrential rains aided the French, playing havoc with Brunswick's lines of communication, and dysentery felled many men.

The government in Paris ordered Dumouriez, who believed the best way to thwart the invasion would be to invade the Austrian Netherlands, to move south and block Brunswick. On 1 September, along with the bulk of his army, he moved from Sedan and took up position in the passes of the Argonne. Although Dumouriez's men fought well and bought valuable time, Brunswick's troops took a lightly defended pass at Croix-aux-Bois, turning the

The Battle of Valmy. While constituting little more than a cannonade, the event is widely regarded as one of history's most decisive engagements, for its outcome saved Paris and, by definition, the Revolution. (The Art Archive/Musée du Château de Versailles/Dagli Orti)

French. Dumouriez then withdrew to Sainte-Manehould and Valmy, where he could threaten Brunswick's flank. Kellermann joined him at Valmy south of the river Bionne on 19 September. The village of Valmy lay between hills to its north, west, and south.

The French generals had planned to withdraw farther west, but the appearance of Brunswick's army early on the tenth from the north had cut off that route. Brunswick was now closer to Paris than were Dumouriez and Kellermann, but he needed to remove the French threat to his supply lines, and he had only about 30,000–34,000 men to accomplish this. Dumouriez's exhausted force of 18,000 men formed a second line east of Valmy. Kellermann commanded the first French line of some 36,000 men, drawn up along a ridge topped by a windmill just west of Valmy. Kellermann's force consisted of an equal mix of trained prewar soldiers and untrained but enthusiastic volunteers. Among French officers on the field that day was young Louis-Philippe, later king of the French.

Early morning fog on 20 September soon dissipated, and once he had identified the French positions, Brunswick positioned his own men on high ground some 2,500

yards to the west and prepared to attack. Brunswick had fifty-four guns; Kellermann only thirty-six. Brunswick was confident of victory, for his troops were far better trained.

The "Battle" of Valmy of 20 September was more a cannonade than anything else. It opened that morning when King Frederick William ordered the Prussian guns to bombard the French positions prior to an infantry assault. The French artillery, well handled by men of the pre-Revolutionary army, replied. A distance of some 2,500 yards between the two sides and soft ground from recent heavy rains meant that the exchange of fire inflicted little damage on either side. Nonetheless, the Prussians had expected the green French troops to break and run at the first volley and were amazed when they stood their ground.

The Prussian infantry then began an advance as if on parade across the soggy ground. Perhaps Brunswick hoped the French would bolt, but when they failed to do so, he halted his troops after about 200 yards. One French battalion after another took up the cry of "Vive la nation!" About 2:00 P.M. a lucky hit from a Prussian shell exploded an ammunition wagon near the windmill, and the French guns

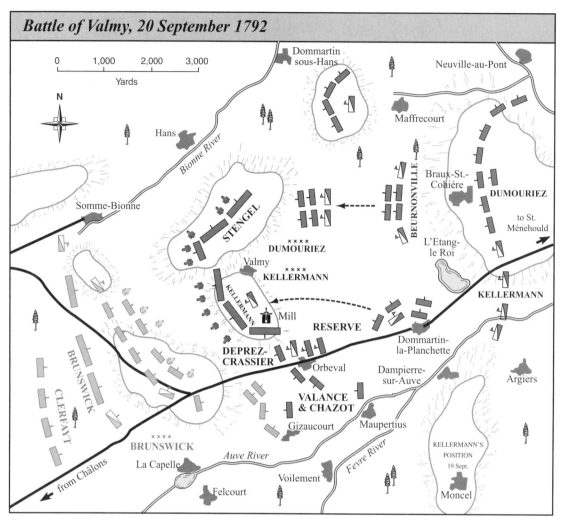

Battle of Valmy, 20 September 1792

Adapted from Chandler 1987, 188.

momentarily fell silent; then the battle resumed. Brunswick ordered a second advance, but his men got no farther than about 650 yards from the French. Brunswick then ordered a halt, followed by a retirement. At 4:00 P.M. he summoned a council of war and announced, "We do not fight here."

Losses on both sides were slight: The Prussians lost 164 men, the French about 300. Brunswick had not been enthusiastic about the offensive that culminated at Valmy. He had wanted only to secure positions east of the Argonne in preparation for a major campaign the following spring. The movement farther west had been at the insistence of the king, and Brunswick now used the rebuff as an excuse to halt the offensive. The dispirited Prussian forces lingered in the area for ten days, but on the night of 30 September–1 October they broke camp and withdrew, recrossing the French border on 23 October.

Although, even had he won at Valmy, Brunswick would probably not have immediately moved against Paris,

the battle ended any Allied hopes of crushing the French Revolution in 1792. The government in Paris then authorized Dumouriez to carry out his plan to conquer the Austrian Netherlands, and on 6 November forces under his command defeated the Austrians at Jemappes.

The Battle of Valmy marked the recovery of the French Army from its disastrous state early in the Revolution. It was important not only as a military and political event but also as marking the end of the age of dynastic armies with no stake in, nor understanding of the political purpose of, wars being fought, and the arrival of the new age of patriotic "national" armies. The poet Johann Wolfgang von Goethe, who was present that day, understood this. When some Prussian officers asked him what he thought of the battle, he reportedly replied, "From this place, and from this day forth, commences a new era in the world's history; and you can all say that you were present at its birth" (Creasy 1987, 179).

Spencer C. Tucker

See also Belgium, Campaign in (1792); Brunswick Manifesto; Brunswick, Charles William Ferdinand, Duke of; Dumouriez, Charles François Dupérier; Emigrés; First Coalition, War of the; Frederick William II, King; Goethe, Johann Wolfgang von; Jemappes, Battle of; Kellermann, François Etienne Christophe "the Elder"; Louis XVI, King

References and further reading

Bertaud, Jean Paul. 1970. Valmy: La Démocratie en armes. Paris: Julliard.

Blanning, T. C. W. 1996. The French Revolutionary Wars, 1787–1802. London: Arnold.

Creasy, Edward S. 1987. The Fifteen Decisive Battles of the World: From Marathon to Waterloo. New York: Dorset.

Davis, Paul K. 1999. 100 Decisive Battles: From Ancient Times to the Present. Santa Barbara, CA: ABC-CLIO.

Fremont-Barnes, Gregory. 2001. The French Revolutionary Wars. Oxford: Osprey.

Fuller, J. F. C. 1995. A Military History of the Western World. Vol. 2. New York: Funk and Wagnalls.

Griffith, Paddy. 1998. The Art of War of Revolutionary France, 1789–1802. London: Greenhill.

Lynn, John. 1992. "Valmy." MHQ: The Quarterly Journal of Military History 5, no. 1 (Autumn): 88–96.

Phipps, Ramsay Weston. 1980. The Armies of the First French Republic and the Rise of the Marshals of Napoleon I. Vol. 2, The Armées de la Moselle, du Rhin, de Sambre-et-Meuse, de Rhin-et-Moselle. London: Greenwood. (Orig. pub. 1926–1939.)

Valutino, Battle of

See Russian Campaign

Vandamme, Dominique-Joseph-René (1770–1830)

Dominique-Joseph-René Vandamme, comte de Unsebourg, général de division, was born on 5 November 1770, at Cassel, in the Nord département. He enlisted in the army in 1788 and rose to the rank of général de brigade in 1793. Vandamme served with the Army of the North and on the Rhine during the French Revolutionary Wars. Named général de division in 1799, he fought at the battles of Austerlitz and Eggmühl in 1805 and 1809, respectively. In 1813 his I Corps was surrounded and destroyed at Kulm, and he was made a prisoner of war. In 1815 he commanded a corps at the Battle of Ligny. Exiled after the decisive defeat at Waterloo, Vandamme lived two years in the United States before returning to France, where he died at Cassel on 15 July 1830.

Vandamme's father, Maurice Joseph van Damme, was a licensed surgeon from the Flemish town of Poperinghe, in present-day Belgium. He married Barbara Françoise Baert of Ghent. After their marriage they moved to Cassel, where their three children were born: Dominique, Louis François, and Valentine Barbara. Dominique, whose first language was Flemish, received a basic education at the Collège de Récollets in Cassel and then spent two years at the military school of Marshal de Biron. He quit school in June 1788 and on 27 July enlisted in the army. Vandamme served fourteen months on the island of Martinique before deserting and returning to France. In 1791 he again enlisted in the army and, because of his previous military training, he was promoted to captain.

When war with Austria and Prussia began in the spring of 1792, Vandamme distinguished himself while serving with the Army of the North. The Revolution, which had begun three years before, moved into its republican phase in September 1792. Vandamme enthusiastically supported the cause, and as a dedicated republican he rose rapidly in rank. Promoted to lieutenant colonel on 5 September 1793, he was named général de brigade on the twenty-seventh of the same month. For the next four years he served with various armies on the northern front and on the Rhine.

Vandamme fought at the Battle of Hondschoote, 7–8 September 1793, and commanded a brigade during the invasion of the Austrian Netherlands (Belgium) that followed. In the fall of 1795, he was transferred to the Army of the Rhine and Moselle and took part in the campaigns in Germany in 1796–1797. When General Napoleon Bonaparte's victories in Italy broke up the First Coalition with the Treaty of Campo Formio, concluded in October 1797, Vandamme was assigned to the (French) Army of England established on the Channel coast to prepare for a possible invasion of Britain. The formation of the Second Coalition, however, brought a renewal of hostilities on the Rhine; and in September 1798, Vandamme joined the Army of Mayence (Mainz). Promoted to général de division on 5 February 1799, he led the left wing of the Army of the Danube in the unsuccessful spring invasion of southern Germany. Accused of the misappropriation of funds in Germany and Alsace, Vandamme was relieved of his command. Exonerated, he was returned to the army in September to command a division of the Army of Batavia (Holland) under General Guillaume-Marie-Anne Brune. An expeditionary force of British and Russian troops had landed late in the summer of 1799 in the Batavian Republic, and Vandamme played an active role in Brune's army as it forced the enemy to withdraw from the Continent. Back with the Army of the Rhine in January 1800, he commanded a division under General Jean Moreau in the last phase of the War of the Second Coalition.

The Treaty of Lunéville, signed in February 1801, brought peace with Austria, and the Treaty of Amiens, concluded in March 1802, ended the war with Britain.

Vandamme was given command of the 16th Military Division at Lille. In May 1803, however, war between France and Britain was renewed, and Vandamme was given command of a division in the corps of General Nicolas Soult at Boulogne. On 18 May 1804 Napoleon was proclaimed Emperor of the French, and the next day, Soult, along with seventeen other generals of division, was raised to the dignity of Marshal of the Empire.

The formation of the Third Coalition in the summer of 1805 brought Russia and Austria into the war with Britain against France. To meet the advancing Austrian army in southern Germany, Napoleon ordered his Grande Armée, which was quartered along the English Channel preparing to invade Britain, to march across the Rhine into southern Germany. Vandamme, commanding the 2nd Division of Soult's IV Corps, crossed the Danube at Neuburg. An Austrian army, commanded by *Feldmarschalleutnant* Karl Mack Freiherr von Leiberich, was surrounded at Ulm and forced to surrender. Vandamme's division had captured the towns east and south of Ulm and sealed off the city to the south. Following Mack's capitulation, the French army marched down the Danube to Vienna.

The Russian army advancing from the east arrived in central Europe too late to save the Austrians at Ulm. Therefore, General Mikhail Kutuzov, who commanded the tsar's army, withdrew into Moravia, where he received reinforcements. With the advantage of numerical superiority, an Austro-Russian army decided to give battle at Austerlitz. On 2 December the two armies met in one of the most decisive battles of the Napoleonic Wars. Soult's IV Corps held the center of the French position with the divisions of generals Vandamme and Louis-Vincent St. Hilaire. Marshal Louis Davout held the French right wing and Marshal Jean Lannes the left. When Kutuzov weakened his center to attack the French right, Napoleon ordered Soult's division up the slopes of the Heights of Pratzen. Vandamme and St. Hilaire broke the Russian center and wheeled right to take the Russian corps on their flank that were attacking Davout. The Russian center and left wing were crushed and suffered heavy casualties as they were driven from the field of battle. Only the enemy's right wing retreated in good order. It was Napoleon's greatest triumph on the battlefield. Vandamme and his division distinguished themselves on that occasion, and in appreciation the Emperor gave the general a pension of 20,000 francs.

In the campaign against Prussia in 1806–1807, Napoleon at Jena and Davout at Auerstädt (14 October) decisively defeated the Prussian army. Following the battle, Vandamme forced the city of Magdeburg to surrender and then served as part of IX Corps under Napoleon's youngest brother, King Jérôme of Westphalia. He besieged and captured the principal fortified cities of Silesia: Glogau, Breslau, Schweidnitz, Glatz, and Neiss. The Treaty of Tilsit ended the fighting in July 1807. Once again Napoleon showed his appreciation for Vandamme's services by naming him comte de Unsebourg on 19 March 1808. Then in the spring of 1809, Vandamme was, for the first time, given command of VIII Corps (Württemberg troops) of the Grande Armée when Austria again chose war with France. He fought at the Battle of Eggmühl (22 April), but he was protecting the army's rear and flanks during the Battle of Aspern-Essling (21–22 May) and Wagram (5–6 July). The Treaty of Pressburg brought an end to the war, and Vandamme was given leave to return to his family at Cassel.

He commanded the camp at Boulogne in 1810–1811. In the spring of 1812 he was given command of VIII Corps of the Grande Armée and was again placed under King Jérôme, whose three army corps formed the right wing of the army that was preparing to invade Russia. Vandamme and Jérôme, who had not worked well together in Silesia, again clashed. Within weeks of the march into Russia, Jérôme relieved the general of his command; Napoleon ordered him back to France, where he spent the months of the disastrous campaign in Russia.

Napoleon was not pleased with Vandamme's insubordination: He had a history of conflict with Soult and Jérôme, under both of whom he had served. However, in 1813 the Emperor was in need of good field commanders, and Vandamme had an excellent record. Napoleon therefore gave him two divisions and placed him under Davout's orders. Davout's reputation as a stern taskmaster was well known to Vandamme, and the general took, and carried out, orders without his usual insolence and insubordination. In the late spring of 1813, Davout assigned him the task of capturing the city of Hamburg, which had rebelled against its French occupiers. With the successful completion of that task, Vandamme was given command of I Corps of the newly organized army in eastern Germany.

Napoleon had won battles at Lützen on 2 May and Bautzen on 13 May while Vandamme besieged Hamburg. A truce followed in the summer months. When the fighting resumed in mid-August, Austria joined Russia, Prussia, Sweden, and Britain to form the Sixth Coalition against France. On 26–27 August Napoleon defeated an Allied army at Dresden. Vandamme was ordered to move onto the enemy's line of retreat. At the Battle of Kulm, his single corps faced a superior force of Austrians, Prussians, and Russians. When he was forced to retreat, General Friedrich Heinrich von Kleist's Prussian corps, retreating from Dresden, stumbled on to Vandamme's rear, surrounding I Corps. Half of Vandamme's command was killed, wounded, or taken prisoner. The rest scattered and found their way back to the main army. Vandamme remained with his troops and was captured by the Russians. He was first taken to Moscow, where he spent several months, and then was sent east to Vyatka, where he lived until the war ended with the abdication of Napoleon in April 1814. Vandamme arrived back in France two months later.

Exiled to the island of Elba, Napoleon returned to France in March 1815. Once again the nations of Europe formed a coalition (the seventh), and on 15 June Napoleon marched north into Belgium to meet the Anglo-Allied and Prussian armies. On the sixteenth the Emperor attacked and defeated the Prussians at Ligny led by Field Marshal Gebhard Lebrecht Fürst Blücher von Wahlstatt. Vandamme commanded the left wing at Ligny, and led the vanguard of Marshal Emmanuel, marquis de Grouchy's force that pursued the Prussians to the north. At Wavre, two days later, Vandamme caught up and engaged the Prussian rear guard, while at the same time Napoleon was fighting the Duke of Wellington and Blücher at Waterloo. When, on the nineteenth, Grouchy learned of the defeat at Waterloo, he led his two corps south to Paris. Following Napoleon's second abdication and the restoration of the Bourbon monarchy, Vandamme was exiled. He took refuge in Philadelphia from 1816 to 1819, at which time he was allowed to return to France. Vandamme lived quietly at Cassel until his death on 15 July 1830.

John Gallaher

See also Amiens, Treaty of; Aspern-Essling, Battle of; Austerlitz, Battle of; Bautzen, Battle of; Blücher von Wahlstatt, Gebhard Lebrecht Fürst; Bonaparte, Jérôme; Brune, Guillaume-Marie-Anne; Campo Formio, Treaty of; Davout, Louis Nicolas; Dresden, Battle of; Eggmühl, Battle of; England, French Plans for the Invasion of; Fifth Coalition, War of the; First Coalition, War of the; Flanders, Campaigns in; Fourth Coalition, War of the; Germany, Campaign in; Grouchy, Emmanuel, marquis de; Hamburg, Defense of; Hondschoote, Battle of; Italian Campaigns (1792–1797); Kleist von Nollendorf, Friedrich Heinrich Ferdinand Emil Graf; Kulm, Battle of; Kutuzov, Mikhail Golenischev-, Prince; Lannes, Jean; Ligny, Battle of; Lunéville, Treaty of; Lützen, Battle of; Mack, Karl Freiherr von Leiberich; Magdeburg, Siege of; Marshalate; Moreau, Jean Victor; North Holland, Campaign in (1799); Pressburg, Treaty of; Rhine Campaigns (1792–1797); Rhine Campaigns (1799–1800); Russian Campaign; Second Coalition, War of the; Soult, Nicolas Jean de Dieu; St. Hilaire, Louis Vincent Joseph le Blond; Third Coalition, War of the; Tilsit, Treaties of; Ulm, Surrender at; Wagram, Battle of; Waterloo Campaign; Wavre, Battle of; Wellington, Arthur Wellesley, First Duke of

References and further reading
Arnold, James R. 1990. *Crisis on the Danube: Napoleon's Austrian Campaign of 1809.* New York: Paragon House.
Becke, A. F. 1966. *Napoleon and Waterloo: The Emperor's Campaign with the Armée du Nord.* Philadelphia: University of Pennsylvania Press.
Chandler, David G. 1995. *The Campaigns of Napoleon.* London: Weidenfeld and Nicolson.
Du Casse, Albert. 1851. *Opérations du neuvième corps de la Grande Armée en Silésie sur le commandement de S.A.I. le Prince Jérôme Napoléon—1806 et 1807.* 2 vols. Paris: J. Corréard.
———. 1870. *Le général Vandamme et sa correspondance.* 2 vols. Paris: Didier.
Duffy, Christopher. 1977. *Austerlitz: 1805.* London: Seeley Service.
Hofschröer, Peter. 1998. *1815, The Waterloo Campaign: Wellington, his German Allies and the Battles of Ligny and Quatre Bras.* London: Greenhill.
———. 2001. *Lützen & Bautzen 1813.* Oxford: Osprey.
Kelly, W. Hyde. 1993. *The Battle of Wavre and Grouchy's Retreat.* Felling, UK: Worley.
Kolzakov, Paul Andreyevich. 2005. *Memoir of Admiral Paul Andreyevich Kolzakov on the Capture of General Vandamme, 1813.* Trans. Alexander Mikaberidze. http://www.napoleon-series.org/research/russianarchives/c_kolzakov.html (accessed April 7, 2006). (Orig. pub. in *Russkaya Starina* 1 [1870]: 208–217.)
Maude, Frederic Natusch. 1908. *The Leipzig Campaign, 1813.* New York: Macmillan.
———. 1912. *The Ulm Campaign.* London: Swan, Sonnenschein.
Nafziger, George. 1994. *Napoleon's Dresden Campaign: The Battles of August 1813.* Chicago: Emperor's.
Petre, F. Loraine. 1992. *Napoleon's Last Campaign in Germany, 1813.* London: Greenhill.

Vauchamps, Battle of (14 February 1814)

Napoleon's victory in the Battle of Vauchamps marked the end of the Six Days campaign in February 1814 and very nearly led to a rout of the Allied forces under Field Marshal Gebhard Lebrecht von Blücher, commander of the Army of Silesia (Russians and Prussians). Following this battle, the Allied leadership reconsidered their previous offers of peace to France, and renewed their intention to fight all the way to Paris in order to defeat Napoleon definitively.

Following his victory at Château-Thierry on 12 February, Napoleon received word that the Army of Bohemia (mostly Austrians) under the command of *Feldmarschall* Karl Philipp Fürst zu Schwarzenberg was gaining ground against the French forces under the command of Marshal Claude Victor along the Seine. He immediately made plans to send his troops south, but was thwarted by the approach of Blücher from the east, who was attempting to prevent Napoleon's movement. Blücher's forces pushed back Marshal Auguste de Marmont's troops, who had been placed in Blücher's path after the Battle of Champaubert on 10 February. Marmont delayed the Prussian advance, and Napoleon was able to put together an attack. Splitting his forces, he sent Marshal Jacques Macdonald and General François Kellermann to help Victor near

Montereau, and took himself and the cavalry under General Emmanuel Grouchy to the east to support Marmont.

Blücher's early success against Marmont's troops was not long lasting: on the morning of the fourteenth, Grouchy's cavalry arrived on the field and successfully broke up the Allied right flank, obliging Blücher to retreat further east. Blücher managed to escape the full brunt of Grouchy's first attack, but as he retreated, Grouchy discovered him again, largely because he had taken a parallel road and had passed Blücher in order to attack from the east. Grouchy was able to cut off Blücher's retreat, but the Allied forces managed to fight their way through the French cavalry, whose artillery was still caught in the muddy roads. Blücher continued his retreat to Châlons, with Marmont in pursuit, while Napoleon and Grouchy proceeded south to meet up with the French troops on the Seine. By the end of the day, Allied losses were severe: Blücher had lost 7,000 men, several guns, and a significant amount of his transport. The French had lost around 600 men.

Napoleon's turn to the south gave Blücher the breathing room he needed to reconstitute his forces; he was also finally in contact with the Army of the North (Russians, Prussians, and Swedes), under the command of General Ferdinand Winzegorode, and the combined might of these armies proved ready to take up the offensive against Napoleon once again.

Korcaighe P. Hale

See also Blücher von Wahlstatt, Gebhard Lebrecht Fürst; Champaubert, Battle of; Château-Thierry, Battle of; France, Campaign in; Grouchy, Emmanuel, marquis de; Kellermann, François Etienne "the Younger," comte; Macdonald, Jacques Etienne Joseph Alexandre; Marmont, Auguste Frédéric Louis Viesse de; Montereau, Battle of; Schwarzenberg, Karl Philipp Fürst zu; Six Days Campaign; Victor, Claude Perrin; Winzegorode, Ferdinand Fedorovich, Baron

References and further reading
Chandler, David G. 1995. *The Campaigns of Napoleon.* London: Weidenfeld and Nicolson.
Delderfield, R. F. 2004. *The March of the Twenty-Six.* London: Leo Cooper.
Lawford, James. 1977. *Napoleon: The Last Campaigns, 1813–1815.* London: Roxby.
Petre, F. Loraine. 1994. *Napoleon at Bay: 1814.* London: Greenhill.

Vendée, Revolts in the (1793–1800)

On 24 February 1793 the National Convention ordered a levy of 300,000 men in response to the mounting pressures of war, intensifying as the anti-French coalition expanded to include the maritime powers of Britain, Holland, and Spain. A week later, in the country town of Cholet, hundreds of young men assaulted recruiting officers sent to enlist them. Thus began a bitter and long-running insurrection that became known as the war of the Vendée, or simply La Vendée. The label is somewhat misleading, because the Vendée was just one of the western departments involved. Another three were profoundly affected, with substantial segments of the Maine-et-Loire (where Cholet is actually located), Deux-Sèvres, and Loire-Inférieure also embroiled. There were, in fact, a series of civil wars, the first and greatest of which, the so-called *grande guerre* (Big War) in 1793, mobilized much of the rural population in these four departments, in an area south of the river Loire. Conflict flared up again from 1794 until Bonaparte's pacification in 1800 (the *petite guerre*, Little War), while there were uprisings during the Hundred Days in 1815 and, finally, surrounding the duchesse de Berry's conspiracy in 1832. This major and enduring hostility to the Republic became notorious, not only for the severity of the uprising, unparalleled elsewhere, but also for the brutality with which it was conducted and repressed; over a third of the official victims of the Terror were executed here, not to mention thousands more who died in the fighting or as a consequence of atrocities committed by both sides.

In the spring of 1793, the rebels, or *Vendéens,* achieved significant success. Organized in bands, with leaders drawn from the nobility or middle classes who possessed some military expertise, this essentially peasant army numbered some 30,000. Poorly equipped, with little training or heavy weaponry, they compensated for material weakness with bravery and an intimate knowledge of the local terrain, taking control of the wooded, hilly countryside (the *bocage*) and also some smaller towns, such as Cholet or La Roche-sur-Yon. By summer the revolt had spread to larger towns on the periphery of the area, such as Thouars or Fontenay-le-Comte. Having established a sort of central command for their Catholic and Royal Army, which began issuing its own decrees, the "whites" (from the color of their flags) ventured further afield, storming Saumur and Angers in June, and laying siege to Nantes, albeit unsuccessfully, losing one of their "generals," Jacques Cathelineau, in the process.

The Vendéens returned to their homes, partly demoralized, partly to harvest their crops. They were forced into battle afresh by the arrival of republican troops ("blues," from the hue of their uniforms), detached from the eastern frontier of France, whom they defeated at Torfou in September. A more solid Armée de l'Ouest was now created by the government in Paris, which was finally persuaded of the magnitude of the problem, and the rebels were crushed at Cholet in a murderous encounter between 15 and 17 October. The vanquished Vendéens, their women, children, and priests in train, set out for the coast of Normandy where they hoped to obtain British assistance, but having arrived at Granville in mid-November, they were disappointed to find no ships awaiting them. Turning back in disorderly fashion toward their native terrain, they were repulsed at both Angers and Le Mans early the next month. The shattered remnants of the Royal and Catholic Army then straggled westward along the Loire, and, on 23 December, they were massacred in the marshlands at Savenay, on the Loire estuary.

This was the end of the grande guerre, and repression quickly followed with the infamous drowning of captured rebels by Jean-Baptiste Carrier at Nantes, when hundreds of prisoners were loaded on to barges and sunk in the freezing waters of the Loire. Meanwhile, General Louis-Marie Turreau's "infernal columns" began sweeping the Vendée in the early months of 1794, laying waste to the land as they went. It is difficult to estimate the numbers who were killed on both sides: There were at least 150,000, perhaps 200,000 victims. Some localities lost almost half of their population, though it is unwise to put too much faith in figures, given the unreliability or destruction of documentation. It is not, in any case, simply a matter of quantity; rather it is the extreme brutality with which both sides inflicted reprisals that appalls: the republicans exacted terrible revenge, but the Vendéens slaughtered republicans at Machecoul, for example. One historian has written of a "Franco-French genocide" (Secher 2003). Although this terminology has been contested, the Vendée bore all the hallmarks of a vicious civil war, which included women and children among its victims.

The question that has generated particular historical debate, as opposed to ongoing recrimination between the adversaries, is why this particular area of France should produce such potent and stubborn resistance to the Republic. The participants issued conflicting interpretations, which cannot be taken at face value. The Vendéens presented their rebellion as an uprising that united peasants, priests, and nobles against the godless Republic and aimed to restore the old rustic order. For the government in Paris, by contrast, simple country folk were led astray by counterrevolutionary priests and nobles, who exploited peasant gullibility to pursue their own agenda against the Revolution. Research over the past half-century suggests that the reality was far more complex and that it is impossible to reduce the conflict to a single cause. Many of the issues that affected the Vendée, such as resistance to the military draft, were evident elsewhere, yet nowhere was the outcome so serious. There was nothing inevitable about this dreadful civil war, which was turned into a far more deadly conflict by the insensitive manner in which it was handled and perceived.

Local inhabitants were by no means content with the ancien régime, as demands for reform in their cahier de doléances (list of grievances; these were drawn up throughout France in 1789) clearly show. They welcomed the Revolution and were expecting a good deal from it. It was their increasing disappointment with what emerged that explains their willingness to rebel, not some desire to return to an earlier golden age. Some historians have coined the phrase resistance to the Revolution to replace the term counterrevolution, in order to demonstrate that if peasants turned to nobles as leaders, it was only after the rebellion had started and the latter were persuaded to assume command. There is a general consensus that the Vendée was a spontaneous popular uprising against what had come to be regarded as an oppressive Revolution.

Material grievances have been accorded an important place in explaining the Vendéens' deep-seated discontent. They profited relatively little from the changes made after 1789. Many were lease-holders, not owner-occupiers, and the abolition of the tithe and seigneurial dues was of scant advantage to them. Moreover, an area that had been lightly taxed before 1789 now began to bear a heavier fiscal burden, especially after the outbreak of war. Nor was the sale of national lands, former property of the Church, of great benefit. These opportunities, like administrative posts in the new system of local government, were grasped by wealthy elements from the towns, which rural dwellers judged unsympathetic to their interests. The long-standing tension between town and country was reinforced in the area around Cholet, where entrepreneurs put out textile manufacturing into the surrounding countryside; animosity was only exacerbated by the economic depression that accompanied the Revolution. A substantial contingent of weavers, and other artisans, thus fought alongside peasants in the rebel army.

This is not to deny the importance of the religious dimension to the uprising, though it should be viewed in a cultural as well as a purely confessional sense. Reform of the Church, summed up in the Civil Constitution of the Clergy and adopted by the National Assembly in 1790, caused unrest elsewhere, but it produced significant disaffection in the west of France. The amalgamation of parishes into larger units hit hard in areas of dispersed habitation, where the church was a social, not simply a religious institution, and gave identity to the different communities. The overwhelming majority of parish priests refused to swear an oath of allegiance to this new order, and later in 1791, they began to be removed from their livings. Their replacements were outsiders, strangers to the language and customs of the area, bitterly resisted as intruders, often with violence, in widespread riots involving women. Matters were made worse when these constitutional clergy were imposed by alien urban administrators, backed up by militia (the National Guard). The injection of a faith element into the conflict, symbolized by the Sacred Heart emblazoned on the Vendéens' banners, deepened divisions, encouraged martyrdom, and rendered compromise all the more difficult.

The Vendée was a tinderbox, set aflame by the efforts of recruiting officers who arrived in the spring of 1793. The inhabitants were in no mood to sacrifice still more for a regime that had short-changed them and decided to die fighting the Revolution at home, rather than on a distant frontier. The local authorities were hopelessly unprepared for the concerted insurrection that confronted them (it was a different story in the equally unsettled areas north of the Loire, where discontent was confined to the sporadic unrest known as *chouannerie*), and their National Guard units were quickly overwhelmed. It took too long for the government in Paris to respond effectively to the uprising in the Vendée, and this tardiness constitutes a key factor in explaining why rebellion became so deep-rooted. When troops were finally diverted from the foreign front, they were hampered by the nature of the terrain—literally bogged down. The Royal and Catholic Army was beaten in set-piece battles, but fighting on their home turf, in a *bocage* environment ideally suited to guerrilla warfare, the peasant irregulars proved much more difficult to defeat. The resultant frustration contributed significantly to the brutality of the repression, which in turn only stiffened the resistance of the so-called fanatics the republican army confronted.

After suffering major defeats in December 1793, the Vendéens waged a protracted guerrilla war, or petite guerre, which lasted for the next year or so, until a less beleaguered post-Thermidorian government felt able to offer an amnesty and brokered truces with the main leaders in 1795. The following year, however, when a sizable band of émigrés, with British backing, contrived a landing at Quiberon Bay in Brittany, the guerrilla campaign in the Vendée reignited. Though the attempted invasion was a fiasco, the Vendéens sustained further resistance until General Jean-Nicolas Stofflet was killed and his colleague François Athanase de la Contrie Charette was executed. It was once again a deteriorating military situation for the Republic, and renewed requisitions, which provoked further insurrection in the Vendée in 1799. It ended after Bonaparte came to power as First Consul and brought effective security measures into force. The truce signed in 1800 proved more lasting, sealed by the Concordat of 1801 with the Church, and a more sensitive attitude toward the official burdens placed on this battered area.

The end of the Empire and the Hundred Days, when the British brought fresh arms for the peasants, saw a recrudescence of unrest, and the Vendée was a natural target for those seeking to undermine the July Monarchy in 1832. The Vendéens themselves have preserved a vivid memory of these horrendous events, and the area still supports a pronounced conservative political tradition. It has also acquired a strong sense of regional identity, precisely as a result of the shared suffering that the Revolution inflicted.

Malcolm Crook

See also Chouans; Concordat; Conscription (French); Convention, The; Emigrés; Guerrilla Warfare; Hoche, Louis Lazare; Jacobins; Kléber, Jean-Baptiste; Levée en Masse; National Guard (French); Public Safety, Committee of; Quiberon, Expedition to; Terror, The; Thermidor Coup; Toulon, Siege of

References and further reading
Hampson, Norman. 1974. *A Social History of the French Revolution.* Toronto: University of Toronto Press.
Hutt, Maurice. 1983. *Chouannerie and Counter-Revolution: Puisaye, the Princes and the British Government in the 1790s.* 2 vols. Cambridge: Cambridge University Press.
Martin, Jean-Clément. 2001. *Blancs et Bleus dans la Vendée Déchirée.* Paris: Gallimard.
Mitchell, Harvey. 1968. "The Vendée and Counter-revolution: A Review Essay." *French Historical Studies* 5, no. 4 (Fall): 405–429.
Paret, Peter. 1961. *Internal War and Pacification: The Vendée, 1789–1796.* Princeton: Princeton University Press.
Petitfrère, Claude. 1981. *La Vendée et les Vendéens.* Paris: Gallimard.
———. 1988. "The Origins of the Civil War in the Vendée." *French History* 2: 187–207.
Ragon, Michel. 1992. *1793: L'Insurrection Vendéenne et les malentendus de la liberté.* Paris: A. Michel.
Roberts, James. 1990. *The Counter-Revolution in France 1787–1830.* Basingstoke, UK: Macmillan.
Secher, Reynald. 2003. *A French Genocide: The Vendée.* Trans. George Holoch. South Bend, IN: University of Notre Dame Press. (Orig. pub. as *Le génocide franco-français: la Vendée-Vengé,* 4th ed. Paris: Presses universitaires de France, 1992.)
Sutherland, Donald. 1982. *The Chouans: The Social Origins of Popular Counter-revolution in Upper Brittany, 1770–1796.* Oxford: Clarendon.
Tackett, Timothy. 1982. "The West in France in 1789: The Religious Factor in the Origins of Counter-Revolution." *Journal of Modern History* 54: 715–745.
Tilly, Charles. 1964. *The Vendée.* Cambridge, MA: Harvard University Press.

Vendémiaire Coup (5 October 1795)

In October 1795 the French Republic was confronted by a fresh uprising in Paris; Napoleon Bonaparte's role in its repression served as another stepping-stone on his road to power. There had been frequent insurrections in the capital since 1789, but that of 13 Vendémiaire Year IV (to employ the Republican calendar then in force) was unusual, for it involved members of the middle classes, from well-heeled western sections of the capital, rather than sans-cu-lottes. Though it would be a mistake to label the revolt royalist, as opponents did, its conservatism was a reflection of the reaction that developed after the ending of the Terror. The rebels were not seeking to overthrow the Republic but instead to oust the National Convention, the parliament that had been sitting for the past three years. In fact, the Convention was about to make way for a new regime, enshrined in the Constitution of 1795, endorsed by means of a plebiscite in which over a million Frenchmen had voted. However, members of the Convention, the so-called *conventionnels,* were concerned that forthcoming elections would return a majority of deputies of a more reactionary hue. In order to prevent this outcome they passed the decree of "two-thirds," which prescribed that two-thirds of deputies to the new Legislative Councils must come from the old Convention.

This proposition had been put when the constitution was voted, but most people had ignored it, unlike the politically aware citizens of the capital and adjacent areas. Determined opposition was galvanized at electoral assemblies in Paris, which declared themselves in a state of insurrection and refused to accept the perpetuation of the conventionnels, whose period of office conjured up such bad memories. As in the past, this defense of popular sovereignty was supported by members of the Parisian National Guard, far more numerous than regular troops. The Convention appointed Paul Barras to organize resistance, and he turned to Bonaparte, whom he had met at the siege of Toulon, but whose career had been languishing since Thermidor on account of his association with the Jacobins.

Bonaparte acted in a characteristically vigorous fashion. When the rebels attacked the Tuileries (where the Convention met), he turned his cannons against them; though his famous "whiff of grapeshot," which saved the day for the conventionnels, was actually a hard-fought affair. The *journées* (days) of Vendémiaire relaunched his military career: he was "re-habilitated" and returned to active service, soon to be given command of the (French) Army of Italy. The political situation after Vendémiaire also had a significant bearing on Bonaparte's future, for the insurrection and its suppression marked a difficult birth for the new regime, the Directory. This was the first, but not the last time that moderate republicans were obliged to turn to the army for support when faced with a hostile verdict at the polls.

Malcolm Crook

See also Barras, Paul Jean François Nicolas, vicomte de; Constitutions (French); Consulate, The; Convention, The; Directory, The; France; French Revolution; Jacobins; National Guard (French); Republican Calendar; Terror, The; Thermidor Coup; Toulon, Siege of

References and further reading
Crook, Malcolm. 1996. *Elections in the French Revolution: An Apprenticeship in Democracy, 1789–1799.* Cambridge: Cambridge University Press.
Rudé, George. 1959. *The Crowd in the French Revolution.* Oxford: Oxford University Press.

Venetian Republic

Following the outbreak of the French Revolution, the Venetian Republic, which was ruled by an oligarchy of patricians, welcomed French émigrés, including Louis XVI's brother, the comte de Provence (Louis XVIII). Venice lacked military force and, like Genoa, remained neutral during the War of the First Coalition. During his Italian campaigns of 1796–1797, Bonaparte occupied parts of the Veneto (the territory that the city of Venice ruled beyond the city itself). He resented Venetian neutrality and was aware that the Venetian patricians opposed and were afraid of Revolutionary France. Shortly after the truce of Leoben, he decided to eliminate the Venetian oligarchy. At the same time he feared that an attack on Venice would entangle him in a prolonged siege of the city, thereby encouraging other Italians to resist the French.

The Venetian government gave Bonaparte the excuse he needed to attack Venice when it supported the fierce anti-French insurrection in the city of Verona, the so-called Veronese Passover (*Le Pasque veronesi*). During 17–23 April 1797 the Veronese population attacked the French garrison in the city and killed several hundred soldiers. The revolt was harshly suppressed. An attack on a French ship that entered the port of Venice only increased Bonaparte's determination to punish Venice. Efforts by the Venetian government to appease the French commander and to convince the Directory to order him to leave Venice alone failed. In early May, Bonaparte demanded that the Venetian government dissolve itself and ordered his troops to attack the city. On 12 May a demoralized Great Council, including the last Doge, Ludovico Manin, resigned, thereby ending centuries-old aristocratic rule in Venice. Power was handed over to a pro-French provisional municipality composed of democrats. Thousands of French troops entered the city and plundered it. Among the treasures they sent to Paris were the four bronze horses of St. Mark's. The Venetian fleet was sent to Toulon. The French soon occupied the Ionian islands of Cefalonia, Corfu, and Zante, which had belonged to Venice.

Representatives from Venice and other cities in the Veneto asked Bonaparte to annex the region to the Cisalpine Republic, but to no avail. The French general was determined to use Venice as a bargaining card in his negotiations with the Austrians. In the Treaty of Campo Formio

(17 October 1797), Bonaparte delivered Venice and the Veneto east of the river Adige to the Austrians, in return for the latter's recognition of French supremacy over northern Italy and the Cisalpine Republic. This act, which officially ended the existence of Venice as an independent state, provoked enormous indignation among Italian nationalists, who condemned it vociferously.

Eight years after transferring Venice to Austria, Napoleon took it back. In the Treaty of Schönbrunn (December 1805), the Austrians ceded Venice and the Veneto to the Kingdom of Italy. The Continental System (the French-imposed embargo on trade with Britain) drastically limited maritime activity in the Venetian port, causing economic hardship. Venice remained part of the Kingdom of Italy until 1814, when the Austrians regained control of it, a reality ratified by the Congress of Vienna the following year.

Alexander Grab

See also Art Treasures (Plundered by the French); Campo Formio, Treaty of; Cisalpine Republic; Continental System; Directory, The; Emigrés; Ionian Islands; Italian Campaigns (1792–1797); Italy, Kingdom of; Leoben, Preliminaries of; Ligurian Republic; Louis XVI, King; Louis XVIII, King; Schönbrunn, Treaty of; Vienna, Congress of

References and further reading

Alberti, Anibale, and Roberto Cessi , eds. 1928–1940. *Verbali delle sedute della municipalità provvisoria di Venezia.* Bologna: Zanichelli.
Dumas, Guy. 1964. *La fin de la république de Venise.* Paris: Presses universitaires de France.
Tessitori, Paula. 1997. *Basta che finissa 'sti cani: Democrazia e polizia nella Venezia dell 1797.* Venice: Istituto Veneto di Scienze, Lettere ed Arti.

Venice

See Venetian Republic

Vera, Battles of
(1 September and 7 October 1813)

The battles for the bridge at Vera over the Bidassoa River were fought on two separate occasions and are sometimes referred to as the Battles of the Bidassoa. Vera is located in the extreme northwest of Spain, close to the Bay of Biscay and the French border.

The initial engagement was the result of General Bertrand, baron Clausel's attempt, while pursued by Allied forces, to rejoin the main French forces under Marshal Nicolas Soult on the northern side of the Bidassoa River after the abortive second counteroffensive against the Marquis of (later the Duke of) Wellington's forces at San Sebastian. While Major General John Byne Skerrett's brigade of

the Light Division was located a short distance away, a company-sized detachment of the 95th Rifles guarded the bridge under the command of Captain Daniel Cadoux. General Lubin Martin Vandermaesen's French force consisted of approximately 10,000 troops, but rains and a swollen river, which prevented him bypassing the bridge through fords, hampered him. Cadoux's riflemen, sheltered in buildings on the northern side of the river, were able to keep up an accurate and constant fire that defeated repeated attempts to storm the bridge. Some accounts state that Cadoux was ordered to withdraw; however, knowing that Clausel's force had no other way to reach the northern side of the river, he refused to withdraw and held the bridge throughout the night of 1 September, withdrawing only when his unit had expended its ammunition.

Vandermaesen, the senior French officer present, was killed attempting to lead an assault on the bridge. While Cadoux's company had only lost two men in the initial French rush of the bridge, they were nearly wiped out as they withdrew under heavy pressure, with Cadoux himself among the dead. Nevertheless, they had delayed Clausel's retreat, nearly causing his surrender to the superior Allied forces closing in. In the end, however, he crossed the river, leaving behind numerous casualties as well as his artillery and baggage.

The second and much larger action at Vera on the banks of the Bidassoa was fought about a month later on 7 October, as an action covering Wellington's crossing of the Bidassoa on fords closer to the sea. Major General Charles, Baron von Alten's Light Division, reinforced by Spanish units, was assigned the task of clearing the heights above the river and the town of Vera, thus distracting the French forces under Soult from the main attacks being launched farther north. Soult had determined that Wellington would attack farther east—inland along the line of the Bidassoa. Accordingly, Wellington was totally successful in his deception. While the main crossings in the estuary of the river were swiftly made—resulting in the turning of the Bidassoa position and allowing Wellington to advance into France—the covering attacks around Vera were costlier, due in large measure to the nature of the rough hilly terrain.

The Light Division attacked with one brigade under Lieutenant Colonel John Colborne, advancing on the left along a spur known as the Bayonette, and another brigade, under Major General James Kempt, attacking on the right along the main northern road, the Puerto De Vera. While in the main attack Wellington's forces had approximately a 2.5 to 1 advantage; Alten's force numbered 6,500 against the defending French forces of Clausel, which numbered approximately 4,000 and held a very strong prepared position. The French forces were, however, unwilling or unable to provide sustained or effective resistance to the advancing British and Portuguese light troops and retreated off the heights in disorder.

While not the main attack of the day, the offensive at Vera both achieved its tactical objective of preventing French reinforcement at the main crossings, and also facilitated Wellington's further advance by breaking the strongest portion of Soult's line of defense along the Bidassoa.

John T. Broom

See also Bidassoa, Crossing of the; Peninsular War; Soult, Nicolas Jean de Dieu; Wellington, Arthur Wellesley, First Duke of
References and further reading
Esdaile, Charles J. 2003. *The Peninsular War: A New History.* New York: Palgrave Macmillan.
Gates, David. 1986. *The Spanish Ulcer: A History of the Peninsular War.* New York: Norton.
Robertson, Ian. 2003. *Wellington Invades France: The Final Phase of the Peninsular War, 1813–1814.* London: Greenhill.

Verling, James Roch (1787–1858)

Verling was a military doctor, most noted for his service on St. Helena while Napoleon was in exile on that island. Verling was born in Queenstown, Ireland, on 27 February 1787. By age twenty-three he had graduated as a Doctor of Medicine at Edinburgh University and henceforth went into military service. He served in the Peninsular War, where he earned the high rank of assistant surgeon. Verling was unusual for military medical men at that time, in that he actually held a degree in medicine.

On 9 August 1815 Napoleon and his entourage sailed into exile aboard the HMS *Northumberland,* with their destination the remote island of St. Helena. On board the ship was a company of the Royal Artillery, with Verling as its medical officer. Verling met Napoleon and his fellow exiles.

Little is known of Verling's service on the island until 25 July 1818, when the governor of the island, Sir Hudson Lowe, ordered him to go to Napoleon's residence, Longwood, to offer his medical assistance to Napoleon and all who were with him. This selection was popular with Napoleon's entourage, who recognized that Verling was the most qualified medical man on the island and encouraged Napoleon to accept Verling as his doctor. It was also wise in terms of the politics of the island, as it was critical that the British not be seen as withholding any proper medical care from their "guest," the term used by the British to describe their famous prisoner.

Napoleon, however, was willing to accept Verling as his doctor only if Verling preserved some medical confidentiality and did not report everything to Lowe. Lowe and Napoleon had become embroiled in a feud, based largely on Lowe's unwillingness to treat Napoleon as the former emperor he was, and Lowe had responded by wanting full and complete control over and information on everything concerning Napoleon. As a result, Napoleon was unwilling to accept any doctor appointed by Lowe on Lowe's terms. Instead, he wanted a doctor who would serve as his own man, with only the minimum required ties to the British military. The kind of arrangement Napoleon wanted ended by destroying the careers of two doctors, Barry O'Meara and John Stokoe. When members of Napoleon's staff suggested a similar arrangement to Verling, he declined and reported the request to Lowe.

Verling did serve as doctor to Napoleon's entourage, a situation that eventually led to tension between him and Lowe. When Dr. Francesco Antommarchi arrived in September of 1819, Verling was pleased to get out of what had become a messy situation for all concerned. Verling left the island on 25 April 1820. He continued to pursue a fine military career, becoming full surgeon in 1827, senior surgeon in 1843, and deputy and full inspector general of the ordnance medical department. He died in 1858 at the age of seventy-one.

One of Verling's most important contributions was the daily journal that he kept during the time he was directly involved with Napoleon. This journal offers exceptional insight into the politics of St. Helena, and it has recently been published for the first time.

J. David Markham

See also Antommarchi, Francesco; Lowe, Sir Hudson; Medical Services; O'Meara, Barry Edward; Peninsular War; St. Helena; Stokoe, John
References and further reading
Chaplin, Arnold. 1919. *A St. Helena Who's Who, or, A Directory of the Island during the Captivity of Napoleon.* 2nd ed. New York and London: Dutton.
Markham, J. David. 2005. *Napoleon and Doctor Verling on St. Helena.* London: Pen and Sword.

Verona, Battle of (26 March 1799)

Opening, indecisive engagement of the War of the Second Coalition in northeast Italy. The Austrian army of 59,000 troops in Venetia under *Feldmarschalleutnant* Paul Kray Freiherr von Krajova faced a French army under General Barthélemy Schérer comprising six divisions totaling 58,000, including 10,000 allied troops. While Kray was awaiting the arrival of 25,000 reinforcements and the first Russian contingent under Field Marshal Alexander Suvorov, Schérer was ordered by the Directory to seize Verona and drive the Austrians from Venetia to support General André Masséna in Switzerland. Both army commanders decided to launch their attacks on the same day—26 March. With their forces massed on their respective left wings, each side was victorious where it had superior numbers, but the result was indecisive. They were to fight again at Magnano on 5 April.

Until he was reinforced, Kray was to stay in position and then march on the vital fortress of Mantua, but he opted for an early attack to unsettle his French opponents on 26 March, the same day Schérer planned to cross the Adige. The Austrian right (northern) flank with 8,000 troops was protected by eighteen redoubts in the Adige–Lake Garda gap around Pastrengo. Two pontoon bridges were thrown over the Adige. Two divisions were in the vicinity of Verona with 20,000 troops and another two divisions (also 20,000 strong) stood to the south around Bevilaqua. Kray's headquarters were on his right wing, and he planned to halt any French advance on Verona in the flank. The French had massed 23,000 men in three divisions on their left, where Schérer had his headquarters. He planned to attack Pastrengo, cross the Adige, and march on Verona. Two divisions with 15,000 men faced Verona, and one division of 9,000 troops covered the right flank.

The French attack in the north began at 3:00 A.M. on 26 March, quickly driving the Austrians over the Adige, but sustaining heavy losses. As they retreated, the Austrians had broken only one bridge, so Schérer's men could cross the river in force. However, when the second bridge was smashed by a riverboat, necessitating five hours' repair work, Schérer halted his right wing, as he believed he could not take Verona without those troops still on the west bank.

It was only at 6:00 P.M. that he ordered his center under General Jean Moreau forward toward Verona. In fierce fighting with *Feldmarschalleutnant* Konrad Freiherr von Kaim's Austrians, which lasted three hours, positions were won and lost, without any clear outcome. In the south, General Joseph Perruquet de Montrichard with his one French division was ordered to watch the Adige, but decided to launch the first attack. Kray soon counterattacked in overwhelming numbers. Crossing the Adige, three Austrian columns drove the French back on St. Pietro and by nightfall had put them to flight. After losing 4,500 men, Schérer withdrew across the Adige on the following day, while Kray, who had sustained 6,500 losses, concentrated his army in Verona.

David Hollins

See also Directory, The; Italian Campaigns (1799–1800); Kray, Paul Freiherr von Krajova; Magnano, Battle of; Masséna, André; Moreau, Jean Victor; Schérer, Barthélemy Louis Joseph; Second Coalition, War of the; Suvorov, Alexander Vasilievich; Switzerland, Campaign in

References and further reading
Phipps, Ramsay Weston. 1980. *The Armies of the First French Republic and the Rise of the Marshals of Napoleon I.* Vol. 5, *The Armies on the Rhine, in Switzerland, Holland, Italy, Egypt, and the Coup d'Etat of Brumaire, 1797 to 1799.* London: Greenwood. (Orig. pub. 1926–1939.)
Wurzbach, C. von. 1856–1891. *Biographische Lexikon des Kaiserthums Österreich* [Biographical Encyclopedia of the Austrian Empire]. 60 vols. Vienna: Zarmarski and Dillmarsch.
Zima, H. 2001. "Magnano 1799." *Pallasch* 10: 2–18.

Victor, Claude Perrin (1764–1841)

Claude-Victor Perrin, later known as Claude Perrin Victor, duc de Bellune, Marshal of the Empire, and Peer of France, was born on 7 December 1764 in La Marche, Lorraine, and died in Paris on 1 March 1841. Although one of the most active and distinguished French generals of the Revolutionary and Napoleonic Wars, Victor appears to have had an unsteady relationship with Napoleon, who never admitted him into his inner circle. Although vilified after the wars for his persecution of former comrades, his performances at Marengo, Friedland, and the crossing of the Berezina in 1812 were equal to any of those of Napoleon's subordinates.

Born the son of a court usher, Victor joined the 4th Artillery Regiment (16 October 1781) initially as a clarinetist. After ten years' service, he obtained his discharge (1 March 1791), settling in Valence. Working as a grocer, he married Jeanne-Marie-Josephine Muguet (16 May 1791), with whom he had four children over the next decade. Victor joined the National Guard as a grenadier (12 October 1791), and volunteered to defend the frontier, becoming adjutant in the 3rd battalion of Drôme Volunteers (21 February 1792). When Victor transferred to the 5th Bouches-du-Rhône battalion (4 August 1792), he was promoted to the post of adjutant major, with the rank of captain, swiftly becoming a lieutenant colonel on 15 September.

Through the course of 1792–1793 he served with the (French) Army of Italy, before taking part in the siege of Toulon (August–December 1793). Twice promoted for bravery by the political commissars Antonio Salicetti and Thomas Gasparin, Victor was appointed *adjutant général* with the rank of *chef de brigade* (the republican equivalent of colonel) on 1 December 1793 and, after receiving a wound while seizing the "little Gibraltar" fortress from the British (17 December), was promoted to *général de brigade* (20 December). In this last attack, Victor encountered Napoleon Bonaparte, who was also wounded and promoted equally with Victor. After recovering from his wounds, Victor served with the Army of the Eastern Pyrenees, receiving confirmation of his grade on 13 June 1795. Victor returned to the Army of Italy and fought at Loano (22–25 November 1795). General Barthélemy Schérer gave him an advance guard command before the arrival of Bonaparte in the spring of 1796.

Taking part in Bonaparte's first Italian campaign (1796–1797), Victor was particularly distinguished at the action of Saint-Georges (15 February 1797), where he led a ferocious attack at the head of the 57th Line. After this action Bonaparte dubbed the 57th "The Terrible," giving Victor a field promotion to *général de division,* which was confirmed on 10 March. After the Treaty of Campo Formio he returned to France and was assigned to the proposed Army of England (12 January 1798). He was made commander of the 12th Military Division (Nantes) on 18 March before being recalled to the Army of Italy (3 May). Victor therefore missed out on the expedition to Egypt, which left him outside the tight nucleus of generals Bonaparte trusted most.

In Italy, Victor fought against the Austro-Russian forces in 1799 and was wounded at the Battle of the Trebbia (18–19 June). In January 1800 General André Masséna intrigued against Victor, telling Bonaparte that Victor openly opposed the Brumaire coup and was encouraging his troops to desert. On 3 February Masséna successfully recommended that Victor be replaced. However, Victor met the First Consul in March, seemingly without any hostility, and was rewarded with the post of *général de division* in the Army of the Reserve (1 April).

On 9 June 1800 Victor came to the assistance of General Jean Lannes and won the Battle of Montebello. Arguably, Victor's best performance came at Marengo (14 June), where he skillfully resisted the first shock of the Austrian army. Ordering General Gaspard Amédée Gardanne's division to make a fighting withdrawal, Victor lured the Austrians into a killing ground around the Fontanone Brook. After two hours, Lannes came up to support his right, and it was only after 2:00 P.M. that Victor's troops began to fall back, delaying the Austrian outbreak long enough to give time for reserves under General Louis Desaix to arrive.

After Marengo, Victor was made lieutenant to the commander in chief of the Army of Batavia (the forces of a French satellite republic, formerly Holland) on 25 July 1801, before being appointed on 9 August 1802 as commander of a military expedition to Louisiana that never sailed. Instead, after having divorced his first wife in 1801, he married Julie Vosch van Avesaat, the seventeen-year-old daughter of a Dutch rear admiral, in June 1803. On 14 June 1804 he was made a Grand-Officer of the Legion of Honor and made president of the Maine-et-Loire Electoral College. He was not included in the first promotions to Marshal of the Empire, but was sent as plenipotentiary to the court of Denmark on 19 February 1805.

After missing the campaign of 1805, Victor was recalled to the Grande Armée in 1806, serving as chief of

staff to Marshal Lannes. He saw action at Saalfeld (10 October) and Jena (14 October), where he was wounded. He signed the capitulation of Spandau (25 October), and was again in action at Pultusk (26 December). Victor was given command of X Corps in Poland (5 January 1807) but was captured and made a prisoner of war on 20 January while en route to take up his post. Exchanged on 8 March, he was sent to besiege Graudetz. Victor then took command of I Corps in Marshal Jean-Baptiste Bernadotte's absence and arrived in time to support Marshal Michel Ney's faltering corps at Friedland (14 June), driving into the Russians and securing the French victory. After Friedland, Victor at last entered the ranks of the Imperial Marshalate (13 July).

After the Peace of Tilsit, Victor was appointed governor of Berlin. He was made a duke in September 1808, receiving the obscure title of duc de Bellune. Legend has it that his ducal title was the result of a pun by the Emperor's sister, Pauline. In his early career, Victor had served under the nom de guerre "Beau Soleil" (beautiful sun). When spoken, the title Bellune sounded like the French words for "beautiful moon." After fifteen months in the Prussian capital, he received orders to proceed to Spain.

Commanding I Corps, Victor won at Espinosa de los Monteros (10–11 November 1808) and Somosierra (30 November). After Madrid was captured (2 December), Victor went on to fight at the battles of Uclés (13 January 1809) and Medellín (28 March). He was ordered to support Marshal Nicolas Soult against Lieutenant General Sir Arthur Wellesley's British troops in Portugal, but was forced onto the retreat. As the British pursued Soult into Spain, Victor joined with King Joseph Bonaparte and General Horace Sébastiani, meeting the British at Talavera (27–28 July). Seizing the initiative, Victor ordered a bold night attack that only narrowly failed. The following day the French were beaten and forced to retreat. However, Wellesley also retreated, and so Victor was able to retrace his steps and belatedly take Talavera. Here Victor demonstrated a generous side to his character, ensuring that captured British wounded were cared for with the same attention as his own soldiers. In October 1809 Victor began operations in the Sierra Morena, advancing into Andalusia and entering Seville on 1 February. He then pushed on to Cádiz (5 November) and began what proved to be a costly, fruitless thirty-month siege.

Victor was recalled to the Grande Armée (3 April 1812) and given command of IX Corps. Occupying the land between the Elbe and Oder rivers until August, Victor moved eastward to support the advance into Russia. When the army retreated from Moscow, Victor moved up in support, most notably at Studienka (27–28 November). While the shattered remains of the army crossed the frozen Berezina River, Victor's troops acted as a rear guard, launching counterattacks to keep the Russians away from the packed bridges. Crossing the Niemen with the wreck of the army, Victor took command of II Corps in Germany, fighting at the battles of Lützen (2 May 1813), Dresden (26–27 August), Wachau (16 October), and Leipzig (16–19 October).

As the fighting entered France, Victor fought at Brienne (29 January 1814), La Rothière (1 February), and Valjouan (17 February). En route to Montereau, Victor saw his son-in-law mortally wounded. Already pushed to the limit, Victor allowed his troops to rest at Salins, enabling the Allied troops he was pursuing to escape. Napoleon was furious and dismissed Victor from his command. Disgraced, Victor refused to quit the army and declared he would take up a musket and serve as a grenadier. This display of dedication mellowed Napoleon's wrath. Having already given Victor's corps to General Maurice, comte Gérard, the Emperor instead offered Victor two brigades of the Imperial Guard. As a proof of his courage, Victor was wounded at Craonne (7 March), struck in the thigh by a round shot (cannonball).

During the First Restoration, Victor was made a Chevalier de Saint-Louis (2 June 1814) and given command of the 2nd Military Division (6 December). Victor dedicated himself to supporting the Bourbons and was unwilling to support Napoleon on his unexpected return to France (1 March 1815). Leaving Paris on 19 March, Victor proceeded to Châlons, where he hoped to employ his troops to block Bonaparte's advance on the capital. However, Victor found their sympathies had turned against the king in favor of their former Emperor. Fearing reprisal, Victor decided to flee from France, following Louis XVIII to Ghent, where he remained in dedicated service until after Waterloo, fought on 18 June. This fidelity to the monarch was rewarded on their return to France in July. On 17 August Victor was called to the Chamber of Peers and made major general of the Royal Guard (6 September). On 12 October he was made president of the notorious commission charged with investigating officers' conduct during the "usurpation" of the Hundred Days. In this role, Victor forever tarnished his reputation among former comrades, in particular for having voted for the death penalty for Marshal Ney.

On 10 January 1816 Victor was made governor of the 16th Military Division. On 14 December 1821 he was appointed minister of war, making an unsuccessful attempt to gain a command in the (French) Army of Spain in 1823. In 1824 he turned down the role of ambassador to Austria (30 November) and retired to his estates. During the coronation of Charles X, Victor was made a member of the Superior War Council. During the July Revolution of 1830, he swore an oath to the new government but distanced himself from public affairs. He died in Paris and was buried at Père-Lachaise cemetery.

Terry Crowdy

See also Berezina, Actions and Crossing at the; Bernadotte, Jean-Baptiste-Jules; Bonaparte, Joseph; Bonaparte, Pauline; Brienne, Treaty of; Brumaire, Coup of; Cádiz, Siege of; Campo Formio, Treaty of; Craonne, Battle of; Desaix, Louis-Charles-Antoine, chevalier de Veygoux; Dresden, Battle of; England, French Plans for the Invasion of; Espinosa de los Monteros, Battle of; Fourth Coalition, War of the; France, Campaign in; Friedland, Battle of; Gérard, Maurice Etienne, comte; Germany, Campaign in; Imperial Guard (French); Italian Campaigns (1792–1797); Italian Campaigns (1799–1800); Jena, Battle of; Jena-Auerstädt Campaign; La Rothière, Battle of; Lannes, Jean; Leipzig, Battle of; Loano, Battle of; Louis XVIII, King; Lützen, Battle of; Madrid, Action at; Marengo, Battle of; Marshalate; Masséna, André; Medellín, Battle of; Montebello, Battle of; National Guard (French); Ney, Michel; Peninsular War; Pultusk, Battle of; Russian Campaign; Saalfeld, Action at; Somosierra, Action at; Soult, Nicolas Jean de Dieu; Talavera, Battle of; Tilsit, Treaties of; Toulon, Siege of; Trebbia, Battle of the; Wellington, Arthur Wellesley, First Duke of

References and further reading
Boycott-Brown, Martin. 2001. *The Road to Rivoli. Napoleon's First Campaign.* London. Cassell.
Chandler, David G., ed. 1987. *Napoleon's Marshals.* London: Weidenfeld and Nicolson.
Cugnac, Jean de. 1900–1901. *Campagne de l'armée de réserve en 1800.* 2 vols. Paris: R. Chapelot.
Delderfield, R. F. 2004. *The March of the Twenty-Six.* London: Leo Cooper.
Derode, Victor. 1839. *Nouvelle Relation de la Bataille de Friedland.* Paris: Bourgogne et Martinet.
Esposito, Vincent J., and John R. Elting. 1999. *A Military History and Atlas of the Napoleonic Wars.* London: Greenhill.
Fabry, Gabriel. 1900–1912. *Campagne de Russie, 1812.* 5 vols. Paris: Gougy.
Humble, Richard. 1973 *Napoleon's Peninsular Marshals: A Reassessment.* New York: Taplinger.
Lievyns, Verdot, and Régat. 1844. *Fastes de la Légion-d'Honneur, Biographie de tous les décorés.* Vol. 2. Paris: Bureau de l'Administration.
Macdonnell, A. G. 1996. *Napoleon and His Marshals.* London: Prion.
Oman, Charles William Chadwick. 1995–1997. *A History of the Peninsular War.* 7 vols. London: Greenhill.
Victor, Maréchal. 1846. *Extraits des Mémoires inédits de feu C.-V. Perrin, duc de Bellune . . . Campagne de l'armée de réserve en l'an VIII (1800).* Paris: Dumaine.
———. 1847. *Mémoires de C.-V. Perrin . . . mis en ordre par son fils aîné.* Paris: Dumaine.
Weinzierl, John F. 1997. *The Military and Political Career of Claude-Victor Perrin.* Ph.D. diss., Florida State University.
Young, Peter. 1973a. *Napoleon's Marshals.* London: Osprey.
———. 1973b. *Napoleon's Marshals.* New York: Hippocrene.

Vienna

Capital city of the Habsburg Empire (from 1804, the Austrian Empire) and until 1806, the seat of the Holy Roman

Emperor, Vienna was the largest city in central Europe with a population of over 200,000. On the south bank of the Danube, the old city was confined within the city walls, with suburbs sprawling in all directions, and beyond, new industrial areas. It was occupied twice by the French, in 1805 and 1809, but became the base of the postwar settlement in its famous Congress.

Largely rebuilt in Rococo style after the Turkish siege of 1683, Vienna was the political and cultural center of Mitteleuropa (central Europe), among the last Alpine foothills before the Hungarian plain. Its wealth was based on its position as the capital of the Habsburg Empire and Lower Austria. The walls of the city were destroyed by Napoleon in late 1809, and at its heart was the great Stephansdom (St. Stephen's Cathedral), which looked out over more than fifty churches, the Hofburg Palace, and the many palaces of wealthy magnates. Around the Hofburg were the government offices, including the Foreign Ministry on the Ballhausplatz and the Albertina Palace with its famous art collection. Home of the composers Mozart, Haydn, and Beethoven, Vienna enjoyed a rich cultural heritage, which included the State Opera House (built in 1776) and the Theater an der Wien musical theatre, as well as many museums and art galleries. In the north lay the Prater, a large green space open to the public. The wider streets and squares were adorned with fountains and statues, although the Kärntnerstrasse was a notorious bottleneck. The shops displayed the wide variety of fine goods imported into the city.

The road north to Bohemia crossed the Danube via the Tabor bridges, while the road south ran down the Wiednerstrasse and out through the Kärntnertor (Carinthian Gate). Beyond the bastioned walls lay the 600-meter-wide glacis, an open area bounded on the east by the noxious river Wien, but now increasingly surrounded by a mix of palaces (including Prince Eugene's Belvedere) and affluent suburbs, which were increasingly served by regular public carriage services. Outside their outer limits, guarded by the defensive works of the Linie (now the Gürtel), lay the unregulated industrial areas and the local villages. Three miles to the south of the city was the new imperial summer palace at Schönbrunn with its famous gardens.

Vienna comprised 6,159 houses in 1790, rising to 7,540 in 1820, following an 1802 commission that relaxed the building rules. Population movements caused fluctuations in the area's population, which by 1790 stood at 215,000 rising to 240,000 by 1805, before falling to 225,000 in 1809 and then rising again steadily.

David Hollins

See also Austria; Beethoven, Ludwig van; Fifth Coalition, War of the; Francis I, Emperor; Haydn, Joseph; Holy Roman Empire; Third Coalition, War of the; Vienna, Congress of

References and further reading
Macartney, C. A. 1969. *The Habsburg Empire, 1790–1918.* London: Weidenfeld and Nicolson.
Musulin, Stella. 1975. *Vienna in the Age of Metternich: From Napoleon to Revolution, 1805–48.* London: Faber.

Vienna, Congress of (15 September 1814–9 June 1815)

A conference of representatives of European states at Vienna to redraw the Continent's political map following the defeat of Napoleonic France.

While fighting Napoleon in 1814, Austria, Britain, Prussia, and Russia concluded a special alliance with the Treaty of Chaumont (1 March 1814), which clarified Allied war aims and made provision for a future European settlement. The later Treaty of Paris (30 May 1814) provided for the convening of a conference at Vienna to create a new political order in Europe based on the principles of legitimacy (generally on a hereditary basis) and the balance of power. Invitations to the Congress were extended to "All the Powers engaged on either side in the present War." However, Article I of the secret agreement between Britain, Austria, Prussia, and Russia stated that these states would reserve the de facto decision-making process to themselves and decide "a system of real and permanent balance of power in Europe." Minor powers were unaware of this arrangement and remained under the impression that they would be given a chance to contribute to the new European order.

Delegates from European states began to arrive in Vienna toward the end of September 1814. Austria was represented by Klemens Fürst Metternich, the foreign minister, and his deputy, Johann Philipp Freiherr von Wessenberg. Friedrich von Gentz was Metternich's personal secretary, Freiherr von Binder advised him on Italian issues, state councillor Hudelist served on the statistical committee, and Johann Graf Radetzky von Radetz on military matters. The British foreign secretary, Viscount Castlereagh, took part in negotiations in 1814, but Britain was later represented by the Duke of Wellington and Richard Le Poer Trench, second Earl of Clancarty. The Prussian delegation was led by Karl Fürst von Hardenberg, the chancellor, representing King Frederick William III, who was also present in Vienna. Other principal Prussian delegates were Wilhelm von Humboldt, General Karl Friedrich von dem Knesebeck, Johann Gottfried Hoffman, and Heinrich Freiherr vom und zum Stein. French foreign minister Prince Charles-Maurice de Talleyrand was sent on behalf of the French monarchy, while the Russian delegation included Tsar Alexander I and his advisers, including Karl Nessel-

The Congress of Vienna. Delegations, including many led by prominent heads of state, assemble in the Austrian capital to reshape the European political landscape and establish a system for future security and cooperation. (Library of Congress)

rode, Count Giovanni Antonio Capo d'Istria, and Charles André (Carlo Andreo) Pozzo di Borgo.

In addition, representatives from Spain, the Papal States, Portugal, Sweden, Hanover, Bavaria, Württemberg, and some thirty-two minor states attended the conference. Two delegations represented Naples, one of them charged with the interests of King Joachim Murat, the former French marshal, the other acting on behalf of the Bourbon dynasty. Initial meetings of the representatives of the major powers—Metternich, Castlereagh, Hardenberg, and Nesselrode—began on 15 September 1814 and led to the adoption of procedural rules for the Congress, which officially opened on 1 October 1814.

The Congress faced daunting problems from the very beginning. The Great Powers failed to realize in advance how much minor powers would resent their exclusion from the initial meetings. Secret articles of the Treaty of Paris were not communicated to the minor powers, depriving the Great Powers of the legal and moral basis for their claims. France, which was also excluded from discussions, took advantage of this circumstance to claim leadership of the minor powers and drive a wedge among the

Great Powers. Furthermore, the Great Powers were mistrustful of each other's designs and intentions, and Talleyrand brilliantly exploited their differences. On 30 September he and the Spanish representative Don Pedro de Labrador received an invitation to a preliminary meeting of the plenipotentiaries. At this meeting, the proposals made by the four Great Powers were presented, and Talleyrand challenged them at once. He questioned his solitary representation of the French delegation and was told that only the head of each cabinet had been invited. Talleyrand retorted that Humboldt, who had accompanied Hardenberg, headed no cabinet; when informed that Humboldt was present because of Hardenberg's deafness, the lame Talleyrand said, "We all have our infirmities and can exploit them when necessary" (quoted in Nicolson 1973, 141).

Talleyrand thus made the Great Powers agree that each country could be represented by two delegates at the meetings. He then attacked the reference to "Allies" in the protocol. When he was told that the term was used for the sake of brevity, he famously responded, "Brevity should not be purchased at the price of accuracy" (quoted in Cooper

2001, 250). He argued that the Quadruple Alliance was obsolete after the signing of the Treaty of Paris; that all powers that had taken part in the Napoleonic Wars had the right to participate in Congress proceedings; and that the Great Powers had no legal or moral justification for their actions. He refused to recognize their authority to discuss issues without the Congress as a whole.

Talleyrand's challenges were supported by minor powers, forcing the Great Powers to withdraw their proposals. Talleyrand then contended that a directing body of eight powers signatory to the Treaty of Paris had to be established and that the whole Congress must confirm its authority in a plenary session. He thus succeeded in reducing the control that Austria, Prussia, Russia, and Britain had arrogated to themselves and ensured the inclusion of France, Spain, Sweden, and Portugal in the Committee of Eight. Furthermore, Talleyrand demanded that all discussions and procedures of the Congress be based upon the principle of legitimacy and public law. In his characteristic wily fashion, Talleyrand, having succeeded in including France in the Big Eight (9 January 1815), abandoned the minor powers and concentrated on his next objectives.

Two separate bodies directed the Congress. The Council of Ministers of eight powers (France, Britain, Austria, Prussia, Spain, Portugal, Sweden, and Russia) organized ten separate committees to deal with specific issues. The committees varied in their composition and status: the German Committee, the Slave Trade Committee (also known as Conference), the Swiss Committee, the Committee on International Rivers, the Committee on Diplomatic Precedence, the Statistical Committee, the Drafting Committee, and three Committees on Tuscany, Sardinia and Genoa, and the Duchy of Bouillon. At the same time, the Allied sovereigns held their daily meetings, in which they often discussed and agreed on issues in ways contrary to instructions given to their negotiators. These inconsistencies often complicated the talks and led to unexpected difficulties.

The first major crisis threatening the unity of the Congress was over the Polish-Saxon issue. Back in 1808, Napoleon had established the Duchy of Warsaw and promised eventual independence to the Poles. Now, Tsar Alexander of Russia wanted to create a larger Kingdom of Poland that would include the Polish territory then in Prussian possession and place it under Russian sovereignty. Prussia agreed to surrender territory if compensated with territory from Saxony, whose king had supported Napoleon and therefore had to be penalized. Austria and Britain immediately objected to these designs as threatening their interests. Metternich, the Austrian chancellor, tried to settle this complex matter by assuring Alexander that Austria would support his Polish claim if he would prevent Prussia from expanding into Saxony; he then approached the Prussian representative, Hardenberg, promising to support the Prussian claim in Saxony if Prussia opposed Russian designs in Poland. However, Saxony was then under Russian occupation, inducing Prussia to heed Alexander's offer. Metternich's intrigue was eventually exposed, and Alexander was so enraged by it that he challenged the Austrian chancellor to a duel and refused to speak with him for three months.

As tensions between the four Great Powers increased, Talleyrand skillfully played them off against one another. Citing the principle of legitimacy, he argued that Russia and Prussia had no authority to deprive the lawful king of Saxony of his territory and throne. On 3 January 1815, he negotiated a secret military alliance with Britain and Austria against Russia and Prussia. Article I of this secret treaty pledged the mutual support of the signatory parties in the event of any one of them becoming involved in a war. In Article II, France and Austria promised to deploy 150,000 men, while Britain would supply them with subsidies. Article III stated that Britain would consider any attack on Hanover or the Low Countries as a casus belli. Article IV considered inviting minor powers (Hanover, Sardinia, Bavaria, and Hesse Darmstadt) to join the alliance. Thus, less than a year after being defeated, France assumed a major role at the Congress, divided the Great Powers, and created a new axis of political alliances.

The diplomatic struggle in Vienna was briefly interrupted by Napoleon's departure from Elba in March 1815. Returning to Paris, Napoleon found a copy of the secret alliance of 3 January 1815 in King Louis XVIII's study and had it delivered to Alexander, hoping this would break up the anti-French coalition. Despite his frustration, the Russian sovereign supported the Seventh Coalition and ordered his forces to France.

On 9 June 1815, nine days before the Battle of Waterloo, the representatives of Austria, Britain, Prussia, France, Russia, and Sweden signed the Final Act of the Congress of Vienna; eventually thirty-three other states acceded to it, excluding only the Ottoman Empire and the Papal States of the original thirty-five minor states. The treaty contained 121 articles and 17 annexes, which together outlined significant changes to the political map of Europe. Facing a new balance of power in Europe, both Prussia and Russia had to make concessions. Alexander agreed to a smaller Polish state (127,000 square kilometers with a population of some 3,200,000 people), with Prussia surrendering Warsaw but retaining Posen and Thorn; Austria kept the province of Galicia, but Kraków was declared a free city. Prussia received two-fifths of Saxony with a population of some 900,000 people, but the rest of Saxony was left under its legitimate ruler.

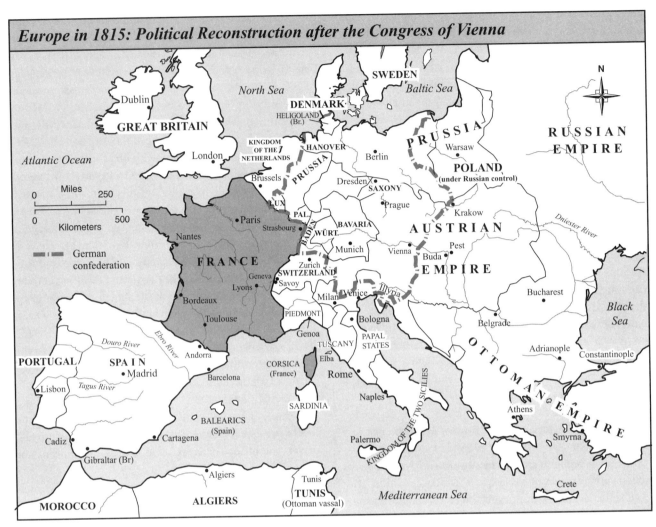

Europe in 1815: Political Reconstruction after the Congress of Vienna

Adapted from Fremont-Barnes 2002B, 87.

Britain succeeded in securing its maritime rights and received the former Dutch colonies of Ceylon (Sri Lanka), Guyana (or Guiana, now Surinam), and Cape Colony (on the southern coast of Africa), agreeing to pay half of Holland's debt to Russia and provide substantial subsidies to the Dutch; all other Dutch colonies in the East Indies were restored to the Netherlands. British also kept Malta and Heligoland and obtained a protectorate over the Ionian Islands. The main British goal of creating an independent state in the Low Countries, closely allied to Britain, was achieved when Belgium (the former Austrian Netherlands) was united with the Kingdom of the Netherlands under the House of Orange.

The Congress also confirmed the Russian conquest of Finland as well as the transfer of Norway from Denmark to Sweden. Western Pomerania was given to Prussia, which compensated Denmark with the Duchy of Lauenbourg. The restoration of Louis XVIII in France and of Ferdinand VII in Spain was confirmed.

Italy was dealt with as a geographic rather than a political entity, and its hopes for unity, revived under Napoleon, were dashed. The Papal States were restored to the pope and the duchies of Parma, Piacenza, and Guastalla were awarded to Napoleon's wife, Empress Marie Louise, for her lifetime. Naples and Sicily were reunited under Bourbon rule, while the House of Habsburg-Lorraine returned to Tuscany and Modena. Austria received Lombardy, Venice, and Dalmatia to compensate for its loss of the Austrian Netherlands (Belgium). The Kingdom of Sardinia was restored and given Savoy, Nice, Piedmont, and Liguria, with Genoa. Switzerland was represented by separate delegations from its nineteen cantons, and the Swiss Committee spent much time discussing their future. It was agreed that an enlarged Switzerland of twenty-one cantons would be established under the rotating leadership of Zürich, Lucerne, and Berne. On 20 November 1815 the five Great Powers recognized the permanent neutrality of Switzerland.

One of the most important changes concerned the Germanic states. Initially, the German Committee consisted of Austria, Prussia, Bavaria, Württemberg, and Hanover, but was later enlarged to include Saxony, Hesse-Darmstadt, the Netherlands, and Denmark. Metternich had great success in seeing to the creation of the Austrian-dominated German Confederation of thirty-eight states and four free cities, which replaced the Confederation of the Rhine. A federal Diet, under the presidency of Austria, was established at Frankfurt to draft the laws and regulations of the Confederation.

Besides territorial divisions, the Final Act of the Congress addressed other important issues. Britain, for instance, sought the total abolition of the slave trade. In early February 1815, the Slave Trade Committee adopted a declaration unanimously condemning the slave trade. Although it was later included in the Final Act, the declaration had no binding provisions for signatory powers and did not prescribe when or how the slave trade should be abolished. Therefore, Britain eventually concluded separate agreements with states engaged in the slave trade. The Jewish community in Germany succeeded in lobbying the Prussian delegation to place the issue of Jewish rights on the agenda of the German Committee, which formally confirmed them in some German states and made a recommendation to extend them to others.

The Committee on International Rivers, established on 14 December 1814, discussed the question of navigation on the major rivers of Europe. It was agreed that navigation on key waterways, including the Rhine, Moselle, Neckar, and Meuse, would be free. The Rhine Commission was established to eliminate trade barriers and standardize navigational regulations, police ordinances, and emergency procedures on rivers. One of the lasting achievements of the Congress of Vienna was agreement on diplomatic precedence and rank. It was agreed that the precedence of diplomatic representatives in a given country would be determined by the date of the official notification of their arrival to their mission. Diplomatic officials were organized into four classes: ambassadors and papal legates, ministers plenipotentiary, resident ministers, and chargés d'affaires. French was selected as the language of international diplomacy, confirming a state of affairs that had existed since the reign of Louis XIV.

An interesting aspect of the Congress of Vienna was the social life surrounding the conference. European emperors, kings, and princes were accompanied by numerous courtiers and pleasure seekers, and the Austrian court did its best to cater to their wishes. Many crucial decisions regarding the future of Europe were achieved at such balls and dinners. Women, the most famous of whom were the Duchess Wilhelmine Biron of Sagan and Princess Catherine Bagration, played an important role in the work of the Congress, where the leaders of European nations competed for their attention. The Parisian court painter Jean-Baptiste Isabey established a thriving practice painting portraits of the Congress participants. The Austrian court used an intricate system of espionage that employed housemaids, porters, coachmen, and servants to procure bits of information.

Not a part of the Congress, but directly stemming from it, the Holy Alliance was suggested by Tsar Alexander as a means to maintain the conservative order and to encourage monarchs to rule according to Christian principles. Some Congress participants downplayed its relevance, with Castlereagh describing it as "a piece of sublime mysticism and nonsense" (quoted in Yonge 1868, 2:229) and Metternich calling it a "loud-sounding nothing" (Metternich 1970, 1:165). Nevertheless, the Holy Alliance was supported by many European sovereigns and eventually became associated with the forces of reaction in Europe, and particularly with the policies of Metternich.

The Congress of Vienna had a significant impact on European history. It established a new political system, also known as the Concert of Europe, which maintained the balance of power on the Continent for the next thirty-three years. The Quadruple Alliance and the Holy Alliance continued to uphold the decisions of the Congress, settled disputes and problems by means of conferences, and maintained conservative order in Europe. The system proved its effectiveness and resilience when it successfully suppressed liberal revolutions throughout Europe in the 1820s and 1830s.

Alexander Mikaberidze

See also Alexander I, Tsar; Austria; Bavaria; Castlereagh, Robert Stewart, Viscount; Chaumont, Conference and Treaty of; Confederation of the Rhine; Denmark; Elba; Ferdinand VII, King; Finland; France; Francis I, Emperor; Frederick William III, King; Gentz, Friedrich von; Great Britain; Hanover; Hardenberg, Karl August Fürst von; Holy Alliance; Humboldt, Wilhelm Christian Karl Ferdinand Freiherr von; Ionian Islands; Louis XVIII, King; Marie Louise, Empress; Metternich, Klemens Wenzel Lothar Fürst von; Murat, Joachim; Naples; Netherlands, The; Norway; Ottoman Empire; Papal States; Paris, First Treaty of; Poland; Portugal; Pozzo di Borgo, Charles André; Prussia; Quadruple Alliance; Radetzky von Radetz, Johann Joseph Wenzel Graf; Russia; Sardinia; Saxony; Sicily; Slave Trade; Spain; Stein, Heinrich Friedrich Karl Freiherr vom und zum; Sweden; Switzerland; Talleyrand-Périgord, Charles-Maurice de, Prince; Wellington, Arthur Wellesley, First Duke of; Württemberg

References and further reading

Alsop, Susan. 1984. *The Congress Dances*. New York: Harper and Row.

Chapman, Tim. 1998. *The Congress of Vienna: Origins, Process and Results*. London: New York: Routledge.

Cooper, Duff. 2001. *Talleyrand.* London: Weidenfield and Nicolson.

Dallas, Gregor. 1997. *The Final Act: The Roads to Waterloo.* New York: Holt.

Ferrero, Guglielmo. 1963. *The Reconstruction of Europe: Talleyrand and the Congress of Vienna, 1814–1815.* New York: Norton.

Gullick, Edward. 1955. *Europe's Classical Balance of Power: A Case History of the Theory and Practice of One of the Great Concepts of European Statecraft.* Ithaca, NY: Cornell University Press.

Kissinger, Henry A. 2000. *A World Restored: Metternich, Castlereagh and the Problems of Peace, 1812–22.* London: Weidenfeld and Nicolson.

Lockhart, John. 1932. *The Peacemakers.* London: Duckworth.

Metternich, Prince. 1970. *Memoirs of Prince Metternich.* 5 vols. Ed. Prince Richard Metternich. New York: Fertig.

Nicolson, Harold. 1973. *The Congress of Vienna: A Study in Allied Unity: 1812–1822.* Gloucester, MA: Smith.

Schroeder, P. W. 1996. *The Transformation of European Politics, 1763–1848.* Oxford: Clarendon.

Sédouy, Jacques-Alain de. 2003. *Le congrès de Vienne: L'Europe contre la France, 1812–1815.* Paris: Perrin.

Spiel, Hilde, ed. 1968. *The Congress of Vienna: An Eyewitness Account.* Philadelphia: Chilton.

Strauss, Hannah. 1949. *The Attitude of the Congress of Vienna toward Nationalism in Germany, Italy, and Poland.* New York: Columbia University Press.

Talleyrand-Périgord, Charles-Maurice de, prince de Bénévent. 1973. *Memoirs of the Prince de Talleyrand.* Ed. duc de Broglie. 5 vols. New York: AMS.

Webster, Charles. 1969. *The Congress of Vienna, 1814–1815.* New York: Barnes and Noble.

Yonge, Charles Duke. 1868. Viscount Castlereagh to Lord Liverpool, 28 September 1815, in *The Life and Administration of Robert Banks, Second Earl of Liverpool.* 2 vols. London: Macmillan.

Villaret-Joyeuse, Louis Thomas (1747–1812)

Born on 29 May 1747 in Auch, France, Villaret-Joyeuse (often shortened to Villaret) initially joined the *gendarmes du Roi,* but reportedly left after killing an adversary in a duel. He joined the navy in 1765 as a *volontaire* (midshipman). During his early naval career, Villaret made numerous voyages to both the Caribbean and the Indian Ocean. During the American Revolutionary War (1775–1783), Villaret served aboard the fleet under the command of the famous admiral, Pierre André de Suffren. Villaret participated in most of the battles fought in the Indian Ocean in 1782–1783. Suffren recognized young Villaret's talent and promoted him to *lieutenant de vaisseau* in 1784 for his service. After the war, Villaret went on to serve a number of years on shore in the port of Lorient.

Villaret returned to active naval command in 1791, when he was ordered to transport troops to St. Domingue aboard his frigate *La Prudente.* Arriving in early August, he was present in St. Domingue when a massive slave revolt broke out, at which time the local governor used Villaret to transport local forces around the colony. In 1792 he was promoted to *capitaine de vaisseau* and given the command of a ship of the line, *Le Trajan.* In 1793 he commanded a small squadron to patrol the coast of the Vendée. When the rest of the Brest squadron sailed down, a mutiny broke out. Villaret was one of the few officers who maintained order aboard his ship.

Due to his record of discipline, Villaret was made commander in chief of the Brest fleet, the most important naval force of the French Navy, and promoted to *contre-amiral* (rear admiral). He held this important position for nearly three years during the tumultuous Revolutionary Wars. In the summer of 1794 Villaret sailed with twenty-five ships of the line to protect a grain shipment arriving from the United States. In order to protect this shipment, he was forced to engage a British fleet in the Battles of Prairial (so-called by the French, in deference to the Republican calendar), the main engagement of which is known to the British as the "Glorious First of June" or simply "First of June." Although defeated, he bravely rallied his remaining ships and rescued vessels that had surrendered. In September 1794 he was promoted to *vice-amiral* (vice admiral). In December 1794 he was ordered to sail out to attack British commerce in what is known as the *Coisière du Grande Hiver* (literally, Cruise of the Great Winter). Battered by storms, several of his ships were sunk, and all suffered damage.

In June 1795 Villaret was ordered to sail with nine ships to relieve a small squadron held up near Belle Isle. During the Battle of Belle Isle on 17 June, he chased away a small British squadron. Unable to bring them to battle, he tried to return to Brest, but contrary winds forced him to sail toward Lorient. Close to Lorient, Villaret was discovered by a British squadron under Sir Alexander Hood, Lord Bridport, which was guarding the royalist expedition to Quiberon. During the Battle of Ile de Groix on 23 June, several of Villaret's ships disobeyed his orders and sailed away under full sail, abandoning three slower ships to the British.

In 1796 Villaret was finally removed from command, not due to his defeats, however, but rather to his opposition to the Directory's plan for an invasion of Ireland, as he had instead advocated a campaign in the Indian Ocean. In 1796 he was elected to the Council of Five Hundred as a representative of Morbihan. As a member of the Clichy Club, he made several speeches about the colonies, speaking out against the emancipation of slaves. Exiled to Ile d'Oléron after the coup of 18 Fructidor in September 1797, Villaret was eventually reinstated by Bonaparte in 1801, who had taken power as First Consul in a coup staged two years before.

In December of that year, Villaret commanded the Brest fleet that carried the major portion of General Charles-Victor Leclerc's expedition to St. Domingue. Conflicts over command led to Villaret returning to France with the bulk of the fleet. In April 1802, Bonaparte named him *capitaine-général* of Martinique. Taking control of Martinique in September, he governed the island under extremely trying circumstances, facing various threats including slave uprisings, yellow fever, and British invasion.

Villaret cooperated with the fleets of admirals Edouard Jacques Burgues de Missiessy and Pierre de Villeneuve, who sailed into the Caribbean in 1805 as the preliminary stage of Bonaparte's plan—aborted in the summer—to invade England. In January 1809 a large British expedition invaded Martinique and laid siege to the fortress at Fort-de-France. The month-long siege ended on 24 February, once the British were able to bring in heavy artillery. Upon his return to France, Napoleon had Villaret court-martialed for surrendering the island. Initially found guilty, Villaret pleaded his case and eventually received a pardon from the Emperor. As Napoleon prepared for the invasion of Russia, he named Villaret governor of Venice in April 1811, where he was occupied with maritime affairs. Villaret retained this position until 24 July 1812, when he died of dropsy (edema).

Kenneth Johnson

See also Belle Isle, Battle of; Council of Five Hundred; Directory, The; England, French Plans for the Invasion of; Glorious First of June, Battle of the; Haiti; Hood, Alexander, First Viscount Bridport; Ile de Groix, Action off; Leclerc, Charles-Victor Emmanuel; Martinique; Quiberon, Expedition to; Republican Calendar; Slave Trade; Slavery; Villeneuve, Pierre Charles Jean Baptiste Silvestre de

References and further reading
Clowes, William Laird. 1997. *The Royal Navy: A History from the Earliest Times to 1900.* 7 vols. Vol. 4. London: Chatham. (Orig. pub. 1898.)
Duffy, Michael, and Roger Morriss, eds. 2001. *The Glorious First of June: A Battle in Perspective.* Exeter: University of Exeter Press.
Gardiner, Robert, ed. 2001. *Fleet Battle and Blockade: The French Revolutionary War, 1793–1797.* London: Caxton.
———, ed. 2002. *The Campaign of Trafalgar, 1803–1805.* London: Caxton.
Warner, Oliver. 1961. *The Glorious First of June.* London: Batsford.

Villeneuve, Pierre Charles Jean Baptiste Silvestre de (1763–1806)

A courageous and competent naval commander, Villeneuve proved unable to influence Napoleon to introduce more sensible naval policies. At Trafalgar, he conducted a futile battle, well aware that Nelson would win.

Villeneuve was born on 31 December 1763 at Valensole (Basses Alpes). Of a noble family, he joined the Guard Marines in 1778 during the American Revolutionary War and fought the British until 1783. In February 1778 he went aboard the frigate *Flore*, attached to Admiral Jean-Baptiste, comte d'Estaing's squadron, and left for American waters in March 1778. Villeneuve then joined the frigate *Montréal* (32 guns), which was captured by the *Bourgogne* (74) on 4 May 1779. After his return to Brest in December of that year, he shipped out as an ensign aboard the *Marseillais* (74) as part of Admiral François Joseph, comte de Grasse's squadron.

The *Marseillais* won fame at the Chesapeake on 5 September 1781 and later in the naval actions against Rear Admiral Sir Samuel Hood off St. Kitts on 25 January 1782, as well as at Les Saintes on 12 April. The *Marseillais* returned to France while escorting a large convoy and was laid up at Brest on 5 September 1782. Villeneuve then shipped out on the *Destin* (74), which joined the French naval force assembling off Cádiz in December 1782, as part of an invasion force intended to attack Jamaica. The invasion did not take place, and the *Destin* was laid up in March 1783. Villeneuve then joined the corvette *La Blonde*. He was made lieutenant in May 1786, served on the frigate *Alceste* in 1787–1788 and then on the corvette *Badine* in 1792. Despite the upheaval caused by the Revolution within the officer corps, Villeneuve refused to emigrate and remained in the navy.

In 1793 Villeneuve was promoted to captain, the same year he lost his status as a member of the nobility. He rejoined the navy in 1795 and became deputy chief of staff at Toulon, the principal French port on the Mediterranean. His competence and the experience he had gained in the American Revolutionary War earned him rapid promotion. He became a rear admiral in 1796 at the age of thirty-three and was assigned the task of taking a force of five ships from Toulon to Brest. At the time of the expedition to Egypt in 1798, Villeneuve, aboard the *Bucentaure* (80), commanded the rear guard of Admiral François, comte de Brueys's fleet. He participated in the capture of Malta en route and then in the landing of Bonaparte's army in Egypt. He was not able to assist Brueys at the Battle of the Nile but managed to get back to Malta and join Rear Admiral Denis Decrès, Napoleon's future minister of the navy.

In September 1800 Villeneuve became a prisoner of war at Malta with the fall of that island to the British. After being freed, he received command of a naval force out of the Italian port of Taranto (April 1801). After the Peace of Amiens in 1802, Villeneuve was put in charge of a force in the Antilles, and subsequently of the squadron based at Rochefort. On 30 May 1804 he was promoted to vice admiral, the same day as Decrès and Honoré Ganteaume. He was the youngest officer to hold that rank.

When Admiral Louis-René de Latouche-Tréville, who had defeated Horatio, Viscount Nelson at Boulogne, died at Toulon, Villeneuve succeeded to command of the Mediterranean fleet. Its mission was to lure Nelson's fleet to the Antilles, in the West Indies, and then to return to European waters to free up the Brest squadron in order eventually to allow the army to cross the Channel and land in England. Villeneuve left Toulon on 17 January 1805, aboard the *Bucentaure*, in the company of eleven ships of the line (four of 80 guns, seven of 74), seven frigates, and 6,400 troops, but a storm and the ships' poor condition forced him to return to port on the twenty-first. He asked Decrès to replace him, but the latter refused. With the Spanish fleet able to cooperate with Villeneuve, Napoleon ordered Villeneuve to rejoin Admiral Missiessy in Martinique and then to return to the English Channel. Villeneuve left Toulon on 30 March. On 14 April he was at Cádiz, where he joined the Spanish commander, Admiral Don Federico Gravina (with six ships of the line of 64 to 80 guns each, and one frigate). A month later, Villeneuve reached Martinique, but Missiessy had already left, and Ganteaume was still blockaded in Brest.

On 9 June, assuming that Ganteaume would not be able to emerge from Brest, and after learning of the arrival of Nelson's and Admiral Sir Alexander Cochrane's squadrons in the West Indies, Villeneuve decided not to attack Barbados and left to return to Europe. He gained a slight advantage against Vice Admiral Sir Robert Calder's squadron off Cape Finisterre on 22 July, and reached Vigo on 28 July, where he left three damaged vessels and 1,200 sick men. On 1 August, he was off Ferrol, then made for Corunna on the northwest coast of Spain, where on 11 August he joined 5 French ships commanded by Admiral Adrien-Louis Gourdon and eleven ships commanded by Admiral Domingo Grandallana. Due to the serious state of damage of his ships, he took refuge in Cádiz on 20 August. By early August, and probably well before that, Napoleon had abandoned his plan for the invasion of England.

While Villeneuve fought the diseases that raged aboard his vessels, Napoleon, on 19 August, left the camp at Boulogne with the Grande Armée for his campaign against the Austrians and Russians, who were to be decisively defeated at Austerlitz on 2 December. Napoleon, who knew little of naval strategy, cared little for the fortunes of Villeneuve's fleet, and decided to replace him. By the time his successor reached Cádiz, however, Villeneuve had already fought Nelson at Trafalgar on 21 October, losing eighteen out of thirty-three ships of the line either captured or destroyed.

Villeneuve was taken prisoner and brought to Britain, where he was allowed to attend Nelson's funeral and was later released. He returned to Paris, where he was imprisoned, and died on 22 April 1806 in mysterious circumstances—his body discovered with six deep knife wounds through and around his heart. A supposed suicide note, addressed to his wife, was found beside the body. The police undertook no investigation into an almost-certain case of homicide, possibly committed on minister of police Joseph Fouché's orders.

Patrick Villiers

See also Amiens, Treaty of; Austerlitz, Battle of; Brueys d'Aigailliers, François Paul; England, French Plans for the Invasion of; Fouché, Joseph, duc d'Otrante; French Navy; Ganteaume, Honoré Joseph Antoine, comte de; Malta, Operations on; Martinique; Middle East Campaign; Nelson, Horatio, First Viscount; Nile, Battle of the; Third Coalition, War of the; Trafalgar, Battle of

References and further reading

Adkin, Mark. 2005. *The Trafalgar Companion: The Complete Guide to History's Most Famous Sea Battle and the Life of Admiral Lord Nelson.* London: Aurum.
Clayton, Tim, and Phil Craig. 2004. *Trafalgar: The Men, the Battle, the Storm.* London: Hodder and Stoughton.
Schom, Alan. 1992. *Trafalgar: Countdown to Battle, 1803–1805.* London: Penguin.
Six, Georges. 1934. *Dictionnaire Biographique des Généraux et Amiraux Français de la Révolution et de L'Empire (1792–1814).* 2 vols. Paris: Librairie Historique et Nobiliaire.

Vilna, Battle of (9–10 December 1812)

A series of military operations around Vilna (present-day Vilnius, the capital of Lithuania) during the French invasion of Russia in the 1812 campaign.

In June, with the Grande Armée at the start of operations, Napoleon hoped to take advantage of his numerical superiority to destroy the 1st Western Army around Vilna, then surround the 2nd Western Army and force Tsar Alexander to sue for peace. The Grande Armée crossed the Niemen River on 23–25 June and advanced through Kovno toward Vilna. On 25 June, General Mikhail Barclay de Tolly ordered his 1st Western Army to retreat along predetermined routes and concentrated his forces around Vilna two days later. Napoleon, meanwhile, gathered some 180,000 men (I and III Corps, I and II Reserve Cavalry Corps, and the Imperial Guard) and planned to attack the Russian army at Vilna. Early on the morning of 28 June, however, Barclay de Tolly withdrew his army toward Sventsyani, and Marshal Joachim Murat's cavalry occupied Vilna later that day.

Napoleon established large supply depots, the army treasury, and hospitals at Vilna under the command of General Antoine Henri Jomini. In November, following the

French army's retreat from Moscow, French authorities began the evacuation of the city. Following the fighting on the Berezina, the survivors straggled into Vilna on 8 December, where they initially found enormous supplies of food and ammunition. In the ensuing chaos, however, supply stores were ravaged and many stragglers trampled to death. The following day, Russian troops under Colonel Alexander Seslavin engaged the French rear guard under Marshal Michel Ney and briefly seized one of the suburbs of Vilna. Murat, who was instructed by Napoleon to rest troops in the city, became concerned about the proximity of Russian forces and ordered the evacuation of Vilna on the night of 9 December, abandoning thousands of wounded in the hospitals.

On 10 December a detachment led by General Vasily Orlov-Denisov, supported by Ataman Matvei Platov's Cossacks, attacked the French rear guard near Vilna, capturing some 2,000 men and forcing the French to withdraw to the Ponarskaya hill, about 4 miles west of Vilna. Ney deployed his troops (some 4,000 men) at the bottom of the hill, and after a brief combat with Cossacks, he withdrew toward Kovno. At the same time, detachments under generals Paul Golenischev-Kutuzov, Yefim Chaplits, and Mikhail Borozdin attacked Vilna from different directions and seized the town. The precise number of casualties is difficult to verify. The Russians captured all the remaining supply depots and over 14,000 men, including 7 generals, 242 staff officers, and more than 5,000 sick. Many of these soldiers died of malnutrition, disease, and exposure to the elements. Early in 2002, municipal workers uncovered a mass grave of Napoleonic soldiers in Vilnius. Further archaeological excavations revealed several thousand contorted skeletons, who were later given a proper burial.

Alexander Mikaberidze

See also Alexander I, Tsar; Barclay de Tolly, Mikhail Andreas; Berezina, Actions and Crossing at the; Cossacks; Imperial Guard (French); Jomini, Antoine Henri, Baron; Murat, Joachim; Ney, Michel; Platov, Matvei Ivanovich, Count and Ataman; Russian Campaign

References and further reading
Barclay de Tolly, Mikhail. 1912. *Izobrazhenie voennikh deistvii 1812 g.* St. Petersburg: N.p.
Bonnal, H. 1905. *Le manoevre de Vilna.* Paris: Chapelot.
Kudrinsky, F. 1912. *Vilna v 1812 g.* Vilna: N.p.
Mikhailovsky-Danilevsky, Alexander. 1839. *Opisanie otechestvennoi voiny 1812 g.* St. Petersburg: Voeynnaya.
Voensky, K. 1912. *Vilna v 1812 g. Iz vospominanii grafa Gogendorpa.* St. Petersburg: N.p.

Vimeiro, Battle of (21 August 1808)

Fought a short distance from Lisbon, Vimeiro was the first major battle of the Peninsular War. Four days after the ac-

tion at Roliça, General Jean Andoche Junot, with 13,000 men and twenty-four guns, marched north from Lisbon to attack the British at Vimeiro, a few miles south of Roliça. Lieutenant General Sir Arthur Wellesley (the future Duke of Wellington) had been reinforced by a further 4,000 men, belonging to the brigades of Brigadier General Robert Anstruther and Brigadier General Wroth Palmer Acland, who had come ashore at the mouth of the Maceira River, about 15 miles south of Roliça. These troops, which brought the number of men under Wellesley's command to 17,000, were welcome reinforcements. Not so welcome, however, was the fifty-three-year-old Lieutenant General Sir Harry Burrard, who had arrived off the mouth of the Maceira on 20 August.

Burrard had arrived in Portugal to assume command of the army, although this came as no great surprise to the thirty-nine-year-old Wellesley, who had been forewarned of his coming by Lord Castlereagh, the secretary of state for war. It was entirely a political move, a fact from which Wellesley could take little comfort. Furthermore, two more British officers, Lieutenant General Sir Hew Dalrymple and Lieutenant General Sir John Moore, both of whom were senior to him, were also on their way to Portugal. Nevertheless, Wellesley joined Burrard aboard his ship; having been apprised of the situation, Burrard decided that it would be unwise to take any further offensive action before the arrival of Moore's reinforcements, which were known to be due shortly. Having been informed of this, Wellesley returned to his troops, determined to do his best as long as he remained in command, while Burrard remained on his ship for the night.

When Wellesley retired for the evening, he did so having placed six of his infantry brigades with eight guns on the western ridge lying on the south of and running parallel to the Maceira River, while a single battalion was placed on the eastern ridge as guard. The river itself flowed south through a defile between the two ridges and continued on to the rear of the village of Vimeiro, which itself was situated on a flat-topped, round hill. Here, Wellesley had placed his other two infantry brigades as well as six guns. The village was separated from the two ridges not only by the Maceira but also by a tributary that flowed along the southern foot of the eastern ridge.

The hush of night had hardly descended upon the British camp when reports came in that the French were advancing in force from the south. In fact, the French under Junot numbered around 13,000 men (the 1st Division under General Henri François Delaborde, and the 2nd Division under General Louis Henri Loison), 4,000 fewer than Wellesley but with five more guns. Long before dawn showed itself on the morning of 21 August, Wellesley was up on the western ridge, peering through his telescope, but

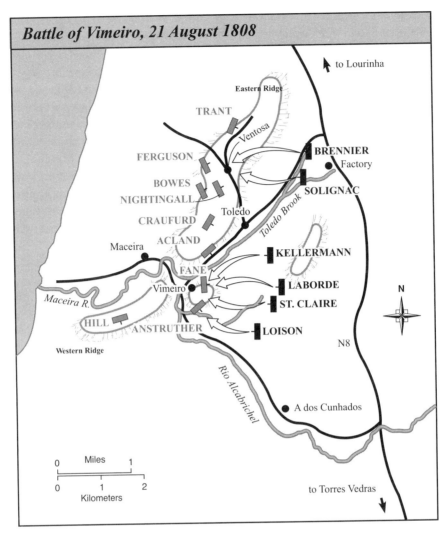

Battle of Vimeiro, 21 August 1808

Adapted from Paget 1997, 66.

as yet no French troops were to be seen, leaving the British troops to while away the early morning cooking their breakfasts. At about nine o'clock, however, clouds of rising dust were spotted away to the east, and soon the glint of bayonets, shako plates, and other accoutrements could be seen as they sparkled in the shimmering sunlight.

From the direction of Junot's approach, it was obvious that Wellesley's left flank was being threatened, which prompted a hasty redeployment of his forces, mainly involving the transfer of three of his brigades from the western ridge to the eastern ridge, leaving Major General Rowland Hill's brigade and two guns alone on the western ridge. Wellesley himself also moved to the eastern ridge, from where he controlled the battle.

The village of Vimeiro itself was held by the brigades of Brigadier General Henry Fane and Brigadier General Robert Anstruther, and it was against this position that the main French thrust appeared to be heading. The British troops here consisted of four companies of the second bat-

talion of the 95th Rifles (2/95th) and the fifth battalion of the 60th Rifles (5/60th), all deployed in a heavy skirmishing line in front of Vimeiro Hill, while on the crest itself were the musket-armed 1/50th (50th Foot), the 2/97th, and the 2/52nd. Behind them, on the reverse slope of the hill, were the 2/9th and the 2/43rd, both in support. These troops were themselves supported by twelve guns. Heading toward these 900 British infantrymen were some 2,400 French troops under General Jean Guillaume Thomières, who were formed into two columns supported by cavalry and artillery and screened by a cloud of skirmishers. The ensuing clash between the two sides marked a significant point in the Napoleonic Wars and set the pattern for a whole series of actions fought in the Peninsula between the British and French armies.

As the French columns advanced against the British infantry on Vimeiro Hill, they did so in the traditional, and up until this point the all too successful, style that had swept Napoleon's armies to victory after victory. Cavalry cantered along on the flanks, field artillery bounded along over the broken ground, while in front of the columns hundreds of light infantrymen engaged the British skirmish line as a prelude to the assault on the main British line. The formula had been tried and tested, and it had proved successful. And yet here, on the slopes of the hill in front of Vimeiro, Wellesley's skirmishers turned the tables, for so effective was his light infantry screen that the men of the 5/60th and the 95th were only forced back following the intervention of the main French columns. The columns themselves were suffering at the hands of the British artillery, which dealt out death in a new form, shrapnel, which swept the French troops with dozens of musket balls from exploding cases. But it was the clash between the British line and the French column that was to become the standard form of combat and perhaps the most enduring image of the war in the Peninsula.

At Vimeiro, this scenario was premiered with devastating results. The French columns, 30 ranks deep by 40 wide, advanced noisily and confidently against the 900 British troops, formed in a silent, two-deep line. As the French approached to within 100 yards, the British troops, in this case the 1/50th, leveled their muskets and delivered a crashing volley into the tightly packed ranks of Frenchmen. As the column came on, so the effects of each of the succeeding volleys, fired at fifteen-second intervals, increased. The French ranks thinned at each discharge while they themselves were able to bring only 200 of their own muskets—those in front and on the flanks—to bear on the British. It was a rather simple mathematical equation that the French commanders were never quite to comprehend during the war, and when they did try to deploy their men into line, the effects of concentrated British musketry made it almost impossible. Thomières did his best to get his men into line, but it was hopeless. The columns melted away to the rear with Fane's riflemen close on their heels.

To the south of this first column, Thomières's second column was making progress toward the British line. This column, also some 1,200-strong, suffered less from artillery fire, owing to the nature of the terrain over which it passed, but when it neared the British line it began to suffer the same fate as the column on its right. Anstruther's brigade duly dealt the decisive blows, the precise, controlled volleys of the 2/97th rolling from one end of its line to the other, ripping great gaps in the French column, and when the 2/52nd and 2/9th closed in on each side of them, the French resolve disappeared, and once again Fane's riflemen enjoyed a brief chase after them before being called back. In their panic, the French abandoned all seven of the guns they had brought forward with them, the horses and gunners falling victims earlier to the accurate fire of the Baker rifles.

With the initial French attacks having been repulsed, Burrard picked his moment to appear on the battlefield. There appeared little danger to the British at this time, however, and Burrard allowed Wellesley to finish the battle himself.

No sooner had Burrard satisfied himself as to the progress of the fighting than the French committed two more columns to the attack. Once again the village of Vimeiro was the focus of the assault, carried out by two columns, each of two battalions of grenadiers. The British line steadied itself once more and braced itself for yet another onslaught. Lieutenant Colonel William Robe's gunners worked furiously at their guns as they poured shot and shell into the leading French column. Enemy artillery attempted to reply, but their fire was ineffective, and there was a real danger of firing into their own men who were skirmishing with Fane's riflemen. In spite of the fire being directed into the column, it pushed on, moving across the ground lying between the routes of the last two French attacks. Gradually, the enveloping fire from 2,000 British muskets of the 2/9th, the 1/50th, and the 2/97th brought the column shuddering to a halt, and as Wellesley's men advanced down the hill, the French column finally gave way and scattered, abandoning four guns that had been brought forward with it.

While this last attack had been in progress, the second column of grenadiers had managed to move round the left flank of the 1/50th and soon had a clear run into the village of Vimeiro itself. The French incurred heavy losses as they swept into the village through a hail of lead and cannon shot. Here, in the narrow, jumbled maze of houses—a sort of prelude to the fighting at Fuentes de Oñoro in 1811—the French came face to face with the 2/43rd, which Anstruther had thrown forward. The ensuing fighting was chaotic and confused, and bayonets were bent and bloodied. The British troops, in spite of their inferior numbers, managed to thrust the French from the village, and the British line was restored.

Wellesley had just 240 British cavalry available to him, all from the 20th Light Dragoons under Lieutenant Colonel Charles Taylor, but with all of the French attacks until now having been repulsed, he chose the moment to launch them in a counterattack. Taylor's men, having dispersed a French infantry square, quickly became intoxicated with their success and rode on at speed, outdistancing their own supporting guns and doing little damage to the French. Almost half the light dragoons were either killed, wounded, or taken prisoner—including Taylor himself, who was mortally wounded—when they collided with fresh, and more numerous, French cavalry. The charge was just the first in a series of misadventures of the British cavalry in the Peninsula, punctuated by rare but notable triumphs.

On the eastern ridge above Ventosa, which lay at the eastern end of the ridge, the French were again attacking in strength with 3,000 infantry under General Jean-Baptiste Solignac, who was supported by a small number of cavalry and three guns, and a further 3,200 infantry, supported by dragoons, under General Antoine François Brennier. The first of these two forces advanced on Ventosa itself, while the second force passed to the north with the intention of attacking the ridge from the northeast.

The results of both of these attacks were predictably similar to the earlier French attacks elsewhere on the battlefield, as both Solignac and Brennier advanced in column against their British adversaries, who waited for them in line. The first force, consisting of three columns, struck that part of the line held by Major General Ronald Craufurd Ferguson's brigade. The French were met by a devastating series of volleys, fired by platoons, which blasted away the heads of the columns and prevented Solignac, desperately trying to deploy his own men into line, from making any progress at all. After a few minutes the French were in full retreat, once more abandoning their guns.

No sooner had Solignac's attack come to grief than Brennier's columns fell upon the rear and flank of three of Ferguson's battalions, the 1/71st, 1/82nd, and 1/29th. By the time the first two of these battalions adjusted their positions to meet them, Brennier's men closed on them, and in a confused fight, both the 71st and 82nd were pushed back, the French retaking the guns that had been abandoned by Solignac. However, the 1/29th had sufficient time to alter its position and was soon setting about the right flank of the attacking French columns, which were forced to halt in the face of the 29th's musketry. Ferguson's other two battalions re-formed, and together the three British units forced Brennier's men back. The French appeared to have little stomach for the fight and were soon fleeing in a disorderly fashion, leaving behind them their commander, Brennier, who was wounded and taken prisoner. The three guns retaken briefly by the French were once again in Wellesley's hands, along with a further three guns that had accompanied Brennier.

It was barely noon, and every single French infantry battalion present at Vimeiro had been thrown into the attack, only to be seen off by the devastating effects of British musketry. Of the British troops, 720 had been either killed or wounded, whereas the French had suffered three times that number of casualties, including 450 killed. Now was the time to advance and pursue the defeated French, who had been all but routed that morning. The road to Lisbon now lay open, a fact that should have spelled the end for Junot and his army, but Burrard decided that any further action was unnecessary, and the opportunity went begging, despite the impassioned pleas of a very frustrated and angry Wellesley. Junot's force, therefore, was allowed to retreat to Lisbon without any hindrance.

Burrard himself did not enjoy the position of commander in chief for long, for the very next day an even older general, Sir Hew Dalrymple, superseded him. Dalrymple also decided that any further action was unnecessary, and together the two elderly generals, devoid of any real military experience and totally failing to grasp the advantageous military situation facing them, agreed to the notorious Convention of Cintra, whereby it was agreed that Junot and his army, along with their arms and accumulated plunder, would be given free passage back to France unmolested. Following this, Burrard, Dalrymple, and Wellesley were recalled to Britain to explain before a Court of Enquiry how they had allowed the French army to escape. Wellesley himself had not even been privy to the treaty but signed it nevertheless, when ordered to do so by Dalrymple.

With all three men having returned home, command of the 30,000 British troops in Portugal devolved upon the 47-year-old Moore, who was about to lead the army through one of the most tragic episodes in the Peninsular War, an episode that was ultimately to cost him his life—the retreat to Corunna.

Ian Fletcher

See also Castlereagh, Robert Stewart, Viscount; Cintra, Convention of; Corunna, Retreat to; Fuentes de Oñoro, Battle of; Hill, Sir Rowland; Junot, Jean Andoche; Moore, Sir John; Peninsular War; Roliça, Battle of; Shrapnel; Wellington, Arthur Wellesley, First Duke of

References and further reading
Chartrand, René. 2001. *Vimeiro 1808: Wellesley's First Victory in the Peninsula*. Oxford: Osprey.
Esdaile, Charles J. 2003. *The Peninsular War: A New History*. London: Palgrave Macmillan.
Gates, David. 2001. *The Spanish Ulcer: A History of the Peninsular War*. New York: Da Capo.
Glover, Michael. 2001. *The Peninsular War, 1807–1814: A Concise Military History*. London: Penguin.
Napier, W. F. P. 1992. *A History of the War in the Peninsula*. 6 vols. London: Constable. (Orig. pub. 1828.)
Oman, Sir Charles. 2005. *A History of the Peninsular War*. 7 vols. London: Greenhill. (Orig. pub. 1902–1930.)
Paget, Julian. 1992. *Wellington's Peninsular War: Battles and Battlefields*. London: Cooper.
Uffindell, Andrew. 2003. *The National Army Museum Book of Wellington's Armies: Britain's Triumphant Campaigns in the Peninsula and at Waterloo, 1808–1815*. London: Sedgwick and Jackson.
Weller, Jac. 1992. *Wellington in the Peninsula*. London: Greenhill.

Vinkovo, Battle of (18 October 1812)

An engagement between Napoleon's cavalry screen outside Moscow, led by Marshal Joachim Murat, and Russian forces under Field Marshal Mikhail Kutuzov, which caused Napoleon to finalize his decision to leave Moscow. It is known in the Russian historiography as the Battle of Tarutino.

When Napoleon took Moscow, he left several major formations outside the city to provide a defensive screen. Among these formations was Murat's cavalry, which, along with Prince Józef Poniatowski's V Corps, was stationed south of Moscow, near the towns of Vinkovo and Voronovo. Troops of these formations had a most unusual situation. On the one hand, their living conditions were extraordinarily poor. They were 50 miles from Moscow and therefore unable to go into the city for needed supplies and food. They had very little in the way of permanent shelter, with their campsites completely exposed to the bitter Russian wind.

On the other hand, the French and Russian troops were posted quite close to each other. Both sides were convinced that peace would soon be declared, and some even thought that the two armies would march together to India to drive the British out of that key economic center. As a result, security was lax, and the two sides would often spend their days fraternizing and even cooperating in the quest for food. Even Murat, who was also the King of Naples and Napoleon's brother-in-law, would parade before the Cossacks, who, out of great respect, would decline to attempt to kill him.

Kutuzov might have been content to continue this way indefinitely, but he was under great pressure from Tsar Alexander to attack the French.

General Horace Sébastiani, commander of the French II Cavalry Corps, received the brunt of the action. General Vasili Denisov's cavalry swept into Sébastiani's camp on the French right flank while most of the French were still asleep. The cavalry was completely surprised and routed, with many killed or captured. The Russians had gained a tremendous advantage, but rather than pursue the fleeing French, the Cossacks instead began to loot the camp.

Russian general Karl Fedorovich Baggovut attacked Murat's left flank and center. Murat was surrounded and in danger of being completely overrun or even captured. But the Russians did not press their advantage, and the French soon rallied. Poniatowski held his position and soon the French were pushing back. Russian resistance collapsed, needed reinforcements failed to materialize, and the French seized the opportunity to turn a likely defeat into a significant victory.

On the Russian side, recriminations soon followed, and the quarreling between the generals intensified. While Kutuzov claimed a great victory, he was only fooling himself. Russian losses were estimated at over 1,000, including Baggovut, with French losses a quarter of that total.

The battle was technically a Russian victory, but the loss of a Russian general was not insubstantial, and the action was all Napoleon needed to cause him to finalize his plans to leave Moscow. It was now clear that, niceties aside, there would be no peace. Some units departed that very night, and the main body of the French army left the next day.

J. David Markham

See also Alexander I, Tsar; Cossacks; Kutuzov, Mikhail Golenischev-, Prince; Moscow, Occupation of; Murat, Joachim; Poniatowski, Józef Anton, Prince; Russian Campaign
References and further reading
Chandler, David G. 1995. *The Campaigns of Napoleon.* London: Weidenfeld and Nicolson.
Zamoyski, Adam. 2004. *1812: Napoleon's Fatal March on Moscow.* London: HarperCollins.

Vitebsk, Battle of (28 July 1812)

A minor battle in Russia between Napoleon's forces and the rear guard of General Mikhail Barclay de Tolly's army. Napoleon's primary goal in the campaign of 1812 was to force a major battle between his Grande Armée and either of the two Russian armies of the west, commanded by generals Barclay de Tolly and Prince Peter Bagration, respectively. He had reason to believe that he had trapped Barclay's army at Vilna, but delays in his attack allowed the Russians to retreat in good order. Napoleon waited eighteen days before moving forward.

After some misdirected activity, Napoleon discovered that Barclay de Tolly was in Vitebsk with the 1st Army of the West (or 1st Western Army). Napoleon had successfully kept his army between the two Russian counterparts and it therefore seemed that he was in a position to swing his forces to Vitebsk and crush Barclay before Bagration could arrive in support.

Napoleon's desire to deal a devastating blow to the Russians led him to delay his attack by one day in order to bring up reinforcements. As was the case with previous and future delays in this campaign, that decision proved disastrous. Barclay had expected to confront the French, but this decision was based on his belief that Bagration would arrive in time to support him by attacking Napoleon's rear. Marshal Louis Davout had blocked this move, however, and when Barclay realized that, he decided to withdraw. He moved in the direction of Smolensk, where he hoped to join forces with Bagration's army.

After minor skirmishes, Napoleon entered Vitebsk on 28 July, only to discover that the Russians were already gone. His delay had cost him a major opportunity to achieve his goals. Even though he now controlled significant territory and had inflicted not insignificant casualties on the Russian armies, he had done nothing to force Tsar Alexander to sue for peace.

There was now a good argument for calling a halt to the operations. The French army was exhausted from the long march in extremely hot weather. The summer heat was having a devastating effect on the Grande Armée, with many of its troops ill. The weather had also been especially hard on the horses, and a disturbingly large number of them had been lost.

Napoleon's staff argued the point as best they could. Pierre Bruno, Count Daru tried to convince Napoleon to consolidate his victory, summon reinforcements, and bring the campaign to a halt. If Alexander refused to agree to peace terms, a refreshed and reinforced army could always take up the campaign in the spring. Meanwhile, Poland could be organized: the country put on a war footing, the government and military organized to operate in closer support of the Grande Armée, and Napoleon's support there solidified. In the end, however, Napoleon became convinced that he needed either to withdraw altogether or press the campaign forward. Withdrawal was considered but ultimately ruled out, so on 13 August he left Vitebsk along the road to Smolensk.

J. David Markham

See also Alexander I, Tsar; Bagration, Peter Ivanovich, Prince; Barclay de Tolly, Mikhail Andreas; Davout, Louis Nicolas; Ostrovno, Battle of; Poland; Russian Campaign; Smolensk, Battle of
References and further reading
Austin, Paul Britten. 1993. *1812: The March on Moscow.* London: Greenhill.
Chandler, David G. 1995. *The Campaigns of Napoleon.* London: Weidenfeld and Nicolson.
Zamoyski, Adam. 2004. *1812: Napoleon's Fatal March on Moscow.* London: HarperCollins.

Vitoria, Battle of (21 June 1813)

The year of 1812 had positively glowed with success for the Anglo-Portuguese forces in the Iberian Peninsula, but it ended inauspiciously, with the failure to take the castle of Burgos, besieged by the Marquis of (later the Duke of) Wellington in September and October. The Allied siege operations provided one of the more unhappy sides to Wellington's campaign in the Peninsula, but at least the army was successful on three occasions (at Ciudad Rodrigo, Badajoz, and Salamanca), albeit after some tremendous bludgeoning, which cost the lives of thousands of British soldiers. At Burgos, however, the operation was flawed from the start, and a combination of bad weather, inadequate siege train, and plain mismanagement caused a despondent Wellington to abandon the dreary place on 19 October.

The outcome of the whole sad episode was a retreat that, to those who survived it, bore too many shades of the retreat to Corunna almost four years earlier. Once again the discipline of the army broke down, drunkenness was rife, and hundreds of Wellington's men were left floundering in the mud to die or be taken prisoner by the French. It was little consolation to Wellington that while his army limped back to Portugal, Napoleon too was about to see his own army disintegrate in the Russian snows. The retreat to Portugal finally ended in late November when the Allied army concentrated on the border, close to Ciudad Rodrigo. The year had thus ended in bitter disappointment for Wellington, but nothing could alter the fact that taken as a whole 1812 had seen the army achieve some of its greatest successes, and once it had recovered it was to embark on the road to even greater success.

During the winter of 1812–1813, Wellington contemplated his strategy for the forthcoming campaign. His army received reinforcements, which brought it up to a strength of around 80,000 men, of whom 52,000 were British. The French believed that any Allied thrust would have to be made through central Spain, an assumption Wellington fostered by sending Lieutenant General Sir Rowland Hill, with 30,000 men and six brigades of cavalry, in the direction of Salamanca. Wellington, in fact, accompanied Hill as far as Salamanca to help deceive the French further. The main Allied advance, however, was to be made to the north, by the left wing of the army, some 66,000-strong, under Lieutenant General Sir Thomas Graham, who would cross the river Douro and march through northern Portugal and the Tras-o-Montes before swinging down behind the French defensive lines. The advance would be aimed at Burgos before moving on to the Pyrenees and finally into southern France. If all went well, Wellington would be able to shift his supply bases from Lisbon to the northern coast of Spain and in so doing, avoid overextending his lines of communication.

The advance began on 22 May 1813. Wellington left Hill's force on the twenty-eighth and joined Graham the following day. By 3 June his entire force, numbering around 80,000 men, was on the northern side of the river Douro, much to the surprise of the French, who began to hurry north to meet them. Such was the speed of Wellington's advance that the French were forced to abandon Burgos, this time without any resistance, and the place was blown up by the departing garrison on the thirteenth. Wellington passed the town and on the nineteenth was just a short distance to the east of Vitoria, which lay astride the great road to France.

The battlefield of Vitoria lay along the floor of the valley of the river Zadorra, some 6 miles wide and 10 miles in

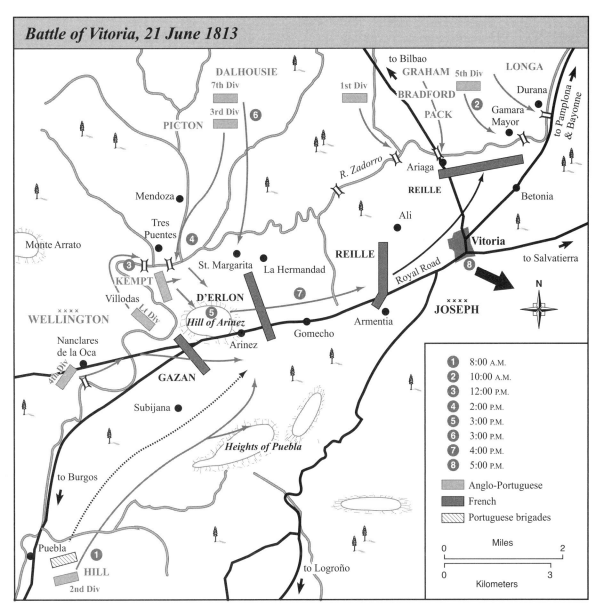

Battle of Vitoria, 21 June 1813

Adapted from Fremont-Barnes 2002A, 66.

length. The eastern end of this valley was open and led to Vitoria itself, while the other three sides of the valley consisted of mountains, although those to the west were heights rather than mountains. The Zadorra itself wound its way from the southwest corner of the valley to the north, where it ran along the foot of the mountains overlooking the northern side of the valley. The river was impassable to artillery but was crossed by four bridges to the west of the valley and four more to the north.

Wellington devised an elaborate plan of attack that involved dividing his army into four columns. On the right, Hill, with 20,000 men consisting of the 2nd Division and Major General Pablo Morillo's Spaniards, was to gain the heights of Puebla on the south of the valley and force the

Puebla pass. The two center columns were both under Wellington's personal command. The right center column consisted of the Light and 4th Divisions, together with four brigades of cavalry, who were to advance through the village of Nanclares. The left center column consisted of the 3rd and 7th Divisions, which were to advance through the valley of the Bayas at the northwest corner of the battlefield and attack the northern flank and rear of the French position. The fourth column, under Graham, consisted of the 1st and 5th Divisions, General Francisco Longa's Spaniards, and two Portuguese brigades. Graham was to march around the mountains to the north and by entering the valley at its northeastern corner, was to sever the main road to Bayonne.

King Joseph Bonaparte's French army numbered 66,000 men with 138 guns, but although another French force under General Bertrand, baron Clausel was hurrying up from Pamplona, it did not arrive in time, and Joseph had to fight the battle with about 14,000 fewer men than Wellington.

On the morning of 21 June Wellington peered through his telescope and saw Joseph, Marshal Jean-Baptiste Jourdan, and General Honoré Théophile, comte Gazan and their staffs gathered together on top of the hill of Arinez, a round eminence that dominated the center of the French line. It was a moist, misty morning, and through the drizzle he saw, away to his right, Hill's troops as they made their way through the Heights of Puebla. It was here that the battle opened at about 8:30 A.M., when Hill's troops drove the French from their positions and took the heights.

Two hours later, away to the northeast, the crisp crackle of musketry signaled Graham's emergence from the mountains, as his men swept down over the road to Bayonne, thus cutting off the main French escape route. Thereafter, Graham's troops probed warily westward and met with stiff resistance, particularly at the village of Gamara Mayor. Moreover, Wellington's instructions bade him proceed with caution, orders that Graham obeyed faithfully. Although his column engaged the French in several hours of bloody fighting on the north bank of the Zadorra, it was not until the collapse of the French army late in the day that he unleashed the full power of his force upon the French.

There was little fighting on the west of the battlefield until about noon, when, acting upon information from a Spanish peasant, Wellington ordered Major General James Kempt's brigade of the Light Division to take the undefended bridge over the Zadorra at Tres Puentes. This was duly accomplished and brought Kempt to a position just below the hill of Arinez, and while the rest of the Light Division crossed the bridge of Villodas, Lieutenant General Sir Thomas Picton's "Fighting" 3rd Division stormed across the bridge of Mendoza on their right. Picton was faced by two French divisions supported by artillery, but these guns were taken in flank by Kempt's riflemen and were forced to retire having fired just a few salvoes. Picton's men rushed on, and, supported by the Light Division and by Cole's 4th Division, which had also crossed at Villodas, the 3rd Division rolled over the French troops on this flank like a juggernaut. A brigade of the 7th Division (Lieutenant General George Ramsay, ninth Earl of Dalhousie) joined them in their attack, and together they drove the French from the hill of Arinez. Soon afterward, what was once Joseph's vantage point was being used by Wellington to direct the battle.

It was just after 3:00 P.M., and the 3rd, 7th, and Light Divisions were fighting hard to force the French from the

village of Margarita. This small village marked the right flank of the first French line, and after heavy fighting the defenders were thrust from it in the face of overwhelming pressure from Picton's division. To the south of the hill of Arinez, Gazan's divisions were still holding firm and, supported by French artillery, were more than holding their own against Lieutenant General Sir Lowry Cole's 4th Division. With Margarita gone, however, the right flank of the French was left unprotected.

It was a critical time for Joseph's army. On its right, Jean-Baptiste Drouet, comte d'Erlon's division was being steadily pushed back by Picton, Dalhousie, and Kempt, whose divisions seemed irresistible. Away to his left, Joseph saw Hill's corps streaming from the heights of Puebla, while behind him Graham's corps barred the road home. Only Gazan's divisions held firm, but when Cole's 4th Division struck at about 5:00 P.M., the backbone of the French army snapped. Wellington thrust the 4th Division into the gap between d'Erlon and Gazan, as a sort of wedge, and as the British troops on the French right began to push d'Erlon back, Gazan suddenly realized he was in danger of being cut off. At this point Joseph finally realized that he was left with little choice but to give the order for a general retreat.

The resulting disintegration of the French army was as sudden as it was spectacular. The collapse was astonishing, as every man, from Joseph downward, looked to his own safety. All arms and ammunition, equipment, and packs were thrown away by the French in an effort to hasten their flight. It was a case of every man for himself. Only General Honoré, comte Reille's corps, which had been engaged with Graham's forces, managed to maintain some sort of order, but even Reille's men could not avoid being swept along with the tide of fugitives streaming back toward Vitoria. With the collapse of all resistance, Graham swept down upon what units remained in front of him, though there was little more to be done but round up prisoners, who were taken in their hundreds. The French abandoned the whole of their baggage train, as well as 415 caissons, 151 of their 153 guns, and 100 wagons. Two thousand prisoners were taken.

More incredible, however, was the fantastic amount of treasure abandoned by Joseph as he fled. The accumulated plunder he had acquired in Spain was abandoned to the eager clutches of the Allied soldiers, who could not believe what they found. Never before nor since in the history of warfare has such an immense amount of booty been captured by an opposing force. Ironically, this treasure probably saved what was left of Joseph's army, for while Wellington's men stopped to fill their pockets with gold, silver, jewels, and valuable coins, the French were making good their escape toward Pamplona. Such was Wellington's disgust at the behavior of his men afterward that he was prompted to write to the Earl Bathurst, the secretary of state for war and the colonies. It was the letter in which he used the famous expression "scum of the earth" to describe his men.

The Allies suffered 5,100 casualties during the battle, while the French losses were put at around 8,000. The destruction of Joseph's army is hardly reflected in this figure, however, and the repercussions of the defeat were far reaching. News of Wellington's victory galvanized the Allies in northern Europe—still smarting after defeats at Lützen and Bautzen—into renewed action and even helped induce Austria to enter the war on the side of the Allies. In Britain, meanwhile, there were wild celebrations the length of the country, while Wellington himself was created field marshal. In Spain, Napoleon's grip on the country was severely loosened, and there was now little but a few French-held fortresses between Wellington's triumphant army and France.

Ian Fletcher

See also Badajoz, Third Siege of; Bautzen, Battle of; Bonaparte, Joseph; Burgos, Siege of; Ciudad Rodrigo, Second Siege of; Corunna, Retreat to; Drouet, Jean-Baptiste, comte d'Erlon; Graham, Sir Thomas; Hill, Sir Rowland; Jourdan, Jean-Baptiste; Lützen, Battle of; Peninsular War; Picton, Sir Thomas; Reille, Honoré Charles Michel Joseph, comte; Salamanca, Battle of; Wellington, Arthur Wellesley, First Duke of

References and further reading
Esdaile, Charles J. 2003. *The Peninsular War: A New History.* London: Palgrave Macmillan.
Fletcher, Ian. 1998. *Vittoria 1813: Wellington Sweeps the French from Spain.* Oxford: Osprey.
Gates, David. 2001. *The Spanish Ulcer: A History of the Peninsular War.* New York: Da Capo.
Glover, Michael. 1996. *Wellington's Peninsular Victories: The Battles of Busaco, Salamanca, Vitoria and the Nivelle.* London: Weidenfeld and Nicolson.
———. 2001. *The Peninsular War, 1807–1814: A Concise Military History.* London: Penguin.
Napier, W. F. P. 1992. *A History of the War in the Peninsula.* 6 vols. London: Constable. (Orig. pub. 1828.)
Oman, Charles. 2005. *A History of the Peninsular War.* 7 vols. London: Greenhill. (Orig. pub. 1902–1930.)
Paget, Julian. 1992. *Wellington's Peninsular War: Battles and Battlefields.* London: Cooper.
Uffindell, Andrew. 2003. *The National Army Museum Book of Wellington's Armies: Britain's Triumphant Campaigns in the Peninsula and at Waterloo, 1808–1815.* London: Sedgwick and Jackson.
Weller, Jac. 1992. *Wellington in the Peninsula.* London: Greenhill.

Vosges, Battle of the (13 July 1794)

The Battle of the Vosges was actually a series of battles that opened the summer and autumn campaign on the Rhine in 1794. The actions forced the Prussian and Austrian armies back to the Rhine and helped convince the Prussian government to make peace with Revolutionary France by the Treaty of Basle.

During the winter of 1793–1794, the French were able to increase the size of the Army of the Rhine, thanks to the mobilization of the nation's manpower under the war minister Lazare Carnot. Many of the troops were untrained, and weapons were in short supply. In February 1794, General Claude Ignace François Michaud assumed command of the Army of the Rhine. Michaud was a solid, if not spectacular, soldier. He received additional reinforcements to boost his army to a paper strength of over 115,000 men. Michaud's key subordinates were General Laurent Gouvion St. Cyr, commanding the left, or northern, flank, and General Louis Desaix, commanding the right, or southern, flank. His opponents were a mixture of Prussian, Austrian, and Saxon troops, with only limited cooperation existing between the different nationalities. The Allies totaled about 70,000 men.

Preliminary skirmishing during the spring showed the outnumbered Prussians and Austrians to be skillful and aggressive. To prevent them from sending reinforcements north to Flanders and the more critical parts of the front, St. Cyr and Desaix convinced Michaud to launch an offensive all along his front. At a conference on 17 June, Desaix persuaded Michaud to make the greater effort on the right. On 2 July the offensive began. At first Desaix made good progress. He reached the Rhine and tried to drive up the left bank, to turn the Allied positions. A counterattack by Prussian cavalry under General Gebhard von Blücher defeated the French cavalry, stopped Desaix's advance cold, and forced Desaix to retreat to his original positions. French losses totaled 1,000.

Under orders from the central government in Paris, another offensive was organized, and opened on 13 July. St. Cyr attacked the anchor of the Allied right at Kaiserslautern, attracting Allied reserves. The main effort was in the center, where General Alexandre Camille Taponier's corps drove the Prussians back. Fighting in the mountainous ravines and ridges prevented the disciplined Prussians from using their advantages of tighter formations and steadier fire against the French, who, moreover, made use of the individual initiative of their light infantry and their ability to swarm around the Prussian formations. The Prussians under *Feldmarschalleutnant* Friedrich Prinz zu Hohenlohe-Kirchberg (generally referred to as Hohenlohe) abandoned Tripstadt and retreated out of the mountains to the Rhine, the Austrians having failed to give any support to Hohenlohe during the battle. Desaix's role was limited to a diversionary bombardment of the Allied left.

The day's fighting cost the Allies approximately 3,000 men, nearly all of them Prussians. On 16 July the Prussians fell back to Worms, separating themselves from the Austrians.

Tim J. Watts

See also Basle, Treaties of; Blücher von Wahlstatt, Gebhard Lebrecht Fürst; Carnot, Lazare Nicolas Marguerite; Desaix, Louis-Charles-Antoine, chevalier de Veygoux; Gouvion St. Cyr, Laurent, comte; Rhine Campaigns (1792–1797)

References and further reading
Blanning, T. C. W. 1996. *The French Revolutionary Wars, 1787–1802.* London: Arnold.
Phipps, Ramsay Weston. 1980. *The Armies of the First French Republic and the Rise of the Marshals of Napoleon I.* Vol. 2, *The Armées de la Moselle, du Rhin, de Sambre-et-Meuse, de Rhin-et-Moselle.* London: Greenwood. (Orig. pub. 1926–1939.)
Ross, Steven T. 1973. *Quest for Victory: French Military Strategy, 1792–1799.* New York: Barnes.

W

Wagram, Battle of (5–6 July 1809)

The Battle of Wagram (also known as Deutsch-Wagram) witnessed more than 300,000 men locked in combat in what was at the time the largest engagement ever fought. The French victory at this hard-fought battle did not immediately bring the War of the Fifth Coalition to an end, but with the French having gained the upper hand, a further battle four days later at Znaim resulted in an armistice and eventually the signing of the Peace of Schönbrunn.

With Austria's offensive into Bavaria in April 1809 having failed, the army fell back to a position north of Vienna. Napoleon accepted the surrender of Vienna on 13 May, but, eager to defeat the Austrian army and bring the war to an end, he threw his army over the Danube with little preparation and suffered defeat at the Battle of Aspern-Essling on 21–22 May. Archduke Charles, the Austrian army commander, declined to follow up, hoping for a peaceful settlement.

Stung by the defeat, Napoleon had no intention of seeking peace and prepared a second, meticulously planned attack over the river. Everything was in place by 4 July, and that evening, as pontoon bridges swung into position, the first French troops stepped onto the north bank. Napoleon could call on 190,000 men, while against him Archduke Charles mustered 138,000. Two corps and the Cavalry Reserve occupied positions close to the river to delay any French advance, while another three corps held positions a few miles back on a low plateau beyond the Russbach stream, at the northern extreme of a vast flat plain, the Marchfeld. Three more corps and the Grenadier Reserve occupied positions farther to the northeast.

The French launch their attack. The first three French corps to cross, under marshals Nicolas Oudinot (II), André Masséna (IV), and Louis Davout (III), opened the battle around 5:00 A.M. on 5 July. Masséna attacked the village of Gross-Enzersdorf, and the two Austrian advanced corps, under *Feldmarschalleutnant* Johann Graf Klenau and *Feldmarschalleutnant* Armand von Nordmann, fell back slowly as the French advance fanned out across the Marchfeld. Masséna, on the left, advanced toward Breitenlee; Oudinot marched for the Russbach near Baumersdorf; Davout, on the right, targeted Markgrafneusiedl. As a gap opened between Masséna and Oudinot, the Army of Italy under Prince Eugène de Beauharnais and Marshal Jean-Baptiste Bernadotte's IX Corps (Saxons) moved forward to fill it. Some skirmishing took place near Raasdorf in midafternoon, but generally the Austrians fell back on their main position.

The first stage of Napoleon's plan was now complete, as his army occupied a great sweeping position extending from Aspern on the left, through Breitenlee toward Aderklaa, before turning along the Russbach toward Markgrafneusiedl. The Austrian front, occupying the outside line of this great arc, extended for nearly 12 miles. Charles now expected Napoleon to occupy these positions for the night and prepare for battle in the morning; however, uncertain of Austrian intentions and strength, the Emperor decided instead on an immediate attack. At about 7:00 P.M., Bernadotte, Eugène, Oudinot, and Davout launched assaults against the villages on the Deutsch-Wagram/Markgrafneusiedl line.

In the center, Baumersdorf, defended by elements of *Feldmarschalleutnant* Prinz Friedrich zu Hohenzollern-Hechingen's II Korps, witnessed a number of vigorous attacks by Oudinot's II Corps. Some French troops entered the village, but others, advancing onto the plateau, were thrown back, forcing the whole group back to Raasdorf. To the left of Baumersdorf, Eugène's Army of Italy crested the plateau and despite some initial panic among *General der Kavallerie* Heinrich Graf Bellegarde's I Corps, the Austrian troops rallied and repulsed the attack, causing the French to open fire on their Saxon allies in the confusion. The attack by Bernadotte's Saxons against Deutsch-Wagram was another confusing affair. In the fading light, Saxon reinforcements, unable to discern friend from foe in the burning village, opened fire on a body of their own men, and the whole force, believing themselves attacked by Austrians

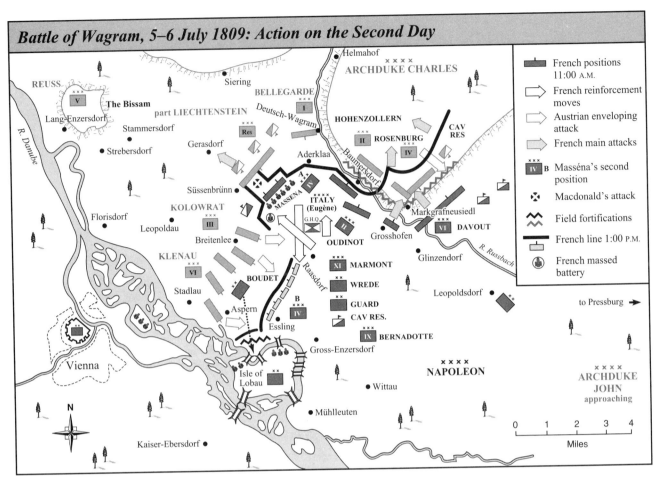

Battle of Wagram, 5–6 July 1809: Action on the Second Day

Adapted from Chandler 1966, 720–721.

on all sides, abandoned the village and fled back to Aderklaa. Davout's attack on the far right of the French line was less eventful and gradually petered out.

Although his attacks were repelled, Napoleon was pleased. It appeared the Austrian army was in strength and prepared to fight. His fear that they would retire northward abated. During the night he moved all but one division of Masséna's corps toward Aderklaa to help strengthen his left. His plan for the following day was to hold the Austrians all along the front while Davout attacked on the right and rolled up the line.

Charles, pleased by the performance of his army and with a significant portion of it still uncommitted, also made plans for the morning. Aware of the weakness of the French left, he planned to advance on his right with Klenau's VI Korps pushing toward Aspern and into the French rear. On Klenau's left *Feldzeugmeister* Johann Karl Graf Kolowrat-Krakowsky's III Korps would advance toward Breitenlee, keeping in line with the Grenadier Reserve advancing through Süssenbrunn. To their left, the Reserve Cavalry would fill the gap toward Aderklaa where they would encounter *General der Kavallerie* Bellegarde's I Korps, wheeling out from behind Deutsch-Wagram and advancing along the Russbach. Hohenzollern's II Korps would act as support to I Korps, while *Feldmarschalleutnant* Franz Fürst von Rosenberg-Orsini's IV Korps and Nordmann's Advance Guard would attack Davout, hopefully with the support of Archduke John, whom Charles urgently ordered to the battlefield. The plan required excellent coordination between the corps, but with the army extended over such a wide area, those on the right, farthest from headquarters, received their orders too late to adhere to the strict timetable.

The Austrian counterattack. Rosenberg's IV Korps, on the Austrian left, moved first, at about 4:00 AM on the morning of 6 July. Pushing back French outposts, the slow-moving Austrian columns faced heavy musketry from three of Davout's infantry divisions, while cavalry from both sides clashed on the open flank toward Ober Siebenbrunn. In his headquarters at Raasdorf, the sound of firing on the far French right convinced Napoleon that Archduke John had finally arrived on the battlefield. Immediately he marched with the Imperial Guard and Marshal Auguste de Marmont's XI Corps—his infantry reserve—and two heavy cavalry divisions to Davout's support.

Although Rosenberg moved forward on time, it was clear to Charles that his right, III and VI Korps, was not yet in motion. Unwilling to proceed with an unsupported attack, he ordered Rosenberg back to his start line. Aware now that Archduke John had not made an appearance, Napoleon ordered the reserve back to Raasdorf.

Back at headquarters, Napoleon was shocked to learn that Bernadotte's Saxon corps had withdrawn from Aderklaa during the night without orders. Delighted by this good fortune, Bellegarde's I Korps occupied the village and the ground between it and Deutsch-Wagram without a fight. Determined to retake the village, Napoleon ordered Masséna, who had moved up during the night, to attack at once. Masséna's men swept forward against the village, with the Saxons moving on their right. The French stormed through the village but fell back when confronted by the firepower of the Austrian second line, although some established themselves in Aderklaa. The Saxons' retreat left the flank of the Army of Italy uncovered, forcing Eugène to realign.

The Austrian offensive slowly gained momentum as the Grenadier Reserve appeared to the right of I Korps at about 8:00 A.M. Attacking Aderklaa, the grenadiers captured the village, although it changed hands again before the Austrians finally secured it, extending their line to the village of Süssenbrunn. Only now, at about 9:00 A.M., did Kolowrat's III Korps come into view to the right of the Grenadier Reserve. Beyond them a cloud of rising dust announced the arrival of more Austrian troops, Klenau's VI Korps—his path opposed only by General Jean Boudet's single division of Masséna's corps. Klenau's attack on Boudet, close to Aspern, drove the outnumbered French division back and left the Austrian commander an open route into the French rear. However, his orders were clear: the whole Austrian line was to advance in concert, and until III Korps moved forward, he must wait.

Napoleon redeploys the army. From his central position at Raasdorf, Napoleon observed the Austrian attack developing and, taking advantage of his shorter inner lines of communication, began to issue orders to defend his open left flank and launch the main attack. By about 10:00 A.M. these crucial movements began. Davout was to attack the Austrian left at Markgrafneusiedl, while Oudinot continued to occupy the attention of the Austrians along the plateau beyond the Russbach. To block any further Austrian advance into the rear, Napoleon ordered Masséna, reforming outside Aderklaa, to march back toward Aspern. As this move required Masséna to march across the front of the now-advancing Grenadier Reserve and III Korps, Napoleon ordered Marshal Jean-Baptiste Bessières, his cavalry commander, to attack the Austrian line. The attack was not well coordinated, but it succeeded in halting the Austrian advance.

As the cavalry assault developed, a grand artillery battery of 112 guns formed to cover the area between Aderklaa and Breitenlee. With the cavalry withdrawn, the guns opened fire with such a weight of firepower that Kolowrat had no option but to pull his men back out of canister range. Under such a combined onslaught, the Austrians were unable to oppose Masséna's redeployment, and by about midday, with cavalry support, he engaged Klenau, who was still waiting for the opportunity to advance. Behind the grand battery, Napoleon ordered Marshal Jacques Etienne Macdonald to prepare three divisions of the Army of Italy for an advance.

Storming the plateau. On the French right, after an artillery bombardment, Davout launched his attack. Opposed to him, Rosenberg's corps and the advance guard under Nordmann put up a determined resistance against the unrelenting French attacks. Slowly Davout's men gained a foothold on the plateau behind Markgrafneusiedl. Charles arrived with reinforcements, and a vast cavalry battle developed northeast of the village. The advantage swung back and forth until the Austrian cavalry eventually fell back on their infantry.

Napoleon closely observed Davout's progress and began to issue orders for a general advance. Masséna was to attack Klenau vigorously, Oudinot's II Corps was to storm the plateau, and Macdonald was to lead the Army of Italy, supported by cavalry and artillery, against III Korps and the Grenadier Reserve. Macdonald's divisions formed in a massive square formation and edged slowly toward the Austrian line, from which they received devastating close-range musketry. However, the success of Davout and Masséna prevented any Austrian exploitation of the situation, as Napoleon committed all his reserves, except two regiments of the Old Guard, to relieve the pressure on Macdonald.

At about 2:00 P.M. Charles received the deflating news that John's long overdue appearance was to be delayed until 5:00 P.M. His men had fought well, but now Rosenberg was in danger of being outflanked by Davout's cavalry, Oudinot was slowly pushing Hohenzollern back, Bellegarde's exhausted men were under attack by fresh French reserves, and Klenau was falling back before Masséna. At about 2:30 P.M., Charles issued orders to commence a phased withdrawal. Retaining a steady discipline, the Austrian formations deflected all French attempts to disrupt this movement. By nightfall contact had been broken, and the battle was over.

Casualties were heavy on both sides. Figures vary, but 23,750 Austrians killed and wounded, 10,000 missing, and 7,500 prisoners, along with the loss of 10 standards and 20 guns appears likely. French losses can be taken as about 27,500 killed and wounded, with 10,000 allowed for those missing or taken prisoner, along with the loss of 12 eagles or standards and 21 guns.

Ian Castle

See also Aspern-Essling, Battle of; Bellegarde, Heinrich Graf; Bernadotte, Jean-Baptiste-Jules; Bessières, Jean-Baptiste; Charles, Archduke of Austria, Duke of Teschen; Davout, Louis Nicolas; Beauharnais, Eugène Rose de; Fifth Coalition, War of the; Imperial Guard (French); John, Archduke; Macdonald, Jacques Etienne Joseph Alexandre; Marmont, Auguste Frédéric Louis Viesse de; Masséna, André; Oudinot, Nicolas Charles; Saxon Army; Schönbrunn, Treaty of; Standards, Flags, and Eagles; Znaim, Battle of

References and further reading

Castle, Ian. 1994. *Aspern and Wagram 1809*. London: Osprey.

Epstein, Robert M. 1994. *Napoleon's Last Victory and the Emergence of Modern War*. University Press of Kansas.

Gill, John H. 1992. *With Eagles to Glory: Napoleon and his German Allies in the 1809 Campaign*. London: Greenhill.

Hourtoulle, F. G. 2002. *Wagram: At the Heyday of the Empire*. Paris: Histoire and Collections.

Müller, W. 1986. *Relation of the Operations and Battles of the Austrian and French Armies in the Year 1809*. Cambridge: Trotman. (Orig. pub. 1810.)

Petre, F. Loraine. 1991. *Napoleon and the Archduke Charles: A History of the Franco-Austrian Campaign in the Valley of the Danube in 1809*. London: Greenhill. (Orig. pub. 1909.)

Rothenberg, Gunther E. 1982. *Napoleon's Great Adversaries: The Archduke Charles and the Austrian Army, 1792–1814*. London: Batsford.

———. 2004. *The Emperor's Last Victory: Napoleon and the Battle of Wagram*. London: Weidenfeld and Nicolson.

Tarbox, Charles, and Scott Bowden. 1990. *Armies on the Danube: Napoleon's Austrian Campaign of 1809*. New York: Paragon.

Tranie, J., and J. C. Carmigniani. 1979. *Napoléon et L'Autriche: La Campagne de 1809*. Paris: Copernic.

Wagram Campaign

See Fifth Coalition, War of the

Walcheren, Expedition to (July–August 1809)

In 1808 and 1809, French forces were being drained by operations conducted in the Iberian Peninsula. Even though the British had been forced to withdraw a small army from the Peninsula, its retreat and stand at Corunna in January 1809 had bloodied the French under Marshal Nicolas Soult. Austria viewed this campaign and the French necessity to maintain a large army in Spain as an opportunity for action. Austrian forces attacked the French in southern Germany but soon found themselves on the defensive. The British assured the Austrians that they would conduct diversionary operations in order to distract the French and divide their forces. The largest of these operations involved an invasion of a Dutch island during the summer of 1809.

The British selected Walcheren as its target due to the island's location in the Scheldt estuary. Several French vessels were either located or being constructed in the area. A British attack in the area could be utilized to destroy these warships and offer some relief to the Austrians. However, news of the Austrian defeat at the Battle of Wagram arrived prior to the launching of the Walcheren expedition. British officials realized the battle probably spelled total defeat for the Austrian army, but they nevertheless opted to continue with the expedition to Holland. John Pitt, second Earl of Chatham led the 45,000-man army being conveyed and escorted by 618 transports and warships. British forces began landing on Walcheren on 30 July, and seized Flushing, the largest town on the island, within two weeks. At this point, the British campaign began to flounder, though some have speculated that they could have seized Antwerp.

The British army stagnated on the island, suffering logistical problems and "Walcheren fever," another name for the malaria carried by the many mosquitoes living in the low-lying areas of recently reclaimed land. Meanwhile, French reinforcements arrived at Antwerp, thwarting any future British plans to capture that important port town. The majority of Chatham's force reembarked aboard their vessels at the end of September. While only approximately 100 men had died in combat, a staggering 4,000 had succumbed to malaria and other diseases. A small garrison left on Walcheren was evacuated back to Britain by the end of the year.

Debate raged in the government and the press over who was to blame for the failed expedition. In September, the cabinet dissolved, and Viscount Castlereagh (secretary of state for war and the colonies) and George Canning (foreign secretary) resigned their respective positions. The two men later fought a scandalous duel over the affair. Parliament convened a formal inquiry to examine the causes of the failure of the expedition. The Medical Board, targeted for not anticipating the health problems on the island, in turn blamed the medical crisis on inadequate and inefficient supply. Chatham, another target for criticism, noted that his force had been too decimated by disease and too small to undertake sustained operations on the Dutch mainland. In the end, the expedition needlessly cost Britain 4,000 men. In return, British forces managed to burn or capture several French vessels—a minor success—though they did force France to increase its garrison troops along the North Sea.

Terry M. Mays

See also Canning, George; Castlereagh, Robert Stewart, Viscount; Fifth Coalition, War of the; Medical Services; Peninsular War; Sickness and Disease; Wagram, Battle of
References and further reading
Bond, Gordon C. 1979. *The Grand Expedition: The British Invasion of Holland in 1809.* Athens: University of Georgia Press.
Fortescue, Sir John. 2004. *History of the British Army.* 13 vols. Uckfield, UK: Naval and Military Press.

War Finance (French)

The French Revolution began partly because of a colossal failure of the French monarch's system of war finance. Louis XVI's immense expenditures on the Seven Years' War (1756–1763) and on French intervention in the American Revolutionary War between 1778 and 1783 had created crushing postwar debts that his government could not repay. The king's ministers proposed a series of fiscal reforms throughout the 1780s, but all failed. By 1788 France was on the brink of financial collapse, and the king was forced to attempt a broader financial solution by involving an assembly—first an assembly of nobles, then the Estates-General—directly in governmental decision making on taxation and debt maintenance. When deputies assembled, however, many wanted political concessions and guarantees before addressing the king's war debts.

The formation of the National Assembly and the fall of the Bastille, in June and July 1789, respectively, made military finances truly a national concern. The National Assembly soon created the National Guard and enshrined the principle of citizen-soldiers. During 1790 the National Assembly increasingly took control of military affairs and war finance, weakening the monarch's hold on the army and the state. Following Louis's flight to Varennes in 1791, a series of new laws further centralized the budgetary procedures of war finance under the legislature's control.

As France faced war against Europe's monarchies, the legislature, now known as the Legislative Assembly, had to struggle to meet the costs of war preparations, including clothing, arms, equipment, wages, and food for the troops. Artillery, munitions, fortifications, and ships all had to be maintained. The Assembly issued sweeping calls for volunteers in 1791 and early 1792, bringing more than a hundred thousand new soldiers to the ranks. After war broke out in April 1792, administrators scurried to supply the composite army, formed of a mixture of troops from the old royal army and the new recruits, and the hurried preparations forced the Revolutionary government to rely on a decentralized supply of troops. An Austro-Prussian army invaded France in the summer of 1792, and the Legislative Assembly declared, "*La patrie est en danger!*"

Supplying the 450,000 citizen-soldiers serving in Revolutionary armies in the fall of 1792 tested the Revolutionary government's new system of war finance. In the initial chaos of the Revolution, most French people simply ceased to pay taxes, and the tax mechanisms that provided funds for military finance crumbled. On the other hand, the Assembly gradually ended elites' tax exemptions and established more egalitarian principles of tax distribution. New procedures for tax collection emphasized direct taxation and eliminated most indirect taxes. Through a massive reorganization of local and regional government, taxation became centralized and more efficient. By 1792 the Treasury was delivering funds directly to the various military administrations, when authorized to do so by the War Ministry.

The Revolutionary government also attempted to use monetary policy to meet the needs of war. Church lands and the properties of émigré nobles were seized and sold to raise money for the government. The Assembly created a fluctuating paper currency, known as assignats, to deal with the shortage of cash. Mounting inflation forced currency depreciation, despite attempts to refinance debts and convert government bonds. While the Assembly attempted to nationalize war finance by making the contractors who handled military logistics and finances into public servants, war finance actually remained only partially public. These wartime financiers could make huge profits on war, but they could also incur great losses, and they sought to protect themselves. The Revolutionary reorganization of war supply did not end corruption and waste, then, and the appointment of new administrators through political patronage only worsened the problem.

More troops were needed in the spring of 1793 to face foreign armies and an expanding war, so the new National Convention issued a call for 300,000 more men. Tens of thousands of new soldiers were armed locally and sent to the front, but the increasing taxation and limited conscription led to protests and civil war within France. In a climate of national emergency, the Committee of Public Safety gradually appropriated powers from the War Ministry and began to direct the entire war effort. Lazare Carnot became the key "organizer of victory" during this crisis of war administration. The Revolutionary armies still lacked sufficient troops, so in August 1793 citizen-soldiers began to be recruited by universal conscription, the *levée en masse*. The levée en masse implied the mobilization of the entire society as a nation-in-arms and demanded an amalgamation of the ad hoc components of the Revolutionary armies. A staggering 750,000 citizen-soldiers were now fighting for the nation.

Arming all these men strained the munitions and arms industries. In the summer of 1793, the Committee of

Public Safety had created a series of workshops known as the Manufacture of Paris to mass-produce muskets and bayonets for the nation's troops. Arms were manufactured in the Luxembourg Gardens and also at the Tuileries and the Invalides. In the spring of 1794 the arms industry employed over 3,000 workers, who could produce more than 600 musket barrels a day. The Committee of Public Safety invested massive funds in the Manufacture of Paris and in arms production in the provinces, to make muskets and artillery for the Revolutionary armies. As one historian has argued, this arms industry "was an armory, and simultaneously a vast public works program" (Alder 1997, 262). The arms workshops created jobs for Paris's unemployed, many of whom were given strong work incentives, such as being paid a fixed wage per piece produced. The Law of the Maximum of September 1793 represented an attempt by the Revolutionary government to control prices and wages so as to make war finance more efficient.

The administration of the war under the direction of the Committee of Public Safety emphasized centralization and the professional management of war finance and supply. By September 1794, the Committee of Public Safety had committed the state to paying fixed salaries to soldiers and to assuming all responsibility for providing food, clothing, and supplies to the nation's troops through government agencies. As the war lengthened, the Revolutionary government would have to pay for regularized soldiers' pay and pensions, and for hospitals. Yet centralization brought problems too. The complex bureaucratic organizations underwent constant reform and evolution, resulting in overlapping responsibilities for different administrations and confusion for bureaucrats responsible for war finance and supply. Further, members of the Committee of Public Safety used their political influence and patronage to place their associates in administrative posts, leading to factionalism and a politicization of the bureaucracy.

Nevertheless, the system of war finance created by the Committee of Public Safety successfully organized the French nation for war and contributed significantly to the battlefield victories of the Revolutionary armies. After the Thermidorian reaction of July 1794, the Convention and its successor government, known as the Directory (1795–1799), continued to rely heavily on the bureaucratic organizations created by the Committee of Public Safety. The administrations that financed and supplied the armies had become more stable than other government agencies. The army and its support services increasingly influenced government policies and asserted political power within the state.

As French armies carried the war to their enemies, they began to export the costs of fighting. The citizen-soldiers of the Revolution were motivated by nationalism

and pride in their *patrie*. The loyalty of these soldiers allowed their commanders to release their troops to forage for themselves, since they could trust the men to return to the ranks. What was known as living off the land—foraging and requisitioning supplies locally rather than relying on fixed depots and baggage trains—transformed logistics, allowing French armies to make rapid marches without the extensive regular supply services on which monarchical armies had to rely.

Within France, the gradual militarization of society was confirmed by the Jourdan Law of 1798, which formalized conscription. Under Napoleon, the military bureaucracy became even more stable and hierarchical but continued to conduct war finance largely using the system inherited from the Revolutionary period. Napoleon established a national bank and stabilized the currency, but his armies increasingly conducted war finance through contributions, making conquered populations throughout Europe pay for the costs incurred by the Grande Armée.

Brian Sandberg

See also Carnot, Lazare Nicolas Marguerite; Conscription (French); Convention, The; Directory, The; Emigrés; French Army; French Revolution; Levée en Masse; Louis XVI, King; National Guard (French); Public Safety, Committee of; Thermidor Coup

References and further reading
Alder, Ken. 1997. *Engineering the Revolution: Arms and Enlightenment in France, 1763–1815.* Princeton: Princeton University Press.
Bertaud, Jean-Paul. 1988. *The Army of the French Revolution: From Citizen-Soldiers to Instrument of Power.* Trans. R. R. Palmer. Princeton: Princeton University Press.
Blanning, T. C. W. 1996. *The French Revolutionary Wars, 1787–1802.* London: Arnold.
Brown, Howard G. 1995. *War, Revolution, and the Bureaucratic State: Politics, and Army Administration in France, 1791–1799.* Oxford: Clarendon.
Holtman, Robert B. 1967. *The Napoleonic Revolution.* Philadelphia: Lippincott.
Lynn, John A. 1984. *The Bayonets of the Republic: Motivation and Tactics in the Army of Revolutionary France, 1791–1794.* Urbana: University of Illinois Press.
———, ed. 1993. *Feeding Mars: Logistics in Western Warfare from the Middle Ages to the Present.* Boulder, CO: Westview.
Tilly, Charles. 1986. *The Contentious French: Four Centuries of Popular Struggle.* Cambridge, MA: Belknap.

War of 1812 (1812–1815)

The War of 1812 fought between Britain and the United States occurred as a direct result of British attempts to break the Continental System imposed by Napoleon and arguments over the Canadian border. The U.S. government anticipated a swift victory over the numerically inferior British. The initial American attacks on Canada failed, due to inadequacies in the U.S. Army and a lack of aggressiveness on the part of its generals.

Following the abdication of Napoleon in April 1814, the British were able to reinforce their small force in North America with many veterans from the Peninsular War. Despite this, they were unable to achieve a decisive victory. Although Washington was attacked, the Americans were able to keep the British at bay, culminating in a famous, though pointless, victory at the Battle of New Orleans. The war was also fought at sea and on the Great Lakes, and during hostilities many Native Americans allied themselves with the British in order to arrest the westward expansion of the United States.

Many causes led to the steady breakdown in relations between the United States and Britain, which flared into war in June 1812. The principal one was the threat to the trading rights of American shipping imposed by the British interpretation of maritime law and the definition of contraband. Specifically, Britain asserted its right to search for any goods that could benefit Napoleon's war effort in Europe—what the Admiralty in London designated as contraband. If a vessel wished to trade with either France or its allies, it was forced to obtain a license. In practice this policy favored British colonial trading interests.

These instructions were enforced in the Orders in Council that were instituted in November and December 1807. They were a direct response to the Berlin Decrees of 1806, which had sought to restrict trade between the Continent and Britain. Many American seamen had also been pressed into the Royal Navy on the basis that some were in fact deserters from, or were otherwise evading, British service, while the nation remained desperately short of qualified sailors. Innocent Americans found themselves caught up in the Royal Navy's efforts to maintain its numbers, though the U.S. government contributed to the problem by granting instant citizenship to Britons, in the clear knowledge that naturalization was not recognized by the authorities in London.

The causes of the war cannot be solely attributed to Britain, however. There were some in the American government, particularly politicians from the West, who wanted to annex Canada and believed that many within that dominion of the British Crown would support this action. The United States was also concerned about the confederation that the Shawnee leader, Chief Tecumseh, had built up among the Native Americans in the northwest of the country (roughly, modern Ohio, Michigan, and Indiana). This confederation was aimed at stopping the further expansion of the United States. It was generally believed in government circles that in some way the British govern-

ment was supporting Tecumseh, and in fact he did ally himself to the British from the start of the war. Throughout the early months of 1812, tension continued to build, and the situation was not helped by the decision to increase the size of the U.S. Army.

On 18 June 1812 the United States declared war. The American plan centered on a rapid invasion and occupation of Canada and the destruction of British naval forces on the Great Lakes. There was a general belief within the United States that, with their numerically superior forces, these objectives would take little time to attain. The Americans were, however, unprepared to confront the experienced British forces or to react quickly to events, and in general British commanders were much more aggressive in their actions. The first actions of the war constituted a succession of defeats for the United States. In the middle of July, Fort Michilimackinac in Michigan surrendered. On 15 August, Fort Dearborn (present-day Chicago) fell, and General William Hull surrendered his force of 200 troops at Detroit to Major General Sir Isaac Brock. Tecumseh had been active in forcing Hull to surrender, and his forces now began a series of raids on settlements in the Northwest Territory.

American forces were largely able to hold back any further advance, and General William Henry Harrison, governor of Indiana Territory, having been able to rebuild U.S. forces in the area, in November felt strong enough to launch an offensive into the Indian confederation. This attack culminated in the engagement at Mississinewa in present-day Alabama. The U.S. force captured the Indian village there and then was counterattacked. Despite this victory for the Americans, their losses and the cold weather forced them to withdraw to Greenville. The expedition had secured the flank of Harrison's force from further interference by the Delaware tribes.

The principal actions were, however, fought along the U.S.-Canadian border. The Battle of Queenstown Heights, in present-day Ontario, took place on 13 October. Here the British, although outnumbered, made a series of attacks upon the American force composed of regular troops and eventually defeated them. This defeat would probably not have occurred if a large force of volunteers had not refused to take part in the battle. The British victory, however, was tempered by the death of General Brock.

Harrison hoped to open a winter campaign at the start of 1813. His plans, however, were thwarted when an enemy force under Colonel Henry Proctor destroyed a brigade led by General James Winchester at Frenchtown on the river Raisin on 22 January. After the battle, American prisoners were killed by the Indians led by Tecumseh. Harrison was forced onto the defensive, and in April he was besieged at Fort Meigs by Proctor's forces. However, the British were unable to take the fort and abandoned the siege in early May. On 27 April U.S. forces had taken York (present-day Toronto), which they burned, yet they were soon to retreat from this position. On 27 May General Henry Dearborn captured Fort George on the Niagara frontier. Nevertheless, the Americans allowed most of the British garrison, under Brigadier General John Vincent, to escape. During the pursuit, the Americans became a little overconfident, and the British were able to attack their pursuers at Stony Creek.

Vincent was encouraged to attack the Americans, as he had been informed by supporters in the area that the U.S. force was widely scattered. The attack was made early in the morning, and in a short space of time four U.S. regiments were in full retreat. Although some American dragoons were able to stabilize the situation for a short time, in the confusion they were fired on by their own side and were forced to withdraw. American generals John Chandler and William Winder were captured, and the ranking officer, the commander of the dragoons, ordered a withdrawal, in the process destroying a large number of vital provisions. The British action at Stony Creek reversed a difficult strategic position. On 29 May a British force attempted to take Sackets Harbor on Lake Ontario, but the small American force there successfully repulsed the attack.

American commanders now made a further attempt to invade Canada. General James Wilkinson advanced down the St. Lawrence River, hoping to link up with another American force led by General Wade Hampton moving from Lake Champlain, the objective being to take Montreal. At Montreal the British were building up a substantial force. Hampton, however, fooled into believing that the forces confronting him were much larger than they actually were, retreated to Plattsburg. Wilkinson, with 8,000 men, continued his advance alone, but was routed at Chrysler's Farm on 11 November by a much smaller force of 800 British regulars and Native Americans.

The scene of the conflict now passed into the area of the Great Lakes. Here U.S. naval forces had been placed under the command of Commodore Oliver Hazard Perry, who had gained experience fighting in the Tripolitan War against Barbary pirates. Perry had been given control of the squadron based on Lake Erie in early 1813, but his command was still in the process of being constructed at that time. By September, however, Perry felt that he was in a position to attack the British. On the tenth he engaged a British flotilla of six vessels, and despite being outgunned he was able to sink or capture the whole enemy force, with the loss of only his flagship. U.S. control of Lake Erie forced the British to evacuate Detroit within a week, and by the end of the month the British were back in Ontario.

After Perry's victory, Harrison was free to embark on a further invasion of Canada. By now the U.S. Army totaled nearly 6,000 men. Harrison had reached Canadian territory by 27 September. A few days later, on 5 October, Proctor decided to turn to face the pursuing U.S. forces, anchoring his position on the Thames River. Mounted volunteers from Kentucky led the first attack. The initial British volley was unable to check the charge, and, confident in close quarter fighting, the frontiersmen broke their opponents, and many of the British surrendered. Tecumseh and his warriors were able to hold out longer, but they too were defeated. It was rumored that Tecumseh had been killed by the commander of the Kentuckian volunteers, Colonel Richard Johnson. For a small loss, the Americans had completely destroyed the British force. This defeat ensured that the area west of the Thames and the Northwest Territory were securely under U.S. control for the remainder of the war.

During this period, General Andrew Jackson defeated the Creeks at Tallushatchee and Talledega in present-day Alabama. The Americans had been angered by the earlier Creek massacre of the garrison of Fort Mimms on 30 August.

In the last months of the year, the Americans tried to take Montreal with a force under Wilkinson's command. This campaign culminated in the Battle of Chrysler's Farm, along the St. Lawrence River, on 11 November. In poor weather, the American attacks were unsuccessful, and Wilkinson was forced to withdraw. His poor performance in this campaign led to his replacement by General Jacob Brown early in 1814. On 18 December, Fort Niagara fell to the British, and Buffalo was burned on 29 December.

Brown was able to reorganize U.S. forces and in early July 1814 crossed the Niagara River and took Fort Erie. On 5 July Brown's troops were able to inflict a defeat on the British forces led by Major General Phineas Riall at Chippewa, along the U.S.-Canadian border. Riall had moved out from his defensive position and had deployed to face the Americans. In this action, General Winfield Scott's brigade of regular troops wore gray uniforms, which Riall mistook for militia, since the normal uniform color of U.S. regular troops was blue. In the ensuing action, Scott's troops performed well and, in honor of this, gray was thereafter to be worn by West Point graduates. The British government was unnerved by this defeat, and after the abdication of Napoleon, the War Office in London made plans to reinforce British forces in Canada with veterans from Wellington's campaigns in Spain and France.

Once these reinforcements had arrived, the British assumed the offensive. Along the U.S.-Canadian border at Lundy's Lane, on 25 July, General William Drummond led 3,000 troops against the U.S. forces. The British had established themselves on a hill in front of the American force, whose vanguard was commanded by Winfield Scott. He realized that, although his brigade was outnumbered, it had to maintain its position, because otherwise the whole U.S. force could be placed in jeopardy. Scott ordered his troops to attempt to capture the British guns to their front. The assault was carried out toward the end of the day, and much of the action took place in growing darkness. As a result the fighting occurred at close quarters, negating the numerical advantage of the British. In a hard-fought action, losses were equal, at around 1,000 casualties. Both commanders were injured, and Riall was captured.

The battle was tactically a draw, but the Americans conceded the strategic advantage and fell back to Fort Erie. Nevertheless, the engagement had shown that the American regular troops were able to fight on equal terms with their British counterparts. Drummond then placed Fort Erie under siege. The Americans were able to lift the siege on 17 September when a determined sortie from the fort broke through the British cordon. After a short time, however, the Americans abandoned Fort Erie.

The strategic initiative had now firmly passed to the British. On 19 August Major General Robert Ross, commanding a punitive expedition, had landed in Chesapeake Bay, with the objective of advancing on Washington. His force consisted of 5,000 Peninsular veterans, and although they were faced by numerically superior forces, the British were able to advance the 40 miles to Washington. The American command seemed paralyzed at this time, and President James Madison was forced to flee the capital. Nevertheless, a mixed force of marines from the naval yards and 6,000 militia under the command of General William Winder attempted to halt the British advance at Bladensburg, in Maryland. The U.S. position was strong, with their forces uphill of the British. Ross would also have to cross a stream to reach the enemy line. Initially, the British suffered from American artillery fire as they advanced, but Ross had with him a battery of Congreve rockets that, though they inflicted very few casualties, had a strong psychological impact on the enemy, whom the British then charged.

Unable to withstand the assault, the American militia started to break. Winder's force began to disintegrate, and the only serious resistance offered was by the naval gun crews who had dragged their cannon from the naval yard. This resistance was, however, short-lived, and Ross was able to complete his advance on Washington. There he burned many of the new buildings in the capital, including the White House. Still, Ross realized that he could not continue with his offensive, as supplies were low and communications back to the coast were vulnerable to attack. He also hoped to repeat his success by launching a similar assault on Baltimore. He therefore reembarked his forces and

landed near Baltimore on 12 September. His attack on this well-defended city failed, and Ross himself was mortally wounded. At the same time, Fort McHenry was bombarded by a British flotilla. The resistance of the fort inspired the writing of the "Star-Spangled Banner," the future anthem of the United States.

During the period in which the major engagements were fought on the Canadian frontier, there had been a protracted series of naval encounters in which the Royal Navy fought to maintain control of the main trading routes. Despite the numerical superiority of the British fleet on the North American station, it was unable to prevent U.S. ships from roaming the Atlantic and disrupting British trade. In the course of the war, 800 British vessels were taken or sunk, and American ships were even able to enter the shipping lanes of the English Channel. Despite the fact that there were no fleet actions (the Americans having no ships of the line and possessing nothing larger than a squadron of vessels, though including heavy frigates), the American captains won a series of ship-to-ship actions, chiefly involving frigates, sloops, and brigs.

Captain Isaac Hull, in the *Constitution* (44 guns), thoroughly drubbed and captured the *Guerrière* (38) off the coast of Nova Scotia (19 August 1812); the 18-gun sloop USS *Wasp* pounded HMS *Frolic* (18) into a defenseless wreck off Virginia (18 October 1812); conducting a murderous long-range bombardment, Commodore Stephen Decatur's USS *United States* (44) forced the *Macedonian* (38) to strike her colors off Madeira (25 October 1812); and Captain William Bainbridge, in the *Constitution*, left HMS *Java* an utter wreck after a two-hour slogging match off the Brazilian coast (29 December 1812).

Notwithstanding some minor defeats of their own, the Americans continued this series of successes over the next two years: the sloop USS *Hornet* sank HMS *Peacock* off Brazil in less than 15 minutes (24 February 1813), though HMS *Shannon*, after a savage encounter, pummeled and captured the USS *Chesapeake* off the New England coast (1 June 1813). American victories at sea were surpassed on the Great Lakes, where, as described earlier, Perry defeated and captured the entire British squadron on Lake Erie (10 September 1813); while a year later, on Lake Champlain, Lieutenant Thomas Macdonough repeated the feat by accepting the surrender of the British squadron after a closely matched 2-hour struggle (11 September 1814). These U.S. successes, though comparatively minor, nevertheless had a significant effect in maintaining support for the war.

By the middle of 1814 the war appeared to be moving toward a negotiated settlement with plenipotentiaries meeting to discuss terms. In late 1814, however, the British were preparing to make one further effort in the south. Jackson, it will be recalled, had led a successful campaign against the Creeks, who had benefited from the support of British agents. Later, when the Americans learned of a British expedition sent to take New Orleans, Jackson was given command of the city. The British were led by Major General Sir Edward Pakenham, the brother-in-law of the Duke of Wellington. Pakenham landed on 13 December and advanced on New Orleans. Among the low-lying swamps, Jackson had constructed an earthwork, behind which his inferior forces awaited the British assault. Jackson's mixed force included rifle-armed frontiersmen from Tennessee and Kentucky, a group of privateers under the command of a local pirate, Jean Lafitte, and a small contingent of militia and army regulars.

On 8 January 1815, Pakenham realized the U.S. position was quite strong and planned to move troops against both flanks before launching a frontal assault. These flanking forces were however delayed by a combination of difficult terrain, including a swamp on the American left and the Mississippi on the right, and American fire, much of it extremely accurate rifle fire. Pakenham, undaunted, decided to continue with his main assault, which was delivered by a force of 5,300 veterans. Due to the nature of the terrain, the attack had mainly to be made frontally against the earthwork. The advance was stopped short of the defenses by the fierce American fire. The British lost 2,000 men, and Pakenham was killed along with his two immediate subordinates. American losses were extremely light, and the British withdrew from the position.

In fact, the Battle of New Orleans need not have been fought, as the Treaty of Ghent had been signed on 24 December 1814. The main clauses stated that the course of the Canadian border should be finally settled and that other territorial issues should be resolved based on the situation as it stood prior to the outbreak of war (that is, the *status quo ante bellum*). Ironically, only days before the American declaration of war in 1812, the British government had abolished the Orders in Council, which had been a fundamental cause of the war. Anglo-American relations rapidly improved with the cessation of hostilities.

Ralph Baker

See also Berlin Decrees; Bladensburg, Battle of; Chippewa, Battle of; Congreve Rockets; Continental System; Frigates; Lundy's Lane, Battle of; New Orleans, Battle of; Orders in Council; Pakenham, Sir Edward; Peninsular War; Tripolitan War; United States; United States Army; United States Navy; Wellington, Arthur Wellesley, First Duke of

References and further reading
Antal, Sandy. 1997. *A Wampum Denied: Proctor's War of 1812.* East Lansing: Michigan State University Press.
Barbuto, Richard V. 2000. *Niagara, 1814: America Invades Canada.* Lawrence: University Press of Kansas.
Benn, Carl. 2002. *The War of 1812.* Oxford: Osprey.
Borneman, Walter. 2004. *1812: The War That Forged a Nation.* London: HarperCollins.
Coles, Harry L. 1965. *The War of 1812.* Chicago: University of Chicago Press.
Gardiner, Robert. 2003. *The Naval War of 1812.* London: Chatham.
Graves, Donald E. 1993. *The Battle of Lundy's Lane on the Niagara, 1814.* Baltimore, MD: Nautical and Aviation Publishing.
———. 1994. *Red Coats and Grey Jackets: The Battle of Chippewa, 5 July 1814.* Toronto, Dundurn.
Heidler, David, and Jeanne Heidler. 2002. *The War of 1812.* Westport, CT: Greenwood.
Hickey, Donald R. 1989. *The War of 1812: A Forgotten Conflict.* Urbana: University of Illinois Press.
Hitsman, J. Mackay. 1965. *The Incredible War of 1812: A Military History.* Toronto: University of Toronto Press.
Katcher, Philip. 1994. *The American War, 1812–1814.* London: Osprey.
Kochan, James. 2000. *The United States Army, 1812–1815.* Oxford: Osprey.
Mahon, John K. 1972. *The War of 1812.* Gainesville: University of Florida Press.
Malcomson, Robert. 1999. *Lords of the Lake: The Naval War on Lake Ontario, 1812–1814.* Annapolis, MD: Naval Institute Press.
Muller, Charles. 2003. *The Darkest Day: The Washington-Baltimore Campaign during the War of 1812.* Philadelphia: University of Pennsylvania Press.
Paine, Ralph. 2002. *The Fight for a Free Sea.* Honolulu, HI: University Press of the Pacific.
Perkins, Bradford. 1962. *The Causes of the War of 1812: National Honor or National Interest?* New York: Holt, Rinehart and Winston.
———. 1964. *Castlereagh and Adams: England and the United States, 1812–1823.* Berkeley: University of California Press.
Pickles, Tim. 1993. *New Orleans 1815.* London: Osprey.
Reilly, Robin. 2002. *The British at the Gates: The New Orleans Campaign in the War of 1812.* Staplehurst, UK: Spellmount.
Remini, Robert. 2001. *The Battle of New Orleans.* London: Pimlico.
Scaggs, David, and Gerard Altoff. *A Signal Victory: The Lake Erie Campaign, 1812–1813.* Annapolis, MD: Naval Institute Press.
Sonneborn, Liz. 2004. *The War of 1812: A Primary Source History of America's Second War with Britain (Primary Sources in American History).* New York: Rosen Central.
Stagg, J. C. A. 1983. *Mr. Madison's War: Politics, Diplomacy, and Warfare in the Early American Republic, 1783–1830.* Princeton: Princeton University Press, 1983.
Stefof, Rebecca. 2001. *The War of 1812 (North American Historical Atlases).* Salt Lake City: Benchmark.
Wait, Eugene M. 1999. *America and the War of 1812.* Commack, NY: Kroshka.

Warsaw, Duchy of

See Poland

Wartenburg, Battle of

See Germany, Campaign in

Waterloo, Battle of (18 June 1815)

The last and most decisive battle of the Napoleonic Wars, Waterloo led to Napoleon's final downfall and ushered in an era of nearly four decades of peace in Europe. Few battles in history can rival Waterloo in terms of its sheer drama, not to mention its political significance.

On 26 February 1815 Napoleon emerged from exile on the island of Elba, landed in the south of France, and marched on Paris, gathering adherents and winning the loyalty of the army as he went. Two Allied forces in the Low Countries (present-day Belgium) were of immediate concern: an Anglo-Allied army of 90,000 men under the Duke of Wellington, and 120,000 Prussians under Field Marshal Gebhard Fürst Blücher von Wahlstatt (generally shortened to "Blücher"). Napoleon's plan was to strike at each in turn, thus preventing them from joining forces. On 15 June he crossed the river Sambre with his Armée du Nord of 125,000 men and moved through Charleroi on the Brussels road. Two battles were fought on the following day, at Ligny and at Quatre Bras. At the former the Prussians were defeated with serious losses but managed to withdraw north to Wavre.

At Quatre Bras, Wellington, though forced to retire to protect Brussels, had not been crushed, with the result that though the two Allied armies had been kept apart, they were capable of fighting another day. On 17 June Wellington marched north and deployed his tired army on a ridge just south of Mont St. Jean. Having detached Marshal Emmanuel, marquis de Grouchy, with 33,000 men, to keep the Prussians occupied at Wavre, 12 miles east of Wellington's position, Napoleon established his army, now 72,000-strong, on a ridge just south of the Anglo-Allied position.

Wellington had 68,000 men, comprising mainly mixed Anglo-Hanoverian, and some Dutch-Belgian, divisions. Most of these he placed along a 2-mile crescent-shaped ridge, though 18,000 were detached 5 miles west at Tubize, to prevent the French from making a wide sweep around to the west and so threatening his right flank. On Wellington's left stood the villages of Papelotte and La Haye. In his center stood the farm of La Haye Sainte near the crossroads formed by the Ohain and Charleroi-Brussels roads. On his right, and somewhat forward of his main line, lay the château of Hougoumont, which included woods, farm buildings, and a garden. Wellington recognized the tactical importance of Hougoumont and La Haye Sainte, and placed strong garrisons in each. These strongpoints pre-

sented obstacles to a French attack on the Allied right and center, and could offer enfilading fire to any opposing troops that sought to bypass them. Hougoumont was large enough, moreover, to make a sweep around Wellington's right more difficult, though not impossible.

Wellington had chosen the ground beforehand, and the topography naturally favored him, for with many folds and dips the ground offered a degree of protection from the numerically superior French artillery, as did the mud, the result of the previous night's downpour, which prevented round shot from bouncing after first impact. Added to this, much of the field was covered with grain, some of it chest high. Some defenders concealed themselves behind the grain, which in some places also encumbered the advance of the attackers.

As mentioned earlier, in his efforts to keep the Prussians and Anglo-Allies separated, on the morning of 17 June Napoleon had detached Grouchy to pursue the Prussians who, after their defeat at Ligny, had moved east toward Wavre. The Emperor was not aware that, though Grouchy would indeed engage part of the Prussian army on the eighteenth, Blücher, along with several corps, was then on the march to bolster Wellington's defense at Waterloo. Had Napoleon known this, perhaps he would not have opened the battle so late—around 11:30 A.M.—as his plan to keep the Allied armies apart and defeat them in turn would have dictated that he defeat Wellington as early on the eighteenth as possible, before the Prussians could arrive to reinforce him. In the event, Napoleon waited for the ground to harden before opening his frontal attack, in spite of the presence of the heavily fortified farms at La Haye, Hougoumont, and elsewhere. Wellington's dispositions might have suggested a different course to a more cautious attacker: either to withdraw and fight Wellington another day on a field of Napoleon's choosing, or to execute a wide outflanking maneuver so as to rob the duke of the advantages of his strong defensive position on the ridge. Instead, Napoleon sought to pierce the Anglo-Allied center and take control of the slopes of Mont St. Jean, thus dividing Wellington's force in two and wresting control of the vital Brussels road—Wellington's main line of retreat and communication.

Napoleon opened the battle at 11:30 with an attack by General Honoré Charles, comte Reille's corps on Hougoumont, whose capture was vital if the Emperor were to achieve victory, for so long as the Anglo-Allies held it, the French could not confidently threaten Wellington's right or center-right. Situated 500 yards in front of the Allied line, along the crest of the ridge, Hougoumont remained a formidable obstacle to any major French advance. Reille's attack was intended as a diversion to force Wellington to weaken his line in order to reinforce the beleaguered farm complex.

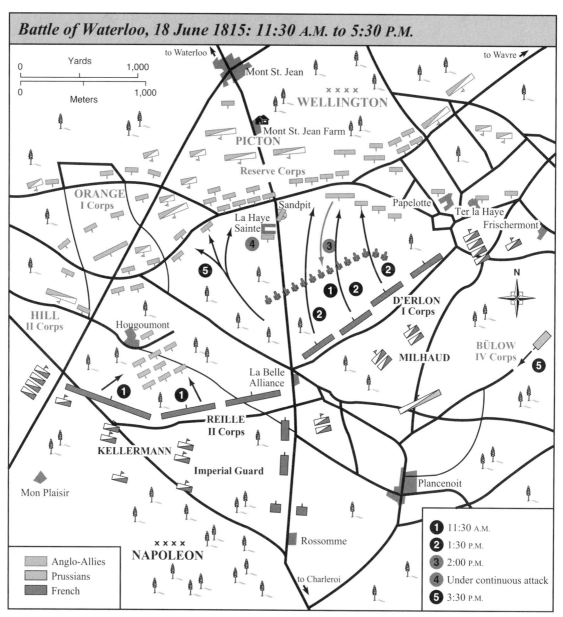

Battle of Waterloo, 18 June 1815: 11:30 A.M. to 5:30 P.M.

Adapted from Fremont-Barnes 2002B, 78.

Ironically, the French attack throughout the day drew in more and more French troops in a fruitless effort to take the stronghold. In the course of the battle, fewer than 3,000 British, Hanoverians, and Nassauers fended off almost 13,000 French troops, making Hougoumont a virtually separate engagement within the greater context of the battle. The French briefly managed to force open the gate of the farmyard, but a handful of men from the 2nd (Coldstream) Foot Guards shut it before the assailants could break in and overwhelm the defenders. In the course of the day, the French lost large numbers of troops outside the walls and in the woods adjacent during the eight hours of fighting that took place there.

By 1:30 Prussian troops under General Friedrich Graf Bülow von Dennewitz began to arrive, at first in small numbers, on Wellington's left flank. Napoleon, unaware of precisely how many Prussians Grouchy had held up at Wavre, decided that no more time could be lost, and ordered General Jean-Baptiste Drouet, comte d'Erlon to advance with his corps of 16,000 men against the Allied center-left. The troops marched 1,300 yards under artillery fire and captured the hamlet of Papelotte, while a detached brigade attacked La Haye Sainte, seizing its garden and orchard from the King's German Legion. The French made no attempt to set fire to the roof with their howitzers or bring up enough artillery to make a breach in the wall; the defenders therefore clung on, though heavily outnumbered. D'Erlon's men had reached as far as the crest of the ridge, driving off a Dutch-Belgian brigade in the process, when Lieutenant General Sir Thomas Picton, commanding the 5th Division, ordered a bayonet attack in the wake of a destructive fusillade. Picton was killed, but his infantry was supported by a strong body of cavalry, including the Union and Household brigades, sent forward by Lieutenant General Henry Paget, second Earl of Uxbridge (best known simply as Lord Uxbridge).

The attacking cavalry pushed aside opposing horsemen protecting d'Erlon's left flank and, surprising the infantry, fell upon it with great ferocity, driving them back down the slope in total confusion and taking 2,000 prisoners. Yet, as had happened on several occasions in Spain, the British failed to maintain proper discipline, and rather than stop, re-form, and return to friendly lines, they galloped on in unrestrained excitement, sabering many of the gunners of the grand battery the French had established at the beginning of the battle, but penetrating perilously deep into enemy lines. Major General Sir William Ponsonby found himself unable to control his men, and the French pounced on them with lancers and cuirassiers from both flanks, leaving more than a third of the British cavalry wounded or killed, including Ponsonby himself. Only 1,000 troopers returned of a force of 2,500. While much of the British cavalry had been put out of action for the remainder of the day, d'Erlon's force, which represented a quarter of the French at Waterloo, had been disastrously repulsed, with 25 percent losses and 2,000 men captured. Had he succeeded, d'Erlon might have won the day then and there. Napoleon now had to find another method.

Meanwhile, the defenders of Hougoumont continued to fend off the ferocious attacks of Jérôme Bonaparte's infantry, while at the same time Major George Baring's Hanoverians clung on at La Haye Sainte. The Prussians began to arrive in gradually increasing numbers from Wavre, and Picton's division withdrew back to friendly lines, not making the same mistake as the cavalry. By 3:00 P.M., apart from the fighting around Hougoumont and La Haye Sainte, the battle entered a lull, as both sides needed a respite in which to consider their next moves. About this time Grouchy began to hear the sound of the guns at Waterloo. Strictly adhering to his instructions to pursue the Prussians to Wavre, and ignoring the entreaties of his staff officers to march immediately to the sound of the guns—where it was correctly presumed the Emperor was engaging Wellington—Grouchy continued to engage the Prussian contingent of 15,000 men left at Wavre. This was to prove a fatal error for the French, for by 4:30 P.M. the bulk of Blücher's forces were arriving on Wellington's left in large numbers, those numbers increasing hourly.

The French now attempted another grand stroke—this time with their cavalry—at about 3:30, once d'Erlon's corps had regrouped and assembled itself back in the line. A renewed attempt at seizing La Haye Sainte, this time under the personal direction of Marshal Michel Ney, failed. With the grand battery's losses from Uxbridge's attack now replaced, the French resumed their bombardment of the Allied lines, where many regiments were ordered to lie down for protection. Even still, artillery fire took a heavy toll on Wellington's men on the ridge. Ney now sought to clear the ridge by launching a massive cavalry attack, unsupported by infantry, totaling about 5,000 men.

The attack fell on the infantry deployed between Hougoumont and La Haye Sainte. But the defenders had formed square—the classic formation for defense against mounted attack—with several ranks of infantry deployed back-to-back in the form of a square, bristling with bayonets presented in the direction of the enemy on all sides, and thus virtually immune from direct assault by men on horseback. Whereas a square was extremely vulnerable to combined-arms attack, particularly artillery at close range, the French cavalry appeared on the ridge practically unaccompanied, there to confront a wall of impenetrable bayonets behind which stood men beyond the reach of sword and saber, firing their muskets with virtual impunity. More and more cavalry—in the end amounting to some 80 squadrons or 10,000 men—were committed to these futile attacks. So ineffective were they, that many British soldiers were relieved to hear the sound of cavalry trumpets announcing each fresh attack, since approaching cavalry forced the French to cease the fire of their artillery lest they should strike their own advancing horsemen. Still, some Anglo-Allied squares suffered heavy casualties at the hands of the few batteries of horse artillery that did manage to accompany the cavalry, together with some skirmishers.

Yet it was the attackers who suffered the most, for wave after wave could do little more than swirl ineffectively around the squares before receding back down the slope, their horses blown and many men and their mounts lost to musket and artillery fire. Indeed, British gunners often discharged their cannon at short range before taking refuge inside the squares. Once the attackers withdrew, the gunners would re-man their guns and prepare for the next onslaught. These attacks—perhaps a dozen or more—continued for about two hours, between 4:00 and 6:00 P.M., but all in vain, for not only did the cavalry fail to penetrate the squares, the bodies of their fallen comrades and horses choked the field and impeded the progress of the regiments behind. Wellington's squares all held fast, and the French grew weary, with many regiments executing the last charges at hardly more than a trot.

A British square at Waterloo puts up dogged resistance against attacking French cavalry. (Print after P. Jazet from Cassell's *Illustrated History of England*, Century Edition. London: Cassell, n.d., vol. 5)

While Ney's cavalry fruitlessly assaulted the infantry squares, the Prussians under Bülow and General August Graf Neidhardt von Gneisenau were arriving on Napoleon's right flank, particularly around Frischermont, where General Georges Mouton, comte Lobau was sent to hold them back while the main French effort continued to concentrate on breaking Wellington's center. Bülow's 30,000 men engaged Lobau's 10,000 defenders in furious fighting in and around the Bois de Paris and Frischermont, out of which Lobau was driven toward the village of Plancenoit. Overwhelmed by superior numbers, Lobau was eventually ejected from Plancenoit as well, obliging Napoleon to send in the Young Guard to retake the place, which they did shortly before 7:00 P.M.

By this time the corps of generals Georg von Pirch and Wieprecht Graf von Zieten had also arrived from the east, on Wellington's flank, boosting the morale of the battered Anglo-Allies, disheartening those of the French who were aware of the Prussians' arrival, and drawing away more of Napoleon's reserves that might have been used against Wellington's center. With the tide turning in the duke's favor and the Prussians arriving to bolster his left, Wellington was able to withdraw some of his forces from his ex-

treme left and shift them to his vulnerable center. This was all the more necessary as infantry from the French reserve were beginning to mass around La Belle Alliance, readying themselves for another great attack on the Anglo-Allied center and center-right; specifically, against the tiny garrison still holding out in La Haye Sainte.

Baring and his King's German Legion (KGL) infantry had been reinforced periodically with Nassauers, but in the course of six hours of fighting, his riflemen had received no new stocks of ammunition, and by six o'clock they were desperately short and unable to continue to resist their assailants with anything more than sword bayonets and musket butts. The French, moreover, had set the roof of the farmhouse on fire, and sometime between 6:00 and 6:30 the remaining 42 KGL infantry out of the original 400 defenders were obliged to abandon the post. This was an important tactical victory for the French, for La Haye Sainte stood firmly in the Anglo-Allied center, offering possession of the strategically important Charleroi-Brussels road. The moment was a critical one for Wellington, for if the French could exploit this opportunity before the full force of the Prussians could be felt, Napoleon still stood a chance of seizing the day. Ney

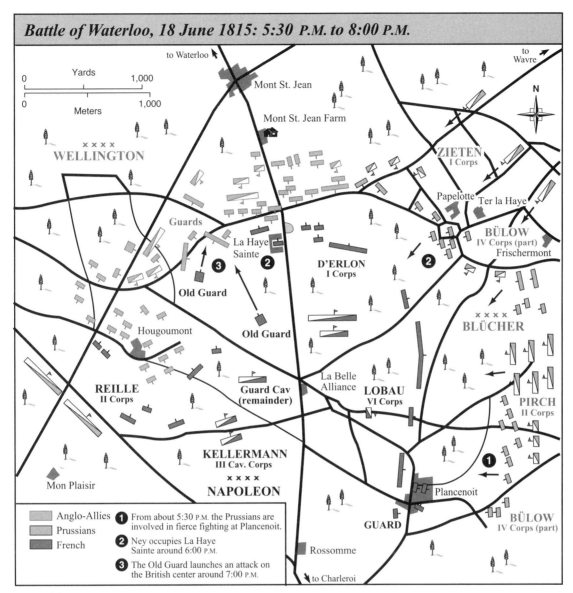

Battle of Waterloo, 18 June 1815: 5:30 P.M. to 8:00 P.M.

Adapted from Fremont-Barnes 2002B, 82.

therefore brought up artillery and pounded the line at close range, repulsed an attempt to retake the farmhouse, and forced out riflemen deployed in the sandpit near La Haye.

The moment had arrived for the French to appear in force. Yet they could not do so. Thousands were still engaged around Hougoumont and could not be withdrawn quickly enough, even if the order had been issued. D'Erlon's formation, though certainly not eliminated from the fighting, was exhausted and in no state to switch to the offensive. Meanwhile, to the southeast, Bülow's corps had by now retaken Plancenoit, ejecting the Young Guard in bitter house-to-house fighting that exposed the French right flank and brought the Prussians to within a mile of La Belle Alliance in the French center. There were no available

reserves for Ney, despite his pleas, apart from the Old Guard, which Napoleon refused to commit.

Wellington for his part remained in a perilous state, riding up and down the line reassuring his men and ordering no withdrawals for any reason lest it cause a panic and general retreat. While gaps—some of them quite large—appeared along Wellington's line, Napoleon declined to gamble on striking a potentially deadly blow, notwithstanding the pounding his artillery had inflicted on the Anglo-Allies throughout the day. Many regiments were but shadows of their original strengths.

The Prussians, meanwhile, carried on pushing forward into Napoleon's right flank, bringing their artillery close enough even to hit the Charleroi road down which any French retreat was likely to pass. Napoleon sensed the crisis and ordered two battalions of the Old Guard to re-capture Plancenoit with the bayonet. Within half an hour this elite infantry had evicted many times their number of Prussians, enabling the Young Guard to reestablish their former positions in the devastated village, by then choked with dead and wounded. When the Old Guard carried on beyond Plancenoit, however, Bülow's superior numbers began to tell, and the French were driven back. Neverthe-less, the Emperor's favorites had given him a respite, and this, with the fall of La Haye Sainte and the wavering Anglo-Allied center, left one last opportunity for Napoleon to defeat Wellington.

Time was short for the French, for much as the Imper-ial Guard could halt, if temporarily, the Prussian advance against the French right, they were powerless to stop the tide of Prussians linking up with the Anglo-Allies on Wellington's left. If he was to deliver a decisive blow against his opponent, Napoleon had to strike soon. He still had at his disposal 5,000 fresh infantry of the Old and Middle Guard. Brought forward at the right point along the Allied line, the Guard might yet have turned the tide of victory in Napoleon's favor. First, in order to bolster his men's morale, the Emperor circulated false reports that the troops arriving on the French right were in fact Grouchy's and not Prussians. Then, at around 7:00 P.M. the Guard in-fantry was sent forward—five battalions in the first wave and three in the second, under Ney. The first wave received support from troops of d'Erlon's corps, plus cavalry and artillery of the Guard. Aware of the impending attack and with 15 minutes in which to prepare to receive it, Welling-ton closed up his line and deployed cavalry to the rear to prevent any possible breakthrough.

As the sun was setting at about 7:30, the Guard marched in columns up the ridge and attacked a point about equidistant between Hougoumont and La Haye Sainte. At the top of the ridge thirty cannon stood to re-ceive them; the grapeshot fired exacted a heavy toll on the attackers. Undeterred, the Guard continued its advance, driving off Brunswickers and British infantry, and captur-ing some artillery. Yet when a Dutch-Belgian battery fired at close range, followed by a bayonet attack made by 3,000 Dutch-Belgian infantry, a battalion of the Guard was driven back down the slope. Another battalion of the Grenadiers of the (Old) Guard struck Major General Sir Colin Halkett's brigade, but its two British regiments re-mained steadfast and then repulsed their assailants with musket fire and the support of a nearby battery of horse artillery. The first French wave had thus failed.

Now came the turn of three battalions of the Chas-seurs of the (Middle) Guard. These had been subjected to intense artillery fire since they had begun their advance from La Belle Alliance and ascended the ridge toward the Ohain road. Suddenly, on Wellington's command, from out of the corn rose the 1st Foot Guards, who had been lying prone. The ensuing devastating volley stopped the Chasseurs in their tracks. At the same time they were sub-jected to grapeshot at under 200 yards' distance. After 10 minutes of this intense fire, the French began to waver, whereupon Wellington ordered the Foot Guards to charge with the bayonet. On this, the Chasseurs retreated down the slopes past Hougoumont and back whence they had come. Finally, another battalion of Chasseurs of the Guard advanced up the ridge, to be met by various units, includ-ing Major General Frederick Adam's brigade, Halkett's brigade, the Foot Guards, and Hanoverians out of Hougoumont, all of whom fired on the attackers from var-ious directions. But the final straw came when the 52nd Light Infantry appeared on the Middle Guard's left flank and fired a volley at point-blank range. The remainder of Adam's brigade then charged with the bayonet, driving the Chasseurs away.

Wellington, seeing that the moment of victory had ar-rived, rode to the top of the ridge and waved his hat in the air to signal a general advance across the entire front. With the repulse of the Guard, the fatal words "*La Garde recule!*" (The Guard recoils!) spread like wildfire down the French ranks, and Napoleon's army rapidly began to dissolve into a fleeing mass. Some of the hitherto uncommitted units of the Guard stood firm in square, but after taking severe punishment from musket and artillery fire at close range, these too broke and ran, following their comrades in head-long flight. The fate of the Armée du Nord was sealed by pursuing Prussian cavalry, who rode down thousands of men before darkness set in.

Napoleon, protected by a small mounted escort and a battalion of the Guard, retreated down the Charleroi road and eventually reached Paris. With his main force shattered and with several Allied armies poised to invade France, Na-poleon abdicated for a second time, surrendered himself to the British, and ended his years in exile on St. Helena.

Gregory Fremont-Barnes

See also Blücher von Wahlstatt, Gebhard Lebrecht Fürst; Bonaparte, Jérôme; Bülow von Dennewitz, Friedrich Wilhelm Graf; Drouet, Jean-Baptiste, comte d'Erlon; Elba; Gneisenau, August Wilhelm Anton, Graf Neidhardt von; Grouchy, Emmanuel, marquis de; Imperial Guard (French); Ligny, Battle of; Ney, Michel; Picton, Sir Thomas; Quatre Bras, Battle of; Reille, Honoré Charles Michel Joseph, comte; St. Helena; Uxbridge, Henry William Paget, Second Earl of; Waterloo Campaign; Wavre, Battle of; Wellington, Arthur Wellesley, First Duke of; Zieten, Wieprecht Hans Karl Friedrich Ernst Heinrich Graf von
References and further reading
Adkin, Mark. 2001. *The Waterloo Companion: The Complete Guide to History's Most Famous Land Battle.* London: Aurum.

Barbero, Alessandro. 2005. *The Definitive History of the Battle of Waterloo*. London: Atlantic Books.

Becke, A. F. 1914. *Napoleon and Waterloo*. Vol. 2. London: Kegan Paul, Trench, Trubner.

Bernard, Giles, and Gérard Lachaux. 2005. *Waterloo*. Paris: Histoire and Collections.

Bowden, Scott. 1983. *Armies at Waterloo*. Arlington, TX: Empire Games.

Brett-James, Antony. 1964. *The Hundred Days*. London: Macmillan.

Chalfont, Lord, ed. 1979. *Waterloo: Battle of Three Armies*. London: Sedgwick and Jackson.

Chandler, David G. 1981. *Waterloo: The Hundred Days*. New York: Macmillan.

———. 1995. *The Campaigns of Napoleon*. London: Weidenfeld and Nicolson.

Chesney, Charles C. 1997. *Waterloo Lectures*. London: Greenhill.

Davies, Paul. 1971. *The Field of Waterloo*. London: Pan.

Esposito, Vincent J., and John R. Elting. 1978. *A Military History and Atlas of the Napoleonic Wars*. New York: AMS.

Fletcher, Ian. 2003. *"A Desperate Business": Wellington, the British Army and the Waterloo Campaign*. Staplehurst, UK: Spellmount.

Fremont-Barnes, Gregory. 2002. *The Napoleonic Wars: The Fall of the French Empire, 1813–1815*. Oxford: Osprey.

Gillespie-Payne, Jonathan. 2004. *Waterloo: In the Footsteps of the Commanders*. London: Leo Cooper.

Hamilton-Williams, David. 1993. *Waterloo: New Perspectives, The Great Battle Reappraised*. London: Arms and Armour.

Haythornthwaite, Philip. 1996. *Uniforms of Waterloo*. London: Weidenfeld and Nicolson.

———. 1999. *Waterloo Men: The Experience of Battle, 16–18 June 1815*. Ramsbury, UK: Crowood.

Herold, J. Christopher. 1967. *The Battle of Waterloo*. London: Cassell.

Hibbert, Christopher. 2004. *Waterloo: Napoleon's Last Campaign*. Blue Ridge Summit, PA: Cooper Square.

Hofschröer, Peter. 1997. *1815, The Waterloo Campaign: Wellington, His German Allies and the Battles of Ligny and Quatre Bras*. London: Greenhill.

———. 1999. *1815, The Waterloo Campaign: The German Victory*. London: Greenhill.

———. 2004. *Wellington's Smallest Victory: The Duke, the Model Maker and the Secret of Waterloo*. London: Faber and Faber.

Houssaye, Henry. 2005. *Napoleon and the Campaign of 1815: Waterloo*. Uckfield, UK: Naval and Military.

Howarth, David. 2003. *Waterloo: A Near Run Thing*. London: Weidenfeld and Nicolson.

Keegan, John. 1976. *The Face of Battle*. London: Cape.

Lachouque, Henry. 1978a. *Waterloo*. London: Arms and Armour.

———. 1978b. *The Anatomy of Glory*. Trans. Anne S. K. Brown. London: Arms and Armour.

Longford, Elizabeth. 1973. *Wellington: The Years of the Sword*. London: Weidenfeld and Nicolson.

Naylor, John. 1960. *Waterloo*. London: Batsford.

Nofi, Albert. 1998. *The Waterloo Campaign: June 1815*. New York: Da Capo.

Paget, Julian. 1992. *Hougoumont*. London: Leo Cooper.

Pericoli, Ugo. 1973. *1815: The Armies at Waterloo*. London: Seeley Service.

Roberts, Andrew. 2005. *Waterloo: Napoleon's Last Gamble*. London: HarperCollins.

Schom, Alan. 1993. *One Hundred Days: Napoleon's Road to Waterloo*. Oxford: Oxford University Press.

Siborne, William. 1990. *History of the Waterloo Campaign*. London: Greenhill.

Uffindell, Andrew, and Michael Corum. 1996. *On the Fields of Glory: The Battlefields of the Waterloo Campaign*. London: Greenhill.

Weller, Jac. 1992. *Wellington at Waterloo*. London: Greenhill.

Wooten, Geoffrey. 1992. *Waterloo 1815*. Oxford: Osprey.

Waterloo Campaign (1815)

The final act of the Napoleonic Wars, the Waterloo campaign took place in Belgium in 1815. It was the military aspect of Napoleon's attempt to seize power in France and reestablish his empire after his short exile on the Mediterranean island of Elba. This period is also known as the Hundred Days. The Waterloo campaign included the "four-day war," which featured the action at Charleroi, and the battles of Quatre Bras, Ligny, Waterloo, and Wavre; the race for Paris; the besieging of a number of fortresses in northern France; and the fall of Paris. The military forces directly involved included the Army of the North (Armée du Nord) under the command of Napoleon, the (Prussian) Army of the Lower Rhine under Field Marshal Gebhard Fürst Blücher von Wahlstatt, and an Anglo-Allied army under the Duke of Wellington consisting of contingents from various German states, the Netherlands, and Britain. The Waterloo campaign marked the end of the Napoleonic Wars, with Napoleon being exiled to the island of St. Helena, where he died six years later.

Napoleon's first abdication had taken place on 6 April at the end of the campaign of 1814. The Bourbons had been restored as the rulers of France, with Louis XVIII becoming king. While much of France breathed a sigh of relief at the end of a long period of warfare, the unemployed soldiers were dissatisfied and restless. The restoration of a dynasty that had not been in power in France for a generation also caused friction. The bitter disputes over the spoils of war between the victorious Allies at the Congress of Vienna did not escape Napoleon's attention either. Judging the moment right, he left Elba (contrary to popular belief, the Treaty of Paris did not confine him there or ban him from leaving; thus he did not "escape" as is often asserted) with a handful of supporters and landed in the south of France on 1 March 1815. This snowball soon turned into an avalanche that swept Napoleon to Paris and back into power. He owed his success to the support of the army, but the country was divided. Open rebellion broke out in the royalist stronghold in the Vendée.

News of Napoleon's return reached Vienna a few days later, galvanizing the Allies into action. They declared Napoleon an outlaw and prepared for war, forming the Seventh Coalition. The great powers joining it included Russia, Austria, Britain, and Prussia. Much of the rest of Europe supported the Allies, although Napoleon's Marshal Joachim Murat, who was concurrently King of Naples, declared for him. The nations of Europe now prepared for the forthcoming conflict. An Austrian army decisively defeated Murat at Tolentino on 2–3 May, while larger forces concentrated along France's northwestern border.

Napoleon's forces were so outnumbered that, at least on paper, he did not have a chance. However, he was a gambler and hoped that an early success would cause the fragile coalition to collapse. After all, the erstwhile Allies had all but gone to war with each other in January 1815, and they had different political aims. While Britain sought an equitable balance of power in post-Napoleonic Europe, the Prussians in particular had territorial ambitions that the Vienna settlement had not satisfied. The new Kingdom of the Netherlands, consisting of modern-day Netherlands, Belgium, and Luxembourg, was an unstable mixture of Dutchmen, Flemings, and Walloons, many of whom had been under French rule for the last generation. Here, Napoleon could count on popular support. There were also strong Bonapartist sympathies in Britain, and any military failure might well have led to the fall of the government, led by Lord Liverpool. As Britain was paymaster of the coalition, a change of ministry was likely to cause a change of policy. Napoleon selected the Low Countries as the target for his military adventure.

The Netherlands had been a disputed territory at the Congress of Vienna. It was occupied by both Prussian forces and an Anglo-Allied (British, Dutch, Belgian, and contingents from various small German states) army. On Napoleon's return to Paris, these forces set about preparing for the forthcoming war. Specifically, they brought in reinforcements and formulated a strategy. The Prussians favored an early intervention in France, but the Anglo-Allies, under Wellington's command from early April, urged greater caution, wanting both the Austrians and the Russians to join them for an invasion of France. The Prussians wanted to grab as much of the glory as possible for themselves to underline their territorial claims. Wellington wanted to see that the balance of power so carefully established at Vienna was maintained. In any case, the defense of the Netherlands was the priority of the armies based there, and Brussels could not be allowed to fall to Napoleon, as that might well destabilize the Kingdom of the Netherlands. They decided on a defense of that great city

to its fore, that is, they resolved to move to meet any invading forces. Against a commander known for his rapid movements, that was a highly risky enterprise.

Napoleon had several choices of routes to Brussels. The shortest way was via Mons, the route Wellington considered he would most likely take. While concentrating his forces along the frontier, Napoleon also undertook a number of movements around Lille, teasing Wellington's sensitive right and his line of communication via the Channel ports. The Allies needed to spread their forces to cover all eventualities, while Napoleon could concentrate at the point of his choice, achieving a local superiority in numbers. The legal situation here was a little unusual. The Allies recognized the legitimacy of Louis XVIII's government-in-exile and had declared war on Napoleon, but not France. Accordingly, the border between France and the Netherlands was open. It was business as usual, and the international postal system was operating normally. The Allies were receiving good information from their informants in Paris, who were making use of the post.

This openness made it difficult for Napoleon to achieve the element of surprise, although he later maintained that his invasion astonished the Allies. However, they were aware of the concentration of French forces in the area of Maubeuge, and from 9 June the Allied troops on the frontier were placed on alert. From Maubeuge, Napoleon had two routes to Brussels: that via Mons, where Wellington's army was waiting for him, or that via Charleroi, where Blücher's Prussians were in position. While it was clear to all that Napoleon was likely to strike soon, the date was not certain and the route not definite. Napoleon played those doubts to his advantage, remaining in Paris for as long as he could before leaving to join his army. He did so on 13 June, the Allies hearing this news only hours later. During the course of the next day, it became evident that hostilities were going to commence the coming morning and that the line of attack was going to be via Charleroi. Wellington had already assured the Prussians that in such an eventuality he would move to their support.

The strategic situation on the outbreak of hostilities on the night of 14–15 June was that Napoleon's army, 120,000 men, was concentrated in the area of Beaumont. The Prussian army under Blücher's command, 120,000 men, was deployed over the southeastern Netherlands. The Prussian I Army Corps under General Wieprecht Graf von Zieten, 30,000 men, was facing Napoleon's troops in the area of Charleroi. Wellington, with his headquarters in Brussels, commanded a mixed force of 90,000 Germans, Dutch-Belgians, and British troops deployed in southwestern Netherlands. The quality of Napoleon's troops was generally higher than Blücher's, two-thirds of his Prussians being raw levies, so Napoleon was considered more than a match for either of the Allied armies in this theater. Should they, however, combine their forces, Napoleon would be overwhelmed by their superiority in numbers. Not surprisingly, he chose to strike at the juncture of their forces, hitting first the Prussians, whom he expected to defeat easily, before moving against Wellington.

After some initial confusion, the Army of the North clashed with the Prussian outposts from 3:30 A.M. on 15 June. The warning cannon woke Zieten, who waited for an hour until the sound of musketry, indicating a serious confrontation, could be heard. He then sent reports to Blücher in Namur and Wellington in Brussels, informing them of this. The Allied outposts along the frontier and adjacent to the Prussians were also informed. While the timing of the arrival of this news in Namur and its movement up the lines of communication of the Allied forces is a matter of record, Wellington made a number of conflicting statements on the subject. However, it is most likely he received this news at 9:00 A.M. Having assured the Prussians that he would come to their assistance rapidly, Wellington did nothing and waited until 6:00 P.M., after receiving several confirmations of this news, before starting to issue orders. Even then, he only ordered his troops to concentrate at their assembly points and waited until that night before finally issuing any orders to move. Wellington had lost a whole day in circumstances that required immediate action. The Prussians were now in danger of being crushed by Napoleon before assistance could arrive.

Blücher's reaction on receipt of this news was to order his army to concentrate in the Sombreffe position, a defensible point on the Namur-to-Brussels road, where he intended to confront Napoleon the next day. He informed Wellington of this. Thanks to a misunderstanding, IV Army Corps under General Friedrich Wilhelm Graf Bülow von Dennewitz, one-quarter of Blücher's forces, did not move off on time. The Prussians were to face Napoleon the next day with fewer men than anticipated. Now more than ever was Wellington's assistance necessary.

Napoleon pushed on in the face of a spirited rearguard action from Zieten, reaching most of his objectives by the evening of 15 June. He had driven a wedge between Wellington and Blücher, with his forces now standing between the two Allied armies. Moreover, his patrols had reached as far as Quatre Bras on the highway to Brussels, putting him in a position to cut the direct line of communication between Brussels and Namur. Blücher had reacted correctly, but did not yet know that Bülow would be delayed. Wellington had now issued orders to his army to move, but had yet to select a single point of concentration. Instead, he left his options open, awaiting developments. That is not, however, what he told the Prussians.

On the morning of the sixteenth, Wellington rode from Brussels to the front. He passed his troops resting near the village of Waterloo before stopping for a moment at the road junction just south of this village to enquire where the two forks of the road led. He then rode through Genappe and on to Quatre Bras. Fortunately, this vital crossroads was still in Allied hands, as the local commander had used his initiative and held his position, despite having been ordered by Wellington the previous evening to move to Nivelles. Once here, Wellington observed the situation and saw little French activity. He then wrote a report for Blücher, the Frasnes Letter, giving misleading information on his positions, before riding to Prussian headquarters at the windmill of Bussy, near Ligny.

Meanwhile, Napoleon was moving the larger part of his army toward the Prussians, whom he intended to crush that day. He placed his left wing under the command of Marshal Michel Ney, expecting him to brush the handful of Allied troops at Quatre Bras out of the way.

When Wellington met Blücher, he saw that the bulk of Napoleon's forces were drawing up to attack the Prussians. Wellington repeated his earlier promises of coming to their support, but in reality knew he was not in a position to do so with the numbers promised. On his return to Quatre Bras, he was surprised to find the French attacking his forces there. Fortunately, his commander on the spot, the Prince of Orange, had ordered up reinforcements, and Wellington was able to hold his position that day.

The Battle of Ligny commenced about 2:30 P.M. and continued until darkness. For much of the day, the Prussians held their own in vicious street fighting, but the final French assault that evening broke through their center, leaving the scattered remnants falling back. Blücher went missing, having led a desperate cavalry charge in an attempt to hold on. General August Graf Neidhardt von Gneisenau, the Prussian chief of staff, attempted to have his men rally at Tilly, near to Wellington's position, but control broke down. Most of the defeated Prussians fell back toward Wavre, 12 miles east of Waterloo, and part toward Namur.

Despite this success, Napoleon had let his one real chance of a decisive victory in the campaign slip. Although he had allocated the corps of General Jean-Baptiste Drouet, comte d'Erlon to Ney's wing, Napoleon recalled it without reference to Ney. The Prussians were holding on at Ligny with greater tenacity than Napoleon had expected, so he ordered d'Erlon to move to confront their right flank. That could well have resulted in a crushing defeat. Ney, too, could have defeated Wellington had d'Erlon arrived at Quatre Bras. When Ney found that d'Erlon had inexplicably turned around, he sent him urgent orders to retrace his steps. Thus, a substantial part of the Army of the North spent the day wandering around aimlessly.

Since the French shot the Prussian messenger to Wellington, the duke did not hear of Blücher's defeat until the following morning. Instead of continuing the battle as expected, Wellington fell back to the ridge of Mont St. Jean, south of the village of Waterloo, where he set up his headquarters.

During the early hours of the morning, some sort of control was reestablished over the Prussian army and Wavre selected as the point for it to rally. Napoleon waited for most of the morning before sending off Marshal Emmanuel, marquis de Grouchy with 33,000 men to pursue the Prussians. By then, the trail had gone cold, and it was some time before he caught up with them. Napoleon believed the Prussians had ceased to be an effective force.

The Emperor now took charge of Ney's wing, adding to it most of the troops that had fought at Ligny. He followed up, although the pursuit of Wellington was not particularly vigorous. Napoleon was losing the initiative.

Heavy rain showers during the night of 17–18 June did not make the going easy. The French supply system broke down, and many of Napoleon's men left their units to look for food. Order was restored the next morning.

The Prussian forces rallied at Wavre, and when the missing ammunition trains were located, Gneisenau confirmed his intention of moving a substantial part of his army the next day to support Wellington. The Prussian march was delayed for several reasons. One was the fact that the freshest corps—Bülow's—was designated to lead the march, even though it was the farthest from Wellington. Then a fire broke out in Wavre, blocking the narrow streets. Finally, the rain had turned the country paths on the route to Plancenoit into mudslides that particularly delayed wheeled vehicles. The much-needed artillery would be the last to arrive. Nevertheless, Wellington observed the leading Prussian posts shortly before the start of the battle.

The battle itself commenced around 11:30 A.M., when men of General Honoré Charles, comte Reille's corps first attacked the château of Hougoumont on Wellington's right. The fighting here continued for most of the day. D'Erlon's corps then assaulted the farmhouse of La Haye Sainte in Wellington's center, before staging a general attack at that point. A charge from the Earl of Uxbridge's cavalry drove this off, and the remainder of the day's action in this area consisted of a heavy artillery bombardment, several attempts to storm La Haye Sainte before its defenders ran out of ammunition and finally withdrew, and cavalry charges

Napoleon addresses the Old Guard as it prepares to attack the Anglo-Allied center at Waterloo. (Print by Ernest Croft from *Life of Napoleon Bonaparte* by William M. Sloane, New York: Century, 1906, vol. 4)

against infantry squares. Losses on both sides were severe, and the situation for Wellington was precarious.

At 4:30 P.M. the Prussians staged their first of three attacks on the village of Plancenoit to Napoleon's right rear. This sucked in a substantial part of the Emperor's last reserves of infantry, particularly elements of the Imperial Guard, depriving him of the opportunity of using these crack troops in the final assault on Wellington's center. This final assault took place at 7:30 P.M., but the elite of the elite was thrown back in disorder. About the same time, Plancenoit fell to the Prussians, endangering Napoleon's line of retreat. Resistance collapsed, and the French fled the field, leaving behind a substantial part of their artillery and ammunition wagons. Blücher and Wellington met at the inn of La Belle Alliance about 9:00 P.M., their symbolic handshake marking the end of the battle.

At Wavre, the Prussians resisted determined assaults from Grouchy's men into the morning of the nineteenth, when news of Waterloo arrived. The French here fell back. Blücher headed rapidly for Paris, wanting to be the first there, so that he could exact revenge without restraint. Several combats were fought during the pursuit, and a number of the French-held fortresses along their northern frontier either capitulated or were stormed, this phase of the action being undertaken largely by the Prussians, with some support from forces of the German Confederation (the newly formed body of central European states created by the Great Powers at the Congress of Vienna). Paris fell to the Allies on 7 July. Although Napoleon had surrendered to the British, a number of fortresses with pro-Bonapartist garrisons continued to resist until well into the autumn.

The surrender of Napoleon marked the end of his final attempt at reestablishing his power in Europe, while his exile to the isolated Atlantic island of St. Helena ended an era. The balance of power established at the Congress of Vienna withstood several tests during the nineteenth century, so demonstrating that the Allied reconstruction of Europe made possible by Napoleon's defeat in the Waterloo campaign stood on a firm foundation.

Peter Hofschröer

See also Blücher von Wahlstatt, Gebhard Lebrecht Fürst; Bülow von Dennewitz, Friedrich Wilhelm Graf; Drouet, Jean-Baptiste, comte d'Erlon; Elba; Gneisenau, August Wilhelm Anton Graf Neidhardt von; Grouchy, Emmanuel, marquis de; Imperial Guard (French); "Italian Independence," War of; Ligny, Battle of; Liverpool, Robert Banks Jenkinson, Second Earl of; Louis XVIII, King; Murat, Joachim; Ney, Michel; Orange, William, Prince of; Paris, First Treaty of; Quatre Bras, Battle of; Reille, Honoré Charles Michel Joseph, comte; St. Helena; Uxbridge, Henry William Paget, Second Earl of; Vienna, Congress of; Waterloo, Battle of; Wavre, Battle of; Wellington, Arthur Wellesley, First Duke of; Zieten, Wieprecht Hans Karl Friedrich Ernst Hans Heinrich Graf von

References and further reading
Adkin, Mark. 2001. *The Waterloo Companion: The Complete Guide to History's Most Famous Land Battle.* London: Aurum.
Bowden, Scott. 1983. *Armies at Waterloo.* Arlington, TX: Empire Games.
Brett-James, Antony. 1964. *The Hundred Days.* London: Macmillan.
Chalfont, Lord, ed. 1979. *Waterloo: Battle of Three Armies.* London: Sedgwick and Jackson.
Chandler, David G. 1980. *Waterloo: The Hundred Days.* London: Osprey.
———. 1995. *The Campaigns of Napoleon.* London: Weidenfeld and Nicolson.
Chesney, Charles C. 1997. *Waterloo Lectures.* London: Greenhill.
Dallas, Gregor. 2001. *1815: The Road to Waterloo.* London: Pimlico.
De Bas, F., and T'Serclaes de Wommersom. 1908. *La campagne de 1815 aux Pay-Bas.* Vol. 1, *Quatre-Bras.* Brussels: Dewit.
Delhaize, Jules, and Winand Aerts. 1915. *Etudes relatives à la campagne de 1815 en Belgique.* Vol. 1. Brussels: De Boeck.
Fletcher, Ian. 2001. *"A Desperate Business": Wellington, the British Army and the Waterloo Campaign.* Staplehurst, UK: Spellmount.
Gillespie-Payne, Jonathan. 2004. *Waterloo: In the Footsteps of the Commanders.* London: Leo Cooper.
Hamilton-Williams, David. 1993. *Waterloo: New Perspectives, The Great Battle Reappraised.* London: Arms and Armour.
Haythornthwaite, Philip. 1996. *Uniforms of Waterloo.* London: Weidenfeld and Nicolson.
Hibbert, Christopher. 2004. *Waterloo: Napoleon's Last Campaign.* Blue Ridge Summit, PA: Cooper Square.
Hofschröer, Peter. 1998. *1815, The Waterloo Campaign: Wellington, his German Allies and the Battles of Ligny and Quatre Bras.* London: Greenhill.
———. 1999. *1815, The Waterloo Campaign: The German Victory.* London: Greenhill.
Houssaye, Henry. 2005. *Napoleon and the Campaign of 1815: Waterloo.* Uckfield, UK: Naval and Military.
Lachouque, Henry. 1972. *Waterloo.* London: Arms and Armour.
Lettow-Vorbeck, Oscar von. 1904. *Napoleons Untergang 1815.* Vol. 1, *Elba–Belle-Alliance.* Berlin: Mittler.
Nofi, Albert. 1993. *The Waterloo Campaign: June 1815.* Harrisburg, PA: Combined.
Pflugk-Harttung, Julius von. 1915. *Belle Alliance.* Berlin: Eisenschmidt.
Ropes, John Codman. 1906. *The Campaign of Waterloo.* New York: Scribner's.
Siborne, William. 1990. *History of the Waterloo Campaign.* London: Greenhill.
Uffindell, Andrew, and Michael Corum. 2002. *On the Fields of Glory: The Battlefields of the 1815 Campaign.* London: Greenhill.
Wooten, Geoffrey. 1992. *Waterloo 1815.* Oxford: Osprey.

Wattignies, Battle of (15–16 October 1793)

The Battle of Wattignies was a hard-fought two-day battle that occurred when a French army tried to repel an Austrian invasion in October 1793. Revolutionary France actually faced two invasions from the Austrian Netherlands that year. An Anglo-Hanoverian army under Frederick Augustus, the Duke of York, advanced along the English Channel to besiege Dunkirk. Meanwhile, an Austro-Dutch army under the command of *Feldmarschall* Friedrich Josias Graf Saxe-Coburg-Saalfeld (generally known as Saxe-Coburg), had crossed into northeastern France, taking the fortresses of Valenciennes and Condé, then besieging Le Quesnoy during the summer.

General Jean-Nicholas Houchard led the Armée du Nord against the Duke of York's forces at Hondschoote on 8 September 1793. Here, Houchard's troops won a victory that forced the Anglo-Hanoverians to withdraw and secured the northern approaches from the Austrian Netherlands. However, the general's failure to pursue the enemy army led the Committee of Public Safety to remove him from command on 22 September. Houchard was later tried and executed, providing a warning to future commanders of French Revolutionary armies.

Although the British invasion had been halted, the Austro-Dutch army continued to advance unimpeded. Saxe-Coburg's troops forced Le Quesnoy to surrender on 11 September, before advancing against Maubeuge, a major fortified town on a key road to Paris that also served as a major encampment for about 20,000 French troops. About 26,000 Dutch and Austrian troops invested the town and began formal siege operations, hoping to capture this substantial French force and clear the way for an advance on Paris at the same time. Saxe-Coburg positioned a covering force of about 37,000 men, under the command of *Feldzeugmeister* Franz Sebastian de Croix Graf von Clerfayt, around Wattignies to protect the besieging troops.

General Jean-Baptiste Jourdan took command of the Armée du Nord and the Armée des Ardennes in September and hurried to meet the invading Austrian and Dutch forces. Jourdan, a former private in the French royal army, may have seemed a surprising choice as the commander to face the most serious remaining military threat to Revolutionary France in 1793. Yet Jourdan proved capable at organizing his troops, and Lazare Carnot, who joined the Armée du Nord as a *représentant en mission* during the Wattignies campaign, ably assisted him. Carnot, soon to be known as the great "Organizer of Victory" in his capacity as minister of war, seems to have been convinced by this experience subsequently to advise all field commanders "on every occasion [to] engage in combat with the bayonet" (Lynn 1984, 189). Jourdan and Carnot decided to attempt

to relieve the siege of Maubeuge and ordered the army of about 45,000 men to advance against the Austrian covering force, which was strung out along a wide front. Jourdan reported to the Committee of Public Safety, "I have only time to tell you that my country will be triumphant, or I shall perish in defending it" (Phipps 1980, 1:252).

Austrian commanders were aware of French preparations to attack them, but Saxe-Coburg supposedly was so confident of victory that he said he would become a sansculotte if the French defeated him. Clerfayt's troops were strung out in a wide cordon south of Maubeuge that would allow him to gather only some 21,000 men to face directly the impending French attack at Wattignies. Further, the Austrians were deployed in fairly wooded terrain that would effectively inhibit the use of cavalry and that would put his force at a potential disadvantage if attacked, since the Austrian cavalry far outclassed their French counterparts.

On 15 October, the French army deployed facing their Austrian counterpart around Wattignies with General Florent Joseph Duquesnoy's division on the right, General Antoine Balland's division in the center, and General Jacques Pierre Fromentin's on the left. Jourdan launched attacks on both wings of the Austrian army, with Duquesnoy's troops attacking the village of Wattignies and Fromentin advancing on the left. After both of the wings made initial progress, the French center began an attack on the Austrian troops posted around the village of Dourlers. In the wake of these intial French successes, Austrian artillery fire checked the French infantry in the center and repulsed Duquesnoy's troops at Wattignies. Meanwhile, Austrian cavalry counterattacked Fromentin's division, driving off its cavalry and cutting down many infantrymen. The French suffered at least 1,500 casualties during the first day's battle.

During the night, Jourdan reorganized his troops and prepared a new plan of attack for the next day. He decided to shift some of the infantry from the French center to the right and to concentrate his attacks on Wattignies and the Austrian left wing. Meanwhile, Saxe-Coburg strengthened the Austrian left, expecting a renewed French effort to take Wattignies.

Fog covered the fields on the morning of 16 October, as the French infantry under Jourdan, Duquesnoy, and General Claude Jacques Lecourbe advanced in columns of attack against the Austrian defenses at Wattignies. French artillery batteries prepared the way for the infantry by battering the enemy lines. The French center and left remained largely passive as the main attack developed. The defenders repulsed the first assault on the village, and Austrian cavalry disrupted some French infantry coming up to assist Duquesnoy's division. After rallying some of the disorganized troops, Jourdan led another coordinated attack on the enemy positions, breaking into Wattignies and pushing the Austrian defenders back. The victorious French then swept beyond the village, completing the victory.

The Austro-Dutch army abandoned its siege of Maubeuge and withdrew northward, but the Armée du Nord was unable to pursue. Instead, Jourdan prepared encampments for his troops, since his army had suffered approximately 8,000 casualties in the fighting, while the Austrians had lost about 5,000. In Paris, the government, known as the Convention, removed Jourdan from command of the Armée du Nord in January 1794 over his refusal to pursue the Austrians along the river Sambre. Still, Jourdan had established a victorious reputation and was not executed. He later served again as a Revolutionary general and then as a marshal under Napoleon.

The French rightly greeted the victory at Wattignies as another Valmy, halting an invasion and saving the Revolution. Historian Jean-Paul Bertaud emphasizes that Wattignies "marked a turning point in the state of military education of the army.... For the first time the army maneuvered well" (Bertaud 1988, 238). Wattignies revealed the growing effectiveness of the French Revolutionary military system and paved the way for a new series of French offensives into the Austrian Netherlands in 1794.

Brian Sandberg

See also Carnot, Lazare Nicolas Marguerite; Convention, The; First Coalition, War of the; Flanders, Campaigns in; Hondschoote, Battle of; Jourdan, Jean-Baptiste; Public Safety, Committee of; Valmy, Battle of; York and Albany, Frederick Augustus, Duke of

References and further reading
Bertaud, Jean-Paul. 1988. *The Army of the French Revolution: From Citizen-Soldiers to Instrument of Power.* Trans. R. R. Palmer. Princeton: Princeton University Press.
Blanning, T. C. W. 1996. *The French Revolutionary Wars, 1787–1802.* London: Arnold.
Glover, Michael. 1987. "The True Patriot: Jourdan." In *Napoleon's Marshals,* ed. David G. Chandler, 156–175. New York: Macmillan.
Griffith, Paddy. 1998. *The Art of War of Revolutionary France, 1789–1802.* London: Greenhill.
Lynn, John A. 1984. *The Bayonets of the Republic: Motivation and Tactics in the Army of Revolutionary France, 1791–94.* Urbana: University of Illinois Press.
Phipps, Ramsay Weston. 1980. *The Armies of the First French Republic and the Rise of the Marshals of Napoleon I.* 5 vols. Vol. 1: *The Armée du Nord.* London: Greenwood. (Orig. pub. 1926–1939.)

Wavre, Battle of (18–19 June 1815)

The Battle of Wavre took place during the Waterloo campaign in and around the town of Wavre on the river Dyle in the southern Netherlands, now Belgium. Here, the Prussian III Army Corps (General Johann Freiherr von Thielmann) held up the right wing of Napoleon's Army of the North, which was commanded by Marshal Emmanuel, marquis de Grouchy, preventing it from participating in the Battle of Waterloo, then simultaneously underway 12 miles to the west. This action helped to decide the day at Waterloo.

Once the remainder of the Prussian army had marched through Wavre on their way to Waterloo on the morning of 18 June, Thielmann set about preparing the town for defense with the 15,000 men he had available. Grouchy had more than double that at his disposal (33,000), including III Corps (under General Dominique Vandamme) and IV Corps (under General Maurice Etienne, comte Gérard), as well as generals Claude Pajol and Isidore Exelmans's cavalry corps.

Wavre was situated on the left bank of the Dyle, with a suburb on the opposite bank. Stone bridges joined them, and there were several more bridges along the river. The recent heavy rain had made the river unfordable.

Vandamme's men started to draw up for the attack on the afternoon of 18 June, attempting to seize the bridges at 4:00 P.M. Grouchy then came up and assumed command. Fierce fighting raged around the bridge at Limale, before the French eventually penetrated as far as the town itself. The ensuing street fighting continued into the night, with counterattacks following each attack.

Vandamme also moved against the village of Bas-Wavre, downstream from the town. He made scant progress here, taking a few houses south of the river, but not capturing the bridge.

That evening, Napoleon's letter, sent to Grouchy at 1:00 P.M. ordering him to move on Waterloo, arrived. It was simply too late for Grouchy to comply that day. Napoleon had to fight this great battle with a third of his men not available where they were needed.

Grouchy ordered Pajol to move rapidly to Limal and awaited the arrival of the divisions of Gérard's IV Corps. He then personally led them to Limal, where they arrived at 11:00 P.M. Pajol was holding the bridges, so they crossed the Dyle and climbed the heights to its north. Here, they clashed with Prussian troops and were forced to retire. Recognizing the importance of the crossing at Limal, Grouchy ordered Vandamme to move there, leaving behind only enough men to cover the bridges. Grouchy was now in a position to move toward Napoleon the next day.

That night, Thielmann received unconfirmed reports of an Allied victory at Waterloo. Confirmation arrived in the morning. Nevertheless, the battle around Wavre recommenced early on 19 June. Grouchy's superiority in numbers told, forcing the Prussians to retire. At 10:30 A.M., learning of Napoleon's defeat, Grouchy called off his attack and decided on a withdrawal to Namur. Thielmann did not follow up immediately, and Grouchy was able to break off the combat under the cover of a screen of cavalry.

Peter Hofschröer

See also Gérard, Maurice Etienne, comte; Grouchy, Emmanuel, marquis de; Pajol, Claude Pierre; Thielmann, Johann Adolph Freiherr von; Vandamme, Dominique Joseph René; Waterloo, Battle of; Waterloo Campaign
References and further reading
Hofschröer, Peter. 1999. *1815, The Waterloo Campaign: The German Victory.* London: Greenhill.
———. 2006. *Waterloo 1815: Wavre, Plancenoit and the Race to Paris.* London: Leo Cooper.

Weissenburg, Battle of (13 October 1793)

Weissenburg, one of many battles fought in the various campaigns on the Rhine front during the War of the First Coalition, displayed many characteristics of the early phase of the Revolutionary Wars: French lack of preparedness, Allied dissension and dithering, and the growing ability of the French government to organize the national defense through a unique combination of terror and professionalism. The focus of the clash was the famous Weissenburg Lines, a series of entrenchments created by Claude-Louis-Hector, duc de Villars in 1706 and extending for some 52 miles along the river Lauter, supporting nearby permanent fortifications and protecting Alsace against invasion from the north. The protection was sorely needed following the fall of Mainz in late July 1793.

Admittedly, the 100,000 Allied troops under the Duke of Brunswick advanced both late and slowly. Brunswick's Prussians, suspicious of Austrian political aims, soon stopped moving altogether and settled into camps at Pirmasens and Kaiserslautern. Farther south, *Feldmarschalleutnant* Dagobert Graf Würmser's Austrians blockaded Landau and established themselves opposite the weak left of the Weissenburg Lines, to which 25,000 troops of the Army of the Rhine under the inexperienced Carlen had retreated after several defeats. Eventually, the Allies agreed to a joint assault. On the night of 12–13 October, Waldeck attacked from behind the French right, whereupon Würmser's forces assaulted the center in three places. Condé's émigrés took Bergzabern. More skillful French leadership might have stemmed the tide, for the complex Allied attacks were only loosely coordinated. Fearful of being cut in half by Brunswick's 10,000 Prussians advancing from the southwest, however, the French retreated in disorder to Strasbourg (ironically, Würmser's native city).

The French public and leadership viewed the defeat as a terrifying disaster, and indeed, the Austrians threatened to annex Alsace, but the blow was more psychological than real—and perhaps even a blessing in disguise. French losses were only about 2,000, whereas those of the Allies were more than twice as heavy. In addition, the Allies failed to capitalize on their victory, whereas the defeat spurred the French government, known as the Convention, to decisive action. After quarreling again with the Austrians, the Prussians stopped to besiege outlying French positions, thus allowing Strasbourg to organize its defenses.

Barely two weeks after the rout, St. Just and Le Bas, *représentants en mission* from the Committee of Public Safety, arrived to restore order. By requisitioning goods and funds from civilians and imposing draconian punishments for infractions of military discipline, they supplied the troops with both new resources and new motivation. The arrival and increasing cooperation of two new generals, Louis Lazare Hoche (Army of the Moselle) and Jean-Charles Pichegru (Army of the Rhine), completed the turnaround: By the end of the year, the French were in control of the Rhine front.

James Wald

See also Brunswick, Charles William Ferdinand, Duke of; Convention, The; First Coalition, War of the; Geisberg, Battle of the; Hoche, Louis Lazare; Mainz, Siege of; Pichegru, Jean-Charles; Public Safety, Committee of; Rhine Campaigns (1792–1797); Würmser, Dagobert Sigismund Graf
References and further reading
Blanning, T. C. W. 1996. *The French Revolutionary Wars, 1787–1802.* London: Arnold.
Chuquet, A. M. 1886–1896. *Les guerres de la Révolution.* 11 vols. Vol. 8. Paris: Léopold Cerf.
Griffith, Paddy. 1998. *The Art of War of Revolutionary France, 1789–1802.* London: Greenhill.
Palmer, R. R. 1970. *Twelve Who Ruled: The Year of the Terror in the French Revolution.* Princeton: Princeton University Press.
Phipps, Ramsay Weston. 1980. *The Armies of the First French Republic and the Rise of the Marshals of Napoleon I.* 5 vols. Vol. 2, *The Armées de la Moselle, du Rhin, de Sambre-et-Meuse, de Rhin-et-Moselle.* London: Greenwood. (Orig. pub. 1926–1939.)

Wellesley, Arthur

See Wellington, Arthur Wellesley, First Duke of

Wellesley, Richard Colley Wellesley, First Marquis (1760–1842)

British diplomat and eldest brother of the victor of the Peninsular War and the Waterloo campaign, Arthur Wellesley, First Duke of Wellington. The son of Garret

Wesley, the first Earl of Mornington, Richard Wellesley (styled Viscount Wellesley until 1781) was born 20 June 1760 in County Meath, Ireland. Educated at Eton and at Christ Church, he left Oxford in 1781 to assume the Mornington peerage as the second earl upon his father's death.

Wellesley was elected a Member of Parliament in 1784 and became a junior Lord of the Treasury in 1786, the same year he started his brother Arthur's military career by enrolling him at the Royal Academy of Equitation at Angers in France. He later purchased for his brother a series of army commissions. Wellesley's growing interest in India moved him to the Board of Control for India, and led to his surprise appointment as governor-general of Bengal in 1797.

When Wellesley arrived in India, the East India Company faced growing unrest in various provinces, the leaders of which controlled large military forces backed by French officers. Wars with Mysore (1799) and a campaign against the Marathas (1803), combined with Wellesley's diplomacy, cemented British domination over much of India. He established Fort William College in Calcutta in 1799 to train British civil servants in the administration of the subcontinent. His success in India earned him the marquisate of Wellesley in December 1799, thus granting to him the title for which he is best known, first Marquis Wellesley.

Having successfully opposed the French threat in India, Wellesley was recalled from India in 1805, largely due to the dissatisfaction of the East India Company, which was saddled with war debts. Returning home in 1806, Wellesley accepted the ambassadorship to the Spanish provisional government, the Junta Central, in Seville, in 1809. Wellesley cooperated with his brother Arthur in prosecuting the war in the Iberian Peninsula and spent most of his time seeking support for his brother's army. Wellesley also found himself at odds with the junta over opening the representative assembly, the Cortes. Frustrated with the lack of support, Wellesley tendered his resignation, which led to renewed vows of support for Wellington's campaign from foreign secretary George Canning.

From 1810 until his resignation in early 1812, Wellesley served as foreign secretary in the ministry of Spencer Perceval. After Perceval's assassination in May 1812, the Prince Regent asked Wellesley to form a government. Few were willing to serve under Wellesley, however, largely because of his strong support for Catholic emancipation and what was seen as undue attention paid in seeking support for his brother's campaign in Spain. Instead, Lord Liverpool formed a government.

Wellesley accepted the post of Lord Lieutenant of Ireland in 1821, largely because his support of Catholic emancipation seemed politically expedient during the period of unrest that followed the Napoleonic Wars. When his brother, since 1814 the Duke of Wellington, became prime minister in 1828, Wellesley resigned over their differences over Catholic emancipation. Wellesley held several other government jobs, including another brief stint as Lord Lieutenant of Ireland from 1832 to 1834, after Catholic emancipation had been approved, before finally retiring from public life in 1835. Wellesley died on 26 September 1842 at Kingston House, Brompton.

Thomas D. Veve

See also Cádiz, Cortes of; Canning, George; Catholic Emancipation; India; Ireland; Junta Central; Liverpool, Robert Banks Jenkinson, Second Earl of; Peninsular War; Perceval, Spencer; Wellington, Arthur Wellesley, First Duke of

References and further reading
Butler, Iris. 1973. *Eldest Brother: The Marquess Wellesley, the Duke of Wellington's Eldest Brother*. London: Hodder and Stoughton.
Hutton, William Holden. 1893. *The Marquess Wellesley, K.G.* Oxford: Clarendon.
Muir, Rory. 1996. *Britain and the Defeat of Napoleon, 1807–1815*. New Haven: Yale University Press.
Severn, John K. 1981. *A Wellesley Affair: Richard Marquess Wellesley and the Conduct of Anglo-Spanish Diplomacy, 1809–1812*. Tallahassee: University Presses of Florida.
Weller, Jac. 2000. *Wellington in India*. London: Greenhill.

Wellington, Arthur Wellesley, First Duke of (1769–1852)

Arguably, Britain's greatest soldier, yet incontestably the principal figure responsible for the Allied victories in both the Peninsular War and the Waterloo campaign. During the course of the French Revolutionary and Napoleonic Wars, no other commander enjoyed greater success against the French than did the Duke of Wellington, who defeated a string of Napoleon's subordinates in Portugal, Spain, and southern France between 1808 and 1814, before finally confronting and vanquishing the Emperor himself at Waterloo in 1815.

The fourth son of impoverished Anglo-Irish aristocrats, Garret Wesley (the family surname being changed to Wellesley in 1789), first Earl of Mornington, and Anne, eldest daughter of Arthur Hill, first Viscount Dungannon, Arthur Wesley was born on 1 May 1769 and variously educated—at Eton, through private tuition in Brussels, and at a military academy at Angers, in France. He was not athletic, nor indeed particularly strong in health, but reasonably accomplished in music and mathematics, both of which he preferred to outdoor or other academic pursuits, and showed no particular interest in, nor aptitude for, military affairs, unlike his elder brother, Richard, the future Marquis Wellesley. With money loaned to him by Richard, who became head of the family upon Mornington's death in 1781, Arthur purchased his commission in March 1787, joining the 73rd Foot as an ensign before exchanging first into the 41st Foot in January 1788, next into the 12th Light Dragoons in June 1789, and finally into the 18th Light Dragoons in October 1792.

From 1787 to 1793 he was aide-de-camp to the Lord Lieutenant of Ireland, and was elected to the Irish Parliament as the member for Trim, County Meath, in 1790, serving for five years. In an age when promotion could be obtained through wealth alone, Wellesley advanced rapidly up the ranks through lavish spending and family connection, becoming lieutenant colonel of the 33rd Foot in 1793. He served in the Duke of York's campaign in Holland in the following year, fighting at Boxtel on 14 September. Wellesley's disappointment at the poor record of the army and the incompetence displayed by senior officers during the campaign led him to make a careful study of military affairs, seeking lessons to be learned from the debacle.

In 1797 his regiment was sent to India, where he benefited greatly from his brother Richard's position as governor-general. As a brigadier, Wellesley commanded a division of British and Indian troops in the campaign against Tipu Sultan of Mysore in 1799, when he distinguished himself at the siege of Seringapatam, which fell on 4 May. Thereafter, Wellesley proved himself adept at the civil administration of both the city and the region as a whole. Despite the fact that poor health obliged him to remain behind when Sir David Baird led an expedition to Egypt in 1801, Wellesley received a promotion to major general the following year at the remarkably young age of thirty-three.

During the campaign against the Mahrattas, he scored two celebrated victories at which he was heavily outnumbered: at Assaye, on 23 September 1803, and Argaum (Argoan), on 29 November. His time in India toughened Wellesley, enabled him to appreciate the connection between tactics and topography, and to grasp the importance of adequate logistics and reconnaissance. He maintained austere domestic habits—being abstemious and taking very little sleep in a narrow campaign cot—all of which were to stand him in good stead during his later years fighting the French in Iberia. Wellesley also showed himself a very competent civil administrator during his years on the subcontinent.

Battle-hardened and experienced, Wellesley left India on 10 March 1805, now as Sir Arthur Wellesley—and returned to Ireland. He was given command of a brigade stationed along the Channel coast while Britain stood poised to receive a threatened French invasion which, in the end, never materialized. In 1806 he was elected to Parliament as the member for Rye, and later for other constituencies. On 10 April he married Catherine Pakenham, with whom his partnership never properly developed. From 1807 to 1809

The Duke of Wellington, commander in chief of the Anglo-Portuguese and Spanish armies, which he led to victory in the Peninsula. He later commanded the Anglo-Allied army during the Waterloo campaign in 1815. (Engraving by W. Say after Thomas Phillips from *British Military Prints* by Ralph Nevill, London: Connoisseur, 1909)

he served as chief secretary for Ireland in the Duke of Portland's government, though he took leave from Dublin in 1807 to lead a division in the expedition to Copenhagen, where he defeated the Danes at Kjoge on 29 August.

Wellesley was promoted to lieutenant general in the summer of 1808 and given command of an expedition dispatched to Portugal, which the French had occupied the year before. He defeated the French at Roliça (16 August) and Vimeiro (21 August), for which he became widely popular at home, though he was superseded by lieutenant generals Sir Harry Burrard and Sir Hew Dalyrmple, who refused Wellesley's pleas to pursue General Jean Andoche Junot and force the surrender of the entire French army in Portugal.

When on 31 August his superiors signed the Convention of Cintra, by whose lenient terms the French were to be evacuated from Portugal in British ships, Wellesley was ordered by his superiors to sign the agreement, much to his own distaste. All three generals were recalled to Britain to account for themselves before a court of inquiry that, however, on 22 December exonerated Wellesley from any misconduct connected with this unauthorized agreement with the vanquished enemy. Meanwhile, in November and December, Lieutenant General Sir John Moore was caught in the midst of his disastrous Corunna campaign, which ended with a horrendous fighting retreat to the northwest coast of Spain, where in January 1809 a Royal Navy squadron evacuated the shattered remains of his army.

Moore having been killed in battle at Corunna, Wellesley assumed command of British forces in Portugal upon his arrival in Lisbon on 22 April. Wasting no time, he opened an offensive, surprising and defeating Marshal Nicolas Soult at Oporto on 12 May, and temporarily ejecting his forces from Portugal. On the basis of help promised by the Spanish, Wellesley then crossed the border into Spain and, on 27–29 July, with nominal help from Spanish general Gregorio García de la Cuesta, confronted the French under Napoleon's brother King Joseph and Marshal Jean-Baptiste Jourdan at Talavera, for which defensive victory Wellesley was raised to the peerage as Viscount Wellington on 4 September. Without adequate support from the Spanish, however, he was obliged to retire back into Portugal, where the army did not fight again between August 1809 and February 1810.

Wellington completely reorganized the army, forming permanent divisions and integrating Portuguese brigades—trained, armed, and clothed under British auspices—into his forces. During the campaign of 1810 Wellington defeated the French at Busaco on 27 September, thus halting the enemy's advance on Lisbon, around which Wellington directed the construction of a remarkable series of fortifications, entrenchments, and outposts known as the Lines of Torres Vedras. Marshal André Masséna, discovering that he could not penetrate these formidable defenses and unable to feed his army as a result of Wellington's scorched-earth policy, retreated on 16 November toward the border fortress of Almeida, with the Anglo-Portuguese army in pursuit.

Wellington confronted Masséna again in a bitterly fought struggle for Fuentes de Oñoro on 3–5 May 1811, while his subordinate, Marshal (his rank in the Portuguese Army) Sir William Beresford, defeated Soult at Albuera on the sixteenth. By this time Wellington's army had evolved into a highly effective fighting force, supported by the diversionary activities of Spanish guerrillas who were tying down substantial numbers of French troops throughout the Peninsula, so relieving some of the pressure from the British army. His achievements thus far earned for Wellington an earldom on 18 February 1812.

In order to advance into Spain, Wellington had to secure the border fortresses of Badajoz and Ciudad Rodrigo, his siege of the former of which he had to raise owing to

the advance of marshals Auguste de Marmont and Soult. On 20 January 1812, however, he assaulted and carried the fortress of Ciudad Rodrigo, followed on 6 April by Badajoz, though at a terrible cost to his infantry, for whom Wellington wept in the wake of the fighting. Still, the path into Spain now lay open, with even greater advantages accruing to Wellington as a result of the withdrawal of substantial numbers of French forces for service in Napoleon's forthcoming campaign against Russia. In his great summer offensive, Wellington scored a remarkable success at Salamanca on 22 July against Marmont, dispelling the myth that the earl was a "defensive" general.

Even so, his subsequent occupation of Madrid in August proved but temporary after his failure in September and October at besieging Burgos—his only major setback in the Peninsula. Pursued by Soult and General Joseph, comte Souham, Wellington conducted an exhausting, costly retreat to the Spanish-Portuguese border before establishing winter quarters. Nevertheless, he was the toast of both Spain and Portugal, received numerous titles and decorations from their respective governments, and was appointed commander in chief of the Spanish Army in October. On behalf of his own nation, Wellington received a marquisate on the third of that month from the Prince Regent.

By the time the new campaign season opened in the spring of 1813, the army had been bolstered by substantial numbers of reinforcements from Britain. With these swelling his existing force, Wellington—for the first time able to deploy superior numbers against the French—opened a new, carefully planned offensive that led to a crushing victory at Vitoria on 21 June. This proved the decisive battle of the war, and forced the French to evacuate most of what they still controlled of Spain. Nevertheless, the fortresses at San Sebastian and Pamplona still remained in French hands, and Soult proceeded to pursue a skillful campaign along the Pyrenees, with fighting at Sorauren (28–30 July), Vera (1 September), and elsewhere. Yet, with the French no longer able to launch offensives of their own, Wellington took San Sebastian—like Ciudad Rodrigo and Badajoz, stormed at heavy cost—on 31 August before crossing the Bidassoa River on 7 October and entering France itself. On native soil, Soult continued to prove himself a formidable opponent, yet consistently obliged to give ground, the heaviest fighting taking place at the Nivelle (10 November), St. Pierre (13 December), the Nive (9–13 December), Orthez (27 February 1814), Tarbes (20 March), and, finally, at Toulouse (10 April), a tragically pointless battle fought before news arrived that Napoleon had already abdicated at Fontainebleau four days earlier.

After an absence from Britain of five years, Wellington received a hero's homecoming, whereupon the Prince

Regent appointed him ambassador to France on 21 April and made him a duke on 3 May. On 15 February 1815 Wellington arrived at the Congress of Vienna as a delegate, joining the British foreign secretary, Viscount Castlereagh, who had been representing his nation's interests in the negotiations for the political reconstruction of postwar Europe that had begun the previous November.

When Napoleon returned from Elba and landed in France on 1 March, Wellington took command of the Anglo-Allied army in the Netherlands and narrowly defeated Marshal Michel Ney at Quatre Bras on 16 June, before, two days later and in conjunction with the Prussian army under the command of Field Marshal Gebhard Fürst Blücher von Wahlstatt, vanquishing Napoleon—against whom Wellington had never personally fought before—at the historic encounter at Waterloo. In the subsequent occupation of France Wellington served as commander in chief of Allied forces, an appointment that marked the end of his active military career, though he remained commander in chief until his death.

Wellington's appointment as Master General of the Ordnance from 1818 to 1827 inaugurated a long political career, during which he led several diplomatic missions to the Continent. He became prime minister in 1828, pushing through legislation granting Catholic emancipation, a cause he reluctantly supported if only to avoid civil war in Ireland. He resigned from office in November 1830 owing to objections against political reforms proposed for the House of Commons, but returned briefly as prime minister in 1834, and later as home secretary.

Wellington's politics were marked by ultraconservatism and a staunch opposition to social and political reform, for which he made himself unpopular during various stages of his postwar career. With his public standing largely restored by 1841, the duke took up in that year a cabinet post as minister without portfolio, and by the time he retired from public life five years later he had achieved an exalted status in British society. He died of stroke, aged eighty-three, at Walmer Castle in Kent on 14 September 1852, mourned by all ranks of society. Wellington's funeral procession, which passed through London to St. Paul's Cathedral on 18 November, was watched by an estimated 1.5 million people.

In assessing Wellington's leadership qualities, one must inevitably examine his record in the Peninsular War, Waterloo merely marking the climax of a career whose foundations were laid in India before maturing in Iberia. The high professional standards that the army achieved in Spain and Portugal were a testament to Wellington's abilities not only as a superb commander in the field, but also as a highly skilled administrator. His constant concern for the welfare of his men earned him his troops' respect and,

later, devotion, though it could not be said that Wellington was loved, unlike his great nemesis, Napoleon.

Indeed, the duke stood largely aloof socially, dressed in sober fashion, demanded strict discipline, never hesitated to order punishments—including death—for infractions, worked extremely long hours, and expected the same commitment to duty of his staff, who for the most part rendered him excellent service. Wellington also possessed remarkable stamina and made industrious use of his time. He would rise at 6:00 A.M. and work until midnight, writing large numbers of orders and dispatches, and rode between 30 and 80 miles a day. In the six years he spent in the Peninsula he never once went on leave.

Wellington's supreme self-confidence about his plans and his abilities was tempered by an understanding of his limitations based on clear-sighted forward planning and good use of intelligence. He began the war with a well-conceived and effective long-term strategy in mind and he adapted his tactics—usually but not always, defensive—to suit the ground, his opponents' strengths and weaknesses, and the capabilities of his men. He possessed the sort of intelligent mind that could quickly assess a situation, whether at the strategic or tactical level. He laid his plans carefully and often anticipated those of his enemy. He had a good grasp of logistics and understood that an effective army required regular supplies of food, equipment, and ammunition. As such, he recognized the importance of an efficiently run commissariat.

Wellington seldom delegated authority to his subordinates in order to maintain personal control of affairs whenever possible, particularly on the battlefield. His orders were clear and he saw to it that they were carried out precisely. While his failure to delegate may be seen as a fault, his consistent battlefield successes owed much to his presence on the scene, where by exposing himself to fire he encouraged his men and could see at first hand where action needed to be taken: sending reinforcements, exploiting a success, withdrawing, and so on. Proof of his constant presence in the thick of things is shown by his narrow escape from capture on three occasions and the three times when he was hit by musket balls—though without receiving serious injury.

Wellington recognized—and acknowledged early in the war—that with only one army, and a small one at that, he could not afford to be defeated: He simply could not enjoy that luxury. Criticisms leveled against him as a strategically "defensive" general should be analyzed in this light. He spent three years in a largely defensive posture and seldom took risks, fighting only when circumstances were favorable and then with positive results. By preventing the French from concentrating their massive numbers against him, he could fight their armies separately on reasonable terms and wait for the time to switch to the offensive.

Thus, though the French had several hundred thousand men in the Peninsula at any given time, Wellington normally fought battles with about 50,000 men on each side. Napoleon's invasion of Russia in 1812, in particular, enabled him to do so, since that campaign not only required some French troops to transfer east, but would later deny to French commanders in the Peninsula much-needed reinforcements. From then on the French were obliged to fight a two-front war, thereby emboldening Wellington to move to the offensive. While it is true that at the tactical level he largely fought on the defensive, this was by no means always the case, as demonstrated at Oporto, Salamanca, Vitoria, and elsewhere.

Wellington understood that the war in the Peninsula would be long, and where other commanders might have regarded the odds as hopeless, he persisted. If his campaigns failed, he would accept responsibility, and he understood his dependence on the goodwill and cooperation of his hosts. He never gave in to what he called "the croakers," officers in his own army who suggested, often behind the scenes, that the war was a lost cause, particularly in the period between Talavera and the withdrawal of Masséna from the Lines of Torres Vedras.

He inherited an army that, though it had undergone reforms under competent men like Sir Ralph Abercromby and Sir John Moore, had a poor military record. Yet in the course of a few years he organized and trained the finest army of its size in Europe. And, whatever one may say about the contribution made by the Spanish—both regulars and guerrillas—the balance of Allied victory or defeat in the Peninsula ultimately hung on the ability of Wellington's army to defeat the French in the field. This he did consistently with small numbers that usually varied between 30,000 and 60,000 men, of mixed nationality, but men of exceptionally high caliber, training, and leadership.

In short, Wellington's consistent victories owed much to his careful planning, his personal supervision of the fighting, and his ability to react appropriately as circumstances changed. He anticipated the actions of his adversaries, who were often experienced generals, and so could plan accordingly. Finally, he commanded an army, composed, in the main, of competent general officers and well-trained men, probably the best Britain has ever produced. His victories were not entirely unbroken: Burgos stands out as the exception, but few commanders of any age enjoyed the succession of victories for which Wellington may rightfully claim credit.

Gregory Fremont-Barnes

See also Abercromby, Sir Ralph; Albuera, Battle of; Almeida, Sieges of; Badajoz, Second Siege of; Badajoz, Third Siege of; Beresford, Sir William Carr; Bidassoa, Crossing of the; Blücher von Wahlstatt, Gebhard Lebrecht Fürst; Bonaparte, Joseph; Burgos, Siege of; Busaco, Battle of; Castlereagh, Robert Stewart, Viscount; Cintra, Convention of; Ciudad Rodrigo, Second Siege of; Copenhagen, Attack on; Corunna, Retreat to; Flanders, Campaigns in; Fuentes de Oñoro, Battle of; García de la Cuesta, Gregorio; India; Jourdan, Jean-Baptiste; Kjoge, Battle of; Marmont, Auguste Frédéric Louis Viesse de; Masséna, André; Moore, Sir John; Ney, Michel; Nive, Battle of the; Nivelle, Battle of the; Oporto, Battle of; Orthez, Battle of; Pamplona, Siege of; Peninsular War; Quatre Bras, Battle of; Roliça, Battle of; Salamanca, Battle of; San Sebastian, Siege of; Sorauren, Battle of; Souham, Joseph, comte; Soult, Nicolas Jean de Dieu; St. Pierre, Battle of; Talavera, Battle of; Tarbes, Battle of; Torres Vedras, Lines of; Toulouse, Battle of; Vera, Battles of; Vienna, Congress of; Vimeiro, Battle of; Waterloo, Battle of; Waterloo Campaign; Wellesley, Richard Colley Wellesley, First Marquis; York and Albany, Frederick Augustus, Duke of

References and further reading

Chandler, David G. 1980. *Waterloo: The Hundred Days.* New York: Macmillan.

———. 1994. *On the Napoleonic Wars: Collected Essays.* London: Greenhill.

Cooper, Leonard. 1967. *The Age of Wellington: The Life and Times of the Duke of Wellington, 1769–1852.* New York: Dodd, Mend.

Corrigan, Gordon. 2000. *Wellington: A Military Life.* London: Hambledon Continuum.

Esdaile, Charles J. 1990. *The Duke of Wellington and the Command of the Spanish Army, 1812–14.* London: Macmillan.

———. 2003. *The Peninsular War: A New History.* London: Penguin.

Fortescue, Sir John. 1925. *Wellington.* London: Williams and Norgate.

Gates, David. 1986. *The Spanish Ulcer: A History of the Peninsular War.* New York: Norton.

Glover, Michael. 1963. *Wellington's Peninsular Victories.* London: Batsford.

———. 1968. *Wellington as Military Commander.* London: Batsford.

———. 1974. *The Peninsular War, 1807–14: A Concise Military History.* Newton Abbot, UK: David and Charles.

Griffith, Paddy. 1985. *Wellington Commander.* Chichester, UK: Bird.

Guedalla, Philip. 1997. *The Duke.* Ware, Hertfordshire, UK: Wordsworth.

Hibbert, Christopher. 1998. *Wellington: A Personal History.* London: HarperCollins.

Holmes, Richard. 2003. *Wellington: The Iron Duke.* London: HarperCollins.

James, Lawrence. 2002. *The Iron Duke: A Military Biography of Wellington.* London: Pimlico.

Longford, Elizabeth. 1969. *The Years of the Sword.* London: Harper and Row.

———. 1972. *Wellington: Pillar of State.* London: Harper and Row.

Neillands, Robin. 1994. *Wellington and Napoleon: Clash of Arms, 1807–1815.* London: John Murray.

Paget, Julian. 1996. *Wellington's Peninsular War: Battles and Battlefields.* London: Cooper.

Rathbone, Julian. 1984. *Wellington's War: His Peninsular Dispatches.* London: Joseph.

Roberts, Andrew. 2003. *Napoleon and Wellington: The Long Duel.* London: Weidenfeld and Nicolson.

Robertson, Ian. 2003. *Wellington Invades France: The Final Phase of the Peninsular War, 1813–1814.* London: Greenhill.

Strachan, Hew. 1984. *Wellington's Legacy: The Reform of the British Army, 1830–54.* Manchester: Manchester University Press.

Thompson, Neville. 1986. *Wellington after Waterloo.* London: Routledge and Kegan Paul.

Weller, Jac. 1992. *Wellington in the Peninsula, 1808–1814.* London: Greenhill.

———. 1998. *Wellington at Waterloo.* London: Greenhill.

———. 2000. *Wellington in India.* London: Greenhill.

West Indies, Operations in the (1793–1810)

Between 1793 and 1810, the West Indies became a major theater of the French Revolutionary and Napoleonic Wars. Operations in the Caribbean were complicated by the necessity for cooperation between the army and navy, the large number of casualties caused by disease, and the ever-growing threat of slave revolts.

When the French Revolutionary government declared war on Britain on 1 February 1793, the conflict thus far involving (principally) France, Austria, and Prussia, evolved from a European conflict to a global war. Prior to the outbreak of the Anglo-French phase of the conflict, the Caribbean was already in turmoil, as the ideals of liberty and equality had sparked civil unrest and slave rebellions across the French Caribbean islands. France's richest colony, St. Domingue, the western portion of the island of Hispaniola (the eastern part being the Spanish possession of Santo Domingo), was plagued with continual warfare after a slave revolt began in August 1791.

In the spring of 1793 Britain began offensive operations in the West Indies, but attention was diverted to the campaigns in Europe. The first conquest was the French island of Tobago, which surrendered on 15 April after the British landed a small force from Barbados. Meanwhile, the French governor of Martinique, General Donatien Rochambeau, had difficulty putting down a royalist revolt. The local British commander sailed in June with 1,100 troops to Martinique. By the time the British arrived, Rochambeau had already captured the main royalist camp. Despite being supported by 800 royalists, the British attack on St. Pierre on 18 June failed after running into a republican ambush. The British withdrew and evacuated over 5,000 royalist refugees.

Meanwhile, the British secretary of war, Henry Dundas, prepared plans for a large expedition to the Caribbean during the fall of 1793 to be commanded by Lieutenant General Sir Charles Grey and Vice Admiral Sir John Jervis. Events in Europe put the expedition in jeopardy, as troops were sent to halt the French offensive in Flanders and protect the captured city of Toulon. In addition, the governor of Jamaica decided to support French planters on St. Domingue, reducing the available British force to a total of around 7,000 men. The expedition left on 26 November and straggled into Barbados by early January 1794.

On 2 February the expedition left Barbados to attack Martinique. Armed with detailed plans of the French defenses provided by royalists, Grey devised a strategy to carry out multiple landings in order to confuse and disperse the French garrison. To defend Martinique, Rochambeau had only around 2,000 men, including regulars and the mulatto national guard. While the British quickly gained control of most of Martinique, Rochambeau consolidated his forces in the forts protecting Fort-de-France. Due to the stubborn defense of the French garrison and the rains that hindered the progress of the British siege, Rochambeau was able to hold out until 25 March. While the British succeeded in capturing this important island, the persistence of the French defense had cost the British nearly a month and half of the campaign season.

The British quickly prepared to continue their sweep of the West Indies. The next target was the smaller French island of St. Lucia to the south. After leaving several regiments on Martinique, the British landed around 5,000 men at various points on St. Lucia on 1 April. The several-hundred-man French garrison quickly surrendered on 4 April after the British had made a strong show of force. After leaving 1,000 troops on St. Lucia, the British continued their offensive and invaded Guadeloupe, where the French garrison surrendered on 22 April 1794 after two weeks of resistance.

Meanwhile, to leeward, in mid-September 1793, a British squadron, loaded with troops from Jamaica, ran into some French white planters who offered the British control of Mole St. Nicolas. The British seized the offer, thereby beginning the British occupation of St. Domingue. Slowly the British increased their control over the southern province of the colony.

June 1794 marked a major turning point in operations in the West Indies. On 2 June nine French ships carrying over a thousand troops anchored off Guadeloupe near Point-à-Pitre. The local British commander did not possess sufficient forces to oppose their landing and called on the governor for aid. Messengers were sent out to Grey and Jervis, who were about to depart from the Caribbean. However, the governor had died that day, and the second in

Operations in the West Indies

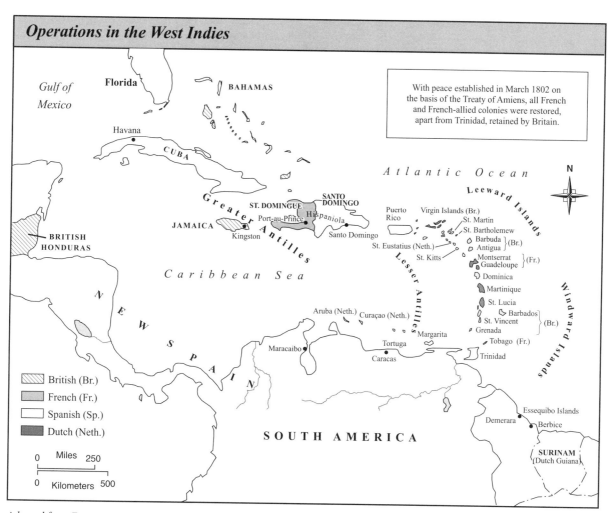

With peace established in March 1802 on the basis of the Treaty of Amiens, all French and French-allied colonies were restored, apart from Trinidad, retained by Britain.

British (Br.)

French (Fr.)

Spanish (Sp.)

Dutch (Neth.)

Adapted from Fremont-Barnes 2001, 35.

command took several days to send reinforcements to Point-à-Pitre. After the French stormed Fort d'Epée, the British retreated across to the other half of the island, Basse Terre. Even the arrival of Grey and Jervis did little to improve the situation for the British. The French squadron was safely anchored in the port of Point-à-Pitre under the protection of the harbor forts, while Grey did not have many troops available to deal with this new threat, as sickness had ravaged his ranks and his reinforcements had been sent on to St. Domingue.

Leadership of the French fell to the republican commissioner Victor Hugues, as all of the other generals and government leaders were killed or incapacitated in the initial fighting or subsequent onset of yellow fever. Hugues published the French declaration of emancipation, which bolstered his disease-ravaged ranks with ex-slaves and free blacks. In late June Grey decided to attempt to storm the French forts, as there was little time available before the sickly season arrived. Hugues had around 3,000 men to face Grey's 3,500. The British assault on 1 July became

bogged down in the town, where the veteran British units were mauled by the French, breaking British morale. Grey evacuated all his troops back to Basse Terre. Disease continued to whittle down the British force and the European troops of the French. Hugues responded by conscripting and training an additional 2,000 black recruits.

When Jervis's ships drifted off their station in September, the French launched an invasion of Basse Terre on 27 September. Most of the British troops surrendered on 6 October, leaving the British in control of only the town of Basseterre. Hugues laid siege to the place, which eventually surrendered in December 1794.

Then, both in Europe and the Caribbean, the British stood on the defensive. In January 1795 Hugues was reinforced with another 2,000 troops, which he used to assume the offensive, sending representatives to St. Lucia, St. Vincent, and Grenada. To Grenada, an ex-French colony, Hugues sent the mulatto planter Julien Fédon to lead the local French population, which had grown discontented with British rule. The local British commander had only

100 troops at his disposal. On St. Vincent, Hugues aided the French population and the native Caribs, who eventually took over control of most of the island. Hugues also sent aid to the French insurgents on St. Lucia who had been harassing the British since their invasion. Losing control over the island and fearing defeat, the British evacuated St. Lucia in June. Only on Dominica, where the old French population failed to rise, did Hugues's efforts prove unsuccessful. To the leeward, the British were not faring much better, as they were under pressure on St. Domingue, and a revolt among the native Maroons broke out on Jamaica.

The loss of its continental allies and the threat posed by Hugues's use of emancipation as an incentive to encourage resistance to British occupation led Britain to prepare a major expedition to the Caribbean. Initially the goal of the operations planned for 1795–1796 was to reconquer Guadeloupe, in the belief that by cutting off French support from the island, they would weaken the resolve of republican forces on the other islands. The British prime minister, William Pitt, hoped that a victory in the West Indies would lead to the conclusion of hostilities with France without the need for continental allies. These operations constituted the largest overseas expedition ever mounted by Britain, even though it was only able to muster 22,000 of the planned 30,000 troops. Even so, combined with the forces already in the West Indies, this force accounted for almost half of the entire British Army. The expedition, commanded by Major General Ralph Abercromby and Rear Admiral Hugh Christian, was to reinforce St. Domingue. The expedition was ready by November, but poor weather forced nearly two-thirds of the vessels to return to port. Dundas then changed the plan: First, recapture St. Lucia, then secure St. Vincent and Grenada, and then occupy Demerara.

Abercromby was sent ahead to begin preparations, while the ships undertook repairs. When he arrived in Barbados in March 1796, Abercromby found that some of the troops that had arrived early had already been sent to reinforce Grenada. Before the rest of the expedition arrived, Abercromby decided to detach small forces to capture the Dutch colonies of Curaçao and Demerara, both of which had offered to place themselves under British control. In mid-April part of the expedition arrived, giving him a total of 7,000 available troops. On 25 April Abercromby landed on St. Lucia. The French garrison put up stiff resistance, forcing Abercromby to lay siege to the island. With the arrival of an additional 5,500 men, he completely encircled the garrison. Although the French black troops put up a stubborn defense, the lack of rain enabled the besiegers to make progress without delays due to weather or disease, while the defenders' own water supplies ran dry. On 25 May the garrison of 2,000 troops

surrendered, although a number of men took to the hills to continue their former guerrilla campaign against the British.

Leaving 3,000 men to garrison St. Lucia, Abercromby dispatched 2,500 troops to both St. Vincent and Grenada. By June both Fédon's revolt on Grenada and the French-Carib uprising on St. Vincent had been suppressed. Although the British Windward Islands were secured, no new advances were made, as the situation was the same as in 1794, with the French still in control of Guadeloupe. Meanwhile, the occupation of St. Domingue fell from the list of priorities, and fewer reinforcements, many of them worthless cavalry, were sent to the island. Meanwhile, in May, a French squadron landed 3,000 troops, as well as a number of guns and ammunition for the republicans.

During the summer of 1796 the British made little progress in the West Indies, as disease killed over two-fifths (6,500) of their troops and confined another one-fifth (4,000 men) to the hospitals, having left only 6,500 men fit for duty by January 1796. Meanwhile, in Europe, France had knocked Prussia and Spain out of the war in 1795, the latter power switching sides to oppose Britain, and thus forcing the Pitt government to end its offensive in the Caribbean.

When Spain declared war on Britain on 8 October 1796, Britain decided to launch a new offensive to attack the vulnerable Spanish Empire, hoping to capture both Buenos Aires and Trinidad. While the expedition to Buenos Aires was dropped due to lack of available ships, the expedition to Trindad was delayed until January 1797 by the difficulty in obtaining shipping and then the news of General Louis Lazare Hoche's expedition to Ireland. Meanwhile, a small Spanish squadron had reinforced Trinidad with another 1,500 troops.

When the British expedition arrived in February, Abercromby collected around 3,700 troops aboard five ships of the line and eight smaller vessels. As the fleet made its way around Trinidad, the British discovered a small Spanish squadron. With insufficient numbers of men to crew his ships, the Spanish admiral set fire to them and led his men across the island toward Puerta de España. During the morning of 17 February, the British disembarked, and the Spanish governor surrendered the next day. Leaving 1,000 men to garrison the island, Abercromby gathered 4,000 troops to launch an attack on Puerto Rico, which Abercromby hoped would surrender quickly like Trinidad.

The British landed east of Puerto Rico's principal port of San Juan on 18 April. The Spanish governor, Don Ramón de Castro, refused the British demand to surrender and reinforced his already formidable defenses. After several failed attempts to advance on the fortifications of San Juan, Abercromby abandoned his plans and evacuated his forces during the night of 30 April.

After the failed attack on Puerto Rico, Britain focused on retaining its conquests rather than continuing its offensives. As part of that plan, Britain started to withdraw its troops from St. Domingue. In the spring of 1798 troops were evacuated from nearly all of southern St. Domingue, with the exception of Mole St. Nicholas and Jeremie. However, even these two locations proved too difficult and costly to defend, obliging the British to withdraw completely in August, leaving St. Domingue for good.

Meanwhile, things were calm in the Windward Islands, as a British squadron blockaded Guadeloupe and Hugues was running low on supplies. While there were no major British operations, several minor expeditions were undertaken. On 20 August 1799 the governor of Dutch Guyana (alternatively, Guiana, now Surinam), surrendered the colony to the British upon the arrival of a small naval squadron. Similarly, Curaçao capitulated to passing British frigates on 13 September 1800.

With the failure of the British expedition to Holland in 1799, Dundas returned to his colonial strategy. Although projects for large-scale expeditions against Cuba, New Orleans, and Buenos Aires were scrapped, the British decided to seize the Swedish and Danish colonies in a pre-emptive strike, to prevent the formation of a new League of Armed Neutrality of the Baltic States, as had been organized in 1780 during the American Revolutionary War.

While 5,000 reinforcements sailed to the Caribbean in February 1801, Lieutenant General Thomas Trigge and Rear Admiral John Duckworth had opened an offensive the preceding month with the 2,000 troops available. On 20 March 1801 the British quickly captured the Swedish colony of St. Bartholomew; the Franco-Dutch island of St. Martin (24 March); and the Danish islands of St. Thomas, St. John's (both 29 March), and St. Croix (31 March). Meanwhile, on 16 April, the French evacuated the Dutch colonies of St. Eustatius and Saba, which were quickly seized by the British.

By the same year, however, France had once again defeated Britain's continental allies, Austria and Russia. In order to save the situation in Europe, the new British prime minister, Henry Addington, agreed to establish peace with France according to the Treaty of Amiens whose preliminary terms were signed in October 1801, later to be definitively settled in March 1802. In conformance with Amiens, Britain returned all of the captured colonies except the Dutch and Spanish possessions of Ceylon (now Sri Lanka) and Trinidad, respectively.

The Peace of Amiens gave Bonaparte free rein to carry out his plan to rebuild the French West Indian empire, a plan that included the reestablishment of slavery. The key part of his plan involved the reassertion of France's authority over St. Domingue, which was now controlled by the ex-slave general, Toussaint Louverture, who had liberated the entire island of Hispaniola and renamed the place Haiti. Napoleon secretly instructed his brother-in-law, General Charles-Victor Leclerc, to eliminate black leaders, disarm the black population, and eventually reenslave them.

Even before the Peace of Amiens was fully ratified, Napoleon had dispatched Leclerc and Admiral Louis Thomas Villaret-Joyeuse with over 20,000 men to St. Domingue. The main force sailed from Brest and Rochefort in mid-December 1801 and arrived off the island in late January 1802. The fleet divided into smaller squadrons, each contingent sent to capture one of the numerous coastal towns of St. Domingue. While some black commanders quickly defected to the French, Toussaint and others resisted and withdrew into the interior of the island to fight. By May Leclerc had persuaded almost all of the black leaders to return to the service of France with promises of maintaining their ranks or positions. Even so, Leclerc's position was deteriorating, as yellow fever decimated his ranks and news of the restoration of slavery in Guadeloupe reached Haiti. During the summer, as Leclerc tried to disarm the black population, resistance movements sprang up across St. Domingue, and by October, many of the black officers joined the rebellion. In November Leclerc died from yellow fever, and command of the troops in St. Domingue passed to Rochambeau, who fought in vain to maintain control.

The Peace of Amiens proved little more than a cease-fire, and hostilities resumed upon Britain's declaration of war on 18 May 1803. Bonaparte's aspirations for a French empire in the Caribbean were quickly ended. A British squadron blockaded the newly independent Haiti, preventing badly needed reinforcements and supplies from reaching the besieged French garrison, portions of which soon began surrendering to the British in order to escape from black forces. Finally, in November, Rochambeau surrendered to the blockading British fleet, leaving only the French garrison of the town of Santo Domingo, on the southeastern coast of the island, to hold out.

In the Windward Islands, Lieutenant General William Grinfeld and Commodore Samuel Hood gathered 3,000 troops in June 1803 to attack St. Lucia. The outnumbered French garrison, led by General Jean François Xavier Noguès, surrendered a few days later on 22 June. The British quickly continued on to Tobago, which surrendered on 30 June. On 20 September the Dutch colonies of Demerara, Essequibo, and Berbice surrendered to the British after Grinfeld made a strong show of force. On 25 April 1804 a British force of 2,000 men invaded Dutch Guyana, which surrendered in early May after a short siege.

In 1805 France resumed the offensive in the Caribbean. As part of the planned invasion of England, Napoleon wanted his various fleets to rendezvous in the West

Indies, where they would divert Vice Admiral Horatio, Viscount Nelson's fleet from European waters and wreak havoc before returning to seize control of the English Channel. On 11 January 1805 Admiral Edouard de Missiessy left Rochefort with 3,500 men aboard five ships of the line and three frigates. Arriving at Martinique in February, Missiessy quickly proceeded to attack the nearby British island of Dominica. General Joseph Lagrange landed his troops on the twenty-second and captured one of the British forts, but the commander had withdrawn the majority of his forces to the safety of another fort in the interior of the island. Having little time available, and expecting Admiral Pierre de Villeneuve, with the combined French and Spanish fleets, to arrive soon, Missiessy and Lagrange decided to abandon the attack on Dominica after collecting a contribution of 100,000 francs. After disembarking reinforcements on Guadeloupe, Missiessy sailed to St. Christopher (St. Kitts), Nevis, and Montserrat, where he collected another 300,000 francs in contributions. In March, upon learning that Villeneuve's initial attempt to sail from Toulon had failed, Missiessy completed his mission by leaving 500 troops for the French garrison of Santo Domingo before returning to France.

Unbeknownst to Missiessy, Villeneuve had successfully slipped out of Toulon on 17 January with a large French fleet carrying 3,300 troops. Arriving in Martinique on 14 May, these troops were used on 31 May to assault Diamond Rock, a little islet off the southern coast of Martinique that had been fortified by the British. Although the terrain made the assault difficult, the British garrison, having expended nearly all its ammunition and weakened by extreme thirst, surrendered on 2 June. When two ships arrived from France, Villeneuve learned that the Brest fleet had not left and that Missiessy had already returned to France. Villeneuve thereupon opted to attack Barbados in June and collected troops from both Martinique and Guadeloupe. On the way, however, Villeneuve learned of the presence of a British fleet nearby and decided to call off the attack. The troops recently taken aboard were then loaded onto frigates to be disembarked on Guadeloupe, while Villeneuve sailed for Spain. This was to be the last French offensive in the West Indies. Despite the presence of two French fleets, little had been accomplished.

In December 1805 Admiral Corentin de Leissègues sailed from Brest with a small squadron of five ships of the line and two frigates to transport 1,000 reinforcements and additional munitions to the besieged garrison in Santo Domingo. While Leissègues reached Santo Domingo in late January 1806 and disembarked the troops and supplies, his ships needed repairs before they could get under way. In early February a large British fleet commanded by Vice Admiral Sir John Duckworth spotted and destroyed

them at the Battle of Santo Domingo on 6 February 1806. Following this defeat, Napoleon sent only frigates, either singly or in small squadrons, to carry reinforcements to the Caribbean.

In 1807 the British returned to the offensive in the West Indies. On 1 January four British frigates sailed into the harbor of St. Ann and quickly overwhelmed the surprised Dutch garrison of Curaçao. After a British fleet attacked the neutral Danish fleet at Copenhagen (2–5 September 1807), the British moved to capture the Danish colonies in the Caribbean. Accordingly, on 21 December the islands of St. Thomas and St. John's, followed on the twenty-fifth by St. Croix, surrendered to the British after the attackers made a strong show of force. In March 1808 the British stormed two of Guadeloupe's dependencies, Marie-Galante on the second, and Désirade on the thirtieth, in order to deprive French privateers of their safe anchorages. During the summer the British intercepted French documents reporting the weakness of the garrison on Martinique. The British assembled on Barbados 8,000 men from various colonial garrisons, while 4,000 men were shipped down from Canada for the attack. Meanwhile, on 14 January 1809, the French colony of Guiana surrendered to a small Anglo-Portuguese expedition of 500 men.

On 30 January the British invaded Martinique with around 12,000 men. As in the 1793 invasion the British disembarked their troops at several points in an attempt to divide the attentions of the French garrison. Slowly the overwhelming number of British troops forced the French to fall back toward the fortifications around Fort-de-France. On 10 February the British began their siege of Fort Desaix (formerly Fort Bourbon). After holding out for two weeks and with no sign of a relief force, Captain General Louis Thomas Villaret-Joyeuse surrendered on the twenty-fourth.

Having learned from their previous experiences, the British quickly reembarked the troops brought from Canada and shipped them back to Halifax before they could be ravaged by disease. On 17 April, the British stormed the remaining dependency of Guadeloupe, the Iles des Saintes. Furthermore, the remnants of the French garrison of Santo Domingo surrendered to the British on 6 July. Napoleon had belatedly organized a fleet to relieve Martinique, but the British had shattered it through the use of fire ships near the Basque and Aix Roads, near Rochefort, on 11–16 April 1809.

In early 1810 the British ended their offensive in the West Indies. While the British had made numerous raids on Guadeloupe since 1809, they launched a full-scale invasion with 7,000 troops on 28 January 1810. Abandoned by most of his black troops and colonial militia, General Manuel Ernouf surrendered on 6 February. From Guadeloupe, the British then dispatched a small force to capture the Franco-Dutch island of St. Martin and the Dutch colonies of St. Eustatius and Saba. Thus, by 1810, the French and Dutch had lost the whole of their West Indian colonial possessions.

Kenneth Johnson

See also Abercromby, Sir Ralph; Addington, Henry; Amiens, Treaty of; Armed Neutrality, League of; Basque Roads, Attack on; Copenhagen, Attack on; England, French Plans for the Invasion of; First Coalition, War of the; Flanders, Campaigns in; Haiti; Hoche, Louis Lazare; Leclerc, Charles-Victor Emmanuel; Martinique; Medical Services; Melville, Henry Dundas, First Viscount; Nelson, Horatio, First Viscount; North Holland, Campaign in (1799); Pitt, William; Santo Domingo; Santo Domingo, Battle of; Second Coalition, War of the; Sickness and Disease; Slave Trade; Slavery; St. Lucia; St. Vincent, John Jervis, First Earl of; Third Coalition, War of the; Toulon, Siege of; Toussaint Louverture; Trinidad, Expedition to; Villaret-Joyeuse, Louis Thomas; Villeneuve, Pierre Charles Jean Baptiste Silvestre de

References and further reading
Buckley, Roger Norman. 1998. *The British Army in the West Indies: Society and the Military in the Revolutionary Age.* Gainesville: University of Florida Press.
Chartrand, René. 1989. *Napoleon's Overseas Army.* London: Osprey.
———. 1996. *British Forces in the West Indies, 1793–1815.* London: Osprey.
Chevalier, E. 1886. *Histoire de la marine française sous le Consulat et l'Empire.* Paris: Hachette.
Clowes, William Laird. 1997. *The Royal Navy: A History from the Earliest Times to 1900.* Vols. 4 and 5. London: Chatham. (Orig. pub. 1898.)
Duffy, Michael. 1987. *Soldiers, Sugar, and Seapower: British Expeditions to the West Indies and the War against Revolutionary France.* Oxford: Clarendon.
———. 1990. "The Caribbean Campaigns of the British Army, 1793–1815." In *The Road to Waterloo: The British Army and the Struggle Against Revolutionary and Napoleonic France, 1793–1815,* 23–31. London: National Army Museum.
Fortescue, Sir John. 2004. *History of the British Army.* Vols. 4, 5, and 7. Uckfield, UK: Naval and Military.
Gardiner, Robert, ed. 2001a. *Fleet Battle and Blockade: The French Revolutionary War, 1793–1797.* London: Caxton.
———. 2001b. *Nelson against Napoleon: From the Nile to Copenhagen, 1798–1801.* London: Caxton.
———. 2002. *The Campaign of Trafalgar, 1803–1805.* London: Caxton.
Poyen-Bellisle, Henry de. 1896. *Les Guerres des Antilles, 1793–1815.* Paris: Berger-Levrault.
Woodman, Richard, ed. 2001. *The Victory of Seapower: Winning the Napoleonic War, 1806–1814.* London: Caxton.

Westphalia

Westphalia was one of a number of kingdoms created by Napoleon from the residue of the Holy Roman Empire to support the hegemony of France in Europe. These kingdoms were of two categories: satellite kingdoms ruled by Napoleon and his family, and independent kingdoms allied with the French Empire. Westphalia was in the first category. A good example of a kingdom in the second category was Bavaria.

Westphalia has traditionally been a geographic term referring to the particular region of Germany east of the Rhine but west of the river Elbe, encompassing Brunswick, Hesse, and parts of Hanover. Napoleon created the Kingdom of Westphalia as a political entity as a result of the Peace of Tilsit (July 1807), mostly from the former domains of the Duke of Brunswick and the Elector of Hesse-Cassel. These individuals had supported Prussia in its losing effort against Napoleon during the War of the Fourth Coalition, and to some degree the kingdom's creation also served as punishment. The Emperor named his youngest brother Jérôme (who was only twenty-three at the time) as king, and Cassel was designated as the capital. To further legitimize his brother, Napoleon had Jérôme marry a princess from the royal family of Württemberg.

Napoleon's intention was to create a kingdom ruled by the Bonaparte family that could also serve to dominate a larger political entity, also Napoleon's creation, known as the Confederation of the Rhine (Rheinbund). Alongside Bavaria, Württemberg, Saxony, and other German principalities, Westphalia would serve as a model of French ideas in law and governance. It would also serve as a military and political counterweight in the western part of Germany.

According to specific instructions provided by Napoleon, the country was structured as a constitutional monarchy. The Napoleonic Code served as its law, with an independent judiciary (appointed by the king, however). Jérôme Bonaparte was to rule as king through a council of state overseen by a parliament. Administratively the new country was organized, as in France, into departments (eight in all). All the feudal vestiges and taxes of the Holy Roman Empire were effectively eliminated. Had there not been continued war and strife in Europe, the chances would have been good for a long and stable government on a liberal model. However, Westphalia was almost immediately subjected to Napoleon's "blood tax" by being required to raise an army of 25,000 men to add to the overall contributions of the Confederation of the Rhine to Napoleon's military adventures.

The Westphalian Army was constructed almost exactly on the French model, relying, like its French counterpart, on conscription. The army was composed of both line and guard units. The Royal Guard closely resembled Napoleon's Imperial Guard, although it was smaller in number, and it was meant to provide a solid core of loyal troops. The Westphalian Guard included cavalry, infantry, and artillery as well as specialists and some of the finest light troops at that time in Europe, due to the abundance of *Jäger* (literally, "hunters"; riflemen) who had served the Holy Roman princes in the Hessian, Hanoverian, and Brunswick forest preserves. The Guard also included a regiment styled the *Hussars Jérôme Napoléon*, paid for by Jérôme's father-in-law, the king of Württemberg. The line units included the same basic three branches. The cavalry was well mounted and included both heavy and light regiments. The artillery was organized according to the Gribeauval system, with standardized and excellent guns. Napoleon's hope was that the natural martial ability of the Hessians and Brunswickers who made up the majority of the population would permeate the army (Westphalia's population was almost 2 million).

Almost immediately, though, Jérôme had problems filling out the regiments of his army. Napoleon's involvement in Spain soon resulted in Westphalia's "fair share" being sent south—including the line chevauléger (light horse) regiment, which remained for almost the entire war. During the War of the Fifth Coalition in 1809, Jérôme and his army were charged with defending parts of the Confederation of the Rhine against incursions by the Austrians and British and were forced to deal with attempts to cause a popular uprising in Westphalia itself. It is a measure of some success of French proxy rule that only a few Westphalian officers and troops supported the revolts of 1809 led by the former Duke of Brunswick (most of whose troops were Bohemian), the turncoat General Wilhelm von Dornberg (a colonel in the Guard), and the hot-headed Prussian major Ferdinand von Schill. Schill was killed in fighting in Stralsund, and both Dornberg and Brunswick were driven from the Continent. Jérôme's kingdom had survived its first major crisis, but not without a cost.

The real problem for Westphalia turned out to be not so much the men but the finances to pay for them. Additionally Jérôme had to pay for the upkeep of fortresses and their provisioning for French troops. Until the dissolution of the kingdom in late 1813, Jérôme and his subjects constantly struggled to meet his older brother's force requirements and always came up short in manpower and money. Nevertheless, Westphalia managed to produce a prodigious number of troops for the campaigns in Spain, Russia, and Germany—eventually over 100,000 Westphalians served in Napoleon's armies between 1808 and 1813. The real disaster occurred, as for most of the German kingdoms and for Napoleon himself, in Russia in 1812; out of over 22,000 Westphalian troops with the Grande Armée (nearly all in Jérôme's VIII Corps), only 1,500 returned. Yet in spite of all this, the kingdom remained relatively loyal until late into 1813. The most notable instance of disloyalty was the defection of the two line hussar regiments at the start of the

fall 1813 campaign. Nevertheless, the Guard Hussars followed Jérôme out of Germany to fight on in 1814 as the 13th (French) Hussars.

As for Jérôme, his skill at military command was probably limited to no higher than corps command. As a wing commander he did poorly, and he abandoned the army early during the Russian campaign. As a ruler he did better; both traditional and more recent scholarship give him high marks for just the sort of enlightened liberal governance that Napoleon had originally intended. There is no other way to explain the remarkable performance of this satellite kingdom than to give Jérôme his fair credit as a ruler.

John Kuehn

See also Bavaria; Bonaparte, Jérôme; Civil Code; Confederation of the Rhine; Fifth Coalition, War of the; Fourth Coalition, War of the; Germany, Campaign in; Hanover; Holy Roman Empire; Imperial Guard (French); Peninsular War; Russian Campaign; Schill, Ferdinand Baptista von; Saxony; Tilsit, Treaties of; Württemberg
References and further reading
Chandler, David G. 1995. *The Campaigns of Napoleon.* London: Weidenfeld and Nicolson.
Connelly, Owen. 1965. *Napoleon's Satellite Kingdoms.* New York: Free Press.
Funcken, Fred, and Liliane Funcken. 1973. *Arms and Uniforms of the Napoleonic Wars, Part II.* Englewood Cliffs, NJ: Prentice-Hall.
Gill, John H. 1992. *With Eagles to Glory: Napoleon and His German Allies in the 1809 Campaign.* London: Greenhill.
Lamar, Glenn J. 2000. *Jerome Bonaparte: The War Years, 1800–1815.* Westport, CT: Greenwood.
Partridge, Richard, and Michael Oliver. 2002. *Napoleonic Army Handbook: The French Army and Her Allies.* Vol. 2. London: Constable and Robinson.
Pivka, Otto von. 1979. *Armies of the Napoleonic Era.* New York: Taplinger.
———. 1992. *Napoleon's German Allies.* Vol. 1, *Westfalia and Kleve-Berg.* London: Osprey.

Westphalian Army

See Westphalia

Wetzlar, Battle of

See Rhine Campaigns (1792–1797)

Wilberforce, William (1759–1833)

William Wilberforce was the most important leader of his generation—or indeed of any period—in the campaign against slavery within the British Empire. The gregarious son of a wealthy merchant family in Hull, Yorkshire, he had an evangelical religious experience in 1785 that convinced him to commit himself to the service of God in a way that would benefit humanity. Although slavery is nowhere condemned in the Bible, Wilberforce and other evangelicals, both those who like him remained in the Anglican Church and those who broke away as Methodists, believed that it was an evil that they had a divine mission to redress. In 1787 he and others formed the Society for the Abolition of the Slave Trade, expecting that ending the trade would lead to better treatment of slaves already in the colonies.

As a Member of Parliament (MP) since 1780 and a friend of the prime minister William Pitt, Wilberforce could gather the support of cabinet ministers and others in the House of Commons. Persuading Parliament to abolish the slave trade, however, proved more difficult than he expected, though the struggle might have taken far longer without the well-connected Wilberforce. Almost every year from 1789 he tried but failed to get a majority in the House of Commons, his only success being a resolution for gradual abolition in 1792, which had no practical effect. The French Revolution and the slave revolt in French St. Domingue (Haiti) in 1791 gave pause to some of those who were well disposed toward abolition, but the 100 Irish MPs sent to Parliament after the union with Britain in 1801 increased the support. In the meantime Wilberforce had helped in 1791 to found the Sierra Leone Company to resettle freed slaves in West Africa. The slave trade in the British Empire was finally abolished in 1807 as the major achievement of Lord Grenville's so-called Ministry of All the Talents. Wilberforce received great praise but was bitterly disappointed that international abolition did not follow the Congress of Vienna, which merely condemned the slave trade. He now turned his attention to the condition of British-owned slaves, which had not improved since 1807. By 1819 slave registers, with one copy in the colony and one in London, had been introduced to prevent illegal imports and curb the harsh punishments employed by the owners.

In the early 1820s, complete abolition of slavery had become the greatest moral and reform cause in Britain, but Wilberforce's health was too poor to lead the Anti-Slavery Society, formed in 1823. In the same year, without opposition, Parliament passed resolutions calling for amelioration in the treatment of slaves and their eventual freedom. This reform foundered on the refusal of the West Indian assemblies to enact legislation and the preoccupation of British governments after 1827 with other issues. In 1833, as Wilberforce lay dying, Lord Grey's government passed an act emancipating the slaves after a seven-year "apprenticeship" (later ended in 1838) to their former owners, who received £20 million in restitution. The triumph was celebrated in Wilberforce's funeral in Westminster Abbey, though some radicals criticized him for overlooking the deprivation of British workers and indeed supporting repressive legislation during and after the wars against France.

Neville Thompson

See also Grenville, William Wyndham Grenville, Baron; Haiti; Pitt, William; Slave Trade; Slavery; Union, Act of; Vienna, Congress of
References and further reading
Anstey, Roger. 1975. *The Atlantic Slave Trade and British Abolition, 1760–1810.* London: Macmillan.
Furneaux, Robin. 1974. *William Wilberforce.* London: Hamilton.
Pollock, John. 1977. *Wilberforce.* London: Constable.

Winter, Johan Willem de (1767–1812)

Dutch admiral best known for his determined leadership against the British at the hard-fought Battle of Camperdown in 1797. Johan Willem de Winter was born on 31 March 1767 in Kampen as a scion of a military family, whose tradition he upheld, as he joined the army as a cadet at the age of nine. After service in the Garde du Corps of Prince William V of Orange and in the colonial army in Demerara, he joined the navy as a midshipman. As a lieutenant he saw action at Dogger Bank on 5 August 1781.

When in the late 1780s the Dutch Republic was torn between reformist Patriots and the Regent patriciate, which by that time had made common cause with the Prince of Orange, de Winter was a staunch Patriot, an exception in the traditionally Orangist navy, and in 1787 he joined one of the small Patriot bands that patrolled the borders of the Dutch Republic. The rebellion was quelled with Prussian support, however, and de Winter fled to France, probably to Dunkirk. In 1792 he joined the Légion Batave (Légion Franche Étrangère) as a lieutenant colonel and received rapid promotion in the Army of the North through his personal bravery. On 18 January 1795 troops under his command captured the Batavian fleet at Den Helder, although the fleet had already surrendered before he arrived. When the Dutch Republic became the Batavian Republic in 1795, de Winter was attached to the Marine Committee, and on 26 June he was promoted to commander of the Batavian Navy, though he had never commanded a ship or a fleet and had not been on active service in the navy since 1789. However, being Dutch by origin yet loyal to them, de Winter was an excellent ally for the French.

De Winter immediately set about to reinforce the fleet, which was in a sorry state. His career as its commander is as closely linked to the fleet's tragic fate, as his name is bound to the terrible Dutch defeat at Camperdown (Kamperduin), when on 11 October 1797 de Winter, commanding the main body of the Batavian fleet, met a British fleet under Admiral Adam Duncan. De Winter's fleet was largely destroyed, shattering any prospect for a Franco-Batavian invasion of Ireland as well as the last remnants of Dutch naval prestige. His flagship *De Vrij-heid* was the last to surrender, and de Winter showed remarkable bravery and tenacity. He was taken captive and was eventually exchanged. Until that time he was allowed to travel home on parole yet honor-bound not to hold any military commission or exercise command. Despite his defeat at Camperdown, he was hailed as a hero and exonerated by a later inquiry.

In 1800 de Winter was sent on a diplomatic mission to France to press the First Consul, Bonaparte, to support Dutch interests in the East Indies, but failed, both through Bonaparte's intransigence as well as through his own naïveté and lack of tact. In 1801 he regained his command, a position he retained during the reign of King Louis Bonaparte (1806–1809), but from that point on he had to share his post with Carel Hendrik Ver Heull, a favorite of Napoleon and probably a more capable commander. De Winter was not involved in any further major action, however, as during the British invasion of Walcheren in 1809 he was passed over in favor of Ver Heull on account of the Emperor's preference for the latter.

When the Netherlands were annexed by France in 1810, de Winter's work became largely administrative, as there was only a vestige of a fleet left and Napoleon's attention was focused on Russia. While suffering from poor heath, de Winter traveled to Paris and died there on 2 June 1812. His body was buried in the Panthéon, his heart in Amsterdam. In 1821 the latter was brought to Kampen, where it was placed in the Bovenkerk.

M. R. van der Werf

See also Bonaparte, Louis; Camperdown, Battle of; Dutch Navy; Flanders, Campaigns in; Netherlands, The; Texel, Capture of the Dutch Fleet off; Walcheren, Expedition to
References and further reading
Fehrmann, C. N. 1969. *Onze vloot in de Franse Tijd, de admiraals De Winter en Verheull*. The Hague: Kruseman.

Winzegorode (Wintzingerode), Ferdinand Fedorovich, Baron (1770–1818)

Russian general and corps commander. Winzegorode was born to a prominent Hessian family and studied at the Cassel Cadet Corps from 1778 to 1785 before joining the Hessian Guard. However, he soon took a discharge, and over the next few years, he served in the armies of various lesser German states. Winzegorode served in the Austrian army in the Austrian Netherlands (Belgium) in 1790 and on the Rhine in 1792–1793 and again in 1795–1796. He entered Russian service with the rank of major in the Military Order Cuirassier Regiment on 19 June 1797. He became lieutenant colonel in the Life Guard Izmailovsk Regiment and adjutant to Grand Duke Constantine in early 1798, and he earned promotion to colonel on 5 June 1798. However, on 14 February 1799, Winzegorode was allowed to leave the Russian and join the Austrian service to take command of the Archduke Ferdinand's Dragoon Regiment and participate in operations against the French in 1799. Winzegorode returned to Russia on 24 November 1801 and was appointed to the Quartermaster Section of the Imperial Retinue. He rose to major general and adjutant general on 24 April 1802. Between 28 May and 23 September 1803, he served as *chef* (colonel proprietor) of the Odessa Hussar Regiment.

In early 1805, Winzegorode served on a diplomatic mission to the Prussian court in Berlin and took part in the drafting of the Allied plan of operations against France. During the 1805 campaign, he served at Russian headquarters, and distinguished himself at Dürnstein (Krems). At Hollabrunn (Schöngrabern), he and Prince Peter Bagration tricked Marshal Joachim Murat into a one-day armistice and helped General Mikhail Kutuzov to rescue his army. Winzegorode then fought at Austerlitz, though after the battle he was held responsible for the defeat. He left the Russian service on 15 January 1807, and in 1807–1811, Winzegorode served in the Austrian Army. In 1809, he distinguished himself at Aspern-Essling, where he was severely wounded and received promotion to *Feldmarschalleutnant* on 5 June 1809. He returned to the Russian Army on 23 May 1812.

During the 1812 campaign, Winzegorode commanded a partisan detachment in the Smolensk *gubernia* (province) and covered the route to St. Petersburg. For his actions, he received a promotion to lieutenant general on 18 September. On 22 October, as the French withdrew from Moscow, Winzegorode entered the city with his adjutant to negotiate with the enemy and prevent them from destroying the Kremlin. He was, however, detained by the French and Napoleon initially wanted to court-martial him for treason, claiming Winzegorode, as a Hessian, was his subject (Hesse had became part of the Confederation of the Rhine in July 1806). As he was transported from Moscow, however, Winzegorode was rescued by Cossacks near Radoshkevichi, between Minsk and Vilna. He assumed command of a corps at Grodno and distinguished himself pursuing the French. In 1813, he took part in the actions at Kalisch, Lützen, Grossbeeren, Dennewitz, and

Leipzig, for which he was promoted to general of cavalry on 20 October 1813.

In 1814, Winzegorode commanded a corps and fought at Soissons, Craonne, Laon, and St. Dizier. In late 1814, he led the 2nd Independent Corps, and after returning to Russia, he took command of the 2nd Cavalry Corps, with which he marched back to France during the Hundred Days in 1815. After the war, Winzegorode took command of 2nd Corps (21 April 1816) and later of the Independent Lithuanian Corps on 7 July 1817. In May 1818, he traveled to Germany to recuperate from wounds but died at Wisbaden on 30 June 1818.

Alexander Mikaberidze

See also Aspern-Essling, Battle of; Austerlitz, Battle of; Bagration, Peter Ivanovich, Prince; Confederation of the Rhine; Cossacks; Craonne, Battle of; Dennewitz, Battle of; Dürnstein, Battle of; France, Campaign in; Germany, Campaign in; Grossbeeren, Battle of; Hollabrunn, Action at; Kutuzov, Mikhail Golenischev-, Prince; Laon, Battle of; Leipzig, Battle of; Lützen, Battle of; Moscow, Occupation of; Murat, Joachim; Russian Campaign; St. Dizier, Battle of; Third Coalition, War of the

References and further reading
Mikaberidze, Alexander. 2005. *The Russian Officer Corps in the Revolutionary and Napoleonic Wars, 1792–1815.* New York: Savas Beatie.

Wittgenstein, Peter Khristianovich (Peter Ludwig Adolf) Graf zu (Sayn-) (1769–1843)

Prominent Russian general of German descent, commander of the Allied forces in 1813. Wittgenstein was born as Peter Ludwig Adolf Sayn-Wittgenstein-Berleburg on 5 January 1769 in Pereyaslavl, in the Poltava province in Ukraine. His father was a Westphalian nobleman who himself had risen to the rank of lieutenant general in the Russian Army. In April 1781 at the age of twelve he enlisted as a sergeant in the Life Guard Semeyonovsk Regiment. In 1789 he transferred to the Horse Guards, becoming a cornet the following year. By 1793 he served as a major in the Ukraine Light Horse Regiment. He first saw action in the campaign of 1794 against the Polish uprising, distinguishing himself at the Battle of Ostrolenka and the assault on Praga (a district of Warsaw). In 1796 he participated in General Varelian Zubov's Persian campaign along the Caspian Sea and, after the capture of the fortress of Derbent, he delivered its keys to St. Petersburg.

After serving in three cavalry regiments, Wittgenstein was promoted to colonel of the Akhtyrsk Hussar regiment on 9 February 1788, became commander of the Akhtyrsk Hussars on 5 May 1799, and rose to the rank of major gen-

eral and commander of the Mariupol Hussars on 1 July 1799. He commanded these units until 29 October 1807, except for three months (October 1801–January 1802), when he led the Elizabetgrad Hussar Regiment. He distinguished himself commanding this unit during the War of the Third Coalition (1805), when he participated in the battles at Amstetten, Wishau, and Austerlitz. In the following year, his regiment was transferred to the Danubian Principalities of Moldavia and Wallachia (in present-day Romania), where he took part in the initial Russian operations of the Russo-Turkish War (1806–1812) before returning to central Europe to take part in the War of the Fourth Coalition (1806–1807), fighting the French at Ostrolenka in February 1807. On 10 November 1807, he received command of the Life Guard Hussar Regiment, which he commanded until 22 April 1818. On 24 December 1807 he was promoted to the rank of lieutenant general and commanded a corps in southern Finland for the next three years, during which time Russia fought a brief war against Sweden.

During the Russian campaign in 1812, Wittgenstein commanded the 1st Corps that, reinforced by *opolchenye* (untrained militia) and garrison regiments, covered the approaches to St. Petersburg. In July and August, he engaged Marshal Nicolas Oudinot's troops at Wilkomir, Klyastitsy, Kokhanovichi, and two battles at Polotsk. For his success in the latter battle, he was promoted to the rank of general of cavalry on 3 November. After Polotsk, in November, he earned the sobriquet the Savior of St. Petersburg. During the French retreat from Moscow, Wittgenstein pursued Oudinot's forces and participated in the bloody crossing of the Berezina, where he was partially responsible for allowing the remnants of Napoleon's forces to escape. From February to April 1813, he occupied Berlin and received several awards for services performed the previous year.

After the death of Prince Mikhail Kutuzov in April 1813, Wittgenstein became commander in chief of the Russian Army and commanded the (Russo-Prussian) Army of Silesia at Lützen and Bautzen, where he was defeated. This promotion, thus, proved beyond his capabilities, and so on 26 May he was succeeded by General Mikhail Barclay de Tolly. Wittgenstein was present at the battles of Dresden and Leipzig, during the autumn campaign in Germany, and, during the 1814 campaign in France, at Nancy and Bar-sur-Aube, at the latter of which he was severely wounded.

In 1818 Wittgenstein was appointed commander of the 2nd Army and became a member of the State Council. In February 1826 he again received command of the Mariupol Hussars, becoming its regimental *chef* (colonel proprietor). On 3 September he was given the rank of general field marshal. During the Russo-Turkish War of 1828–1829, Wittgenstein commanded the Russian army, capturing Macin and Bralia in 1828. The following year, however, he retired from the army on grounds of ill health. That was the formal reason; in reality, he was ignored and circumvented by his own general staff, led by the young and ambitious General Ivan Diebitch, who corresponded directly with Tsar Nicholas I. After retiring, Wittgenstein settled on his estate, where he led a quiet life; in 1834 the king of Prussia elevated him to the rank of prince for his role in the 1813 campaign, and two years later Nicholas conferred on him the title of His Highness Prince. Wittgenstein died on 11 June 1843 in Lemberg (now L'vov).

Laurence Spring

See also Amstetten, Battle of; Austerlitz, Battle of; Barclay de Tolly, Mikhail Andreas; Bar-sur-Aube, Battle of; Bautzen, Battle of; Berezina, Actions and Crossing at the; Dresden, Battle of; Fourth Coalition, War of the; France, Campaign in; Germany, Campaign in; Kutuzov, Mikhail Golenishev-, Prince; Leipzig, Battle of; Lützen, Battle of; Oudinot, Nicolas Charles; Polotsk, Battle of; Russian Campaign; Russo-Polish War; Russo-Swedish War; Russo-Turkish War; Third Coalition, War of the

References and further reading
Hachenburg, Alexander Graf von. 1934. *Ludwig Adolf Peter, Fürst zu Sayn und Wittgenstein, Kaiserlich Russischer General-Feldmarschall, 1768/69–1843.* Hanover: W. Dorn.
Mikaberidze, Alexander. 2005. *The Russian Officer Corps in the Revolutionary and Napoleonic Wars, 1792–1815.* New York: Savas Beatie.

Wordsworth, William (1770–1850)

One of the greatest English poets of the nineteenth century and Poet Laureate (1843–1850), who laid the foundation for the English Romantic movement.

Wordsworth was born, the second of five children, to the family of John Wordsworth, a relatively prosperous lawyer and estate manager, in the Lake District of northern England. His mother, Anne Cookson, died when he was only seven, followed by his father's death six years later. Orphaned and placed with his siblings under guardianship of their uncles, Wordsworth studied at the Hawkshead School where his teacher, William Tyler, encouraged his various interests in classics, literature, and mathematics. His rural explorations profoundly impressed his psyche, affecting him throughout his life. In his autobiographical *The Prelude, or Growth of a Poet's Mind*, he reminisced, "Fair seed-time had my soul, and I grew up / Fostered alike by beauty and by fear" (Wordsworth 1996, 52, I:305–306).

In 1787 Wordsworth enrolled at St. John's College, Cambridge, but the stringent atmosphere of the college did not appeal to him and "a feeling that I was not for that

hour, nor for that place" haunted him (ibid., 106, III:80–81). Still, he persevered and completed his education with a degree in 1791. His student years were noteworthy for the publication of his first sonnet in *The European Magazine* in 1787 and his memorable trip to France in 1790, where he observed ongoing Revolutionary turmoil and became an ardent republican sympathizer. After his graduation, he returned to France in 1791 and grew to admire French Revolutionary principles. "Bliss was it in that dawn to be alive, / But to be young was very Heaven," wrote the young poet (440, X:692). He delighted in French victories over Britain and denounced hereditary monarchy, hoping "to equalize in God's pure sight Monarch and peasant" (233, VI:456).

While in France, he fell in love with Marie Annette Vallon, a surgeon's daughter, who gave birth to his daughter, Anne Caroline, in 1792. He reflected this relationship in his poem *Vaudracour and Julia* and confessed in *The Prelude* his desire to "turn aside / From law and custom" (ibid., 378, XI:603) to gain happiness with her. However, as France declared war on Britain and the rest of Europe, Wordsworth was compelled to return to England that year, leaving his common-law wife and their newborn child. Over the next decade, Wordsworth and Vallon struggled to maintain a relationship despite distance and political unrest. Vallon was actively engaged in the royalist cause and was under surveillance by the Revolutionary government up to the time of the Consulate.

By 1802, with his passion already withered, Wordsworth was finally able to visit Annette and Caroline for four weeks. Yet the new series of wars on the Continent prevented him from seeing them again for nearly two decades. In 1816, he did not attend his daughter's wedding, and his next meeting with Annette and Caroline was only in October 1820, when Wordsworth had already long been married to Mary Hutchinson. Annette would live for another twenty-one years, while Caroline lived until 1862. He continued to support them in later life.

Back in 1792, upon his return to England, Wordsworth faced some of the most difficult years of his life as he struggled with poverty and his pro-republican sentiments. His first poems, *Descriptive Sketches* and *An Evening Walk* (1793) were ill-received. During this period, he was influenced in his radicalism by William Godwin, Mary Wollstonecraft, and Tom Paine. The privation of these years ended when in 1795 his friend Raisley Calvert bequeathed him £900, allowing him to pursue his literary interests. Wordsworth settled at Alfoxden House, near Bristol, with his sister Dorothy, who served as his housekeeper, nursemaid, friend, and secretary. That same year, Wordsworth met Samuel Taylor Coleridge, and their partnership blossomed over the next few years. As they "together wantoned in wild Poesy" (ibid., 534, XIII:414), Coleridge made a lasting influence on Wordsworth, who abandoned his earlier, socially conscious poems in favor of the more lyrical and dramatic works that earned him fame.

Another consequence of Wordsworth's friendship with Coleridge was his decision to start working on an ambitious poem that eventually developed into his masterpiece, *The Prelude.* In 1798 Wordsworth and Coleridge published *Lyrical Ballads,* an event often considered the beginning of the English Romantic movement. Wordsworth then wintered in Germany during 1798–1799 where he wrote some of his most poignant poetry, including the "Lucy" and "Matthew" poems. Returning to England, he produced a new edition of *Lyrical Ballads* in 1800 and received an inheritance from his father's estate, allowing him to marry his childhood friend Mary Hutchinson in 1802. The couple would have five children.

Wordsworth's *Poems, in Two Volumes* was published in 1807 and received scathing reviews. Wordsworth had chosen to disregard contemporary conventions and instead write about common people and events in such poems as "The Old Cumberland Beggar," "The Thorn," "Alice Fell," and "Michael," while firmly repudiating his critics by establishing the parameters of his work. Wordsworth was also disparaged by his critics for having discarded his youthful idealism. By 1804 Wordsworth had become dismayed by the social degeneration that he believed had resulted from the French Revolution. He accepted that some societal improvement warranted revolutionary activity, but the emerging Napoleonic tyranny completely soured him on republicanism. The death of his favorite brother in 1805 had a deep impact on him and made his poetry more somber and restrained. By 1807 he was a Tory, advocating parliamentary reform and confirming his allegiance to Britain. He also established the *Quarterly Review,* a Tory periodical.

Wordsworth's appointment in 1813 as official Distributor of Stamps for Westmorland assured the family a solid income and warranted a move to Rydal Mount, Ambleside, for his family and Dorothy. *The Excursion* was published in 1814 and a revised *Poems* in 1815, followed by *The White Doe of Rylstone* (1815), *Thanksgiving Ode* (1816), *Peter Bell* (1819), and *Guide through the Distsrict of the Lakes* (1820). He resigned his position as Distributor when he succeeded his friend Robert Southey as Britain's Poet Laureate in 1843. He was not required to write: this was in honor of past literary contributions, his critics having long since accepted him.

Wordsworth died of pleurisy on 23 April 1850 and was buried in the churchyard at St. Oswald's Church, Grasmere. *The Prelude,* having gone through four distinct manuscript versions (1798–1799, 1805–1806, 1818–1820, and 1832–1839), was published posthumously in 1850. Wordsworth sought to place poetry—"the first and last of

all knowledge . . . immortal as the heart of man" (ibid., 445)—at the center of human experience. He introduced new attitudes toward nature and its relation with man and set new standards of sensibility and psychological understanding.

Annette E. Richardson

See also Blake, William; Byron, George Noel Gordon, Lord; Coleridge, Samuel Taylor; Consulate, The; Keats, John; Paine, Tom; Romanticism; Scott, Sir Walter; Shelley, Percy Bysshe; Southey, Robert
References and further reading
Davies, Hunter. 1997. *William Wordsworth.* 2nd ed. London: Sutton.
Gill, Stephen. 1990. *William Wordsworth: A Life.* Oxford: Oxford Paperbacks.
Mahoney, Charles. 2003. *Romantics and Renegades: The Poetics of Political Reaction.* New York: Palgrave Macmillan.
Mahoney, John L. 2001. *Wordsworth and the Critics: The Development of a Critical Reputation.* Rochester, NY: Camden.
Reid, Ian. 2004. *Wordsworth and the Formation of English Studies.* Aldershot, UK: Ashgate.
Rieder, John. 1997. *Wordsworth's Counterrevolutionary Turn: Community, Virtue, and Vision in the 1790s.* Newark: University of Delaware Press.
Williams, John. 2002. *William Wordsworth.* New York: Palgrave
Wordsworth, William. 1996. *The Prelude: The Four Texts (1798, 1799, 1805, 1850).* New York: Penguin.

Wrede, Karl Philipp Freiherr von (1767–1838)

Bavarian general who fought against the French Republic and then commanded Bavarian troops allied to the French until 1812. In 1813–1815 he fought against Napoleon and later rose to the rank of field marshal in the Bavarian Army.

Wrede's first major command was that of an infantry brigade at the Battle of Hohenlinden, in December 1800, covering the retreat of the Austrian army. After the peace of Lunéville the following year, Bavarian forces became allied to the French. Wrede faced the Austrians in 1805 and took part in the encirclement of their forces under *Feldmarschalleutnant* Karl Mack Freiherr von Leiberich at Ulm. In 1806–1807, during the War of the Fourth Coalition, Bavarian forces took part in a number of sieges of Prussian fortresses, at which Wrede was present. In 1809, during the War of the Fifth Coalition, he commanded a division in the Bavarian corps led by Marshal François Lefebvre. He fought at Abensberg and at Neumarkt, where his division held off a superior force under the Austrian commander Johann von Hiller. Wrede was then sent with the rest of the Bavarian troops to the Tyrol to put down the rebellion there. When his division was then ordered to rejoin the main French army, Wrede made a forced march of

170 miles in four days. During the Battle of Wagram, Wrede was ordered to attack the Austrian line where Marshal Jacques Etienne Macdonald's attack had failed. Using his artillery to good effect, he was able to break the weakened enemy, though he himself was wounded by an artillery shell. Wrede was sent back to the Tyrol to help complete the destruction of forces supporting the Austrians. He was later made a Count of the Empire as a reward for his service.

In the campaign in Russia in 1812, he commanded a division in the (Bavarian) VI Corps under the command of General (from August, Marshal) Laurent Gouvion St. Cyr. The Bavarians of VI Corps guarded the northern flank of the Grande Armée and were engaged in two battles at Polotsk. After the retreat from Russia, Wrede helped to reorganize the shattered Bavarian Army. By 1813 Wrede commanded the Army of the River Inn. However, the king of Bavaria was turning against Napoleon. Wrede was duly instructed to make peace with the Allies, which he did at Reid (8 October), by which agreement, after the Battle of Leipzig (16–19 October), Bavarian forces joined the Allies. On 30 October Wrede commanded at the Battle of Hanau, where he attempted to trap the retreating French army. Due, however, to faulty deployment, by which his force was split by a river spanned only by a single bridge, Wrede was badly defeated. At La Rothière, during the 1814 campaign in France, his force arrived on the flank of the French and nearly succeeded in destroying the bulk of the enemy. He then went on to defeat Marshal Nicolas Oudinot at Bar-sur-Aube. After Napoleon's abdication, Wrede took part in the Congress of Vienna, representing the views of the Bavarian government. Although Bavarian forces were mobilized against Napoleon during the campaign of the Hundred Days in 1815, Wrede did not see action.

Ralph Baker

See also Abensberg, Battle of; Bar-sur-Aube, Battle of; Bavaria; Bavarian Army; Fifth Coalition, War of the; Fourth Coalition, War of the; France, Campaign in; Germany, Campaign in; Gouvion St. Cyr, Laurent, comte; Hanau, Battle of; Hohenlinden, Battle of; La Rothière, Battle of; Lefebvre, François Joseph; Leipzig, Battle of; Lunéville, Treaty of; Macdonald, Jacques Etienne Joseph Alexandre; Mack, Karl Freiherr von Leiberich; Oudinot, Nicolas Charles; Polotsk, Battle of; Russian Campaign; Third Coalition, War of the; Tyrol, Uprising in the; Ulm, Surrender at; Vienna, Congress of; Wagram, Battle of

References and further reading
Gill, John. 1993. *With Eagles to Glory.* Novato CA: Presidio.
Hamilton-Williams, David. 1994. *The Fall of Napoleon: The Final Betrayal.* London: Arms and Armour.
Pivka, Otto von. 1980. *Napoleon's German Allies.* Vol. 4, *Bavaria.* London: Osprey.
Zamoyski, Adam. 2004. *1812: Napoleon's Fatal March on Moscow.* London: HarperCollins.

Würmser, Dagobert Sigismund Graf (1724–1797)

Veteran Austrian commander of Alsatian origin, who was defeated by Bonaparte at Castiglione and Bassano during the 1796 Italian campaign. He commanded French and Austrian hussars, as well as being *Inhaber* (honorary colonel) of two Austrian hussar regiments in the 1790s and a Balkan *Freikorps* (irregular volunteers). His determined defense of Mantua delayed Bonaparte's advance across Italy in 1796 for several months.

Born in Strasbourg, Würmser came from an old Alsatian family and joined the French army as a hussar officer, distinguishing himself in advance-guard and outpost work. In 1762 he and his irregular legion transferred to the Austrian army, and after further distinguished service, he was promoted to *Generalmajor* in the following year and to *Feldmarschalleutnant* in 1778. During the War of the Bavarian Succession (1778–1779), he led his hussars against Prussian troops attempting to assault the right wing of the Jaromirz fortified camp and repelled them. Over the winter, he directed *Oberst* (colonel) Wilhelm Klebek's *Grenzers* in a raid on Ditterbach, taking eight flags, and the following January, he destroyed Prinz Wilhelm von Hessen-Philippstal's force near Glatz, leading the third of a five-column assault. For his exploits, he was appointed *General Kommandant* of Galicia in 1788.

As commander of the Army of the Upper Rhine in 1793, he defeated the French army of General Adam de Custine and then halted a French attempt to relieve Mainz in July by defeating them at Offenbach. From early September to mid-October, he smashed through the fortified Lautersburg and Weissenburg Lines, previously considered impregnable defenses. He directed the capture of Fort Louis on 27 October, but was later forced by numerically superior French forces to withdraw across the Rhine. Forced to remain on the defensive in early 1795, when the Prussians left the First Coalition, Würmser briefly resigned his command, but after being reappointed to command the Upper Rhine army in August 1795, he resumed the offensive and took Mannheim in November.

Promoted to *Feldmarschall,* he was transferred to Italy in June 1796 to shore up the shattered army facing Bonaparte's advance. Tasked with relieving Mantua, his three-pronged assault enabled him to break through on 2 August and destroy the French siege works, but Bonaparte's counterattack against *Feldmarschalleutnant* Vitus Freiherr von Quosdanovich led to a French victory at Castiglione on 5 August. A second attempt during the first half of September was defeated at Bassano, although Würmser had again broken through to Mantua with his cavalry. This time, he had to seek safety in the fortress and endure the remainder of the siege as its commander. Despite his directing of several breakout attempts, the supplies ran out, and after the field army's defeat at Rivoli, he was forced to surrender on 2 February 1797. His health had been shattered by the siege, and he died six months later.

David Hollins

See also Bassano, Battle of; Castiglione, Battle of; First Coalition, War of the; Italian Campaigns (1792–1797); Mainz, Siege of; Mannheim Offensive; Mantua, Sieges of; Rhine Campaigns (1792–1797); Rivoli, Battle of; Weissenburg, Battle of
References and further reading
Hirtenfeld, Jaromir. *Der Militär-Maria-Theresien-Orden und seine Mitglieder.* 1857. Vienna: Staatsdruckerei.
Hollins, David. 2004. *Austrian Commanders of the Napoleonic Wars.* Oxford: Osprey.

Württemberg

Württemberg, the dominant power in the Swabian Circle of the Holy Roman Empire, was anomalous in that a traditional representative body, the Territorial Estates, still exercised an authority parallel to that of the ruler in domestic and foreign affairs. Its history nonetheless exemplifies the perils and opportunities that the Revolution presented to German states of the second rank.

Duke Carl Eugen (ruled 1744–1793) advocated neutrality in the war with France, but his brothers, Ludwig Eugen (ruled 1793–1795) and Friedrich Eugen (ruled 1795–1797), had no such reservations, and a decade of conflict proved devastating. Württemberg sued for peace in 1796, and suffered crushing exactions, first from the conquering French and then from the returning and vengeful Austrians. Both the Estates and Duke Friedrich II (ruled 1797–1816) exploited the resultant fiscal-political crisis by flexing their muscles and pressing their versions of reform.

Content to use Austria against the Estates, but humiliated when it dragged him down to defeat and exile in the War of the Second Coalition, Friedrich turned from the weak Habsburg ally to the strong French enemy. He thereby acquired territory and protection, undercut the separate diplomacy of the Estates, and crushed their resistance to centralization. The Imperial Recess of 1803 raised Württemberg to an electorate and exchanged its lost French possessions for German ecclesiastical territories and imperial cities. Overawed by Napoleon in 1805, Friedrich concluded an alliance (solidified in 1807 by marrying his daughter Katharina to Jérôme Bonaparte). After Austerlitz, Württemberg was rewarded with Habsburg lands in Swabia and the status of a kingdom in the new Confederation of the Rhine (1806). Friedrich abolished the Estates, imposing an absolutist administration. Moderni-

zation was initiated and carried out by the sovereign rather than, as elsewhere, by bureaucrats.

By 1810 Württemberg had doubled the population and territory it had possessed before the Revolution. One price was supplying troops for Napoleon's campaigns (some 20,000 in 1809 and 16,000 in 1812). One paradoxical result was to instill both pride in service for the Emperor and a new national consciousness that could be directed against France in the "War of German Liberation" of 1813.

Following the Battle of Leipzig (16–19 October 1813), Friedrich returned to the Allied side. The Congress of Vienna confirmed the kingdom's borders but rejected Friedrich's attempt to dictate a constitution, forcing him to restore the Estates. Tension between the latter and the crown were resolved in 1819 under the popular King William I (reigned 1816–1864), when a constitution blending elements of the "Good Old Law" and the new order was promulgated.

Württemberg's elite educational system produced generations of outstanding intellectual talent—including the poets Friedrich von Schiller and Friedrich Hölderlin and the philosophers Georg Hegel and Friedrich Wilhelm von Schelling—whose work, which entered the canon of a German national literature, reflected their encounter with the upheaval of revolution.

James Wald

See also Austerlitz, Battle of; Bonaparte, Jérôme; Confederation of the Rhine; Germany, Campaign in; Hegel, Georg Wilhelm Friedrich; Holy Roman Empire; Imperial Recess; Leipzig, Battle of; Schiller, Friedrich von; Second Coalition, War of the; Third Coalition, War of the; Vienna, Congress of
References and further reading
Gill, John H. 1992. *With Eagles to Glory: Napoleon and His German Allies in the 1809 Campaign.* London: Greenhill.
Sheehan, James J. 1989. *German History, 1770–1866.* Oxford: Oxford University Press.
Württembergisches Landesmuseum Stuttgart, ed. 1987. *Baden und Württemberg im Zeitalter Napoleons* [Baden and Württemberg in the Age of Napoleon]. 2 vols. Stuttgart: Württembergisches Landesmuseum.

Würzburg, Battle of (3 September 1796)

Decisive Austrian victory over the French, which ended the campaign on the Rhine during the War of the First Coalition. After initially withdrawing, Archduke Charles had defeated French general Jean-Baptiste Jourdan at Amberg and driven him west to Würzburg. The battle gradually extended northward until Charles massed his cavalry to destroy the French center. Jourdan withdrew across the Rhine, allowing Charles to turn south and force General Jean Moreau to retreat hastily from Bavaria.

After victory at Amberg, Charles drove Jourdan's Army of the Sambre and Meuse toward the key crossroads at Würzburg. On 1 September, Charles pushed two divisions (under *Feldmarschalleutnant* Johann Freiherr von Hotze and *Generalmajor* Anton Graf Sztáray) toward the city. Jourdan had reached Schweinfurt, 40 kilometers to the northeast and, leaving General François Lefebvre's division, marched to preempt the Austrians on 2 September. General Jacques-Philippe Bonnaud's reserve cavalry and General Edouard François Simon's infantry division were soon driving Hotze toward the city, but Sztáray secured the Repperndorf hills, east of the city, to cover the archduke's advance. Jourdan arrived with General Jean Etienne Championnet's division and General Dominique Klein's cavalry, who evicted Sztáray from Kurnach village. General Paul Grenier's division brought the French total to 30,000. Charles massed 31,000 infantry and 13,000 cavalry.

On 3 September, thick fog disguised the archduke's advance. Sztáray and Hotze attacked Simon around Lengfeld at dawn, driving the French out of the Kurnach valley. Jourdan counterattacked around 10:00 A.M. to split Sztáray from Charles, whose troops were arriving. Championnet attacked Sztáray frontally, while Simon retook Lengfeld toward noon, and from the north, Bonnaud and Grenier attempted to outflank Sztáray's right. Charles rushed *Feldmarschalleutnant* Paul Kray Freiherr von Krajova's light cavalry division forward, and they moved north to face Bonnaud. Kray's infantry followed, while *Feldzeugmeister* Ludwig Graf Wartensleben's heavy cavalry forded the river and turned north. Around noon, Grenier's advance was halted by Kray's cavalry, and Championnet was making no progress against Sztáray. By 1:00 P.M. Kray's infantry were engaging Grenier, and Wartensleben's cavalry had reached Euerfeld. As the two armies formed up along a southwest to northeast alignment, Jourdan massed Bonnaud's cavalry on Championnet's left, allowing Klein's light cavalry to attack Kray. Frantic orders were dispatched to Lefebvre to send reinforcements, but Kray's cavalry had cut the road.

As Klein attacked, *Generalmajor* Johannes Fürst zu Liechtenstein's light cavalry countercharged, only to be repulsed by Bonnaud, while Sztáray was joined by Austrian grenadiers at 3:00 P.M. Bonnaud counterattacked, but Charles halted him with some heavy cavalry, while others attacked Grenier's right. As Kray drove Grenier northward, Austrian cavalry massed in the center and in a single charge swept Bonnaud away. Jourdan ordered a retreat to the northwest, pursued by the grenadiers and light infantry into the Gramschatzer Forest, near where Austrian cavalry broke four French squares. The French lost 6,000 troops, compared with an Austrian total of 1,469. It was Charles's greatest victory and rewarded his daring campaign strategy.

David Hollins

See also Amberg, Battle of; Charles, Archduke of Austria, Duke of Teschen; First Coalition, War of the; Jourdan, Jean-Baptiste; Kray, Paul Freiherr von Krajova; Lefebvre, François Joseph; Moreau, Jean Victor; Rhine Campaigns (1792–1797)

References and further reading
Blanning, T. C. W. 1996. *The French Revolutionary Wars, 1787–1802*. London: Arnold.
Charles, Archduke. 1816. *Grundsätze der Strategie erlautert durch die Darstellung des Feldzuges in Deutschland 1796* [Principles of Strategy Explained by a Description of the 1796 campaign in Germany]. Vienna: Strauss.
Hollins, David. 1996. "Decided by Cavalry: Würzburg 1796." *Age of Napoleon* 20 (Spring): 12–17.
Phipps, Ramsay Weston. 1980. *The Armies of the First French Republic and the Rise of the Marshals of Napoleon I*. Vol. 2, *The Armées de la Moselle, du Rhin, de Sambre-et-Meuse, de Rhin-et-Moselle*. London: Greenwood. (Orig. pub. 1926–1939.)

Y

Yorck von Wartenburg, Johann David Ludwig Graf (1759–1830)

Prussian general and important instructor of Prussian light troops. On 30 December 1812 he signed on his own initiative the Convention of Tauroggen, which declared the Prussian auxiliary corps under his command neutral and prepared the uprising of Prussia against France. In 1813–1814 his I Corps was the backbone of the Army of Silesia under General Gebhard von Blücher. Most famous were his crossing of the river Elbe at Wartenburg (3 October 1813) and his attack on Möckern (16 October) during the Battle of Leipzig. He was made *Graf* (count) Yorck von Wartenburg on 3 June 1814.

Born on 26 November 1759, Yorck, like many other noblemen destined for military service, entered a Prussian infantry regiment at a young age. He began his career on 1 December 1772 as a corporal, his subsequent promotions being to ensign (4 March 1775) and second lieutenant (11 June 1777). He served during the War of the Bavarian Succession (1778–1779) and, in spite of being brave, his refusal to take orders from an officer who had plundered during this conflict ended his career. On 10 January 1780 he was dishonorably discharged and held under arrest for a year for insubordination. On 1 June 1781, through recommendations, he succeeded in being employed as a company commander in the Swiss infantry regiment Meuron in Dutch service, spending 1783–1784 in the East Indies (present-day Indonesia). He however left in 1785 out of discontent with political developments there. On 7 May 1787 Yorck was allowed to reenter Prussian service as a captain (the patent being antedated to 30 May 1786, the day after King Frederick William II had first rejected his request) in a newly raised fusilier battalion.

His subsequent promotions were to major (27 November 1792); lieutenant colonel (11 June 1800); colonel (2 June 1803); major general (18 June 1807); lieutenant general (24 March 1812); general of infantry (8 December 1813); and, finally, general field marshal (5 May 1821).

Because of his distinguished service during the 1794–1795 campaign in Poland, he was appointed commander of a newly raised fusilier battalion on 12 September 1797. On 16 November 1799 he became commander of the Prussian rifle regiment. Leading his regiment, he distinguished himself in the 1806 campaign, above all in the combat at Altenzaun (26 October), but was severely wounded and taken prisoner at Lübeck (6 November). In 1807 he was exchanged and employed in East Prussia. In the following years he was given command of different brigades and made governor-general of a succession of different provinces. Owing to his abilities in instructing light troops, he became inspector of the Prussian rifle battalions on 16 November 1808 and inspector general of all Prussian light troops (hussar regiments and fusilier and rifle battalions) on 16 February 1810.

On 12 March 1812 Yorck was appointed second in command of the Prussian auxiliary corps and became commander of this corps on 12 October, having already taken over de facto command as of 17 August, from General Julius von Grawert, who had fallen ill. On 11 March 1813 Yorck was exonerated for his part in the capitulation at Tauroggen. In the campaign in Saxony in the spring of 1813, his corps was part of the Russo-Prussian army under the command of the Russian general Peter Graf zu Wittgenstein. On 12 July it was designated I Corps, and assigned to the Army of Silesia under Blücher's command. Yorck's corps distinguished itself in the autumn campaign in Saxony and in the campaign of 1814 in northern France. On 8 May 1814, a week after the conclusion of peace, II and III Corps were also placed under Yorck's command, and on 18 June he became commander of the Prussian troops in Silesia. On 15 April 1815 he was appointed commander of V Corps, which, however, did not see action in the Waterloo campaign, and returned to his post in Silesia on 3 October 1815.

On his own request, Yorck was pensioned on 26 December 1815; he died on 4 October 1830.

Oliver Schmidt

See also Blücher von Wahlstatt, Gebhard Lebrecht Fürst; Fourth Coalition, War of the; Germany, Campaign in; Leipzig, Battle of; Tauroggen, Convention of; Russian Campaign; Wittgenstein, Peter Khristianovich (Peter Ludwig Adolf) Graf zu (Sayn-)
References and further reading
Paret, Peter. 1966. *Yorck and the Era of Prussian Reform 1807–1815*. Princeton: Princeton University Press.
Priesdorff, Kurt von. 1937–1942. *Soldatisches Führertum* [Military Leadership]. 10 vols. 3: 248–263 (no. 1120). Hamburg: Hanseatische Verlagsanstalt.

York and Albany, Frederick Augustus, Duke of (1763–1827)

Second son of George III of Great Britain, the Duke of York led three unsuccessful campaigns in the Low Countries (1793–1799) and served twice as commander in chief of British forces.

Groomed to join the British Army, the Duke of York trained in Prussia under Frederick the Great and his successor Frederick William II, eventually marrying the latter's daughter Frederica, in 1791. On the outbreak of war between Britain and France in 1793, York commanded troops as a major general at the siege of Valenciennes in the campaign of 1793, but failed to take Dunkirk. The following year, he held the center of the Anglo-Austrian army under *Feldmarschall* Friedrich Josias Graf Saxe-Coburg-Saalfeld (generally known as Saxe-Coburg), but faltered at Tourcoing because of poor logistical supply and insufficient Austrian support. Promoted to field marshal and commander in chief, York was recalled in 1795. A final campaign in 1799 in conjunction with Hanoverian and Russian troops ended in disaster on the Helder, in North Holland, inspiring the nursery rhyme "The Grand Old Duke of York."

Proving a far better administrator than a general, York implemented needed reforms, pulling underage officers out of the field and establishing the Military Colleges at Woolwich (1800) and High Wycombe (1802), the forerunner to Sandhurst. Unfortunately, York's mistress Mary Ann Clarke used his office to sell commissions, promotions, and army supply contracts, a scandal that surfaced in 1806 and was investigated by the House of Commons in 1809. Although cleared by a Commons vote of 278 to 196, York resigned and was replaced by Sir David Dundas until reinstated in 1811.

As heir to the throne (1817–1827) after the death of George IV's only child, York lived extravagantly at his manor, Oatlands, and in London with a series of mistresses and was an important member of Regency high society and the House of Lords. A friend and supporter of the Duke of Wellington, York used his political patronage to oppose Catholic emancipation and push Wellington toward accepting the prime ministership in 1828. York predeceased his elder brother King George IV, dying on 17 January 1827 in London.

Margaret Sankey

See also Catholic Emancipation; Flanders, Campaigns in; George III, King; North Holland, Campaign in (1799); Prince Regent and the Regency Period; Tourcoing, Battle of; Wellington, Arthur Wellesley, First Duke of
References and further reading
Burne, Alfred. 1949. *The Noble Duke of York: The Military Life of Frederick, Duke of York and Albany*. London: Staples.
Fulford, Roger. 1968. *The Wicked Uncles*. Freeport, NY: Books for Libraries.
Marples, Morris. 1972. *Wicked Uncles in Love*. London: Joseph.
Priestley, J. B. 2002. *The Prince of Pleasure and His Regency 1811–20*. London: Penguin.
Redman, Alvin. 1960. *The House of Hanover*. New York: Funk and Wagnall.

Young Guard

See Imperial Guard (French)

Z

Zaragoza, Sieges of

See Saragossa, Sieges of

Zieten, Wieprecht Hans Karl Friedrich Ernst Heinrich Graf von (1770–1848)

Prussian general. In the Battle of Waterloo (18 June 1815), the support of the Duke of Wellington's left wing by I Corps under Zieten's command was vital to the outcome of the battle. From 1815 to 1819, he commanded the Prussian corps of occupation in France. He was made *Graf* (count) on 3 September 1817.

Zieten entered military service on 26 May 1785, becoming a corporal. On 2 February 1788 he became a cornet, a second lieutenant on 10 June 1790, a captain of the army on 7 December 1793 (that is, without assignment to a unit), a major on 12 June 1800, a lieutenant colonel on 21 June 1807, and a colonel on 20 May 1809 (the patent being postdated to 1 June). On 12 Decmber of that year he was promoted to brigadier general, rising to major general on 14 March 1813 (the patent being postdated to 30 March). He was made a lieutenant general on 13 December 1813, a general of cavalry on 18 June 1825, and a general field marshal on 6 June 1839. He fought in the campaigns of 1792–1794 on the Rhine, and in the campaigns of 1813, 1814, and 1815 in Germany, France, and Belgium, respectively.

Born 3 March 1770, Zieten joined the hussar regiment of his distant relative, the famous General Hans Joachim von Zieten, at the age of fifteen. From 1793 to 1806, he was adjutant to General Friedrich Adolf Graf von Kalckreuth (or Kalkreuth). In 1806 he reentered service in the line, commanding different hussar brigades and regiments, until, on 12 December 1809, he was given charge of the Upper Silesian brigade. In 1811 he was a member of the commission that prepared the new regulations for cavalry exercise. In the spring of 1813 his brigade was part of the army corps commanded by General Gebhard von Blücher, distinguishing himself especially in the combat at Haynau on 26 June. After the armistice he commanded the 11th Brigade in II Corps.

On 10 April 1814, Zieten took command of II Corps from General Friedrich Graf Kleist von Nollendorf. On 19 March 1815 he was made commander of I Corps, which bore the main burden of fighting on 15 June, and at Ligny on the following day. He also fought at the Battle of Waterloo on the eighteenth and took part in the advance on Paris. On 3 October he became chief of the Prussian corps of occupation in France. After the return of this formation to Prussia, he was made commanding general of VI Corps on 11 February 1819. Zieten was pensioned on 2 June 1839 and died on 3 May 1848.

Oliver Schmidt

See also Blücher von Wahlstatt, Gebhard Lebrecht Fürst; France, Campaign in; Germany, Campaign in; Kleist von Nollendorf, Friedrich Heinrich Ferdinand Emil Graf; Ligny, Battle of; Waterloo, Battle of; Waterloo Campaign; Wellington, Arthur Wellesley, First Duke of

References and further reading

Priesdorff, Kurt von. 1937–1942. *Soldatisches Führertum* [Military leadership]. 10 vols. 4: 253–260 (no. 1315). Hamburg: Hanseatische Verlagsanstalt.

Znaim, Battle of (10–11 July 1809)

This battle, the last fought during the War of the Fifth Coalition, occurred as a result of the French pursuit of the defeated Austrians after the Battle of Wagram (5–6 July 1809). Marshal Auguste de Marmont began the action on the tenth and was soon in difficulty. Early on the eleventh, however, Napoleon and Marshal André Masséna arrived to shift the balance. The fighting was ended by the announcement of a cease-fire toward the end of the day.

The immediate cause of the two-day Battle of Znaim was the decision of the Austrian commander in chief, Archduke Charles, to stage a rearguard action near the town of Znaim (now Znojmo, in the Czech Republic), about 80 kilometers north of Vienna, in order to give his army time to withdraw its baggage train in safety toward Moravia. Marmont's two combined French and Bavarian corps were the first of Napoleon's troops to arrive on the field following the course of the river Thaya. Believing that he faced only a rear guard, Marmont ordered his Bavarian troops to take the village of Tesswitz south of Znaim, while the rest of his troops attacked the village of Zuckerhandel.

The Bavarians succeeded in storming Tesswitz but were then thrown out by Austrian reinforcements. Marmont renewed the Bavarian attack, and Tesswitz was retaken, only to be lost soon after. The village changed hands a number of times during the day, this contest constituting the heaviest fighting the Bavarians saw in the whole campaign. Marmont had hoped to swing his cavalry in behind the Austrian rear guard, but on reaching high ground above Tesswitz, they were faced with five enemy corps. The French cavalry was forced to withdraw in the face of a large body of Austrian cuirassiers.

Marmont was now engaged by 40,000 Austrian troops and was heavily outnumbered. His men nevertheless managed to hold onto both Tesswitz and Zuckerhandel overnight. Archduke Charles withdrew his forces into a strong defensive position situated so as to hold the north bank of the Thaya and Znaim. Napoleon arrived at Tesswitz at 10:00 A.M., and despite the fact that he had brought with him reinforcements of cavalry and artillery, he believed that his force was too weak to launch a full-scale attack. His plan therefore was to employ Masséna's corps to pin the Austrians throughout the day and to await the corps of marshals Louis Davout and Nicolas Oudinot, which would be able to arrive early on the twelfth. Masséna launched his attack on the extreme right of the Austrian position during midmorning and quickly seized the main bridge across the Thaya south of Znaim. His troops took two small villages and then advanced directly on Znaim. Charles meanwhile reinforced the Austrian position with two grenadier brigades, which advanced during a thunderstorm and initially threw the French back.

The situation was stabilized by a body of French cavalry at approximately 7:00 P.M., when French and Austrian staff officers rode along the opposing lines announcing a cease-fire, which led to the signature of an armistice on the twelfth. Znaim was to prove the last action of the 1809 campaign. The two sides signed a treaty of peace at Pressburg on 26 December.

Ralph Baker

See also Charles, Archduke of Austria, Duke of Teschen; Davout, Louis Nicolas; Fifth Coalition, War of the; Masséna, André; Marmont, Auguste Fréderic Louis Viesse de; Oudinot, Nicolas Charles; Pressburg, Treaty of; Wagram, Battle of

References and further reading
Gill, John. 1992. *With Eagles to Glory: Napoleon's German Allies in the Campaign of 1809.* London: Greenhill.

Zürich, First Battle of (4–6 June 1799)

Indecisive Austrian victory during the War of the Second Coalition, which forced the French on to the defensive in Switzerland. After defeating General Jean-Baptiste Jourdan's French army at the first Battle of Stockach in Germany, Archduke Charles had been left on the defensive for two months by the political leaders in Vienna. In June he marched to Zürich, the last defensive line in northern Switzerland before the Rhine valley and a key junction on the road to Italy. Over three days, he attempted to dislodge Masséna's (French) Army of Helvetia (Switzerland) from the 650-meter Zürichberg hill. Masséna eventually withdrew, but the Austrians could not exploit their success.

The Austrian *Feldmarschalleunant* Johann Freiherr von Hotze had foiled French general André Masséna's attack on the Austrian Tyrol in March 1799 and advanced into the Graubünden (eastern Switzerland) in May. On the pretext of supporting him, Archduke Charles led 40,000 men south from Germany to seize what he considered the key strategic area. Joined by Hotze's 15,000 troops south of Lake Constance in late May, he defeated Masséna at Winterthur, following which the French army withdrew to concentrate 45,000 men in the fortified position on the Zürichberg, east of Zürich, which Charles believed to be virtually impregnable.

Unable to cross the river Limmat to the north, which was protected by extensive marshes, the Austrians had to take the Zürichberg. On 4 June the main assault was mounted in four columns totaling twenty-one battalions (as cavalry was useless) with a reserve. By midday all were engaged in a near stationary line on the steep slopes, the Austrian advance halted by French artillery set up in redoubts, together with musketry from French infantry dug in on the wooded slopes. To the south, additional columns under *Generalmajor* Franz Jellacic Freiherr von Buzim and *Generalmajor* Graf Bey reached the southern city gate, but were driven back. French general Nicolas Soult described the hill as "an enormous volcano vomiting flame" (Phipps 1980, 5:130).

After bridges were thrown over the river Glatt on the northern flank around 2:00 P.M., the Austrian columns under *Feldmarschalleutnant*s Karl Graf Hadik, Prinz Joseph von Lothringen, and Heinrich Fürst zu Reuss-Plauen resumed their attacks, but could make no further progress. *Feldzeugmeister* Olivier Graf Wallis's column (center and reserve) penetrated the French defenses and attacked their main camp, but was driven out by 8:00 P.M. by a French counterattack. Heavy rain prevented any activity on 5 June, but the Austrian army regrouped. As the assault resumed at 2:00 A.M. on the following day, it soon became clear that Masséna had evacuated his positions and withdrawn to new defenses around the Albisrieden ridge, west of Zürich. Unwilling to risk further heavy casualties after sustaining more than 2,000, but having secured the city, Charles had to await further directions from Vienna.

Allied forces had cleared northern Italy and, following their victory at Novi, the Russians under Field Marshal Alexander Suvorov marched north to take over in Switzerland, while on 19 July Charles was ordered back to Germany. Masséna exploited the opportunity to defeat General Alexander Rimsky-Korsakov and Hotze at the second Battle of Zürich.

David Hollins

See also Charles, Archduke of Austria, Duke of Teschen; Italian Campaigns (1799–1800); Jourdan, Jean-Baptiste; Masséna, André; Novi, Battle of; Rimsky-Korsakov, Alexander Mikhailovich; Second Coalition, War of the; Soult, Nicolas Jean de Dieu; Stockach, First Battle of; Suvorov, Alexander Vasilievich; Switzerland, Campaign in; Zürich, Second Battle of
References and further reading
Blanning, T. C. W. 1996. *The French Revolutionary Wars, 1787–1802.* London: Arnold.
Phipps, Ramsay Weston. 1980. *The Armies of the First French Republic and the Rise of the Marshals of Napoleon I.* Vol. 5, *The Armies on the Rhine, in Switzerland, Holland, Italy, Egypt, and the Coup d'état of Brumaire, 1797 to 1799.* London: Greenwood. (Orig. pub. 1926–1939.)
Shadwell, L. 1875. *Mountain Warfare.* London: Henry S. King.

Zürich, Second Battle of (25–26 September 1799)

A decisive French victory over a combined Austro-Russian force, which turned the tide of the War of the Second Coalition and prompted the Russians to abandon their allies. When, after the breakdown of the Treaty of Campo Formio the French Revolutionary Wars restarted in 1799, Switzerland's key strategic position between southern Germany and northern Italy made it an important battleground. The Austrians under Archduke Charles defeated the French at the first Battle of Zürich in early June, but political blunders led to the main Austrian force being ordered north before Russian reinforcements could arrive. The French under General André Masséna took advantage of the Allied weakness to defeat the small remaining Austro-Russian force in late September. Political tensions within the Allied coalition worsened as the Russians made a difficult retreat into Austria, and they left the coalition at the end of the year.

The French had established a puppet Helvetic (Swiss) Republic in 1798 and occupied most of Switzerland, although Austria controlled the eastern Graubünden (Grisons). When the military phase of the War of the Second Coalition began in March 1799 (the coalition having been formed the previous December), the (French) Army of Helvetia under Masséna was halted on the Austrian border by *Feldmarschalleutnant* Johann Freiherr von Hotze's Austrian Vorarlberg Korps, which drove the French back on Zürich, supported by 40,000 troops under Archduke Charles from Germany. The Austrian forces combined to defeat Masséna at the first Battle of Zürich over 4–6 June, but Masséna secured his defensive positions behind the river Limmat, and Archduke Charles had been ordered to remain in position pending the arrival of Russian troops, under Field Marshal Alexander Suvorov, from Italy.

The Russian advance guard, 27,000 men under General Alexander Rimsky-Korsakov, began arriving at Austrian headquarters at Kloten on 12 August, and sixteen days later Archduke Charles marched away with 30,000 men, heading for the central Rhine. He left 16,000 troops under Hotze, but it would be mid-September before Suvorov's main body even entered Switzerland. Hotze and Rimsky-Korsakov were facing Masséna's 76,000 troops, hoping that Suvorov's 21,000 men would arrive from the south in time to form the third component of a renewed assault on Zürich. By 20 September Suvorov could anticipate reaching Schwyz, 40 kilometers south of Zürich, six days later, when the assault would begin and his men would march on Lucerne to cut the French line of retreat.

A proficient mountain warfare commander, Masséna saw his chance: on 25 September he seized the initiative by crossing the Limmat, which flows north-east from the Zürichsee (Lake Zürich). His attack comprised three thrusts: Masséna with 35,000 troops would attack Rimsky-Korsakov around Zürich; 10,000 under General Nicolas Soult would attack Hotze on the river Linth, to the south of the Zürichsee; and another 10,000 troops under General Gabriel Molitor would tackle the Austrian left, to separate it from Suvorov. First, Masséna feigned attacks on Rimsky-Korsakov's right and left wings before launching his main assault on the Russian center at a bend in the Limmat, 10 kilometers from Zürich, which allowed French artillery to provide effective supporting fire.

Rimsky-Korsakov was initially concerned with launching counterattacks by his left wing under General Peter Essen against the French divisions under generals Adolphe Edouard Mortier and Dominique Klein around the Albisberg on the western side of the lake, but by 2:00 P.M. Masséna's main body was approaching the city. Separated from his right wing, Rimsky-Korsakov attempted to mass his forces in front of Zürich, but they made easy targets for the French, and by 9:00 P.M. the Russians had been driven back into the city.

To the south, Soult's troops had begun crossing the river Linth between the two lakes, the Zürichsee and the Walensee, around 4:00 A.M. on the morning of the twenty-sixth. This French advance gained an early advantage: During an early morning reconnaissance ride near Weesen on the Walensee, Hotze was killed by French outpost fire. Under cover of fog, the French crossed the upper Zürich-see and the Linth, splitting the 8,000 demoralized Austrian troops in two and quickly driving them back to Lichten-steig. The Austrian left wing under *Feldmarschalleutnant* Franz Jellacic Freiherr von Buzim made progress toward Glarus and reached the Panixer Pass, but was then marching away from Suvorov. Indecisive fighting with Molitor was only resolved on 29 September when French reinforcements and news of the defeat forced Jellacic to withdraw in line with the other Allied forces.

The Russians held the Zürichberg during the night of 25–26 September, but Rimsky-Korsakov recognized the precariousness of his position, and in some disorder his troops began their retreat toward the upper Rhine on the following morning. Abandoning 8,000 casualties, Rimsky-Korsakov lost another 3,800 men as he was forced to take a longer route, which subjected them to regular French raids. As the battle was being fought, Suvorov was approaching the Chinzig Pass, 45 kilometers to the south, so on receipt of the news of Rimsky-Korsakov's defeat, he had to turn east to retreat into Austria.

Massena's victory had saved the crumbling French Republic and reduced the impact of Bonaparte's return to France on 8 October, as the news reinvigorated the Directory. Nevertheless, Bonaparte would seize power a month later in the coup of Brumaire (9–10 November), and Switzerland would become the essential mounting area for the two French armies, which would advance north into Germany and south into Italy in the decisive campaign of 1800. The recriminations between the Austrian and Russian governments over the defeat led to Tsar Paul I of Russia effectively abandoning the coalition by the end of 1799 and subsequently seeking better relations with the new French government, the Consulate.

David Hollins

See also Brumaire, Coup of; Campo Formio, Treaty of; Charles, Archduke of Austria, Duke of Teschen; Consulate, The; Directory, The; Italian Campaigns (1799–1800); Masséna, André; Mortier, Adolphe Edouard Casimir Joseph; Paul I, Tsar; Rhine Campaigns (1799–1800); Rimsky-Korsakov, Alexander Mikhailovich; Second Coalition, War of the; Soult, Nicolas Jean de Dieu; Suvorov, Alexander Vasilievich; Switzerland, Campaign in; Zürich, First Battle of

References and further reading
Blanning, T. C. W. 1996. *The French Revolutionary Wars, 1787–1802*. London: Arnold.
Duffy, Christopher. 1999. *Eagle over the Alps: Suvorov in Italy and Switzerland, 1799*. Chicago: Emperor's.
Gray, Wilbur. 1993. "Alpine Thunder: The Battle for Zürich 1799." *Empires, Eagles & Lions* 2 (no. 4): 8–15.
Phipps, Ramsay Weston. 1980. *The Armies of the First French Republic and the Rise of the Marshals of Napoleon I*. Vol. 5, *The Armies on the Rhine, in Switzerland, Holland, Italy, Egypt, and the Coup d'état of Brumaire, 1797 to 1799*. London: Greenwood. (Orig. pub. 1926–1939.)
Rodger, A. B. 1964. *The War of the Second Coalition: A Strategic Commentary*. New York: Oxford University Press.
Shadwell, L. 1875. *Mountain Warfare*. London: Henry S. King.

Primary Source Documents

1. William Pitt's Speech to the House of Commons, 1 February 1793

Coupland, R., ed. 1916. *The War Speeches of William Pitt the Younger.* Oxford: Clarendon, 24–51.

In laying out his country's grievances against Revolutionary France in a long address to Parliament, Pitt produced one of the greatest speeches of his long and distinguished career as prime minister.

The Speaker of the House of Commons opened the session with the following statement:

His Majesty has given directions for laying before the House of Commons, copies of several papers which have been received from M. Chauvelin, late minister plenipotentiary from the Most Christian King, by His Majesty's Secretary of State for Foreign Affairs, and of the answers returned thereto; and likewise a copy of an Order by His Majesty in Council, and transmitted by His Majesty's commands to the said M. Chauvelin, in consequence of the accounts of the atrocious act recently perpetrated at Paris.

In the present situation of affairs, His Majesty thinks it indispensably necessary to make a further augmentation of his forces by sea and land; and relies on the know affection and zeal of the House of Commons to enable His Majesty to take the most effectual measures, in the present important conjuncture, for maintaining the security and rights of his own dominions; for supporting his allies; and for opposing views of aggrandizement and ambition on the part of France, which would be at all times dangerous to the general interests of Europe, but are peculiarly so, when connected with the propagation of principles, which lead to the violation of the most sacred duties and are utterly subversive of the peace and order of all civil society.

G. R. [George Rex (King)]

The Speaker having read the message, Pitt rose.

Sir—I shall now submit to the House some observations on the many important objects which arise out of the communication of His Majesty's message and out of the present situation of this country. And in proceeding to the consideration of that message, the attention of the House should, in the first instance, be strongly directed to that calamitous event, to that dreadful outrage against every principle of religion, of justice, and of humanity, which has created one general sentiment of indignation and abhorrence in every part of this island, and most undoubtedly has produced the same effect in every civilized country.

At the same time I am aware, that I should better consult not only my own feelings, but those of the House, if considerations of duty would permit me to draw a veil over the whole of this transaction, because it is, in fact, in itself, in all those circumstances which led to it, in all that attended it, and in all which have followed, or which are likely to follow it hereafter, so full of every subject of grief and horror, that it is painful for the mind to dwell upon it. It is a subject which, for the honour of human nature, it would be better, if possible, to dismiss from our memories, to expunge from the page of history, and to conceal it, both now and hereafter, from the observation of the world.

Excidat ille dies aevo, neu postera credant
Secula; nos certe taceamus, et obruta mula
Nocte tegi nostrae patiamur criminal gentis.

[Let that day be blotted out of Time,
and let not after ages believe the story;
let us at least be silent and suffer the sins
of our race to be hid and buried deep in night.]

These, Sir, are the words of a great historian of France in a former period, and were applied to an occasion which has always been considered as an eternal reproach to the French nation [the St. Bartholomew Massacre]: and the atrocious acts lately perpetrated at Paris are, perhaps, the only instances that furnish any match to that dreadful and complicated scene of proscription and blood. But whatever may be our feelings on this subject, since, alas! it is not possible that the present age should not be contaminated with its guilt; since it is not possible that the knowledge of it should not be conveyed by the breath of tradition to posterity, there is a duty which we are called upon to perform—to enter our solemn protestation, that, on every principle by which men of justice and honour are actuated, it is the foulest and most atrocious deed which the history of the world has yet had occasion to attest.

There is another duty immediately relating to the interest of this and of every other country. Painful as it is to dwell upon this deed, since we cannot conceal what has happened, either from the view of the present age or of posterity, let us not deprive this nation of the benefit that may be derived from reflecting on some of the dreadful effects of those principles which are entertained and propagated with so much care and industry by a neighbouring country. We see in this one instance concentrated together the effect of principles, which originally rest upon grounds that dissolve whatever has hitherto received the best sanctions of human legislation, which are contrary to every principle of law, human and divine. Presumptuously relying on their deceitful and destructive theories, they have rejected every benefit which the world has hitherto received from the effect either of reason, experience, or even of Revelation itself. The consequences of these principles have been illustrated by having been carried into effect in the single person of one whom every human being commiserates. Their consequences equally tend to shake the security of commerce, to rob the meanest individual in every country of whatever is most dear and valuable to him. They strike directly against the authority of all regular government and the inviolable personal situation of every lawful sovereign. I do feel it, therefore, not merely a tribute due to humanity, not merely an effusion of those feelings which I possess in common with every man in this country, but I hold it to be a proper subject of reflection to fix our minds on the effect of those principles which have been thus dreadfully attested, before we proceed to consider of the measures which it becomes this country to adopt, in order to avert their contagion and to prevent their growth and progress in Europe.

However, notwithstanding that I feel strongly on this subject, I would, if possible, entreat of the House to consider even that calamitous event rather as a subject of reason and reflection than of sentiment and feeling. Sentiment is often unavailing, but reason and reflection will lead to that knowledge which is necessary to the salvation of this and of all other countries. I am per-

suaded the House will not feel this as a circumstance which they are to take upon themselves, but that they will feel it in the manner in which I state it, as a proof of the calamities arising out of the most abominable and detestable principles; as a proof of the absence of all morals, of all justice, of all humanity, and of every principle which does honour to human nature; and, that it furnishes the strongest demonstration of the dreadful outrage which the crimes and follies of a neighbouring nation have suggested to them. I am persuaded the House will be sensible that these principles, and the effects of them, are narrowly to be watched, that there can be no leading consideration more nearly connected with the prospect of all countries, and most of all, that there can be no consideration more deserving the attention of this House, than to crush and destroy principles which are so dangerous and destructive of every blessing this country enjoys under its free and excellent constitution.

We owe our present happiness and prosperity, which has never been equalled in the annals of mankind, to a mixture of monarchical government. We feel and know we are happy under that form of government. We consider it as our first duty to maintain and reverence the British constitution, which, for wise and just reasons of lasting and internal policy, attaches inviolability to the sacred person of the Sovereign, though, at the same time, by the responsibility it has annexed to government, by the check of a wise system of laws, and by a mixture of aristocratic and democratical power in the frame of legislation, it has equally exempted itself from the danger arising from the exercise of absolute power on the one hand, and the still more dangerous contagion of popular licentiousness on the other. The equity of our laws and the freedom of our political system have been the envy of every surrounding nation. In this country no man, in consequence of his riches or rank, is so high as to be above the reach of the laws, and no individual is so poor or inconsiderable as not to be within their protection. It is the boast of the law of England, that it affords equal security and protection to the high and the low, to the rich and the poor.

Such is the envied situation of England, which may be compared, if I may be allowed the expression, to the situation of the temperate zone on the surface of the globe, formed by the bounty of Providence for habitation and enjoyment, being equally removed from the polar frosts on the one hand and the scorching heat of the torrid zone on the other; where the vicissitude of the seasons and the variety of the climate contribute to the vigour and health of its inhabitants and to the fertility of the soil; where pestilence and famine are unknown, as also earthquakes, hurricanes, and the like, with all their dreadful consequences. Such is the situation, the fortunate situation of Britain: and what a splendid contrast does it form to the situation of that country which is exposed to all the tremendous consequences of that ungovernable, that intolerable and destroying spirit, which carries ruin and desolation wherever it goes!

Sir, this infection can have no existence in this happy land, unless it is imported, unless it is studiously and industriously brought into this country. These principles are not the natural produce of Great Britain, and it ought to be our first duty and principal concern, to take the most effectual measures in order to stop their growth and progress in this country, as well as in the other nations of Europe.

Under this impression, I wish to bring the House to the consideration of the situation in which we stand with respect to France, and with respect to the general state of the different Powers of Europe. This subject was very much discussed on the first day of the present session, and I had the good fortune to concur with a very large majority of the House in the address that was presented to His Majesty, for his most gracious speech to both houses of Parliament. Gentlemen then drew their inferences from those notorious facts which every man's observation presented to him: and those circumstances were supposed to excite every sentiment of jealousy and precaution. They induced the House to arm His Majesty and the executive Government with those powers which were indispensably necessary for effectually providing for the safety of the country. Many weeks have now elapsed since the beginning of the session, when the country appeared to be in a critical situation. Let us consider what are the circumstances now to attract our attention at the moment when the message of His Majesty calls on us for farther decision.

The papers which contain the communication between this country and France, consist of two different parts. The one comprehends the communication between this country and France, prior to the period which attracted those sentiments of jealousy I have stated. This part also contains those comments which have taken place since, and those explanations which have been entered into by His Majesty's permission, with a view, if possible, that our jealousy might be removed in consequence of some step that might be taken. The other part consists, either of what were notorious facts at the meeting of Parliament, or of those notorious facts which, though not officially communicated by His Majesty, were very generally known to the public.

The first part of these papers has never before been made public. The date of the first communication is May 12, 1792. And the communication from that period till July 8 contains the system on which His Majesty acted between France and the other European Powers. From that period down to the meeting of Parliament, His Majesty had most scrupulously observed the strictest neutrality with respect to France. He had taken no part whatever in the regulation of her internal government. He had given her no cause of complaint; and therefore the least return he might expect was that France would be cautious to avoid every measure that could furnish any just ground of complaint to His Majesty. He might also well expect that France would have felt a proper degree of respect for the rights of himself and his allies [Prussia and Holland]. His Majesty might most of all expect, that, in the troubled state of that country, they would not have chosen to attempt an interference with the internal government of this country, for the sole purpose of creating dissension among us, and of disturbing a scene of unexampled felicity. But fortunately for this country, they did not succeed. The express assurances contained in the papers which have been printed and are now on the table, the very compact on the part of France does distinctly and precisely apply to every one of these points.

I have no doubt but gentlemen have applied the interval in perusing these papers with sufficient attention to make it unnec-

essary for me to trouble them with more than the leading points. You will perceive that the very first communication is from M. Chauvein [the French ambassador to Britain], May 12, 1792, and contains this passage:

Thus the King (of France) saw himself forced into a war, which was already declared against him; but, religiously faithful to the principles of the constitution, whatever may finally be the fate of arms in this war, France rejects all ideas of aggrandizement. She will preserve her limits, her liberty, her constitutions, her unalienable right of reforming herself whenever she may think proper: she will never consent that, under any relation, foreign Powers should attempt to dictate, or even dare to nourish a hope of dictating laws to her. But this very pride, so natural and so great, is a sure pledge to all the Powers from whom she shall have received no provocation, not only of her constantly pacific dispositions, but also of the respect which the French well know how to show at all times for the laws, the customs, and all the forms of government of different nations.

The King indeed wishes it to be known, that he would publicly and severely disavow all those of his agents at foreign courts in peace with France, who should dare to depart an instant from that respect, either by fomenting or favouring insurrections against the established order, or by interfering in any manner whatever in the interior policy of such States, under pretence of a proselytism, which, exercised in the dominions of friendly Powers, would be a real violation of the law of nations.

This paper, therefore, contains a declaration, that whatever might be the fate of arms, France rejected all ideas of aggrandizement; she would preserve her rights, she would preserve her limits and her liberty. This declaration was made in the name of the King.

Gentlemen must remember, after the first revolution, and after the establishment of what they called the model of a government of liberty, the King wished it to be known, that he would publicly disavow all those of his agents at foreign courts, in peace with France, who should dare to depart an instant from that respect, either by fomenting or raising insurrections, or by interfering in any manner whatever in the internal government of such States, under pretence of proselytism, which would be a real violation of the law of nations. They have therefore passed, by anticipation, that sentence on their own conduct; and whether we shall pass a different sentence, is one of the objects of this day's consideration.

In the passage I have read, two distinct principles are laid down: the one, that whatever might be the fate of arms, France renounced all ideas of aggrandizement, and declared she would confine herself within her own territories; the other, that to foment and raise insurrections in neutral States, under pretence of proselytism, was a violation of the law of nations. It is evident to all Europe, her conduct has been directly the reverse of those principles, both of which she had trampled under foot, in every instance where it was in her power. In the answer to that Note of

M. Chauvelin, His Majesty expresses his concern for the war that had arisen, for the situation of His Most Christian Majesty, and for the happiness of his dominions. He also gives him a positive assurance of his readiness to fulfil, in the most exact manner, the stipulations of the Treaty of Navigation and Commerce [of 1786]; and concludes with these words:

> Faithful to all his engagements, His Majesty will pay the strictest attention to the preservation of the good understanding which so happily subsists between him and His Most Christian Majesty, expecting with confidence, that, animated with the same sentiments, His Most Christian Majesty will not fail to contribute to the same end, by causing, on his part, the rights of His Majesty and his allies to be respected, and by rigorously forbidding any step which might affect the friendship which His Majesty has ever desired to consolidate and perpetuate, for the happiness of the two Empires.

We may also see what general assurances France thought fit to make to Great Britain, from a Note from M. Chauvelin to Lord Grenville [the Foreign Secretary] dated June 8, 1792; where it is said,

> The King of the French is happy to renew to the King of Great Britain the formal assurance, that everything which can interest the rights of His Britannic Majesty will continue to be the object of his most particular and most scrupulous attention.
>
> He hastens, at the same time, to declare to him, that the rights of all the allies of Great Britain, who shall not have provoked France by hostile measures, shall by him be no less religiously respected.
>
> In making, or rather renewing this declaration, the King of the French enjoys the double satisfaction of expressing the wish of a people, in whose eyes every war, which is not rendered necessary by a due attention to its defence, is essentially unjust, and of joining particularly in the wishes of His Majesty, for the tranquillity of Europe, which would never be disturbed, if France and England would unite in order to preserve it.

Such then, Sir, is the situation in which His Majesty stands with respect to France. During the transactions of the last summer, when France was engaged in a war against the Powers of Austria and Prussia, His Majesty departed in no shape from that neutrality. His Majesty did no one act from which it could be justly inferred that he was friendly to that system. But what, let me ask the House, has been the conduct of France as to those express reiterated assurances, applied to the public concerns which I have now detailed?

These assurances went to three points: to a determination to abstain from views of aggrandizement; not to interfere with the government of neutral nations, which they admitted to be a violation of the law of nations; and to observe the rights of His Majesty and his allies. What has been the conduct of France on these three points, under the new system? She has, both by her words and actions, manifested a determination, if not checked by force, to act on principles of aggrandizement. She has completely disclaimed that maxim, "that whatever was the fate of their arms in war, France rejected all ideas of aggrandizement." She has made use of the first moment of success to publish a contradiction to that declaration. She has made use of the first instance of success in Savoy, without even attempting the ceremony of disguise (after having professed a determination to confine herself within her ancient limits), to annex it for ever as an eighty-fourth department to the present sovereignty of France. They have by their decree announced a determination to carry on a similar operation in every country into which their arms can be carried, with a view, in substance, if not in name, to do the same thing in every country where they can with success.

Their decree of the 15th of December contains a fair illustration and confirmation of their principles and designs. They have by that decree expressly stated the plan on which they mean to act. Whenever they obtain a temporary success, whatever be the situation of the country into which they come, whatever may have been its antecedent conduct, whatever may be its political connexions [sic], they have determined not to abandon the possession of it, till they have effected the utter and absolute subversion of its form of government, of every ancient, every established usage, however long they may have existed and however much they may have been revered. They will not accept, under the name of liberty, any model of government, but that which is conformable to their own opinions and ideas; and all men must learn from the mouth of their cannon the propagation of their system in every part of the world. They have regularly and boldly avowed these instructions, which they sent to the commissioners who were to carry these orders into execution. They have stated to them what this House could not believe, they have stated to them a revolutionary principle and order, for the purpose of being applied in every country in which the French arms are crowned with success. They have stated, that they would organize every country by a disorganizing principle; and afterwards, they tell you all this is done by the will of the people. Wherever our arms come, revolutions must take place, dictated by the will of the people. And then comes this plain question, what is this will of the people? It is the power of the French. They have explained what that liberty is which they wish to give to every nation; and if they will not accept of it voluntarily, they compel them. They take every opportunity to destroy every institution that is most sacred and most valuable in every nation where their armies have made their appearance; and under the name of liberty, they have resolved to make every country in substance, if not in form, a province dependent on themselves, through the despotism of Jacobin societies. This has given a more fatal blow to the liberties of mankind than any they have suffered, even from the boldest attempts of the most aspiring monarch. We see, therefore, that France has trampled under foot all laws, human and divine. She has at last avowed the most insatiable ambition and greatest contempt for the law of nations, which all independent States have hitherto professed most religiously to observe; and unless she is stopped in her career, all Europe must soon learn their ideas of justice—law of nations—models of government—and principles of liberty from the mouth of the French cannon.

I gave the first instance of their success in Savoy as a proof of their ambition and aggrandizement. I wish the House to attend to the practical effect of their system, in the situation of the Netherlands. You will find, in some of the correspondence between France and this country, this declaration on the part of France:

> "She has renounced, and again renounces every conquest, and her occupation of the Low Countries shall only continue during the war and the time which may be necessary to the Belgians to ensure and consolidate their liberty; after which they will be independent and happy. France will find her recompense in their felicity."

I ask whether this can mean anything else, than that they hope to add the Netherlands, as an eighty-fourth or eighty-fifth department, to the French Republic; whether it does not mean a subjugation of the [Austrian] Netherlands [i.e., Belgium] to the absolute power of France, to a total and unequalled dependence on her? If any man entertains doubts upon the subject, let him look at the allegations of [General Charles] Dumouriez, enforced by martial law. What was the conduct of this general, when he arrived at Brussels? Did he not assemble the inhabitants in the most public part of their city to elect the primary assemblies? How agreeable must have been his arrival in the [Austrian] Netherlands, by his employing threats to procure a general illumination of his entrance into Brussels! A hollow square of the French troops was drawn round the tree of liberty, to prevent the natives from pulling down the emblem of French freedom. This shows how well disposed the people were to receive the French system of liberty! This is the manner in which their principles are carried into effect in the different countries of Europe.

I may here mention the conduct of the Convention [the French government], on the occasion of an address from the people of Mons, in which they desire that the province of Hainault might be added as an eighty-fifth department of France. The Convention referred the address to a committee, to report the form in which countries, wishing to unite with France, were to be admitted into the union. The Convention could not decide upon it, and therefore they sent it to a committee to point out the manner in which they were to make their application for that purpose, so that the receiving of them was to be a fixed and standing principle, which in its consequences, if not timely prevented, must destroy the liberties and independence of England, as well as of all Europe.

I would next proceed to their confirmed pledge, not to interfere in the government of other neutral countries. What they have done here is in countries which, under some pretence or other, they have made their enemies. I need not remind the House of the decree of the 19th of November, which is a direct attack on every Government in Europe, by encouraging the seditious of all nations to rise up against their lawful rulers, and by promising them their support and assistance. By this decree, they hold out an encouragement to insurrection and rebellion in every country in the world. They show you they mean no exception, by ordering this decree to be printed in all languages. And therefore I might ask any man of common sense, whether any nation upon earth could be out of their contemplation at the time they passed it? And whether it was not meant to extend to England, whatever might be their pretences to the contrary? It is most manifest they mean to carry their principles into every nation, without exception, subvert and destroy every government, and to plant on their ruins their sacred tree of liberty.

Some observations, to which they have affected to give the name of explanations, have been applied to this decree, and are these: "Now to come to the three points which can alone make an object of difficulty at the Court of London, the executive council observe respecting the first, which is the decree of the 19th of November, that we have not been properly understood by the Ministry of His Britannic Majesty, when they accuse us of having given an explanation *which announces to the seditious of all nations, what are the cases in which they may previously count on the support and assistance of France.* Nothing could be more foreign than this reproach to the sentiments of the National Convention, and to the explanation we have given of them; and we did not think it was possible we should be charged with the open design of favouring the *seditious,* at the very moment when we declare that it would be *wronging the National Convention, if they were charged with the project of protecting insurrections, and with the commotions that may break out in any corner of a State, of joining the ringleaders, and of thus making the cause of a few private individuals that of the French nation.*

> "We have said, and we desire to repeat it, that the decree of the 19th of November could not have any application, unless to the single case in which the GENERAL WILL of a nation clearly and unequivocally expressed, should call the French nation to its assistance and fraternity. Sedition can certainly never be construed into the GENERAL WILL. These two ideas mutually repel each other, since a sedition is not and cannot be any other than the movement of a small number against the nation at large. And this movement would cease to be seditious, provided all the members of a society should at once rise, either to reform its Government, or to change its form *in toto,* or for any other object.
>
> "The Dutch were assuredly not seditious when they formed the general resolution of shaking off the yoke of Spain; and when the general will of that nation called for the assistance of France, it was not reputed a crime in Henry IV, or in Elizabeth of England, to have listened to them. The knowledge of the *general will* is the only basis of the transactions of nations with each other; and we can only treat with any Government whatever on this principle, that such a Government is deemed *the organ of the general will of the nation governed.*
>
> "Thus when by this natural interpretation, the decree of the 19th of November is reduced to what it truly implies, it will be found, that it announces nothing more than an act of the general will, and that beyond any doubt so effectually founded in right, that it was scarcely worth the trouble to express it. On this account, the executive council think that

the evidence of this right might, perhaps, have been dispensed with, by the National Convention, and did not deserve to be made the object of a particular decree; but, with the interpretation that precedes it, it cannot give uneasiness to any nation whatever."

To all this I shall only observe, that in the whole context of their language, on every occasion, they show the clearest intention to propagate their principles all over the world. Their explanations contain only an avowal and repetition of the offence. They have proscribed royalty as a crime, and will not be satisfied but with its total destruction. The dreadful sentence which they have executed on their own unfortunate monarch applies to every sovereign now existing. And lest you should not be satisfied that they mean to extend their system to this country, the conduct of the National Convention has applied itself, by repeated acts, to yourselves by name, which make any explanation on their part unsatisfactory and unavailing. There is no society in England, however, contemptible in their numbers, however desperate in their principles and questionable in their existence, who possessed treason and disloyalty, who were not cherished, justified, and applauded, and treated even with a degree of theatrical extravagance at the bar of the National Convention. You have also a list of the answers given to them at the bar. And, after all this, am I to ask you, whether England is one of the countries into which they wish to introduce a spirit of proselytism, which, exercised in the dominions of friendly Powers, they themselves admit, would be a violation of the law of nations?

On the third point it is unnecessary for me to expatiate—I mean on the violation of the rights of His Majesty, or of his allies.

To insist upon the opening of the River Scheldt, is an act of itself, in which the French nation had no right to interfere at all, unless she was the sovereign of the Low Countries, or boldly professed herself the general arbitress of Europe. This singular circumstance was an aggravation of their case, because they were bound by the faith of solemn and recent treaties to secure to the Dutch the exclusive navigation of the Scheldt, and to have opposed the opening of that river if any other Power had attempted it. If France were the sovereign of the Low Countries, she would only succeed to the rights which were enjoyed by the House of Austria: and if she possessed the sovereignty, with all its advantage, she must also take it with all its encumbrances, of which the shutting up of the Scheldt was one. France can have no right to annul the stipulations relative to the Scheldt, unless she has also the right to set aside, equally, all the other treaties between all the Powers of Europe, and all the other rights of England, or of her allies. England will never consent that France shall arrogate the power of annulling at her pleasure, and under the pretence of a natural right of which she makes herself the only judge, the political system of Europe, established by solemn treaties, and guaranteed by the consent of all the Powers. Such a violation of rights as France has been guilty of, it would be difficult to find in the history of the world. The conduct of that nation is in the highest degree arbitrary, capricious, and founded upon no one principle of reason or justice. They declare this treaty was antiquated, and extorted by despotism, or procured by corruption. But what hap-

pened recently in the last year? This new and enlightened nation renewed her assurances of respecting all the rights of all His Majesty's allies, without any exception, without any reservation, so that the advancement of this claim is directly contrary to their recent professions. From the Treaty of Munster down to the year 1785, the exclusive navigation of the Scheldt has been one of the established rights of Holland.

We are told it is to be said, no formal requisition has been made by Holland for the support of this country. I beg gentlemen to consider, whether ships going up the Scheldt, after a protest of the States-General [the Dutch Government], was not such an act as to have justified them in calling upon this country for a contingent of men. If this House means substantial good faith to its engagements, if it retains a just sense of the solemn faith of treaties, it must show a determination to support them. Without entering too far upon this subject, let me call to their attention, for a moment, one circumstance—I mean the sudden effect and progress of French ambition and of French arms. If from that circumstance Holland had just reason to be afraid to make a formal requisition; if she had seen just reason not to do what she might have been well justified in doing, that was no reason why we should not observe our treaty. Are we to stand by as indifferent spectators, and look at France trampling upon the ancient treaties of the allies of this country? Are we to view with indifference the progress of French ambition and of French arms, by which our allies are exposed to the greatest danger? This is surely no reason for England to be inactive and slothful. If Holland has not immediately called upon us for our support and assistance, she may have been influenced by motives of policy, and her forbearance ought not to be supposed to arise from her indifference about the River Scheldt. If Holland had not applied to England when Antwerp was taken, the French might have overrun her territory. And unless we wish to stand by, and to suffer State after State to be subverted under the power of France, we must now declare our firm resolution effectually to oppose those principles of ambition and aggrandizement, which have for their object the destruction of England, of Europe, and of the world.

The next thing is, whether we see anything in these papers which furnishes an answer to the past, or gives any security for the future? What does the explanation amount to on the subject of the treaty of our allies? It refers to the possibility of negotiation at an indefinite period. She says, "she (France) has renounced, and again renounces every conquest, and her occupation of the Low Countries shall only continue during the war, and the time which may be necessary to the Belgians to ensure and consolidate their liberty; after which, they will be independent and happy, and France will find her recompense in their felicity." What is this but an avowal of their former declarations?

On the subject of interference with neutral nations, there are one or two explanations of the decree of the 19th of November, which has been so often discussed. We are, indeed, told it is injurious to suppose the National Convention could have intended to apply this decree to any country by where, by the public will, they have been called to give assistance and fraternity. This is in fact to advertise for treason and rebellion. Is there any man who could give credit to the reception which the English societies received in

France? Though their numbers are too contemptible for the animadversion of the law, or the notice of our own Executive Government, they were considerable enough for the National Convention. They tell you they are the clear, undisputed, constituted organ of the will of the people at large. What reliance can be placed on all their explanations, after the avowal of principles to the last degree dangerous to the liberty, the constitution, the independence, and the very existence of this country?

My time and my strength would fail me, if I were to attempt to go through all those various circumstances which are connected with this subject. I shall take the liberty of reading a passage from a publication which came into my hands this morning, and I am extremely glad to have seen collected together so many instances in which the conduct of France is detected. In a Note from M. Chauvelin, dated December 27, 1792, he complains of the harsh construction which the British Ministry had put on the conduct of France, and professes the strongest friendship for Great Britain. And yet, on the 31st of December, 1792, that is in four days after, one of the members of the Executive Council, who had given these assurances to England, wrote this letter to the friends of liberty and equality in all the seaports of France:

"The Government of England is arming, and the King of Spain, encouraged by this, is preparing to attack us. These two tyrannical Powers, after persecuting the patriots in their own territories, think, no doubt, that they shall be able to influence the judgement to be pronounced on the tyrant Louis. They hope to frighten us. But no! a people who has made itself free; a people who has driven out of the bosom of France, and as far as the distant borders of the Rhine, the terrible army of the Prussians and Austrians; the people of France will not suffer laws to be dictated to them by a tyrant.

"The King and his Parliament mean to make war against us! Will the English republicans suffer it? Already these free men show their discontent and the repugnance which they have to bear arms against their brothers, the French. Well! We will fly to their succour; we will make a descent on the island; we will lodge there fifty thousand caps of liberty; we will plant there the sacred tree, and we will stretch out our arms to our republican brethren; *the tyranny of their Government will soon be destroyed.* Let every one of us be strongly impressed with this idea!—MONGE."

Such is the declaration of the sentiments of the Minister of the Marine [Navy]; a declaration which separates not only the King, but the King and Parliament of Great Britain from the people, who are called republicans. What faith can be put in assurances given on the part of France by M. Chauvelin, on the 27th of December, when, in four days after, we find the Minister of the Marine writing such a letter? It was to be hoped we might have seen reasons, perhaps, in consequence of friendly explanations, for not going to war. But such explanations as this communication contains have been justly rejected. I shall not detain the House longer on this subject.

I shall state now what appears to be the state of the negotiations. I take the conduct of France to be inconsistent with the peace and liberty of Europe. They have not given us satisfaction with respect to the question in issue. It is true, what they call explanations have taken place; but their principles, and the whole manner of their conduct, are such, that no faith can be put in their declarations. Their conduct gives the lie to their public professions; and, instead of giving satisfaction on the distinct articles, on which you have a right to claim a clear and precise explanation, and showing any desire to abandon those views of conquest and aggrandizement, to return within their ancient limits, and to set barriers to the progress of their destructive arms, and to their principles still more destructive; instead of doing so, they have given—explanations I cannot call them, but an avowal of those very things you complain of. And in the last paper from M. Chauvelin, which may therefore be considered as the *ultimatum,* are these words:

"After so frank a declaration, which manifests such a sincere desire of peace, His Britannic Majesty's Ministers ought not to have any doubts with regard to the intentions of France. If her explanations appear insufficient, and if we are still obliged to hear a haughty language; if hostile preparations are continued in the English ports, after having exhausted every means to preserve peace, we will prepare for war with the sense of the justice of our cause, and of our efforts to avoid this extremity. We will fight the English, whom we esteem, with regret—but we will fight them without fear."

This is an *ultimatum* to which you cannot accede. They have neither withdrawn their armies from the neighbouring nations, nor shown the least disposition to withdraw them. If France is really desirous of maintaining friendship and peace with England, she must show herself disposed to renounce her views of aggression and aggrandizement, and to confine herself within her own territory, without insulting other governments, without disturbing their tranquillity, without violating their rights. And unless she consents to these terms, whatever may be our wishes for peace, the final issue must be war. As to the time, as to the moment when war is to commence, if there is yet any possibility of satisfactory explanation and security for the future, it is not to the last moment precluded. But I should disguise my sentiments to the House, if I stated, that I thought it in any degree probable. This country has always been desirous of peace. We desire it still, but such as may be real and solid, and consistent with the interests and dignity of Britain, and with the general security of Europe. War, whenever it comes, will be preferable to peace without honour, without security, and which is incompatible either with the external safety or the internal happiness of this country.

I have endeavoured to comprehend as much as possible, though I am sensible I have left a great deal untouched. If any topic should afterwards arise, I trust I shall meet with the indulgence of the House in stating it. I shall now move,

"That an humble address be presented to His Majesty, to return His Majesty the thanks of this House for his most gracious message and the communication of the papers, which, by His Majesty's command, have been laid before us.

"To offer His Majesty our heartfelt condolence on the atrocious act lately perpetrated at Paris, which must be viewed by every nation in Europe as an outrage on religion, justice, and humanity, and as a striking and dreadful example of the effects of principles which lead to the violation of the peace and order of all civil society.

"To represent to His Majesty, that it is impossible for us not to be sensible of the views of aggrandizement and ambition which, in violation of repeated and solemn professions, have been openly manifested on the part of France, and which are connected with the propagation of principles incompatible with the existence of all just and regular government; that under the present circumstances, we consider a vigorous and effectual opposition to those views as essential to the security of everything that is most dear and valuable to us as a nation, and to the future tranquillity and safety of all other countries.

"That impressed with these sentiments, we shall, with the utmost zeal and alacrity, afford His Majesty the most effectual assistance, to enable His Majesty to make a further augmentation of his forces by sea and land, and to act as circumstances may require in the present important conjuncture, for maintaining the security and honour of his crown, for supporting the just rights of his allies, and for preserving to his people the undisturbed enjoyment of the blessings, which, under the Divine Providence, they receive from the British Constitution!"

2. Battle of the Glorious First of June, 1 June 1794

Dillon, Sir William Henry. 1953. *Dillon's Narrative:* Vol. 1, *1790–1802.* London: Navy Records Society, vol. 93.

At the age of fourteen Dillon served as a midshipman aboard the British 74-gun Defence, *which fought in the first fleet engagement of the French Revolutionary Wars.*

On the morning of the 30th we had foggy weather. Our feet not being in very good order, the signals were made from [Admiral] Lord Howe's ship to form in line of battle. The *Caesar* happened at that moment to be close to us, pumping out quantities of water, the effect of the shot she had received below. We heard that one of her guns had burst on the previous day, by which 18 men were killed and wounded. The fog partially clearing away, the enemy was seen to leeward. The admiral instantly made the signal to prepare for action, upon which the *Caesar* threw out the signal of inability to do so. Our fleet formed in line of battle as well as circumstances would allow, but the hazy weather rendered our evolutions uncertain, and there did not appear any probability, that day, of any more fighting. Finally, the fog becoming thicker, we lost sight of the French, so that we could not close upon the enemy.

The morning of the 31st was still misty, with favourable symptoms of its clearing away, the wind in the S.W. quarter. In the afternoon, the fog disappearing, we beheld the enemy some

distance to leeward. We prepared for action, and made sail to close upon him. By 7 o'clock we had reached within five miles of the French fleet. The weather became fine, and we enjoyed one of the most splendid sights ever witnessed—the two fleets close to each other in line of battle, only waiting for the signal to commence the work of destruction, the repeating frigates [signal ships] of the two nations within gunshot. However, all passed off in quietness. Lord Howe, having placed his fleet in exact line with that of the enemy, he drew off for the night, which we passed in extreme anxiety. We could not reckon on more than six hours of darkness, and therefore concluded that we should commence operations with the dawn. Very few of the *Defences* took off any clothing, and the hammocks were not piped down [opened]. Our whole thoughts hung upon the approaching event. As to your humble servant, being rather fatigued, I preferred, it being a beautiful starlight night, to remain on deck. I selected one of the topsail halyard tubs in the forecastle, and coiled myself as well as I could inside it, where I took a snooze which I enjoyed, and felt more refreshed when awoke by the tars than I should have done had I gone to bed: at least I thought so. I felt an elasticity beyond expression.

Rising then from my tub, I beheld the enemy about 10 miles off to leeward, on the starboard tack. There was a fine breeze and lovely weather. It was Sunday, and I thought the Captain would not have much time for prayers, as the work in hand would be of a very different nature. Lord Howe drew up the fleet in capital order. He made several changes in the disposition of the ships, to render every part of his line equal. The *Defence* was the seventh ship in the van. When his Lordship had completed his arrangements for attacking the enemy, he made the signal for the different divisions, that is the van, centre and rear, to engage the opposite divisions of the French: then for each ship in the English line to pass through the enemy and attack his opponent to leeward. Next, the fleet was hove to, that the crews might have their breakfasts. This was going to work in a regular methodical manner. His Lordship knew that John Bull did not like fighting with an empty stomach; but it was a sorry meal, scarcely deserving the name. We had not had much time for a fire in the range for cooking since the 28th of last month. All the tables and conveniences were stowed below; all the partitions taken down; nothing to be seen on the decks but powder, shot, ramrods and instruments of destruction. Whilst the ship's Company were making the best of the time allowed for refreshment, the Captain collected most of his officers in the cabin, where a short prayer suitable to the occasion was offered to the Almighty for protection against the impending event. The half hour having elapsed, up went the signal for the fleet to bear down and bring the enemy to action, it being then near 9 o'clock. What an awful moment! How shall I describe it? A scene of magnificence and importance, not of common occurrence, and not often equalled on the ocean—upwards of 50 sail of the line viewing each other, and preparing to pour out their thunder destructive of the human species, which would decide the fate of either fleet, and probably that of the nation.

Our Captain went round the ship and spoke to all the men at their guns in terms of encouragement, to fight for their country. The replies he received were gratifying in the highest degree.

The noblest feelings of patriotism were proclaimed, with expressions of the warmest enthusiasm: in short, a determination to conquer prevailed throughout the ship—and, I may as well say, throughout the British fleet. As we neared the French up went our colours. . . .

The *Defence*, being a good sailer, made rapid speed through the waves, going under double reefed topsails with a commanding breeze. Twysden, noticing that we had advanced too far beyond our line, hastened on to the quarter deck to point out to his Captain, with becoming respect, that he was exposing his ship to the utmost danger by going on singlehanded without support, and that he ran the risk of being either sunk or totally disabled. The maintopgallant sail had been set by us, the only ship in the line to have done so. In fact, when the signal had been made to bear down, the ship came before the wind, and the Captain, anxious to obey orders, was striving to commence the action as soon as he could. Lord Howe had observed this action of Capt. [James] Gambier's, and mentioned it to the officers near him, saying, "Look at the *Defence*. See how nobly she is going into action!" His Lordship then turning round and casting his eyes over the fleet, said, "I believe I cannot make any more signals. Every ship has had instructions what to do"; then, shutting his signal book, left the poop to take his chance on the quarter deck. Lieut. Twysden prevailed on his Captain to take in the maintopgallant sail, but the ship still proceeded, and extended her distance beyond the British line. Then the mizen topsail was braced aback, by which more wind filled the maintopsail. Therefore, instead of retarding her motion, it was accelerated. The lieutenant mentioned this, but the Captain would not make any more reduction of sail. He said, "I am acting in obedience to the admiral's signal. Fill the mizen topsail again. It may probably be thought that I have no wish to do so if I shorten sail." This last reply quieted Twysden. As I happened to be present at that particular moment, I heard every word that passed. The mizen topsail was braced round to receive the wind, and our whole attention was then directed to the ship in the enemy's line—the 7th—that we were to engage.

The French fleet had their maintopsails to the mast, and were waiting for our attack. Shortly after 9 o'clock we were getting very near to our opponents. Up went their lower deck ports, out came the guns, and the fire on us commenced from several of the enemy's van ships. Twysden then went to his quarters on the main deck, and your humble servant went below to his station. We retained our fire till in the act of passing under the Frenchman's stern, then, throwing all our topsails aback, luffed up and poured in a most destructive broadside. We heard most distinctly our shot striking the hull of the enemy. The carved work over his stern was shattered to pieces. Then, ranging up alongside of him within half pistol shot distance, our fire was kept up with the most determined spirit. When we had measured our length with that of our adversary, we backed the maintopsail. In that position the action was maintained for some time. We had instructions below to lower the ports whilst loading the guns, that the enemy's musketry might not tell upon our men, and also to fire with a slight elevation, as the upper deck guns would be depressed a few degrees, thus making a cross fire upon the Frenchman. After the two or three first broadsides, I became anxious to have a good view of the ship we were engaging. To effect this object, I requested the men at the foremost gun to allow me a few seconds, when the port was hauled up, to look out from it. They complied with my wishes. The gun being loaded, I took my station in the centre of the port; which being held up, I beheld our antagonist firing away at us in quick succession. The ship was painted a dark red, as most of the enemy's fleet were, to denote (as previously mentioned) their sanguinary feelings against their adversaries. I had not enjoyed the sight long—only a few seconds—when a rolling sea came in and completely covered me. The tars, noticing this, instantly let down the port, but I got a regular soaking for my curiosity. The men cheered me, and laughingly said, "We hope, Sir, you will not receive further injury. It is rather warm work here below: the salt water will keep you cool."

One of these, John Polly, of very short stature, remarked that he was so small the shot would all pass over him. The words had not been long out of his mouth when a shot cut his head right in two, leaving the tip of each ear remaining on the lower part of the cheek. His sudden death created a sensation among his comrades, but the excitement of the moment soon changed those impressions to others of exertion. There was no withdrawing from our situation, and the only alternative was to face the danger with becoming firmness. The head of this unfortunate seaman was cut so horizontally that anyone looking at it would have supposed it had been done by the blow of an axe. The body was committed to the deep.

The action was kept up with the utmost determination. At 1/2 past 10 our mizen mast was shot away, and our ship drifted to leeward. Several of my men were wounded. Holmes, the Captain of one of the guns, a powerful fine fellow, had his arm carried away close to the shoulder. By this time it was evident that the French were getting the worst of it, as we were obliged to go over to the starboard side to defend ourselves against an enemy's ship. At 1/2 past 11 the main mast came down on the starboard side of the poop with a terrible crash. This information was conveyed to us below by some of the seamen who had been in the tops. As they could no longer be useful in consequence of two of the masts being shot away, they were ordered down to the guns. They reported the upper end of the quarter deck to be dreadfully shattered. The lower deck was at times so completely filled with smoke that we could scarcely distinguish each other, and the guns were so heated that, when fired, they nearly kicked the upper deck beams. The metal became so hot that, fearing some accident, we reduced the quantity of powder, allowing also more time to elapse between the loading and firing of them.

One of the Captains of my guns was a Swede, by name John West. I noticed his backwardness, but before I could take any steps in his behalf, we had to change sides, a ship engaging us on our left. We had not been long occupied with her when we were called over to the right. After firing a broadside, John Lee, second captain of West's gun, told me that he had deserted his quarters. "Why didn't you knock him down?" I asked. "I did, Sir," was the reply, "with this handspike," showing it to me. However, West had absconded, and I was too much taken up with the pressing events of the moment to look after him. The ship we were engaging was very close, and the shot from him did us considerable injury. One of my guns was dismounted. This disaster created some confusion, more especially as the ship, from the loss of her masts, was rolling deeply; and we had considerable difficulty in securing the gun. Whilst we were occupied about this job, Lieut. Beecher thought that he observed a disinclination on the part of the seamen to exert themselves. All of a sudden he drew his sword from the scabbard, and began flourishing it about with threats that he would cut the first man down that did not do his duty. The tars were rather astonished at this proceeding of their officer as, hitherto, he had approved of their conduct. They had been fighting hard for upwards of two hours, and naturally were fatigued. They explained their anxiety to do their best. This pacified the heroic lieutenant. He sheathed his sword, and the men went on at the guns as before.

Just as this scene terminated, two of the men were blown down from the wind of a shot from the ship we were engaging, and I was carried away with them by the shock. I thought myself killed, as I became senseless, being jammed between these men. So soon as the smoke cleared away, our companions noticed my situation. They came, lugged me out, and began rubbing my limbs. This brought me to my senses. They lifted me up, enquiring if I felt myself hurt. I called out for water to drink. They handed to me a bowl with water. When I drank of it, it was quite salt. There were some salt bags hanging up close by, belonging to the men of that particular mess. These had been shot down, and had impregnated the water placed there to be used as required by those that were thirsty. Recovering myself, I felt considerable pain in my head and shoulders. My left cheek was cut by a splinter and bled profusely. I then examined the two men with whom I had been knocked down. In outward appearance they were dead; but as I did not consider myself a sufficient judge of these matters, I desired a couple of seamen to take them below to the surgeon. Whilst I was giving these directions, we were called over to the larboard side to repel the attack of an enemy. After a few broadsides he passed us. From him we received no injury at my quarters. Not long after, another Frenchman ranged up on the starboard side. Away we turned to, and pelted him as hard as we could. In crossing over I beheld the two wounded men still lying in the same position I had left them. Then, calling upon those to whom I had given orders to take the disabled men below, I insisted upon their immediately complying with my directions. They were then conveyed to the cockpit. After a few broadsides exchanged with our opponent, he made sail to leeward, and we had a few minutes' rest. This gave me an opportunity of looking out of the ports, but there was not much to be seen from that low situation. All that we could make out, in our conjectures, led us to believe that the action was nearly over. We could plainly at times distinguish the French ships sailing off and forming to leeward, engaging our ships as they passed by.

We had not long been quiet, when we received orders from the quarter deck for all hands to lie down, as an enemy three decker was coming to rake us. This ship closed gradually upon us with only her foremast standing, the sail of which enabled him to make way at a very slow pace. This was, to me, the most awful part of the battle. We could not defend ourselves from the stern, and here was an immense overpowering ship of upwards of 100

guns going to pour in her broadside into the weakest and most exposed part of our ship. It was a moment of extreme anxiety, as there was a chance of our being sunk. As he neared us there was an appearance of intending to board, and the boarders were called to repulse the attempt. But when he altered his course to rake, we were again ordered to lie down. We waited the coming event with a silent suspense not easily described. At length the enemy in passing across our stern, to our astonishment, only fired a few random shot, which brought down our disabled foremast. We were now completely dismasted and quite unmanageable. The three decker, ranging up on our larboard side, gave us an opportunity of sending some well directed shot into him. In watching the motions of this ship, I noticed that the Frenchmen, in many instances, loaded their guns from the outside. One man I distinctly saw riding upon a lower deck gun, loading it. He was stripped from the waist upwards, and had we been sufficiently near, our marines could have picked him off with their muskets. This three decker soon got out of range, leaving us free of further molestation.

It was past 12 o'clock, and I concluded the fighting part of our duty to be at an end. My clothes were still damp: my shoes, to which I had small buckles, were covered with blood; my face and hand smutched [sic] with power and blood. At my quarters I had 14 men killed and wounded (if I included myself I should say 15); and a gun. I now ascertained that no part of the lower deck had suffered so much as mine. On my way aft I shook hands with other mids[hipmen] who had escaped. Of these I shall never forget Ritchie. He was in his shirt upwards, with a bandage round his head. These were all bloody, and I thought he had been hurt. On my inquiring of him if it were the case, he gave me a hearty shake by the hand, telling me he was strong and hearty, and ready to continue the action when required. The bloody spots on his linen were occasioned by his having assisted some wounded men below. He gave the strongest symptoms of a bold and daring spirit, and had it not been for the bloody marks upon him, one might have supposed he had been at a merry and jovial party instead of a destructive battle. The next person I came in contact with was one of my mess-mates, Consitt. He also had taken off his coat and waistcoat, and his linen too was all bloody, which led me to suppose that he had been injured. However, upon enquiry, I found that he was safe and sound. In a few words he gave me an interesting account of what had been going on upon the quarter deck, as he was one of the Captain's aide-de-camps. He had been sent down to the lower deck to ascertain its state and condition. Among the informations received from him, he stated that the Royal Sovereign, one of our three deckers, had fired into us and wounded some of our men. Upon further inquiry his assertion turned out to be true.

I now hastened up to the quarter deck. In attempting to do so I was prevented by the splinter netting which, from its lying across the quarter deck under the mainmast, had turned the place into a sort of cage. There was no getting on it until the netting had been cut away. Whilst on the ladder, Mr. Hawtayne, the clergyman, came to me. From my appearance he thought that I had been seriously injured, but I soon set his mind at rest on that subject. Leaving him, I at length reached the poop, where I met my

Captain. He noticed me very kindly, and in replying to his questions I related to him what had happened at my quarters. Whilst in conversation with him, the second lieutenant, Mr. Dickson, began firing some of the starboard main deck guns. He was drunk. By this rash act he set the ship on fire, as the foretopsail was lying over the side. But in due time the fire was extinguished, and our alarms at an end.

The cannonade of the hostile fleets had lulled the wind, but the swell of the sea was still paramount, and our ship, without sails or masts to balance her motion, laboured in a most annoying manner. The first object that attracted my notice of the quarter deck was the immense quantity of the enemy's musket shot lying there. On the starboard side, which had at the commencement of the action been the lee one, they were at least three or four tier deep, and the rest of the deck completely covered with them. How could it be possible, thought I, for anyone to escape being hit where so many thousand instruments of death had fallen? But so it was; and the Captain, with many of those around him, came off without injury. The only officers of the ship that were killed were the master, Webster, and the boatswain, Mr. Fitzpatrick. Lieut. Boycott of the 2nd Regiment, Queen's, was severely wounded. He was a remarkably fine young man. The effect of his wounds obliged him to quit the ship upon our arrival at Spithead, to the regret of all who knew him. Looking around me, I saw the Queen, 98, some distance to leeward of us, still engaged with the enemy's ships which had formed a line on the starboard tack. That ship had lost her main mast, but it soon became evident that she would rejoin us, and there was no apprehension on her account. But the *Brunswick,* 74, was to leeward of the French, and we were uneasy about her fate. She had lost her mizen mast. By one o'clock all firing was at an end.

The next thing to be done was to attend to the disabled ships. We made the signal for assistance from the stump of our mizen mast. In clearing away the lumber on the poop, a marine was found stowed away under the hen coops. Those who lugged him out thought him dead. However, he soon came to life. This was the Fugleman of that Corps, one of the finest limbed men I ever beheld, and the most perfect in his exercise. All hands laughed at him when they saw he had not been hurt. He was also, like my friend West, a foreigner.

There was no walking the quarter deck till the small shot had been cleared away. The next object of consequence was to get rid of the main mast, which with some difficulty was finally rolled overboard. The quantity of damaged spars, with rigging, that was floating about gave proofs of the severity of the contest in which we had been engaged. The *Queen Charlotte,* Lord Howe's flagship, passed close to leeward of us. She had lost all her topmasts, which prevented his following the French admiral. We gave his Lordship three hearty cheers, at which moment, we were afterwards told, Lord Howe observed, "If every ship of the fleet had followed Capt. Gambier's example, the result of this action would have been very different from what it is." The flagship having stood on a little while longer, signals were made to form on the starboard tack. While these things were passing, an opinion existed on board of us that action would be renewed, as it became clear that the French were fairly beaten.

But that signal was not made. There were 14 sail of the line dismasted, 12 French and two English—ourselves and the *Marlborough,* 74, Capt. The Hon. George Berkeley. Capt. Gambier, giving me his spy glass (which had been hit by a shot) desired me to let him know the number of ships in the British fleet with topgallant yards across; and as Mr. Twysden overheard that order, he said he would assist me in the counting. We accordingly set to work, and after a strict examination, twice repeated, we made out 18 sail of the line in our fleet with topgallant yards across, and in appearance fit to go into battle. We had 7 disabled ships; the French more than 12. What astonished us most at his critical moment was the want of instructions. No signal had as yet been made to take possession of the enemy's disabled ships. Capt. [Thomas] Troubridge, who had been captured in the *Castor,* already mentioned, was a prisoner of war on board the *Sanspareil,* 80. He was quite lost at this apparent inactivity. Had that signal been made at the close of the action, we might with ease have captured their 12 disabled ships; instead of which upwards of an hour was allowed to elapse before such a signal was thrown out. In that hour 5 French ships contrived to slip though our line under their spritsails, and join their own to leeward, leaving 7 with us, which were then taken possession of. I hardly know how to restrain my feelings on this subject even now, 26 years after the event. Had Lord Howe been a younger man, there is every probability—I ought to say *no* doubt—but the action would have been renewed. We were 200 miles away from the land, with plenty of sea room for evolutions. His Lordship was clever at naval tactics: therefore, had the French been brought to action that afternoon, the result would have been the most splendid victory every achieved on the ocean over our enemy. On our way into port, the many officers that visited the *Defence* expressed the same opinions as I have herewith written down.

Many years afterwards, I heard from the best authority that the Captain of the fleet, Sir Roger Curtis, who had been selected by Lord Howe to assist him in his naval duties, when consulted by his Lordship after the action, replied, "You have gained a victory. Now make sure of it. If you renew the action, who knows what may be the result? Make sure of what you have got. Your Lordship is tired. You had better take some rest, and I will manage the other matters for you." Lord Howe accordingly went below, to bed I believe, leaving the Captain of the fleet to make signals as he thought necessary.

To return to the *Defence:* whilst we were hard at work in clearing the wreck, the *Invincible,* 74, the Hon. Capt. Thomas Pakenham, came up and hailed us. These two Captains were very intimate. "Jemmy," said Capt. Pakenham, "whom the Lord loveth He chasteneth"—in allusion to the shattered condition we were in. Our Captain made a suitable reply, then asked if he had lost many men: to which question he answered, "Damn[ed] me if I know. They won't tell me, for fear I should stop their grog." A few more words passed, when Capt. Pakenham sent an officer on board to inquire if any help was required. I shall never forget that gentleman. When he came alongside he was dressed in a Guernsey jacket with a welch wig, and had not the slightest appearance of an officer, as all the boat's crew were similarly attired. When he reached the quarter deck, we ascertained by the buttons on his smalls that he was a lieutenant—McGuire. He was presented to the Captain, to whom he said he had been sent to offer us assistance. Capt. Gambier naturally put many questions to him relating to the action. His replies were delivered with many oaths, which so disgusted our chief that he turned his back and left him. The lieutenant then, very quietly folding his arms, seated himself on the stump of the main mast; but as none of the *Defences* seemed inclined to take further notice of him after his rudeness, he left the ship. Capt. Pakenham, it seems, had given directions that his officers and Ship's Company, all Irish, should all be dressed alike: of which Mr. McGuire was a specimen. The Hon. Thos. Pakenham, brother to Lord Longford, was a regular character, and established a discipline on board the *Invincible* in direct opposition to the established rules of the Navy. But as I shall have to bring him again into notice, I take my leave of the Honourable Captain for the present.

We had scarcely done with the *Invincible* when the *Phaeton* Frigate, Capt. George Bentinck, came to take us in tow. This ship had been commanded by Sir Andrew Douglas. Several of my messmates of the *Alcide* were on board her, from whom I received many hearty congratulations at having escaped with my life. I little thought then that I should command that frigate. It is not many months since I paid her off. She was, without exception, one of the best sea boats I have ever had my foot on board. Whilst the frigate was taking us in tow, up came another line of battle ship, the *Valiant* (I believe Capt. [Thomas] Pringle). Her Captain overloaded ours with compliments upon the noble example he had shown to the whole fleet: and among other sayings he insisted that we had sunk an enemy's ship. This we could not make out. However, it was for a long time the general opinion that we had sent a French 74 [-gun ship] to the bottom. But time set this matter at rest. The ship we engaged in breaking the line was called *l'Eole.* She arrived safe at Brest: consequently, she could not have been sunk by us.

So soon as the Surgeon could make his report, it appeared that we had 91 men killed and wounded on this day: altogether, in the two actions of May 29 and June 1, twenty killed and eighty wounded. One of our Mates, Mr. Elliot, was severely wounded in the thigh by a grape shot. He was in the first instance moved into the Captain's cabin, where I saw him resting on a sofa in great agony, until he could be taken below to the doctor. He had served in the American [Revolutionary] War, and was a very superior young man. The havoc on board us was terrific. Two of the ports on the larboard side of the main deck were knocked into one by a shot. Only one shot penetrated between wind and water. It came into the bread room on the larboard side and smashed some of the lanterns there, without any serious injury to the ship. The spars upon our brooms were sadly cut up. One of our boats, smashed to atoms, was thrown overboard and, I am sorry to say, many other things were cast into the sea that might have been turned to good account. My duty, I thought, was to obey orders, and not to point out the acts of wastefulness I witnessed. No doubt there were many similar ones on board of the other ships. The expense in refitting the fleet must have been immense.

The number of men thrown overboard that were killed, without ceremony, and the sad wrecks around us taught those who, like myself, had not before witnessed similar scenes that war was the greatest scourge of mankind. The first leisure I had, I went to see the Captain of my gun, who had lost his arm. He was in good spirits, and when I told him we had gained the victory, he replied, "Then I don't mind the loss of my arm. I am satisfied." Leaving him, I met a young man who had lost a part of his arm. When I spoke to him he was quite cheerful, not seeming to mind his misfortune. He was eating a piece of buttered biscuit as if nothing had happened. It was a very gratifying circumstance to witness so many acts of heroic bravery that were displayed on board our ship. Patriotic sentences were uttered that would have done honour to the noblest minds: yet these were expressed by the humblest class of men.

Many of our ships that had slightly suffered in their yards, sails and rigging were all to rights in the afternoon. But the ship that astonished us all by her extraordinary exertions was the *Queen.* She had lost her main mast. This was replaced in a most able manner before the evening of this day: all her sides were scrubbed, her paintwork looking as clean as if nothing had happened—a good proof of what can be done with good discipline and management. In the evening, boats were sent to remove the crew from the French prize *le Vengeur,* 74. She was in a sinking state, and went to the bottom about 10 o'clock. 259 of her men were saved.

So soon as I could get hold of the surgeon, I enquired the fate of the two men I had sent him from my quarters. He told me they were both killed! One of them was without the slightest mark of a wound on any part of his body: the other had a bruise across his loins, supposed to have been occasioned by his having come in contact with the bitts [timbers] in his fall. It is therefore clear that they were killed by the wind of a shot. Few persons will believe that the wind of a shot can take away life. But here was proof that it could, and the surgeon was a witness to its having happened. My next question to the doctor was whether he recollected anything of West: if such a person had been to him. He replied that he had; and, upon examining him, he noticed a bruise on the neck. "Yes," said I, "that was a blow he received from the second captain of his gun with a handspike, for deserting his quarters." So the Swede told a good story to the surgeon, and remained snug in the cockpit for the remainder of the action.

3. Battle of St. Vincent, 14 February 1797

Nicolas, Sir Nicholas Harris, ed. 1846. *The Dispatches and Letters of Vice Admiral Lord Viscount Nelson.* London: Henry Colburn, 2: 340–343.

Although not in command of the British squadron at St. Vincent, Commodore Horatio Nelson attained widespread public recognition for his intrepidity in not only cutting the Spanish line, but in boarding and capturing two enemy ships. The following is his account of the action.

At one P.M., the *Captain* having passed the sternmost of the Enemy's Ships which formed their van and part of their centre, consisting of seventeen Sail of the Line, they on the larboard, we on the starboard tack, the Admiral made the signal to "tack in succession;" but I, perceiving the Spanish Ships all to bear up before the wind, or nearly so, evidently with an intention of forming their line going large, joining their separated Division, at that time engaged with some of our centre Ships, or flying from us—to prevent either of their schemes from taking effect, I ordered the ship to be wore, and passing between the *Diadem* and *Excellent,* at a quarter past one o'clock, was engaged with the headmost, and of course leeward-most of the Spanish division. The Ships which I know were, the *Santissima Trinidad,* 126 [guns]; *San Josef,* 112; *Salvador del Mundo,* 112; *San Nicolas,* 80; another First-rate, and [a] Seventy-four, names not known. I was immediately joined and most nobly supported by the *Culloden,* Captain [Thomas] Troubridge. The Spanish Fleet, from not wishing (I suppose) to have a decisive battle, hauled to the wind on the starboard tack, which brought the Ships afore-mentioned to be the leeward-most and sternmost Ships in their Fleet. For near an hour, I believe, (but do not pretend to be correct as to time,) did the *Culloden* and *Captain* support this apparently, but not really, unequal contest; when the *Blenheim,* passing between us and the Enemy, gave us a respite, and sickened the Dons [Spanish]. At this time, the *Salvador del Mundo* and *San Isidro* dropped astern, and were fired into in a masterly style by the *Excellent,* Captain Collingwood, who compelled the *San Isidro* to hoist English colours, and I thought the large Ship *Salvador del Mundo* had also struck; but Captain Collingwood, disdaining the parade and taking possession of beaten enemies, most gallantly pushed up, with every sail set, to save his old friend and messmate, who was to appearance in a critical state. The *Blenheim* being ahead, and the *Culloden* crippled and astern, the *Excellent* ranged up within ten feet of the *San Nicolas,* giving a most tremendous fire, The *San Nicolas* luffing up, the *San Josef* fell on board her, and the *Excellent* passing on for the *Santissima Trinidad,* the *Captain* resumed her situation abreast of them, and close alongside. At this time the *Captain* having lost her foretop-mast, not a sail, shroud, or rope left, her wheel shot away, and incapable of further service in the line, or in chase, I directed Captain [Ralph] Miller to put the helm a-starboard, and calling for the Boarders, ordered them to board.

The Soldiers of the 69th Regiment, with an alacrity which will ever do them credit, and Lieutenant Pierson of the same Regiment, were amongst the foremost on this service. The first man who jumped into the Enemy's mizzen-chains was Captain [Edward] Berry, late my First Lieutenant; (Captain Miller was in the very act of going also, but I directed him to remain;) he was supported from our spritsail-yard, which hooked in the mizzen-rigging. A soldier of the 69th regiment having broke[n] the upper quarter-gallery window, jumped in, followed by myself and others as fast as possible. I found the cabin-doors fastened, and some Spanish Officers fired their pistols; but having broken open the doors, the soldiers fired, and the Spanish Brigadier (Commodore with a Distinguishing Pendant) fell, as retreating to the quarter deck, on the larboard side, near the wheel. Having pushed on [to] the quarter-deck, I found Captain Berry in possession of the poop, and the Spanish ensign hauling down. I passed with my people and Lieutenant Pierson on the larboard gangway to the forecastle, where I met two or three Spanish Officers prisoners to my seamen, and they delivered me their swords.

At this moment, a fire of pistols or muskets opened from the Admiral's stern gallery of the *San Josef,* I directed the soldiers to fire into her stern; and, calling to Captain Miller, ordered him to send more men into the *San Nicolas,* and directed my people to board the First-rate, which was done in an instant, Captain Berry assisting me into the main chains. At this moment a Spanish Officer looked over the quarter-deck rail, and said—"they surrendered;" from this most welcome intelligence it was not long before I was on the quarter-deck, when the Spanish Captain, with a bow, presented me his Sword, and said the Admiral was dying of his wounds below. I asked him, on his honour, if the Ship were surrendered? he declared she was; on which I have him my hand, and desired him to call to his Officers and Ship's company, and tell them of it—which he did; and on the quarter-deck of a Spanish First-rate, extravagant as the story may seem, did I receive the Swords of vanquished Spaniards; which, as I received, I gave to William Fearney, one of my bargemen, who put them with the greatest sangfroid under his arm. I was surrounded by Captain Berry, Lieutenant Pierson, 69th Regiment, John Sykes, John Thomson, Francis Cook, all old *Agamemnons,* and several other brave men, seamen and soldiers: thus fell these Ships.

4. Battle of the Nile, 1 August 1798

Nicolas, Sir Nicholas Harris, ed. 1846. *The Dispatches and Letters of Vice Admiral Lord Viscount Nelson.* London: Henry Colburn, 3: 48–53.

The destruction of the French fleet in Aboukir Bay left Napoleon's army stranded, without hope of either reinforcement or evacuation. For Rear Admiral Sir Horatio Nelson, the Nile marked the beginning of official recognition of his brilliance as an independent naval commander. The following account was written by Edward Berry, captain of the 74-gun Vanguard, *aboard which Nelson directed the battle.*

From Syracuse the Squadron proceeded with all expedition to the Morea [the contemporary name for the southern Greek peninsula now known as the Peloponnese], and nothing particular occurred on the passage except that, on the 28th of July, being near the Morea, the *Culloden* was sent into the Gulf of Coron for intelligence, and on her return, the next day, she brought with her a French brig, a prize, and information that the Enemy's Fleet had been seen steering to the S. E. from Candia [Crete] about four weeks before. The *Alexander,* Captain [Alexander] Ball, on the same day obtained similar intelligence from a Vessel passing close to the Fleet, and Nelson immediately bore up, under all sail, for Alexandria. At seven in the evening, of the 31st of July, the Admiral made the signal for the Fleet to close, and early in the morning of the 1st of August, the *Alexander* and *Swiftsure* were sent ahead to look out. . . .

The utmost joy seemed to animate every breast on board the Squadron, at sight of the Enemy; and the pleasure which the Admiral himself felt, was perhaps more heightened than that of any other man, as he had now a certainty by which he could regulate his future operations. The Admiral had, and it appeared most justly, the highest opinion of, and placed the firmest reliance on, the valour and conduct of every Captain in his Squadron. It had been his practice during the whole of the cruise, whenever the weather and circumstances would permit, to have his Captains on board the *Vanguard,* where he would fully develop to them his own ideas of the different and best modes of attack, and such plans as he proposed to execute upon falling in with the Enemy, whatever their position or situation might be, by day or by night. There was no possible position in which they could be found, that he did not take into his calculation, and for the most advantageous attack of which he had not digested and arranged the best possible disposition of the force which he commanded. With the masterly ideas of their Admiral, therefore, on the subject of Naval tactics, every one of the Captains of his Squadron was most thoroughly acquainted; and upon surveying the situation of the Enemy, they could ascertain with precision what were the ideas and intentions of their Commander, without the aid of any further instructions; by which means signals became almost unnecessary, much time was saved, and the attention of every Captain could almost undistractedly be paid to the conduct of his own particular Ship, a circumstance from which, upon this occasion, the advantages to the general service were almost incalculable. It cannot here be thought irrelevant, to give some idea of what were the plans which Admiral Nelson had formed, and which he explained to his Captains with such perspicuity, as to render his ideas completely their own. To the Naval service, at least, they must prove not only interesting, but useful. Had he fallen in with the French Fleet at sea, that he might make the best impression upon any part of it that should appear the most vulnerable, or the most eligible for attack, he divided his force into three Sub-squadrons, viz.

Vanguard,	*Orion,*	*Culloden,*
Minotaur,	*Goliath,*	*Theseus,*
Leander,	*Majestic,*	*Alexander,*
Audacious,	*Bellerophon,*	*Swiftsure.*
Defence,		
Zealous,		

Two of these Sub-squadrons were to attack the Ships of War, while the third was to pursue the Transports, and to sink and destroy as many as it could. The destination of the French armament was involved in doubt and uncertainty; but it forcibly struck the Admiral, that, as it was commanded by the man whom the French had dignified with the title of the Conqueror of the Italy [General Napoleon Bonaparte], and as he had with him a very large body of troops, an expedition had been planned which the land force might execute without the aid of their Fleet, should the Transports be permitted to make their escape, and reach in safety their place of rendezvous; it therefore became a material consideration with the Admiral so to arrange his force as at once to engage the whole attention of their Ships of War, and at the same time materially to annoy and injure their convoy. It will be fully admitted, from the subsequent information which has been received upon the subject, that the ideas of the Admiral upon this

occasion were perfectly just, and that the plan which he had arranged was the most likely to frustrate the designs of the Enemy. It is almost unnecessary to explain his projected mode of attack at anchor, as that was minutely and precisely executed in the Action which we now come to describe. These plans, however, were formed two months before an opportunity presented itself of executing any of them, and the advantage now was, that they were familiar to the understanding of every Captain in the Fleet.

We saw the Pharos of Alexandria at noon on the first of August. The *Alexander* and *Swiftsure* had been detached a-head on the preceding evening, to reconnoitre the Ports of Alexandria, while the main body of the Squadron kept in the offing. The Enemy's Fleet was first discovered by the *Zealous,* Captain [Samuel] Hood, who immediately communicated, by signal, the number of Ships, sixteen, laying at anchor in Line of Battle, in a Bay upon the larboard bow, which we afterwards found to be Aboukir Bay. The Admiral hauled his wind that instant, a movement which was immediately observed and followed by the whole Squadron; and at the same time he recalled the *Alexander* and *Swiftsure.* The wind was at this time N.N.W., and blew what seamen call a top-gallant breeze. It was necessary to take in the royals when we hauled upon a wind. The Admiral made to signal to prepare from battle, and that it was his intention to attack the Enemy's van and centre, as they lay at anchor, and according to the plan before developed. His idea, in this disposition of his force was, first to secure the victory, and then to make the most of it according to future circumstances. A bower cable of each Ship was immediately got out abaft, and bent forward. We continued carrying sail, and standing in for the Enemy's Fleet in a close Line of Battle. As all the officers of our Squadron were totally unacquainted with Aboukir Bay, each Ship kept sounding as she stood in. The Enemy appeared to be moored in a strong and compact Line of Battle, close in with the shore, their line describing an obtuse angle in its form, flanked by numerous Gun-boats, four frigates, and a battery of guns and mortars, on an Island in their Van. This situation of the Enemy seemed to secure to them the most decided advantages, as they had nothing to attend to but their artillery, in their superior skill in the use of which the French so much pride themselves, and to which indeed their splendid series of land victories are in a great measure to be imputed.

The position of the Enemy presented the most formidable obstacles; but the Admiral viewed these with the eye of a seaman determined on attack, and it instantly struck his eager and penetrating mind, *that where there was room for an Enemy's Ship to swing, there was room for one of ours to anchor.* No further signal was necessary, than those which had already been made. The Admiral's designs were as fully known to his whole Squadron, as was his determination to conquer, or perish in the attempt. The *Goliath* and *Zealous* had the honour to lead inside, and to receive the first fire from the Van ships of the Enemy, as well as from the Batteries and Gun-boats with which their van was strengthened. These two Ships, with the *Orion, Audacious,* and *Theseus,* took their stations inside of the Enemy's Line, and were immediately in close action. The *Vanguard* anchored the first on the outer side of the Enemy, and was opposed within half pistol-shot of *Le Spartiate,* the third in the Enemy's Line. In standing in, our leading Ships were unavoidably obliged to receive into their bows the whole fire of the broadsides of the French line, until they could take their respective stations; and it is but justice to observe, that the Enemy received us with great firmness and deliberation, no colours having been hoisted on either side, nor a gun fired, till our Van ships were within half gun shot. At this time the necessary number of our men were employed aloft in furling sails, and on deck, in hauling the braces, &c. preparatory to our casting anchor. As soon as this took place, a most animated fire was opened from the *Vanguard,* which Ship covered the approach of those in the rear, which were following in a close line. The *Minotaur, Defence, Bellerophon, Majestic, Swiftsure,* and *Alexander,* came up in succession, and passing within hail of the *Vanguard,* took their respective stations opposed to the Enemy's line. All our Ships anchored by the stern, by which means the British line became inverted from van to rear. Captain [Thomas] Thompson, of the *Leander,* of 50 guns, with a degree of skill and intrepidity highly honourable to his professional character, advanced towards the Enemy's line on the outside, and most judiciously dropped his anchor athwart hause of the *Le Franklin,* raking her with great success, the shot from the *Leander*'s broadside which passed that Ship all striking *L'Orient,* the Flag Ship of the French Commander in Chief [Vice Admiral François Paul Brueys d'Aigailliers].

The action commenced at sun-set, which was at thirty-one minutes past six P.M., with an ardour and vigour which it is impossible to describe. At about seven o'clock total darkness had come on, but the whole hemisphere was, with intervals, illuminated by the fire of the hostile Fleets. Our Ships, when darkness came on, had all hoisted their distinguishing lights, by a signal from the Admiral. The Van ship of the Enemy, *Le Guerrier,* was dismasted in less than twelve minutes, and, in ten minutes after, the second ship, *Le Conquérant,* and the third, *Le Spartiate,* very nearly at the same moment were almost dismasted, *L'Aquilon* and *Le Souverain Peuple,* the fourth and fifth Ships of the Enemy's line, were taken possession of by the British at half-past eight in the evening. Captain Berry, at that hour, sent Lieutenant Galwey, of the *Vanguard,* with a party of marines, to take possession of *Le Spartiate,* and that officer returned by the boat, the French Captain's sword, which Captain Berry immediately delivered to the Admiral, who was then below, in consequence of the severe wound which he had received in the head during the heat of the attack. At this time it appeared that victory had already declared itself in our favour, for although *L'Orient, L'Heureux,* and *Tonnant* were not taken possession of, they were considered as completely in our power, which pleasing intelligence Captain Berry had likewise the satisfaction of communicating in person to the Admiral. At ten minutes after nine, a fire was observed on board *L'Orient,* the French Admiral's Ship, which seemed to proceed from the after part of the cabin, and which increased with great rapidity, presently involving the whole of the after part of the Ship in flames. This circumstance Captain Berry immediately communicated to the Admiral, who, though suffering severely from his wound, came up upon deck, where the first consideration that struck his mind was concern for the danger of so many

lives, to save as many as possible of whom he ordered Captain Berry to make every practicable exertion. A boat, the only one that could swim, was instantly dispatched from the *Vanguard,* and other Ships that were in a condition to do so, immediately followed the example; by which means, from the best possible information, the lives of about seventy Frenchmen were saved. The light thrown by the fire of *L'Orient* upon the surrounding objects, enabled us to perceive with more certainty the situation of the two Fleets, the colours of both being clearly distinguishable. The cannonading was partially kept up to leeward of the Centre till about ten o'clock, when *L'Orient* blew up with a most tremendous explosion. An awful pause and death-like silence for about three minutes ensued, when the wreck of the masts, yards, &c. which had been carried to a vast height, fell down into the water, and on board the surrounding Ships. A port fire from *L'Orient* fell into the main royal of the *Alexander,* the fire occasioned by which was, however, extinguished in about two minutes, by the active exertions of Captain Ball.

After this awful scene, the firing was recommenced with the Ships to leeward of the Centre, till twenty minutes past ten, when there was a total cessation of firing for about ten minutes; after which it was revived till about three in the morning, when it again ceased. After the victory had been secured in the Van, such British ships as were in a condition to move, had gone down upon the fresh Ships of the Enemy, which occasioned these renewals of the fight, all of which terminated with the same happy success in favour of our Flag. At five minutes past five in the morning, the two Rear ships of the Enemy, *Le Guillaume Tell* and *Le Généreux,* were the only French ships of the Line that had their colours flying. At fifty-four minutes past five, a French frigate, *L'Artemise,* fired a broadside and struck her colours; but such was the unwarrantable and infamous conduct of the French Captain [Pierre Standelet], that after having thus surrendered, he set fire to his Ship, and with part of his crew, made his escape on shore. Another of the French frigates, *La Sérieuse,* had been sunk by the fire from some of our Ships; but as her poop remained above water, her men were saved upon it, and were taken off by our boats in the morning. The *Bellerophon,* whose masts and cables had been entirely shot away, could not retain her situation abreast of *L'Orient,* but had drifted out of the line to the lee side of the Bay, a little before that Ship blew up. The *Audacious* was in the morning detached to her assistance. At eleven o'clock, *Le Généreux* and *Guillaume Tell,* with the two Frigates, *La Justice* and *La Diane,* cut their cables and stood out to sea, pursued by the *Zealous,* Captain [Samuel] Hood, who, as the Admiral himself has stated, handsomely endeavoured to prevent their escape: but as there was no other Ship in a condition to support the *Zealous,* she was recalled. The whole day of the 2nd was employed in securing the French ships that had struck, and which were now all completely in our possession, *Le Tonnant* and *Timolèon* excepted; as these were both dismasted, and consequently could not escape, they were naturally the last of which we thought of taking possession. On the morning of the third, the *Timoléon* was set fire to, and *Le Tonnant* had cut her cable and drifted on shore, but that active officer, Captain Miller, of the *Theseus,* soon got her off again, and secured her in the

British line. The British force engaged consisted of twelve Ships of 74 guns, and the *Leander,* of 50.

From the over anxiety and zeal of Captain [Thomas] Troubridge to get into action, his Ship, the *Culloden,* in standing in for the Van of the Enemy's line, unfortunately grounded upon the tail of a shoal running off from the Island, on which were the mortar and gun batteries of the Enemy; and notwithstanding all the exertions of that able officer and his Ship's company, she could not be got off. This unfortunate circumstance was severely felt at the moment by the Admiral and all the officers of the Squadron, but their feelings were nothing compared to the anxiety and even anguish of mind which the Captain of the *Culloden* himself experienced, for so many eventful hours. There was but one consolation that could offer itself to him in the midst of the distresses of his situation, a feeble one it is true—that his ship served as a beacon for three other Ships, viz., the *Alexander, Theseus,* and *Leander,* which were advancing with all possible sail set close to his rear, and which otherwise might have experienced a similar misfortune, and thus in greater proportion still have weakened our force. It was not till the morning of the second, that the Culloden could be got off, and it was found she had suffered very considerable damage in her bottom, that her rudder was beat off, and the crew could scarcely keep her afloat with all pumps going. The resources of Captain Troubridge's mind availed him much, and were admirably exerted upon this trying occasion. In four days he had a new rudder made upon his own deck, which was immediately shipped; and the *Culloden* was again in a state for actual service, though still very leaky.

The Admiral, knowing that the wounded of his own Ships had been well taken care of, bent his first attention to those of the Enemy. He established a truce with the Commandant of Aboukir, and through him made a communication to the Commandant of Alexandria, that it was his intention to allow all the wounded Frenchmen to be taken ashore to proper hospitals, with their own surgeons to attend them—a proposal which was assented to by the French, and which was carried into effect on the following day. The activity and generous consideration of Captain Troubridge were again exerted at this time for the general good. He communicated with the shore, and had the address to procure a supply of fresh provisions, onions, &c. which were served out to the sick and wounded, and which proved of essential utility. On the 2nd [of August], the Arabs and Mamelukes, who during the Battle had lined the shores of the Bay, saw with transport that the victory was decisively ours, an event in which they participated with an exultation almost equal to our own; and on that and the two following nights, the whole coast and country were illuminated as far as we could see, in celebration of our victory. This had a great effect upon the minds of our prisoners, as they conceived that this illumination was the consequence, not entirely of our success, but of some signal advantage obtained by the Arabs and Mamelukes over Buonaparte. Although it is natural to suppose that the time and attention of the Admiral, and all the officers of his Squadron, were very fully employed in repairing the damages sustained by their own Ships, and in securing those of the Enemy, which their valour had subdued, yet the mind of that great and good man felt the strongest emotions of the most pious

gratitude to the Supreme Being for the signal success, which, by his Divine favour, had crowned his endeavours in the cause of his Country. . . . At two o'clock accordingly on that day, public service was performed on the quarter-deck of the *Vanguard* by the Rev. Mr. Comyn, the other Ships following the example of the Admiral, though perhaps not all at the same time. This solemn act of gratitude to Heaven seemed to make a very deep impression upon several of the prisoners, both officers and men, some of the former of whom remarked, that it was no wonder we could preserve such order and discipline, when we could impress the minds of our men with such sentiments after a victory so great, and at a moment of such seeming confusion.

5. Treaty of Lunéville, 9 February 1801

Reproduced by kind permission of the editors of the Napoleon Series (www.napoleon-series.org).

With Austria knocked out the War of the Second Coalition, Britain remained the only major power opposing France. Lunéville reaffirmed French possession of the Austrian Netherlands as agreed at Campo Formio in 1797, extended the territory of the French satellite, the Cisalpine Republic, restored the King of Naples to his mainland possessions, and confirmed the pope's rule over the Papal States. Lunéville signified the end of further Habsburg resistance to French political and territorial ambitions during the Revolutionary Wars.

Treaty of Peace concluded at Lunéville, 9 February 1801, between the French Republic, and the Emperor and the Germanic Body [Holy Roman Empire].

His majesty, the emperor and the king of Hungary and Bohemia, and the First Consul of the French republic, in the name of the French people, having equally at heart to put an end to the miseries of war, have resolved to proceed to the conclusion of a definite treaty of peace and amity.

His said imperial and royal majesty, not less anxiously desirous of making the Germanic [Holy Roman] empire participate in the blessings of peace, and the present conjecture not allowing the time necessary for the empire to be consulted, and to take part by its deputies in the negotiation; his said majesty having, besides, regard to what has been agreed upon by the deputation of the empire at he preceding congress at Rastadt [Rastatt], has resolved, in conformity with the precedent of what has taken place in familiar circumstances, to stipulate in the name of the Germanic body.

In consequence of which the contracting parties have appointed as their plenipotentiaries, to it,

His imperial and royal majesty, the sieur Louis Cobentzel [Cobenzl], count of the holy Roman empire, knight of the golden fleece, grand cross of the royal order of St Stephen and of the order of St. John of Jerusalem, chamberlain, and privy counsellor of his imperial and royal majesty, his minister for the conference, and vice-chancellor of the court of state;

And the First Consul of the French republic, in the name of the French people, has appointed citizen Joseph Bonaparte, counsellor of state; who, after having exchanged their full powers, have agreed to the following articles:

Art. I. There shall be henceforth and forever, peace, amity, and good understanding, between his majesty the emperor, king of Hungary and Bohemia, stipulating, as well in his own name as that of the Germanic empire, and the French republic, is said majesty engaging to cause the empire to give ratification in good and due form to the present treaty. The greatest attention shall be paid on both sides to the maintenance of perfect harmony, to preventing all hostilities by land and by sea, for whatever cause, or on whatever pretence, and to carefully endeavouring to maintain the union happily established. No assistance or protection shall be given, either directly or indirectly, to those who would do any thing to the prejudice of either of the contracting parties.

II. The cession of the ci-devant Belgic provinces to the French republic, stipulated by the 3rd article of the treaty of Campo Formio, is renewed there in the most formal manner, so that his imperial and royal majesty, for himself and his successors, as well in his own name as that of the Germanic empire, renounces all his right and title to the said provinces, which shall be possessed henceforth as its sovereign right and property by the French republic, with the territorial property dependent on it. There shall also be given up to the French republic by his imperial and royal majesty, and with the formal consent of the empire:

1st, The comté of Falkenstein, with its dependencies.

2d, The Frickthall, and all belonging to the house of Austria in the left bank of the Rhine, between Zarsach and Basle; the French republic reserving to themselves the right of ceding the latter country to the Helvetic republic [Switzerland].

III. In the same manner, in renewal and confirmation of the 6th article of the treaty of Campo Formio [1797], his majesty the emperor and the king shall possess in sovereignty, and as his right, the countries below enumerated, viz. Istria, Dalmatia, and the Venetian isles in the Adriatic dependant upon those countries, the Bocca de Cattaro, the city of Venice, the canals and the country included between the hereditary state of his majesty the emperor and king; the Adriatic sea, and the Adige, from its leaving the Tyrol to the mouth of the said sea; the towing path of the Adige serving as the line of limitation. And as by this line the cites of Verona and of Porto Legnano will be divided, there shall be established, on the middle bridges of the said cities, drawbridges to mark the separation.

IV. The 18th article of the treaty of Campo Formio is also renewed thus far, that his majesty the emperor and king binds himself to yield to the Duke of Modena, as an indemnity for the countries which this prince and his heirs had in Italy, the Brisgau, which he shall hold on the same terms as those by virtue of which he possesses the Modenese.

V. It is moreover agreed, that his royal highness the grand duke of Tuscany shall renounce, for himself and his successors, having any right to it, the grand duchy of Tuscany, and that part of the isle of Elba which is dependent upon it, as well as all right and title resulting from his rights on the said states, which shall be henceforth possessed in complete sovereignty, and as his own

property, by his royal highness the infant duke of Parma. The grand duke shall obtain in Germany a full and complete indemnity for his Italian states. The grand duke shall dispose at pleasure of the goods and property which he possesses in Tuscany, either by personal acquisition, or by descent from his late father, the emperor Leopold II, or from his grandfather the emperor Francis I. It is also agreed, that other property of the grand duchy, as well as the debts secured on the country, shall pass to the new grand duke.

VI. His majesty the emperor and king, as well as in his own name as in that of the Germanic empire, consents that the French republic shall possess henceforth in complete sovereignty, and as their property, the country and domains situated on the left bank of the Rhine, and which formed part of the Germanic empire: so that, in conformity with what had been expressly consented to at the congress of Rastadt, by the deputation of the empire, and approved by the emperor, the towing path of the Rhine will henceforth be the limit between the French republic and the Germanic empire; that is to say, from the place where the Rhine leaves the Helvetic territory, to that where it enters the Batavian [Dutch] territory.

In consequence of this, the French republic formally renounces all possession whatever on the right bank of the Rhine, and consents to restore to those whom it may belong, the fortresses of Dusseldorff, Ehrenbreitstein, Philipsburgh, the fort of Cassel, and other fortifications opposite to Mentz, on the right bank, the fort of Kehl, and Old Brisach, on the express condition that these places and fortresses shall continue and remain in the state in which they were at the time of their evacuation.

VII. And as, in consequence of the cession which the empire makes to the French republic, several princes and states of the empire will be dispossessed, either altogether or in part, whom it is incumbent upon the Germanic empire collectively to support, the losses resulting from the stipulations in the present treaty, it is agreed between his majesty the emperor and king, as well in his own name as in that of the Germanic empire, and the French republic, that in conformity with the principles formally established at the congress of Rastadt, the empire shall be bound to give to the hereditary princes who shall be dispossessed on the left bank of the Rhine, an indemnity, which shall be taken from the whole of the empire, according to arrangements which on these bases shall be ultimately determined upon.

VIII. In all the ceded countries, acquired or exchanged by the present treaty, it is agreed, as had already been done by the 4th and 10th articles of the treaty of Campo Formio, that those to whom they shall belong shall take them, subject to the debts charged on the said countries; but considering the difficulties which have arisen in this respect, with regard to the interpretation of the said articles of the treaty of Campo Formio, it is expressly understood, that the French republic will not take upon itself any thing more that the debts resulting from the loans formally agreed to by the state so the ceded countries, or by the actual administrations of such countries.

IX. Immediately after the change of the ratifications of the present treaty, the sequestration imposed on the property, effects, and revenues of the inhabitants or proprietors, shall be taken off.

The contracting parties oblige themselves to pay all they may owe for money lent them by individuals, as well as by the public establishments of the said countries and to pay and reimburse all annuities created for their benefit on every one of them. In consequence of this, it is expressly admitted, that the holders of stock in the bank of Vienna, become French subjects, shall continue to enjoy the benefit of their funds, and shall receive the interest accrued, or to accrue, not withstanding the infringement which the holders aforesaid, become French subjects, sustained by not being able to pay the 30 and 100 percent demanded by his imperial and royal majesty, of all creditors of the bank of Vienna.

X. The contracting parties shall also cause all the sequestrations to be taken off, which have been imposed on account of the war, on the property, the rights, and revenues of the emperor, or of the empire, in the territory of the French republic, and of the French citizens in the states of the said majesty or the empire.

XI. The present treaty of peace, and particularly the 8th, 9th, 10th and 15th articles, are declared to extend to, and to be common to the Batavian, Helvetic, Cisalpine and Ligurian republics [the latter two situated in northern Italy]. The contracting parties mutually guaranty the independence of the said republics, and the right of the people who inhabit them to adopt what form of government they please.

XII. His imperial and royal majesty renounces for himself and his successors, in favour of the Cisalpine republic, all rights and titles arising from those rights, which his majesty might claim on the countries of the 8th article of the treaty of Campo Formio, now form part of the Cisalpine republic, which shall possess them as their sovereignty and property, with all the territorial property dependent upon it.

XIII. His imperial and royal majesty, as well in his own name as in that of the Germanic empire, confirms the agreement already entered into by the treaty of Campo Formio, for the union of ci-devant imperial fiefs to the Ligurian republic, and renounces all rights and titles arising from these rights on the said fiefs.

XIV. In conformity with the 2d article of the treaty of Campo Formio, the navigation of the Adige, which serves as the limits between his majesty the emperor and king, and the navigation of the rivers in the Cisalpine republic, shall be free, nor shall any toll be imposed, nor any ship of war kept there.

XV. All prisoners of war on both sides, as well as hostages given or taken during the war, who shall not be yet restored, shall be so within forty days from the time of the signing of the present treaty.

XVI. The real and personal property unalienated to this royal highness the archduke Charles, and of the heirs of her royal highness the archduchess Christina, deceased, situated in the countries ceded to the French republic, shall be restored to them on condition of their selling them within three years. The same shall be the case also with the landed and personal property of their royal highnesses the archduke Ferdinand and the archduchess Beatrice, his wife, in the territory of the Cisalpine republic.

XVII. The 12th, 13th, 15th, 16th 17th, and 23d articles of the treaty of Campo Formio, are particularly renewed, and are to be executed according to their form and effect, as if they were here repeated verbatim.

XVIII. The contributions, payments, and war impositions, of whatever kind, shall cease from the day of the exchange of the ratifications of the present treaty on the one hand, by his imperial majesty and the Germanic empire, and on the other by the French republic.

XIX. The present treaty shall be ratified by his majesty the emperor and king, by the empire, and by the French republic, in the space of thirty days or sooner if possible; and it is agreed that the armies of the two powers shall remain in the present positions, both in Germany and in Italy, until the ratification shall be respectively, and at the same moment, exchanged at Lunéville.

It is also agreed, that ten days after the exchange of ratifications, the armies of his imperial and royal majesty shall enter the hereditary possessions, which shall, within the same space of time, be evacuated by the French armies; and thirty days after the said ratifications shall be exchanged, the French armies shall evacuate the whole of the territory of the said empire.

Executed at Lunéville, Feb. 9, 1801
Louis Count Cobentzel.
Joseph Bonaparte.

6. Treaty of Amiens, 25 March 1802

Reproduced by kind permission of the editors of the Napoleon Series (www.napoleon-series.org).

The terms of Amiens, which heavily favored France, brought a formal end to the French Revolutionary Wars. Britain agreed to restore virtually all the colonial possessions seized from France and her allies, in return for the French evacuation of Naples, the Papal States, and the British evacuation of Egypt. Observers on both sides of the Channel recognized that the agreement was at best tenuous, and indeed hostilities between Britain and France were to resume little more than a year later over the questions of French expansion on the Continent and Britain's refusal to evacuate its troops from Malta.

Definitive Treaty of Peace between the French Republic, his Majesty the King of Spain and the Indies, and the Batavian Republic (on the one Part); and his Majesty, the King of the United Kingdom of Great Britain and Ireland (on the other Part).

The First Consul of the French republic, in the name of the French people, and his majesty the king of the united kingdom of Great Britain and Ireland, being equally animated with a desire to put an end to the calamities of war, have laid the foundation of peace, by the preliminary articles, which were signed in London the 9th Vendemaire, (or the first of October 1801).

And as by the 15th article of the preliminaries it has been agreed on, "that plenipotentiaries should named on the part of each government, who should repair to Amiens, and there proceed to arrange a definitive treaty, in concert with the allies of the contracting powers."

The First Consul of the French republic, in the name of the French people, has named as plenipotentiary the citizen Joseph Buonaparte, counsellor of state:

His majesty the king of the United Kingdom of Great Britain and Ireland has named the marquis Cornwallis, knight of the most noble order of the garter, one of his majesty's privy council, general in his majesty's army, &c. &c.

His majesty the king of Spain and the Indies, and the government of the Batavian republic [Holland], have appointed the following plenipotentiaries, to wit, his catholic majesty has named Don Joseph Nicolas d'Azara, his counsellor of state, grand cross of the order of Charles III, ambassador extraordinary of his majesty to the French republic &c. &c.:

And the government of the Batavian republic, Jean Schimmelpennick its ambassador extraordinary to the French republic, &c.:

Which said plenipotentiaries having duly communicated to each other their respective Powers, which are transcribed at the conclusion of the present treaty, have agreed the following articles:

Article I. There shall be peace, friendship, and good understanding between the French republic, his majesty the king of Spain, his heirs and successors, and the Batavian republic, on the one part, and his majesty the king of the United Kingdom of Great Britain and Ireland, his heirs and successors, on the other part.

The contracting parties shall use their utmost efforts to preserve a perfect harmony between their respective countries, without permitting any act of hostility whatever by sea or by land, for any cause, or under any pretext.

They shall carefully avoid every thing which might for the future disturb the happy union now re-established between them, and shall not give any succour or protection, directly or indirectly, to those who wish to injure any of them.

II. All the prisoners made on one side and the other, as well by land as by sea, and the hostages carried off, or delivered up during the war, and up to the present day, shall be restored without ransom in six weeks at the latest, to be reckoned from the day when the ratifications of the present treaty are exchanged, and on paying the debts which they shall have contracted during their captivity. Each of the contracting parties shall respectively discharge the advances which shall have been made by any of the contracting parties, for the support and maintenance of prisoners in the countries where they have been detained. There shall be appointed by mutual consent for this purpose a commission, especially empowered to ascertain and determine the compensation which may be due to any one of the contracting parties. . . . The time and the place shall likewise be fixed, by mutual consent, for the meeting of the commissioners, who shall be entrusted with the execution of this article, and who shall take into account, not only the expenses incurred on account of the prisoners of the respective nations, but likewise on account of the foreign troops, who, before being taken, were in the pay, and at the disposal of one of the contracting parties.

III. His Britannic majesty restores to the French republic and its allies, viz. his Catholic majesty and the Batavian republic, all the possessions and colonies which respectively belonged to them, and which have been either occupied or conquered by the British forces, during the course of the present war, with the exception of the island of Trinidad, and of the Dutch possessions on the island of Ceylon.

IV. His Catholic majesty cedes and guarantees, in full property and sovereignty, the island of Trinidad to his Britannic majesty.

V. The Batavian republic cedes and guarantees, in full property and sovereignty, to his Britannic majesty, all the possessions and establishments in the island of Ceylon, which previous to the war belonged to the republic of the united provinces, or to the Dutch East India company.

VI. The port of the Cape of Good Hope remains to the Batavian republic in full sovereignty, in the same manner as it did previous to the war.

The ships of every kind belonging to the other contracting parties, shall be allowed to enter the said ports, and there to purchase what provisions they may stand in need of heretofore, without being liable to pay any other imposts than such as the Batavian republic compels the ships of its own nation to pay.

VII. The territories and possessions of his most Faithful majesty are maintained in their integrity, such as they were antecedent to the war. However the boundaries of French and Portuguese Guiana are fixed by the river Arroway, which empties itself into the ocean above Cape North, near the islands Nuovo and Penetentia, about a degree and a third of north latitude. These boundaries shall run along the river Arroway, from its mouth, the most distant from Cape North, to its source, and afterwards on a right line, drawn from that source, to the Rio Brunco, towards the west.

In consequence, the northern bank of the river Arroway, from its said mouth to its source, and the territories that lie to the north of the line of boundaries laid down as above, shall belong in full sovereignty to the French republic.

The southern bank of the said river, from the same mouth, and all the territories to the south of the said line, shall belong to her most Faithful majesty.

The navigation of the river Arroway, along the whole of its course, shall be common to both nations.

The arrangements which have been agreed upon between the courts of Madrid and Lisbon, respecting the settlement of their boundaries in Europe, shall nevertheless be adhered to conformably to the stipulations of the treaty of Badajos.

VIII. The territories, possessions, and rights of the sublime Porte, are maintained in their integrity, as they were before the war.

IX. The republic of the Seven [Ionian] Islands is recognised.

X. The islands of Malta, Gozo, and Comino, shall be restored to the order of St. John of Jerusalem to be held on the same conditions, on which it possessed them before the war, and under the following stipulations.

The knights of the order whose Langues shall continue to subsist after the exchange of the ratification of the present treaty, are invited to return to Malta, as soon as the exchange shall have taken place. They shall there form a general chapter, and proceed to the election of a grand master, chosen from among the natives of those nations which are to preserve their Langues, unless that election has been already made since the exchange of the preliminaries.

It is understood that an election made subsequent to that epoch, shall alone be considered valid, to the exclusion of any other that have taken place at any period prior to that epoch.

The governments of the French republic, and of Great Britain, desiring to place the order and island of Malta in a state of entire independence with respect to themselves, agree that there shall not be in future either a French or an English Langue; and that no individual belonging to either the one or to the other of these powers shall be admitted into the order.

There shall be established a Maltese Langue, which shall be supported by the territorial revenues and commercial duties of the island. This Langue shall have its peculiar dignities, an establishment and a mansion-house. Proofs of nobility shall not be necessary for the admission of knights of the Langue; and they shall be moreover admissible to all offices, and shall enjoy all privileges, in the same manner as the knights of the other Langues. At least half of the municipal, administrative, civil, judicial, and other employments depending on the government, shall be filled by inhabitants of the islands of Malta, Gozo, and Comino.

The forces of his Britannic majesty shall evacuate the island, and its dependencies, within three months from the exchange of the ratifications, or sooner if possible. At that epoch it shall be given up to the order in its present state, provided the grand master, or commissaries, fully authorized according to the statutes of the order, shall be in the island to take possession, and that the force which is to be provided by his Sicilian majesty, as is hereafter stipulated, shall have arrived there.

One half of the garrison at least shall always be composed of native Maltese; for the remainder, the order may levy recruits in those countries only which continue to possess the Langues. The Maltese troops shall have Maltese officers. The commandership in chief of the garrison, as well as the nomination of the officers, shall pertain to the grand master, and this right he cannot resign even temporarily, except in favour of a knight, and in concurrence with the advice of the council of the order.

The independence of the isles Malta, of Gozo, and Comino, as well as the present arrangement, shall be placed under the protection and guarantee of France, Great Britain, Austria, Spain, Russia, and Prussia.

The neutrality of the order and of the island of Malta, with its dependencies, is hereby proclaimed.

The ports of Malta shall be opened to the commerce and the navigation of all nations, who shall there pay equal and moderate duties: these duties shall be applied to the maintenance of the Maltese Langue, as specified in paragraph 3, to that of the civil and military establishments of the island, as well as to that of a general lazaret, open to all colours.

The states of Barbary [Morocco, Algiers, Tunis, and Tripoli] are excepted from the conditions of the preceding paragraphs, until, by means of an arrangement to be procured by the contracting parties, the system of hostilities, which subsists between the states of Barbary, and the order of St. John, or the powers possessing the Langue, or concurring in the composition of the order, shall have ceased.

The order shall be governed, both with respect to spirituals and temporals, by the same statutes which were in force when the knights left the isle, as far as the present treaty does not abrogate them.

The regulations contained in the paragraphs 3, 5, 7, 8, and 10, shall be converted into laws, and perpetual statutes of the order, in the customary manner; and the grand master, or, if he shall not be in the island, at the time of its restoration to the order, his representative, as well as his successors, shall be bound to take an oath for their punctual observance.

His Sicilian majesty shall be invited to furnish 2000 men, natives of his states, to serve as a garrison in the different fortresses of the said islands. That force shall remain one year, to bear date from their restitution to the knights; and if, at the expiration of this term, the order should not have raised a force sufficient, in the judgement of the guarantying powers to garrison the island and its dependencies, as is specified in the 5th paragraph, the Neapolitan troops shall continue there until they shall be replaced by a force deemed sufficient by the said powers.

The different powers designated in the 6th paragraph, to wit, France, Great Britain, Austria, Spain, Russia, and Prussia, shall be invited to accede to the present stipulations.

XI. The French troops shall evacuate the kingdom of Naples and the Roman states; the English forces shall also evacuate Porto Ferrajo [on Corsica], and generally all the ports and islands, that they occupy in the Mediterranean or the Adriatic.

XII. The evacuations, cessions, and restitutions, stipulated by the present treaty, shall be executed in Europe within a month; on the continent and seas of America and Africa in three months; on the continent and seas of Asia in six months, which shall follow the ratification of the present definitive treaty, except in case of a special reservation.

XIII. In all cases of restitution, agreed upon by the present treaty, the fortifications shall be restored in the condition they were in at the time of signing the preliminaries; and all the works which shall have been constructed since their occupation shall remain untouched.

It is agreed besides that in all the stipulated cases of cessions, there shall be allowed to the inhabitants, of whatever rank or nation they may be, a term of three years, reckoning from the notification of the present treaty, to dispose of all their properties, whether acquired by them before or during the continuance of the present war; during which term of three years, they shall have free and entire liberty to exercise their religion, and to enjoy their fortunes. The same power is granted in the countries that are hereby restored, to all persons, whether inhabitants or not, who shall have formed any establishments there, during the time that those countries were in the possession of Great Britain.

As to the inhabitants of the countries restored or ceded, it is hereby agreed, that no person shall, under any pretence, be prosecuted, disturbed, or molested, either in person or property, on account of his political conduct or opinion, or for his attachment to any of the contracting parties, on any account whatever except for debts contracted with individuals, or for acts subsequent to the present treaty.

XIV. All the sequestrations laid on either side on funds, revenues, and credits, of what nature soever they may be, belonging to any of the contracting powers, or to their citizens or subjects, shall be taken off immediately after the signature of this definitive treaty.

The decision of all chains among the individuals of the respective nations, for debts, property, effects, or rights, of any nature whatsoever, which should, according to received usages, and the law of nations, be preferred at the epoch of the peace shall be referred to the competent tribunals: in all those cases speedy and complete justice shall be done in the countries wherein those claims shall be respectively preferred.

XV. The fisheries on the coasts of Newfoundland, and of the adjacent islands, and in the gulf of St. Laurence [St. Lawrence], are placed on the same footing as they were before the war.

The French fishermen of Newfoundland, and the inhabitants of the islands of St. Pierre and Miquelon, shall have liberty, to cut such wood as may be necessary for them in the bays of Fortune and Despair during the first year, reckoning from the ratification of the present treaty.

XVI. To prevent all grounds of complaint and disputes which might arise on account of captures which may have been made at sea subsequent to the signing of the preliminaries [1 October 1801], it is reciprocally agreed that the ships and property which may have been taken in the channel, and in the north seas, after a space of twelve days, reckoning from the exchange of the ratifications of the preliminary articles, shall be restored on the one side and the other; that the term shall be one month for the space, from the channel and the north seas, as far as the Canary islands inclusively, as well in the ocean as in the Mediterranean; two months from the Canary islands to the equator; and, finally five months in all other parts of the world, without any further exceptions or distinction of time or place.

XVII. The ambassadors, ministers, and other agents of the contracting powers, shall enjoy respectively in the states of the said powers the same rank, privileges, prerogative, and immunities, which were enjoyed before the war by agents of the same class.

XVIII. The branch of the house of Nassau, which was established in the ci-devant republic of the united provinces, now the Batavian republic, having experienced some losses, as well with respect to private property as by the change of constitution adopted in those countries, an equivalent compensation shall be procured for the losses which it shall be proved to have sustained.

XIX. The present definitive treaty of Peace is declared common to the sublime Ottoman Porte [the government of the Ottoman Empire], the ally, of his Britannic majesty; and the sublime Porte shall be invited to transmit its act of accession as soon as possible.

XX. It is agreed that the contracting parties, upon requisitions made by them respectively, or by their ministers, or officers duly authorized for that purpose, shall be bound to deliver up to justice persons accused of murder, forgery, or fraudulent bankruptcy, committed within the jurisdiction of the requiring party,

provided that this shall only be done in cases in which thee evidence of the crime shall be such, that the laws of the place in which the accused persons shall be discovered, would have authorized the detaining and bringing him to trial, had the offence been committed there. The expenses of the arrest and prosecution shall be defrayed by the party making the requisition; but this article has no sort of reference to crimes of murder, forgery, or fraudulent bankruptcy, committed before the conclusion of this definitive treaty.

XXI. The contracting parties promise to observe sincerely and faithfully all the articles contained in the present treaty, and will not suffer any sort of counteraction, direct or indirect, to be made to it by their citizens, or respective subjects; and the contracting parties guaranty, generally and reciprocally, all the stipulations of the present treaty.

XXII. The present treaty shall be ratified by the contracting parties, as soon as possible, and the ratifications shall be exchanged in due form in Paris.

In testimony whereof, we, the undersigned plenipotentiaries, have signed with our hands, and in virtue of our respective full powers, the present definitive treaty, causing it to be sealed with our respective seals.

Done at Amiens, the 4th Germinal, in the year 10 (March 25, 1802)

(Signed) Bonaparte.
Cornwallis.
Azara, and
Schimmelpennick.
(A correct copy) J. Bonaparte

7. Pitt's State Paper, 19 January 1805

Webster, C. K., ed. 1921. *British Diplomacy, 1813–1815: Select documents dealing with the reconstruction of Europe.* London: Bell, 389–394.

Pitt's State Paper, in which he outlined the political reconstruction of postwar Europe, stands as one of the key documents of nineteenth-century British foreign policy. The collapse of the Third Coalition prevented its implementation, but it served as the basis for Lord Castlereagh's negotiating position during the critical years of 1813–1815 and contributed many of the ideas that saw practical expression in the Vienna settlement.

Official Communication made to the Russian Ambassador at London [Count Simon Vorontsov], on the 19th January 1805, explanatory of the views which His Majesty and the Emperor of Russia formed for the deliverance and security of Europe.

The result of the communications which have been made by Prince Czartoryski [the Russian foreign minister] to [Britannic] His Majesty's Ambassador at St. Petersburgh [Lord Granville Leveson Gower], and of the confidential explanations which have been received from your Excellency, has been laid before the King [George III]; and His Majesty has seen with inexpressible satisfaction, the wide, dignified, and generous policy, which the Emperor of Russia [Alexander I] is disposed to adopt, under the present calamitous situation of Europe. His Majesty is also happy to perceive, that the views and sentiments of the Emperor respecting the deliverance of Europe, and providing for its future tranquillity and safety, correspond so entirely with his own. He is therefore desirous of entering into this great object, and of forming the closest union of councils, and concert of measures, with his Imperial Majesty, in order, by their joint influence and exertions, to insure the co-operation and assistance of other Powers of the Continent, on a scale adequate to the magnitude and importance of an undertaking, on the success of which the future safety of Europe must depend.

For this purpose, the first step must be, to fix as precisely as possible, the distinct objects to which such a concert is to be directed.

These, according to the explanation given of the sentiments of the Emperor, in which His Majesty entirely concurs, appear to be three:—

1. To rescue from the dominion of France those countries which it has subjugated since the beginning of the Revolution, and to reduce France within its former limits, as they stood before that time.
2. To make such an arrangement with respect to the territories recovered from France, as may provide for their security and happiness, and may at the same time constitute a more effectual barrier in future against encroachments on the part of France.
3. To form, at the restoration of peace, a general agreement and Guarantee for the mutual protection and security of different Powers, and for re-establishing a general system of public law in Europe.

The first and second objects are stated generally, and in their broadest extent; but neither of them can be properly considered in detail without reference to the nature and extent of the means by which they may be accomplished. The first is certainly that to which, without any modification or exception, his Majesty's wishes, as well as those of the Emperor, would be preferably directed, and nothing short of it can completely satisfy the views which both Sovereigns form for the deliverance and security of Europe. Should it be possible to unite in concert with Great Britain and Russia, the two other great military Powers of the Continent [Austria and Prussia], there seems little doubt that such a union of force would enable them to accomplish all that is proposed. But if (as there is too much reason to imagine may be the case) it should be found impossible to engage Prussia in the Confederacy, it may be doubted whether such operations could be carried on in all the quarters of Europe, as would be necessary for the success of the whole of this project.

The chief points, however, to which His Majesty considers this doubt as applicable, relate to the question of the entire recovery of the [former Austrian] Netherlands [i.e., Belgium] and the countries occupied by France on the left bank of the Rhine. His Majesty considers it essential even on this supposition to include nothing less than the evacuation of the North of Germany and

Italy, the re-establishment of the independence of the United Provinces [Holland] and of Switzerland, the Restoration of the dominions of the King of Sardinia and security of Naples; but on the side of the Netherlands it might perhaps be more prudent in this case to confine the views of the Allies to obtaining some moderate acquisitions for the United Provinces calculated (according to the principle specified under the second head) to form an additional barrier for that country. His Majesty, however, by no means intends to imply if very brilliant and decisive success should be obtained, and the power of France broken and overcome by operations in other quarters, the Allies might not in such a case, extend their views to the recovery of the whole or the greater part of these territories, but, as in the first instance it does not appear possible that they can be reconquered by the operations of the war without the aid of Prussia, His Majesty is inclined to think that this object ought in any Treaty of Concert to be described in such terms as would admit of the modifications here stated.

The second point of itself involves in it many important considerations. The views and sentiments by which His Majesty and the Emperor of Russia are equally animated in endeavouring to establish this concert, are pure and disinterested.

The insular situation and extensive resources of Great Britain, aided by its military exertions and naval superiority, and the immense power, the established Continental ascendancy and remote distance of Russia already give to the territories of the two Sovereigns a security against the attacks of France—even after all her acquisitions of influence, a power and dominion—which cannot be the lot of any other country. They have therefore no separate objects of their own in the arrangements which are in question, no personal interest to consult in this Concert but that which grows out of the general interest and security of Europe, and is inseparably connected with it. Their first view, therefore, with respect to any of the countries which may be recovered from France, must be to restore, as far as possible, their ancient rights, and provide for the internal happiness of their inhabitants; but in looking at this object, they must not lose sight of the general security of Europe, on which even that separate object must principally depend.

Pursuant to this principle, there can be no question that, whenever any of these countries are capable of being restored to their former independence, and of being placed in a situation in which they can protect it, such an arrangement must be most congenial to the policy and the feelings on which this system is founded: but there will be found to be other countries among those now under the dominion of France, to which these considerations cannot apply, where either the ancient relations of the country are so completely destroyed that they cannot be restored, or where independence would be merely nominal and alike inconsistent with the security for the country itself, or for Europe; happily, the larger number is of the first description. Should the arms of the Allies be successful to the full extent of expelling France from all the dominions she has acquired since the Revolution, it would certainly be the first object, as has already been stated, to re-establish the republics of the United Provinces and Switzerland, the territories of the King of Sardinia, Tuscany,

Modena, of the Italian Republic, including the three Legations, Parma, and Placentia; and on the other side of Europe, the Austrian Netherlands, and the States which have been detached from the German [Holy Roman] Empire on the left bank of the Rhine, evidently belong to the second class. With respect to the territories enumerated in Italy, experience has shown how little disposition existed in some, and how little means in any, to resist the aggression or influence of France. The King of Spain was certainly too much a party to the system of which so large a part of Europe has been a victim, to entitle the former interests of his family in Italy to any consideration; nor does the past conduct of Genoa, or any of the other States, give them any claim, either of justice or liberality. It is also obvious that these separate petty sovereignties would never again have any solid existence in themselves, and would only serve to weaken and impair the force which ought to be, as much as possible, concentrated in the hands of the chief Powers of Italy.

It is needless to dwell particularly on the state of the Netherlands. Events have put out of the question the restoration of them to the House of Austria; they are therefore necessarily open to new arrangements, and evidently can never exist separate and independent. Nearly the same considerations apply to the Ecclesiastical Electorates, and the other territories on the left bank of the Rhine, after their being once detached from the Empire, and the former possessors of them indemnified. There appears, therefore, to be no possible objection, on the strictest principles of justice and public morality, to making such a disposition with respect to any of these territories as may be most conducive to the general interests; and there is evidently no other mode of accomplishing the great and beneficent object of re-establishing (after so much misery and bloodshed) the safety and repose of Europe on a solid and permanent basis. It is fortunate too that such a plan of arrangement as in itself essential to the end proposed, is also likely to contribute, in the greatest degree, to secure the means by which that great end can best be promoted.

It is evidently of the utmost importance, if not absolutely indispensable for this purpose, to secure the vigorous and effectual co-operation both of Austria and Prussia; but there is little reason to hope that either of these Powers will be brought to embark in the common cause, without the prospect of obtaining some important acquisition to compensate for its exertions. On the grounds which have been already stated, his Majesty conceives that nothing fresh remains of resisting the views of France on the side of Italy, and placing Prussia in a similar situation with respect to the Low Countries; and the relative situations of the two Powers would naturally make those the quarters to which their views would respectively be directed.

In Italy, sound policy would require, that the power and influence of the King of Sardinia should be augmented, and that Austria should be replaced in a situation which may enable her to afford an immediate and effectual support to his dominions, in case of their being attacked. His Majesty sees with satisfaction, from the secret and confidential communications recently received through your Excellency, that the views of the Court of Vienna are perfectly conformable to this general principle, and that the extension at which she aims, might not only safely be

admitted, but might even be increased, with advantage to the general interest. In other respects His Majesty entirely concurs in the outline of the arrangement which he understands the Emperor of Russia to be desirous of seeing effected in this quarter. His Majesty considers it as absolutely necessary for the general security, that Italy should be completely rescued both from the occupation and influence of France, and that no Powers should be left within it, who are not likely to enter into a general system of defence for maintaining its independence. For this purpose, it is essential that the countries now composing what is called the Italian Republic, should be transferred to other Powers. In distributing these territories, an increase of wealth and power should undoubtedly be given to the King of Sardinia; and it seems material that his possessions, as well as the Duchy of Tuscany (which it is proposed to restore to the Grand Duke), should be brought into immediate contact, or ready communication with those of Austria. On this principle the part of the Milanese to the South West of the Adda, and the whole of the territories which no compose the Ligurian Republic, as well as perhaps Parma and Placentia, might, it is conceived, be annexed to Piedmont.

The Three Legations might in His Majesty's opinion be annexed to the territories of Austria, and the addition which may be made to the acquisitions proposed for that Power, with advantage to the common cause. And the Duchy of Modena, placed as it would be between the new acquisitions of Sardinia and the Duchy of Tuscany (which may be considered under this arrangement as virtually Austrian) might safely be restored to its former possessors.

The observations which have been stated respecting the situation of Sardinia in Italy seem, in a great measure, to apply to that of Holland and Prussia, in relation to the Low Countries; with this difference, however, that the Piedmontese dominions, affording in themselves considerable means of defence, they may be perhaps sufficiently secure in the possession of the King of Sardinia, supported by Austria, whereas the Netherlands being more open and exposed seem scarcely capable of being secured unless by annexing a considerable part of them to Prussia, and placing Holland in a second line of defence. With this view (supposing France to be reduced within its ancient [pre-1792] limits) it might be proposed to annex to the United Provinces, as an additional Barrier, the part of Flanders lying within a military line to be drawn from Antwerp to the Meuse at Maestricht, and the remainder of the [former Austrian] Netherlands, together with the Duchies of Luxembourg and Juliers, and the other territories between the Meuse and the Moselle to Prussia.

His Majesty indeed feels so strongly the importance both of augmenting the inducements to Prussia to take part and of rendering it a powerful and effectual Barrier for the defence not only of Holland but of the North of Germany against France, that he should even consider it as adviseable in addition to what has been already proposed, to put into possession of that Power the territories which may be recovered from France on the left bank of the Rhine, eastward of the Moselle, and His Majesty entertains a strong conviction that this arrangement (if it not in other respects be thought liable to insuperable objections) would be infinitely more effective for the protection of the North of Europe than any other than can be devised.

His Majesty is, however, aware that great difficulties may arise in regulating the proportionate acquisitions of Austria and Prussia, in such a way as to prevent their being the source of mutual jealousy, and this consideration it is which, amongst others, has operated as a great additional inducement of acquisition for Austria on the side of Italy.

He thinks it also important to remark that the acquisition to be held to Prussia ought not to be measured merely by what would be in itself desirable but by the consideration of what may be necessary to outweigh the temptations which France will not fail to offer to that Power, to secure its co-operation. These will probably be on an extensive scale, and in a quarter much more calculated to produce effects injurious to the interests of Austria and of Russia herself while, on the other hand, if the ambition of Prussia can be gratified in the manner proposed at the expense of France, it will be diverted from the views which it will otherwise form towards the North, the accomplishment of which would tend to increase, to an alarming degree, its influence both in Germany and over the secondary Powers of the Baltic. But, if notwithstanding these powerful considerations, it should still be thought by His Imperial Majesty that the augmentation here proposed to the territories of Prussia is greater than ought to be admitted, His Majesty will, (though not without reluctance) concur in any other arrangement that may be thought preferable by which a larger portion of the [former Austrian] Netherlands may be allotted to the United Provinces [Holland], and the acquisitions of Prussia confined within narrower limits; but he trusts that at any rate, it will not be necessary to reduce them to anything less than the territories on the left bank of the Rhine between the Meuse and the Moselle, and it will in this case, require much consideration, in what hands the territories on the left bank of the Rhine, east of the Moselle can best be placed or whether they may be safely left in the possession of France.

In the event of Prussia not being prevailed upon to enter into the concert, I have already stated His Majesty's conviction, that the views of the Allies on this side of Europe must be more limited; and in that case probably nothing more can be expected than to obtain the complete evacuation of the North of Germany, and the re-establishment of the independence of Holland, together with the Barrier here stated within the line drawn from Antwerp to Maestricht, leaving the other territories on the left bank of the Rhine in the possession of France. . . .

Supposing the efforts of the Allies to have been completely successful, and the two objects already discussed to have been fully obtained, His Majesty would nevertheless consider this salutary work as still imperfect, if the restoration of peace were not accompanied by the most effectual measures for giving solidity and permanence to the system which shall thus have been established. Much will undoubtedly be effected for the future repose of Europe by these territorial arrangements, which will furnish a more effectual barrier than has before existed against the ambition of France. But in order to render this security as complete as possible, it seems necessary, at the period of a general pacification, to form a Treaty to which all the principal Powers of Europe

should be parties, by which their respective rights and possessions, as they then have been established, shall be fixed and recognized; and they should all bind themselves mutually to protect and support each other, against any attempt to infringe them:—It should re-establish a general and comprehensive system of public law in Europe, and provide, as far as possible, for repressing the future attempts to disturb the general tranquillity; and above all, for restraining any projects of aggrandizement and ambition similar to those which have produced all the calamities inflicted on Europe since the disastrous era of the French Revolution.

This Treaty should be put under the special Guarantee of Great Britain and Russia, and the two Powers should by a separate engagement, bind themselves to each other jointly to take an active part in preventing its being infringed. Such a Treaty might also be accompanied by more particular and specific provisions, by which the several Powers of Italy might be united in a closer alliance for their own defence. How far any similar system could be adopted for giving additional security for the Germanic Body is well deserving of consideration. Their present state is certainly very unsatisfactory with a view either to their own immediate interests, or to the safety of Europe. At the same time it appears to His Majesty very doubtful whether from local circumstances and other causes, it would ever be possible to consolidate them into any effectual system. Should this be found to be the case, the evils to be apprehended from their weak and exposed state might (as far as relates to the danger from France) perhaps be remedied by adopting a system (but on a larger scale) similar to that formerly established by the Barrier Treaty for the protection of the Netherlands. It might not be difficult to settle some general plan for maintaining at the joint expense of the different Powers of the Empire, fortresses of sufficient strength, and properly garrisoned, along the course of the Rhine from Basle to Ehrenbreiten, commanding the principal approaches from France to the most exposed parts of Germany, and the military custody of these fortresses (without infringing in other respects on the territorial rights of the Power in whose dominions they might be placed) might be confided to the two great Powers of Germany [Austria and Prussia], according to their respective means of occupying them.

It seems also desirable, in order to give further security to the United Provinces (under any of the arrangements which have already been discussed) that they should be called upon to enter into an engagement jointly with Great Britain and Russia to maintain at all times their army on such a footing as may be thought necessary to provide for their defence against sudden attacks. In addition to this stipulation His Majesty in his Electoral capacity, might perhaps be induced to keep a considerable force (in consequence of arrangements with the British Government) ready to be employed on the first alarm for the defence of the United Provinces; and His Majesty would also be ready to enter into a Concert with other Powers for defraying the expense of maintaining at all times an adequate and effective garrison to consist of German troops for garrisoning any fortresses now existing, or hereafter to be established, on whatever may be the line ultimately fixed as the Dutch frontier.

Having thus stated what more immediately relates to the specific objects of the Concert and of the means to be employed to give effect, there still remains one great and important question for consideration, and that is how far, either now or here-after, the views of the Allies ought to be directed towards the re-establishment of monarchy in France, and the restoration of the Bourbon Family on the throne. His Majesty agrees entirely with the Emperor of Russia in thinking that such a settlement is in it-self highly desirable for the future both of France and Europe, and that no fair occasion ought to be neglected of promoting it. But he at the same time thinks, that it ought to be considered only a secondary object in the Concert now to be established and one which could in no case justify the prolongation of the war if a Peace could be obtained on the principles which have been stated. It is one with a view to which no active or decided measures can be taken, unless a series of great and signal successes shall previ-ously have been obtained by the Allies, and a strong and prevail-ing disposition for the return of the Monarch, shall then manifest itself in the interior of France. In the meantime in order to afford every reasonable chance for the attainment of this object, His Majesty entirely agrees with the Emperor of Russia, that it is highly important that in the conduct of the war, and in the public declarations and language of the Allied Courts, the greatest care should be taken to prevent any apprehension in the minds of any part of the French nation of any design either to dictate to them by force any particular form of government, or to attempt to dis-member the ancient territories of France.

Such are the sentiments and observations which His Majesty is desirous of offering to the consideration of the Emperor on the great outlines of the important system which they are equally anxious to establish.

His Majesty will receive with the utmost attention and satis-faction, every fresh communication of the opinion of His Impe-rial Majesty on all the details connected with so extensive a sub-ject. In the meanwhile from an anxiety to lose no time in laying the foundation of this great work, His Majesty has directed a project to be prepared of a Provisional treaty conformable to the sentiments which appear to be entertained both by the Emperor and himself; and which, if it should meet with His Imperial Majesty's concurrence, he is ready immediately to conclude.

8. Battle of Trafalgar, 21 October 1805

Robinson, William. 2002. *Jack Nastyface: Memoirs of an English Seaman.* London: Chatham, 42–63. (Orig. pub. 1836.)

Trafalgar rightly holds its place amongst the most decisive battles in history. It not only saved Britain from the prospect of Napoleonic in-vasion, but in leaving the French Navy impotent for many years to come, it set the stage for the long, virtually unchallenged, period of imperial and commercial hegemony that Britain would enjoy dur-ing the Victorian era. The following account was written by William Robinson, who wrote under the pseudonym of "Jack Nastyface," and served aboard the 74-gun Revenge.

During this time each ship was making the usual prepara-tions, such as breaking away the captain and officers' cabins, and sending all the lumber below—the doctors, parson, purser and loblolly men [surgeon's assistants], were also busy, getting the medicine chests and bandages out; and sails prepared for the wounded to be placed on, that they might be dressed in rotation, as they were taken down to the after cock-pit. In such a bustling, and it may be said, trying as well as serious time, it is curious to notice the different dispositions of the British sailor. Some would be offering a guinea for a glass of grog, whilst others were making a sort of mutual verbal will, such as, if one of Johnny Crapeau's shots (a term given to the French,) knocks my head off, you will take all my effects; and if you are killed, and I am not, why, I will have yours, and this is generally agreed to. During this momen-tous preparation, the human mind had ample time for medita-tion and conjecture, for it was evident that the fate of England rested on this battle; therefore well might Lord Nelson make the signal, "England expects each man will do his duty."

Here, if I may be indulged the observation, I will say that, could England but have seen her sons about to attack the enemy on his own coast, within sight of the inhabitants of Spain, with an inferior force, our number of men being not quite twenty thou-sand, whilst theirs was upwards of thirty thousand; from the zeal which animated every man in the fleet, the bosom of every inhab-itant of England would have glowed with an indescribable patri-otic pride; for such a number of line-of-battle ships have never met together and engaged, either before or since. As we drew near, we discovered the enemy's line was formed with a Spanish ship between two French ones, nearly all through their line; as I suppose, to make them fight better; and it must be admitted that the Dons [Spanish] fought as well as the French in that battle; and, if praise was due for seamanship and valour, they were well entitled to an equal share. We now began to hear the enemy's can-non opening on the *Royal Sovereign,* commanded by Lord Collingwood, who commenced the action; and, a signal being made by the admiral to some of our senior captains to break the enemy's line at different points, it fell to our lot to cut off the five stern-most ships; and, while we were running down to them, of course we were favoured with several shots, and some of our men were wounded. Upon being thus pressed, many of our men thought it hard that the firing should be all on one side, and be-came impatient to return the compliment: but our captain had given orders not to fire until we got close in with them, so that all our shots might tell;—indeed, these were his words: "We shall want all our shot when we get close in: never mind their firing: when I fire a carronade from the quarter-deck, that will be a sig-nal for you to begin, and I know you will do your duty as English-men." In a few minutes the gun was fired, and our ship bore in and broke the line, but we paid dead for our temerity, as those ships we had thrown into disorder turned round, and made an attempt to board. A Spanish three-decker ran her bowsprit over our poop, with a number of her crew on it, and, in her fore rig-ging, two or three hundred men were ready to follow; but they caught a Tartar, for their design was discovered, and our marines with their small arms, and the carronades on the poop, loaded with canister shot, swept them off so fast, some into the water, and some on the decks, that they were glad to sheer off. While this was going on aft, we were engaged with a French two-deck ship on our starboard side, and on our larboard bow another, so that many of their shots must have struck their own ships, and done severe execution. After being engaged about an hour, two other ships fortunately came up, received some of the fire intended for us, and we were now enabled to get at some of the shot-holes between wind and water, and plug them up:—this is the duty performed by the carpenter and his crew. We were now unable to work the ship, our yards, sails, and masts being disabled, and the braces completely shot away. In this condition we lay by the side of the enemy, firing away, and now and then we received a good raking from them, passing under our stern. This was a busy time with us, for we had not only to endeavour to repair our damage, but to keep to our duty. Often during the battle we could not see for the smoke, whether we were firing at a foe or friend, and as to hearing, the noise of the guns had so completely made us deaf, that we were obliged to look only to the motions that were made. In this manner we continued the battle till nearly five o'clock, when it ceased.

It was shortly after made known by one of our boat's crew, that Lord Nelson had received a fatal shot: had this news been communicated through the fleet before the conflict was over, what effect it might have had on the hearts of our seamen I know not, for he was adored, and in fighting under him, every man thought himself sure of success; a momentary but naturally melancholy pause among the survivors of our brave crew ensued.

We were now called to clear the decks, and here might be witnessed an awful and interesting scene, for as each officer and seaman would meet, (oh! what an opportunity for the Christian and man of feeling to meditate on the casualty of fate in this life,) they were inquiring for their mess-mates. Orders were now given to fetch the dead bodies from the after cock-pit, and throw them over-board; these were the bodies of men who were taken down to the doctor during the battle, badly wounded, and who by the time of the engagement was ended were dead. Some of these, perhaps, could not have recovered, while others might, had timely assistance been rendered, which was impossible; for the rule is, as order is requisite, that every person shall be dressed in rotation as they are brought down wounded, and in many instances some have bled to death.

The next call was, "all hands to splice the main brace," which is the giving out a gill of rum to each man, and indeed they much needed it, for they had not ate or drank from breakfast time: we had now a good night's work before us; all our yards, masts, and sails were sadly cut, indeed the whole of the sails were obliged to be unbent, being rendered completely useless, and by the next morning we were partly jury-rigged: we now began to look for our prizes, as it was coming on to blow hard on the land, and Admiral Collingwood made signals for each ship that was able, to take a prize in tow, to prevent them drifting into their own harbour, as they were complete wrecks and unmanageable.

We took an eighty gun Spanish ship in tow for a day and night, but were obliged to cast her off, it blew so hard, and our ship being so very much disabled, indeed we were obliged to scuttle a few of them; some we contrived to take into Gibraltar; some we contrived to take into Gibraltar; some were wrecked near Cadiz harbour; and others drifted into the harbour from whence they had only come out two days before. It was a mortifying sight to witness the ships we had fought so hard for, and had taken as

prizes, driven by the elements from our possession, with some of our own men on board as prize masters, and it was a great blight to our victorious success; but, in justice to the enemy, it may with truth be recorded, that, however contrary to the Spanish character as an enemy generally, yet, upon this occasion, they used our men well.

In order to shew the crippled state in which our ships must have been, it will be requisite to mention that, in preparing to engage the enemy closely, and protect ourselves as much as possible, the seamen's hammocks with the bedding and blankets were lashed to the shrouds, which served much to save our rigging, as was very evident from examination on the second night after the battle; for when our men got their hammocks down, many were found to have received a great deal of damage, being very much cut with the large shot, and some were found to have had grape or canister shot lodged in them. The most destructive shot to us appeared to be the thirty-two pounds double-headed; two of these deafeners we observed to be sticking in our main-mast, which miraculously and fortunately for us, was not carried away,

I will now call the reader's attention to some occurrences during and after the battle, which, although they may not regularly belong to a seaman's log, yet they may be found interesting.

The advantage of learning to dance

As we were closely engaged throughout the battle, and the shots were playing their pranks pretty freely, grape as well as canister, with single and double headed thunderers all joining in the frolic; what was termed a *slaughtering one,* came in at one of the lower deck ports, which killed and wounded nearly all at the gun, and amongst them, a very merry little fellow, who was the very life of the ship's company, for he was ever the mirth of his mess, and on whatever duty he might be ordered, his spirits made light the labour. He was the ship's cobbler, and withall a very good dancer; so that when any of his messmates would *sarve* us out a tune, he was sure to trip it on light fantastic toe, and find a step to it. He happened to be stationed at the gun where this messenger of death and destruction entered, and the poor fellow was so completely stunned by the head of another man being knocked against his, that no one doubted but that he was dead. As it is customary to throw overboard those, who, in an engagement are killed outright, the poor cobbler, amongst the rest, was taken to the port-hole to be committed to the deep, without any other ceremony than showing him through the port: but, just as they were about to let him slip from their hands into the water, the blood began to circulate, and he commenced kicking. Upon this sign of returning life, his shipmates soon hauled the poor snob in again, and, though wonderful to relate, he recovered so speedily, that he actually fought the battle out; and, when he was afterwards joked about it, he would say, "it was well that I learned to dance; for if I had not shown you some of my steps, when you were about to throw me overboard, I should not be here now, but safe enough in Davy Jones's Locker."

The danger of giving too much power into the hands of young officer

If an officer is of a tyrannical disposition on board a ship, whatever accident may happen to him, he will never receive pity or commiseration from any of the ship's crew;—as, for instance.—We had a mid-shipman on board our ship of a wickedly mischievous disposition, whose sole delight was to insult the feelings of the seamen, and furnish pretexts to get them punished. His conduct made every man's life miserable that happened to be under his orders. He was a youth not more than twelve or thirteen years of age; but I have often seen him get on the carriage of a gun, call a man to him, and kick him about the thighs and body, and with his fist would beat him about the head; and these, although prime seamen, at the same time dared not murmur. It was ordained, however, by Providence, that this reign of terror and severity should not last; for during the engagement, he was killed on the quarter-deck by a grape-shot, his body greatly mutilated, his entrails being driven and scattered against the larboard side; nor were there any lamentation for his fate!—No! for when it was known that he was killed, the general exclamation was, "Thank God, we are rid of the young tyrant!" His death was hailed as the triumph over an enemy. . . .

The Day after the Battle

Some of our men were sent on board of the Spanish ship before alluded to, in order to assist at the pumps, for she was much shattered in the hull, between wind and water. The slaughter and havoc our guns had made, rendered the scene of carnage horrid to behold: there were a number of their dead bodies piled up in the hold; many, in a wounded or mutilated state, were found lying amongst them; and those who were so fortunate as to escape our shot, were so dejected and crest-fallen, that they could not, or would not, work at the pumps, and of course the ship was in a sinking state.

The gale at this time was increasing so rapidly, that manning the pumps was of no use, and we were obliged to abandon our prize, taking away with us all our men, and as many of the prisoners as we could. On the last boat's load leaving the ship, the Spaniards who were left on board, appeared on the gangway and ship's side, displaying their bags of dollars and doubloons, and eagerly offering them as reward for saving them from the expected and unavoidable wreck; but, however well inclined we were, it was not in our power to rescue them, or it would have been effected without the proffered bride.

Here a very distressing and affecting scene took place; it was a struggle between inclination and duty. On quitting the ship, our boats were overloaded in endeavouring to save all the lives we could, that it is a miracle they were not upset. A father and his son came down the ship's side to get on board one of our boats; the father had seated himself, but the men in the boat, thinking, from the load and the boisterous weather, that all their lives would be in peril, could not think of taking the boy; as the boat put off, the lad, as though determined not to quit his father, sprung from the ship into the water, and caught hold of the gunwale of the boat; but his attempt was resisted, as it risked all their lives, and some of the men resorted to their cutlasses to cut his fingers off, in order to disentangle the boat from his grasp; at the same time the feelings of the father were so worked upon, that he was about to leap overboard, and perish with his son: Britons could face an enemy, but could not witness such a scene of self-devotion; as it were, a simultaneous thought burst forth from the crew, which said "let us save both father and son, or die in the attempt." The Almighty

aided them in their design; they succeeded, and brought both father and son safe on board of our ship, where they remained, until, with other prisoners, they were exchanged at Gibraltar.

9. Admiral Collingwood's Dispatch, 22 October 1805

Nicolas, Sir Nicholas Harris, ed. 1846. *The Dispatches and Letters of Vice Admiral Lord Viscount Nelson.* London: Henry Colburn, 7: 212–214.

With Nelson's death at Trafalgar, command devolved upon Vice Admiral Cuthbert Collingwood, who took the opportunity not only to provide a brief account of the action, but also to produce a moving tribute to his fallen superior. Within hours of receiving the dispatch in Whitehall, the Admiralty supplied the text to the press.

To William Marsden, Esq. Admiralty.

Euryalus, off Cape Trafalgar, October 22nd, 1805

Sir,

The ever to be lamented death of Vice-Admiral Lord Viscount Nelson, who, in the late conflict with the Enemy, fell in the hour of victory, leaves to me the duty of informing my Lord Commissioners of the Admiralty, that on the 19th instant it was communicated to the Commander in Chief from the Ships watching the motions of the Enemy in Cadiz, that the Combined Fleet had put to sea. As they sailed with light winds westerly, his Lordship concluded their destination was the Mediterranean, and immediately made all sail for the Streights' [of Gibraltar] entrance with the British squadron, consisting of twenty-seven Ships, three of them sixty-fours, where his Lordship was informed by Capt. [Henry] Blackwood, (whose vigilance in watching, and giving notice of the enemy's movements, has been highly meritorious,) that they had not yet passed the Streights.

On Monday the 21st instant, at daylight, when Cape Trafalgar bore E[ast]. by S[outh]. about seven leagues, the Enemy was discovered six or seven miles to the eastward, the wind about west, and very light; the Commander in Chief immediately made the signal for the fleet to bear up in two columns, as they are formed in order of sailing; a mode of attack his Lordship had previously directed, to avoid the inconvenience and delay in forming a line of battle in the usual manner. The Enemy's line consisted of thirty-three Ships (of which eighteen were French and fifteen Spanish), commanded in chief by Admiral [Pierre de] Villeneuve; the Spaniards, under the direction of [Admiral Don Federico] Gravina, wore, with their heads to the northward, and formed their line of battle with great closeness and correctness; but as the mode of attack was unusual, so the structure of their line was new;—it formed a crescent convexing to leeward – so that, in leading down to their centre, I had both their van and rear abaft the beam. Before the fire opened, every alternate Ship was about a cable's length to windward of her second a-head and a-stern, forming a kind of double line, and appeared, when on their beam, to leave a very little interval between them; and this without crowding their Ships. Admiral Villeneuve was in the *Bucentaure* in the centre, and the *Prince of Asturias* bore Gravina's flag in the rear; but the French and Spanish Ships were mixed without any apparent regard to order of National squadron.

As the mode of our attack had been previously determined on, and communicated to the Flag-officers and Captains, few signals were necessary, and none were made except to direct close order as the lines bore down.

The Commander in Chief in the *Victory* led the weather column; and the *Royal Sovereign,* which bore my flag, the lee.

The Action began at twelve o'clock, by the leading Ships of the columns breaking through the Enemy's line, the Commander in Chief [Nelson] about the tenth Ship from the van, the Second in Command [Collingwood] about the twelfth from the rear, leaving the van of the Enemy unoccupied; the succeeding Ships breaking through in all parts, a-stern of their leaders, and engaging the Enemy at the muzzles of their guns, the conflict was severe. The Enemy's Ships were fought with a gallantry highly honourable to their Officers, but the attack on them was irresistible; and it pleased the Almighty Disposer of all events to grant His Majesty's arms a complete and glorious victory. About three P.M. many of the Enemy's Ships having struck their colours, their line gave way; Admiral Gravina, with ten Ships, joining their Frigates to leeward, stood towards Cadiz. The five headmost Ships in their van tacked, and standing to the southward to windward of the British line, were engaged, and the sternmost of them taken; the others went off, leaving to His Majesty's squadron nineteen Ships of the line, (of which two are first-rates, the *Santissima Trinidad* and the *Santa Anna,*) with three Flag Officers; viz. Admiral Villeneuve, the Commander in Chief; Don Ignatio Maria d'Alava. Vice-Admiral, and the Spanish Rear-Admiral, Don Baltazar Hidalgo Cisneros.

After such a victory it may appear unnecessary to enter into encomiums on the particular parts taken by the several Commanders; the conclusion says more on the subject than I have language to express; the spirit which animated all was the same: when all exert themselves zealously in their country's service, all deserve that their high merits should stand recorded; and never was high merit more conspicuous than in the battle I have described.

The *Achille* (a French 74), after having surrendered, by some mismanagement of the Frenchmen took fire, and blew up; two hundred of her men were saved by the Tenders.

A circumstance occurred during the Action, which so strongly marks the invincible spirit of British seamen, when engaging the enemies of their country, that I cannot resist the pleasure I have in making it known to their Lordships. The *Temeraire* was boarded by accident, or design, by a French Ship on one side, and a Spaniard on the other: the contest was vigorous; but in the end the Combined ensigns were torn from the poop, and the British hoisted in their places.

Such a Battle could not be fought without sustaining a great loss of men. I have not only to lament, in common with the British Navy and the British Nation, in the fall of the Commander-in-Chief, the loss of a hero whose name will be immortal, and his memory ever dear to his Country; but my heart is rent with the most poignant grief for the death of a friend, to whom, by many years' intimacy, and a perfect knowledge of the virtues of his mind, which inspired ideas superior to the common

race of men, I was bound by the strongest ties of affection;—a grief to which even the glorious occasion in which he fell, does not bring the consolation which perhaps it ought: his Lordship received a musket ball in his left breast about the middle of the Action, and sent an Officer to me immediately with his last farewell, and soon after expired.

I have also to lament the loss of those excellent Officers, Captains Duff of the *Mars* and Cooke of the *Bellerophon:* I have yet heard of none others.

I fear the numbers that have fallen will be found very great when the returns come to me; but it having blown a gale of wind ever since the Action, I have not yet had it in my power to collect any reports from the Ships.

The *Royal Sovereign* having lost her masts, except the tottering foremast, I called the *Euryalus* to me, while the Action continued, which Ship lying within hail, made my signals, a service Captain Blackwood performed with great attention. After the Action I shifted my flag to her, that I might more easily communicate my orders to, and collect the Ships, and towed the Royal Sovereign out to seaward. The whole fleet were now in a very perilous situation; many dismasted; all shattered; in thirteen fathoms of water, off the shoals of Trafalgar; and when I made the signal to prepare to anchor, few of the Ships had an anchor to let go, their cables being shot; but the same good Providence which aided us through such a day preserved us in the night, by the wind shifting a few points, and drifting the Ships off the land, except four of the captured dismasted Ships, which are now at anchor off Trafalgar, and I hope will ride safe until those gales are over.

Having thus detailed the proceedings of the fleet on this occasion, I beg to congratulate their Lordships on a victory which, I hope, will add a ray to the glory of His Majesty's crown, and be attended with public benefit to our country.

10. Documents concerning the Continental System, 1806–1810

Reproduced by kind permission of the editors of the Napoleon Series (www.napoleon-series.org).

The first five (A–E) of these documents demonstrate methods employed to destroy neutral maritime trade during the Anglo-French conflict that formed just one aspect of the Napoleonic Wars. Document F reveals a subsequent adjustment in British policy. Document G illustrates the methods employed by Napoleon in the application of his Continental System. The idea of conquering Britain by destroying her commerce was an old French conception that the Directory had begun to apply. Napoleon resumed the policy on the renewal of the war in 1803, and his measures led to Document A.

A.   British Note to the Neutral Powers, 16 May 1806
B.   The Berlin Decree, 21 November 1806
C.   British Order in Council, 10 January 1807
D.   British Order in Council, 11 November 1807
E.   The Milan Decree, 17 December 1807
F.   British Order in Council, 26 April 1809
G.   The Rambouillet Decree, 23 March 1810

A. British Note to the Neutral Powers, 16 May 1806

Downing Street [location of the Foreign Office in London]

The undersigned, His Majesty's principal Secretary of State for Foreign Affairs [Charles James Fox], has received His Majesty's commands to acquaint Mr. Monroe [the American minister plenipotentiary to Britain], that the King, taking into consideration the new and extraordinary means resorted to by the enemy for the purpose of distressing the commerce of his subjects, has thought fit to direct that the necessary measures should be taken for the blockade of the coast, rivers and ports, from the river Elbe to the port of Brest, both inclusive; and the said coast, rivers and ports are and must be considered as blockaded; but that His Majesty is pleased to declare that such blockade shall not extend to prevent neutral ships and vessels laden with goods not being the property of His Majesty's enemies, and not being contraband of war, from approaching the said coast, and entering into and sailing from the said rivers and ports (save and except the coast, rivers and ports from Ostend to the river Seine, already in a state of strict and rigorous blockade, and which are to be considered as so continued), provided the said ships and vessels so approaching and entering (except as aforesaid), shall not have been laden at any port belonging to or in the possession of any of His Majesty's enemies; and that the said ships and vessels so sailing from said rivers and ports (except as aforesaid) shall not be destined to any port belonging to or in possession of any of His Majesty's enemies, nor have previously broken the blockade.

Mr. Monroe is therefore requested to apprise the American consuls and merchants residing in England, that the coast, rivers and ports above mentioned, must be considered as being in a state of blockade, and that from this time all the measures authorised by the law of nations and the respective treaties between His Majesty and the different neutral powers, will be adopted and executed with respect to vessels attempting to violate the said blockade after this notice.

The undersigned requests Mr. Monroe, etc.

C. J. FOX.

B. The Berlin Decree, 21 November 1806

From our Imperial Camp at Berlin, November 21, 1806.

Napoleon, Emperor of the French and King of Italy, in consideration of the fact:

That England does not recognize the system of international law universally observed by all civilized nations.

That she regards as an enemy every individual belonging to the enemy's state, and consequently makes prisoners of war not only of the crews of armed ships of war but of the crews of ships of commerce and merchantmen, and even of commercial agents and of merchants traveling on business.

That she extends to the vessels and commercial wares and to the property of individuals the right of conquest, which is applicable only to the possessions of the belligerent power.

That she extends to unfortified towns and commercial ports, to harbors and the mouths of rivers, the right of blockade, which, in accordance with reason and the customs of all civilized nations, is applicable only to strong places. That she declares places in a state of blockade before which she has not even a single ship of war, although a place may not be blockaded except it be so completely guarded that no attempt to approach it can be made without imminent danger. That she has declared districts in a state of blockade which all her united forces would be unable to blockade, such as entire coasts and the whole of an empire.

That this monstrous abuse of the right of blockade has no other aim than to prevent communication among the nations and to raise the commerce and the industry of England upon the ruins of that of the continent.

That, since this is the obvious aim of England, whoever deals on the continent in English goods, thereby favors and renders himself an accomplice of her designs.

That this policy of England, worthy of the earliest stages of barbarism, has profited that power to the detriment of every other nation.

That it is a natural right to oppose such arms against an enemy as he makes use of, and to fight in the same way that he fights. Since England has disregarded all ideas of justice and every high sentiment, due to the civilization among mankind, we have resolved to apply to her the usages which she has ratified in her maritime legislation.

The provisions of the present decree shall continue to be looked upon as embodying the fundamental principles of the Empire until England shall recognize that the law of war is one and the same on land and sea, and that the rights of war cannot be extended so as to include private property of any kind or the persons of individuals unconnected with the profession of arms, and that the right of blockade should be restricted to fortified places actually invested by sufficient forces.

We have consequently decreed and do decree that which follows:

The British Isles are declared to be in a state of blockade.

All commerce and all correspondence with the British Isles are forbidden. Consequently letters or packages directed to England or to an Englishman or written in the English language shall not pass through the mails and shall be seized.

Every individual who is an English subject, of whatever state or condition he may be, who shall be discovered in any country occupied by our troops or by those of our allies, shall be made a prisoner of war.

All warehouses, merchandise or property of whatever kind belonging to a subject of England shall be regarded as a lawful prize.

Trade in English goods is prohibited, and all goods belonging to England or coming from her factories or her colonies are declared lawful prize.

Half of the product resulting from the confiscation of the goods and possessions declared a lawful prize by the preceding articles shall be applied to indemnify the merchants for the losses they have experienced by the capture of merchant vessels taken by English cruisers.

No vessel coming directly from England or from the English colonies or which shall have visited these since the publication of the present decree shall be received in any port.

Any vessel contravening the above provision by a false declaration shall be seized, and the vessel and cargo shall be confiscated as if it were English property.

Our Court of Prizes at Paris shall pronounce final judgment in all cases arising in our Empire or in the countries occupied by the French Army relating to the execution of the present decree. Our Court of Prizes at Milan shall pronounce final judgment in the said cases which may arise within our Kingdom of Italy.

The present decree shall be communicated by our minister of foreign affairs to the King of Spain, of Naples, of Holland and of Etruria, and to our other allies whose subjects, like ours, are the victims of the unjust and barbarous maritime legislation of England.

Our ministers of foreign affairs, of war, of the navy, of finance and of the police and our Directors-General of the port are charged with the execution of the present decree so far as it affects them.

NAPOLEON.

C. British Order in Council, 10 January 1807

Note communicated by Lord Howick [the Foreign Secretary] to Mr. Monroe [the American minister plenipotentiary to Britain], dated Downing Street, January 10, 1807.

The undersigned, His Majesty's principal Secretary of State of Foreign Affairs, has received His Majesty's commands to acquaint Mr. Monroe that the French Government having issued certain orders, which, in violation of the usages of war, purport to prohibit the commerce of all neutral nations with His Majesty's dominions, and also to prevent such nations from trading with any other country in any articles, the growth, produce, or manufacture of His Majesty's dominions. And the said Government having also taken upon itself to declare all His Majesty's dominions to be in a state of blockade, at a time when the fleets of France and her allies are themselves confined within their own ports by the superior valor and discipline of the British navy.

Such attempts, on the part of the enemy, giving to His Majesty an unquestionable right of retaliation, and warranting His Majesty in enforcing the same prohibition of all commerce with France, which that Power vainly hopes to effect against the commerce of His Majesty's subjects, a prohibition which the superiority of His Majesty's naval forces might enable him to support, by actually investing the ports and coasts of the enemy with numerous squadrons and cruisers, so as to make the entrance or approach thereto manifestly dangerous.

His Majesty, though unwilling to follow the example of his enemies by proceeding to an extremity so distressing to all nations not engaged in the war, and carrying on their accustomed trade, yet feels himself bound, by a due regard to the just defence of the rights and interests of his people, not to suffer such measures to be taken by the enemy, without taking some steps, on his part, to restrain this violence, and to retort upon them the evils of their own injustice. Mr. Monroe is, therefore, requested to apprise the American consuls and merchants residing in England, that His Majesty has, therefore, judged it expedient to order that no vessel shall be permitted to trade from one port to another, both which ports shall belong to, or be in the possession of, France or her allies, or shall be so far under their control as that British vessels may not freely trade thereat [sic]; and that the commanders of His Majesty's ships of war and privateers have been instructed to warn every neutral vessel coming from any such port, and destined to another port, to discontinue her voyage, and not to proceed to any such port; and every vessel after being so warned, or any vessel coming from any such port, after a reasonable time shall have been afforded for receiving information of this His Majesty's order, which shall be found proceeding to another such port, shall be captured and brought in, and, together with her cargo, shall be condemned as lawful prize. And that, from this time, all the measures authorised by the law of nations, and the respective treaties between His Majesty and the different neutral Powers, will be adopted and executed with respect to vessels attempting to violate the said order after this notice.

HOWICK.

D. British Order in Council, 11 November 1807

At the Court at the Queen's Palace, the 11th of November, 1807: Present, the King's Most Excellent Majesty in Council.

Whereas certain orders establishing an unprecedented system of warfare against this kingdom, and aimed especially at the destruction of its commerce and resources, were some time since issued by the Government of France, by which "the British islands were declared to be in a state of blockade," thereby subjecting to capture and condemnation all vessels, with their cargoes, which should continue to trade with His Majesty's dominions:

And, whereas, by the same order, "all trading in English merchandise is prohibited, and every article of merchandise belonging to England, or coming from her colonies, or of her manufacture, is declared lawful prize:"

And, whereas, the nations in alliance with France, and under her control, were required to give, and have given, and do give, effect to such orders:

And, whereas, His Majesty's order of the 7th of January last has not answered the desired purpose, either of compelling the enemy to recall those orders, or of inducing neutral nations to interpose, with effect, to obtain their revocation, but on the contrary, the same have been recently enforced with increased rigor:

And, whereas, His Majesty, under these circumstances, finds himself compelled to take further measures for asserting and vindicating his just rights, and for supporting that maritime power which the exertions and valor of his people have, under the blessings of Providence, enabled him to establish and maintain; and the maintenance of which is not more essential to the safety and prosperity of His Majesty's dominions, than it is to the protection of such states as still retain their independence, and to the general intercourse and happiness of mankind:

His Majesty is therefore pleased, by and with the advice of his privy council, to order, and it is hereby ordered, that all the ports and places of France and her allies, or of any other country at war with His Majesty, and all other ports or places in Europe, from which, although not at war with His Majesty, the British flag is excluded, and all ports or places in the colonies belonging to His Majesty's enemies, shall, from henceforth, be subject to the same restrictions in point of trade and navigation, with the exceptions hereinafter mentioned, as if the same were actually blockaded by His Majesty's naval forces, in the most strict and rigorous manner: And it is hereby further ordered and declared, that all trade in articles which are of the produce or manufacture of the said countries or colonies shall be deemed and considered to be unlawful; and that every vessel trading from or to the said countries or colonies, together with all goods and merchandise on board and all articles of the produce or manufacture of the said countries or colonies, shall be captured and condemned as a prize to the captors.

But, although His Majesty would be fully justified by the circumstances and considerations above recited, in establishing such system of restrictions with respect to all the countries and colonies of his enemies, without exception or qualification, yet His Majesty being, nevertheless, desirous not to subject neutrals to any greater inconvenience than is absolutely inseparable from the carrying into effect His Majesty's just determination to counteract the designs of his enemies, and to retort upon his enemies themselves the consequences of their own violence and injustice; and being yet willing to hope that it may be possible (consistently with that object) still to allow to neutrals the opportunity of furnishing themselves with colonial produce for their own consumption and supply, and even to leave open, for the present, such trade with His Majesty's enemies as shall be carried on directly with the ports of His Majesty's dominions, or of his allies, in the manner hereinafter mentioned:

His Majesty is, therefore, pleased further to order and it is hereby ordered, that nothing herein contained shall extend to subject to capture or condemnation any vessel, or the cargo of any vessel, belonging to any country not declared by this order to be subjected to the restrictions incident to a state of blockade, which shall have cleared out with such cargo from some port or place of the country to which she belongs, either in Europe or America, or from some free port in His Majesty's colonies, under circumstances in which such trade, from such free ports, is permitted, direct to some port or place in the colonies of His Majesty's enemies, or from those colonies direct to the country to which such vessel belongs, or to some free port in His Majesty's colonies, in such cases, and with such articles, as it may be lawful to import into such free port; nor to any vessel, or the cargo of any vessel, belonging to any country not at war with His Majesty, which shall have cleared out under such regulations as His Majesty may think fit to prescribe, and shall be proceeding direct from some port or place in this kingdom, or from Gibraltar, or Malta, or from any port belonging to His Majesty's allies, to the port specified in her clearance; nor to any vessel, or the cargo of any vessel, belonging to any country not at war with His Majesty, which shall be coming from any port or place in Europe which is declared by this order to be subject to the restrictions incident to a state of blockade, destined to some port or place in Europe belonging to His Majesty, and which shall be on her voyage direct thereto; but these exceptions are not to be understood as exempting from capture or confiscation any vessel or goods which shall be liable thereto in respect to having entered or departed from any port or place actually blockaded by His Majesty's squadrons or ships of war, or for being enemy's property, or for any other cause than the contravention of his present order.

And the commanders of His Majesty's ships of war and privateers, and other vessels acting under His Majesty's commission, shall be, and are hereby, instructed to warn every vessel which shall have commenced her voyage prior to any notice of this order, and shall be destined to any port of France or of her allies or of any other country at war with His Majesty or any port or place from which the British flag, as aforesaid, is excluded, or to any colony belonging to His Majesty's enemies, and which shall not have cleared out as is herein before allowed, to discontinue her voyage, and to proceed to some port or place in this kingdom, or to Gibraltar, or Malta; and any vessel which, after having been so warned or after a reasonable time shall have been afforded for the arrival of information of this His Majesty's order at any port or place from which she sailed, or which, after having notice of this order, shall be found in the prosecution of any voyage contrary to the restrictions contained in this order, shall be captured, and, together with her cargo, condemned as lawful prize to the captors.

And, whereas, countries not engaged in the war have acquiesced in these orders of France, prohibiting all trade in any articles the produce or manufacture of His Majesty's dominions; and the merchants of those countries have given countenance and effect to those prohibitions by accepting from persons, styling themselves commercial agents of the enemy, resident at neutral ports, certain documents, termed "certificates of origin," being certificates obtained at the ports of shipment, declaring that the articles of the cargo are not of the produce or manufacture of His Majesty's dominions, or to that effect.

And, whereas, this expedient has been directed by France, and submitted to by such merchants, as part of the new system of warfare directed against the trade of this kingdom, and as the most effectual instrument of accomplishing the same, and it is therefore essentially necessary to resist it.

His Majesty is therefore pleased, by and with the advice of his privy council, to order, and it is hereby ordered, that if any vessel, after reasonable time shall have been afforded for receiving notice of this His Majesty's order, at the port or place from which such vessel shall have cleared out, shall be found carrying any such certificate or document as aforesaid, or any document referring to or authenticating the same, such vessel shall be adjudged lawful prize to the captor, together with the goods laden therein, belonging to the person or persons by whom, or on whose behalf, any such document was put on board.

And the right honourable the Lords Commissioners of His Majesty's Treasury, His Majesty's principal Secretaries of State, the Lords Commissioners of the Admiralty, and the Judges of the High Court of Admiralty, and Courts of Vice-Admiralty, are to take the necessary measures herein as to them shall respectively appertain.

W. Fawkener.

E. The Milan Decree, 17 December 1807

At Our Royal Palace at Milan, December 17, 1807.

Napoleon, Emperor of the French, King of Italy, Protector of the Confederation of the Rhine. In view of the measures adopted by the British government on the 11th of November last by which vessels belonging to powers which are neutral or are friendly and even allied with England are rendered liable to be searched by British cruisers, detained at certain stations in England, and subject to an arbitrary tax of a certain per cent upon their cargo to be regulated by English legislation.

Considering that by these acts the English government has denationalized the vessels of all the nations of Europe, and that no government may compromise in any degree its independence or its rights—all the rulers of Europe being jointly responsible for the sovereignty and independence of their flags,—and that, if through unpardonable weakness which would be regarded by posterity as an indelible stain, such tyranny should be admitted and become consecrated by custom, the English would take steps to give it the force of law, as they have already taken advantage of the toleration of the governments to establish the infamous principle that the flag does not cover the goods and to give the right of blockade an arbitrary extension which threatens the sovereignty of every state: We have decreed and do decree as follows:

Every vessel of whatever nationality which shall submit to be searched by an English vessel or shall consent to a voyage to England, or shall pay any tax whatever to the English government is *ipso facto* declared denationalized, loses the protection afforded by its flag and becomes English property.

Should such vessels which are thus denationalized through the arbitrary measures of the English government enter our ports or those of our allies or fall into the hands of our ships of war or of our privateers they shall be regarded as good and lawful prizes.

The British Isles are proclaimed to be in a state of blockade both by land and by sea. Every vessel of whatever nation or whatever may be its cargo, that sails from the ports of England or from those of the English colonies or of countries occupied by English troops, or is bound for England or for any of the English colonies or any country occupied by English troops, becomes, by violating the present decree, a lawful prize, and may be captured by our ships of war and adjudged to the captor.

These measures, which are only a just retaliation against the barbarous system adopted by the English government, which models its legislation upon that of Algiers, shall cease to have any effect in the case of those nations which shall force the English to respect their flags. They shall continue in force so long as that government shall refuse to accept the principles of international law which regulate the relations of civilized states in a state of war. The provisions of the present decree shall be *ipso facto* abrogated and void so soon as the English government shall abide again by the principles of the law of nations, which are at the same time those of justice and honor.

All our ministers are charged with the execution of the present decree, which shall be printed in the *Bulletin des lois.*

F. British Order in Council, 26 April 1809

At the Court at the Queen's Palace, the 26th of April, 1809; Present, the King's Most Excellent Majesty in council.

Whereas, His Majesty, by his order in council of the 11th of November, 1807, was pleased, for the reasons assigned therein, to order that "all the ports and places of France and her allies, or of any other country at war with His Majesty, and all other ports or places in Europe, from which, although not at war with His Majesty, the British flag is excluded, and all ports or places in the colonies belonging to His Majesty's enemies, should from henceforth be subject to the same restrictions in point of trade or navigation as if the same were actually blockaded in the most strict and vigorous manner; and also to prohibit "all trade in articles which are the produce or manufacture of the said countries or colonies; "and whereas, His Majesty, having been nevertheless desirous not to subject those countries which were in alliance or amity with His Majesty to any greater inconvenience than was absolutely inseparable from carrying into effect His Majesty's just determination to counteract the designs of his enemies, did make certain exceptions and modifications expressed in the said order of the 11th of November, and in certain subsequent orders of the 25th of November, declaratory of the aforesaid order of the 11th of November and of the 18th of December, 1807, and of the 30th of March, 1808;

And whereas, in consequence of diverse events which have taken place since the date of the first-mentioned order, affecting the relations between Great Britain and the territories of other Powers, it is expedient that sundry parts and provisions of the said orders should be ordered or revoked;

His Majesty is therefore pleased, by and with the advice of his privy council, to revoke and annul the said several orders, except as hereinafter expressed; and so much of the said orders, except as aforesaid, is hereby revoked accordingly. And His Majesty is pleased, by and with the advice of his privy council, to order, and it is hereby ordered, that all the ports and places as far north as the river Ems, inclusively, under the government styling itself the Kingdom of Holland, and all ports and places under the Government of France, together with the colonies, plantations, and settlements in the possession of those Governments, respectively, and all ports and places in the northern parts of Italy, to be reckoned from the ports of Orbitello and Pesaro, inclusively, shall continue, and be subject to the same restrictions, in point of trade and navigation, without any exception, as if the same were actually blockaded by His Majesty's naval forces in the most strict and rigorous manner; and that every vessel trading from and to the said countries or colonies, plantations or settlements, together with all goods and merchandise on board, shall be condemned as prize to the captors.

And His Majesty is further pleased to order, and it is hereby ordered, that this order shall have effect from the day of the date thereof with respect to any ship, together with its cargo, which may be captured subsequent to such day, on any voyage which is and shall be rendered legal by this order, although such voyage, at the time of the commencement of the same, was unlawful, and prohibited under the said former orders; and such ships, upon being brought in, shall be released accordingly; and with respect to all ships, together with their cargoes, which may be captured in any voyage which was permitted under the exceptions of the orders above mentioned, but which is not permitted according to the provisions of this order, His Majesty is pleased to order, and it is hereby ordered that such ships and their cargoes shall not be liable to condemnation, unless they shall have received actual notice of the present order, as were allowed for constructive notice in the orders of the 25th of November, 1807, and the 18th of May, 1808, at the several places and latitudes therein specified.

And the right honorable the Lords Commissioners of His Majesty's Treasury, His Majesty's principal Secretary of State, the Lords Commissioners of the Admiralty, and the Judge of the High Court of Admiralty, and Judges of the Courts of Vice-admiralty, are to give the necessary directions herein as to them may respectively appertain.

Stephen Cottrell.

G. The Rambouillet Decree, 23 March 1810

[The Emperor] Napoleon . . . considering that the Government of the United States, by an act dated March 1, 1809, which forbids the entrance of the ports, harbors and rivers of the said States to all French vessels, orders:

1st. That, dating from the 20th of May following, the vessels under the French flag which shall arrive in the United States shall be seized and confiscated, as well as their cargoes;

2d. That, after the same date no merchandise and productions coming from the soil or manufactures of France or of its colonies can be imported into the said United States, from any port or foreign place whatsoever, under penalty of seizure, confiscation and fine of three times the value of the merchandise;

3d. That American vessels cannot repair to any port of France, its colonies or dependencies;

We have decreed and do decree as follows:

That all vessels navigating under the flag of the United States, or possessed in whole or in part by any citizen or subject of that Power, which, dating from May 20, 1809, may have entered or shall enter into the ports of our Empire, our colonies or the countries occupied by our armies, shall be seized, and the products of the sales shall be deposited in the surplus fund.

Vessels which may be charged with despatches or commissions of Government of the said States and which have not cargo or merchandise on board are excepted from this provision.

Our grand judge, minister of justice, and our minister of finance, are charged with the execution of the present decree.

11. Documents concerning the formation of the Confederation of the Rhine, 1806

Reproduced by kind permission of the editors of the Napoleon Series (www.napoleon-series.org).

The destruction of the Holy Roman Empire, begun by the terms of the treaties of Basle (1795) and Campo Formio (1797), was finally completed by the organization of the Confederation of the Rhine (1806), which survived until the Allies defeated Napoleon at the Battle of Leipzig in 1813.

A.　Treaty for Establishing the Confederation, 12 July 1806
B.　Note of Napoleon to the Diet, 1 August 1806
C.　Declaration of the Confederated States, 1 August 1806
D.　Abdication of Francis II, 7 August 1806; in *Le Moniteur*, 14 August 1806

A. Treaty for Establishing the Confederation, 12 July 1806

His Majesty the Emperor of the French [Napoleon I], King of Italy, on the one part, and on the other part their Majesties the Kings of Bavaria and of Württemberg and Their Serene Highnesses the Electors, the Archchancellor of Baden, the Duke of Berg and of Cleves, the Landgrave of Hesse-Darmstadt, the Princes of Nassan-Usingen and Nassau-Weilburg, the Princes of Hohenzollern-Heckingen and Hohenzollern-Sigmaringen, the Princes of Salm-Salm and Salm-Kirburg, the Prince of Isneburg-Birstein, the Duke of Aremberg and the Prince of Lichenstein, and the Count of Leyen, wishing, by suitable stipulations, to assure the internal peace of the south of Germany, for which experience for a long time past and quite recently still more has shown that the Germanic Constitution can no longer offer any sort of guarantee. . . .

The States of . . . [names of the parties of the second part] shall be forever separated from the territory of the Germanic [Holy Roman] Empire and united among themselves by a separate Confederation, under the name of the Confederated States of the Rhine.

. . . .

Each of the Kings and Confederated Princes shall renounce those of his titles which express any relations with the Germanic Empire; and on the 1st of August next he shall cause the Diet to be notified of his separation from the Empire.

His Serene Highness the Archchancellor shall take the titles of Prince Primate and Most Eminent Highness. The title of Prince Primate does not carry with it any prerogative contrary to the plenitude of sovereignty which each of the Confederates shall enjoy.

. . . .

The common interests of the Confederated States shall be dealt with in a Diet, of which the seat shall be at Frankfort, and which shall be divided into two Colleges, to wit: the College of Kings and the College of Princes.

. . . .

His Majesty the Emperor of the French shall be proclaimed Protector of the Confederation, and in that capacity, upon the decease of each Prince Primate, he shall appoint the successor of that one.

. . . .

There shall be between the French Empire and the Confederated States of the Rhine, collectively and separately, an alliance in virtue of which every continental war which one of the High Contracting Parties may have to carry on shall immediately become common to all the others.

. . . .

The contingent to be furnished by each of the Allies in case of war is as follows: France shall furnish 200,000 men of all arms: the Kingdom of Bavaria 30,000 men of all arms; the Kingdom of Württemberg 12,000; the Grand Duke of Baden 8,000; the Grand Duke of Berg 5,000; the Grand Duke of Darmstadt 4,000; Their Serene Highnesses the Dukes and the Prince of Nassau, together with the other Confederated Princes, shall furnish a contingent of 4,000 men.

The High Contracting Parties reserve to themselves the admission at a later time into the new Confederation of other Princes and States of Germany whom it shall be found for the common interest to admit thereto.

B. Note of Napoleon to the Diet, 1 August 1806

The undersigned, *charge d'affaires* of His Majesty the Emperor of the French and King of Italy at the general Diet of the German Empire, has received orders from His Majesty to make the following declarations to the diet:

Their Majesties the Kings of Bavaria and of Württemberg, the Sovereign Princes of Regensburg, Baden, Berg, Hesse-Darmstadt and Nassau, as well as the other leading princes of the south and west of Germany have resolved to form a confederation between themselves which shall secure them against future emergencies, and have thus ceased to be states of the Empire.

The position in which the Treaty of Pressburg has explicitly placed the courts allied to France, and indirectly those princes whose territory they border or surround, being incompatible with the existence of an empire, it becomes a necessity for those rulers to reorganize their relations upon a new system and to remove a contradiction which could not fail to be a permanent source of agitation, disquiet and danger.

France on the other hand, is directly interested in the maintenance of peace in Southern Germany and yet must apprehend that, the moment she shall cause her troops to recross the Rhine, discord, the inevitable consequence of contradictory, uncertain and ill-defined conditions, will again disturb the peace of the people and reopen, possibly, the war on the continent. Feeling it incumbent upon her to advance the welfare of her allies and to assure them the enjoyment of all the advantages which the Treaty of Pressburg secures them and to which she is pledged, France cannot but regard the confederation that they have formed as a natural result and a necessary sequel to that treaty.

For a long period successive changes have, from century to century, reduced the German constitution to a shadow of its former self. Time has altered all the relations in respect to size and importance which originally existed among the various members of the confederation, both as regards each other and the whole of which they have formed a part.

The Diet has no longer a will of its own. The sentences of the superior courts can no longer be executed. Everything indicates such serious weakness that the federal bond no longer offers any

protection whatever and only constitutes a source of dissension and discord between the powers. The results of three coalitions have increased this weakness to the last degree. An electorate has been suppressed by the annexation of Hanover to Prussia. A king in the north has incorporated with his other lands a province of the Empire. The Treaty of Pressburg assures complete sovereignty to their majesties the Kings of Bavaria and of Württemberg and to His Highness the Elector of Baden. This is a prerogative which the other electors will doubtless demand, and which they are justified in demanding; but this is in harmony neither with the letter nor the spirit of the constitution of the Empire.

His Majesty the Emperor and King is, therefore, compelled to declare that he can no longer acknowledge the existence of the German Constitution, recognizing, however, the entire and absolute sovereignty of each of the princes whose states compose Germany today, maintaining with them the same relations as with the other independent powers of Europe.

His Majesty the Emperor and King has accepted the title of Protector of the Confederation of the Rhine. He has done this with a view only to peace, and in order that by his constant mediation between the weak and the powerful be may obviate every species of dissension and disorder.

Having thus provided for the dearest interests of his people and of his neighbors, and having assured, so far as in him lay, the future peace of Europe and that of Germany in particular, heretofore constantly the theatre of war, by removing a contradiction which placed people and princes alike under the delusive protection of a system contrary both to their political interests and to their treaties, His Majesty the Emperor and King trusts that the nations of Europe will at last close their ears to the insinuations of those who would maintain an eternal war upon the continent. He trusts that the French armies which have crossed the Rhine have done so for the last time, and that the people of Germany will no longer witness, except in the annals of the past, the horrible pictures of disorder, devastation and slaughter which war invariably brings with it.

His Majesty declared that he would never extend the limits of France beyond the Rhine, and he has been faithful to his promise. At present his sole desire is so to employ the means which Providence has confided to him as to free the seas, restore the liberty of commerce and thus assure the peace and happiness of the world.

[signed] BACHER. *Regensburg, August 1, 1806*

C. Declaration of the Confederated States, 1 August 1806

The undersigned, Ministers Plenipotentiary to the General Diet of the Germanic Empire, have received orders to communicate to Your Excellencies, in the name of their most high Principals, the following declaration:

The events of the last three wars which almost without interruption have disturbed the repose of Germany, and the political changes which have resulted therefrom, have put in broad daylight the sad truth that the bond which ought to unite the different Members of the Germanic Body is no longer sufficient for that purpose, or rather that it is already broken in fact; the feeling of this truth has been already a long time in the hearts of all Germans; and however painful may have been the experience of latter years, it has in reality served only to put beyond doubt the senility of a constitution respectable in its origin, but become defective through the instability inherent in all human institutions; Doubtless it is to that instability alone that the scission which was effected in the Empire in 1795 [Prussia's separate peace with France by the Treaty of Basle, 5 April] must be attributed, and which had for result the separation of the interests of the North from those of the South of Germany. From that moment all idea of a fatherland and of common interests was of necessity bound to disappear; the words *war of the Empire* and *peace of the Empire* became devoid of meaning; one sought in vain for Germany in the midst of the Germanic Body; The Princes who bordered upon France; left to themselves and exposed to all the evils of a war to which they could not seek to put an end by constitutional means, saw themselves forced to free themselves from the common bond by separate peace arrangements.

The Treaty of Lunéville [8 February 1801], and still more the *Recez* of the Empire [Imperial Recess] of 1803, should no doubt have appeared sufficient to give new life to the Germanic Constitution, by causing the feeble parts of the system to disappear and by consolidating its principal supports. But the events which have occurred in the last six months; under the eyes of the entire Empire, have destroyed that hope also and have again put beyond doubt the complete insufficiency of the existing Constitution. The urgency of these important considerations has determined the Sovereigns and Princes of the South and West of Germany to form a new Confederation suited to the circumstances of the time. In freeing themselves, by this declaration, from the bonds which have united them up to the present with the Germanic Empire, they are only following the systems established by anterior facts, and even by the declarations of the leading States of the Empire. It is true, they might have preserved the empty shadow of an extinct constitution; but they have believed that it was more in conformity with their dignity and with the purity of their intentions to make frank and open declaration of their resolution and of the motives which have influenced them.

Moreover, they would flatter themselves in vain upon attaining the desired aim, if they were not at the same time assured of a powerful protection. The Monarch whose views are always found to be in conformity with the true interests of Germany charges himself with that protection. A guarantee so powerful is tranquilizing under a double aspect. It offers the assurance that His Majesty the Emperor of the French [Napoleon I] will have at heart, as well for the interest of his glory as for the advantage of his own French Empire, the maintenance of the new order of things and the consolidation of the internal and external tranquility. That precious tranquility is the principal object of the Confederation of the Rhine, of which the Co-States of the sovereigns in whose name the present declaration is made will see the proof in the opportunity which is left to each of them to accede to it, if his position makes it desirable for him to do so.

In discharging this duty, we have the honor to be, . . .
[Signed by the representatives of thirteen sovereigns.]

D. Abdication of Francis II, 7 August 1806; in Le Moniteur, *14 August 1806*

We, Francis the Second, by the Grace of God Roman Emperor Elect, Ever August, Hereditary Emperor of Austria; etc., King of Germany, Hungary, Bohemia, Croatia, Dalmatia, Slavonia, Galizia, Lodomeria and Jerusalem; Archduke of Austria, etc.

Since the peace of Pressburg [26 December 1805] all our care and attention has been directed towards the scrupulous fulfillment of all engagements contracted by the said treaty, as well as the preservation of peace so essential to the happiness of our subjects, and the strengthening in every way of the friendly relations which have been happily reestablished. We could but await the outcome of events in order to determine whether the important changes in the German [Holy Roman] Empire resulting from the terms of the peace would allow us to fulfill the weighty duties which, in view of the conditions of our election, devolve upon us as the head of the Empire. But the results of certain articles of the Treaty of Pressburg, which showed themselves immediately after and since its publication, as well as the events which, as is generally known, have taken place in the German Empire, have convinced us that it would be impossible under these circumstances farther to fulfill the duties which we assumed by the conditions of our election. Even if the prompt readjustment of existing political complications might produce an alteration in the existing conditions, the convention signed at Paris, July 12th, and approved later by the contracting parties, providing for the complete separation of several important states of the Empire and their union into a separate confederation, would entirely destroy any such hope.

Thus, convinced of the utter impossibility of longer fulfilling the duties of our imperial office, we owe it to our principles and to our honor to renounce a crown which could only retain any value in our eyes so long as we were in a position to justify the confidence reposed in us by the electors, princes, estates and other members of the German Empire, and to fulfill the duties devolving upon us.

We proclaim, accordingly, that we consider the ties which have hitherto united us to the body politic of the German Empire as hereby dissolved; that we regard the office and dignity of the imperial headship as extinguished by the formation of a separate union of the Rhenish States, and regard ourselves as thereby freed from all our obligations toward the German Empire; herewith laying down the imperial crown which is associated with these obligations, and relinquishing the imperial government which we have hitherto conducted.

We free at the same time the electors, princes and estates and all others belonging to the Empire, particularly the members of the supreme imperial courts and other magistrates of the Empire, from the duties constitutionally due to us as the lawful head of the Empire. Conversely, we free all our German provinces and imperial lands from all their obligations of whatever kind, towards the German Empire.

In uniting these, as Emperor of Austria, with the whole body of the Austrian state we shall strive, with the restored and existing peaceful relations with all the powers and neighboring states, to raise them to the height of prosperity and happiness, which is our keenest desire, and the aim of our constant and sincerest efforts.

Done at our capital and royal residence, Vienna, August 6, 1806, in the fifteenth year of our reign as Emperor and hereditary ruler of the Austrian lands.

[signed] FRANCIS.

12. Documents concerning the Peace of Tilsit, 1807–1808

Reproduced by kind permission of the editors of the Napoleon Series (www.napoleon-series.org).

By the Peace of Tilsit—one of the fundamentally important treaties of the whole era—France broke up the Fourth Coalition, based principally around the cooperation of Russia and Prussia, leaving herself at peace save with Britain. The first three of these documents show the arrangements made at Tilsit as the basis for continental peace. Document D shows the manner in which certain of the provisions in document C were finally carried out. Among the numerous features that call for notice are: (1) the character of the alliance made between Russia and France; (2) the recent changes in Europe effected by Napoleon and sanctioned by these treaties; and (3) the humiliation of Prussia through the loss of territory, the payment of a heavy indemnity, and the reduction of its army, among other harsh terms.

A.　Treaty of Peace between France and Russia, 7 July 1807
B.　Secret Treaty of Alliance between France and Russia, 7 July 1807
C.　Treaty of Peace between France and Prussia, 9 July 1807
D.　Treaty between France and Prussia, 8 September 1808

A. *Treaty of Peace between France and Russia, 7 July 1807*

His Majesty the Emperor of the French [Napoleon I], King of Italy, Protector of the Confederation of the Rhine and His Majesty the Emperor of all the Russias [Alexander I], being prompted by an equal desire to put an end to the calamities of war. . . .

. . . .

There shall be, dating from the day of the exchange of the ratifications of the present treaty, perfect peace and amity between His Majesty the Emperor of the French, King of Italy, and His Majesty the Emperor of all the Russias.

. . . .

His Majesty the Emperor Napoleon, out of regard for His Majesty the Emperor of all the Russias, and wishing to give a proof of his sincere desire to unite the two nations by the bonds of an unalterable confidence and friendship, consents to restore to His Majesty the King of Prussia [Frederick William III], the ally of His Majesty the Emperor of all the Russias, all the conquered countries, cities and territories denominated hereinafter, to wit: . . . . [The omitted passage is practically identical with article 2 of document C.]

The provinces which on the 1st of January, 1772, made up part of the former Kingdom of Poland and which have since passed at different times under Prussian domination, with the exception of the countries that are named or designated in the preceding article and of those specified in Article 9 hereinafter, shall be possessed in complete ownership and sovereignty by His Majesty the King of Saxony [Frederick Augustus I], under the title of the Duchy of Warsaw, and shall be governed by constitutions which, while assuring the liberties and privileges of the peoples of this Duchy, are consistent with the tranquility of the neighboring States.

The city of Danzig, with a territory of two leagues radius from its circumference, shall be re-established in its independence, under the protection of His Majesty the King of Prussia and His Majesty the King of Saxony and shall be governed by the laws which governed it at the time when it ceased to govern itself.

. . . .

Their Serene Highnesses the Dukes of Saxe-Coburg Oldenburg, and Mechlinburg [Mecklenburg]-Schwerin shall each be replaced in the complete and peaceable possession of his States; but the ports of the Duchies of Oldenburg and Mechlinburg shall continue to be occupied by French garrisons until the exchange of the ratifications of the future definitive treaty of peace between France and England.

His Majesty the Emperor Napoleon accepts the mediation of His Majesty the Emperor of all the Russias for the purpose of negotiating and concluding a definitive treaty of peace between France and England, upon the supposition that this mediation will also be accepted by England, one month after the exchange of the ratifications of the present treaty.

On his side, His Majesty the Emperor of all the Russias, wishing to prove how much he desires to establish the most intimate and enduring relations between the two Empires, recognizes His Majesty the King of Naples, Joseph Napoleon, and His Majesty the King of Holland, Louis Napoleon.

His Majesty the Emperor of all the Russias likewise recognizes the Confederation of the Rhine, the actual state of possession of each of the Sovereigns who compose it, and the titles given to several of them, whether by the Act of Confederation or by the subsequent treaties of accession. His said Majesty promises to recognize, upon the notifications which shall be made to him on the part of His Majesty the Emperor Napoleon, the Sovereigns who shall subsequently become members of the Confederation, in the capacity which shall be given them in the documents which shall bring about their entrance to it.

. . . .

The present treaty of peace and amity is declared common to their Majesties the Kings of Naples and of Holland, and to the Confederated Sovereigns of the Rhine, Allies of His Majesty the Emperor Napoleon.

His Majesty the Emperor of all the Russias also recognizes His Imperial Highness, Prince Jerome Bonaparte, as King of Westphalia.

The Kingdom of Westphalia shall be composed of the provinces on the left of the Elbe ceded by His Majesty the King of Prussia and of other States actually possessed by His Majesty the Emperor Napoleon.

His Majesty the Emperor of all the Russias promises to recognize the arrangement which, in consequence of Article 19 above and of the cessions of His Majesty the King of Prussia, shall be made by His Majesty the Emperor Napoleon (which shall be announced to His Majesty the Emperor of all the Russias) and the resulting state of possession for the Sovereigns for whose profit it shall have been made.

. . . .

The Russian troops shall retire from the provinces of Wallachia and Moldavia [now Romania], but the said provinces can be occupied by the troops of His Highness until the exchange of the ratifications of the future definitive treaty of peace between Russia and the Ottoman Porte [the Ottoman Empire].

His Majesty the Emperor of all the Russias accepts the mediation of His Majesty the Emperor of the French, King of Italy, for the purpose of negotiating and concluding a peace advantageous and honorable to the two Empires. The respective Plenipotentiaries shall repair to the place which the interested parties shall have agreed upon in order to open and to pursue the negotiations.

. . .

His Majesty the Emperor of the French, King of Italy, and His Majesty the Emperor of all the Russias mutually guarantee the integrity of their possessions and those of the Powers included in the present treaty of peace, such as they now are or shall be in consequence of the above stipulations.

. . . .

The ceremonial of the two Courts of the Tuileries and of Saint Petersburg between themselves and with respect to the Ambassadors, Ministers and Envoys whom they shall accredit to each other shall be established upon the principle of a perfect reciprocity and equality.

SEPARATE AND SECRET ARTICLES.

. . . .

The Seven [Ionian] Islands shall be possessed in complete proprietorship and sovereignty by His Majesty the Emperor Napoleon.

. . . .

His Majesty the Emperor of all the Russias engages to recognize His Majesty the King of Naples, Joseph Napoleon, as King of Sicily as soon as King Ferdinand IV shall have an indemnity such as the Balearic islands or the island of Candia [Crete], or any other of like value.

If, at the time of the future peace with England, Hanover should come to be united with the Kingdom of Westphalia, a territory formed from the countries ceded by His Majesty the King of Prussia upon the left bank of the river Elbe, and having a population of from three to four hundred thousand souls, shall cease to make part of that Kingdom and shall be retroceded to Prussia.

B. Secret Treaty of Alliance between France and Russia, 7 July 1807

His Majesty the Emperor of the French, King of Italy, Protector of the Confederation of the Rhine [Napoleon I], and His Majesty the Emperor of all the Russias [Alexander I], having particularly at heart to re-establish the general peace in Europe upon substantial and, if it be possible, immovable foundations, have for that purpose resolved to conclude an offensive and defensive alliance. . . .

. . . .

His Majesty the Emperor of the French, King of Italy, and His Majesty the Emperor of all the Russias, undertake to make common cause, whether by land or by sea, or indeed by land and by sea, in every war which France or Russia may be under the necessity of undertaking against any European Power.

The occasion for the alliance occurring, and each time that it shall occur, the High Contracting Parties shall regulate, by a special convention, the forces which each of them shall employ against the common enemy, and the points at which these forces shall act; but for the present they undertake to employ, if the circumstances require it, the totality of their land and sea forces.

All the operations of the common wars shall be carried on in concert, and neither of the Contracting Parties in any case can treat for peace without the concurrence and consent of the other.

If England does not accept the mediation of Russia or if having accepted it she does not by the first of November next consent to conclude peace, recognizing therein that the flags of all the Powers shall enjoy an equal and perfect independence upon the seas and restoring therein the conquests made by it from France and its Allies since the year eighteen hundred and five, when Russia made common cause with it, a note shall be sent to the cabinet of St. James [the British government] in the course of the said month of November by the Ambassador of His Majesty the Emperor of all the Russias. This note, expressing the interest that his said Imperial Majesty takes in the tranquility of the world and the purpose which he has of employing all the forces of his Empire to procure for humanity the blessing of peace, shall contain the positive and explicit declaration that, upon the refusal of England to conclude peace upon the aforesaid conditions, His Majesty the Emperor of all the Russias will make common cause with France, and, in case the Cabinet of St. James shall not have given upon the 1st of December next a categorical and satisfactory reply, the Ambassador of Russia shall receive the contingent order to demand his passports on the said day and to leave England at once.

If the case provided for by the preceding article occurs, the High Contracting Parties shall act in concert and at the same moment summon the three courts of Copenhagen, Stockholm and Lisbon to close their ports to the English, to recall their Ambassadors from London, and to declare war upon England. That one of the three Courts which refuses this shall be treated as an enemy by the two High Contracting Parties, and, if Sweden refuses it, Denmark shall be constrained to declare war upon it.

The two High Contracting Parties shall likewise act in concert and shall urge with force upon the Court of Vienna that it adopt the principles set forth in article four above, that it close its ports to the English, recall its Ambassador from London and declare war on England.

If, on the contrary, within the period specified above, England makes peace upon the aforesaid conditions [and His Majesty the Emperor of all the Russias shall employ all his influence to bring it about], Hanover shall be restored to the King of England [George III] in compensation for the French, Spanish and Dutch colonies.

Likewise, if in consequence of the changes which have just occurred at Constantinople, the Porte should not accept the mediation of France [to bring about peace between Russia and Turkey, at war since 1806], or if after it has been accepted it should happen that, within the period of three months after the opening of the negotiations, they have not led to a satisfactory result, France will make common cause with Russia against the Ottoman Porte, and the two High Contracting Parties shall come to an agreement to remove all the provinces of the Ottoman Empire in Europe, the city of Constantinople and the Province of Roumalia excepted, from the yoke and the vexations of the Turks.

The present treaty shall remain secret and shall not be made public nor communicated to any Cabinet by one of the two Contracting Parties without the consent of the other. It shall be ratified and the ratifications thereof exchanged at Tilsit within the space of four days.

Done at Tilsit, July 7, 1807

C. Treaty of Peace between France and Prussia, 9 July 1807

His Majesty the Emperor of the French, King of Italy, Protector of the Confederation of the Rhine [Napoleon I], and His Majesty the King of Prussia [Frederick William III], being prompted by an equal desire to put an end to the calamities of war. . . .

There shall be, dating from the day of the exchange of the ratifications of the present Treaty, perfect peace and amity between His Majesty the Emperor of the French, King of Italy; and His Majesty the King of Prussia.

The portion of the Duchy of Magdeburg situated to the right of the Elbe; the Mark of Prignitz, the Unker-Mark, the middle and the new Mark of Brandenburg, with the exception of the Cotbuser-Kreis or circle of Cotbus in lower Lusace; the duchy of Pomerania; upper, lower and middle Silesia, with the county of Glatz; the portion of the district of Netze situated to the north of the causeway running from Driesen to Schneidemühl and of a line running from Schneidemühl to the Vistula at Waldau, following the limits of the circle of Bromberg; Pommerellen; the island of Nogat; the countries to the right of Nogat and the Vistula, to the east of Old Prussia and to the north of the circle of Kulm; Ermeland; and, lastly, the Kingdom of Prussia, such as it was on January 1, 1772, shall be restored to His Majesty the King of Prussia, with the places of Spandau, Stettin, Küstrin, Glogau, Braslan, Schweidnitz, Neisse, Brieg, Kosel, and Glatz, and generally all the places, citadels, chateaux, and strongholds of the countries denominated above in the condition in which the said places, citadels, chateaux and strongholds now are. The cities and citadels of Graudenz, with the villages of Neudorf, Parschken and Swirkorzy, shall also be restored to His Majesty the King of Prussia.

His Majesty the King of Prussia recognizes His Majesty the King of Naples, Joseph Napoleon; and His Majesty the King of Holland, Louis Napoleon.

His Majesty the King of Prussia likewise recognizes the Confederation of the Rhine, the actual state of possession of each of the sovereigns who compose it, and the titles given to several of them, whether by the Act of Confederation or by the subsequent treaties of accession. His Majesty promises to recognize the Sovereigns who shall subsequently become members of the said Confederation, in the capacity which shall be given them by the documents which shall bring about their entrance to it.

The present Treaty of peace and amity is declared common to His Majesty the King of Naples, Joseph Napoleon, to His Majesty the King of Holland, and the Confederated Sovereigns of the Rhine; allies of His Majesty the Emperor Napoleon.

His Majesty the King of Prussia likewise recognizes His Imperial Highness Prince Jerome Napoleon as King of Westphalia.

His Majesty the King of Prussia cedes in complete ownership and sovereignty to the Kings, Grand Dukes, Dukes or Princes who shall be designated by His Majesty the Emperor of the French, King of Italy, all the Duchies, Marquisdoms, Principalities, Counties, Lordships and generally all the territories or parts of any territories, as well as all the domains and landed estates of every nature which His Said Majesty the King of Prussia possessed by any title whatsoever between the Rhine and the Elbe at the commencement of the present war.

The Kingdom of Westphalia shall be composed of provinces ceded by His Majesty the King of Prussia and of other States actually possessed by His Majesty the Emperor Napoleon.

The disposition which shall be made by His Majesty the Emperor Napoleon of the countries designated in the two preceding articles and the state of possession resulting therefrom to the Sovereigns for whose profit it shall have been made, shall be recognized by His Majesty the King of Prussia, in the same manner as if it were already effected and were contained in the present Treaty.

His Majesty the King of Prussia, for himself, his heirs and successors, renounces all present or contingent right which he can have or lay claim to: 1st. Upon all the territories, without exception, situated between the Rhine and the Elbe other than those designated in article 7; 2d. Upon those of the possessions of His Majesty the King of Saxony [Frederick Augustus I] and of the House of Anhalt which are upon the right of the Elbe; reciprocally, every present or contingent right and every claim of the States included between the Elbe and the Rhine upon the possessions of His Majesty the King of Prussia, as they shall be in consequence of the present Treaty, are and shall remain forever extinguished.

All Agreements, Conventions or Treaties of Alliance, open or secret, which may have been concluded between Prussia and any of the states situated to the left of the Elbe, and which the present war shall not have dissolved, shall remain without effect and shall be regarded as null and void.

His Majesty the King of Prussia cedes in complete ownership and sovereignty to His Majesty the King of Saxony the Cotbuser-Kreis or Circle of Cotbus in lower Lusatia.

His Majesty the King of Prussia renounces in perpetuity the possession of all the provinces which, having belonged to the Kingdom of Poland subsequent to the 1st of January, 1807, have passed at various times under the domination of Prussia, with the exception of Ermeland and the countries situated to the west of old Prussia, to the east of Pomerania and the new Mark, to the north of the circle of Kulm and of a line running from the Vistula to Schneidemühl through Waldau, following the limits of the circle of Bomberg and of the causeway running from Schneidemühl to Drisen, which, with the city and citadel of Graudenz and the villages of Neudorf, Parschken, and Swierkorzy, shall continue to be possessed in complete ownership and sovereignty by His Majesty the King of Prussia.

His Majesty the King of Prussia likewise renounces in perpetuity the possession of Dantzig.

The Provinces which His Majesty the King of Prussia renounces by Article 13 above (with the exception of the territory specified in Article 18 above) shall be possessed in complete ownership and sovereignty by His Majesty the King of Saxony, under the title of the Duchy of Warsaw, and shall be governed by constitutions which, while assuring the liberties and privileges of the peoples of this duchy, are consistent with the tranquility of the neighboring States.

. . . .

The city of Dantzig, with a territory of two leagues radius from its circumference, shall be re-established in its independence, under the protection of His Majesty the King of Prussia and of His Majesty the King of Saxony and shall be governed by the laws which governed it at the time when it ceased to govern itself.

. . . .

The city, port and territory of Dantzig, shall be closed during the continuance of the present maritime war to the commerce and navigation of the English.

. . . .

Until the day of the exchange of the ratifications of the future definitive Treaty of peace between France and England, all the countries under the domination of His Majesty the King of Prussia, without exception, shall be closed to the navigation and commerce of the English. No shipment can be made from Prussian ports for the British islands, nor can any vessel coming from England or its colonies be received in the said ports.

. . . .

SECRET ARTICLES

. . . .

His Majesty the King of Prussia engages to make common cause with France against England, if, on the 1st of December, England has not consented to conclude a peace upon conditions reciprocally honorable to the two nations and conformable to the true principles of maritime law; in such case, there shall be a special convention made to regulate the execution of the above stipulation.

D. Treaty between France and Prussia, 8 September 1808

His Majesty the Emperor of the French, King of Italy, Protector of the Confederation of the Rhine [Napoleon I] and His Majesty the King of Prussia [Frederick William III], wishing to remove the difficulties which have occurred in the execution of the treaty of Tilsit, ...

The amount of the sums due from the Prussian States to the French army, as well for extraordinary contribution as for arrears of revenues, is fixed at 140 million francs; and by means of the payment of the said sum, every claim of France upon Prussia, on the ground of war contributions, shall be extinguished. This sum of 140 millions shall be deposited within twenty days from the exchange of the ratifications of the present Treaty in the counting house of the Receiver General of the army, to wit: half in ready money or in good and acceptable bills of exchange, payable at the rate of 6 millions per month dating from the day of the exchange of the ratifications and the payment of which shall be guaranteed by the Prussian treasury. The other half [shall be] in land notes of privileged mortgage upon the royal domains, which shall be reimbursable within the space of from one year to eighteen months after the exchange of the ratifications of the present treaty.

. . . .

The places of Glogau, Stettin and Custrin shall remain in the power of the French army until the entire discharge of the bills of exchange and the land notes given in payment of the contribution mentioned in the first article. . . .

. . . .

His Majesty the Emperor and King guarantees to His Majesty the King of Prussia the integrity of his territory, on condition that His Majesty the King of Prussia remains the faithful ally of France.

His Majesty the King of Prussia recognizes as King of Spain and of the Indies His Majesty Joseph—Napoleon [Joseph Bonaparte], and as King of the Two Sicilies His Majesty Joachim—Napoleon [Joachim Murat].

SEPARATE ARTICLES

His Majesty the King of Prussia, wishing to avoid everything which can give umbrage to France, makes engagement to maintain for ten years, dating from January 1, 1809, only the number of troops specified below, to wit:

10 Regiments of infantry, forming at most an effective [force] of	22,000 men
8 Regiments of cavalry or 32 squadrons forming at most an effective [force] of	8,000 men
A Corps of artillerymen, miners and sappers, at most of	6,000 men
Not included the Guard of the King estimated, infantry and cavalry, at most	6,000 men
TOTAL:	42,000 men

At the expiration of the ten years, His Majesty the King of Prussia shall re-enter into the common right and shall maintain the number of troops which shall seem to him suitable, according to circumstances.

During these ten years there shall not be any extraordinary levy of militia or of citizen guards, nor any mustering that tends to augment the forces above specified.

. . . .

In return for the guarantee stipulated in the Treaty of this day, and as security of the alliance contracted with France, His Majesty the King of Prussia promises to make common cause with His Majesty the Emperor of the French if war comes to be declared between him and Austria, and in that case, to place at his disposal a division of 16,000 men, infantry as well as cavalry and artillery.

The present engagement shall continue for ten years. Nevertheless, the King of Prussia, not having been able yet to form his military establishment, shall not be held for any contingent during the present year, and shall be bound to furnish in the year 1809, if war should break out, which the present amicable relations between France and Austria in no wise give occasion to fear, only a contingent of 12,000 men, infantry as well as cavalry.

13. Encounter between the frigates HMS *Macedonian* and USS *United States*, 25 October 1812

Leech, Samuel. 1999. *A Voice from the Main Deck: Being a Record of the Thirty Years Adventures of Samuel Leech.* London: Chatham Publishing, 69–77. (Orig. pub. 1857.)

Very few firsthand accounts of the naval actions of this period exist, largely the consequence of the poor state of literacy among a ship's company. The reminiscences of Samuel Leech, a seaman aboard the British frigate Macedonian, *stand as particularly insightful and entertaining.*

At Plymouth we heard some vague rumours of a declaration of war against America. More than this, we could not learn, since the utmost care was taken to prevent our being fully informed. The reason of this secrecy was, probably, because we had several Americans in our crew, most of whom were pressed men, as before stated. These men, had they been certain that war had broken out, would have given themselves up as prisoners of war, and claimed exemption from that unjust service, which compelled them to act with the enemies of their country. This was a privilege which the magnanimity of our officers ought to have offered them. They had already perpetrated a grievous wrong upon them in impressing them; it was adding cruelty to injustice, to compel their service in a war against their own nation. But the difficulty with naval officers is, that they do not treat with a sailor as with a man. They know what is fitting between each other as officers; but they treat their crews on another principle; they are apt to look at them as pieces of living mechanism, born to serve, to obey their orders, and administer to their wishes without complaint. This is alike a bad morality and a bad philosophy. There is often more real manhood in the forecastle [i.e., among the ordinary seamen] than in the ward-room [i.e., among the officers]; and until the common sailor is treated as a man, until every feeling of human nature is conceded to him in naval discipline – perfect, rational subordination will never be attained in ships of war, or in merchant vessels. It is needless to tell of an intellectual degradation of the mass of seamen. "A man's man for a' that;" and it is this very system of discipline, this treating them as automatons, which keeps them degraded. When will human nature put more confidence in itself?

Leaving Portsmouth, we next anchored, for a brief space, at Torbay, a small port in the British [English] Channel. We were or-

dered thence to convoy a huge East India merchant vessel, much larger than our frigate, and having five hundred troops on board, bound to the East Indies, with money to pay the troops stationed there. We set sail in a tremendous gale of wind. Both ships stopped two days at Madeira to take in wine and a few other articles. After leaving this island, we kept her company two days more; and then, according to orders, having wished her success, we left her to pursue her voyage, while we returned to finish our cruise.

Though without any positive information, we now felt pretty certain that our government was at war with America [declared 18 June 1812]. Among other things, our captain appeared more anxious than usual; he was on deck almost all the time; the "look-out" aloft was more rigidly observed; and every little while the cry of "Mast-head there!" arrested our attention.

It is customary in men of war to keep men at the fore and main mast-heads, whose duty it is to give notice of every new object that may appear. They are stationed in the royal yards, if there are up, but if not, on the top-gallant yards: at night a look-out is kept on the fore yard only.

Thus we passed several days; the captain running up and down, and constantly hailing the man at the mast-head: early in the morning he began his charge "to keep a good look-out," and continued to repeat it until night. Indeed, he seemed almost crazy with some pressing anxiety. The men felt there was something anticipated, of which they were ignorant; and had the captain heard all their remarks upon his conduct, he would not have felt very highly flattered. Still, everything went on as usual; the day was spent in the ordinary duties of man-of-war life, and the evening in telling stories of things most rare and wonderful; for your genuine old tar is an adept in spinning yarns, and some of them, in respect to variety and length, might safely aspire to a place beside the great magician of the north, Sir Walter Scott, or any of those prolific heads that now bring forth such abundance of fiction to feed a greedy public, who read as eagerly as our men used to listen. To this yarn-spinning was added the most humorous singing, sometimes dashed with a streak of the pathetic, which I assure my readers was most touching; especially on very plaintive melody, with a chorus beginning with,

> *Now if our ship should be cast away,*
> *It would be our lot to see old England no more,*

Which made rather a melancholy impression on my boyish mind, and gave rise to a sort of presentiment that the *Macedonian* would never return home again; a presentiment which had its fulfilment in a manner totally unexpected to us all. The presence of a shark for several days, with its attendant pilot fish, tended to strengthen this prevalent idea.

The Sabbath came, and it brought with it a stiff breeze. We usually made a sort of holiday of this sacred day. After breakfast it was common to muster the entire crew on the spar deck, dressed as the fancy of the captain might dictate; sometimes in blue jackets and white trowsers, or blue jackets and blue trowsers; at other times in blue jackets, scarlet vests, and blue or white trowsers; with our bright anchor buttons glancing in the sun, and our black, glossy hats, ornamented with black ribbons, and with the name of our ship painted on them. After muster, we frequently had church service read by the captain; the rest of the day was devoted to idleness. But we were destined to spend the Sabbath, just introduced to the reader, in a very different manner.

We had scarcely finished breakfast, before the man at the mast-head shouted, "Sail ho!"

The captain rushed upon deck, exclaiming, "Mast-head there!"

"Sir!"

"Where away is the sail?"

The precise answer to this question I do not recollect, but the captain proceeded to ask, "What does she look like?"

"A square-rigged vessel, sir," was the reply of the look-out.

After a few minutes, the captain shouted again, "Mast-head there!"

"Sir!"

"What does she look like?"

"A large ship, sir, standing toward us!"

By this time, most of the crew were on deck, eagerly straining their eyes to obtain a glimpse of the approaching ship, and murmuring their opinions to each other on her probable character. Then came the voice of the captain, shouting, "Keep silence, fore and aft!" Silence being secured, he hailed the look-out, who, to his question of "What does she look like?" replied, "A large frigate, bearing down upon us, sir!"

A whisper ran along the crew that the stranger ship was a Yankee frigate. The thought was confirmed by the command of "All hands clear the ship for action, ahoy!" The drum and fife beat to quarters; bulk-heads were knocked away; the guns were released from their confinement; the whole dread paraphernalia of battle was produced; and after the lapse of a few minutes of hurry and confusion, every man and boy was at his post, ready to do his best service for his country, except the band, who, claiming exemption from the affray, safely stowed themselves away in the cable tier. We had only one sick man on the list, and he, at the cry of battle, hurried from his cot, feeble as he was, to take his post of danger. A few of the junior midshipmen were stationed below, on the berth deck, with orders, given in our hearing, to shoot any man who attempted to run from his quarters.

Our men were all in good spirits; though they did not scruple to express the wish that the coming foe was a Frenchman rather than a Yankee. We had been told, by the Americans on board, that frigates in the American service carried more and heavier metal [guns] than ours. This, together with our consciousness of superiority over the French at sea, led us to a preference for a French antagonist.

The Americans among our number felt quite disconcerted at the necessity which compelled them to fight against their own countrymen. One of them, named John Card, as brave a seaman as every trod a plank, ventured to present himself to the captain, as a prisoner, frankly declaring his objections to fight. That officer, very ungenerously, ordered him to his quarters, threatening to shoot him if he made the request again. Poor fellow! He obeyed the unjust command, and was killed by a shot from his own countrymen. This fact is more disgraceful to the captain of

the *Macedonian*, than even the loss of his ship. It was a gross and a palpable violation of the rights of man.

As the approaching ship showed American colours, all doubt of her character was at an end. "We must fight her," was the conviction of every breast. Every possible arrangement that could insure success was accordingly made. The guns were shotted; the matches lighted; for, although our guns were furnished with first-rate locks, they were also provided with matches, attached by lanyards, in case the lock should miss fire. A lieutenant then passed through the ship, directing the marines and boarders, who were furnished with pikes, cutlasses, and pistols, how to proceed if it should be necessary to board the enemy. He was followed by the captain, who exhorted the men to fidelity and courage, urging upon their consideration the well-known motto of the brave Nelson, "England expects every man to do his duty." In addition to all these preparations on deck, some men were stationed in the tops with small-arms, whose duty it was to attend to trimming the sails, and to use their muskets, provided we came to close action. There were others also below, called sail trimmers, to assist in working the ship, should it be necessary to shift her position during the battle.

My station was at the fifth gun on the main deck. It was my duty to supply my gun with powder, a boy being appointed to each gun in the ship on the side we engaged for this purpose. A wooden screen was placed before the entrance to the magazine, with a hole in it, through which the cartridges were passed to the boys; we received them there, and covering them with our jackets, hurried to our respective guns. These precautions are observed to prevent the powder taking fire before it reaches the gun.

Thus we all stood, awaiting orders, in motionless suspense. At last we fired three guns from the larboard side of the main deck; this was followed by the command, "Cease firing; you are throwing away your shot!"

Then came the order to "wear ship," and prepare to attack the enemy with our starboard guns. Soon after this I heard a firing from some other quarter, which I at first supposed to be a discharge from our quarter deck guns; though it proved to be the roar of the enemy's cannon.

A strange noise, such as I had never heard before, next arrested my attention; it sounded like the tearing of sails, just over our heads. This I soon ascertained to be the wind of the enemy's shot. The firing, after a few minutes' cessation, recommenced. The roaring of cannon could now be heard from all parts of our trembling ship, and, mingling as it did with that of our foes, it made a most hideous noise. By-and-by I heard the shot strike the sides of our ship; the whole scene grew indescribably confused and horrible; it was like some awfully tremendous thunderstorm, whose deafening roar is attended by incessant streaks of lighting, carrying death in every flash, and strewing the ground with the victims of its wrath; only, in our case, the scene was rendered more horrible than that, by the presence of torrents of blood which dyed our decks.

Though the recital may be painful, yet, as it will reveal the horrors of war, and show at what a fearful price a victory is won or lost, I will present the reader with things as they met my eye during the progress of this dreadful fight. I was busily supplying my gun with powder, when I saw blood suddenly fly from the arm of a man stationed at our gun. I saw nothing strike him; the effect alone was visible; in an instant, the third lieutenant tied his handkerchief round the wounded arm, and sent the groaning wretch below to the surgeon.

The cries of the wounded now rang through all parts of the ship. These were carried to the cockpit as fast as they fell, while those more fortunate men, who were killed outright, were immediately thrown overboard. As I was stationed but a short distance from the main hatchway, I could catch a glimpse at all who were carried below. A glance was all I could indulge in, for the boys belonging to the guns next to mine were wounded in the early part of the action, and I had to spring with all my might to keep three or four guns supplied with cartridges. I saw two of these lads fall nearly together. One of them was struck in the leg by a large shot; he had to suffer amputation above the wound. The other had a grape or canister shot sent through his ancle [sic]. A stout Yorkshireman lifted him in his arms, and hurried him to the cockpit. He had his foot cut off, and was thus made lame for life. Two of the boys stationed on the quarter deck were killed. They were both Portuguese. A man, who saw one of them killed, afterwards told me that his powder caught fire and burnt the flesh almost off his face. In this pitiable situation, the agonized boy lifted up both hands, as if imploring relief, when a passing shot instantly cut him in two.

I was an eye-witness to a sight equally revolting. A man named Aldric had one of his hands cut off by a shot, and almost at the same moment he received another shot, which tore open his bowels in a terrible manner. As he fell, two or three men caught him in their arms, and, as he could not live, threw him overboard.

One of the officers in my division also fell in my sight. He was a noble-hearted fellow, named Nan Kivell. A grape or canister shot struck him near the heart: exclaiming, "Oh! My God!" he fell, and was carried below, where he shortly after died.

Mr Hope, our first lieutenant, was also slightly wounded by a grummet, or small iron ring, probably torn from a hammock clew by a shot. He went below, shouting to the men to fight on. Having had his wound dressed, he came up again, shouting to us at the top of his voice, and bidding us fight with all our might. There was not a man in the ship but would have rejoiced had he been in the place of our master's mate, the unfortunate Nan Kivell.

The battle went on. Our men kept cheering with all their might. I cheered with them, though I confess I scarcely knew for what. Certainly there was nothing very inspiriting in the aspect of things where I was stationed. So terrible had been the work of destruction round us, it was termed the slaughter-house. Not only had we had several boys and men killed or wounded, but several of the guns were disabled. The one I belonged to had a piece of the muzzle knocked out; and when the ship rolled, it struck a beam of the upper deck with such force as to become jammed and fixed in that position. A twenty-four pound shot had also passed through the screen of the magazine, immediately over the orifice through which we passed our powder. The schoolmaster received a death wound. The brave boatswain, who came from the sick bay to the din of battle, was fastening a stopper on a back-stay which had been shot away, when his head was smashed to pieces by a cannon-ball; another man, going to complete the unfinished task, was also struck down. Another of our midshipmen also received a severe wound. The unfortunate wardroom steward, who, the reader will recollect, attempted to cut his throat on a former occasion, was killed. A fellow named John, who, for some petty offence, had been sent on board as a punishment, was carried past me, wounded. I distinctly heard the large blood-drops fall pat, pat, pat, on the deck; his wounds were mortal. Even a poor goat, kept by the officers for her milk, did not escape the general carnage; her hind legs were shot off, and poor Nan was thrown overboard.

Such was the terrible scene, amid which we kept on our shouting and firing. Our men fought like tigers. Some of them pulled off their jackets, others their jackets and vests; while some, still more determined, had taken off their shirts, and, with nothing but a handkerchief tied round the waistbands of their trowsers, fought like heroes. Jack Sadler . . . was one of these. I also observed a boy, named Coop, stationed at a gun some distance from the magazine. He came to and fro on the full run, and appeared to be as "merry as a cricket." The third lieutenant cheered him along, occasionally, by saying, "Well done, my boy, you are worth your weight in gold!"

I have often been asked what were my feelings during this fight. I felt pretty much as I suppose every one does at such a time. That men are without thought when they stand amid the dying and the dead, is too absurd an idea to be entertained a moment. We all appeared cheerful, but I know that many a serious thought ran through my mind: still, what could we do but keep up a semblance, at least, of animation? To run from our quarters would have been certain death from the hands of our own officers; to give way to gloom, or to show fear, would do no good, and might brand us with the name of cowards, and ensure certain defeat. Our only true philosophy, therefore, was to make the best of our situation, by fighting bravely and cheerfully. I thought a great deal, however, of the other world; every groan, every falling man, told me that the next instant I might be before the Judge of all the earth. For this, I felt unprepared; but being without any particular knowledge of religious truth, I satisfied myself by repeating again and again the Lord's prayer, and promising that if spared I would be more attentive to religious duties than ever before. This promise I had no doubt, at the time, of keeping; but I have learned since that it is easier to make promises amidst the roar of the battle's thunder, or in the horrors of shipwreck, than to keep them when danger is absent, and safety smiles upon our path.

While these thoughts secretly agitated my bosom, the din of battle continued. Grape and canister shot were pouring through our portholes like leaden rain, carrying death in their trail. The large shot came against the ship's side like iron hail, shaking her to the very keel, or passing through her timbers, and scattering terrific splinters, which did a more appalling work than even their own death-giving blows. The reader may form an idea of the effect of grape and canister, when he is told that grape shot is formed by seven or eight balls confined to an iron and tied in a cloth. These balls are scattered by the explosion of the powder.

Canister shot is made by filling a powder canister with balls, each as large as two or three musket balls; these also scatter with direful effect when discharged. What then with splinters, cannon balls, grape and canister poured incessantly upon us, the reader may be assured that the work of death went on in a manner which must have been satisfactory even to the King of Terrors himself.

Suddenly, the rattling of the iron hail ceased. We were ordered to cease firing. A profound silence ensued, broken only by the stifled groans of the brave sufferers below. It was soon ascertained that the enemy had shot ahead to repair damages, for she was not so disabled but she could sail without difficulty; while we were so cut up that we lay utterly helpless. Our head braces were shot away; the fore and main top-masts were gone; the mizzen mast hung over the stern, having carried several men over in its fall: we were in the state of a complete wreck.

A council was now held among the officers on the quarter deck. Our condition was perilous in the extreme: victory or escape was alike hopeless. Our ship was disabled; many of our men were killed, and many more wounded. The enemy would without doubt bear down upon us in a few moments, and as she could now choose her own position, would without doubt rake us fore and aft. Any further resistance was therefore folly. So, in spite of the hot-brained lieutenant, Mr Hope, who advised them not to strike, but to sink alongside, it was determined to strike our bunting. This was done by the hands of a brave fellow named Watson, whose saddened brow told how severely it pained his lion heart to do it. To me it was a pleasing sight, for I had seen fighting enough for one Sabbath; more than I wished to see again on a week day. His Britannic Majesty's frigate *Macedonian* was now the prize of the American frigate *United States*.

14. Treaty of Chaumont, 1 March 1814

Reproduced by kind permission of the editors of the Napoleon Series (www.napoleon-series.org).

Although dated 1 March the treaty was not actually signed until 9 March. The terms alluded to in Article 1 were those offered to Napoleon at the Congress of Châtillon. As the most comprehensive of the series of treaties that established the Sixth Coalition against France, the terms of Chaumont continued the pattern of alliance based on British subsidies, mutual war aims, and the principle of no separate peace with the enemy. It diverged from all previous treaties of alliance, however, in establishing the principle of defensive obligations between the signatories even after the conclusion of hostilities—in this case for a period of twenty years.

His Imperial Majesty and Royal Highness the Emperor of Austria, King of Hungary and of Bohemia [Francis I], His Majesty the Emperor of all the Russias [AlexanderI], His Majesty the King of the United Kingdom of Great Britain and Ireland [George III], His Majesty the King of Prussia [Frederick William III], having forwarded to the French Government proposals for the conclusion of a general peace, and desiring, in case France should refuse the conditions of that peace, to draw

closer the bonds which unite them for the vigorous prosecution of a war undertaken with the salutary purpose of putting an end to the misfortunes of Europe by assuring future repose through the re-establishment of a just equilibrium of the Powers, and wishing at the same time, if Providence blesses their pacific intentions, to settle the methods of maintaining against every attack the order of things which shall have been the happy result of their efforts, have agreed to sanction by a solemn Treaty, signed separately by each of the four Powers with the other three, this double engagement.

. . . .

The High Contracting Parties above named solemnly engage by the present Treaty, and in the event of France refusing to accede to the Conditions of Peace now proposed, to apply all the means of their respective States to the vigorous prosecution of the War against that Power, and to employ them in perfect concert, in order to obtain for themselves and for Europe a General Peace, under the Protection of which the Rights and Liberties of all Nations may be established and secured.

This engagement shall in no respect affect the Stipulations which the several Powers have already contracted relative to the number of Troops to be kept against the Enemy; and it is understood that the Courts of England, Austria, Russia, and Prussia engage by the present Treaty to keep in the field, each of them, 150,000 effective men, exclusive of garrisons, to be employed in active service against the common Enemy.

The High Contracting Parties reciprocally engage not to treat separately with the common Enemy, nor to sign Peace, Truce, nor Convention, but with common consent. They, moreover, engage not to lay down their Arms until the object of the War, mutually understood and agreed upon, shall have been attained.

In order to contribute in the most prompt and decisive manner to fulfill this great object, His Britannic Majesty engages to furnish a Subsidy of £5,000,000 for the service of the year 1814, to be divided in equal proportions amongst the three Powers; and His said Majesty promises, moreover, to arrange before the 1st of January in each year, with their imperial and Royal Majesties, the further succours to be furnished during the subsequent year, if (which God forbid) the War should so long continue.

. . . .

The High Contracting Parties, reserving to themselves to concert together, on the conclusion of a peace with France, as to the means best adapted to guarantee to Europe, and to themselves reciprocally, the continuance of the Peace, have also determined to enter, without delay, into defensive engagements for the Protection of their respective States in Europe against every attempt which France might make to infringe the order of things resulting from such Pacification.

To effect this, they agree that in the event of one of the High Contracting Parties being threatened with an Attack on the part of France, the others shall employ their most strenuous efforts to prevent it, by friendly interposition.

In case of these endeavours proving ineffectual, the High Contracting Parties promise to come to the immediate assistance of the Power attacked, each with a body of 60,000 men.

As the situation of the Seat of War, or other circumstances, might render it difficult for Great Britain to furnish the stipulated succours in English troops within the term prescribed, and to maintain the same on a War establishment, His Britannic Majesty reserves the right of furnishing his contingent to the requiring Power in Foreign Troops in his pay, or to pay annually to that Power a sum of money, at the rate of £20 per man for infantry, and of £30 for cavalry, until the stipulated succour shall be complete.

. . . .

The High Contracting Parties mutually promise, that in case they shall be reciprocally engaged in hostilities, in consequence of furnishing the stipulated Succours, the party requiring and the parties called upon, and acting as Auxiliaries in the War, shall not make Peace but by common consent.

. . . .

In order to render more effectual the Defensive Engagements above stipulated, by uniting for their common defence the Powers the most exposed to a French invasion, the High Contracting Parties engage to invite those Powers to accede to the present Treaty of Defensive Alliance.

The present Treaty of Defensive Alliance having for its object to maintain the equilibrium of Europe, to secure the repose and Independence of its States, and to prevent the Invasions which during so many years have desolated the World, the High Contracting Parties have agreed to extend the duration of it to 20 years, to take date from the day of its signature; and they reserve to themselves to concert upon its ulterior prolongation three years before its expiration, should circumstances require it.

. . . .

Secret Articles

The re-establishment of an equilibrium of the powers and a just distribution of the forces among them being the aim of the present war, their Imperial and Royal Majesties obligate themselves to direct their efforts toward the actual establishment of the following system in Europe, to wit:

Germany composed of sovereign princes united by a federative bond which assures and guarantees the independence of Germany.

The Swiss Confederation in its former limits and in an independence placed under the guarantee of the great powers of Europe, France included.

Italy divided into independent states, intermediaries between the Austrian possessions in Italy and France.

Spain governed by King Ferdinand VII in its former limits.

Holland, [a] free and independent state, under the sovereignty of the Prince of Orange, with an increase of territory and the establishment of a suitable frontier.

The high confederated parties agree, in execution of Article 15 of the open treaty, to invite the accession to the present treaty of defensive alliance of the monarchies of Spain, Portugal, Sweden, and His Royal Highness the Prince of Orange, and to admit to it likewise other sovereigns and states according to the exigency of the case.

Considering the necessity which may exist after the conclusion of a defensive treaty of peace with France, to keep in the field during a certain time sufficient forces to protect the arrangements which the allies must make among themselves for the re-establishment of the situation of Europe, the high confederated powers have decided to concert among themselves, not only over the necessity, but over the sum and the distribution of the forces to be kept upon foot, according to the need of the circumstances. None of the high confederated powers shall be required to furnish forces, for the purpose set forth above, during more than one year, without its express and voluntary consent, and England shall be at liberty to furnish its contingent in the manner stipulated in article 9.

15. (First) Treaty of Paris, 30 May 1814

Reproduced by kind permission of the editors of the Napoleon Series (www.napoleon-series.org).

By this agreement peace finally returned to Europe after—with the exception of the brief period of peace from March 1802 to May 1803—more than two decades of war. The terms were remarkably lenient, reflecting the Allies' desire that France return as a responsible member of the community of nations, a circumstance thought to be more likely with the restoration of the Bourbon line and a minimal call for territorial concessions.

May 30, 1814.

In the Name of the Most Holy and Undivided Trinity.

His Majesty, the King of the United Kingdom of Great Britain and Ireland [George III], and his Allies on the one part, and His Majesty the King of France and Navarre [Louis XVIII] on the other part, animated by an equal desire to terminate the long agitations of Europe, and the sufferings of Mankind, by a permanent Peace, founded upon a just repartition of force between its States, and containing in its Stipulations the pledge of its durability, and His Britannic Majesty, together with his Allies, being unwilling to require of France, now that, replaced under the paternal Government of Her Kings, she offers the assurance of security and stability to Europe, the conditions and guarantees which they had with regret demanded from her former Government, Their said Majesties have named Plenipotentiaries to discuss, settle, and sign a Treaty of Peace and Amity; namely,

There shall be from this day forward perpetual Peace and Friendship between His Britannic Majesty and his Allies on the one part, and His Majesty the King of France and Navarre on the other, their Heirs and Successors, their Dominions and Subjects, respectively.

The High Contracting Parties shall devote their best attention to maintain, not only between themselves, but, inasmuch as depends upon them, between all the States of Europe, that harmony and good understanding which are so necessary for their tranquility.

The Kingdom of France retains its limits entire, as they existed on the 1st of January, 1792. It shall further receive the increase of Territory comprised within the line established by the following Article:

On the side of Belgium. Germany, and Italy, the Ancient Frontiers shall be re-established as they existed on the 1st of January, 1792, extending from the North Sea, between Dunkirk and Nieuport to the Mediterranean between Cagnes and Nice, with the following modifications:

. . . .

France on her part renounces all rights of Sovereignty, Suzerainty, etc., and of possession, over all the Countries, Districts, Towns, and places situated beyond the Frontier above described, the Principality of Monaco being replaced on the same footing on which it stood before the 1st of January, 1792.

The Allied Powers assure to France the possession of the Principality of Avignon, of the Comitat Venaissin, of the Comté of Montébliard, together with the several insulated Territories which formerly belonged to Germany, comprehended within the Frontier above described, whether they have been incorporated with France before or after the 1st of January, 1792.

. . . .

To secure the communications of the town of Geneva with other parts of the Swiss territory situated on the Lake, France consents that the road by Versoy shall be common to the two countries.

The Navigation of the Rhine, from the point where it becomes navigable unto the sea, and vice versa, shall be free, so that it can be interdicted to no one:—and at the future Congress [opened in Vienna on 1 November 1814] attention shall be paid to the establishment of the principles according to which the duties to be raised by the States bordering on the Rhine may be regulated, in the mode the most impartial and the most favourable to the commerce of all Nations.

The future Congress, with a view to facilitate the communication between Nations and continually to render them less strangers to each other, shall likewise examine and determine in what manner the above provisions can be extended to other Rivers which, in their course, separate or traverse different States.

Holland, placed under the sovereignty of the House of Orange, shall receive an increase of Territory. The title and exercise of that Sovereignty shall not in any case belong to a Prince wearing, or destined to wear, a Foreign Crown.

The States of Germany shall be independent, and united by a Federative Bond.

Switzerland, Independent, shall continue to govern herself.

Italy, beyond the limits of the countries which are to revert to Austria, shall be composed of Sovereign States.

The Island of Malta and its Dependencies shall belong in full right and Sovereignty to His Britannic Majesty.

His Britannic Majesty, stipulating for himself and his Allies, engages to restore to His Most Christian Majesty, within the term which shall be hereafter fixed, the Colonies, Fisheries Factories, and Establishments of every kind which were possessed by France on the 1st of January, 1792, in the Seas and on the Continents of America, Africa, and Asia; with the exception, however, of the Islands of Tobago and St. Lucia, and of the Isle of France and its Dependencies [in the Indian Ocean], especially Rodrigues and Les Séchelles, which several Colonies and possessions His Most Christian Majesty cedes in full right and Sovereignty to His Bri-

tannic Majesty, and also the portion of St. Domingo [Santo Domingo, the eastern portion of the West Indian island of Hispaniola] ceded [by Spain] to France by the Treaty of Basle [12 July 1795], and which His Most Christian Majesty [Louis XVIII] restores in full right and Sovereignty to His Catholic Majesty [Ferdinand VII].

His Majesty the King of Sweden and Norway [Charles XII], in virtue of the arrangements stipulated with the Allies, and in execution of the preceding Article, consents that the island of Guadeloupe be restored to His Most Christian Majesty, and gives up all the rights he may have acquired over that island.

Her Most Faithful Majesty [Maria I of Portugal], in virtue of the arrangements stipulated with her Allies, and in execution of the VIIIth Article, engages to restore French Guiana as it existed on the 1st of January 1792, to His Most Christian Majesty, within the term hereafter fixed.

The renewal of the dispute which existed at that period on the subject of the frontier, being the effect of this stipulation, it is agreed that that dispute shall be terminated by a friendly arrangement between the two Courts, under the mediation of His Britannic Majesty.

The places and forts in those colonies and settlements, which, by virtue of the VIIIth, IXth and Xth Articles, are to be restored to His Most Christian Majesty, shall be given up in the state in which they may be at the moment of the signature of the present Treaty.

His Britannic Majesty guarantees to the subjects of His Most Christian Majesty the same facilities, privileges, and protection, with respect to commerce, and the security of their persons and property within the limits of the British Sovereignty on the Continent of India, as are now, or shall be granted to the most favoured nations.

His Most Christian Majesty, on his part, having nothing more at heart than the perpetual duration of peace between the two Crowns of England and of France, and wishing to do his utmost to avoid anything which might affect their mutual good understanding, engages not to erect any fortifications in the establishments which are to be restored to him within the limits of the British sovereignty upon the Continent of India, and only to place in those establishments the number of troops necessary for the maintenance of the police.

The French right of fishery upon the Great Bank of Newfoundland, upon the coasts of the island of that name, and of the adjacent islands in the Gulf of St. Lawrence, shall be replaced upon the footing on which it stood in 1792.

Those colonies, factories [trading posts] and establishments which are to be restored to His Most Christian Majesty or his Allies in the Northern Seas, or in the Seas on the Continents of America and Africa, shall be given up within the 3 months, and those which are beyond the Cape of Good Hope within 6 months which follow the ratification of the present Treaty.

The High Contracting Parties having, by the IVth Article of the Convention of the 23rd of April last, reserved to themselves the right of disposing, in the present Definitive Treaty of Peace, of the arsenals and ships of war, armed and unarmed, which may be found in the maritime places restored by the IInd Article of the said Convention, it is agreed that the said vessels and ships of war, armed and unarmed, together with the naval ordnance and naval stores, and all materials for building and equipment shall be divided between France and the countries where the said places are situated, in the proportion of two-thirds for France and on-third for the Power to whom the said places shall belong.

Antwerp shall for the future be solely a Commercial Port.

The High Contracting Powers, desirous to bury in entire oblivion the dissensions which have agitated Europe, declare and promise that no individual, of whatever rank or condition he may be, in the countries restored and ceded by the present Treaty, shall be prosecuted, disturbed, or molested in his person or property, under any pretext whatsoever, either on account of his conduct or political opinions, his attachment either to any of the Contracting Parties or to any Government which has ceased to exist, or for any other reason, except for debts contracted towards individuals, or acts posterior to the date of the present Treaty.

The native inhabitants and aliens, of whatever nation and condition they may be, in those countries which are to change Sovereigns, as well in virtue of the present Treaty as of the subsequent arrangements to which it may give rise, shall be allowed a period of six years, reckoning from the exchange of the Ratifications, for the purpose of disposing of their property, if they think fit, whether acquired before or during the present War, and retiring to whatever country they may choose.

The Allied Powers, desiring to offer His Most Christian Majesty a new proof of their anxiety to arrest, as far as in them lies, the bad consequences of the disastrous epoch fortunately terminated by the present Peace, renounce all the sums which their Governments claim from France, whether on account of contracts, supplies, or any other advances whatsoever to the French Government, during the different Wars which have taken place since 1792.

His Most Christian Majesty, on his part, renounces every claim which he might bring forward against the Allied Powers on the same grounds.

The French Government engages to liquidate and pay all debts it may be found to owe in countries beyond its own territory, on account of contracts, or other formal engagements between individuals, or private establishments, and the French authorities, as well for supplies, as in satisfaction of legal engagements.

The High Contracting Parties, immediately after the exchange of the Ratifications of the present Treaty, shall name Commissioners to direct and superintend the execution of the whole of the stipulations contained in the XVIIIth and XIXth Articles. These Commissioners shall undertake the examination of the claims referred to in the preceding Article, the liquidation of the sums claimed, and the consideration of the manner in which the French Government may propose to pay them.

The debts which in their origin were specifically mortgaged upon the countries no longer belonging to France, or were contracted for the support of their internal administration, shall remain at the charge of the said countries.

The French Government shall remain charged with the reimbursement of all sums paid by the subjects of said countries into French coffers, whether under the denomination of surety, deposit or consignment.

. . . .

National domains acquired for valuable considerations by French subjects in the late departments of Belgium, and of the left bank of the Rhine, and the Alps, beyond the ancient limits of France, and which now cease to belong to her, shall be guaranteed to the purchasers.

. . . .

All the Powers engaged on either side in the present War, shall, within the space of two months, send Plenipotentiaries to Vienna, for the purpose of regulating, in General Congress, the arrangements which are to complete the provisions of the present Treaty.

The present Treaty shall be ratified, and the Ratifications shall be exchanged within the period of 15 days, or sooner if possible.

In witness whereof, the respective Plenipotentiaries have signed and affixed to it the seals of their arms.

[Lord] Castlereagh.
[Lord] Aberdeen.
[Lord] Cathcart.
Charles Stewart, Lieut.-Genl.
Le Prince de Benevent [Charles-Maurice de Talleyrand].

Separate and Secret Articles between France and Great Britain, Austria, Prussia, and Russia. Paris, 30 May 1814

The disposal of the territories given up by His Most Christian Majesty, under the IIIrd Article of the Public Treaty, and the relations from whence a system of real and permanent balance of power in Europe is to be derived, shall be regulated at the Congress upon the principles determined upon by the Allied Powers among themselves, and according to the general provisions contained in the following Articles.

The possessions of His Imperial and Royal Apostolic Majesty in Italy shall be bounded by the Po, the Tessino, and Lago Maggiore. The King of Sardinia shall return to the possession of his ancient dominions, with the exception of that part of Savoy secured to France by the IIIrd Article of the present Treaty. His Majesty shall receive an increase of territory from the State of Genoa. The Port of Genoa shall continue to be a Free Port; the Powers reserving to themselves the right of making arrangements upon this point with the King of Sardinia.

France shall acknowledge and guarantee, conjointly with the Allied Powers, and on the same footing, the political organisation which Switzerland shall adopt under the auspices of the said Allied Powers, and according to the basis already agreed upon with them.

The establishment of a just balance of power in Europe requiring that Holland should be so constituted as to be enabled to support her independence through her own resources, the countries comprised between the sea, the frontiers of France, such as they are defined by the present Treaty, and the Meuse, shall be given up for ever to Holland.

The frontiers upon the right bank of the Meuse shall be regulated according to the military convenience of Holland and her neighbours.

The freedom of the navigation of the Scheldt shall be established upon the same principle which has regulated the navigation of the Rhine, in the Vth Article of the present Treaty.

The German territories upon the left bank of the Rhine, which have been united to France since 1792, shall contribute to the aggrandisement of Holland, and shall be further applied to compensate Prussia and other German states.

Additional Articles between France and Great Britain. Paris, 30 May 1814

His Most Christian Majesty, concurring without reserve in the sentiments of His Britannic Majesty, with respect to a description of traffic repugnant to the principles of natural justice and of the enlightened age in which we live, engages to unite all his efforts to those of His Britannic Majesty, at the approaching Congress, to induce all the Powers of Christendom to decree the abolition of the Slave Trade, so that the said Trade shall cease universally, as it shall cease definitely, under any circumstances, on the part of the French Government, in the course of 5 years; and that, during the said period, no slave merchant shall import or sell slaves, except in the colonies of the State of which he is a subject.

16. Declaration of the Powers against Napoleon, 13 March 1815

Reproduced by kind permission of the editors of the Napoleon Series (www.napoleon-series.org).

No sooner had the delegates at the Congress of Vienna learned of Napoleon's arrival in France from Elba that they issued this declaration branding him an outlaw. The Allies were careful to express their personal hostility toward the former emperor, in distinction to France itself, which was the de jure domain of Louis XVIII.

The Powers who have signed the [First] Treaty of Paris [30 May 1814] reassembled in Congress at Vienna, having been informed of the escape of Napoleon Bonaparte and of his entrance into France [1 March] with an armed force, owe to their dignity and the interest of social order a solemn Declaration of the sentiments which that event has inspired in them.

In thus violating the convention which established him in the Island of Elba, Bonaparte destroyed the only legal title for his existence. By reappearing in France with projects of disorder and destruction, he has cut himself off from the protection of the law and has shown in the face of the world that there can be neither peace nor truce with him.

Accordingly, the Powers declare that Napoleon Bonaparte is excluded from civil and social relations, and, as an Enemy and Disturber of the tranquility of the World, that he has incurred public vengeance.

At the same time, being firmly resolved to preserve intact the Treaty of Paris of May 30, 1814, and the arrangements sanctioned

by that treaty, as well as those which have been or shall be arranged hereafter in order to complete and consolidate it, they declare that they will employ all their resources and will unite all their efforts in order that the General Peace, the object of the desires of Europe and the constant aim of their labors, may not be again disturbed, and in order to secure themselves from all attempts which may threaten to plunge the world once more into the disorders and misfortunes of revolutions.

And although fully persuaded that all France, rallying around its legitimate sovereign, will strive unceasingly to bring to naught this last attempt of a criminal and impotent madman, all the Sovereigns of Europe, animated by the same feeling and guided by the same principles, declare that if, contrary to all expectation, there shall result from that event any real danger, they will be ready to give to the King of France and the French Nation or to any government which shall be attacked, as soon as shall be required, all the assistance necessary to re-establish the public tranquility, and to make common cause against all who may attempt to compromise it.

The present Declaration, inserted in the protocol of the Congress assembled at Vienna, March 13, 1815, shall be made public.

17. Holy Alliance Treaty, 26 September 1815

Reproduced by kind permission of the editors of the Napoleon Series (www.napoleon-series.org).

This treaty, drawn up by Tsar Alexander, reflects the return to conservative politics in Europe after the long struggle against Revolutionary and Napoleonic France. It was subsequently acceded to by all the monarchs of Europe except the British Prince Regent, who declined to sign it on constitutional grounds: Pope Pius VII, who refused to deal with Protestant monarchs; and the sultan of the Ottoman Empire, who refused to put his name to a document that expressly championed Christian principles. Both Castlereagh and Metternich dismissed the wording of the treaty as largely meaningless, and it had little influence on the policies of the signatories. Liberals and nationalists hated the alliance as a symbol of the reactionary Restoration.

Treaty between Austria, Prussia, and Russia. Signed at Paris 26th September 1815.

In the name of the Most Holy and Indivisible Trinity.

Holy Alliance of Sovereigns of Austria, Prussia, and Russia.

Their Majesties the Emperor of Austria [Francis I], the King of Prussia [Frederick William III], and the Emperor of Russia [Alexander I], having, in consequence of the great events which have marked the course of the three last years in Europe, and especially of the blessings which it has pleased Divine Providence to shower down upon those States which place their confidence and their hope on it alone, acquired the intimate conviction of the necessity of settling the steps to be observed by the Powers, in their reciprocal relations, upon the sublime truths which the Holy Religion of our Saviour teaches:

GOVERNMENT AND POLITICAL RELATIONS

They solemnly declare that the present Act has no other object than to publish, in the face of the whole world, their fixed resolution, both in the administration of their respective States, and in their political relations with every other Government, to take for their sole guide the precepts of that Holy Religion, namely, the precepts of Justice, Christian Charity, and Peace, which, far from being applicable only to private concerns, must have an immediate influence on the councils of Princes, and guide all their steps, as being the only means of consolidating human institutions and remedying their imperfections. In consequence, their Majesties have agreed on the following Articles:

PRINCIPLES OF THE CHRISTIAN RELIGION

ART. I. Conformably to the words of the Holy Scriptures, which command all men to consider each other as brethren, the Three contracting Monarchs will remain united by the bonds of a true and indissoluble fraternity, and considering each other as fellow countrymen, they will, on all occasions and in all places, lend each other aid and assistance; and, regarding themselves towards their subjects and armies as fathers of families, they will lead them, in the same spirit of fraternity with which they are animated, to protect Religion, Peace, and Justice.

FRATERNITY AND AFFECTION

ART. II. In consequence, the sole principle of force, whether between the said Governments or between their Subjects, shall be that of doing each other reciprocal service, and of testifying by unalterable good will the mutual affection with which they ought to be animated, to consider themselves all as members of one and the same Christian nation; the three allied Princes looking on themselves as merely designated by Providence to govern three branches of the One family, namely, Austria, Prussia, and Russia, thus confessing that the Christian world, of which they and their people form a part, has in reality no other Sovereign than Him to whom alone power really belongs, because in Him alone are found all the treasures of love, science, and infinite wisdom, that is to say, God, our Divine Saviour, the Word of the Most High, the Word of Life. Their Majesties consequently recommend to their people, with the most tender solicitude, as the sole means of enjoying that Peace, which arise from a good conscience, and which alone is more durable, to strengthen themselves every day more and more in the principles and exercise of the duties which the Divine Saviour has taught to mankind.

ACCESSION OF FOREIGN POWERS

ART. III. All the powers who shall choose solemnly to avow the sacred principles which have dictated the present Act, and shall acknowledge how important it is for the happiness of nations, too long agitated, that these truths should henceforth exercise over the destinies of mankind all the influence which belongs to them, will be received with equal ardour and affection into this Holy Alliance.

Done in triplicate, and signed at Paris, the year of Grace 1815, 26th September.

(L. S.) Francis (L. S.) Frederick William (L. S.) Alexander

18. (Second) Treaty of Paris, 20 November 1815

Reproduced by kind permission of the editors of the Napoleon Series (www.napoleon-series.org).

The Allied settlement after Waterloo imposed much harsher terms on France than had been the case with the first Treaty of Paris, concluded the previous year. This new, punitive, treaty imposed heavy indemnity payments and further territorial losses, as well as a period of occupations.

In the Name of the Most Holy and Undivided Trinity.

The Allied Powers having by their united efforts, and by the success of their arms, preserved France and Europe from the convulsions with which they were menaced by the late enterprise of Napoleon Bonaparte, and by the revolutionary system reproduced in France, to promote its success; participating at present with His Most Christian Majesty [Louis XVIII] in the desire to consolidate, by maintaining inviolate the Royal authority, and by restoring the operation of the Constitutional Charter, the order of things which had been happily re-established in France, as also in the object of restoring between France and her neighbours those relations of reciprocal confidence and good will which the fatal effects of the Revolution and of the system of Conquest had for so long a time disturbed: persuaded, at the same time, that this last object can only be obtained by an arrangement framed to secure to the Allies proper indemnities for the past and solid guarantees for the future, they have, in concert with His Majesty the King of France, taken into consideration the means of giving effect to this arrangement; and being satisfied that the indemnity due to the Allied Powers cannot be either entirely territorial or entirely pecuniary, without prejudice to France in one or other of her essential interests, and that it would be more fit to combine both the modes, in order to avoid the inconvenience which would result, were either resorted to separately, their Imperial and Royal Majesties have adopted this basis for their present transactions; and agreeing alike as to the necessity of retaining for a fixed time in the Frontier Provinces of France, a certain number of allied troops, they have determined to combine their different arrangements, founded upon these bases, in a Definitive Treaty.

. . . .

The frontiers of France shall be the same as they were in the year 1790, save and except the modifications on one side and on the other, which are detailed in the present Article.

. . . .

The pecuniary part of the indemnity to be furnished by France to the Allied Powers is fixed at the sum of 700,000,000 Francs. . . .

The state of uneasiness and fermentation, which after so many violent convulsions, and particularly after the last catastrophe, France must still experience, notwithstanding the paternal intentions of her King, and the advantages secured to every class of his subjects by the Constitutional Charter, requiring for the security of the neighbouring States, certain measures of precaution and of temporary guarantee, it has been judged indispensable to occupy, during a fixed time, by a corps of Allied Troops, certain military positions along the frontiers of France, under the express reserve, that such occupation shall in no way prejudice the Sovereignty of His Most Christian Majesty, nor the state of possession, such as it is recognized and confirmed by the present Treaty. The number of these troops shall not exceed 150,000 men. . . .

As the maintenance of the army destined for this service is to be provided by France, a Special Convention shall regulate everything which may relate to that object. . . .

The utmost extent of the duration of this military occupation is fixed at 5 years. It may terminate before that period if, at the end of 3 years, the Allied Sovereigns, after having, in concert with His Majesty the King of France, maturely examined their material situation and interests, and the progress which shall have been made in France in the re-establishment of order and tranquility, shall agree to acknowledge that the motives which led them to that measure have ceased to exist. But whatever may be the result of this deliberation, all the Fortresses and Positions occupied by the Allied troops shall, at the expiration of 5 years, be evacuated without further delay, and given up to His Most Christian Majesty, or to his heirs and successors.

. . . .

The [First] Treaty of Paris of the 30th of May, 1814, and the Final Act of the Congress of Vienna of the 9th of June, 1815, are confirmed, and shall be maintained in all such of their enactments which shall not have been modified by the Articles of the present Treaty.

Bibliography

A

Abbott, John Stevens C. 1897. *History of Joseph Bonaparte, King of Naples and of Italy*. New York: Harper and Brothers.

Abella, Rafael. 1997. *José Bonaparte*. Barcelona: Planeta.

Abercromby, James (Lord Dunfermline). 1861. *Lieutenant-General Sir Ralph Abercromby, K. B., 1793–1801*. Edinburgh: Edmonston and Douglas.

Abrantès, Laure Junot, duchesse d'. 1967. *Mémoires complets et authentiques de Laure Junot duchesse d'Abrantès. Souvenirs historiques sur Napoléon, la Révolution, le Directoire, le Consulat, l'Empire, le Restauration, la Révolution de 1830 et les premières années du règne de Louis-Philippe*. 10 vols. Paris: J. Bonnot.

Abrantès, Laure Junot, duchesse d'. 1989. *At the Court of Napoleon: Memoirs of the Duchess d'Abrantès*. New York: Doubleday.

Ackroyd, Peter. 1995. *Blake*. London: Sinclair-Stevenson.

Acton, Harold. 1998. *The Bourbons of Naples*. London: Trafalgar Square.

Acúrsio das Neves, José. N.d. *História geral da invasão dos franceses em Portugal e da restauração deste reino*. 2 vols. Porto: Afrontamento.

Adalbert, Prinz von Bayern. 1957. *Max I, Joseph von Bayern, Pfalzgraf, Kurfürst und König*. Munich: Bruckmann.

Adams, Ephraim Douglass. 1904. *The Influence of Grenville on Pitt's Foreign Policy, 1787–1798*. Washington, DC: Carnegie Institution.

Adams, Henry. 1986. *History of the United States of America during the Administrations of Thomas Jefferson*. New York: Library of America.

Adams, John Quincy. 1847. *Life of General Lafayette*. New York: Nafis and Cornish.

Adams, Max. 2005. *Admiral Collingwood: Nelson's Own Hero*. London: Weidenfeld and Nicolson.

Addington, Larry H. 1994. *The Patterns of War since the Eighteenth Century*. Bloomington: Indiana University Press.

Adkin, Mark. 2001. *The Waterloo Companion: The Complete Guide to History's Most Famous Land Battle*. London: Aurum.

Adkin, Mark. 2005. *The Trafalgar Companion: The Complete Guide to History's Most Famous Sea Battle and the Life of Admiral Lord Nelson*. London: Aurum.

Adkins, Roy. 2004. *Trafalgar: The Biography of a Battle*. London: Little, Brown.

Afanas'ev, A. 1992. *1812–1814: Lichnaia perepiska Nikolaia Rayevskogo*. Moscow: Terra.

Aglamov, S. 1912. *Otechestvennaya voina 1812 goda: Istoricheskie materialy Leib-Gvardii Semyenovskogo polka*. Poltava, Ukraine: N.p.

Al Jabarti, Abd al-Rahman. 1994. *Abd al-Rahman al-Jabarti's History of Egypt*. 4 vols. Ed. Moshe Perlmann and Thomas Philipp. Stuttgart: Steiner.

Al Jabarti, 'Abd al-Rahman Jabarti. 2004. *Napoleon in Egypt: Al-Jabarti's Chronicle of the French Occupation, 1798*. Princeton: Wiener.

Alberti, Anibale, and Roberto Cessi, eds. 1928–1940. *Verbali delle sedute della municipalità provvisoria di Venezia*. Bologna: Zanichelli.

Albertini, Paul. 1966. *Pozzo di Borgo contre Napoleon*. Paris: Peyronnet.

Alberts, A. 1964. *Koning Willem II*. Den Haag: Kruseman.

Alder, Ken. 1997. *Engineering the Revolution: Arms and Enlightenment in France, 1763–1815*. Princeton: Princeton University Press.

Aldington, Richard. 1943. *The Duke*. New York: Viking.

Aldington, Richard. 1946. *Wellington*. London: Heinemann.

Aldridge, Alfred O. 1984. *Thomas Paine's American Ideology*. Newark: University of Delaware Press.

Aleksandrov, G. 1874. "Cherti iz zhizni S.A. Tuchkova." *Russkii Arkhiv*, no. 5.

Alekseyev, Vladimir. 1976. *Russkie i sovetskie moriaki na Sredizemnom more*. Moscow: Voeniszdat.

Alexander, Don W. 1985. *Rod of Iron: French Counterinsurgency Policy in Aragon during the Peninsular War*. Wilmington, DE: Scholarly Resources.

Alexander, John T. 1989. *Catherine the Great: Life and Legend*. Oxford: Oxford University Press.

Alexander, R. S. 2001. *Napoleon*. London: Arnold.

Alger, John Goldworth. 1904. *Napoleon's British Visitors and Captives, 1801–1815*. New York: Pott.

Alger, John I. 1975. *Antoine-Henri Jomini: A Bibliographical Survey*. West Point, NY: United States Military Academy.

Allen, James Smith. 1981. *Popular French Romanticism: Authors, Readers and Books in the Nineteenth Century*. Syracuse, NY: Syracuse University Press.

Allison, Robert J. 2000. *The Crescent Obscured: The United States and the Muslim World, 1776–1815*. Chicago: University of Chicago Press.

Alombert-Goget, Paul Claude. 1897. *Le corps d'armée aux orders du maréchal Mortier, combat du Dürrenstein*. Paris: Berger-Levrault.

Alombert-Goget, Paul Claude. 2002. *La campagne de 1805 en Allemagne*. 3 vols. Paris: Editions historiques Teissèdre.

Alombert-Goget, Paul Claude, and Jean Lambert Alphonse Colin. 1902. *La campagne de 1805 en Allemagne*. 4 vols. Paris: Librarie Militaire R. Chapelot.

Alsop, Susan. 1984. *The Congress Dances*. New York: Harper and Row.

Amo, Emilio. 1972. *Da Montenotte a Cherasco* [From Montenotte to Cherasco]. Fossano: Tec.

Anderson, M. S. 1966. *The Eastern Question, 1774–1923*. New York: St. Martin's.

Anderson, Troyer Steele. 1972. *The Command of the Howe Brothers during the American Revolution*. New York: Octagon.

Andersson, Ingvar. 1956. *A History of Sweden*. London: Weidenfeld and Nicolson.

Andress, David. 2005. *The Terror: Civil War in the French Revolution*. London: Little, Brown.

Angeli, Moritz Edler v. 1896–1898. *Erzherzog Carl von Österreich als Feldherr und Heeresorganisator* [Archduke Charles as a General and Army Reformer]. 5 vols. Vienna: K. u. K. Hof-universitäts-Buchhändler.

Anna, Timothy E. 1983. *Spain and the Loss of America*. Lincoln: University of Nebraska Press.

Ansari, A. A. 2001. *William Blake's Minor Prophecies*. Lewiston, NY: Mellen.

Anstey, Roger. 1975. *The Atlantic Slave Trade and British Abolition, 1760–1810*. London: Macmillan.

Antal, Sandy. 1997. *A Wampum Denied: Proctor's War of 1812*. East Lansing: Michigan State University Press.

Antelava, I. 1849. "Generali Iashvili v Otechestvennoi voine 1812 g." In *Trudi Sukhumskogo gos. ped. Instituta*. Sokhumi.

Antommarchi, Francesco. 1826. *The Last Days of Napoleon: Memoirs of the Last Two Years of Napoleon's Exile*. London: Colburn.

Appleyard, Rollo. 1962. *Pioneers of Electrical Communication*. Freeport, N.Y.: Books for Libraries.

Aretz, Gertrude Kuntze-Dolton. 1929. *Queen Louise of Prussia, 1776–1810*. Trans. Ruth Putnam. New York: Putnam's.

Arkhiv Rayevskikh. 1908–1915. 5 vols. St. Petersburg: Raevskago.

Arnold, Eric A. 1969. *Administrative Leadership in a Dictatorship: The Position of Joseph Fouché in the Napoleonic Police, 1800–1810*. New York: Arnold.

Arnold, Eric A. 1979. *Fouché, Napoleon, and the General Police*. Washington, DC: University Press of America.

Arnold, James A. 2005. *Marengo and Hohenlinden: Napoleon's Rise to Power*. London: Leo Cooper.

Arnold, James R. 1990. *Crisis on the Danube: Napoleon's Austrian Campaign of 1809*. New York: Paragon House.

Arnold, James R. 1995. *Napoleon Conquers Austria: The 1809 Campaign for Vienna*. Westport, CT: Praeger.

Arnold, James. 2005. *Marengo and Hohenlinden*. London: Leo Cooper.

Arthur, Charles B. 1986. *The Remaking of the English Navy by Admiral St. Vincent: The Great Unclaimed Naval Revolution (1795–1805)*. Lanham, MD: University Press of America.

Artom, Guido. 1970. *Napoleon Is Dead in Russia: The Extraordinary Story of One of History's Strangest Conspiracies*. Trans. Muriel Grindrod. New York: Atheneum.

Askenazy, Szymon. 1905. *Książę Józef Poniatowski 1763–1813*. Warsaw: Gebethner and Wolff.

Aspinall-Oglander, Cecil Faber. 1956. *Freshly Remembered: The Story of Thomas Graham, Lord Lynedoch*. London: Hogarth.

Asprey, Robert. 2001. *The Rise of Napoleon Bonaparte*. New York: Basic.

Assereto, Giovanni. 1975. *La Rupubblica Ligure. Lotte politiche e problemi finanziari*. Turin: Fondazione Luigi Einaudi.

Aston, Nigel. 2004. *The French Revolution, 1789–1804: Authority, Liberty and the Search for Stability*. Basingstoke, UK: Palgrave Macmillan.

Atteridge, Andrew Hillard. 1909. *Napoleon's Brothers*. London: Methuen; New York: Brentano's.

Atteridge, Andrew Hillard. 2001. *Marshal Murat: King of Naples*. Uckfield, East Sussex, UK: Naval and Military.

Atteridge, Andrew Hillard. 2005. *Marshal Ney: The Bravest of the Brave*. London: Cooper.

Aubry, J. T. 1889. *Souvenirs du 12e Chausseurs*. Paris: Maison Quantin.

Augoyat, Antoine Marie. 1840. *Rélation de la défence de Torgau par les troupes françaises en 1813*. Paris: Leneveu.

Augoyat, Antoine Marie. 1860–1864. *Aperçu historique sur les fortifications, les ingénieurs, et sur le corps du génie en France*. 3 vols. Paris: Dumaine.

Aulard, F. A., ed. 1889–1951. *Recueil des Actes du Comité de Salut Public*. Paris: Impr. nationale.

Aumale, Henri d'Orleans. 1872. *History of the Princes de Condé in the XVIth and XVIIth Centuries*. London: Bentley.

Austin, Paul Britten. 1995. *1812: Napoleon in Moscow*. London: Greenhill.

Austin, Paul Britten. 1996. *1812: The Great Retreat*. London: Greenhill.

Austin, Paul Britten. 2000. *1812: Napoleon's Invasion of Russia*. London: Greenhill.

Austin, Paul Britten. 2002. *1815: The Return of Napoleon*. London: Greenhill.

Austrian General Staff. 1904–1905. *Kriege gegen die französische Revolution*. Vol. 2, *Die Feldzuge von 1792*. Vienna: L. Seidel.

Austrian Kriegsarchiv, Abtheilung für Kriegsgeschichte. 1902–1905. *Krieg gegen die französische Revolution* [War against the French Revolution]. Vol. 1. Vienna: Seidel.

Austrian Kriegsarchiv, Abtheilung für Kriegsgeschichte. 1910. *Krieg 1809* [War 1809]. Vol. 1, *Regensburg*. Vienna: Seidel.

Auvray, Michel. 1983. *Objecteurs, insoumis, déserteurs: Histoire des réfractaires en France*. Paris: Stock.

Avout, Auguste, Baron Auguste-Richard d'. 1896. "La defense de Hamburg en 1813–1814." In *Mémoires de la Société bourguignonne de Géographie et d'Histoire*. Vol. 12. Dijon: Darantière.

Ayling, Stanley Edward. 1972. *George the Third*. New York: Knopf.

Azan, Paul, and Ernest Picard. 1907–1909. *Campagne de 1800 en Allemagne* [Campaign of 1800 in Germany]. Paris: Chapelot.

B

Bagration, Peter. 1945. *Sbornik dokumentov i materialov* [General Bagration: Compilation of Documents and Materials]. Ed. S. N. Golubov. Moscow: OGIZ.

Bagration, Peter. 1949. *Bagration v Dunaiskikh kniazhestvakh: Sbornik Dokumentov* [Bagration in the Danubian Principalities: Compilation of Documents]. Chi(ineu: Gos. izd. Moldavii.

Bailey, Anthony. 1997. *Standing in the Sun: A Life of J. M. W. Turner*. London: Sinclair-Stevenson.

Bailey, Brian J. 1998. *The Luddite Rebellion*. New York: New York University Press.

Bainbridge, Simon John Julian. 1995. *Napoleon and English Romanticism*. Cambridge: Cambridge University Press.

Baker, Keith M. 1975. *Condorcet: From Natural Philosophy to Social Mathematics*. Chicago: University of Chicago Press.

Baker, Keith M., Colin Lucas, François Furet, and Mona Ozouf, eds. 1987–1994. *The French Revolution and the Creation of Modern Political Culture*. 4 vols. New York: Pergamon.

Baker, Keith M., Colin Lucas, François Furet, and Mona Ozouf, eds. 1994. *The French Revolution and the Creation of Modern Political Culture*. Vol. 4, *The Terror*. New York: Pergamon.

Balazs, Eva. 1997. *Hungary and the Habsburgs 1765–1800*. Budapest: Central European University Press.

Balcombe, Betsy. 2005. *To Befriend an Emperor: Betsy Balcombe's Memoirs of Napoleon on St Helena*. Introduction by J. David Markham. Welwyn Garden City, UK: Ravenhall.

Bancalari, Gustav. 1882. *Feldmarschall Carl Philip Fürst Schwarzenberg*. Salzburg: Dieter.

Barbero, Alessandro. 2005. *The Definitive History of the Battle of Waterloo*. London: Atlantic Books.

Barbuto, Richard V. 2000. *Niagara, 1814: America Invades Canada*. Lawrence: University Press of Kansas.

Barclay, Charles Wright. 1924–1934. *History of the Barclay Family with Full Pedigree from 1066 to 1933*. London: St. Catherine.

Barclay, Robert. 1812. *Genealogical Account of the Barclays of Urie*. London: Herbert.

Barclay de Tolly, Mikhail. 1912. *Izobrazhenie voennikh deistvii 1812 g.* St. Petersburg.

Barnes, Donald G. 1939. *George III and William Pitt, 1783–1806*. Stanford, CA: Stanford University Press.

Barnett, Corelli. 1978. *Bonaparte*. London: Allen and Unwin.

Barras, Paul. 1895–1896. *Memoirs of Barras, Member of the Directorate*. Ed. George Duruy. 4 vols. New York: Harper and Brothers.

Barrister of the Inner Temple, A. 1999. *Code Napoleon, or The French Civil Code*. Washington, DC: Beard. (Orig. pub. 1804.)

Barteau, H. C. 1996. *Historical Dictionary of Luxembourg*. London: Scarecrow.

Barthorp, Michael. 1990. *Wellington's Generals*. Oxford: Osprey.

Barthorp, Michael. 1992. *Napoleon's Egyptian Campaigns, 1798–1801*. London: Osprey.

Bartlett, C. J. 1966. *Castlereagh*. London: Macmillan.

Bartlett, Thomas, ed. 2003. *1798: A Bicentenary Perspective*. Dublin: Four Courts.

Barton, H. Arnold. 2003. *Sweden and Visions of Norway: Politics and Culture 1814–1905*. Carbondale: Southern Illinois University Press.

Bassford, Christopher. 1994. *Clausewitz in English: The Reception of Clausewitz in Britain and America 1815–1945*. Oxford: Oxford University Press.

Bate, Walter Jackson. 1967. *John Keats*. London: Oxford University Press.

Bates, Jennifer Ann. 2004. *Hegel's Theory of Imagination*. Albany: State University of New York Press.

Bath, B. H. Slicher van. 1963. *The Agrarian History of Western Europe, 500–1850*. London: Arnold.

Baticle, Jeannine. 1999. *Goya: Painter of Terror and Splendour*. London: Thames and Hudson.

Batiza, Rodolfo. 1973. *Domat, Pothier, and the Code Napoleon: Some Observations Concerning the Actual Sources of the French Civil Code*. N.p.: N.p.

Baye, Joseph. 1912. *Smolensk; les origines, l'épopée de Smolensk en 1812; d'après des documents inédits*. Paris: Perrin.

Bear, Joan. 1972. *Caroline Murat: A Biography*. London: Collins.

Beatson, F. C. 1995. *Wellington: Crossing the Gaves and the Battle of Orthez*. London: Donovan.

Beatson, F. C. 1995. *Wellington: The Bidassoa and the Nivelle*. London: Donovan.

Beau, André. 1998. *Talleyrand: L'apogée du sphinx: La Monarchie de Juillet*. Paris: Royer.

Beaucour, Fernand, Yves Laissus, and Chantal Orgogozo. 1990. *The Discovery of Egypt: Artists, Travelers and Scientists*. Trans. Bambi Ballard. Paris: Flammarion.

Beauharnais, Eugène Rose de. 1858–1860. *Mémoires et correspondance politique et militaire du prince Eugène*. Ed. Albert Du Casse. 10 vols. Paris: Michel Levy frères.

Becke, A. F. 1914. *Napoleon and Waterloo*. Vol. 2. London: Kegan Paul, Trench, Trubner.

Becke, A. F. 1966. *Napoleon and Waterloo: The Emperor's Campaign with the Armée du Nord*. Philadelphia: University of Pennsylvania Press.

Beer, Adolf. 1877. *Die Finanzen Osterreichs im XIX Jahrhundert* [Austria's Finances in the Nineteenth Century]. Prague: Tempsky.

Begunova, A. 1992. *Sabli ostri, koni bistri . . . Iz istorii russkoi kavalerii*. Moscow: Molodaia gvardiia.

Behrens, C. B. A. 1967. *The Ancien Regime*. New York: Harcourt, Brace.

Belloc, Hilaire. 1912. *Tourcoing*. London: Swift.

Belloc, Hilaire. 1926. *Napoleon's Campaign of 1812 and the Retreat from Moscow*. New York: Harper.

Belmas, Jacques. 1836–1837. *Journaux des sièges faites ou soutenus par les français dans la Peninsule de 1807 à 1814*. 4 vols. Paris: Didot Frères.

Bemis, Samuel. 1936. *A Diplomatic History of the United States*. Holt: New York.

Benckendorff, Alexander. N.d. *The Liberation of the Netherlands (November–December 1813): From Memoirs of Alexander Benckendorf*. Trans. and ed. A. Mikaberidze. Napoleon Series Web site. http://www.napoleon-series.org/research/c_russianarchives.html.

Benn, Carl. 2002. *The War of 1812*. Oxford: Osprey.

Bennett, Geoffrey. 2002. *Nelson the Commander*. London: Penguin.

Bennett, Geoffrey. 2004. *The Battle of Trafalgar*. Barnsley, UK: Wharncliffe.

Bennigsen, Levin. 1907. *Mémoires du général Bennigsen, avec une introduction, des annexes et des notes de E. Cazalas*. Paris: Charles-Lavauzelle.

Benot, Yves. 2004. *La révolution française et la fin des colonies*. Paris: Découverte.

Bentley, G. E. 2001. *The Stranger from Paradise: A Biography of William Blake*. New Haven: Yale University Press.

Berckman, Evelyn. 1962. *Nelson's Dear Lord: A Portrait of St. Vincent*. London: Macmillan.

Berdahl, Robert M. 1988. *The Politics of the Prussian Nobility: The Development of a Conservative Ideology, 1770–1848*. Princeton: Princeton University Press.

Beretti, Francis. 1988. *Pascal Paoli et l'image de la Corse au dix-huitième siècle.* Oxford: Voltaire Foundation at the Taylor Institution.

Bergeron, Louis. 1981. *France under Napoleon.* Trans. R. R. Palmer. Princeton: Princeton University Press.

Berghahn, Klaus L. 1992. "*Gedankenfreiheit.* From Political Reform to Aesthetic Revolution in Schiller's Works." In *The Internalized Revolution: German Reactions to the French Revolution, 1789–1989,* ed. Ehrhardt Bahr and Thomas P. Saine, 99–118. New York: Garland.

Bernard, Giles, and Gérard Lachaux. 2005. *Waterloo.* Paris: Histoire and Collections.

Bernard, H. 1969. *Education and the French Revolution.* Cambridge: Cambridge University Press.

Bernard, Jack F. 1973. *Talleyrand: A Biography.* New York: Putnam.

Bernède, Allain. 1994. *Aux avant-postes de Charleroi: Fleurus, 1794.* Le Mans: Cénomane.

Bernier, Oliver. 1983. *Lafayette: Hero of Two Worlds.* New York: Dutton.

Bertaud, Jean-Paul. 1970. *Valmy: La Démocratie en armes.* Paris: Julliard.

Bertaud, Jean-Paul. 1988. *The Army of the French Revolution: From Citizen-Soldiers to Instrument of Power.* Trans. R. R. Palmer. Princeton: Princeton University Press.

Bertaud, Jean-Paul. 2001. *Le duc d'Enghien.* Paris: Fayard.

Berthier, Alexandre. 1827. *Campagne d'Egypte. 1re partie, Mémoires du maréchal Berthier.* Paris: Baudoin.

Bertier de Sauvigny, Guillaume de. 1966. *The Bourbon Restoration.* Trans. Lynn M. Case. Philadelphia: University of Pennsylvania Press.

Bertrand, Pierre, ed. 1890. *Projet de mariage de Napoléon Ier avec la grande-duchesse Anne de Russie: Correspondance secrète et inédite de Champagny et de Caulaincourt.* Paris: N.p.

Beskrovny, L., ed. 1954. *M. I. Kutusov: Sbornik Dokumentov.* Vol. 2. Moscow: Voennoe izd-vo.

Beskrovny, L. 1974. *Russkoe voennoe iskusstvo XIX v.* Moscow: Nauk.

Beskrovny, L. 1996. *The Russian Army and Fleet in the Nineteenth Century.* Gulf Breeze, FL: Academic International.

Besson, André. 2002. *Malet: l'homme qui fit trembler Napoléon.* Paris: France-Empire.

Best, Geoffrey. 1982. *War and Society in Revolutionary Europe, 1770–1870.* New York: St. Martin's.

Best, Nicholas. 2005. *Trafalgar: The Untold Story of the Greatest Sea Battle in* History. London: Weidenfeld and Nicolson.

Bestuzhev, N. A. 1961. *Opyt istorii rosiiskogo flota.* Leningrad: Gos. soiuznoe izd-vo sudostroit. Promyshl.

Bezotosny, V. 1999. *Donskoi generalitet i ataman Platov v 1812 g.* Moscow: Rosspen.

Bezotosny, V. 2000. *Russkaia armia, 1812–1814.* Moscow: Vlados.

Bibl, Viktor. 1938. *Kaiser Franz.* Vienna: Gunther.

Bibl, Viktor. 1942. *Erzherzog Karl: Der Bharrliche Kämpfer für Deutschlands Ehre.* Vienna: Gunther.

Bienvenue, Richard. 1970. *The Ninth of Thermidor.* Oxford: Oxford University Press.

Bieri, James. 2004. *Percy Bysshe Shelley, A Biography: Youth's Unextinguished Fire, 1792–1816.* Newark: University of Delaware Press.

Bieri, James. 2005. *Percy Bysshe Shelley, A Biography: Exile of Unfulfilled Renown, 1816–1822.* Newark: University of Delaware Press.

Bierman, Irene A., ed. 2003. *Napoleon in Egypt.* Portland, OR: Ithaca Press.

Billard, Max. 1910. *The Marriage Ventures of Marie Louise.* Trans. Evelyn, Duchess of Wellington. London: Nash.

Billinger, Robert D. 1991. *Metternich and the German Question: States' Rights and Federal Duties, 1820–1834.* Newark: University of Delaware Press.

Biot, H. F. 1901. *Souvenirs anecdotique et militaries.* Paris: Henri Vivien.

Birkett, Jennifer, and James Kearns. 1997. *A Guide to French Literature: From Early Modern to Postmodern.* Basingstoke, UK: Macmillan.

Bishop, Lloyd. 1989. *Romantic Irony in French Literature from Diderot to Beckett.* Nashville, TN: Vanderbilt University Press.

Black, Jeremy. 1998. *Britain as a Military Power, 1688–1815.* London: Routledge.

Black, Jeremy. 2001. *Western Warfare, 1775–1882.* Bloomington: Indiana University Press.

Black, Jeremy. 2002. *European International Relations, 1648–1815.* New York: Palgrave.

Black, Jeremy, and Philip Woodfine, eds. 1988. *The British Navy and the Use of Naval Power in the Eighteenth Century.* Atlantic Highlands, NJ: Humanities.

Blackbourn, David. 2002. *History of Germany, 1780–1918: The Long Nineteenth Century.* Oxford: Blackwell.

Blackburn, Julia. 1993. *The Emperor's Last Island: A Journey to St. Helena.* New York: Vintage.

Blackburn, Robin. 1988. *The Overthrow of Colonial Slavery, 1776–1848.* London: Verso.

Blackmore, Howard L. 1994. *British Military Firearms, 1650–1850.* London: Greenhill.

Blake, Nicholas. 2005. *Steering to Glory: A Day in the Life of a Ship of the Line.* London: Chatham.

Blake, Nicholas, and Richard Lawrence. 2003. *The Illustrated Companion to Nelson's Navy.* London: Chatham.

Blanc, Olivier. 1995. *Les espions de la Revolution et de l'Empire.* Paris: Perrin.

Blanco, Richard L. 1974. "The Development of British Military Medicine, 1793–1814." *Military Affairs* 38 (Feb.): 4–10.

Blanco, Richard L. 1974. *Wellington's Surgeon General, Sir James McGrigor.* Durham, NC: Duke University Press.

Blanning, T. C. W. 1974. *Reform and Revolution in Mainz, 1743–1803.* New York: Cambridge University Press.

Blanning, T. C. W. 1980. "German Jacobins and the French Revolution." *Historical Journal* 23: 985–1002.

Blanning, T. C. W. 1983. *The French Revolution in Germany: Occupation and Resistance in the Rhineland, 1792–1802.* Oxford: Clarendon.

Blanning, T. C. W. 1987. *The Origins of the French Revolutionary Wars.* London: Longman.

Blanning, T. C. W. 1996. *French Revolutionary Wars, 1787–1802.* London: Arnold.

Blocqueville, Adélaïde-Louise. 1879–1880. *Le maréchal Davout prince d'Eckmühl: Raconté par les siens et par lui-même.* 4 vols. Paris: Didier.

Bluhm, Raymond K. 2005. *U.S. Army: A Complete History.* Westport, CT: Hugh Lauter Levin Associates.

Blumenthal, Henry. 1970. *France and the United States: Their Diplomatic Relations, 1789–1914.* Chapel Hill: University of North Carolina Press.

Blythe, LeGette. 1937. *Marshal Ney: A Dual Life.* New York: Stackpole.

Bodart, Gaston. 1916. *Losses of Life in Modern Wars: Austria-Hungary, France.* Oxford: Clarendon.

Bogdanov, L. 1979. *Russkaia armia v 1812 g.* Moscow: Voennoe izd-vo Ministerstva oborony.

Boime, Albert. 1987. *A Social History of Modern Art.* Vol. 1, *Art in an Age of Revolution 1750–1800.* Chicago: University of Chicago Press.

Bonaparte, Joseph. 1854. *Mémoires.* Vols. 8 and 9. Paris: Perrotin.

Bond, Gordon C. 1979. *The Grand Expedition: The British Invasion of Holland in 1809.* Athens: University of Georgia Press.

Bonnal, Henri. 1905. *Le manœvre de Vilna.* Paris.

Bonnal, Henri. 1910. *La vie militaire du maréchal Ney: duc d'Elchingen, prince de la Moskowa.* 3 vols. Paris: Librairie Militaire R. Chapelot.

Bonnal, M. E. 1881. *Histoire de Desaix: Armées du Rhin, expédition d'Orient, Marengo; D'après les archives du dépôt de la guerre.* Paris: Dentu.

Bonnet, Jean-Claude. 2004. *L'Empire des muses: Napoléon, les arts et les lettres.* Paris: Belin.

Borel, Jean. 1929. *Gênes sous Napoléon.* Paris: Attinger.

Borisevich, A. 1912. *General ot kavalerii N. N. Rayevsky.* St. Petersburg: Raevskago.

Borneman, Walter. 2004. *1812: The War That Forged a Nation.* London: HarperCollins.

Borodkin, Mikhail. 1909. *Istoriia Finliandii: Vremia Imperatora Aleksandra I* [History of Finland: The Reign of Emperor Alexander I]. St. Petersburg: Gosudarstvennaia tipografiia.

Bosher, J. F. 1988. *The French Revolution.* New York: Norton.

Boston Consulting Group. 2001. *Clausewitz on Strategy: Inspiration and Insight from a Master Strategist.* London: Wiley.

Both, Carl von. 1807. *Relation de la bataille de Friedland le 14 juin 1807.* Berlin: Schropp.

Botzenhart, Erich. 1931–1937. *Freiherr vom Stein: Briefwechsel, Denkschriften und Aufzeichnungen.* Berlin: Heymann.

Boulay de la Meurthe, Alfred. 1920. *Histoire de la negociation du concordat de 1801.* Tours: Mame.

Boulger, Demetrius Charles. 1915. *The Belgians at Waterloo.* New York: Scribner.

Bouloiseau, Marc. 1968. *Le Comité de Salut Public.* Paris: Presses universitaires de France.

Bourgogne, Sergeant A. J. 1996. *Memoirs of Sergeant Bourgogne.* London: Constable.

Bourrienne, L. A. F. de. 1903. *Memoirs of Napoleon Bonaparte.* London: Hutchinson.

Bouzet, Eugène du, ed. 1862. *Mémoires de l'amiral Tchitchagoff.* Leipzig: Franck.

Bowden, Scott. 1983. *Armies at Waterloo.* Arlington, TX: Empire Games.

Bowden, Scott. 1990. *Napoleon's Grande Armée of 1813.* Chicago: Emperor's Press.

Bowden, Scott. 1997. *Napoleon and Austerlitz.* Chicago: Emperor's.

Boyce, Myrna M. 1918. "The Diplomatic Relations of England with the Quadruple Alliance 1815–1830." *University of Iowa Studies in the Social Sciences* 7: no. 1. Iowa City: University of Iowa.

Boycott-Brown, Martin. 2002. *The Road to Rivoli: Napoleon's First Campaign.* London: Weidenfeld and Nicolson.

Boyden, Peter B., ed. 2000. *Ashes and Blood: The British Army in South Africa, 1795–1914.* Staplehurst, UK: Spellmount.

Boyle, Nicholas. 1991–2000. *Goethe: The Poet and the Age.* 2 vols. New York: Oxford University Press.

Bradford, Ernle. 1999. *Nelson: The Essential Hero.* London: Macmillan.

Bragin, Mikhail. 1944. *Field Marshal Kutuzov: A Short Biography.* Moscow: Foreign Language.

Brandes, Georg. 1960. *Revolution and Reaction in Nineteenth-Century French Literature.* New York: Russell.

Brandt, Heinrich von. 1999. *In the Legions of Napoleon: The Memoirs of a Polish Officer in Spain and Russia, 1808–1813.* London: Greenhill.

Braudel, Ferdinand. 1979. *The Wheels of Commerce: Civilization and Capitalism, 15th–18th Century.* New York: Harper and Row.

Breazeale, Daniel, and Tom Rockmore, eds. 1994. *Fichte: Historical Contexts/Contemporary Controversies.* New York: Prometheus.

Breen, Jennifer, ed. 1966. *The French Romantics.* New York: Russell.

Breen, Jennifer, ed. 1992. *Women Romantic Poets, 1785–1832: An Anthology.* Rutland, VT: Tuttle.

Breen, Jennifer. 1996. *Women Romantics, 1785–1832: Writing in Prose.* London: Orion.

Brégeon, Jean-Joël. 2002. *Kléber.* Paris: Perrin.

Bressonnet, Pascal. 1909. *Etudes tactiques sur la campagne de 1806.* Paris: Chapelot.

Brett-James, Antony. 1959. *General Graham, Lord Lynedoch.* London: Macmillan.

Brett-James, Antony. 1964. *The Hundred Days.* London: Macmillan.

Brett-James, Antony. 1966. *1812: Eyewitness Accounts of Napoleon's Defeat in Russia.* New York: Harper.

Brett-James, Antony. 1995. *Life in Wellington's Army.* London: Donovan.

Breunig, Charles. 1977. *The Age of Revolution and Reaction, 1789–1850.* New York: Norton.

Brewer, John. 1990. *Sinews of Power: War, Money and the English State, 1688–1783.* Cambridge, MA: Harvard University Press.

Brice, Leon. 1907. *Le corps de santé militaire en france: sa evolution, ses campagnes, 1708–1882.* Paris: Berger-Levrault.

Brindle, Rosemary, trans. and ed. 2002. *Guns in the Desert: General Jean-Pierre Doguereau's Journal of Napoleon's Egyptian Expedition.* Westport, CT: Praeger.

Britt, Albert Sidney, III. 1985. *The Wars of Napoleon.* Wayne, NJ: Avery.

Brnardic, Vladimir. 2004. *Napoleon's Balkan Troops.* Oxford: Osprey.

Brock, Michael. 1973. *The Great Reform Act.* London: Hutchinson.

Brock, W. R. 1941. *Lord Liverpool and Liberal Toryism.* Cambridge: Cambridge University Press.

Brockliss, Laurence. 2005. *Nelson's Surgeon: William Beatty, Naval Medicine, and the Battle of Trafalgar.* Oxford: Oxford University Press.

Broers, Michael. 1996. *Europe under Napoleon, 1799–1815*. London: Arnold.

Broers, Michael. 1997. *Napoleonic Imperialism and the Savoyard Monarchy, 1773–1821: State Building in Piedmont*. Lampeter, UK: Mellen.

Broers, Michael. 2002. *The Politics of Religion in Napoleonic Italy: The War against God, 1801–1814*. London: Routledge.

Broers, Michael. 2005. *The Napoleonic Empire in Italy, 1796–1814: Cultural Imperialism in a European Context?* New York: Palgrave Macmillan.

Broglie, Albert duc de. 1893. *Concordat*. Paris: Levy.

Bronowski, J. 1972. *William Blake and the Age of Revolution*. London: Routledge and Kegan Paul.

Brooke, John. 1972. *King George III*. New York: McGraw-Hill.

Brookner, Anita. 1980. *Jacques-Louis David*. New York: Thames and Hudson.

Brooks, Richard. 2002. *The Royal Marines: A History*. London: Constable and Robinson.

Brose, Eric Dorn. 1997. *German History, 1789–1871: From the Holy Roman Empire to the Bismarckian Reich*. Providence, RI: Bergham.

Brown, Anne S. K., and Howard C. Rice, eds. and trans. 1972. *The American Campaigns of Rochambeau's Army 1780, 1781, 1782, 1783*. Vol. 1. Princeton: Princeton University Press; Providence, RI: Brown University Press.

Brown, Gordon S. 2005. *Toussaint's Clause: The Founding Fathers and the Haitian Revolution*. Jackson: University Press of Mississippi.

Brown, H. G. 1997. "From Organic Society to Security State: The War on Brigandage in France, 1797–1802." *Journal of Modern History* 69: 661–695.

Brown, Howard G. 1995. *War, Revolution and the Bureaucratic State: Politics and Army Administration in France, 1791–1799*. Oxford: Clarendon.

Brown, Julia Prewitt. 1979. *Jane Austen's Novels: Social Change and Literary Form*. Cambridge, MA: Harvard University Press.

Brown, Michael, Patrick M. Geoghegan, and James Kelly, eds. 2003. *The Irish Act of Union 1800: Bicentennial Essays*. Dublin: Irish Academic.

Brown, Richard. 2000. *Revolution, Radicalism, and Reform: England, 1780–1846*. Cambridge: Cambridge University Press.

Brown, Wilburt. 1969. *The Amphibious Campaign for West Florida and Louisiana, 1814–1815: A Critical Review of Strategy and Tactics at New Orleans*. University, AL: University of Alabama Press.

Browne-Olf, Lillian. 1970. *Their Name Is Pius: Portraits of Five Great Popes*. Freeport, NY: Books for Libraries.

Browning, Oscar, ed. 1889. *England and Napoleon in 1803: Being the Despatches of Lord Whitworth and Others*. London: Longmans.

Bruce, Evangeline. 1996. *Napoleon and Josephine: An Improbable Marriage*. London: Weidenfeld and Nicolson.

Bruijn, J. R., and C. B. Wels. 2003. *Met man en macht, de militaire geschiedenis van Nederland 1550–2000*. Amsterdam: Balans.

Bryant, Arthur. 1942. *The Years of Endurance, 1793–1802*. New York: Harper.

Bryant, Arthur. 1945. *The Years of Victory, 1802–1812*. New York: Harper.

Bryant, Arthur. 1950. *The Age of Elegance, 1812–1822*. London: Collins.

Bucholz, Arden. 1991. *Moltke, Schlieffen, and Prussian War Planning*. New York: Berg.

Buckland, C. S. 1932. *Metternich and the British Government*. London: Macmillan.

Buckley, Roger Norman. 1998. *The British Army in the West Indies: Society and the Military in the Revolutionary Age*. Gainesville: University of Florida Press.

Bukhari, Emir. 1977. *Napoleon's Line Chasseurs*. London: Osprey.

Bukhari, Emir. 1978. *Napoleon's Guard Cavalry*. London: Osprey.

Bukhari, Emir. 1978. *Napoleon's Hussars*. London: Osprey.

Bukhari, Emir. 1992. *Napoleon's Dragoons and Lancers*. London: Osprey.

Bukhari, Emir. 1994. *Napoleon's Cuirassiers and Carabiniers*. London: Osprey.

Bullocke, John Greville. 1938. *Sailors' Rebellion: A Century of Naval Mutinies*. London: Eyre and Spottiswood.

Burke, Edmund. 1999. *Reflections on the Revolution in France*. Oxford: Oxford University Press. (Orig. pub. 1790.)

Burkhardt, Richard W, Jr. 1977. *The Spirit of System: Lamarck and Evolutionary Biology*. Cambridge, MA: Harvard University Press.

Burkholder, Mark A., and Lyman L. Johnson. 2001. *Colonial Latin America*. 4th ed. Oxford: Oxford University Press.

Burne, A. H. 1949. *The Noble Duke of York: The Military Life of Frederick, Duke of York and Albany*. New York: Staples.

Burton, R. G. 2003. *From Boulogne to Austerlitz*. Cambridge: Trotman. (Orig. pub. 1912.)

Bushnell, David, and Neil Macaulay. 1994. *The Emergence of Latin America in the Nineteenth Century*. 2nd ed. Oxford: Oxford University Press.

Busse, Winfried, and Jürgen Trabant. 1986. *Les Idéologues*. Amsterdam: Benjamins.

Butler, Iris. 1973. *Eldest Brother: The Marquess Wellesley, the Duke of Wellington's Eldest Brother*. London: Hodder and Stoughton.

Butlin, Martin, and Evelyn Joll. 1977. *The Paintings of J. M. W. Turner*. New Haven: Yale University Press.

Butterfield, Herbert. 1929. *The Peace Tactics of Napoleon, 1806–1808*. Cambridge: Cambridge University Press.

Butterfield, Herbert. 1961. *Charles James Fox and Napoleon*. London: Athlone.

Buturlin, Dmitri. 1838. *Istoriya nashestviya Imperatora Napoleona na Rossiyu v 1812 godu*. St. Petersburg: Pechat. v voen. tip.

Byrne, Paula. 2005. *Perdita: The Literary, Theatrical, Scandalous Life of Mary Robinson*. London: Random House.

Byron, Lord. 1973–1982, 1995. *Byron's Letters and Journals*. 13 vols. Ed. Leslie A. Marchand. London: John Murray.

Byron, Lord. 1986. *Byron: A Critical Edition of the Major Works*. Ed. Jerome J. McGann. Oxford: Oxford University Press.

C

Cable, James. 1998. *The Political Influence of Naval Force in History*. New York: St. Martin's.

Cadbury, Deborah. 2002. *The Lost King of France*. New York: St. Martin's.

Caird, Edward. 1881. *Hegel*. Philadelphia: Lippincott.

Callahan, William J. 1984. *Church, Politics, and Society in Spain, 1750–1874*. Cambridge, MA: Harvard University Press.

Callo, Joseph F. 2001. *Nelson Speaks: Admiral Lord Nelson in His Own Words*. London: Chatham.

Calvert, Michael, with Peter Young. 1979. *A Dictionary of Battles: 1715–1815*. New York: Mayflower.

Campbell, Sir Neil. 2004. *Napoleon on Elba: Diary of an Eyewitness to Exile*. Welwyn Garden City, UK: Ravenhall.

Campredon, Jacques. 1889. *La Defense du Var et le passage des Alpes 1800*. Paris: Charles Auriol.

Cannadine, David. 2005. *Admiral Lord Nelson: Context and Legacy*. London: Palgrave Macmillan.

Cannadine, David, ed. 2006. *Trafalgar in History: A Battle and Its Afterlife*. New York: Palgrave Macmillan.

Canney, Donald L. 2001. *Sailing Warships of the U.S. Navy*. London: Chatham.

Cantlie, Sir Neil. 1974. *A History of the Army Medical Department*. London: Longmans.

Caravale, Mario, and Alberto Caracciolo. 1978. *Lo Stato Pontificio da Martino V a Pio IX*. Torino: UTET.

Cardoza, Thomas. 2001. "Stepchildren of the State: Educating *Enfants de Troupe* in the French Army." *Paedegogica Historica* 37, no. 3: 551–568.

Cardoza, Thomas. 2002. "Exceeding the Needs of the Service: The French Army and the Suppression of Female Auxiliaries, 1871–1906." *War and Society* 20, no. 1: 1–22.

Cardoza, Thomas. 2002. "These Unfortunate Children: Sons and Daughters of the Regiment in Revolutionary and Napoleonic France." In *Children and War: A Historical Anthology*, ed. James Marten, 205–215. New York: New York University Press.

Cardwell, Donald. 1994. *The Norton History of Technology*. New York and London: Norton.

Carnall, Geoffrey. 1960. *Robert Southey and His Age: The Development of a Conservative Mind*. Oxford: Clarendon Press.

Carnot, Hippolyte. 1861–1864. *Mémoires sur Carnot par son fils*. 2 vols. Paris: Education de la jeunesse.

Carpenter, Kirsty, and Philip Mansel, eds. 1999. *The French Emigrés in Europe and the Struggle against the Revolution, 1789–1814*. Basingstoke, UK: Macmillan.

Carpenter, Scott. 1996. *Acts of Fiction: Resistance and Resolution from Sade to Baudelaire*. University Park: Pennsylvania State University Press.

Carr, Raymond. 1945. "Gustavus IV and the British Government, 1804–09." *English Historical Review* 60, no. 1: 36–66.

Carrington, Dorothy. 1990. *Napoleon and His Parents on the Threshold of History*. New York: Dutton.

Carsten, F. L. 1959. *Princes and Parliaments in Germany*. Oxford: Oxford University Press.

Carsten, F. L. 1989. *A History of the Prussian Junkers*. Brookfield, VT: Gower.

Caruana, Adrian B. 1997. *The History of English Sea Ordnance, 1523–1875*. Vol. 2, *The Age of the System, 1715–1815*. Ashley Lodge, UK: Boudriot.

Casaglia, Gherardo. 1998. *Le Partage du Monde: Napoleon et Alexandre à Tilsit, 25 juin 1807*. Paris: S.P.M.

Casanova, Antoine, and Ange Rovère. 1989. *La Révolution française en Corse, 1789–1800*. Toulouse: Privat.

Cassin-Scott, Jack. 1976. *Scandinavian Armies in the Napoleonic Wars*. London: Osprey.

Cassirer, Ernst. 1983. *Kant's Life and Thought*. New Haven: Yale University Press.

Castelot, André. 1960. *Napoleon II, King of Rome: A Biography of Napoleon's Tragic Son*. New York: Harper.

Castelot, André. 1967. *Josephine*. New York: Harper and Row.

Castle, Ian. 1998. *Aspern and Wagram, 1809: Mighty Clash of Empires*. Oxford: Osprey.

Castle, Ian. 1998. *Eggmühl 1809: Storm over Bavaria*. Oxford: Osprey.

Castle, Ian. 2002. *Austerlitz 1805: The Fate of Empires*. Oxford: Osprey.

Castle, Ian. 2002. "The Rise of 'the Unfortunate Mack.'" *Osprey Military Journal* 4, no. 2: 3–6.

Castle, Ian. 2005. *Austerlitz: Napoleon and the Eagles of Empire*. London: Leo Cooper.

Castlereagh, Robert Stewart, Viscount. 1848–1853. *Memoirs and Correspondence of Viscount Castlereagh, Second Marquess of Londonderry*. Ed. his brother, Charles Vane. 12 vols. London: Colburn.

Castries, duc de. 1979. *The Lives of the Kings and Queens of France*. New York: Knopf.

Cate, Curtis. 1985. *The War of Two Emperors: The Duel between Napoleon and Alexander: Russia 1812*. New York: Random House.

Caulaincourt, Armand-Augustine-Louis de, duc de Vicence. 1933. *Mémoires du général de Caulaincourt, duc de Vicence, grand écuyer de l'empereur*. Paris: Plon.

Caulaincourt, Armand-Augustin-Louis de, duc de Vicence. 1935. *With Napoleon in Russia: The Memoirs of General de Caulaincourt, Duke of Vincenza*. Ed. George Libaire. New York: Grosset and Dunlap.

Caulaincourt, General Armand-Augustin-Louisde, duc de Vicence. 1936. *Memoirs*. From the original edition by Jean Hanoteau (ed. George Libaire). New York: Morrow.

Cauna, Jacques de, ed. 2004. *Toussaint Louverture et l'indépendance d'Haïti: Témoignages pour un bicentenaire*. Paris: Karthala; Saint-Denis: Société française d'histoire d'outre-mer.

Cazamian, Louis. 1959. *A History of French Literature*. London: Oxford University Press.

Center for Louisiana Studies. 1995–2003. *The Louisiana Purchase Bicentennial Series in Louisiana History*. Lafayette: University of Southwestern Louisiana Press.

Cerami, Charles A. 2003. *Jefferson's Great Gamble: The Remarkable Story of Jefferson, Napoleon, and the Men Behind the Louisiana Purchase*. Naperville, IL: Sourcebooks.

Cetre, F. O. 1991. "Beresford and the Portuguese Army, 1809–1814." In *New Lights on the Peninsular War*, ed. Alice Berkeley, 149–155. Lisbon: British Historical Society of Portugal.

Chalfont, Lord, ed. 1979. *Waterloo: Battle of Three Armies*. London: Sedgwick and Jackson.

Chamberlain, Paul. 1991. "Marching into Captivity: Prisoners of War during the Peninsular Campaign, 1808–1814." In *New Lights on the Peninsular War: International Congress on the Iberian Peninsula, Selected Papers 1780–1840*, ed. Alice D. Berkeley, 221–229. Almada, Portugal: British Historical Society of Portugal.

Championnet, Jean-Etienne. 1904. *Souvenirs du général Championnet (1792–1800)*. Paris: Flammarion.

Chandler, David G. 1981. *Waterloo: The Hundred Days*. New York: Macmillan.

Chandler, David G. 1990. *Austerlitz 1805: Battle of the Three Emperors*. Oxford: Osprey.

Chandler, David G. 1993. *Jena 1806: Napoleon Destroys Prussia.* London: Osprey.

Chandler, David G. 1994. "Column versus Line: The Case of Maida, 1806." In *On the Napoleonic Wars: Collected Essays,* 130–144. London: Greenhill.

Chandler, David G. 1994. *On the Napoleonic Wars: Collected Essays.* London: Greenhill.

Chandler, David G. 1995. *The Campaigns of Napoleon.* London: Weidenfeld and Nicolson. (Orig. pub. 1966.)

Chandler, David G. 1999. *Dictionary of the Napoleonic Wars.* Ware, UK: Wordsworth.

Chandler, David G. 2001. *Napoleon.* London: Pen and Sword.

Chandler, David G. 2002. *The Military Maxims of Napoleon.* London: Greenhill.

Chandler, David G., ed. 1987. *Napoleon's Marshals.* London: Macmillan.

Chapell, Michael. 2004. *Wellington's Peninsula Regiments.* Vol. 2, *The Light Infantry.* Oxford: Osprey.

Chaplin, Arnold. 1919. *A St. Helena Who's Who, or a Directory of the Island During the Captivity of Napoleon.* London: Humphrey's.

Chaplin, Arnold. 2002. *Napoleon's Captivity on St Helena, 1815–1821.* London: Savannah.

Chapman, Tim.1998. *The Congress of Vienna: Origins, Process and Results.* London, New York: Routledge.

Chappell, Mike. 2000. *The King's German Legion.* Vol. 1, *1803–1812.* Oxford: Osprey.

Chappell, Mike. 2000. *The King's German Legion.* Vol. 2, *1812–1816.* Oxford: Osprey.

Chappell, Mike. 2003. *Wellington's Peninsula Regiments.* Vol. 1, *The Irish.* Oxford: Osprey.

Chappell, Mike. 2004. *Wellington's Peninsula Regiments.* Vol. 2, *The Light Infantry.* Oxford: Osprey.

Chapuisat, Edouard. 1908. *Le commerce et l'industrie à Genève pendant la domination française, 1798–1813.* Geneva, Paris: Julien.

Charles, Archduke. 1814. *Grundsätze der höheren Kriegskunst.* 2 vols. Vienna: Strauss. Volume 2 translated by George Nafziger as *Archduke Charles's 1796 Campaign in Germany* (West Chester, OH: Self-published).

Charles, Archduke. 1816. *Grundsätze der Strategie erlautert durch die Darstellung des Feldzuges in Deutschland 1796* [Principles of Strategy Explained by a Description of the 1796 Campaign in Germany]. Vienna: Strauss.

Charles, Archduke. 1893. *Geschichte des Feldzuges in Deutschland in Ausgewählte Schriften.* Vol. 3. Vienna: Braumüller.

Charles, Archduke. 1893–1894. *Ausgewählte Schriften* [Selected Writings]. 6 vols. Vienna: Malcher.

Charles, Napoleon. 2000. *Napoléon Bonaparte et Paoli: Aux origines de la question corse.* Paris: Perrin.

Charnay, Jean-Pierre. 1990. *Lazare Carnot, ou Le savant-citoyen.* Paris: Presses de l'Université de Paris-Sorbonne.

Charras, Lt. Col. 1870. *Histoire de la guerre de 1813 en Allemagne.* Paris: Armand le Chevalier.

Charrié, Pierre. 1982. *Drapeaux et Étendards de la Révolution et de l'Empire* [Flags and Standards of the Revolution and the Empire]. Paris: Copernic.

Chartrand, René. 1989. *Napoleon's Overseas Army.* London: Osprey.

Chartrand, René. 1990. *Napoleon's Sea Soldiers.* London: Osprey.

Chartrand, René. 1996. *Napoleonic Wars, Napoleon's Army.* London: Brassey's.

Chartrand, René. 1998. *Spanish Army of the Napoleonic Wars.* Vol. 1: *1793–1808.* Oxford: Osprey.

Chartrand, René. 2000. *The Portuguese Army of the Napoleonic Wars.* 3 vols. Oxford: Osprey.

Chartrand, René. 2001. *Bussaco 1810: Wellington Defeats Napoleon's Marshals.* Oxford: Osprey.

Chartrand, René. 2001. *Vimeiro 1808.* London: Osprey.

Chartrand, René. 2001. *Wellesley's First Victory in the Peninsula.* Oxford: Osprey.

Chartrand, René. 2002. *Fuentes de Oñoro: Wellington's Liberation of Portugal.* Oxford: Osprey.

Chartrand, René. 2003. *Napoleon's Guns, 1792–1815.* Vol. 1, *Field Artillery.* Oxford: Osprey.

Chartrand, René. 2003. *Napoleon's Guns, 1792–1815.* Vol. 2, *Heavy and Siege Artillery.* Oxford: Osprey.

Chartrand, René. 2004. *Spanish Guerrillas in the Peninsular War, 1808–14.* Oxford: Osprey.

Charvet, Patrick. 1967. *A Literary History of France.* Vol 4, *The Nineteenth Century, 1789–1870.* London: Benn.

Chateaubriand, François-René de. 1999. *Vie de Napoléon.* Ed. Marc Fumaroli. Paris: Fallois.

Chatel de Brancion, Laurence. 2001. *Cambacérès: Maître d'œuvre de Napoléon.* Paris: Perrin.

Cheke, Marcus. 1947. *Carlotta Joaquina.* London: Sidgwick and Jackson.

Chernishev, Alexander. 1839. *Voennie deistvia otriada gen. Adjutant Chernisheva v 1812, 1813 i 1814 gg.* St. Petersburg: N.p.

Chesney, Charles C. 1997. *Waterloo Lectures.* London: Greenhill.

Chevalier, E. 1886. *Histoire de la marine française sous le Consulat et l'Empire.* Paris: Hachette.

Chevrier, Edmond. 1884. *Le général Joubert, d'après sa correspondance: Etude historique.* Paris: Fischbacher.

Chibiryaev, S. A. 1989. *Velikii russkii reformator. Zhizn, deyatelnost, politicheskie vzgliadi M.M. Speranskogo.* Moscow: N.p.

Childress, Diana. 2004. *The War of 1812.* Minneapolis: Lerner.

Chinard, Gilbert. 1979. *Jefferson et les Ideologues.* Manchester, NH: Ayer.

Chrisawn, Margaret Scott. 2001. *The Emperor's Friend: Marshal Jean Lannes.* Westport, CT: Greenwood.

Christie, Ian R. 1982. *Wars and Revolutions: Britain, 1760–1815.* Cambridge, MA: Harvard University Press.

Christie, Ian R. 1984. *Stress and Stability in Late Eighteenth-Century Britain: Reflections on the British Avoidance of Revolution.* Oxford: Clarendon.

Christophe, Robert. 1964. *Napoleon on Elba.* Trans. Len Ortzen. London: Macdonald.

Christophe, Robert. 1968. *Le maréchal Marmont.* Paris: Hachette.

Chuquet, Arthur. 1886–1896. *Les guerres de la révolution.* 11 vols. Vol. 4, *Jemappes.* Paris: Leópold Cerf.

Chuquet, Arthur. 1886–1896. *Les guerres de la révolution.* 11 vols. Vol. 5, *La traison de Dumouriez.* Paris: Leópold Cerf.

Chuquet, Arthur. 1886–1896. *Les guerres de la révolution.* 11 vols. Vol. 7, *Mayence.* Paris: Leópold Cerf.

Chuquet, Arthur. 1886–1896. *Les guerres de la révolution.* 11 vols. Vol. 8, *Wissembourg.* Paris: Leópold Cerf.

Chuquet, Arthur. 1886–1896. *Les guerres de la révolution.* 11 vols. Vol. 10, *Valenciennes.* Paris: Leópold Cerf.

Chuquet, Arthur. 1886–1896. *Les guerres de la révolution.* 11 vols. Vol. 11, *Hondschoote.* Paris: Leópold Cerf.

Chuquet, Arthur. 1911–1926. *Quatre généraux de la révolution: Hoche & Desaix, Kléber et Marceau. Lettres et notes inédites. Suivies d'annexes historiques et biographiques.* Paris: Fontemoing.

Chuquet, Arthur. 1914. *Dumouriez.* Paris: Hachette.

Clapham, J. H. 1899. *The Causes of the War of 1792.* Cambridge: Cambridge University Press.

Clark, L. 1984. *Schooling the Daughters of Marianne.* Albany: State University of New York Press.

Clausewitz, Carl von. 1833. *Die Feldzuge von 1799 in Italien und der Schweiz.* Berlin: F. Dümmler.

Clausewitz, Carl von. 1976. *De la guerre* [On War]. Paris: Minuit.

Clausewitz, Carl von. 1979. *Verstreute kleine Schriften.* Osnabrück: Biblio.

Clausewitz, Carl von. 1980. *Vom Kriege.* Bonn: Dümmler.

Clausewitz, Carl von. 1984. *On War.* Princeton: Princeton University Press.

Clausewitz, Carl von. 2003. *Principles of War.* Mineola, NY: Dover.

Clausewitz, Carl von. 1992. *The Campaign of 1812 in Russia.* London: Greenhill.

Clausewitz, Carl von. 1984. *On War.* Princeton: Princeton University Press.

Clay, Matthew, and Gareth Glover, eds. 2006. *A Narrative of the Battles of Quatre-Bras and Waterloo, with the Defence of Hougoumont.* Huntingdon, UK: Ken Trotman.

Clayton, Tim, and Phil Craig. 2004. *Trafalgar: The Men, the Battle, the Storm.* London: Hodder and Stoughton.

Clement, Lt. 1890. *Historique du 4e Régiment d'Artillerie.* Paris: N.p.

Clement, Nemours Honoré. 1939. *Romanticism in France.* New York: Modern Language Association of America.

Clercq, Alexandre J. H. de, and Jules de Clercq, eds. 1864–1882. *Recueil des traités de la France, publié sous les auspices du ministère des affaires étrangères.* Paris: Pédone.

Clerget, C. 1905. *Tableaux des armées révolutionnaires.* Paris: Chapelot.

Clowes, William Laird. 1997. *The Royal Navy: A History from the Earliest Times to 1900.* 7 vols. London: Chatham. (Orig. pub. 1898.)

Clubbe, John. 1997. "Between Emperor and Exile, Byron and Napoleon, 1814–1816." *Napoleonic Scholarship: The Journal of the International Napoleonic Society* (ed. J. David Markham) 1, no. 1 (April): 70–84.

Clubbe, John, and Ernest J. Lovell Jr. 1983. *English Romanticism: The Grounds of Belief.* London: Macmillan.

Cobb, Richard. 1970. *The Police and the People: French Popular Protest, 1789–1820.* Oxford: Oxford University Press.

Cobb, Richard. 1975. *Paris and Its Provinces, 1792–1802.* London: Oxford University Press.

Cobb, Richard, ed. 1988. *The French Revolution: Voices from a Momentous Epoch.* London: Simon and Schuster.

Cobb, Richard. 1998. *The French and Their Revolution: Selected Writings.* London: Murray.

Cobb, Richard, and Colin Jones, eds. 1988. *Voices of the French Revolution.* Topsfield, MA: Salem House.

Cobban, Alfred. 1954. *Ambassadors and Secret Agents: The Diplomacy of the First Earl of Malmesbury at the Hague.* London: Cape.

Cobban, Alfred. 1965. *A History of Modern France.* New York: Braziller.

Cobbett, William. 2001. *Rural Rides.* London: Penguin. (Orig. pub. 1830.)

Cochrane, Admiral Lord. 2000. *The Autobiography of a Seaman.* London: Chatham.

Cockburn, Lord Henry. 1852. *Life of Lord Jeffrey.* 2 vols. Edinburgh: A. and C. Black.

Cole, G. D. H. 1966. *The Life of Robert Owen.* Hamden, CT: Archon.

Cole, Hubert. 1971. *Fouché: The Unprincipled Patriot.* London: Eyre and Spottiswoode.

Cole, Hubert. 1972. *The Betrayers: Joachim and Caroline Murat.* New York: Saturday Review.

Coleman, Terry. 2002. *Nelson: The Man and the Legend.* London: Bloomsbury.

Coles, Harry L. 1965. *The War of 1812.* Chicago: University of Chicago Press.

Colin, Jean. 1902. *La tactique de la discipline dans les armées de la révolution.* Paris: Chapelot.

Colin, Jean Lambert Alphonse. 1906. "Campagne de 1805." *Revue historique* 71.

Colletta, Pietro. 1982. *La campagna d'Italia di Gioacchino Murat (1815)* [Joachim Murat's Italian Campaign (1815)]. Turin: UTET.

Colley, Linda. 1992. *Britons: Forging the Nation, 1707–1837.* New Haven: Yale University Press.

Comarin, Elio. 1998. *La mort de Venise: Bonaparte et la cité des doges, 1796–1797.* Paris: Perrin.

Compton, H. 1892. *A Particular Account of the European Military Adventurers of Hindustan, from 1784 to 1803.* London: T. Fisher Unwin.

Compton-Hall, Richard. 1977. *The Submarine Pioneers.* Stroud, UK: Sutton.

Connelly, Owen. 1966. *Napoleon's Satellite Kingdoms.* New York: Free Press.

Connelly, Owen. 1968. *The Gentle Bonaparte: A Biography of Joseph, Napoleon's Elder Brother.* New York: Macmillan.

Connelly, Owen. 1991. *The French Revolution and Napoleonic Era.* New York: Harcourt Brace.

Connelly, Owen. 1999. *Blundering to Glory: Napoleon's Military Campaigns.* Wilmington, DE: Scholarly Resources.

Conner, Tom. 1995. *Chateaubriand's "Mémoires d'outre-tombe": A Portrait of the Artist as Exile.* New York: Lang.

Consalvi, Ercole. 1866. *Mémoires du Cardinal Consalvi, avec une introduction et des notes par J. Cretineau-Joly.* Paris: Plon.

Cookson, J. E. 1975. *Lord Liverpool's Administration: The Crucial Years, 1815–1822.* Edinburgh: Scottish Academic Press.

Cookson, J. E. 1982. *The Friends of Peace: Anti-War Liberalism in England, 1793–1815.* Cambridge: Cambridge University Press.

Cookson, J. E. 1997. *The British Armed Nation, 1793–1815.* Oxford: Clarendon.

Coombs, Heather. 1978. *The Age of Keats and Shelley.* Glasgow: Blackie.

Cooper, Anna Julia. 1988. *Slavery and the French Revolutionists.* New York: E. Mellen.

Cooper, Barry. 2000. *Beethoven.* Oxford: Oxford University Press.

Cooper, Duff. 2001. *Talleyrand.* London: Weidenfeld and Nicolson.

Cooper, Leonard. 1967. *The Age of Wellington: The Life and Times of the Duke of Wellington, 1769–1852.* New York: Dodd, Mend.

Cooper, Randolf. 2004. *The Anglo-Maratha Campaigns and the Contest for India: The Struggle for Control of the South Asian Military Economy.* Cambridge: Cambridge University Press.

Corbett, Julian. 1972. *Some Principles of Maritime Strategy.* Mineola, NY: Dover. (Orig. pub. 1912.)

Corbett, Julian. 1976. *The Campaign of Trafalgar.* 2 vols. New York: AMS.

Cordingly, David. 2003. *Billy Ruffian: His Majesty's Ship "Bellerophon" and the Downfall of Napoleon: A Biography of a Ship of the Line, 1782–1836.* London: Bloomsbury.

Cormack, William S. 1995. *Revolution and Political Conflict in the French Navy, 1789–1794.* Cambridge: Cambridge University Press.

Cornwallis-West, G. 1928. *The Life and Letters of Admiral Cornwallis.* London: Holden.

Corrigan, Gordon. 2000. *Wellington: A Military Life.* London: Hambledon Continuum.

Corsi, Pietro. 1988. *The Age of Lamarck: Evolutionary Theories in France, 1790–1830.* Trans. Jonathan Mandelbaum. Berkeley: University of California Press.

Corvisier, André, and Jean Delmas. 1992. *Histoire militaire de la France: de 1715 à 1871* [Military History of France: 1715 to 1871]. Paris: Presses Universitaires de France.

Costeloe, Michael P. 1986. *Response to Revolution: Imperial Spain and the Spanish American Revolutions, 1810–1840.* Cambridge: Cambridge University Press.

Couëdic, Stéphane le, ed. 1997. *L'Etat-major de Kléber en Egypte.* Paris: Vouivre.

Coupland, R., ed. 1916. *The War Speeches of William Pitt.* Oxford: Clarendon.

Coutanceau, H., H. Lepus, and Clement La Jonquière. 1903. *La Campagne de 1794 a l'Armée du Nord.* Paris: Chapelot.

Craig, Gordon A. 1961. *Europe since 1815.* New York: Holt, Rinehart and Winston.

Craig, Gordon A. 1964. *The Politics of the Prussian Army: 1640–1945.* London: Oxford University Press.

Craig, Gordon A. 1965. *Problems of Coalition Warfare: The Military Alliance against Napoleon, 1813–1814.* The Harmon Memorial Lectures in Military History, no. 7. Colorado Springs, CO: United States Air Force Academy.

Craig, Gordon A. 1984. *The End of Prussia.* Madison: University of Wisconsin Press.

Creasy, Edward S. 1987. *The Fifteen Decisive Battles of the World: From Marathon to Waterloo.* New York: Dorset.

Crecelius, Daniel. 1998. "The Mamluk Beylicate in the Last Decades before Its Destruction by Muhammad Ali Pasha in 1811." In *Mamluks in Egyptian Politics and Society,* ed. Thomas Philip and Ulrich Haarmann, 128–153. Cambridge: Cambridge University Press.

Crecelius, Daniel, and Gotcha Djaparidze. 2002. "Relations of the Georgian Mamluks of Egypt with Their Homeland in the Last Decades of the Eighteenth Century." *Journal of the Economic and Social History of the Orient* 45, part 3: 320–341.

Creston, Dormer. 1946. *In Search of Two Characters: Some Intimate Aspects of Napoleon and His Son.* London: Macmillan.

Crimmin, P. K. 2000. "John Jervis, Earl of St. Vincent." In *Precursors of Nelson: British Admirals of the Eighteenth Century,* ed. Peter Le Fevre and Richard Harding, 325–350. London: Chatham.

Crimmins, James E. 1994. "Bentham's Political Radicalism Reexamined." *Journal of the History of Ideas* 55, no. 2: 259–281.

Criste, Oskar. 1905. *Feldmarschall Johannes Fürst von Liechtenstein.* Vienna: Seidel.

Criste, Oskar. 1912. *Erzherzog Carl von Österreich.* 3 Vols. Vienna: Braumüller.

Croce, Benedetto. 1970. *History of the Kingdom of Naples.* Chicago: University of Chicago Press.

Croker, John Wilson. 1823. *An Answer to O'Meara's Napoleon in Exile, or, A Voice from St. Helena: From the Quarterly Review for February, 1823.* New York: T. and J. Swords.

Cronin, Vincent. 1972. *Napoleon Bonaparte: An Intimate Biography.* New York: Morrow.

Cronin, Vincent. 1976. *Louis and Antoinette.* New York: Morrow.

Crook, Joseph M. 1972. *The Greek Revival: Neo-classical Attitude in British Architecture, 1760–1870.* London: John Murray.

Crook, Malcolm. 1991. *Toulon in War and Revolution: From the Ancien Regime to the Restoration, 1750–1820.* Manchester: Manchester University Press.

Crook, Malcolm. 1996. *Elections in the French Revolution: An Apprenticeship in Democracy, 1789–1799.* Cambridge: Cambridge University Press.

Crook, Malcolm. 1998. *Napoleon Comes to Power: Democracy and Dictatorship in Revolutionary France, 1795–1804.* Cardiff: University of Wales Press.

Crosby, Travis L. 1977. *English Farmers and the Politics of Protection, 1815–1852.* Hassocks, UK: Harvester.

Crosland, Maurice P. 1967. *The Society of Arcueil: A View of French Science at the Time of Napoleon I.* Cambridge, MA: Harvard University Press.

Crosland, Maurice. 1978. *Gay-Lussac: Scientist and Bourgeois.* Cambridge: Cambridge University Press.

Crouzet, François. 1958. *L'economie britannique et le blocus continental, 1806–1813.* Paris: Presses Universitaires de France.

Crouzet, François. 1964. "Wars, Blockade and Economic Change in Europe, 1792–1815." *Journal of Economic History* 24, no. 4: 567–588.

Crouzet, François. 1980. "England and France in the 18th Century: A Comparative Analysis of Two Economic Growths." In *The Causes of the Industrial Revolution,* ed. R. M. Hartwell, 139–174. New York: Routledge.

Crouzet, François. 1989. "The Impact of the French Wars on the British Economy." In *Britain and the French Revolution, 1789–1815,* ed. H. T. Dickinson, 189–209. London: Macmillan.

Crouzet, François. 2001. *A History of the European Economy, 1000–2000.* Charlottesville: University of Virginia Press.

Crowdy, Terry. 2002. *French Napoleonic Infantryman, 1803–1815.* Oxford: Osprey.

Crowdy, Terry. 2003. *French Revolutionary Infantryman, 1791–1802.* Oxford: Osprey.

Crowdy, Terry. 2003. *French Soldier in Egypt, 1798–1801.* Oxford: Osprey.

Crowdy, Terry. 2004. *French Revolutionary Infantry.* Oxford: Osprey.

Crowdy, Terry. 2005. *French Warship Crews, 1789–1815: From the French Revolution to Trafalgar.* Oxford: Osprey.

Crowhurst, Patrick. 1989. *The French War on Trade: Privateering 1793–1815.* Aldershot, UK: Gower.

Cubberly, Ray Ellsworth. 1969. *The Role of Fouché during the Hundred Days.* Madison: State Historical Society of Wisconsin.

Cuccia, Phillip. 2001. "The Key to the Quadrilateral: An Analysis of the Sieges of Mantua During the Napoleonic Wars." Ph.D. diss., Florida State University.

Cugnac, Jean de. 1900–1901. *Campagne de l'armée de réserve en 1800.* 2 vols. Paris: R. Chapelot.

Curry, Kenneth. 1974. *Southey.* London: Routledge and Keegan Paul.

Curtin, Philip D. 1969. *The Atlantic Slave Trade: A Census.* Madison: University of Wisconsin Press.

Curtin, Philip D. 1998. *The Rise and Fall of the Plantation Complex.* Cambridge: Cambridge University Press.

Cutler, William H. 1920. *The Enclosure and Redistribution of Our Land.* Oxford: Clarendon.

D

D'Archimbaud, Nichola, et al. 2001. *Louvre: Portrait of a Museum.* New York: Abrams.

Dagre, Tor. "History of Norway." In *Norway: The Official Site in the United States.* www.norway.org (accessed April 6, 2006).

Daiches, David. 1971. *Sir Walter Scott and his World.* London: Thames and Hudson.

Dallas, Gregor. 1997. *The Final Act: The Roads to Waterloo.* New York: Henry Holt.

Dallas, Gregor. 2001. *1815: The Road to Waterloo.* London: Pimlico.

Dane, Clemence. 1942. *The Nelson Touch: An Anthology of Lord Nelson's Letters.* London: Heinemann.

Danielson, Johann Richard. 1896. *Suomen sota ja Suomen sotilaat vuosina, 1808–1809.* Helsinki: Weilin ja Göös.

Daston, Lorraine. 1990. "Nationalism and Scientific Neutrality under Napoleon." In *Solomon's House Revisited: The Organization and Institutionalization of Science,* ed. Tore Frangsmyr, 95–119. Canton, MA: Science History Publications.

Davenport, Hester. 2004. *The Prince's Mistress: A Life of Mary Robinson.* Stroud, UK: Sutton.

David, Saul. 1999. *Prince of Pleasure: The Prince of Wales and the Making of the Regency.* London: Abacus.

Davidov, Denis. 1999. *In the Service of the Tsar against Napoleon: The Memoirs of Denis Davidov, 1806–1814.* Trans. and ed. Gregory Troubetzkoy. London: Greenhill.

Davies, David. 1996. *Fighting Ships: Ships of the Line, 1793–1815.* London: Constable.

Davies, Hunter. 1997. *William Wordsworth.* 2nd ed. London: Sutton.

Davies, Paul. 1971. *The Field of Waterloo.* London: Pan.

Davies, Paul. 1972. *The Battle of Trafalgar.* London: Pan.

Davis, David Brion. 1999. *The Problem of Slavery in the Age of Revolution, 1770–1823.* New York: Oxford University Press.

Davis, Paul K. 1999. *100 Decisive Battles: From Ancient Times to the Present.* Santa Barbara, CA: ABC-CLIO.

Davis, Ralph. 1973. *The Rise of the Atlantic Economies.* Ithaca: Cornell University Press.

Davis, William C. 2005. *The Pirates Laffite: The Treacherous World of the Corsairs of the Gulf.* Orlando, FL: Harcourt.

Davout, Louis Nicolas. 1885. *Correspondance du maréchal Davout, prince d'Eckmühl, ses commandements, son ministère, 1801–1815.* Paris: Plon, Nourrit.

Davout, Louis Nicolas, duc d'Auerstädt et prince d'Eckmühl. 1896. *Operations de 3e Corps, 1806–1807. Raport du maréchal Davout, duc d'Auerstädt.* Paris: Calmann Lévy.

Day, Roger William. 2002. *The Life of Sir John Moore: "Not a Drum Was Heard."* London: Pen and Sword.

De Bas, F., and T'Serclaes de Wommersom. 1908. *La campagne de 1815 aux Pay-Bas.* Vol. 1, *Quatre-Bras.* Brussels: Dewit.

De Bernardy, Françoise. 1973. *Eugène de Beauharnais, 1781–1821.* Paris: Librairie Académique Perrin.

De Cugnac, Gaspar. 1901. *Campagne de l'Armée de Reserve en 1800.* Paris: Librairie militaire R. Chapelot.

De Kay, James T. 2004. *A Rage for Glory: The Life of Commodore Stephen Decatur, USN.* New York: Free Press.

De la Jonquiere, C. F. 1889–1902. *L'expédition d'Egypte.* 5 vols. Paris: Charles-Lavauzelle.

De Madariaga, Isabel. 1981. *Russia in the Age of Catherine the Great.* New Haven: Yale University Press.

De Nanteuil, Luc. 1990. *Jacques-Louis David.* New York: Abrams.

Dean, Martin C. 1993. *Austrian Policy during the French Revolutionary Wars, 1796–1802.* Vienna: Military History Institute.

DeConde, Alexander. 1958. *Entangling Alliance: Politics and Diplomacy under George Washington.* Durham, NC: Duke University Press.

DeConde, Alexander. 1966. *The Quasi-War: The Politics and Diplomacy of Undeclared War with France, 1797–1801.* New York: Scribner.

Dederfield, R. F. 2001. *Imperial Sunset: The Fall of Napoleon, 1813–1814.* New York: Cooper Square Press.

Dedrej, Piotr. 2000. *Zieleńce-Mir-Dubienka 1792.* Warsaw: Bellona.

Defranceschi, Jean. 1991. *La Corse et la Révolution française.* Ajaccio, Corsica: Cyrnos et Mediterranée.

Delavoye, Alexander M. 1880. *Life of Thomas Graham, Lord Lynedoch.* London: Richardson.

Delbrück, Hans. 1902. "Erzherzog Carl." In *Ernnerungen, Aufsätze und Reden,* 582–605. Lincoln: University of Nebraska Press.

Delderfield, R. F. 1965. *The Golden Millstones.* New York: Harper and Row.

Delderfield, R. F. 2001. *Imperial Sunset: The Fall of Napoleon, 1813–1814.* Lanham, MD: Cooper Square.

Delderfield, R. F. 2004. *The March of the Twenty-Six.* London: Leo Cooper.

Delhaize, Jules, and Winand Aerts. 1915. *Études realtives à la campagne de 1815 en Belgique.* Vol. 1. Brussels: A. de Boeck.

Della Peruta, Franco. 1988. *Esercito e società nell'Italia napoleonica* [Army and Society in Napoleonic Italy]. Milan: Franco Angeli.

Delorme, Eleanor P. 2002. *Josephine: Napoleon's Incomparable Empress.* New York: Abrams.

Demian, Johann. 1804. *Darstellung der oesterreichischen Monarchie nach den neuesten statistischen Beziehungen* [Description of the Austrian Empire Based on the Most Recent Statistical Surveys]. Vienna: Camesina.

Dempsey, Guy C. 2002. *Napoleon's Mercenaries: Foreign Units in the French Army under the Consulate and Empire, 1799–1814.* London: Greenhill.

Denisov, Adrian. 2000. *Zapiski donskogo atamana Denisova.* St. Petersburg: VIRD.

Dennis, Alfred. 1901. *Eastern Problems at the Close of the Eighteenth Century.* Cambridge, MA: The University Press.

Denon, Vivant. 1973. *Travels in Upper and Lower Egypt during the Campaigns of General Bonaparte.* New York: Arno. (Orig. pub. 1803.)

Denon, Vivant. 1986. *Travels in Egypt.* London: Darf. (Orig. pub. 1802.)

Derode, M. 1839. *Nouvelle relation de la bataille de Friedland.* Paris: Anselin et Laguionie.

Derry, John W. 1972. *Charles James Fox.* London: St. Martin's.

Derry, John W. 1990. *Politics in the Age of Fox, Pitt, and Liverpool: Continuity and Transformation.* Basingstoke, UK: Macmillan.

Derry, Thomas Kingston. 1960. *A Short History of Norway.* London: Allen and Unwin.

Derry, Thomas Kingston. 2000. *A History of Scandinavia: Norway, Sweden, Denmark, Finland, and Iceland.* Minneapolis: University of Minnesota Press.

Dershowitz, Nachum, and Edward Reingold. 2002. *Calendrical Calculations.* New York: Cambridge University Press.

Desbrière, Edouard. 1900–1902. *Projets et tentatives de debarquement aux iles britanniques, 1792–1805.* 4 vols. Paris: Chapelot.

Desbrière, Edouard. 1933. *The Naval Campaign of 1805: Trafalgar.* Trans. and ed. Constance Eastwick. 2 vols. Oxford: Clarendon.

Desmarest, Pierre Marie. 1900. *Quinze ans de haute police sous le Consulat et de l'Empire.* Paris: Garnier frères.

Desormeaux, H. Bagueniel. 1907. *Kléber en Vendée (1793–1794).* Paris: Picard.

Desvernois, Nicolas Philibert. 1898. *Mémoires du General Bon. Desvernois.* Paris: Plon.

Detlov, K. 1888. "J. P. Kulnev in Actions of 20 and 21 July 1812 g." *Russkaia Starina* 5.

Deutsch, Harold C. 1938. *The Genesis of Napoleonic Imperialism.* Cambridge, MA: Harvard University Press.

Deutschland in seiner tiefsten Erniedrigung. Anonyme Flugschrift, für deren. Nuremberg, 1806.

Dhombres, Jean, and Nicole Dhombres. 1997. *Lazare Carnot.* Paris: Fayard.

Dible, James H. 1970. *Napoleon's Surgeon.* London: Heinemann Medical.

Dickinsen, Henry Winram. 1987. *Robert Fulton, Engineer and Artist: His Life and Works.* Freeport, NY: Books for Libraries.

Dickinson, H. T. 1985. *British Radicalism in the French Revolution, 1789–1815.* Oxford: Blackwell.

Dickson, H. T., ed. 1989. *Britain and the French Revolution, 1789–1815.* New York: St. Martin's.

Diesbach, Ghislain de. 1998. *Histoire de l'émigration, 1789–1814.* Paris: Perrin.

Dietze, Anita, and Walter Dietze, eds. 1991. *Ewiger Friede? Dokumente einer deutschen Diskussion um 1800.* Munich: Beck.

Ditchfield, G. M. 2002. *George III: An Essay in Monarchy.* New York: Palgrave Macmillan.

Dixon, C. Willis. 1968. *The Colonial Administration of Sir Thomas Maitland.* London: Cass.

Dixon, Peter. 1976. *Canning: Politician and Statesman.* London: Weidenfeld and Nicolson.

Dixon, Pierson. 1965. *Pauline, Napoleon's Favorite Sister.* New York: McKay.

Dixon, S. 1999. *Russia in the Age of Modernization, 1676–1825.* Cambridge: Cambridge University Press.

Djanelidze, D. 1967. *Qartveli mamluqebi egvipteshi* [Georgian Mamelukes in Egypt]. Tbilisi: N.p.

Doguereau, Jean-Pierre. 2002. *Guns in the Desert: General Jean-Pierre Doguereau's Journal of Napoleon's Egyptian Expedition.* Westport, CT: Praeger.

Dokhturov, D. S. 1874. "Pisma D. S. Dokhturova k ego supruge" [D. S. Dokhturov's Letters to His Wife]. *Russkii arkhiv* 12.

Dolleczek, Anton. 1887. *Monographie der k.u.k. österr.-ung. blanken und Handfeuer-Waffen, Kriegsmusik, Fahnen und Standarten seit Errichtung des stehenden Heeres bis zur Gegenwart* [Essay on the Imperial and Royal Austro-Hungarian Swords and Firing Weaponry, Military Musical Instruments, Flags and Standards from the Raising of the Standing Army to the Present]. Vienna: Kreisel und Gröger.

Donskoe kazachestvo v Otechestvennoi voine 1812 goda. 1942. Moscow: Gospolitizdat.

Doughty, Robert A., et al. 1996. *Warfare in the Western World.* Vol. 1, *Military Operations from 1600 to 1871.* Lexington, MA: Heath.

Dowden, Edward. 1879. *Southey.* London: Macmillan.

Doyle, William. 1999. *Origins of the French Revolution.* 3rd ed. New York: Oxford University Press.

Doyle, William. 2002. *The French Revolution: A Very Short Introduction.* Oxford: Oxford University Press.

Doyle, William. 2003. *The Oxford History of the French Revolution.* Oxford: Oxford University Press.

Draexler, Hans-Dieter. 1996. *Die Idéologie in Deutschland.* Münster: Nodus.

Drescher, Seymour. 1987. *Capitalism and Antislavery: British Mobilization in Comparative Perspective.* New York: Oxford University Press.

Driault, Edouard. 1927. *Napoléon et l'Europe: La legende de Napoléon (1812–1815).* Paris: Librairie Felix Alcan.

Drinkwater, John. 1928. *Charles James Fox.* London: Benn.

Drouet d'Erlon, Jean-Baptiste. 1844. *Le maréchal Drouet, comte d'Erlon: Vie militaire écrite par lui-même et dédiée à ses amis.* Paris: Barba.

Droysen, Johann Gustav. 1913. *Das Leben des Feldmarschalls Grafen Yorck von Wartenburg.* 2 vols. Leipzig: Insel.

Du Casse, Albert. 1851. *Opérations du neuvième corps de la Grande Armée en Silésie sur le commandement de S.A.I. le Prince Jérôme Napoléon—1806 et 1807.* 2 vols. Paris: J. Corréard.

Du Casse, Albert. 1870. *Le général Vandamme et sa correspondance.* 2 vols. Paris: Didier.

Duane, William. 1824. *Two Americas, Great Britain, and the Holy Alliance.* Washington, DC: DeKrafft.

Dubois, Laurent. 1998. *Les esclaves de la république: L'histoire oubliée de la première émancipation, 1789–1794.* Paris: Calmann-Lévy.

Dubois, Laurent. 2004. *A Colony of Citizens: Revolution and Slave Emancipation in the French Caribbean, 1787–1804.* Chapel Hill: University of North Carolina Press.

Dubois, Laurent. 2004. *Avengers of the New World: The Story of the Haitian Revolution.* Cambridge, MA: Harvard University Press.

Dubois, Laurent. 2004. *A Colony of Citizens: Revolution and Slave Emancipation in the French Caribbean, 1787–1804.* Chapel Hill: University of North Carolina Press.

Dubois, Laurent, and John D. Garrigus. 2006. *Slave Revolution in the Caribbean, 1789–1804: A Brief History with Documents.* London: Palgrave Macmillan.

Ducere, Edouard. 1881. *L'Armée des Pyrénées Occidentales avec éclaircissements historiques sur les campagnes de 1793, 1794, 1795.* Bayonne: Hourquet.

Duckworth, Colin. 1986. *The d'Antraigues Phenomenon: The Making and Breaking of a Revolutionary Royalist Espionage Agent.* Newcastle, UK: Avero.

Dudley, William S. 1985. *The Naval War of 1812: A Documentary History.* Washington, DC: Naval Historical Center, Department of the Navy.

Duffy, Christopher. 1972. *Borodino and the War of 1812.* London: Seeley Service.

Duffy, Christopher. 1977. *Austerlitz 1805.* London: Seeley Service.

Duffy, Christopher. 1979. *Siege Warfare: The Fortress in the Early Modern World, 1494–1660.* London: Routledge.

Duffy, Christopher. 1981. *Russia's Military Way to the West: Origins and Nature of Russian Military Power, 1700–1800.* London: Routledge.

Duffy, Christopher. 1985. *The Fortress in the Age of Vauban and Frederick the Great, 1660–1789.* London: RKP.

Duffy, Christopher. 1996. *Fire and Stone.* London: Greenhill.

Duffy, Christopher. 1999. *Eagle over the Alps: Suvorov in Italy and Switzerland, 1799.* Chicago: Emperor's.

Duffy, Michael. 1987. *Soldiers, Sugar, and Seapower: British Expeditions to the West Indies and the War against Revolutionary France.* Oxford: Clarendon.

Duffy, Michael. 1989. "British Diplomacy and the French Wars." In *Britain and the French Revolution,* ed. H. T. Dickinson. New York: St. Michael's.

Duffy, Michael. 1990. "The Caribbean Campaigns of the British Army, 1793–1815." In *The Road to Waterloo: The British Army and the Struggle Against Revolutionary and Napoleonic France, 1793–1815,* 23–31. London: National Army Museum.

Duffy, Michael. 2000. *The Younger Pitt.* New York: Longman.

Duffy, Michael, and Roger Morriss, eds. 2001. *The Glorious First of June: A Battle in Perspective.* Exeter, UK: University of Exeter Press.

Dugan, James. 1965. *The Great Mutiny.* New York: Putnam.

Düller, Eduard. 1847. *Erzherzog Karl von Oesterreich.* Vienna: Kaulfuß Witwe.

Dumas, Guy. 1964. *La fin de la république de Venise.* Paris: Presses universitaires de France.

Dumas, Samuel, and K. O. Vedel-Petersen. 1923. *Losses of Life Caused by Wars.* Oxford: Clarendon.

Dumont, Franz. 1993. *Die Mainzer Republik von 1792/93: Studien zur Revolutionierung in Rheinhessen und der Pfalz* [The Mainz Republic of 1792/93: Studies on the Revolutionizing of Rhenish Hesse and the Palatinate]. 2nd ed. Alzey: Verlag der Rheinhessischen Druckwerkstätte.

Dupont, Maurice. 1991. *L'amiral Decrès et Napoléon.* Paris: Economica.

Dupre, Huntley. 1940. *Lazare Carnot, Republican Patriot.* Oxford, OH: Mississippi Valley.

Dupuis, V. 1906–1909. *La campagne de 1793 à l'Armée du Nord et des Ardennes.* 2 vols. Paris: Chapelot.

Dupuy, Colonel T. N. 1984. *A Genius for War: The German Army and General Staff, 1807–1945.* Fairfax, VA: Hero.

Dupuy, Trevor N. 1968. *The Battle of Austerlitz: Napoleon's Greatest Victory.* New York: Macmillan.

Durant, Will, and Ariel Durant. 1975. *The Age of Napoleon: A History of European Civilization from 1789 to 1815.* New York: Simon and Schuster.

Dwyer, Philip G. 1996. *Charles-Maurice de Talleyrand, 1754–1838: A Bibliography.* Westport, CT: Greenwood.

Dwyer, Philip G. 2001. *Napoleon and Europe.* New York: Longman.

Dyck, Ian. 1992. *William Cobbett and Rural Popular Culture.* Cambridge: Cambridge University Press.

Dyer, Denys. 1977. *The Stories of Kleist: A Critical Study.* New York: Holmes and Meier.

Dziewanowski, M. 1990. *Alexander I: Russia's Mysterious Tsar.* New York: Hippocrene.

E

Ebert, Jens-Florian, and Roland Kessinger. 2003. "The First Battle of Biberach, 1796." *First Empire* (Bridgnorth, UK) 70: 12–20.

Edginton, Harry. 1981. *Nelson, the Hero and Lover.* London: Hamlyn.

Edmonds, W. D. 1990. *Jacobinism and the Revolt of Lyon 1789–1793.* Oxford: Clarendon.

Edwards, Peter. 2005. *Talavera: Wellington's Early Peninsula Victories, 1808–09.* Ramsbury, UK: Crowood.

Edwards, Thomas Joseph. 1953. *Standards, Guidons and Colours of the Commonwealth Forces.* Aldershot, UK: Gale and Polden.

Egan, Clifford L. 1983. *Neither Peace nor War: Franco-American Relations, 1803–1812.* Baton Rouge: Louisiana State University Press.

Egger, Rainer. 1965. *Das Gefecht bei Dürnsten-Loiben 1805.* Heft [Series] 3. Vienna: Militärhistorische Schriftenreihe.

Egger, Rainer. 1982. *Das Gefecht bei Hollabrunn und Schöngrabern 1805.* Militärhistorische Schriftenreihe, Heft [Ser.] 27. Vienna: Österreichischer Bundesverlag.

Ehrman, John. 1969. *The Younger Pitt.* Vol. 1, *The Years of Acclaim.* New York: Dutton.

Ehrman, John. 1983. *The Younger Pitt.* Vol. 2, *The Reluctant Transition.* London: Constable.

Ehrman, John. 1996. *The Younger Pitt.* Vol. 3, *The Consuming Struggle.* London: Constable.

Eidahl, Kyle Orlan. 1990. "The Military Career of Nicholas Charles Oudinot (1767–1847)." Ph.D. diss., Florida State University.

Ekshtut, Semyon. 2000. "Suvorov." *Russian Life* 43, no. 3: 40–48.

Elgström, Ole. 2000. *Images and Strategies for Autonomy: Explaining Swedish Security Policy Strategies in the 19th Century.* Dordrecht, Netherlands: Kluwer.

Elkan, Sofie. 1913. *An Exiled King: Gustaf Adolf IV of Sweden.* London: Hutchinson.

Elliott, Marianne. 1982. *Partners in Revolution: The United Irishmen and France.* New Haven: Yale University Press.

Elliott, Marianne. 1989. *Wolfe Tone, the Prophet of Irish Independence.* New Haven: Yale University Press.

Ellis, Geoffrey. 1981. *Napoleon's Continental Blockade: The Case of Alsace.* Oxford: Clarendon.

Ellis, Geoffrey J. 1989. *Continental Blockade: The Case of Alsace.* Oxford: Oxford University Press.

Ellis, Geoffrey J. 1991. *The Napoleonic Empire.* Atlantic Highlands, NJ: Humanities Press International.

Elting, John R. 1997. *Swords around a Throne: Napoleon's Grande Armée*. London: Weidenfeld and Nicolson.

Emerson, Donald Eugene. 1969. *Metternich and the Political Police: Security and Subversion in the Hapsburg Monarchy, 1815–1830*. The Hague: Nijhoff.

Emsley, Clive. 1979. *British Society and the French Wars, 1793–1815*. London: Macmillan.

Emsley, Clive. 2000. *Britain and the French Revolution*. New York: Longman.

Enghien, Louis-Antoine-Henri de Bourbon, duc d'. 1904–1913. *Correspondance du duc d'Enghien (1801–1804) et documentes sur son enlèvement et sa mort*. Ed. Alfred Boulay de la Meurthe. Paris: Picard et fils.

Englund, Steven. 2004. *Napoleon: A Political Life*. New York: Scribner.

Epstein, Robert M. 1984. *Prince Eugene at War, 1809*. Arlington TX: Empire Games.

Epstein, Robert M. 1994. *Napoleon's Last Victory and the Emergence of Modern War*. Lawrence: University Press of Kansas.

Epton, Nina. 1975. *Josephine: The Empress and Her Children*. London: Weidenfeld and Nicolson.

Erdem, Y. Hakan. 1996. *Slavery in the Ottoman Empire and Its Demise, 1800–1909*. New York: St. Martin's.

Erickson, Carolly. 1994. *Great Catherine: The Life of Catherine the Great, Empress of Russia*. New York: Crown.

Erickson, Carolly. 1998. *Josephine: A Life of the Empress*. New York: St. Martin's.

Ermolov, Alexander. 1912. *A. P. Ermolov: Biograficheskii ocherk*. St. Petersburg: Izd. Imp. russkago voenno-istoricheskago ob-va.

Ernstberger, Anton. 1957. "Ferdinand von Schills Nachlass." *Bayerische Akademie der Wissenshaften*. No. 11.

Escalle, Charles-Pierre. 1912. *Des marches dans les armées de Napoléon*. Paris: Chapelot.

Escande, G. 1888. *Hoche en Irlande, 1795–1798*. Paris: Alcan.

Esdaile, Charles J. 1988. *The Spanish Army in the Peninsular War*. Manchester, UK: Manchester University Press.

Esdaile, Charles J. 1990. *The Duke of Wellington and the Command of the Spanish Army, 1812–14*. London: Macmillan.

Esdaile, Charles J. 1995. *The Wars of Napoleon*. London: Longman.

Esdaile, Charles J. 2000. *Spain in the Liberal Age: From Constitution to Civil War, 1808–1939*. Oxford: Blackwell.

Esdaile, Charles J. 2001. *The French Wars: 1792–1815*. New York: Routledge.

Esdaile, Charles J. 2003. *The Peninsular War: A New History*. New York: Palgrave Macmillan.

Esdaile, Charles J. 2004. *Fighting Napoleon: Guerrillas, Bandits and Adventurers in Spain, 1808–14*. New Haven, CT. Yale University Press.

Esdaile, Charles J., ed. 2004. *Popular Resistance in Napoleonic Europe*. Houndmills, UK: Palgrave Macmillan.

Esdaile, Charles J. 2007. *From Amiens to Waterloo: An International History of the Napoleonic Wars*. London: Penguin.

Esposito, Vincent J., and John R. Elting. 1999. *A Military History and Atlas of the Napoleonic Wars*. London: Greenhill.

Esquer, G., ed. 1914. *Correspondance du duc de Rovigo, commandant en chef le corps d'occupation d'Afrique (1831–1833)*. Algiers: Carbonel.

Eugene of Württemberg. 1849. "Vospominania o kampanii 1812 g v Rossii." *Voennii zhurnal* 3.

Eyck, Erich. 1950. *Pitt versus Fox: Father and Son, 1735–1806*. Trans. Eric Northcott. London: Bell and Sons.

Eysturlid, Lee W. 2000. *The Formative Influences, Theories and Campaigns of the Archduke Carl of Austria*. Westport, CT: Greenwood.

F

Fabb, John, and Jack Cassin-Scott. 1977. *The Uniforms of Trafalgar*. London: Batsford.

Fabre, Marc-Andre. 1947. *Hoche L'enfant de la Victoire, 1768–1797*. Paris: Hachette.

Fabry, Gabriel. 1900–1912. *Campagne de Russie, 1812*. 5 vols. Paris: Gougy.

Fairweather, Maria. 2006. *Madame de Staël*. London: Constable and Robinson.

Fangier, Maurice. 1971. *Recherche sur les Héraultais morts aux armées de 1803 à 1810* [Studies on the Héraultais Who Died in the Army, 1803–1810]. Montpellier, France: Mémoire Maîtrise Histoire.

Farrington, F. 1910. *French Secondary Schools: An Account of the Origin, Development and Present Organization of Secondary Education in France*. New York: Longmans, Green.

Faure, Gabriel, and Marcel Deléon. 1929. *Napoléon à Laffrey*. Grenoble: F. Dardelet.

Fedorak, Charles J. 2002. *Henry Addington: Prime Minister, 1801–1803; Peace, War, and Parliamentary Politics*. Akron, OH: University of Akron Press.

Fedorov, V. A. 1997. *M. M. Speransky and A. A. Arakcheyev*. Moscow: N.p.

Fehrenbach, Elisabeth. 2001. *Vom Ancien Régime zum Wiener Kongress* [From the *Ancien Régime* to the Congress of Vienna]. 4th ed. Munich: Oldenbourg.

Fehrmann, C. N. 1969. *Onze vloot in de Franse Tijd, de admiraals De Winter en Verheull*. The Hague: Kruseman.

Feichtinger, Josef, ed. 1984. *Tirol 1809 in der Literatur*. Vienna: Athesia.

Feldbaek, Ole. 1980. *Denmark and the Armed Neutrality, 1800–1801: Small Power Policy in a World War*. Copenhagen: Akademisk.

Feldbaek, Ole. 2002. *The Battle of Copenhagen, 1801*. London: Pen and Sword.

Feldmarschalleutnant Ferdinand von Schill: Freiheitskämpfer und Held: Dramtisches Gedicht in fünf Akten. N.d. Breslau: Lützow.

Fergusson, Priscilla Pankhurst. 1994. *Paris as Revolution: Writing the Nineteenth-Century City*. Berkeley and Los Angeles: University of California Press.

Ferrero, Guglielmo. 1961. *The Gamble: Bonaparte in Italy, 1796–1797*. New York: Walker.

Ferrero, Guglielmo. 1963. *The Reconstruction of Europe: Talleyrand and the Congress of Vienna, 1814–1815*. New York: Norton.

Ferval, N. N. 1861. *Campagnes de la revolution française dans les Pyrenées-Orientales*. Paris: Dumaine.

Fezensac, Raymond-Aymery-Philippe-Joseph de Montesquiou. 1988. *A Journal of the Russian Campaign of 1812*. Cambridge: Ken Trotman.

Fichte, Johann Gottlieb. 1968. *Addresses to the German Nation*. Ed. George A. Kelly. New York: Harper and Row.

Fiedler, Siegfried. 1978. *Grundriss der Militär- und Kriegsgeschichte.* Vol. 3, *Napoleon gegen Preussen.* Munich: Schild.

Fiedler, Siegfried. 2002. *Taktik und Strategie der Revolutionskriege 1792–1848* [Tactics and Strategy of the Revolutionary Wars]. Bonn: Bernhard and Graefe.

Field, Alexander J. 1994. "French Optical Telegraphy, 1793–1855: Hardware, Software, Administration." *Technology and Culture* 35: 315–347.

Figgis, John Neville. 1965. *The Divine Right of Kings.* New York: Harper and Row.

Finley, Gerald. 1981. *Turner and George the Fourth in Edinburgh, 1822.* London: Tate Gallery and Edinburgh University Press.

Finley, Milton. 1994. *The Most Monstrous of Wars: Napoleonic Guerrilla War in Southern Italy, 1806–1811.* Columbia: University of South Carolina Press.

Fisher, Todd. 2001. *The Napoleonic Wars.* Vol. 1: *The Rise of the Emperor, 1805–1807.* Oxford: Osprey.

Fisher, Todd. 2001. *The Napoleonic Wars.* Vol. 2: *The Empires Fight Back, 1808–1812.* Oxford: Osprey.

Flayhart, William. 1992. *Counterpoint to Trafalgar: The Anglo-Russian Invasion of Naples, 1805–06.* Columbia: University of South Carolina Press.

Fleming, Thomas. 2003. *The Louisiana Purchase.* Hoboken, NJ: Wiley.

Fletcher, Ian. 1991. *The Waters of Oblivion: The British Invasion of the Rio de la Plata, 1806–07.* Staplehurst, UK: Spellmount.

Fletcher, Ian. 1994. *Wellington's Regiments: The Men and Their Battles, 1808–1815.* Staplehurst, UK: Spellmount.

Fletcher, Ian. 1995. *Craufurd's Light Division: The Life of Robert Craufurd and His Command of the Light Division.* New York: Da Capo.

Fletcher, Ian. 1997. *Salamanca 1812: Wellington Crushes Marmont.* Oxford: Osprey.

Fletcher, Ian. 1998. *In Hell before Daylight: The Siege and Storming of the Castle of Badajoz.* Staplehurst, UK: Spellmount.

Fletcher, Ian. 1998. *The Peninsular War: Aspects of the Struggle for the Iberian Peninsula.* Staplehurst, UK: Spellmount.

Fletcher, Ian. 1998. *Vittoria 1813: Wellington Sweeps the French from Spain.* Oxford: Osprey.

Fletcher, Ian. 1999. *Badajoz 1812: Wellington's Bloodiest Siege.* Oxford: Osprey.

Fletcher, Ian. 1999. *Galloping at Everything: The British Cavalry in the Peninsular War and at Waterloo 1808–1815.* Mechanicsburg, PA: Stackpole.

Fletcher, Ian. 2000. *Bloody Albuera: The 1811 Campaign in the Peninsula.* Ramsbury, UK: Crowood.

Fletcher, Ian. 2001. *Voices from the Peninsula: Eyewitness Accounts by Soldiers of Wellington's Army, 1808–1814.* London: Greenhill.

Fletcher, Ian. 2003. *"A Desperate Business": Wellington, the British Army and the Waterloo Campaign.* Staplehurst, UK: Spellmount.

Fletcher, Ian. 2003. *Fortresses of the Peninsular War, 1808–14.* Oxford: Osprey.

Fletcher, Ian. 2003. *The Lines of Torres Vedras, 1809–11.* Oxford: Osprey.

Fletcher, Robert. 2002. "A Tapestry of Kings, Fools and Traitors." *First Empire* 64: 32–39; 65: 33–35.

Fletcher, Robert. 2004. "The Last Neapolitan Battle: Gaeta." *First Empire* 79: 4–10.

Forczyk, Robert A. 2005. *Toulon 1793: Napoleon's First Great Victory.* Oxford: Osprey.

Ford, Guy S. 1922. *Stein and the Era of Reform in Prussia, 1807–15.* Princeton: Princeton University Press.

Foreman, Laura, and Eileen Blue Phillips. 1999. *Napoleon's Lost Fleet: Bonaparte, Nelson, and the Battle of the Nile.* London: Discovery.

Forrest, Alan. 1989. *Conscripts and Deserters: The Army and French Society during the Revolution and Empire.* New York: Oxford University Press.

Forrest, Alan. 1991. *The Soldiers of the French Revolution.* Durham, NC: Duke University Press.

Forrest, Alan. 1995. *The French Revolution.* Cambridge, MA: Blackwell.

Forrest, Alan. 2002. *Napoleon's Men: The Soldiers of the Revolution and Empire.* New York: Hambledon and London.

Forshufvud, Sten, and Ben Weider. 1995. *Assassination at St. Helena Revisited.* London: Wiley.

Forssell, Nils. 1970. *Fouché: The Man Napoleon Feared.* New York: AMS.

Forsyth, William. 1853. *History of the Captivity of Napoleon at St. Helena; From the Letters and Journals of the late Lieut.-Gen. Sir Hudson Lowe, and Official Documents Not Before Made Public.* 3 vols. London: John Murray.

Fortescue, J. W. 1918. *British Campaigns in Flanders, 1690–1794.* London: Macmillan.

Fortescue, J. W. 2004. *History of the British Army.* Vol. 5. Uckfield, UK: Naval and Military Press.

Fortescue, J. W. 1925. *Wellington.* London: Williams and Norgate.

Fortescue, J. W. 2002. *The County Lieutenancies and the Army, 1803–1814.* Uckfield, UK: Naval and Military Press.

Fortescue, J. W. 2004. *History of the British Army.* 19 vols. Uckfield, UK: Naval and Military. (Orig. pub. 1899–1920.)

Fosten, Bryan. 1982. *Wellington's Heavy Cavalry.* London: Osprey.

Fosten, Bryan. 1982. *Wellington's Light Cavalry.* London: Osprey.

Fosten, Bryan. 1992. *Wellington's Infantry.* 2 vols. London: Osprey.

Foucart, Paul. 1887–1895. *Campagne de Prusse (1806): Iéna, d'après les archives de la guerre.* 2 vols. Paris: Berger-Levrault.

Foucart, Paul, and Jules Finot. 1893. *La défense nationale dans le Nord de 1792 à 1802.* Vol. 2. Lille: Lefebvre-Ducrocq.

Fouché, Joseph. 1992. *Mémoires de Joseph Fouché, duc d'Otrante.* Ed. Michel Vovelle. Paris: Imprimerie nationale.

Fowler, William M. 1984. *Jack Tars and Commodores: The American Navy, 1783–1815.* Boston: Houghton Mifflin.

Fox, Ruth. 1947. *Great Men of Medicine.* New York: Random House.

Foy, Maximilien Sebastien, comte. 1827. *Histoire de la guerre de la Peninsule sous Napoléon, précédée d'un tableau politique et militaire des puissances belligérantes.* 4 vols. Ed. Mme la comtesse Foy. Paris: Baudouin frères.

France, Peter, ed. 1995. *The New Oxford Companion to Literature in French.* Oxford: Clarendon.

Franklin, Alexandra. 2003. *Napoleon and the Invasion of Britain.* Oxford: Bodleian Library.

Fraser, Antonia. 1989. *The Warrior Queens.* New York: Knopf.

Fraser, Antonia. 2001. *Marie Antoinette: The Journey.* New York: Doubleday.

Fraser, Edward. 1914. *Napoleon the Gaoler: Personal Experiences and Adventures of British Sailors and Soldiers during the Great Captivity.* New York: Brentano's.

Fraser, Edward, Marianne Cznik, and Michael Nash. 2004. *The Enemy at Trafalgar: Eyewitness Narratives, Dispatches and Letters from the French and Spanish Fleets.* London: Chatham.

Fraser, Flora. 2003. *Beloved Emma: The Life of Emma, Lady Hamilton.* London: John Murray.

Fraser, Flora. 2004. *The Unruly Queen: The Life of Queen Caroline.* London: John Murray.

Fraser, Flora. 2005. *Princesses: The Six Daughters of George III.* London: John Murray.

Frazier, Nancy. 2000. *The Penguin Concise Dictionary of Art History.* New York: Penguin Reference.

Fregosi, Paul. 1990. *Dreams of Empire: Napoleon and the First World War, 1792–1815.* Secaucus, NJ: Carol.

Fremont-Barnes, Gregory. 2001. *The French Revolutionary Wars.* Oxford: Osprey.

Fremont-Barnes, Gregory. 2002a. *The Peninsular War, 1807–1814.* Oxford: Osprey.

Fremont-Barnes, Gregory. 2002b. *The Fall of the French Empire, 1813–1815.* Oxford: Osprey.

Fremont-Barnes, Gregory. 2005a. *Nelson's Sailors.* Oxford: Osprey.

Fremont-Barnes, Gregory. 2005b. *Trafalgar 1805: Nelson's Crowning Victory.* Oxford: Osprey.

Fremont-Barnes, Gregory. 2006. *The Wars of the Barbary Pirates.* Oxford: Osprey.

Fremont-Barnes, Gregory, and Todd Fisher. 2004. *The Napoleonic Wars: The Rise and Fall of an Empire.* Oxford: Osprey.

Frick, Carolyn E. 1990. *The Making of Haiti: The Saint Domingue Revolution from Below.* Knoxville: University of Tennessee Press.

Friedenberg, Zachary B. 2002. *Medicine under Sail.* London: Chatham.

Friedenthal, Richard. 1965. *Goethe: His Life and Times.* London: Weidenfeld and Nicolson.

Friederich, Rudolf. 1903–1906. *Geschichte des Herbstfeldzuges 1813.* Berlin: Mittler.

Fruchtman, Jack. 1994. *Thomas Paine: Apostle of Freedom.* New York: Four Walls Eight Windows.

Fry, Howard Tyrrell. 1970. *Alexander Dalrymple (1737–1808) and the Expansion of British Trade.* London: Cass for the Royal Commonwealth Society.

Fry, Michael. 1992. *The Dundas Despotism.* Edinburgh: Edinburgh University Press.

Frye, Northrop. 2004. *Fearful Symmetry: A Study of William Blake.* Toronto: Toronto University Press.

Fuchs, Karl. 1907. *Erzherzog Karl.* Graz: Styria.

Fulford, Roger. 1960. *Hanover to Windsor.* London: Batsford.

Fulford, Roger. 1968. *The Wicked Uncles.* Freeport, NY: Books for Libraries.

Fuller, J. F. C. 1970. *A Military History of the Western World.* Vol. 2, *From the Defeat of the Spanish Armada to the Battle of Waterloo.* London: Paladin.

Funcken, Fred, and Liliane Funcken. 1973. *Arms and Uniforms of the Napoleonic Wars, Part II.* Englewood Cliffs, NJ: Prentice-Hall.

Funcken, Liliane, and Fred Funcken. 1984. *The Napoleonic Wars: Arms and Uniforms.* 2 vols. New York: Prentice-Hall.

Furber, H. 1976. *Rival Empires of Trade in the Orient, 1600–1800.* Minneapolis: Biniversity of Minnesota Press.

Furet, François. 1996. *The French Revolution, 1770–1814.* Trans. Antonia Neville. Oxford: Blackwell.

Furneaux, Robin. 1974. *William Wilberforce.* London: Hamilton.

Furse, George Armand. 1993. *Marengo and Hohenlinden.* [Facsimile. of 1903 ed.] Felling, UK: Worley.

Furse, George Armand. 1995. *Campaigns of 1805: Ulm, Trafalgar and Austerlitz.* Tyne and Wear: Worley. (Orig. pub. 1905.)

G

Gabaev, G. 1912. *Rospis rus. Polkam 1812 g.* Kiev: N.p.

Gabriel, Richard A., and Karen S. Metz. 1992. *A History of Military Medicine.* Vol. 2, *From the Renaissance through Modern Times.* New York: Greenwood.

Gachot, Edouard. 1903. *Les Campagnes de 1799: Souvarow en Italie.* Paris: Perrin.

Gachot, Henri. 1967. *Le télégraphe optique de Claude Chappe, Strasbourg, Metz, Paris, et ses embranchements.* Saverne: Savernoises.

Gagliardo, John G. 1980. *Reich and Nation: The Holy Roman Empire as Idea and Reality, 1763–1806.* Bloomington: Indiana University Press.

Gallagher, Louis N. 1976. *The Iron Marshal: A Biography of Louis N. Davout.* Carbondale and Edwardsville: Southern Illinois University Press.

Gallaher, John. 2000. *The Iron Marshal: A Biography of Louis N. Davout.* London: Greenhill.

Gallina, Johann. 1872. *Beiträge zur Geschichte des österreichschen Heerwesens.* Vienna: N.p.

Gallo, Max. 2004. *Napoleon.* London: Macmillan.

Gambles, Anna, ed. 1999. *Protection and Politics: Conservative Economic Discourse, 1815–1852.* Woodbridge, UK: Boydell, for the Royal Historical Society.

Gândara Terenas, Gabriela. 2000. *O Portugal da guerra Peninsular.* Lisbon: Colibri Lisbon.

Gardiner, Robert. 2000. *Frigates of the Napoleonic Wars.* London: Chatham.

Gardiner, Robert. 2002. *The Campaign of Trafalgar, 1803–1805.* London: Caxton.

Gardiner, Robert. 2003. *The Naval War of 1812.* London: Chatham.

Gardiner, Robert. 2003. *Warships of the Napoleonic Era.* London: Chatham.

Gardiner, Robert, ed. 1992. *The Line of Battle: The Sailing Warship, 1650–1840.* London: Conway Maritime.

Gardiner, Robert, ed. 2001. *Fleet Battle and Blockade: The French Revolutionary War, 1793–1797.* London: Caxton.

Gardiner, Robert, ed. 2001. *Nelson against Napoleon: From the Nile to Copenhagen, 1798–1801.* London: Chatham.

Garfield, Leon. 1976. *The House of Hanover: England in the 18th Century.* London: Deutsch.

Garlick, Kenneth, ed. 1989. *Sir Thomas Lawrence: A Complete Catalogue of the Oil Paintings.* Oxford: Phaidon.

Garnier, Jean Paul. 1970. *Barras, Le roi du Directoire.* Paris: Perrin.

Garrison, Fielding H. 1929. *History of Medicine.* Washington, DC: Saunders.

Gascoigne, John. 1998. *Science in the Service of Empire: Joseph Banks, the British State and the Uses of Science in the Age of Revolution.* Cambridge and New York: Cambridge University Press.

Gash, Norman. 1984. *Lord Liverpool*. London: Weidenfeld and Nicolson.

Gaspar, David Berry, and David Patrick Geggus, eds. 1997. *A Turbulent Time: The French Revolution and the Greater Caribbean*. Bloomington: Indiana University Press.

Gates, David. 1987. *The British Light Infantry Arm, c. 1790–1815*. London: Batsford.

Gates, David. 1997. *The Napoleonic Wars, 1803–1815*. London: Arnold.

Gates, David. 2001. *Warfare in the Nineteenth Century*. Basingstoke, UK: Palgrave Macmillan.

Gates, David. 2002. *The Spanish Ulcer: A History of the Peninsular War*. London: Pimlico.

Gavrilov, I. 1998. *Tuchkovy*. Moscow: N. p.

Gay, Peter. 1965. *Voltaire's Politics: The Poet as Realist*. New York: Random House.

Gearey, John. 1968. *Heinrich von Kleist: A Study in Tragedy and Anxiety*. Philadelphia: University of Pennsylvania Press.

Geisman, P. 1902. "Istoricheskii ocherk vozniknovenia i razvitia v Rossii Generalnogo shtaba do kontsa tsarstvovania Aleksandra I." In *Stoletie Voennogo Ministerstva*, vol. 4, part 2: sect. 1. St. Petersburg: Voennoe Ministerstvo.

Gengembre, Gérard. 2003. *Napoleon: History and Myth*. London: Hachette Illustrated.

Gentz, Friedrich von. 1836–1838. *Ausgewählte Schriften von Friedrich von Gentz* [Writings of Frederick von Gentz]. 5 vols. Stuttgart: Rieger.

Geoghegan, Patrick M. 1999. *The Irish Act of Union: A Study in High Politics, 1798–1801*. Dublin: Gill and Macmillan.

George, Albert Joseph. 1955. *The Development of French Romanticism: The Impact of the Industrial Revolution on Literature*. Syracuse, NY: Syracuse University Press.

Germain, Pierre. 1985. *J.-B. Drouet d'Erlon: Maréchal de France, général comte d'Empire, premier gouverneur de l'Algérie*. Paris: Lanore.

Gershoy, Leo D. 1957. *The Era of the French Revolution: The Era That Shook the World*. Malabar, FL: Krieger.

Gershoy, Leo D. 1960. *The French Revolution: 1789–1799*. New York: Holt, Rinehart and Winston.

Gershoy, Leo D. 1964. *The French Revolution and Napoleon*. New York: Meredith.

Ghirelli, Antonio. 1981. *Storia di Napoli* [History of Naples]. Torino: Einaudi.

Ghisalberti, Alberto Maria, ed. 1960. *Dizionario Biografico degli Italiani*. Vol. 27. Istituto dell'Enciclopedia Italiana. Rome: Treccani.

Gibbs, N. H. 1957. "Armed Forces and the Art of War." In *The New Cambridge Modern History*, ed. C. W. Crawley. Vol. 9: 473 ff. Cambridge: Cambridge University Press.

Gierowski, Józef Andrzej. 1996. *The Polish-Lithuanian Commonwealth in the XVIIIth Century*. Kraków: Polska Akademia Umiejętno_ci.

Giesselmann, Werner. 1977. *Die brumairianische Elite*. Stuttgart: Klett.

Giles, Frank. 2001. *Napoleon Bonaparte: England's Prisoner*. New York: Carroll and Graf.

Gill, Conrad. 1913. *The Naval Mutinies of 1797*. Manchester, UK: Manchester University Press.

Gill, John, 1993. *With Eagles to Glory: Napoleon and His German Allies in the 1809 Campaign*. Novato, CA: Presidio.

Gill, John H. 1998. "Vermin, Scorpions and Mosquitoes: The Rheinbund in the Peninsula." In *The Peninsular War: Aspects of the Struggle for the Iberian Peninsula*, ed. Ian Fletcher. Staplehurst, UK: Spellmount.

Gill, Stephen. 1990. *William Wordsworth: A Life*. Oxford: Oxford Paperbacks.

Gillespie-Payne, Jonathan. 2004. *Waterloo: In the Footsteps of the Commanders*. London: Leo Cooper.

Gillispie, Charles Coulston. 1971. *Lazare Carnot, Savant: A Monograph Treating Carnot's Scientific Work*. Princeton: Princeton University Press.

Gillispie, Charles Coulston. 1980. *Science and Polity in France at the End of the Old Regime*. Princeton: Princeton University Press.

Gillispie, Charles Coulston, and Michel Dewachter, eds. 1987. *The Monuments of Egypt: The Napoleonic Edition*. Princeton: Princeton Architectural Press.

Gillispie, Charles Coulston, with Robert Fox and Ivor Grattan-Guiness. 1997. *Pierre Simon Laplace, 1749–1827: A Life in Exact Science*. Princeton: Princeton University Press.

Gilmour, Ian H. 2002. *The Making of the Poem: Byron and Shelley in Their Time*. London: Chatto and Windus.

Girod de l'Ain, Felix Jean. 1873. *Dix ans de mes Souvenirs militaires (de 1805 à 1815)*. Paris: N.p.

Gittings, Robert. 1978. *John Keats: The Living Year, 21 September 1818 to 21 September 1819*. Westport, CT: Greenwood.

Glaser, Hubert, ed. 1980. *Krone und Verfassung, Konig Max I. Joseph und der neue Staat*. Munich: Hirmer.

Glendon, Mary Ann, Michael Wallace Gordon, and Paolo G. Carozza. 1999. *Comparative Legal Traditions in a Nutshell*. 2nd ed. St. Paul, MN: West Group.

Glinka, Fedor. 1814. *Podvigi grafa Mikhaila Andreyevich Miloradovicha v Otechestvennuiu voinu 1812 goda, s prisovokupleniem nekotorikh pisem ot raznikh osob* [Exploits of Count Mikhail Andreyevich Miloradovich during the Patriotic War of 1812, annexed with Some Additional Letters from Various Persons]. St. Petersburg: V tip. S. Selivanovskago.

Glinka, Fedor. 1818. *Kratkoe obozrenie voennoi zhizni i podvigov grafa Miloradovicha* [A Brief Description of the Military Career and Exploits of Count Miloradovich]. St. Petersburg: N.p.

Glinka, V. M., and A. V. Pomarnatskii. 1981. *Voennaya Galereya Zimnego Dvortsa*. Leningrad: Iskusstvo.

Glinoetskii, N. 1874. *Russkii Generalnii Shtab v tsarstvovanie Aleksandra I*. St. Petersburg: V Tip. Departamenta udielov.

Glover, Michael. 1970. *Britannia Sickens: Sir Arthur Wellesley and the Convention of Cintra*. London: Cooper.

Glover, Michael. 1971. *Legacy of Glory: The Bonaparte Kingdom of Spain, 1808–1813*. New York: Scribner's Sons.

Glover, Michael. 1977. *Wellington's Army in the Peninsula, 1808–1814*. New York: Hippocrene.

Glover, Michael. 1979. *The Napoleonic Wars: An Illustrated History, 1792–1815*. New York: Hippocrene.

Glover, Michael. 1987. "The True Patriot: Jourdan." In *Napoleon's Marshals*, ed. David G. Chandler, 156–175. New York: Macmillan.

Glover, Michael. 1996. *Wellington's Peninsular Victories: The Battles of Busaco, Salamanca, Vitoria and the Nivelle*. London: Weidenfeld and Nicolson.

Glover, Michael. 2001. *The Peninsular War, 1807–1814: A Concise Military History.* London: Penguin.

Glover, Michael. 2001. *Wellington as Military Commander.* London. Penguin.

Glover, Michael. 2003. *Warfare in the Age of Bonaparte.* London: Pen and Sword.

Glover, Richard. 1963. *Peninsular Preparation: Reform of the British Army, 1795–1809.* Cambridge: Cambridge University Press.

Glover, Richard. 1973. *Britain at Bay: Defence against Bonaparte, 1803–14.* London: Allen and Unwin.

Gneisenau, August Wilhelm. 1815. *Memoirs of the Life and Campaigns of Marshal Blücher.* Trans. J. E. Marston. London: Sherwood, Neely and Jones.

Gneisenau, August Wilhelm. 1996. *The Life and Campaigns of Field-Marshal Prince Blücher.* London: Constable.

Godechot, Jacques. 1983. *La Grande Nation: L'Expansion révolutionnaire de la France dans le monde de 1789 à 1799.* Paris: Aubier Montaigne.

Godechot, Jacques. 1986. *Le comte d'Antraigues.* Paris: Fayard.

Godfrey, Richard. 2002. *James Gillray: The Art of Caricature.* London: Tate Gallery.

Goerlitz, Walter. 1953. *History of the German General Staff: 1657–1945.* New York: Praeger.

Goethe, Johann Wolfgang von. 1983–1989. *Collected Works.* 12 vols. New York: Suhrkamp; Cambridge, MA: Insel.

Goetz, Robert. 2005. *1805, Austerlitz: Napoleon and the Destruction of the Third Coalition.* London: Greenhill.

Golinski, Jan. 1992. *Science as Public Culture: Chemistry and Enlightenment in Britain, 1760–1820.* Cambridge: Cambridge University Press.

Golitsyn, N. 1892. *Rod kniazei Golitsynikh.* St. Petersburg: I. N. Skorokhodov.

Goltz, Colmar Freiherr von der. 1913. *Jena to Eylau: The Disgrace and Redemption of the Old Prussian Army.* New York: Dutton.

Gonner, E. C. K. 1966. *Common Land and Inclosure.* 2nd ed. New York: Kelley.

Gooch, G. P, and Sir A. W. Ward. 1970. *The Cambridge History of British Foreign Policy, 1783–1919.* 3 vols. Vol. 1, *1783–1815.* New York: Octagon. (Orig. pub. 1923.)

Goodspeed, D. J. 1965. *Napoleon's Eighty Days.* Boston: Houghton Mifflin.

Goodspeed, Donald J. 1965. *Bayonets at St. Cloud: The Story of the 18th Brumaire.* New York: Hart-Davis.

Goodwin, G. 1997. *The Janissaries.* London: Saqi.

Goodwin, Peter. 2004. *Men O'War: The Illustrated Story of Life in Nelson's Navy.* London: National Maritime Museum.

Goodwin, Peter. 2004. *Nelson's Victory: 101 Questions and Answers about HMS* Victory, *Nelson's Flagship at Trafalgar 1805.* London: Brassey's.

Goodwin, Peter. 2005. *The Ships of Trafalgar: The British, French and Spanish Fleets, 21 October 1805.* London: Conway Maritime.

Gordon, Stewart. 1993. *The Marathas, 1600–1818.* Cambridge: Cambridge University Press.

Gotteri, Nicole. 1997. *La police secrète du Premier Empire.* Paris: Perrin.

Gottschalk, Louis Reichental, and Margaret Maddox. 1969. *Lafayette in the French Revolution.* Chicago: University of Chicago Press.

Gotwals, Vernon, ed. 1968. *Haydn: Two Contemporary Portraits.* Madison: University of Wisconsin Press.

Gough, Hugh. 1988. *The Newspaper Press in the French Revolution.* London: Routledge.

Gough, Hugh, 1998. *The Terror in the French Revolution.* Basingstoke, UK: Macmillan.

Gould, Cecil. 1965. *Trophy of Conquest: The Musée Napoléon and the Creation of the Louvre.* London: Faber and Faber.

Grab, Alexander. 2003. *Napoleon and the Transformation of Europe.* New York: Palgrave Macmillan.

Grabbe, Pavel Khristoforovich. *Iz zapisok grafa A. F. Lanzherona, Russkii Arkhiv.* 1895. No. 3. St. Petersburg: N.p.

Grainger, John D., ed. 1996. *The Royal Navy in the River Plate, 1806–1807.* Brookfield, VT: Ashgate.

Grainger, John D. 2004. *The Amiens Truce: Britain and Bonaparte, 1801–1803.* Rochester, NY: Boydell.

Grand Duke Nikolay Mikhailovich. 1913. *General Adjutanti imperatora Aleksandra I.* St. Petersburg: Ekspeditsiia zagotovleniia gos. bumag.

Grant, Charles. 1971. *Foot Grenadiers.* London: Osprey.

Graves, Donald E. 1993. *The Battle of Lundy's Lane on the Niagara, 1814.* Baltimore, MD: Nautical and Aviation.

Graves, Donald E. 1994. *Red Coats and Grey Jackets: The Battle of Chippewa, 5 July 1814.* Toronto: Dundurn.

Gray, Collin S. 1999. *Modern Strategy.* Oxford: Oxford University Press.

Gray, Denis. 1963. *Spencer Perceval: The Evangelical Prime Minister 1762–1812.* Manchester: Manchester University Press.

Gray, Marion W. 1986. *Prussia in Transition: Society and Politics under the Stein Reform Ministry of 1808.* Philadelphia: American Philosophical Society.

Gray, Wilbur. 1993. "Alpine Thunder: The Battle for Zürich 1799." *Empires, Eagles & Lions* 2 (no. 4): 8–15.

Great Britain. War Office, Intelligence Division. 1884. *British Minor Expeditions, 1746–1814.* London: Her Majesty's Stationery Office.

Greer, Donald. 1935. *The Incidence of the Terror in the French Revolution: A Statistical Study.* Cambridge, MA: Harvard University Press.

Greer, Donald. 1951. *The Incidence of the Emigration during the French Revolution.* Cambridge, MA: Harvard University Press.

Gregory, Desmond. 1988. *Sicily: The Insecure Base: A History of the British Occupation of Sicily, 1806–15.* Madison, NJ: Fairleigh Dickinson University Press.

Gregory, Desmond. 1996. *Malta, Britain, and the European Powers, 1793–1815.* Madison, NJ: Fairleigh Dickinson University Press.

Gregory, Desmond. 1996. *Napoleon's Jailer: Lt. Gen. Sir Hudson Lowe: A Life.* Madison, NJ: Fairleigh Dickinson University Press.

Gregory, Desmond. 2001. *Napoleon's Italy.* Madison, NJ: Fairleigh Dickinson University Press.

Grehan, John. 2004. *The Lines of Torres Vedras: The Cornerstone of Wellington's Strategy in the Peninsular War, 1809–1812.* Staplehurst, UK: Spellmount.

Grenier, E. 1911. *Etude sur 1807: Manoeuvres d'Eylau et Friedland.* Paris: Lavauzelle.

Grenville, William Wyndham Grenville, Baron. 1891–1927. *The Manuscripts of J. B. Fortescue, Esq., Preserved at Dropmore.* 10 vols. London: Eyre and Spottiswoode.

Gribanov, V. 1979. *Bagration v Peterburge* [Bagration in St. Petersburg]. Leningrad: Lenizdat.

Griffin, Andrew. 2004. *Cuthbert Collingwood: The Northumbrian Who Saved the Nation.* Durham, UK: Mouth of the Tyne.

Griffith, Patrick [Paddy]. 1976. *French Artillery.* London: Almark.

Griffith, Paddy. 1985. *Wellington Commander.* Chichester, UK: Bird.

Griffith, Paddy. 1998. *The Art of War of Revolutionary France, 1789–1802.* London: Greenhill.

Griffiths, Arthur. 1891. *French Revolutionary Generals.* London: Chapman and Hall.

Grimble, Ian. 2001. *The Sea Wolf: The Life of Admiral Cochrane.* Edinburgh: Birlinn.

Grimsted, Patricia K. 1969. *The Foreign Ministers of Alexander I: Political Attitudes and the Conduct of Russian Diplomacy, 1801–1825.* Berkeley and Los Angeles: University of California Press.

Grimsted, Patricia K. 1970. "Czartoryski's System for Russian Foreign Policy, 1803: A Memorandum." *California Slavic Studies* 5: 19–91.

Griswold, Rufus. 1855. *Napoleon and the Marshals of the Empire.* Philadelphia: Lippincott.

Grosser Generalstab, Kriegsgeschichtliche Abteilung, II. 1906. *1806: Das Preussische Offizierkorps und die Untersuchung der Kriegsereignisse.* Berlin: Mittler.

Grosskurth, Phyllis. 1997. *Byron: The Flawed Angel.* Boston: Houghton Mifflin.

Gruber, Ira D. 1972. *The Howe Brothers and the American Revolution.* Published for the Institute of Early American History and Culture at Williamsburg, VA. Chapel Hill: University of North Carolina Press.

Grunwald, Constantin de. 1953. *Metternich.* Trans. Dorothy Todd. London: Falcon.

Gruppe. Henry, ed. 1979. *The Frigates.* New York: Time-Life Books.

Guedalla, Philip. 1997. *The Duke.* Ware, UK: Wordsworth.

Guillon, Edouard. 1888. *La France et l'Irlande pendant la revolution: Hoche et Humbert.* Paris: Colin.

Guillon, Edouard. 1910. *Napoleon et la Suisse, 1803–1815.* Paris: Lausanne Plon.

Gullick, Edward. 1955. *Europe's Classical Balance of Power: A Case History of the Theory and Practice of One of the Great Concepts of European Statecraft.* Ithaca, NY: Cornell University Press.

Gurney, Gene. 1982. *Kingdoms of Europe.* New York: Crown.

Guttridge, Leonard F. 1992. *Mutiny: A History of Naval Insurrection.* New York: Berkley.

Guy, Alan J., ed. 1990. *The Road to Waterloo: The British Army and the Struggle against Revolutionary and Napoleonic France, 1793–1815.* London: National Army Museum.

H

Hachenburg, Alexander Graf von. 1934. *Ludwig Adolf Peter, fürst zu Sayn und Wittgenstein, kaiserlich russischer general-feldmarschall, 1768/69–1843.* Hanover: W. Dorn.

Haffner, Sebastian. 1980. *Preussen ohne Legende.* Hamburg: Gruner and Jahr.

Hague, William. 2004. *William Pitt the Younger.* London: HarperCollins.

Hahn, Roger. 1971. *The Anatomy of a Scientific Institution: The Paris Academy of Sciences, 1666–1803.* Berkeley and Los Angeles: University of California Press.

Haiman, Miecislaus. 1977. *Kosciuszko: Leader and Exile.* New York: Kosciuszko Foundation.

Haines, Simon. 1997. *Shelley: The Divided Self.* Basingstoke, UK: Macmillan.

Hales, E. E. Y. 1962. *Napoleon and the Pope: The Story of Napoleon and Pius VII.* London: Eyre and Spottiswoode.

Hales, Edward. 1966. *Revolution and Papacy, 1769–1846.* Notre Dame, IN: University of Notre Dame Press.

Halévy, Elie. 1972. *The Growth of Philosophical Radicalism.* Trans. from the French by Mary Morris. London: Faber and Faber.

Hall, Christopher D. 1992. *British Strategy in the Napoleonic Wars, 1803–15.* Manchester: Manchester University Press.

Hall, Christopher D. 2004. *Wellington's Navy: Sea Power and the Peninsular War, 1807–1814.* London: Chatham.

Hall, John. 1915. *General Pichegru's Treason.* New York: Dutton.

Hallows, Ian S. 1991. *Regiments and Corps of the British Army.* London: Arms and Armour.

Hamilton, Emma. 2001. *Memoirs of Emma, Lady Hamilton, the Friend of Lord Nelson, and the Court of Naples.* Honolulu: University Press of the Pacific. (Orig. pub. 1910.)

Hamilton-Williams, David. 1993. *Waterloo, New Perspectives: The Great Battle Reappraised.* New York: Wiley.

Hamilton-Williams, David. 1994. *The Fall of Napoleon: The Final Betrayal.* London: Arms and Armour.

Hampson, Norman. 1974. *The Life and Opinions of Maximilien Robespierre.* London: Duckworth.

Hampson, Norman. 1974. *A Social History of the French Revolution.* Toronto: University of Toronto Press.

Hampson, Norman. 1982. *Will and Circumstance: Montesquieu, Rousseau and the French Revolution.* London: Duckworth.

Handel, Michael I. 2000. *Masters of War: Classical Strategic Thought.* London: Cass.

Handelsman, M. 1948–1950. *Adam Czartoryski.* 2 vols. Warsaw: Historyczne Towarzystwo.

Hankins, Thomas L. 1985. *Science and the Enlightenment.* Cambridge: Cambridge University Press.

Harbron, John. 2004. *Trafalgar and the Spanish Navy: The Spanish Experience of Sea Power.* London: Conway Maritime.

Harding, Richard. 1999. *Sea Power and Naval Warfare, 1650–1830.* Annapolis, MD: Naval Institute Press.

Hardman, John. 1981. *The French Revolution: The Fall of the Ancien Régime to the Thermidorian Reaction, 1785–1795.* London: Arnold.

Hardman, John. 1999. *Robespierre.* London: Longman.

Hardman, William, and J. Holland Rose, eds. 1994. *A History of Malta during the Period of the French and British Occupations, 1798–1815.* Valletta: Midsea. (Orig. pub. 1909.)

Harland, John. 1984. *Seamanship in the Age of Sail.* London: Conway Maritime.

Harrison, J. F. C. 1969. *Robert Owen and the Owenites in Britain and America: The Quest for the New Moral World.* London: Routledge and Kegan Paul.

Hart, Roger. 1972. *England Expects.* London: Wayland.

Hartley, Janet M. 1994. *Alexander I.* London: Longman.

Hartley, Janet M. 1995. "'It Is the Festival of the Crown and Sceptres': The Diplomatic, Commercial and Domestic Significance of the Visit of Alexander I to England in 1814."

Slavonic and East European Review 73, no. 2 (April): 126–168.

Hartley, Janet M. 1999. *A Social History of the Russian Empire, 1650–1825.* London and New York: Longman.

Harvey, A. D. 1978. *Britain in the Early Nineteenth Century.* London: Batsford.

Harvey, Robert. 2000. *Liberators.* London: Constable and Robinson.

Harvey, Robert. 2002. *Cochrane: The Life and Exploits of a Fighting Captain.* London: Constable and Robinson.

Haswell, Jock. 1969. *The First Respectable Spy: The Life and Times of Colquhoun Grant, Wellington's Head of Intelligence.* London: Hamilton.

Hattersley, Roy. 1974. *Nelson.* London: Purcell.

Hauterive, Ernest d'. 1922–1964. *Police secrète du Ier Empire.* 5 vols. Paris: Perrin.

Hauterive, Ernest d'. 1944. *Napoléon et sa police.* Paris: Flammarion.

Havard, Robert. 1996. *Wellington's Welsh General: A Life of Sir Thomas Picton.* London: Aurum.

Hawke, David Freeman. 1955. *Paine.* New York: Harper and Row.

Hayman, Peter. 1990. *Soult: Napoleon's Maligned Marshal.* London: Arms and Armour.

Haythornthwaite, Philip J. 1976. *Uniforms of the Retreat from Moscow, 1812, in Color.* New York: Hippocrene.

Haythornthwaite, Philip J. 1981. *Uniforms of the French Revolutionary Wars, 1789–1802.* Poole, UK: Blandford.

Haythornthwaite, Philip J. 1983. *Napoleon's Line Infantry.* London: Osprey.

Haythornthwaite, Philip J. 1984. *Napoleon's Guard Infantry.* Vol. 1. Oxford: Osprey.

Haythornthwaite, Philip J. 1985. *Uniforms of the Napoleonic Wars, 1796–1814.* Poole, UK: Blandford.

Haythornthwaite, Philip J. 1986. *Austrian Army of the Napoleonic Wars.* Vol. 1, *Infantry.* London: Osprey.

Haythornthwaite, Philip J. 1986. *Austrian Army of the Napoleonic Wars.* Vol. 2, *Cavalry.* London: Osprey.

Haythornthwaite, Philip J. 1987. *The Russian Army of the Napoleonic Wars.* Vol. 1, *Infantry, 1799–1814.* London: Osprey.

Haythornthwaite, Philip J. 1987. *The Russian Army of the Napoleonic Wars.* Vol. 2, *Cavalry.* London: Osprey.

Haythornthwaite, Philip J. 1988. *Napoleon's Specialist Troops.* London: Osprey.

Haythornthwaite, Philip J. 1989. *Wellington's Military Machine.* London: Guild.

Haythornthwaite, Philip J. 1990. *Austrian Specialist Troops of the Napoleonic Wars.* London: Osprey.

Haythornthwaite, Philip J. 1990. *The Napoleonic Sourcebook.* London: Cassell.

Haythornthwaite, Philip J. 1993. *Napoleon's Campaigns in Italy.* London: Osprey.

Haythornthwaite, Philip J. 1995. *The Colonial Wars Sourcebook.* London: Arms and Armour.

Haythornthwaite, Philip J. 1995. *Uniforms of the Peninsular War, 1807–1814.* London: Weidenfeld Military.

Haythornthwaite, Philip J. 1996. *The Armies of Wellington.* London: Arms and Armour.

Haythornthwaite, Philip J. 1996. *British Infantry of the Napoleonic Wars.* London: Weidenfeld and Nicolson.

Haythornthwaite, Philip J. 1996. *Uniforms of Waterloo.* London: Weidenfeld and Nicolson.

Haythornthwaite, Philip J. 1997. *Imperial Guardsman, 1799–1815.* London: Osprey.

Haythornthwaite, Philip J. 1999. *Nelson's Navy.* Oxford: Osprey.

Haythornthwaite, Philip J. 1999. *Waterloo Men: The Experience of Battle, 16–18 June 1815.* Ramsbury, UK: Crowood.

Haythornthwaite, Philip J. 1999. *Weapons and Equipment of the Napoleonic Wars.* London: Arms and Armour.

Haythornthwaite, Philip J. 2001. *Corunna 1809.* Oxford: Osprey.

Haythornthwaite, Philip J. 2001. *Die Hard: Famous Napoleonic Battles.* London: Cassell.

Haythornthwaite, Philip J. 2001. *Napoleonic Cavalry.* London: Weidenfeld and Nicolson.

Haythornthwaite, Philip J. 2001. *Napoleon's Commanders.* 2 vols. Vol. 1, *c. 1792–1809.* Oxford: Osprey.

Haythornthwaite, Philip J. 2002. *British Rifleman, 1797–1815.* Oxford: Osprey.

Haythornthwaite, Philip J. 2002. *Napoleon's Commanders.* 2 vols. Vol. 2, *c. 1809–15.* Oxford: Osprey.

Haythornthwaite, Philip J. 2005. *Corunna 1809: Sir John Moore's Fighting Retreat.* Westport, CT: Greenwood.

Haythornthwaite, Philip J., James R. Arnold, Ian Castle, Guy C. Dempsey Jr., Tim Hicks, J. David Markham, Peter G. Tsouras, and Andrew Uffindel. 1998. *Napoleon: The Final Verdict.* London: Weidenfeld and Nicolson.

Hayward, Joel. 2003. *For God and Glory: Lord Nelson and His Way of War.* Annapolis, MD: Naval Institute Press.

Hazareesingh, Sudhir. 2004. *The Legend of Napoleon.* London: Granta.

Headley, J. T. 1900. *Napoleon and His Marshals.* Vol. 1. New York: Burt.

Headley, J. T. 1910. *Napoleon and His Marshals.* Vol. 2. New York: Hurst.

Heathcote, T. A. 2005. *Nelson's Trafalgar Captains and Their Battles.* London: Pen and Sword.

Heckscher, E. F. 1964. *The Continental System: An Economic Interpretation.* Gloucester, MA: Peter Smith.

Hedley, Douglas. 2000. *Coleridge, Philosophy and Religion.* Cambridge: Cambridge University Press.

Hegel, Georg Wilhelm Friedrich. 1956. *The Philosophy of History.* New York: Dover.

Heidler, David, and Jeanne Heidler. 2002. *The War of 1812.* Westport, CT: Greenwood.

Heinl, Michael, Robert Heinl, and Nancy Heinl. 1996. *Written in Blood: The Story of the Haitian People, 1492–1995.* New York: University Press of America.

Heitz, Louis. 1892. *Le général Duroc, duc de Frioul.* Grenoble: Baratier.

Helfert, Baron J. A. 1887. *Kaiser Franz und die österreichischen Befreiungs-Kriege.* Vienna: Prandel und Ewald.

Henderson, Ernest F. 1911. *Blücher and the Uprising of Prussia against Napoleon.* New York: Putnam's Sons.

Henderson, James. 1998. *The Frigates.* London: Wordsworth.

Henderson, James. 2005. *Frigates, Sloops and Brigs.* London: Leo Cooper.

Henry, Chris. 2002. *British Napoleonic Artillery, 1793–1815.* Vol. 1, *Field Artillery.* Oxford: Osprey.

Henry, Chris. 2003. *British Napoleonic Artillery, 1793–1815.* Vol. 2, *Siege and Coastal Artillery.* Oxford: Osprey.

Henry, Chris. 2004. *Napoleonic Naval Armaments, 1792–1815.* Oxford: Osprey.

Henry, Isabel. 2002. *Dumouriez: Général de la Révolution (1739–1823); Biographie.* Paris: L'Harmattan.

Hereford, George B. 2002. *Napoleon's Invasion of Russia.* London: Empiricus.

Heriot, Angus. 1957. *The French in Italy, 1796–1799.* London: Chatto and Windus.

Herman, Arthur. 2005. *To Rule the Waves: How the British Navy Shaped the Modern World.* London: Hodder and Stoughton.

Herold, J. Christopher. 1964. *Mistress to an Age: A Life of Madame de Staël.* New York: Time.

Herold, J. Christopher. 1967. *The Battle of Waterloo.* London: Cassell.

Herold, J. Christopher. 1987. *The Age of Napoleon.* New York: Houghton Mifflin.

Herold, J. Christopher. 2005. *Bonaparte in Egypt.* London: Leo Cooper.

Herr, Richard. 1959. *The Eighteenth Century Revolution in Spain.* Princeton: Princeton University Press.

Herr, Richard. 1989. *Rural Change and Royal Finances in Spain at the End of the Old Regime.* Berkeley and Los Angeles: University of California Press.

Hertenberger, H., and F. Wiltscheck. 1938. *Erzherzog Karl: Der Sieger von Aspern.* Vienna: Styria.

Hibbert, Christopher. 1973. *George IV: Regent and King, 1811–1830.* New York: Harper and Row.

Hibbert, Christopher. 1980. *The French Revolution.* London: Lane.

Hibbert, Christopher. 1995. *Nelson: A Personal History.* London: Penguin.

Hibbert, Christopher. 1998. *George III: A Personal History.* London: Viking.

Hibbert, Christopher. 1998. *Wellington: A Personal History.* London: HarperCollins.

Hibbert, Christopher. 2003. *Corunna.* London: Weidenfeld and Nicolson.

Hibbert, Christopher. 2003. *Napoleon: His Wives and Women.* London: HarperCollins.

Hibbert, Christopher. 2004. *Waterloo: Napoleon's Last Campaign.* Blue Ridge Summit, PA: Cooper Square.

Hickey, Donald R. 1989. *The War of 1812: A Forgotten Conflict.* Urbana: University of Illinois Press.

Higonnet, Patrice. 1998. *Goodness beyond Virtue: Jacobins during the French Revolution.* Cambridge, MA: Harvard University Press.

Hill, Brian. 1985. *British Parliamentary Parties, 1742–1832.* London: Allen and Unwin.

Hill, David. 1985. *Constable's English Landscapes Scenery.* London: John Murray.

Hill, Peter P. 2005. *Napoleon's Troublesome Americans: Franco-American Relations, 1804–1815.* Washington, DC: Potomac.

Hill, Richard. 1998. *The Prizes of War: The Naval Prize System in the Napoleonic Wars, 1793–1815.* Stroud, UK: Sutton.

Hilt, Douglas. 1987. *The Troubled Trinity: Godoy and the Spanish Monarchs.* Tuscaloosa: University of Alabama Press.

Hilton, Boyd. 1977. *Corn, Cash, Commerce: The Economic Policies of the Tory Governments, 1815–1830.* Oxford: Oxford University Press.

Hilton, Boyd. 1988. *The Political Arts of Lord Liverpool.* Transactions of the Royal Historical Society, 5th ser., 38. London: Royal Historical Society.

Hinde, Wendy. 1981. *Castlereagh: A Political Biography.* London: Collins.

Hinde, Wendy. 1989. *George Canning.* Oxford: Blackwell.

Hinde, Wendy. 1992. *Catholic Emancipation: A Shake to Men's Minds.* Oxford: Blackwell.

Hirtenfeld, Jaromir. 1856–1857. *Der Maria Theresienorden und seine Mitglieder.* Vienna: Staatsdruckerei.

Hitsman, J. Mackay. 1999. *The Incredible War of 1812: A Military History.* Toronto: Robin Brass.

Hittle, J. D., ed. 1947. *Jomini and His Summary of the Art of War.* Harrisburg, PA: Military Service.

Hobsbawm, Eric John. 1996. *The Age of Revolution, 1789–1848.* New York: Vintage.

Hochschild, Adam. 2006. *Bury the Chains: The British Struggle to Abolish Slavery.* London: Pan.

Hodge, Jane Aiken. 1972. *The Double Life of Jane Austen.* London: Hodder and Stoughton.

Hodges, R. 1992. *The Eagle and the Spade: Archaeology of Rome during the Napoleonic Era, 1809–14.* Cambridge: Cambridge University Press.

Hoeven, Marco van der, Graddy Boven, and Annelies Aerts-van Bueren. 1999. *1799! Strijd achter de Duinen: Brits-Russische invasie en Noord-Holland.* Den Helder, Netherlands: Marinemuseum.

Hofschröer, Peter. 1984. *Prussian Light Infantry, 1792–1815.* London: Osprey.

Hofschröer, Peter. 1985. *Prussian Cavalry of the Napoleonic Wars.* 2 vols. London: Osprey.

Hofschröer, Peter. 1987. "The Good Officer." In *Napoleon's Marshals,* ed. David G. Chandler, 176–189. New York: Macmillan.

Hofschröer, Peter. 1987. *Prussian Reserve, Militia and Irregular Troops, 1806–15.* London: Osprey.

Hofschröer, Peter. 1989. *The Hanoverian Army of the Napoleonic Wars, 1793–1816.* London: Osprey.

Hofschröer, Peter. 1998. *1815, The Waterloo Campaign: Wellington, His German Allies and the Battles of Ligny and Quatre Bras.* London: Greenhill.

Hofschröer, Peter. 1999. *1815, The Waterloo Campaign: The German Victory from Waterloo to the Fall of Napoleon.* London: Greenhill.

Hofschröer, Peter. 2000. *Leipzig 1813: The Battle of the Nations.* Oxford: Osprey.

Hofschröer, Peter. 2001. *Lützen and Bautzen 1813: The Turning Point.* Oxford: Osprey.

Hofschröer, Peter. 2003. *Prussian Staff and Specialist Troops, 1791–1815.* Oxford: Osprey.

Hofschröer, Peter. 2004. *Wellington's Smallest Victory: The Duke, the Model Maker and the Secret of Waterloo.* London: Faber and Faber.

Hofschröer, Peter. 2005. *Waterloo 1815: Quatre Bras and Ligny.* London: Leo Cooper.

Hofschröer, Peter. 2006. *Wavre, Plancenoit and the Race to Paris.* London: Leo Cooper.

Hogg, O. F. 1970. *Artillery: Its Origin, Heyday, and Decline.* Camden, CT: Archon.

Höhne, Horst. 2000. *In Pursuit of Love: The Short and Troublesome Life and Work of Percy Bysshe Shelley.* New York: Peter.

Holleben, Albert Hermann Ludwig von, and Rudolf von Caemmerer. 1904–1909. *Geschichte des Frühjahrsfeldzuges 1813 und seine Vorgeschichte.* 2 vols. Berlin: Mittler.

Hollins, David. 1996. *Austrian Auxiliary Troops, 1792–1816.* London: Osprey.

Hollins, David. 1996. "Decided by Cavalry: Würzburg 1796." *Age of Napoleon* 20 (Spring): 12–17.

Hollins, David. 1998. *Austrian Grenadiers and Infantry, 1788–1816.* Oxford: Osprey.

Hollins, David. 2000. *The Battle of Marengo.* Oxford: Osprey.

Hollins, David. 2003. *Austrian Napoleonic Artillery, 1792–1815.* Oxford: Osprey.

Hollins, David. 2003. *Hungarian Hussar, 1756–1815.* Oxford: Osprey.

Hollins, David. 2004. *Austrian Commanders of the Napoleonic Wars, 1792–1815.* Oxford: Osprey.

Hollins, David. 2004. "The Battle of Jemappes." *First Empire* 77: 7–13; 78: 32.

Holme, Thea. 1976. *Prinny's Daughter.* London: Hamish Hamilton.

Holme, Thea. 1979. *Caroline: A Biography of Caroline of Brunswick.* London: Hamish Hamilton.

Holmes, Richard. 1990. *Coleridge: Early Visions.* New York: Viking.

Holmes, Richard. 1998. *Coleridge: Darker Reflections.* London: HarperCollins.

Holmes, Richard. 2001. *Redcoat: The British Soldier in the Age of Horse and Musket.* London: HarperCollins.

Holmes, Richard. 2003. *Wellington: The Iron Duke.* London: HarperCollins.

Holt, Edgar. 1971. *The Making of Italy: 1815–1870.* New York: Atheneum.

Holtman, Robert B. 1950. *Napoleonic Propaganda.* Baton Rouge: University of Louisiana Press.

Holtman, Robert B. 1967. *The Napoleonic Revolution.* Philadelphia: Lippincott.

Holzman, Gerard J., and Björn Pehrson. 1995. *The Early History of Data Networks.* Los Alamitos, CA: IEEE Computer Society Press.

Honor, Hugh. 1968. *Neo-Classicism.* Harmondsworth, UK: Penguin.

Hoobler, Thomas, and Dorothy Hoobler. 1990. *Toussaint Louverture.* New York: Chelsea House.

Höpfner, Eduard von. 1991. *Der Krieg von 1806 und 1807: Ein Beitrag zur Geschichte der Preussischen Armee nach den Quellen des Kriegs-Archivs bearbeitet.* 1850–1851. 4 vols. Berlin: LTR-Verlag GmbH.

Hopton, Richard. 2002. *The Battle of Maida 1806: Fifteen Minutes of Glory.* London: Leo Cooper.

Hore, Peter. *The Habit of Victory: The Story of the Royal Navy from 1545 to 1945.* London: Pan.

Hornborg, Erik. 1955. *När Riket Sprängdes: Fälttågen I Finland och Västerbotten, 1808–1809.* Stockholm: Norstedt.

Horne, Alistair. 1979. *Napoleon, Master of Europe, 1805–1807.* London: Weidenfeld and Nicolson.

Horne, Alistair. 1996. *How Far from Austerlitz? Napoleon, 1805–1815.* London: Macmillan.

Horricks, Raymond. 1988. *Marshal Ney: The Romance and the Real.* London: Archway.

Horricks, Raymond. 1994. *Military Politics from Bonaparte to the Bourbons: The Life and Death of Michel Ney, 1769–1815.* New Brunswick, NJ: Transaction.

Horricks, Raymond. 1995. *Napoleon's Elite.* London: Transaction.

Horsetzky, A. von. 1888. *Kriegsgeschichtliche Ubersicht der wichtigsten Feldzüge in Europa seit 1792* [Military-Historical Overview of the Most Important Campaigns in Europe since 1792]. Vienna: L. Seidel.

Horsman, Reginald. 1962. *The Causes of the War of 1812.* Philadelphia: University of Pennsylvania Press.

Horward, Donald. 1965. *The Battle of Bussaco.* Tallahassee: Florida State University Press.

Horward, Donald, ed. 1973. *The French Campaign in Portugal: 1810–1811.* Minneapolis: University of Minnesota Press.

Horward, Donald. 1994. *Napoleon and Iberia: The Twin Sieges of Ciudad Rodrigo and Almeida.* London: Greenhill.

Houdaille, Jacques. 1972. "Pertes de l'armée française sous le premier empire" [French Army Losses during the First Empire]. *Population* (janvier–février): 27–50.

Houlding, J. A. 1981. *Fit for Service: Training of the British Army, 1715–95.* Oxford: Oxford University Press.

Hourtoulle, F. G. 1998. *Jena-Auerstaedt: The Triumph of the Eagle.* Paris: Histoire and Collections.

Hourtoulle, F. G. 2000. *Borodino, the Moskova: The Battle for the Redoubts.* Paris: Histoire and Collections.

Hourtoulle, F. G. 2002. *Battle of Jena, 1806.* Paris: Histoire et Collections.

Hourtoulle, F. G. 2002. *Wagram: At the Heyday of the Empire.* Paris: Histoire and Collections.

Hourtoulle, F. G. 2003. *Austerlitz: The Empire at Its Zenith.* Paris: Histoire and Collections.

Hourtoulle, F. G. 2005. *1814: The French Campaign.* Paris: Histoire et Collections.

Houssaye, Henry. 1900. *1815 Waterloo.* London: Adam and Charles Black.

Houssaye, Henry. 1912. *Iéna et la campagne de 1806.* Paris: Perrin.

Houssaye, Henry. 1927. *1815.* Paris: Perrin.

Houssaye, Henry. 2005. *Napoleon and the Campaign of 1814: France.* Uckfield, UK: Naval and Military.

Howard, Frank. 1979. *Sailing Ships of War, 1400–1860.* London: Conway Maritime.

Howard, Martin. 2002. *Wellington's Doctors: The British Army Medical Services in the Napoleonic Wars.* Staplehurst, UK: Spellmount.

Howard, Martin. 2006. *Napoleon's Doctors.* Staplehurst, UK: Spellmount.

Howard, Michael. 2002. *Clausewitz: A Very Short Introduction.* Oxford: Oxford Paperbacks.

Howarth, David. 2003. *Waterloo: A Near Run Thing.* London: Weidenfeld and Nicolson.

Howarth, David, and Stephen Howarth. 1998. *Nelson: The Immortal Memory.* London: S. M. Dent.

Hubatsch, Walter, and Erich Botzenhart, eds. 1957–1974. *Freiherr vom Stein: Briefe und amtliche Schriften.* 10 vols. Stuttgart: Kohlhammer.

Hudson, Roger, ed. 1994. *Nelson and Emma.* London: Folio Society.

Hufeld, Ulrich, ed. 2003. *Der Reichsdeputationshauptschluss von 1803: Eine Dokumentation zum Untergang des Alten Reiches* [The Imperial Recess of 1803: Documents Concerning the End of the Old Reich]. Stuttgart: UTB. (Orig. pub. 1913.)

Hüffer, Hermann. 1900–1901. *Quellen zur Geschichte der Kriege von 1799 und 1800* [Sources Related to the History of the Wars of 1799 and 1800]. Vol. 2. Leipzig: B. G. Teuber.

Hughes, B. P. 1974. *Firepower: Weapons Effectiveness on the Battlefield, 1630–1850.* London: Arms and Armour.

Hughes, Edward, ed. 1957. *The Private Correspondence of Admiral Lord Collingwood.* London: Navy Records Society.

Hulot, Frédéric. 2001. *Le général Moreau: Adversaire et victime de Napoléon.* Paris: Pygmalion.

Humble, Richard. 1973 *Napoleon's Peninsular Marshals: A Reassessment.* New York: Taplinger.

Hunt, Lynn Avery. 1984. *Politics, Culture and Class in the French Revolution.* Berkeley and Los Angeles: University of California Press.

Hunt, Lynn Avery, ed. and trans. 1996. *The French Revolution and Human Rights: A Brief Documentary History.* New York: St. Martin's.

Hurst, Michael, ed. 1972. *Key Treaties for the Great Powers, 1814–1914.* Vol. 1, *1814–1870.* Newton Abbot, UK: David and Charles.

Husayn, Afandi. 1964. *Ottoman Egypt in the Age of the French Revolution.* Ed. and trans. Stanford J. Shaw. Cambridge, MA: Harvard University Press.

Hutchinson, Wallace. 1981. *Robert Fulton, Pioneer of Undersea Warfare.* Annapolis, MD: Naval Institute.

Hutt, Maurice. 1983. *Chouannerie and Counter-Revolution: Puisaye, the Princes and the British Government in the 1790s.* 2 vols. Cambridge: Cambridge University Press.

Hutton, William Holden. 1893. *The Marquess Wellesley, K.G.* Oxford: Clarendon.

Hyde Kelly, W. 1905. *The Battle of Wavre and Grouchy's Retreat.* London: John Murray.

I

Ilari, Virgilio, Piero Crociani, and Ciro Paoletti. 2000. *La guerra delle Alpi, 1792–1796* [The Alps War, 1792–1796]. Rome: Stato Maggiore dell'Esercito, Ufficio Storico.

Ilari, Virgilio, Piero Crociani, and Ciro Paoletti. 2001. *Storia militare dell'Italia giacobina: Dall'armistizio di Cherasco alla pace di Amiens (1796–1802).* [A Military History of Jacobin Italy]. 2 vols. Rome: Stato Maggiore dell'Esercito, Ufficio Storico.

Ingrams, Richard. 2005. *The Life and Adventures of William Cobbett.* London: HarperCollins.

Inostrantsev. 1914. *Otechestvennaya voina 1812 goda, Operatsii 2-oi Zapadnoi armii kniazya Bagrationa ot nachala voini do Smolenska.* St. Petersburg: N.p.

Ireland, Bernard. 2000. *Naval Warfare in the Age of Sail: War at Sea, 1756–1815.* New York: Norton.

Ireland, Bernard. 2005. *The Fall of Toulon: The Royal Navy and the Royalist Stand against the French Revolution.* London: Weidenfeld and Nicolson.

Irwin, David J. 1997. *Neoclassicism.* London: Phaidon.

Israel, Jonathan I. 1998. *The Dutch Republic: Its Rise, Greatness, and Fall, 1477–1806.* Oxford: Clarendon.

J

Jackson, T. Sturges. 1899. "Howe." In *From Howard to Nelson: Twelve Sailors,* ed. John Knox Laughton. London: Lawrence and Bullen.

Jacques, Henri-Robert. 1990. *Dictionnaire des diplomates de Napoléon.* Paris: H. Veyrier.

James, Cyril L. 1963. *The Black Jacobins.* 2nd ed. New York: Vantage.

James, Lawrence. 2002. *The Iron Duke: a Military Biography of Wellington.* London: Pimlico.

James, William. 2002. *The Naval History of Great Britain during the French Revolutionary and Napoleonic Wars.* 6 vols. Mechanicsburg, PA: Stackpole. (Orig. pub. 1837.)

Janelidze, D. 1967. *Qartveli mamluqebi egyipteshi* [Georgian Mamelukes in Egypt]. Tbilisi: N.p.

Janson, H. W., and Anthony F. Janson. 1997. *History of Art.* 5th ed. Upper Saddle River, NJ: Prentice-Hall.

Jany, Curt. 1967. *Geschichte der Preussischen Armee vom 15. Jahrhundert bis 1914* [History of the Prussian Army from the 15th Century to 1914]. 4 vols. 2nd ed. Osnabrueck: Biblio.

Jarrett, Derek. 1974. *Pitt the Younger.* New York: Scribner.

Jeanneney, John R., ed. 1995. *The French Revolution of 1789 and Its Impact.* Westport, CT: Greenwood.

Jenkins, Ernest H. 1973. *A History of the French Navy from Its Beginnings to the Present Day.* Annapolis, MD: Naval Institute Press.

Jenkins, M. 1969. *Arakcheev: Grand Visier of the Russian Empire.* London: Faber and Faber.

Jespersen, Knud J. 2004. *A History of Denmark.* New York: Palgrave Macmillan.

John, Wilhelm. 1913. *Erzherzog Karl, der Feldherr und seine Armee.* Vienna: Braumüller.

Johns, Christopher M. S. 1998. *Antonio Canova and the Politics of Patronage in Revolutionary and Napoleonic Europe.* Berkeley and Los Angeles: University of California Press.

Johnson, David. 1989. *The French Cavalry 1792–1815.* London: Belmont.

Johnson, David. 1999. *Napoleon's Cavalry and Its Leaders.* Charlottesville, VA: Howell.

Johnson, Edgar. 1970. *Sir Walter Scott: The Great Unknown.* London: Hamish Hamilton.

Johnson, Hubert C. 1986. *The Midi in Revolution: A Study of Regional Political Diversity, 1789–1793.* Princeton: Princeton University Press.

Johnson, William E. 1994. *The Crescent among the Eagles: The Ottoman Empire and the Napoleonic Wars 1792–1815.* Ocean Springs, MS: Johnson.

Johnston, Edith Mary. 1974. *Ireland in the Eighteenth Century.* Dublin: Gill and Macmillan.

Johnston, Robert M. 1904. *The Napoleonic Empire in Southern Italy and the Rise of the Secret Societies.* 2 vols. London: Macmillan.

Jomini, Baron Antoine Henri de. 1996. *The Art of War.* London: Greenhill.

Jones, Colin. 1990. *The Longman Companion to the French Revolution.* London: Longman.

Jones, Peter, ed. 1995. *Reform and Revolution in France: The Politics of Transition, 1774–1791.* Cambridge: Cambridge University Press.

Jones, Peter, ed. 1996. *The French Revolution in Social and Political Perspective*. London: Hodder Arnold.

Jones, Peter. 2003. *The French Revolution, 1787–1804*. Harlow, UK: Pearson-Longman.

Jones, Proctor, ed. 1992. *Napoleon: An Intimate Account of the Years of Supremacy, 1800–1814*. San Francisco: Random House.

Jones, Proctor, ed. 2004. *Napoleon: How He Did It; The Memoirs of Baron Fain, First Secretary of the Emperor's Cabinet*. London: Greenhill.

Jones, R. Ben. 1968. *The French Revolution*. New York: Funk and Wagnalls.

Jones, R. Ben. 1977. *Napoleon: Man and Myth*. New York: Holmes and Meier.

Jonge, J. C. de. 1869. *Geschiedenis van het Nederlandse Zeewezen*. Zwolle: Hoogstratenen Gorter.

Jonquière, C. E. de la. 1902. *La bataille de Jemappes*. Paris: Chapelot.

Jonquière, C. E. de la. 1902. *L'expédition d'Egypte*. 5 vols. Paris: Lavauzelle.

Jontes, Günther. 1997. *Der Vorfriede von Leoben und die Ereignisse der ersten französischen Invasion in der Steiermark, 1797*. Leoben: Obersteirischer.

Jordan, David P. 1985. *The Revolutionary Career of Maximilien Robespierre*. New York: Free Press.

Jörgensen, Christer. 2004. *The Anglo-Swedish Alliance against Napoleonic France*. New York: Palgrave Macmillan.

Joubert, André. 1873. *Révolte du Major Schill d'après de documents noveaux et inédits*. Paris: Angers.

Jourdan, Annie. 1999. *Napoléon, héros, imperator, mécène*. Paris: Aubier.

Journal Voennykh Deystviy Imperatorskoy Rossiiskoi Armii. 1807. St. Petersburg: N.p.

Juillet, Jacques. 1989. "Desaix, Louis-Charles-Antoine, 1768–1800, général." *Revue du Souvenir Napoléonien*, no. 363 (February): 2–13.

Junkelman, Marcus. 1985. *Napoleon und Bayern den Anfängen des Königreiches*. Regensburg: F. Pustet.

Junot, Mme Laure, duchesse d'Abrantès. 1831–1835. *Mémoires de Madame la duchesse d'Abrantès*. 18 vols. Paris: Ladvocat.

Jupp, P. 1985. *Lord Grenville: 1759–1834*. Oxford: Clarendon; New York: Oxford University Press.

Jupp, P. J. 2004. "Perceval, Spencer (1762–1812)." In *Oxford Dictionary of National Biography*. Oxford: Oxford University Press.

Jussila, Osmo, Seppo Hentilä, and Jukka Nevakivi. 1999. *From Grand Duchy to a Modern State: A Political History of Finland since 1809*. London: Hurst.

K

Kafker, Frank A., and James M. Laux, eds. 1991. *Napoleon and His Times: Selected Interpretations*. Malabar, FL: Krieger.

Kagan, F. W. 1999. *The Military Reforms of Nicholas I: The Origins of the Modern Russian Army*. London: Macmillan.

Kalinovsky, A. 1887. "J. P. Kulnev (1766–1812)." *Russkaia Starina* 2.

Kann, Robert A. 1977. *A History of the Habsburg Empire, 1526–1918*. Berkeley and Los Angeles: University of California Press.

Kant, Immanuel. 1991. *Kant: Political Writings*. Ed. H. S. Reiss. Cambridge: Cambridge University Press.

Kant, Immanuel. 2003. *To Perpetual Peace: A Philosophical Sketch*. Ed. Ted Humphrey. New York: Hackett.

Kaplan, Herbert H. 1962. *The First Partition of Poland*. New York: Columbia University Press.

Karamzin, Nikolai Mikhailovich. 2002. "Letters from Paris, 1790." In *In Old Paris: An Anthology of Source Descriptions, 1323–1790*, ed. Robert W. Berger. New York: Italica.

Karger, Johann. 1998. *Die Entwicklung der Adjustierung, Rüstung und Bewaffnung der österreich-ungarische Armee, 1700–1809* [The Development of the Uniforms, Equipment and Weaponry of the Austro-Hungarian Army, 1700–1809]. Hamburg: LTR.

Karvyalisa, V. A., and A. E. Solovyeova, eds. 1951. *Dokumenti shtaba M. I. Kutusova, 1805–1806*. Vilnius: Gos. izd-vo polit lit-ry.

Kastor, Peter J. 2004. *The Nation's Crucible: The Louisiana Purchase and the Creation of America*. New Haven: Yale University Press.

Katcher, Philip. 1994. *The American War, 1812–1814*. London: Osprey.

Kauffman, Jean-Paul. 1999. *The Black Room at Longwood: Napoleon's Exile on Saint Helena*. London: Four Walls Eight Windows.

Kaufman, Matthew, and Allan Carswell. 2003. *Musket-Ball and Sabre Injuries from the First Half of the Nineteenth Century*. London: Royal College of Surgeons.

Kaufmann, William. 1967. *British Policy and the Independence of Latin America, 1804–1828*. Hamden, CT: Archon.

Kavtaradze, A. 1977. *General A. P. Ermolov*. Tula, Russia: Priokskoe knizhnoe izd-vo.

Keane, John. 1995. *Tom Paine: A Political Life*. Boston: Little, Brown.

Keegan, John. 1976. *The Face of Battle*. London: Cape.

Keen, Benjamin, and Keith Haynes. 2000. *A History of Latin America*. 6th ed. New York: Houghton Mifflin.

Keenan, Dennis King, ed. 2004. *Hegel and Contemporary Continental Philosophy*. Albany: State University of New York Press.

Keevil, John, Christopher Lloyd, and Jack Coulter. 1957–1963. *Medicine and the Navy, 1200–1900*. 4 vols. Edinburgh: E. & S. Livingstone.

Kelly, Ian. 2006. *Beau Brummell: The Ultimate Dandy*. London: Hodder.

Kelly, W. Hyde. 1993. *The Battle of Wavre and Grouchy's Retreat*. Felling, UK: Worley.

Kennedy, Emmet. 1989. *A Cultural History of the French Revolution*. New Haven: Yale University Press.

Kennedy, Ludovic. 2001. *Nelson and His Captains*. London: Penguin.

Kennedy, Michael L. 1982–2000. *The Jacobin Clubs in the French Revolution*. 3 vols. Princeton: Princeton University Press.

Kennedy, Paul. 1987. *The Rise and Fall of the Great Powers: Economic Change and Military Conflict From 1500–2000*. New York: Vintage.

Kennedy, Paul. 1991. *Grand Strategies in War and Peace*. New Haven: Yale University Press.

Kennedy, Paul. 2004. *The Rise and Fall of British Naval Mastery*. London: Penguin.

Keogh, Dáire, and Kevin Whelan, eds. 2001. *Acts of Union: The Causes, Contexts, and Consequences of the Acts of Union*. Dublin: Four Courts.

Kerchnawe, Hugo. 1904. *Kavallerieverwendung, Aufklärung und Armeeführung bei der Hauptarmee in den entscheidenden Tagen vor Leipzig.* Vienna: Seidel.

Kerchnawe, Hugo, and Alois Veltze. 1913. *Feldmarschall Karl Fürst Schwarzenberg, der Führer der Verbündeten in den Befreiungskriegen.* Vienna: Gesellschaft für neuere Geschichte Osterreichs.

Kersnovskii, A. 1992. *Istoriia russkoi armii.* Moscow: Golos.

Kessinger, Roland. 2001. "The Battle of Engen." *First Empire* 60.

Kessinger, Roland. 2002. "The Battle of Ostrach." *First Empire* 66: 24–32.

Kessinger, Roland. 2002. "The Battle of Stockach." *First Empire* 66.

Kharkevich, V. 1893. *Berezina.* St. Petersburg: Voennaia tipographia.

Kharkevich, V. 1901. *Deistvia Platova v ariergarde Bagrationa v 1812 g.* St. Petersburg: N.p.

Kharkevich, V. 1901. *Voina 1812 goda. Ot Nemana do Smolenska.* Vilna: Izd. Nikolaevskoi akademii general'nago shtaba.

Kiaiviarianen, I. 1965. *Mezhdunarodnie otnoshenia na severe Evropi v nachale XIX veka i prisoedinenie Finlandii k Rossii v 1809 godu.* Petrozavodsk: N.p.

Kikkert, J. G. 1981. *Koning van Holland, Louis Bonaparte, 1778–1848.* Rotterdam: Donker.

Kikkert, J. G. 2002. *De misstappen van een koning, Willem II, 1792–1849.* Soesterberg: Aspekt.

Kiley, Kevin. 2004. *Artillery of the Napoleonic Wars.* London: Greenhill.

Kirchberger, Joe H. 1989. *The French Revolution and Napoleon: An Eyewitness History.* New York: Facts on File.

Kissinger, Henry A. 2000. *A World Restored: Metternich, Castlereagh and the Problems of Peace, 1812–1822.* London: Weidenfeld and Nicolson.

Kitchen, Martin. 1996. *The Cambridge Illustrated History of Germany.* Cambridge: Cambridge University Press.

Kitson, Michael, and Felicity Owen. 1991. *From Gainsborough to Constable: The Emergence of Naturalism in British Landscape Painting, 1750–1819.* Sudbury, UK: Gainsborough's House Society.

Kitzen, Michael L. 1993. *Tripoli and United States at War: A History of American Relations with the Barbary States, 1785–1805.* Jefferson, NC: McFarland.

Klingender, Francis. 1968. *Goya in the Democratic Tradition.* London: Sidgwick and Jackson.

Knapton, Ernest John. 1939. *The Lady of the Holy Alliance: The Life of Julie de Krüdener.* New York: Columbia University Press.

Knight, David. 1992. *Humphry Davy: Science and Power.* Oxford: Blackwell.

Knight, Roger. 2000. "Richard, Earl Howe." In *Precursors of Nelson: British Admirals of the Eighteenth Century,* ed. Peter Le Fevre and Richard Harding, 279–299. London: Chatham.

Knight, Roger. 2005. *The Pursuit of Victory: The Life and Achievement of Horatio Nelson.* London: Allen Lane.

Kobell, L. von. 1894. *Unter den vier ersten Königen Bayerns: Nach Briefen und eigenen Erinnerungen.* Munich: N.p.

Kochan, James. 2000. *The United States Army, 1812–1815.* Oxford: Osprey.

Kolzakov, Paul Andreyevich. 2005. *Memoir of Admiral Paul Andreyevich Kolzakov on the Capture of General Vandamme, 1813.* Trans. Alexander Mikaberidze. http://www.napoleon-series.org/research/russianarchives/c_kolzakov.html (accessed April 7, 2006). (Orig. pub. in *Russkaya Starina* 1 [1870]: 208–217.)

Konigs, Philip. 1993. *The Hanoverian Kings and Their Homeland: A Study of the Personal Union, 1714–1837.* Lewes, UK: Book Guild.

Konstam, Angus. 2001. *British Napoleonic Ship-of-the-Line.* Oxford: Osprey.

Konstam, Angus. 2003. *Historical Atlas of the Napoleonic Era.* Guilford, CT: Lyons.

Korngold, Ralph. 1945. *Citizen Toussaint.* Boston: Little, Brown.

Kozłowski, Eligiusz, and Mieczysław Wrzosek. 1974. *Dzieje oręża polskiego 1794–1938.* Warsaw: Wydawnictwo MON.

Kraehe, E. E. 1963. *Metternich's German Policy.* Vol. 1, *The Contest with Napoleon, 1799–1814.* Princeton: Princeton University Press.

Kraivanova, I. 1972. *General A. I. Osterman-Tolstoi.* Moscow: Moskovskii rabochii.

Kramers, J. H. 1936. "Selim III." In *The Encyclopedia of Islam,* ed. M. T. Houtsma, 4: 219–222. Leiden: Brill.

Krasnov, P. 1912. *Dontsy i Platov v 1812.* Moscow: N.p.

Krotkov, A. 1889. *Russkii flot v tsarstvovanie imperatritsy Ekateriny II s 1772 g. po 1783 God.* St. Petersburg: Morskago ministerstva.

Kukla, Jon. 2004. *A Wilderness So Immense: The Louisiana Purchase and the Destiny of America.* New York: Anchor.

Kuroedov, Mikhail, and Konstantin Masov. 2001. *Sfinks Rossiiskoi istorii.* Omsk: Omsk State Pedagogical University.

Kutuzov, M. I. 1956. *Dokumenti.* Vol. 5. Ed. Liubormir Beskrovny. Moscow: Voennoe Izdatelstvo.

Kutuzov, M. I. 1995. *I Russkaia armia na 2-m etape Otechestvennoi voini 1812 g.* Maloyaroslavets: Maloyaroslavets Museum.

Kwiatkowski, Ernst. 1908. *Die Kämpfe bei Schöngrabern und Oberhollabrunn 1805 und 1809, Mitteilungen des K.K. Archivs für Niederösterrich, I.* Vienna: Im Selbstverlage des Verfassers.

L

La Jonquiere, C. F. de. 1889–1902. *L'expédition d'Egypte.* 5 vols. Paris: H. Charles-Lavauzelle.

La Paix de Vienne conclué entre la France, ses Alliées, et l'Autriche le 14 octobre 1809. 1809. Weimar.

La Tourt, Jean de. 2004. *Duc de Frioul, grand maréchal du palais impérial, 1772–1813.* Paris: Nouveau monde.

Lachouque, Henry. 1967. *Napoleon's Battles: A History of His Campaigns.* Trans. Roy Monkcom. New York: Dutton.

Lachouque, Henry. 1972. *Waterloo.* London: Arms and Armour.

Lachouque, Henry, and Anne S. K. Brown. 1997. *The Anatomy of Glory: Napoleon and His Guard—A Study in Leadership.* London: Greenhill.

Lachouque, Henry, Jean Tranie, and J.-C. Carmigniani. 1982. *Napoleon's War in Spain: The French Peninsular Campaigns, 1807–1814.* London: Arms and Armour.

Lacour-Gayet, G. 1928–1934. *Talleyrand, 1754–1838.* 4 vols. Paris: Payot.

Lacour-Gayet, Michel. 1990. *Marie-Caroline, Reine de Naples: 1752–1814.* Paris: Tallandier.

Lacroix, D. 1898. *Bonaparte en Egypte.* Paris: Garnier.

Laing, Margaret. 1974. *Josephine and Napoleon.* New York: Mason/Charter.

Lamar, Glenn J. 2000. *Jérôme Bonaparte: The War Years, 1800–1815.* Westport, CT: Greenwood.

Lambert, Andrew. 2000. *War at Sea in the Age of Sail, 1650–1850.* London: Cassell.

Lambert, Andrew. 2004. *Nelson: Britannia's God of War.* London: Faber and Faber.

Lambert, David. 2005. *White Creole Culture, Politics and Identity during the Age of Abolition.* Cambridge: Cambridge University Press.

Lambert, Frank. 2005. *The Barbary Wars: American Independence in the Atlantic World.* New York: Hill and Wang.

Lambert, Henri. 2004. *Accusé Pichegru, Levez-vous: gloire et misère d'un grand soldat: Jean-Charles Pichegru, 1761–1804.* Bordeaux: Les Dossiers d'Aquitaine.

Lambert, Ray. 2005. *John Constable and the Theory of Landscape Painting.* Cambridge: Cambridge University Press.

Landon, H. R. Robbins, and David Wyn Jones. 1988. *Haydn: His Life and Music.* Bloomington: Indiana University Press.

Lane, Jason. 2003. *General and Madame Lafayette: Partners in Liberty's Cause in the American and French Revolutions.* New York: Taylor.

Langendorf, Jean-Jacques. 2002. *Faire la guerre: Antoine-Henri Jomini.* Geneva: Georg.

Langeron, Alexander Andrault. 1998. *Journal inédit de la campagne de 1805.* Paris: La Vouivre.

Langley, Harold D. 1995. *A History of Medicine in the Early U.S. Navy.* Baltimore, MD: Johns Hopkins University Press.

Langsam, Walter C. 1930. *The Napoleonic Wars and German Nationalism in Austria.* New York: AMS.

Langsam, Walter C. 1949. *Francis the Good: The Education of an Emperor, 1768–1792.* New York: Macmillan.

Lanzerac, Colonel. 1904. *La manœuvre de Lützen 1813.* Paris: Berger-Levrault.

Lardas, Mark. 2003. *American Heavy Frigates, 1794–1826.* Oxford: Osprey.

Larrey, Baron. 1983–1984. *Mémoires et campagnes du baron Larrey.* 5 vols. Paris: Remanence. (Orig. pub. 1812, 1817, and 1841.)

Larrey, Dominique Jean, Baron. 1832. *Memoirs of the Campaigns of Russia, Germany, and France.* Trans. John C. Mercer. Philadelphia: Carey and Lea.

Las Cases, Marie Joseph Emmanuel Auguste. 1818. *Memoirs of Emanuel Augustus Dieudonné Count de Las Cases.* London: Colburn.

Las Cases, Marie Joseph Emmanuel Auguste. 1823. *Mémorial de Sainte-Hélène, ou journal se trouve consigné, jour par jour, ce qu'a dit et fait Napoléon durant dix-huit mois, du 20 juin 1815–25 novembre 1816.* 8 vols. Paris: L'Auteur.

Lauerma, Matti. 1956. *L'Artillerie de campagne française pendant les guerres de la Révolution.* Helsinki: Suomalainen Tiedeakatemia.

Lavallette, Antoine-Marie Chamans. 1831. *Mémoires et souvenirs.* Paris: Fournier jeune.

Lavery, Brian. 1983. *The Ship of the Line: Design, Construction, and Fittings.* 2 vols. London: Conway Maritime.

Lavery, Brian. 1987. *The Arming and Fitting of English Ships of War, 1600–1815.* London: Conway Maritime.

Lavery, Brian. 1991. *Building the Wooden Walls: The Design and Construction of the 74-gun Ship* Valiant. London: Conway Maritime.

Lavery, Brian. 1992. *Nelson's Navy: The Ships, Men and Organisation, 1793–1815.* London: Conway Maritime.

Lavery, Brian. 2003. *Nelson and the Nile: The Naval Campaign against Bonaparte, 1798.* London: Caxton.

Lavery, Brian, ed. 2004. *The Line of Battle: Sailing Warships, 1650–1840.* London: Conway Maritime.

Lavery, Brian. 2004. *Nelson's Fleet at Trafalgar.* Annapolis, MD: Naval Institute Press.

Law de Lauriston, Napoléon, comte. 1858. *Quelques observations sur les Mémoires du duc de Raguse.* Paris: E. Dentu.

Lawford, James Philip. 1973. *Wellington's Peninsular Army.* London: Osprey.

Lawford, James Philip. 1977. *Napoleon: The Last Campaigns, 1813–1815.* New York: Crown.

Lawford, James Philip, and Peter Young. 1972. *Wellington's Masterpiece: The Battle and Campaign of Salamanca.* London: Allen and Unwin.

Le Boterf, Hervé. 1984. *Le brave général Cambronne.* Paris: France Empire.

Le Couëdic, Stéphane, ed. 1997. *L'état-major de Kléber en Egypte.* Paris: La Vouivre.

Le Fevre, Peter, and Richard Harding, eds. 2005. *British Admirals of the Napoleonic Wars: The Contemporaries of Nelson.* London: Chatham.

Le Nebour, Eric. 1982. *Barras: Le vicomte rouge.* Paris: Lattes.

Lecène, Paul. 1885. *Les marins de la république et de l'empire, 1793–1815.* Paris: Librairie Centrale.

Lechartier, G. 1910. *Les Services de l'Arrière à la Grande Armée, 1806–07.* Paris: Chapelot.

Lecomte, Ferdinand. 1860. *Le général Jomini, sa vie et ses écrits.* Paris: C. Tanera.

Lee, Christopher. 2005. *Nelson and Napoleon: The Long Haul to Trafalgar.* London: Headline.

Lefebvre, Georges. 1964. *The French Revolution from 1793 to 1799.* Trans. J. Hall and J. Friguglietti. New York: Columbia University Press.

Lefebvre, Georges. 1964. *The Thermidorians and the Directory: Two Phases of the French Revolution.* New York: Random House.

Lefebvre, Georges. 1969. *Napoleon from 18 Brumaire to Tilsit, 1799–1807.* Trans. H. Stockhold. New York: Columbia University Press.

Lefebvre, Georges. 1969. *Napoleon from Tilsit to Waterloo, 1807–1815.* Trans. J. Anderson. New York: Columbia University Press.

Lefebvre, Georges. 2001. *The French Revolution.* London: Routledge.

Legg, Stuart. 1966. *Trafalgar: An Eyewitness Account of a Great Battle.* London: David.

Leggiere, Michael V. 1997. "The Life, Letters and Campaigns of Friedrich Wilhelm Graf Bülow Von Dennewitz, 1755–1816." 2 vols. Ph.D. diss., Florida State University.

Leggiere, Michael V. 2002. *Napoleon and Berlin: The Franco-Prussian War in North Germany, 1813.* Norman: University of Oklahoma Press.

Lehmann, Hans Friedrich Gottlieb. 1867. *Der Tugendbund, aus den hinterlassenen Papieren des Mitstifters Professor Dr. Hans*

Friedrich Gottlieb Lehmann, herausgegeben von Professor Dr. August Lehmann. Berlin: Weidling.

Lehmann, Max. 1902–1905. *Freiherr vom Stein.* 3 vols. Leipzig: Hirzel.

Lejeune, Louis François. 1897. *Memoirs of Baron Lejeune, Aide-de-camp to Marshals Berthier, Davout and Oudinot.* London: Longmans.

Lemaire, Jean-François. 1992. *Napoléon et la médecine.* Paris: Bourin.

Lemaire, Jean-François. 1999. *Les blessés dans les armées napoléoniennes.* Paris: Lettrage.

Lemaire, Jean-François. 2003. *La médecine napoléonienne.* Paris: Fondation Napoléon.

Lemonofides, Dino. 1971. *British Infantry Colours.* London: Almark.

Lenman, Bruce. 1992. *Integration and Enlightenment: Scotland 1746–1832.* Edinburgh: Edinburgh University Press.

Lentz, Thierry. 1999. *Le Grand Consulat, 1799–1804.* Paris: Fayard.

Lentz, Thierry. 2001. *Savary: Le séide de Napoléon.* Paris: Fayard.

Lerchenfeld, Freiherr von. 1854. *Gesch. Bayerns unter König Maximilian Joseph I.* Berlin: N.p.

Lesch, John E. 1984. *Science and Medicine in France: The Emergence of Experimental Physiology, 1790–1855.* Cambridge, MA, and London: Harvard University Press.

Leslie, Shane. 1926. *George the Fourth.* London: Ernest Benn.

Lettow-Vorbeck, Oscar von. 1896. *Der krieg von 1806 und 1807.* Berlin: Mittler und Sohn.

Lettow-Vorbeck, Oscar von. 1904. *Napoleons Untergang 1815.* Vol. 1. *Elba. Belle-Alliance.* Berlin: Mittler.

Levchenko, V. 1987. *Geroi 1812 goda.* Moscow: Molodaia gvardiia.

Levey, Michael. 1979. *Sir Thomas Lawrence, 1769–1830.* London: National Portrait Gallery.

Lewis, Gwynne. 1993. *The French Revolution: Rethinking the Debate.* London: Routledge.

Lewis, James E. 2003. *The Louisiana Purchase: Jefferson's Noble Bargain?* Charlottesville, VA: Thomas Jefferson Foundation.

Lewis, Michael A. 1962. *Napoleon and His British Captives.* London: Allen and Unwin.

Lewis, Michael A. 2004. *A Social History of the Navy, 1793–1815.* London: Chatham.

Leyland, John, ed. 1899–1902. *Dispatches and Letters Relating to the Blockade of Brest, 1803–1805.* 2 vols. London: Navy Records Society.

Lievyns, Verdot, and Régat. 1844. *Fastes de la Légion-d'Honneur, Biographie de tous les décorés.* Vol. 2. Paris: Bureau de l'Administration.

Lilencro. L. K. C. von. 1810. *Schilliana: das ist, Züge und Thatsachen aus dem Leben und Charakter des preussischen Major von Schill. Von einem Unpartheischen.* Hamburg: Herold.

Lincoln, Margarette. 2002. *Representing the Royal Navy: British Sea Power, 1750–1815.* Aldershot, UK: Ashgate.

Lincoln, Margarette, ed. 2005. *Nelson and Napoleon.* London: National Maritime Museum.

Lincoln, W. Bruce. 1981. *The Romanovs.* New York: Dial.

Lindsay, Jack. 1971. *J. M. W. Turner: His Life and Work: A Critical Biography.* New York: Harper and Row.

Linzen, Karl. 1937. *Johann Philipp Palm: Glühen und Sterben.* Salzburg: Otto Müller.

Liss, Peggy. 1982. *Atlantic Empires: The Network of Trade and Revolution, 1714–1826.* Baltimore: Johns Hopkins University Press.

Litschel, Roland. 1968. *Militärhistorische Schriftenreihe.* Vol. 9, *Das Gefecht bei Ebelsberg.* Vienna: Heeresgeschichtliches Museum.

Livermore, Harold V. 1966. *A New History of Portugal.* Cambridge: Cambridge University Press.

Livermore, Harold V. 1999. "Beresford and the Reform of the Portuguese Army." In *A History of the Peninsular War.* Vol. 9, *Modern Studies of the War in Spain and Portugal, 1808–1824,* ed. Paddy Griffith, 121–144. London: Greenhill.

Livesley, James. 2001. *Making Democracy in the French Revolution.* Cambridge, MA: Harvard Universty Press.

Lloyd, Christopher. 1963. *St. Vincent and Camperdown.* London: Batsford.

Lloyd, Peter. 1991. *The French Are Coming! The Invasion Scare, 1803–1805.* Staplehurst, UK: Spellmount.

Lobanov-Rostovsky, Andrei A. 1947. *Russia and Europe.* Durham, NC: Duke University Press.

Locke, John. 1965. *John Locke: Two Treatises of Government.* Ed. Peter Laslett. New York: New American Library. (Orig. pub. 1690.)

Lockhart, John. 1932. *The Peacemakers.* London: Duckworth.

Lockwood, Lewis. 2003. *Beethoven: The Music and the Life.* New York: Norton.

London, Joshua. 2005. *Victory in Tripoli: How America's War with the Barbary Pirates Established the U. S. Navy and Shaped a Nation.* Hoboken, NJ: John Wiley.

Longford, Elizabeth. 1972. *Wellington: Pillar of State.* London: Harper and Row.

Longford, Elizabeth. 1973. *Wellington: The Years of the Sword.* London: Weidenfeld and Nicolson.

Longworth, Philip. 1965. *The Art of Victory: The Life and Achievements of Field-Marshal Suvorov, 1729–1800.* New York: Holt, Rinehart and Winston.

Lopatin, V. S. 2001. *Zhizn' Suvorova, rasskazannaia im samim i ego sovremennikami: Pis'ma, dokumenty, vospominaniia, ustnye predaniia.* Moscow: Terra-Knizhnyi klub.

Lord, Robert Howard. 1915. *The Second Partition of Poland: A Study in Diplomatic History.* Cambridge, MA: Harvard University Press.

Lord, Walter. 1972. *The Dawn's Early Light.* New York: Norton.

Lorenz, Reinhold. 1941. "Erzherzog Carl als Denker." In *Das Bild des Kriegs im deutschen Denken,* 235–276. Stuttgart: Tempsky.

Lovett, Gabriel H. 1965. *Napoleon and the Birth of Modern Spain.* 2 vols. New York: New York University Press.

Low, Donald A. 1999. *The Regency Underworld.* Stroud, UK: Sutton.

Lowe, John. 1991. *The Concert of Europe: International Relations, 1814–70.* London: Hodder and Stoughton.

Lowry, James. 2006. *Fiddlers and Whores: Memoirs of a Surgeon in Nelson's Fleet.* London: Chatham.

Lucas-Dubreton, Jean. 1941. *Le maréchal Ney, 1769–1815.* Paris: Fayard.

Lucas-Dubreton, Jean. 1948. *Soldats de Napoléon.* Paris: Flammarion.

Lucas-Dubreton, Jean. 1962. *Le comte d'Artois; Charles X; le prince; l'émigré; le roi.* Paris: Hachette.

Lukowski, Jerzy. 1991. *Liberty's Folly.* New York: Routledge.

Lukowski, Jerzy. 1999. *The Partitions of Poland, 1772, 1793, 1795.* New York: Longman.

Lydon, James. 1998. *The Making of Ireland: From Ancient Times to the Present.* New York: Routledge.

Lynch, John. 1986. *The Spanish American Revolutions, 1808–1826.* 2nd ed. New York: Norton.

Lynch, John. 1989. *Bourbon Spain, 1700–1808.* Oxford: Blackwell.

Lynch, John, ed. 1994. *Latin American Revolutions, 1808–1826: Old and New World Origins.* Norman: University of Oklahoma Press.

Lynn, John. A. 1989. "Toward an Army of Honor: The Moral Evolution of the French Army, 1789–1815." *French Historical Studies* 16, no. 1 (Spring): 152–173.

Lynn, John A. 1992. "Valmy." *MHQ: The Quarterly Journal of Military History* 5, no. 1 (Autumn): 88–96.

Lynn, John A., ed. 1993. *Feeding Mars: Logistics in Western Warfare from the Middle Ages to the Present.* Boulder, CO: Westview.

Lynn, John. A. 1996. *The Bayonets of the Republic: Motivation and Tactics in the Army of Revolutionary France, 1791–94.* Boulder, CO: Westview.

Lyon, David. 1996. *Sea Battles in Close-up: The Age of Nelson.* Annapolis, MD: Naval Institute Press.

Lyons, Martyn. 1975. *France under the Directory.* Cambridge: Cambridge University Press.

Lyons, Martyn. 1994. *Napoleon Bonaparte and the Legacy of the French Revolution.* New York: St. Martin's.

M

Macartney, Carlile Aylemer. 1969. *The Habsburg Empire, 1790–1918.* New York: Macmillan.

Macaulay, Rose. 1990. "King Beresford: Este Britânico Odioso." In *They Went to Portugal Too,* ed. L. C. Taylor, 98–232. Manchester: Carcanet.

Macdonald, Janet. 2004. *Feeding Nelson's Navy: The True Story of Food at Sea in the Georgian Era.* London: Chatham.

Macdonnell, A. G. 1998. *The March of the Twenty-Six.* London: Prion.

Machin, G. I. T. 1964. *The Catholic Question in English Politics, 1820 to 1830.* Oxford: Clarendon.

Mack Smith, Denis. 1968. *Modern Sicily after 1713.* London: Chatto and Windus.

Mackay, Charles Hugh. 1995. "The Tempest: The Life and Career of Jean Andoche Junot, 1771–1813." Ph.D. diss., Florida State University.

Mackay, David. 1985. *In the Wake of Cook: Exploration, Science and Empire, 1780–1801.* London: Helm.

MacKenzie, Norman. 1982. *The Escape from Elba: The Fall and Flight of Napoleon, 1814–1815.* New York: Oxford University Press.

Mackenzie, Robert Holden. 2004. *The Trafalgar Roll: The Officers, the Men, the Ships.* London: Chatham.

Mackesy, Piers. 1957. *The War in the Mediterranean, 1803–1810.* New York: Longmans, Green.

Mackesy, Piers. 1974. *Statesmen at War: The Strategy of Overthrow, 1798–1799.* London: Longman.

Mackesy, Piers. 1984. *War without Victory: The Downfall of Pitt, 1799–1802.* Oxford: Clarendon.

Mackesy, Piers. 1995. *British Victory in Egypt, 1801: The End of Napoleon's Conquest.* London: Routledge.

Madden, Lionel. 1972. *Robert Southey: The Critical Heritage.* London: Routledge and Keegan Paul.

Madelin, Louis. 1901. *Fouché.* 2 vols. Paris: Plon.

Maffeo, Steven. 2000. *Most Secret and Confidential: Intelligence in the Age of Nelson.* Annapolis, MD: Naval Institute Press.

Magenschab, Hans. 1984. *Andreas Hofer: Zwischen Napoleon und Kaiser Franz.* Graz: Styria.

Magenschab, Hans. 1995. *Erzherzog Johann.* Vienna: Deutsch Heyne.

Mahan, Alfred Thayer. 1905. *Sea Power in Its Relation to the War of 1812.* Boston: Little, Brown.

Mahan, Alfred Thayer. 1982. *The Influence of Sea Power upon the French Revolution and Empire.* Boston: Little, Brown.

Mahon, John K. 1972. *The War of 1812.* Gainesville: University of Florida Press.

Mahoney, Charles. 2003. *Romantics and Renegades: The Poetics of Political Reaction.* New York: Palgrave Macmillan.

Mahoney, John L. 2001. *Wordsworth and the Critics: The Development of a Critical Reputation.* Rochester, NY: Camden.

Maine, René. 1957. *Trafalgar: Napoleon's Naval Waterloo.* London: Thames and Hudson.

Malcomson, Robert. 1999. *Lords of the Lake: The Naval War on Lake Ontario, 1812–1814.* Annapolis, MD: Naval Institute Press.

Mamishev, V. 1904. *Gen. Lieutenant D. V. Davydov.* St. Petersburg: N.p.

Manceron, Claude. 1966. *Austerlitz: The Story of a Battle.* Trans. George Unwin. New York: Norton.

Mann, Golo. 1946. *Secretary of Europe: The Life of Friedrich von Gentz, Enemy of Napoleon.* New Haven: Yale University Press.

Mansel, Philip. 1981. *Louis XVIII.* London: Blond and Briggs.

Manwaring, George. 1935. *The Floating Republic: An Account of the Mutinies at Spithead and the Nore in 1797.* London: Bles.

Marcelli, Umberto. 1967. *La vendita dei beni nazionali nella Repubblica Cisalpina.* Bologna: Patron.

Marchioni, Jean. 2003. *Place à monsieur Larrey: Chirurgien de la garde impériale.* Paris: Actes Sud.

Marcus, Geoffrey Jules. 1971. *The Age of Nelson: The Royal Navy, 1793–1815.* New York: Viking.

Marek, George. 1974. *The Eagles Die: Franz Joseph, Elisabeth and Their Austria.* New York: Harper and Row.

Margadant, Ted W. 1992. *Urban Rivalries in the French Revolution.* Princeton: Princeton University Press.

Marguerit-Montmeslin, N. G. 1814. *De l'assassinat de Monseigneur le duc d'Enghien et de la justification de M. de Caulaincourt.* Paris: Chez les Marchands de Nouveautés.

Markham, Felix. 1963. *Napoleon.* New York: New American Library.

Markham, Felix. 1975. *The Bonapartes.* London: Weidenfeld and Nicolson.

Markham, J. David. 1994. "Following in the Footsteps of Glory: Stendhal's Napoleonic Career." In *Selected Papers of the Twenty-Fourth Consortium on Revolutionary Europe,* 415–425.

Markham, J. David. 1996. "Prisoners and Writers: Napoleon's British Captives and Their Stories." In *Consortium on Revolutionary Europe: Selected Papers,* eds. Charles Crouch, Kyle Eidahl, and Donald Horward, 121–134. Tallahassee: Florida State University.

Markham, J. David. 1998. "Napoleon and the Romantic Poets." Consortium on Revolutionary Europe. *Selected Papers*, 651–663.

Markham, J. David. 1999–2000. "Wellington's Lost Soldiers: British Prisoners of War." In *The Journal of the Royal United Services Institute for Defence Studies*. Part 1: 144: 6, December 1999, 83–89. Part 2: 145: 1, February 2000, 84–91. London: Royal United Services Institute.

Markham, J. David. 2003. *Imperial Glory: The Bulletins of Napoleon's Grande Armée*. London: Greenhill.

Markham, J. David. 2003. *Napoleon's Road to Glory: Triumphs, Defeats and Immortality*. London: Brassey's.

Markham, J. David. 2005. *Napoleon and Doctor Verling on St. Helena*. London: Pen and Sword.

Markov, Walter. 1990. *Grand Empire: Virtue and Vice in the Napoleonic Era*. Trans. Peter Underwood. New York: Hippocrene.

Marmont, Marshal Auguste F. L. V. de, Duke of Ragusa. 1857. *Mémoires*. Paris: Perrotin.

Marmont, Marshal Auguste F. L. V. de, Duke of Ragusa. 1864. *The Spirit of Military Institutions*. Columbia, SC: Evans and Cosgwell.

Marples, Morris. 1972. *Wicked Uncles in Love*. London: Joseph.

Marquant, R. 1973. "La fortune de Cambacérès." *Revue de l'Institut Napoléon*, no. 127 (avril–mai): 43–52.

Marques, A. H. de Oliveira. 1972. *History of Portugal*. 2 vols. New York: Columbia University Press.

Marques, A. H. de Oliveira. 1972. "Invasoes franceseas." In *História de Portugal*. 2 vols. Lisbon: Palas.

Marshall, P. J., ed. 2001. *The Oxford History of the British Empire: The Eighteenth Century*. Oxford: Oxford University Press.

Marshall-Cornwall, James. 1965. *Marshal Masséna*. London: Oxford University Press.

Marshall-Cornwall, James. 2002. *Napoleon as Military Commander*. New York: Penguin.

Martens, Fedor. 1885. *Sobranie traktatov i konventsii, zakliuchennykh Rossieiu sinostrannymi derzhavami*. Vol. 7. St. Petersburg: A. Benke.

Martin, Jean-Clément. 2001. *Blancs et Bleus dans la Vendée Déchirée*. Paris: Gallimard.

Martin, Kingsley. 1962. *French Liberal Thought in the Eighteenth Century: A Study of Political Ideas from Bayle to Condorcet*. New York: Harper and Row.

Martineau, Gilbert. 1991. *Caroline Bonaparte: Princesse Murat, Reine de Naples*. Paris: France-Empire.

Masefield, John. 1971. *Sea Life in Nelson's Time*. London: Conway Maritime.

Mason, Laura, and Tracey Rizzo, eds. 1999. *The French Revolution: A Document Collection*. Boston: Houghton Mifflin.

Masséna, André, prince d'Essling. 1966–1967. *Mémoires d'André Masséna*. 7 vols. Ed. Gen. Koch. Paris: J. de Bonnet (Orig. pub. 1848–1850.)

Masson, Frédéric. 2004. *Aventures de la guerre, 1792–1809*. Paris: Boussod, Valdon. (Orig. pub. 1894.)

Mathiez, Albert. 1931. *After Robespierre: The Thermidorian Reaction*. New York: Knopf

Maude, Frederic Natusch. 1908. *The Leipzig Campaign 1813*. London: Allen and Unwin.

Maude, Frederic Natusch. 1912. *The Ulm Campaign*. London: Swan, Sonnenschein.

Maude, Frederic Natusch. 1998. *The Jena Campaign, 1806*. London: Greenhill. (Orig. pub. 1909)

Maurois, André. 1969. *Chateaubriand: Poet, Statesman, Lover*. New York: Greenwood.

May, Arthur James. 1963. *Age of Metternich, 1814–1848*. New York: Holt, Reinhart and Winston.

May, Gita. 1977. *Stendhal and the Age of Napoleon*. New York: Columbia University Press.

Maycock, F. W. O. 1912. *The Napoleonic Campaign of 1805*. London: Gale and Polden.

Mayer, Jacob Peter. 1970. *Political Thought: The European Tradition*. Freeport, NY: Books for Libraries.

Mayerhoffer von Vedropolje, Eberhard, et al. 1907–1910. *Krieg 1809*. Vol. 1. Vienna: Seidel.

Mayhead, Robin. 1973. *Walter Scott*. Cambridge: Cambridge University Press.

Maynard, C., ed. 2004. *A Nelson Companion: A Guide to the Royal Navy of Jack Aubrey*. London: O'Mara.

Mayol de Lupé, Henri de. 1912. *La captivité de Pie VII: d'après des documents inédits*. Paris: Emile-Paul.

McClain, James. 1977. *The Economic Writings of DuPont de Nemours*. Newark: University of Delaware Press.

McClellan, George B. 1931. *Venice and Bonaparte*. Princeton: Princeton University Press.

McConnell, A. 1970. *Tsar Alexander I: Paternalistic Reformer*. New York: Crowell.

McEarlean, John. 1996. *Napoleon and Pozzo di Borgo in Corsica and after, 1764–1821: Not Quite a Vendetta*. Lewiston, NY: Mellen.

McGowan, Alan. 1999. *HMS Victory: Her Construction, Career and Restoration*. London: Chatham.

McGrew, Roderick E. 1992. *Paul I of Russia, 1754–1801*. Oxford: Oxford University Press.

McGrigor, Mary, ed. 2000. *The Scalpel and the Sword: The Autobiography of the Father of Army Medicine*. Dalkeith, Scotland: Scottish Cultural Press.

McGrigor, Mary. 2005. *Wellington's Spies*. London: Leo Cooper.

McLynn, Frank. 1997. *Napoleon: A Biography*. London: Cape.

McMaster, Juliet, ed. 1976. *Jane Austen's Achievements: Papers Delivered at the Jane Austen Bicentennial Conference at the University of Alberta*. London: Macmillan.

McNiece, Gerald. 1992. *The Knowledge That Endures*. London: Macmillan.

McPhee, Peter. 2002. *The French Revolution 1789–1799*. Oxford: Oxford University Press.

Melchior-Bonnet, Bernadine. 1961. *Un policier dans l'ombre de Napoléon: Savary, duc de Rovigo*. Paris: Perrin.

Melchior-Bonnet, Bernadine. 1978. *Jérôme Bonaparte, Ou l'envers de l'épopée*. Paris: Perrin.

Melvin, Frank E. 1970. *Napoleon's Navigation System: A Study of Trade Control during the Continental Blockade*. New York: AMS. (Orig. pub. 1919)

Menais, G-P. 1970. *Napoleon et l'argent*. Paris: Lepargne.

Méneval, Claude François. 1893–1894. *Mémoires*. Ed. Baron Napoleon Joseph de Méneval. 3 vols. Paris: Dentu.

Menning, Bruce W. 1986. "Train Hard, Fight Easy: The Legacy of A. V. Suvorov and His 'Art of Victory.'" *Air University Review*, November–December: 79–88.

Merryman, John Henry. 1985. *The Civil Law Tradition: An Introduction to the Legal Systems of Western Europe and Latin America*. 2nd ed. Stanford: Stanford University Press.

Metternich, Clemens Wenzel Lothar Fürst von. 1970. *Memoirs of Prince Metternich.* 5 vols. Ed. by Prince Richard Metternich. New York: Fertig.

Metternich, Clemens Wenzel Lothar Fürst von. 2004. *Metternich: The Autobiography, 1773–1815.* Welwyn Garden City, UK: Ravenhall.

Metz, Jean de. 1911. *Aux pays de Napoléon, l'Italie 1796–97–1800. D'Albenga à Leoben. Passage des Alpes. Marengo.* Grenoble: J. Rey.

Meyer, Jean, and Martine Acerra.1994. *Histoire de la marine française: des origines à nos jours.* Rennes: Ouest-France.

Meyerson, Daniel. 2005. *The Linguist and the Emperor: Napoleon and Champollion's Quest to Decipher the Rosetta Stone.* New York: Random House.

Mézière, Henri. 1990. *Le Général Leclerc (1772–1802) et l'expédition de Saint-Domingue.* Paris: Tallandier.

Michel, Lt. Col. 1909. *Etude sur la période du 5 au 14 juin de la campagne de 1807.* Paris: Berger-Levrault.

Mignet, François Auguste Marie. 1939. *The History of the French Revolution.* London: Dent.

Mikaberidze, Alexander. 2003. "Lion of the Russian Army: Life and Military Career of General Prince Peter Bagration." 2 vols. Ph.D. diss., Florida State University.

Mikaberidze, Alexander, ed. 2005. *Czar's General: Memoirs of Napoleonic Wars by General Aleksey Ermolov.* London: Ravenhall.

Mikaberidze, Alexander. 2005. *The Russian Officer Corps in the Revolutionary and Napoleonic Wars, 1792–1815.* New York: Savas Beatie

Mikhailosvky-Danilevsky, Alexander. 1839. *Opisanie Otechestvennoi voini 1812 g.* St. Petersburg: Pechat v voen. tip.

Mikhailovsky-Danilevsky, Alexander. 1845. *Imperator Aleksandr I i ego spodvizhniki v 1812, 1813, 1814, 1815 godakh: Voennaia galereia Zimnego Dvortsa.* St. Petersburg: N.p.

Mikhailovsky-Danilevsky, Alexander. 1849. *Opisanie vtoroi voini Imperatora Aleksandra s Napoleonom v 1806–1807 godakh.* St. Petersburg: N.p.

Mikhailovsky-Danilevsky, Alexander. 2001. *Memuary 1814–1815.* St. Petersburg: National Library of Russia.

Mikhailovsky-Danilevsky, Alexander. 2002. *Russo-Turkish War of 1806–1812.* 2 vols. Trans. and ed. Alexander Mikaberidze. West Chester, OH: Nafziger Collection.

Mikhailovsky-Danilevsky, Alexander, and Dmitri Miliutin. 1852. *Istoriia voini Rossii s Frantsiei v 1799 godu.* St. Petersburg: Tip. Shtaba voenno-uchebnykh zavedenii.

Mikhalov, B. 1991. "K. O. Pozzo di Borgo: Diplomat restavratsii na sluzhbe Rossiiskoi imperii." In *Portrety rossiiskikh diplomatov,* ed. A. V. Ignatiev. Moscow: Institut istorii SSSR.

Millar, Simon. 2006. *Assaye 1803: Wellington's Bloodiest Battle.* Oxford: Osprey.

Miller, Marion S. 1977–1978. "Italian Jacobinism." *Eighteenth-Century Studies* 11: 246–252.

Milne, Andrew. 1975. *Metternich.* Totowa, NJ: Rowman and Littlefield.

Miloradovich, G. A. 1871. *O rode dvorian i grafa Miloradovich.* Kiev: N.p.

Mingay, G. E. 1968. *Enclosure and the Small Farmer in the Age of the Industrial Revolution.* London: Macmillan.

Mintz, Sidney. 1995. *Sweetness and Power: The Place of Sugar in Modern History.* New York: Viking.

Miot de Melito, André François, comte. 1881. *Memoirs of Count Miot de Melito, Minister, Ambassador, Councillor of State and Member of the Institute of France between the Years 1788 and 1815.* Ed. General Fleischmann. Trans. from the French by Cashel Hoey and John Lillie. New York: Scribner's Sons.

Miquel, Pierre. 2005. *Austerlitz.* Paris: Michel.

Mitchell, Donald W. 1974. *A History of Russian and Soviet Sea Power.* New York: Macmillan.

Mitchell, Harvey. 1965. *The Underground War against Revolutionary France: The Missions of William Wickham, 1794–1800.* Oxford: Clarendon.

Mitchell, Harvey. 1968. "The Vendée and Counter-revolution: A Review Essay." *French Historical Studies* 5, no. 4 (Fall): 405–429.

Mitchell, Leslie George. 1971. *Charles James Fox and the Disintegration of the Whig Party, 1782–1794.* London: Oxford University Press.

Mitchell, Leslie George. 1992. *Charles James Fox.* Oxford: Oxford University Press.

Mitton, Geraldine Edith. 1905. *Jane Austen and Her Times.* Port Washington, NY: Kennikat.

Moalla, Asma. 2003. *Tunisian Regency and the Ottoman Porte (1777–1814): Army and Government of a North-African Eyalet at the end of the Eighteenth Century.* New York: Routledge Curzon.

Moffat, Mary Maxwell. 1906. *Queen Louise of Prussia.* New York: Dutton.

Moiret, Captain Joseph-Marie. 2001. *Memoirs of Napoleon's Egyptian Expedition, 1798–1801.* Trans. Rosemary Brindle. London: Greenhill.

Moïse, Claude. 2001. *Le projet national de Toussaint Louverture et la Constitution de 1801.* Montréal: CIDIHCA.

Mollien, Comte Nicolas. 1898. *Mémoires d'un ministre du trésor public.* Vol. 3. Paris: Guillaumin.

Molnar, Miklos. 2001. *A Concise History of Hungary.* Cambridge: Cambridge University Press.

Monaque, Rémi. 2000. *Latouche-Tréville, l'amiral qui défiait Nelson.* Paris: Kronos.

Mongin, Jean-Marie. 2005. *Officers and Soldiers of the French Imperial Guard.* Vol. 2, Part 2, *Cavalry, 1804–1815.* Paris: Histoire and Collections.

Montalcini, Camillo, et al., eds. 1917–1948. *Assemblee della Repubblica Cisalpina.* 11 vols. Bologna: Zanichelli.

Montesquiou-Fezensac, Raymond-Aymery-Philippe-Joseph de. 1863. *Souvenirs Militaires de 1804 à 1814.* Paris: Librairie Militaire.

Montgomery Hyde, H. 1959. *The Strange Death of Lord Castlereagh.* London: Heinemann.

Montholon, Charles Jean Tristan, marquis de. 1823. *Memoirs of the History of France during the Reign of Napoleon, dictated by the Emperor at Saint Helena to the Generals Who Shared His Captivity; and Published from the Original Manuscripts Corrected by Himself.* 3 vols. London: Colburn and Bossange.

Moon, David. 1999. *The Russian Peasantry, 1600–1900: The World the Peasants Made.* London and New York: Longman.

Moon, Penderel. 1989. *The British Conquest and Dominion of India.* London: Duckworth.

Moran, Daniel, and Arthur Waldron. 2003. *The People in Arms: Military Myth and National Mobilization since the French Revolution.* Cambridge: Cambridge University Press.

Mordvinov, R. N. 1951. *Admiral Ushakov.* Moskva: Voenno-morskoe izd-vo Voenno- morskogo ministerstva Soiuza SSR.

Moreau, Jean V. 1997. *Memoirs of General Moreau.* Ed. and trans. John Philippart. London: Valpy. (Orig. pub. 1814)

Morgan, Kenneth. 2001. *Slavery, Atlantic Trade and the British Economy, 1660–1800.* Cambridge: Cambridge University Press.

Morgan, Kenneth O., ed. 1999. *The Oxford History of Britain.* Rev. ed. Oxford: Oxford University Press.

Mori, Jennifer. 1997. *William Pit and the French Revolution, 1785–1795.* Edinburgh: Keele University Press.

Mori, Jennifer. 2000. *Britain in the Age of the French Revolution, 1785–1820.* London: Longman.

Morriss, Roger. 1983. *The Royal Dockyards during the Revolutionary and Napoleonic Wars.* Leicester, UK: Leicester University Press.

Morriss, Roger, 1996. *Nelson: The Life and Letters of a Hero.* London: Collins and Brown.

Morton, John B. 1958. *Marshal Ney.* London: Barker.

Mosley, Charles, ed. 1999. *Burke's Peerage and Baronetage.* 106th ed., 2 vols. Crans, Switzerland: Burke's Peerage.

Motion, Andrew. 1998. *Keats.* New York: Farrar, Straus and Giroux.

Mouravieff, Boris. 1954. *L'Alliance Russo-Turque au milieu des guerres Napoléoniennes.* Neuchâtel: Éditions de la Baconière.

Mowat, R. B. 1924. *The Diplomacy of Napoleon.* New York: Russell and Russell.

Müffling, Baron Carl von. 1997. *The Memoirs of Baron von Müffling: A Prussian Officer in the Napoleonic Wars.* 1853. London: Greenhill.

Muir, Rory. 1996. *Britain and the Defeat of Napoleon, 1807–1815.* New Haven: Yale University Press.

Muir, Rory. 2000. *Tactics and the Experience of Battle in the Age of Napoleon.* New Haven, CT: Yale University Press.

Muir, Rory. 2001. *Salamanca 1812.* New Haven, CT: Yale University Press.

Muller, Charles. 2003. *The Darkest Day: The Washington-Baltimore Campaign during the War of 1812.* Philadelphia: University of Pennsylvania Press.

Müller, W. 1986. *Relation of the Operations and Battles of the Austrian and French Armies in the Year 1809.* Cambridge: Trotman. (Orig. pub. 1810.)

Murray, Christopher John, ed. 2003. *Encyclopedia of the Romantic Era, 1760–1850.* New York: Dearborn.

Murray, Venetia. 1998. *High Society: A Social History of the Regency Period, 1788–1830.* London: Viking.

Musulin, Stella. 1975. *Vienna in the Age of Metternich: From Napoleon to Revolution, 1805–48.* London: Faber.

Myatt, Frederick. 1980. *Peninsular General: Sir Thomas Picton, 1758–1815.* London: David and Charles.

Myatt, Frederick. 1987. *British Sieges of the Peninsular War, 1811–13.* Staplehurst, UK: Spellmount.

N

Nafziger, George F. 1991. *Poles and Saxons of the Napoleonic Wars.* Chicago: Emperor's.

Nafziger, George F. 1992. *Lutzen and Bautzen: Napoleon's Spring Campaign of 1813.* Chicago: Emperor's.

Nafziger, George F. 1995. *Napoleon at Dresden: The Battles of 1813.* Chicago: Emperor's.

Nafziger George F. 1996. *Imperial Bayonets: Tactics of the Napoleonic Battery, Battalion and Brigade as Found in Contemporary Regulations.* London: Greenhill.

Nafziger, George F. 1996. *Napoleon at Leipzig: The Battle of Nations, 1813.* Chicago: Emperor's.

Nafziger, George F. 1998. *Napoleon's Invasion of Russia.* New York: Presidio.

Nafziger, George F., and Marco Gioannini. 2002. *The Defense of the Napoleonic Kingdom of Northern Italy, 1813–1814.* Westport, CT: Praeger.

Napier, W. F. P. 1992. *A History of the War in the Peninsula.* 6 vols. London: Constable. (Orig. pub. 1828.)

Napoleon I. 1856. *The Confidential Correspondence of Napoleon Bonaparte with His Brother Joseph, Sometime King of Spain.* 32 vols. New York: Appleton.

Napoleon I, Emperor of the French. 1858–1869. *Correspondance de Napoléon Ier; publiée par ordre de l'empereur Napoléon III.* 32 vols. Paris: Impr. Impériale.

Napoleon I. 2002. *In the Words of Napoleon: The Emperor Day by Day.* Ed. R. M. Johnston. London: Greenhill.

Napoleon I. 2004. *The Letters of Napoleon to Josephine.* Welwyn Garden City, UK: Ravenhall.

Naylor, John. 1960. *Waterloo.* London: Batsford.

Neillands, Robin. 1994. *Wellington and Napoleon: Clash of Arms, 1807–1815.* London: John Murray.

Nemetz, Walter. 1960. "Erzherzog Karl." In *Klassikerder Kriegkunst,* ed. Werner Hahlweg, 285–303. Vienna: Wehr und Wissen.

Nemoianu, Virgil. 1984. *The Taming of Romanticism: European Literature and the Age of Beidermeier.* Cambridge, MA: Harvard University Press.

Neue Deutsche Biographie. 1969. Vol. 8. Berlin: Duncker und Humboldt.

Neumann, Hans-Joachim. 1997. *Friedrich Wilhelm II: Preussen unter den Rosenkreuzern.* Berlin: Edition Q.

Newitt, Malyn, and Martin Robson. 2004. *Lord Beresford and British Intervention in Portugal, 1807–1820.* Lisbon: Instituto de Ciências Sociais.

Nicolas, Jean. 1989. *La Révolution française dans les Alpes, Dauphiné et Savoie, 1789–1799.* Toulouse: Privat.

Nicolas, Sir Nicholas Harris, ed. 1998. *The Dispatches and Letters of Vice Admiral Lord Viscount Nelson.* 7 vols. London: Chatham.

Nicolle, David. 1998. *Armies of the Ottoman Empire, 1775–1820.* Oxford: Osprey.

Nicolson, Adam. 2005. *Men of Honour: Trafalgar and the Making of the English Hero.* London: HarperCollins.

Nicolson, Harold. 1973. *The Congress of Vienna: A Study in Allied Unity: 1812–1822.* Gloucester, MA: Smith.

Nicolson, Nigel. 1985. *Napoleon, 1812.* London: Weidenfeld and Nicolson.

Nightingale, Joseph. 1978. *Memoirs of the Public and Private Life of Queen Caroline.* London: Folio Society.

Niqula ibn Yusuf al-Turk. 1950. *Chronique d'Égypte, 1798–1804.* Cairo: Institut français d'archéologie orientale.

Niven, Alexander C. 1978. *Napoleon and Alexander I: A Study in Franco-Russian Relations, 1807–12.* Washington, DC: University Press of America.

Nofi, Albert. 1998. *The Waterloo Campaign: June 1815.* New York: Da Capo.

Nora, Pierre. 1998. *Realms of Memory: The Construction of the French Past.* Vol. 3, *The Symbols.* Ed. Laurence D. Kritzman and trans. Arthur Goldhammer. New York: Columbia University Press.

Nordstrom, Byron J. 2002. *The History of Sweden.* Westport, CT: Greenwood.

Norman, Barbara. 1976. *Napoleon and Talleyrand: The Last Two Weeks.* New York: Stein and Day.

Norman, E. R. 1968. *Anti-Catholicism in Victorian England.* New York: Barnes and Noble.

North, Jonathan. 2003. "General Hoche and Counterinsurgency." *Journal of Military History* 26, no. 2 (April): 529–540.

Nosworthy, Brent. 1990. *The Anatomy of Victory: Battle Tactics, 1689–1763.* New York: Hippocrene.

Nosworthy, Brent. 1996. *With Musket, Cannon and Sword: Battle Tactics of Napoleon and His Enemies.* New York: Sarpedon.

Nosworthy, Brent. 1998. *Battle Tactics of Napoleon and His Enemies.* London: Constable.

Nowak, Tadeusz, and Jan Wimmer. 1968. *Dzieje orężapolskiego do roku 1793.* Warsaw: Wydawnictwo MON.

Nowak, Tadeusz, and Jan Wimmer. 1981. *Historia oręża polskiego 963–1795.* Warsaw: Wiedza Powszechna.

O

O'Donnell, Ruán. 2003. *Robert Emmet and the Rebellion of 1798.* Dublin: Irish Academic Press.

O'Dwyer, Margaret M. 1985. *The Papacy in the Age of Napoleon and the Restoration: Pius VII, 1800–1823.* Lanham, MD: University Press of America.

O'Gorman, Frank. 1967. *The Whig Party and the French Revolution.* London: Macmillan; New York: St. Martin's.

O'Gorman, Frank. 1982. *The Emergence of the British Two-Party System, 1760–1832.* London: Arnold.

O'Meara, Barry Edward. 1819. *An Exposition of Some of the Transactions, that Have Taken Place at St. Helena, Since the Appointment of Sir Hudson Lowe as Governor of that Island . . . Various Official Documents, Correspondence, &c.* 2nd ed. London: Ridgway.

O'Meara, Barry Edward. 1822. *Napoleon in Exile, or, A Voice from St. Helena: The Opinion and Reflections of Napoleon on the Most Important Events of His Life and Government, in His Own Words.* Philadelphia: Jehu Burton.

Ogg, David. 1965. *Europe of the Ancien Regime, 1715–1783.* New York: Harper and Row.

Okey, Robert. 2000. *The Habsburg Monarchy, c. 1765–1918: The Improbable Empire.* Basingstoke, UK: Palgrave Macmillan.

Oman, Carola. 1953. *Sir John Moore.* London: Hodder and Stoughton.

Oman, Carola. 1966. *Napoleon's Viceroy Eugène de Beauharnais.* London: Hodder and Stoughton.

Oman, Carola. 1996. *Nelson.* London: Greenhill.

Oman, Charles, 2005. *A History of the Peninsular War.* 7 vols. 1902–1930. London: Greenhill.

Oman, Charles. 2006. *Wellington's Army, 1809–1814.* London: Greenhill. (Orig. pub. 1912.)

Ommen, Heinrich. 1900. *Die Kriegführung des Erzherzog Carl.* Historische Studien 14. Berlin: Matthuesen.

Orlov, Nilolay. 1892. *Suvorov: Razbor voennikh deistvii Suvorova v Itallii v 1799 godu.* St. Petersburg: V. A. Berezovskii.

Orlov, Nikolay. 1895. *Suvorov na Trebbii v 1799 g.* St. Petersburg: N.p.

Orlov, Nikolay, ed. 1898. *Pokhod Suvorova v 1799 g.: Po zapiskam Gryazeva.* St. Petersburg: N.p.

Ortenburg, Georg. 1988. *Waffen der Revolutionskriege, 1792–1848.* Bonn: Bernhard and Graefe.

Ortiz, Jose M. 1998. "The Revolutionary Flying Ambulance of Napoleon's Surgeon." *U.S. Army Medical Department Journal* (Oct.–Dec.): 17–25.

Ortzen, Len. 1974. *Imperial Venus.* New York: Stein and Day.

Osipov, K. 1944. *Alexander Suvorov: A Biography.* London: Hutchinson.

Otechestvennaia voina 1812 g.: Materiali Voenno-Uchebnogo arkhiva Glavnogo Shtaba. 1910. Vol. 24. St. Petersburg: [General Staff of the Russian Army] N.p.

Ott, Thomas O. 1973. *The Haitian Revolution, 1789–1804.* Knoxville: University of Tennessee Press.

Over, Keith. 1976. *Flags and Standards of the Napoleonic Wars.* London: Bivouac.

Owsley, Frank L. 2000. *Struggle for the Gulf Borderlands: The Creek War and the Battle of New Orleans, 1812–1815.* Tuscaloosa: University of Alabama Press.

P

Page, F. C. G. 1986. *Following the Drum: Women in Wellington's Wars.* London: Deutsch.

Paget, Julian. 1992. *Hougoumont.* London: Leo Cooper.

Paget, Julian. 1997. *Wellington's Peninsular War: Battles and Battlefields.* London: Leo Cooper.

Paine, Ralph. 2002. *The Fight for a Free Sea.* University Press of the Pacific.

Paine, Thomas. 1999. *The Rights of Man.* Mineola, NY: Dover. (Orig. pub. 1791–1792)

Pajol, Charles Pierre Victor. 1874. *Pajol: général en chef.* 3 vols. Paris: Firmin Didot frères.

Pakenham, Thomas. 2000. *The Year of Liberty: The Great Irish Rebellion of 1798.* Grand Rapids, MI: Abacus.

Pallain, G. 1889. *La mission de Talleyrand à Londres en 1792.* Paris: Plon.

Pallain, G. 1891. *Correspondance diplomatique: Talleyrand sous le Directoire.* Paris: Plon.

Palluel-Guillard, André. 1999. *L'Aigle et la Croix: Genève et la Savoie, 1798–1815.* Saint-Gingolph: Cabédita.

Palmer, A. 1974. *Alexander I: Tsar of War and Peace.* London: Weidenfeld and Nicolson.

Palmer, Alan Warwick. 1972. *Russia in War and Peace.* London: Weidenfeld and Nicolson.

Palmer, Alan Warwick. 1990. *Bernadotte: Napoleon's Marshal, Sweden's King.* London: John Murray.

Palmer, Alan Warwick. 1990. *Bernadotte: The Crowned Sergeant.* London: John Murray.

Palmer, Alan Warwick. 1997. *Metternich: Councillor of Europe.* London: Weidenfeld and Nicolson.

Palmer, Alan Warwick. 1997. *Napoleon in Russia.* London: Constable.

Palmer, Alan Warwick. 2001. *Napoleon and Marie Louise: The Emperor's Second Wife.* New York: St. Martin's.

Palmer, Dave R. 2001. *Provide for Common Defense: America, Its Army, and the Birth of a Nation.* New York: Presidio.

Palmer, Michael A. 1987. *Stoddert's War: Naval Operations during the Quasi-War with France, 1798–1801.* Columbia: University of South Carolina Press.

Palmer, R. R. 1954. "Much in Little: The Dutch Revolution of 1795." *Journal of Modern History* 26 (March): 15–35.

Palmer, R. R. 1970. *The Age of the Democratic Revolution.* 2 vols. Princeton: Princeton University Press.

Palmer, R. R. 2005. *Twelve Who Ruled: The Year of the Terror in the French Revolution.* Princeton: Princeton University Press. (Orig. pub. 1941.)

Pares, Richard. 1953. *King George III and the Politicians.* Oxford: Clarendon.

Paret, Peter. 1961. *Internal War and Pacification: The Vendée, 1789–1796.* Princeton: Princeton University Press.

Paret, Peter. 1966. *Yorck and the Era of Prussian Reform 1807–1815.* Princeton: Princeton University Press.

Paret, Peter. 1976. *Clausewitz and the State.* Oxford: Oxford University Press.

Paret, Peter, Gordon A. Craig, and Felix Gilbert, eds. 1986. *Makers of Modern Strategy from Machiavelli to the Nuclear Age.* Princeton: Princeton University Press.

Parissien, Steven. 2000. *Palladian Style.* London: Phaidon.

Parker, Harold T. 1983. *Three Napoleonic Battles.* Durham, NC: Duke University Press.

Parker, Richard. 2004. *Uncle Sam in Barbary: A Diplomatic History.* Tallahassee: University Press of Florida.

Parkinson, C. Northcote. 1954. *The War in the Eastern Seas, 1793–1815.* London: Allen and Unwin.

Parkinson, C. Northcote. 1994. *Britannia Rules: The Classic Age of Naval History 1793–1815.* Stroud, UK: Sutton.

Parkinson, Roger. 1970. *Clausewitz.* London: Wayland.

Parkinson, Roger. 1973. *The Peninsular War.* London: Hart-Davis MacGibbon.

Parkinson, Roger. 1975. *The Hussar General: The Life of Blücher, Man of Waterloo.* London: Davies.

Parkinson, Roger. 1976. *Fox of the North: The Life of Kutuzov, General of War and Peace.* New York: McKay.

Parkinson, Roger. 1976. *Moore of Corunna.* London: Hart-Davis MacGibbon.

Parkinson, Wenda. 1978. *"This Gilded African": Toussaint Louverture.* London: Quartet.

Parry, Clive, ed. 1969. *Consolidated Treaty Series.* 231 vols. Dobbs Ferry, NY: Oceana.

Partridge, Richard, and Michael Oliver. 1999. *Napoleonic Army Handbook.* Vol. 1, *The British Army and Her Allies.* London: Constable and Robinson.

Partridge, Richard, and Michael Oliver. 2002. *Napoleonic Army Handbook.* Vol. 2, *The French Army and Her Allies.* London: Constable and Robinson.

Patrick, Alison. 1972. *The Men of the First Republic.* Baltimore: Johns Hopkins University Press.

Patterson, Benton Rain. 2005. *The Generals: Andrew Jackson, Sir Edward Pakenham, and the Road to the Battle of New Orleans.* New York: New York University Press.

Patton, Charles. 2001. *Chalmette: The Battle of New Orleans and How the British Nearly Stole the Louisiana Territory.* Bowling Green, KY: Hickory Tales.

Paulin, Karl. 1996. *Andreas Hofer und der Tiroler Freiheitskampf 1809.* Vienna: Tosa-Verl.

Pawly, Ronald. 2001. *Wellington's Belgian Allies, 1815.* Oxford: Osprey.

Pawly, Ronald. 2002. *Napoleon's Guards of Honour, 1813–14.* Oxford: Osprey.

Pawly, Ronald. 2002. *Wellington's Dutch Allies, 1815.* Oxford: Osprey.

Pawly, Ronald. 2003. *Napoleon's Red Lancers.* Oxford: Osprey.

Pawly, Ronald. 2004. *Napoleon's Imperial Headquarters.* 2 vols. Oxford: Osprey.

Pawly, Ronald. 2005. *Napoleon's Carabiniers.* Oxford: Osprey.

Pawly, Ronald. 2006. *Napoleon's Mamelukes.* Oxford: Osprey.

Peakman, Julie. 2005. *Emma Hamilton.* London: Haus.

Pelet, Jean J. 1824–1826. *Mémoires sur la guerre de 1809 en Allemagne.* Vols. 1–3. Paris: Roret.

Percy, Baron. 2002. *Journal des campagnes du baron Percy.* Paris: Tallandier.

Pericoli, Ugo. 1973. *1815: The Armies at Waterloo.* London: Seeley Service.

Perkin, Harold. 1985. *The Origins of Modern English Society, 1780–1880.* Boston: Ark.

Perkins, Bradford. 1955. *The First Rapprochement: England and the United States, 1795–1805.* Philadelphia: University of Pennsylvania Press.

Perkins, Bradford. 1961. *Prologue to War: England and the United States, 1805–1812.* Berkeley: University of California Press.

Perkins, Bradford. 1962. *The Causes of the War of 1812: National Honor or National Interest?* New York: Holt, Rinehart and Winston.

Perkins, Bradford. 1964. *Castlereagh and Adams: England and the United States, 1812–1823.* Berkeley: University of California Press.

Perkins, David. 1959. *The Quest for Permanence: The Symbolism of Wordsworth, Shelley, and Keats.* Cambridge, MA: Harvard University Press.

Perrin, Jean-Pierre. 1989. *Valmy, 1er victoire de la Nation.* Paris: Grancher.

Pertz, Georg Heinrich. 1848. *Denkschriften des Ministers Freiherrn vom Stein.* Berlin: E. S. Mittler.

Pertz, Georg Heinrich. 1849–1854. *Das Leben des Ministers Freiherrn vom Stein.* 6 vols. Berlin: Mittler.

Peschot, Bernard. 1971. *Recherche sur les Héraultais morts aux armées (1792–1802).* Montpellier, France: Mémoire Maîtrise Histoire.

Peters, Hauptmann von. 1907. "Die Anfänge der Militärluftschiffahrt und ihre erste Anwendung im Feldzug 1794" [The Beginnings of Military Aircraft and Their First Use in the 1794 Campaign]. *Mitteilungen des Kriegsarchivs III* (Vienna) 5: 123–184.

Petitfrère, Claude. 1981. *La Vendée et les Vendéens.* Paris: Gallimard.

Petitfrère, Claude. 1988. "The Origins of the Civil War in the Vendée." *French History* 2: 187–207.

Petre, F. Loraine. 1991. *Napoleon and the Archduke Charles: A History of the Franco-Austrian Campaign in the Valley of the Danube in 1809.* London: Greenhill.

Petre, F. Loraine. 1992. *Napoleon's Last Campaign in Germany, 1813.* London: Greenhill.

Petre, F. Loraine. 1998. *Napoleon at Bay, 1814.* London: Greenhill.

Petre, F. Loraine. 2001. *Napoleon's Campaign in Poland, 1806–1807.* London: Greenhill.

Petrov, A. 1885–1887. *Voina Rossii s Turtsiei, 1806–1812* [Russia's War against Turkey, 1806–1812]. 3 vols. St. Petersburg: Voennaia.

Pflugk-Harttung, Julius von. 1913. *Leipzig 1813*. Gotha: Friedrich Andreas Perthes.

Pflugk-Harttung, Julius von. 1915. *Belle Alliance*. Berlin: Eisenschmidt.

Philip, Cynthia Owen. 1985. *Robert Fulton: A Biography*. New York: Watts.

Philip, Raymond de. 1900. *Etude sur le Service d'Etat Major pendant les guerres du premier empire*. Paris: Chapelot.

Phillips, Michael. 2000. *William Blake: The Creation of the Songs; From Manuscript to Illuminated Printing*. Princeton: Princeton University Press.

Phillips, W. Alison. 1966. *Confederation of Europe: A Study of the European Alliance 1813–1823, as an Experiment in the International Organization of Peace*. New York: Fertig.

Phipps, Ramsay Weston. 1980. *The Armies of the First French Republic and the Rise of the Marshals of Napoleon I*. 5 vols. London: Greenwood. (Orig. pub. 1926–1939.)

Picard, Ernst. 1909. *Hohenlinden*. Paris: Lavauzelle.

Pickles, Tim. 1993. *New Orleans 1815: Andrew Jackson Crushes the British*. London: Osprey.

Piétri, François. 1939. *Lucien Bonaparte*. Paris: Plon.

Pigeard, Alain. 2003. *La conscription au temps de Napoléon, 1798–1814*. Paris: Giovanangeli.

Pillepich, Alain. 2001. *Milan capitale napoléonienne, 1800–1814*. Paris: Lettrage.

Pillepich, Alain. 2003. *Napoléon et les Italiens: République italienne et royaume d'Italie, 1802–1814*. Paris: Fondation Napoléon.

Pils, François. 1895. *Journal de marche du grenadier Pils, 1804–1814*. Ed. Raoul de Cisternes. Paris: Ollendorff.

Pistor, Wilfrid Ritter von. 1882. *Erzherzog Carl: Sein Leben und Wirken als Feldherr und Staatsmann*. Linz: Ewert.

Pitch, Anthony. 1998. *The Burning of Washington: The British Invasion of 1814*. Annapolis, MD: Naval Institute Press.

Pivka, Otto von [Digby Smith]. 1973. *The Black Brunswickers*. London: Osprey.

Pivka, Otto von [Digby Smith]. 1974. *The King's German Legion*. London: Osprey.

Pivka, Otto von [Digby Smith]. 1974. *Napoleon's Polish Troops*. London: Osprey.

Pivka, Otto von [Digby Smith]. 1975. *Spanish Armies of the Napoleonic Wars*. London: Osprey.

Pivka, Otto von [Digby Smith]. 1977. *The Portuguese Army of the Napoleonic Wars*. London: Osprey.

Pivka, Otto von [Digby Smith]. 1979. *Armies of the Napoleonic Era*. New York: Taplinger.

Pivka, Otto von [Digby Smith]. 1979. *Napoleon's German Allies*. Vol. 3, *Saxony, 1806–1815*. London: Osprey.

Pivka, Otto von [Digby Smith]. 1979. *Napoleon's Italian and Neapolitan Troops*. London: Osprey.

Pivka, Otto von [Digby Smith]. 1980. *Napoleon's German Allies*. Vol. 4, *Bavaria*. London: Osprey.

Pivka, Otto von [Digby Smith]. 1980. *Navies of the Napoleonic Era*. New York: Hippocrene.

Pivka, Otto von [Digby Smith]. 1991. *Napoleon's German Allies*. Vol. 2, *Nassau and Oldenburg*. London: Osprey.

Pivka, Otto von [Digby Smith]. 1992. *Dutch-Belgian Troops of the Napoleonic Wars*. London: Osprey.

Pivka, Otto von [Digby Smith]. 1992. *Napoleon's German Allies*. Vol. 1, *Westfalia and Kleve-Berg*. London: Osprey.

Pivka, Otto von [Digby Smith]. 1992. *Napoleon's German Allies*. Vol. 5, *Hesse*. London: Osprey.

Pivka, Otto von [Digby Smith]. 1992. *Napoleon's Italian Troops*. London: Osprey.

Plotho, Carl von. 1811. *Tagebuch während des Krieges zwischen Russland und Preussen einerseits, und Frankreich andrerseits, in den Jahren 1806 und 1807*. Berlin: Braunes.

Plumb, John H. 1974. *The First Four Georges*. London: Hamlyn.

Pocock, Tom. 1980. *The Young Nelson in the Americas*. London: Collins.

Pocock, Tom. 1994. *Horatio Nelson*. London: Pimlico.

Pocock, Tom. 1996. *A Thirst for Glory: The Life of Admiral Sir Sidney Smith*. London: Aurum.

Pocock, Tom. 2002. *Nelson's Women*. London: Deutsch.

Pocock, Tom. 2003. *The Terror before Trafalgar: Nelson, Napoleon and the Secret War*. London: John Murray.

Pocock, Tom. 2004. *Stopping Napoleon: War and Intrigue in the Mediterranean*. London: John Murray.

Pogodin, M. 1844. *Nekrolog kniazia D. V. Golitsyna*. Moscow: N.p.

Pogodin, M. 1863. *A. P. Ermolov*. Moscow: Univ. tip. Potto, V.

Pogodin, M. 1899. *A. P. Ermolov na Kavkaze*. St. Petersburg: N.p.

Pollock, John. 1977. *Wilberforce*. London: Constable.

Polt, John. 1971. *Gaspar Melchor de Jovellanos*. New York: Twayne.

Poniatowski, Michel. 1982. *Talleyrand et le Directoire, 1796–1800*. Paris: Perrin.

Pope, Dudley. 1997. *Life in Nelson's Navy*. London: Chatham.

Pope, Dudley. 1999. *Decision at Trafalgar*. New York: Henry Holt.

Pope, Dudley. 1999. *England Expects: Nelson and the Trafalgar Campaign*. London: Chatham.

Pope, Dudley. 2003. *The Great Gamble: Nelson at Copenhagen*. London: Chatham.

Pope, Stephen. 1998. *Hornblower's Navy: Life at Sea in the Age of Nelson*. London: Welcome Rain.

Pope, Stephen. 1999. *The Cassell Dictionary of the Napoleonic Wars*. London: Cassell.

Popham, Hugh. 1991. *A Damned Cunning Fellow: The Eventful Life of Sir Home Popham*. Tywardreath, UK: Old Ferry.

Popkin, Jeremy D. 1990. *Revolutionary News: The Press in France, 1789–1799*. Durham, NC: Duke University Press.

Popkin, Jeremy D. 1995. *A Short History of the French Revolution*. Upper Saddle River, NJ: Prentice-Hall.

Porch, Douglas. 1974. *Army and Revolution: France, 1815–1848*. London: Routledge and Kegan Paul.

Powell, David. 1989. *Charles James Fox: A Man of the People*. London: Hutchinson.

Poyen-Bellisle, Henry de. 1896. *Les Guerres des Antilles, 1793–1815*. Paris: Berger-Levrault.

Prados de la Escosura, Leandro, ed. 2004. *Exceptionalism and Industrialisaton: Britain and Its European Rivals, 1688–1815*. Cambridge: Cambridge University Press.

Pratt, Michael. 1978. *Britain's Greek Empire: Reflections on the History of the Ionian Islands from the Fall of Byzantium*. London: Collings.

Price, Munro. 2002. *The Fall of the French Monarchy: Louis XVI, Marie Antoinette and the Baron de Breteuil*. London: Pan Macmillan.

Priesdorff, Kurt von. 1937–1942. *Soldatisches Führertum*. 10 vols. Hamburg: Hanseatische Verlagsanstalt.

Priestley, J. B. 2002. *The Prince of Pleasure and His Regency 1811–20*. London: Penguin.

Prokesch-Osten, Anton von. 1823. *Denkwurdigkeiten aus dem Leben des Feld-marschall's Fürsten Schwarzenberg.* Vienna: Strauss.

Pula, James. 1998. *Thaddeus Kosciuszko: The Purest Son of Liberty.* London: Hippocrene.

Puryear, V. 1951. *Napoleon and the Dardanelles.* Cambridge: Cambridge University Press.

Putney, Martha. 1975. "The Slave Trade in French Diplomacy from 1814 to 1815." *Journal of Negro History* 60, no. 3: 411–427.

Q

Quante, Michael. 2004. *Hegel's Concept of Action.* Trans. Dean Moyar. Cambridge: Cambridge University Press.

Quimby, Robert S. 1957. *The Background of Napoleonic Warfare.* New York: Columbia University Press.

Quimby, Robert S. 1997. *The U.S. Army in the War of 1812: An Operational and Command Study.* East Lansing: Michigan State University Press.

R

Raack, R. C. 1965. *The Fall of Stein.* Cambridge, MA: Harvard University Press.

Rabut, Elisabeth. 1989. *La Savoie du Nord et la Révolution.* Annecy: Archives départementales de la Haute-Savoie.

Raeff, Marc. 1956. *Siberia and the Reforms of 1822.* Seattle: University of Washington Press.

Raeff, Marc. 1969. *Michael Speransky: Statesman of Imperial Russia, 1772–1839.* The Hague: Nojhoff.

Raeuber, Charles. 1987. "Duty and Discipline—Berthier." In *Napoleon's Marshals,* ed. David C. Chandler, 42–59. New York: Macmillan.

Ragon, Michel. 1992. *1793: L'Insurrection Vendéenne et les malentendus de la liberté.* Paris: A. Michel.

Ragsdale, Hugh, ed. 1979. *Paul I: A Reassessment of His Life and Reign.* Pittsburgh: University of Pittsburgh Center for International Studies.

Ragsdale, Hugh. 1980. *Détente in the Napoleonic Era: Bonaparte and the Russians.* Lawrence: Regents Press of Kansas.

Ragsdale, Hugh. 1988. *Tsar Paul and the Question of Madness: An Essay in History and Psychology.* New York: Greenwood.

Raine, Kathleen. 2002. *Blake and Tradition.* London: Routledge.

Ranke, Leopold von, ed. 1877. *Denkwürdigkeiten des Staatskanzlers Fürsten von Hardenberg.* 5 vols. Leipzig: Duncker and Humblot.

Rapin, Ami-Jacques. 2002. *Jomini et la Stratégie: Une approche historique de l'oeuvre.* Lausanne, Switzerland: Editions Payot Lausanne.

Rapp, Jean, comte. 1823. *Memoirs of General Count Rapp, First Aide-de-Camp to Napoleon.* London: H. Colburn.

Ratch, V. 1864. *Svedenia o grafe A. A. Arakcheyeve.* St. Petersburg: N. p.

Rath, Reuben John. 1941. *The Fall of the Napoleonic Kingdom of Italy, 1814.* New York: Columbia University Press.

Rathbone, Julian. 1984. *Wellington's War: His Peninsular Dispatches.* London: Joseph.

Rauchensteiner, Manfried. 1972. *Kaiser Franz und Erzherzog Carl.* Vienna: Verlag für Geschichte und Politik.

Raumer, Kurt von. 1960. *Die Autobiographie des Freiherrn vom Stein.* Münster: Aschendorff.

Rawski, Tadeusz, and Andrzej Ajnenkiel. 1994. *Powstanie kosciuszkowskie 1794: dzieje militarne.* Warsaw: Wojskowy Instytut Historyczny.

Rayan, A. N. 1953. "The Causes of the British Attack upon Copenhagen in 1807." *English Historical Review* 68: 37–55.

Rayan, A. N. 1953. "The Navy at Copenhagen in 1807." *Mariner's Mirror* 39: 201–210.

Reddaway, W. F., et al., eds. 1978. *The Cambridge History of Poland.* 2 vols. Vol. 2, *From Augustus II to Pilsudski (1697–1935).* New York: Octagon.

Redman, Alvin. 1960. *The House of Hanover.* New York: Funk and Wagnalls.

Rees, Joan. 1976. *Jane Austen: Woman and Writer.* New York: St. Martin's.

Regele, Oskar. 1966. *Generalstabschefs aus vier Jahrhunderten.* Vienna: Herold.

Regele, Oskar. 1969. "Karl Freiherr von Mack und Johann Ludwig Graf Cobenzl: Ihre Rolle im Kriegsjahr 1805." *Mitteilungen des österreichischen Staatsarchivs* 21: 142–164.

Reich, Jerome. 1968. "The Slave Trade at the Congress of Vienna—A Study in English Public Opinion." *Journal of Negro History* 53:129–143.

Reichel, Daniel. 1975. *Davout et l'art de la guerre.* Neuchâtel, Switzerland: Delachaux and Niestlé.

Reid, Anthony. 1997. "The Crisis of the Seventeenth Century in Southeast Asia." In *The General Crisis of the Seventeenth Century,* ed. Geoffrey Parker and Lesley Smith, 206–234. New York: Routledge.

Reid, Ian. 2004. *Wordsworth and the Formation of English Studies.* Aldershot, UK: Ashgate.

Reid, Stuart. 1992. *Wellington's Highlanders.* Oxford: Osprey.

Reid, Stuart. 1997. *British Redcoat.* Vol. 2, *1793–1815.* London: Osprey.

Reid, Stuart. 2004. *Wellington's Army in the Peninsula, 1809–1814.* Oxford: Osprey.

Reilly, Robin. 1979. *William Pitt the Younger.* New York: Putnam.

Reilly, Robin. 2002. *The British at the Gates: The New Orleans Campaign in the War of 1812.* Staplehurst, UK: Spellmount.

Reinhard, Marcel. 1950–1952. *Le Grand Carnot.* 2 vols. Paris: Hachette.

Remini, Robert V. 2001. *The Battle of New Orleans: Andrew Jackson and America's First Military Victory.* New York: Penguin.

Renier, G. J. 1930. *Great Britain and the Establishment of the Kingdom of the Netherlands, 1813–15.* London: Allen and Unwin.

Reynaud, Jean-Louis. 1992. *Contre-guerilla en Espagne (1808–1814): Suchet pacifie l'Aragon.* Paris: Economica.

Richards, Edward G. 1999. *Mapping Time: The Calendar and Its History.* New York: Oxford University Press.

Richardson, Hubert. 1920. *A Dictionary of Napoleon and His Times.* New York: Cassell.

Richardson, Joanna. 1960. *The Disastrous Marriage.* London: Cape.

Richardson, Robert G. 2001. *Larrey: Surgeon to Napoleon's Imperial Guard.* Harrisburg, PA: Stackpole.

Rieder, John. 1997. *Wordsworth's Counterrevolutionary Turn: Community, Virtue, and Vision in the 1790s.* Newark: University of Delaware Press.

Riehn, Richard K. 1991. *1812: Napoleon's Russian Campaign.* New York: Wiley.

Riley, J. P. 2000. *Napoleon and the World War of 1813: Lessons in Coalition War Fighting.* London: Cass.

Ringoir, H. 1968. *De Nederlandse infanterie.* Bussum, Netherlands: Van Dishoeck.

Ringrose, David R. 1970. *Transportation and Economic Stagnation in Spain, 1750–1850.* Durham, NC: Duke University Press.

Ritter, Gerhard. 1958. *Stein—Eine politische Biographie.* Stuttgart: Deutsche Verlagsanstalt.

Robert, Christian. 1971. *Recherche sur les Héraultais morts aux armées (1811–1815).* Montpellier, France: Mémoire Maîtrise Histoire.

Roberti, Melchiorre. 1946–1947. *Milano capitale napoleonica.* 3 vols. Milan: Fondazione Treccani.

Roberts, Andrew. 2003. *Napoleon and Wellington: The Long Duel.* London: Weidenfeld and Nicolson.

Roberts, Andrew. 2005. *Waterloo: Napoleon's Last Gamble.* London: HarperCollins.

Roberts, J. M. 1997. *The French Revolution.* Oxford: Oxford University Press.

Roberts, James. 1990. *The Counter-Revolution in France 1787–1830.* Basingstoke, UK: Macmillan.

Roberts, Michael. 1939. *The Whig Party, 1807–12.* London: Macmillan.

Roberts, Warren. 1989. *Jacques-Louis David, Revolutionary Artist: Art, Politics, and the French Revolution.* Chapel Hill: University of North Carolina Press.

Roberts, Warren. 1995. *Jane Austen and the French Revolution.* London: Athlone.

Robertson, Charles G. 1911. *England under the Hanoverians.* London: Methuen.

Robertson, Ian. 2000. *Wellington at War in the Peninsula, 1808–1814: An Overview and Guide.* London: Pen and Sword.

Robertson, Ian. 2003. *Wellington Invades France: The Final Phase of the Peninsular War, 1813–1814.* Mechanicsburg, PA: Stackpole.

Robertson, William S. 1967. *France and Latin-American Independence.* New York: Octagon.

Robinson, J. H. 1906. *Readings in European History.* Boston: Ginn.

Robinson, Mike. 2005. *The Battle of Quatre Bras, 1815.* Stroud, UK: Spellmount.

Robson, Martin. 2005. *Battle of Trafalgar.* London: Conway Maritime.

Rockmore, Tom. 2005. *Hegel, Idealism, and Analytic Philosophy.* New Haven: Yale University Press.

Rodger, Alexander B. 1964. *The War of the Second Coalition 1798 to 1801: A Strategic Commentary.* Oxford: Clarendon.

Rodger, N. A. M. 1988. *The Wooden World: An Anatomy of the Georgian Navy.* London: Fontana.

Rodger, N. A. M. 2005. *The Command of the Ocean: A Naval History of Britain, 1649–1815.* London: Penguin.

Rodman, Selden. 1964. *Quisqueya: A History of the Dominican Republic.* Seattle: University of Washington Press.

Rodmell, Graham E. 1990. *French Drama of the Revolutionary Years.* London: Routledge.

Rodner, William S. 1997. *J. M. W. Turner: Romantic Painter of the Industrial Revolution.* Berkeley: University of California Press.

Rodriguez, Junius P., ed. 1997. *The Historical Encyclopedia of World Slavery.* 2 vols. Santa Barbara, CA: ABC-CLIO.

Rogers, H. C. B. 1972. *Weapons of the British Soldier.* London: Sphere.

Rogers, H. C. B. 1974. *Napoleon's Army.* New York: Hippocrene.

Rogers, H. C. B. 1977. *The British Army of the Eighteenth Century.* London: Allen and Unwin.

Rogers, H. C. B. 1979. *Wellington's Army.* London. Ian Allan.

Roider, Karl A. 1987. *Baron Thugut and the Austrian Response to the French Revolution.* Princeton: Princeton University Press.

Roland, Alex. 1978. *Undersea Warfare in the Age of Sail.* Bloomington: Indiana University Press.

Rolo, P. J. V. 1965. *George Canning.* London: Macmillan.

Romanov, D. 1979. *Polkovodets D. S. Dokhturov.* Tula: N.p.

Ropes, John Codman. 1906. *The Campaign of Waterloo: A Military History.* New York: Scribner's. (Orig. pub. 1893)

Ros, Martin. 1994. *The Night of Fire: The Black Napoleon and the Battle for Haiti.* Trans. Karin Ford-Treep. New York: Sarpedon.

Rose, John Holland. 1909. *Dumouriez and the Defence of England against Napoleon.* London and New York: Lane.

Rose, John Holland. 1911. *The Revolutionary and Napoleonic Era: 1789–1815.* Cambridge: Cambridge University Press.

Rose, John Holland. 1922. *Lord Hood and the Defence of Toulon.* Cambridge: Cambridge University Press.

Rosinski, Herbert. 1966. *The German Army.* New York: Praeger.

Ross, Michael. 1977. *Reluctant King: Joseph Bonaparte, King of the Two Sicilies and of Spain.* New York: Mason/Charter.

Ross, Steven T. 1963. *The War of the Second Coalition.* Princeton: Princeton University Press.

Ross, Steven T. 1969. *European Diplomatic History, 1789–1815: France against Europe.* Garden City, NY: Anchor.

Ross, Steven T. 1973. *Quest for Victory: French Military Strategy, 1792–1799.* New York: Barnes.

Ross, Steven T. 1979. *From Flintlock to Rifle: Infantry Tactics, 1740–1866.* Cranbury, NJ: Associated University Presses.

Rosselli, John. 1956. *Lord William Bentinck and the British Occupation of Sicily, 1811–14.* Cambridge: Cambridge University Press.

Rossetti, General. 1998. *Journal d'un compagnon de Murat.* Paris: Librairie Historique F. Teissèdre.

Rössler, Helmut. 1966. *Graf Johann Phillip Stadion. Napoleons deutsche Gegenspieler.* Vienna: Herold.

Rothenberg, Gunther E. 1966. *The Military Border in Croatia, 1740–1881: A Study of an Imperial Institution.* Chicago: University of Chicago Press.

Rothenberg, Gunther E. 1976. "Nobility and Military Careers: The Habsburg Officer Corps, 1740–1914." *Military Affairs* 40 (4): 182–185.

Rothenberg, Gunther E. 1995. *Napoleon's Great Adversaries: The Archduke Charles and the Austrian Army, 1792–1814.* London: Spellmount.

Rothenberg, Gunther E. 1997. *Art of Warfare in the Age of Napoleon.* London: Spellmount.

Rothenberg, Gunther E. 2000. *The Napoleonic Wars.* London: Cassell.

Rothenberg, Gunther E. 2004. *The Emperor's Last Victory: Napoleon and the Battle of Wagram.* London: Weidenfeld and Nicolson.

Rothfels, Hans. 1920. *Carl von Clausewitz—Politik und Krieg.* Berlin: Dümmler.

Roubiçek, Marcel. 1978. *Modern Ottoman Troops, 1797–1915.* Jerusalem: Franciscan Print.

Rousseau, I. J., ed. 1930. *The Peninsular Journal of Major General Sir Benjamin D'Urban.* London: Longman.

Rousseau, Jean-Jacques. 1978. *On the Social Contract: With Geneva Manuscript and Political Economy.* Ed. Roger D. Masters. New York: St. Martin's.

Rousseau, Jean-Jacques. 1999. *Discourse on Political Economy and the Social Contract.* Oxford: Oxford Paperbacks. (Orig. pub. 1762.)

Rousseau. M. F. 1900. *Kléber et Menou en Egypte depuis le départ de Bonaparte, 1799–1801.* Paris: Picard.

Roux, Xavier. 1892. *L'invasion de la Savoie et du Dauphiné par les autrichiens en 1813 et 1814.* Grenoble: Baratier.

Rovigo, Duc de. 1828. *Mémoires du Duc de Rovigo: Pour servir à l'histoire de l'empereur Napoléon.* 8 vols. Paris: Bossange.

Rovigo, Duc de. 1892. *La mission du Général Savary à Saint-Pétersbourg: Sa correspondance avec l'empereur Napoléon et les ministres des relations extérieures, 1807.* St. Petersburg: N.p.

Rowe, Michael. 2003. *Collaboration and Resistance in Napoleonic Europe: State Formation in an Age of Upheaval, 1800–1815.* London: Palgrave.

Royle, Stephen. 1992. "Attitudes and Aspirations on St Helena in the Face of Continued Economic Dependency." *Geographical Journal* 158, no. 1 (March): 31–39.

Rudé, George. 1959. *The Crowd in the French Revolution.* Oxford: Oxford University Press.

Rudé, George, ed. 1967. *Robespierre.* Englewood Cliffs, NJ: Prentice-Hall.

Rudé, George. 1996. *The French Revolution.* London: Phoenix Giant.

Rudé, George. 2000. *Revolutionary Europe, 1783–1815.* Oxford: Blackwell.

Rudorff, Raymond. 1974. *War to the Death: The Twin Sieges of Zaragoza, 1808–1809.* London: Hamilton.

Ruggiero, Michele. 1974. *La rivolta dei Contadini Piemontesi 1796–1802.* Turin: Piemonte in bancarella.

Russell, Jack. 1969. *Nelson and the Hamiltons.* London: Blond.

Russell of Liverpool, Lord. 1964. *Knight of the Sword: The Life and Letters of Admiral Sir William Sidney Smith.* London: Gollancz.

Russkii biograficheskii slovar. 1896–1918. St. Petersburg: Izdanie Imperatorskago Russkago istoricheskago obshchestva.

Rüstow, Friedrich Wilhelm. 1853. *Der Krieg von 1805 in Deutschland und Italien.* Frauenfeld, Switzerland: Reimmann.

Rutherford, Jessica. 1995. *The Royal Pavilion: The Palace of George IV.* Brighton, UK: Royal Pavilion Art Gallery and Museums.

Ryan, Edward. 1999. *Napoleon's Elite Cavalry: Cavalry of the Imperial Guard, 1804–1815.* London: Greenhill.

Ryan, Edward, and Lucien Rousselot. 1999. *Napoleon's Elite Cavalry: Cavalry of the Imperial Guard, 1804–1815.* Mechanicsburg, PA: Stackpole.

S

Sack, James J. 1979. *The Grenvillites, 1801–1829: Party Politics and Factionalism in the Age of Pitt and Liverpool.* Urbana: University of Illinois Press.

Saint-Albin, A. 1860. *Championnet, général des armées de la république française, ou Les campagnes de Hollande, de Rome et de Naples.* Paris: Poulet-Malassis et De Broise.

Saint-Bris, Gonzague. 1995. *Desaix, Le sultan de Bonaparte.* Paris: Perrin.

Saint-Hilaire, Émile Marco de. 1977. *Cadoudal, Moreau et Pichegru.* Paris: Librairie Académique Perrin.

Sainte-Beuve, Charles Augustin. 1869. *Le général Jomini.* Paris: Michel Lévy frères.

Saricks, Ambrose. 1965. *Pierre Samuel du Pont de Nemours.* Lawrence: University Press of Kansas.

Saski, Charles G. L. 1889–1902. *Campagne de 1809 en Allemagne et en Autriche.* Vols. 1–2. Paris: Berger-Levrault.

Saul, Norman E. 1970. *Russia and the Mediterranean, 1797–1807.* Chicago: University of Chicago Press.

Saunders, David. 1992. *Russia in the Age of Reaction and Reform 1801–1881.* London: Longman.

Savary, Anne-Jean-Marie-René, duc de Rovigo. 1828. *Memoirs of the Duke of Rovigo Written by Himself Illustrative of the History of the Emperor Napoleon.* Translated from the French. 4 vols. London: H. Colburn.

Savatier, Rene. 1927. *L'art de Faire les Lois: Bonaparte et le Code Civil.* Paris: Dalloz.

Savinel, Pierre. 1986. *Moreau, rival républicain de Bonaparte.* Rennes: Ouest-France.

Savinkin, A. E., ed. 2001. *Ne chislom, a umeniem!: voennaia sistema A. V. Suvorova.* Moscow: Russkii put'.

Scaggs, David, and Gerard Altoff. 1997. *A Signal Victory: The Lake Erie Campaign, 1812–1813.* Annapolis, MD: Naval Institute Press.

Schama, Simon. 1992. *Citizens: A Chronicle of the French Revolution.* New York: Knopf.

Schama, Simon. 1992. *Patriots and Liberators: Revolution in the Netherlands, 1780–1813.* London: Fontana.

Scheid, Frederick C. 1995. *Soldiers of Napoleon's Kingdom of Italy: Army, State, and Society, 1800–1815.* Oxford: Westview.

Schels, J. B. 1811–1812. "Des Herzogs Albert von Sachsen-Teschen Königliche Hoheit Vertheidigung der Niederlande im Jahre 1792." In *Österreichische Militärische Zeitschrift.* Vienna: L. Seidel.

Schiller, Friedrich. 1959. *An Anthology for Our Time.* Trans. Jane Bannard Greene, Charles E. Passage, and Alexander Gödevon Aesch. Ed. Frederick Ungar. New York: Ungar.

Schmidt, Oliver. 2003. *Prussian Regular Infantryman, 1808–15.* Oxford: Osprey.

Schmitt, Carl. 2004. *The Theory of the Partisan: A Commentary/Remark on the Concept of the Political.* East Lansing: Michigan State University Press.

Schmitt, Jacques. 1999. *Joubert: La vie brève d'un grenadier bressan.* Bourg-en-Bresse: Musnier-Gilbert.

Schneid, Frederick C. 2002. *Napoleon's Italian Campaigns, 1805–1815.* Westport, CT: Greenwood.

Schneid, Frederick C. 2005. *Napoleon's Conquest of Europe: The War of the Third Coalition.* Westport, CT: Praeger.

Schneider, Günter. 2000. *Hohenlinden 1800: Die Vergessene Schlacht* [The Forgotten Battle]. With English translation. Berg-Potsdam: Kurt Vowinckel-Verlag.

Schofield, Philip, and Catherine Pease-Watkin, eds. 2002. *Rights, Representation, and Reform: Nonsense upon Stilts and Other Writings on the French Revolution.* Oxford: Clarendon.

Schom, Alan. 1992. *Trafalgar: Countdown to Battle, 1803–1805.* New York: Oxford University Press.

Schom, Alan. 1993. *One Hundred Days: Napoleon's Road to Waterloo.* Oxford: Oxford University Press.

Schom, Alan. 1997. *Napoleon Bonaparte.* New York: HarperCollins.

Schonhardt-Bailey, Cheryl, ed. 1996. *Free Trade: The Repeal of the Corn Laws.* Bristol, UK: Thomemmes.

Schpecht, A. 1852. *Korolevstvo Westfalskoe I razrushenie ego gen.-adjutantom Chernishevim.* St. Petersburg: N.p.

Schroeder, Paul. W. 1996. *The Transformation of European Politics, 1763–1848.* Oxford: Clarendon.

Schuchart, Max. 1972. *The Netherlands.* New York: Walker.

Schultz, Kirsten. 2001. *Tropical Versailles.* London: Routledge.

Schur, Nathan. 1999. *Napoleon in the Holy Land.* Mechanicsburg, PA: Stackpole.

Schwartz, Bernard, ed. 1956. *The Code Napoleon and the Common Law Tradition.* New York: New York University Press.

Schwarz, Karl. 1878. *Leben des Generals Carl von Clausewitz und der Frau Marie von Clausewitz geb. Gräfin von Brühl.* Berlin: Mittler.

Scicluna, Hannibal P. 1923. *Documents Relating to the French Occupation of Malta in 1798–1800.* Malta: Empire.

Scott, Franklin D. 1935. *Bernadotte and the Fall of Napoleon.* Cambridge, MA: Harvard University Press.

Scott, Franklin D. 1988. *Sweden: The Nation's History.* Carbondale: Southern Illinois University Press.

Scott, Samuel F. 1978. *The Response of the Royal Army to the French Revolution: The Role and Development of the Line Army, 1787–1793.* Oxford: Clarendon.

Scott, Samuel F. 1998. *From Yorktown to Valmy.* Niwot: University Press of Colorado.

Scurr, Ruth. 2006. *Fatal Purity: Robespierre and the French Revolution.* London: Chatto and Windus.

Seaton, Albert. 1979. *The Russian Army of the Napoleonic Wars.* London: Osprey.

Secher, Reynald. 2003. *A French Genocide: The Vendée.* Trans. George Holoch. South Bend, IN: University of Notre Dame Press.

Sédouy, Jacques-Alain de. 2003. *Le congrès de Vienne: L'Europe contre la France, 1812–1815.* Paris: Perrin.

Seeley, J. R. 1879. *Life and Times of Stein.* 2 vols. Boston: Roberts.

Ségur, Louis-Philippe, comte de. 1873. *Histoire et memoirs par le général comte de Ségur.* Paris: Didot.

Ségur, Louis-Philippe, comte de. 1928. *The Memoirs and Anecdotes of the Count de Ségur.* New York: Scribner.

Ségur, Louis-Philippe, comte de. 2003. *Napoleon's Expedition to Russia: The Memoirs of General de Ségur.* London: Constable and Robinson.

Ségur, Philippe Paul, comte de. 1958. *Napoleon's Russian Campaign.* Boston: Houghton Mifflin.

Semanov, S. N., ed. 2000. *Aleksandr Vasil'evich Suvorov.* Moscow: Russkii Mir.

Semmel, Stuart. 2004. *Napoleon and the British.* New Haven: Yale University Press.

Serebryakov, G. 1985. *Denis Davidov.* Moscow: Molodaia gvardiia.

Seton-Watson, Hugh. 1967. *The Russian Empire, 1801–1917.* Oxford: Clarendon.

Severn, John K. 1981. *A Wellesley Affair: Richard Marquess Wellesley and the Conduct of Anglo-Spanish Diplomacy, 1809–1812.* Tallahassee: University Presses of Florida.

Seward, Desmond. 1991. *Metternich: The First European.* New York: Seward.

Sewell, William H. 1995. *A Rhetoric of Bourgeois Revolution: The Abbé Sieyes and What Is the Third Estate?* Durham, NC: Duke University Press.

Shadwell, L. 1875. *Mountain Warfare.* London: Henry S. King.

Shanahan, William O. 1945. *Prussian Military Reforms, 1786–1813.* New York: Columbia University Press.

Shankland, Peter. 1975. *Beware of Heroes: Admiral Sir Sidney Smith's War against Napoleon.* London: Purcell.

Shaw, Stanford Jay. 1962. *The Financial and Administrative Organization and Development of Ottoman Egypt, 1517–1798.* Princeton: Princeton University Press.

Shaw, Stanford Jay. 1965. "The Established Ottoman Army Corps under Selim III." *Der Islam* 40: 142–184.

Shaw, Stanford Jay. 1971. *Between the Old and New: The Ottoman Empire under Sultan Selim III, 1789–1807.* Cambridge, MA: Harvard University Press.

Sheehan, James J. 1989. *German History, 1770–1866.* New York: Oxford University Press.

Shenkman, Gregory. 2003. *General Raevskii i ego semia.* St. Petersburg: Aleteiia.

Shepperd, Alan. 1987. "The Patagonian . . . Brune." In *Napoleon's Marshals,* ed. David G. Chandler, 79–91. New York: Macmillan.

Sherwig, John M. 1969. *Guineas and Gunpowder: British Foreign Aid in the Wars with France, 1793–1815.* Cambridge, MA: Harvard University Press.

Shevirev, S. 1844. *Kniaz D. V. Golitsyn.* Moscow: N.p.

Shilder, Nikolay. 1897. "Graf Shuvalov i Napoleon v 1814 g." *Russkaia Starina,* no. 5.

Shilder, Nikolay. 1901. *Imperator Pavel I.* St. Petersburg: A. S. Suvorin.

Shilder, Nikolay. 1902. "Svetleishii kniaz A. I. Chernishev." *Voennii Sbornik,* nos. 1–4.

Shirokorad, A. 2000. *Russko-Turetskie voini, 1676–1918 gg.* Moscow: AST.

Shishov, A. V. 2002. *Neizvestnyi Kutuzov: Novoe prochtenie biografii.* Moscow: Olma.

Showalter, Dennis E. 1996. *The Wars of Frederick the Great.* London: Longman.

Shumigorsky, E. 1907. *Imperator Pavel I.* St. Petersburg: Surovina.

Shupp, Paul. 1931. *The European Powers and the Near Eastern Question, 1806–07.* New York: Columbia University Press.

Siborne, William. 1848. *History of the War in Belgium and France in 1815.* London: T. and W. Boone.

Siborne, William. 1990. *History of the Waterloo Campaign.* London: Greenhill.

Sichel, Walter. 1907. *Emma, Lady Hamilton.* New York: Dodd, Mead.

Simms, Brendan. 1997. *The Impact of Napoleon: Prussian High Politics, Foreign Policy and the Crisis of the Executive, 1797–1806.* New York: Cambridge University Press.

Simms, Brendan. 1998. *The Struggle for Mastery in Germany, 1779–1850.* London: Macmillan.

Simon, Walter M. 1955. *The Failure of the Prussian Reform Movement. 1807–1819.* Ithaca: Cornell University Press.

Simpson, Colin. 1983. *Emma: The Life of Lady Hamilton*. London: Bodley Head.

Sirotkin, V. 1962. "Franko-russkaia diplomaticheskaya borba na Balkanakh i plany sozdania slaviano-Serbskogo gosudarstva v 1806–1807 gg." In *Uchenie Zapiski Instituta Slavianovedeniia 25*. Moscow: N.p.

Six, Georges. 1934. *Dictionnaire biographique des généraux and amiraux français de la Révolution et de L'Empire (1792–1814)*. 2 vols. Paris: Saffroy.

Six, Georges. 1947. *Les généraux de la Révolution et de l'Empire*. Paris: Bordan.

Sked, Alan, ed. 1979. *Europe's Balance of Power, 1815–1848*. New York: Harper and Row.

Sked, Alan. 1979. *The Survival of the Habsburg Empire: Radetsky, the Imperial Army, and the Class War of 1848*. New York: Longman.

Skeen, Carl E. 1999. *Citizen Soldiers in the War of 1812*. Lexington: University Press of Kentucky.

Skowronek, Jerzy. 1984. *Książę Józef Poniatowski*. Warsaw: Ossolineum.

Skowronek, Jerzy. 1994. *Adam Jerzy Czartoryski, 1770–1861*. Warsaw: Wiedza Powszechna.

Slatta, Richard W., and Jane Lucas De Grummond. 2003. *Simón Bolívar's Quest for Glory*. College Station: Texas A&M University Press.

Small, Stephen. 2002. *Political Thought in Ireland, 1776–1798: Republicanism, Patriotism, and Radicalism*. Oxford: Clarendon.

Smirnov, A. 2002. *General Aleksandr Kutaisov*. Moscow: Reitar.

Smith, David Bonner. 1922–1927. *Letters of Admiral of the Fleet the Earl of St. Vincent, 1801–1804*. 2 vols. London: Navy Records Society.

Smith, Denis. 2001. *The Prisoners of Cabrera: Napoleon's Forgotten Soldiers, 1809–1814*. New York: Four Walls Eight Windows.

Smith, Digby. 1998. *Borodino*. Moreton-in-Marsh, UK: Windrush.

Smith, Digby. 1998. *The Greenhill Napoleonic Wars Data Book: Actions and Losses in Personnel, Colours, Standards and Artillery, 1792–1815*. London: Greenhill.

Smith, Digby. 2000. *Napoleon's Regiments: Battle Histories of the Regiments of the French Army, 1792–1815*. London: Greenhill.

Smith, Digby. 2001. *1813: Leipzig, Napoleon and the Battle of the Nations*. London: Greenhill.

Smith, Digby. 2002. *Armies of 1812: The Grande Armée and the Armies of Austria, Prussia, Russia and Turkey*. Staplehurst, UK: Spellmount.

Smith, Digby. 2003. *Charge! Great Cavalry Charges of the Napoleonic Wars*. London: Greenhill.

Smith, Digby. 2004. *Armies of the Napoleonic Era*. Atglen, PA: Schiffer.

Smith, Digby. 2005. *The Decline and Fall of Napoleon's Empire: How the Emperor Self-Destructed*. London: Greenhill.

Smith, Digby. 2006. *Uniforms of the Napoleonic Wars: An Illustrated Encyclopedia*. London: Lorenz.

Smith, E. A. 1993. *A Queen on Trial: The Affair of Queen Caroline*. Stroud, UK: Sutton.

Smith, E. A. 1999. *George IV*. New Haven, CT: Yale University Press.

Smyth, Jim, ed. 2000. *Revolution, Counter-revolution, and Union: Ireland in the 1790s*. Cambridge: Cambridge University Press.

Soboul, Albert. 1974. *The French Revolution, 1787–1799: From the Storming of the Bastille to Napoleon*. New York: Random House.

Soboul, Albert. 1988. *Understanding the French Revolution*. Trans. A. Knutson. New York: International.

Solé, Robert. 1998. *Les savants de Bonaparte*. Paris: Editions du Seuil.

Solé, Robert, and Dominique Vabelle. 2001. *The Rosetta Stone: The Story of the Decoding of Hieroglyphics*. London: Profile.

Solov'ev, Vladimir. 1960. *Istoricheskie dramy: Velikii gosudar'. Feldmarshal Kutuzov. Denis Davydov. Pobeditelei sudiat*. Moscow: Gosudarstvennoe Izd.atel'stvo.

Soltl, J. M. 1837. *Max Joseph: König von Bayern*. Stuttgart: N.p.

Sonneborn, Liz. 2004. *The War of 1812: A Primary Source History of America's Second War with Britain*. New York: Rosen Central.

Sorel, Albert. 1969. *The Eastern Question in the Eighteenth Century: The Partition of Poland and the Treaty of Kainardji*. New York: Fertig.

Sorel, Albert. 1969. *Europe and the French Revolution*. London: Collins.

Sorkin, David. 1983. "Wilhelm von Humboldt: The Theory and Practice of Self-Formation (*Bildung*), 1791–1810." *Journal of the History of Ideas* 44: 55–73.

Soubiran, André. 1966. *Le baron Larrey, chirurgien de Napoléon*. Paris: Fayard.

Soubiran, André. 1969. *Napoléon et un million de morts*. Paris: Segep.

Sparrow, Elizabeth. 1992. "The Swiss and Swabian Agencies, 1795–1801." *Historical Journal* 35, 4: 861–884.

Sparrow, Elizabeth. 1999. *Secret Service: British Agents in France, 1792–1815*. Rochester, NY: Boydell.

Spater, George. 1982. *William Cobbett: The Poor Man's Friend*. 2 vols. Cambridge: Cambridge University Press.

Spiel, Hilde, ed. 1968. *The Congress of Vienna: An Eyewitness Account*. Philadelphia: Chilton.

Spring, Laurence. 2002. *Russian Grenadiers and Infantry, 1799–1815*. Oxford: Osprey.

Spring, Laurence. 2003. *The Cossacks, 1799–1815*. Oxford: Osprey.

St. Clair, William. 1972. *That Greece Might Still Be Free: The Philhellenes in the War of Independence*. Oxford: Oxford University Press.

Staël, Germaine de. 2000. *Ten Years of Exile*. Trans. Avriel H. Goldberger. De Kalb: Northern Illinois University Press.

Stagg, J. C. A. 1983. *Mr. Madison's War: Politics, Diplomacy and Warfare in the Early American Republic, 1783–1830*. Princeton: Princeton University Press.

Stalker, Archibald. 1921. *The Intimate Life of Sir Walter Scott*. London: Black.

Stamm-Kuhlmann, Thomas. 1992. *König in Preussens grosser Zeit—Friedrich Wilhelm III., der Melancholiker auf dem Thron*. Berlin: Siedler.

Stefof, Rebecca. 2001. *The War of 1812 (North American Historical Atlases)*. Salt Lake City: Benchmark.

Stendhal [Marie-Henri Beyle]. 1953. *Scarlet and Black: A Chronicle of the Nineteenth Century*. Trans. Margaret Shaw. London: Penguin.

Stendhal [Marie-Henri Beyle]. 1954. *The Private Diaries of Stendhal*. Ed. and trans. Robert Sage. New York: Doubleday.

Stendhal [Marie-Henri Beyle]. 1956. *A Life of Napoleon*. London: Rodale.

Stendhal [Marie-Henri Beyle]. 1958. *The Charterhouse of Parma*. Trans. Margaret Shaw. London: Penguin.

Stendhal [Marie-Henri Beyle]. 1986. *The Life of Henry Brulard*. Trans. Jean Steward and B. C. J. G. Knight. Chicago: University of Chicago Press.

Stendhal [Marie-Henri Beyle]. 1986. *To the Happy Few: Selected Letters*. Ed. Boudot-Lamotte and trans. Norman Cameron. London: Soho.

Stenzel, Alfred. 1911. *Seekriegsgeschichte*. 5 vols. Hannover: Pemsel.

Stephen, Alexis. 1949. *Black Liberator: The Life of Toussaint Louverture*. Trans. William Stirling. London: Benn.

Stephenson, Charles. 2004. *The Fortifications of Malta, 1530–1945*. Oxford: Osprey.

Stewart, Charles William Vane, Marquess of Londonderry. 1830. *Narrative of the War in Germany and France in 1813 and 1814*. London: Colburn and Bentley.

Stewart, Richard Winship, ed. 2005. *American Military History*. Vol. 1, *The United States Army and the Forging of a Nation, 1775–1917*. Washington, DC: Department of the Army.

Stinchcombe, William. 1981. *The XYZ Affair*. Westport, CT: Greenwood.

Stine, John E. 1980. "King Frederick William II and the Decline of the Prussian Army, 1786–1797." Ph.D. diss., University of South Carolina.

Stokoe, Dr. John. 1902. *With Napoleon at St. Helena: Being the Memoirs of Dr. John Stokoe, Naval Surgeon*. Translated from the French of Paul Frémeaux by Edith S. Stokoe. London: Lane.

Stone, Alison. 2005. *Petrified Intelligence: Nature in Hegel's Philosophy*. Albany: State University of New York Press.

Stone, Bailey. 2002. *Reinterpreting the French Revolution. A Global-Historical Perspective*. Cambridge: Cambridge University Press.

Stone, Daniel. 2001. *The Polish-Lithuanian State, 1386–1795*. Seattle: University of Washington Press.

Storey, Mark. 1997. *Robert Southey: A Life*. Oxford: Oxford University Press.

Strachan, Hew. 1984. *Wellington's Legacy: The Reform of the British Army, 1830–54*. Manchester: Manchester University Press.

Strachey, Lytton, and Roger Fulford. 1938. *The Greville Memoirs, 1814–1860*. 8 vols. London: Macmillan.

Strauss, Hannah. 1949. *The Attitude of the Congress of Vienna toward Nationalism in Germany, Italy, and Poland*. New York: Columbia University Press.

Strawson, John. 1991. *Beggars in Red: The British Army, 1789–1889*. London: Hutchinson.

Stroud, Patricia Tyson. 2005. *The Man Who Had Been King: The American Exile of Napoleon's Brother Joseph*. Philadelphia: University of Pennsylvania Press.

Stutterheim, Major-General Freiherr Karl von. 1985. *A Detailed Account of the Battle of Austerlitz*. Cambridge: Trotman. (Orig. pub. 1807.)

Suchet, Louis-Gabriel, duc d'Albufera. 1828. *Mémoires du maréchal Suchet: duc d'Albufera, sur ses campagnes en Espagne, depuis 1808 jusqu'en 1814, écrits par lui-même*. Paris: Adolphe Bossange.

Sugden, John. 2004. *Nelson: A Dream of Glory*. Vol. I. London: Cape.

Sukhtelen, Paul. 1854. *Narrative of the Conquest of Finland by the Russians in the Years 1808–9: From an Unpublished Work by a Russian Officer of Rank*. Ed. General Monteith. London: Booth.

Summerville, Christopher. 2003. *March of Death: Sir John Moore's Retreat to Corunna, 1808–1809*. London: Greenhill.

Summerville, Christopher. 2005. *Napoleon's Polish Gamble: Eylau and Friedland, 1807*. London: Leo Cooper.

Sunderland, John. 1975. *John Constable*. London: Phaidon.

Suratteau, Jean. 1969. "Occupation, occupants et occupés en Suisse de 1792 à 1814." In *Occupants, Occupés, 1792–1815*. Brussels: Université Libre de Bruxelles.

Sutherland, Donald M. 1982. *The Chouans: The Social Origins of Popular Counter-Revolution in Upper Brittany, 1770–1796*. New York: Oxford University Press.

Sutherland, Donald M. 1985. *France, 1789–1815: Revolution and Counter-Revolution*. New York: Oxford University Press.

Sutherland, Donald M. 2003. *The French Revolution and Empire: The Quest for a Civic Order*. Malden, MA: Blackwell.

Sutherland, John. 1995. *The Life of Walter Scott: A Biography*. Oxford: Blackwell.

Suvorov, A. V. 1952. *Dokumenti*. Moscow: N.p.

Sweden Armen, Generalstaben. 1890–1922. *Sveriges krig åren 1808 och 1809*. 9 vols. Stockholm: Kongl. boktryckeriet P.A. Norstedt ja söner.

Sweden Armen, Generalstaben. 1906. *Krigshistoriska avdelningen. Shveidskaia voina 1808–1809 g.g. sostavlena voenno-istoricheskim otdelom Shvedskogo Generalnogo Shtaba*. 2 vols. St. Petersburg: Izd. Glavnago upravleniia General'nago shtaba.

Sweet, Paul R. 1941. *Friedrich von Gentz: Defender of the Old Order*. Madison: University of Wisconsin Press.

Sweet, Paul R. 1978–1980. *Wilhelm von Humboldt: A Biography*. 2 vols. Columbus: Ohio State University Press.

Sweetman, John. 1998. *The Enlightenment and the Age of Revolution 1700–1850*. London: Longman.

Sydenham, Michael. 1961. *The Girondins*. London: Athlone.

Sydenham, Michael. 1974. *The First French Republic, 1792–1804*. London: Batsford.

T

Tackett, Timothy. 1982. "The West in France in 1789: The Religious Factor in the Origins of Counter-Revolution." *Journal of Modern History* 54: 715–745.

Tackett, Timothy. 1996. *Becoming Revolutionary: The Deputies of the French National Assembly and the Emergence of a National Culture, 1789–1790*. Princeton: Princeton University Press.

Talleyrand-Périgord, Charles-Maurice de, prince de Bénévent. 1967. *Lettres de Talleyrand à Napoléon*. Ed. Pierre Bertrand. Paris: Bonnot.

Talleyrand-Périgord, Charles-Maurice de, prince de Bénévent. 1973. *Memoirs of the Prince de Talleyrand*. Ed. duc de Broglie. 5 vols. New York: AMS.

Talleyrand-Périgord, Charles-Maurice de, prince de Bénévent. 1989. *Mémoires complets et authentiques de Charles-Maurice de Talleyrand, prince de Bénévent: texte conforme au manuscrit original. Contenant les notes de Monsieur Adolphe*

Fourier de Bacourt, légataire des manuscrits de l'auteur. 6 vols. Paris: Bonnot.

Tarasov, E. 1902. *Donskoi ataman Platov.* St. Petersburg: N.p.

Tarbox, Charles, and Scott Bowden. 1990. *Armies on the Danube: Napoleon's Austrian Campaign of 1809.* New York: Paragon.

Tarle, Evgenii Viktorovich. 1942. *Napoleon's Invasion of Russia, 1812.* New York: Oxford University Press.

Tarle, Evgenii Viktorovich. 1949. *How Mikhail Kutuzov Defeated Napoleon.* London: Soviet War News.

Tarle, Evgenii Viktorovich. 1956. *Tri ekspeditsii russkogo flota.* Moscow: Voennoe izd-vo.

Tarle, Evgenii Viktorovich. 1959. *Tisiacha vosem'sot dvenadtsatyi god.* Moscow: Gosudarstvennoe Isdatel'stvo.

Tarnstrom, Ronald. 2001. *French Arms.* Linsborg, KS: Trogen.

Tate, W. E. 1967. *The English Village Community and the Enclosure Movements.* Oxford: Clarendon.

Tavera, Nedo. 1982. *Elisa Bonaparte Baciocchi, Principessa di Piombino.* Florence: Giuntina.

Taylor, Brian. D. 2003. *Politics and the Russian Army: Civil-Military Relations, 1689–2000.* Cambridge: Cambridge University Press.

Terraine, John. 1998. *Trafalgar.* London: Wordsworth.

Tessitori, Paula. 1997. *Basta che finissa 'sti cani: Democrazia e polizia nella Venezia dell 1797.* Venice: Istituto Veneto di Scienze, Lettere ed Arti.

Thadd, E. 1971. *France and the Eighteenth-Century Corsican Question.* New York: New York University Press.

Thaden, Edward C. 1971. *Russia Since 1801: The Making of a New Society.* New York: Wiley-Interscience.

Thibaudet, Albert. 1938. *French Literature from 1795 to Our Era.* Trans. Charles Lam Markmann. New York: Funk and Wagnalls.

Thielen, Peter Gerrit. 1967. *Karl August von Hardenberg (1750–1822): Eine Biographie.* Cologne: Grote.

Thiessé, Léon. 1816. *Procès du maréchal-de-camp, baron Cambronne: Précédé d'une notice historique très-détaillée, sur la vie et le caractère de cet officier-général.* Paris: N.p.

Thiry, Jean. 1973. *Bonaparte en Egypte: Décembre 1797–24 août 1799.* Paris: Berger-Levrault.

Thomas, Hugh. 1972. *Goya: The Third of May, 1808.* London: Lane.

Thomas, Hugh. 1997. *The Slave Trade.* New York: Simon and Schuster.

Thomas, Peter. 2002. *George III: King and Politicians, 1760–1770.* Manchester, UK: Manchester University Press.

Thomis, Malcolm I. 1970. *The Luddites: Machine-Breaking in Regency England.* Hamden, CT: Archon.

Thompson, E. P. 1963. *The Making of the English Working Class.* New York: Pantheon.

Thompson, J. M. 1958. *Napoleon Bonaparte: His Rise and Fall.* Oxford: Blackwell.

Thompson, J. M. 1988. *Robespierre.* Oxford: Blackwell.

Thompson, Neville. 1986. *Wellington after Waterloo.* London: Routledge and Kegan Paul.

Thompson, Neville. 1999. *Earl Bathurst and the British Empire, 1762–1834.* Barnsley, UK: Cooper.

Thomson, David. 1965. *Europe since Napoleon.* New York: Knopf.

Thornton, John. 1998. *Africa and Africans in the Making of the Atlantic World. 1400–1800.* Cambridge: Cambridge University Press.

Thoumas, Charles Antoine. 1887. *Les transformations de l'armée française.* 2 vols. Paris: Berger-Levrault.

Thoumas, Charles Antoine. 1890–1909. *Les grands cavaliers du premier empire: notice biographiques.* 3 vols. Paris: Berger-Levrault.

Tilly, Charles. 1964. *The Vendée.* Cambridge, MA: Harvard University Press.

Tilly, Charles. 1986. *The Contentious French: Four Centuries of Popular Struggle.* Cambridge, MA: Belknap.

Timiriazev, V. 1895. "Chernishev i Michel." *Istoricheskii Vestnik,* no. 2.

Todd, Janet M. 2003. *Rebel Daughters: Ireland in Conflict, 1798.* London: Viking.

Todorov, Tzvetan. 1999. *A Passion for Democracy: Benjamin Constant.* Trans. Alice Seberry. New York: Algora.

Tolstoy, M. 1894. "Svetleishii kniaz D. V. Golitsyn." *Russkii arkhiv* 7.

Tomalin, Claire. 1997. *Jane Austen: A Life.* London: Viking.

Tomsinov, V. A. 1991. *Svetilo russkoi biurokratii. Istoricheskii portret M.M. Speranskogo.* Moscow: N.p.

Tone, John Lawrence. 1995. *The Fatal Knot: The Guerrilla War in Navarre and the Defeat of Napoleon in Spain.* Chapel Hill: University of North Carolina Press.

Toussaint du Wast, Nicole. 1985. *Laure Junot duchesse d'Abrantès.* Paris: Fanval.

Townsend, Joyce. 1973. *Turner's Painting Techniques.* London: Tate Gallery.

Tracy, Nicholas. 1996. *Nelson's Battles: The Art of Victory in the Age of Sail.* Annapolis, MD: Naval Institute.

Tracy, Nicolas. 2005. *Who's Who in Nelson's Navy: Two Hundred Heroes.* London: Chatham.

Tranié, J., and J.-C. Carmigniani. 1979. *Napoléon et L'Autriche: La Campagne de 1809.* Paris: Copernic.

Tranié, J., and J.-C. Carmigniani. 1982. *Napoleon's War in Spain: The French Peninsular Campaigns, 1807–1814.* London: Arms and Armour.

Tranié, J., and J.-C. Carmigniani. 1984. *Napoléon et l'Allemagne: Prusse 1806.* Paris: Pygmalion/Watelet.

Trausch, Gilbert. 2003. *Histoire du Luxembourg: le destin européen d'un petit pays.* Toulouse: Privat.

Treitschke, Heinrich von. 1975. *History of Germany in the Nineteenth Century: Selections from the Translation of Eden and Cedar Paul.* Chicago: University of Chicago Press.

Tresse, R. 1957. "J. A. Chaptal et l'enseignement technique de 1800–1819." *Revue d'histoire des sciences* 10: 167–174.

Triaire, Paul. 1902. *Dominique Larrey et les campagnes de la Révolution et de l'Empire.* Tours: Mame.

Troitsky, Nikolay. 1988. *1812: Velikii god Rossii.* Moscow: Nauka.

Troyanski, David G. 1991. *The French Revolution in Culture and Society.* New York: Greenwood.

Troyat, Henri. 1980. *Catherine the Great.* Trans. Joan Pinkham. New York: Dutton.

Troyat, Henri. 2002. *Alexander of Russia: Napoleon's Conqueror.* New York: Grove.

Tsintsadze, Zurab. 1997. *Bagration Voennaia Deiatelnost General Petra Ivanovicha Bagrationa, 1782–1812.* Moscow: N.p.

Tuchkov, P. 1873. "Moi vospominania o 1812 g." *Russkii Arkhiv,* no. 10.

Tuchkov, Sergey. 1908. *Zapiski.* St. Petersburg: N.p.

Tucker, Jedediah Stephens. 1844. *Memoirs of the Right Hon. the Earl of St. Vincent.* 2 vols. London: Bentley.

Tucker, Spencer C. 1989. *Arming the Fleet: U.S. Navy Ordnance in the Muzzle-Loading Era.* Annapolis, MD: Naval Institute Press.

Tucker, Spencer C. 1993. *The Jeffersonian Gunboat Navy.* Columbia: University of South Carolina Press.

Tucker, Spencer C. 2005. *Stephen Decatur: A Life Most Bold and Daring.* Annapolis, MD: Naval Institute Press.

Tulard, Jean. 1979. *Napoléon et la noblesse d'Empire.* Paris: Tallandier.

Tulard, Jean. 1992. *Napoléon II.* Paris: Fayard.

Tulard, Jean. 1998. *Joseph Fouché.* Paris: Fayard.

Tunstall, Brian. 1990. *Naval Warfare in the Age of Sail: The Evolution of Fighting Tactics, 1650–1815.* Annapolis, MD: Naval Institute Press.

Turnbull, Patrick. 1971. *Napoleon's Second Empress: A Life of Passion.* New York: Walker.

Turnbull, Patrick. 1976. "1814: The Last Napoleonic Victories." *History Today* 26, no. 8: 499–507.

Turner, Michael. 2002. *Pitt the Younger: A Life.* London: Hambledon and London.

Turner, Wesley B. 1999. *British Generals in the War of 1812.* Ithaca: McGill-Queen's University Press.

Tyson, George F. 1973. *Toussaint Louverture.* Englewood Cliffs, NJ: Prentice-Hall.

U

Uffindell, Andrew. 1994. *The Eagle's Last Triumph: Napoleon's Victory at Ligny, June 1815.* London: Greenhill.

Uffindell, Andrew. 2003. *Great Generals of the Napoleonic Wars and Their Battles, 1805–1815.* Staplehurst, UK: Spellmount.

Uffindell, Andrew. 2005. *National Army Museum Book of Wellington's Armies: Britain's Triumphant Campaigns in the Peninsula and at Waterloo, 1808–1815.* London: Pan.

Uffindell, Andrew, and Michael Corum. 2002. *On the Fields of Glory: The Battlefields of the 1815 Campaign.* London: Greenhill.

Ulianov, I. 1997. *Reguliarnaia pekhota. 1801–1855.* Moscow: OOO Izd-vo AST.

Unger, Harlow G. 2002. *Lafayette.* New York: Wiley.

Updyke, Frank A. 1965. *The Diplomacy of the War of 1812.* Gloucester, MA: Smith.

Urban, Mark. 2001. *The Man Who Broke Napoleon's Codes.* New York: HarperCollins.

Urban, Mark. 2004. *Wellington's Rifles: Six Years to Waterloo with England's Legendary Sharpshooters.* New York: Walker.

Urie (Barony) Scotland Court. 1892. *Court Book of the Barony of Urie in Kincardinshire, 1604–1747.* Edinburgh: University Press; printed by Constable.

Uythoven, Geert van. 1999. *Voorwaarts Bataven! De Engels-Russische invasie van 1799.* Zaltbommel, Netherlands: Europese Bibliotheek.

V

Vachée, J. B. 1995. *Napoleon at Work.* Minneapolis, MN: PDI. (Orig. pub. 1914.)

Vale, Brian. 2001. *A Frigate of King George: Life and Duty on a British Man-of-War.* London: I. B. Tauris.

Valka, S. N., ed. 1961. *M. M. Speranskii: Proiekty i zapiski.* Moscow: N.p.

Valori, Vicomte de. 1839. *Le Grand-duc Ferdinand IV* [sic] *et Toscane.* Paris: Dentu.

Van Creveld, Martin. 1985. *Command in War.* Cambridge, MA: Harvard University Press.

Vaquette, Claude. 1991. *Caulaincourt: Un général diplomate.* Amiens: Martelle.

Vasiliev, I. 2001. *Neskolko gromkikh udarov po khvostu tigra.* Moscow: Reitar.

Vaughan, William, and Helen Weston. 2000. *Jacques-Louis David's Marat.* Cambridge: Cambridge University Press.

Verbreitung der Buchhändler Palm. 1806. *Von franzoesischen Truppen standrechtlich erschossen wurde.* Kiel: Arndt.

Vertray, Captain. 1883. *L'armée française en Egypte, 1798–1801: Journal d'un officier de l'Armée d'Egypte.* Paris: Charpentier.

Vess, David M. 1967. "The Collapse and Revival of Medical Education in France: A Consequence of Revolution and War, 1789–1795." *History of Education Quarterly* 7, no. 1: 71–92.

Vess, David M. 1975. *Medical Revolution in France, 1789–1796.* Gainesville: Florida State University Press.

Vianello, Carlo. 1942. *Le finanze della Repubblica Cisalpina.* Milan: Giuffre.

Vichness, Samuel E. 1976. "Marshal of Portugal: The Military Career of William Carr Beresford." Ph.D. diss., Florida State University.

Victor, Maréchal. 1846. *Extraits des Mémoires inédits de feu C.-V. Perrin, duc de Bellune . . . Campagne de l'armée de réserve en l'an VIII (1800).* Paris: Dumaine.

Victor, Maréchal. 1847. *Mémoires de C.-V. Perrin . . . mis en ordre par son fils aîné.* Paris: Dumaine.

Vidalenc, Jean. 1963. *Les émigrés français, 1789–1825.* Caen: L'Université de Caen.

Vignery, R. 1966. *The French Revolution and the Schools.* Madison: University of Wisconsin Press.

Villar, Constant. 1821. *Campagne des Autrichiens contre Murat en 1815.* Brussels: Wahlen.

Villiers, Patrick. 1988. "La guerre de course de Louis XIV à Napoléon 1er." In *Marine et Technique au XIXe siècle,* Actes du colloque international, Paris, Ecole Militaire, 10–12 juin 1987: 91–141. Paris: Service Historique de la Marine.

Villiers, Patrick. 2002. "Premiers résultats d'une recherche sur les corsaires français en Méditerranée sous l'Empire." In *Mélanges de recherches en l'honneur du professeur George Jehel.* Vol. 13. Amiens: Presses de l'université de Picardie.

Vincent, Edgar. 2004. *Nelson: Love and Fame.* New Haven: Yale University Press.

Viskovatov, A. V. 1841–1862. *Istoricheskoe opisanie odezhdi i vooruzheniia Rossiiskikh voisk.* 30 vols. St. Petersburg: Voennaya.

Vivenot, Alfred Ritter von. 1870. *Thugut und sein politisches System.* Vienna: K. Gerold's Sohn.

Voensky, K. 1912. *Vilna v 1812 g. Iz vospominanii grafa Gogendorpa.* St. Petersburg: N.p.

Voronovskii, V. M. 1912. *Otechestvennaya voina 1812 g. v predelakh Smolenskoi gubernii.* St. Petersburg: Tip. A. S. Suvorina.

Vovelle, Michel. 1984. *The Fall of the French Monarchy, 1787–1792.* Cambridge: Cambridge University Press.

Voykowitsch, Bernhard. 1998. *Castiglione 1796: Napoleon Repulses Würmser's First Attack.* Maria Enzersdorf: Helmet Military Publications.

Vries, Jan de, and Ad van der Woude. 1997. *The First Modern Economy: Success, Failure and Perseverance of the Dutch*

Economy, 1500–1850. Cambridge: Cambridge University Press.

W

Wagner, Anton H. 1981. *Der Feldzug der K. Preussischen Armee am Rhein im Jahre 1793.* Wiesbaden: LTR. (Orig. pub. 1831)

Wagner, Anton H. 1984. *Militärhistorische Schriftenreihe 51: Das Gefecht bei St. Michael-Leoben am 25. Mai 1809.* Vienna: Heeresgeschichtliches Museum.

Wait, Eugene M. 1999. *America and the War of 1812.* Commack, NY: Kroshka.

Waliszewski, Kazimierz. 1913. *Paul the First of Russia.* Philadelphia: Lippincott.

Walsh, Henry H. 1933. *The Concordat of 1801: A Study of the Problem of Nationalism in the Relations of Church and State.* New York: Columbia University Press.

Walsh, John, Herbert Zima, and David Hollins. "Birth of a Legend: The Bridge of Lodi." In *Age of Napoleon,* 34: 21–27; 35: 11–20. Leigh-on-Sea, UK: Partizan.

Walter, Dierk. 2001. *A Military Revolution? Prussian Military Reforms before the Wars of German Unification.* Forsvarsstudier 2/2001. Oslo: Norwegian Institute for Defence Studies.

Walter, Dierk. 2003. *Preussische Heeresreformen 1807–1870: Militaerische Innovation und der Mythos der "Roonschen Reform."* Paderborn: Schoeningh.

Walvin, James. 2001. *Black Ivory: Slavery in the British Empire.* Oxford: Blackwell.

Wandycz, Piotr. 1975. *The Lands of Partitioned Poland, 1795–1918.* Seattle: University of Washington Press.

Wangensteen, Owen H., et al. 1972. "Wound Management of Ambroise Paré and Dominique Larrey, Great French Military Surgeons of the 16th and 19th Centuries." *Bulletin of the History of Medicine* 46, no. 3: 207–234.

War Office, London. 2003. *Treatise on Ammunition.* Uckfield: Naval and Military Press; London: Imperial War Museum. (Orig. pub. 1877.)

Ward, Adolphus William, Sir, and G. P. Gooch, eds. 1970. *The Cambridge History of British Foreign Policy, 1783–1919.* Vol. 1, *1783–1815.* New York: Octagon.

Ward, Aileen. 1986. *John Keats: The Making of a Poet.* Rev. ed. New York: Farrar, Straus and Giroux.

Ward, S. G. P. 1957. *Wellington's Headquarters.* Oxford: Oxford University Press.

Wareham, Tom. 2003. *The Star Captains: Frigate Command in the Napoleonic Wars.* London: Chatham.

Wareham, Tom. 2004. *Frigate Commander.* London: Cooper.

Warner, Oliver. 1958. *A Portrait of Lord Nelson.* London: Chatto and Windus.

Warner, Oliver. 1960. *The Battle of the Nile.* New York: Macmillan.

Warner, Oliver. 1961. *The Glorious First of June.* London: Batsford.

Warner, Oliver. 1965. *Nelson's Battles.* London: Batsford.

Warner, Oliver. 1966. *Trafalgar.* London: Pan.

Warner, Oliver. 1968. *The Life and Letters of Vice-Admiral Lord Collingwood.* London: Oxford University Press.

Wartenburg, General Yorck von. 1902. *Napoleon as a General.* London: Kegan Paul Trubner.

Warwick, Peter. 2005. *Voices from Trafalgar.* London: David and Charles.

Wassef, Amin Sami. 1975. *L'information et la presse officielle en Egypte jusquà la fin de l'occupation française.* Cairo: Institut français d'archéologie orientale du Caire.

Watkins, Frederick M. 1964. *The Age of Ideology: Political Thought 1750 to the Present.* Englewood Cliffs, NJ: Prentice-Hall.

Watson, J. S. 1960. *Oxford History of England: The Reign of George III.* Oxford: Oxford University Press.

Watts de Peyster, J., trans. 1895. *Marshal Blücher as Portrayed by His Correspondence.* New York: Ludwig.

Waxman, Percy. 1931. *The Black Napoleon: The Story of Toussaint Louverture.* New York: Harcourt, Brace.

Webster, Charles. 1921. *British Diplomacy, 1813–1815: Select Documents Dealing with the Reconstruction of Europe.* London: Bell.

Webster, Charles. 1931. *The Foreign Policy of Castlereagh, 1812–1815: Britain and the Reconstruction of Europe.* London: Bell.

Webster, Charles. 1969. *The Congress of Vienna, 1814–1815.* New York: Barnes and Noble.

Weibull, Jörgen. 1997. *Swedish History in Outline.* Trelleborg, Sweden: Skogs Boktryckeri AB.

Weider, Ben, and Stan Forshufvud. 1995. *Assassination at St. Helena Revisited.* New York: Wiley.

Weigley, Russell F. 1991. *The Age of Battles: The Quest for Decisive Warfare from Breitenfeld to Waterloo.* Bloomington: Indiana University Press.

Weil, Maurice. 1902. *Le prince Eugène et Murat, 1813–1814. Operations militaires, negociations diplomatiques.* Paris: Fontemoing.

Weiner, Margery. 1964. *The Parvenu Princesses.* New York: Morrow.

Weiner, Margery. 1973. *Sovereign Remedy: Europe after Waterloo.* New York: St. Martin's.

Weinstein, Leo. 1989. *The Subversive Tradition in French Literature.* Vol. 1, *1721–1870.* Boston: Twayne.

Weinzierl, John F. 1997. *The Military and Political Career of Claude-Victor Perrin.* Tallahassee: Florida State University.

Weissmann, Nahoum. 1964. *Les janissaires: Etude de l'organisation militaire des Ottomans.* Paris: Librairie Orient.

Welch, Cheryl. 1984. *Liberty and Utility: The French Ideologues and the Transformation of Liberalism.* New York: Columbia University Press.

Weller, Jac. 1996. *British Forces in the West Indies, 1793–1815.* London: Osprey.

Weller, Jac. 1998. *Wellington at Waterloo.* London: Greenhill.

Weller, Jac. 1999. *Wellington in the Peninsula, 1808–1814.* London: Greenhill.

Weller, Jac. 2000. *Wellington in India.* London: Greenhill.

Wels, P. Forbes. 1963. *De Nederlande cavalerie.* Bussum, Netherlands: Van Dishoeck.

Welschinger, Henri. 1888. *Le duc d'Enghien, 1772–1804.* Paris: Plon, Nourrit.

Welschinger, Henri. 1905. *Le pape et l'empereur, 1804–1815.* Paris: Plon-Nourrit.

Welsh, William Jeffrey, and David Curtis, eds. 1991. *War on the Great Lakes: Essays Commemorating the 175th Anniversary of the Battle of Lake Erie.* Kent, OH: Kent State University Press.

Wende, Peter. 2005. *A History of Germany.* New York: Palgrave Macmillan.

Wescher, Paul. 1988. *I furti d'arte: Napoleone e la nascita del Louvre.* Turin: Giulio Eiraudi.

Westwood, David. 2004. *The Military Rifle.* Santa Barbara, CA: ABC-CLIO.

Wetzler, Peter. 1985. *War and Subsistence: The Sambre and Meuse Army in 1794.* New York: Lang.

Wheelan, Joseph. 2003. *Jefferson's War: America's First War on Terror, 1801–1805.* New York: Carroll and Graf.

Whipple, A. B. C. 1991. *To the Shores of Tripoli: The Birth of the U. S. Navy and Marines.* Annapolis, MD: Naval Institute Press.

White, Colin, ed. 1995. *The Nelson Companion.* Stroud, UK: Sutton.

White, Colin. 2001. *1797: Nelson's Year of Destiny.* Stroud, UK: Sutton.

White, Colin. 2003. *The Nelson Encyclopedia.* Mechanicsburg, PA: Stackpole.

White, Colin. 2005. *Nelson the Admiral.* Stroud, UK: Sutton.

White, Colin, ed. 2005. *Nelson: The New Letters.* Woodbridge, UK: Boydell.

White, Colin, ed. 2005. *The Trafalgar Captains: Their Lives and Memorials.* London: Chatham.

White, R. J. 1963. *Life in Regency England.* London: Batsford.

Wiarda, Howard J., and Michael J. Kryzanek. 1982. *The Dominican Republic: A Caribbean Crucible.* Boulder, CO: Westview Press.

Wickwire, Franklin B. 1980. *Cornwallis: The Imperial Years.* Chapel Hill: University of North Carolina Press.

Wilcken, Patrick. 2005. *Empire Adrift: The Portuguese Court in Rio de Janeiro, 1808–1821.* London: Bloomsbury.

Wilkinson, Spenser. 1930. *The Rise of General Bonaparte.* Oxford: Clarendon.

Wilkinson-Latham, Robert. 1975. *Napoleon's Artillery.* London: Osprey.

Willbold, Franz. 1987. *Napoleons Feldzug um Ulm.* Ulm: Süddeutsche Verlagsgesellschaft.

Williams, John. 2002. *William Wordsworth.* New York: Palgrave.

Williamson, Audrey. 1973. Thomas Paine: *His Life, Work and Times.* London: Allen and Unwin.

Wilson, A. N. 1982. *The Lord of Abbotsford: A View of Sir Walter Scott.* Oxford: Oxford University Press.

Wilson, David A. 1998. *United Irishmen, United States: Immigrant Radicals in the Early Republic.* Ithaca: Cornell University Press.

Wilson, General Sir Robert. 1861. *Private Diary of General Sir Robert Wilson.* Vol. 2. London: John Murray.

Wilson, Peter H. 1998. *German Armies—War and German Politics, 1648–1806.* London: UCL.

Wilson, Peter H. 1999. *The Holy Roman Empire, 1495–1806.* London: Macmillan.

Wilson, Sir Robert. 2000. *Campaigns in Poland.* Felling, UK: Worley (Orig. pub. as *Brief Remarks on the Character and Composition of the Russian Army, and a Sketch of the Campaigns in Poland in the Years 1806–1807.* London: Roworth and Egerton, 1810.)

Wilson-Smith, Timothy. 1996. *Napoleon and His Artists.* London: Constable.

Wilson-Smith, Timothy. 2002. *Napoleon: Man of War, Man of Peace.* London: Constable.

Wilton, Andrew. 1987. *Turner in His Time.* London: Thames and Hudson.

Wimberley, Douglas. 1903. *Barclays of Barclay of Grantuly or Garly and Towie Barclay.* Aberdeen, Scotland: Barclays.

Winegarten, Renée. 1985. *Mme. de Staël.* Dover, NH: Berg.

Winfield, Riff. 2005. *British Warships in the Age of Sail, 1792–1815: Design, Construction, Career and Fates.* London: Chatham.

Wise, Terence. 1977. *Military Flags of the World, 1618–1900.* Poole, UK: Blandford.

Wise, Terence. 1979. *Artillery Equipments of the Napoleonic Wars.* Oxford: Osprey.

Wise, Terence. 1990–1991. *Flags of the Napoleonic Wars.* 3 vols. London: Osprey.

Wöber, Ferdi I. 2001. *1809 Schlacht bei Raab.* Maria Anzbach: Self-published.

Wohlfeil, Rainer. 1964. *Handbuch zur deutschen Militärgeschichte.* Vol. 2, *Vom stehenden Heer des Absolutismus zur Allgemeinen Wehrpflicht (1789–1814).* München: Bernhard and Graefe.

Wojciech, Mikula. 1991. *Maciejowice, 1794.* Warsaw: Wydawn, Bellona.

Woloch, Isser. 1986. "Napoleonic Conscription: State Power and Civil Society." *Past and Present* 111: 101–129.

Woloch, Isser. 2002. *Napoleon and His Collaborators: The Making of a Dictatorship.* New York: Norton.

Woltanowski, Andrzej, and Tadeusz Rawski. 1994. *Bitwa pod Maciejowicami 10.X.1794 r.* Bialystok: Instytut Historii Filii UW.

Wood, Dennis. 1993. *Benjamin Constant: A Biography.* New York: Routledge.

Woodman, Richard. 2002. *The Sea Warriors: Fighting Captains and Frigate Warfare in the Age of Nelson.* New York: Carroll and Graf.

Woodman, Richard. 2003. *The Victory of Seapower: Winning the Napoleonic War, 1806–1814.* London: Chatham.

Woolf, S. J. 1991. *Napoleon's Integration of Europe.* London: Routledge.

Wooten, Geoffrey. 1999. *Waterloo 1815.* Oxford: Osprey

Wordsworth, William. 1851. *The Complete Poetical Works of William Wordsworth.* Ed. Henry Reed. Philadelphia: Porter and Coates.

Wordsworth, William. 1893. *The Poetical Works of William Wordsworth.* Ed. Edward Dowden. Vol. 7. London: George Bell.

Wordsworth, William. 1970. *The Prelude, or Growth of a Poet's Mind (Text of 1805).* Ed. Ernest de Selincourt. Oxford: Oxford University Press.

Woronoff, Denis. 1984. *The Thermidorean Regime and the Directory: 1794–1799.* Cambridge: Cambridge University Press.

Wrede, Alphons Freiherr von. 1898–1903. *Geschichte der k.u.k. Wehrmacht. Die Regimenter, Corps, Branchen und Anstalten von 1618 bis Ende des 19. Jahrhunderts.* 5 vols. Vienna: Kriegsarchiv.

Wright, Constance. 1969. *Beautiful Enemy: A Biography of Queen Louise of Prussia.* New York: Dodd, Mead.

Wright, D. G. 1991. *Revolution and Terror in France, 1789–95.* London: Longman.

Wright, J. Leitch, Jr. 1975. *Britain and the American Frontier, 1783–1815.* Athens: University of Georgia Press.

Württembergisches Landesmuseum Stuttgart, ed. 1987. *Baden und Württemberg im Zeitalter Napoleons.* 2 vols. Stuttgart: Württembergisches Landesmuseum.

Wurzbach, Constant von. 1966. *Biographische Lexikon des Kaiserthums Österreich, 1856–1891.* 60 vols. New York: Johnson.

Y

Yemetz, Yu. 1912. *Geroi Otechestvennoi voini Kulnev.* Moscow: N.p.

Yepanchin, Yu. 1999. "N. N. Rayevsky." *Voprosi istorii,* no. 3.

Yermolov, Aleksey. 2005. *Czar's General: Memoirs of Napoleonic Wars by General Aleksey Yermolov.* Trans. Alexander Mikaberidze. London: Ravenhall.

Yonge, Charles Duke. 1868. "Viscount Castlereagh to Lord Liverpool, 28 September 1815." In *The Life and Administration of Robert Banks, Second Earl of Liverpool, K.G., Late First Lord of the Treasury.* 2 vols. London: Macmillan.

Young, Norwood. 1914. *Napoleon in Exile at Elba (1814–1815).* Philadelphia: Winston.

Young, Peter. 1971. *Chasseurs of the Guard.* London: Osprey.

Young, Peter. 1972. *Blücher's Army, 1813–15.* London: Osprey.

Young, Peter. 1972. *Wellington's Masterpiece: The Battle and Campaign of Salamanca.* London: Allen and Unwin.

Young, Peter. 1973. *Napoleon's Marshals.* New York: Hippocrene.

Young, Peter. 1999. *Eagles over the Alps: Suvorov in Italy and Switzerland, 1799.* New York: Emperor's Press.

Z

Zacks, Richard. 2005. *The Pirate Coast: Thomas Jefferson, the First Marines, and the Secret Mission of 1805.* New York: Hyperion.

Zaghi, Carlo. 1956. *Bonaparte e il Direttorio dopo Campolorimo; il problema italiano nella diplomazia europea, 1797–1798.* Naples: Edizioni scientifiche italiane.

Zaghi, Carlo. 1986. *L'Italia di Napoleone dalla Cisalpina al Regno.* Turin: UTET.

Zamoyski, Adam. 2004. *1812: Napoleon's Fatal March on Moscow.* London: HarperCollins.

Zanca, Massimo. 2005. *Dal Mincio al Piave: Pozzolo 1800* [From the Mincio to the Piave]. Mantua: Sommetti.

"Zapiski grafa Lanzherona. Voina s Turtsei v 1806–1812 gg." *Russkaia Starina,* [1907] No. 7; [1908] Nos. 4–6; [1910] Nos. 7–10; [1911] Nos. 7–8. St. Petersburg: N.p.

Zawadzki, W. H. 1993. *A Man of Honour: Adam Czartoryski as a Statesman of Russia and Poland, 1795–1831.* Oxford: Clarendon.

Zeissberg, Heinrich von. 1883. *Aus der Jugendzeit des Erzherzogs Karl.* Vienna: Hölder.

Zeissberg, Heinrich von. 1892. *Aldenhofen, Neerwinden, Löwen.* Vienna: W. Braumüller.

Zhilin, Paul. 1988. *Gibel' Napoleonovskoi armii v Rossii.* Moscow: Nauka.

Zhizn i podvigi Gen. leitenanta D. P. Neverovskogo. 1912. Moscow: N.p.

Zhurnal Voennikh Deistvii Otriada Kn. P.I. Bagrationa (s 9 Aprelia po 28 Sentiabria 1799). 1903. St. Petersburg: N.p.

Ziegler, Philip. 1965. *Addington: A Life of Henry Addington, First Viscount Sidmouth.* New York: Day.

Zieseniss, C. O. 1980. *Napoléon et la cour impériale.* Paris: Tallandier.

Zima, H. 2000. "Magnano." *First Empire* 49: 27–35.

Zima, H. 2001. "Magnano 1799." *Pallasch* 10: 2–18.

Zimmerman, Jürg. 1965. *Militärverwaltung und Heeresaufbringung in Osterreich bis 1806.* Frankfurt: Bernard und Graefe.

Zins, Ronald. 1999. *Journal de voyage du Général Desaix, Suisse et Italie.* Reyrieux, France: Cardon. (Orig. pub. 1797.)

Zweig, Stephen. 1930. *Joseph Fouché: The Portrait of a Politician.* New York: Viking.

List of Contributors

Ralph Ashby
Elmwood Park, Illinois

Jean-Jacques Arzalier
SAMU 83
Toulon
France

Rolando Avila
University of Texas, Pan American
Edinburg, Texas

Ralph Baker
Newport, Shropshire
United Kingdom

C.N. Bartlett
Horry-Georgetown Technical College
Conway, South Carolina

Jakub Basista
Jagiellonian University
Krakow
Poland

John T. Broom
Park University
Parkville, Missouri

Dino E. Buenviaje
University of California, Riverside
Riverside, California

William E. Burns
Howard University
Washington, DC

Melanie S. Byrd
Valdosta State University
Valdosta, Georgia

Thomas Cardoza
Truckee Meadows Community College
Reno, Nevada

Ian Castle
London
United Kingdom

Pauline Chakmakjian
London
United Kingdom

Paul Chamberlain
International Napoleonic Society
Luton, Bedfordshire
United Kingdom

William L. Chew III
Vesalius College
Brussels
Belgium

Elvio Ciferri
Leopoldo and Alice Franchetti Institute
Città di Castello
Italy

Craig T. Cobane II
Western Kentucky University
Bowling Green, Kentucky

Samuel Cohen
University of Toronto
Toronto, Ontario
Canada

Llewellyn D. Cook Jr.
Jacksonville State University
Jacksonville, Alabama

Malcolm Crook
Keele University
Keele, Staffordshire
United Kingdom

Terry Crowdy
Kent
United Kingdom

Laura Cruz
Western Carolina University
Cullowhee, North Carolina

Charles M. Dobbs
Iowa State University
Ames, Iowa

William E. Doody
Indiana Area School District
Indiana, Pennsylvania

Charles J. Esdaile
University of Liverpool
Liverpool, Merseyside
United Kingdom

Lee Eysturlid
Illinois Mathematics and Science Academy
Aurora, Illinois

Rachel Finley-Bowman
Delaware Valley College
Doylestown, Pennsylvania

Ian Fletcher
Kent
United Kingdom

Alan Forrest
University of York
York
United Kingdom

Gregory Fremont-Barnes
Oxford
United Kingdom

John G. Gallaher
Southern Illinois University at
    Edwardsville
Edwardsville, Illinois

Marco Gioannini
European Centre for Research and Studies
  on the Napoleonic Age
Alessandria
Italy

Philippe Girard
McNeese State University
Lake Charles, Louisiana

Alexander Grab
University of Maine
Orono, Maine

Christine Grafton

Kevin R. C. Gutzman
Western Connecticut State University
Danbury, Connecticut

Korcaighe P. Hale
Ohio University
Zanesville, Ohio

Clifford D. Harmon
Virginia Military Institute
Staunton, Virginia

Janet Hartley
London School of Economics and Political
  Science
London
United Kingdom

Oliver Benjamin Hemmerle
Mannheim
Germany

Neil M. Heyman
San Diego State University
San Diego, California

Peter Hofschröer
Gaishorn am See
Austria

David Hollins
Stamford, Lincolnshire
United Kingdom

Arthur Holst
Widener University
Chester, Pennsylvania

John T. Kuehn
U.S. Army Command and General Staff
  College
Fort Leavenworth, Kansas

Eve-Marie Lampron
Université de Montréal
Montréal, Quebec
Canada

Tom Lansford
University of Southern Mississippi
Long Beach, Mississippi

J. David Markham
International Napoleonic Society
Olympia, Washington

Terry M. Mays
The Citadel
Charleston, South Carolina

James R. Mc Intyre
Moraine Valley Community College
Palos Hills, Illinois

Alexander Mikaberidze
ABC-CLIO
Santa Barbara, California

Ian Morley
Ming Chuan University
Gwei-Shan
Taiwan

Jason R. Musteen
United States Military Academy
West Point, New York

Malyn Newitt
King's College London
London
United Kingdom

Jaime Ramon Olivares
Houston Community College-Central
Houston, Texas

Eric W. Osborne
Charlottesville, Virginia

Kenneth Pearl
Queensborough Community College
Bayside, New York

Barbara Bennett Peterson
Oregon State University
Corvallis, Oregon

J. Ward Regan
New York, New York

Robert V. Ricadela
Virgina Military Institution
Lexington, Virginia

Annette Richardson
University of Alberta
Edmonton, Alberta
Canada

Marie H. Weller
Paoli, Pennsylvania

Brian Sandberg
Medici Archive Project
Firenze, Italy

Margaret Sankey
Minnesota State University, Moorhead
Moorhead, Minnesota

Rohan Saravanamuttu
London
United Kingdom

Kenneth G. Johnson
Florida State University
Tallahassee, Florida

Shannon Schedlich-Day
Flinders University
Adelaide
Australia

Oliver Schmidt
Heidelberg
Germany

Orianne Smith
University of Maryland
Baltimore, Maryland

Mark G. Spencer
Brock University
St. Catharines, Ontario
Canada

Laurence Spring
Surrey
United Kingdom

Charles Steele
United States Military Academy
West Point, New York

Arthur Steinberg
Salisbury, North Carolina

Stephen Stewart
The Herald
Glasgow
Scotland

Gordon Stienburg
University of Toronto
Toronto, Ontario
Canada

Richard Taws
University College London
London
United Kingdom

Neville Thompson
University of Western Ontario
London, Ontario
Canada

Spencer C. Tucker
Lexington, Virginia

Dallace W. Unger Jr.
Fort Collins, Colorado

M. R. van der Werf
Amsterdam
Netherlands

Thomas D. Veve
Dalton State College
Dalton, Georgia

Patrick Villiers
Université du Littoral-côte d'Opale
Boulogne-sur-mer
France

Irena Vladimirsky
Achva Academic College
Beer Tuvia
Israel

Roderick S. Vosburgh
La Salle University
Philadelphia, Pennsylvania

James Wald
Hampshire College
Amherst, Massachusetts

Dierk Walter
Hamburger Institut fuer Sozialforschung
Hamburg
Germany

Andrew Jackson Waskey
Dalton State College
Dalton, Georgia

Tim J. Watts
Kansas State University
Manhattan, Kansas

Grant T. Weller
US Air Force Academy
Colorado Springs, Colorado

John Beresford Welsh
Olympia, Washington

David Westwood
MLRS Books
Buxton, Derbyshire
United Kingdom

Leigh Whaley
Acadia University
Wolfville, Nova Scotia
Canada

Brett F. Woods
American Public University
Manassas, Virginia

Ronald Young
Canterbury School
Fort Myers, Florida

Index